STREET

Lancashire

C000156127

First published in 1997 by

Philip's, a division of
Octopus Publishing Group Ltd
2-4 Heron Quays, London E14 4JP

Third colour edition 2004
Second impression with revisions 2006
LANCB

ISBN-10   0-540-08657-6 (spiral)
ISBN-13   978-0-540-08657-3 (spiral)

© Philip's 2006

OS Ordnance Survey®

This product includes mapping data licensed
from Ordnance Survey® with the permission of
the Controller of Her Majesty's Stationery Office.
© Crown copyright 2006. All rights reserved.
Licence number 100011710.

To the best of the Publishers' knowledge, the
information in this atlas was correct at the time
of going to press. No responsibility can be
accepted for any errors or their consequences.

The representation in this atlas of a road, track
or path is no evidence of the existence of a right
of way.

Ordnance Survey and the OS Symbol are
registered trademarks of Ordnance Survey, the
national mapping agency of Great Britain.

Printed by Toppan, China

Contents

III	**Key to map symbols**
IV	**Key to map pages**
VI	**Route planning**
X	**Administrative and Postcode boundaries**
1	**Street maps** at 3½ inches to 1 mile
226	**Street maps** at 1¾ inches to 1 mile
244	**Index** of towns and villages
247	**Index** of streets, hospitals, industrial estates, railway stations, schools, shopping centres, universities and places of interest

Digital Data

The exceptionally high-quality mapping found in this atlas is available as digital data in TIFF
format, which is easily convertible to other bitmapped (raster) image formats.

The index is also available in digital form as a standard database table. It contains all the details
found in the printed index together with the National Grid reference for the map square in which
each entry is named.

For further information and to discuss your requirements, please contact Philip's on
020 7644 6932 or james.mann@philips-maps.co.uk

45, Riverglen.

	Motorway with junction number (22a)
	Primary route – dual/single carriageway
	A road – dual/single carriageway
	B road – dual/single carriageway
	Minor road – dual/single carriageway
	Other minor road – dual/single carriageway
	Road under construction
	Tunnel, covered road
	Rural track, private road or narrow road in urban area
	Gate or obstruction to traffic (restrictions may not apply at all times or to all vehicles)
	Path, bridleway, byway open to all traffic, road used as a public path
	Pedestrianised area
DY7	**Postcode boundaries**
	County and unitary authority boundaries
	Railway, tunnel, railway under construction
	Tramway, tramway under construction
	Miniature railway
Walsall	**Railway station**
	Private railway station
South Shields	**Metro station**
	Tram stop, tram stop under construction
	Bus, coach station

◆	**Ambulance station**
◆	**Coastguard station**
◆	**Fire station**
◆	**Police station**
✚	**Accident and Emergency entrance to hospital**
H	**Hospital**
✛	**Place of worship**
i	**Information Centre** (open all year)
	Shopping Centre
P P&R	**Parking, Park and Ride**
PO	**Post Office**
Δ	**Camping site**
	Caravan site
▶	**Golf course**
⊠	**Picnic site**
Prim Sch	**Important buildings, schools, colleges, universities and hospitals**
River Medway	**Water name**
	River, weir, stream
	Canal, lock, tunnel
	Water
	Tidal water
	Woods
	Built up area
Church	**Non-Roman antiquity**
ROMAN FORT	**Roman antiquity**
94 / 164	**Adjoining page indicators and overlap bands** The colour of the arrow and the band indicates the scale of the adjoining or overlapping page (see scales below)

Abbr	Full	Abbr	Full	Abbr	Full
Acad	**Academy**	Inst	**Institute**	Recn Gd	**Recreation Ground**
Allot Gdns	**Allotments**	Ct	**Law Court**		
Cemy	**Cemetery**	L Ctr	**Leisure Centre**	Resr	**Reservoir**
C Ctr	**Civic Centre**	LC	**Level Crossing**	Ret Pk	**Retail Park**
CH	**Club House**	Liby	**Library**	Sch	**School**
Coll	**College**	Mkt	**Market**	Sh Ctr	**Shopping Centre**
Crem	**Crematorium**	Meml	**Memorial**	TH	**Town Hall/House**
Ent	**Enterprise**	Mon	**Monument**	Trad Est	**Trading Estate**
Ex H	**Exhibition Hall**	Mus	**Museum**	Univ	**University**
Ind Est	**Industrial Estate**	Obsy	**Observatory**	W Twr	**Water Tower**
IRB Sta	**Inshore Rescue Boat Station**	Pal	**Royal Palace**	Wks	**Works**
		PH	**Public House**	YH	**Youth Hostel**

■ The small numbers around the edges of the maps identify the 1 kilometre National Grid lines

■ The dark grey border on the inside edge of some pages indicates that the mapping does not continue onto the adjacent page

The scale of the maps on the pages numbered in blue is 5.52 cm to 1 km • 3½ inches to 1 mile • 1: 18103

0   ¼   ½   ¾   1 mile
0   250m   500m   750m   1 kilometre

The scale of the maps on pages numbered in green is 2.76 cm to 1 km • 1¾ inches to 1 mile • 1: 36206

0   ¼   ½   ¾   1 mile
0   250m 500m 750m 1 kilometre

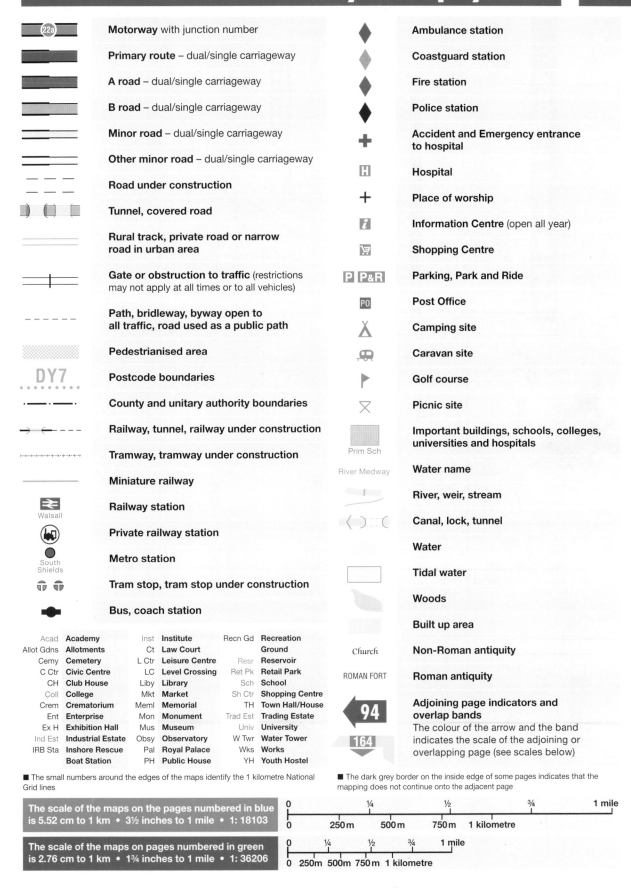

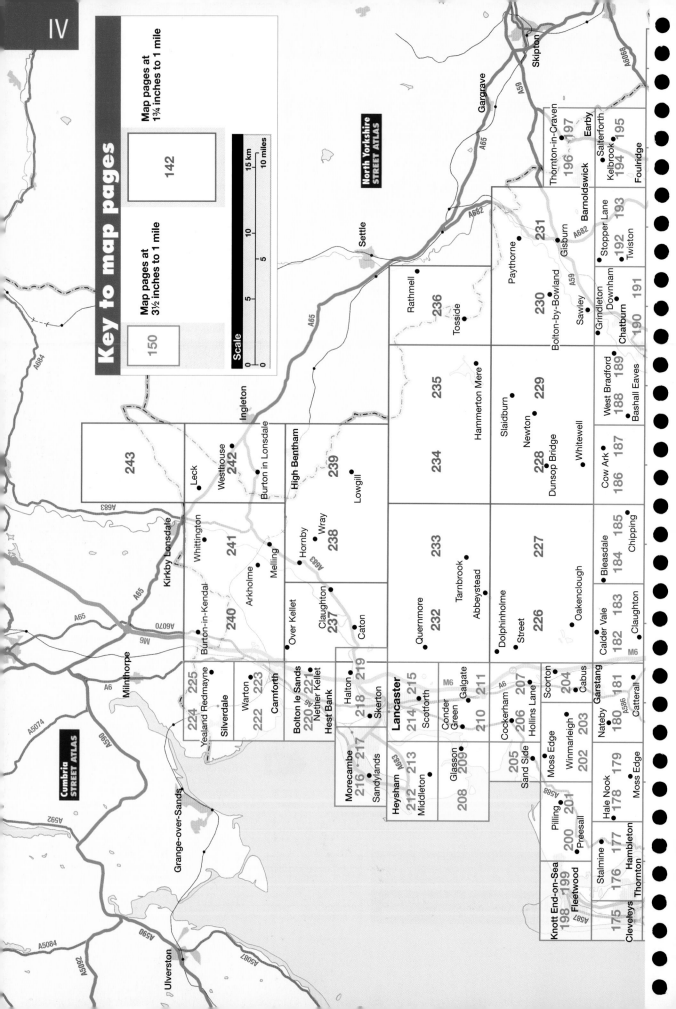

Key to map pages

Map pages at 1¾ inches to 1 mile

142

Map pages at 3½ inches to 1 mile

150

Scale

| 0 | 5 | 10 | 15 km |
| 0 | 5 | 10 miles |

Cumbria STREET ATLAS

North Yorkshire STREET ATLAS

Ulverston
Grange-over-Sands
Milnthorpe
Kirkby Lonsdale
Burton-in-Kendal
Whittington
Arkholme
Melling
Leck
Westhouse 242
Burton in Lonsdale
Ingleton
Settle
Gargrave
Skipton

243

Yealand Redmayne 225
Silverdale 224
Warton 223
Carnforth 222
Bolton le Sands 220 221
Nether Kellet
Hest Bank
Over Kellet
Claughton 237
Caton
High Bentham
Lowgill 239
Wray 238
Hornby

241

240

Thornton-in-Craven 196 197
Earby
Salterforth 195
Kelbrook 194
Foulridge
Barnoldswick
Stopper Lane 192 193
Twiston
Gisburn 231
Grindleton 190 191
Downham
Chatburn
Paythorne
Bolton-by-Bowland 230
Sawley
A682
A59

Rathmell 236
Tosside
Hammerton Mere 235
Slaidburn
Newton 229
Dunsop Bridge 228
Whitewell
West Bradford 188 189
Bashall Eaves
Cow Ark 186 187

234

Tarnbrook 233
Abbeystead
Dolphinholme
Street 226
Oakenclough
Bleasdale 184 185
Chipping
Calder Vale 182 183
Claughton

Quernmore 232

Lancaster 214 215
Scotforth
Conder Green 210 211
Galgate
M6
Cockerham 206 207
Hollins Lane
Sand Side 205
Moss Edge
Winmarleigh 202 203
Scorton 204
Cabus
Garstang 181
Nateby 180
Catterall
Glasson 209
208
Heysham 212 213
Middleton
Morecambe 216 217
Sandylands
Halton 218 219
Skerton

Hale Nook 178 179
Pilling 200 201
Preesall
Moss Edge
Knott End-on-Sea 198 199
Fleetwood
Stalmine 176 177
Hambleton
Thornton
Cleveleys 175

A684
A683
A65
A590
A6
A5074
A5084
A5092
A592
A5087
M6
A6070
A6068

V

West Yorkshire STREET ATLAS
Greater Manchester STREET ATLAS
Cheshire STREET ATLAS
Merseyside STREET ATLAS

Laneshaw Bridge 174
Wycoller 173
Trawden 172
150 151
170 171 Colne
Barrowford 170
Nelson 148 149 Haggate
Brierfield 148
Worsthorne 129
Hurstwood 128
Holme Chapel 108 109
Cornholme
Portsmouth 88
Sharneyford
Bacup 71 Broadley 52
Shawforth 70 Whitworth Syke
Nun Hills
Waterfoot 69
Rawtenstall 86 87
Helmshore 68 Edenfield
Ramsbottom 50 51
Summerseat
Todmorden
Littleborough
Rochdale
Manchester
Oldham
Ashton-under-Lyne
Stalybridge
Denton
Stretford
Salford
Prestwich
Bury Chesham 33
Heywood

Barley 168 169 Fence
Newchurch in Pendle 168
Higham 146 147
Padiham 126 127
Walk Mill 106 107
Love Clough
Crawshawbooth 86
Haslingden 84 85
Rising Bridge
Goodshaw Fold 104 105
Accrington 104
Rishton
Clayton-le-Moors 124 125
Great Harwood
Read 144 145
Whalley 144
Barrow
Pendleton 166 167
Clitheroe 166
Walker Fold 164 165
Great Mitton
Langho
York 122 123 Sunny Bower
Wilpshire 122
Ribchester
Knowle Green 162 163
Hesketh Lane 162
Longridge 140 141
Grimsargh 138 139
Goosnargh
Inglewhite 160 161
Whitechapel
Bilsborrow 158 159
Barton 136 137
Broughton
Cottam 116 117 Fulwood
Ribbleton 118 119
Samlesbury
Nab's Head 98 99
Gregson Lane
Mellor 120 121
Balderstone
Blackburn 100 101
Cherry Tree
Ewood 80 81
Abbey Village
Darwen
Belgrave 64 65
Cadshaw 66 67
Edgworth 48 49
Greenmount
Belmont
Egerton
Belthorn 82 83
Hoddlesden
Daisyfield 102 103
Oswaldtwistle
Bolton
Farnworth
Leigh
Wigan
Horwich 45
Blackrod 32
Adlington 30 31
Aspull
Brindle 78 79
Higher Wheelton
Brinscall 62
Whittle-le-Woods 60 61
Euxton
Chorley 42 43
Coppull
Standish 28 29
Limbrick 44
Rivington 45
Lostock Hall 76 77
Leyland
Bamber Bridge 96 97
Preston 95
Bottom of Hutton 94
Hutton
New Longton 74 75
Much Hoole
Croston 58 59
Shaw Green
Eccleston 40 41
Mawdesley
Mossy Lea 28
Parbold 26 27
Hoscar
Appley Bridge 18 19
Skelmersdale
Orrell 10
Longshaw 9
Digmoor 8
Stanley 17
Westhead 16
Ormskirk 14 15
Downholland Cross
Aughton 6 7
Bickerstaffe
St Helen's
Rainford 1 Kirkby
Rainford Junction
Billinge
Newton-le-Willows
Ashton-in-Makerfield
Holmeswood 38 39
Rufford
Tarlscough
Bispham Green 24 25
Burscough
Bescar 24
Tarleton 56 57
Sollom
Banks 54 55
Churchtown
High Park 36 37
Brown Edge
Shirdley Hill 22 23
Halsall
Lydiate 4 5
Maghull
Haskayne 12 13
Great Altcar
Formby 11
Hightown 3
Ince Blundell 2
Southport
Birkdale 34 35
Blowick
Ainsdale 20 21
Marshside 53
Litherland
Bootle
Liverpool
Wallasey

Norbreck 152 153
Poulton-le-Fylde
Whin Lane End 154 155
Singleton
St Michael's on Wyre 156 157
Great Eccleston
Inskip
Thistleton 132 133
Weeton
Catforth 134 135
Wharles
Kirkham 114 115
Clifton
Great Plumpton 112 113
Wrea Green
Blackpool 130 131
Staining
Sandham's Green 110 111
Moss Side
Lytham St Anne's 90 91
Lytham
St Annes 89
Warton 92 93
Freckleton
Hesketh Bank 73
Hundred End 72

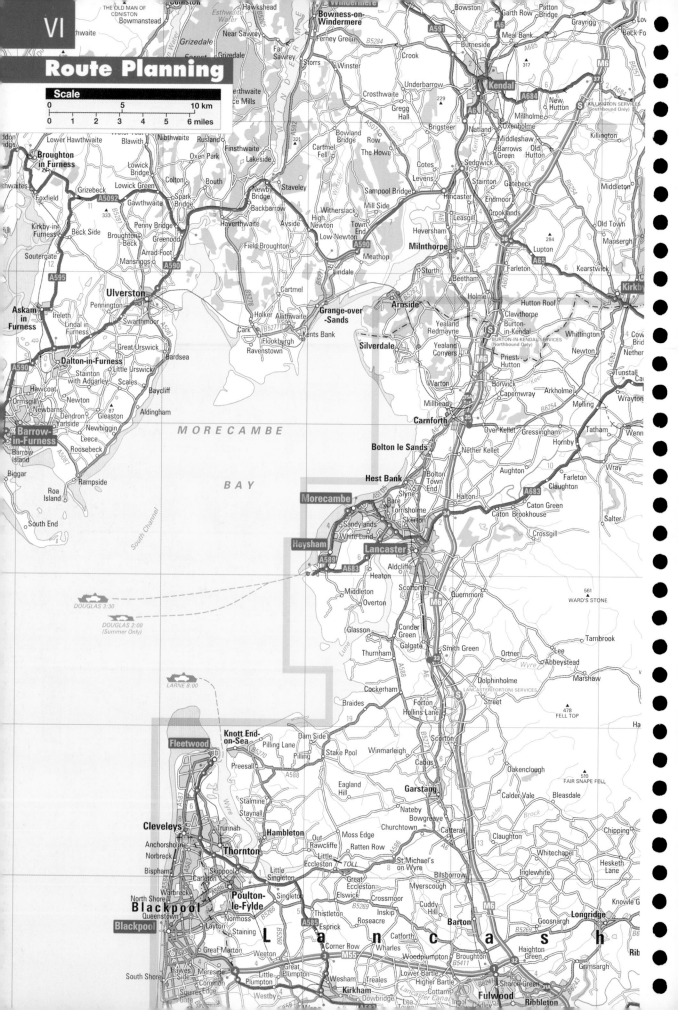

Route Planning

Scale

0   5   10 km

0   1   2   3   4   5   6 miles

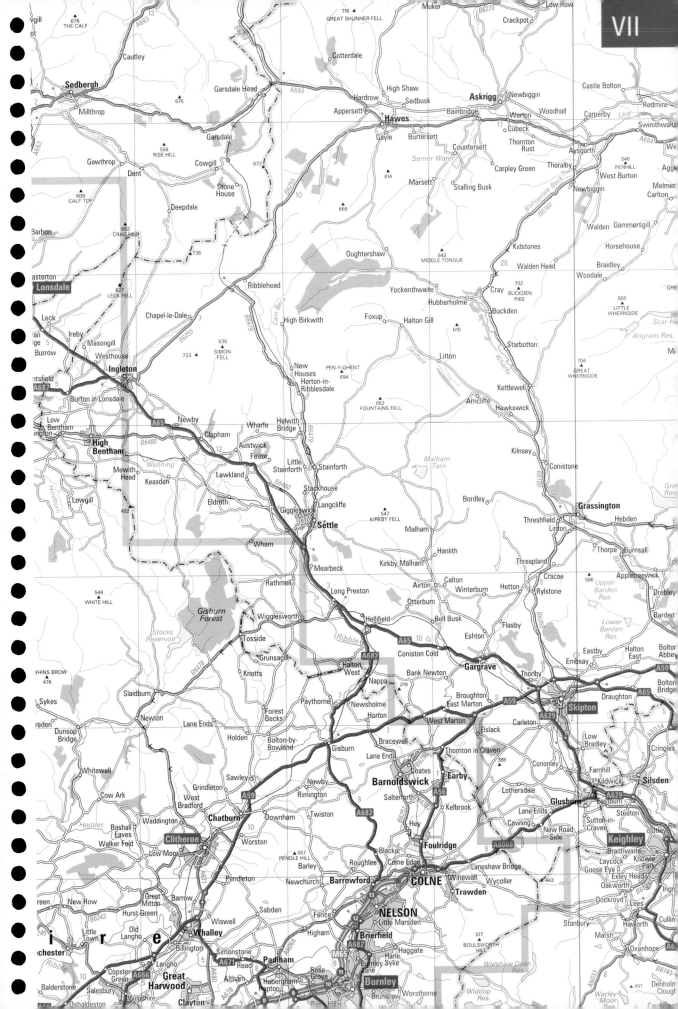

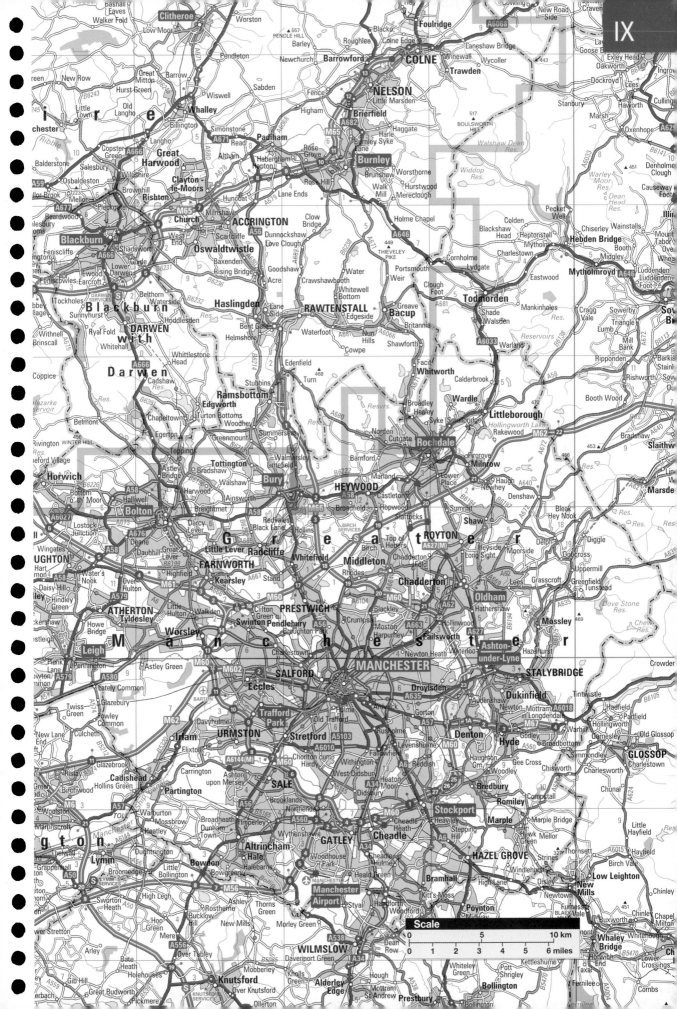

Major administrative and Postcode boundaries

County and unitary authority boundaries

District boundaries

Postcode boundaries

Area covered by this atlas

Scale

| 0 | | 5 | | 10 | | 15 km |
| 0 | | | 5 | | | 10 miles |

Cumbria

LA10

LA7

Silverdale

Burton-in-Kendal

LA5

LA6

Burton in Lonsdale

Carnforth

Hornby

High Bentham

North Yorkshire

Morecambe

LA4

Caton

Lancaster

Heysham

LA1

LA3

Lancaster

LA2

BD24

Overton

Glasson

Galgate

Dolphinholme

Tosside

BD23

Slaidburn

Dunsop Bridge

Gisburn

Fleetwood

FY7

Pilling

Scorton

BB7

Barnoldswick

Earby

Garstang

Ribble Valley

BB18

FY6

Wyre

PR3

Chipping

Clitheroe

BB9

Pendle

BB8

BD22

Cleveleys

FY5

Hambleton

Great Eccleston

Bilsborrow

Lancashire

Colne

Trawden

FY2

Poulton-le-Fylde

Nelson

Bradford

Blackpool

FY3

Longridge

Whalley

BB12

HX7

Blackpool

FY1

Fylde

Fulwood

PR2

BB6

Padiham

BB10

Burnley

FY4

Kirkham

Mellor

Great Harwood

Burnley

FY8

Preston

PR1

BB1

Hyndburn

BB11

OL14

Lytham St Anne's

Warton

PR4

PR5

Blackburn

BB2

Accrington

Holme Chapel

South Ribble

Bamber Bridge

BB5

BB4

OL13

Bacup

Calderdale

Walmer Bridge

Leyland

PR25

Darwen

BB3

Haslingden

Rossendale

OL12

Banks

Tarleton

PR26

Brinscall

Blackburn with Darwen

Whitworth

Croston

Chorley

PR6

BL10

Southport

Eccleston

Chorley

Belmont

Ramsbottom

OL10

PR9

PR7

BL7

BL8

Ainsdale

PR8

L40

Burscough

WN1

Adlington

BL6

BL9

Bury

Rochdale

West Lancashire

Parbold

WN6

Horwich

Formby

L37

Haskayne

Ormskirk

WN8

Standish

WN2

Bolton

Bury

Oldham

L39

Aughton

Skelmersdale

Orrell

Wigan

Hightown

L38

L31

Maghull

WN5

Salford

L29

WA11

SD

Sefton

L33

SJ

St Helens

Manchester

Tameside

Liverpool

Knowsley

Warrington

Trafford

Stockport

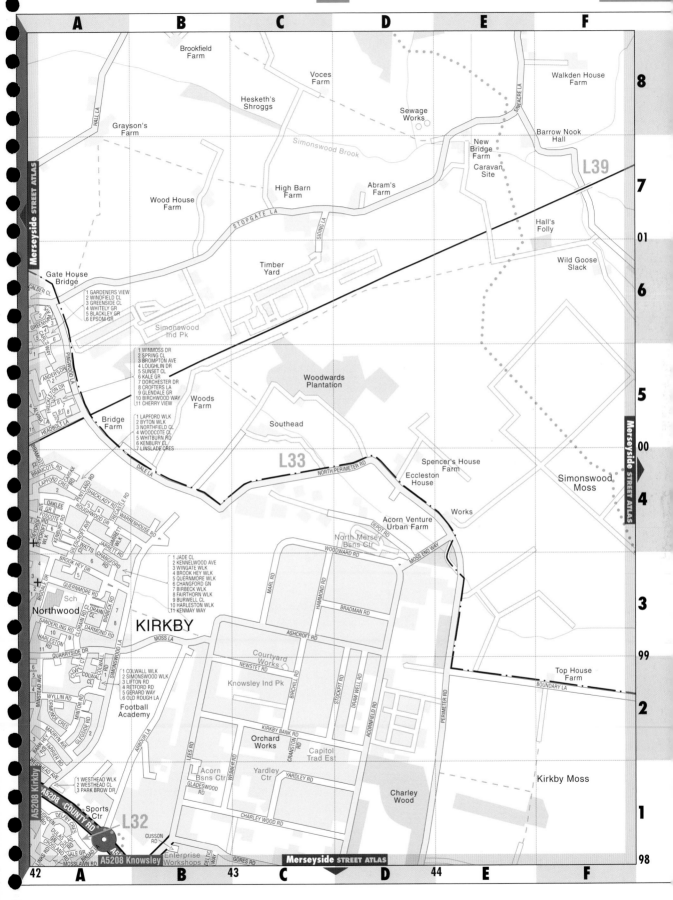

A B C D E F

8

Brookfield
Farm

Voces
Farm

Walkden House
Farm

Hesketh's
Shroggs

Sewage
Works

Barrow Nook
Hall

Grayson's
Farm

New
Bridge
Farm

L39

7

Caravan
Site

Simonswood Brook

High Barn
Farm

Abram's
Farm

Hall's
Folly

Wood House
Farm

01

STOPGATE LA

SIDING LA

SPINACRE LA

Gate House
Bridge

Timber
Yard

Wild Goose
Slack

6

CALDER CL

1 GARDENERS VIEW
2 WINDFIELD CL
3 GREENSIDE CL
4 WHITELY GR
5 BLACKLEY GR
6 EPSOM GR

Simonswood
Ind Pk

1 WINMOSS DR
2 SPRING CL
3 BROMPTON AVE
4 LOUGHLIN DR
5 SUNSET CL
6 KALE GR
7 DORCHESTER DR
8 CROFTERS LA
9 GLENDALE GR
10 BIRCHWOOD WAY
11 CHERRY VIEW

Woodwards
Plantation

5

Woods
Farm

Southead

Bridge
Farm

1 LAPFORD WLK
2 BYTON WLK
3 NORTHFIELD CL
4 WOODCOTE CL
5 WHITBURN RD
6 KENBURY CL
7 LINSLADE CRES

00

DALE LA

L33

NORTH PERIMETER RD

Spencer's House
Farm

Eccleston
House

Simonswood
Moss

4

Acorn Venture
Urban Farm

Works

North Mersey
Bsns Ctr

DEPOT RD

MOSS END WAY

BRAMCOTE RD
BRAKEFAX

WARRENHOUSE RD

1 JADE CL
2 KENNELWOOD AVE
3 WINGATE WLK
4 BROOK HEY WLK
5 QUERNMORE WLK
6 CHANGFORD GN
7 BIRBECK WLK
8 FAIRTHORN WLK
9 BURWELL CL
10 HARLESTON WLK
11 KENMAY WAY

WOODWARD RD

MARL RD

HAMMOND RD

BRADMAN RD

3

Northwood

KIRKBY

MOSS LA

ASHCROFT RD

Courtyard
Works

NEWSTET RD

BIRCHILL RD

STOCKPIT RD

DRAW WELL RD

PERIMETER RD

Top House
Farm

BOUNDARY LA

99

1 COLWALL WLK
2 SIMONSWOOD WLK
3 LIFTON RD
4 RETFORD RD
5 GERARD WAY
6 OLD ROUGH LA

Knowsley Ind Pk

ACORNFIELD RD

2

Football
Academy

KIRKBY BANK RD

CRANSTON RD

Orchard
Works

Capitol
Trad Est

Kirkby Moss

LEES RD

WEBBER RD

Acorn
Bsns Ctr

Yardley
Ctr

YARDLEY RD

GLADESWOOD
RD

Charley
Wood

1 WESTHEAD WLK
2 WESTHEAD CL
3 PARK BROW DR

1

A5208 Kirkby

A5208 COUNTY RD

Sports
Ctr

L32

CUSSON
RD

CHARLEY WOOD RD

GORES RD

98

A5208 Knowsley

Enterprise
Workshops

42 A B 43 C D 44 E F

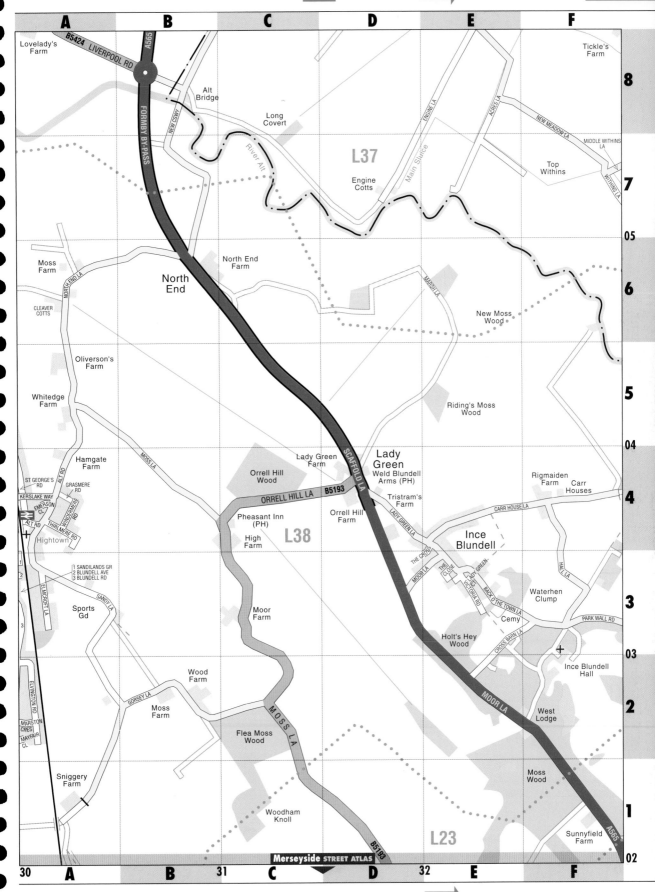

	A	B	C	D	E	F

8

Oliver's Farm
BROAD LA
RYE MOSS LA
Sewage Works
L39
Holland's Farm
CHURCH LA
INTAKE LA

MIDDLE WITHINS LA
LINACRE LA
Lydiate Brook
L37
Lydiate Wood
ACRES LA

7
The Withins

WITHINS LA
LOWER CARR LA

05

MONKS CARR LA
Altcar Meadows
Carr Wood
Maghull Hey Cop
Trans Pennine Trail
Gore House Farm
PUNNELL'S LA

6

Carr Sluice

5
L38
P CARR LA
LYDIATE STATION RD
ALTCAR LA

04
Searchlight Plantation
L31

4

Carr Side Farm
BLACKCAR LA
River Alt
CABIN LA

3
CARRS SIDE LA
L29

03

2
Tower Wood
East Lodge Farm
EAST LA
Huntsbrook Farm
Broad Farm
BROAD LA
PARK WALL RD

Ince Blundell Park

1
L23
Homer Green
LUNT RD
LONG LA
GATES LA
MOOR LA
LUNT LA

02
L23

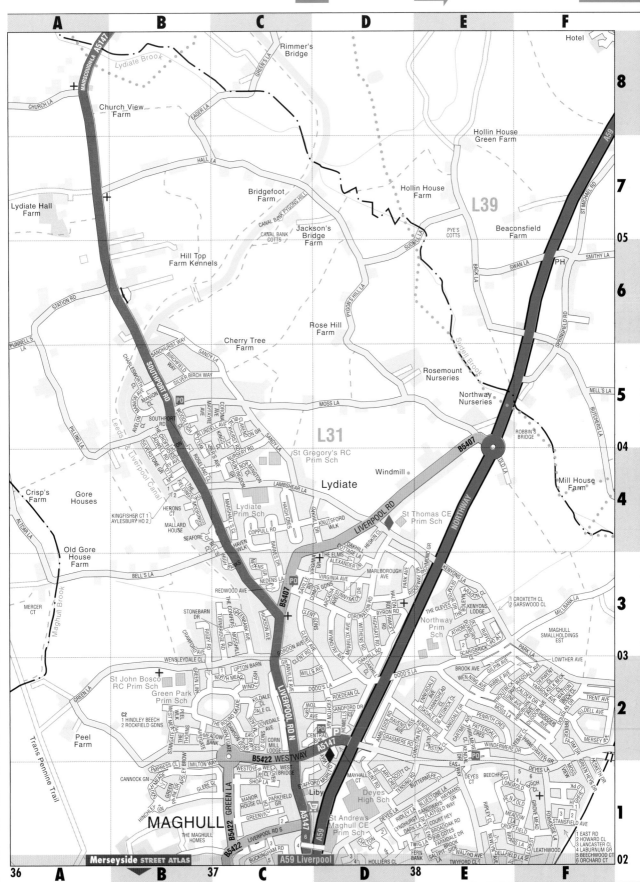

A B C D E F

8

7

05

6

L39

Hotel

Hollin House
Green Farm

Hollin House
Farm

Beaconsfield
Farm

PH

SMITHY LA

SWAN LA

PYE'S
COTTS

BACK LA

NELL'S LA

Rosemount
Nurseries

Northway
Nurseries

Robbin's
Bridge

Mill House
Farm

B5407

MARSCOUGH LA A5147

Lydiate Brook

Rimmer's
Bridge

GREEN'S LA

EAGER LA

HALL LA

Church View
Farm

CHURCH LA

Lydiate Hall
Farm

PUNNELL'S
LA

STATION RD

Bridgefoot
Farm

CANAL BANK PYGON'S HILL LA

CANAL BANK
COTTS

Jackson's
Bridge
Farm

Hill Top
Farm Kennels

PYGON'S HILL LA

SUDELL LA

Rose Hill
Farm

MOSS LA

Sudell Brook

Cherry Tree
Farm

L31

Windmill

SOUTHPORT RD

PO

SANDHURST WAY

BIRCHFIELD
WAY

SILVER BIRCH WAY

SANDY LA

Leeds & Liverpool Canal

CHARLESWORTH CT

MUNCASTER CL

AVELON

MANOR

THE CROFT

SOUTHPORT
RD

CORONAL
AVE

MATTAFIELD
AVE

BLUNDELL AVE

CLARENDON GR

WOOD END

KINGSLEY AVE

CLARENCE AVE

SANDY LA

CLENT GR

NURSERY RD

NORMINGTON

HUNTINGDON

ROSLAND CL

St Gregory's RC
Prim Sch

LAMBSHEAR LA

Lydiate

St Thomas CE
Prim Sch

LIVERPOOL RD

NORTHWAY

B5407

Crisp's
Farm

Gore
Houses

PILLING LA

ALTCAR LA

SILVERSTONE GR

KINGFISHER CT 1
AYLESBURY HO 2

HERONS
CT

MALLARD
HOUSE

SEAFORE CL

FIELDING RD

LONG MEADOWS

THE CROFT

Lydiate
Prim Sch

MARSHALL'S CL

HAIGH CRES

COPPULL RD

KNUTSFORD
WLK

OAKHILL DR

HESKIN CL

OAKHILL

COTTAGE LA

THE ELMS

VIRGINIA
WLK

ALEXANDER DR

Marlborough
Ave

PARK AVE

RIDGEWAY DR

RICHMOND GR

KENTONS LA

KENYON'S LA

Northway
Prim Sch

THE CLEVES

KENYONS
LODGE

1 CROXTETH CL
2 GARSWOOD CL

MILLBANK LA

MAGHULL
SMALLHOLDINGS
EST

LOWTHER AVE

PARK LA

Old Gore
House
Farm

BELL'S LA

REDWOOD AVE

HAVEN WLK

NEDENS LA

ROSE CRES

VIRGINIA AVE

SADDLE

COMER GDNS

ANCASTA

SUNNYMEDE

CORONATION RD

BYRON RD

WITHENS RD

MERRILOX AVE

HIGHGATE RD

Mercer
CT

Gore
La

THE CONIFERS

Stonebarn
Dr

TURNBRIDGE RD

MOSSHILL

RIGBY RD

GORDON AVE

CLENT AVE

CLENT GDNS

WYNDALE

CLENT RD

CORONSON RD

DODD'S LA

ATHOM GR

DIXON DR

SCARISBRICK DR

BROOK AVE

WEN AVE

GILPIN AVE

RIBBLE AVE

DERWENT

KELK BECK

MASDALE CL

CALDER DR

YARROW AVE

WHITTLE

WITTON

TRENT AVE

SUDELL AVE

DOUGLAS AVE

BRIDGE RD

MERSEY AVE

WENSLEYDALE CL

St John Bosco
RC Prim Sch

CRAWFORD
AVE

Green Park
Prim Sch

GREEN LINK

GREEN LA

NORTH MEAD

WINDS

UPTON BARN

KILDALE
CL

DOVEDALE
AVE

DALE CL

WILLS AVE

ROEDEAN CL

SANDFORD DR

LANGDALE DR

PATTERDALE
CRES

ESKDALE DR

KESWICK DR

KENDAL DR

PENRITH CRES

AMBLESIDE

RAVENGLASS
AVE

GRASMERE RD

HAWESWATER GR

RYDAL AVE

WINDERMERE DR

C2
1 HINDLEY BEECH
2 ROCKFIELD GDNS

THE ROUND
MEADOW

THE THORNS

STANGATE

THE SIGNAL

ARMIGEAD
BANK

PEEL
WLK

EAST

GREEN PARK DR

KILDALE

CORN
MILL
LODGE

DEYES LA

PO

EAS

EAST

Peel
Farm

Trans Pennine Trail

GREEN LA

B5422

HINCHLEY GN

EMPRESS CL

LADE

CANNOCK GN

GREEN LA

MANOR
HOUSE CL

PARKFIELD
GR

GLEBE CT

MILTON WAY

WESTWAY

SHOP LA

GREENVILLE

B5422 GREEN LA

LIVERPOOL RD N

GRANVILLE RD

HOKSON AVE

SANDY

B5422 WESTWAY

B5422 Liverpool RD S

BUCKINGHAM RD

A5147

West
Bridge

STAFFORD MOOR

P

HOWELLS

CENTRAL
SQ

A5147

Liby

Deyes
High Sch

Mayhall

LEIGHTON

DODD'S LA

CORONSON
RD

MOI

ST ANDREWS
CL

SCOTT CL

TEESDALE

BLUESTONE LA

SANDIWAYS

HAYMANS
WLK

FLATFIELD WAY

BROADOAK RD

FIR COTES

DARK LA

RIDLEY RD

LYNDHURST

BUTTERMERE

DEYES
CT

BEECHFIELD

LONGFOLD

PEN-Y-GHENT

OLD

MEADOW
FIELD

GROVE MEAD

FOXHOUSE LA

STANSFIELD AVE

1 EAST RD
2 HOWARD CL
3 LANCASTER CL
4 LABURNUM GR
5 BEECHWOOD GT
6 ORCHARD CT

MAGHULL

THE MAGHULL
HOMES

St Andrews
Maghull CE
Prim Sch

COURT HEY

FARMDALE DR

BROOK

SALTPIT
FERN
BANK

TWIG LA

FARNDALE

TWYFORD LA

DELLFIELD LA

WALTHO AVE

LEATHWOOD

A59

A59 Liverpool

ST MICHAEL'S RD

SPRINGFIELD RD

BUTCHERS LA

DUDLA

A59

ST MICHAEL'S RD

C1
1 HOLMEFIELD GR
2 RED LION CL
3 BALMORAL RD
4 ALEXANDER WHARF
5 WINDSOR RD
6 DAMFIELD LA

D1
1 BEECHCROFT
2 CHILTON MEWS
3 THE MEADOWS
4 CHAPEL HO
5 CHILTON CT

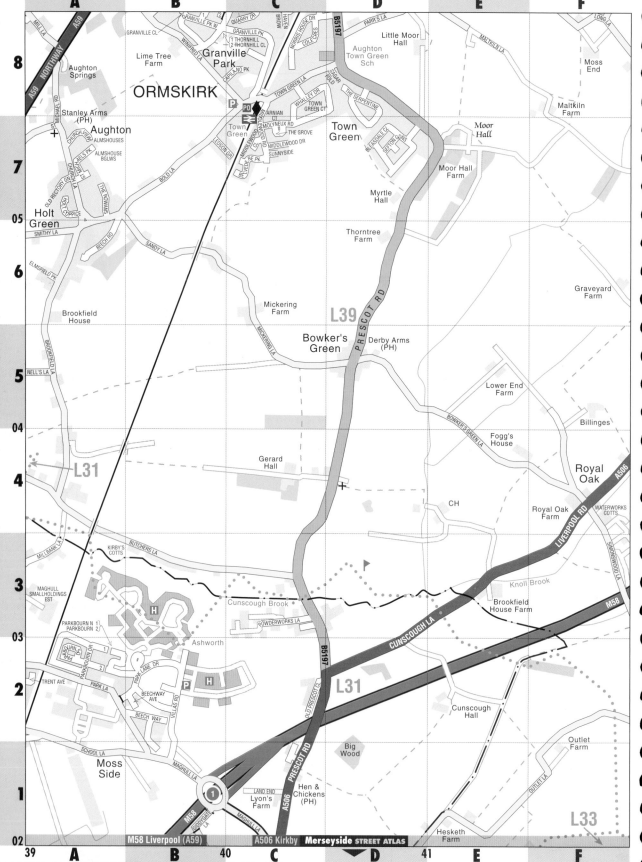

ORMSKIRK

Aughton Springs

Lime Tree Farm

Granville Park

Stanley Arms (PH)

Aughton

Almshouses

Almshouse Bglws

Holt Green

Brookfield House

Little Moor Hall

Aughton Town Green Sch

Town Green

Moor Hall

Moor Hall Farm

Moss End

Maltkiln Farm

Myrtle Hall

Thorntree Farm

Graveyard Farm

L39

Mickering Farm

Bowker's Green

Derby Arms (PH)

L31

Lower End Farm

Billinges

Gerard Hall

Fogg's House

Royal Oak

CH

Royal Oak Farm

Waterworks Cotts

Maghull Smallholdings Est

Knoll Brook

Cunscough Brook

Brookfield House Farm

Ashworth

Trent Ave

L31

Cunscough Hall

Outlet Farm

Moss Side

Big Wood

Hen & Chickens (PH)

Lyon's Farm

L33

Hesketh Farm

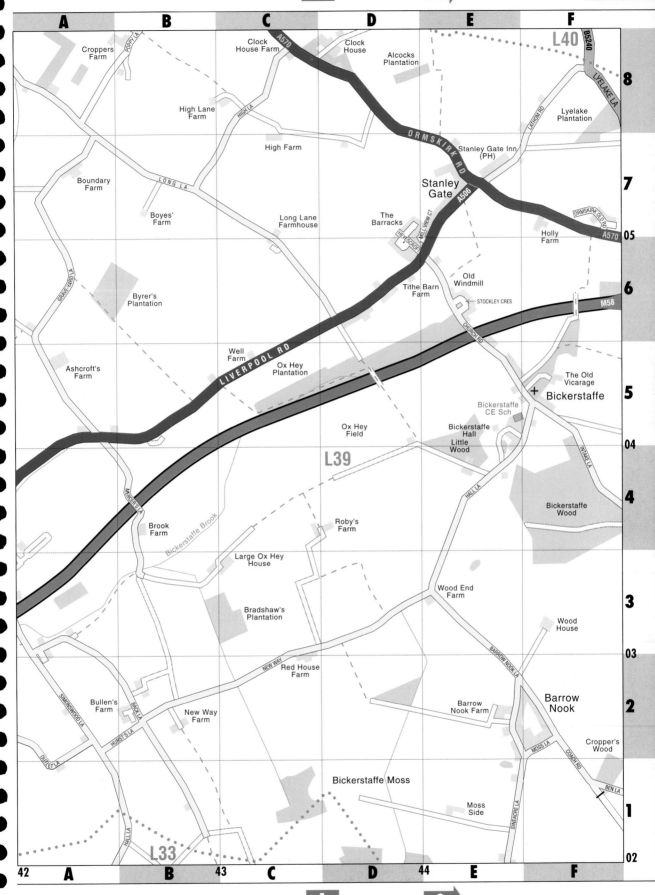

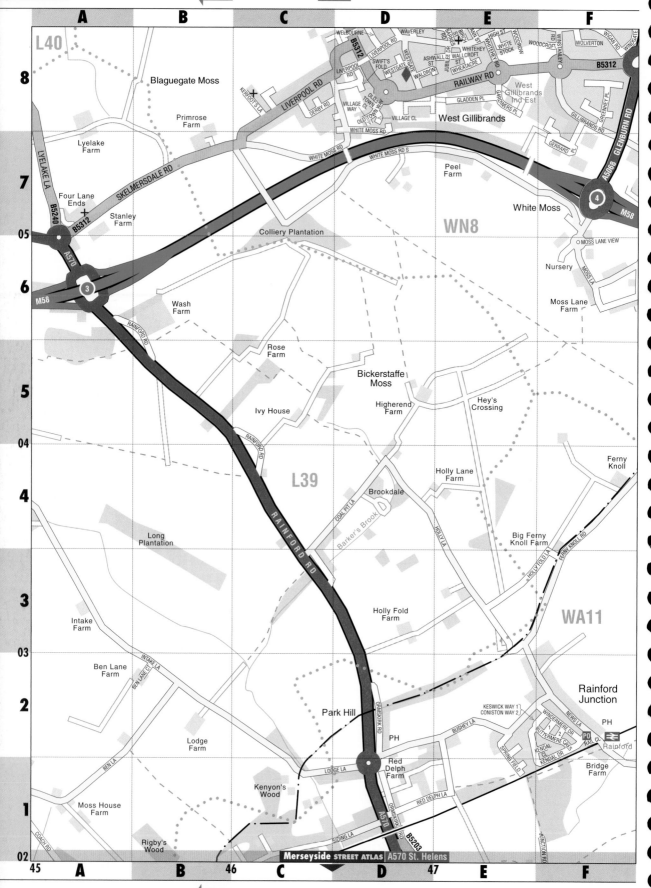

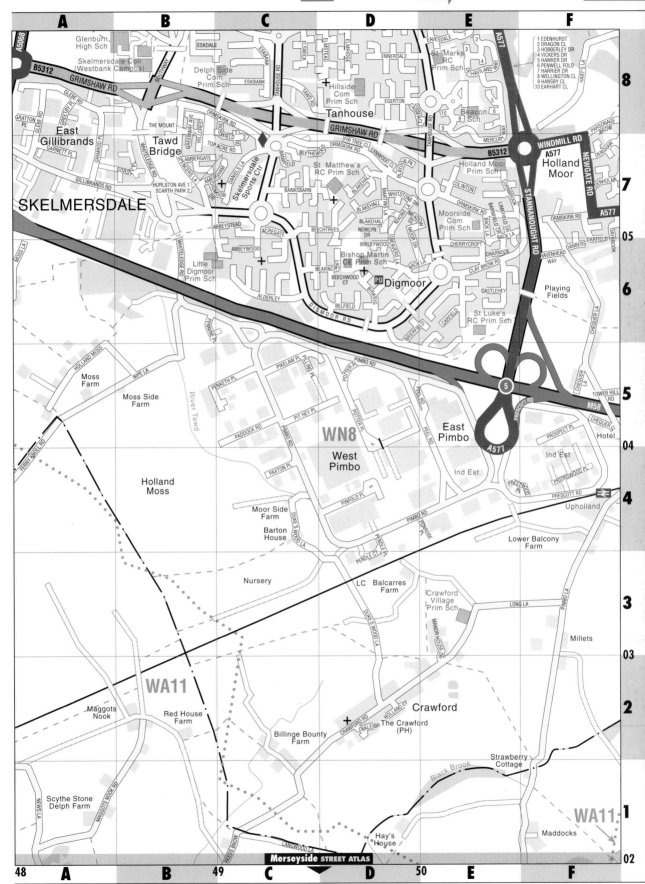

A B C D E F

8

7

05

6

5

04

4

03

3

2

1

02

HART'S LA
Windmill (dis)
Windmill HTS
BEACON HTS
PARSONAGE BROW
MILL LA
WINDSOR RD
MILLERS NOOK
St Thomas Sch
COLLEGE RD
GROVE RD
PARLIAMENT ST
DINGLE RD
CH
Hotel
LAFFORD LA
WOODSIDE
BEAN WOOD AVE
B5206
SPRING RD
ETON WAY
M6
GATHURST RD
DERWENT RD
CAMBRIDGE RD
GRASMERE AVE
HARROW
OXFORD RD
ANNANDALE
BANFORD
DENSHAW
Hall Green
DALTON RD
MORRIS RD
MAYFIELD
DAYFIELD
HIGHGATE
BEACON VIEW DR
GREENHAVEN
DEAN
THIRLMERE AVE
TITHEBARN
ABBEY LA
HALL GN
ALMA HILL
BACK BROW
PRIORY RD
HORSE SHOE WEN
HOPWOOD
NOOK
SPENCER'S LA
ORRELL
F7
1 THIRLMERE AVE
2 LATIMER CL
3 BYRON CL
4 WINCHESTER CL
5 RYDAL AVE
CONISTON AVE
GRASMERE AVE
WINDERMERE AVE
ULLSWATER
THAMES DR
DOUGLAS DR
St Peter's RC High Sch
DORCHESTER CL
CARLTON AVE
MILLGREEN CL
A577
ORMSKIRK RD
THE FELLS
DEXTER WAY
BACK SCHOOL LA
SCHOOL LA
Up Holland
ST THOMAS'S CT
ORRELL RD
Orrell Post
Orrell Post
PO
BROXTON AVE
IRWELL
MERSEY RD
MOUNTFIELD CT
Liby
SUNNY DR
EAST MOUNT
A577
A577 Wigan (A49)
Ravenhead Rd
FIELDVIEW
MEADOWFIELD
HEATLAND
DEVON CL
GALLOWAY
WELLCROSS RD
Newgate
Works
Higher Tower Hill Farm
Well Cross Farm
Mast
TOWER HILL RD
CINNAMON BROW
TONTINE RD
M58
MAJESTIC MEWS
Tontine
GREENLEA CL
SALTDOWFIELDS
BRYONY CL
SEFTON RD
SEFTON VIEW
MOOR RD
LINDEN AVE
LINDEN WLK
NABURN
WILSHAW RD
COSGATE CL
Orrell RU FC
THE ORCHARDS
26
M58
MILTON RD
M6 The Midlands
Greater Manchester STREET ATLAS
WN8
LOWER BROOK
PIMBO LA
Upholland Tunnel
The Lawns Farm
WN5
LAWNS AVE
SANDFORD
QUEENS RD
KILBURN RD
LINDLEY AVE
DELPHSIDE RD
SANDBROOK RD
BROOKLANDS CL
MILLCROFT
ST GEORGE
MILL
CHURCH CL
FOXWOOD
CL
Orrell Holgate Prim Sch
EDGE HALL RD
ST JAMES RD
St James' RC Prim Sch
Orrell
Hewitt Bsns Pk
HALL LA
Lower Pimbo
Up Holland High Sch
DAGHDALE RD
Orrell Newfold Com Prim Sch
NEW TEW
UPHOLLAND RD
GANTLEY RD
CROFTLANDS
Far Moor
ST LUKE'S DR
SANDY LA
VICARAGE RD
LODGE RD
P
Orrell Water Park
Farrar's Farm
Higher Pimbo Farm
Pimbo Bushes
GANTLEY AVE
GANTLEY CRES
CROSS LA
GREEN LA
BELMONT
MARL GR
JUBILEE AVE
DORIS
MOSS AVE
THE CROFT
GREENSIDE
WATERMERE
GREENSLATE RD
LAKESIDE AVE
THE AVENUE
TRACKS LA
Higher End
Greenslate Farm
Winstanley Coll
WINSTANLEY RD
M6
Bispham Hall Bsns Pk
SMETHURST RD
SMETHURST HALL PK
Works
SMETHURST RD
Billinge
Moss Wood
WA11
Mountains Farm
BROWNLOW LA
UPHOLLAND RD
BISPHAM CT
H
COPPICE DR
BANG
CRANK RD
WINCHESTER
COLERIDGE RD
KEATS AVE
TENNYSON RD
MILTON GR
SWINBURN GR
TREVELYAN DR
BURNS CL
COB MOOR AVE
Longshaw
Longshaw Bottom
PARK RD
New House Farm
Heaton House
Bispham Hall
Brownlow Farm
Promised Land Farm
Brownlow
WALLBROOK
COB MOOR RD
LONGSHAW
BEVERLEY AVE
PO
B5206
PARK AVE
NORFOLK AVE
LONGSHAM AVE
OAKSHAW AVE
Longshaw Comm
LONGSHAW CL
Merseyside STREET ATLAS

51 A B 52 C D 53 E F

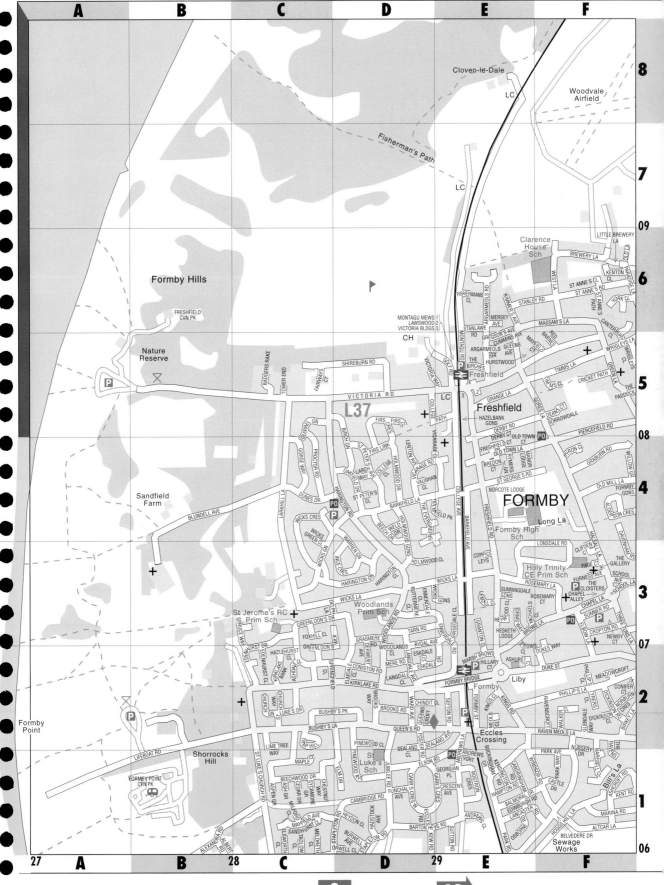

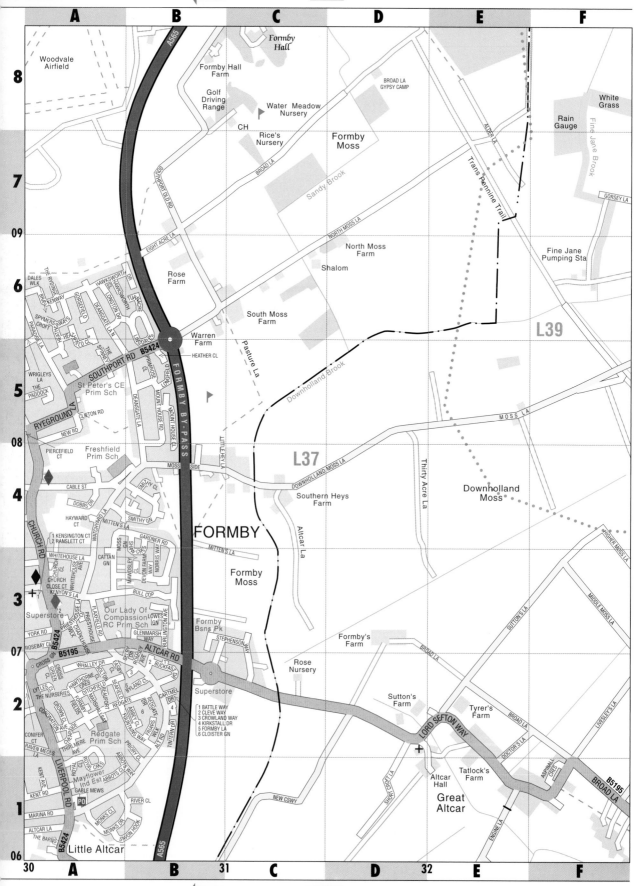

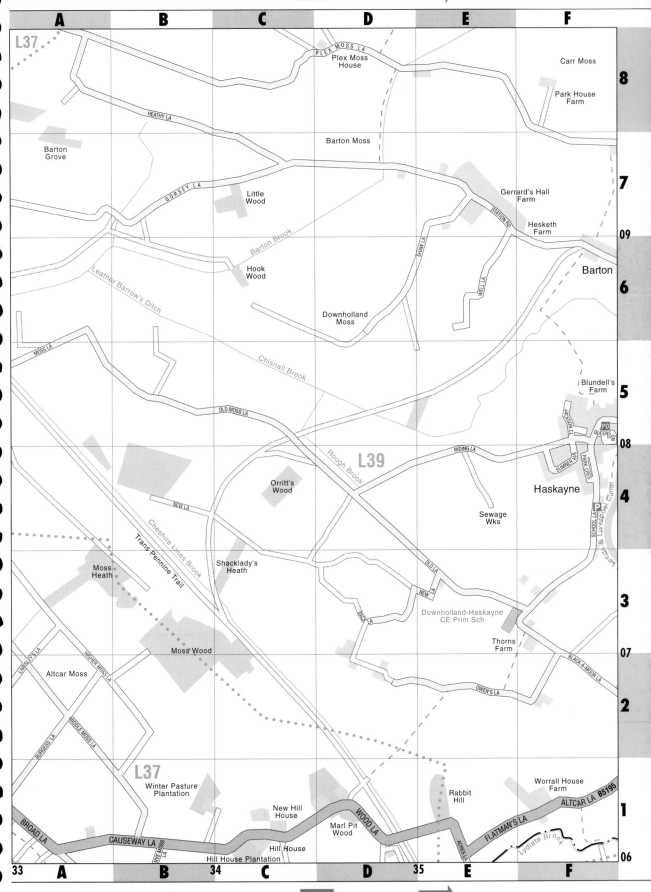

13
23

	A	B	C	D	E	F

8

Halsall

Carr Moss La
Linaker Dr
A5147
New St

Mill House Farm

Mere Lane Farm

Mere La

Summerwood La

Watson House

Big Brick Farm

Clock House

North Moor La
Harridge La

Primrose Hill Farm

L40

Malt House Farm

Asmall La

7

Plex Moss La

Mill Brow

Southport Rd

Trundle Pie La

Bangor's Green

Bangor's Green Farm

Aughton Cliffs Farm

Primrose Hill

Wharton's Farm

Cut La

09

Blue Bell Inn (PH)

Holly Farm

Model Farm

Trundle Pie House

Narrow Lane (Clieves Hills)

6

Station Rd

Smithy La

Wanishar Brook

Plex Lane Farm

Harker's Farm

Plex La

Small La S

Halsall La

Trundle Pie La

Narrow Lane Farm

5

Wanishar La

Moor Farm

Ship Inn (PH)

Gibbon's Farm

Lowland Farm

Dicconson's Farm

Shepherd's Farm

Shepherd's La

Goores Farm

Clieves Hills Farm

Booth's La

08

School La
Delf Cl
Woods Cl

Rosemary La

L39

Firs La

4

Delf La

Rosemary Farm

Blundell House Farm

Dicconson's La

Clieves Hills

Fir Tree La

3

Downholland Hall

Bye La

Poplar Farm

Firs Farm

Firs La

Clieves Hills La

Double Bank Farm

Small La

07

Bank Farmhouse

Broad La

B5195

2

Scarisbrick Arms (PH)

Black-a-moor La

Works

Tanpit Farm

Formby La

1

Altcar La

Downholland Cross

Mairscough La

Leeds & Liverpool Canal

Green's La

L31

Green's Lane Farm

Walsh Hall

Back La

Birches Brow Farm

B5195

Mill La

B5195

Altcar Lane Farm

06

Lydiate Brook

L31

A5147

| 36 | A | B | 37 | C | D | 38 | E | F |

13
5

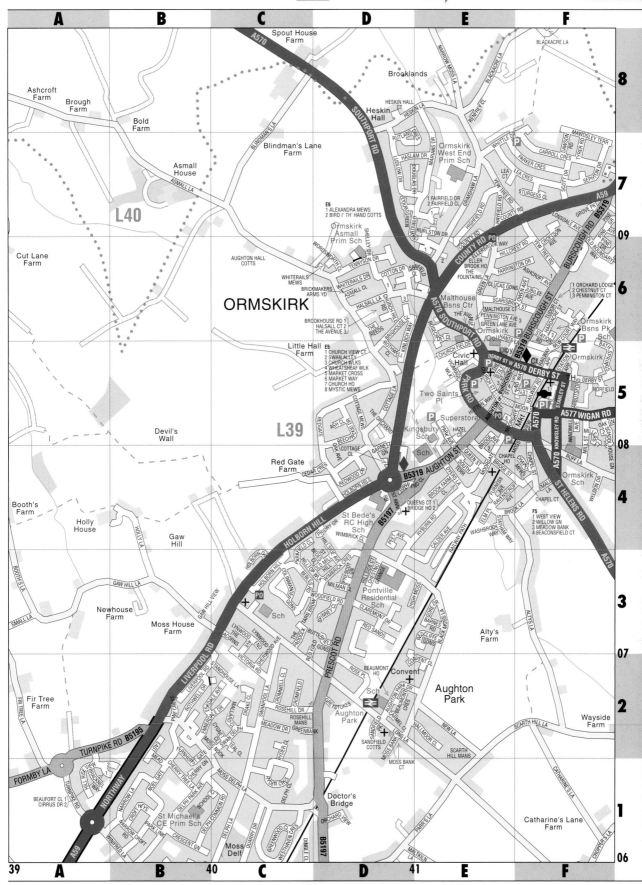

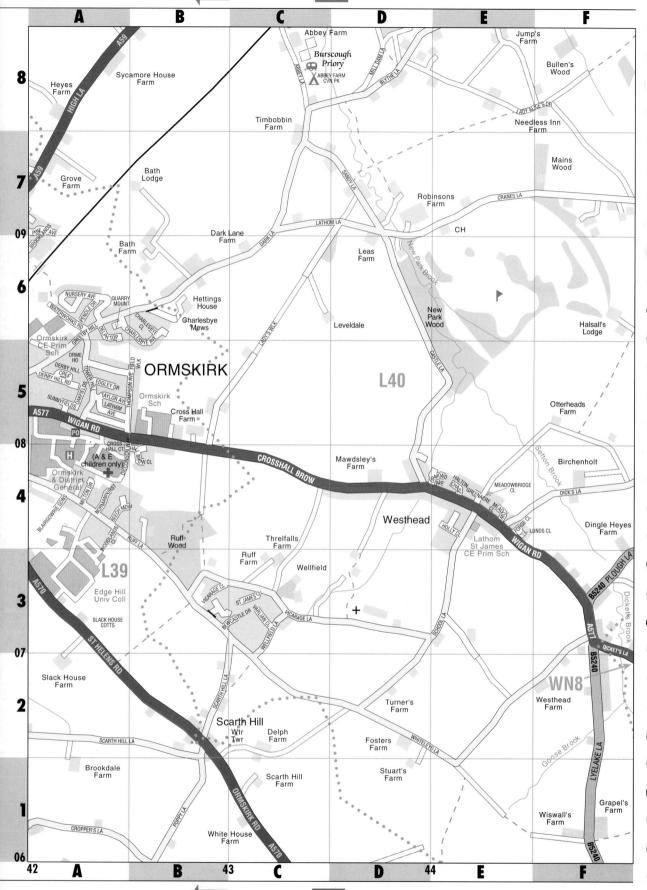

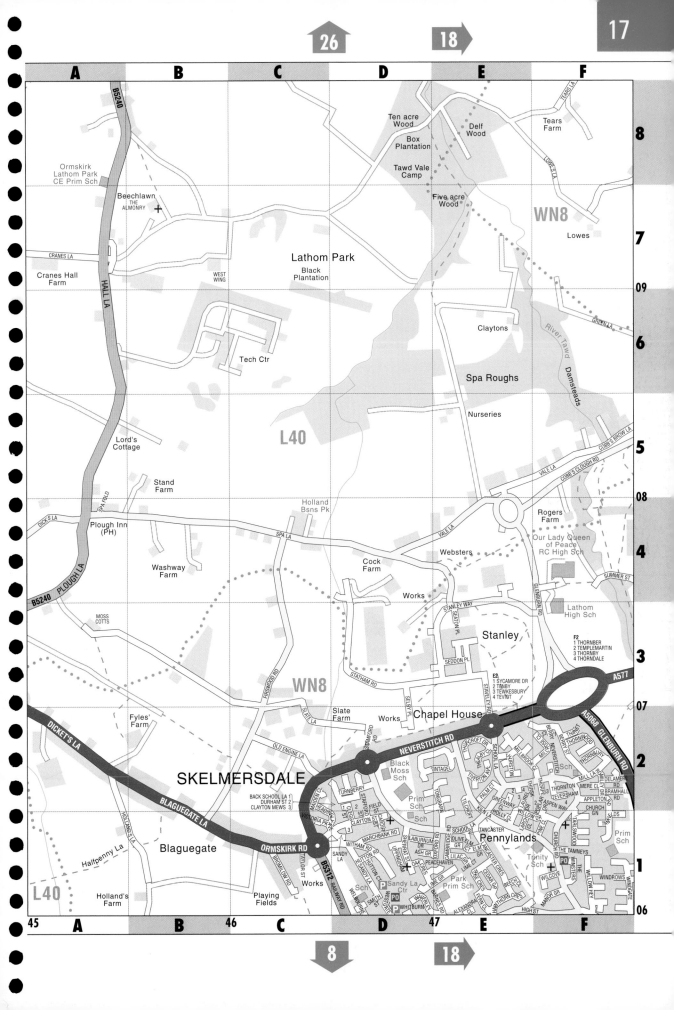

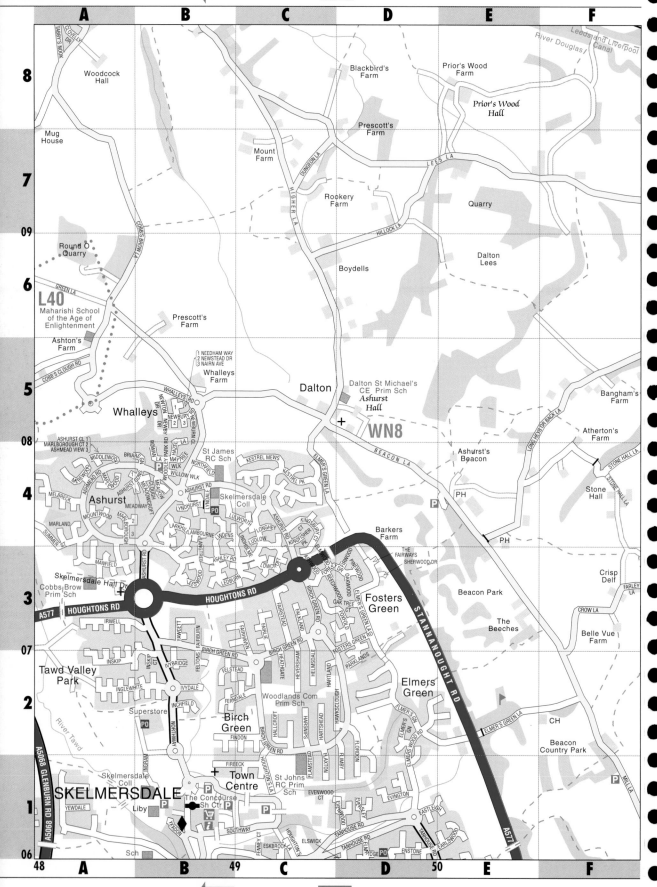

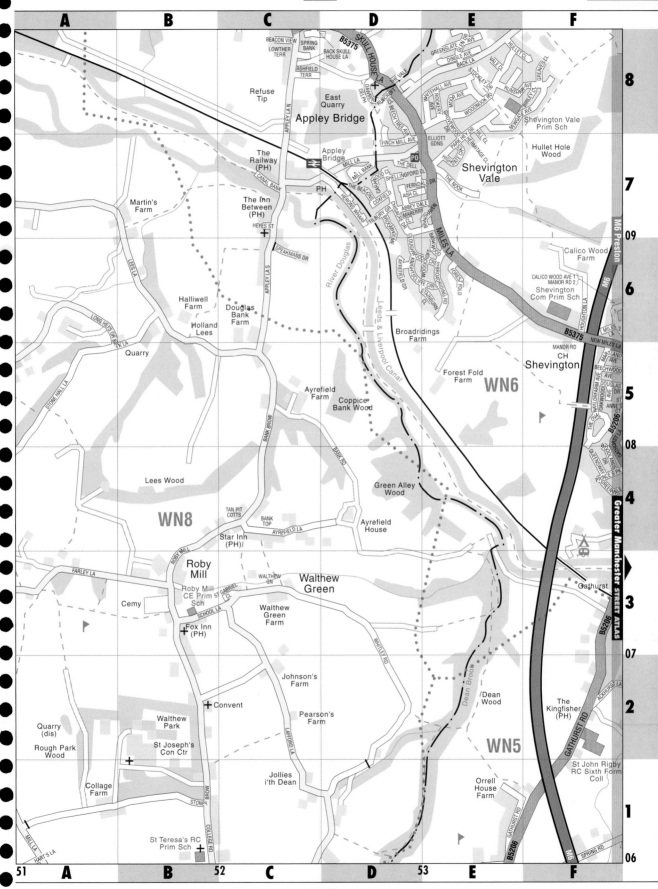

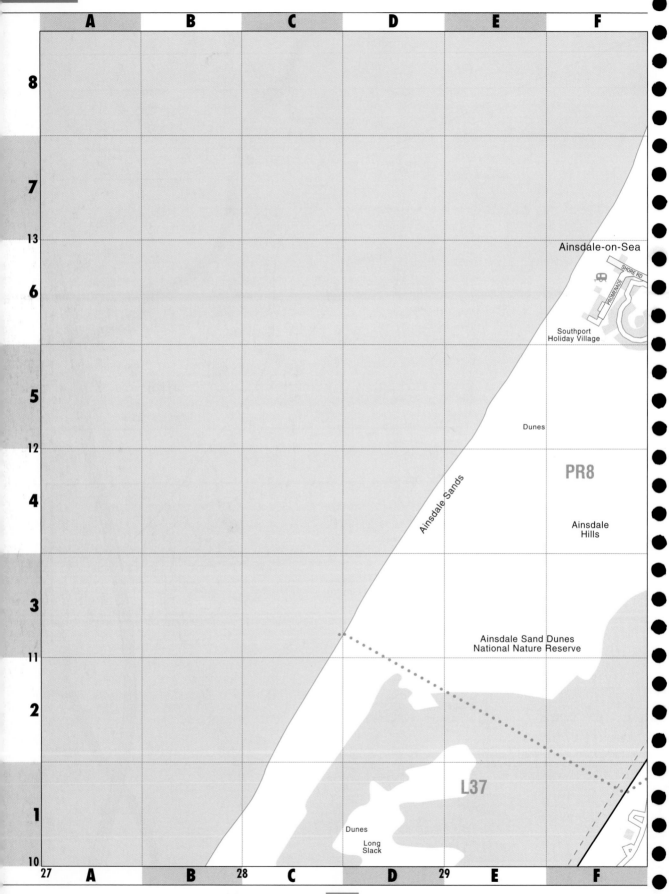

Ainsdale-on-Sea

SHORE RD

PROMENADE

Southport
Holiday Village

Dunes

PR8

Ainsdale Sands

Ainsdale
Hills

Ainsdale Sand Dunes
National Nature Reserve

L37

Dunes

Long
Slack

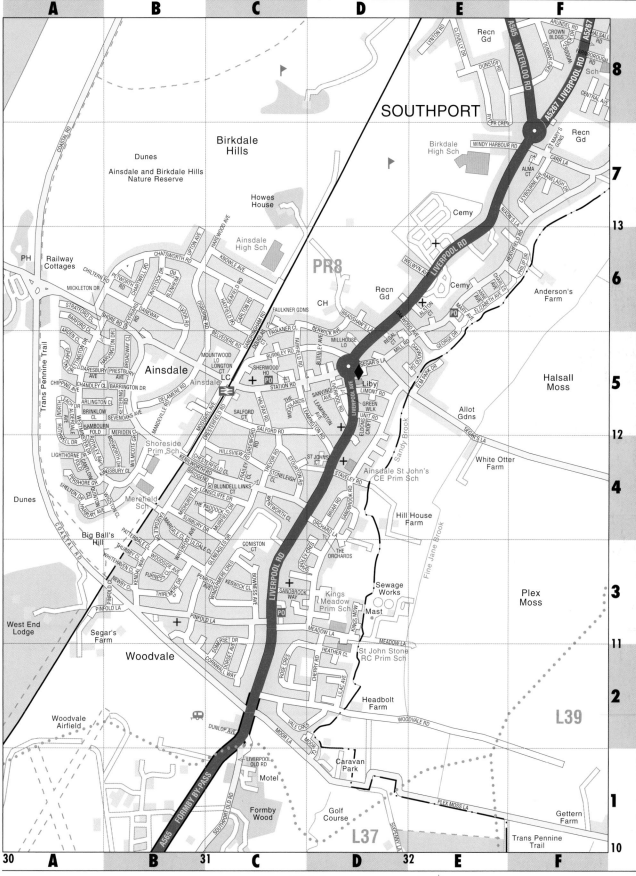

A B C D E F

8

7

13

6

5

12

4

3

11

2

1

10

PR8

White Moss Farm

BIRKDALE COP B5243

Hodge's Farm

Shaftesbury Ave
Halsall Rd
Blythe Mews
Suffolk Rd
Essex Rd
Guildford Rd
New Cut Cl
Central Ave

Farnborough Road Inf & Jun Schs

Gorsehill Farm

Fine Jane's Brook

Boundary Brook

London La

Renacres Moss

East Crantum Farm

London Farm

SHAW CL

King's Covert

The Willows

NEW CUT LA

SHAWS GARTH

New Moss

PENACRES LA

Halsall Moss

Old Canal

Short Ranks Farm

Manor House Farm

BARLOW'S LA

CABIN LA

Olverston House

HEADBOLT LA

L39

SEGAR'S LA

New Cut Brook

Rain Bag

SPENCER'S LA

Barn House Farm

Front Covert

MICHAEL'S LA

Heather Farm

Green Kettle House

PLUMPTON LA

Colonel's Holt

Plex Moss

Gettern Mere Farm

CARR MOSS LA

Holt Farm

Carr Moss

PLEX MOSS LA

33 A B 34 C D 35 E F

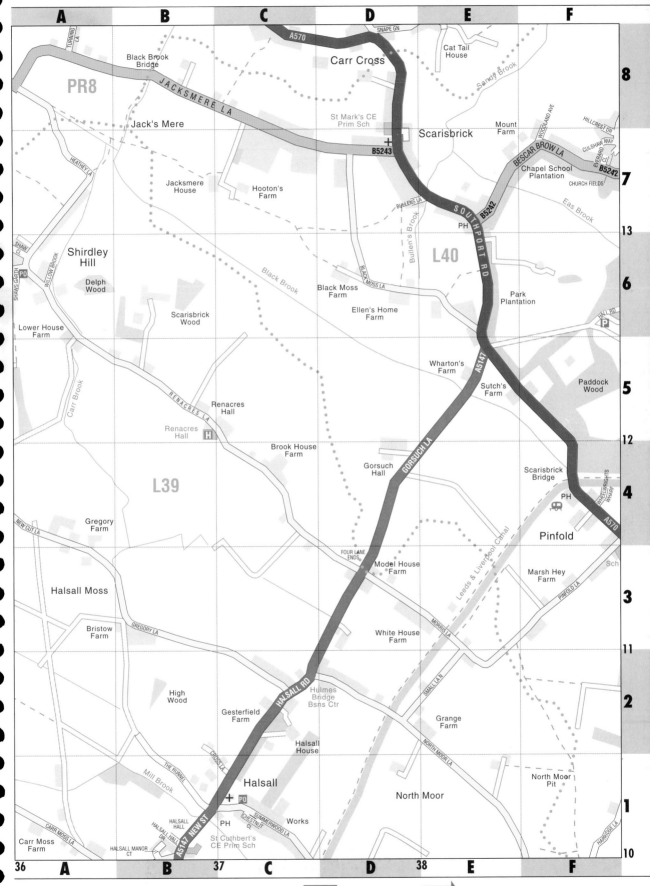

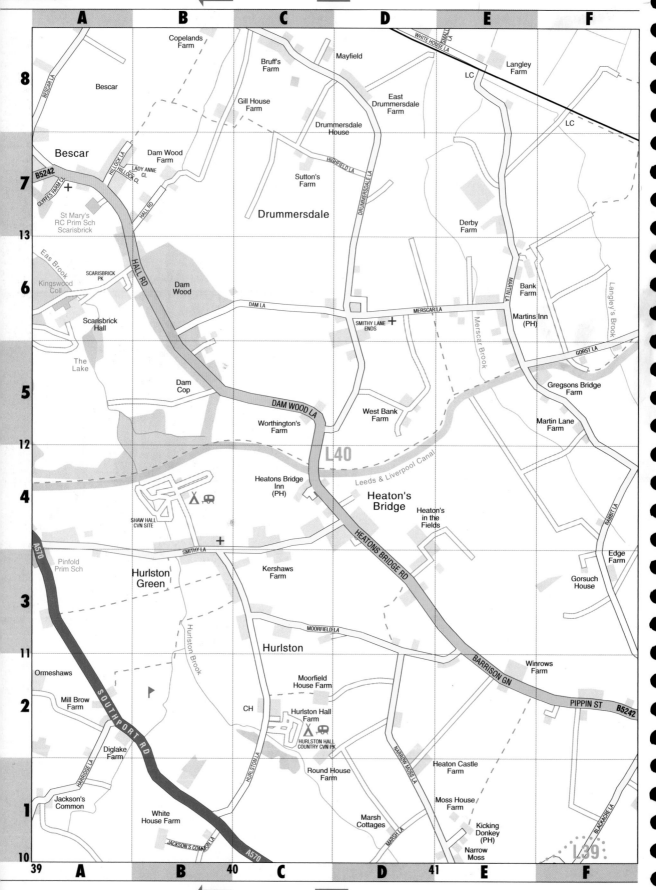

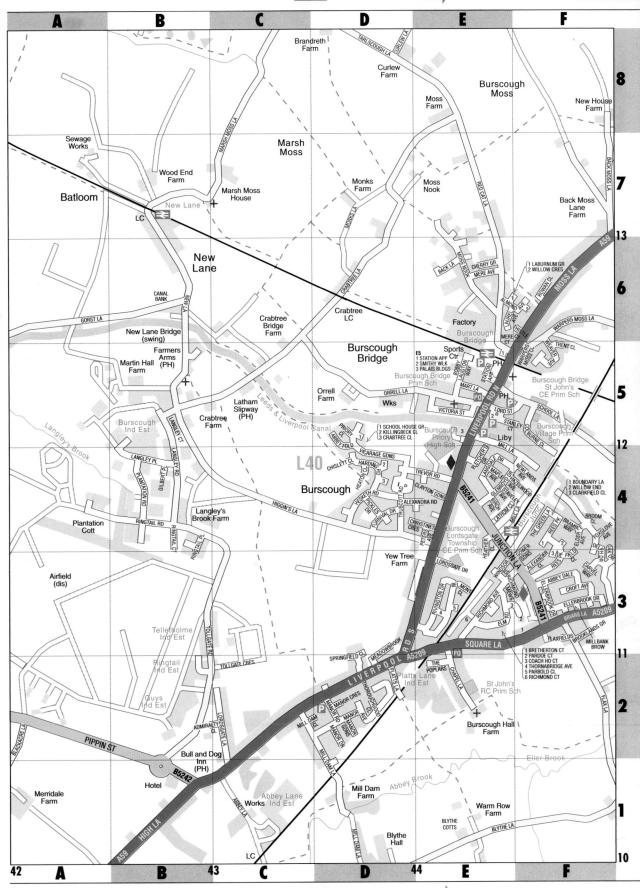

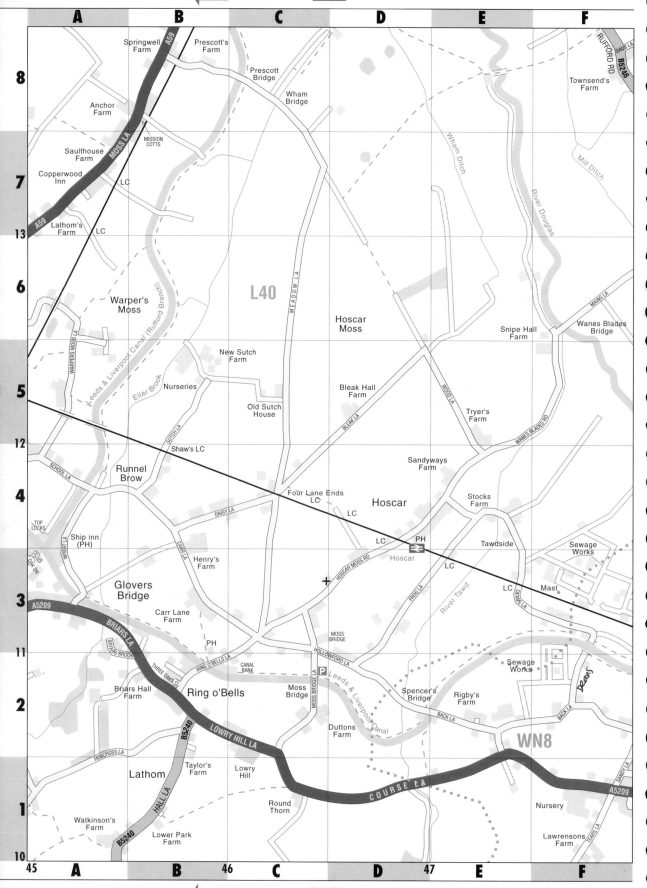

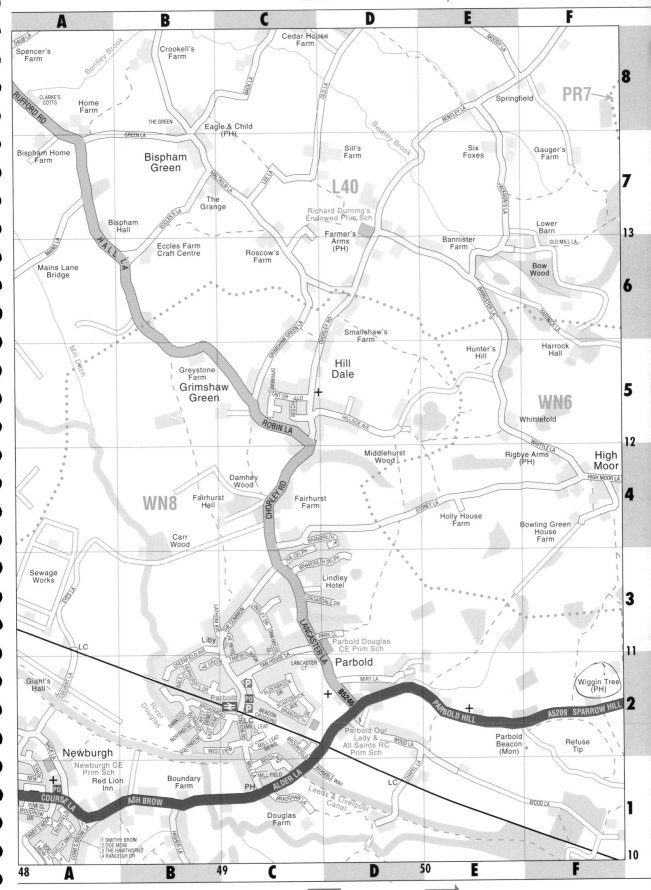

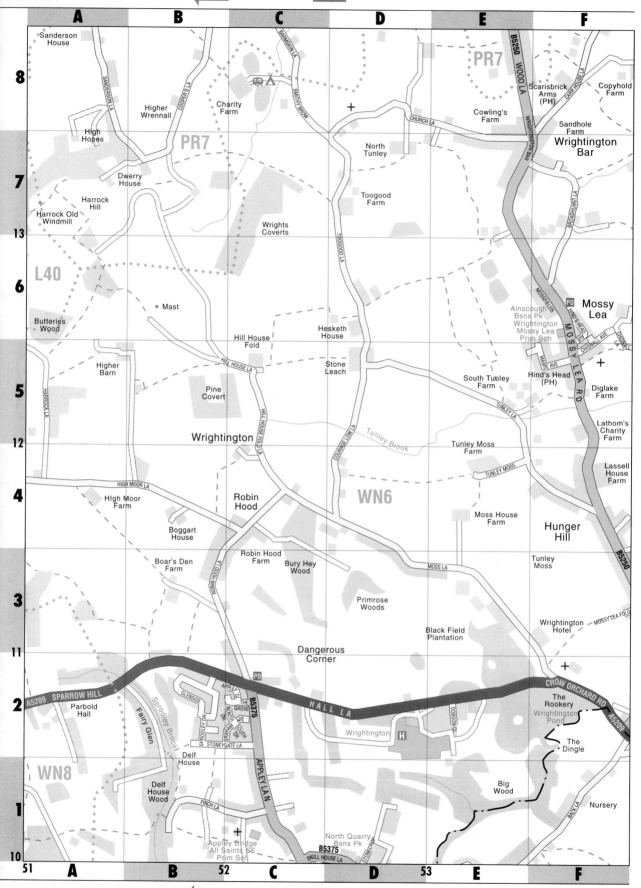

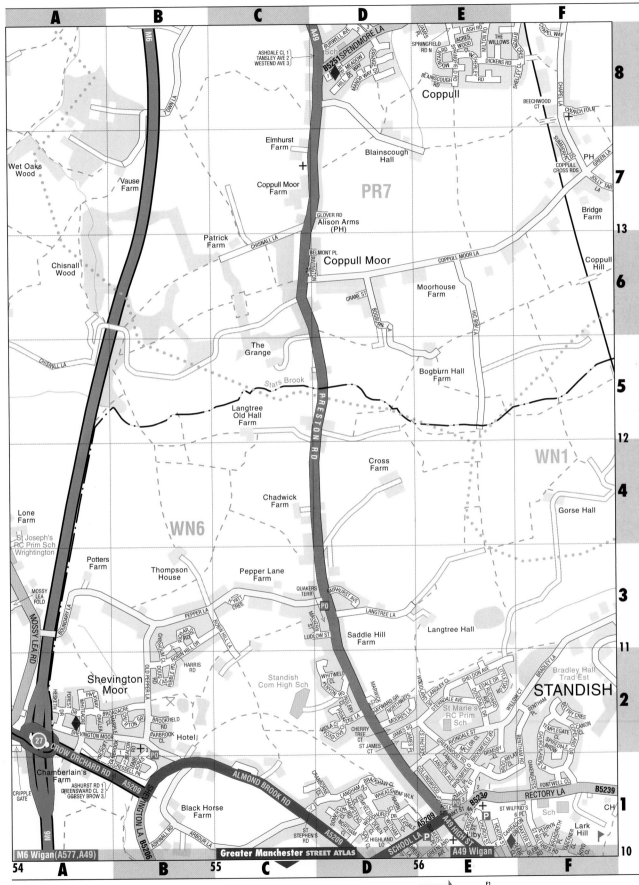

A B C D E F

8
7
13
6
5
12
4
3
11
2
1
10

M6 Wigan (A577, A49)

Greater Manchester STREET ATLAS

A49 Wigan

54 A 55 B C 56 D E F

E1
1 BRADLEY LA
2 BRAMLEY CT
3 WELL CT
4 The Standish Ctr
5 MOODY ST
6 ST WILFRID'S WAY

Coppull

PR7

Coppull Moor

WN1

WN6

STANDISH

Wet Oaks Wood

Vause Farm

Chisnall Wood

Elmhurst Farm

Coppull Moor Farm

Blainscough Hall

Patrick Farm

Alison Arms (PH)

Belmont Pl

Moorhouse Farm

Coppull Hill

Bridge Farm

The Grange

Stars Brook

Bogburn Hall Farm

Langtree Old Hall Farm

Cross Farm

Gorse Hall

Lone Farm

St Joseph's RC Prim Sch Wrightington

Chadwick Farm

Potters Farm

Thompson House

Pepper Lane Farm

Saddle Hill Farm

Langtree Hall

Shevington Moor

Standish Com High Sch

St Marie's RC Prim Sch

Bradley Hall Trad Est

Chamberlain's Farm

Black Horse Farm

Lark Hill

Cripple Gate

ASHDALE CL 1
TANSLEY AVE 2
WESTEND AVE 3

ASHURST RD 1
GREENSWARD CL 2
GOBSEY BROW 3

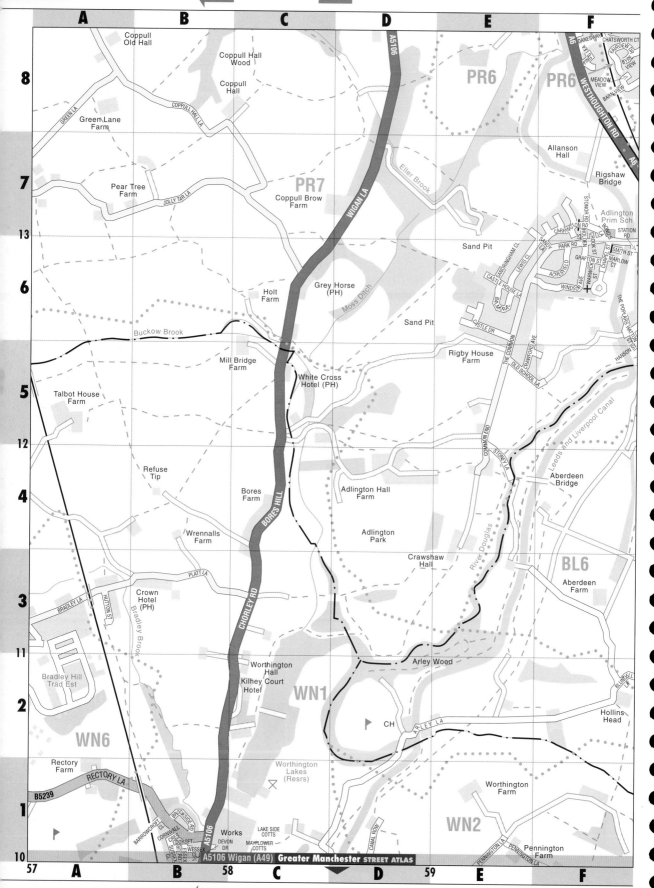

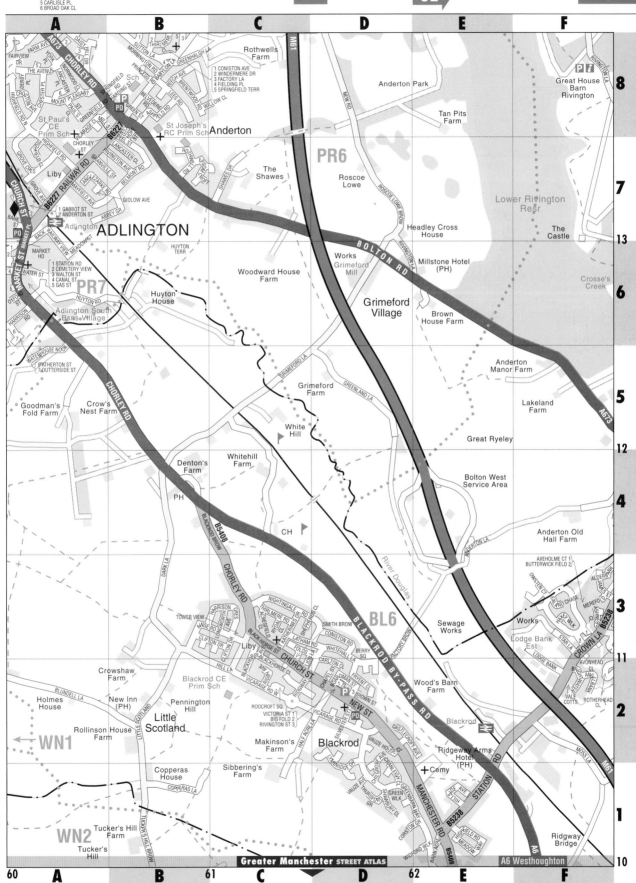

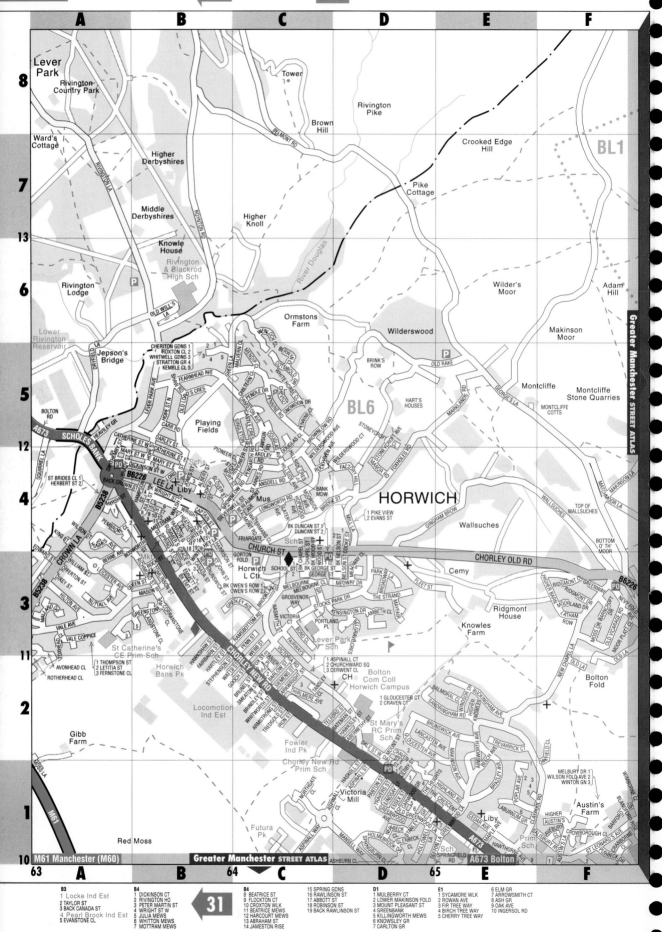

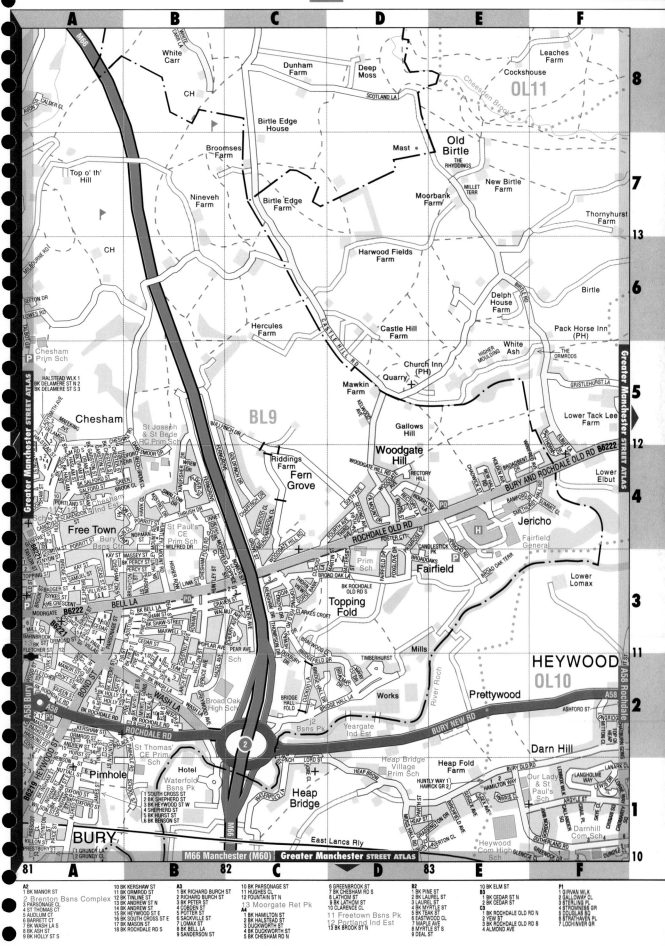

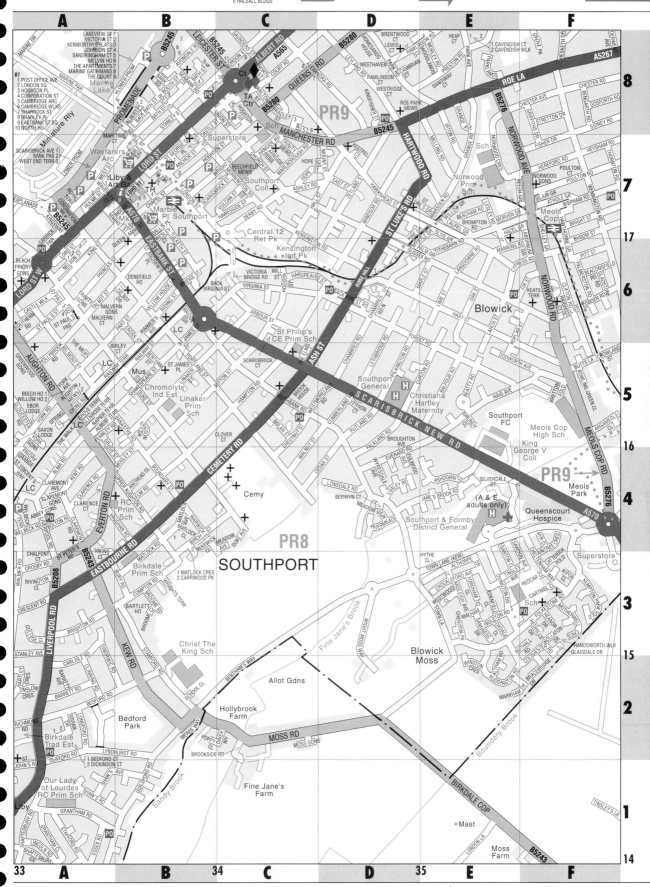

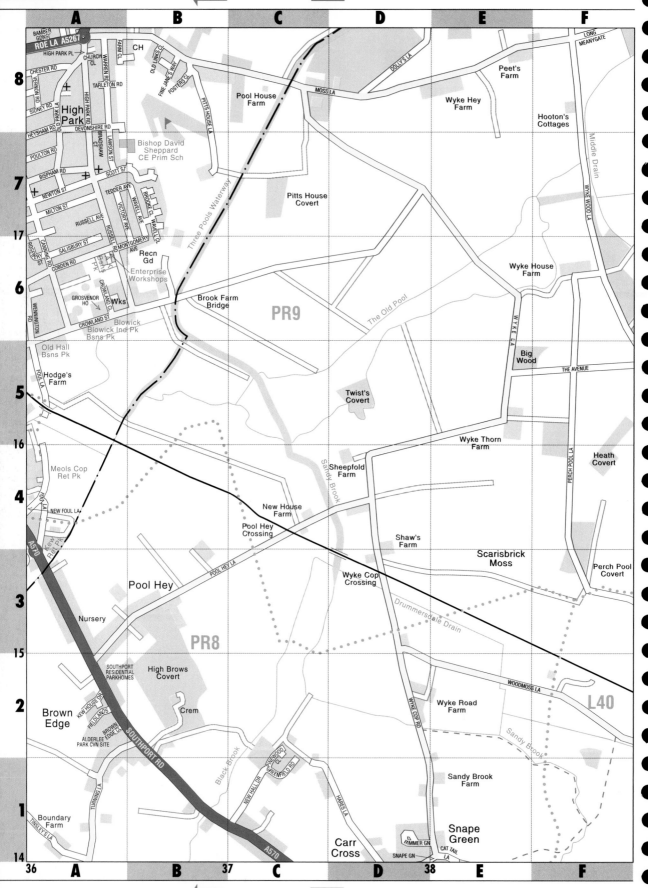

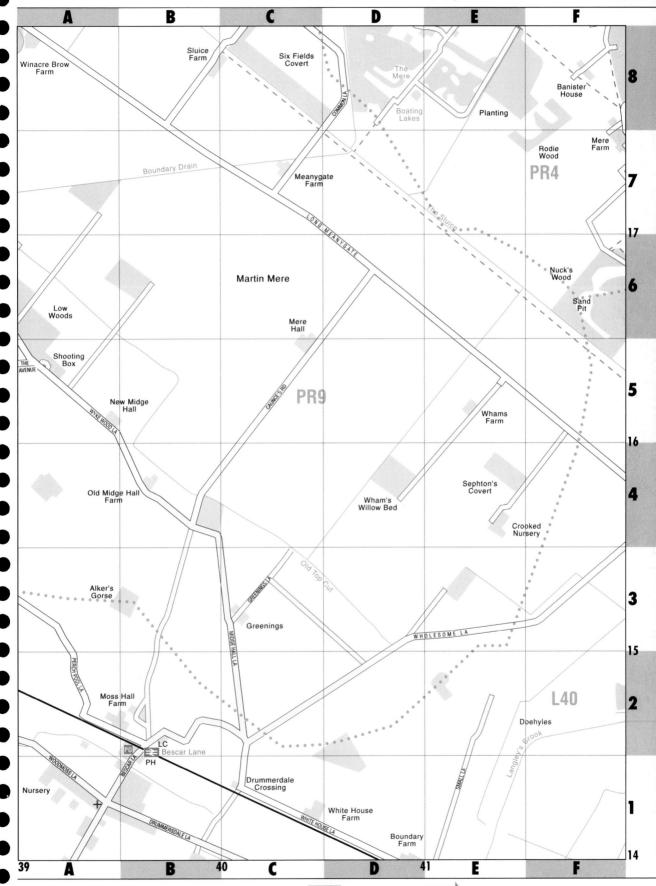

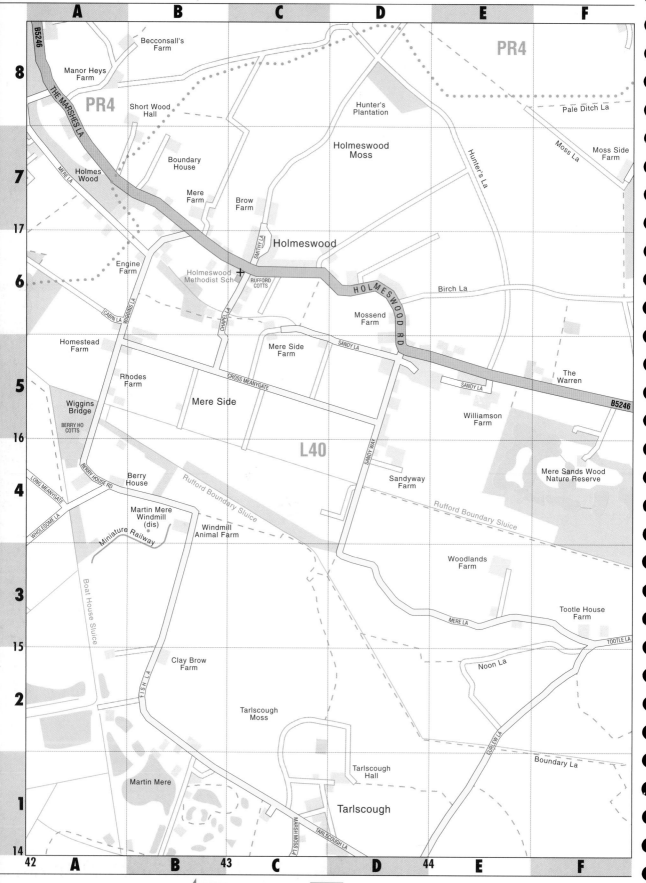

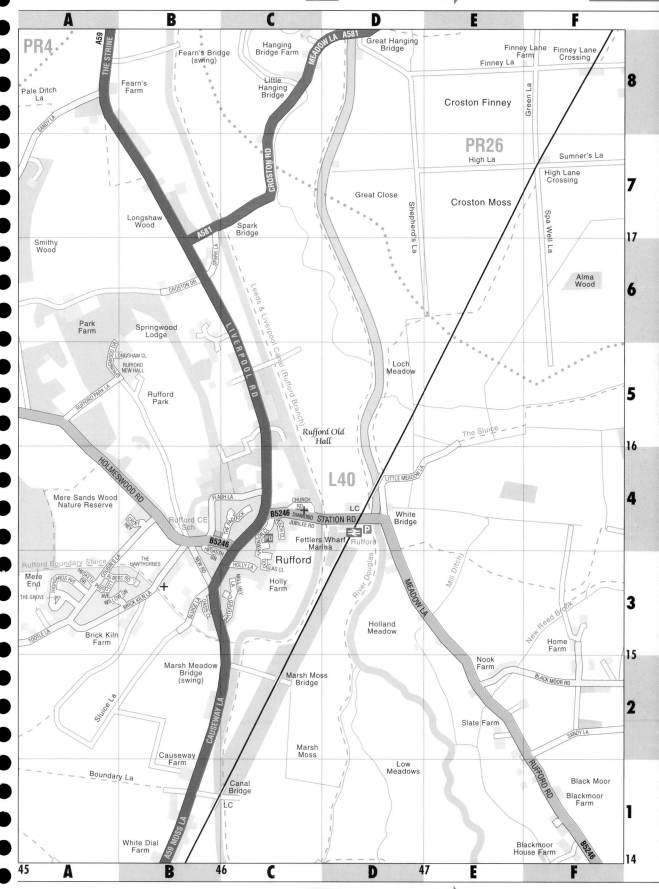

39
58

A | B | C | D | E | F

8

Square's Wood

Gravel Farm

Croston Mill

River Yarrow

Silcock's Wood

CARR LA

MOSS LA

Croston Park

Croston Big Wood

Henrietta Covert

Syd Brook Hall Farm

Sumner's Farm

SUMNER'S LA

PR26

Moss House Farm

7

Keeper's Wood

CARR LA

Moss Wood

Old Wood

NEW RD

Forshaw's Wood

Midge Hall Farm

SYD BROOK LA

PR7

17

Lord's Wood

Hunter's Wood

Syd Brook Lane Farm

Syd Brook

6

Croston Moss

Syd Brook Farm

Tincklers Bridge

TINCKLERS LA

Robin Hood (PH)

Wood Lane Farm

Boundary Farm

WOOD LA

Nook Farm

NOOK LA

TANNERSMITH LA

Mawdesley Moss

5

HAND LA

Caunce Wood

Cliffs Farm

16

Townfield Wood

Moss House

BLUE STONE LA

L40

4

Back House

Rector's Wood

Barretts Farm

Old Reed Brook

GATES LA

New Reed Brook

Brook Farmhouse

Black Bull (PH)

Gouldings Farm

SALT PIT LA

3

Mawdesley St Peter's CE Prim Sch

HALL LA

DARK LA

15

P

GN

PO

SYCAMORE CL

Hurst Green

TANNBECK DR

Mawdesley Hall

Towngate

HURST

NEW ST

THE WILLOWS

ASHTREES

BROOKFIELD

SMITHY LA

BRADSHAW BROW

BRANDRETH

RIDLEY LA

2

Mawdesley

SS Peter & Paul RC Prim Sch

Black Moor

HIGH ST

GORSEY LA

BACK LA

Monk's Farm

MOODY LA

BACK LA E

Tootles Farm

1

Joy Bank Farm

SANDY LA

SCHOOL LA

Four Lane Ends

Cedar Farm Galleries

OLD LA

House Farm

BENTLEY LA

14

DAUB LA

48 | A | B | 49 | C | D | 50 | E | F

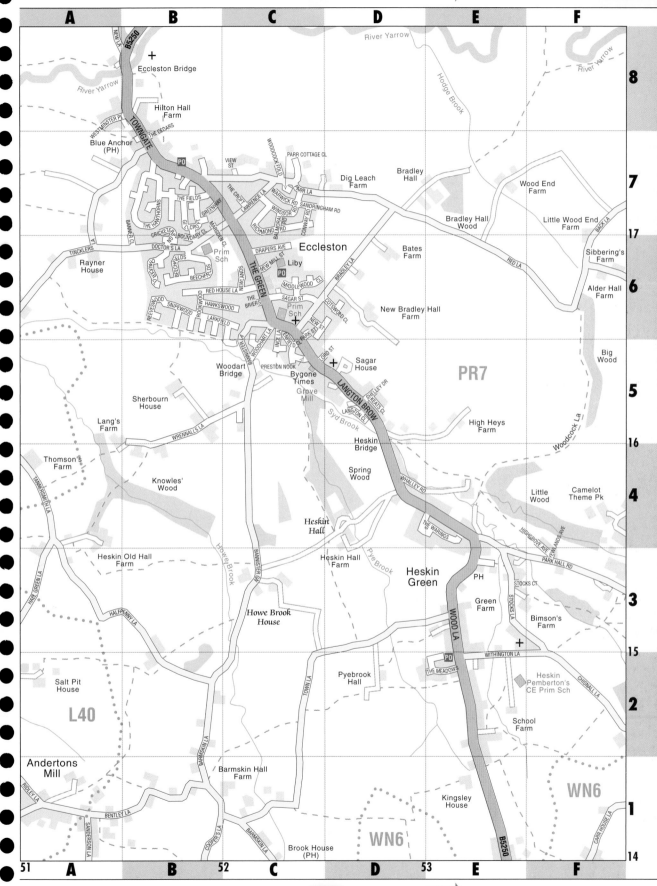

A B C D E F

8

SOUTHPORT RD
A581
Ackhurst Bsns Pk & Ind Est
FOXHOLE RD
ACKHURST RD

River Yarrow

Pincock
Charnock's Farm
PINCOCK ST
PINCOCK BROW
WIGAN RD A49
CROSS BROW
Pincock Bridge
Old House Farm
LUCAS AVE
GERMAN LA
Superstore
Fox Hole Wood
Sewage Works
Common Bank Employment Area
COMMON BANK LA
ACKHURST RD
COPPERWOOD WAY
Chorley West Bsns Pk
JOHNS WOOD CL

Bolton Green

7

Ratho Park Farm
MILL LA
BACK LA
Calderbank Farm
SIBBERING BROW
CHARNOCK BROW
Charnock Brow Farm
Valley Farm
River Yarrow
Common Bank
Wallets Wood
BURGH LA

17

Worsley Farm
Charnock Old Hall
OLD HALL LA
Bowling Green (PH)
Tan House Farm
DELPH LA
Yarrow Farm
GREAT WOOD CL 1
KEEPERS WOOD WAY 2
DENHAM WOOD WAY 3
BEECH HO 4
CEDAR HO 5

6

New Park Hall
Charnock Green
Roscoe House
Willow Tree Farm

Parker's i' th' Fields

5

Charnock House
DELPH LA
Parker's Wood
KINGFISHER CL 1
FIELDFARE CT 2
RAVEN CL 3
WOODLARK DR

16

Dam Wood
Hotel
Fisher's Farm
Iddon House Farm

4

P
Park Hall L Ctr
P
P
PRESTON RD
BROOK LA
Charnock House Farm
FOUR LANE ENDS
DARLINGTON CT
PO
PR7
Charnock Richard
MEADOWLANDS
CHURCH LA
LICHEN CL
ALMA DR
CHURCH FOLD
NURSERY CL PH
LEESON AVE
DOB BROW
Sharrocks Farm
COPPULL RD
B5251
BIRKACRE RD

3

P
PARK HALL RD
P
Charnock Richard Service Area
CHARTER LA
CHORLEY LA
WILLOW DR
ROBIN CL
NEARGATES
WHITE GATE FOLD
FREEMAN'S
ALDER DR
SOUTHGATES
MERE FOLD
SHARRATS PATH
NEW RD
BIRKACRE BROW

15

Welch Farm
Motel
MILL LA
Yew Tree Farm
CROSTON LA
Haydocks Farm
Row High Wood
HOLLY OAKS
BIRCHWOOD DR
THE LAURELS
PEAR TREE AVE
PLANTOLT LA
HOLT AVE
LONGFIELD AVE
THE BRAMBLES
PLEASANT VIEW
OAKWOOD CL
LONGWORTH AVE

2

CARR HOUSE LA
Chisnall House
Guest's Farm
THE FOXWOOD
Hind's Head (PH)
Coppull Ent Ctr
Coppull
NORTHENDEN RD
MOSS BANK
MAVIS DR
MOSS LA
MILL LA
STATION RD
THE HEYS
CLAYGONTATE
PUE HEY DR
HURST BROOK
THE CHESTNUTS
BROOKSIDE
GOOSE GREEN AVE

1

WN6
Knob Farm
TOWN LA
Haydock Farm
Whittle Bridge Farm
PARK RD
ARCON RD
BENTHAM ST
REGENT ST
KIMBERLEY ST
HEWLETT ST
DARLINGTON ST
CHAPEL WLK
Sch
LANCASTER ST
ALDER GR
CHAPEL LA
CHANCERY CL

14

M6
A49
TANSLEY AVE
WESTEND AVE
TANYARD CL
SPENDMORE LA
MILTON CT
B5251
Liby
BIRCH RD
PO
SOUTH RD
BAKER ST
HOLWAY
Sch

54 A 55 B C 56 D E F

E1
1 GERMAN LA
2 CLEVELAND ST
3 SPRINGFIELD RD N
4 MILL ST
5 ARCON HO

C8
1 SPRINGFIELD RD
2 WOODVILLE RD
3 CROWN ST
4 ST THOMAS'S SQ
5 BACK MOUNT
6 MEALHOUSE LA

7 CHORCLIFFE HO
8 KELLETT ST
9 STANLEY PL
10 HIGH ST
11 CANNON ST
12 MARKET PL
13 FAZAKERLEY ST

14 BACK FAZAKERLEY ST
15 FOUNDRY ST
16 ST MARY'S WLK
17 DEVONSHIRE CT

61

D8
1 PORTLAND ST
2 BRUNSWICK ST
3 East Chorley Bsns Ctr
4 MACKAY CROFT
5 MACKENZIE CL
6 CAMERON CROFT

44

D8
7 SANDHAM ST
8 HOUGHTON ST
E8
1 WHIMBERRY CL
2 COLYTON RD E
3 THE CAUSEWAY

4 THE MOORINGS
5 CHATHAM PL
6 HEALD ST
7 BRIGHTON ST
8 TEMPERANCE ST
9 PIKESTONE CT
10 ALBANY CT

43

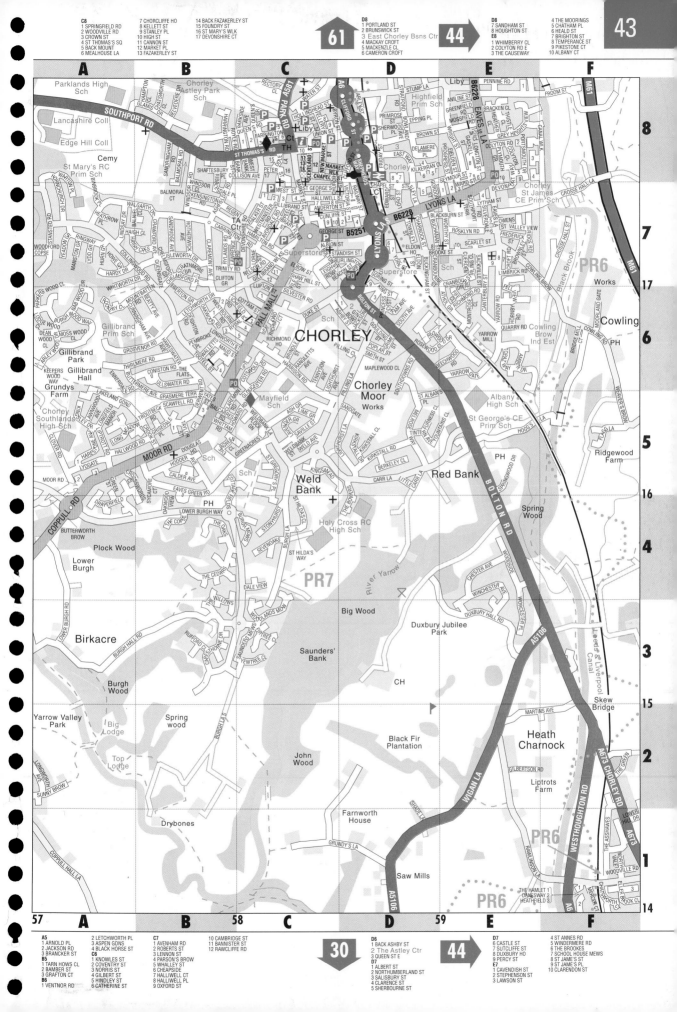

A5
1 ARNOLD PL
2 JACKSON RD
3 BRANCKER ST
B5
1 TARN HOWS CL
2 BAMBER ST
3 GRAFTON CT
B6
1 VENTNOR RD

2 LETCHWORTH PL
3 ASPEN GDNS
4 BLACK HORSE ST
C6
1 KNOWLES ST
2 COVENTRY ST
3 NORRIS ST
4 GILBERT ST
5 HINDLEY ST
6 CATHERINE ST

C7
1 AVENHAM RD
2 ROBERTS ST
3 PARSON'S BROW
4 WHALLEY ST
5 CHEAPSIDE
6 HALLIWELL CT
7 HALLIWELL PL
8 OXFORD ST

10 CAMBRIDGE ST
11 BANNISTER ST
12 RAWCLIFFE RD

30

D6
1 BACK ASHBY ST
2 The Astley Ctr
D7
1 ALBERT ST
2 NORTHUMBERLAND ST
3 SALISBURY ST
4 CLARENCE ST
5 SHERBOURNE ST

44

D7
6 CASTLE ST
7 SUTCLIFFE ST
8 DUXBURY HO
9 PERCY ST
E7
1 CAVENDISH ST
2 STEPHENSON ST
3 LAWSON ST

4 ST ANNES RD
5 WINDERMERE RD
6 THE BROOKES
7 SCHOOL HOUSE MEWS
8 ST JAMES S ST
9 ST JAMES'S PL
10 CLARENDON ST

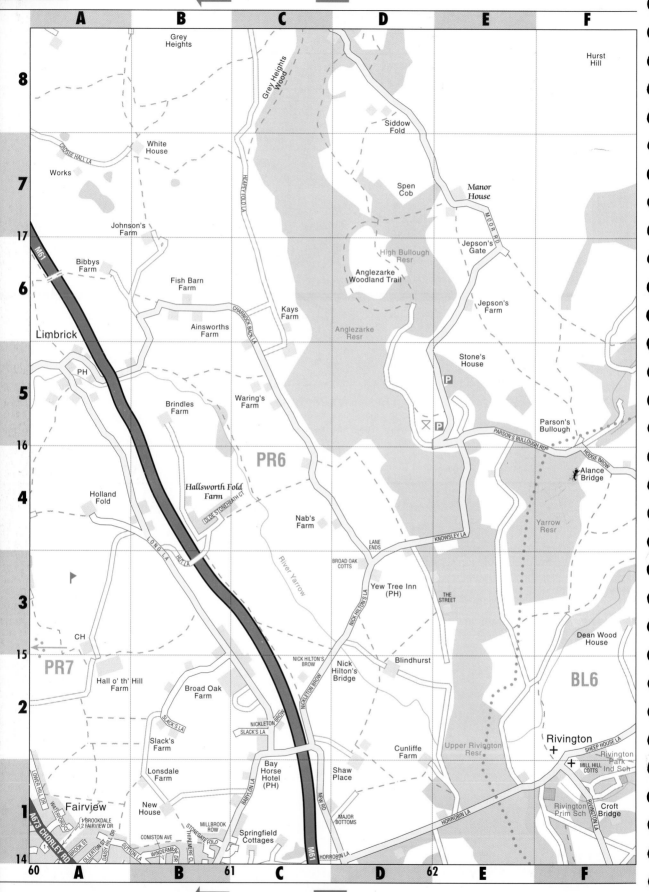

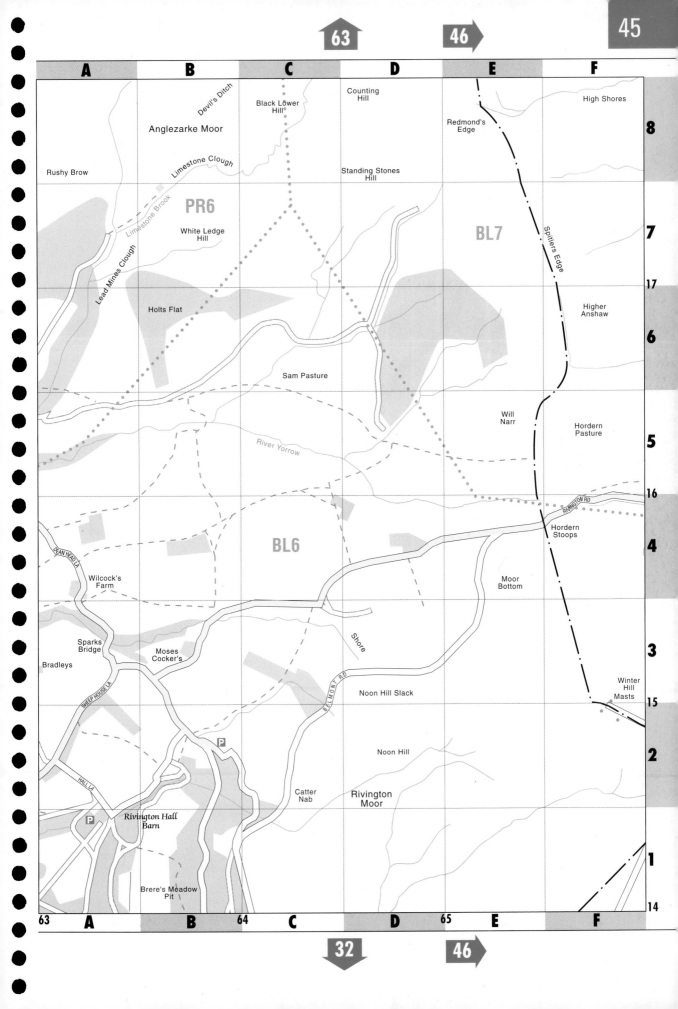

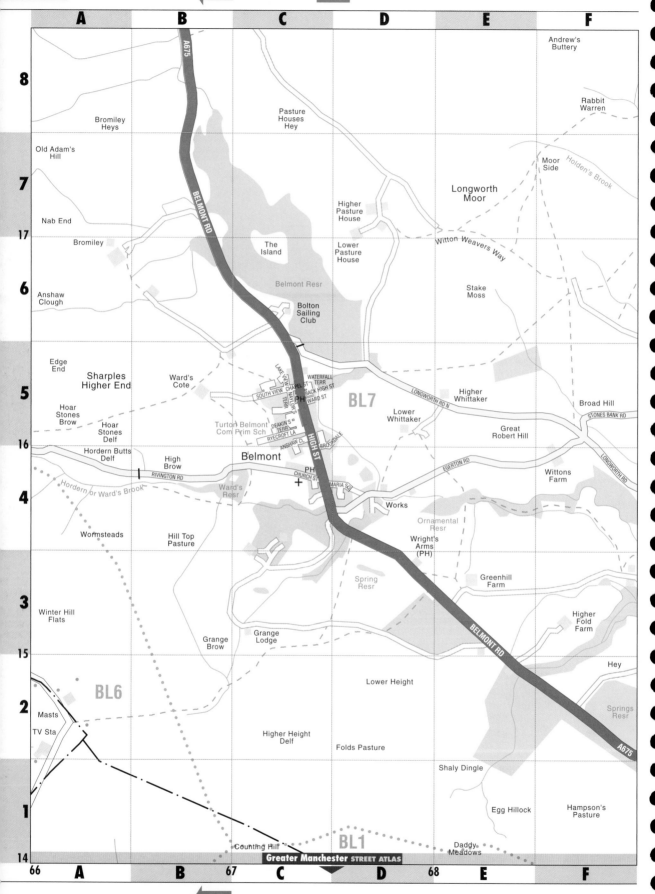

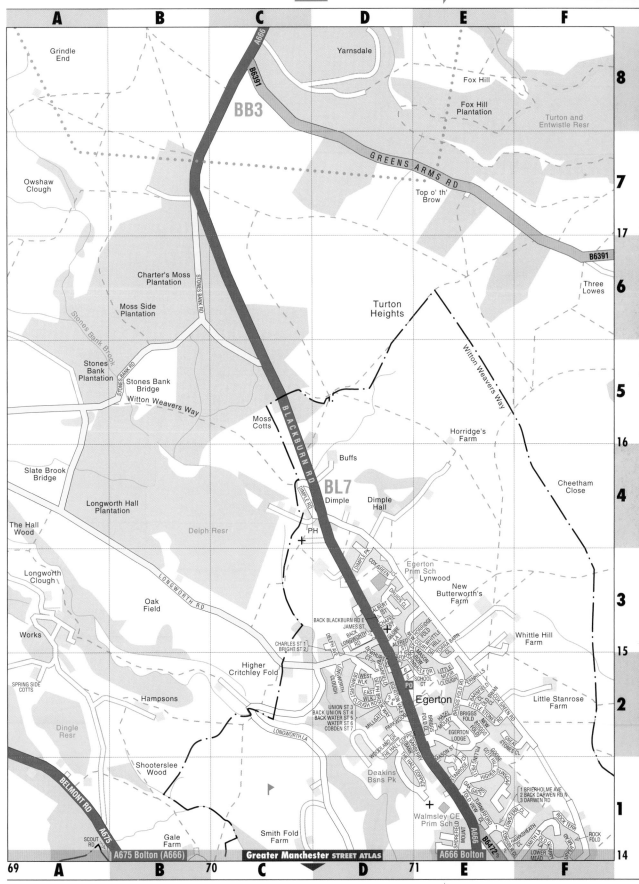

A | B | C | D | E | F

8

Grindle End

Yarnsdale

Fox Hill

Fox Hill Plantation

Turton and Entwistle Resr

BB3

A666

B6391

Owshaw Clough

GREENS ARMS RD

7

Top o' th' Brow

17

B6391

Charter's Moss Plantation

Three Lowes

6

Moss Side Plantation

Turton Heights

Stones Bank Brook

STONES BANK RD

Stones Bank Plantation

Witton Weavers Way

Stones Bank Bridge

Witton Weavers Way

5

Moss Cotts

Horridge's Farm

16

Buffs

BLACKBURN RD

BL7

Slate Brook Bridge

Dimple

Dimple Hall

Cheetham Close

4

DIMPLE RD

Longworth Hall Plantation

Delph Resr

PH

The Hall Wood

LONGWORTH RD

Oak Field

Egerton Prim Sch

Lynwood

New Butterworth's Farm

3

Longworth Clough

ALBERT ST

COY GREEN

Works

Back Blackburn Rd E

JAMES ST

BACK LONGWORTH RD

Whittle Hill Farm

15

CHARLES ST 1

BRIGHT ST 2

Spring Side Cotts

Higher Critchley Fold

DELPH AVE

LONGWORTH CLOUGH

WEST WLK

EAST WLK

Little Stanrose Farm

2

Hampsons

Egerton

UNION ST 3

BACK UNION ST 4

BACK WATER ST 5

WATER ST 6

COBDEN ST 7

MILLGATE

Egerton Lodge

LONGWORTH LA

Shooterslee Wood

WOODLAND GR

THE HALL COPPICE

Deakins Bsns Pk

1 BRIERHOLME AVE
2 BACK DARWEN RD N
3 DARWEN RD

1

A675

BELMONT RD

SCOUT RD

Gale Farm

Smith Fold Farm

Walmsley CE Prim Sch

A666

B6472

ROCK TERR

ROCK FOLD

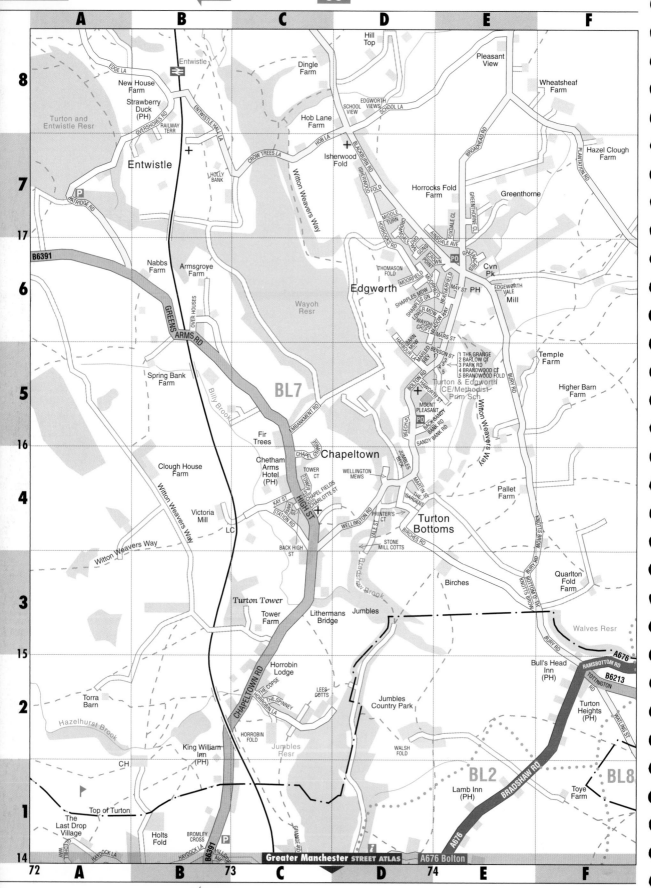

Greater Manchester STREET ATLAS · A676 Bolton

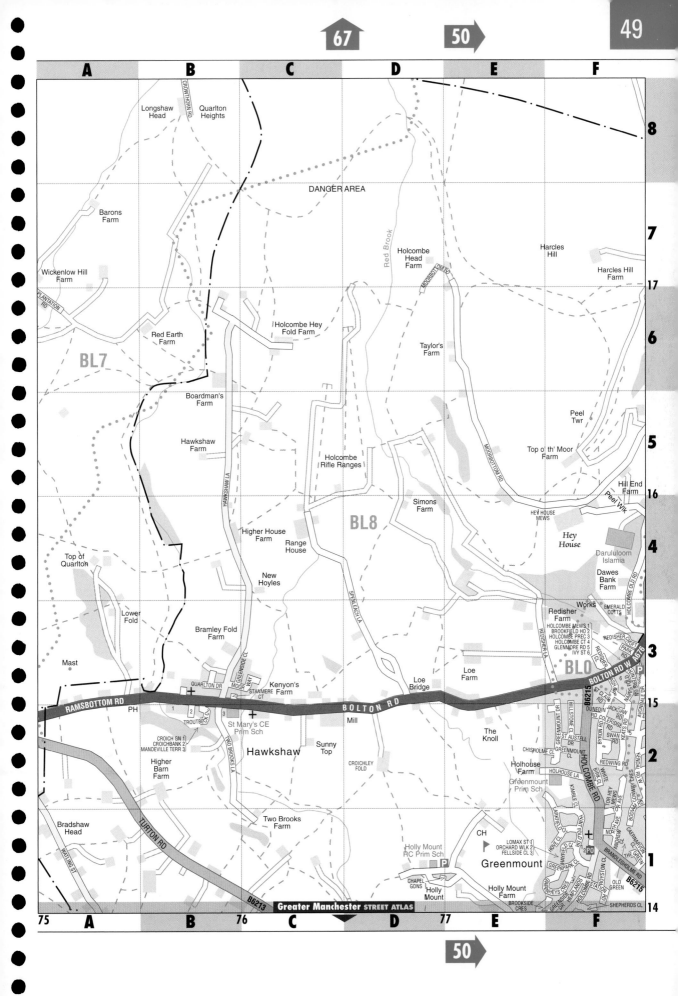

A B C D E F

8
7
17
6
5
16
4
15
3
2
1
14

DANGER AREA

Longshaw Head
Quarlton Heights
CROWTHORN RD

Barons Farm

Wickenlow Hill Farm

PLANTATION RD

BL7

Red Earth Farm

Boardman's Farm

Hawkshaw Farm

HAWKSHAW LA

Top of Quarlton

Lower Fold

Mast

Holcombe Hey Fold Farm

Red Brook

MOORBOTTOM RD

Holcombe Head Farm

Harcles Hill

Harcles Hill Farm

Taylor's Farm

Peel Twr

Top o' th' Moor Farm

Hill End Farm
Peel Wlk

HEY HOUSE MEWS

Hey House

Darululoom Islamia

Dawes Bank Farm

HOLCOMBE OLD RD

Works

EMERALD COTTS

Redisher Farm

HOLCOMBE MEWS 1
BROOKFIELD HO 2
HOLCOMBE PREC 3
HOLCOMBE CT 4
GLENMORE RD 5
IVY ST 6

REDISHER CROFT

REDISHER LA

BLO

BOLTON RD W A676

B6215

Holcombe Rifle Ranges

BL8

Simons Farm

Higher House Farm

Range House

New Hoyles

SPENLEACH LA

Bramley Fold Farm

GREENSIDE CL

QUARLTON DR

MOOR WAY

STANMERE CT

Kenyon's Farm

Loe Bridge

Loe Farm

RAMSBOTTOM RD
PH

TROUTBECK CL

St Mary's CE Prim Sch

BOLTON RD

Mill

The Knoll

HILLSTONE CL

GREENMOUNT DR

St AUSTELL

DUNEDIN
HACKAW
COLERIDGE RD
SWAN ST

AVONDALE RD

BYRON RD
BIRCH RD

Greenmount CL

REDWING RD

WHITE CL

1
2
3

CROICH GN 1
CROICHBANK 2
MANDEVILLE TERR 3

TWO BROOKS LA

Hawkshaw

Sunny Top

CROICHLEY FOLD

Holhouse Farm

HOLCOMBE RD

KIMBLE CL

Greenmount Prim Sch

Higher Barn Farm

Bradshaw Head

TURTON RD

WATLING ST

Two Brooks Farm

Holly Mount RC Prim Sch
P

CH

Greenmount

LOMAX ST 1
ORCHARD WLK 2
FELLSIDE CL 3

HOPE CL

HAYFIELD

GREENPARK CL

GREENPARK CRES

CHAPEL GDNS

Holly Mount

Holly Mount Farm

BROOKSIDE CRES

ROYSTON CL

B6215

OLD GREEN

SHEPHERDS CL

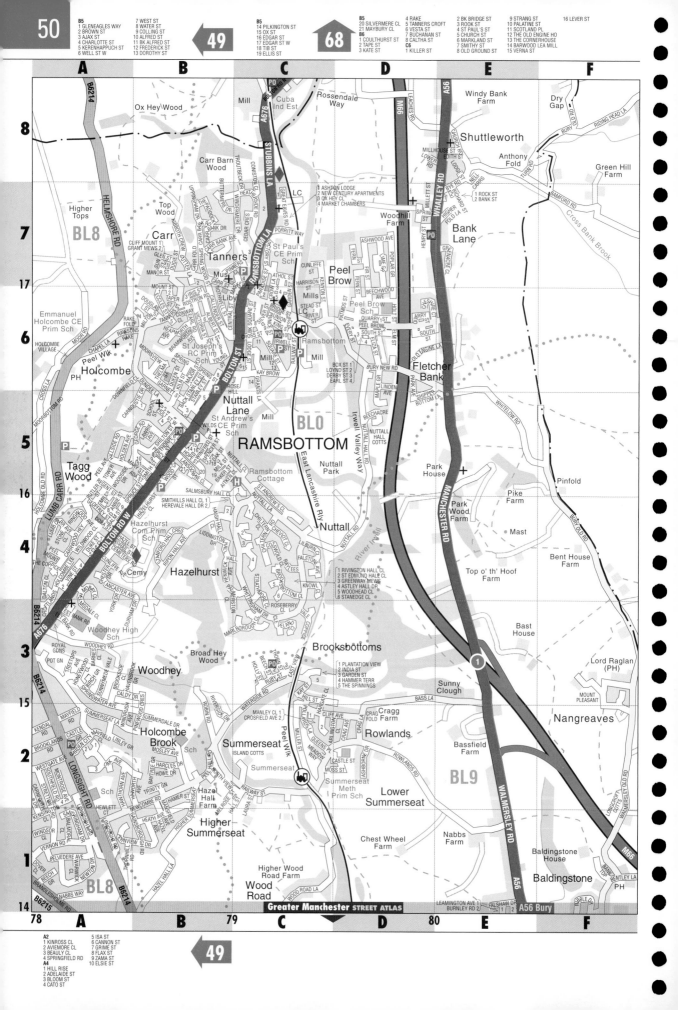

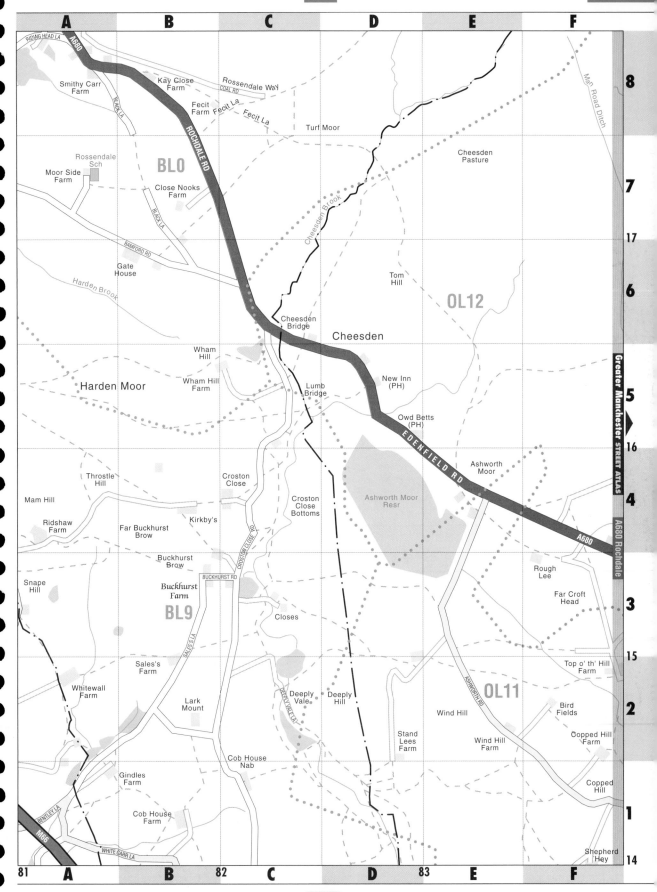

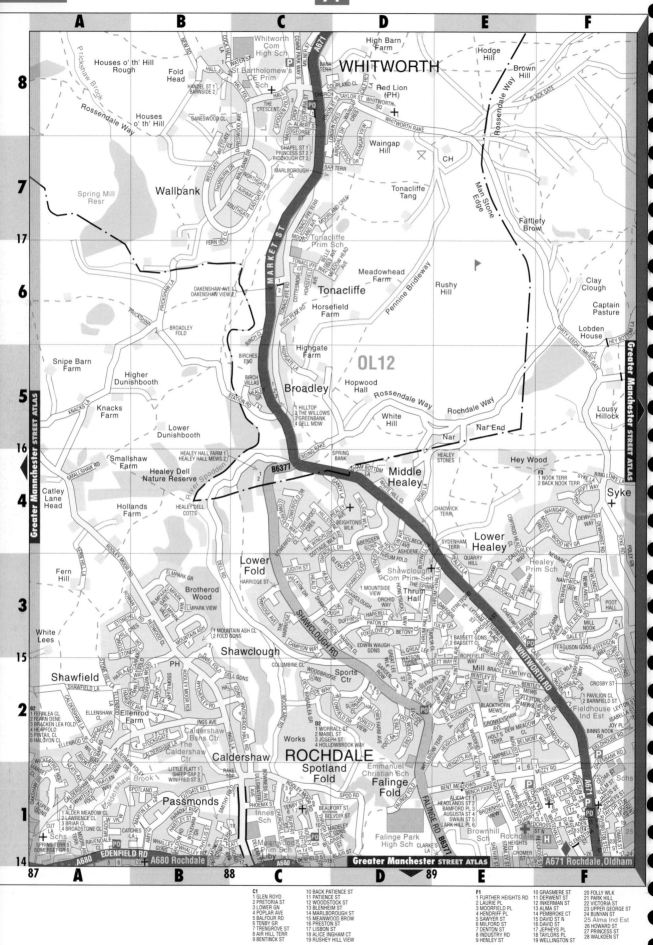

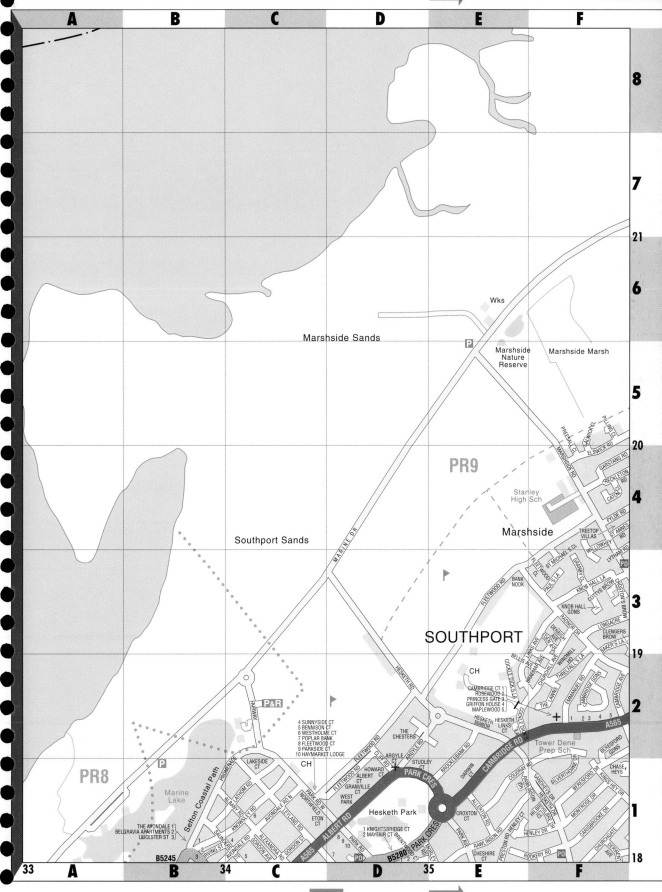

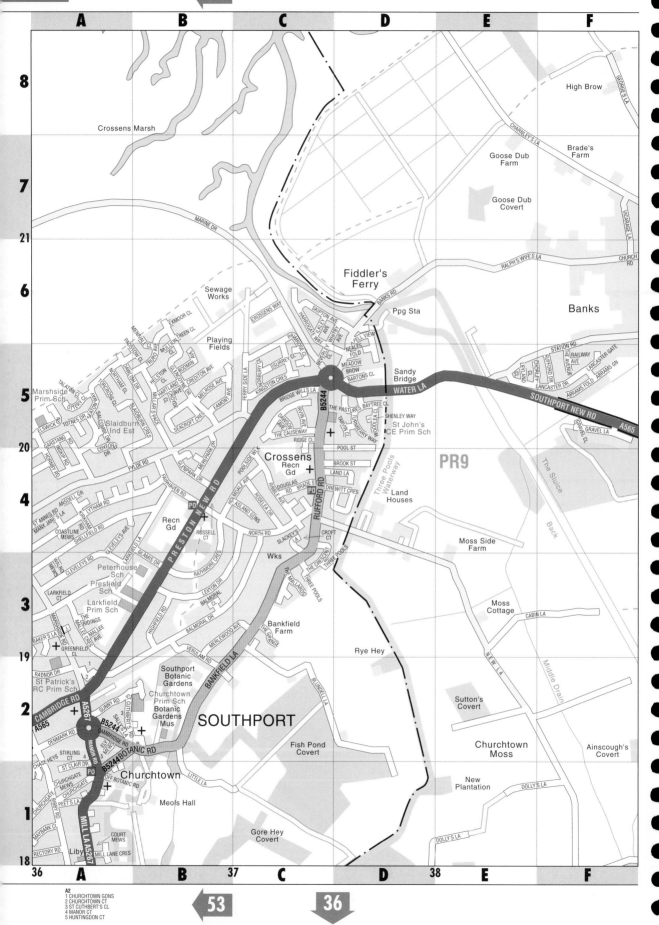

A   B   C   D   E   F

8

7

21

6

Crossens Marsh

High Brow

Goose Dub Farm

Brade's Farm

Goose Dub Covert

CHARNLEY'S LA

GEORGE'S LA

VICARAGE LA

CHURCH RD

Marine Dr

Fiddler's Ferry

RALPH'S WIFE'S LA

Banks

Sewage Works

Ppg Sta

Banks Rd

CROSSENS WAY

SKIPTON AVE

ILKLEY

WHITBY

HARROGATE WAY

BEVERLEY

PRIMROSE CL

FELL VIEW

NEALES FOLD

MEADOW BROW

BARTONS CL

Sandy Bridge

STATION RD

RAILWAY AVE

THE AVENUE

RUFFORD DR

CHORLEY

LEYLAND CL

LANCASTER GATE

ABRAMS FOLD

ABRAMS GN

WATER LA

SOUTHPORT NEW RD   A565

5

Marshside Prim Sch

Playing Fields

TALATON CL

OTTERY CL

AVON

SALCOMBE DR

MENHALE CL

PADSTOW CL

HURD AVE

MULLION

GLEBODMIN

HELSTON

HARTLAND CLOYDE

CREDITON DR

FERRY SIDE LA

TORRY CL

KINGSTON CRES

SURREY CL

PR MORSE CL

B5244

THE PASTURES

BAYTREE CL

SHENLEY WAY

St John's CE Prim Sch

GRAVEL LA

GRAVEL LA

20

ELSWICK RD

TOTNES CT

GARSTANG RD

HORNBY RD

TISKIP RD

NORTHAM CL

TORCROSS CL

CONVEY DR

FYLDE RD

MELROSE AVE

EAMONT AVE

SEACROFT CRES

GLENPARK DR

MEREPARK DR

BRIDGE WILLS LA

IRVIN AVE

DAWSON AVE

THE CAUSEWAY

RIDGE CL

Crossens Recn Gd

DOUGLAS RD

POOL-SIDE WLK

POOL ST

BROOK ST

LAND LA

Three Pools Waterway

Land Houses

PR9

The Sluice

Back

4

St ANNES RD

MARY JANE'S LA

ANSDELL GR

KIRKHAM RD

LYTHAM RD

CLEVELEYS DR

GLAMIS DR

FAIRHAVEN RD

HOLDALE AVE

ASLAND GDNS

ROSELEA DR

RIBBLE AVE

NORTH RD

SLACKEY'S LA

RUFFORD RD

PRESTON NEW RD

PO

Recn Gd

RUSSELL CT

B5244

DREWITT CRES

CROFT CT

PO

BRADE'S

Moss Side Farm

19

COASTLINE MEWS

SHELLFIELD RD

WALK RD

CLEVELEYS RD

Peterhouse Sch

Presfield Sch

RATHMORE DR

LEXTON DR

BALMORAL CL

BALMORAL DR

THE CRESCENT

THREE POOLS

Wks

THE MALLARDS

CABIN LA

Moss Cottage

3

LARKFIELD CT

MARSHSIDE RD

BAKER'S LA

Larkfield Prim Sch

THE RIDINGS

THE MALLEE

MALLEE GRVE

HIGHFIELD RD

VERULAM RD

MERLEWOOD AVE

THE GRANGE

Bankfield Farm

N EW LA

Moss

Rye Hey

Middle Drain

GREENFIELD CL

RADNOR DR

St Patrick's RC Prim Sch

Southport Botanic Gardens

BANKFIELD LA

BLUNDELL LA

Sutton's Covert

Churchtown Moss

Ainscough's Covert

2

CAMBRIDGE RD   A5267

A565

DENMARK RD

SUNNY RD

ST CUTHBERT'S CL

SALIX CL

CAMBRIDGE RD

B5244

Churchtown Prim Sch

Botanic Gardens Mus

SOUTHPORT

Fish Pond Covert

STIRLING CT

ST CLAIR DR

MANOR CT

B5244

BOTANIC RD

OFF BOTANIC RD

BOTANIC RD

LITTLE LA

New Plantation

DOLLY'S LA

1

CHASE HEYS

CHURCHGATE MEWS

CHURCHGATE

BIRBY RD

PEET'S LA

PO

Churchtown

Meols Hall

MILL LA   A5267

18

MAYBANK CL

RECTORY RD

Lib

COURT MEWS

MILL LANE CRES

Gore Hey Covert

DOLLY'S LA

36   A   B   37   C   D   38   E   F

A2
1 CHURCHTOWN GDNS
2 CHURCHTOWN CT
3 ST CUTHBERT'S CL
4 MANOR CT
5 HUNTINGDON CT

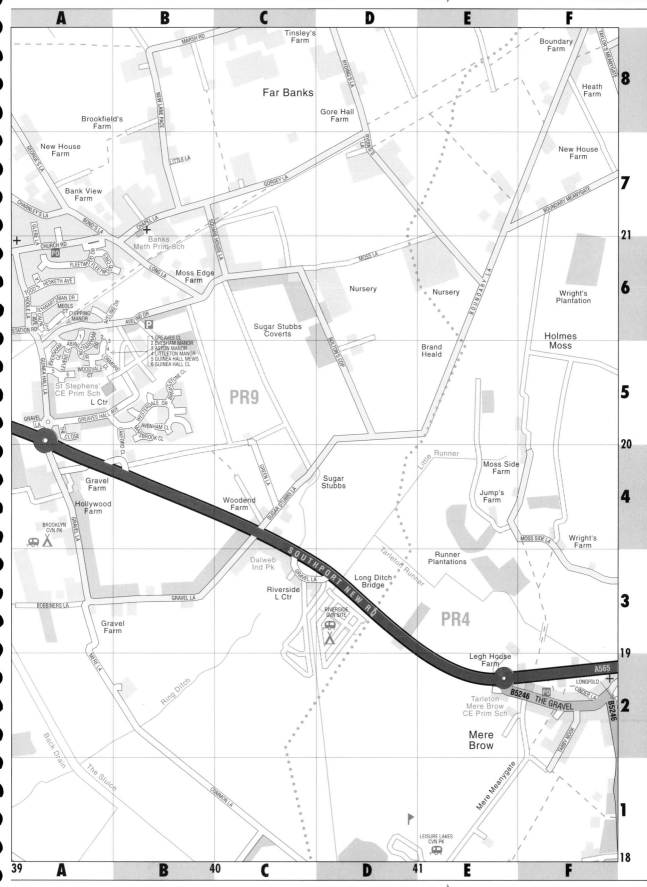

A B C D E F

MOSS LA

Aughton's
Farm

Moss
Farm

Tarleton
Com Prim Sch

Balls Farm

HESKETH LA

8

Blundell's
Farm

Greenfields

NAPIER AVE
PARTINGTON CL

HAZEL
GR

BOUNDARY MEANYGATE

DUCKWORTH LA

Dobson's
Farm

DANDY'S MEANYGATE

MIDDLE MEANYGATE

JOHNSON'S MEANYGATE

Carr Heys

HOWARD DR
HOMER AVE
CARR LA

7

Pribet
Farm

Carr Heys
Plantation

21

Johnson's
Farm

BOLTON'S MEANYGATE

Tarleton Moss

Johnson's
Farm

TAYLOR'S MEANYGATE

6

Chapel House
Farm

Farrington's
Plantation

SWORD MEANYGATE

NEW LA

Meanygate
Farm

Rose
Farm

GORSE LA

Nurseries

SUTTON LA
BYRON CL

OAKGATE CL

5

Crosses
Farm

BLACKGATE LA

Gorse Lane
Farm

20

PR4

LEGH LA

Green Lane
Farm

4

GREEN LA

SOUTHPORT NEW RD

Cookson's
Farm

Jackson's
Farm

Holmes

MOSS SIDE LA

3

MOSS HEY LA

HUNTER'S LA

BLACKGATE LA

Nurseries

TAYLOR'S LA

DOCTOR'S LA

Becconsall
Farm

Tarleton Runner

HIGHER LA

19

A565

MERE BROW LA

Resr

CHARLOTTE'S LA

BARN CL

Taylor's
La

2

PARK LA

Sewage
Farm

GREEN LA

THE MARSHES LA

1

B5246

Ashcroft's
Farm

Pale Ditch La

Smith's La

SMITH'S LA

Moss Side
Farm

18

42 A B 43 C D 44 E F

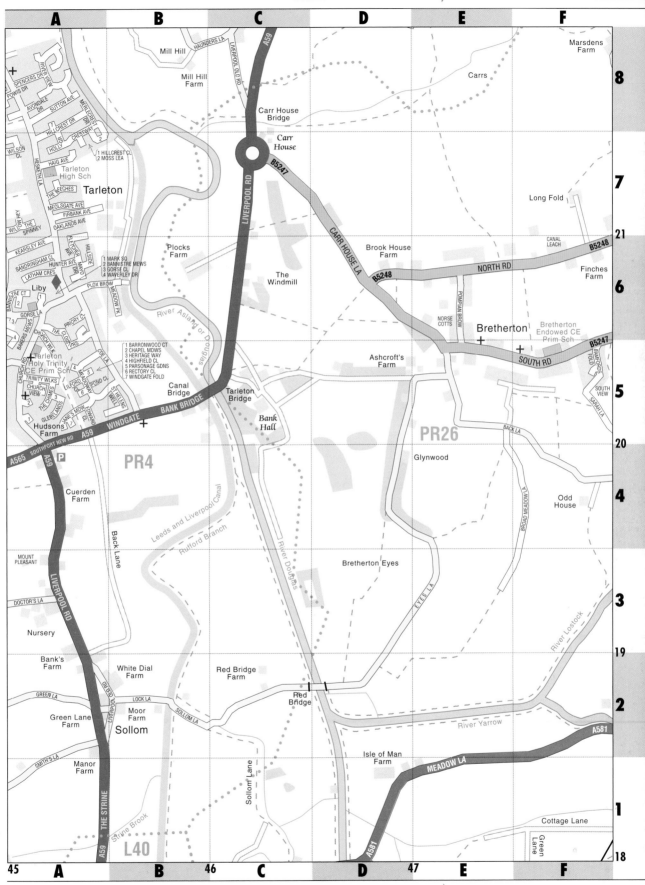

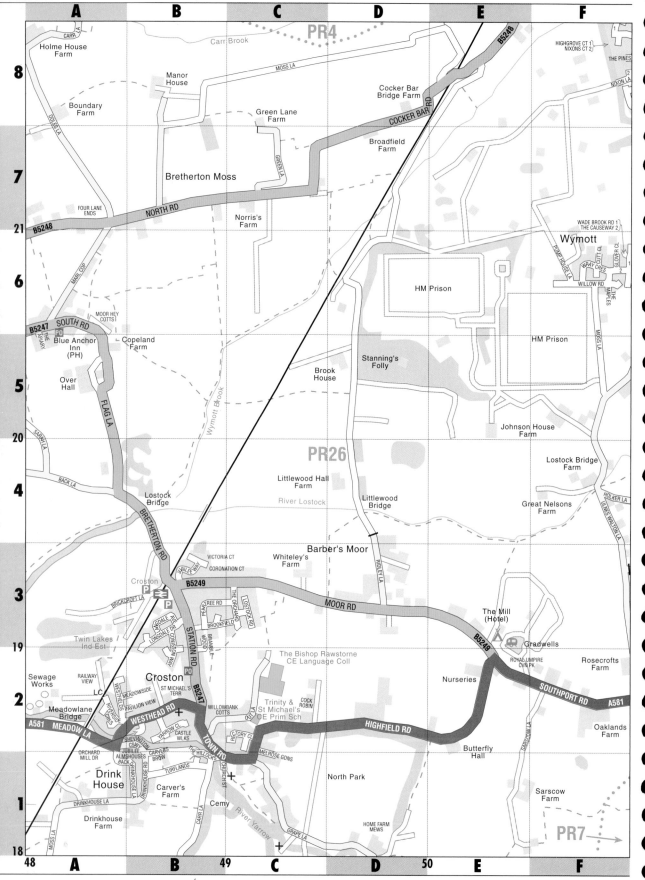

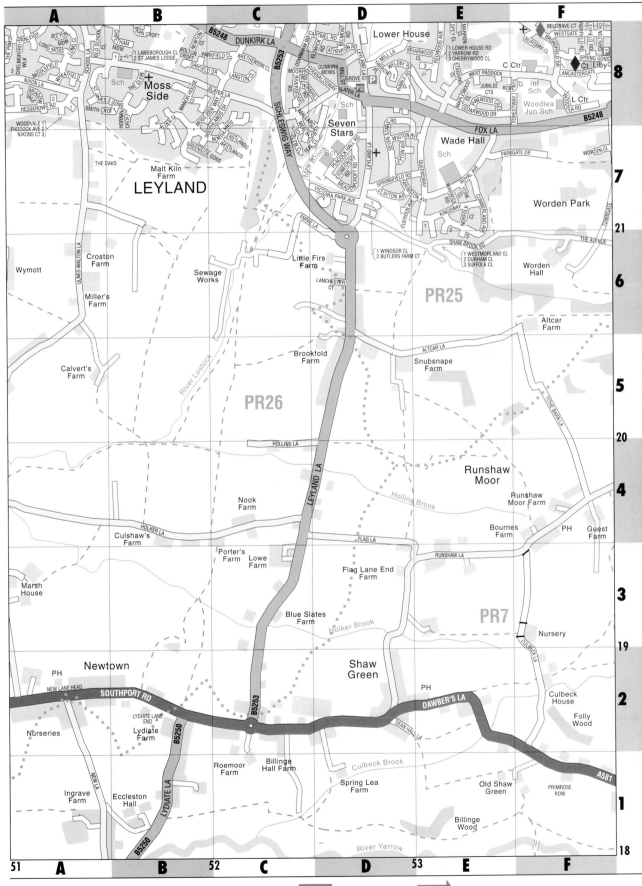

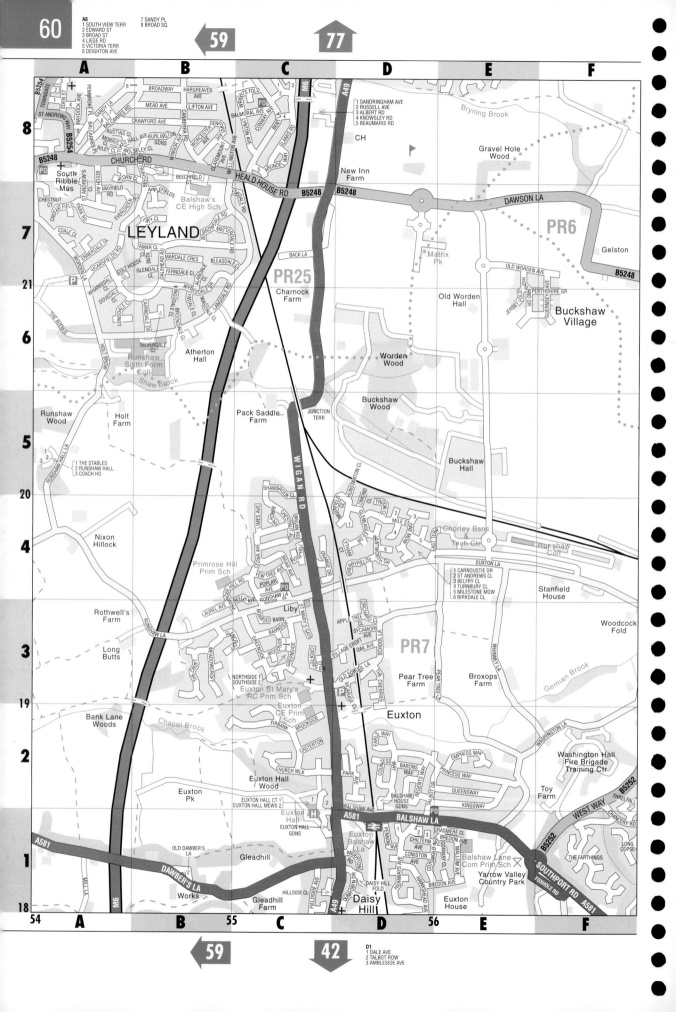

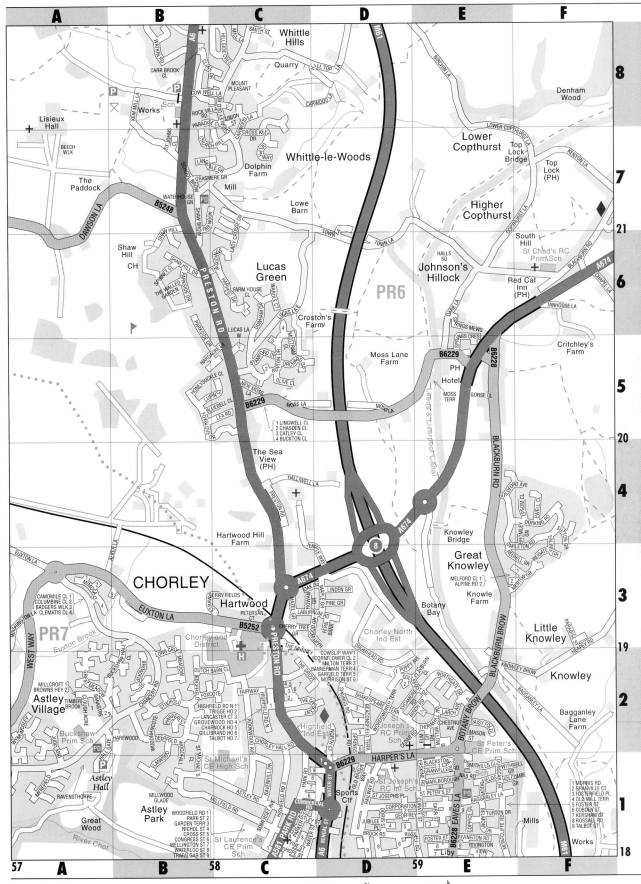

D1
1 PRESTON ST
2 VICTORIA TERR
3 VICARAGE ST
4 WESTWELL RD
5 INGLE CL
6 RUSSELL SQ W
7 WHINFIELD AVE
8 MAYFIELD RD
9 BRIERCLIFFE RD

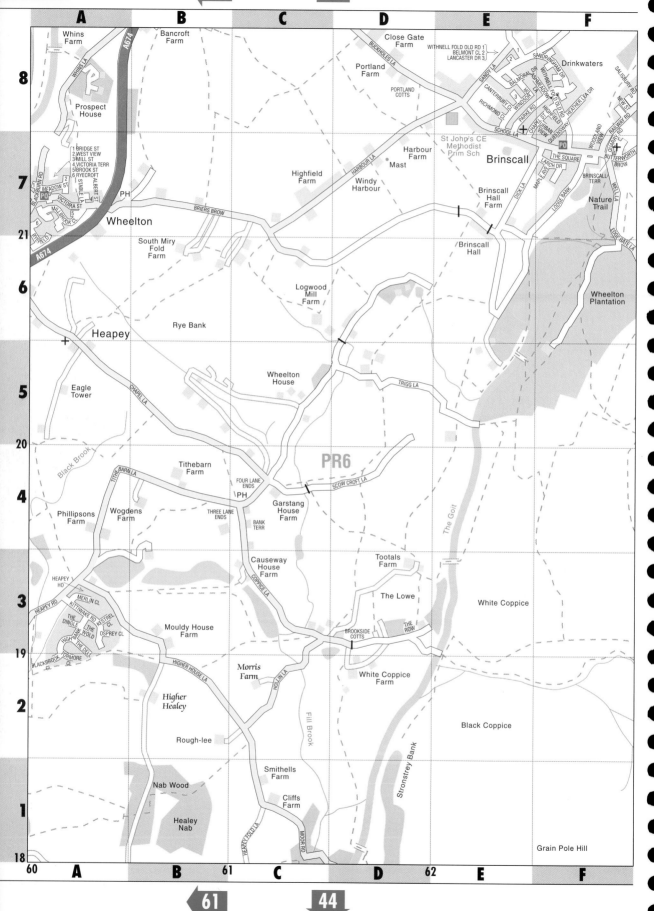

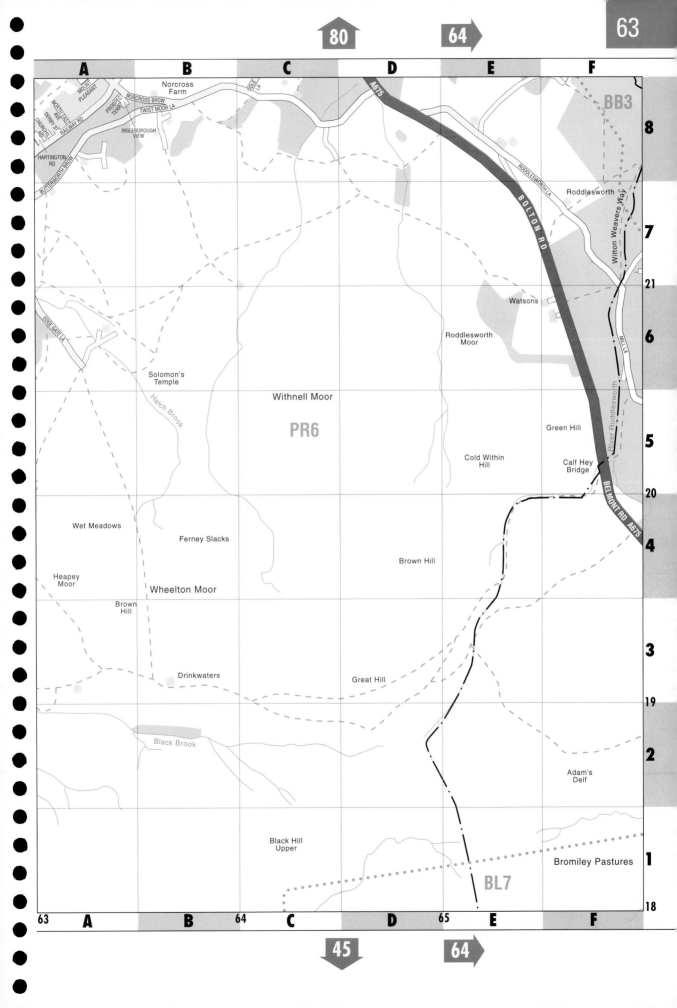

BB3

8

Roddlesworth

Witton Weavers Way

7

21

Watsons

6

Roddlesworth Moor

Solomon's Temple

Withnell Moor

PR6

Green Hill

5

Cold Within Hill

Calf Hey Bridge

20

BELMONT RD A675

Wet Meadows

Ferney Slacks

Brown Hill

4

Heapey Moor

Wheelton Moor

Brown Hill

Drinkwaters

Great Hill

3

19

Black Brook

2

Adam's Delf

Black Hill Upper

Bromiley Pastures

1

BL7

18

Norcross Farm

Mount Pleasant

North East Ave

Railway Rd

Derby's

Churchill Rd

Hartington Rd

Butterworth Brow

Prospect Terr

Ingleborough View

Norcross Brow

Twist Moor La

Dole La

A675

Roddlesworth La

Bolton Rd

Mill La

River Roddlesworth

Edge Gate La

Hatch Brook

63
81

A **B** **C** **D** **E** **F**

8

Ryal Farm

Roddlesworth
Nature Trail

Royal Arms
(PH)
Roddlesworth
Vistor Ctr

HOLLINSHEAD TERR

Sunnyhurst Hey
Resr

SNIDDLE HILL LA

Sniddle Hill
Farm

TURM LA

WESTLAND AVE

GRANVILLE RD

MANOR RD

Belgrave

ARLINGTON RD 1
LIMES AVE 2
RADFIELD HEAD 3

INVERNESS RD

BELGRAVE RD

EAST PK RD

RADFIELD RD

Higher
Wenshead

Jubilee Tower

Tockholes
No 2 Plantation

Darwen
Hill

7

Stepback Brook

Height
Side

21

New Barn

Tockholes
No 3 Plantation

6

BB3

Witton Weavers Way

Green Lowe
Farm House

TOCKHOLES RD

STONY FOLD BROW

DUCKSHAW RD

Duckshaw Clough

SLIPPER LOWE BROW
MILL LA

Darwen Moor

Duckshaw Brook

5

Duckshaw
Farm

Slipper
Lowe

20

Thorny Bank
Plantation

Cartridge Hill

Whitehall
Farm

Piccadilly

Brown Lowe

4

A675

Black Hill

PR6

Conyries
Plantation

Wilding
Fields

Turn Lowe

3

CROOKFIELD RD

Witton Weavers Way

Green Lowe

19

2

Old Man's
Hill

Little Hill

BELMONT RD

Hulton Pasture

BL7

Lower
Pasture Barn

1

Turton Moor

A675

18

Long Lands

66 **A** **B** **67** **C** **D** **68** **E** **F**

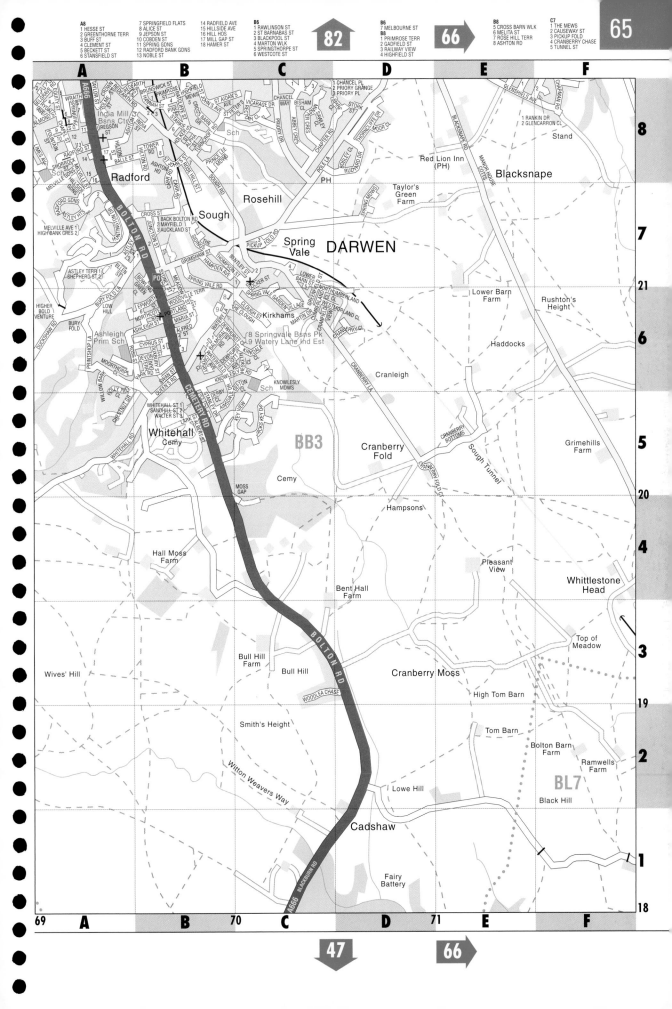

A8
1 HESSE ST
2 GREENTHORNE TERR
3 BUFF ST
4 CLEMENT ST
5 BECKETT ST
6 STANSFIELD ST

7 SPRINGFIELD FLATS
8 ALICE ST
9 JEPSON ST
10 COBDEN ST
11 SPRING GDNS
12 RADFORD BANK GDNS
13 NOBLE ST

14 RADFIELD AVE
15 HILLSIDE AVE
16 MILL HOS
17 MILL GAP ST
18 HAMER ST

B6
1 RAWLINSON ST
2 ST BARNABAS ST
3 BLACKPOOL ST
4 MARTON WLK
5 SPRINGTHORPE ST
6 WESTCOTE ST

B6
7 MELBOURNE ST
B8
1 PRIMROSE TERR
2 GADFIELD ST
3 RAILWAY VIEW
4 HIGHFIELD ST

B8
5 CROSS BARN WLK
6 MELITA ST
7 ROSE HILL TERR
8 ASHTON RD

C7
1 THE MEWS
2 CAUSEWAY ST
3 PICKUP FOLD
4 CRANBERRY CHASE
5 TUNNEL ST

82 →

66 →

A   B   C   D   E   F

47

66 →

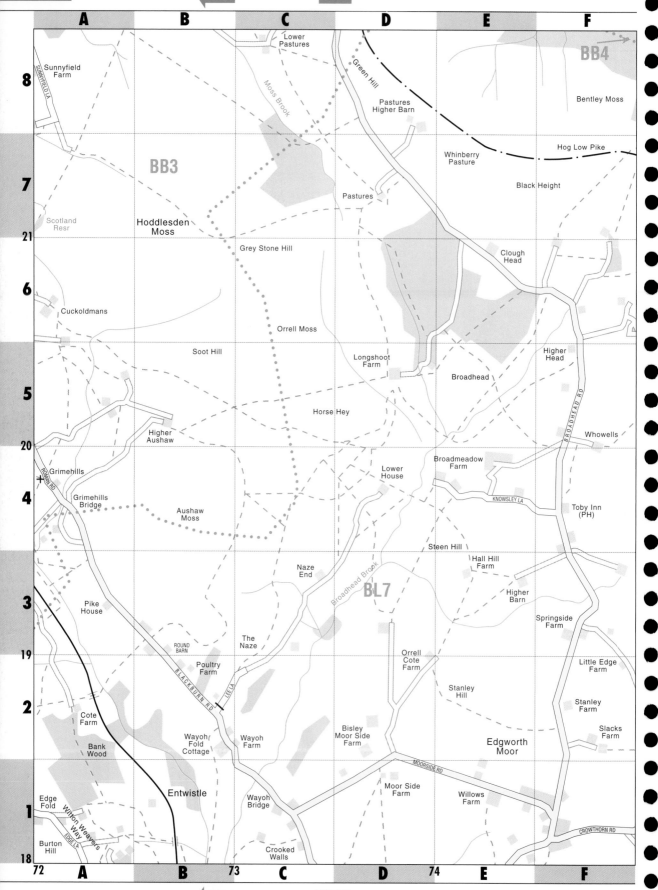

A **B** **C** **D** **E** **F**

Sunnyfield Farm

BB3

BB4

Bentley Moss

Lower Pastures

Moss Brook

Green Hill

Pastures Higher Barn

Hog Low Pike

Whinberry Pasture

Black Height

Scotland Resr

Hoddlesden Moss

Pastures

Grey Stone Hill

Clough Head

Cuckoldmans

Orrell Moss

Soot Hill

Longshoot Farm

Higher Head

Broadhead

Horse Hey

Higher Aushaw

Grimehills

Whowells

Grimehills Bridge

Aushaw Moss

Lower House

Broadmeadow Farm

KNOWSLEY LA

Toby Inn (PH)

Steen Hill

Hall Hill Farm

Pike House

Naze End

Broadhead Brook

BL7

Higher Barn

Springside Farm

ROUND BARN

The Naze

Orrell Cote Farm

Little Edge Farm

Poultry Farm

BLACKBURN RD

Stanley Hill

Stanley Farm

Cote Farm

Slacks Farm

Bank Wood

Wayoh Fold Cottage

Wayoh Farm

Bisley Moor Side Farm

Edgworth Moor

MOORSIDE RD

Edge Fold

Witton Weavers Way

Entwistle

Wayoh Bridge

Moor Side Farm

Willows Farm

Burton Hill

EDGE LA

Crooked Walls

CROWTHORN RD

A **B** **C** **D** **E** **F**

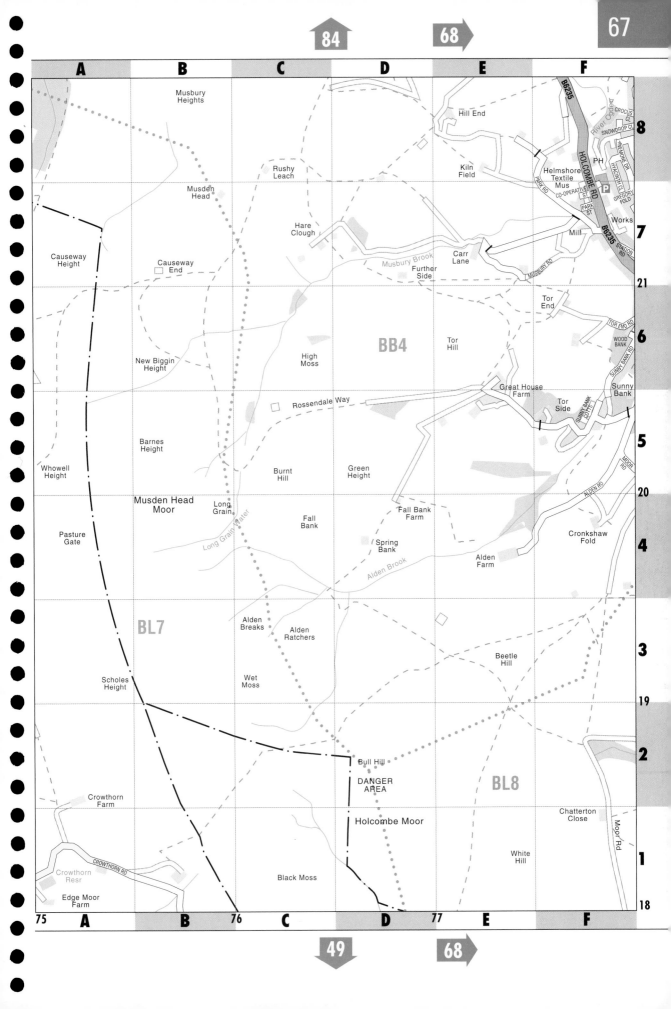

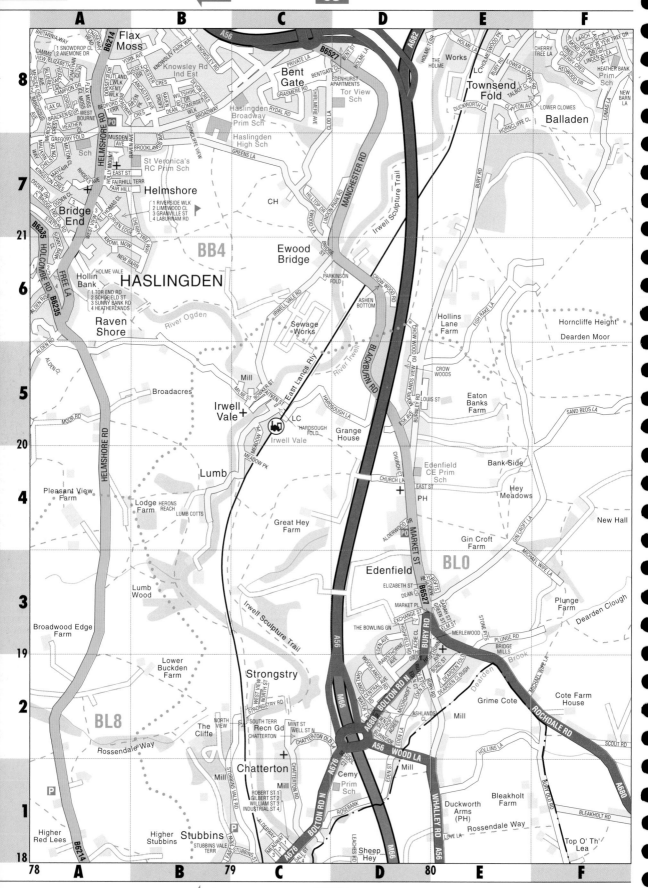

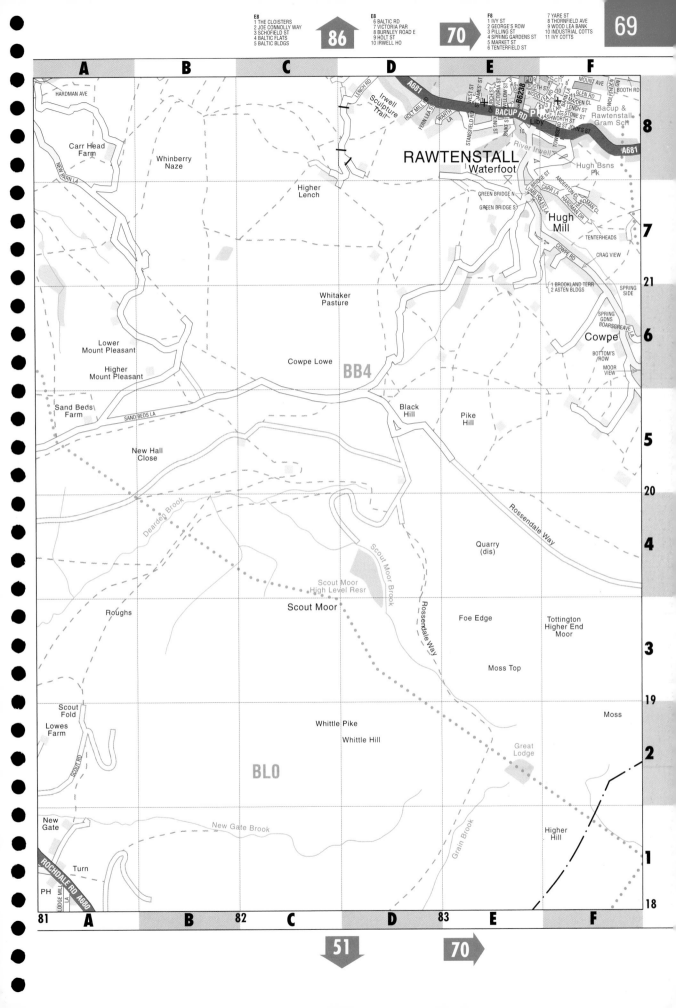

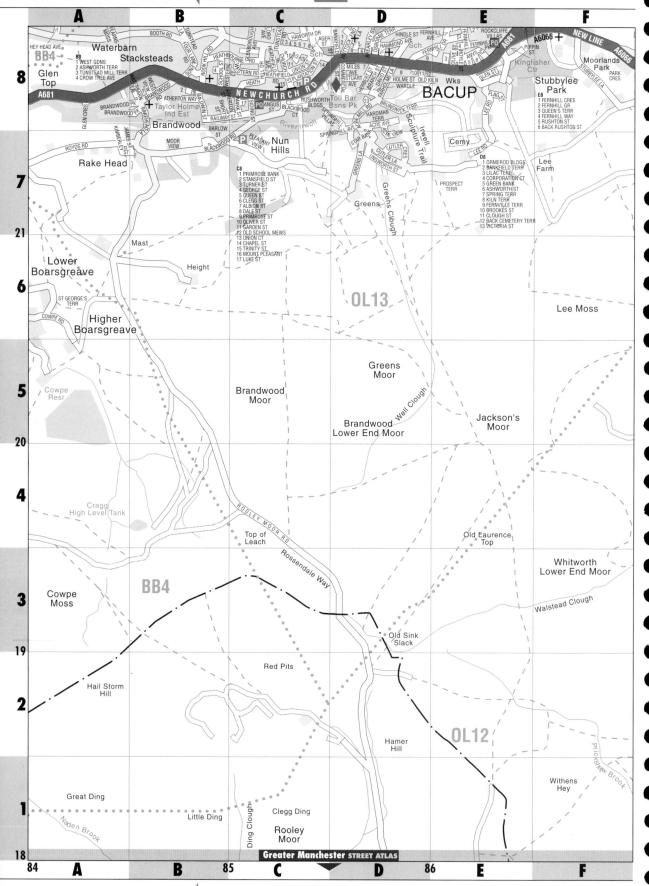

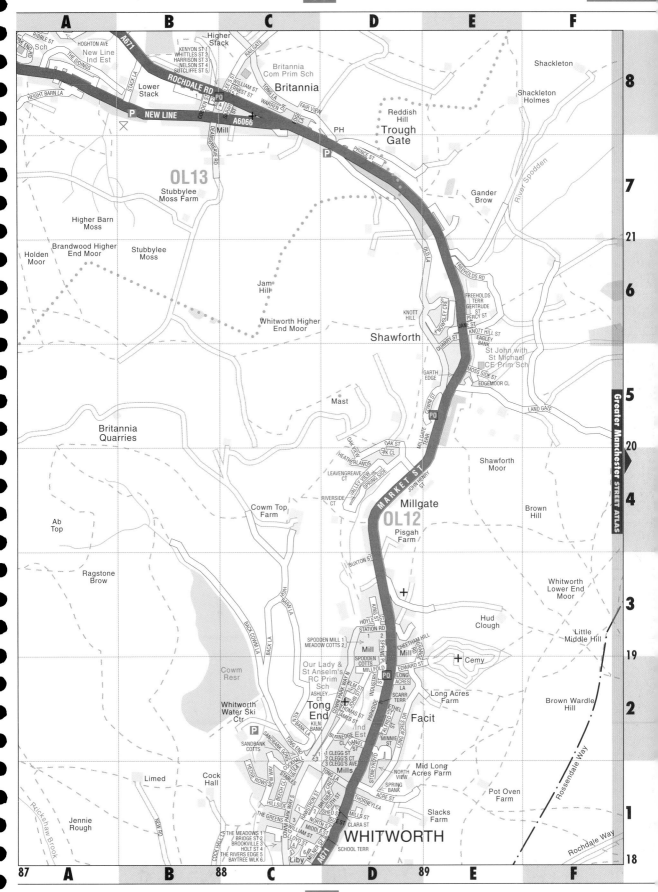

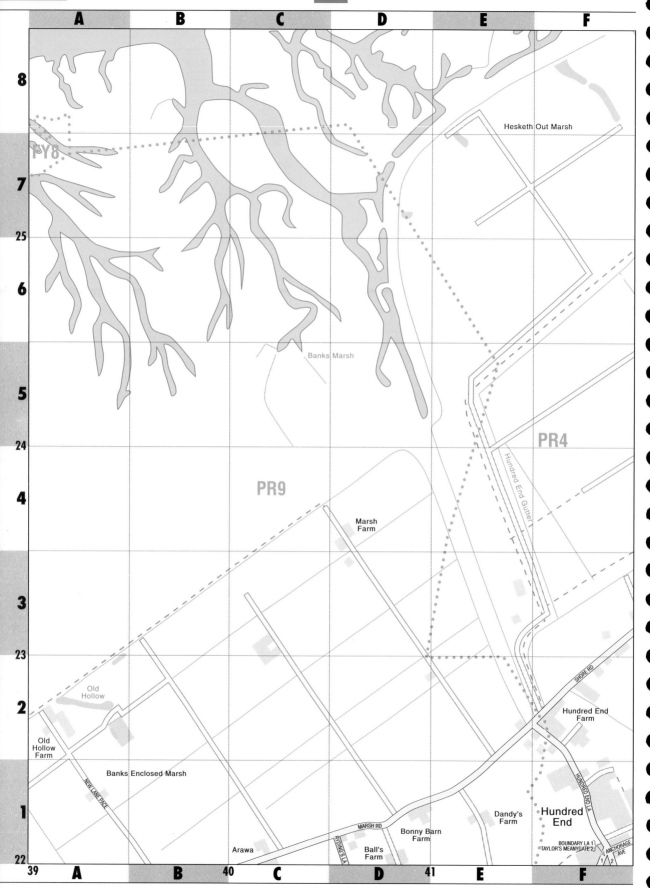

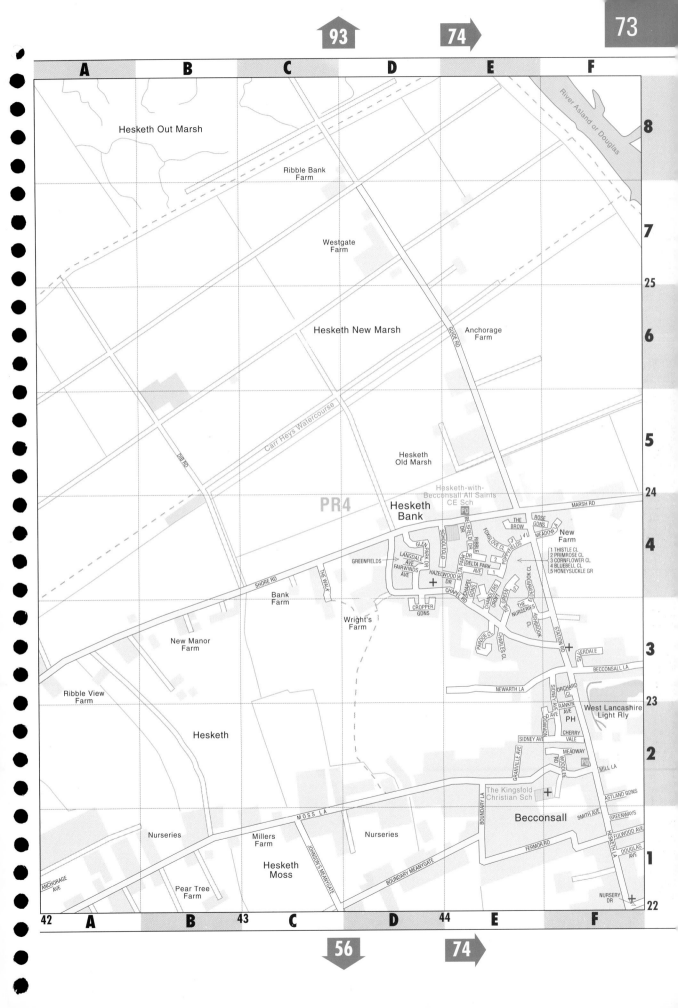

A B C D E F

8
7
25
6
5
24
4
3
23
2
1
22

Hesketh Out Marsh

Ribble Bank Farm

Westgate Farm

River Asland or Douglas

Hesketh New Marsh

Anchorage Farm

GUIDE RD

Carr Heys Watercourse

Hesketh Old Marsh

DIB RD

PR4

Hesketh Bank

Hesketh-with-Becconsall All Saints CE Sch

MARSH RD

New Farm

PO

THE BROW

ROSE GDNS

MEADOW LA

SCHOOL FOLD

BESSFIELD DR

RIBBLE DR

FOXGLOVE CL

POPPY FIELDS

GLEN PARK DR

Greenfields

LANGDALE AVE

FAIRWINDS AVE

DELTA PARK DR

DELTA PARK AVE

1 THISTLE CL
2 PRIMROSE CL
3 CORNFLOWER CL
4 BLUEBELL CL
5 HONEYSUCKLE GR

HAZELWOOD DR

CHAPEL RD

CHAPEL GDNS

CHANDLERS CROFT

THE GREEN

ELDERBROOK CL

THE NURSERIES

ASHBROOK CL

STATION RD

SILVERDALE

SHORE RD

THE WALK

Bank Farm

CROPPER GDNS

Wright's Farm

PARLOE CT

CHARLES CL

New Manor Farm

NEWARTH LA

BECCONSALL LA

Ribble View Farm

Hesketh

ORCHARD CL

SIDNEY AVE

RANKIN AVE

NORWOOD

PH

West Lancashire Light Rly

CHERRY VALE

SIDNEY AVE

MEADWAY

WOODLER RD

PO

MILL LA

GRANVILLE AVE

BOUNDARY LA

The Kingsfold Christian Sch

ASTLAND GDNS

Becconsall

SMITH AVE

GREENWAYS

HESKETH LA

FULWOOD AVE

DOUGLAS AVE

MOSS LA

Nurseries

Millers Farm

JOHNSON'S MEANYGATE

Nurseries

FERMOR RD

BOUNDARY MEANYGATE

Hesketh Moss

ANCHORAGE AVE

Pear Tree Farm

NURSERY DR

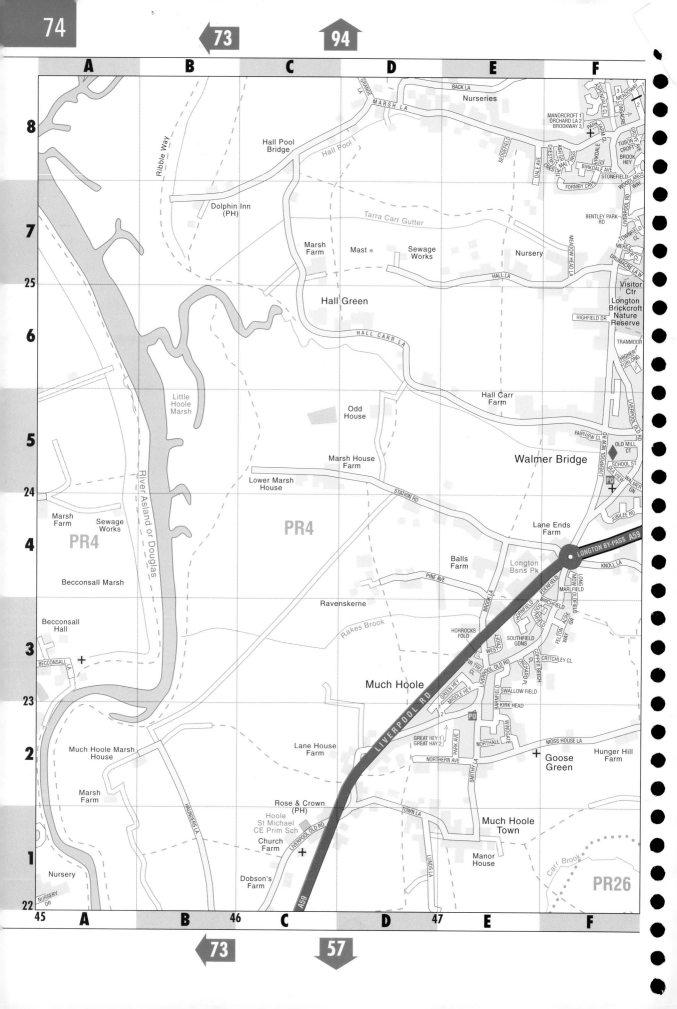

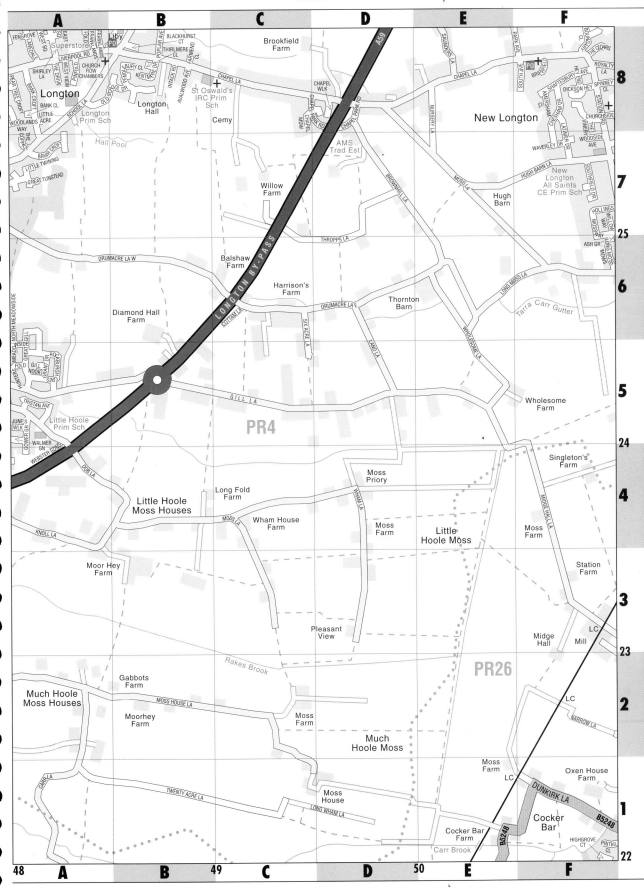

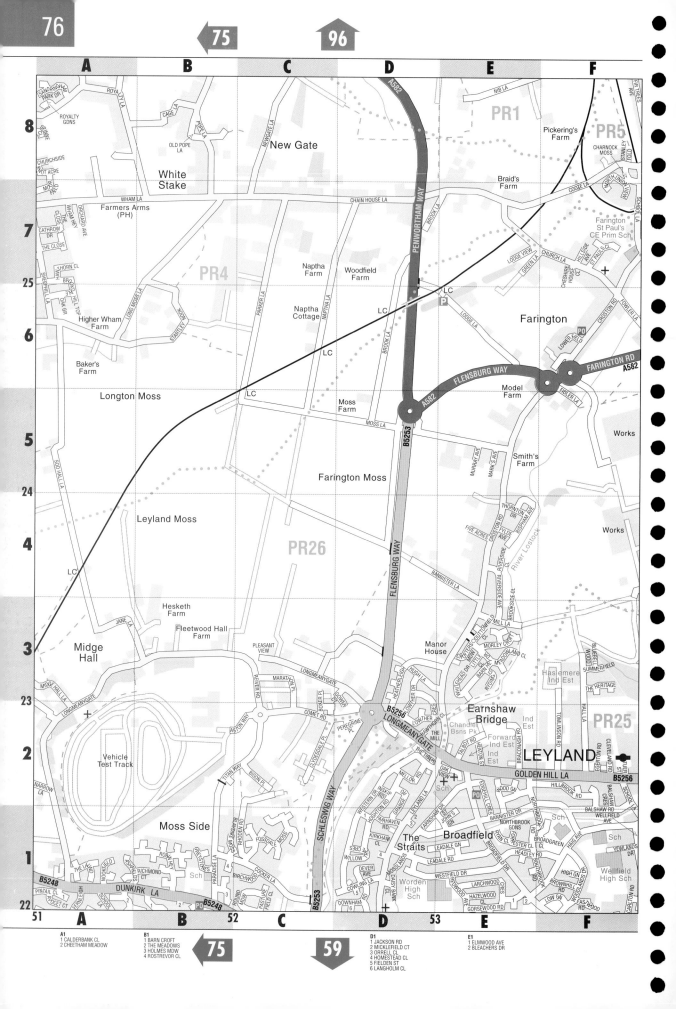

A B C D E F

8

7

25

6

5

24

4

3

23

2

1

22

51 A B 52 C D 53 E F

75

59

White Stake

New Gate

PR1

PR5

Pickering's Farm

Charnock Moss

Farmers Arms (PH)

PR4

Naptha Farm

Woodfield Farm

Farington St Paul's CE Prim Sch

Higher Wham Farm

Naptha Cottage

LC

Farington

Baker's Farm

Longton Moss

LC

Moss Farm

Model Farm

FARINGTON RD

A582

FLENSBURG WAY

A582

Works

Faringon Moss

Smith's Farm

Leyland Moss

PR26

Works

Hesketh Farm

Fleetwood Hall Farm

Pleasant View

Manor House

Haslemere Ind Est

THE HERITAGE

Midge Hall

Vehicle Test Track

Longmeanygate

Earnshaw Bridge

PR25

LEYLAND

GOLDEN HILL LA

B5256

Moss Side

Schleswig Way

The Straits

Broadfield

Worden High Sch

Wellfield High Sch

B5248

DUNKIRK LA

B5248

B5253

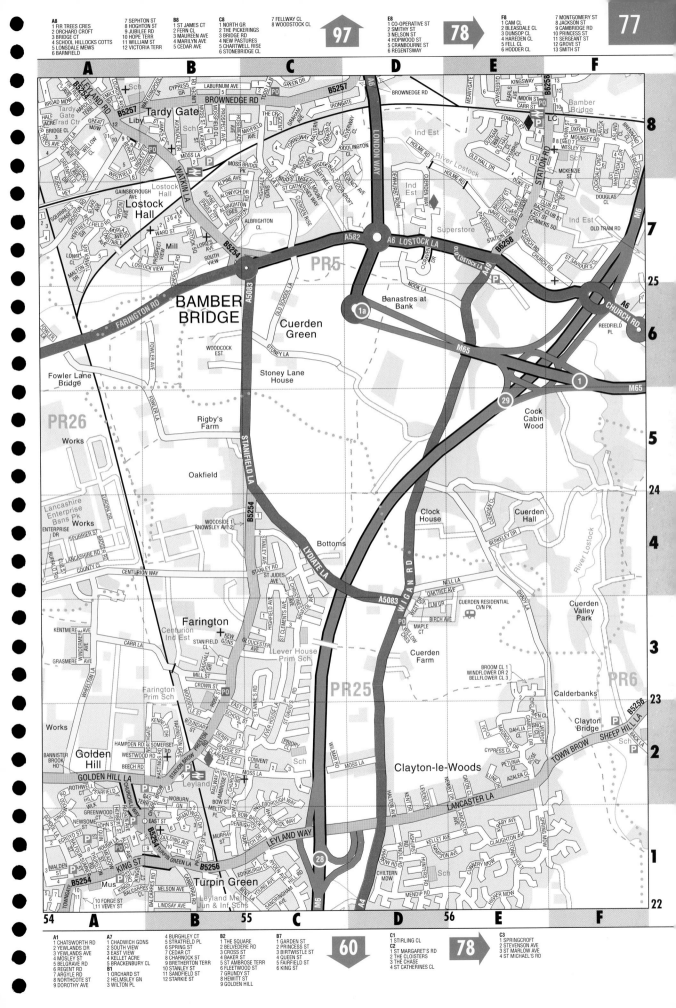

A8
1 FIR TREES CRES
2 ORCHARD CROFT
3 BRIDGE CT
4 SCHOOL HILLOCKS COTTS
5 LONSDALE MEWS
6 BARNFIELD

7 SEPHTON ST
8 HOGHTON ST
9 JUBILEE RD
10 HOPE TERR
11 WILLIAM ST
12 VICTORIA TERR

B8
1 ST JAMES CT
2 FERN CL
3 BRIDGE RD
4 MARILYN AVE
5 CEDAR AVE

C8
1 NORTH GR
2 THE PICKERINGS
3 BRIDGE RD
4 NEW PASTURES
5 CHARTWELL RISE
6 STONEBRIDGE CL

7 FELLWAY CL
8 WOODSTOCK CL

97

78

E8
1 CO-OPERATIVE ST
2 SMITHY ST
3 NELSON ST
4 HOPWOOD ST
5 CRANBOURNE ST
6 REGENTSWAY

F8
1 CAM CL
2 BLEASDALE CL
3 DUNSOP CL
4 HAREDEN CL
5 FELL CL
6 HODDER CL

7 MONTGOMERY ST
8 JACKSON ST
9 CAMBRIDGE RD
10 PRINCESS ST
11 SERGEANT ST
12 GROVE ST
13 SMITH ST

77

A1
1 CHATSWORTH RD
2 YEWLANDS DR
3 MOSLEY ST
4 BELGRAVE RD
5 REGENT RD
6 ARGYLE RD
7 NORTHCOTE ST
8 DOROTHY AVE

A7
1 CHADWICH GDNS
2 SOUTH VIEW
3 EAST VIEW
4 KELLET ACRE
5 BRACKENDALE CL

B1
1 ORCHARD CL
2 HELMSLEY GN
3 WILTON PL

4 BURGHLEY CT
5 STRATFIELD PL
6 SPRING ST
7 CEDAR CT
8 CHARNOCK ST
9 BRETHERTON TERR
10 STANLEY ST
11 SANDFIELD ST
12 STARKIE ST

B2
1 THE SQUARE
2 BELVEDERE RD
3 CROSS ST
4 BAKER ST
5 ST AMBROSE TERR
6 FLEETWOOD ST
7 GRUNDY ST
8 HEWITT ST
9 GOLDEN HILL

B7
1 GARDEN ST
2 PRINCESS ST
3 BIRTWISTLE ST
4 QUEEN ST
5 FAIRFIELD ST
6 KING ST

60

C1
1 STIRLING CL

C2
1 ST MARGARET'S RD
2 THE CLOISTERS
3 THE CHASE
4 ST CATHERINES CL

78

C3
1 SPRINGCROFT
2 STEVENSON AVE
3 ST MARLOW AVE
4 ST MICHAEL'S RD

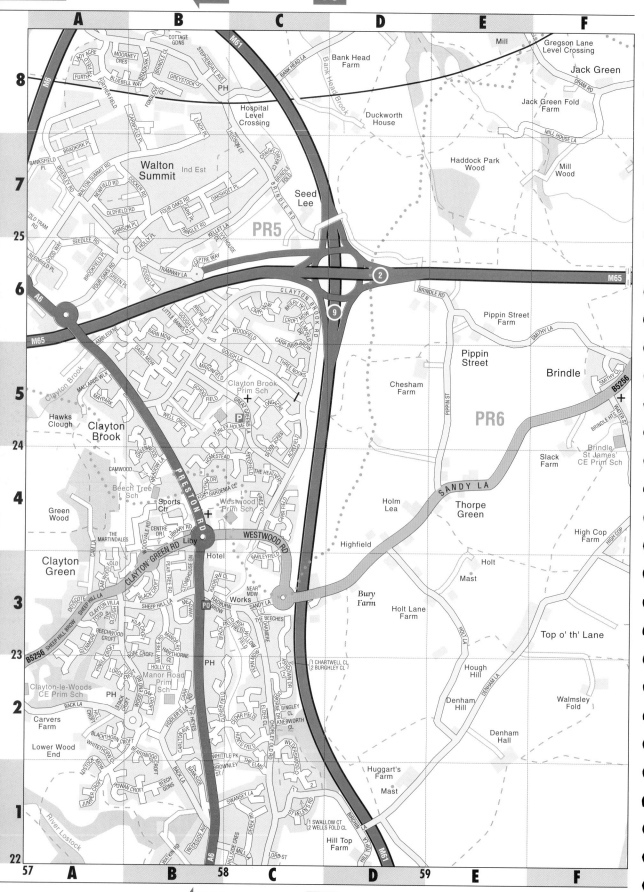

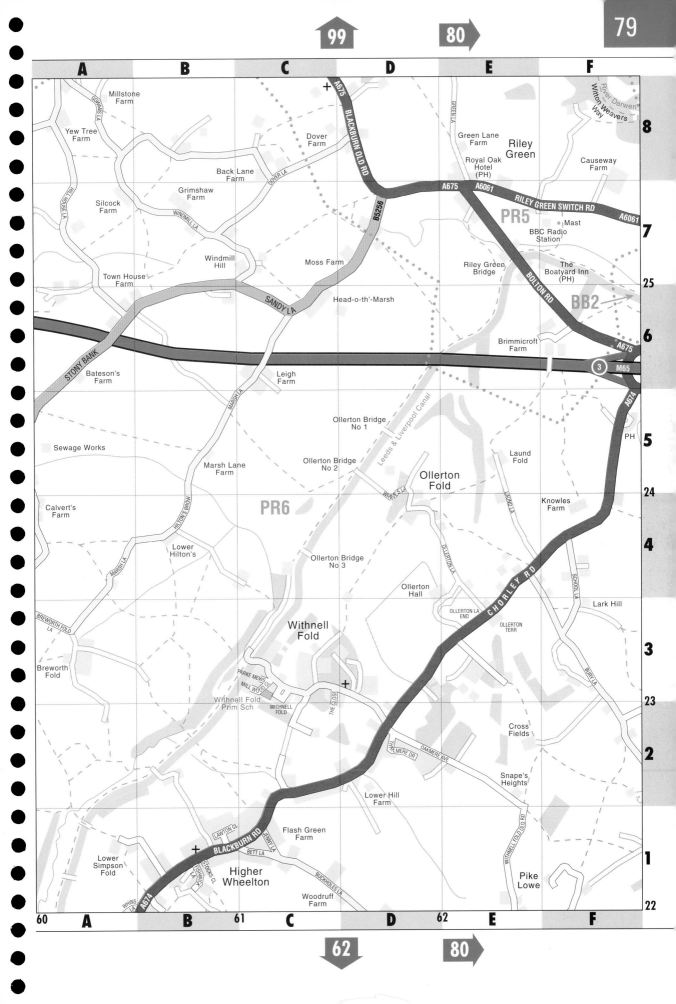

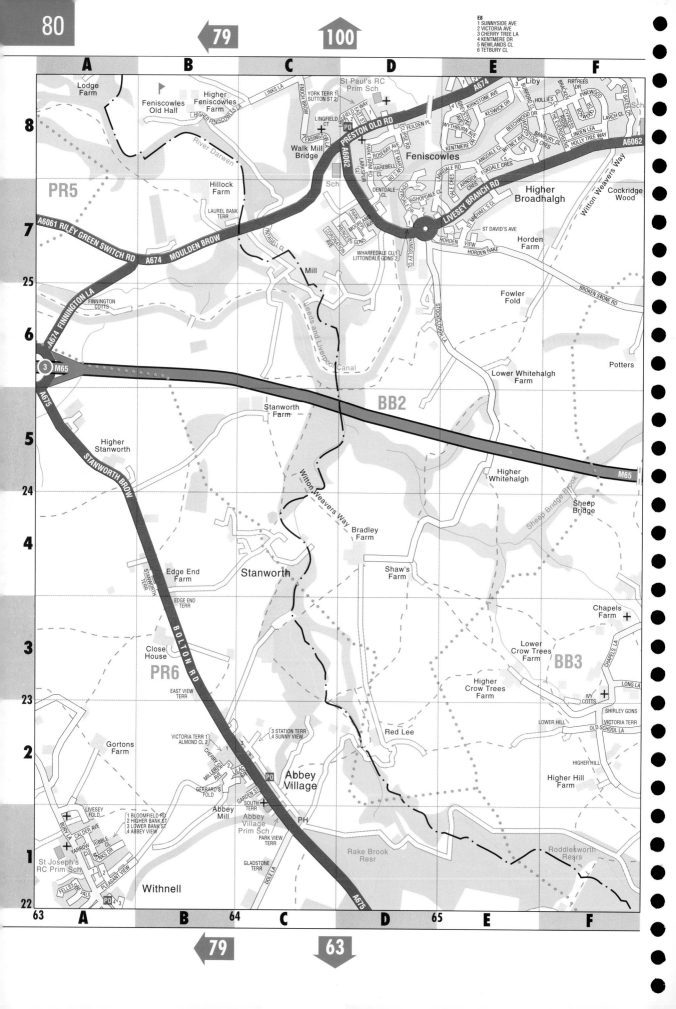

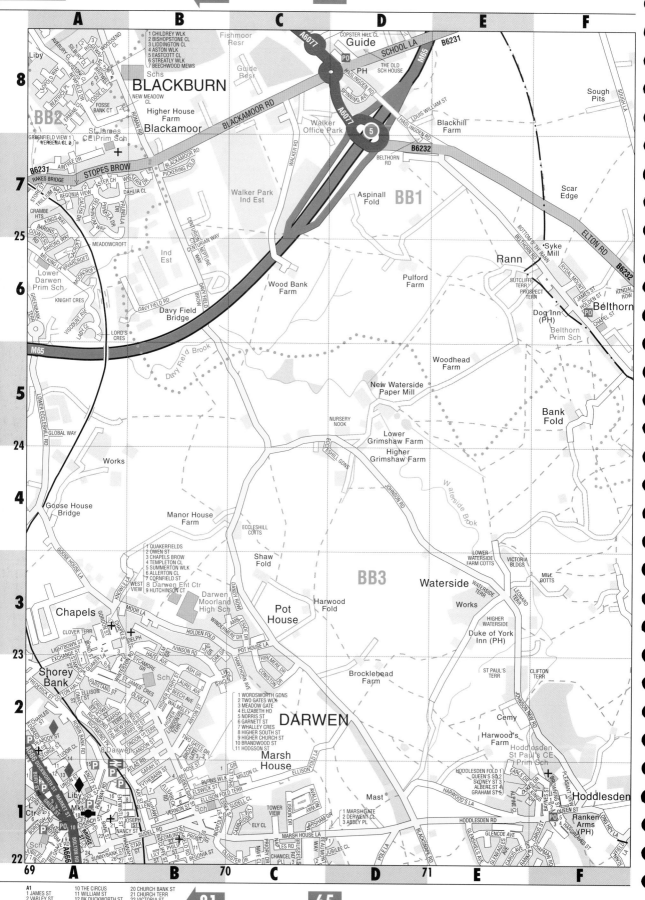

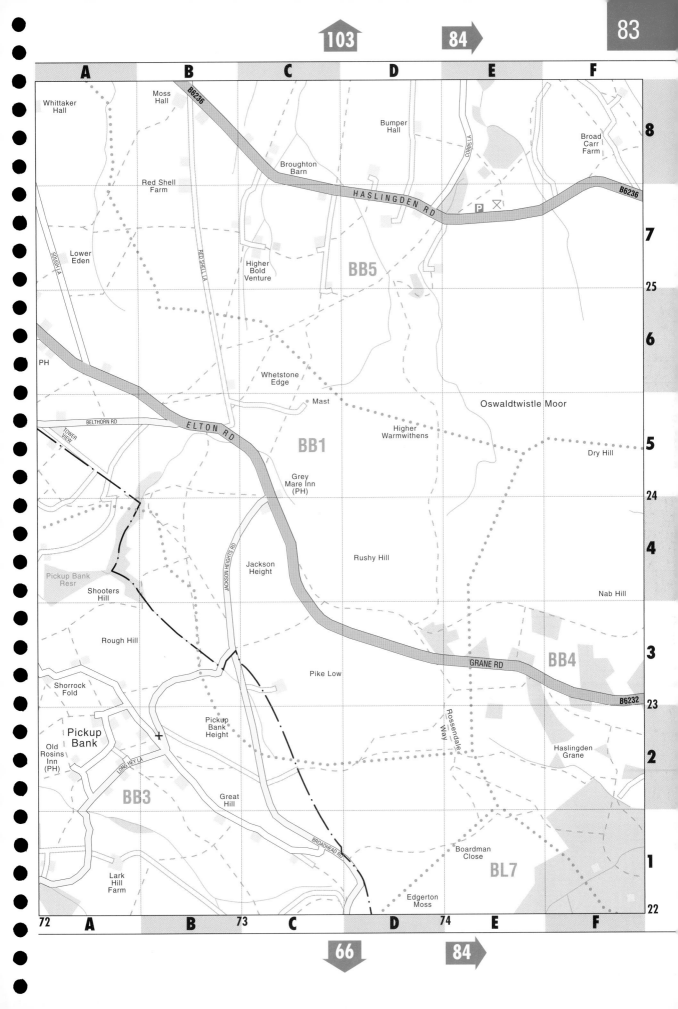

83 104

A B C D E F

8
Mattbridge
Accrington Moor
Meadow Top Farm
Meadow Head Farm
ALMA PL
Turkey Red Ind Est
MANCHESTER RD A680
BACK LA
Red Walls
BROADFIELD
Trees Farm
BRIDGE HOS
BLACKBURN RD

RAMS CLOUGH LA
Coach & Horses Hotel (PH)
Farther Friar Hill Farm
Paragon Works
B6236

7
Rams Clough
Sandybeds Farm
HASLINGDEN RD
Lark Hill Farm

25
ROUNDHILL RD
ROUNDHILL LA
PH
B6236

BB5
High Cockham
Roundhill
Moor Lane Farm
MOOR LA

6
Elm Tree Farm
Rossendale Way
Coldwells

Thirteen Stone Hill

5
Haslingden Moor

Copy Farm

24
Deep Clough
Higher Swineherd Lowe Farm

4
Rossendale Way
Picker Hill
Todd Hall Farm
TODD HALL RD

COB CASTLE RD
Unicorn Carrs Ind Est

3
Clough Head Visitor Ctr
P
Quarry (dis)
Clod Farm
BB4
Windy Harbour Farm
Hutch Bank
UNDERBANK RD

B6232
HEAP CLOUGH

23
Haslingden Grane (Trail)
Cemy
GRANE RD
Leys End
HUTCH BANK RD
Hutch Bank
GREAVES ST
STONE ST

2
CALF HEY RD
P
Haslingden Grane
Duke of Wellington (PH)
Cemy
GAS ST
HOLDEN ST
B6232
Rothwell Fold
Ogden Resr
Holden Wood Resr
B6235
PH
QUARRY BANK

Calf Hey Resr
HOLCOMBE RD
Holden Wood
WARBURTON ST 1
MUSBURY VIEW 2
WARBURTON BLDGS 3
HOLDEN WOOD DR
Cvn Pk

1
Rossendale Way
Tenements Farm
4 MUSBURY MEWS
5 GRANGE PARK WAY
EDINBURGH RD

22
Chy
B6235

75 A B 76 C D 77 E F

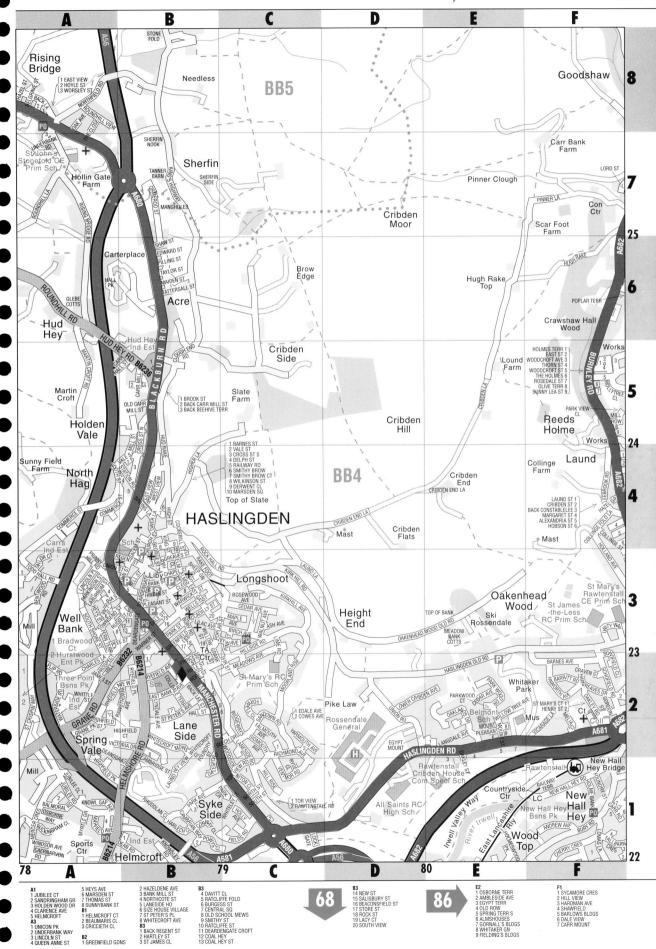

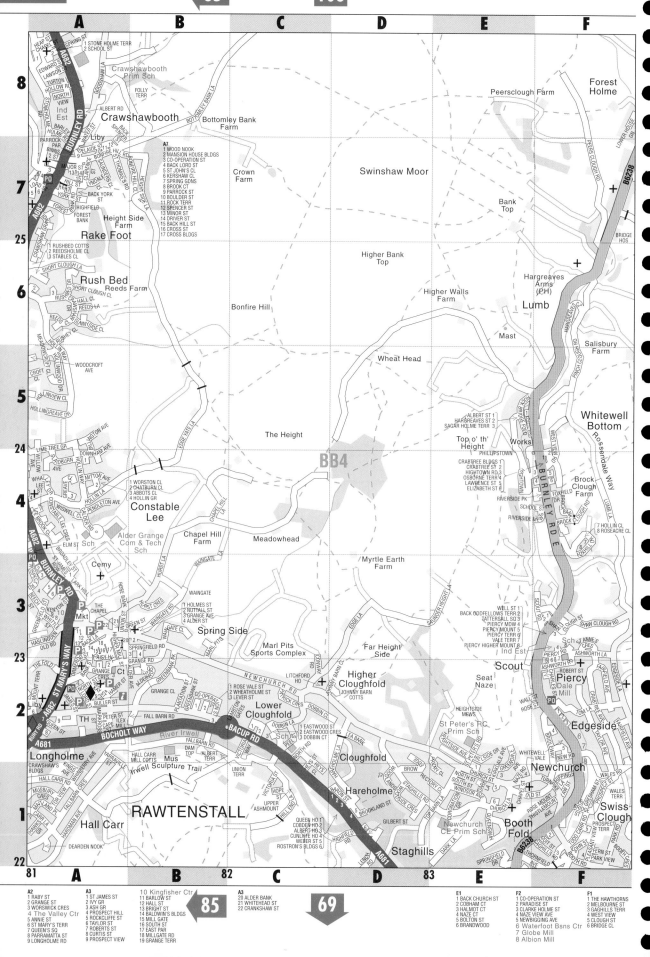

A2
1 RABY ST
2 GRANGE ST
3 WORSWICK CRES
4 The Valley Ctr
5 ANNIE ST
6 ST MARY'S TERR
7 QUEEN'S SQ
8 PARRAMATTA ST
9 LONGHOLME RD

A3
1 ST JAMES ST
2 IVY GR
3 ASH GR
4 PROSPECT HILL
5 ROCKCLIFFE ST
6 TAYLOR ST
7 ROBERTS ST
8 CURTIS ST
9 PROSPECT VIEW

10 KINGFISHER CTR
11 BARLOW ST
12 HALL ST
13 BRIGHT ST
14 BALDWIN'S BLDGS
15 MILL GATE
16 SOUTH ST
17 EAST PAR
18 MILLGATE RD
19 GRANGE TERR

A3
20 ALDER BANK
21 WHITEHEAD ST
22 CRANKSHAW ST

E1
1 BACK CHURCH ST
2 COBHAM CT
3 HALMOT CT
4 NAZE CT
5 BOLTON ST
6 BRANDWOOD

F2
1 CO-OPERATION ST
2 PARADISE ST
3 CLARKE HOLME ST
4 NAZE VIEW AVE
5 NEWBIGGING AVE
6 Waterfoot Bsns Ctr
7 Globe Mill
8 Albion Mill

F1
1 THE HAWTHORNS
2 MELBOURNE ST
3 GAGHILLS TERR
4 WEST VIEW
5 CLOUGH ST
6 BRIDGE CL

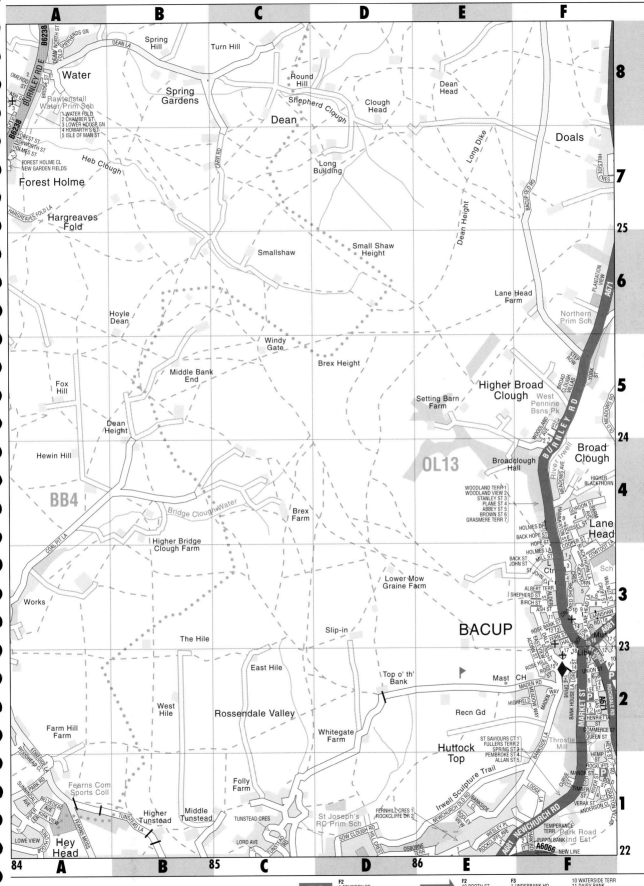

F2
1 FOUNDRY ST
2 Henrietta Street Ind Est
3 FORGE ST
4 INDUSTRIAL PL
5 KING ST
6 AUSTIN ST
7 IRWELL ST
8 KERSHAW ST
9 LUMB SCAR

F2
10 BOOTH ST
11 PICKUP ST
12 IRWELL TERR
13 TOWER ST
14 BANK ST
15 THISTLE ST
16 LILY ST
17 PRINCESS ST
18 MAITLAND ST

F3
1 UNDERBANK HO
2 MOWGRAIN VIEW
3 UNDERBANK CL
4 LAUREL ST
5 ST JOHN'S CT
6 STANLEY MOUNT
7 BENTLEY ST
8 HIGHER CROSS ROW
9 MYRTLE BANK RD

10 WATERSIDE TERR
11 DAISY BANK
12 BAKER ST
13 GOOSE HILL ST
14 HARCOURT ST
15 ST JAMES SQ
16 YORKSHIRE ST
17 HAMMERTON GN
18 EARNSHAW ROW
19 KING GEORGE CT

A B C D E F

8
7
25
6
5
24
4
3
23
2
1
22

The Old Woman

Old Clough
A671
THE MOORLANDS
HEALD LA
HEALD CL
Wambs Farm
Carr & Craggs Moor
Green's Clough

FELL VIEW
SCAR END CL
DOALS GATE
WESLEY TERR
KATEHOLM
PHILIPS RD
BURNLEY RD
ROCHESTER RD
BEAUFORT RD
FIELD TOP
BENT EST

1 RICHARD ST
2 COMET ST
3 WRIGHT ST
4 CAPTAIN ST
5 HALLEY ST

MELROSE TERR
Weir
Scar End Hey
Scar End Brook
Heald Top Farm

A671
River Irwell
Irwell Sculpture Trail
Far Old Meadows Farm
Mean Hey
FLOWER SCAR RD

DOG PITS LA
Old Meadows
OLD MEADOWS RD
Stake Moss
Sharneyford Prim Sch
Sharneyford
Slate Pit Hill
Todmorden Moor
Clough Head
Works
BACUP RD
Holden Gate
Planet Earth Ctr (Observatory & Planetarium)

TODMORDEN OLD RD
OL13
Little Tooter Hill
HIGHER CHANGE VILLAS
Higher Change
TODMORDEN RD
Parrock Farm
Tooter Hill
Rossendale Way
OL14
A687
Midgelden Pasture
LIMERS GATE

West Yorkshire STREET ATLAS A681 Todmorden (A6033)

The Flowers (PH)
COWTOOT LA
COAL PIT LA
HAZEL GR
LANE SIDE
ROSEMOUNT
MOORSIDE
HIGHER CHANGE OLD
GREENS LA
BEECH ST
CARLTON
Greave
Maden Pasture
Sch
GREENSNOOK LA
CLOVER ST
ALBION ST
OAK ST
VALE ST
GROVE
BEECH ST
PO
GREAVE CLOUGH DR
OAKENCLOUGH
INITIAL ST
ARTHUR ST
OAKEN
Pasture Bottom Farm

1 GREAVE RD
2 GREAVE TERR
3 GREAVE CL
4 ROSENDALE CL
Lower Reaps Farm
Reaps Moss
Counting Hill

TONG LA
SPRINGFIELD
20 AVE
SOUTH ST
ALMA ST
INKERMAN ST
CRIMEA ST
BATH ST
QUARRY ST
GLADSTONE
CRES
PENDLE
HAWTHORN
THORN BANK
THORN DR
REED
CLOUGH RD
FAIRVIEW CRES
ROSENDALE CRES
WARCOCK LA
TONG LA

1 THORN GDNS
2 MYRTLE COTTS
3 REGENT ST
4 THORN ST
5 CO-OPERATION ST
6 INDUSTRIAL ST
7 CENTRAL VIEW

Hoyle Hey Clough

Rockliffe
A671
St Mary's RC Prim Sch
PENNINE RD
HANNAH
BACUP
1 GREEN HILL
2 GREEN HILL RD
3 PINE ST
4 MOORLANDS TERR
5 BRIAR ST
6 MERSEY ST
7 LANE END LA
Mast
Higher Hogshead
Hogshead Law Hill
OL12

CRABTREE AVE
METTLE COTE
RANDAL ST
RONALDSWAY
ONGHAN RD
PEEL DR
DOUGLAS RD
CHURCHTOWN
CHURCHTOWN CRES
RAILGATE
Whitworth

ROCHDALE RD
A671
RAMSEY AVE
WALTON
1 LEE VIEW
2 CASTLETOWN DR
A671
89

A3
1 GREENSNOOK TERR
2 SPRING GDNS
3 BEECH IND EST
4 CROSS ST
5 GREENSNOOK MEWS
6 CHRIST CHURCH ST
7 ELM ST
8 THE COURTYARD
9 GREAVE CLOUGH CL
10 GREAVE CRES
11 ARBOUR ST
12 GREEN END CL
13 EDWARD ST
14 BEAVER TERR
15 HANNAH ST
16 ASHWORTH ST
17 COWGILL ST
18 WARKWORTH TERR
19 VENTURE ST
20 TONG HO

90

E6
1 HARDAKER CT
2 CLIFTON CT
3 WHITEHALL CT
4 CONWAY CT
5 DEE ST COTT
6 TWEED ST

89

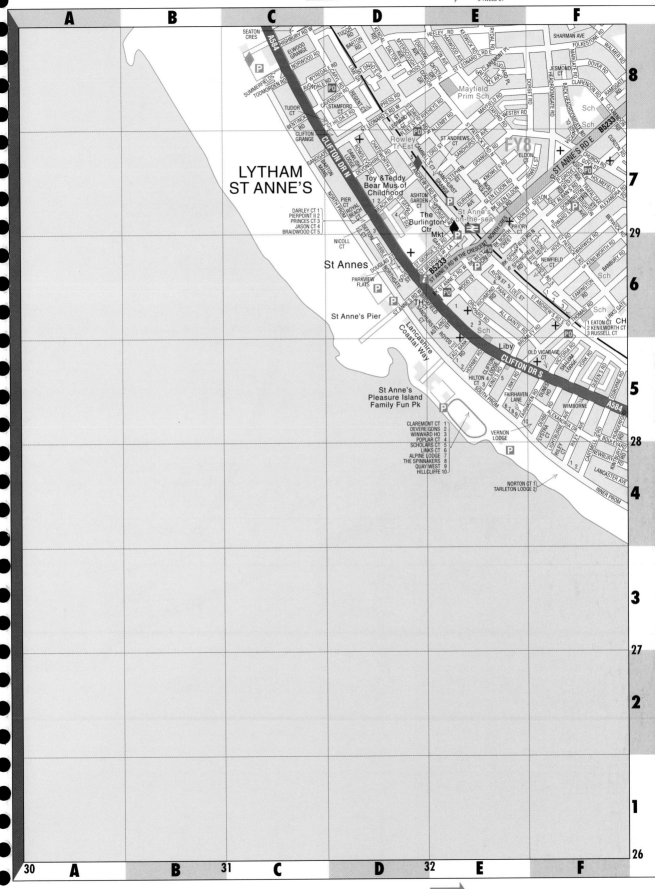

LYTHAM
ST ANNE'S

St Annes

DARLEY CT 1
PIERPOINT II 2
PRINCES CT 3
JASON CT 4
BRAIDWOOD CT 5

St Anne's Pier

Toy &Teddy
Bear Mus of
Childhood

The
Burlington
Ctr

St Anne's-on-the-sea

St Anne's
Pleasure Island
Family Fun Pk

CLAREMONT CT 1
DEVERE GDNS 2
WINWARD HO 3
POPLAR CT 4
SCHOLARS CT 5
LINKS CT 6
ALPINE LODGE 7
THE SPINNAKERS 8
QUAY WEST 9
HILLCLIFFE 10

Lancashire
Coastal Way

VERNON
LODGE

1 EATON CT CH
2 KENILWORTH CT
3 RUSSELL CT

NORTON CT 1
TARLETON LODGE 2

FY8

Mayfield
Prim Sch

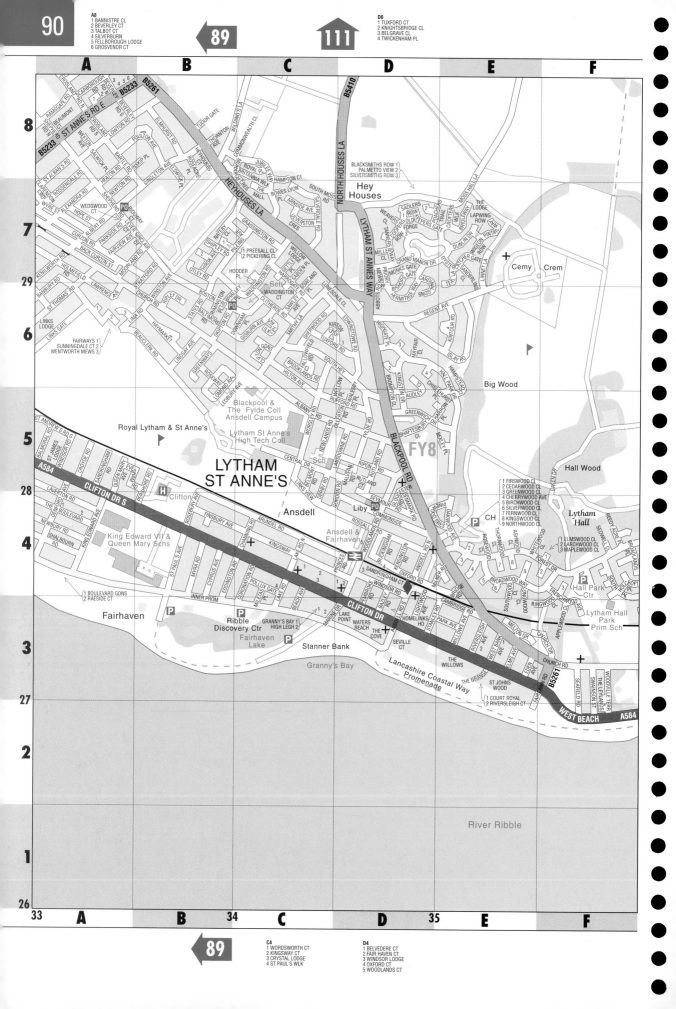

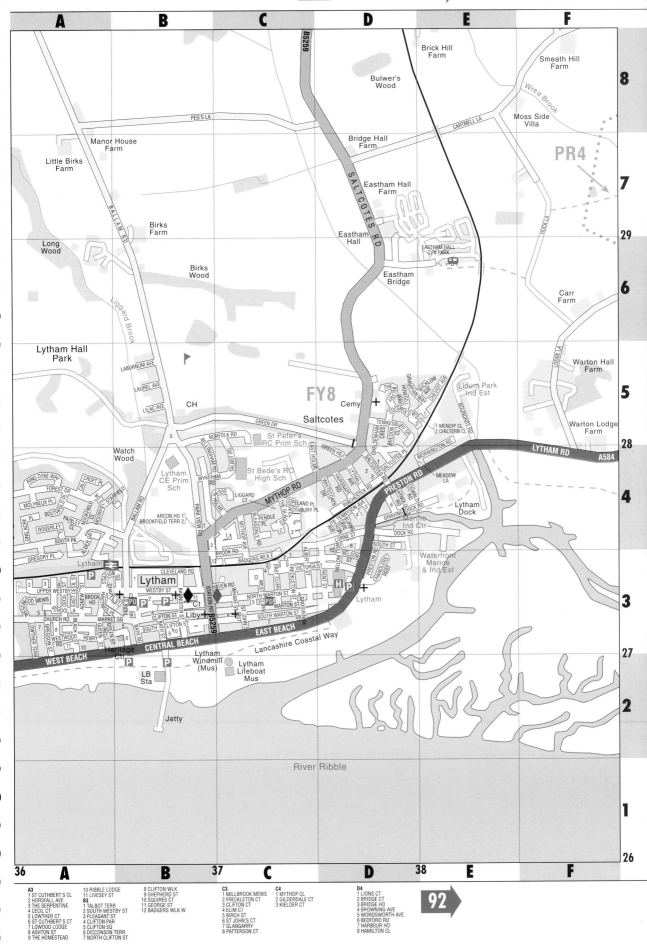

A3
1 ST CUTHBERT'S CL
2 HORSFALL AVE
3 THE SERPENTINE
4 CECIL CT
5 LOWTHER CT
6 ST CUTHBERT'S CT
7 LOWOOD LODGE
8 ASHTON ST
9 THE HOMESTEAD

10 RIBBLE LODGE
11 LIVESEY ST
B3
1 TALBOT TERR
2 SOUTH WESTBY ST
3 PLEASANT ST
4 CLIFTON PAR
5 CLIFTON SQ
6 DICCONSON TERR
7 NORTH CLIFTON ST

8 CLIFTON WLK
9 SHEPHERD ST
10 SQUIRES CT
11 GEORGE ST
12 BADGERS WLK W

C3
1 MILLBROOK MEWS
2 FRECKLETON CT
3 CLIFTON CT
4 ELIM CT
5 BIRCH ST
6 ST JOHN'S CT
7 GLANGARRY
8 PATTERSON CT

C4
1 MYTHOP CL
2 GILDERDALE CT
3 KIELDER CT

D4
1 LIONS CT
2 BRIDGE CT
3 BRIDGE HO
4 BROWNING AVE
5 WORDSWORTH AVE
6 BEDFORD RD
7 HARBOUR HO
8 HAMILTON CL

92

91
113

A   **B**   **C**   **D**   **E**   **F**

8

BRYNING HALL LA

Bryning

Bryning Hall Farm

Hillock Farm

7

Great Carr Side Farm

BRYNING LA

Leyland Farm

Kellamergh

Birley Arms Hotel (PH)

Windy Harbour Farm

HILLOCK LA

RAMSGATE CL
DOVER CL
FOLKESTONE CL

29

CARR LA

Blackfield End Farm

VERNON AVE 1
WORDSWORTH AVE 2

MOORHEAD GDNS

TENNYSON AVE

KEATS BYRON AVE

HASTINGS AVE

HARBOUR LA

QUEENSWAY

CANBERRA WAY

Little Carr Side Farm

SUNNY SIDE
CHURCH RD

CLIFTON AVE

6

LODGE LA

FIR GR
BEECH AVE
ELM AVE
POPLAR AVE

MARLBOROUGH AVE

MAPLE

CHESTNUT DR
BLENHEIM DR

WOOD CL

ALDERVILLE CL

RIBBLE VIEW CL

BUTLERS MDW

A584

LYTHAM RD

Warton

OLIVER GR
ASH DR

CEDAR AVE

THE ORCHARD

HARBOUR AVE

+ Liby

PEG WAY

POST LA

MILL LA

MILLFIELD CL

WEST END LA

MEADOW DR

SANDY CL
WOODS

PO

LILAC CL

HIGHGATE LA

ELDER CL

WESTFIELD DR

Great Birch Wood

Brook Farm

LYTHAM RD

HOLLY CL
CARDS

RAKE LA

GRAHAM AVE

FERRIER BANK

Bryning with Warton St Paul's CE Prim Sch

Works

Holy Family RC Prim Sch

RYDAL AVE

LARCH CL

5

28

A584

Lodge Farm

Sewage Works

Warton Bank

THE CRESCENT

BANK LA

LORENCE AVE

Parles Farm

PR4

Warton Aerodrome

4

FY8

Wrea Brook

3

Lancashire Coastal Way

Warton Brows

27

2

River Ribble

1

26

91
72

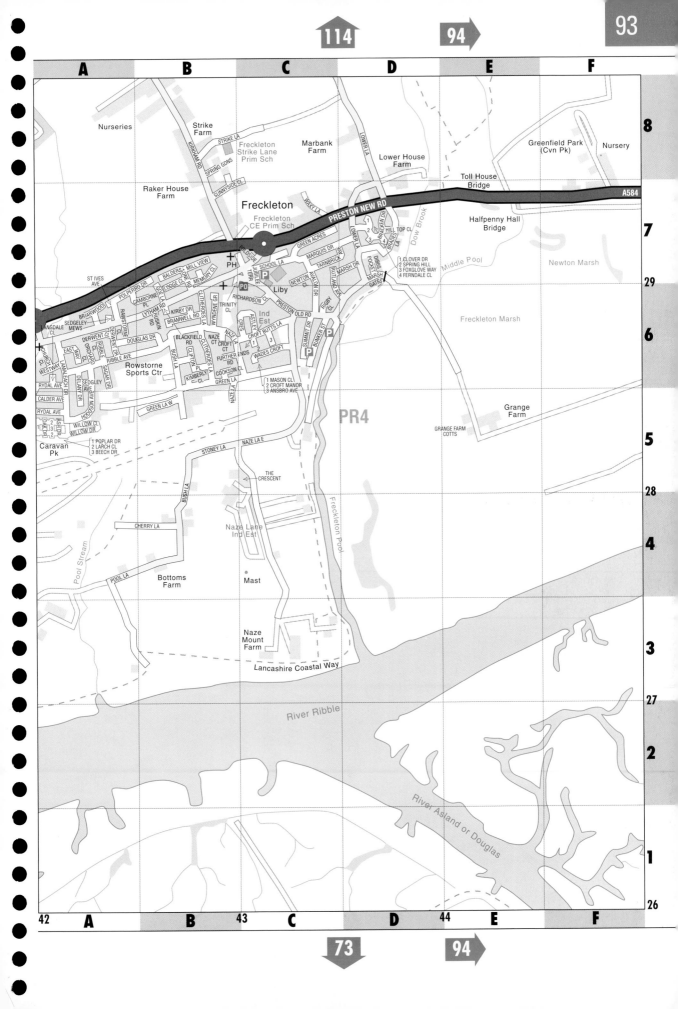

A B C D E F

8

Nurseries

Strike
Farm

Freckleton
Strike Lane
Prim Sch

Marbank
Farm

Lower House
Farm

Greenfield Park
(Cvn Pk)

Nursery

Raker House
Farm

KIRKHAM RD

STRIKE LA

SPRING GDNS

SUNNYSIDE CL

LOWER LA

Toll House
Bridge

A584

7

Freckleton

Freckleton
CE Prim Sch

WAXY LA

GREEN ACRES

PRESTON NEW RD

Dow Brook

BRICK HILL TOP LA

BRADES LA

Halfpenny Hall
Bridge

Middle Pool

Newton Marsh

29

St Ives
Ave

ST IVES
AVE

POL PERRO DR

BALDERS

MILL VIEW

LODGE CL

MEMORY CL

SCHOOL LA

JUBILEE
TERR

NEWTON DR

AVALON DR

MARQUIS DR

TARNBRICK

RUTLAND AVE

MARSH DR

RIGBY CL

DIBBS
POCKET

MARSH
GATES

1 CLOVER DR
2 SPRING HILL
3 FOXGLOVE WAY
4 FERNDALE CL

Freckleton Marsh

6

BRIARWOOD

LANGDALE
MEWS

SEDGELEY
CL

CAMBORNE
PL

LYTHAM RD

RAWSTORNE
CL

RUSKIN
RD

KIRBY DR

WYNDENE GR

CLITHEROES LA

TRINITY
CL

JUSTLEY
CRES

CROFT BUTTS LA

PRESTON OLD RD

SUMMIT DR

BUNKER ST

BRAMWELL RD

Liby

Ind
Est

RICHARDSON

EAST
WAY

CHURCH
CL

WESTWAY

DERWENT CL

DERWENT CL

RIBBLE AVE

DOUGLAS DR

BUSH LA

BLACKFIELD
RD

NAZE
CT

CROFT
CT

FURTHER
ENDS
RD

WADES CROFT

COOKSON CL

GREEN LA

NAZE LA

1 MASON CL
2 CROFT MANOR
3 ANSBRO AVE

Rowstorne
Sports Ctr

CLIFTON

KIMBERLY
CL

SAGAR DR

DELANY DR

HORNBY
AVE

SEDGLEY
AVE

PR4

RYDAL AVE

CALDER AVE

RYDAL AVE

ASH DR

OAK DR

WILLOW CL

WILLOW DR

GREEN LA W

1 POPLAR DR
2 LARCH CL
3 BEECH DR

Caravan
Pk

5

STONEY LA

NAZE LA E

THE
CRESCENT

28

BUSH LA

CHERRY LA

Naze Lane
Ind Est

Freckleton Pool

Grange
Farm

GRANGE FARM
COTTS

Pool Stream

POOL LA

Bottoms
Farm

Mast

4

Naze
Mount
Farm

3

Lancashire Coastal Way

27

River Ribble

2

River Asland or Douglas

1

26

93
115

A B C D E F

8

Eastwood
Plantation

Deepdale Brook

A583

BLACKPOOL RD

LODGE LA

A584

Savick
Bridge

PH

A583

Three
Nooks

Savick Brook
Farm

Savick Brook

A584

PRESTON NEW RD

7

Clifton Marsh
Farm

29

6

Clifton Marsh

River Ribble

5

Sewage
Works

28

PR4

4

Ribble Way

Farrers
Farm

Woodfold
Farm

3

Hutton Marsh

Westlands
Farm

GRANGE LA

Bottom of
Hutton

Middle
Grange

27

GRANGE LA

Old
Grange

Farrer's
Wood

2

Longton Brook

1

Longton Marsh

Pilot's
Cottage

GRANGE LA

SEVEN SANDS

ARKHOLME DR

HAMBLETON CL

TARNACRE

HAMBLEFIELD

GRANGEFIEL

BACK LA

26

45 A B 46 C D 47 E F

93
74

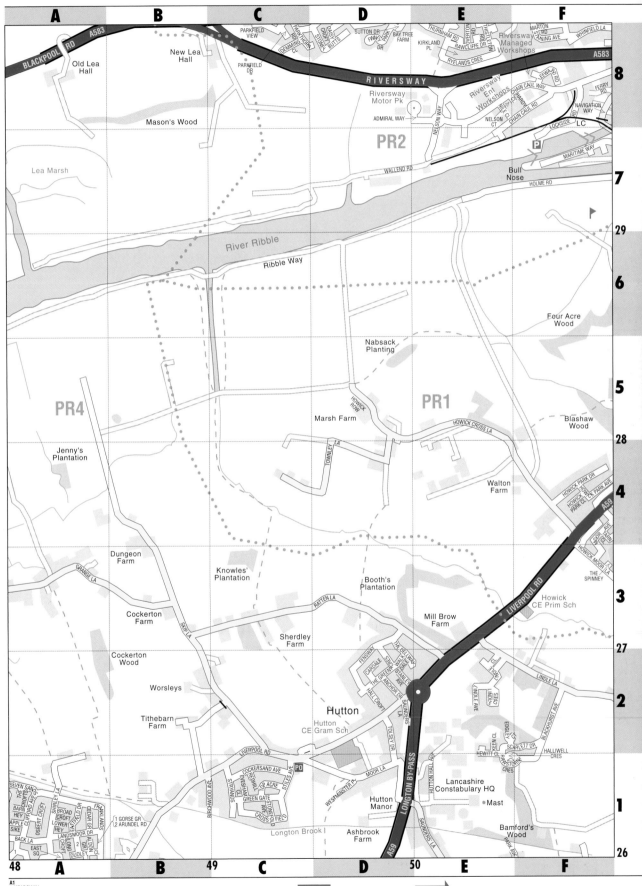

A1
1 MEADOWAY

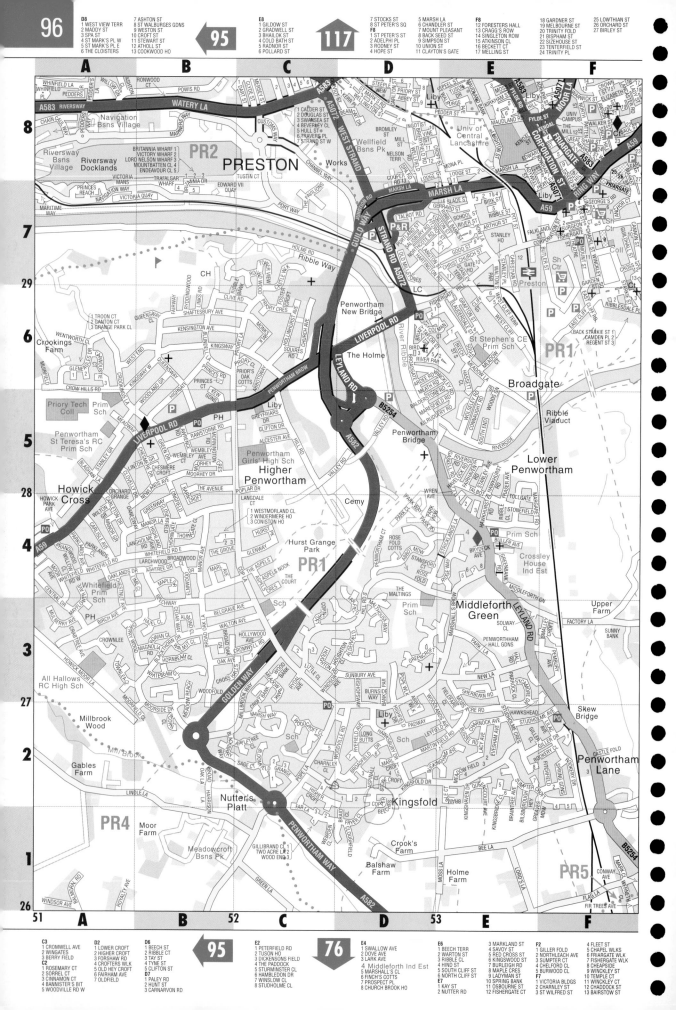

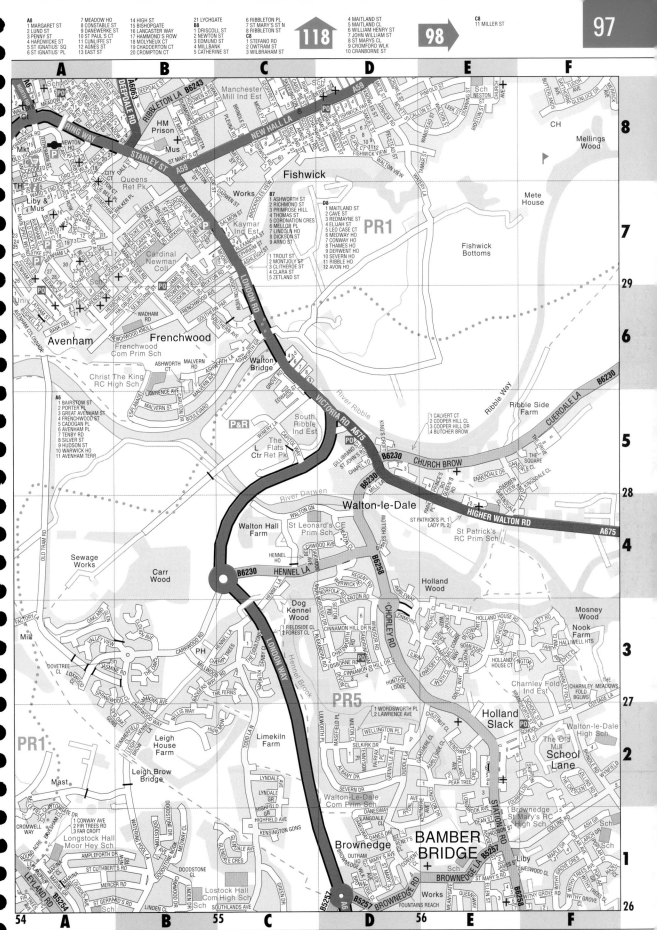

A B C D E F

Eyes Wood
PR2
PR1
RUSSELL AVE
NEWTON AVE
Ribble Way
River Ribble

Preston New Rd
A59
M6
31

Works
Cowell's Farm
B6230
VICARAGE LA

Cuerdale Hall

New Hall Tavern (PH)
Roacher Hall

Cuerdale Wood
Walmsley Fold Farm
New Hall Farm

CUERDALE LA

Roach Bridge Cotts
Mill Roach Bridge
ROACH RD
GREEN LA

Woodhouse Farm
B6230
Silverholme
Smithy House
Roach Bridge

Swaines Fold
Potter Lane Farm
Darwen Side Farm
Fleetwood Hall

POTTER LA

Sallom House
Cottage Farm

Osbaldeston House Wood
PR5
River Darwen
Beeston Wood

Bannister Hall
Carver Fold
Carr Wood
Coupe Green

Higher Walton
Jolly Fold

BANNISTER HALL LA
BANNISTER HALL DR
BANNISTER HALL CRES
DARWEN ST
SHOP LA
PO

1 ROSSALL CL
2 WINSTER CL
3 SILVERDALE CL
4 METHUEN CL
5 MANSFIELD DR

Coupe Green Prim Sch
Cuerdale Hey Farm
Beeston Brook

A675
HIGHER WALTON RD
CANAL BRIDGE ST
Higher Walton Mill
Works
Rass Wood

COUPE GN
GRANGE
LOWICK DR
RUSLAND DR
CARTMEL DR
CODHALL CRES
FOX CL
POULTON CRES
CLEVELEYS RD
HOLKER
METHUEN AVE
MARSBY CL
MANOR

LARK HILL
Swan Inn (PH)
Higher Walton CE Prim Sch
ROSEWOOD DR
ROSEWOOD AVE
HAWTHORNE AVE

HOGHTON LA
Old Oak Inn (PH)
Olive Farm
A675

BLACKBURN RD
BRIDGE ST
BROOK ST
CHURCH ST
KITTLINGBORNE BROW
THE OLD SCHOOL HO
ASHTREE CT

Mast
Prospect Hill
COTTAGE LA
BROWN LA

CHARLES CRES
GREGSON LA
Cooper House Farm
DAUB HALL LA
BELLS LA

30
Tottering Temple Farm
FOUR LANE ENDS
CONWAY CL
SQUIRES CL
RHODESWAY
LYDRIC AVE
CENTRAL AVE
Gregson Lane

LYAL GR
WOODLAND AVE
BROWN LA
SHUTTLING FIELDS LA
Middle Shuttling Fields
Drum Head Brook
Fowler Brook

ARROWSMITH DR
KNOWSLEY DR
KNOWSLEY CL
BROWNHOUSE DR
BROWNHOUSE CL
MINTHOLME AVE
ARROWSMITH CL
FRITHS AVE
PO
LARCH GATE
ALMA ROW
MANY BROOKS HO

Sch
HAZEL AVE
BRINDLE RD
WITHY TREES AVE
BRINDLE AVE

ALDERSLEIGH CRES
ALDER DR
CROSS ROW
OAK BANK
Brindle
Black Horse (PH)
Hewn Gate Farm

Ctr
COTTAGE GDNS
M61
M61
BANK HEAD LA
MAYFIELD AVE
WESTFIELD DR
BOURNES ROW
BOURNESFIELD
BOURNES STOW
GREGSON LA
FRITH'S CT
Frith's Farm
LC

Livesey Green Farm
Gregson Lane Prim Sch
St Joseph's RC Prim Sch

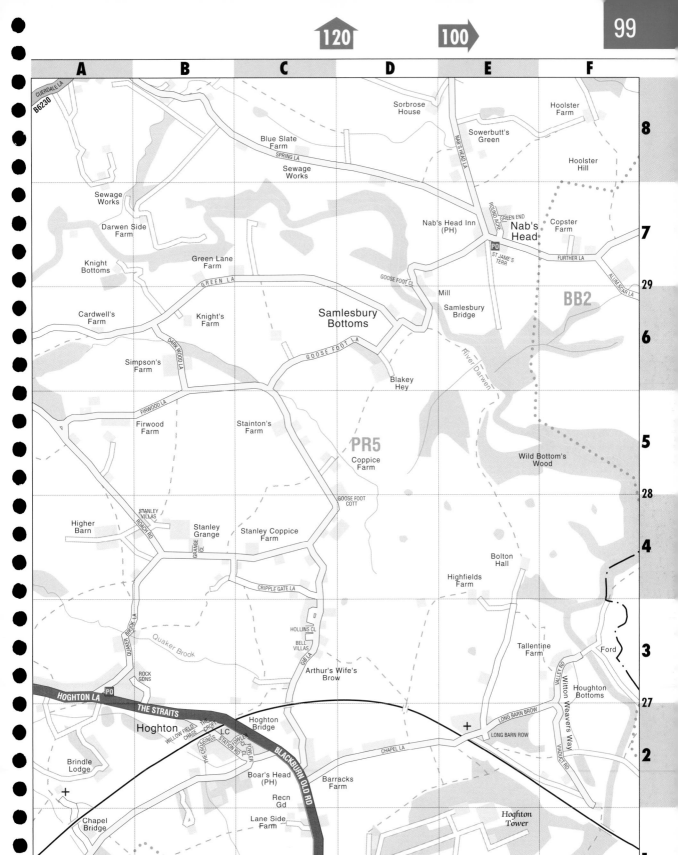

B6230
CUERDALE LA

Sorbrose
House

Hoolster
Farm

Blue Slate
Farm

SPRING LA

Sewage
Works

Sowerbutt's
Green

8

Hoolster
Hill

Sewage
Works

Darwen Side
Farm

NAB'S HEAD LA

Green End

Nab's Head Inn
(PH)

Nab's
Head

Copster
Farm

7

Green Lane
Farm

Knight
Bottoms

ROUND ACRE

PO

ST JAME'S
TERR

FURTHER LA

ALUM SCAR LA

29

GREEN LA

GOOSE FOOT CL

Mill

Samlesbury
Bridge

BB2

Cardwell's
Farm

Knight's
Farm

Samlesbury
Bottoms

6

DARK WOOD LA

Simpson's
Farm

GOOSE FOOT LA

River Darwen

FIRWOOD LA

Blakey
Hey

Firwood
Farm

Stainton's
Farm

PR5

Wild Bottom's
Wood

5

Coppice
Farm

28

GOOSE FOOT
COTT

Higher
Barn

STANLEY
VILLAS

ROACH RD

Stanley
Grange

GRANGE CL

Stanley Coppice
Farm

Bolton
Hall

4

CRIPPLE GATE LA

Highfields
Farm

HOLLINS CL

Tallentine
Farm

Ford

3

QUAKER BROOK LA

Quaker Brook

BELL
VILLAS

GIB LA

Witton Weavers Way

Houghton
Bottoms

ROCK
GDNS

Arthur's Wife's
Brow

VIADUCT RD

27

HOGHTON LA

PO

THE STRAITS

Hoghton
Bridge

Long Barn Brow

2

WILLOW FIELD
CHASE

THE
CROFT

LC

FOWLER
CL

Chapel LA

Long Barn Row

Hoghton

THE
CROSSINGS

STATION RD

BLACKBURN OLD RD

Brindle
Lodge

Boar's Head
(PH)

Barracks
Farm

Hoghton
Tower

Chapel
Bridge

Recn
Gd

Lane Side
Farm

1

GREGSON
LA

GOWANS

PR6

Hatchwood
Farm

A6675

King's
Hill

26

99
121

A · B · C · D · E · F

8

Bolton Fold
Stanley House
Hacking House
A677
PRESTON NEW RD
A6119
YEW TREE DR
Lodge Wood
WILTON CL

Ravenswing Farm
FURTHER LA
Woodfold Park Farm
Arley Brook
Arley Farm
WILTON CT 1
COUNTRY MEWS 2
LEVER CL 3
EDEN PK 4
A677
WYCOLLER AVE

7
Woodfold Hall
Jeffery Wood
Billinge Scarr

29
White House Pond
Lower Bencock Farm
SCARR LA

Middle Shorrock Hey Farm
CARR LA
Stock's Farm

6
Wallbanks House
ALUM SCARR LA
Old Woodfold Farm
Westholme Sch
HEATHFIELD PK
CARRS WOOD

MEINS RD
WOODGATES RD

5
Lower Shorrock Hey Farm
PALL MALL
BILLINGE END RD
BILLINGE SIDE

Alum House Wood
Clog and Billycock (PH)
KILLARD
Billinge Hill

28
River Darwen
Lee Farm
BB2
UNDER BILLINGE LA

4
Close Farm
BILLINGE END RD
Witton Weavers Way
Billinge Nook

Butler's Delf
Witton Country Park

Woodcock Hill
Visitors Ctr

PR5

3
Maiden House Farm
WOODCOCK HILL RD
Lower Fold
Crem

Cemy
Pleasington Nature Reserve

27
Hunter's Hill
STONEFIELD COTTS
LONG LA
Pleasington Old Hall
River Darwen
BILLINGE VIEW

Trout Brook Farm
OLD HALL LA
A674
TOWER RD

2
Higher Park Farm
SANDY LA
OLD HALL LA
Butler's Bridge
TOWER RD
HILL CREST RD
GEDDES ST

PRIORY CL
Witton Weavers Way
CHERRY TREE TERR 1
HUNTERS LODGE 2
GLADSTONE TERR 3
MELFORT CL 4
TORRIDON CL 5
Cherry Tree

Throstle Nest Brow
REGENTS CL
PH
BOWER AVE
Tongue Hill
Playing Fields
PRESTON OLD RD
Leeds and Liverpool Canal
GREEN LA

1
Brownlands Farm
Pleasington
Pleasington
Cherry Tree
LIVESEY HALL CL
THE CRESCENT
A674
St Francis CE Prim Sch

VICTORIA RD
WOODLANDS AVE
SPRINGFIELD AVE
VICTORIA AVE

26
BROWNLOW TERR
CH
ROSE HILL RD
Liby

63 · 64 · 65

A · B · C · D · E · F

99
80

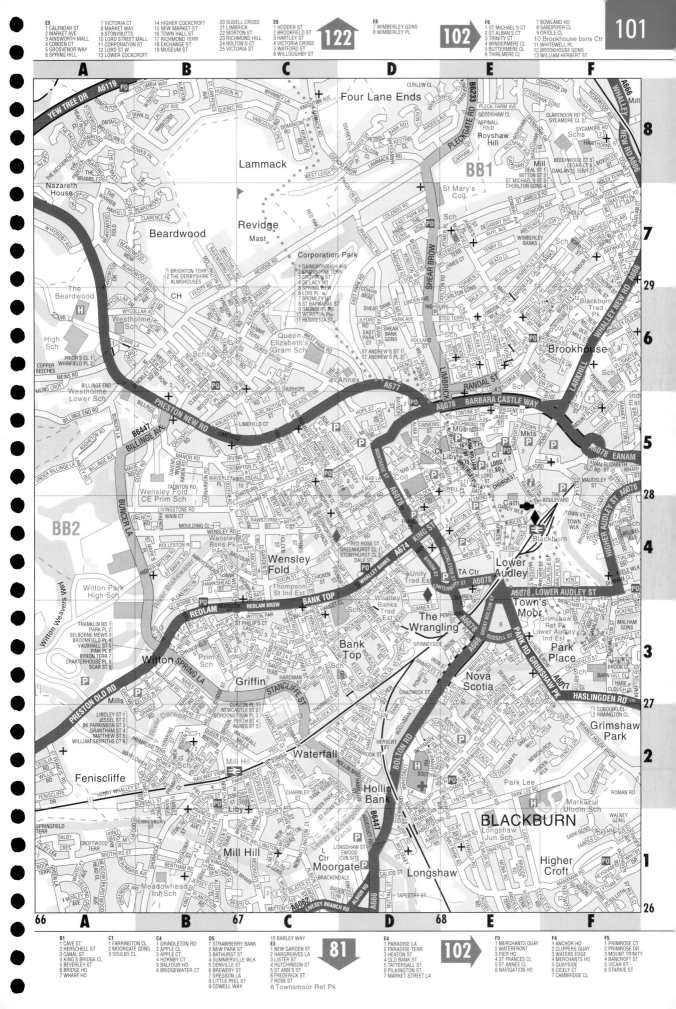

101   123

A   B   C   D   E   F

8 Cemy
Bastwell
Clarendon Mill RD

Whitebirk Ind Est
Little Harwood

BROWNHILL DR A6119
WHITEBIRK DR

Rishton Resr
WOODSIDE AVE
A678

BLACKBURN RD
M65

7 Cob Wall
Ribble Bsns Pk
Glenfield Park Ind Est
Greenbank Tech Pk

Whitebirk Moss Farm

COWHILL LA

29 Daisyfield
Green Bank Bsns Pk
Whitebirk
A6119
A678
WHITEBIRK DR

6
BLACKBURN
Hole House
Leeds & Liverpool Canal
PH
Depot
Cowhill Moss

Green Bank
Furthergate Ind Est
BURNLEY RD
BURNLEY ST
Intack Prim Sch

BB1
Redcap Farm
PH
A679
BLACKBURN RD

5
Fort Street Ind Est
Appleby Bsns Ctr
Daisyfield Mill
Superstore
FURTHERGATE A678
A679
Intack

Knuzden Brook
BALMORAL CRES

28
Higher Eanam
A6078 COPY NOOK
BOTTOMGATE
Sch
ACCRINGTON RD
B6236 BANK LA

4
Higher Audley
Queen's Park
B6130
Seven Houses
Cabin End Row
B6234
STANHILL RD
Knuzden Brook
B6234
St Oswald's CE Prim Sch

3
Audley Inf & Jun Schs
Queen's Park
1 LANGDEN BROOK SQ
2 SKELSHAW CL
3 WHITENDALE CRES
Prim Sch
SHADSWORTH RD
Shadsworth
HASLINGDEN OLD RD
BROOKSIDE LA
Magnoll's Farm

27
A6077
Queen's Park
Crosshill Specl Sch
Martindale CL
Shadsworth Jun Sch
BB5

2
BB2
OLD BANK LA
H
Mast
OLD BANK LA
Shadsworth L Ctr
Queen's Park Tech Coll
Knuzden Brook
Blackburn Small Holdings
Sough Lane Farm
B6236

1
Whinny Heights
HASLINGDEN RD
1 LINDISFARNE AVE
2 DELIUS CL
3 TIPPET CL
4 HOLST GDNS
5 RAVENGLASS CL
6 WHITEHAVEN CL
B6130
SETT END RD W
Shadsworth Bsns Pk
Four Lane Ends
LOTTICE LA
B6231

26
Fishmoor Resr
Sports Ctr
A6077
M65
B6231
SCHOOL LA
DUCKWORTH HILL LA
COLLIER'S ROW

69   A   70   B   C   70   D   71   E   F

101   82

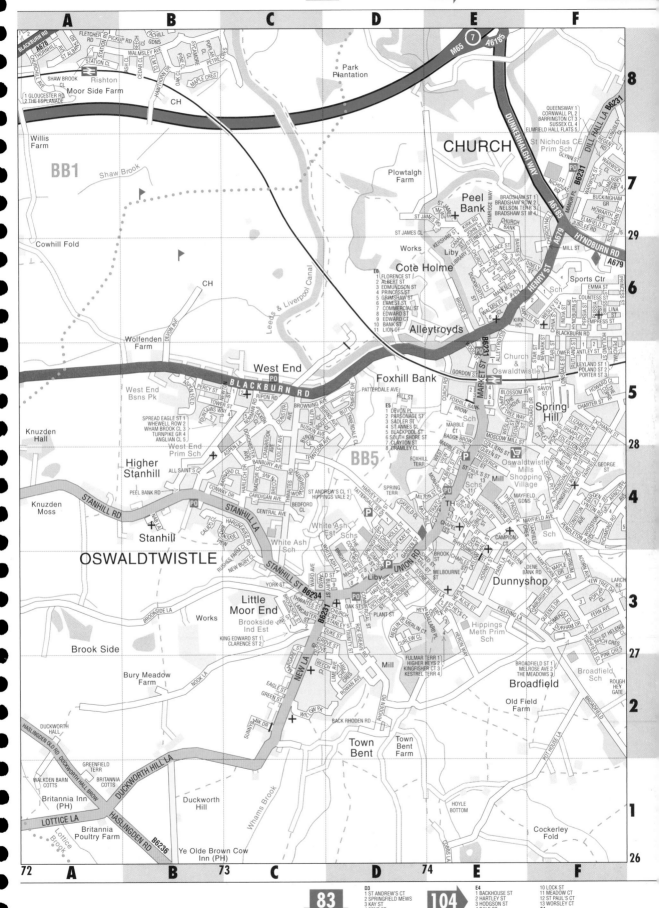

CHURCH

BB1

Shaw Brook

Willis Farm

Cowhill Fold

Moor Side Farm

Rishton

1 GLOUCESTER RD
2 THE ESPLANADE

Park Plantation

St Nicholas CE Prim Sch

Queensway 1
Cornwall Pl 2
Barrington Ct 3
Sussex Cl 4
Elmfield Hall Flats 5

Plowtalgh Farm

Peel Bank

Cote Holme

Alleytroyds

E6
1 FLORENCE ST
2 ALBERT ST
3 EDMUNDSON ST
4 PRINCESS ST
5 GRIMSHAW ST
6 ERNEST ST
7 COMMERCIAL ST
8 EDWARD ST
9 EDWARD CT
10 BANK ST
11 LION ST

Sports Ctr

Wolfenden Farm

West End

BLACKBURN RD

Foxhill Bank

West End Bsns Pk

Spread Eagle St 1
Whewell Row 2
Wham Brook Cl 3
Turnpike Gr 4
Anglian Cl 5

West End Prim Sch

Higher Stanhill

Knuzden Hall

Knuzden Moss

STANHILL RD

Stanhill

OSWALDTWISTLE

BB5

E5
1 DEVON PL
2 PARSONAGE ST
3 SADLER ST
4 ST ANNES CL
5 BLACKPOOL ST
6 SOUTH SHORE ST
7 CLAYTON ST
8 BRAMLEY CL

Spring Hill

Oswaldtwistle Mills Shopping Village

St Andrew's Cl 1
Hippings Vale 2

STANHILL LA

White Ash Est

White Ash Sch

Little Moor End

Brookside Ind Est

King Edward St 1
Clarence St 2

Brook Side

Bury Meadow Farm

Dunnyshop

Hippings Meth Prim Sch

Fulmar Terr 1
Higher Heys 2
Kingfisher Cl 3
Kestrel Terr 4

Broadfield St 1
Melrose Ave 2
The Meadows 3

Broadfield

Broadfield Sch

Rough Hey Gate

Mill

Old Field Farm

Town Bent

Town Bent Farm

Duckworth Hall

Greenfield Terr
Britannia Cotts

Walkden Barn Cotts

Britannia Inn (PH)

LOTTICE LA

Britannia Poultry Farm

Duckworth Hill

HASLINGDEN RD B6236

Whams Brook

Hoyle Bottom

Cockerley Fold

Ye Olde Brown Cow Inn (PH)

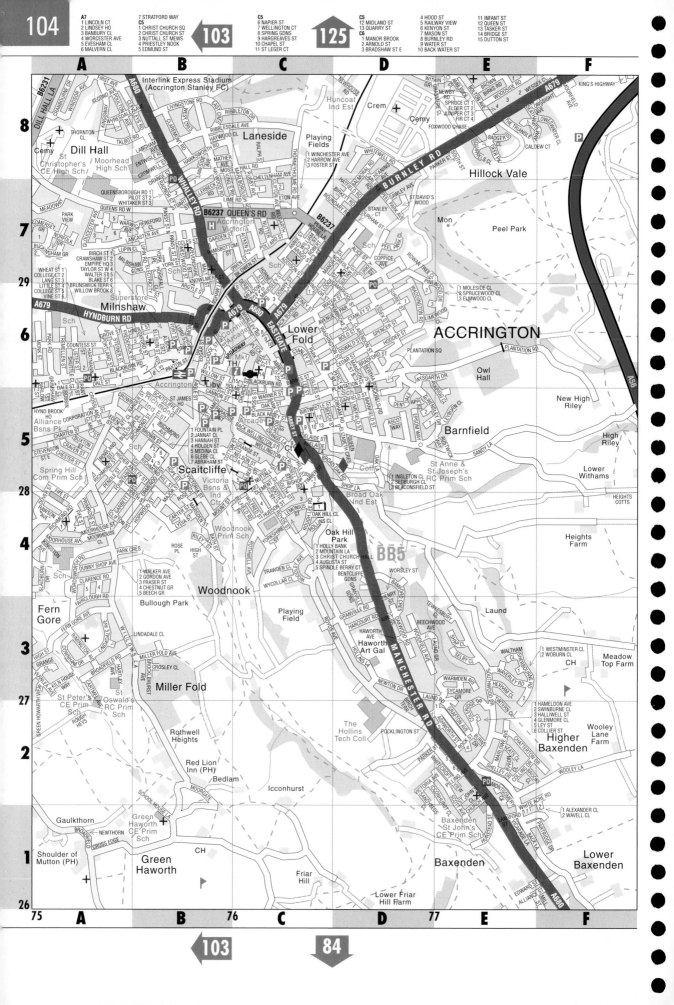

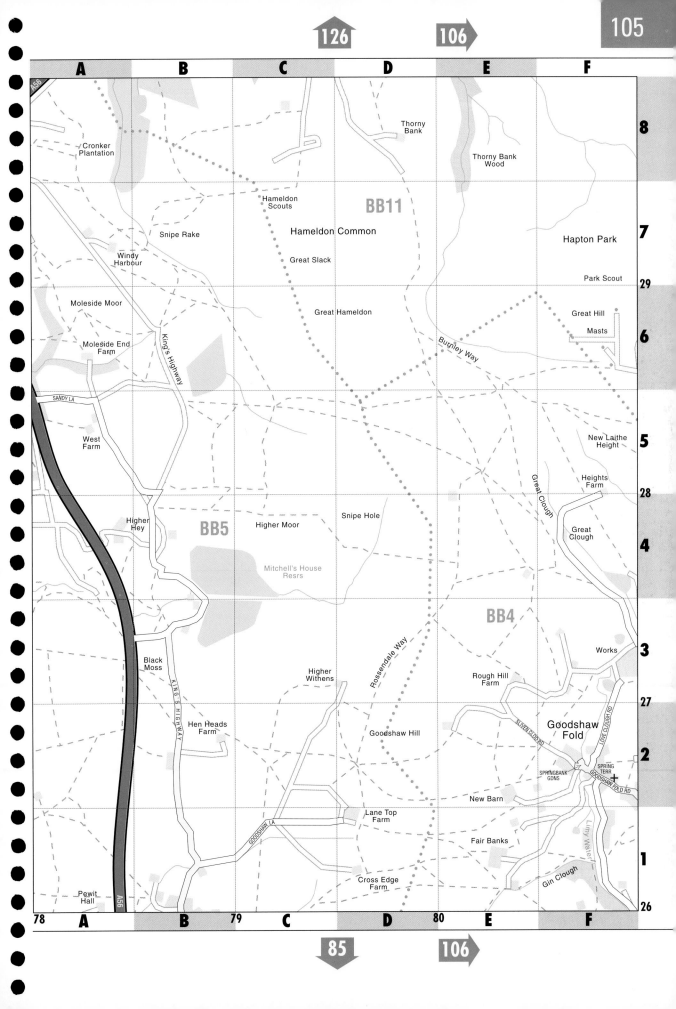

105
127

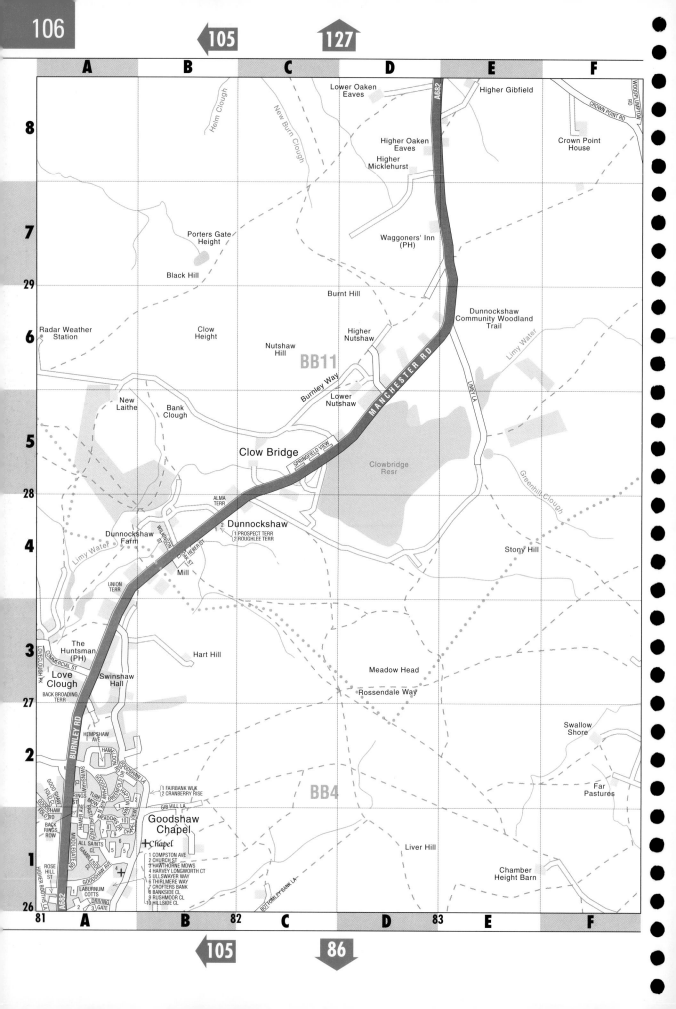

105
86

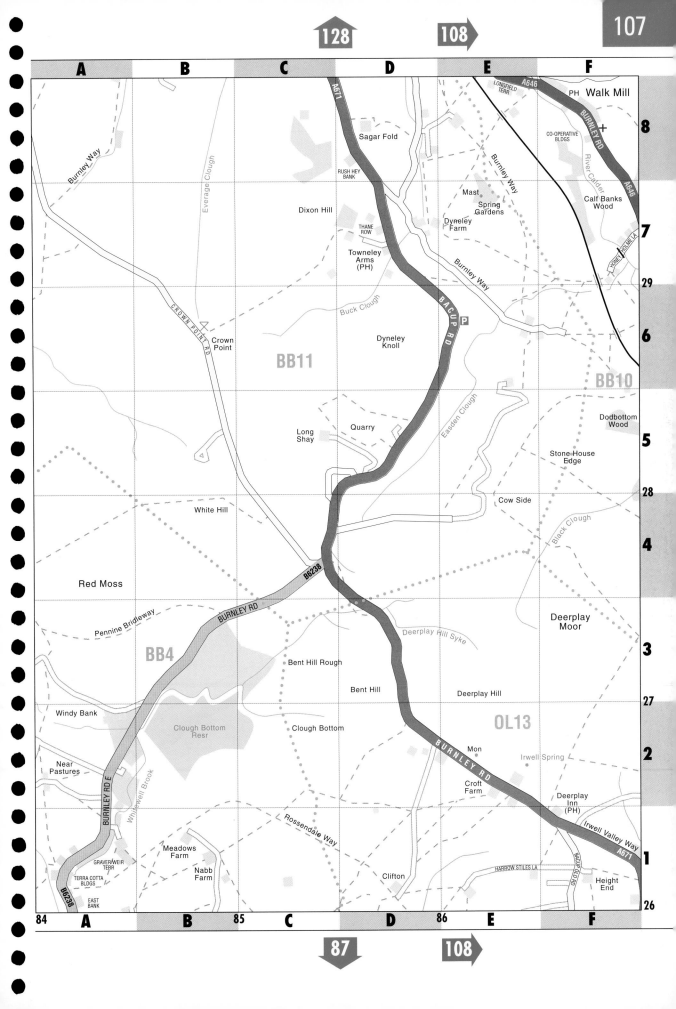

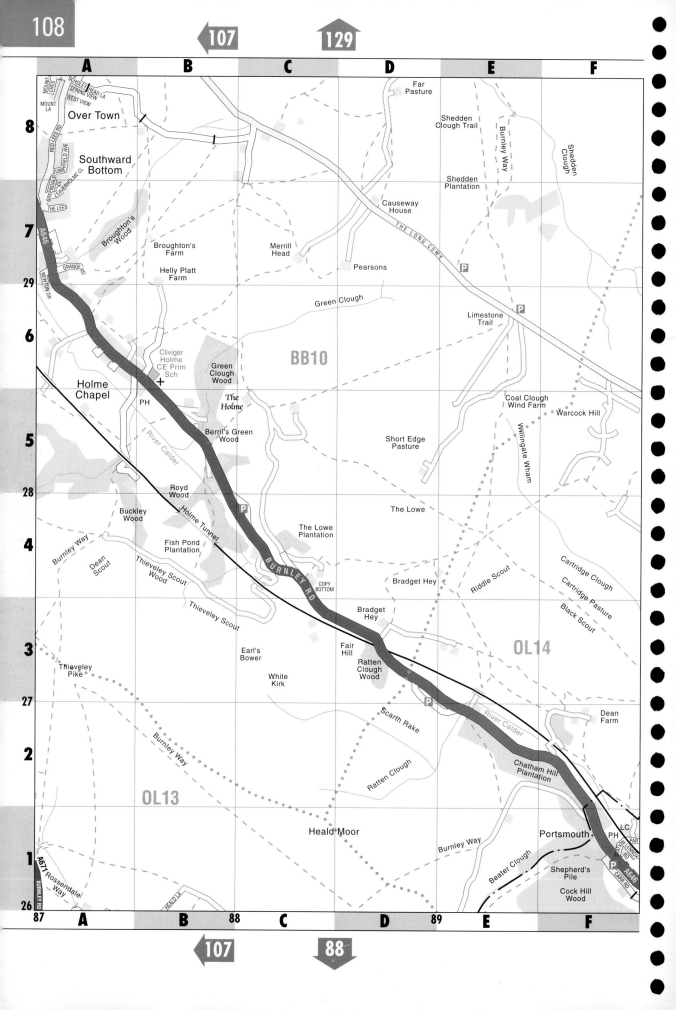

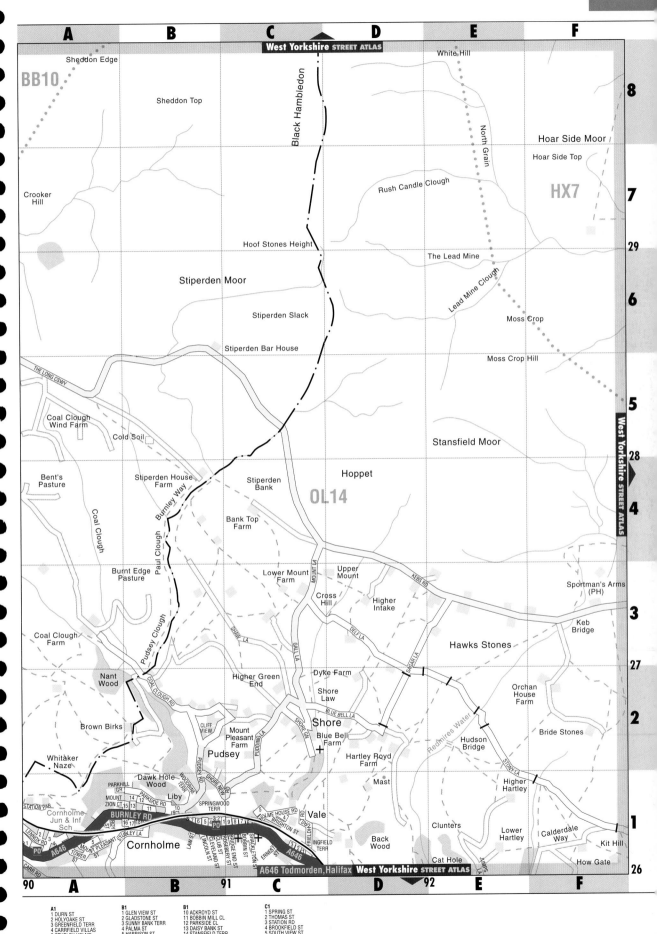

A1
1 DURN ST
2 HOLYOAKE ST
3 GREENFIELD TERR
4 CARRFIELD VILLAS
5 STUBLEY HOLME

B1
1 GLEN VIEW ST
2 GLADSTONE TERR
3 SUNNY BANK TERR
4 PALMA ST
5 HARRISON ST
6 HIRST ST
7 SUN TERR
8 OAKLEIGH TERR
9 CORNHOLME TERR

B1
10 ACKROYD ST
11 BOBBIN MILL CL
12 PARKSIDE CL
13 DAISY BANK ST
14 STANSFIELD TERR
15 BROWN BIRKS ST
16 PEAR PL
17 PEAR ST
18 SPRING VILLAS

C1
1 SPRING ST
2 THOMAS ST
3 STATION RD
4 BROOKFIELD ST
5 SOUTH VIEW ST
6 HUDSON ST
7 COLLEGE ST
8 GARFIELD ST
9 VICTORIA ST

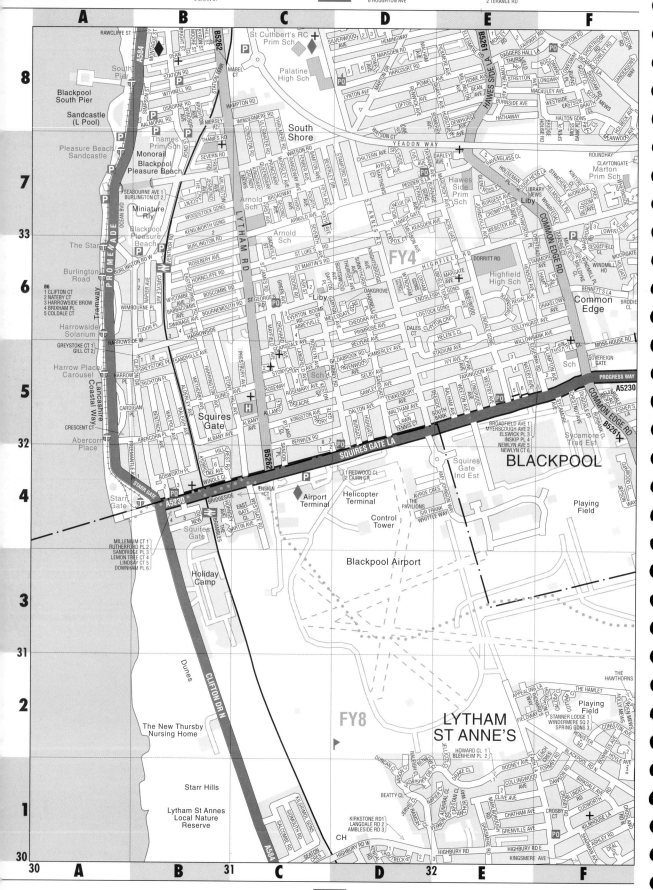

C5
1 COLVILLE AVE
2 STONY CROFT PL
3 ROSEBANK AVE
4 WHITWELL AVE
5 THE SANCTUARY
6 CAIRN CT

C6
1 ST LUKE'S CT
2 PARK VIEW CT
3 LAURIER AVE
4 SUMMERVILLE

7 SQUIRES CT

130

D8
1 SILVERWOOD CT
2 FREDRICK ST
3 NEWBURY AVE
4 CLAUGHTON MANS
5 WALVERDEN AVEW
6 HOUGHTON AVE

7 SWINDON AVE

E7
1 TEENADORE AVE
2 ANNASIDE CL
3 REANEY AVE

E8
1 TROUGHTON CRES
2 TERANCE RD

F7
1 AYSGARTH CT
2 MOORVIEW CT
3 MOSS WAY
4 GREEN WAY
5 GREGSON CL

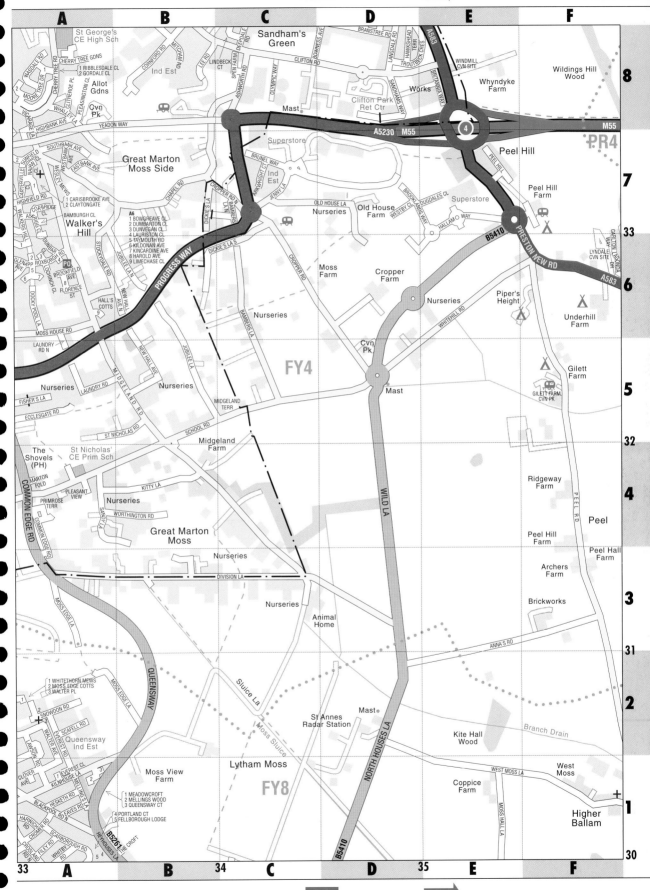

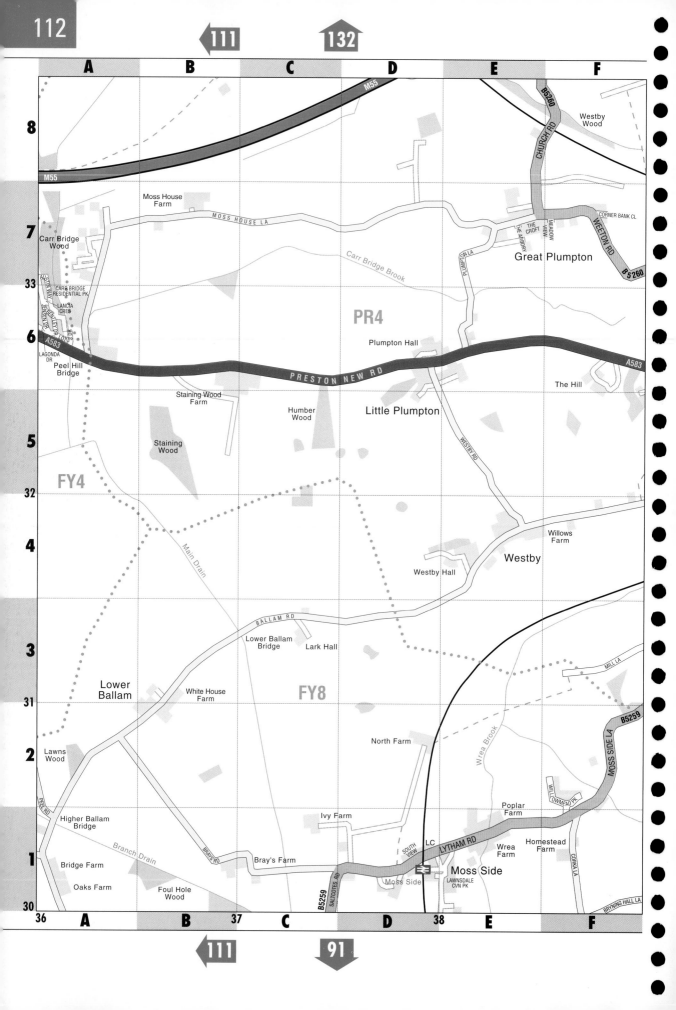

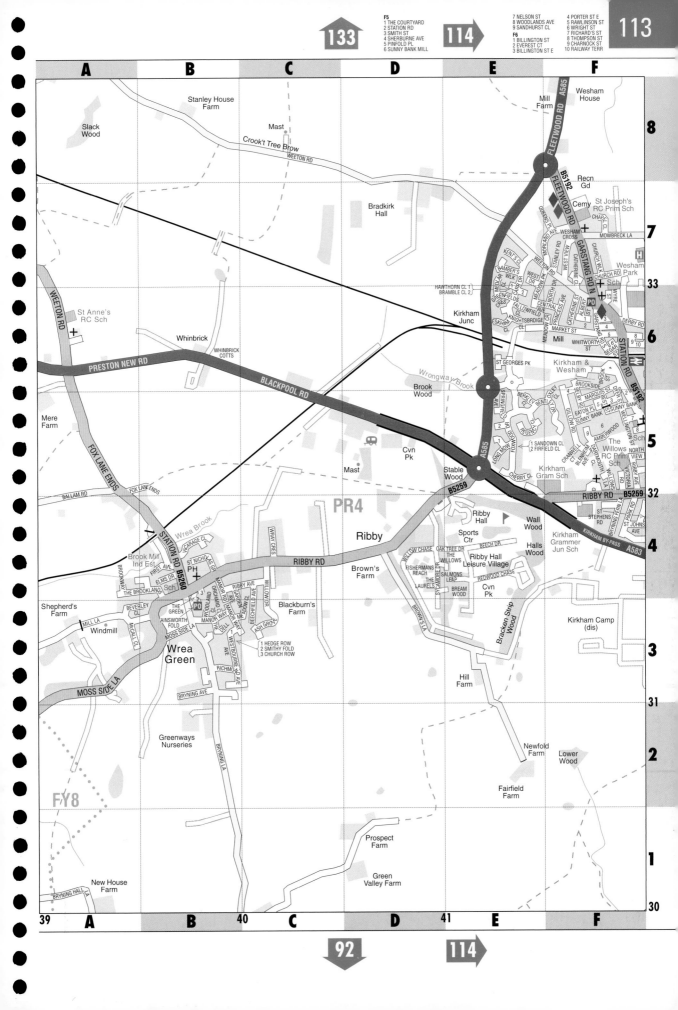

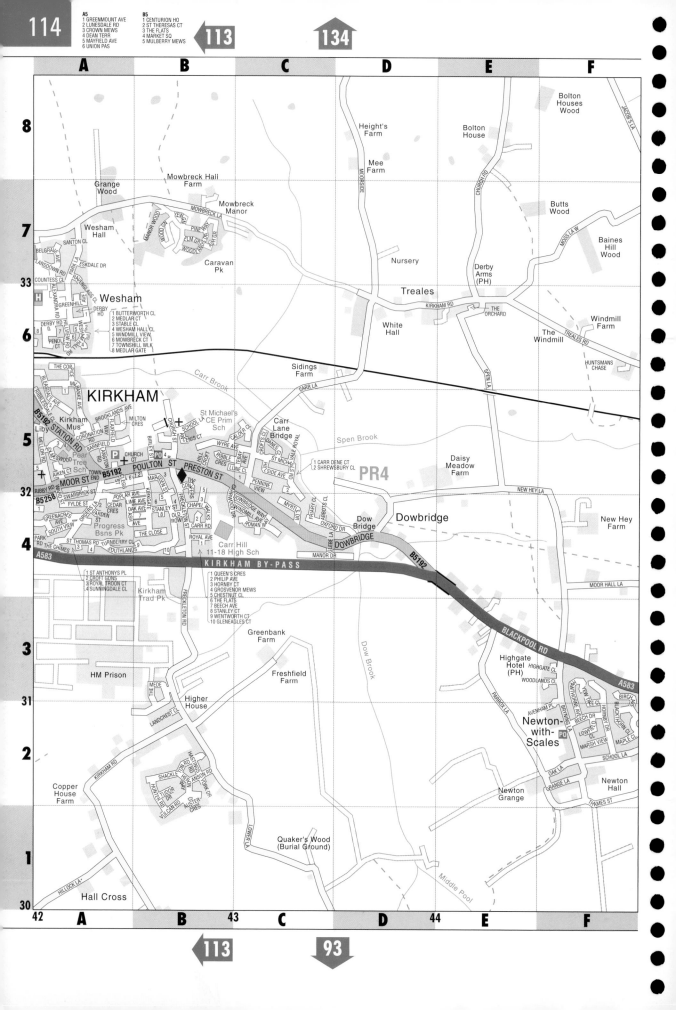

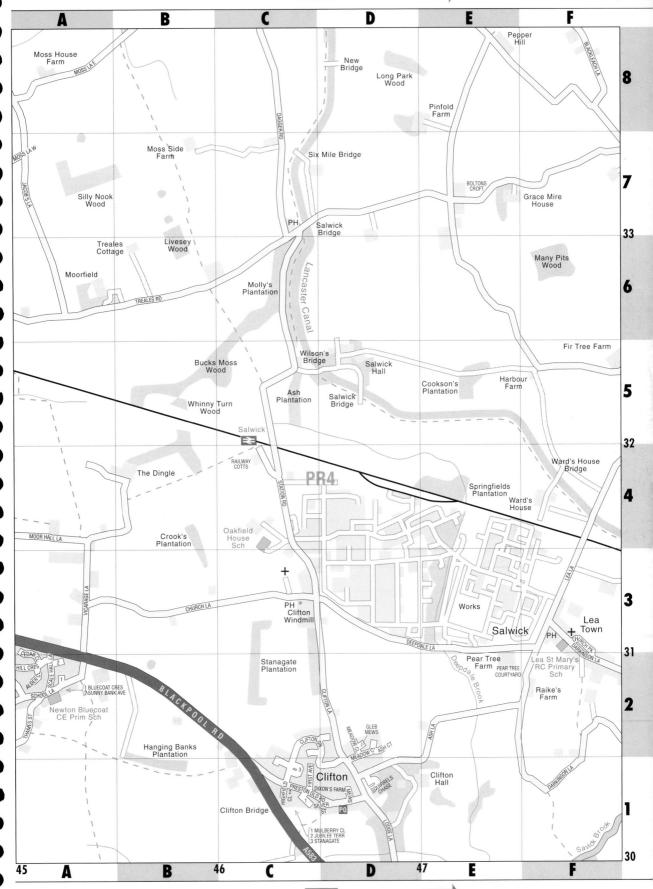

A B C D E F

8
7
33
6
5
32
4
3
31
2
1
30

Moss House Farm

MOSS LA E

New Bridge

Long Park Wood

Pepper Hill

BLACK LEACH LA

Moss Side Farm

DAGGER RD

Six Mile Bridge

Pinfold Farm

BOLTONS CROFT

MOSS LA W

JACOB'S LA

Silly Nook Wood

Livesey Wood

Grace Mire House

Treales Cottage

PH

Salwick Bridge

Many Pits Wood

Moorfield

Molly's Plantation

TREALES RD

Lancaster Canal

Wilson's Bridge

Salwick Hall

Fir Tree Farm

Bucks Moss Wood

Ash Plantation

Salwick Bridge

Cookson's Plantation

Harbour Farm

Whinny Turn Wood

Salwick

Ward's House Bridge

The Dingle

RAILWAY COTTS

STATION RD

PR4

Springfields Plantation

Ward's House

MOOR HALL LA

Crook's Plantation

Oakfield House Sch

LEA LA

Ward's House

VICARAGE LA

CHURCH LA

PH Clifton Windmill

Works

Salwick

CHURCH PK

Lea Town

DARKINSON LA

DEEPDALE LA

PH

CEDAR CL
HILL CRES
ALDER CT
SCALE HALL LA
SCHOOL LA
THAMES ST

1 BLUECOAT CRES
2 SUNNY BANK AVE

Stanagate Plantation

CLIFTON LA

Pear Tree Farm

PEAR TREE COURTYARD

Lea St Mary's RC Primary Sch

Deepdale Brook

Raike's Farm

Newton Bluecoat CE Prim Sch

BLACKPOOL RD

Hanging Banks Plantation

GLEB MEWS

MEADOW CL
MEADOW C' ASH CT

ASH LA

Clifton Hall

DARKINSON LA

CLIFTON GN
FIRST AVE
HIGHFIELD CL
PRESTON OLD RD
SILVER ST
Clifton
DIXON'S FARM MEWS
PO

SQUIRRELS CHASE

LODGE LA

Clifton Bridge

A583

1 MULBERRY CL
2 JUBILEE TERR
3 STANAGATE

Savick Brook

45 A B 46 C D 47 E F 30

115 136

A B C D E F

8
7
33
6
5
32
4
3
31
2
1
30

M55
B5411

Lower Bartle

Higher Bartle

TABLEY LA

Houghton House Farm

ROSEMARY LA

School Farm

BLACKLEACH LA

Bartle Hall

BARTLE LA

Old Vicarage Farm

SANDY LA

Maxey House

Nog Tow

LIGHTFOOT LA

1 BROOK MDW
2 DAISYFIELDS

B6241

Ivy Farm

Sitting Goose Inn (PH)

Moor Hall

Saddle Inn (PH)

LEA LA

Fir Tree Farm

PR4

HOYLES LA

SANDRINGHAM WAY 1
BLENHEIM WAY 2
BIDEFORD WAY 3
BUDE CL 4
BARNSTAPLE WAY 5
ASHFIELD CT 6

Haydock Farm

HONITON WAY

KINGSLEY RD

TANTERTON HALL RD

B5411

TAG LA

Cottam

THE GRAINGS

MILLER LA

THE VILLAGE

SANDYFIELDS
COPSEFIELD
FLOWERFIELD
MEADOWBARN
SWALLOWFIELDS
MOSSBROOK DR
POPPYFIELD
COTTAM LA
GOLDFINCH
KIDSGROVE
MARTHFIELD

WORCESTER GDNS 1
WILTSHIRE MEWS 2

THE WEALD

THE CHASE

MILLER LA

THE GRANGE

MERRY TREES LA

LAPET GR

ROSEWOOD

PH

Cottam Hall

COTTAM HALL LA

TAG CROFT
TAG FARM CT

HOLLYBANK CL

HEREFORD GR
AVON GDNS

HAYDOCKS LA

Sch

SPIRES
GR
VANGE
GR

ANCILA
GR
BERRY
GR

1 CROSIER WLK
2 ROSEDENE CL

EASTBOURNE CL
WATBY AVE

SIDGREAVES LA

Lea Neeld's Endowed CE Prim Sch

GREENSIDE
SWINSIDE

BAMPTON DR

KEN'S WAY

VALENTINES MDW

THE GREENS
THE CABLES
MILLERSGATE

HARGREAVES CT 1
WHITBY PL 2
NEWLYN PL 3

REDCAR AVE

Moor Hey

Earl's Farm

Bryars Farm

THORNTHWAITE RD

OUTGATE RD

COTTAM WAY

COLERIDGE CL

CABERRA LA
FINCH LA

KINNOCK LA

Holy Family RC Prim Sch

Ingol Com Prim Sch

DINWOOD CT
DINWOOD CL

TOM BENSON WAY

Quaker's Bridge

Lancaster Canal

Westleigh

VALENTINES LA

BRIDGEND CT 1
RUTHIN CT 2
NEWPORT CT 3
PENARTH CT 4
MONMOUTH CT 5
PORTHCAWL CT 6
BARDSEA PL 7

CRESSWELL AVE

RAILWAY COTTS

Cotty Brook (PH)

Preston Sports Arena

Works

B6241

Halsall's Farm

DARKINSON LA

LEARD

ALDER COPPICE

WILLOW COPPICE

WEST
VIEW

MALLETFIELD

HAZEL COPPICE

SAVICK WAY

SUMMER TREES AVE

BILSBORROW

WHITE MDW

LIME GR

PR2

New House Farm

Law Head Runnel

SAVICK BROOK

CH

Leyland Bridge

Ashton Prim Sch

LUTON RD

WEST PARK AVE

ELM AVE

QUEENSWAY

KINGSWAY

ALDWYCH DR

BROADWAY

Brewer House Farm

Millennium Ribble Link

NELSON CRES

ARNSIDE CL
CARTMEL RD

AINSDALE RD
DENDON
HENDON AVE

LYNDHURST RD

Ashton-on-Ribble High Sch

Liby

A5085

NORTH SYKE AVE
HACKLANDS AVE

LINCOLN CHASE

GILHOUSE AVE

GREENSIDE AVE

SAVICK AVE

Lea

SHEFFIELD

CHARLES
ST

BLACKPOOL RD
BARTLE
BALSHAW
SALWICK
MYTHOP PL

RIBB
NORBRECK PL
NORCROSS PL

Ashton Park

Larches

1 WESTLEIGH RD
2 STAINING AVE
3 OAKLANDS GR

RIVERWAY

BLACKPOOL RD A5085

115 95

C1
1 FULFORD AVE
2 ROSE BANK
3 MAPLEBANK
4 WHITELENS AVE
5 PARKFIELD CL
6 PARKFIELD CRES
7 HARDWEN AVE

D1
1 THE CRESCENT
2 HOLMFIELD CRES
3 THORNPARK DR
4 WHITETHORN SQ
5 DAISY CROFT

E1
1 CHARLESWAY CT
2 THE PLOUGHLANDS
3 WHITEHOLME PL
4 WEETON PL
5 ROSEACRE PL
6 THE WOODLANDS
7 ALDCLIFFE RD
8 FORTON RD
9 THURNHAM RD

E2
1 GREENDALE MEWS
2 EXETER PL
3 DOWNHAM PL
4 NEWARK PL

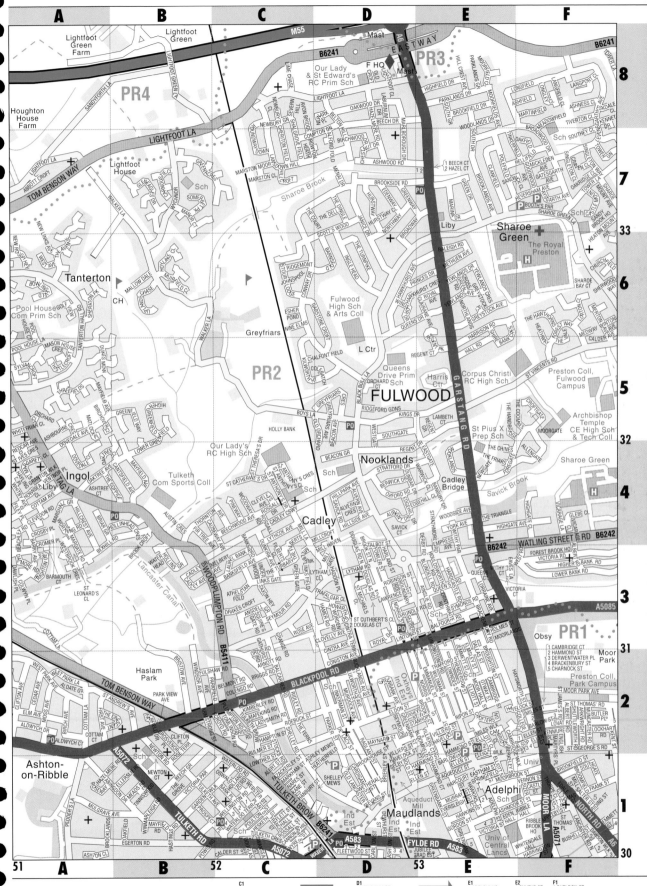

C1
1 THRELFALL ST
2 BRAMPTON ST
3 ELTON ST
4 BRUNSWICK PL
5 PECHELL ST
6 BLANCHE ST
7 HIGHBANK HOTEL

96

D1
1 NEWSHAM ST
2 BATH ST
3 MALTHOUSE CT
4 THE MALTHOUSE

118

E1
1 ADELPHI HO
2 HEYSHAM ST
3 DERWENT HALL
4 DOUGLAS HALL
5 TOWN BROOK HO

E2
1 OXHEYS CT
2 ALMELO HO

F1
1 SHELDON CT
2 AUGHTON WLK
3 BECKETT CT
4 HANOVER CT
5 Preston Ent Ctr

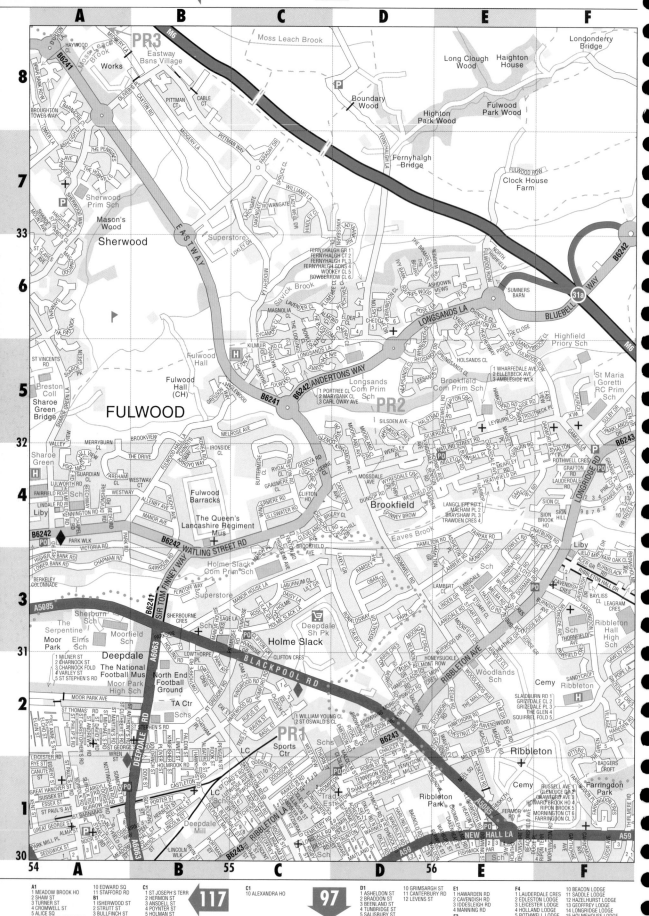

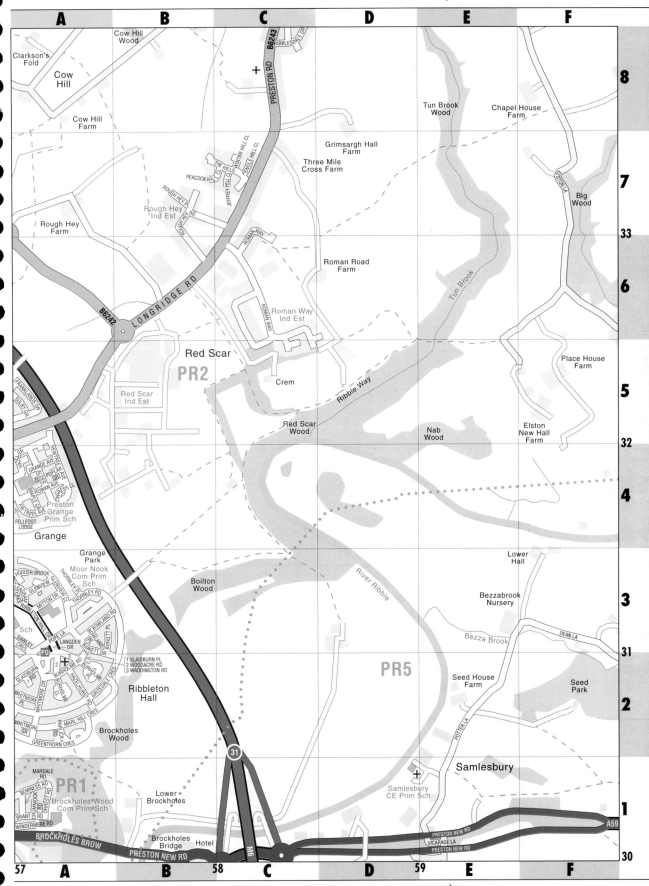

← 119
↑ 140

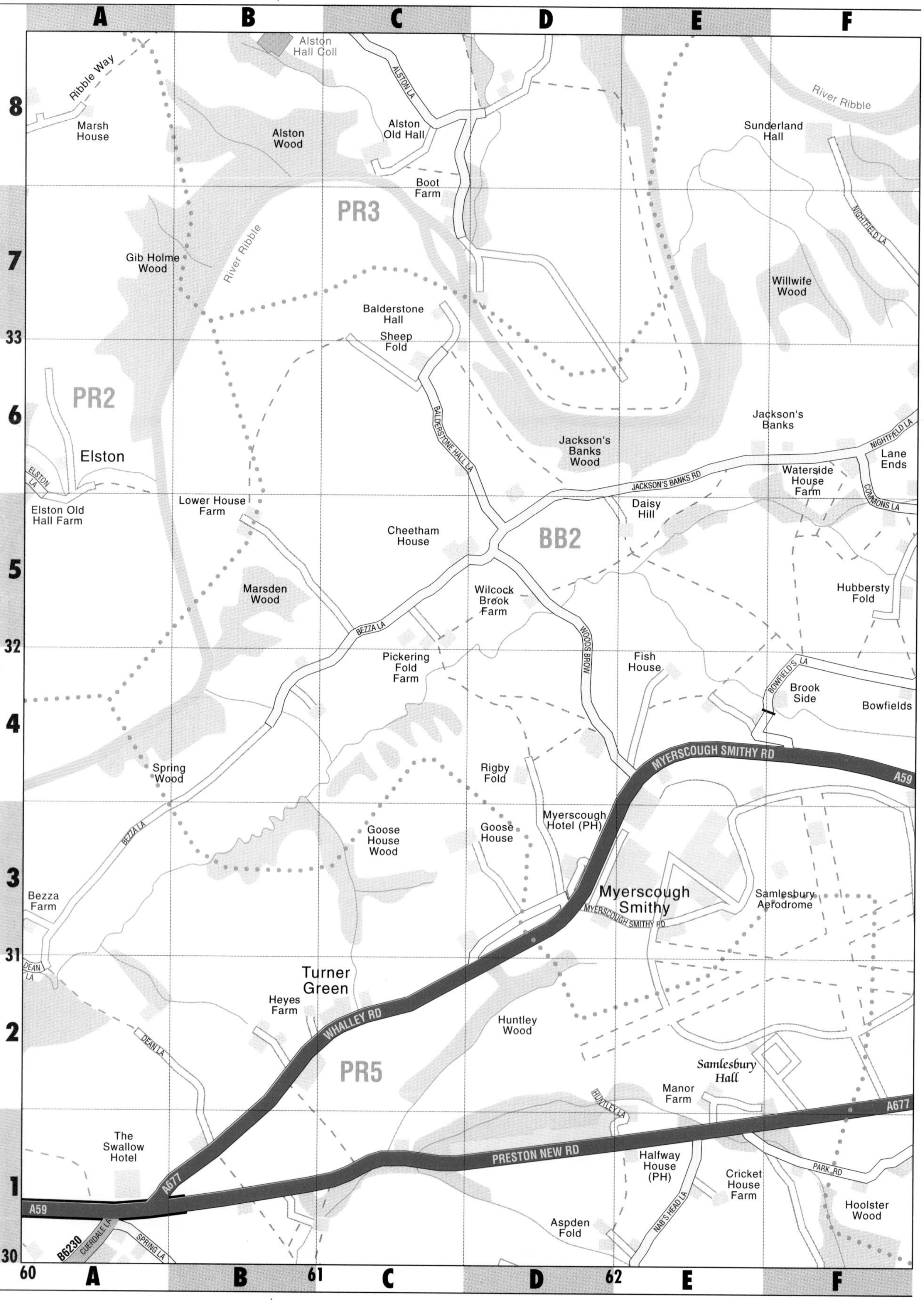

A B C D E F

8

Ribble Way
Marsh House
Alston Hall Coll
Alston Wood
Alston Old Hall
Boot Farm
Sunderland Hall
River Ribble
NIGHTFIELD LA

PR3

7

Gib Holme Wood
River Ribble
Willwife Wood

33

Balderstone Hall
Sheep Fold

PR2

6

Elston
Jackson's Banks Wood
Jackson's Banks
Lane Ends
ELSTON LA
JACKSON'S BANKS RD
Waterside House Farm
COMMONS LA
NIGHTFIELD LA
BALDERSTONE HALL LA

Elston Old Hall Farm
Lower House Farm
Cheetham House
Daisy Hill

BB2

5

Marsden Wood
Wilcock Brook Farm
Hubbersty Fold
BEZZA LA

32

Pickering Fold Farm
Fish House
WOODS BROW
BONFIELD'S LA
Brook Side
Bowfields

4

Spring Wood
Rigby Fold
MYERSCOUGH SMITHY RD
A59
BEZZA LA

Goose House Wood
Goose House
Myerscough Hotel (PH)

3

Bezza Farm
Myerscough Smithy
MYERSCOUGH SMITHY RD
Samlesbury Aerodrome

31

DEAN LA

Turner Green
Heyes Farm
WHALLEY RD
Huntley Wood

2

DEAN LA
PR5
Samlesbury Hall
Manor Farm
HUNTLEY LA
A677

The Swallow Hotel
PRESTON NEW RD
Halfway House (PH)
PARK RD

1

A59
A677
NAB'S HEAD LA
Cricket House Farm
Hoolster Wood
Aspden Fold

30

60 B6230 GUERDALE LA SPRING LA 61 62

A B C D E F

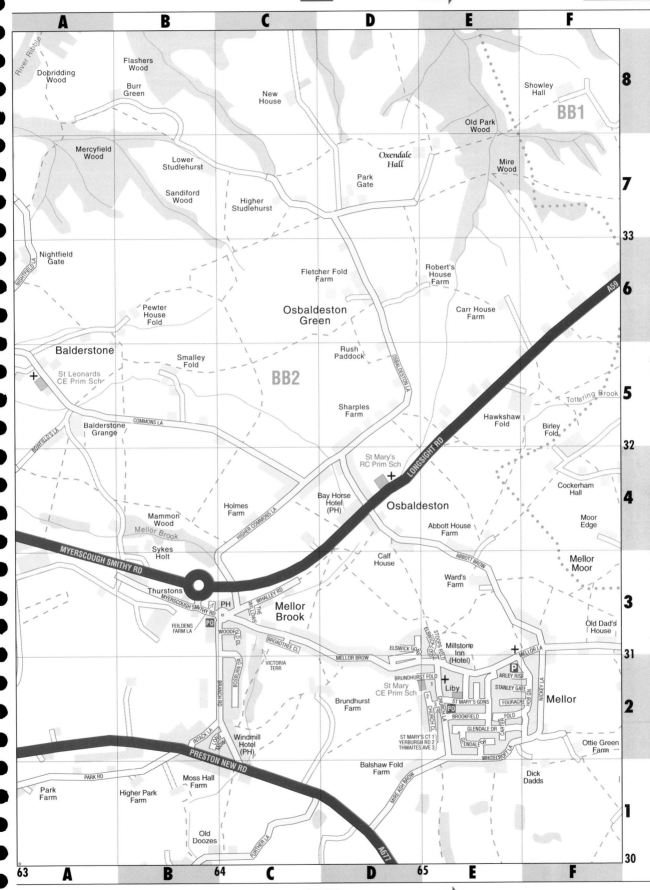

A **B** **C** **D** **E** **F**

8

B6245

Eden Holme

White Holme

RIBCHESTER RD

Oakes Bridge

Oakes Bar

Oaks Farm

ALBANY DR

A59

Copster Green

Dewhurst House

Langho Colony

BB6

Brook Cottage

LONGSIGHT RD

Clayton-Le-Dale

OAKS BROW

Lovely Hall

LOVELY HALL LA

Ashes Farm

7

Low Farm

Mire Fold

Nook House

Salesbury CE Prim Sch

33

Royal Oak Inn (PH)

A59

BB2

SHOWLEY RD

Harwood Fold

CLAYTON GR

PH

PO

1 CHURCH VIEW
2 HAZELMOOR

THE HAZELS

BRYER'S CROFT

DURHAM RD

SHETLAND

BERKSHIRE CL

ELY CL

A666

6

Showley Fold

Tottering Brook

St PETER'S CL

RYDEN AV

Clayton Hey Fold Farm

Salesbury

RIBCHESTER RD

SHOWLEY CT

YEW TREE CL

ART GR

BEECH

MAPLE CL

KNOWSLEY RD W

THE HAWTHORNS

SOMERSET AVE

GLENDENE

VALLEY

B6245

WHALLEY RD

GROSVENOR LODGE

FAIRWAYS CT

CH

Blue Slate Farm

Showley Brook

Wilpshire

BROOKLYN RD

KNOWSLEY RD

WOODCREST

MAYFAIR CRES

HOLLOWHEAD LA

THE GRANGE

BEAVER

EMERALD AVE

HOLLOWHEAD AVE

5

Midge Hall

BB1

Hagg's Hall

Ramsgreave Wood

Bottoms Farm

HOLLOWHEAD CL

WILPSHIRE BANKS

32

Mountain Ash Farm

SACCARY LA

Cunliffe Moss Farm

SHOWLEY BROOK CL 1
CLIFTON GR 2

STATION CL

2

WILPSHIRE

4

Wardfall

Ramsgreave Hall Farm

RAMSGREAVE RD

Ramsgreave & Wilpshire

ISLE OF MAN

WAVERLEY RD

PARIS

SALESBURY VIEW

WALDEN

PARSONAGE RD

Collinson's Farm

MAYFIELD RD

MOORFIELD AVE

GLENGREAVE AVE

BEECH MOUNT

WILLOW

BROWNHILL RD

PENDLE

CAMBRIAN RD

EAST LANCASHIRE RD

YORK RD

Brownhill Farm

REMINGTON AVE

3

Primrose Hill

PRIMROSE HILL

HIGHER RAMSGREAVE RD

Longworth's House

Top of Ramsgreave

WHALLEY NEW RD

HASTON LEE AVE

BANK

PO

31

MELLOR LA

Spread Eagle (PH)

BB2

LONG ROW

BARKER LA

Kingbank Farm

Vine House Farm

WHINNEY LA

LAMMACK RD

Stone's Farm

BROADWAY

PLECKGATE RD

BROWNHILL DR

A6119

Brownhill

Roe Lee Park Prim Sch

OPAL ST

AMETHYST ST

SMITHY ST

EMERALD ST

PEARL ST

GRETNA WLK

BERYL AVE

2

Kay Fold Farm

KAY FOLD LODGE

Further Wilworth

St Gabriel's CE Prim Sch

WILWORTH CRES

Lower Wilworth

Holy Souls RC Prim Sch

CAMPBELL CT

NORTH BANK AVE

SANDRINGHAM

PEMBERTON ST

JASPER ST

CAMPBELL ST

ROYAL OAK AVE

REGENTS VIEW

HARDY ST

SAPPHIRE ST

AGATE ST

HIGH BANK

DOUGLAS PL

Cemy

1

Lower Reaps

Bullion Moss

RAMSGREAVE DR

YEW TREE DR

WHINNEY LA

GRASMERE AVE

WILLOW TREES DR

Pleckgate High Sch

PLECKGATE

PLECKGATE FOLD

Roe Lee

NORTH BANK AVE

BARMOUTH CRES

B6233

ROSEWOOD AVE

GOODSHAW AVE

30

A6119

Lammack Prim Sch

Pleckgate

66 **A** **B** 67 **C** **D** 68 **E** **F**

E1
1 BLENHEIM CL
2 OUTRAM LA
3 HAYDOCK ST
4 CHATSWORTH CL
5 THORNWOOD CL
6 PENSHAW CL
7 HILL VIEW
8 GOODSHAW CL

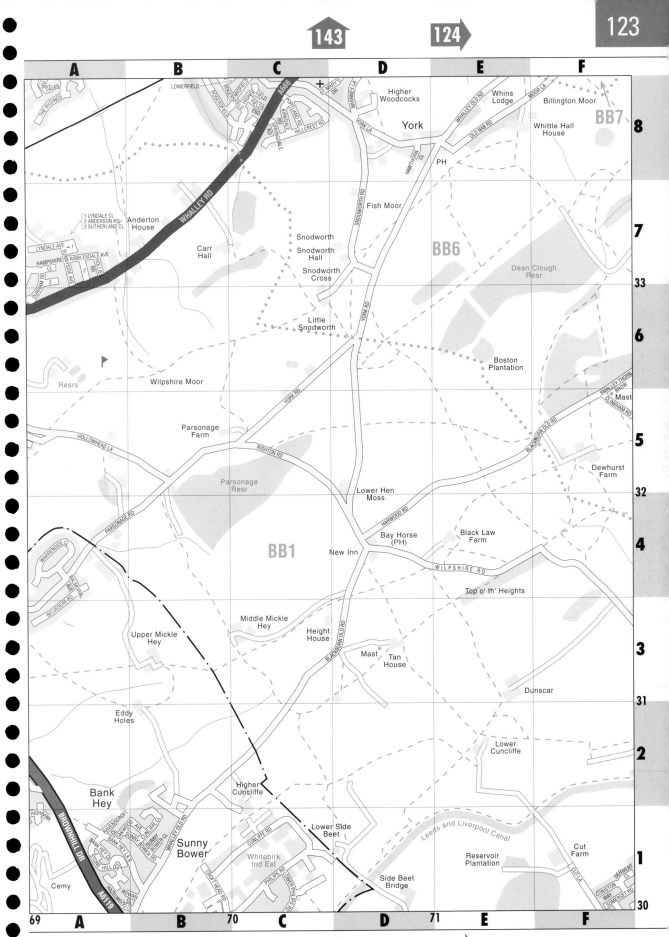

A B C D E F

8
7
33
6
5
32
4
3
31
2
1
30

BB7

BB6
Caravan Site

BB12

Game Cook Inn

Egg Syke

Rodger Hey

Stoops

CH

Harwood Bar

Bradley Hall

Bowley Hill

Back o' Bowley

Dean Farm

Cowden

Allsprings

Squires Farm

Dean Brook

Blackleach

North Cliffe Sch

Kebb House

Laneside

Edge End

Edgeside Farm

Belmont Farm

Lower Fold

Cliffe

Dog & Otter (PH)

Tan House

Coronation St 1
Hallfield Rd 2
Hartley St 3
Robert St 4

Allsprings Cl
Louie Pollard Cres
Premier Bsns Pk 5

Harwood New Rd

PARK LA

HARWOOD LA

Prim Sch

Hyndburn Bridge

Hyndburn Bridge

GREAT HARWOOD

Recn Gd

Liby

1 St Edmund's St
2 St Cecilia St
3 Park St

New Plough Yd

Charter Brook

Station Road Ind Est

Heys Lane Ind Est

Clayton Lodge 1
Pendle Ave 2
Clayton Hall Dr 3

Norden Court

Waverledge

Waverledge Bsns Pk

Trout Beck

Woodlands

The Coppice

Harwood Edge

Smallshaw Hey

St John's CE Prim Sch

Norden Brook

1 WEST ST
2 CHARLES ST
3 CROFT ST
4 VICAR ST
5 WELLINGTON ST

Cemetery Hotel (PH)

Close Nook

Tottleworth Lee

LEE LA

Tottleworth

Hyndburn Brook

Oakenshaw

BB5

Freshfield Ave 1
Cross St 2
Crowther St 3
Alexandra St 4
Ellison Fold 5

Devonshire

Sch

Civic Ctr & Liby

Norden

Leeds & Liverpool Canal

BB1

RISHTON

Norden High Sch

1 WELL ST
2 Bridgefield Cl

Holt Farm

Riverside Ind Est

CLAYTON-LE-MOORS

Brigsteer Cl 1
Grizedale Cl 2
Arnside Cl 3

All Saints CE Prim Sch

Clayton-Le-Moors Ind Est

Norden Prim Sch

A1
1 ST PAUL'S RD
2 ST PETER ST
3 ULLSWATER CL
4 ESSEX RD
5 HIGHFIELD RD
6 ST ALBANS RD
7 THE ESPLANADE

The Old Chapel

HERMITAGE ST

Hanson St

B1
1 Norden Ct
2 Eachill Rd
3 Maple St
4 Talbot Ave
5 Hick's Terr
6 Clarke St
7 Company St
8 Ashworth St

1 Chapel Ho
2 Derby St

Mill Wood

Dunkenhalgh Park

Dunkenhalgh Hotel

BLACKBURN RD

Beech St 1
Ernest St 2

Whin Isle Farm

Leeds & Liverpool Canal

HIGH ST

Liby

72   73   74

A B C D E F

C5
1 HAYDOCK SQ
2 FRANKLIN AINSWORTH HO
3 DELPH CT
4 SOUTH VIEW
5 BACK CHURCH ST
6 BRIDGE ST
7 EDWARD ST
8 TOWN HALL SQ
9 TOWN HALL ST
10 JOINERS ALLEY
11 LOYND ST
12 COMMERCIAL ST
13 NETHERTON HO
14 WESTWELL ST
15 KING ST
16 WESLEY CT
17 NOWELL ST
18 WALMSLEY ST
19 SEGAR ST

F2
1 BARNES SQ
2 GRIMSHAW ST
3 HAZEL GR
4 TALBOT AVE
5 KING ST
6 BURNLEY RD

F3
1 STOPFORD CT
2 BRANCH RD
3 FRANCIS ST
4 ANN ST
5 JACKSON ST
6 DRYDEN ST
7 NORFOLK CL
8 GLOUCESTER AVE
9 ALMA ST
10 DANIEL ST
11 FORT ST
12 JAMES ST
13 GEORGE ST
14 NEW CHURCH CL
15 BACK ARTHUR ST
16 MERCER ST

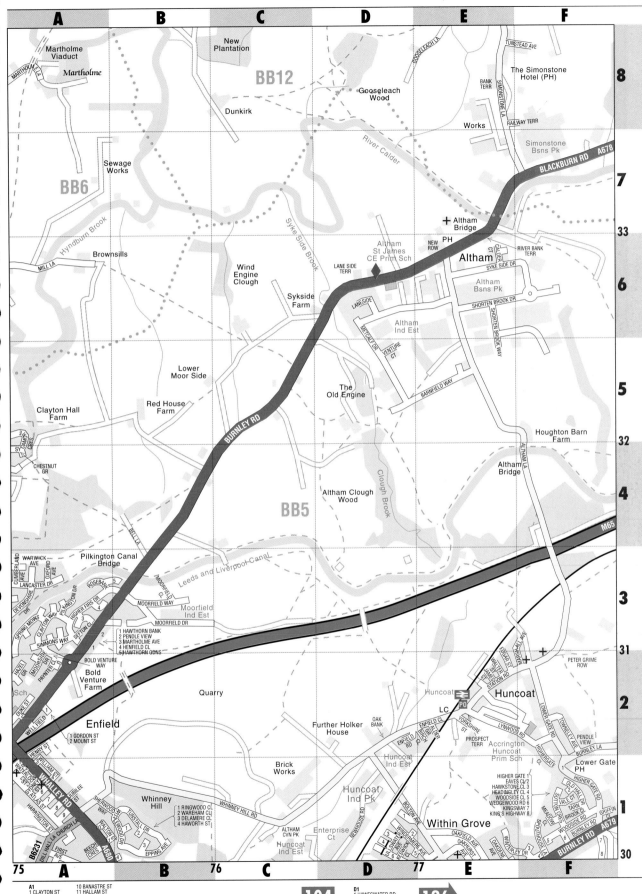

A1
1 CLAYTON ST
2 READ ST
3 HILL ST
4 FRANK ST
5 MERCER HO
6 MELBOURNE ST
7 ADELAIDE ST
8 BRISBANE ST
9 WHINFIELD ST
10 BANASTRE ST
11 HALLAM ST

D1
1 HAWESWATER RD
2 THIRLMERE CL
3 LANGDALE CL
4 BORROWDALE CL
5 RYDAL CL
6 WITHIN GR

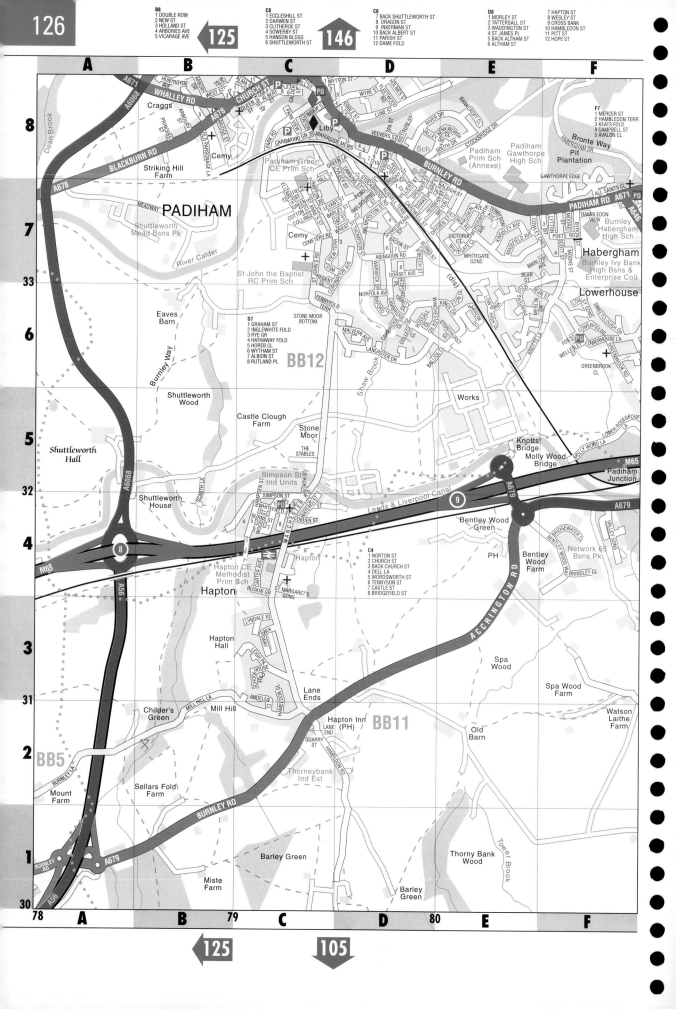

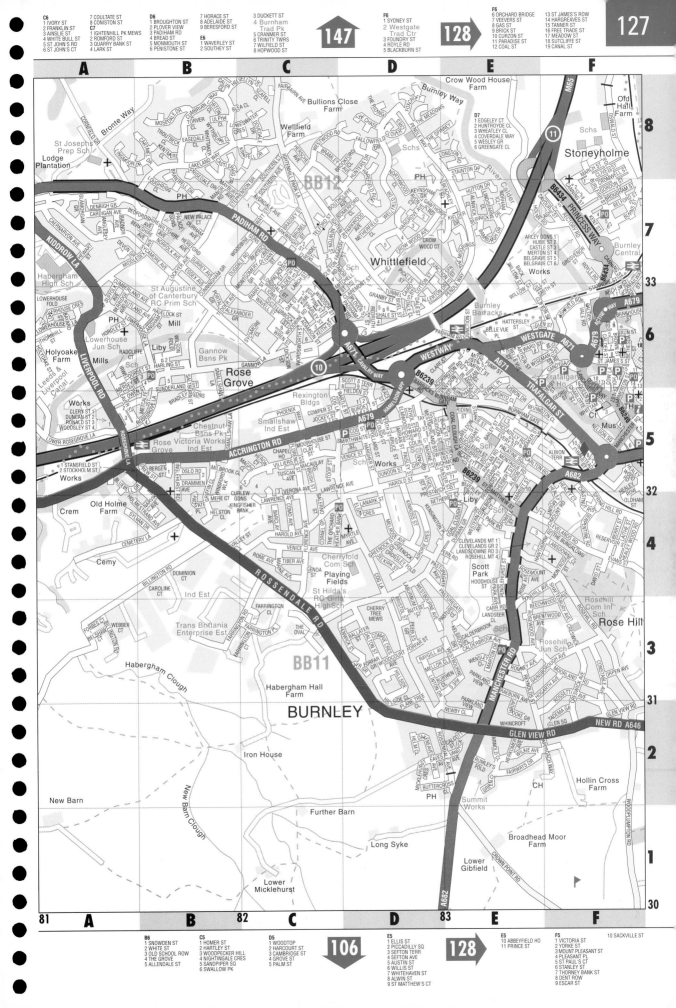

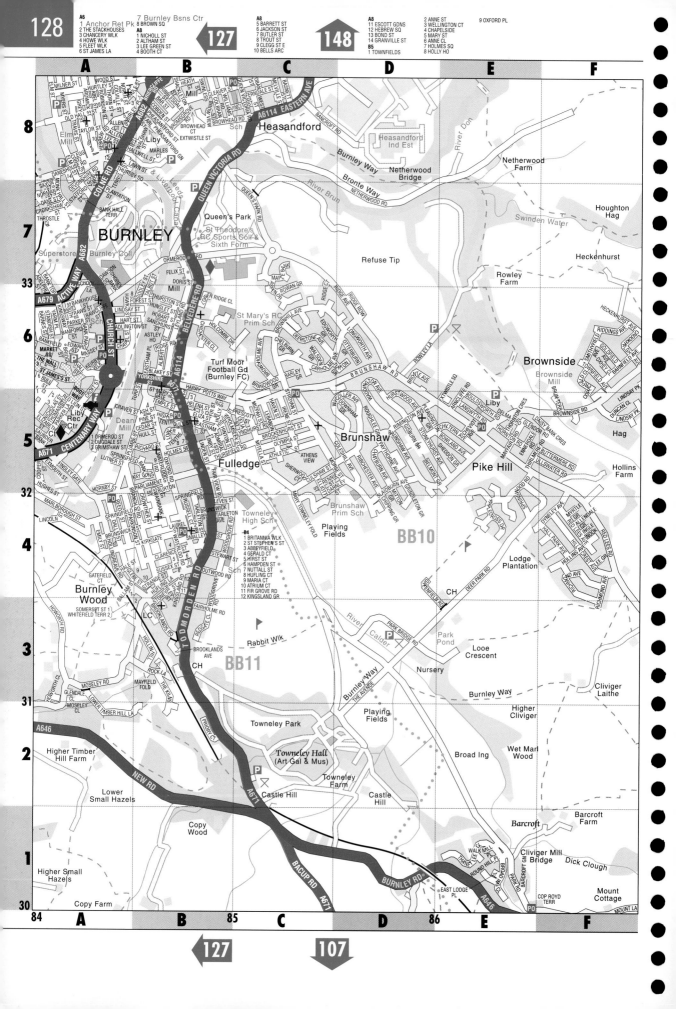

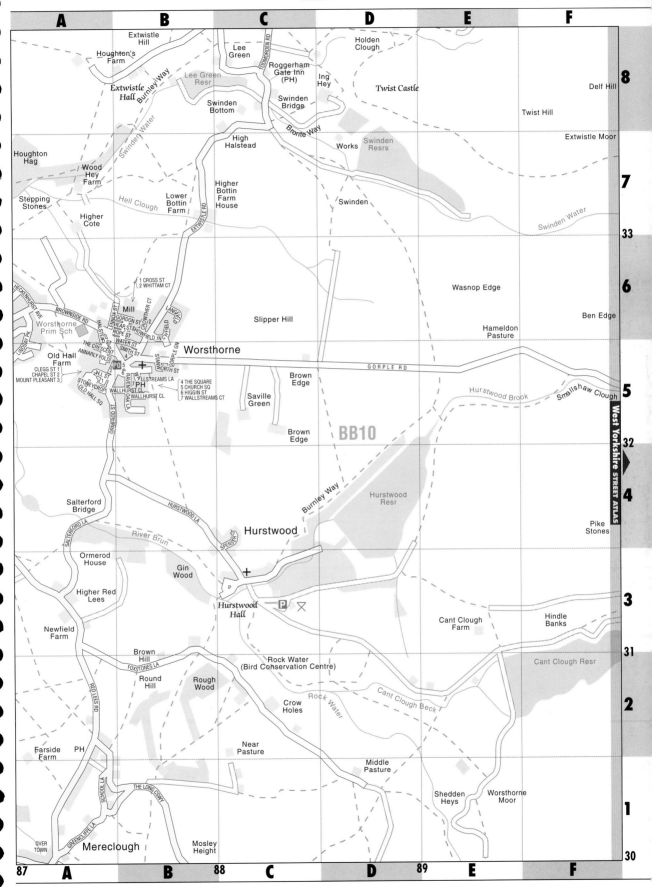

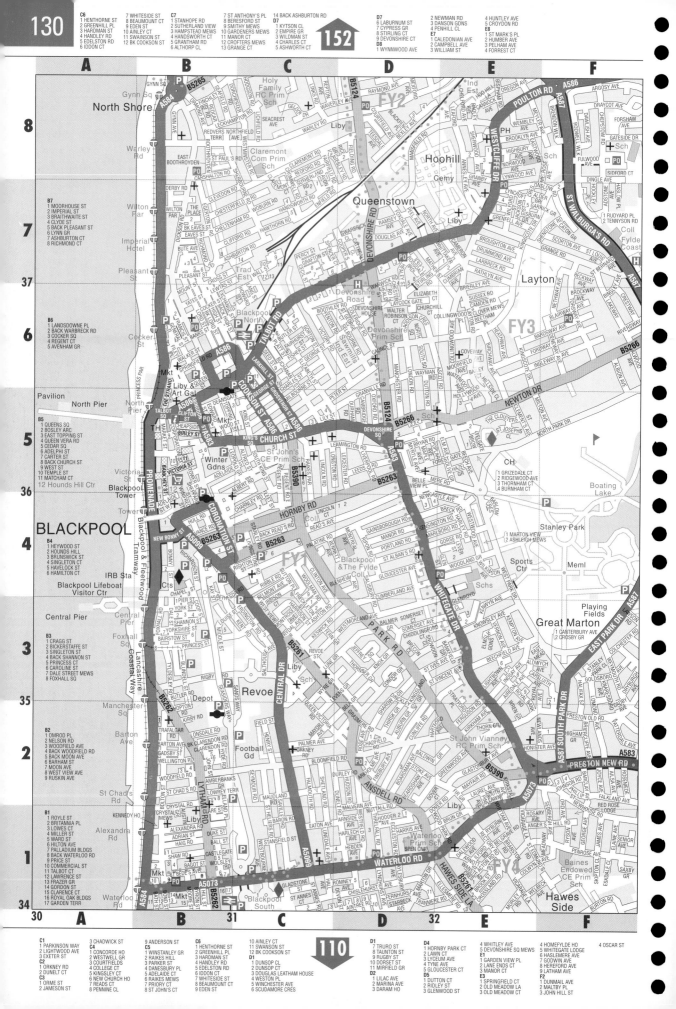

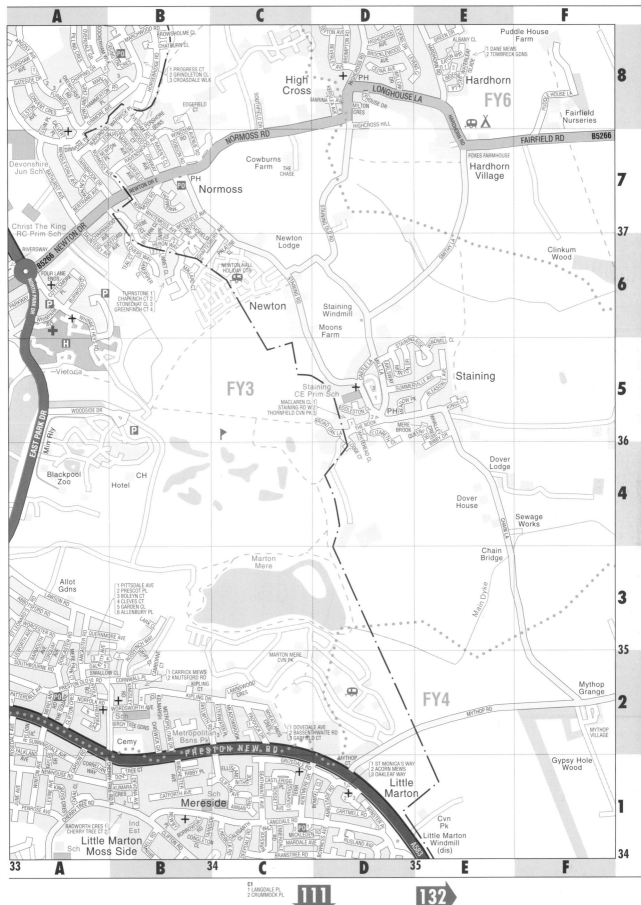

A8
1 ARGOSY CT
2 GATESIDE CT
3 FURNESS CT
4 CHIPPING CT
5 SLAIDBURN WLK

C1
1 LANGDALE PL
2 CRUMMOCK PL

131
154

A   **B**   **C**   **D**   **E**   **F**

B5266

Kennel Wood

Avenham Hall

STATION RD

FY6

Mill Farm

Rogue Wood

8

Fairfield Farm

B5266

FAIRFIELD RD

Avenham Wood

WEETON RD

B5260

Summerer Farm

7

Fairfield Cottage

37

SUMMERER GR

6

Todderstaffe Hall

Lucas Flash Wood

Singleton Rd

GRANTHAM RD

ASTON ST

SUTTON ST

OXFORD ST

HARRISON ST

Playing Fields

INKERMAN RD

Todderstaffe Wood

Weeton Prim Sch

PO

HENDERSON RD

GIBRALTAR RD

ANZIO RD

MINDEN RD

High Moor

Weeton Camp

FY3

LC

5

Crossings Wood

Hawes House Farm

36

Preese Hall

PR4

Hall's House Farm

4

Hill House

3

Mythop Hall

35

Stanley Bank

Mythop

FY4

Eagle & Child (PH)

ELMWOOD CT

Weeton

2

Hillcrest

MYTHOP RD

KIRKHAM RD

WEETON RD

Mythop Moss Wood

MYTHOP RD

THE CLOSE

BRIARWOOD CL

THE GREEN

BACK LA

KNOWSLEY CRES

Weston Lane Heads

CHURCH RD

M55

1

Westfield Cott

Hall Hill

B5260

M55

Weeton St.Michael's CE Prim Sch

34

36   **A**   **B**   **37**   **C**   **D**   **38**   **E**   **F**

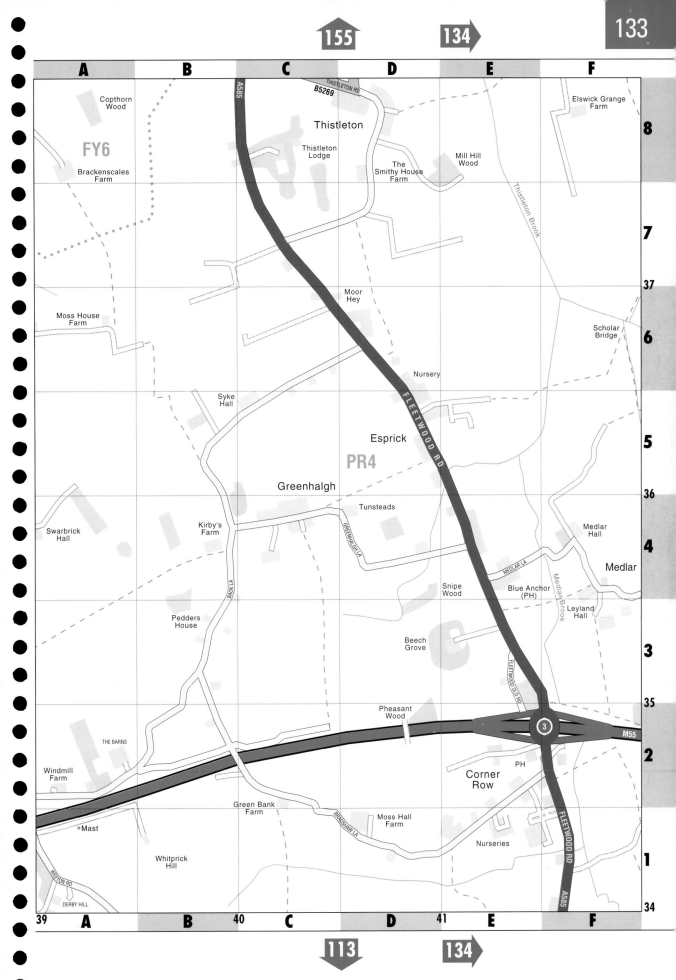

A B C D E F

8
7
37
6
5
36
4
3
35
2
1
34

Copthorn Wood

FY6

Brackenscales Farm

Moss House Farm

Swarbrick Hall

THE BARNS

Windmill Farm

Mast

WESTON RD

DERBY HILL

Whitprick Hill

Green Bank Farm

Pedders House

Kirby's Farm

BACK LA

Syke Hall

Greenhalgh

PR4

Tunsteads

GREENHALGH LA

Snipe Wood

Beech Grove

Pheasant Wood

BRADSHAW LA

Moss Hall Farm

A585

B5269

THISTLETON RD

Thistleton

Thistleton Lodge

The Smithy House Farm

Mill Hill Wood

Thistleton Brook

Moor Hey

Nursery

FLEETWOOD RD

Esprick

Scholar Bridge

Elswick Grange Farm

Medlar Hall

Medlar

MEDLAR LA

Blue Anchor (PH)

Medlar Brook

Leyland Hall

FLEETWOOD OLD RD

3

M55

Corner Row

PH

Nurseries

FLEETWOOD RD

A585

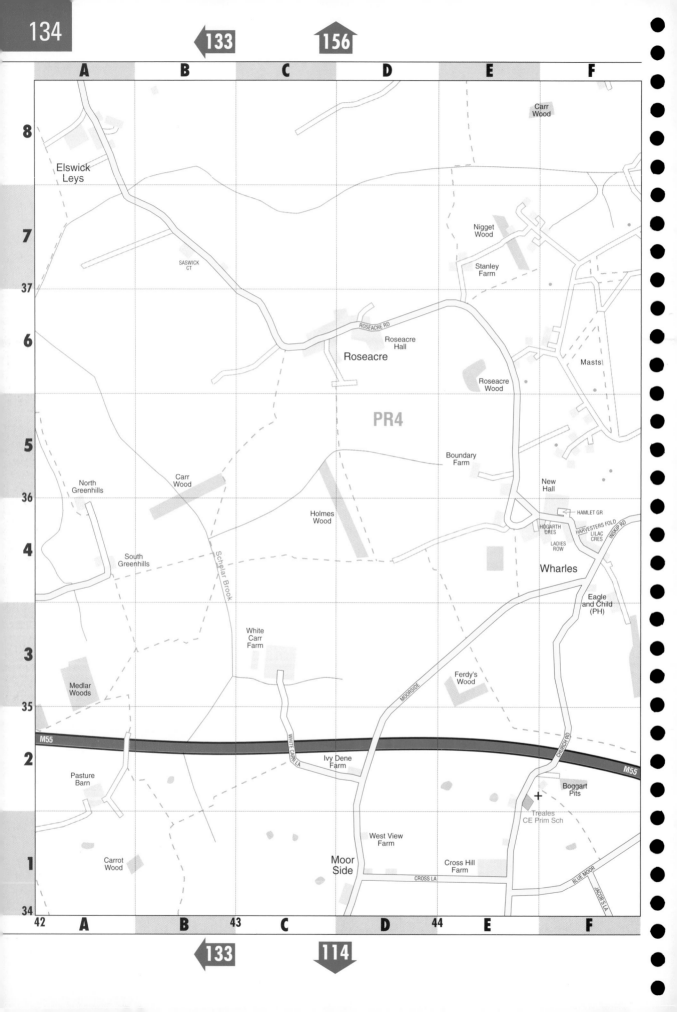

133
156

Carr Wood

Elswick Leys

Nigget Wood

Stanley Farm

SASWICK CT

ROSEACRE RD

Roseacre Hall

Roseacre

Masts

Roseacre Wood

PR4

Boundary Farm

New Hall

North Greenhills

Carr Wood

HAMLET GR

HOGARTH CRES

HARVESTERS FOLD

LILAC CRES

INSKIP RD

Holmes Wood

LADIES ROW

South Greenhills

Scholar Brook

Wharles

Eagle and Child (PH)

White Carr Farm

Ferdy's Wood

Medlar Woods

MOORSIDE

CHURCH RD

M55

WHITE CARR LA

Ivy Dene Farm

M55

Pasture Barn

Boggart Pits

Treales CE Prim Sch

West View Farm

Carrot Wood

Moor Side

Cross Hill Farm

CROSS LA

BLUE MOOR

JACOBS LA

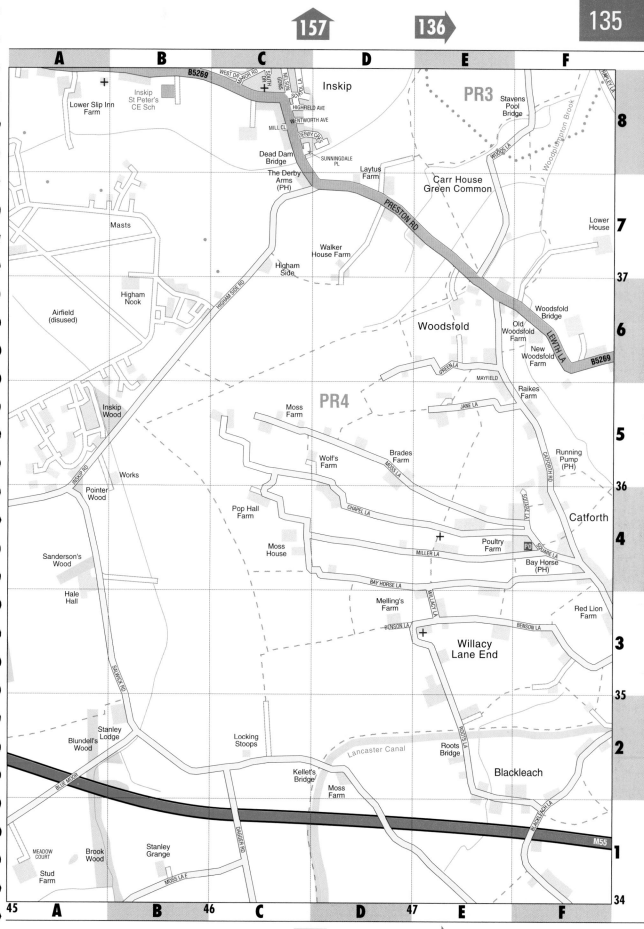

135
158

A B C D E F

8

Myrepole Farm
Singleton's Farm
BRIERLEY LA
MALLEY LA
Plough at Eaves (PH)
BENSON S LA
Willow Nook Farm
PR3
Yew Tree
Higher Park Head

7

RAPLEY LA
Cuddy Hill
EAVES LA
Cross House
Eaves Farm
Lower Park Head
Park Head Bridge

37

Mast
CINDER LA
New Mill Bridge
Higher Hill House
Hankinson House
Hankinson Bridge

6

Lewth Hall
B5269
Lewth
EAVES LA
New Mill Brook
Danson Hill
Hollowforth Hall
STATION LA
Hepgreave Bridge
PR3

5

LEWTH LA
Rolling Pin Farm
Black Pole
Bell Fold
Moon's Bridge
HOLLOWFORTH HILL
Marina

36

PR4
Moor Side
Moorside House Farm

4

SCHOOL LA
Catforth Hall
MOORSIDE LA
Mill
WOODPLUMPTON RD
Bell Fold Bridge
Newsham Lodge
Catforth Prim Sch
Catforth Hall Bridge

3

BENSON LA
CATFORTH RD
Godson House Farm
Woodplumpton Brook
Whinneyfield Bridge
Lancaster Canal
White Hill
Ambrose Hall
B5411
WHITTLE GN
AMBROSE HALL LA
WHITTLE HILL
NEWSHAM HALL LA
B5269

35

BLACKLEACH LA
Willow House Farm

2

Swillbrook
Swillbrook Bridge
Swillbrook House
CROWN LA
Whinneyfield Farm
WHINNEYFIELD LA
WOODPLUMPTON RD
THE HAWTHORNS
PLUMPTON FIELD
PO
Woodplumpton
Toplands Farm

1

M55
ROSEMARY LA
Sergeant Bridge
Woodplumpton St Anne's CE Prim Sch
THE ORCHARD

34

Barnfield Cottage
M55
Woodplumpton Bridge
SANDY LA
TABLEY LA B5411

48 A B 49 C D 50 E F

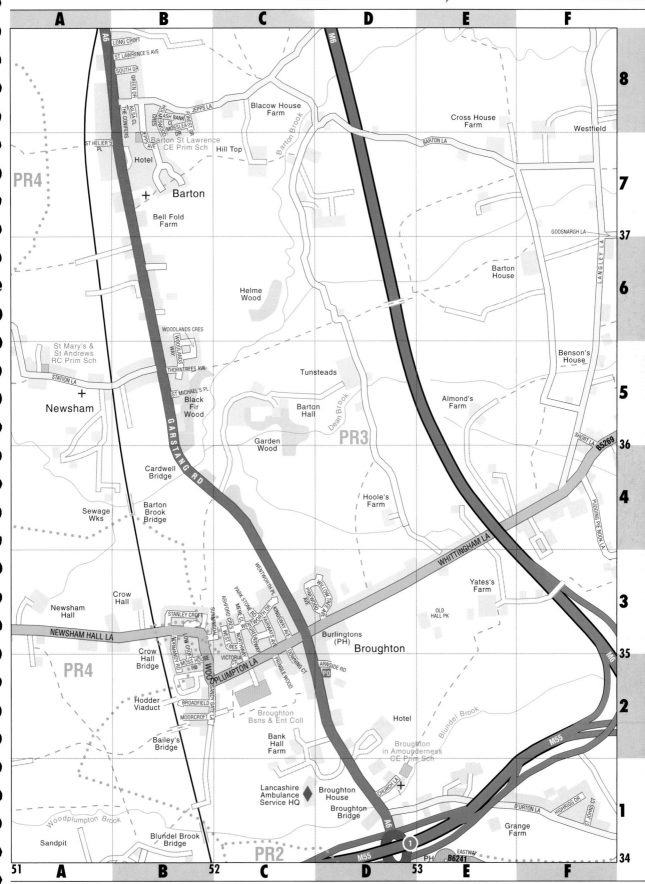

137 160

A **B** **C** **D** **E** **F**

Westfield Brook

Westfield Wood

Rigby Wood

Cross House

8

Eaves Green Hall

EAVES GREEN LA

Middleton Hall

Eaves Green

Little Westfield

7

MILL LA

Field Foot Farm

37

GOOSNARGH LA

Oliverson's CE Prim Sch

H

Bushell's

CAMFORTH HALL LA

MILL LA

6

OAKLEA CT

WILLOW GR

Bushell's Arms (PH)

GRINDLESTONE CT

SOUTH VIEW

Cumeragh Village

GREEN ACRE

NORTHGATE

CHURCHGATE

Goosnargh

HIGHGATE

PARKGATE

THE CROFT

BEACON DR

CARR LA

BLEASDALE RD

THE SQUARE

PR3

BEACON CT

CUMERAGH LA **B5269**

Meadowcroft

Mast

JUBILEE TERR

PO

Cemetery

5

WHITTINGHAM LA

Stags Head (PH)

B5269

Parkinson's House

Whittingham Hall

NOELS VILLA

Guild Park

36

Whittingham House

Dean House

Chingle Hall

H

4

New Field

Cowell's Farm

PUDDING PIE NOOK LA

Works

3

Pudding Pie Nook

Blundle Brook

Cockshoot Wood

35

M55

Haighton Manor

New Chingle Hall

Haighton Green

2

M6

32

PR2

HAIGHTON GREEN LA

Boyse's Farm

Sea Mark

Savick Brook

1

D'URTON LA

Haighton Top

FERNYHALGH LA

M6

34

54 **A** **B** **55** **C** **D** **56** **E** **F**

137 118

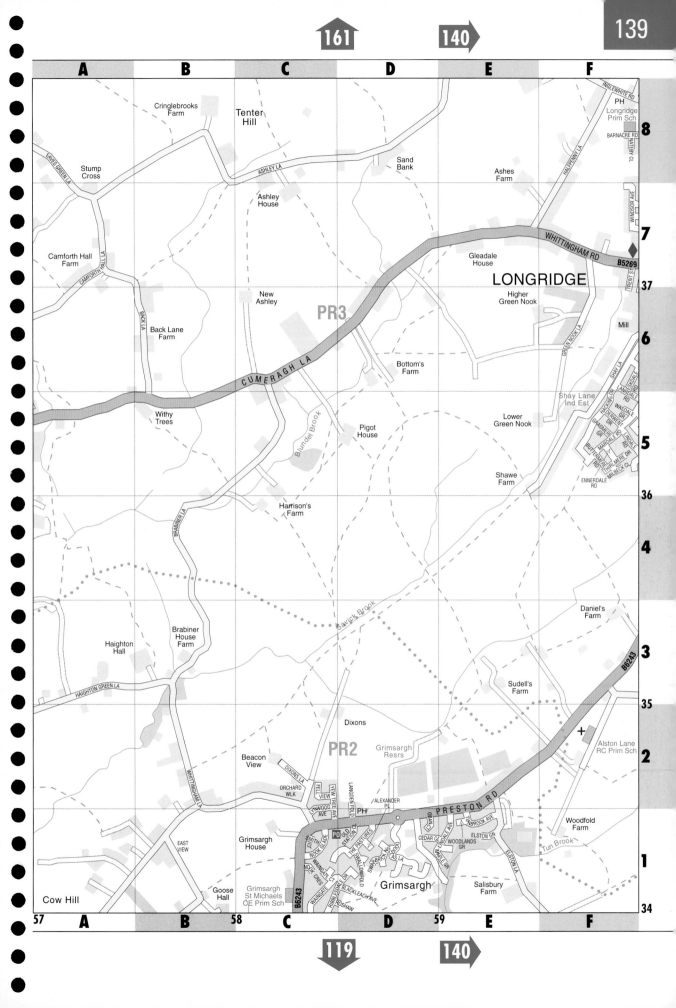

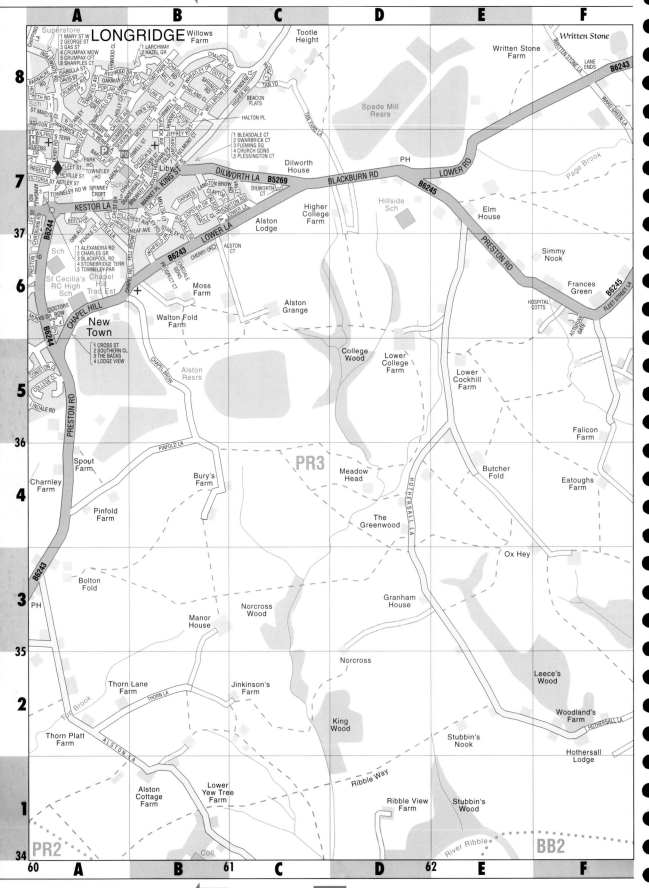

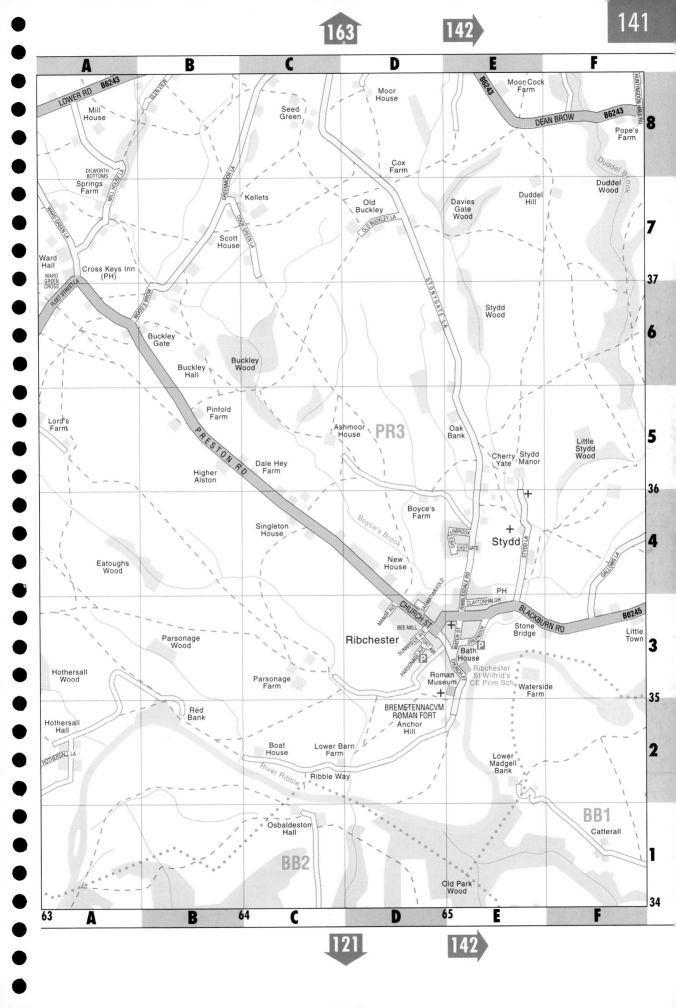

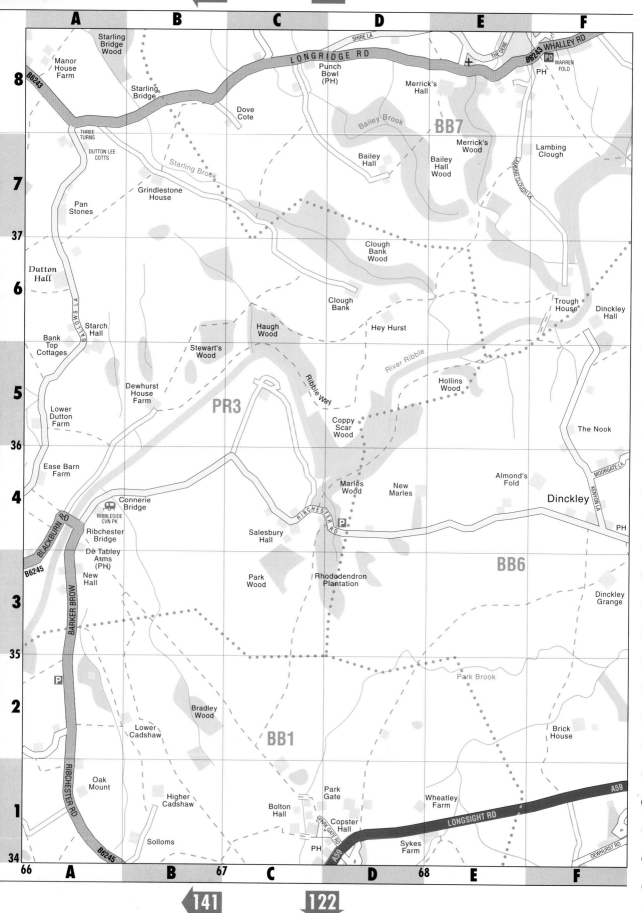

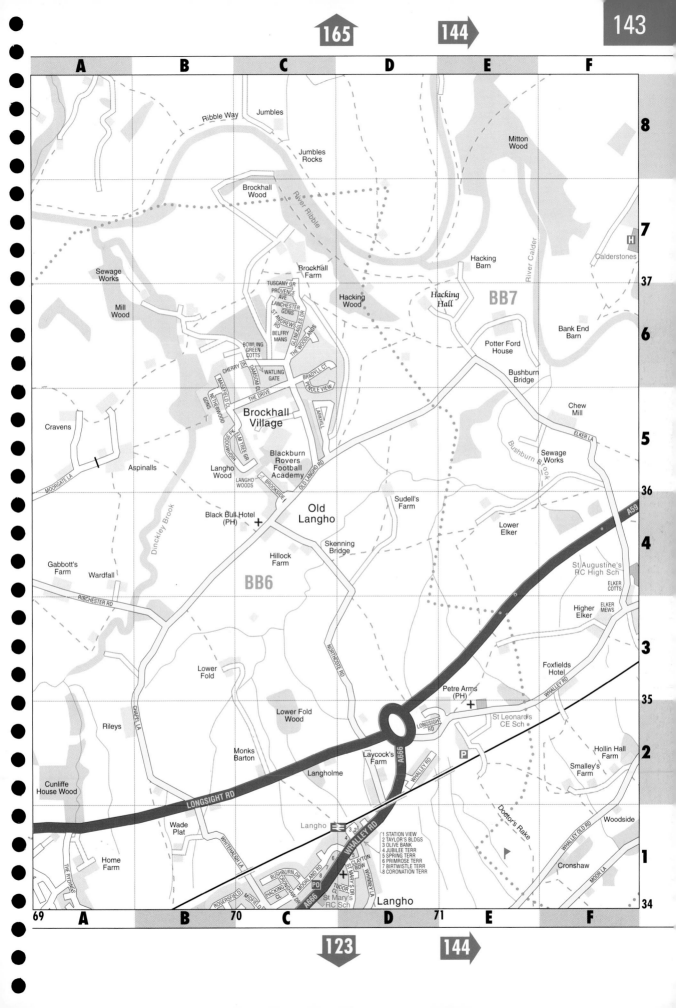

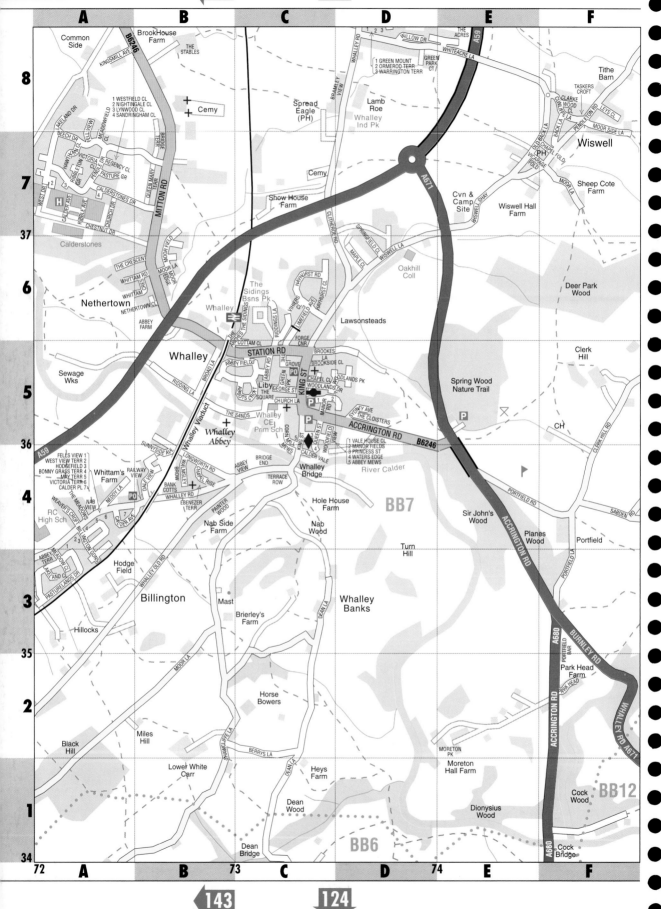

A B C D E F

8

7

37

6

5

36

4

3

35

2

1

34

72 A B 73 C D 74 E F

Common Side
BrookHouse Farm
THE STABLES
KINGSMILL AVE
B6246

1 WESTFIELD CL
2 NIGHTINGALE CL
3 LYNWOOD CL
4 SANDRINGHAM CL
Cemy

LAKELAND DR
BEECH DR
MEADOWFIELD
FELL VIEW
HAWTHORN CL
RIBBLETON
PEARL DR
CULEY
PENDLE
VICTORIA
REGENCY CL
PASTURE GR
CALDERSTONES DR
QUEEN MARY TERR
MITTON RD
BRIDGE TERR

WEST DR
CALDER AVE
RIBBLE AVE
CHURCH DR
CHESTNUT DR
H
CALDERSTONES

37 THE CRESCENT
MOOR FIELD
MOOR LA
MOOR EDGE
WHITTAM RD
WHITTAM
NETHERTOWN CL
Nethertown

Whalley
ABBEY FARM
THE SIDINGS
The Sidings Bsns Pk
Whalley
RIDDING LA
BROAD LA
ABBEY FIELDS
ABBEY RD
STATION RD
COTTAM CL
THE ACRES
THE SIDINGS

Sewage Wks

A59

FELLS VIEW 1
WEST VIEW TERR 2
HODGEFIELD 3
BONNY GRASS TERR 4
MARY TERR 5
VICTORIA TERR 6
CALDER PL 7
Whittam's Farm
SUNNYSIDE AV
LONGWORTH RD
CHAPEL RISE
RAILWAY VIEW
CALDER VIEW
WALMSLEY
BROW
BANK COTTS
EBENEZER TERR
WHALLEY RD
PO

THE MEADOWS
WEAVER'S CROFT
BILLINGTON GDNS
RC High Sch
NAB VIEW
NEDDY LA
CALDER AVE
PO

ABBEY TERR
MEADOW LA
LAKELAND CL
PASTURELANDS DR

Hodge Field
Billington
WHALLEY OLD RD
MOOR LA

Hillocks

Black Hill

Miles Hill

Lower White Carr

SHUTTLEWORTH LA
Mast
Brierley's Farm
DEAN LA
BERRYS LA
Horse Bowers
DEAN LA
Heys Farm
Dean Wood
Dean Bridge

Nab Side Farm
PAINTER WOOD
ABBEY VIEW
TERRACE ROW
BRIDGE END
Whalley Abbey
Whalley Viaduct
Whalley CE Prim Sch
THE SANDS
SCOTS CROFT
THE SQUARE
CHURCH LA
Liby
GEORGE ST
GROVE ST
GREEN PK
KING ST
CHAPEL CL
WOODLANDS DR
QUEEN ST
CORN MILL MEWS
MANOR RD
WOODFIELD
SYDNEY AVE
ACCRINGTON RD
THE CLOISTERS
CALDER VALE
Whalley Bridge

1 VALE HOUSE CL
2 MANOR FIELDS
3 PRINCESS ST
4 WATERS EDGE
5 ABBEY MEWS
River Calder

Hole House Farm
Nab Wood
Whalley Banks

BB7

B6246

Spread Eagle (PH)
WHALLEY RD
BRAMLEY VIEW
Whalley Ind Pk
Lamb Roe
Cemy
Show House Farm
CLITHEROE RD
HAYHURST RD
HAYHURST CL
VIHERS
HAYHURST AVE
LIMEFIELD AVE
RIDINGS LA
FORGE CNR
BROOKES LA
BROOKSIDE CL
SODLANDS PK
Lawsonsteads
SPRINGFIELD CL
MAPLE CL
WISWELL LA

Oakhill Coll

WILLOW DR
WHITEACRE LA
1 GREEN MOUNT
2 ORMEROD TERR
3 WARRINGTON TERR
GREEN PARK CT
A59
A671

THE ACRES
TASKERS CROFT
CLARKE WOOD CL
BACK LA
OLD CHAPEL FOLD
PENDLETON RD
LEYS CL
MOOR SIDE LA
Wiswell
PH
VICARAGE FOLD
WISWELL SHAY
Cvn & Camp Site
Wiswell Hall Farm
MOOR LA
Sheep Cote Farm

Tithe Barn

Deer Park Wood

Clerk Hill

Spring Wood Nature Trail
P
CH
CLERK HILL RD

Sir John's Wood
Planes Wood
PORTFIELD RD
Portfield
SABDEN
ACCRINGTON RD
PORTFIELD LA

Turn Hill

Moreton Pk
MORETON
Moreton Hall Farm
Dionysius Wood

A680
BURNLEY RD
ACCRINGTON RD
PORTFIELD BAR
PARK HEAD
Park Head Farm
WHALLEY RD A671
BB12
Cock Wood
Cock Bridge
A680
BB6

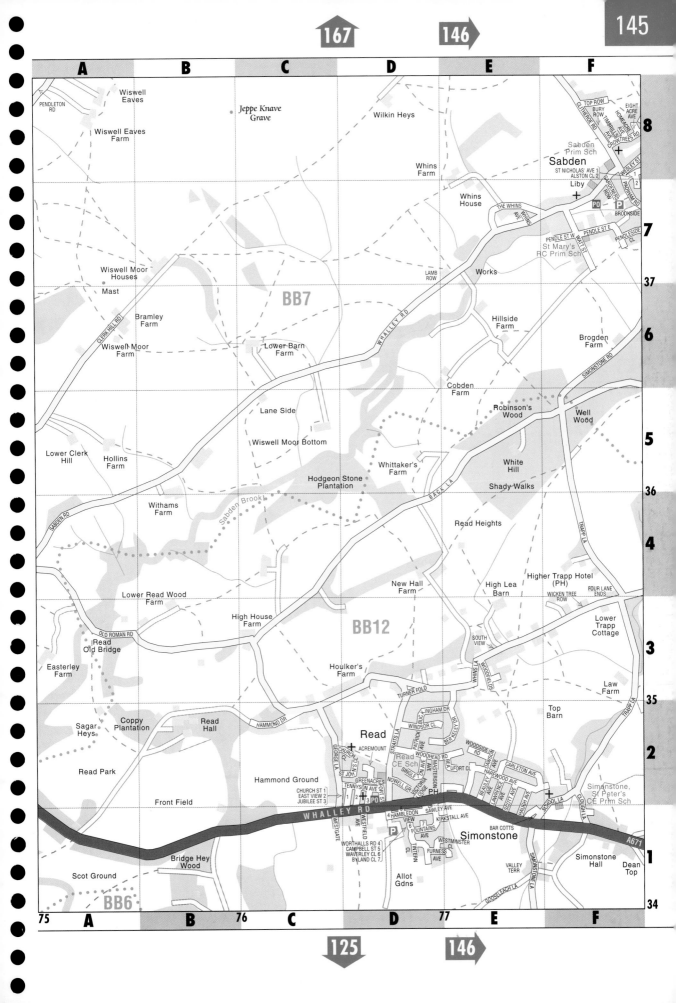

A B C D E F

8

BADGER WELLS COTTS
New York
HEYHOUSES
Hey Barn Farm
Drivers
Dean Farm
Back o' th' Hill

1 SABDEN BROOK CT
2 LITTLEMOOR CL
3 LITTLEMOOR HO
STUBBINS LA
BB7
MOUNT PLEASANT
PENDLESIDE CL
STUBBINS VALE CVN PK
Sabden Brook
Dean Height
Stump Hall
STUMP HALL RD
Hill Top
Sagar Hill

7

THORN ST
Chew Barn
PADIHAM RD
Dry Corner
The Height
BACK LA
BACK LA

37

SIMONSTONE RD
Padiham Heights
Copthurst
PENDLE VIEW 1
HAMBLEDON TERR 2
WESLEY PL 3

6

Black Hill
P
Copthurst
Mill
PH
POP
SABDEN RD
CROFT LA
RAKE TOP AVE

Moor Barn
Copthurst
Higham
ACRESFIELD CL

5

Cavaliers
Old Jeremy's Farm
Holly Brow
1 ANDERTON RD
2 NUTTER CRES
3 HOLLINHURST VIEW
4 CHAPEL ST
5 GARDEN ST
6 WILKINSON ST
7 GAWTHORPE VIEW
8 DAME FOLD

BARROWFORD RD
A6068

36

SABDEN RD
Foulds House
Northwood
Height Side
Northwood
Hencock
West Close

BB12

Priddy Bank Farm

4

FIR TREES BROOK
High House
Northwood Farm
Hollins Farm

3

Trap House
WHINS LA
Wall Green
Huntroyde
WHITTAKER CLOUGH
High Whittaker Farm
Brookfoot Farm

35

HIGHER RD
PENNINE GR
SLADE LA
Hargrove
Mona Bents Plantation
BURNLEY WAY

2

Black Wood
HUNTROYDE BROOK
Higher Slade
Lower Slade
1 ESKDALE GDNS
2 THIRLMERE AVE
Jack Hill
GRASMERE AVE
RYDAL
HARGROVE AVE
Grove Lane Plantation
GROVE LA
RIVER CALDER

1

A671
WHALLEY RD
A6068
PADIHAM
Huntroyde Demesne
Mast
WOODLANDS GR
Sch
P
Works
Playing Fields
Gawthorpe Hall
P

34

Dean Bridge
A671
Home Farm

78 A B 79 C D 80 E F

C1
1 THE MEWS
2 CHAPEL WLK
3 SPRING GARDENS TERR
4 HALL HILL ST
5 CROSSHILLS
6 ST GILES TERR
7 ST GILES ST
8 ST LEONARD'S ST
9 CLAYBANK FOLD

10 CLAYBANK
11 HAVELOCK ST
12 CHURCH LA
13 GAWTHORPE ST
14 BARBON ST
15 JOHN O' GAUNT ST
16 CENTRAL BLDGS
17 FACTORY LA
18 COPTHURST ST
19 HAMBERGHAM ST

C1
20 VICTORIA APARTMENTS
21 CLITHEROE ST

D1
1 KAY ST
2 DEAN ST
3 CHIPPING ST
4 PARTRIDGE HILL
5 PARTRIDGE HILL ST

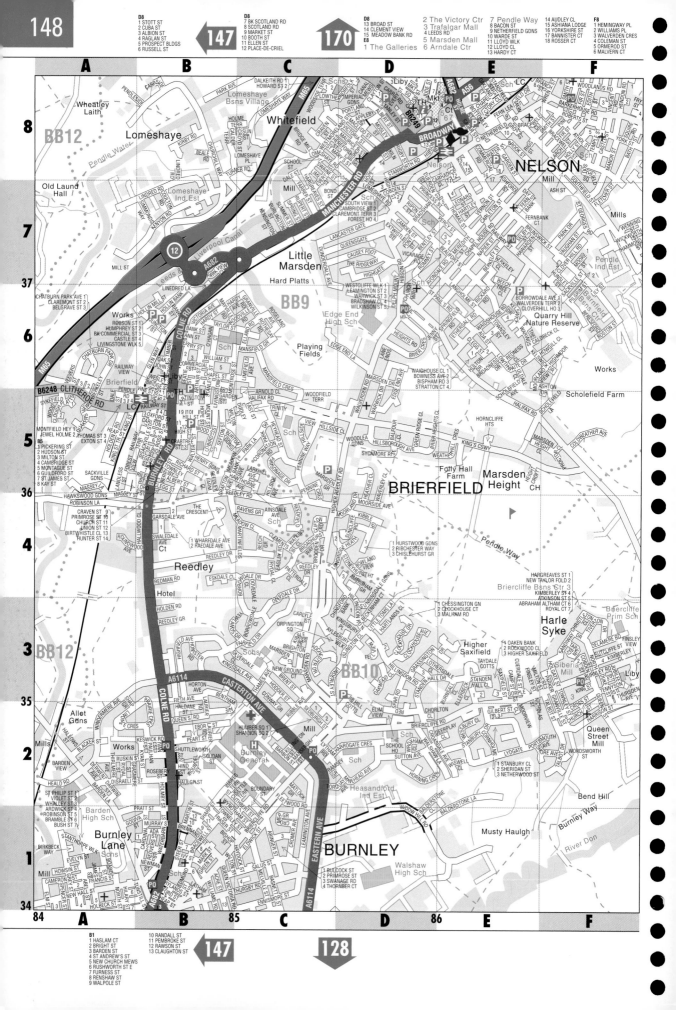

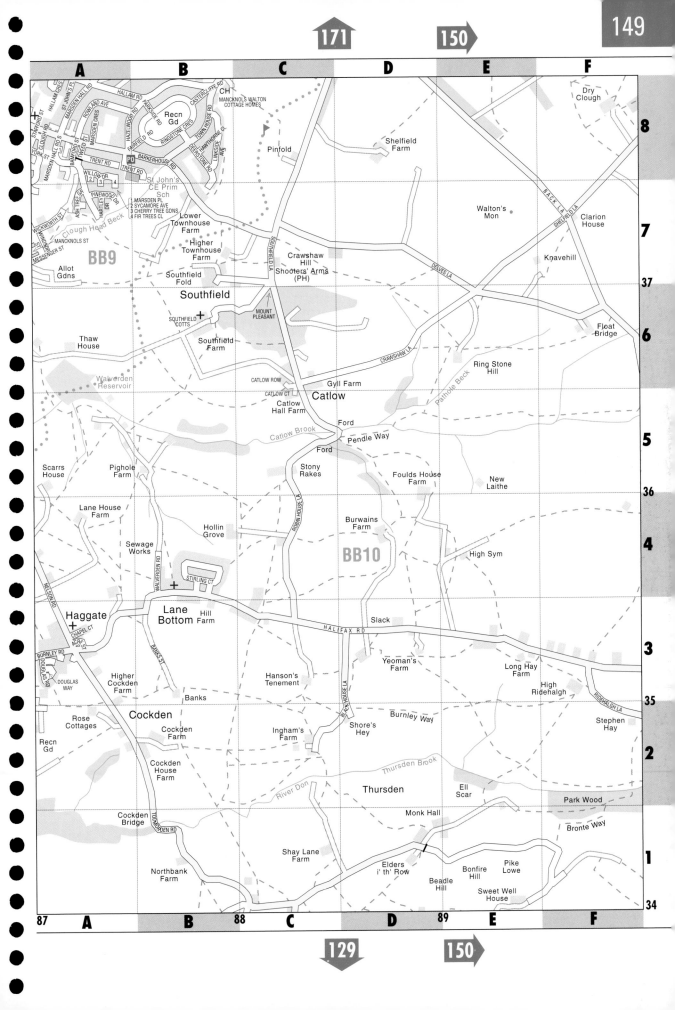

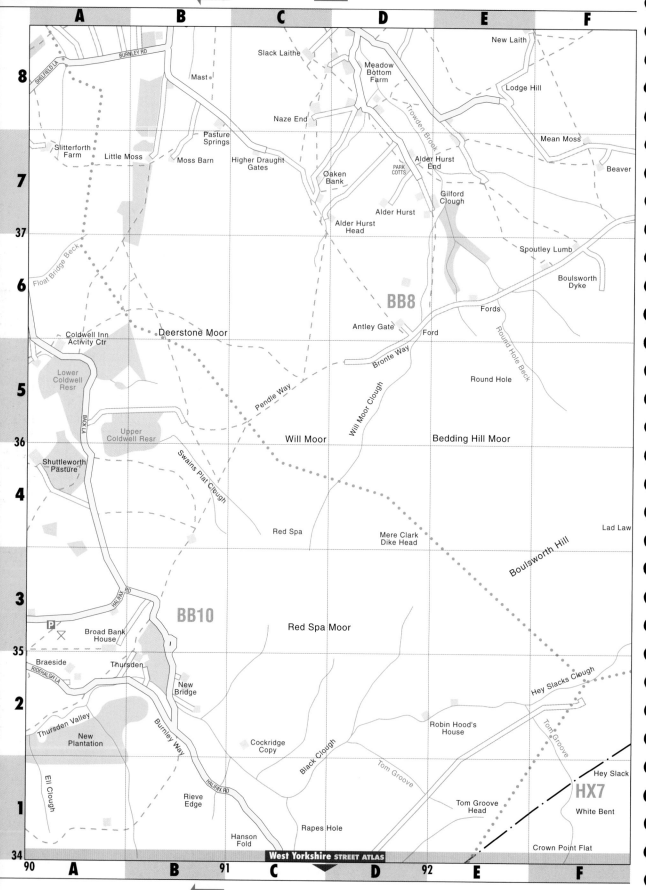

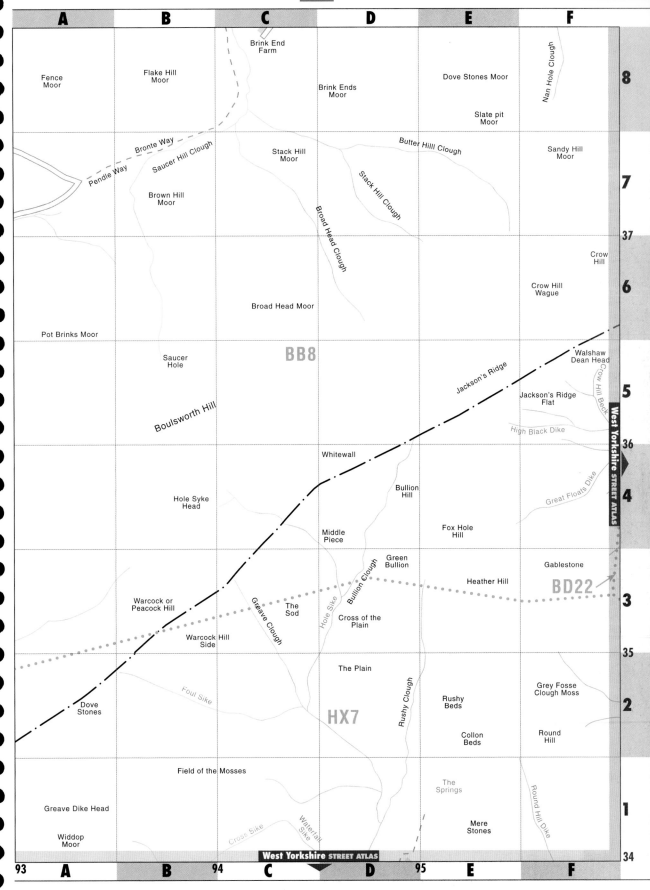

Brink End Farm

Fence Moor

Flake Hill Moor

Brink Ends Moor

Dove Stones Moor

Nan Hole Clough

8

Slate pit Moor

Bronte Way

Pendle Way

Saucer Hill Clough

Stack Hill Moor

Butter Hilll Clough

Sandy Hill Moor

Brown Hill Moor

7

37

Broad Head Clough

Stack Hill Clough

Crow Hill

6

Pot Brinks Moor

Broad Head Moor

Crow Hill Wague

BB8

Saucer Hole

Walshaw Dean Head

Boulsworth Hill

Jackson's Ridge

Jackson's Ridge Flat

Crow Hill Beck

5

High Black Dike

36

Whitewall

Bullion Hill

4

Hole Syke Head

Fox Hole Hill

Great Floats Dike

Middle Piece

Green Bullion

Gablestone

Heather Hill

BD22

3

Warcock or Peacock Hill

Greave Clough

The Sod

Hole Sike

Bullion Clough

Cross of the Plain

Warcock Hill Side

35

Foul Sike

The Plain

Rushy Clough

Rushy Beds

Grey Fosse Clough Moss

2

HX7

Dove Stones

Collon Beds

Round Hill

Field of the Mosses

The Springs

Round Hill Dike

1

Greave Dike Head

Cross Sike

Waterfall Sike

Mere Stones

Widdop Moor

34

West Yorkshire STREET ATLAS

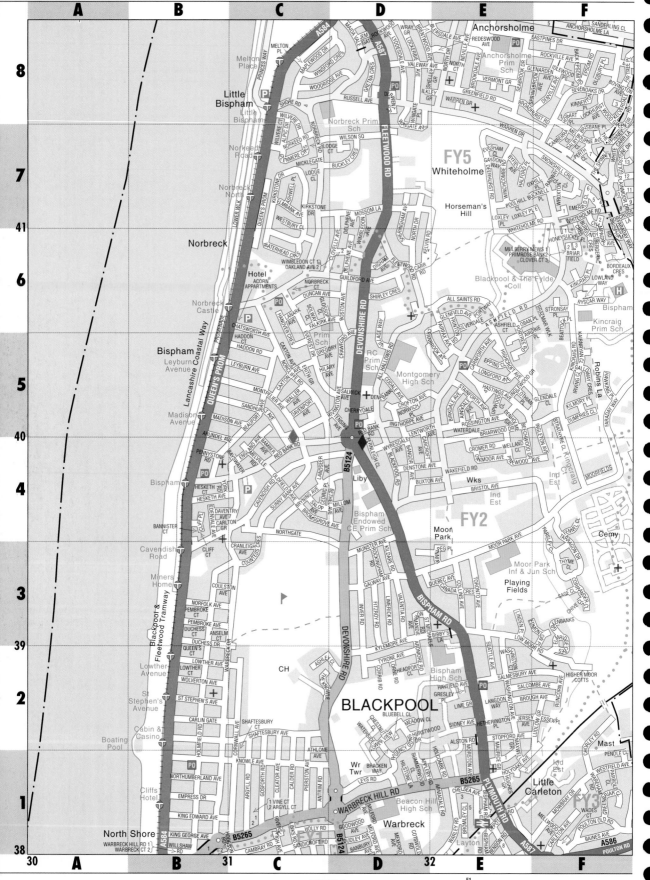

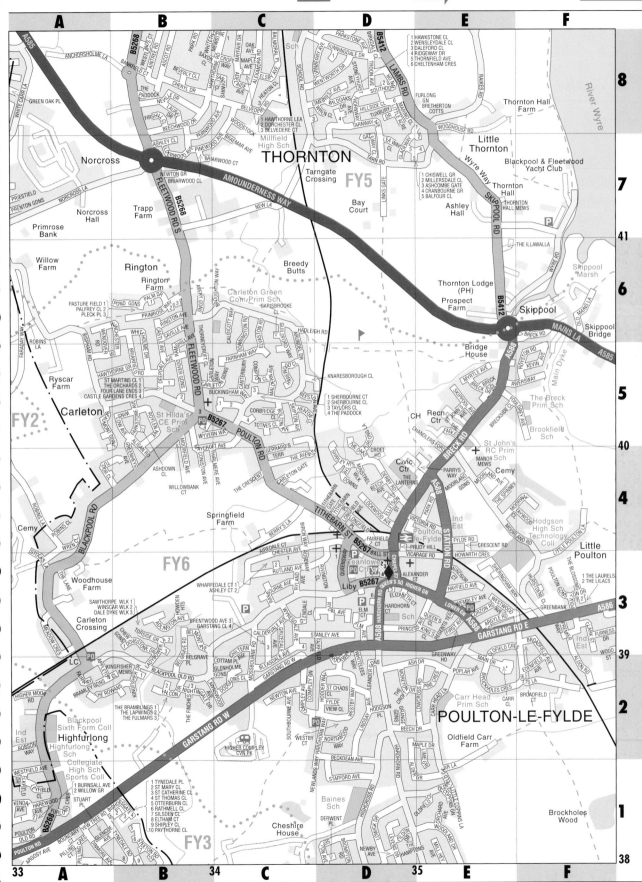

D3
1 BURLINGTON HO
2 CHURCH ST
3 CHAPEL STREET CT
4 MARKET PL
5 STOCKS CT
6 FALKUS CT

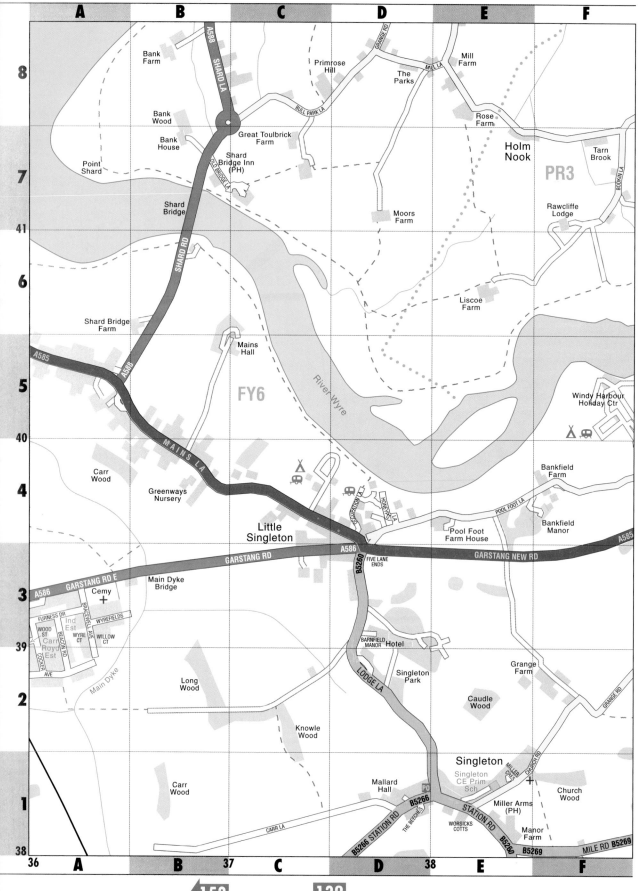

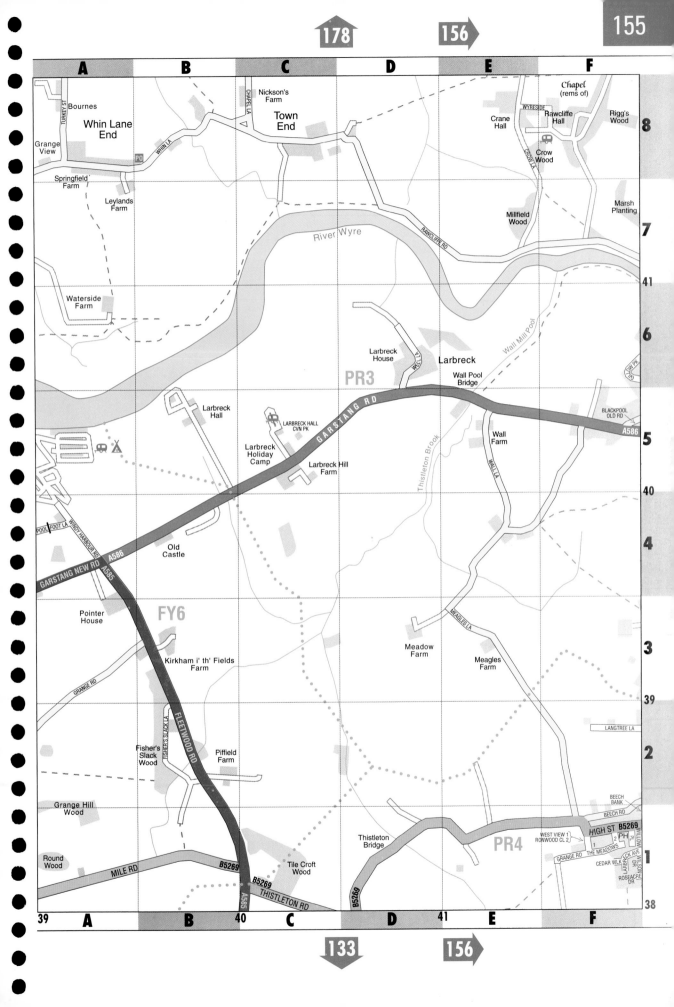

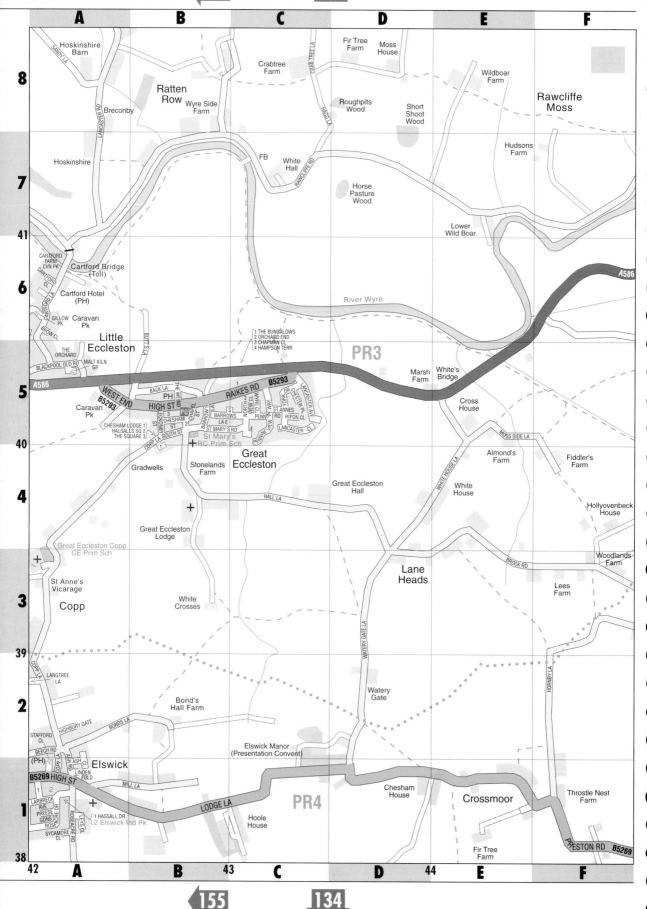

155
179

A B C D E F

8

Hoskinshire Barn

Ratten Row

Crabtree Farm

Fir Tree Farm

Moss House

Wildboar Farm

Rawcliffe Moss

Breconby

Wyre Side Farm

Roughpits Wood

Short Shoot Wood

Hudsons Farm

7

Hoskinshire

FB

White Hall

Horse Pasture Wood

41

Lower Wild Boar

A586

6

Cartford Farm CVN PK

Cartford Bridge (Toll)

Cartford Hotel (PH)

River Wyre

Gillow Pk

Caravan Pk

THE ORCHARD

Little Eccleston

1 THE BUNGALOWS
2 ORCHARD END
3 CHAPMAN CL
4 HAMPSON TERR

PR3

Marsh Farm

White's Bridge

MALT KILN GR

BACK LA

B5293

RAIKES RD

B5293

Cross House

5

A586

WEST END

HIGH ST

PH

PO

CHESHAM ST

BARROWS LA E

LANCASTER AVE

Caravan Pk

CHESHAM LODGE 1
HALSALLS SQ 2
THE SQUARE 3

St Mary's RC Prim Sch

St Mary's Rd

MOSS SIDE LA

40

Gradwells

Stonelands Farm

Great Eccleston

Almond's Farm

Fiddler's Farm

Great Eccleston Hall

White House

4

HALL LA

Hollyovenbeck House

Great Eccleston Lodge

WHITE HOUSE LA

BROCK RD

Woodlands Farm

Great Eccleston Copp CE Prim Sch

Lane Heads

Lees Farm

3

St Anne's Vicarage

Copp

White Crosses

WATERY GATE LA

39

COPP LA

LANGTREE LA

Watery Gate

HORNBY LA

2

Bond's Hall Farm

HIGHBURY GATE

BONDS LA

STAFFORD CL

BEECH RD

Elswick Manor (Presentation Convent)

(PH)

Elswick

MILL LA

Chesham House

Crossmoor

Throstle Nest Farm

B5269

HIGH ST

LINDEN FOLD

1

LODGE LA

PR4

Hoole House

THROSTLE NEST FARM

LARBRECK AVE

PREESE GDNS

ROSE

SYCAMORE CL

ROSACRE RD

1 HASSALL DR
2 Elswick Ind Pk

Fir Tree Farm

PRESTON RD

B5269

38

42 A B 43 C D 44 E F

155
134

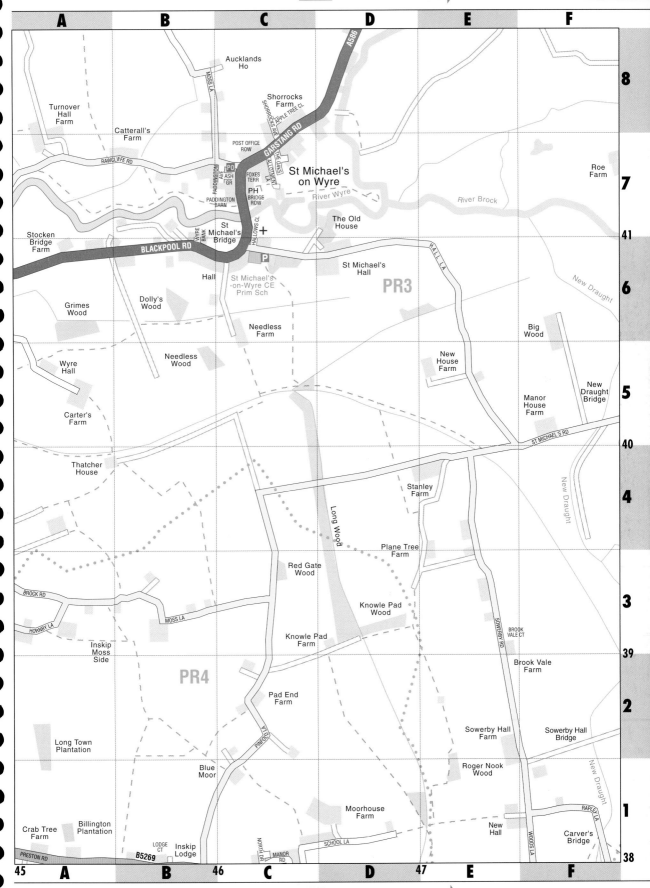

8

Aucklands Ho

Turnover Hall Farm

Catterall's Farm

Shorrocks Farm

MOSS LA

SHORROCKS AVE   APPLE TREE CL

GARSTANG RD

A586

RAWCLIFFE RD

POST OFFICE ROW

PADDINGTON AVE   ASH GR

THE OAKS

ALLOTMENT

PO

FOXES TERR

St Michael's on Wyre

7

PADDINGTON BARN

PH   BRIDGE ROW

River Wyre

River Brock

Roe Farm

Stocken Bridge Farm

WYRE BANK

St Michael's Bridge

HALLOWS CL

The Old House

41

BLACKPOOL RD

Hall

P

St Michael's Hall

HALL LA

PR3

New Draught

6

Grimes Wood

Dolly's Wood

St Michael's -on-Wyre CE Prim Sch

Needless Farm

New House Farm

Big Wood

Needless Wood

New Draught Bridge

5

Wyre Hall

Manor House Farm

Carter's Farm

ST MICHAEL'S RD

40

Thatcher House

Stanley Farm

New Draught

4

Long Wood

Plane Tree Farm

BROCK RD

Red Gate Wood

Knowle Pad Wood

SOWERBY RD

BROOK VALE CT

3

HORNBY LA

MOSS LA

Knowle Pad Farm

Brook Vale Farm

39

Inskip Moss Side

PR4

Pad End Farm

2

Long Town Plantation

PIMFOLD LA

Sowerby Hall Farm

Sowerby Hall Bridge

Blue Moor

Roger Nook Wood

New Draught

RAPLEY LA

1

Crab Tree Farm

Billington Plantation

NORTH DR

MANOR RD

Moorhouse Farm

SCHOOL LA

WOODS LA

New Hall

Carver's Bridge

LODGE CT

Inskip Lodge

B5269

PRESTON RD

38

A B C D E F

Higher Silcock Farm

Shelley Wood

Westfield Square Wood

Bradley Hill

Old Turnpike

Town Croft

A6

PRESTON LANCASTER RD

Lancaster Canal

NEW LA

Claughton Lane Bridge

Nut Wood

Big Wood

Blay Brook

John Hall's Wood

Myerscough House

Eastwood Farm

STANZAKER HALL DR

Stanzaker Hall

A6

41

Roe Bridge

Farther Light Ash

Drive Wood

Banners Farm

Duck Wood

Lancaster Canal

6

Three Pits Wood

Nearer Light Ash

Brock Wood

River Brock

Brock Aqueduct

Light Ash Bridge

5

PR3

Myerscough Coll

Old Brock Bridge

Crow Wood

MYERSCOUGH HALL DR

SUNNYSIDE CVN PK

40

Myerscough

ST MICHAEL'S RD

Primrose Hill

Owd Nells Tavern (PH)

4

Myerscough Lodge

Old River Brock

Myerscough Mill Farm

GARSTANG RD A6

Carefoot

Guys Thatched Hamlet (Craft Ctr)

Duncombe

3

Withney Dyke

Lee Farm

39

Hallidays Farm

MOSS LA

Headnook Farm

2

PR4

Lancaster Canal

Nook Farm

Beech Grove

BENSON'S LA

Fence Foot

1

White Horse Bridge

BRIERLEY LA

MALLEY LA

WHITE HORSE LA

38

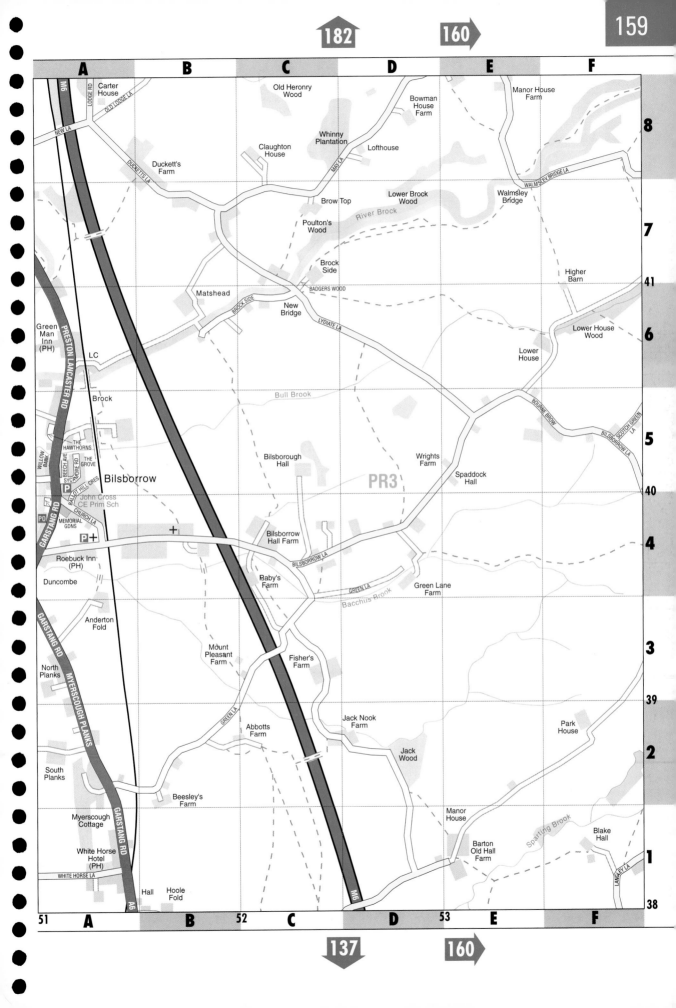

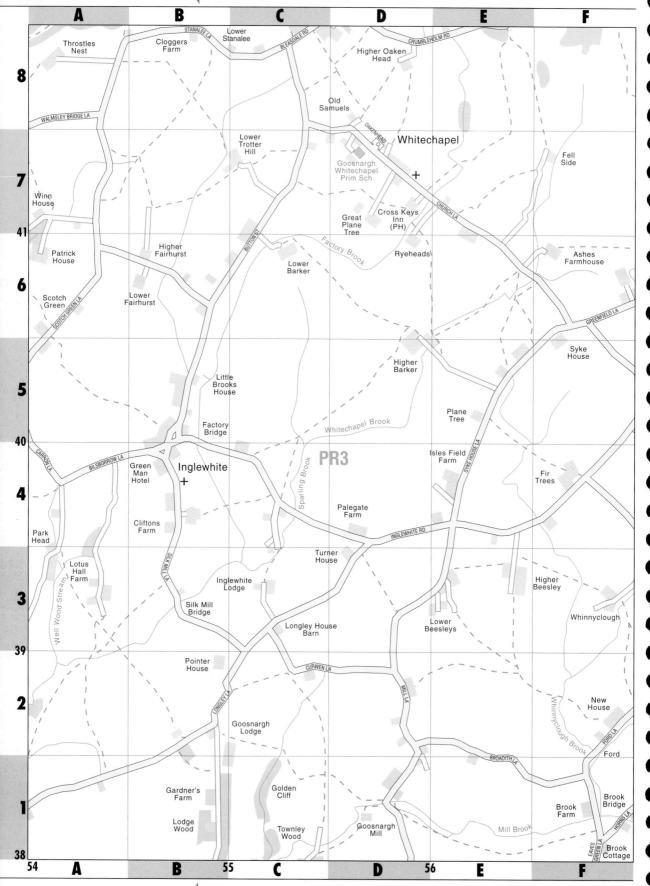

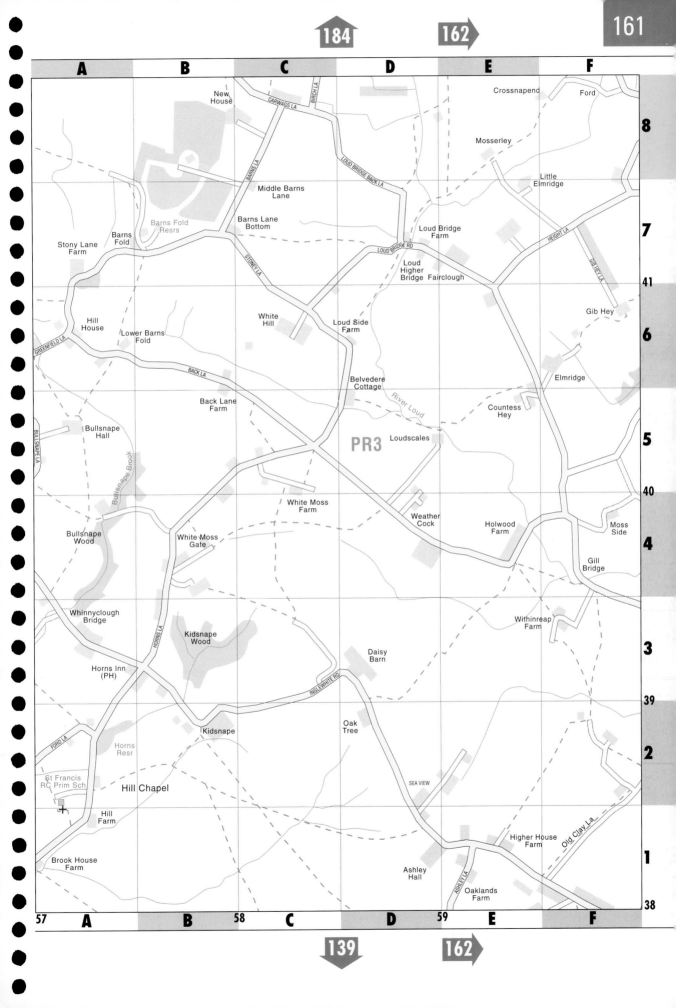

161
185

A | B | C | D | E | F

8

Old Vicarage
PARSONAGE LA
Higher Parsonage
Astley House
CUTLER LA
Fields Farm
Sandy Bank Farm
Pale Farm
Folly
Dobson's Hall

PARKINSON LA
Wallclough
Higher Chipping House
Hesketh Lane
Loud Side
Leach House

MILL LA
HESKETH LA
Dog and Partridge (PH)
Lanshaw Bridge
LONGRIDGE RD

7

Hesketh End
Loud Lower Bridge
ARBOUR LANE END
CADGELEY LA

Crow Trees Farm
JUDD HOLMES LA
Judd Holmes
Loud Lower Bridge

41

Black Moss House
Arbour Farm

6

Elmridge Wood
Rose Grove
LONGRIDGE RD
Lyme House Farm

Black Moss
Black Moss Wood
Knott
River Loud
HOPE LA
Dale House

5

Lea House Bridge
✛
PR3
FOUR ACRE LA

40

Clap Gate
Woodhill
ELM BROW
Wheatley Farm
Turnley's

4

Blackmoss House
Elm Wood
Bradleys Farm

Moss Gate Farm
Derby Arms (PH)
White Fold

Priest Hill
LONGRIDGE RD
Little Town
Oaks Barn
BINNS BROW
CH

3

BEACON VIEW
Higher Birks

39

Higher Cockleach
Curtis House
Sharple's House
FORTY ACRE LA

COCKLEACH LANE ENDS
HILL TOP
Stone Croft
Hills

2

Lower Cockleach
LORD'S LA
Old Rhodes
HIGHER RD
Dilworth Brows

Jenkinsons
Cottam House Farm

1

Billingtons
Nook Fold
WRITTEN STONE LA

CHIPPING LA
Tootle Height
BEACON FELL CVN PK

38

60 | A | B | 61 | C | D | 62 | E | F

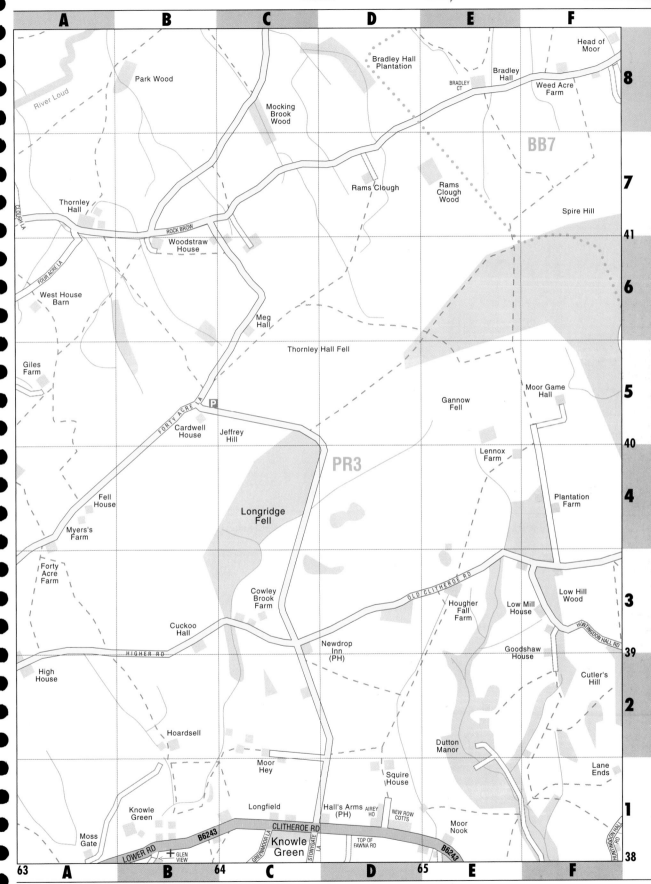

River Loud

Park Wood

Mocking Brook Wood

Bradley Hall Plantation

BRADLEY CT

Bradley Hall

Head of Moor

Weed Acre Farm

BB7

8

Rams Clough

Rams Clough Wood

7

Thornley Hall

Spire Hill

CLOUGH LA

ROCK BROW

Woodstraw House

41

FOUR ACRE LA

West House Barn

Meg Hall

6

Giles Farm

Thornley Hall Fell

Moor Game Hall

5

FORTY ACRE LA

P

Cardwell House

Jeffrey Hill

Gannow Fell

40

Lennox Farm

PR3

Plantation Farm

4

Fell House

Longridge Fell

Myers's Farm

Forty Acre Farm

Cowley Brook Farm

OLD CLITHEROE RD

Houlgher Fall Farm

Low Mill House

Low Hill Wood

HUNTINGDON HALL RD

3

Cuckoo Hall

HIGHER RD

Newdrop Inn (PH)

Goodshaw House

Cutler's Hill

39

High House

2

Hoardsell

Dutton Manor

Lane Ends

Moor Hey

Squire House

1

Knowle Green

Longfield

Hall's Arms (PH)

AIREY HO

NEW ROW COTTS

Moor Nook

Moss Gate

LOWER RD

GREENMOOR LA

Knowle Green

B6243

CLITHEROE RD

STONYGATE LA

TOP OF FAWNA RD

B6243

HUNTINGDON HALL RD

38

GLEN VIEW

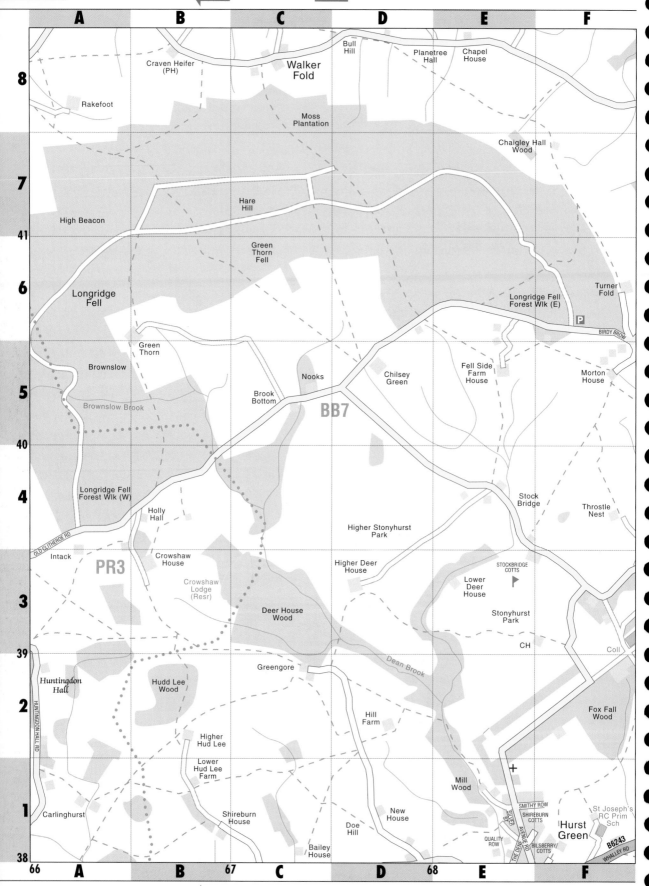

A   B   C   D   E   F

8   Rakefoot
Craven Heifer (PH)   Walker Fold   Bull Hill   Planetree Hall   Chapel House
Moss Plantation   Chaigley Hall Wood

7   High Beacon   Hare Hill
41   Green Thorn Fell
6   Longridge Fell   Longridge Fell Forest Wlk (E)   Turner Fold
Green Thorn   BIRDY BROW
Brownslow   Nooks   Chilsey Green   Fell Side Farm House   Morton House
5   Brook Bottom   BB7
Brownslow Brook
40   Stock Bridge   Throstle Nest
4   Longridge Fell Forest Wlk (W)   Higher Stonyhurst Park
Holly Hall
Intack   Crowshaw House   Higher Deer House   STOCKBRIDGE COTTS
PR3   Crowshaw Lodge (Resr)   Lower Deer House   Stonyhurst Park
3   Deer House Wood   CH   Coll
39   Dean Brook
Huntingdon Hall   Greengore   Fox Fall Wood
2   Hudd Lee Wood   Hill Farm
Higher Hud Lee   Mill Wood
Lower Hud Lee Farm   SMITHY ROW
1   Carlinghurst   Shireburn House   New House   SHIREBURN COTTS   St Joseph's RC Prim Sch
Doe Hill   QUALITY ROW   Hurst Green   B6243
Bailey House   BILSBERRY COTTS   WHALLEY RD
38   66   A   67   B   C   68   D   E   F
OLD CLITHEROE RD
HUNTINGDON HALL RD
THE AVENUE
CARRS LANE
THE DENE

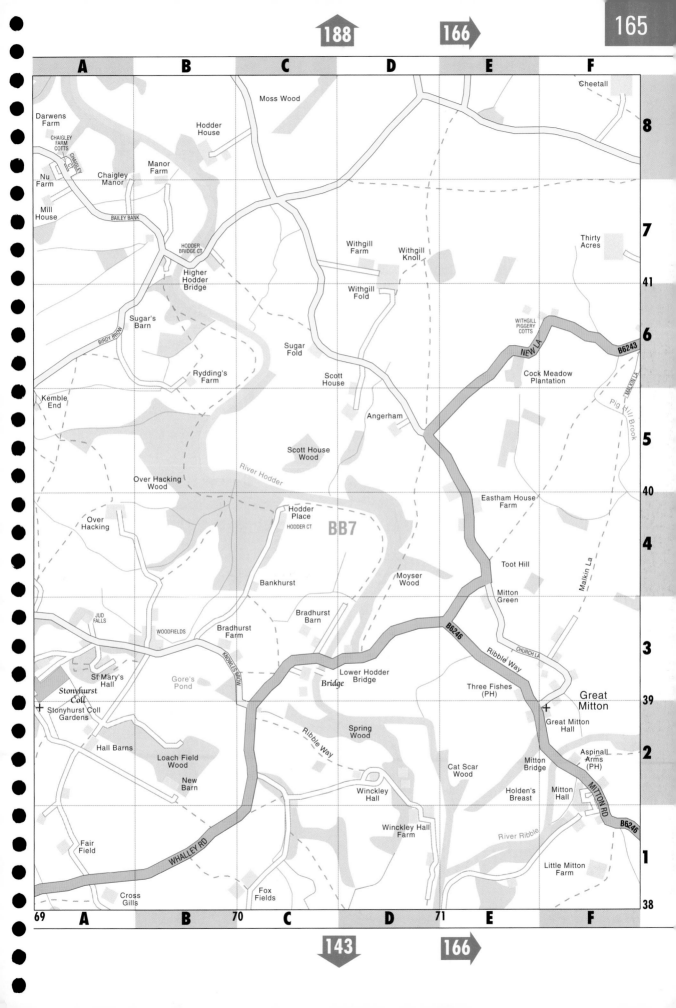

A B C D E F

8
7
41
6
5
40
4
3
39
2
1
38

Cheetall

Darwens Farm

CHAIGLEY FARM COTTS

Nu Farm

Mill House

Chaigley Manor

Manor Farm

Hodder House

Moss Wood

BAILEY BANK

HODDER BRIDGE CT.

Higher Hodder Bridge

BIRDY BROW

Sugar's Barn

Rydding's Farm

Kemble End

Over Hacking Wood

Over Hacking

Withgill Farm

Withgill Knoll

Withgill Fold

Sugar Fold

Scott House

Angerham

Scott House Wood

River Hodder

Hodder Place

HODDER CT.

BB7

Bankhurst

Moyser Wood

Bradhurst Barn

Bradhurst Farm

WOODFIELDS

JUD FALLS

KNOWLES BROW

Gore's Pond

St Mary's Hall

Stonyhurst Coll

Stonyhurst Coll Gardens

Hall Barns

Loach Field Wood

New Barn

Fair Field

WHALLEY RD

Cross Gills

Fox Fields

Ribble Way

Bridge

Lower Hodder Bridge

Spring Wood

Winckley Hall

Winckley Hall Farm

Cat Scar Wood

Thirty Acres

WITHGILL PIGGERY COTTS

NEW LA

B6243

Cock Meadow Plantation

MALKIN LA

Pig Hill Brook

Eastham House Farm

Toot Hill

Malkin La

Mitton Green

B6246

Ribble Way

CHURCH LA

Three Fishes (PH)

Great Mitton

Great Mitton Hall

Mitton Bridge

Holden's Breast

Mitton Hall

Aspinall Arms (PH)

MITTON RD

B6246

River Ribble

Little Mitton Farm

69 A B 70 C D 71 E F

165 189

D7
1 CURZON ST
2 MONK ST
3 BARN CROFT
4 HENTHORN CL
5 DEAN MEADOW
6 MAPLE AVE

D7
7 VICTORIA MEWS
D8
1 CARDIGAN CL
2 ALBEMARLE CT
3 BALDWIN HILL
4 MONTAGUE ST

5 WHALLEY ST
6 CORPORATION ST
7 MOSS ST
8 JOHN WALL CT
9 MILLTHORNE HO
E8
1 CHURCH ST

2 HARRIS CT
3 MARKET PL
4 BOWLAND CT
5 SADDLERS MEWS
6 WILKIN SQ
7 THE EMPORIUM
8 OLD STATION CT

9 PARSONAGE COTTS
10 CARDIGAN AVE
11 CASTLE VIEW HO
F8
1 ALBION ST
2 DUCK ST
3 CANDLEMAKERS CROFT

4 SHAW BRIDGE ST
5 PENDLE CT
6 BOLLAND CL
7 BROTHERTON MDWS

CLITHEROE

Low Moor
Stephen Bridge
Meadowlands
Riverside
Waddow Gn
Throstle Nest Farm
Edisford Bridge Inn (PH)
Edisford Prim Sch
Edisford Bridge
Edisford Hall
Rose Cottage
Bawdlands
Clitheroe Castle (rems of)
Mus
Windermere Ave
Ennerdale Cl
Hargreaves Ct
St James's CE Prim Sch
Primrose
Siddows Hall
Henthorn Rd
Siddows
Lower Standen
Little Moor
Higher Standen
Depot
Little Moor
Ribble Way
River Ribble
Sewage Works
Barrow Clough
Standen Cottage
Standen Hall
Fulshaw Wood
Barraclough House
Oak Wood
Whalley Rd
Brown Hill Barn
Barra Clough Wood
BB7
Fishes and Peggy Hill
Limehouse Farm
Shuttleworth Farm
Lower Standen Hey Farm
Higher Standen Hey Farm
CH
Barrow Gardens
A671
Park Farm
A59
Barrow Nurseries
Barrow Brook
Birch View
Barrow Sch
1 PAYNTER CL
2 TRAFFORD GDNS
3 CATLOW TERR
4 MILL BROOK PL
5 CHORLTON TERR
6 ABBEY TERR
7 COCKERILL TERR
8 OLD ROW
B6246
Mitton Rd
Lane Side
B6246
Barrow
Chestnut
Oak Cl
Ash Cl
Birch Gr

1 HAYHURST FARM TERR
2 MEARLEY BROOK FOLD
3 STANDEN ROAD BGLWS

Brookside Prim Sch

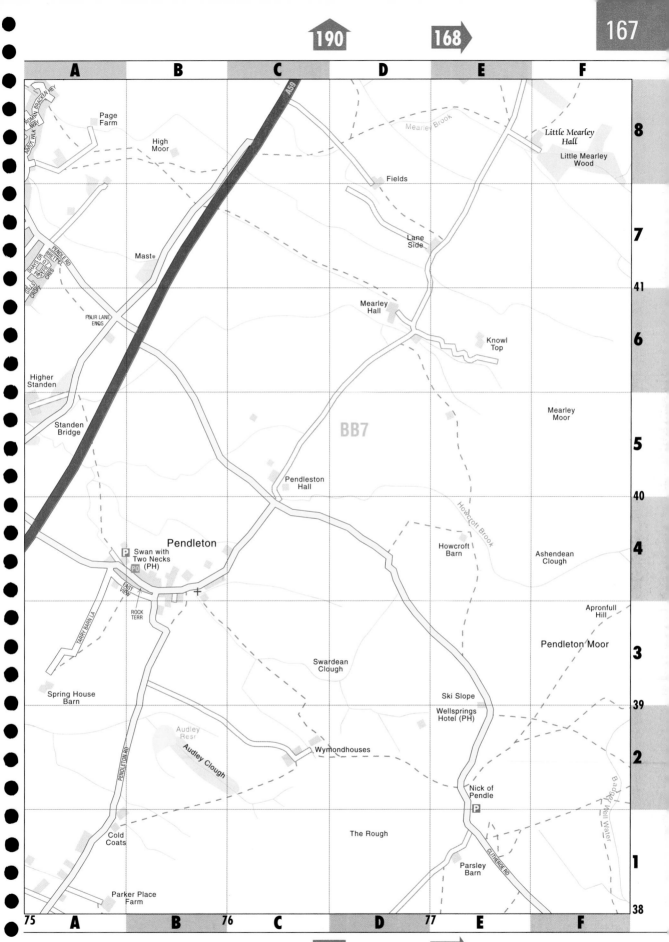

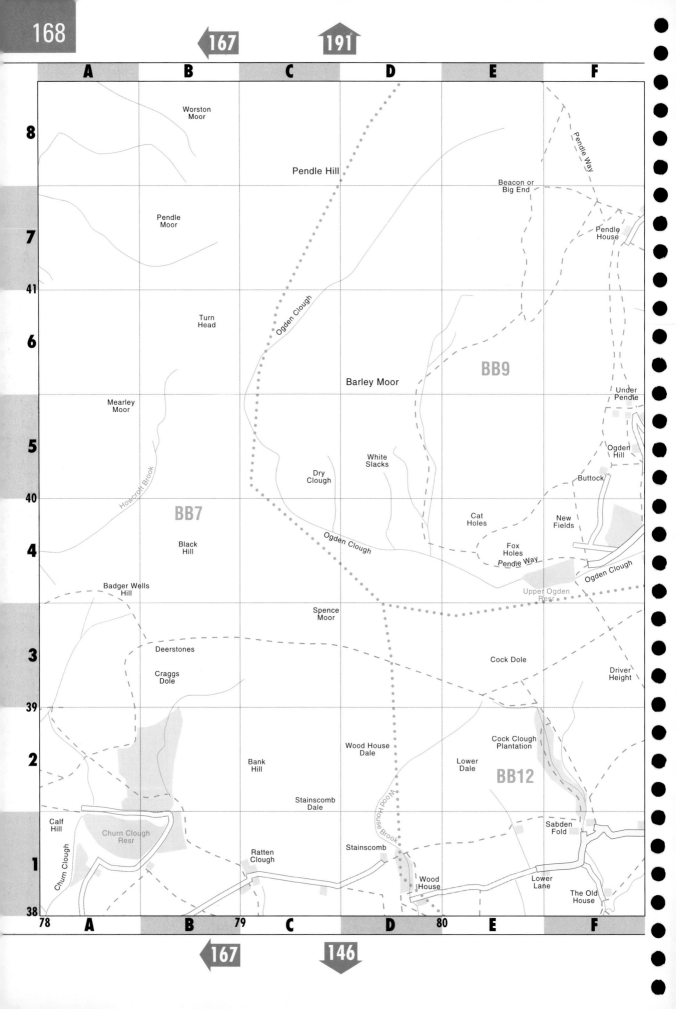

A   B   C   D   E   F

8   Worston
Moor

Pendle Hill

Pendle Way

Beacon or
Big End

7   Pendle
Moor

Pendle
House

41

Turn
Head

Ogden Clough

6   BB9

Barley Moor

Under
Pendle

Mearley
Moor

5   White
Slacks

Ogden
Hill

Dry
Clough

Buttock

40   Howcroft Brook

Cat
Holes

New
Fields

BB7

Ogden Clough

Fox
Holes

4   Black
Hill   Pendle Way   Ogden Clough

Upper Ogden
Resr

Badger Wells
Hill

Spence
Moor

3   Deerstones

Cock Dole

Driver
Height

Craggs
Dole

39   Cock Clough
Plantation

Wood House
Dale

2   Bank
Hill   Lower
Dale   BB12

Stainscomb
Dale

Sabden
Fold

Calf
Hill

Churn Clough
Resr

Ratten
Clough

Stainscomb

Lower
Lane

1   Wood
House

The Old
House

Churn Clough

Wood House Brook

38   **78   A   B   79   C   D   80   E   F**

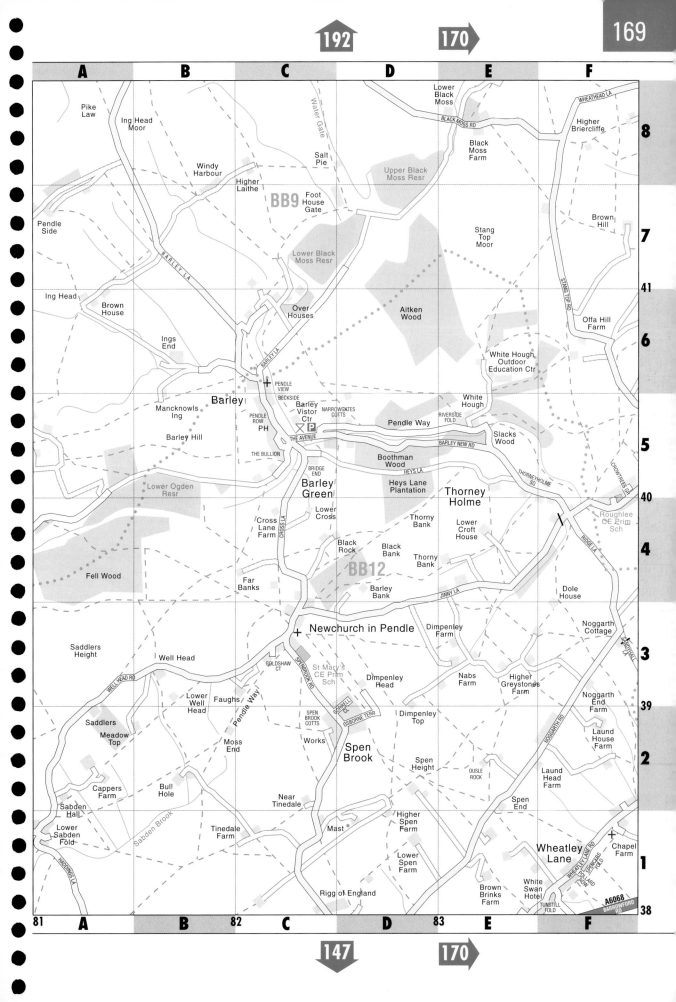

A B C D E F

8
7
41
6
5
40
4
3
39
2
1
38

Pike Law
Ing Head Moor
Windy Harbour
Higher Laithe
Salt Pie
Water Gate
Foot House Gate
BB9
Lower Black Moss
BLACK MOSS RD
WHEATHEAD LA
Higher Briercliffe

Pendle Side
Upper Black Moss Resr
Black Moss Farm
Brown Hill

Ing Head
Brown House
BARLEY LA
Lower Black Moss Resr
Stang Top Moor
STANG TOP RD
Offa Hill Farm

Ings End
Over Houses
Aitken Wood
White Hough Outdoor Education Ctr

Mancknowls Ing
Barley
PENDLE VIEW
PENDLE ROW PH
BECKSIDE
Barley Vistor Ctr
NARROWGATES COTTS
Pendle Way
White Hough
RIVERSIDE FOLD
Slacks Wood

Barley Hill
THE AVENUE
BARLEY NEW RD
THORNEYHOLME SQ
CROWTREES CR

THE BULLION
Boothman Wood
HEYS LA

Lower Ogden Resr
BRIDGE END
Barley Green
Lower Cross
Heys Lane Plantation
Thorney Holme
Roughlee CE Prim Sch
40

Cross Lane Farm
CROSS LA
Black Rock
Thorny Bank
Black Bank
Lower Croft House
RIDGE LA

Fell Wood
Far Banks
BB12
Thorny Bank
Dole House

Barley Bank
JINNY LA

Newchurch in Pendle
Dimpenley Farm
Noggarth Cottage
STUMP CR

Saddlers Height
Well Head
GOLDSHAW CT
SPENBROOK RD
St Mary's CE Prim Sch
Dimpenley Head
Nabs Farm
Higher Greystones Farm
Noggarth End Farm

WELL HEAD RD
Lower Well Head
Faughs
Pendle Way
GORRELL CL
OSBORNE TERR
Dimpenley Top
NOGGARTH RD
Laund House Farm

Saddlers
Meadow Top
Moss End
SPEN BROOK COTTS
Works
Spen Brook
Spen Height
OUSLE ROCK
Laund Head Farm

Cappers Farm
Bull Hole
Near Tinedale
Mast
Higher Spen Farm
Spen End
Chapel Farm

Sabden Hall
SABDEN BROOK
Tinedale Farm
Lower Spen Farm
Wheatley Lane
WHEATLEY LANE RD
SPENCERS FOLD
POLLARD ROW

Lower Sabden Fold
HADDINGS LA
Rigg of England
Brown Brinks Farm
White Swan Hotel
TUNSTILL FOLD
A6068
BARROWFORD RD

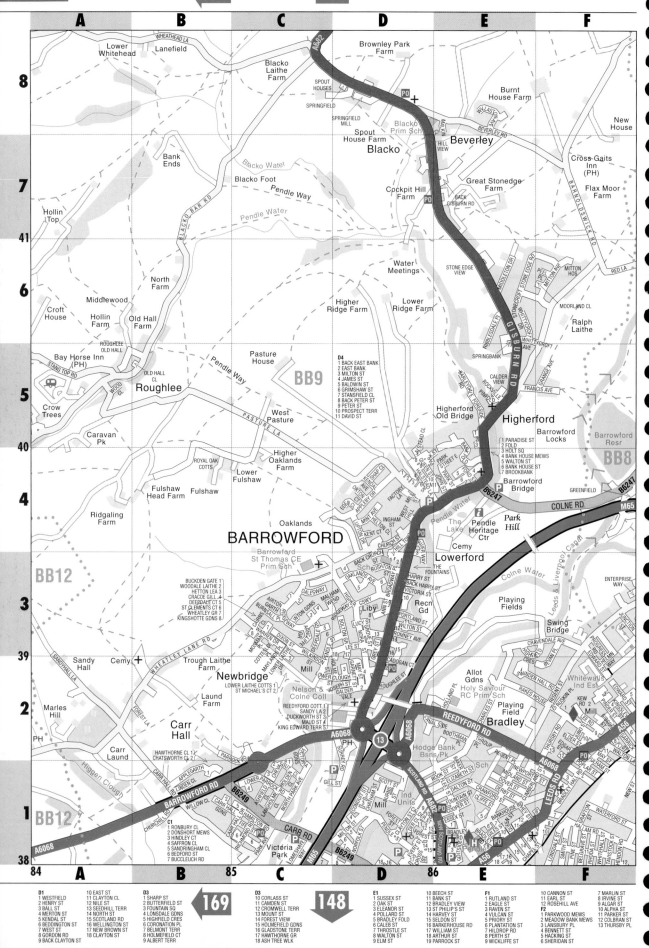

D1
1 WESTFIELD
2 HENRY ST
3 BALL ST
4 MERTON ST
5 KENDAL ST
6 BEDDINGTON ST
7 WEST ST
8 GORDON RD
9 BACK CLAYTON ST
10 EAST ST
11 CLAYTON CL
12 NILE ST
13 SEEDHILL TERR
14 NORTH ST
15 SCOTLAND RD
16 WELLINGTON ST
17 NEW BROWN ST
18 CLAYTON ST

D3
1 SHARP ST
2 BUTTERFIELD ST
3 FOUNTAIN SQ
4 LONSDALE GDNS
5 HIGHFIELD CRES
6 CORONATION PL
7 BELMONT TERR
8 HOLMEFIELD CT
9 ALBERT TERR

D3
10 CORLASS ST
11 CAMDEN ST
12 CROMWELL TERR
13 MOUNT ST
14 FOREST VIEW
15 HOLMEFIELD GDNS
16 GLADSTONE TERR
17 HAWTHORNE GR
18 ASH TREE WLK

E1
1 SUSSEX ST
2 OAK ST
3 ELEANOR ST
4 POLLARD ST
5 BRADLEY FOLD
6 CALEB ST
7 THROSTLE ST
8 WALTON ST
9 ELM ST

10 BEECH ST
11 BANK ST
12 BRADLEY VIEW
13 ST PHILIP'S ST
14 HARVEY ST
15 SELDON ST
16 BARKERHOUSE RD
17 WILLIAM ST
18 ARTHUR ST
19 PARROCK ST

F1
1 RUTLAND ST
2 EAGLE ST
3 RAVEN ST
4 VULCAN ST
5 PRIORY ST
6 PLANTATION ST
7 HILDROP RD
8 PERTH ST
9 WICKLIFFE ST

10 CANNON ST
11 EARL ST
12 ROSEHILL AVE
F2
1 PARKWOOD MEWS
2 MEADOW BANK MEWS
3 LANSBURY PL
4 BENNETT ST
5 HACKING ST
6 SHERIDAN ST

7 MARLIN ST
8 IRVINE ST
9 ALGAR ST
10 ALPHA ST
11 PARKER ST
12 COLBRAN ST
13 THURSBY PL

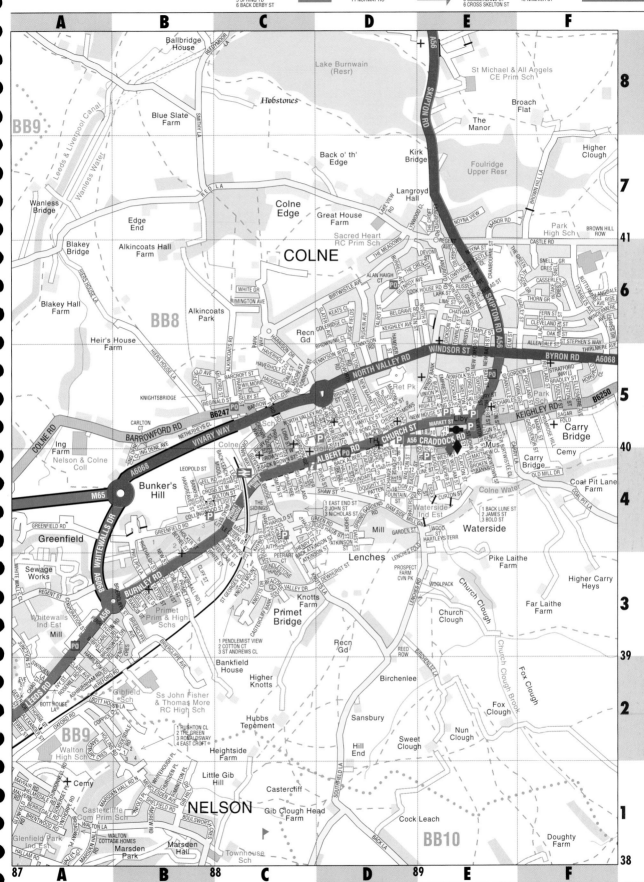

194

172

C5
1 FOTHERGILL ST
2 MOORHEAD ST
3 MELLING CT

D5
1 WALLACE HARTLEY MEWS
2 THE EXCHANGE
3 BIRTWISTLE HYDE PK
4 MITCHELL ST
5 SPRING YD
6 BACK DERBY ST

D5
7 NELSON ST
8 ARGYLE ST
9 TURNEY CROOK MEWS
10 SPRING PL
11 NORWAY HO

E5
1 WATER ST
2 DOCKRAY CT
3 ANGEL WAY
4 DOCKRAY YD
5 CUMBERLAND ST
6 CROSS SKELTON ST

7 BIRTWISTLE FOLD
8 POST OFFICE YD
9 ARCADIA
10 MARKET PL
11 PARLIAMENT ST
12 NINEVEH ST

B4
1 Garden Vale Bsns Ctr
2 Holker Bsns Ctr
3 Riverside Mill
4 Primet Bsns Ctr

D4
1 BACK DUKE ST
2 BACK EARL ST
3 KNOWSLEY ST
4 BACK CHAPEL ST
5 CROSS SCHOOL ST
6 LOWER SCHOOL ST
7 WEST EXCHANGE ST
8 RAGLAN ST
9 CAMBRIDGE ST

D4
10 BACK CAMBRIDGE ST
11 SELDON ST
12 CHAPEL FOLD
13 BLASCOMAY SQ
14 BACK BOUNDARY ST
15 BURRANS MDW
16 BACK ZION ST
17 CROSS HELLIWELL ST

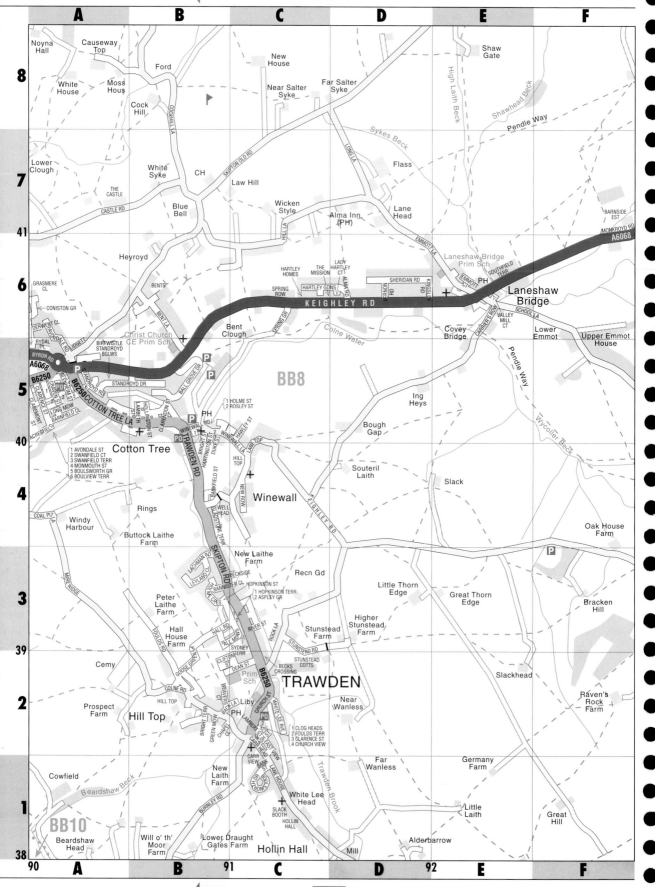

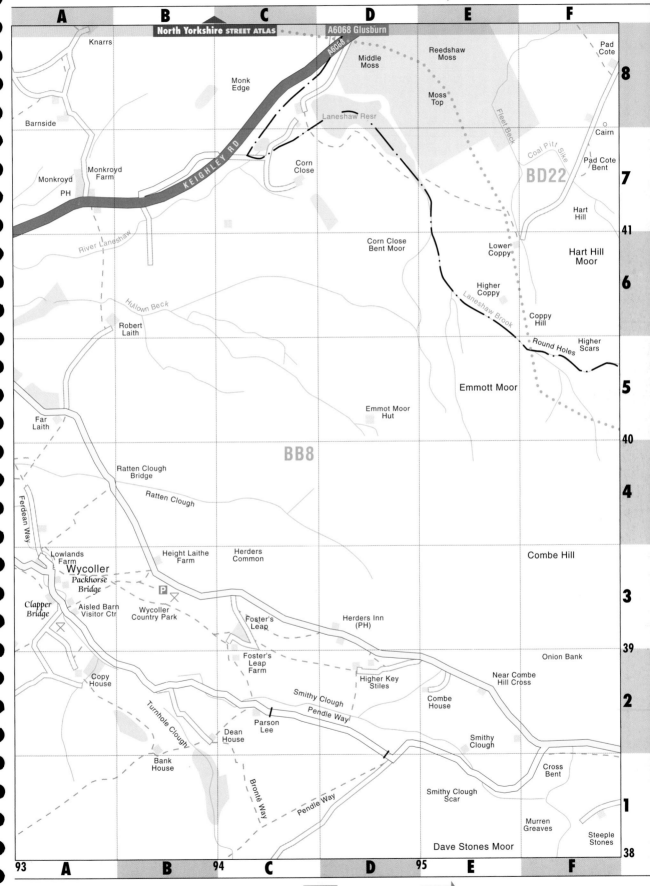

A   B   C   D   E   F

North Yorkshire STREET ATLAS

A6068 Glusburn

Knarrs

Middle Moss

Reedshaw Moss

Pad Cote

Monk Edge

Moss Top

8

Barnside

Laneshaw Resr

Cairn

Corn Close

Fleet Beck

BD22

Pad Cote Bent

Monkroyd Farm

KEIGHLEY RD

Hart Hill

7

Monkroyd PH

A6068

41

River Laneshaw

Corn Close Bent Moor

Lower Coppy

Hart Hill Moor

Hulown Beck

Higher Coppy

6

Robert Laith

Laneshaw Brook

Coppy Hill

Higher Scars

Round Holes

Far Laith

Emmott Moor

5

Emmot Moor Hut

40

BB8

Ratten Clough Bridge

4

Ferdean Way

Ratten Clough

Lowlands Farm

Height Laithe Farm

Herders Common

Combe Hill

Wycoller

Packhorse Bridge

P ✕

Clapper Bridge

Aisled Barn Visitor Ctr

Wycoller Country Park

Foster's Leap

Herders Inn (PH)

3

Onion Bank

39

Foster's Leap Farm

Higher Key Stiles

Near Combe Hill Cross

Copy House

Smithy Clough

Combe House

2

Turnhole Cloughv

Parson Lee

Pendle Way

Smithy Clough

Dean House

Cross Bent

Bank House

Brontë Way

Pendle Way

Smithy Clough Scar

Murren Greaves

Steeple Stones

1

Dave Stones Moor

38

93   A   B   94   C   D   95   E   F

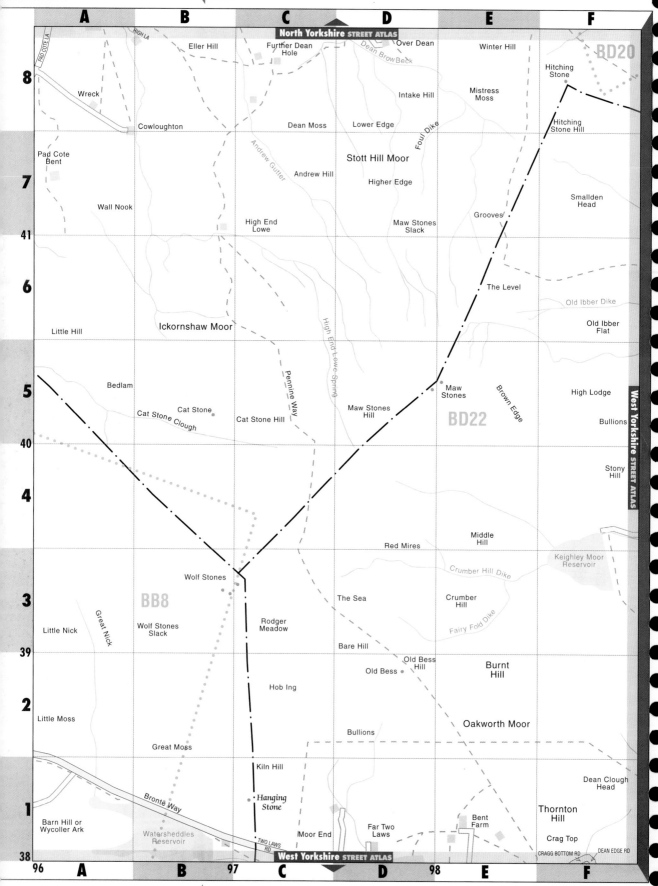

North Yorkshire STREET ATLAS

West Yorkshire STREET ATLAS

BD20

BD22

BB8

A

PAD COTE LA
HIGH LA
Eller Hill
Further Dean Hole
Over Dean
Dean Brow Beck
Winter Hill
Hitching Stone
Wreck
Intake Hill
Mistress Moss
Cowloughton
Dean Moss
Lower Edge
Hitching Stone Hill
Foul Dike
Pad Cote Bent
Andrew Gutter
Stott Hill Moor
Wall Nook
Andrew Hill
Higher Edge
Smallden Head
High End Lowe
Maw Stones Slack
Grooves
The Level
Old Ibber Dike
Ickornshaw Moor
High End Lowe Spring
Little Hill
Old Ibber Flat
Bedlam
Pennine Way
Maw Stones
High Lodge
Cat Stone
Cat Stone Clough
Cat Stone Hill
Maw Stones Hill
Brown Edge
Bullions
Stony Hill
Wolf Stones
Middle Hill
Red Mires
Keighley Moor Reservoir
Great Nick
Crumber Hill Dike
BB8
The Sea
Crumber Hill
Wolf Stones Slack
Rodger Meadow
Fairy Fold Dike
Little Nick
Bare Hill
Old Bess Hill
Hob Ing
Old Bess
Burnt Hill
Little Moss
Bullions
Oakworth Moor
Great Moss
Kiln Hill
Dean Clough Head
Bronté Way
Hanging Stone
Thornton Hill
Barn Hill or Wycoller Ark
Watersheddles Reservoir
TWO LAWS RD
Moor End
Far Two Laws
Bent Farm
Crag Top
CRAGG BOTTOM RD
DEAN EDGE RD

West Yorkshire STREET ATLAS

96   A   B   97   C   D   98   E   F
8   41   7   6   5   40   4   3   39   2   38   1

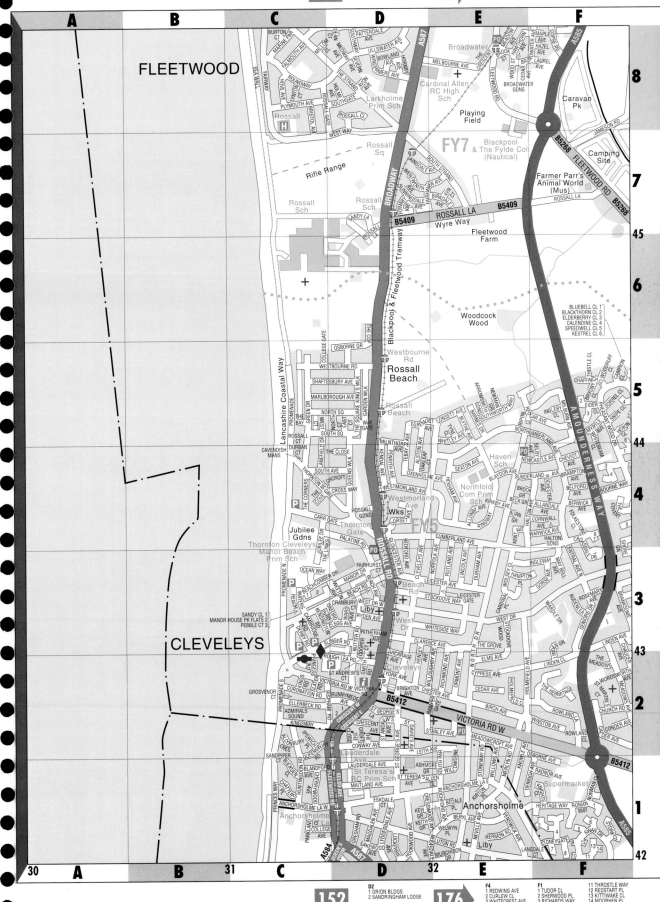

FLEETWOOD

CLEVELEYS

FY7

FM5

D2
1 ORION BLDGS
2 SANDRINGHAM LODGE

F4
1 REDWING AVE
2 CURLEW CL
3 WHITECREST AVE
4 BARNFIELD CL
5 WIDGEON CL
6 COLCHESTER DR
7 PORTSMOUTH CL

F1
1 TUDOR CL
2 SHERWOOD PL
3 RICHARDS WAY
4 GLADSTONE AVE
5 POCHARD PL
6 DOVE CL
7 INGLENOOK CL
8 HERIOT CL
9 BUNTING PL
10 SANDPIPER PL

11 THROSTLE WAY
12 REDSTART PL
13 KITTIWAKE CL
14 MOORHEN PL

BLUEBELL CL 1
BLACKTHORN CL 2
ELDERBERRY CL 3
CALENDINE CL 4
SPEEDWELL CL 5
KESTREL CL 6

SANDY CL 1
MANOR HOUSE PK FLATS 2
PEBBLE CT 3

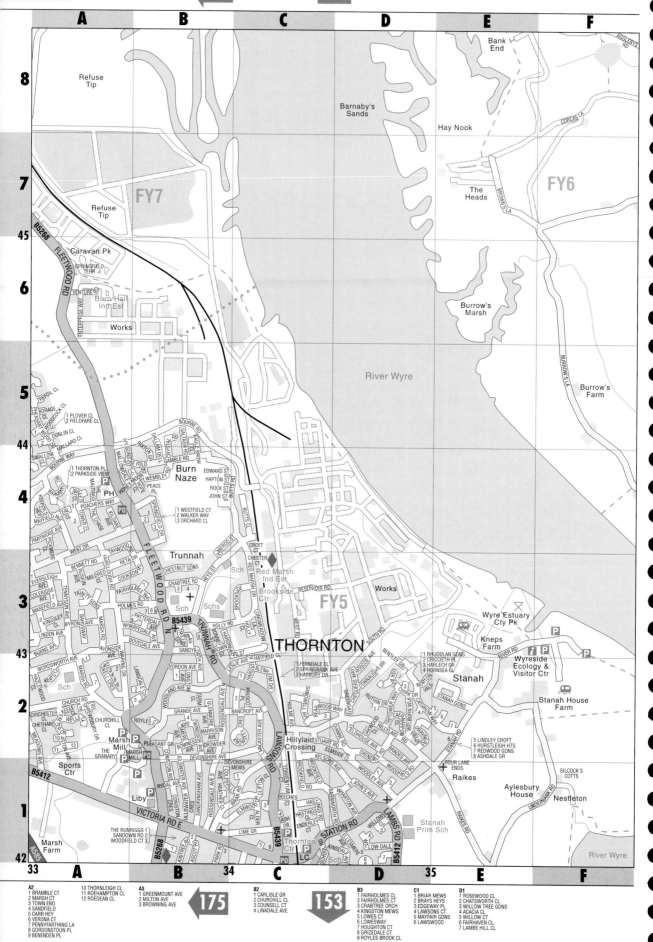

THORNTON

FY7
FY6
FY5

River Wyre

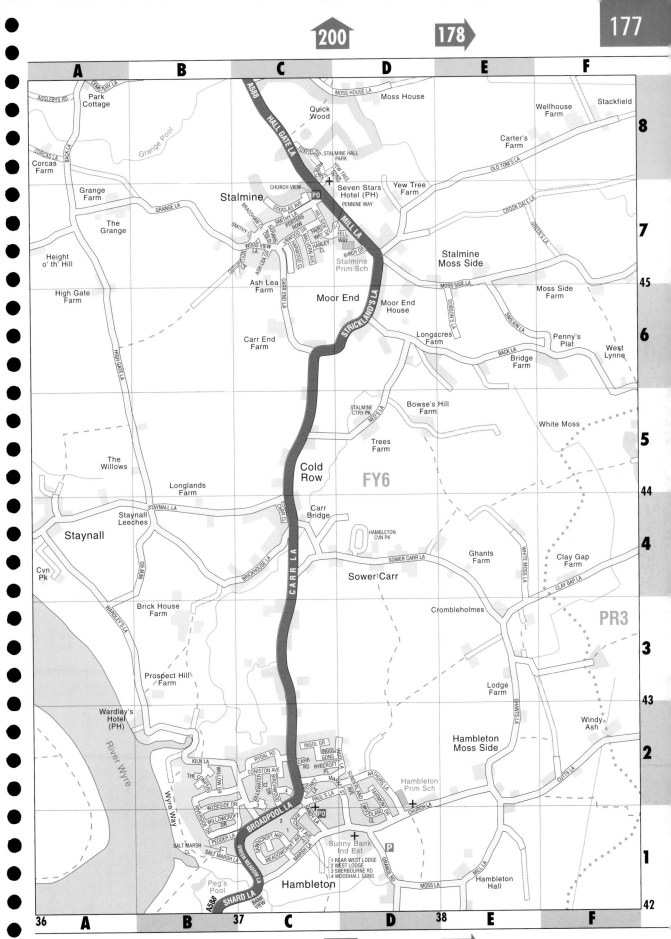

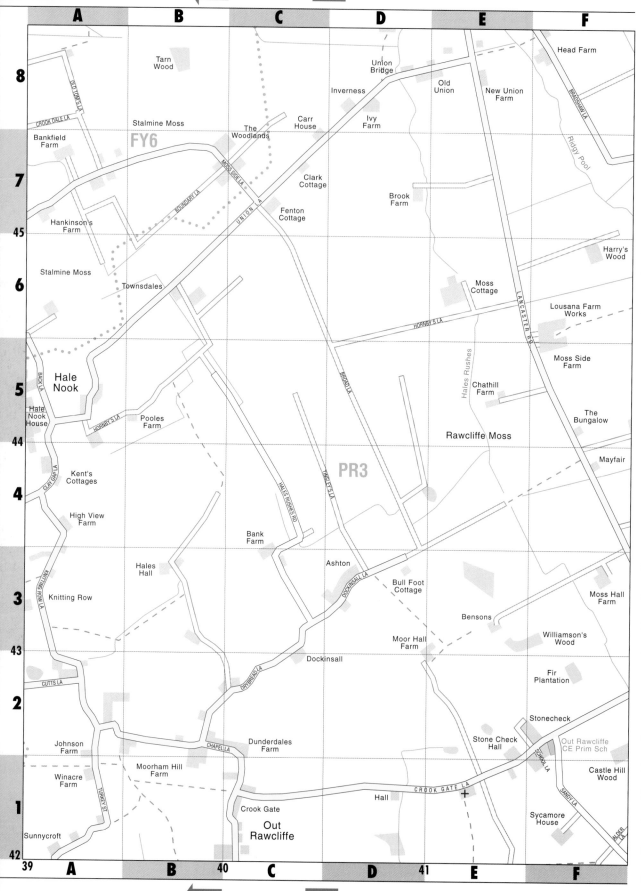

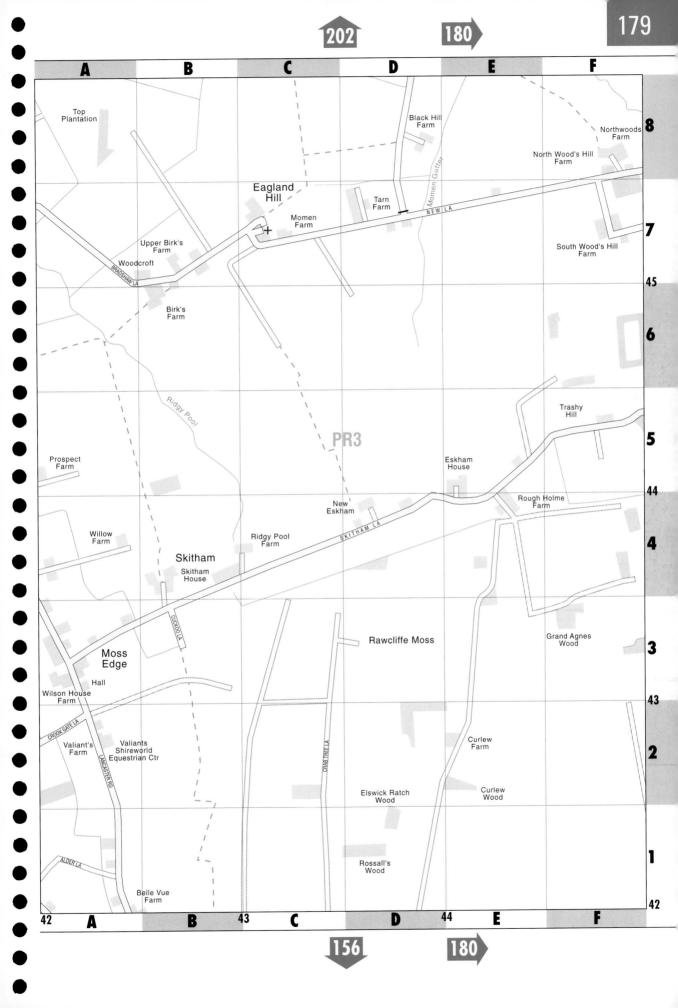

A B C D E F

Top
Plantation

Black Hill
Farm

Northwoods
Farm

8

North Wood's Hill
Farm

Eagland
Hill

Momen
Farm

Tarn
Farm

NEW LA

Momen Gutter

South Wood's Hill
Farm

7

Upper Birk's
Farm

Woodcroft

BRADSHAW LA

45

Birk's
Farm

6

Ridgy Pool

PR3

Trashy
Hill

5

Prospect
Farm

Eskham
House

44

New
Eskham

Rough Holme
Farm

Willow
Farm

Ridgy Pool
Farm

SKITHAM LA

4

Skitham

Skitham
House

Rawcliffe Moss

Grand Agnes
Wood

3

Moss
Edge

CUCKOO LA

Hall

Wilson House
Farm

43

CROOK GATE LA

Valiant's
Farm

Valiants
Shireworld
Equestrian Ctr

LANCASTER RD

CRAB TREE LA

Curlew
Farm

2

Elswick Ratch
Wood

Curlew
Wood

ALDER LA

1

Rossall's
Wood

Belle Vue
Farm

42

42 A B 43 C D 44 E F

179
203

A **B** **C** **D** **E** **F**

8

Black La

Nickytom Woods

Fowler's Farm

Island Farm

Station La

The Bowers

Long Wood

New La

Island Wood

Cartmell La

Hoole Farm

Kilcrash La

Bowerswood

Big Wood

Bowers La

Park Wood

7

Pilling Water

Park Farm

45

Primrose Hill Farm

Nateby Prim Sch

Nook Cotts

PO

Longmoor La

Poulton's Farm

Ains Pool

Woods La

Caton's Farm

Nateby

Cragg Farm

Gibson's Farm

6

Copthorne Farm

Graystones Wood

Nook Farm House

Nateby Lodge

Humblescough La

New Wood

Skitham La

Southfield

Lodge Wood

5

Brook Farm

Hoole La

Greenlands

Poplar Grove Farm

Humblescough Farm

PR3

44

Manor House Farm

Humblescough La

Upper Humblescough Wood

Kirkland Hall Farm

4

Bella's Wood

Shenty's Farm

Watson's Wood

Ains Pool

Ainspool House Farm

Band Wood

Wag Hill

Lower Humblescough Wood

3

Pilling Water

Top Moss Wood

Wag Wood

Ainspool Bridge

A586

43

Cuckoo Wood

Sharples La

Tarnacre House Farm

Works

2

Pancake Wood

Brook House Farm

Tarnacre La

Hamilton House Farm

Band La

Buttfield Wood

Tarnacre Hall Bsns Pk

Land House

River Wyre

Catterall Hall Farm

1

Fairfield Farm

Tarnacre Hall Farm

Tyrer Bridge

Garstang Rd

A586

42

45 **A** **B** **46** **C** **D** **47** **E** **F**

179
157

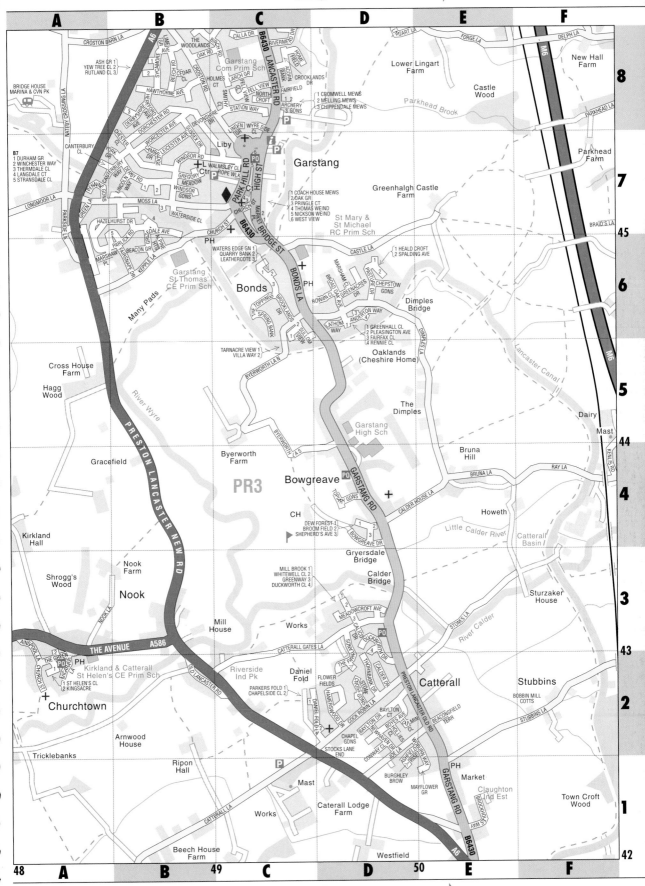

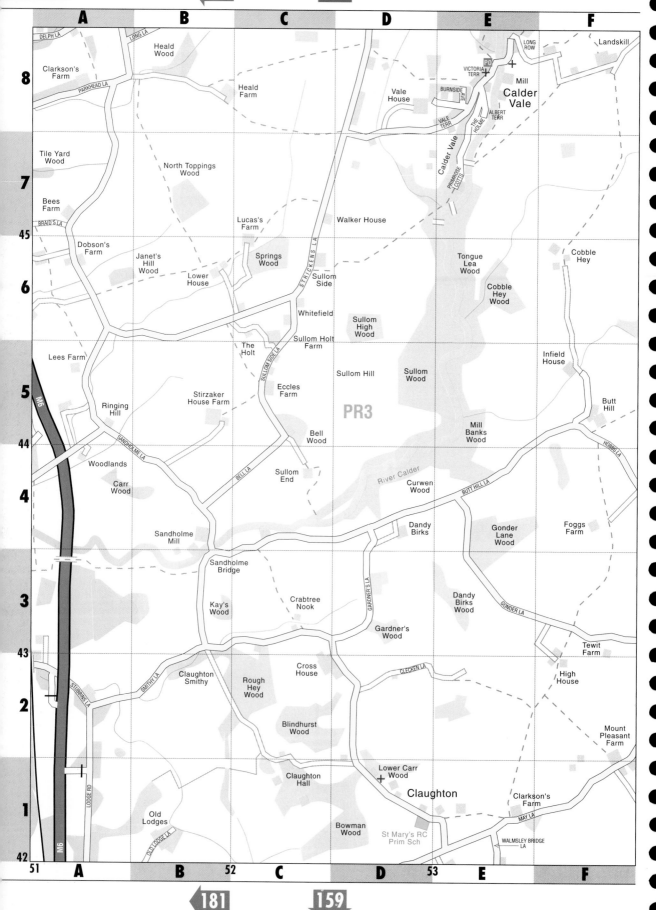

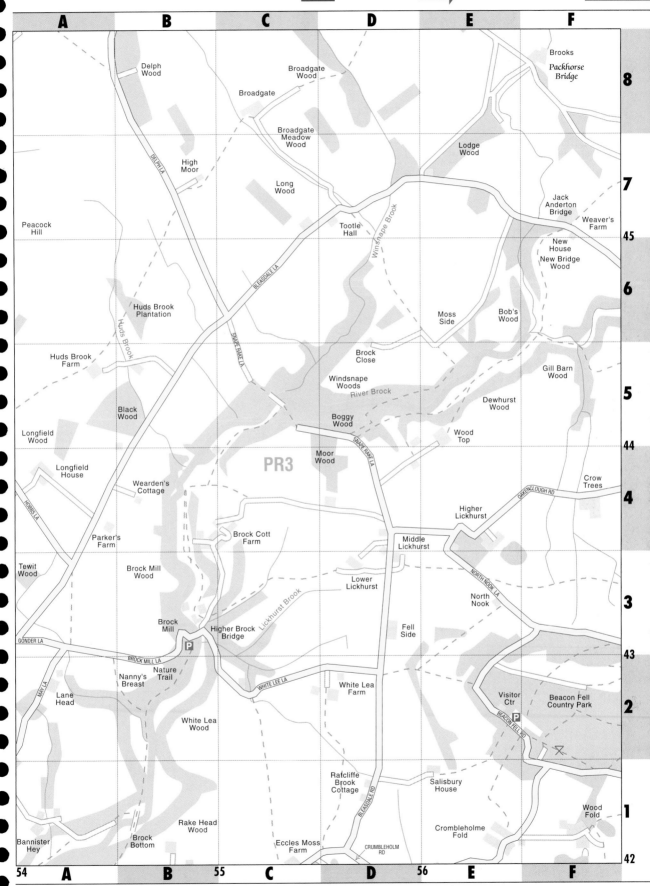

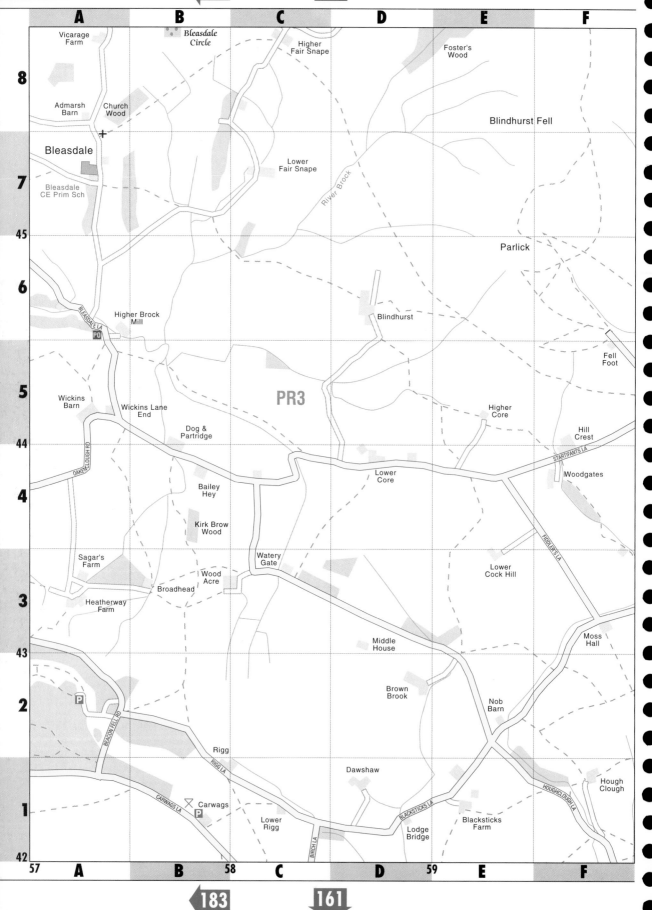

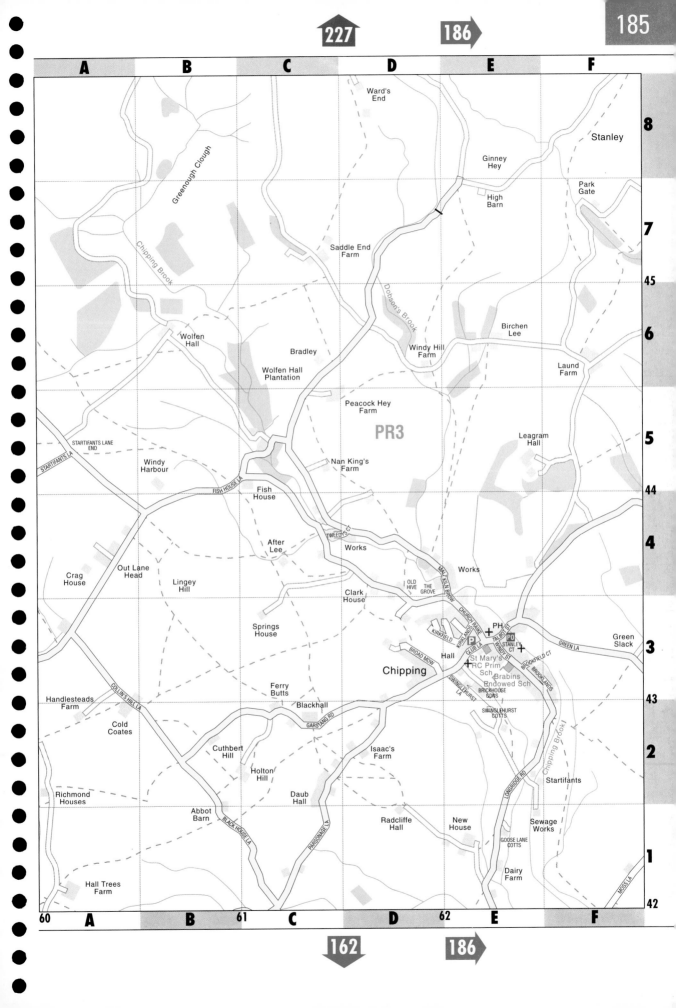

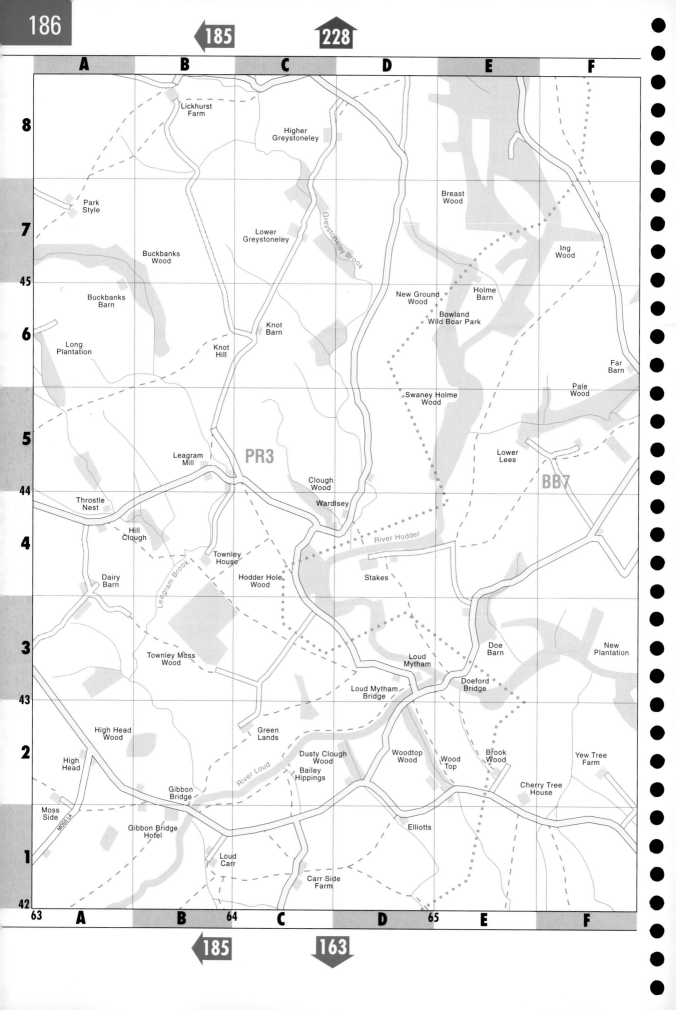

A   B   C   D   E   F

8
Lickhurst Farm
Higher Greystoneley
Park Style
Breast Wood
Ing Wood
7
Lower Greystoneley
Greystoneley Brook
Buckbanks Wood
45
Buckbanks Barn
New Ground Wood
Holme Barn
6
Long Plantation
Knot Barn
Knot Hill
Bowland Wild Boar Park
Far Barn
Swaney Holme Wood
Pale Wood
5
Leagram Mill
PR3
Lower Lees
44
Clough Wood
Wardlsey
BB7
Throstle Nest
Hill Clough
River Hodder
4
Townley House
Dairy Barn
Hodder Hole Wood
Stakes
Leagram Brook
3
Townley Moss Wood
Loud Mytham
Doe Barn
New Plantation
43
Loud Mytham Bridge
Doeford Bridge
High Head Wood
Green Lands
2
High Head
Dusty Clough Wood
Woodtop Wood
Wood Top
Brook Wood
Yew Tree Farm
Bailey Hippings
River Loud
Gibbon Bridge
Cherry Tree House
Moss Side
MOSS LA
Elliotts
Gibbon Bridge Hotel
1
Loud Carr
Carr Side Farm
42
63   A   B   64   C   D   65   E   F

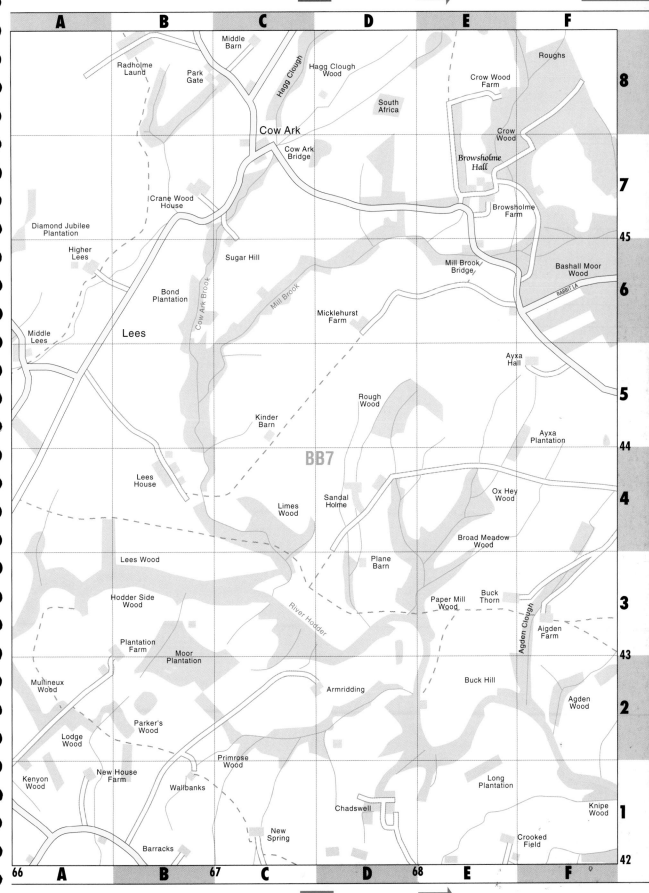

A   **B**   **C**   **D**   **E**   **F**

Middle
Barn

Radholme
Laund

Park
Gate

Hagg Clough

Hagg Clough
Wood

Roughs

Crow Wood
Farm

8

South
Africa

Cow Ark

Cow Ark
Bridge

Crow
Wood

*Browsholme
Hall*

7

Crane Wood
House

Browsholme
Farm

Diamond Jubilee
Plantation

45

Higher
Lees

Sugar Hill

Mill Brook
Bridge

Bashall Moor
Wood

Bond
Plantation

Mill Brook

RABBIT LA

6

Middle
Lees

Lees

Cow Ark Brook

Micklehurst
Farm

Ayxa
Hall

Rough
Wood

5

Kinder
Barn

Ayxa
Plantation

44

BB7

Lees
House

Sandal
Holme

Ox Hey
Wood

4

Limes
Wood

Broad Meadow
Wood

Lees Wood

Plane
Barn

Paper Mill
Wood

Buck
Thorn

Agden Clough

3

Hodder Side
Wood

River Hodder

Aigden
Farm

43

Plantation
Farm

Moor
Plantation

Buck Hill

Mullineux
Wood

Armridding

Agden
Wood

2

Parker's
Wood

Lodge
Wood

Primrose
Wood

Long
Plantation

Kenyon
Wood

New House
Farm

Wallbanks

Knipe
Wood

1

Chadswell

Barracks

New
Spring

Crooked
Field

42

66   **A**   **B**   67   **C**   **D**   68   **E**   **F**

187
229

A **B** **C** **D** **E** **F**

8

Sod Kiln Shoot

Elm Clough

Hodgson Moor

BROWSHOLME RD

Daisy Hill

Buckstall

Flatts

Hare Clough

Bashall Brook

Birch Hill

Braddup Clough

Burbles Hill

FREEHOLDS LA

7

Calf House

T Plantation

45

Blackhill Wood

RABBIT LA

Moor Piece

Sandy Ford Brook

FREEHOLDS LA

6

Braddup Wood

Braddup Farm

WHINNY LA

Hollins Wood

Kitchens

Gannies Farm

Colthurst Hall

5

Talbot Bridge

CROSS LA

Braddup House

44

Marsdens

BB7

Ridge Page Fold

4

Clough Bottom

Page Fold

Lower New House

Coulthurst

Sandy Ford

PO

Rugglesmire

Bashall Brook

Cow Hey Brook

Mason Green

Bashall Eaves

Cow Hey

Backridge Plantation

3

Red Pump Inn (PH)

43

Lower Titherington

2

Horse Hey

Back-Ridge Farm

Moss Barn

Bashall Hall

1

River Hodder

Bashall Lodge Plantation

Bashall Town

42

69 **A** **B** 70 **C** **D** 71 **E** **F**

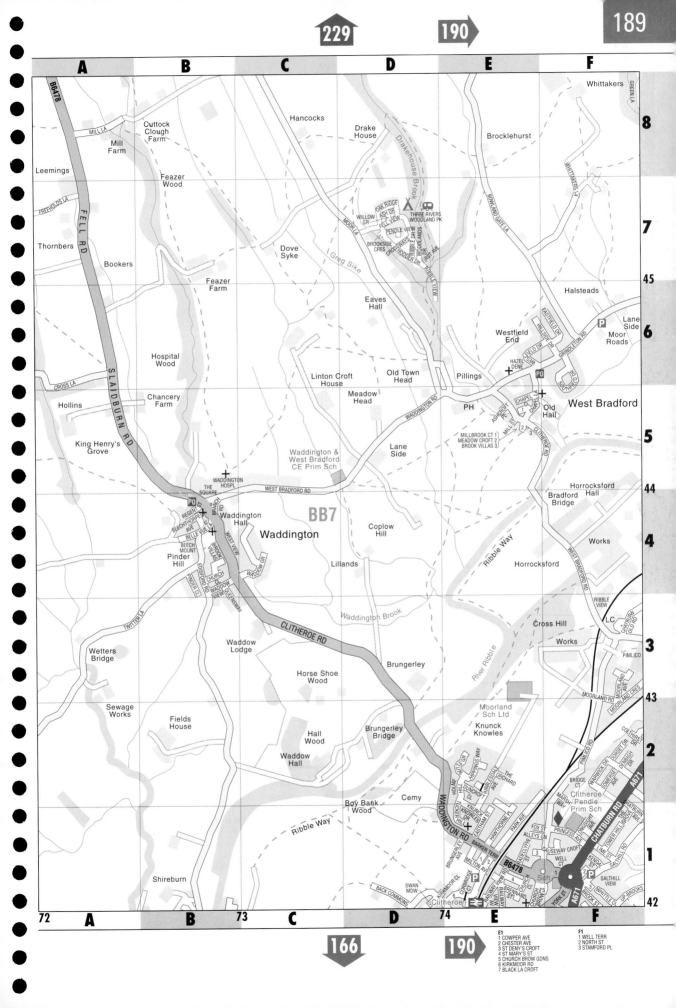

189
230

A B C D E F

8

Stubbin Lathe

HIGHER CHAPEL LA
LOWER CHAPEL LA
Brows House

1 CROSS FOLD
2 HARRISON TERR
3 WEST VIEW
4 GREENDALE VIEW
5 MEADOWSIDE

SAWLEY RD

MARY BROWN COTTS

Smithies Bridge

Beck House

Greendale Mill

PH

Grindleton

Grindleton CE Prim Sch

Fields House

Smithies Brook

BROWGATE

A59

BUCK ST
PENDLE VIEW

7

Green Banks

EAST VIEW 1
THE SPINNEY 2

Skin House

Arnot House

GRINDLETON BROW

GRINDLETON RD

RIBBLE AVE

MAIN ST B 6478

BACK LA

Grindleton Brook

West Clough Brook

GREEN LA

45

Higher West Clough

WEST BRADFORD RD

West Clough Bridge

River Ribble

SAWLEY RD

6

Lower West Clough

Bond Hurst Wood

Ribble Way

Mast

Chapel Laithe

SAWLEY RD

RIBBLE LA

5

BB7

ST CHAD'S AVE

DARKWOOD CRES

GREENFIELD AVE

VICTORIA CT

PARK AVE

QUARRY FARM CT

Chatburn

Chatburn CE Prim Sch

Liby

PH

PO

BRIDGE RD

CROW TREES

CLOUGH BANK

1 ROBINSON ST
2 VICTORIA AVE

RIBBLESDALE VIEW

DOWNHAM RD

KAYLEY LA

PENDLE AVE

WOOD TERR

Chatburn Rd

44

Works

CHATBURN OLD RD

DALE TERR 1
MOUNT PLEASANT 2
EDMUND GENNINGS CT 3
BEECH GR 4

CROW TREES BROW

FERNS

Ashcroft

White Croft Wood

Heys Brook

4

BOLD VENTURE COTTS

Pendle Trad Est

Pendle Hotel (PH)

Piked Acre Wood

Saw Mill

CLITHEROE RD

3

Park House

RYDAL PL

Middlewood

Warren Hill

Worsaw Hill

43

CHATBURN RD

1 CRANGLE FOLD
2 LONG CL

H

Clitheroe

Link 59 Bsns Pk

DEANFIELD

Worsaw End House

Crow Hill

Calf's Head Hotel (PH)

Worston Brook

2

CRINGLE WAY

THURSTAN LA

GREEN DR

DEANFIELD CT

Nature Res

PIMLICO LINK RD

LINCOLN WAY

Salthill Ind Est

Hall Foot

A671

Clitheroe Royal Gram Sch

CHATBURN PARK DR

Worston

SALTHILL RD

LINCOLN WAY

A671

Meadows Farm

1

Tower Hill

Lincoln Pk

Twinbrook Farm

UP BROOKS

Up-Brooks Ind Est

Mearley Brook

Angram Green

Hawthorne Ind Pk

42

75 A **76** B C **77** D E **F**

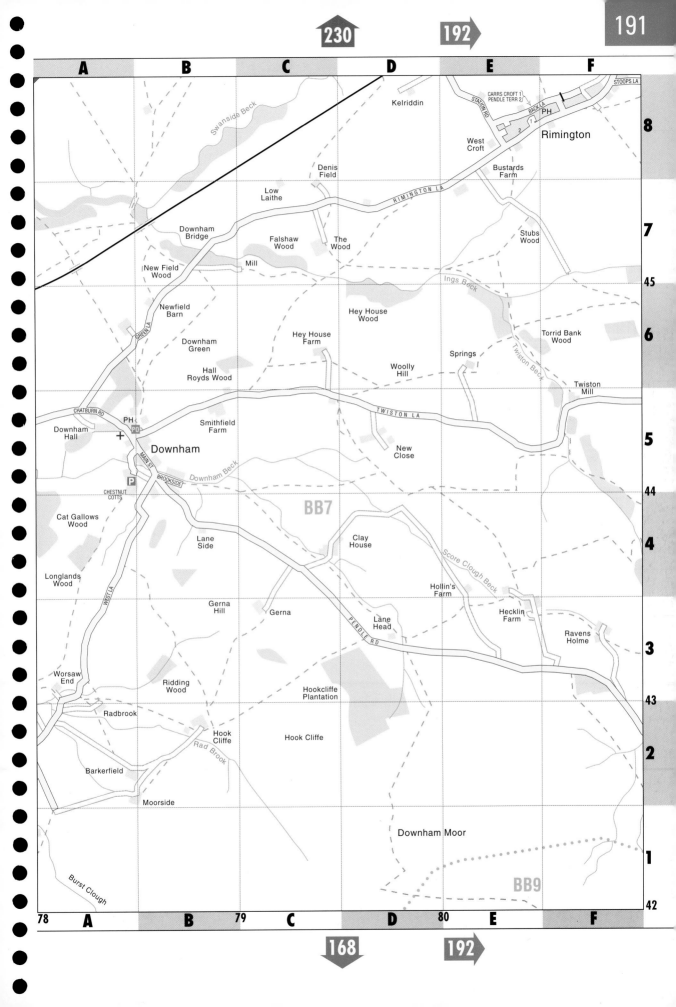

191
231

A682

A **B** **C** **D** **E** **F**

STOORS LA

NEWBY LA

Rakes

LONG LOVER LA

Crag Clough

8

Newby

Middop Wood

Stopper Lane

Whitwell Hill

Howcroft

Cudber Hill

Newby Hill

Howgill Beck

Higher Laithe

STOCKS LA

7

Tewit Hill

STOPPER LA

Ox Close

Martin Top

MARTIN TOP LA

Middop Hall

45

Hollins

Skeleron

SIDE LA

Key Hill

WHYTHA RD

Whytha

Ox Close Clough

SKELERON LA

Moor Close

Lower Gills

6

Ings End

Middop Wood

Lower Gate

Tory Log Clough

TWISTON LA

BB7

White Stones Farm

Lower Laithe

5

Smithy Fold Plantation

Higher Gills

Bale Hill

Hill Top

44

Hill Foot

Manor House

Clough Head

Smithy Fold

4

Twiston

Fern Side

Higher Higson

Higher Smithy Fold

Rimington Moor

3

Brownlow

Coolham

Twiston Moor

Firber House

BB9

Pendle Bridge Wood

43

Earton Hill

Wheathead Height

PENDLE RD

FOUR LANE ENDS

Helliwell Wood

2

Colne Gate

Annel Cross Moor

Higher Black Moss

Mountain Farm

Great Coppy

BARLEY LA

1

Turf Fields

Water Gate

BLACK MOSS RD

42

81 **A** **B** **82** **C** **D** **83** **E** **F**

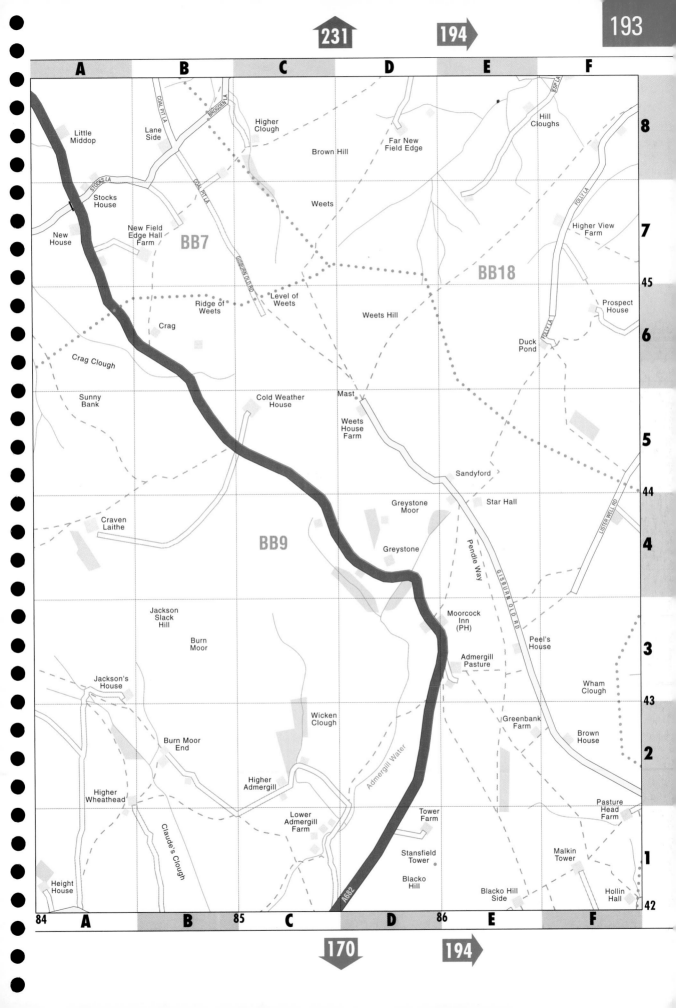

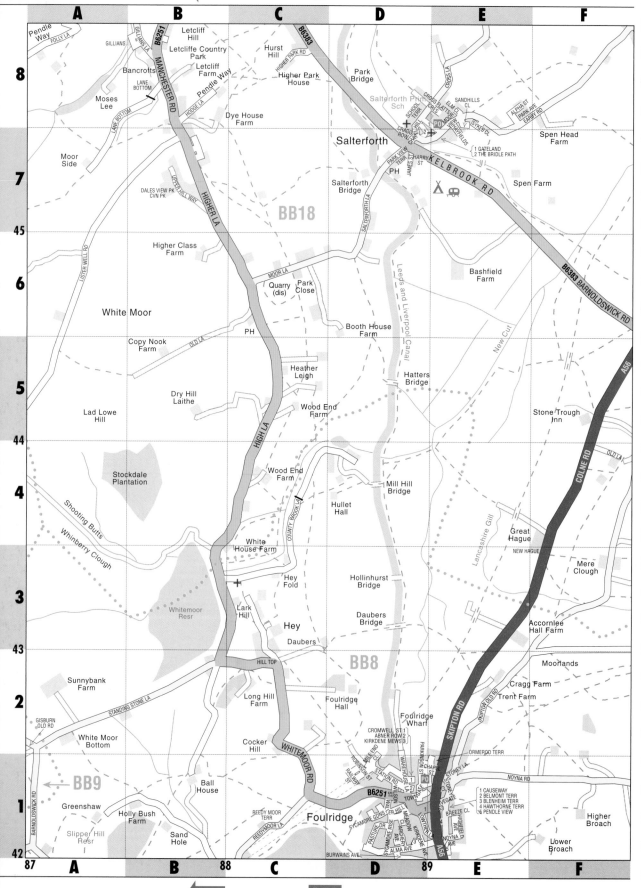

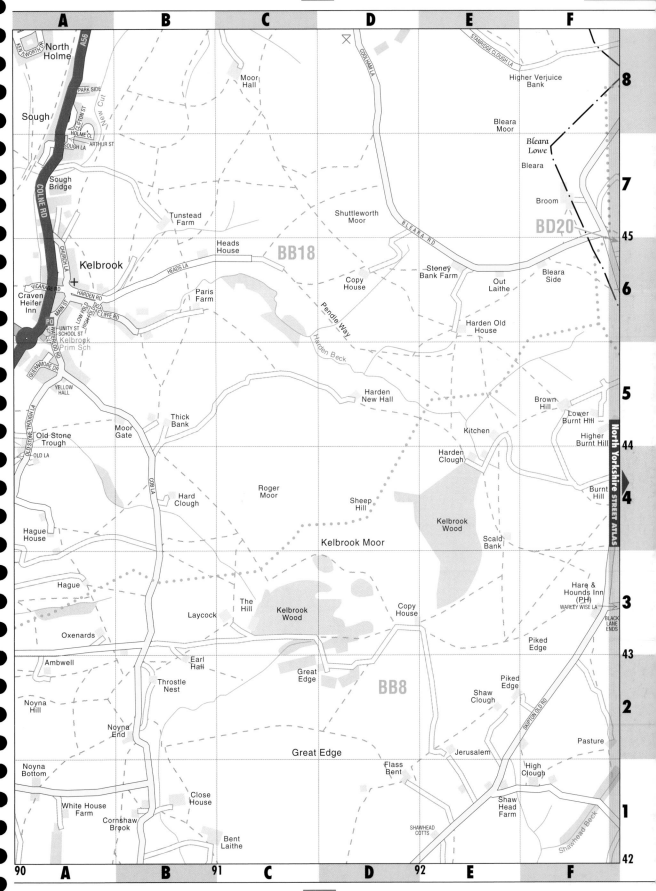

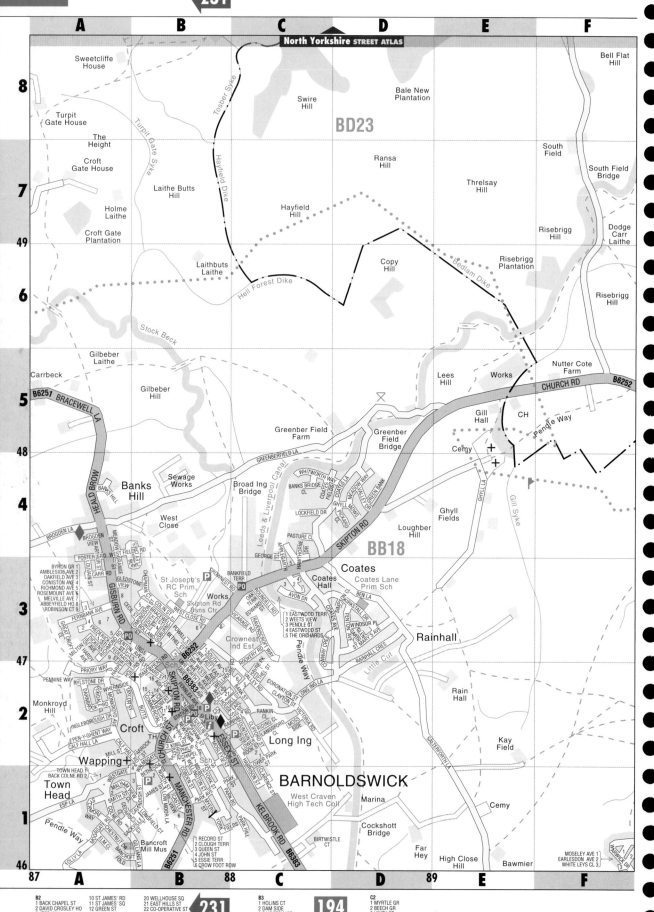

North Yorkshire STREET ATLAS

BD23

BB18

Coates

Rainhall

BARNOLDSWICK

Town Head

Wapping

Croft

Long Ing

231   194

B2
1 BACK CHAPEL ST
2 DAVID CROSLEY HO
3 JEPP HILL
4 BROOK ST
5 ORCHARD ST
6 GARDEN ST
7 MARKET ST
8 BACK SKIPTON RD
9 FORESTER'S BLDGS
10 ST JAMES' RD
11 ST JAMES' SQ
12 GREEN ST
13 BESSIE ST
14 EAST VIEW TERR
15 PLEASANT VIEW
16 FAR EAST VIEW
17 MONTROSE TERR
18 POST OFFICE BLDGS
19 EAST PAR
20 WELLHOUSE SQ
21 EAST HILLS ST
22 CO-OPERATIVE ST
23 RAILWAY ST
24 MAJESTIC BLDGS
25 SUSSEX ST

B3
1 HOLINS CT
2 DAM SIDE
3 BAIRSTOW ST
4 BROGDEN ST
5 BRUCE ST
6 CORNMILL TERR
7 NORTH PAR
8 MASONS WAY

C2
1 MYRTLE GR
2 BEECH GR
3 UNITY ST
4 TURNER ST
5 STUART ST
6 CRAVEN ST

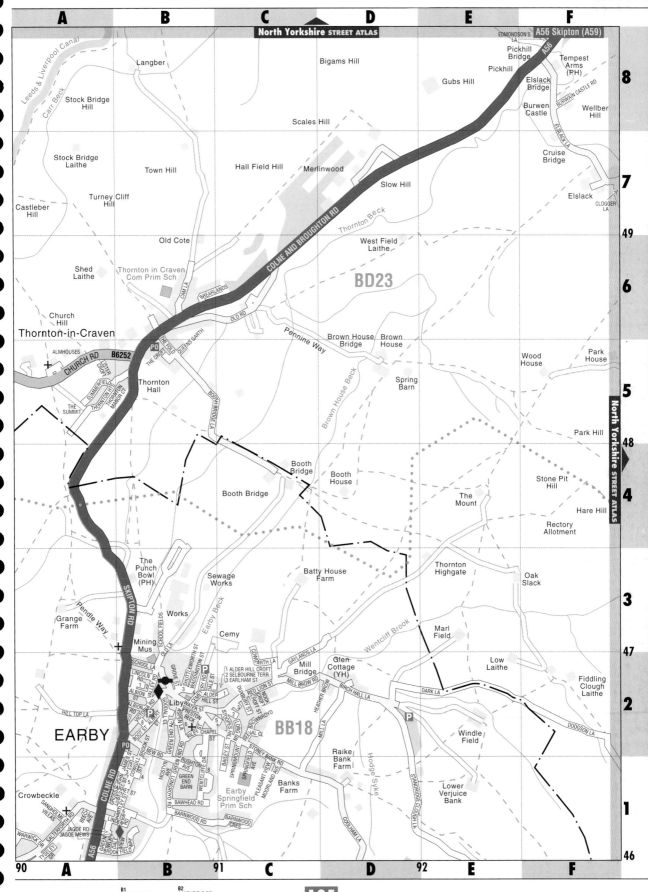

North Yorkshire STREET ATLAS

A56 Skipton (A59)

EDMONDSON'S LA

Pickhill Bridge

Tempest Arms (PH)

Langber

Bigams Hill

Gubs Hill

Pickhill

Elslack Bridge

Wellber Hill

Burwen Castle

BURWAIN CASTLE RD

8

Stock Bridge Hill

Leeds & Liverpool Canal

Carr Beck

ELSLACK LA

Scales Hill

Stock Bridge Laithe

Town Hill

Hall Field Hill

Merlinwood

Cruise Bridge

7

Castleber Hill

Turney Cliff Hill

Slow Hill

Elslack

CLOGGER LA

Old Cote

Thornton Beck

49

COLNE AND BROUGHTON RD

Shed Laithe

West Field Laithe

BD23

6

Thornton in Craven Com Prim Sch

CAM LA

BREARLANDS

OLD RD

Church Hill

Pennine Way

Brown House Bridge

Brown House

Wood House

Park House

Thornton-in-Craven

ALMHOUSES

CHURCH RD

B6252

PO

THE CROFT

QUEEN'S GARTH

Brown House Beck

5

THE SUMMIT

THE TOP

Thornton Hall

Thornton Manor Ct

Spring Barn

Park Hill

48

The Summit

BOOTH BRIDGE LA

Booth Bridge

Booth House

The Mount

Stone Pit Hill

Hare Hill

4

Booth Bridge

Booth House

Rectory Allotment

The Punch Bowl (PH)

Sewage Works

Batty House Farm

Thornton Highgate

Oak Slack

3

Grange Farm

Pendle Way

SKIPTON RD

Works

SCHOOL FIELDS

Earby Beck

Wentcliff Brook

Marl Field

Low Laithe

47

Mining Mus

Cemy

Mill Bridge

Glen Cottage (YH)

Fiddling Clough Laithe

DARK LA

2

EARBY

Libry

BB18

Windle Field

Lower Verjuice Bank

Crowbeckle

COLNE RD

Banks Farm

Earby Springfield Prim Sch

Raike Bank Farm

Hodge Syke

COLEHAM LA

STANDRIDGE CLOUGH LA

DODGSON LA

1

Jagoe Rd

Jagoe Mews

WARWICK DR

TYSELEY GR

46

North Yorkshire STREET ATLAS

B1
1 GEORGE ST
2 CHAPEL MEWS
3 APPLEGARTH ST
4 RIVERSIDE TERR
5 WILLIAM ST
6 ROSTLE TOP RD
7 LINDEN CT
8 THE BUNGALOWS

B2
1 HIGHFIELD RD
2 VALLEY GDNS
3 LOWER CROFT ST
4 SHAW SQ
5 WELBURY CL
6 WILKINSON MOUNT
7 VICTORIA ST
8 EDWARD ST

FLEETWOOD

FY7

Promenade
Rossall
Point

D3
1 CURTIS DR
2 GARLAND GR
3 MONROE DR
4 LAMOUR PL
5 KENTMERE CL
6 HONISTER CL

Fleetwood
Charles Saer
Com Prim Sch

Fleetwood
High Sch

Larkholme

Marine
Gdns

Boating
Pool

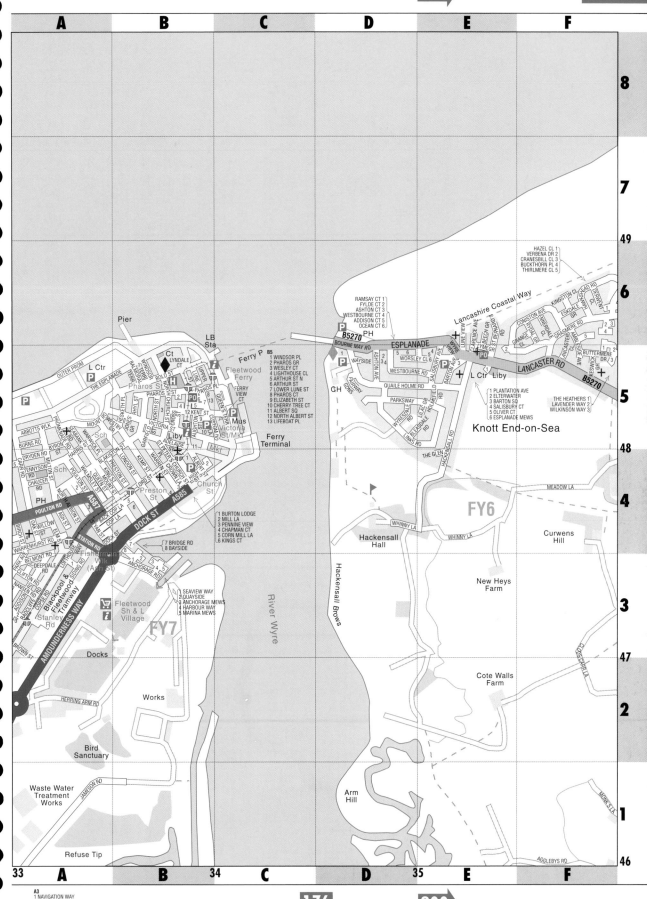

◀ 200
176
200 ▶

A3
1 NAVIGATION WAY
2 STANLEY RD
3 KEATING CT
A4
1 ST MARGARET'S CT
2 DELTA LA
3 POULTON GR
4 LAWRENCE ROW
5 WARREN AVENUE N

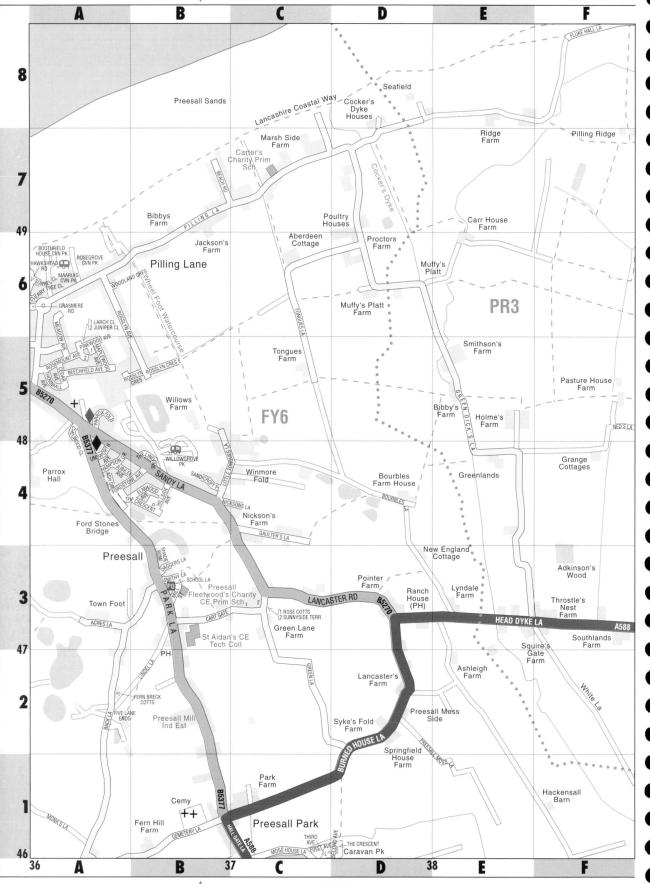

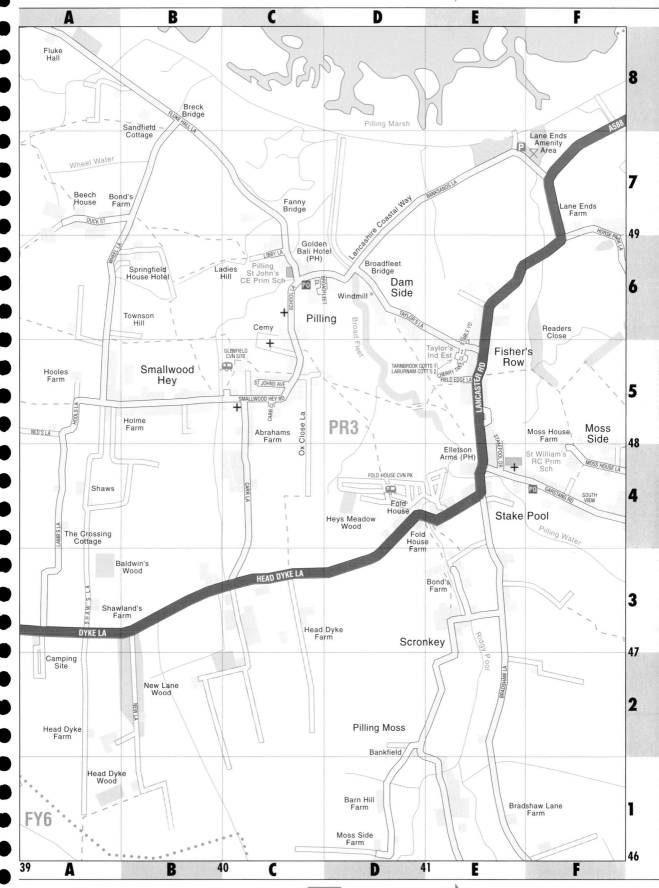

Fluke Hall

Breck Bridge

FLUKE HALL LA

Sandfield Cottage

Pilling Marsh

P

Lane Ends Amenity Area

A588

8

Wheel Water

WHEEL LA

Beech House

Bond's Farm

DUCK ST

Fanny Bridge

Golden Bali Hotel (PH)

LIBBY LA

Lancashire Coastal Way

BANKSANDS LA

Lane Ends Farm

HORSE PARK LA

7

49

Springfield House Hotel

Ladies Hill

SCHOOL LA

Pilling St John's CE Prim Sch

PO

BROADFLEET CL

Broadfleet Bridge

Dam Side

6

Townson Hill

Cemy

Windmill

TAYLOR'S LA

STABLE YD

Readers Close

Smallwood Hey

GLENFIELD CVN SITE

Pilling

Broad Fleet

Taylor's Ind Est

2

Fisher's Row

5

Hooles Farm

HOOLES LA

ST JOHNS AVE

CARR CL

Abrahams Farm

Ox Close La

SMALLWOOD HEY RD

Tarnbrook Cotts 1
Laburnam Cott's 2

CHERRY TREE CL

FIELD EDGE LA

LANCASTER RD

Moss House Farm

Moss Side

48

NED'S LA

Holme Farm

PR3

Elletson Arms (PH)

STAKEPOOL DR

St William's RC Prim Sch

GARSTANG RD

SOUTH VIEW

4

Shaws

CARR LA

FOLD HOUSE CVN PK

Fold House

Heys Meadow Wood

Fold House Farm

PO

Stake Pool

Pilling Water

LAMB'S LA

The Crossing Cottage

Baldwin's Wood

HEAD DYKE LA

Bond's Farm

3

SHAW'S LA

Shawland's Farm

DYKE LA

Scronkey

RIDGY POOL

47

Camping Site

New Lane Wood

NEW LA

Head Dyke Farm

BRADSHAW LA

2

Head Dyke Farm

Pilling Moss

Bankfield

Head Dyke Wood

FY6

Barn Hill Farm

Bradshaw Lane Farm

1

Moss Side Farm

46

A   B   C   D   E   F

Mill House

Wrampool Bridge

A588

8

A588

Gulf Farm

Birch House Farm

Wrampool House

Moss Edge

Lancashire Coastal Way

GULF LA

7

Near Moss Farm

Moss House Farm

Moss Edge Farm

Tarn Farm

Pilling Hall

49

LA2

6

Moss House

Cockerham Moss

Parkfield Farm

Gull Moss

Bond's Farm

5

HORSE PARK LA

Stake Pool

MORLEY LA

48

Crawley's Dyke

MOSS HOUSE LA

4

PEAHALL LA

Works

PR3

Poplar Farm

Winmarleigh Moss

Poplar Grove

Works

3

Jarvis Carr Farm

GARSTANG RD

Brookfield

47

Calcald's Farm

Crookabreast Farm

Carr Bridge

ISLAND LA

Stafford's Farm

Crawley's Cross Farm

Bone Hill Bridge

Cumming Carr

Cogie Hill Farm

2

Pilling Water

Bone Hill Farm

BONE HILL LA

BLACK LA

1

Rushy Slack Farm

Kentucky Farm

46

42   A   B   43   C   D   44   E   F

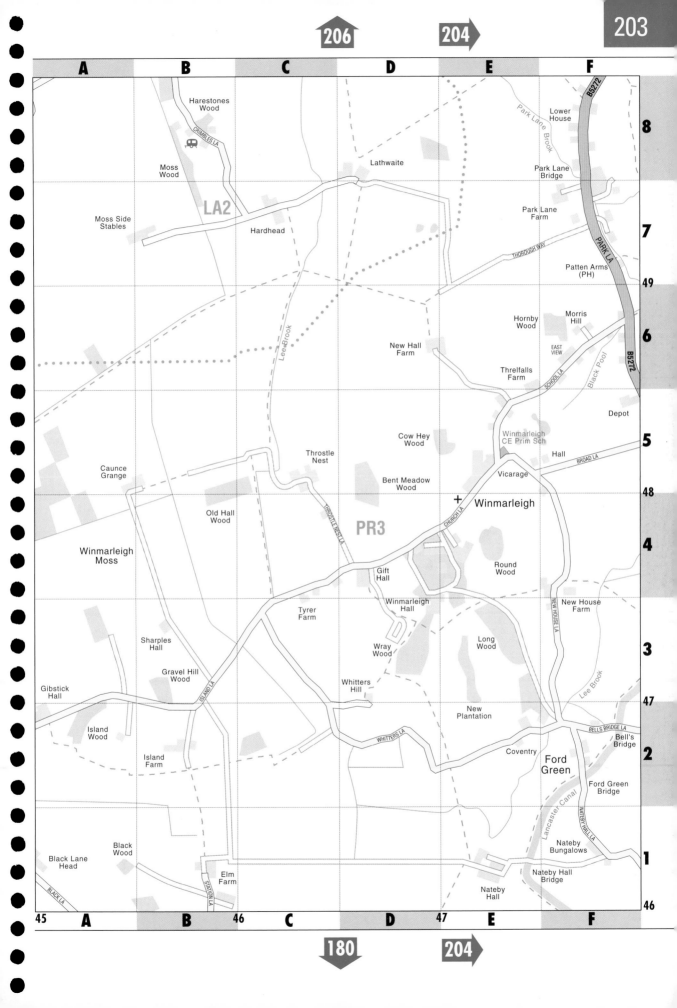

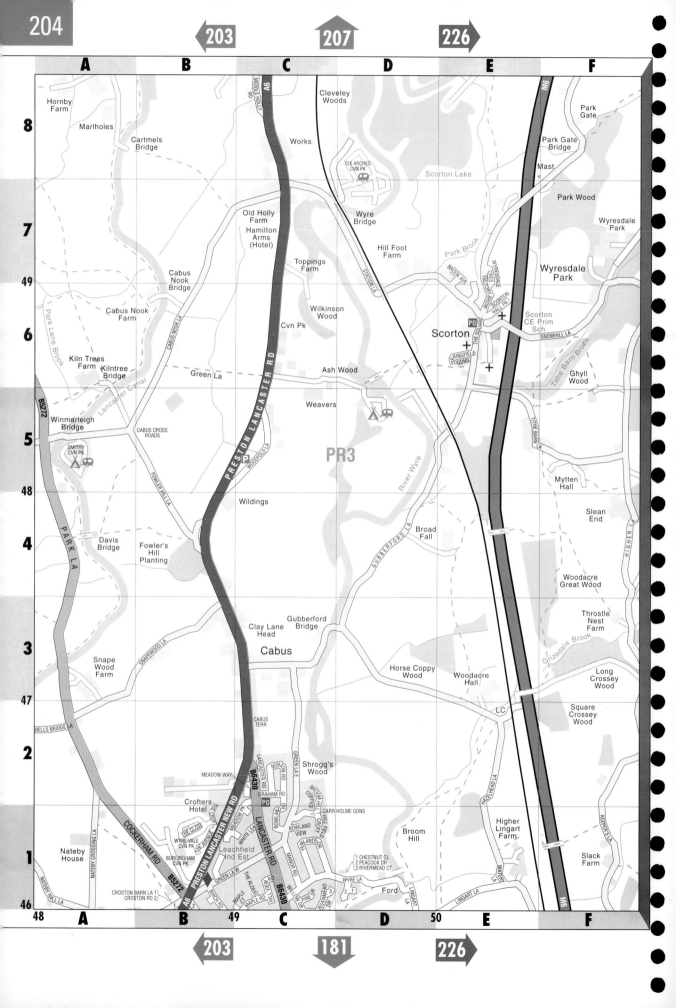

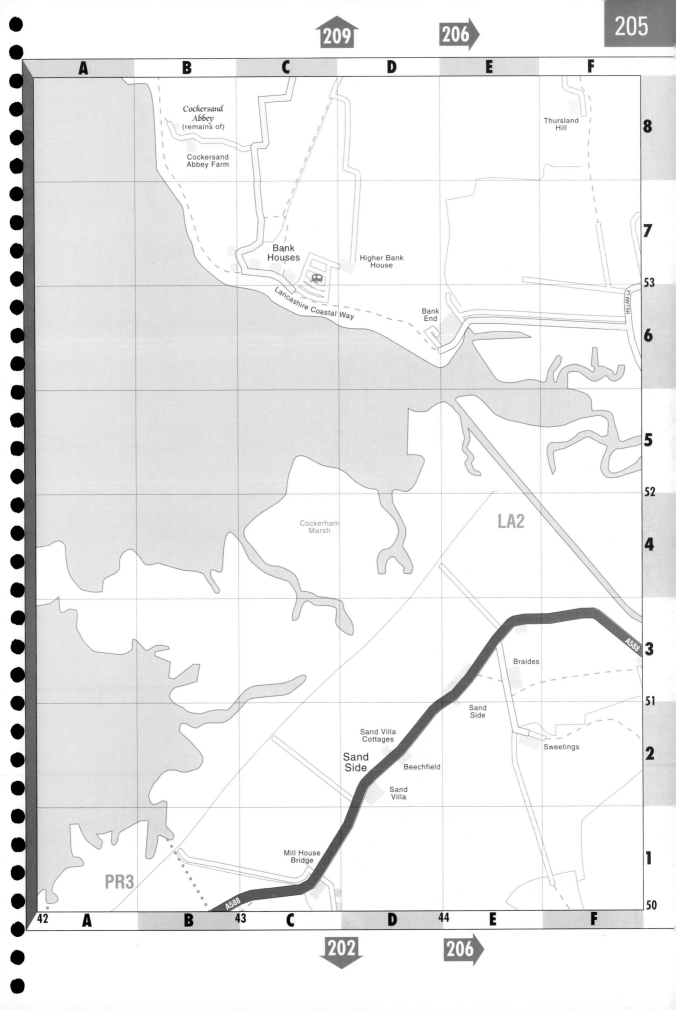

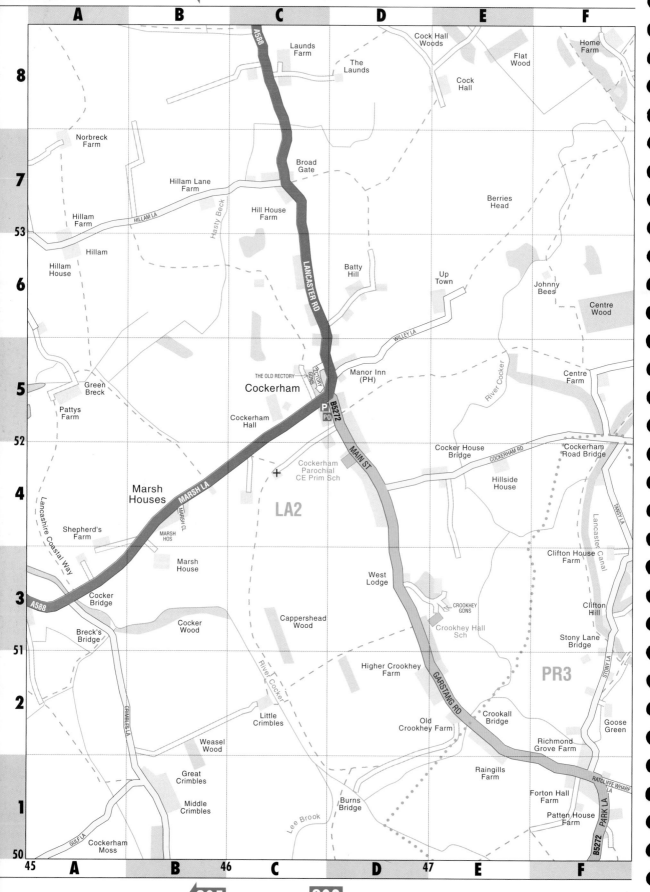

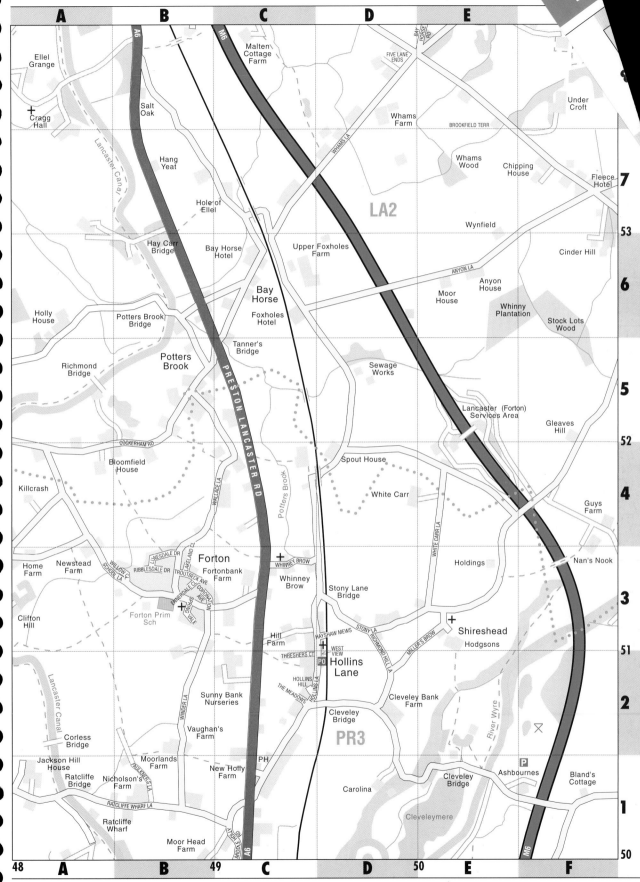

A B C D E

Ellel
Grange

Cragg
Hall

Salt
Oak

Hang
Yeat

Malten
Cottage
Farm

BAY HORSE RD

FIVE LANE
ENDS

Whams
Farm

BROOKFIELD TERR

Under
Croft

Whams
Wood

Chipping
House

Fleece
Hotel

7

Hole of
Ellel

LA2

Wynfield

53

Hay Carr
Bridge

Bay Horse
Hotel

Upper Foxholes
Farm

ANYON LA

Cinder Hill

Moor
House

Anyon
House

6

Bay
Horse

Lancaster Canal

Holly
House

Potters Brook
Bridge

Foxholes
Hotel

Tanner's
Bridge

Whinny
Plantation

Stock Lots
Wood

Richmond
Bridge

Potters
Brook

PRESTON LANCASTER RD

Sewage
Works

Lancaster (Forton)
Services Area

Gleaves
Hill

5

COCKERHAM RD

Bloomfield
House

WALLACE LA

Potters Brook

Spout House

White Carr

52

Killcrash

Guys
Farm

4

Home
Farm

Newstead
Farm

WILLOW C.
SCHOOL LA

MESDALE DR
LAKELAND CL
RIBBLESDALE DR
TROUTBECK AVE
PINNINGTON AVE
GRIZEDALE
CORONATION
AVE

Forton

Fortonbank
Farm

WHINNEY BROW

Whinney
Brow

Stony Lane
Bridge

WHITE CARR LA

Holdings

Nan's Nook

3

Clifton
Hill

Forton Prim
Sch

Hill
Farm

HAYSHAW MEWS

WEST
VIEW

Hollins
Lane

STONY LA
RICHMOND HILL LA
MILLER'S BROW

Shireshead

Hodgsons

51

Lancaster Canal

Corless
Bridge

WINDER LA

Sunny Bank
Nurseries

THRESHERS CT
PO

HOLLINS
HILL

THE MEADOWS

HOLLINS LA

Cleveley Bank
Farm

River Wyre

Ashbournes

P

2

Jackson Hill
House

Ratcliffe
Bridge

Nicholson's
Farm

FAULKNER ST LA

Moorlands
Farm

Vaughan's
Farm

New Hotty
Farm

PH

Cleveley
Bridge

PR3

Cleveley
Bridge

Bland's
Cottage

1

RATCLIFFE WHARF LA

Ratcliffe
Wharf

Moor Head
Farm

OLD VIODUCT RD

A6

Carolina

Cleveleymere

50

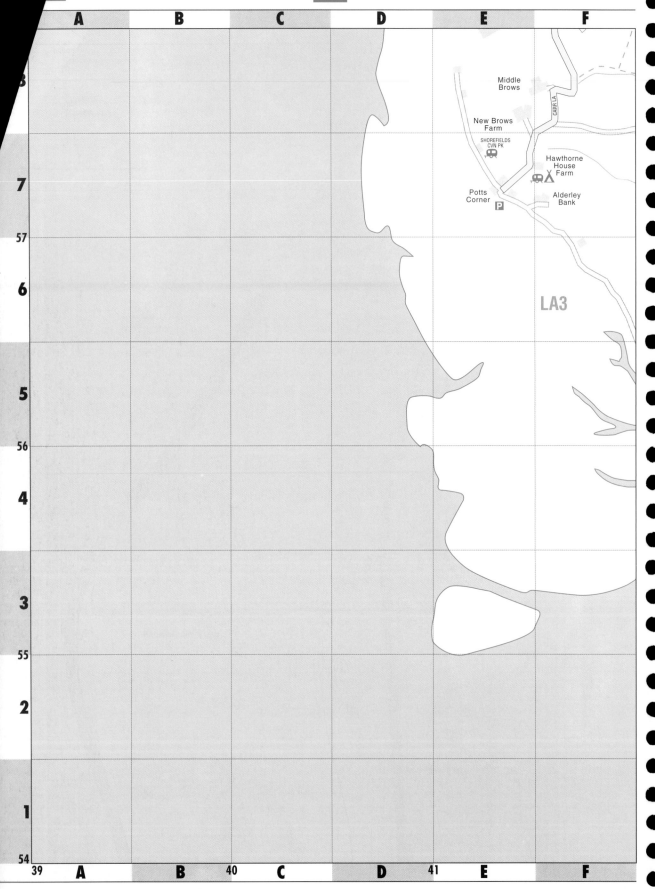

Middle Brows

New Brows Farm

CARR LA

SHOREFIELDS CVN PK

Hawthorne House Farm

Potts Corner

Alderley Bank

LA3

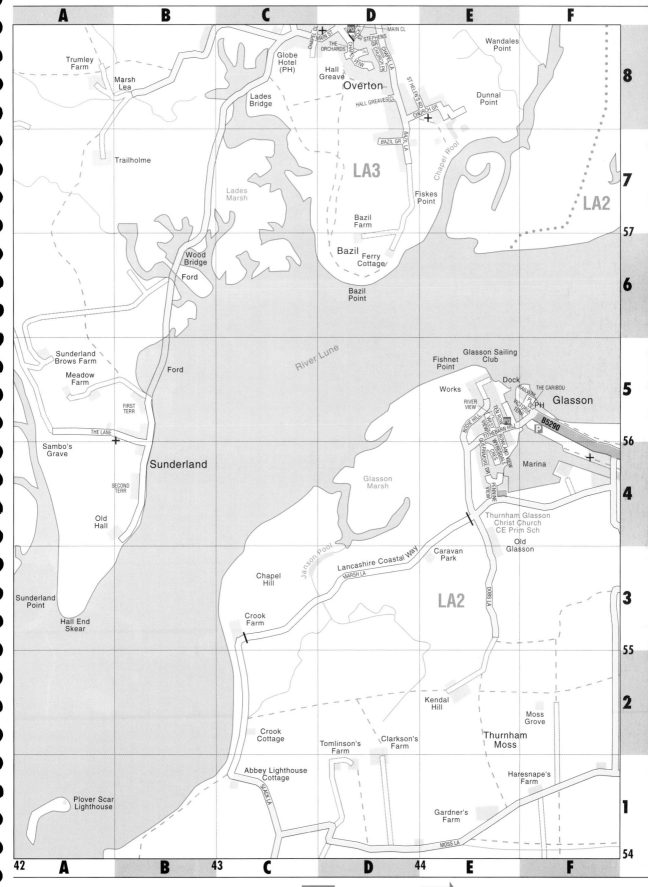

209
214

A B C D E F

8

7

57

6

5

56

4

55

3

2

1

54

River Lune

A588

Burrow Beck Bridge

Burrow Heights

BURROW HEIGHTS LA

A6

FIVE ASHES LA

Ashton Park

Lane End

Tarnwater

Tarnwater La

Crane Wood

Brantbeck Bridge

Five Ashes

Lower Burrow

Meldham Wood

CH

Ashton Hall

CH

Waterloo

Brantbeck Farm

Ashton Park Bridge

Lancaster Canal

New Park Bridge

Park Coppice

Seafield Plantation

Lancashire Coastal Way

Long Plantation

Heronswood Farm

Heronswood

LA2

Shearset Beck Bridge

Old Park Wood

Conder Green Farm

Conder Green

Crow Wood

Parkside

Forerigg Wood

P

The Stork (PH)

B5290

Brows Farm

B5290

Conder Bridge

Webster's Farm

Berry's Farm

Brick Kiln Bridge

Mill Farm

MEADOW PK

ROSE SQ

ELM AVE

ASH AVE

BEECH AVE

LEACHFIELD RD

OAK AVE

BIRCH AVE

BANK CL

CARRWOOD

ELLEL HALL GDNS

CONDER GREEN RD

Ellel Hall Bridge

Ellel Hall

Thurnham Bridge

Lancaster Canal (Glasson Branch)

Thurnham Mill

River Conder

Thurnham Moss

Aspley Farm

Bailey Bridge

Bayley Bridge

Sellerly

Lower Thurnham

Throstle Nest

Upper Thurnham

Thurnham Hall

Forth Lock Bridge

Bamber's Farm

MOSS LA

Brigg's Brow

Back Wood

Third Lock Bridge

Second Lock Bridge

A588

45 46 47

A B C D E F

216

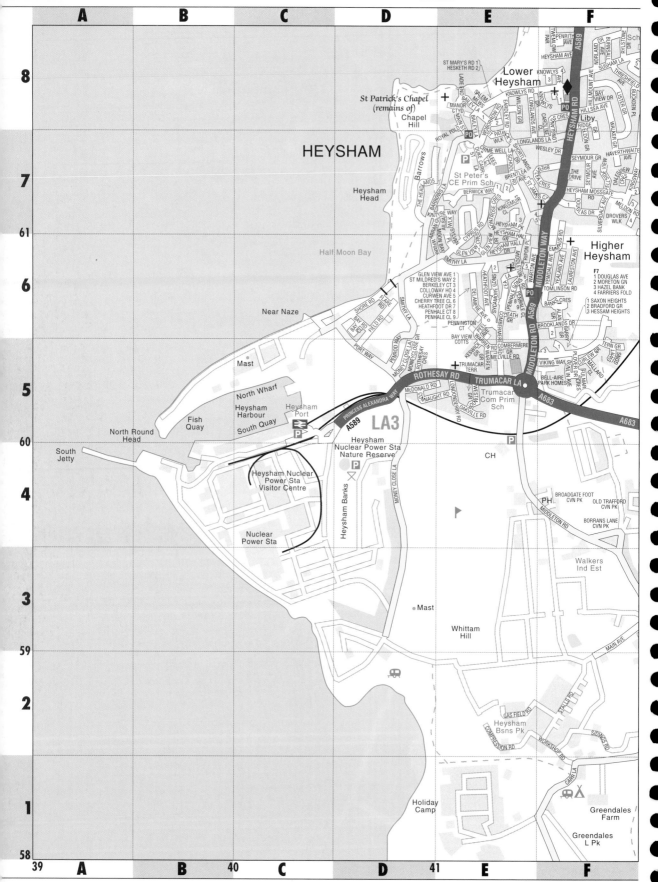

E7
1 WEMYSS CL
2 DUNBAR DR
3 TOWER COTTS
4 HEYSHAM RD
5 MIDDLETON WAY

F8
1 STRAWBERRY MEWS
2 BACK KNOWLYS RD
3 KNOWLYS DR
4 KNOWLYS CRES
5 TARNBROOK RD

HEYSHAM

Lower Heysham

St Patrick's Chapel (remains of)
Chapel Hill

Heysham Head

Higher Heysham

F7
1 DOUGLAS AVE
2 MORETON GN
3 HAZEL BANK
4 FARRIERS FOLD

1 SAXON HEIGHTS
2 BRADFORD GR
3 HESSAM HEIGHTS

Half Moon Bay

Near Naze

St Peter's CE Prim Sch

GLEN VIEW AVE 1
ST MILDRED'S WAY 2
BERKELEY CT 3
COLLOWAY HO 4
CURWEN AVE 5
CHERRY TREE CL 6
HEATHFOOT DR 7
PENHALE CT 8
PENHALE CL 9

LA3

Mast

North Wharf

Heysham Harbour

Heysham Port

South Quay

Fish Quay

North Round Head

South Jetty

Trumacar Com Prim Sch

Heysham Nuclear Power Sta Nature Reserve

Heysham Nuclear Power Sta Visitor Centre

Heysham Banks

Nuclear Power Sta

CH

PH

Broadgate Foot CVN PK
Old Trafford CVN PK
Borrans Lane CVN PK

Walkers Ind Est

Mast

Whittam Hill

Gas Field
Heysham Bsns Pk

Holiday Camp

Greendales Farm

Greendales L Pk

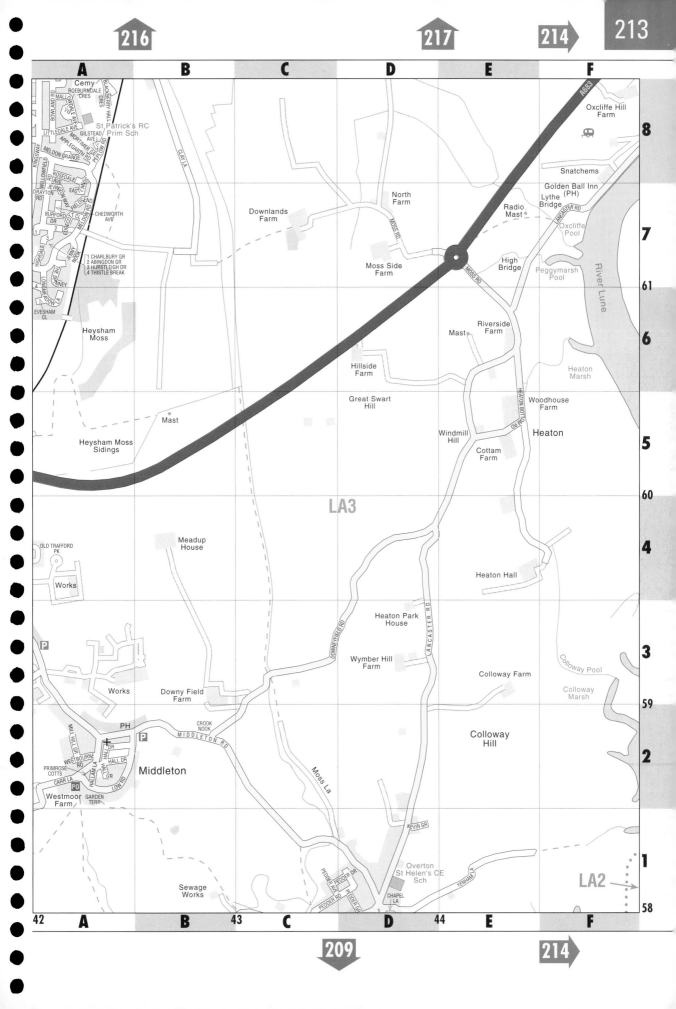

A B C D E F

8
7
61
6
5
60
4
3
59
2
1
58

LA3

Cemy
Roeburndale Cres
Blackberry Hall
Mallowdale Ave
Bowland Rd
Littledale Ave
St Patrick's RC Prim Sch
Gilstead Gr
Mortimer Gr
Applegarth Rd
Peel Rd
Clay La
Kingsway
Willowfield
Rosedale Ave
Jevington Way
Meldon Grange
East Lancs
Fieldend
Edgecote Cl Meldon Rd
Drayton Rd
Burford Dr
Chedworth Ave
Higholdale
Ferny Knoll
The Spinney
Longmeadow
Evesham Cl

1 CHARLBURY GR
2 ABINGDON GR
3 HURSTLEIGH DR
4 THISTLE BREAK

Downlands Farm
North Farm
Moss Rd
Moss Side Farm
Radio Mast
High Bridge
Oxcliffe Pool
Peggymarsh Pool
A683
Oxcliffe Hill Farm
Snatchems
Golden Ball Inn (PH)
Lythe Bridge
Lancaster Rd
River Lune

Heysham Moss
Mast
Riverside Farm
Hillside Farm
Great Swart Hill
Windmill Hill
Cottam Farm
Heaton
Woodhouse Farm
Heaton Marsh
Heaton Bottom Rd

Heysham Moss Sidings
Mast

Old Trafford Pk
Works
Meadup House

Heaton Hall
Colloway Pool
Colloway Marsh

Works
Downy Field Farm
Downeyfield Rd
Heaton Park House
Wymber Hill Farm
Lancaster Rd
Colloway Farm

P
PH
Westbourne Rd
Mill Hill Gr
Hallam La
Hall Dr
Crook Nook
M I D D L E T O N R D
Colloway Hill
Primrose Cotts
Hallam Gr
Low Rd
Carr La
Garden Terr
Middleton
Moss La
Westmoor Farm
PO
Kevin Gr

Sewage Works
Pedder Ave
Pedder Rd
Pedder Gr
Overton St Helen's CE Sch
Chapel La
Yeoman La
LA2

42 A B 43 C D 44 E F 58

217 ← 213 → 218

F8
1 WOOD ST
2 BUTTERFIELD ST
3 CHAPEL ST
4 ALEXANDRA CT
5 NILE ST
6 DYE HOUSE LA

F8
7 CALKELD LA
8 ROSEMARY LA
9 BACK SUN ST
10 MARKET SQ
11 CHEAPSIDE
12 ASHTON WLK

13 St Nicholas Arcs
14 LANCASTER GATE
15 RENDSBURG WAY
16 PERPIGNAN WAY
17 STONEWELL
18 ST ANNE'S PL

19 BREWERY LA
20 GREAT JOHN ST
21 ABBOTS HO
22 BRIDGET ST
23 FRIARS PAS
24 FRIAR ST
25 BRYER ST

F8
26 ST CATHERINES CT
27 ST SIMON'S ARC
28 MARKETGATE
29 SLIP INN LA
30 JAMES ST
31 FFRANCES PAS

32 GAGE ST
33 MOOR ST
34 KINGS ARMS CL
35 ALMSHOUSES
36 WINDMILL
37 KINGS ARC
38 COMMON GARDEN ST

39 RUSSELL ST
40 RUSSELL MEWS
41 SPRING GARDEN ST
42 BREWERY ARC
43 ROBERT ST
44 THE ROUNDHOUSE

E8
1 KELLET CT
2 ST LUKES CT
3 COVELL HO
4 CHENNEL HO
5 CASTLE PAR
6 PRIORY CT
7 KELNE HO
8 WHEATFIELD CT
9 HARDWICKE HO
10 HARDWICKE HO
11 JUBILEE CT

KENSINGTON HO 1
GREAVES MEAD 2
THE HASTINGS 3
CHELTENHAM RD 4
VICTORIA AVE 5
HEATON HO 6
FRANKLIN ST 7
DEVONSHIRE ST 8

CUNNINGHAM CT 1
STOREY HALL 2
ALBERT CT 3

CHARLES CT 1
RIPLEY CT 2
ALMA HO 3
BINYON CT 4
PICKARD ST 5
GROVE CT 6

GREYTHWAITE CT 1
SIZERGH CT 2

ADDENBROOKE CL 1
VISCOUNT DR 2

LARCH GR 1
HOLLY WLK 2
HAZEL GR 3
LIME GR 4
MAPLE GR 5
ROWAN PL 6
ASHBROOK ST 7
STANLEY PL 8
BEECH ST 9

213 ← 210 ↓

F7
1 HIGH MOUNT HO
2 HIGH MOUNT CT
3 GEORGE ST
4 MARTON ST
5 PETER ST
6 VICTORIA PL
7 THURNHAM MEWS
8 ALEXANDRA HALL
9 ELIZABETH CT
10 DIANA CT
11 ROYAL CT
12 BACK QUEEN ST
13 LINDOW CL
14 ALMSHOUSES

Map labels: LANCASTER, Marsh, Abraham Heights, Aldcliffe, Aldcliffe Marsh, Haverbreaks, The Greaves, Heaton Marsh, Colloway Marsh, Arna Wood, Low Wood, Sewage Works, Stodday, Grange Farm, Lunecliffe Hall, Whinney Carr, Jansteval, Waterside Farm, Hamilton Plantation, Burrow Bridge, Burrow Beck Bridge, Lawson's Bridge, Deep Cutting Farm, Deep Cutting Bridge, Cemy, River Lune, Lancaster Canal, LA1, LA2, LA3

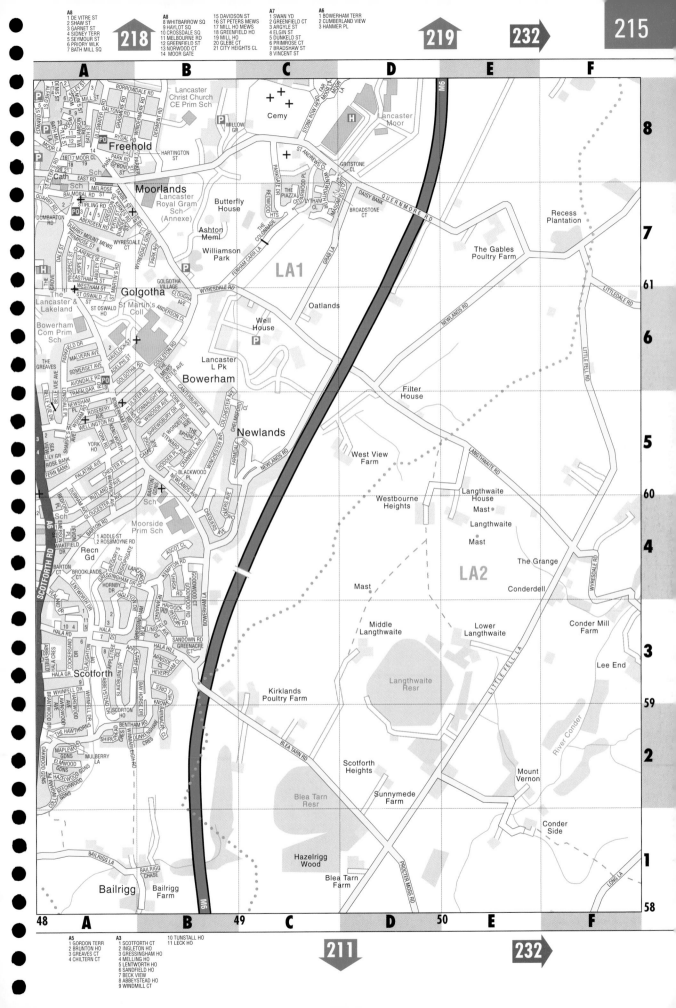

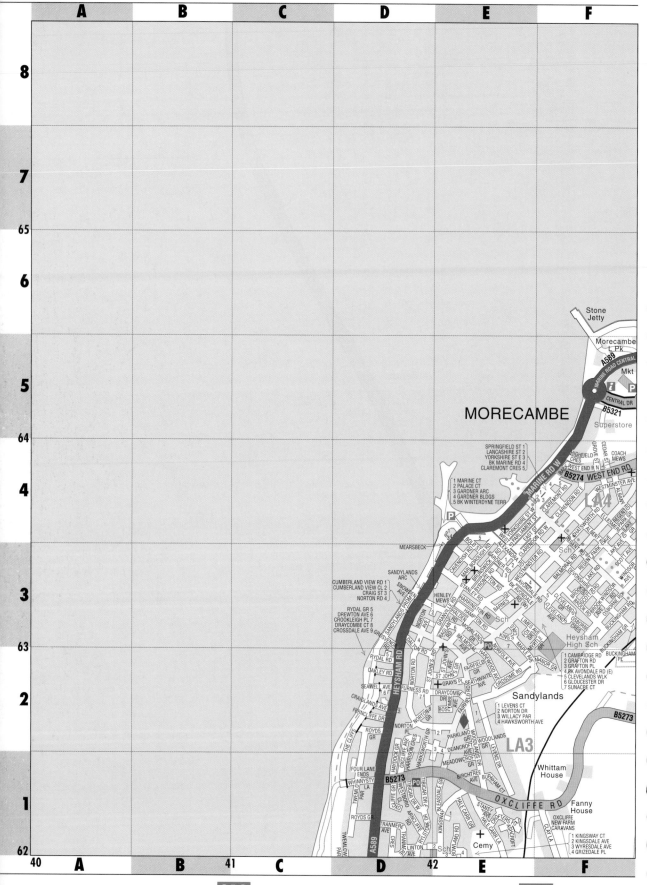

MORECAMBE

Stone Jetty

Morecambe L Pk

Mkt

Superstore

SPRINGFIELD ST 1
LANCASHIRE ST 2
YORKSHIRE ST E 3
BK MARINE RD 4
CLAREMONT CRES 5

1 MARINE CT
2 PALACE CT
3 GARDNER ARC
4 GARDNER BLDGS
5 BK WINTERDYNE TERR

WEST END RD

Mearsbeck

SANDYLANDS ARC

CUMBERLAND VIEW RD 1
CUMBERLAND VIEW CL 2
CRAIG ST 3
NORTON RD 4

RYDAL GR 5
DREWTON AVE 6
CROOKLEIGH PL 7
DRAYCOMBE CT 8
CROSSDALE AVE 9

Heysham High Sch

1 CAMBRIDGE RD
2 GRAFTON RD
3 GRAFTON PL
4 AVONDALE RD (E)
5 CLEVELANDS WLK
6 GLOUCESTER DR
7 SUNACRE CT

Sandylands

1 LEVENS CT
2 NORTON DR
3 WILLACY PAR
4 HAWKSWORTH AVE

LA3

B5273

Whittam House

OXCLIFFE RD

Fanny House

OXCLIFFE NEW FARM CARAVANS

1 KINGSWAY CT
2 KINGSDALE AVE
3 WYRESDALE AVE
4 GRIZEDALE PL

Cemy

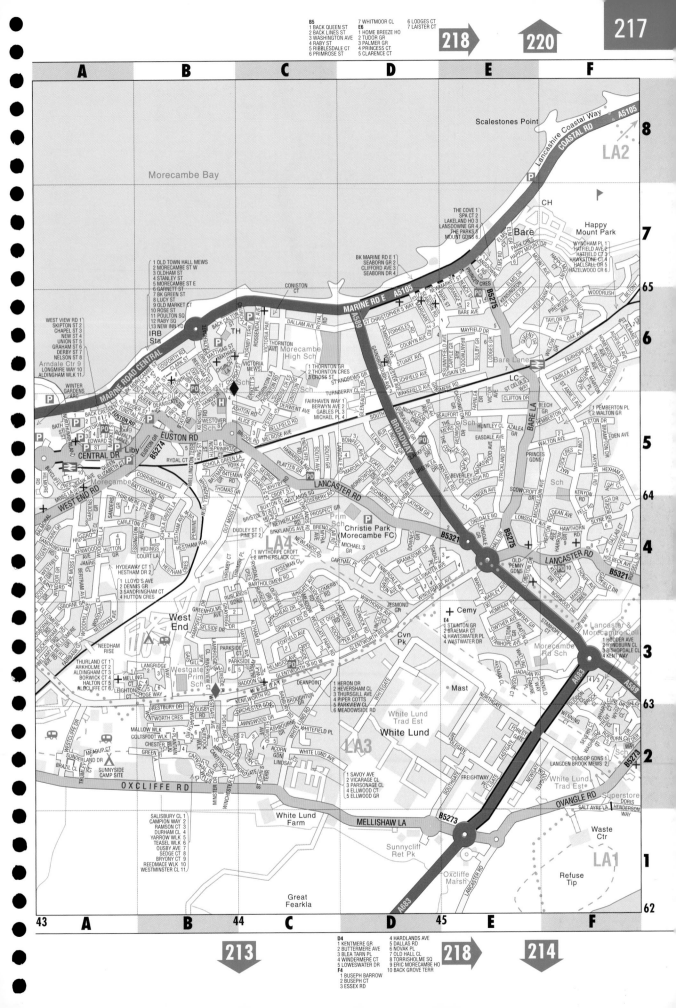

218
220
213
218
214

A B C D E F

8
7
65
6
5
64
4
3
63
2
1
62

Map labels (selection):

COASTAL RD · MARINE DR · A5105 · SEA VIEW CL · RAKES HILL LA · RAKES HEAD Bridge · MANOR CRES · ASCOT GDNS · BOTTOMDALE CVN PK · Cemy · Ancliffe Hall · St Luke's CE Prim Sch · THE KNOLL · GOODWOOD WLK · ORCHARD CL · MANOR AVE · CROFT CL · DALE AVE 1 · MANOR CL 2 · MANOR DR 3 · BAY VIEW RD · WARREN RD · LAWSON AVE · THROSTLE GR · MAIN RD · Cross Keys Hotel (PH) · Slyne · BOTTOMDALE RD · ANCLIFFE LA · KELLET LA · FOUR LANE ENDS

TOWNFIELD LA · SUMMERFIELD DR · ROSEGARTH · ROSEDENE · BEECH GR · LA2 · SLYNEWOODS · Beaumont Grange

Belmount · HASTY BROW RD · Standerlands Farm · Beaumont Gate Farm · LANCASTER RD · GREEN LA · Carus Lodge · Carus House · LITTLEDALE MEWS

LA4 · HAWL AVE · WILLIAMS AVE · RANLEA AVE · WEBSTER GR · FULWOOD DR · Morecambe South Junction · Belmount Bridge · Lancaster Canal · Williamsland Farm · Foley Farm · TURNPIKE FOLD · Halton Road Bridge · POLLARD PL · Halton Training Camp · GREEN LA

Torrisholme Barrow · SLYNE RD · RUSSELL DR · POWDER HOUSE LA · FOLLY RD · Beaumont Coll (The Spastics Society) · 1 GASKELL HO · 2 WORDSWORTH HO · 3 HAMMERTON HALL CL · 4 RUSKIN HO · 5 COLERIDGE HO · Lune Aqueduct · Riverside Park Ind Est · A683 · LUNE VALLEY · CH

Torrisholme · B5321 · ENDSLEIGH GR · Crem · MEADOW VIEW · BIRKDALE CL 1 · MALHAM CL 2 · BELMONT CL 3 · Hammerton Hall Bridge · BARLEY COP LA · RICKTHORN · GREENSET CT · HAMMERTON HALL LA · SHAKESPEARE · Skerton · TEBAY CT · WRAY CT · HORNBY · TALL TREES · BEAUMONT PL · BOLTON RD · RICHMOND AVE · WHALLEY RD · Cemy · Works · Lansil Ind Est · CATON RD

Coll · HAMILTON DR · BURTON RD · LEICESTER DR · LYNN AVE · WINDHAM PL · FENDLE RD · WHERNSIDE RD · INGLEBOROUGH RD · CAST VIEW · JOHN KAY CT · MAYFIELD RD · MORLEY · HARCOURT RD · LONGLANDS AVE · RAVENS CL · ST CHAD'S DR · GRANVILLE RD · VALE RD · OXFORD ST · BAKER ST · ASHBOURNE DR · CLARENDON RD · ALEXANDRA RD · HILL RD · MOUNT RD · Sch · Lune Valley Ramble · Lune Riverside Park · Newton · NEWTON TERR · SCAFELL RD · GRIZEDALE RD · Ridge

A589 · MORECAMBE RD · WINSTER · RICHMOND · SCALE · Scale Hall · PH · The Loyne Sch · Ryelands Prim Sch · LUPTON PL · ASHDALE PL · FOXDALE PL · CONDER PL · LA1 · Ryelands · LANCASTER · Ryelands Park · Carlisle Bridge · B5321 · OWEN RD · SLYNE RD · BROADWAY · NORFOLK ST · PINFOLD LA · THE RAMPARTS · TA Ctr · LANGDALE · Ladies Wlk Ind Est · AMBLESIDE RD · CONISTON RD · ESTHWAITE RD · Central Lancaster High Sch

Sports Hall · Salt Aire Sports Ctr · DORIS HENDERSON WAY · BROWNHOLME · SALT AYRE LA · DERWENT CT · TARNSYKE RD · WENNING · ROEBURN PL · George's QUAY · Mus · Sports Gd · Brunton's Warehouse 4 · PEEL HO 5 · VICTORIA WHARF 6 · BUOYMASTERS 7 · River LUNE · GREYHOUND BRIDGE RD · A6 · Skerton Bridge · KINGSWAY · A683 · Sports Ctr · P · Ridge Prim Sch · Bulk

New Quay · Lancashire Coastal Way · NEW QUAY RD · RIVERSIDE LOFTS 1 · REYNOLDS ST 2 · Works · CARLTON WHARF 3 · WATERSIDE · LUNE STREET · PARLIAMENT ST · A6 CATON RD · A6 GATE · A589 · Bulk

Bottom index:

A2	**B1**	**B2**
1 KEER BANK	1 CHARNLEY ST	1 BURNFELL RD
2 GILPIN CL	2 BRIERY ST	2 TARNBROOK RD
3 BELA CL	3 FURNESS ST	3 RAYGILL PL
4 CRAKE BANK	4 MARSH ST	4 AUSTWICK RD
5 GREGARETH CL	5 HUTTON WAY	5 RAWTHEY RD
6 WINDHOLME	6 BORDER CL	6 MEARBECK RD
7 CROASDALE	7 RICHARDS WLK	7 CROSSGILL PL
8 WHITENDALE	8 COWDREY MEWS	8 BROWGILL PL
9 BRINDLE CL		9 WHITERAY RD

C2	**7** BACK LORD ST	**8** FLEMING HO	**18** BRIDGE HO	**9** RICHMOND HO
1 UDALE PL	8 PHOENIX ST	9 STEWART CT	**D3**	**D4**
2 HINDBURN PL	**D2**	10 RIGG HO	1 BULLER ST	1 RIPON AVE
D1	1 SKERTON	11 ACRE CT	2 RUSKIN RD	2 SELBY AVE
1 KILN CT	2 LABURNUM RD	12 ELLERSHAW HO	3 MILLSTONE CT	3 FARLETON CT
2 HILLS CT	3 KENT ST	13 GREG HO	4 DAISY ST	4 ESKRIDGGE CL
3 CAPTAIN'S ROW	4 RIVERSWAY	14 MILLER CT	5 REGAL TERR	
4 PARK HO	5 MILLRACE CT	15 FRANKLAND HO	6 ALDEN TERR	
5 LUNE HO	6 SKERTON CT	16 CHURCH CT	7 ASHBOURNE CT	
6 DERBY HO	7 GREENWATER CT	17 SHARDS CT	8 LINDETH GDNS	

E1
1 MARDALE RD
2 GREBE WHARF
3 GLADSTONE TERR
4 FACTORY HILL
5 ST LEONARD CT
6 DE VITRE ST
7 SWALLOW WHARF

Central Lancaster High Sch
1 HERLEBECK RISE
2 LINGMOOR RD
3 MONTHALL RISE
4 RIDGE SQ
5 KESWICK RD
6 KESWICK WLK
7 THIRLEMERE CT
8 BUTTERMERE CT

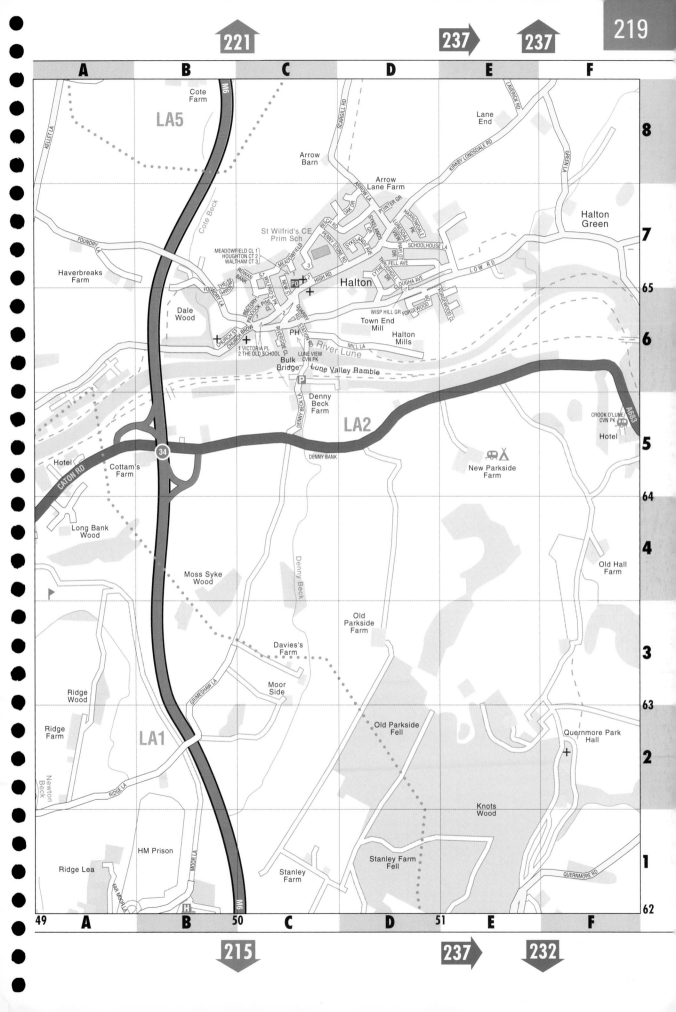

222

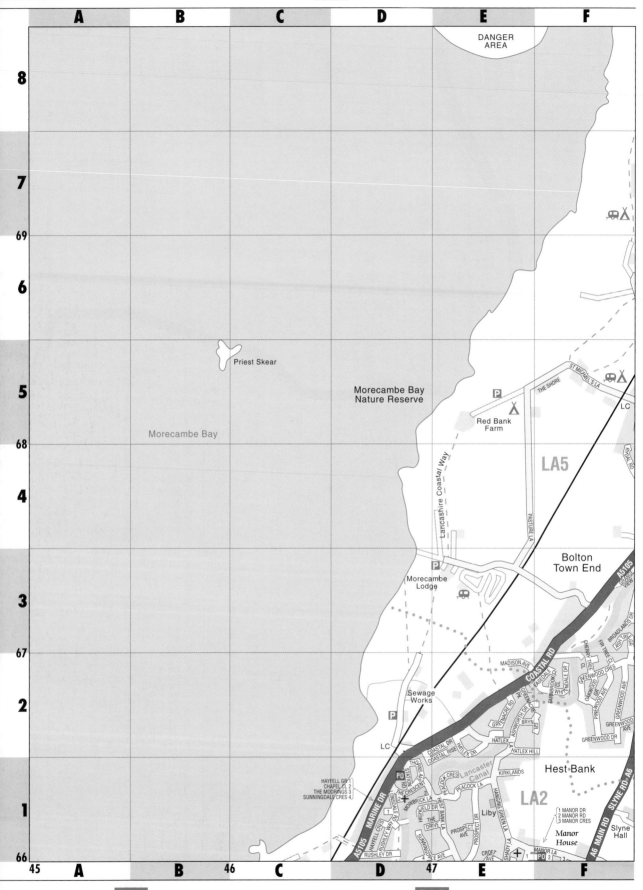

Morecambe Bay

Priest Skear

Morecambe Bay
Nature Reserve

Morecambe Bay

DANGER AREA

Lancashire Coastal Way

Red Bank Farm

THE SHORE

ST MICHAEL'S LA

LC

P

LA5

RYDAL RD

Bolton
Town End

A5105
GRANGE VIEW

Morecambe
Lodge

P

PASTURE LA

COASTAL RD

MADISON AVE

Sewage
Works

P

LC

COASTAL DR
COASTAL RISE

HATLEX DR

HATLEX

Hatlex Hill

Hest Bank

GREENWOOD CRES

GREENWOOD AVE

GREENWOOD DR

KIRKLANDS

Lancaster Canal

HAYFELL GR 1
CHAPEL CL 2
THE MODRINGS 3
SUNNINGDALE CRES 4

MARINE DR

THE CRESCENT

MOWBRICK LA

HEST BANK LA

PEACOCK CRES

PEACOCK LA

HANGING GREEN LA

LA2

1 MANOR DR
2 MANOR RD
3 MANOR CRES

Liby

Manor
House

SLYNE RD A6

Slyne
Hall

A5105

RUSHLEY DR

SUNNINGDALE AVE

THE DRIVE

PROSPECT DR

PROSPECT AVE

SHADY LA

CROFT AVE

A6 MAIN RD

MANOR LA

Manor House

217   218

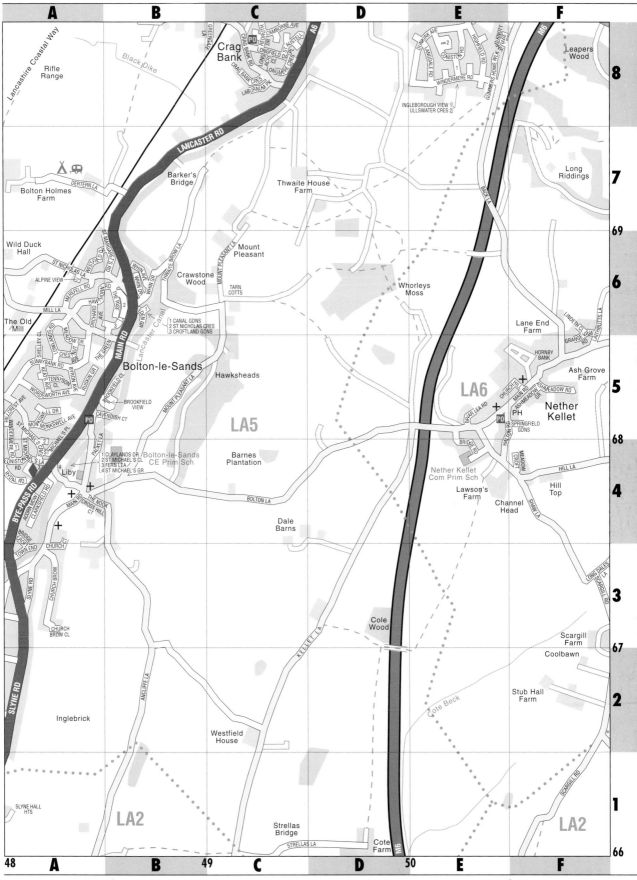

223
237
218
219
237

A B C D E F

Crag Bank

Lancashire Coastal Way

Rifle Range

Black Dike

PO

Camborne Ave

A6

GREENGATE LA
CRAG BANK RD
LONGMERE CRES
LONGFIELD RD
CRAG BANK CRES
HIGHFIELD
CAMBORNE AVE
ST AUSTELL
LONGMERE
LABURNUM LA

DUNIRK AVE
LANGDALE AV
HOWE
GUMMERS
CONISTON RD
HIGHFIELD RD
WINDERMERE WLK
3RD KNOTT
RISE
WINDERMERE RD

Leapers Wood

8

LANCASTER RD

Barker's Bridge

Thwaite House Farm

INGLEBOROUGH VIEW 1
ULLSWATER CRES 2

BACK LA

Long Riddings

7

DERTERN LA

Bolton Holmes Farm

M6

69

Wild Duck Hall

Mount Pleasant

Whorleys Moss

6

Alpine View

ST NICHOLAS LA
ST MARGARE'S RD
WESTFIELD
WHIN LA
WHIN GR
WHIN LA
THWAITE BROW LA
MT NEST

Crawstone Wood

MOUNT PLEASANT LA

TARN COTTS

Lane End Farm

LINDETH LA
GRANGE VIEW
LATHBUTTS LA

MERLFELL RD
MILL LA
THE RISE
HAW
ORCHARD
JOHN

HORNBY BANK

Ash Grove Farm

The Old Mill

1 CANAL GDNS
2 ST NICHOLAS CRES
3 CROFTLAND GDNS

Lancaster Canal

MAIN RD

Bolton-le-Sands

Hawksheads

LA6

CHURCH

BAR LEA RD

PH
PO

Nether Kellet

5

SUNNYBANK RD
LOWLANDS RD
CHES
MEADOW DR
ORCHARD
THE GREEN
BROOKFIELD CL
BROW AVE
RUSKIN GR

BROOKFIELD VIEW

CAVENDISH CT

MOUNT PLEASANT LA

ASHMEADOW RD
ASHMEADOW GR

SPRINGFIELD GDNS

68

SHELLEY CL
KEATS AVE
TENNYSON CL
WORDSWORTH AVE
MONKSWELL AVE
PO

1 CLAYLANDS DR
2 ST MICHAEL'S CL
3 FERN LEA
4 ST MICHAEL'S GR

Bolton-le-Sands CE Prim Sch

Barnes Plantation

HALTON RD
BRIDGE RD

MEADOW CROFT

HILL LA

LA5

Nether Kellet Com Prim Sch

Lawson's Farm

Hill Top

4

CREST AVE
WINDERMERE RD
ST MICHAEL'S LA
ST MICHAEL'S CRES
CONISTON RD
RYDAL RD
PACKET LA
Liby

THE NOOK
CROSS HILL

BOLTON LA

Dale Barns

Channel Head

SHAW LA

BYE-PASS RD
ACORN MON
CLARKSFIELD RD
MAIN RD

BRIDGE
DRIVE
CHURCH
TOWN END

CHURCH BROW

Cole Wood

LONG DALES LA
SCARGILL RD

3

67

CHURCH BROW CL

KELLET LA

Scargill Farm

Coolbawn

SLYNE RD

ANCLIFFE LA

Cote Beck

Stub Hall Farm

2

Inglebrick

Westfield House

SLYNE HALL HTS

LA2

Strellas Bridge

STRELLAS LA

Cote Farm

M6

LA2

1

66

48 A B 49 C D 50 E F

Heald Brow

Lancashire Coastal way

8

Jack Scout

Ridgway Park

Quaker's Stang

Crag Foot

New RD

CRAG RD

Brown's Houses

Quicksands Pool

Jenny Brown's Point

7

73

Morecambe Bay Nature Reserve

6

Warton Sands

LA5

Ings Point

5

72

Cumbria STREET ATLAS

4

3

71

2

1

70

DANGER AREA

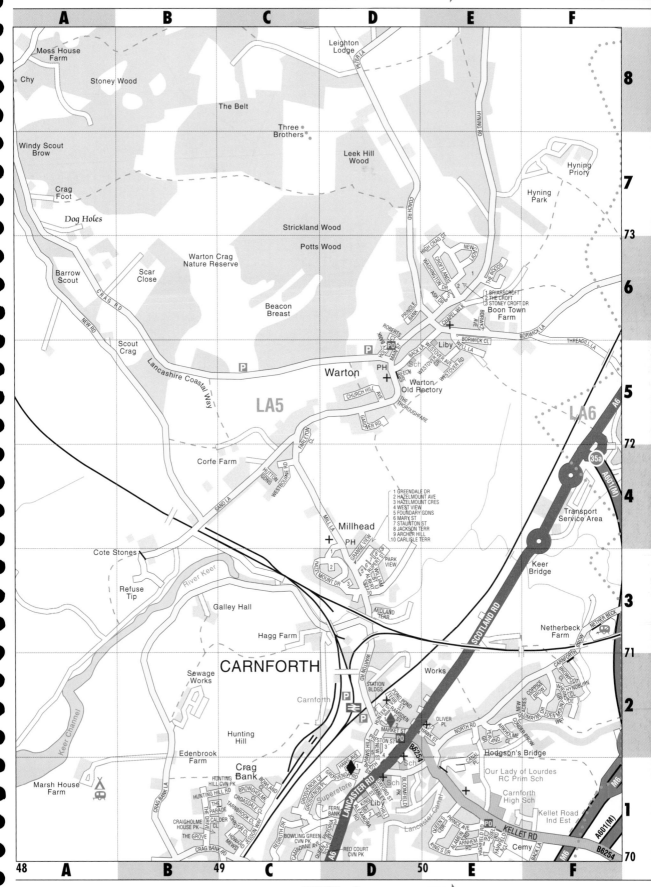

8

A B C D E F

Moss House Farm
Chy
Stoney Wood
The Belt
Leighton Lodge
Three Brothers
Leek Hill Wood
Hyning Priory
Hyning Park
Windy Scout Brow
Crag Foot
Dog Holes
Strickland Wood
Potts Wood
High Crag Ct
Boon Town Farm
Barrow Scout
Scar Close
Warton Crag Nature Reserve
Beacon Breast
Crag Rd
New Rd
Scout Crag
Lancashire Coastal Way
Roberts
Warton
Liby
Sch
Warton Old Rectory
LA5
Borwick Cl
Well La
Borwick La
Threagill La
LA6
A6
Church Hill Ave
Garden Rd
The Thoroughfare
PH
Corfe Farm
Hutton Gdns
Westbourne Rd
Sand La
Mill La
Millhead
Orange View
Park View
1 GREENDALE DR
2 HAZELMOUNT AVE
3 HAZELMOUNT CRES
4 WEST VIEW
5 FOUNDARY GDNS
6 MARY ST
7 STAUNTON ST
8 JACKSON TERR
9 ARCHER HILL
10 CARLISLE TERR
Transport Service Area
Keer Bridge
Cote Stones
Refuse Tip
River Keer
Galley Hall
Hazelmount Dr
Robert St
William St
Midland Terr
Scotland Rd
Netherbeck Farm
Nether Beck
Hagg Farm
CARNFORTH
Station Bldgs
Carnforth
Pond Pond
Marsden
Works
Carnforth Brow
Browfoot
Coppice Brow
Hynburn
Sewage Works
Hunting Hill
Edenbrook Farm
Crag Bank
Oliver Pl
North Rd
Hodgson's Bridge
Canal
Marsh House Farm
Hunting Hill Cvn Pk
Hunting Hill Rd
Browsholme
Carnbrook Cl
Croasdale Way
Boland
Grosvenor Ct
Grosvenor Pl
Haws Ave
Grosvenor Rd
Preston St
Market St
Hunter St
Station Rd
Lancaster Rd
A6
Liby
Sch
Bloomfield Pk
Our Lady of Lourdes RC Prim Sch
Carnforth High Sch
Kellet Road Ind Est
Craigholme House Pk
The Parade
The Drive
Calder Cl
The Grove
Crag Bank Rd
Howard Mews
Bowling Green Cvn Pk
Redruth Dr
Johnson Cl
Victoria St
Claiborne Ave
Queens Dr
Fern Bank
Alexandra
King St
Red Court Cvn Pk
King's Dr
Queens Dr
Arnhem Rd
Kellet Rd
Cemy
A601(M)
B6254
M6

48 49 50 70 71 72 73 2 1 3 4 5 6 7 8

D1
1 WARTONWOOD VIEW
2 TOWPATH WLK
3 ALBERT ST
D2
1 BACK HUNTER ST
2 ASHTREES WAY
3 EDWARD ST
4 JOHN ST
5 BACK NEW ST

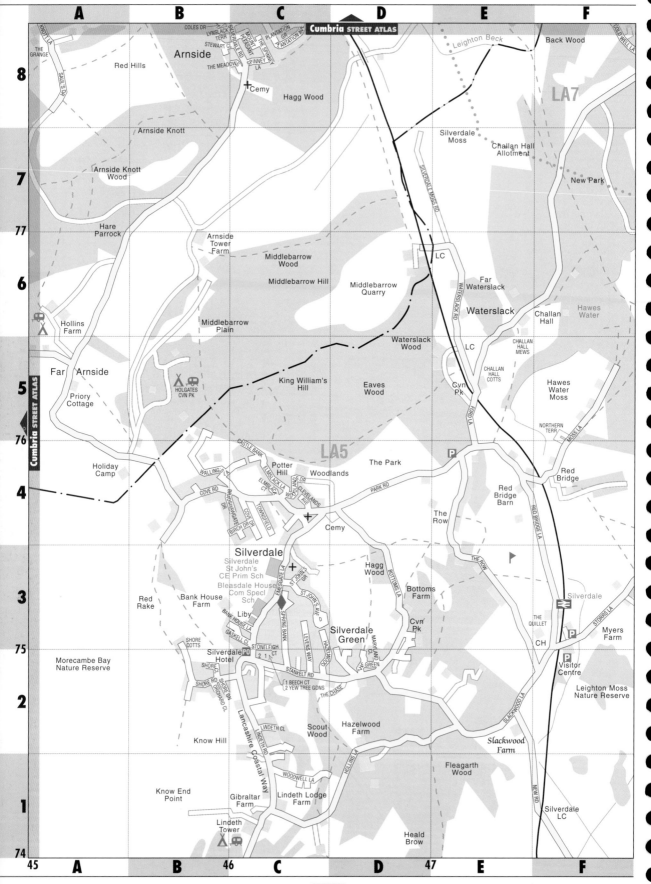

A B C D E F

8

7

77

6

5

76

4

3

75

2

1

74

45 46 47

LA7

Back Wood
Leighton Beck
Silverdale Moss
Challan Hall Allotment
New Park

Arnside
Red Hills
COLES DR
LYNSLACK TERR
STEWART CLOSE RD
MOUNT PLEASANT
THE SPINNEY
PLANTATION GR
PLANTATION AVE
THE MEADOWS
SPINNEY LA
Cemy
Hagg Wood

Arnside Knott

Arnside Knott Wood

Hare Parrock

Arnside Tower Farm

Middlebarrow Wood

Middlebarrow Hill

Middlebarrow Quarry

Middlebarrow Plain

SILVERDALE MOSS RD

LC

WATERSLACK RD

Far Waterslack

Waterslack

Challan Hall

Hawes Water

Hollins Farm

Far Arnside

Priory Cottage

HOLGATES CVN PK

King William's Hill

Eaves Wood

Waterslack Wood

LC

Cvn Pk

FORD LA

CHALLAN HALL MEWS

CHALLAN HALL COTTS

NORTHERN TERR

MOSS LA

Hawes Water Moss

LA5

Holiday Camp

CASTLE BANK

Potter Hill

Woodlands

The Park

P

Red Bridge Barn

Red Bridge

WALLINGS LA

COVE RD

BROADGATE

COVE DR

BIRCH DR

ELMSLACK LA

ELMSLACK CT

TOWNSFIELD

CLEVELANDS AVE

S DR

WOOD

PARK RD

The Row

RED BRIDGE LA

Cemy

Silverdale

Silverdale St John's CE Prim Sch

Bleasdale House Com Specl Sch

Red Rake

Bank House Farm

Liby

EMESGATE LA

ST JOHN'S DR

ST JOHN'S AVE

SPRING BANK

Hagg Wood

BOTTOMS LA

Bottoms Farm

THE ROW

Silverdale

SHORE COTTS

BANK HOUSE LA

GASKELL LA

STONELEIGH CT

LEVENS WAY

HOLLYWOOD

Silverdale Green

Cvn Pk

MARYLAND CL

LYE GREEN

CH

THE QUILLET

P

P

STORRS LA

Myers Farm

Silverdale Hotel

SHORE RD

SHORE CL

ORCHARD CL

STANKELT RD

1 BEECH CT
2 YEW TREE GDNS

THE CHASE

Visitor Centre

Leighton Moss Nature Reserve

Morecambe Bay Nature Reserve

Know Hill

LINDETH CL

LINDETH RD

Scout Wood

Hazelwood Farm

SLACKWOOD LA

Slackwood Farm

Lancashire Coastal Way

Know End Point

Gibraltar Farm

Lindeth Lodge Farm

WOODWELL LA

HOLLINS LA

Fleagarth Wood

NEW RD

Silverdale LC

Lindeth Tower

Heald Brow

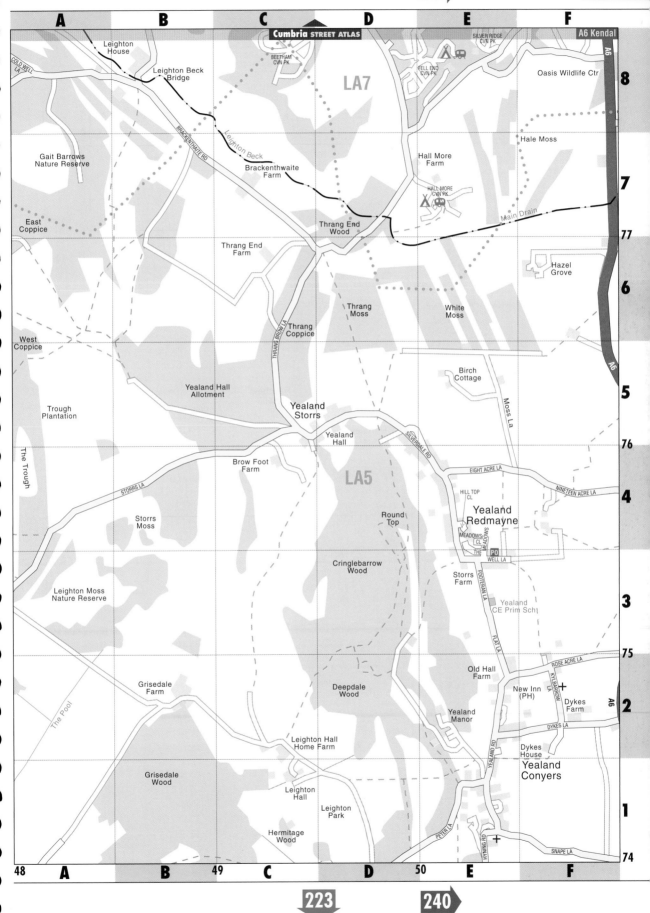

240

Cumbria STREET ATLAS

LA7

Oasis Wildlife Ctr

A6 Kendal

A6

Leighton House

Leighton Beck Bridge

BEETHAM CVN PK

SILVER RIDGE CVN PK

FELL END CVN PK

Leighton Beck

BRACKENTHWAITE RD

Brackenthwaite Farm

Hall More Farm

Hale Moss

8

Gait Barrows Nature Reserve

Thrang End Wood

HALL MORE CVN PK

Main Drain

7

East Coppice

Thrang End Farm

77

Hazel Grove

6

West Coppice

Thrang Coppice

THRANG BROW LA

Thrang Moss

White Moss

Birch Cottage

Trough Plantation

Yealand Hall Allotment

Yealand Storrs

Moss La

5

The Trough

Brow Foot Farm

Yealand Hall

LA5

SILVERDALE RD

76

Storrs La

Storrs Moss

EIGHT ACRE LA

HILL TOP CL

NINETEEN ACRE LA

4

Round Top

Yealand Redmayne

Leighton Moss Nature Reserve

Cringlebarrow Wood

MEADOWS CL

THE MEADOWS

PO

WELL LA

Storrs Farm

FOOTERAN LA

Yealand CE Prim Sch

3

The Pool

Grisedale Farm

Deepdale Wood

FLAT LA

Old Hall Farm

75

ROSE ACRE LA

New Inn (PH)

KYLBARROW LA

Dykes Farm

A6

2

Yealand Manor

DYKES LA

YEALAND RD

Dykes House

Yealand Conyers

Leighton Hall Home Farm

Grisedale Wood

Leighton Hall

Leighton Park

Hermitage Wood

PETER LA

HYNING RD

SNAPE LA

74

1

48   A   B   49   C   D   50   E   F

207
204

232

A   B   C   D   E   F

8

Dolphinholme
Pennine View
Four Lane Ends
Dolphinholme CE Prim Sch
South View
Corless Cotts
PO
Brookside Dr
Abbeystead Rd
Dolphinholme Mill
Rivers View
Springl
Wagon Rd
Damas Gill

River Wyre

Lower Swainshead

River Wyre

Catshaw Hall

Abbeystead Resr

Hawthornthwaite

LA2

53

Belvidere House

Wyreside Hall

Swainshead Hall

Camm House

7

Bantons

Street Bridge

Street Brook

Timber's La

Halls

Waste La

Hall Gill

Fellside Farm

52

Street

Bracken Lea

Stonehead

Yates

Catshaw Greave

6

Foxhouses

Taylor's Farm

Crosshill Four Lane Ends

Kays Farm

Isle of Skye Farm

Catshaw Fell

51

Crosshill Farm

Long La

Grizedale Head

5

Websters

Syke's Farm

Hayshaw Fell

Grizedale Fell

Lea Green

Cliftons

Ford

Harrisend Fell

Stake House Fell

50

4

Sands Bottom

Wyresdale Park

Fell End

Stake House

Arbour

49

Higher La

The Tarn

Nickey Nook

Grizedale Resr

Calder Fell

3

Pedder's Wood

Grize Dale

Grizedale Lea Resr

PR3

Calder Dyke

Bleasdale Moors

48

Woodacre Pasture

Calder Side

Hazelhurst Fell

2

Barnacre Resrs

Oakenclough
Masts

Works

Oakenclough Cotts

Oakenclough Fell

Clough Heads Brook

Higher La

Burns Farm

Bank Farm

Moorcock Inn (PH)

Hazelhurst

47

River Calder

1

Barnacre Lodge

Edisforth La

Birks Farm

Long La

Strickers La

Mast
Kelbrick Farm

Calder Vale St John CE Prim Sch

Rough Moor

Delph La

Fell End

Bleasdale Tower

Clough Heads Cotts

River Brock

46

Delph La

51   A   52   B   53   C   54   D   55   E   56   F

Scale: 1¾ inches to 1 mile

0   ¼   ½ mile
0   250m 500m 750m 1 km

233

228

227

A   B   C   D   E   F

8

53

7

52

6

51

5

50

4

49

3

48

2

47

1

46

Tower
Lodge

Winfold Fell

Blaze Moss

Trough of Bowland

Sniddle
Holes

Marshaw

Marshaw Wyre

Marshaw
Fell

Top of
Blaze Moss

TROUGH RD

Nab
End

Black Clough

Stables Breast

LA2

Holdron Moss

Stake End

Hawthornthwaite Fell

Langden
House

Hawthornthwaite
Fell Top

Langden Head

Holdron
Castle

Johnny Pye's
Clough Top

White Moss

Higher Raven
Scar

Raven
Scar

Lingy Pits
Moss

Langden
Castle
(ruin)

Langden Brook

Miry Ellis

Hunter's Clough

Sykes Fell

BB7

Tom Waring's
Well

Fiendsdale

Bleadale
Nab

Birch
Bank

Bleadale
Ridge

Bleadale Water

Hareden Brook

Luddock's
Fell

Hareden Fell

Shooting
Box

Webster's
Meadow

Bleadale
Moss

PR3

Brown Berry
Plain

Fair Oak
Fell

River Brock

Holme House Fell

Saddle
Fell

Holme
House

Fair Snape
Fell

Wolf Fell

Burnslack
Fell

Burnslack

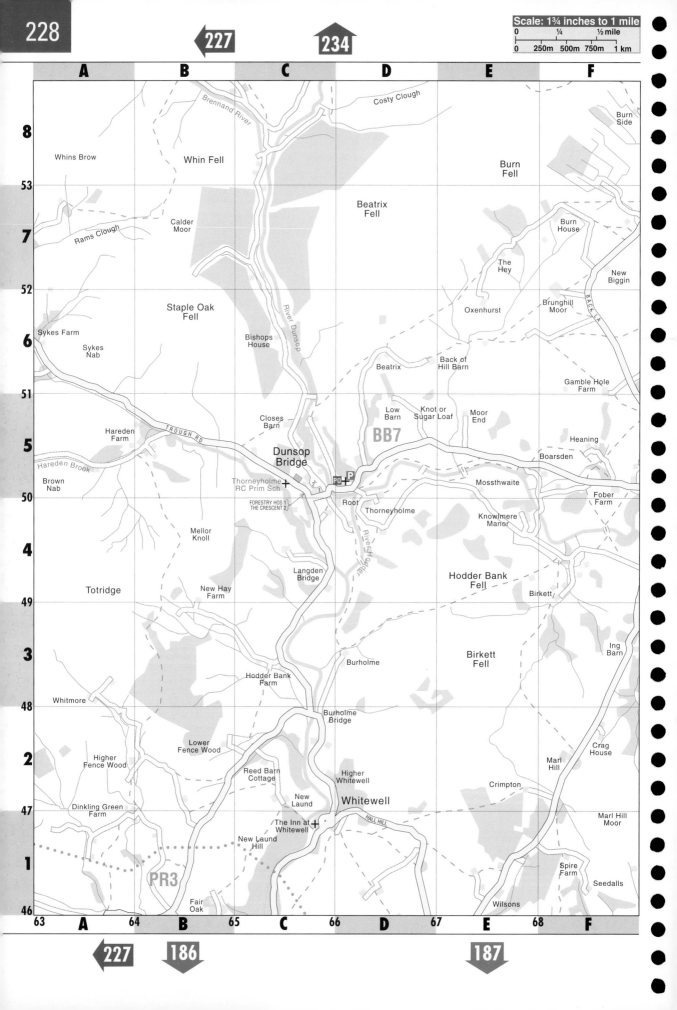

Scale: 1¾ inches to 1 mile

0   ¼   ½ mile

0   250m   500m   750m   1 km

A   **B**   **C**   **D**   **E**   **F**

8

53

7

52

6

51

5

4

49

3

48

2

47

1

46

63   **A**   64   **B**   65   **C**   66   **D**   67   **E**   68   **F**

Costy Clough

Burn Side

Whins Brow

Whin Fell

Burn Fell

Brennand River

Beatrix Fell

Calder Moor

Rams Clough

Burn House

The Hey

New Biggin

BACK LA

Staple Oak Fell

River Dunsop

Oxenhurst

Brunghill Moor

Sykes Farm

Sykes Nab

Bishops House

Beatrix

Back of Hill Barn

Gamble Hole Farm

TROUGH RD

Closes Barn

Low Barn

Knot or Sugar Loaf

Moor End

Heaning

Hareden Farm

BB7

Boarsden

Hareden Brook

Dunsop Bridge

Thorneyholme RC Prim Sch

Mossthwaite

Brown Nab

FORESTRY HOS 1
THE CRESCENT 2

PO P

Root

Thorneyholme

Fober Farm

Mellor Knoll

Knowlmere Manor

River Hodder

Totridge

New Hay Farm

Langden Bridge

Hodder Bank Fell

Birkett

Whitmore

Hodder Bank Farm

Burholme

Birkett Fell

Ing Barn

Lower Fence Wood

Burholme Bridge

Crag House

Higher Fence Wood

Reed Barn Cottage

Higher Whitewell

Marl Hill

Dinkling Green Farm

New Laund

Whitewell

Crimpton

Marl Hill Moor

The Inn at Whitewell

HALL HILL

PR3

New Laund Hill

Spire Farm

Seedalls

Fair Oak

Wilsons

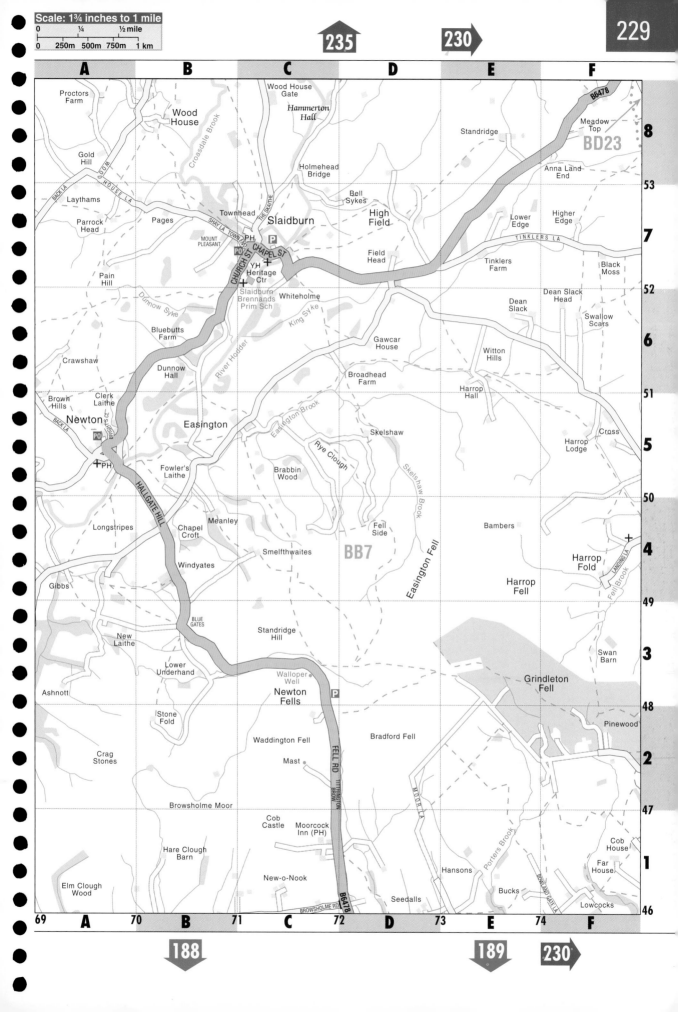

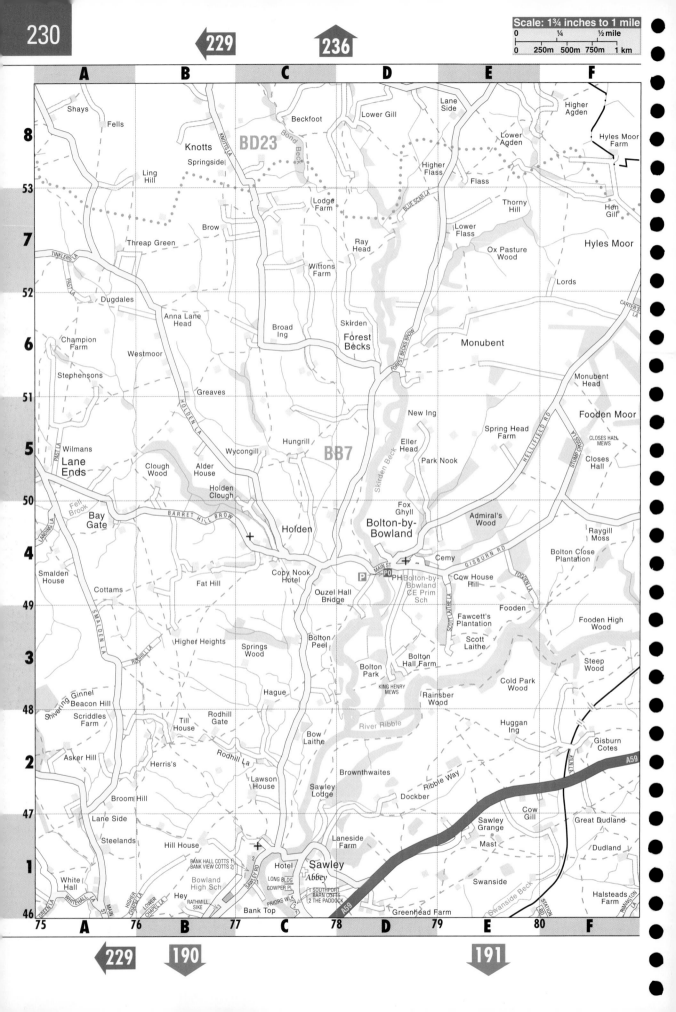

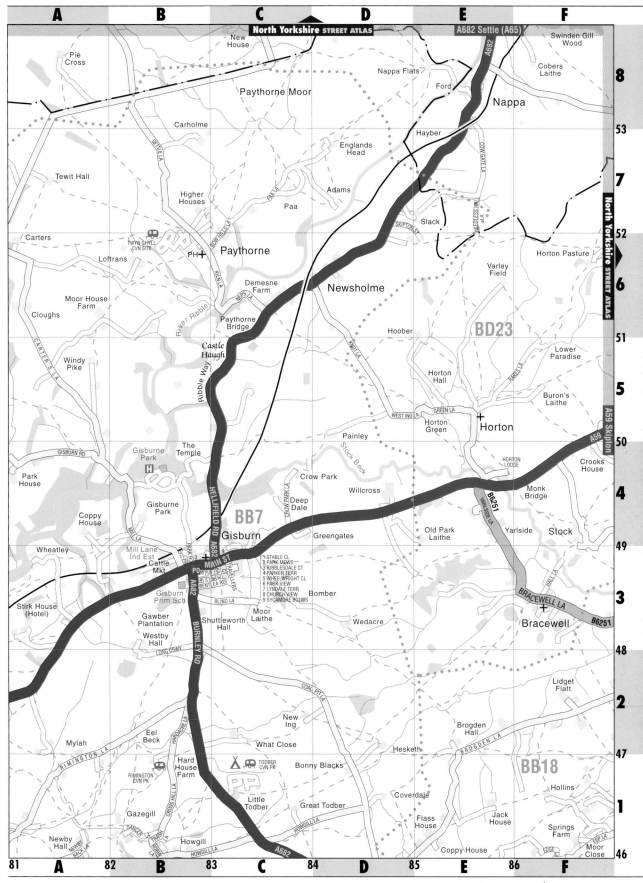

Scale: 1¾ inches to 1 mile

0   ¼   ½ mile
0   250m 500m 750m 1 km

North Yorkshire STREET ATLAS

A682 Settle (A65)

North Yorkshire STREET ATLAS

Swinden Gill Wood

Pie Cross

New House

Nappa Flats

Cobers Laithe

Paythorne Moor

Ford

Nappa

8

Carholme

Hayber

53

Englands Head

Tewit Hall

7

Higher Houses

Adams

Paa

52

Carters

Slack

6

Loftrans

PH

Paythorne

Demesne Farm

Newsholme

TWYN GHYLL CVN SITE

Hoober

BD23

Moor House Farm

Horton Pasture

Varley Field

Cloughs

Paythorne Bridge

Horton Hall

Lower Paradise

51

Castle Haugh

Buron's Laithe

Windy Pike

Horton Green

Horton

5

River Ribble

Ribble Way

WEST ING LA

GREEN LA

RAKES LA

Painley

Carters La

Gisburn Rd

The Temple

Gisburne Park

Crow Park

Stock Beck

HORTON LODGE

A59 Skipton

Crooks House

50

Park House

H

Willcross

Deep Dale

Monk Bridge

Gisburne Park

BB7

Greengates

Old Park Laithe

B6251

Yarlside

Stock

4

Coppy House

Gisburn

Mill Lane Ind Est

Wheatley

Cattle Mkt

PO

MAIN ST

1 STABLE CL
2 PARK MEWS
3 RIBBLESDALE CT
4 PARKER TERR
5 WHEELWRIGHT CL
6 PARK VIEW
7 LYNDALE TERR
8 CHURCH VIEW
9 SYCAMORE BGLWS

Bomber

49

Stirk House (Hotel)

Gisburn Prim Sch

BLIND LA

Moor Laithe

Wedacre

Bracewell La

Bracewell

B6251

3

Gawber Plantation

Shuttleworth Hall

Westby Hall

LONG CSWY

48

BURNLEY RD

COAL PIT LA

Lidget Flatt

2

Mylah

RIMINGTON LA

Eel Beck

HARDACRE LA

New Ing

What Close

Hesketh

Brogden Hall

BROGDEN LA

47

RIMINGTON CVN PK

Hard House Farm

TODBER CVN PK

Bonny Blacks

Coverdale

BB18

Hollins

Gazegill

CROSS HILL LA

Little Todber

Great Todber

HOWGILL LA

Flass House

Jack House

Springs Farm

1

Newby Hall

DANCER LA

RIBBY

NEWBY BACK LA

Howgill

HOWGILL LA

A682

Coppy House

Moor Close

46

81   A   82   B   83   C   84   D   85   E   86   F

192   193   196

215 211
237

A   B   C   D   E   F

8

Quernmore Rd
Postern Gate Rd
Friar's Moss Rd
Corney Hill Farm
Baines Cragg
The Cragg
Littledale Hall
Foxdale Beck
Bellhill Farm
Field Head
Knotts Farm
Friar's Moss Farm
Askew Hill
Cragg Wood

61

Littledale

River Gander
Littledale Rd
Wisp Hill
Udale Beck

7

Stock-a-Bank
Greenlot
Windy Clough
Conder Head

Quernmore CE Prim Sch
Rigg La
Black Fell

60

Far Lodge
Fell End Farm
Clougha Scar

6

Narr Lodge
Clougha
Brownley Hill

Wyresdale Rd
Rowton Brook
Clougha Pike

Quernmore
PO
Rowton Brook Fell
Rowton Brook Fell

59

Long La
Quernmore Brow
Brow Top Farm
Shooters Pile

5

Gibson's Farm
Terrace Farm
Grit Fell

Bay Horse Rd
Middle Brow Top
Hare Appletree Fell
Burrow Hill
Grizedale Head

58

Hare Appletree
LA2

Lower Browtop
Abbeystead Fell
Lee Fell

4

Blackwood End
Damas Gill
Rotten Hill

Twr Westfield House
P

57

Longmoor
Castle o' Trim
Higher Moor Head
High Moor Cross
River Grizedale

3

Yeat House Farm
Grizedale Barn

Gate House Bridge
Procter Moss Rd
Lower Moor Head

56

Damas Gill
Lower Castle o' Trim
Tills Farm
Balderstones
Bakehouse Brow

2

Middle Crag
Borwicks
Brook House
Grizedale Bridge
Lee

Abbeystead La
Summer House Head
Grizedale Bridge
Lee Bridge

55

Hollyhead Farm
Gallows Clough
Plantation La
Chapel House Farm
Abbeystead

Tarnbrook Wyre
Long La

1

Ortner
Cawthorne Prim Sch
Smithy Brow
Strait La
Doeholme Farm

Starbank
Lower Green Bank
Abbeystead Rd
River Wyre
Lentworth Hall
Abbeystead Resr
The Rake
Doeholme Rake

54

51   A   52   B   53   C   54   D   55   E   56   F

215 211
226

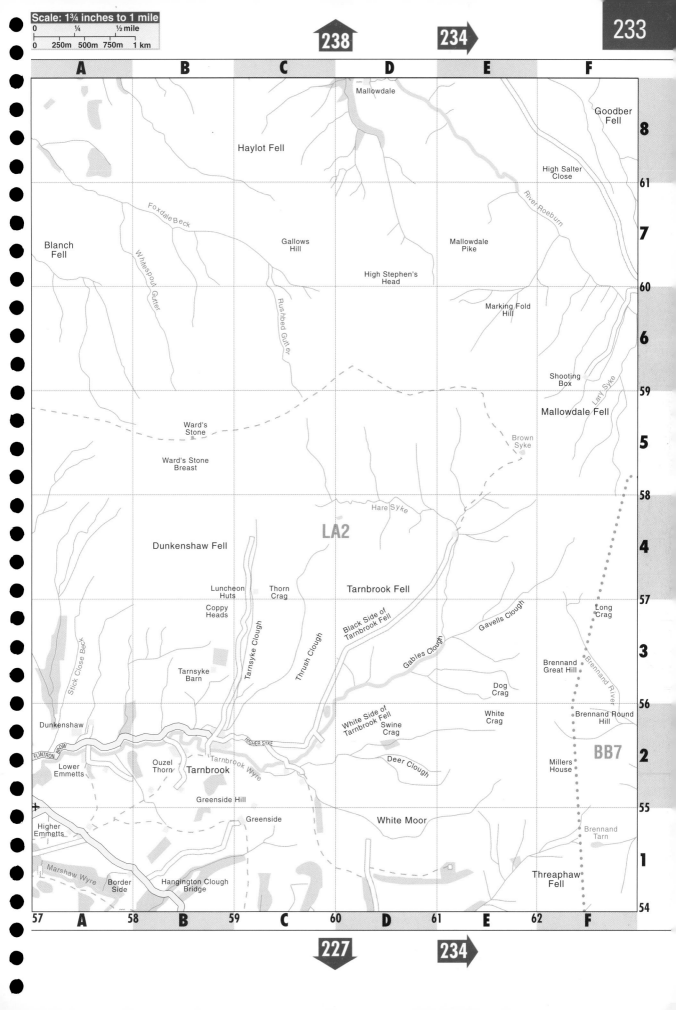

Scale: 1¾ inches to 1 mile

0   ¼   ½ mile
0   250m 500m 750m 1 km

238
234

A **B** **C** **D** **E** **F**

Mallowdale

Goodber
Fell

8

High Salter
Close

61

Haylot Fell

Foxdale Beck

River Roeburn

7

Blanch
Fell

Gallows
Hill

Mallowdale
Pike

Whitespout Gutter

High Stephen's
Head

60

Marking Fold
Hill

6

Rushbed Gutter

Shooting
Box

Lary Syke

59

Mallowdale Fell

Ward's
Stone

Brown
Syke

5

Ward's Stone
Breast

Hare Syke

58

LA2

Dunkenshaw Fell

4

Luncheon
Huts

Thorn
Crag

Tarnbrook Fell

57

Coppy
Heads

Tarnsyke Clough

Thrush Clough

Black Side of
Tarnbrook Fell

Gavells Clough

Long
Crag

3

Tarnsyke
Barn

Gables Clough

Brennand
Great Hill

Brennand River

Stick Close Beck

Dog
Crag

56

White Side of
Tarnbrook Fell

White
Crag

Brennand Round
Hill

Dunkenshaw

Swine
Crag

BB7

FLINTRON BROW

HIGHER SYKE

Millers
House

2

Lower
Emmetts

Ouzel
Thorn

Tarnbrook

Tarnbrook Wyre

Deer Clough

Greenside Hill

55

Higher
Emmetts

Greenside

White Moor

Brennand
Tarn

1

Marshaw Wyre

Border
Side

Hangington Clough
Bridge

Threaphaw
Fell

54

227
234

Scale: 1¾ inches to 1 mile

0   ¼   ½ mile
0   250m 500m 750m 1 km

A   **B**   **C**   **D**   **E**   **F**

Summersgill
Fell

8

Thrushgill
Fell

Lower Green
Bank

Higher Green
Bank

Botton
Head

Whitray
Fell

Whitray Beck

LYTHE FELL RD

61

New
Coppy

Cross of Greet
(rems of)

7

Hawkshead

Greenbank
Fell

Dale Beck

Middle Gill

River Hodder

60

Salter Fell

Botton Head
Fell

LA2

6

Coumes

Far Costy Clough

59

White
Hill

Lamb Hill
Fell

5

Shooters Clough

Esp
Crag

Hard Hill Top

58

Wolfhole
Crag

Little Bull
Stones

Great Bull
Stones

Reeves Edge

4

Croasdale Brook

57

Brown Syke
Hill

Shooting
Box

Croasdale Fell

Higher Stoney Clough

3

Brown Syke

BB7

Whitendale
Fell

Whitendale
Hanging Stones

Whitendale River

Baxton Fell

56

Shooting
Box

Dane Hill
Well

Black Brook

2

Lee End

Brennand
Fell

Calf Clough

Low Fell

55

Whitendale

Brennand River

Dunsop Fell

1

Middle
Knoll

Brennand
Farm

54

63   **A**   **64**   **B**   **65**   **C**   **66**   **D**   **67**   **E**   **68**   **F**

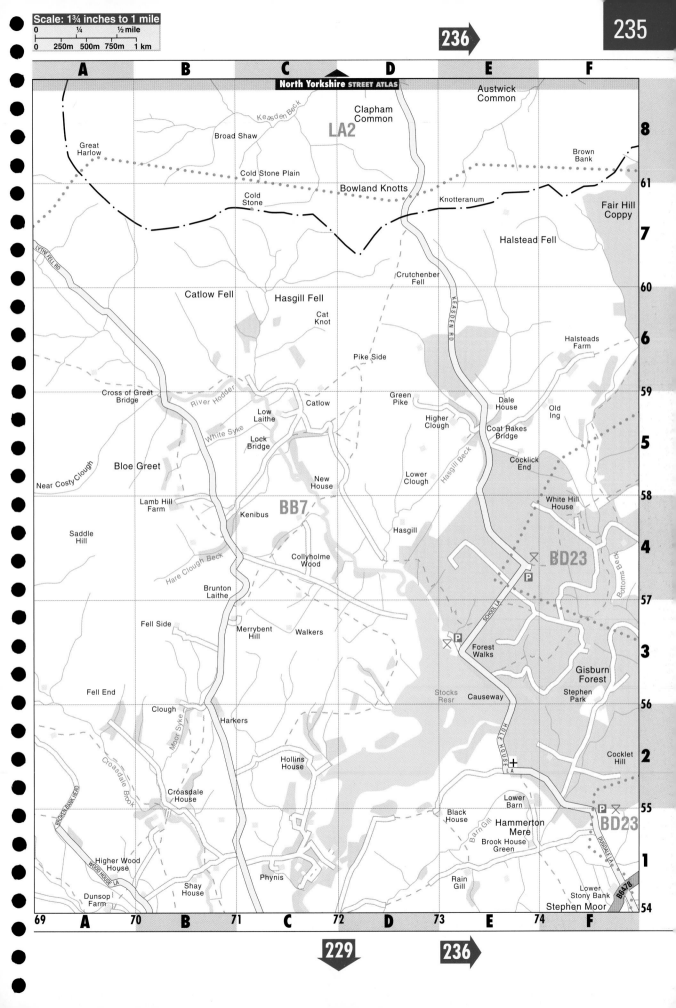

Scale: 1¾ inches to 1 mile

0   ¼   ½ mile
0 250m 500m 750m 1 km

236

North Yorkshire STREET ATLAS

A **B** **C** **D** **E** **F**

Austwick
Common

Clapham
Common

Keasden Beck

Broad Shaw

LA2

Great
Harlow

Cold Stone Plain

Bowland Knotts

Brown
Bank

8

Cold
Stone

Knotteranum

Fair Hill
Coppy

61

7

Halstead Fell

Crutchenber
Fell

Catlow Fell

Hasgill Fell

60

Cat
Knot

KEASDEN RD

Halsteads
Farm

6

Pike Side

Green
Pike

Dale
House

Old
Ing

59

Cross of Greet
Bridge

River Hodder

Low
Laithe

Catlow

Higher
Clough

Coat Rakes
Bridge

5

White Syke

Lock
Bridge

Cocklick
End

Bloe Greet

New
House

Lower
Clough

Hasgill Beck

White Hill
House

58

Near Costy Clough

Lamb Hill
Farm

Kenibus

BB7

Hasgill

BD23

4

Saddle
Hill

Hare Clough Beck

Collyholme
Wood

P

Bottoms Beck

57

Brunton
Laithe

Fell Side

Merrybent
Hill

Walkers

P

Forest
Walks

SCHOOL LA

3

Fell End

Gisburn
Forest

Clough

Harkers

Stocks
Resr

Causeway

Stephen
Park

56

Moor Syke

Hollins
House

HOLE HOUSE LA

Cocklet
Hill

2

Croasdale Brook

Croasdale
House

Lower
Barn

55

BROKEN BANK HEAD

Black
House

Barn Gill

Hammerton
Mere

P

BD23

WOOD HOUSE LA

Higher Wood
House

Brook House
Green

1

Dunsop
Farm

Shay
House

Phynis

Rain
Gill

Lower
Stony Bank

DUGDALE LA

B6478

Stephen Moor

54

69 **A** 70 **B** 71 **C** 72 **D** 73 **E** 74 **F**

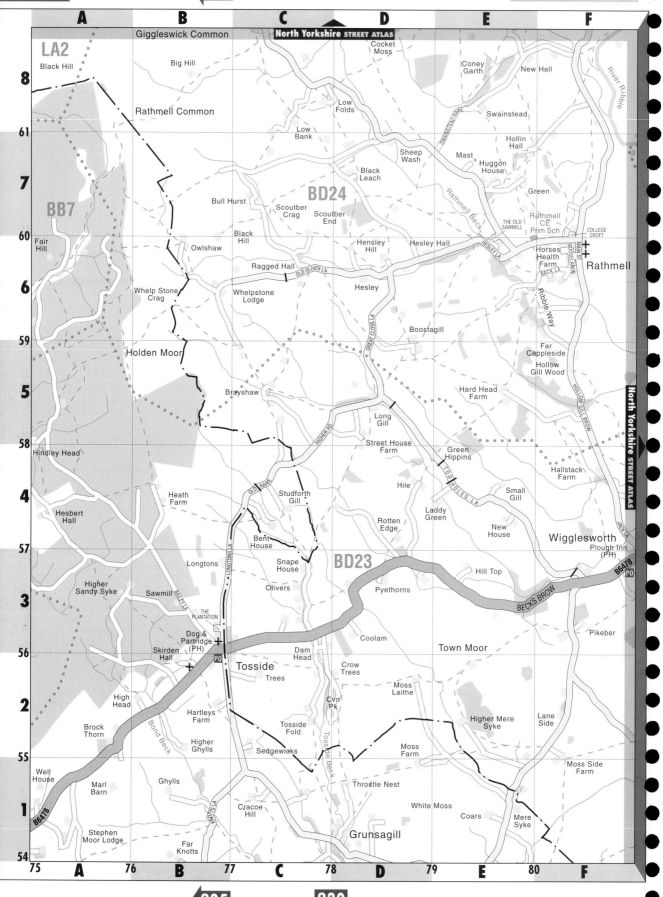

Scale: 1¾ inches to 1 mile
0   ¼   ½ mile
0 250m 500m 750m 1 km

LA2
Black Hill
Giggleswick Common
Big Hill
North Yorkshire STREET ATLAS
Cocket Moss
Coney Garth
New Hall
River Ribble

Rathmell Common
Low Folds
Low Bank
Swainstead
Hollin Hall
Mast
Huggon House
Green

BB7
Fair Hill
Bull Hurst
Scoutber Crag
Scoutber End
BD24
Black Leach
Sheep Wash
Rathmell Beck
THE OLD SAWMILL
Rathmell CE Prim Sch
COLLEGE CROFT
Rathmell

Black Hill
Owlshaw
Ragged Hall
OLD OLIVER LA
Hensley Hill
Hesley Hall
HESLEY LA
Horses Health Farm
BACK LA
MAIN ST
GOOSE LANDS

Whelp Stone Crag
Whelpstone Lodge
Hesley
Ribble Way
Far Cappleside
Hollow Gill Wood

Holden Moor
Brayshaw
GREAT CLOSE LA
Boostagill
Hard Head Farm
HOLLOW GILL BROW

Hindley Head
HIGHER RD
Long Gill
Street House Farm
Green Hippins
Hallstack Farm

Heath Farm
OLD RAIKE
Studforth Gill
Hile
TOD HOLES LA
Small Gill
North Yorkshire STREET ATLAS

Hesbert Hall
Bent House
Rotten Edge
Laddy Green
New House
Wigglesworth
Plough Inn (PH)
JACK LA

Higher Sandy Syke
Sawmill
Longtons
LONGTONS LA
BELLE LA
Snape House
Olivers
BD23
Pyethorns
Hill Top
BECKS BROW
B6478
PO

THE PLANTATION
Dog & Partridge (PH)
Coolam
Town Moor
Pikeber

Skirden Hall
PO
Tosside
Dam Head
Crow Trees
Trees

High Head
Hartleys Farm
Cvn Pk
Moss Laithe
Higher Mere Syke
Lane Side

Brock Thorn
Higher Ghylls
Tosside Fold
Sedgewioks
Moss Farm
Moss Side Farm

Well House
Marl Barn
Ghylls
BOND BECK
TOSSIDE BECK
Throstle Nest
White Moss
Coars
Mere Syke

B6478
Stephen Moor Lodge
KNOTS LA
Cracoe Hill
Far Knotts
Grunsagill

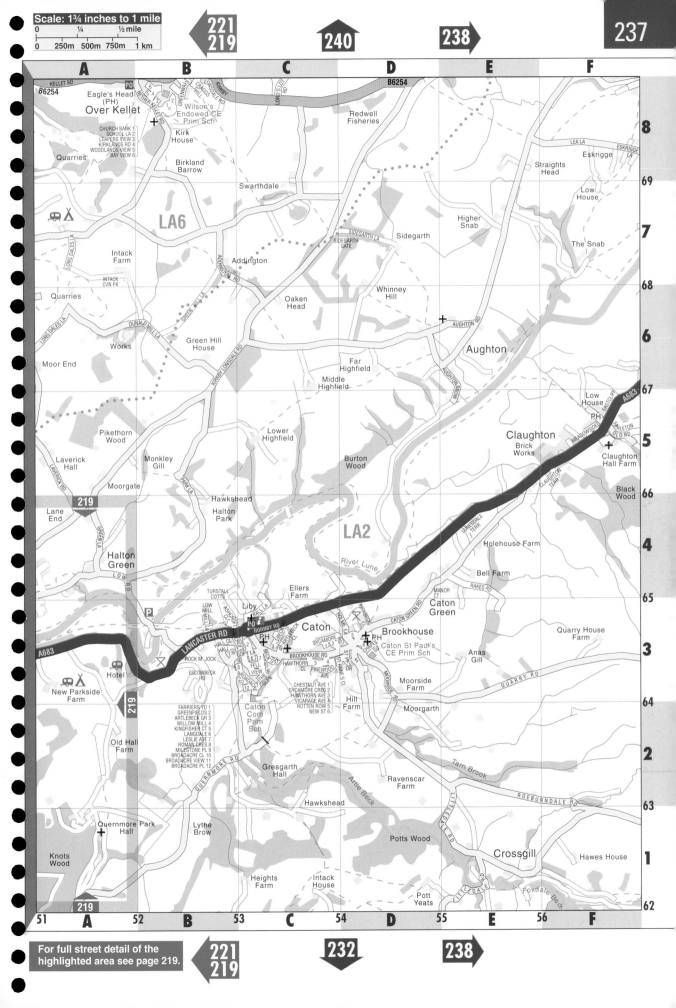

237
241

Scale: 1¾ inches to 1 mile

0   ¼   ½ mile
0   250m 500m 750m 1 km

LA6

LA2

Clintsfield
Wennington
Tatham Bridge Inn (PH)
Wennington Old Farm
Old Moor Rd
Raw Ridding
Park House
Tatham
School Hill
Hornby Park Wood
River Wenning
Park La
Russells
Tatham Hall
Parkside
Perry Moor
Feathermire
Bottom Farm
Meal Bank
Four Score Acres
Trinket La
Mill Houses
Castle Stede
Loyn Bridge
River Lune
Priory Farm
Sandbeds
Hornby High Sch
Royal Oak Mdw
Kennels
Hornby
Prim Sch
Castle Hotel
Post Horse La
1 Stanley Dr
2 Monteagle Dr
3 Monteagle Sq
4 Castle Pk
Strands Farm Ct
Lancaster Rd
Station Way
Ind Est
Ingleborough View
Back La
Camp House
B6480
Butt Yeats
Linesdale Ct
Curwen Hall Farm
Wray with Botton Prim Sch
Kiln La
Gars End
Hornby Rd
The Orchard
PH
School St
Wenning Rd
Wray
Agnes Ho La
River Hindburn
A683
Farleton
Meadow View
Farleton Old Rd
Scale House Barn
Cold Park Wood
Moor La
Above Beck
Higher Broadwood
Cragg Hall
Claughton Hall
Hamstone Gill
Manor House
Alcocks Farm
Bellhurst
Smeer Hall
Claughton Moor
Quarry Rd
Wind Farm
Whit Moor
River Roeburn
LA2
Four Lane Ends
Leyland Farm
Scale
Outhwaite
Outhwaite Wood
Wray Wood Moor
Back Farm
Barkin Gate
Thornbush
Stauvin
Caton Moor
Winder Wood
Harterbeck
Goodber Common
Lower Salter
Middle Salter
Winder
Roeburndale Rd
Ford
Hornby Rd
High Salter
Deep Clough
Raguil Beck
Haylot Farm

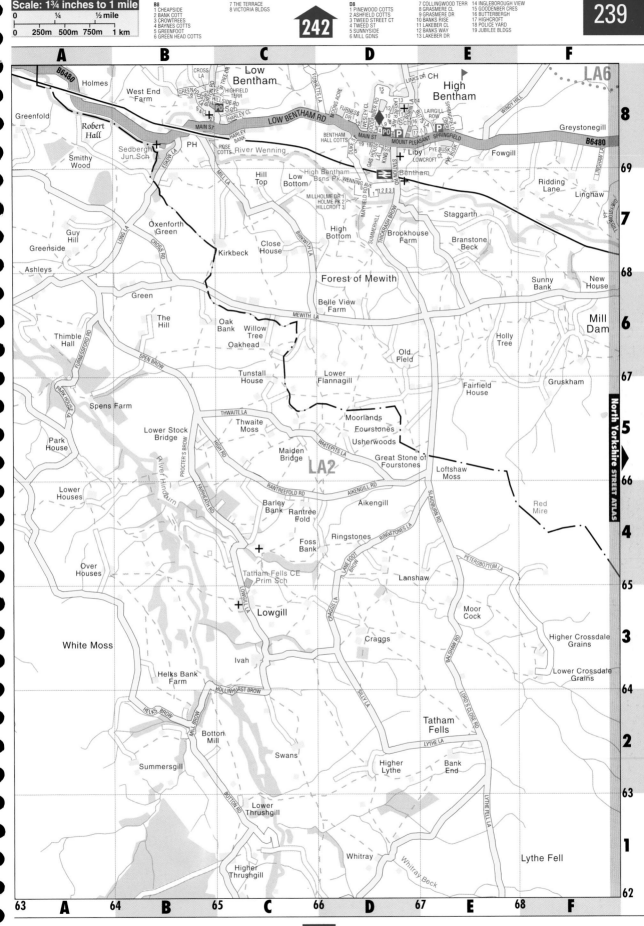

B8
1 CHEAPSIDE
2 BANK COTT
3 CROWTREES
4 BAYNES COTTS
5 GREENFOOT
6 GREEN HEAD COTTS

7 THE TERRACE
8 VICTORIA BLDGS

D8
1 PINEWOOD COTTS
2 ASHFIELD COTTS
3 TWEED STREET CT
4 TWEED ST
5 SUNNYSIDE
6 MILL GDNS

7 COLLINGWOOD TERR
8 GRASMERE CL
9 GRASMERE DR
10 BANKS RISE
11 LAKEBER CL
12 BANKS WAY
13 LAKEBER DR

14 INGLEBOROUGH VIEW
15 GOODENBER CRES
16 BUTTERBERGH
17 HIGHCROFT
18 POLICE YARD
19 JUBILEE BLDGS

242

234

North Yorkshire STREET ATLAS

LA6

LA2

Low Bentham

High Bentham

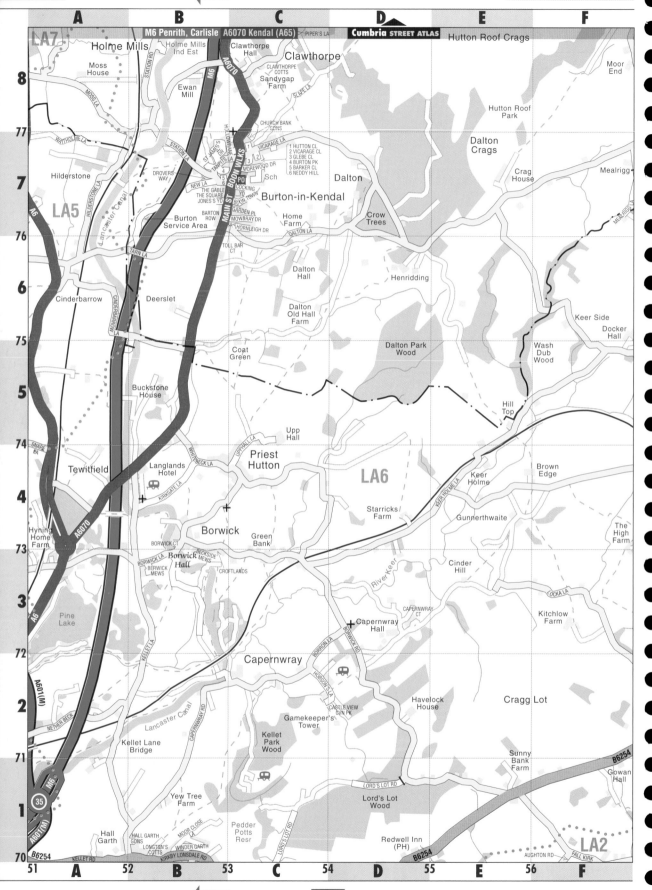

Scale: 1¾ inches to 1 mile

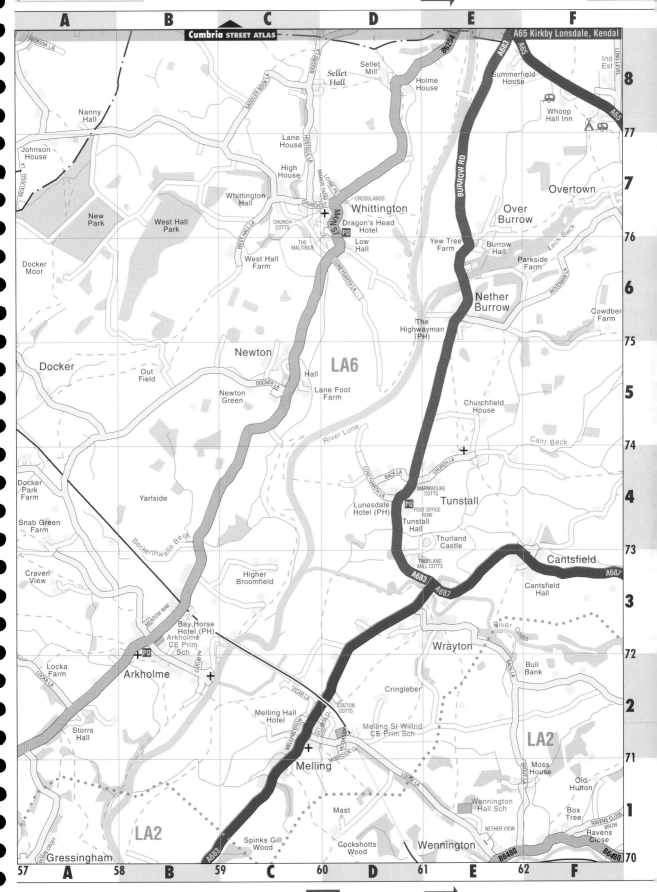

241
243

Scale: 1¾ inches to 1 mile

0   ¼   ½ mile
0   250m 500m 750m 1 km

North Yorkshire STREET ATLAS

Row 8
Notts Pot
Springs Wood
Bank House
Fellside Barn
Ireby Fell Cavern

Row 77
Fairthwaite Park House
Leck Beck
Ford
Over Leck
Low La
Leck
Ireby Fell
Marble Steps Pot
A65
Kail Pot

Row 7
High Gale
PO
Leck St Peter's CE Prim Sch
Leck
Leck Villa Farm
Low Douk Cave
Turbary Rd
North End Scar
Cheese Press Stone
Woodman La
Cowan Bridge
Colter Beck La
Heber Hill

Row 76
Hipping Hall (Hotel)
Green La
Over Hall
Ireby Beck
Masongill Fell Lane
Mill Race or Water Cut
Tow Scar
Tow Scar Rd

Row 6
Low House Farm
Ireby
Masongill Hall
Fell Side
LA6

Row 75
Collingholme
Ireby Hall Farm
Cant Beck
Masongill
Westgate
Westgate La
Mast
Cowgill Farm
Thornton La

Row 5
Laithbutts
Anems House
Moffinber Farm
Kirksteads
Westhouse
Bank House Rd

Row 74
Scaleber
Whaitber
Galegreen
Lower Westhouse
Post Office Row
Smith La
Bank House
Thornton in Lonsdale
A65 Ingleton, Skipton

Row 4
Stainderber
High Threaber Farm
PH Caravan Pk

Row 73
A687
Longber La
Gallaber
Selber
Low Threaber
Gooda
Lowfields
Lund Farm
A687 New Rd
Halsteads
A65
Clarrick Terr
Beech Terr

Row 3
Halfway House
Longber
Burton in Lonsdale
Blind La
Twine Walk
The Croft
4 Coronation Mount
5 Ingle View
Lund Holme
Ingleton
Clarrick House Farm
Tamour Cl
Bentham Rd

Row 72
Lowfields
Richard Thornton's CE Prim Sch
Leeming La
Greta Heath
Burton Hill
Low St
Brookland
PH
High St PO
1 Chapel La
2 Wood View
3 Duke St
Barnoldswick La
River Greta
Kepp House
Park Foot
Wilson Wood
Warth House
Warth La

Row 2
Scaleber Farm
Chalybeate Spring
Clifford Hall
Black Wood
Skipton Gate
Bentham Moor Rd
Barnoldswick
Fourlands Hill
Raygill House
Broats House
Langber

Row 71
Back La
Gill Farm
Bentham Moor
Fourlands House
Over Raygill
Nookdales House
Langber End La
Nookdales Cotts

Row 1
Raths Close Brow
Goodenbergh Farm
Four Lane Ends
Bracken Hill
LA2
Dumb Tom's La
Thornber

Row 70
B6480
The Ridding
Calf Cop
Wards End
Seat Hall
Ghyllhead Farm
Gillhead Brow
Robin La
Tatterthorn

Grid columns: A 63 B 64 C 65 D 66 E 67 F 68

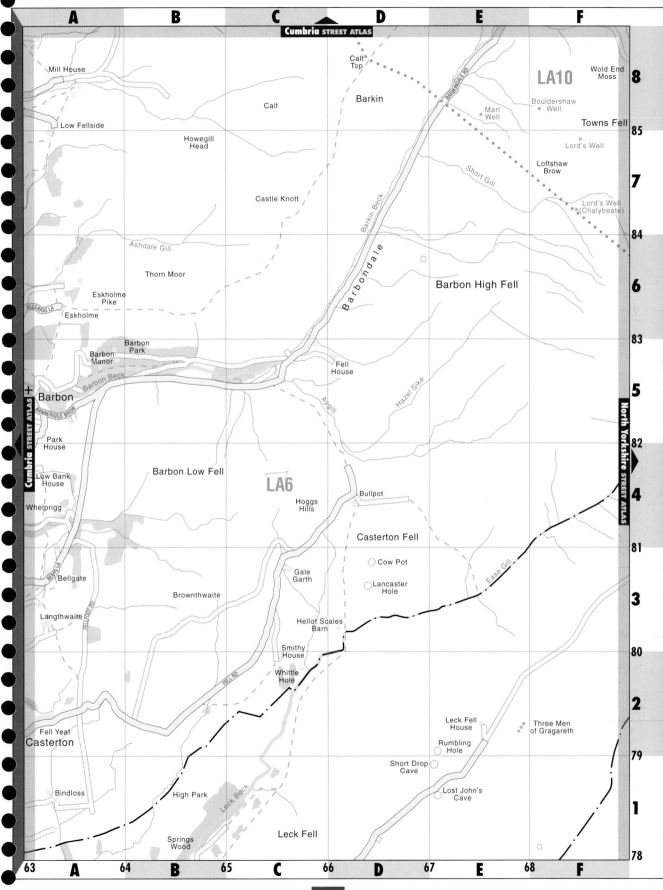

Scale: 1¾ inches to 1 mile

0   ¼   ½ mile
0   250m 500m 750m 1 km

Cumbria STREET ATLAS

LA10

Wold End Moss

Mill House

Calf Top

Barkin

Bouldershaw Well

Low Fellside

Calf

Marl Well

Towns Fell

Howegill Head

Lord's Well

Loftshaw Brow

Castle Knott

Short Gill

Lord's Well (Chalybeate)

Ashdale Gill

Barbondale

Thorn Moor

Barbon High Fell

Eskholme Pike

ELLERGG LA

Eskholme

Barbon Park

Barbon Manor

Fell House

Hazel Sike

Barbon

BANNERIGGS BROW

Park House

Aygill

Low Bank House

Barbon Low Fell

LA6

Whelprigg

Hoggs Hills

Bullpot

Casterton Fell

BEN'S LA

Bellgate

Gale Garth

Cow Pot

Lancaster Hole

Ease Gill

FELLFOOT RD

Brownthwaite

Langthwaite

FELL RD

Hellot Scales Barn

Smithy House

Three Men of Gragareth

Whittle Hole

Leck Fell House

Fell Yeat

Rumbling Hole

Casterton

Short Drop Cave

Bindloss

Lost John's Cave

High Park

Leck Beck

Springs Wood

Leck Fell

Cumbria STREET ATLAS

North Yorkshire STREET ATLAS

8
85
7
84
6
83
5
82
4
81
3
80
2
79
1
78

A   B   C   D   E   F

63   64   65   66   67   68

Index

Church Rd **6** Beckenham BR2..........**53** C6

Place name	**Location number**	**Locality, town or village**	**Postcode district**	**Page and grid square**
May be abbreviated on the map	Present when a number indicates the place's position in a crowded area of mapping	Shown when more than one place has the same name	District for the indexed place	Page number and grid reference for the standard mapping

Public and commercial buildings are highlighted in magenta   **Places of interest** are highlighted in blue with a star★

Abbreviations used in the index

Acad	**Academy**	Comm	**Common**	Gd	**Ground**	L	**Leisure**	Prom	**Promenade**
App	**Approach**	Cott	**Cottage**	Gdn	**Garden**	La	**Lane**	Rd	**Road**
Arc	**Arcade**	Cres	**Crescent**	Gn	**Green**	Liby	**Library**	Recn	**Recreation**
Ave	**Avenue**	Cswy	**Causeway**	Gr	**Grove**	Mdw	**Meadow**	Ret	**Retail**
Bglw	**Bungalow**	Ct	**Court**	H	**Hall**	Meml	**Memorial**	Sh	**Shopping**
Bldg	**Building**	Ctr	**Centre**	Ho	**House**	Mkt	**Market**	Sq	**Square**
Bsns, Bus	**Business**	Ctry	**Country**	Hospl	**Hospital**	Mus	**Museum**	St	**Street**
Bvd	**Boulevard**	Cty	**County**	HQ	**Headquarters**	Orch	**Orchard**	Sta	**Station**
Cath	**Cathedral**	Dr	**Drive**	Hts	**Heights**	Pal	**Palace**	Terr	**Terrace**
Cir	**Circus**	Dro	**Drove**	Ind	**Industrial**	Par	**Parade**	TH	**Town Hall**
Cl	**Close**	Ed	**Education**	Inst	**Institute**	Pas	**Passage**	Univ	**University**
Cnr	**Corner**	Emb	**Embankment**	Int	**International**	Pk	**Park**	Wk, Wlk	**Walk**
Coll	**College**	Est	**Estate**	Intc	**Interchange**	Pl	**Place**	Wr	**Water**
Com	**Community**	Ex	**Exhibition**	Junc	**Junction**	Prec	**Precinct**	Yd	**Yard**

Index of localities, towns and villages

A

Abbeystead 232 F1
Abbey Village 80 C2
Abraham Heights 214 D7
Accrington 104 E6
Acre 85 B6
Adelphi 117 E1
Adlington 31 B7
Ainsdale 21 B5
Ainsdale-on-Sea 20 F6
Alleytroyds 103 D6
Altham 125 E6
Anchor 81 F5
Anchorsholme 175 E1
Anderton 31 C8
Andertons Mill 41 A1
Ansdell 90 C4
Appley Bridge 19 C8
Arkholme 241 B2
Ashton-on-Ribble ...117 A1
Ashurst 18 A4
Astley Village 61 A2
Aughton Lancaster 237 E6
Aughton Maghull 6 A7
Aughton Park 15 E2
Avenham 97 A6

B

Bacup 70 E8
Bailrigg 215 A1
Balderstone 121 A5
Baldingstone 50 F1
Balladen 68 F8
Bamber Bridge 97 E1
Bank Fold 82 F5
Bank Hey 123 A2
Bank Houses 205 C7
Bank Lane 50 E7
Banks 54 F6
Banks Hill 196 A4
Bank Top 101 D3
Barber's Moor 58 D3
Barbon 243 A5
Bare 217 E7
Barley 169 B5
Barley Green 169 C5
Barnfield 104 E5
Barnoldswick Ingleton .242 D2
Barnoldswick Nelson ...196 C1
Barrow 166 D1
Barrowford 170 C4
Barrow Nook 7 F2
Barton Preston 137 B7
Barton Southport 13 F6
Bashall Eaves 188 A3
Bastwell 102 A8
Baxenden 104 E1
Bay Horse 207 C6
Beardwood 101 B7
Becconsall 73 E1
Belgrave 64 E8
Belmont 46 C4
Belthorn 82 F6
Bent Gate 68 C8
Bescar 24 A7

B (continued)

Beverley 170 E7
Bickerstaffe 7 F5
Billington 144 B3
Bilsborrow 159 A5
Birch Green 18 B2
Birch Hall 81 E4
Birkacre 43 A3
Birkdale 34 F2
Bispham 152 B5
Bispham Green 27 B7
Blackamoor 82 B8
Blackburn 101 E1
Blackleach 135 E2
Blacko 170 D7
Black Pole 136 C5
Blackpool 130 A4
Blackrod 31 D2
Blacksnape 65 E8
Blaguegate 17 B1
Bleasdale 184 A7
Blowick 35 E6
Bolton-by-Bowland 230 D4
Bolton Green 42 C8
Bolton-le-Sands 221 B5
Bolton Town End 220 F3
Bonds 181 C6
Booth Fold 86 E1
Borwick 240 B4
Bottom of Hutton 94 F3
Bowerham 215 B6
Bowgreave 181 D4
Bowker's Green 6 D5
Bracewell 231 F3
Bradley 170 E2
Brandwood 70 B8

B (continued)

Bretherton 57 E6
Bridge End 68 A7
Brierfield 148 D5
Brindle 78 F5
Brinscall 62 E7
Britannia 71 C8
Broad Clough 87 F4
Broadfield Leyland 76 E1
Broadfield Oswaldtwistle .103 F2
Broadgate 96 E6
Broadly 52 C4
Brockhall Village 143 C5
Brookfield 118 D4
Brookhouse Blackburn ...101 F6
Brookhouse Lancaster ...237 D3
Brooksbottoms 50 C3
Broughton 137 D3
Brownedge 97 D1
Brown Edge 36 A2
Brownhill 122 F2
Brownlow 10 C1
Brownside 128 F6
Brunshaw 128 D5
Bryning 92 C8
Buckshaw Village 60 F6
Bulk 218 E1
Bunker's Hill 171 B4
Burnley 128 A7
Burnley Lane 148 A1
Burnley Wood 128 A4
Burn Naze 176 B4
Burscough 25 D4
Burscough Bridge 25 D5
Burton-in-Kendal 240 C7
Burton in Lonsdale ...242 C3

B (continued)

Bury 33 A1
Butt Yeats 238 B6

C

Cabus 204 C3
Cadley 117 C4
Cadshaw 65 D1
Caldershaw 52 B2
Calder Vale 182 E8
Cantsfield 241 F3
Capernwray 240 C2
Carleton 153 A5
Carnforth 223 C2
Carr 50 B7
Carr Cross 23 D8
Carr Hall 170 B2
Carry Bridge 171 F5
Casterton 243 A2
Catforth 135 F4
Catlow 149 C5
Caton 237 C3
Caton Green 237 D3
Catterall 181 E2
Chapel House 17 E2
Chapels 82 A3
Chapeltown 48 C4
Charnock Green 42 C6
Charnock Richard 42 D4
Chatburn 190 D5
Chatterton 68 C1
Cheesden 51 D6
Cherry Tree 100 E1

Chesham 33 A5
Chipping 185 D3
Chorley 43 C6
Chorley Moor 43 D6
Church 103 E7
Churchtown Garstang 181 A2
Church Town Southport 54 A1
Claughton Catterall 182 D1
Claughton Lancaster 237 E5
Clawthorpe 240 E8
Clayton Brook 78 A5
Clayton Green 78 A3
Clayton-Le-Dale 122 C7
Clayton-le-Moors 124 D2
Clayton-le-Woods 77 D2
Cleveleys 175 C3
Cliffe 124 C6
Clifton 115 D1
Clitheroe 166 B8
Cloughfold 86 D2
Clow Bridge 106 C5
Coates 196 D3
Cob Wall 102 A7
Cockden 149 B2
Cocker Bar 75 F1
Cockerham 206 C5
Cold Row 177 C5
Colne 171 C6
Colne Edge 171 C7
Common Edge 110 F6
Conder Green 210 C5
Constable Lee 86 B4
Copp 156 A3
Coppull 42 E2
Coppull Moor 29 D6
Copster Green 122 D8
Corner Row 133 C2
Cornholme 109 B1
Cote Holme 103 C6
Cottam 116 D5
Cotton Tree 172 B4
Coupe Green 98 E4
Cowan Bridge 242 A7
Cow Ark 187 C8
Cowling 43 F6
Cowpe 69 F6
Crag Bank 221 C8
Cranberry Fold 65 D5
Crawford 9 D2
Crawshawbooth 86 A8
Croft 196 B2
Crossens 54 C4
Crossgill 237 E1
Croston 58 B2
Cuddy Hill 136 B7
Cuerden Green 77 C6
Cumeragh Village 138 F6

D

Daisyfield 102 A6
Daisy Hill 60 D1
Dalton Burton-in-Kendal 240 D7
Dalton Skelmersdale 18 C3
Dam Side 201 D6
Dangerous Corner 28 C2
Darn Hill 33 F2
Darwen 81 E1
Dean 87 C8
Deepdale 118 A2
Digmoor 9 D6
Dill Hall 104 D4
Doals 87 F7
Docker 241 D4
Dolphinholme 226 A8
Dowbridge 114 D4
Downham 191 B5
Downholland Cross 14 A2
Drink House 58 A1
Drummersdale 24 C7
Duncombe 158 F3
Dunnockshaw 106 B4
Dunnyshop 103 E3
Dunsop Bridge 228 C5

E

Eagland Hill 179 C8
Earby 197 A2
Earcroft 81 E6
Earnshaw Bridge 76 B3
Easington 229 B5
East Gillibrands 9 A8
East Pimbo 9 E5
Eccleston 41 C7
Edenfield 68 D3
Edge End 124 B6
Edgeside 86 F2
Edgworth 48 D6
Egerton 47 E2
Ellel 211 B5
Elmers Green 18 D2

Elston 120 A6
Elswick 156 A1
Elswick Leys 134 A8
Enfield 125 A2
Entwistle 48 B7
Esprick 133 D5
Euxton 60 D3
Ewood 81 D8
Ewood Bridge 68 C6

F

Facit 71 D2
Fairfield 33 D3
Fairhaven 90 A3
Fairview 44 A1
Falinge Fold 52 D1
Far Arnside 224 A5
Far Banks 55 C8
Farington Bamber Bridge 76 F6
Farington Leyland 77 B3
Farleton 238 A6
Far Moor 10 D4
Farringdon Park 118 F1
Fence 147 E7
Feniscliffe 101 A2
Feniscowles 80 D8
Fern Gore 104 A3
Fern Grove 33 C4
Fiddler's Ferry 54 D6
Fisher's Row 201 E5
Fishwick 97 C8
Flax Moss 68 A8
Fleetwood 198 E5
Fletcher Bank 50 D6
Ford Green 203 F2
Forest Becks 230 D6
Forest Holme 87 A7
Formby 11 E4
Forton 207 B3
Foulridge 194 D1
Four Lane Ends 101 D8
Foxhill Bank 103 D5
Freckleton 93 C7
Freehold 215 B8
Free Town 33 A4
Frenchwood 97 B6
Freshfield 11 E5
Fulledge 128 B5
Fulwood 117 D5
Fulwood Row 118 E6

G

Galgate 211 B3
Garstang 181 C7
Gisburn 231 C4
Glasson 209 F5
Glen Top 70 A8
Glovers Bridge 26 A3
Golden Hill 77 C4
Golgotha 215 B6
Goodshaw 85 F8
Goodshaw Chapel 106 B1
Goodshaw Fold 105 F2
Goose Green 74 F2
Goosnargh 138 C6
Granville Park 6 B8
Great Altcar 12 E1
Great Eccleston 156 C4
Great Harwood 124 D4
Great Knowley 61 E3
Great Marton 130 F3
Great Marton Moss 111 B4
Great Marton Moss Side
....111 B2
Great Mitton 165 F3
Great Plumpton 112 E2
Greave 88 B3
Green Bank 102 B6
Greenfield 171 A4
Greenhalgh 133 C5
Green Haworth 104 B1
Green Lane 81 A8
Greenmount 49 E1
Gregson Lane 98 E2
Griffin 101 C3
Grimeford Village 31 D6
Grimsargh 139 D1
Grimshaw Green 27 B5
Grimshaw Park 101 F2
Grindleton 190 B7
Guide 82 D8

H

Habergham 126 F7
Haggate 149 A3
Hale Nook 178 A5
Hall Carr 86 A1

Hall Cross 114 A1
Hall Green Preston 74 C6
Hall Green Skelmersdale 10 A7
Halsall 23 C1
Halton 219 D7
Halton Green 219 F7
Hambleton 177 C1
Hambleton Moss Side 177 E2
Hammerton Mere 235 E1
Hampson Green 211 C1
Hapton 126 B4
Hardhorn 131 E8
Hardhorn Village 131 E7
Hareholme 86 D1
Harle Syke 148 F3
Harrop Fold 229 F4
Hartwood 61 C3
Harwood Bar 124 F6
Haskayne 13 F4
Haslingden 85 B4
Haverbreaks 214 E5
Hawes Side 130 F1
Hawkshaw Blackburn 81 D3
Hawkshaw Ramsbottom 49 C2
Hazelhurst 50 B4
Heap Bridge 33 C1
Heapey 62 A6
Heasandford 128 C8
Heath Charnock 43 E2
Heaton 213 E5
Heaton's Bridge 24 D4
Height End 85 D3
Helmcroft 85 B1
Helmshore 68 B7
Hesketh Bank 73 D4
Hesketh Lane 162 D8
Hesketh Moss 73 C1
Heskin Green 41 D3
Hest Bank 220 F1
Hey Head 87 A1
Hey Houses 90 D7
Heysham 212 D7
Heywood 33 F2
Higham 146 E5
High Bentham 239 E8
High Cross 131 C8
Higher Audley 102 A4
Higher Bartle 116 E7
Higher Baxenden 104 F2
Higher Boarsgreave 70 A6
Higher Broad Clough 87 F5
Higher Broadhalgh 80 E7
Higher Change 88 B4
Higher Cloughfold 86 D2
Higher Copthurst 61 E7
Higher Croft 101 F1
Higher End 10 D3
Higherford 170 E5
Higher Heysham 212 F6
Higher Penwortham 96 C5
Higher Stanhill 103 B4
Higher Summerseat 50 B1
Higher Walton 98 B4
Higher Wheelton 79 B1
Highfurlong 153 A2
High Moor 27 C4
High Park 36 A8
Hightown 2 F3
Hill Dale 27 D5
Hillock Vale 104 E8
Hill Top 172 B2
Hoddlesden 82 F1
Hoghton 99 B2
Holcombe 50 A6
Holcombe Brook 50 B2
Holden 230 C4
Holden Vale 85 A5
Hole House 102 C6
Holland Slack 97 E2
Hollin Bank 101 D2
Hollin Hall 172 C1
Hollins 81 F4
Hollins Grove 81 F3
Hollins Lane 207 D2
Holme Chapel 108 A6
Holme Mills 240 A8
Holmes 56 D3
Holme Slack 118 C3
Holmeswood 38 C6
Holm Nook 154 E7
Holt Green 6 A7
Hoohill 130 D8
Hornby 238 B7
Horton 231 E5
Horwich 32 D4
Hoscar 26 D4
Howick Cross 96 A5
Hud Hey 85 A6
Hugh Mill 69 F7
Huncoat 125 E2
Hundred End 72 F1
Hunger Hill 28 F4
Hurlston 24 C3
Hurlston Green 24 B3

Hurst Green 164 F1
Hurstwood 129 C4
Hutch Bank 84 F2
Huttock Top 86 E2
Hutton 95 D2

I

Ince Blundell 3 E4
Ingleton 242 F3
Inglewhite 160 B4
Ingol 117 A4
Inskip 135 D8
Intack 102 D5
Ireby 242 C6
Irwell Vale 68 B5

J

Jack Green 78 B2
Jericho 33 F4
Johnson's Hillock 61 E6

K

Kelbrook 195 A6
Kellamergh 92 C7
Kingsfold 96 D2
Kirkby 1 A3
Kirkham 114 A5
Knott End-on-Sea 199 C4
Knowle Green 163 C1
Knowley 61 E2
Knuzden Brook 102 F4

L

Lady Green 3 D4
Lammack 101 C8
Lancaster 214 C8
Lane Bottom 149 B3
Lane Ends 230 A5
Lane Head 87 C4
Lane Heads 156 D3
Laneshaw Bridge 172 E6
Laneside 104 C8
Lane Side 85 B2
Langho 143 D1
Larches 116 F1
Larkholme 198 D1
Laund 85 F4
Layton 130 F2
Lea 116 D1
Lea Town 115 F3
Leck 242 B7
Lee 232 F2
Lees 187 B6
Lenches 171 D3
Lewth 136 A4
Leyland 76 F2
Lightfoot Green 117 B8
Limbrick 44 A6
Little Altcar 12 A1
Little Bispham 152 C8
Little Carleton 152 F1
Little Eccleston 156 A6
Little Harwood 102 B8
Little Hoole Moss Houses
....75 B4
Little Knowley 61 F3
Little Marsden 148 C7
Little Marton 131 D1
Little Marton Moss Side
....131 A1
Little Moor End 103 C4
Little Plumpton 112 D5
Little Poulton 153 F4
Little Scotland 31 B2
Little Singleton 154 C4
Little Thornton 153 E7
Livesey Fold 81 F2
Lomeshaye 148 B8
Longholme 86 A2
Long Ing 196 C2
Longridge 140 A8
Longshaw Blackburn 101 C1
Longshaw Skelmersdale 10 E1
Longshoot 85 C3
Longton 75 A8
Lostock Hall 77 A7
Love Clough 106 A3
Lower Audley 101 E4
Lower Ballam 112 A3
Lower Bartle 116 D8
Lower Baxenden 104 F1
Lower Boarsgreave 70 A6
Lower Cloughfold 86 C2

Lower Copthurst 61 E7
Lower Darwen 81 F7
Lower Fold Accrington 104 C6
Lower Fold Great Harwood
....124 C6
Lower Fold Rochdale 52 C5
Lowerford 170 E3
Lower Green Bank 232 B3
Lower Healey 52 E4
Lower Heysham 212 E8
Lowerhouse 126 F6
Lower House 59 D8
Lower Penwortham 96 E5
Lower Summerseat 50 D2
Lower Thurnham 210 B2
Lower Westhouse 242 D4
Lowgill 239 C3
Low Moor 166 C8
Lucas Green 61 C6
Lumb Haslingden 68 B4
Lumb Rawtenstall 86 F6
Lydiate 5 D4
Lytham 91 B3
Lytham St Anne's 90 B5

M

Maghull 5 B1
Marsden Height 148 E5
Marsh 214 C8
Marsh House Blackburn 82 C2
Marsh Houses Lancaster 206 B4
Marshside 53 E4
Masongill 242 D6
Maudlands 117 D1
Mawdesley 40 C2
Medlar 133 F4
Melling 241 E1
Mellor 121 F2
Mellor Brook 121 C3
Mere Brow 55 E2
Mereclough 129 A1
Mereside 131 B1
Middleforth Green 96 E3
Middle Healey 52 D4
Middleton 213 B2
Midge Hall 76 A3
Mill Dam 239 F6
Miller Fold 104 B3
Millgate 71 D4
Millhead 223 D4
Mill Hill 101 B1
Milnshaw 104 A7
Moor End 177 C6
Moorgate 101 C1
Moorlands 215 B7
Moor Side Kirkham 134 C1
Moor Side Preston 136 C4
Morecambe 216 E5
Moss Bridge 81 E5
Moss Edge Fisher's Row 202 C7
Moss Edge Hambleton 179 A3
Moss Side Blackpool 112 E1
Moss Side Fisher's Row 201 F5
Moss Side Leyland 76 B1
Moss Side Maghull 6 A1
Mossy Lea 28 F6
Much Hoole 74 D3
Much Hoole Moss Houses
....75 A2
Much Hoole Town 74 E1
Myerscough 158 C4
Myerscough Smithy 120 D3
Mythop 132 A3

N

Nab's Head 99 E7
Nangreaves 50 F2
Nappa 231 E8
Nateby 180 D6
Nelson 148 E8
Nether Burrow 241 E6
Nether Kellet 221 F5
Newbridge 170 C2
Newburgh 27 A2
Newby 192 B8
Newchurch 86 F1
Newchurch in Pendle 169 C3
Newgate 10 A6
New Gate 76 C8
New Hall Hey 85 F1
Newlands 215 C5
New Lane 25 B6
New Longton 75 E8
Newsham 137 A5
Newsholme 231 D6
Newton Blackpool 131 C6
Newton Kirkby Lonsdale 241 C5
Newton Lancaster 218 E2
Newton Slaidburn 229 A5
Newton-with-Scales 114 F2

Newtown Leyland 59 A2
New Town Longridge 140 A6
Nog Tow 116 F7
Nook 181 B3
Nooklands 117 D4
Norbreck 152 B6
Norcross 153 A7
Norden 124 A2
Normoss 131 B7
North End 3 B6
North Hag 85 A4
North Holme 195 A8
North Shore 130 A8
Northwood 1 A3
Nova Scotia 101 E3
Nun Hills 70 C7
Nuttall 50 C4
Nuttall Lane 50 B5
Nutter's Platt 96 B2

O

Oakenclough 226 C2
Oakenhead Wood 85 E3
Oakenshaw 124 E3
Old Birtle 33 C4
Old Langho 143 C4
Ollerton Fold 79 D5
Ormskirk 15 C6
Orrell 10 E7
Orrell Post 10 E7
Ortner 232 C1
Osbaldeston 121 D4
Osbaldeston Green 121 C6
Oswaldtwistle 103 B3
Out Rawcliffe 178 C1
Over Burrow 241 E7
Over Kellet 237 A8
Overton 209 D8
Overtown Kirkby Lonsdale .241 F7
Over Town Burnley 108 A8

P

Padiham 126 B7
Parbold 27 D2
Park Place 101 F3
Passmonds 52 B1
Paythorne 231 C6
Peel 111 F4
Peel Bank 103 E7
Peel Brow 50 C7
Peel Hill 111 E7
Pendleton 167 B4
Pennylands 17 E1
Penwortham 96 C5
Penwortham Lane 96 F2
Pickup Bank 83 A2
Piercy 86 E5
Pike Hill 128 E5
Pilling 201 C6
Pilling Lane 200 B6
Pimhole 33 A1
Pincock 42 C8
Pinfold 23 F4
Pippin Street 78 E5
Pleasington 100 C1
Pleckgate 122 D1
Pool Hey 36 B3
Portsmouth 108 F1
Pot House 82 C3
Potters Brook 207 B5
Poulton-le-Fylde 153 E2
Preesall 200 A3
Preesall Park 200 C4
Preston 96 C8
Prettywood 33 D2
Priest Hutton 240 C4
Primet Bridge 171 C3
Primrose 166 D6

Pudsey 109 B2

Q

Queen's Park 102 B4
Queenstown 130 D7
Quernmore 232 A6

R

Radford 65 A8
Rainford Junction 8 F2
Rainhill 196 D3
Rake Foot 86 A7
Rake Head 70 A7
Ramsbottom 50 C5
Rann 82 E6
Rathmell 236 F6
Ratten Row 156 B8
Raven Shore 68 A6
Rawtenstall 86 B1
Read 145 D2
Red Bank 43 E5
Red Scar 119 B5
Reedley 148 B4
Reeds Holme 85 F5
Revidge 101 C7
Revoe 130 C3
Ribbleton 118 E2
Ribby 113 D4
Ribchester 141 D3
Ridge 218 F2
Riley Green 79 E8
Rimington 191 F8
Ring o'Bells 26 B2
Rishton 124 C2
Rising Bridge 85 A8
Rivington 44 F2
Roach Bridge 98 F6
Robin Hood 28 C4
Roby Mill 19 B3
Rochdale 52 C2
Rockcliffe 88 A2
Roe Lee 122 E1
Roseacre 134 D6
Rose Grove 127 B6
Rosehill 65 C7
Rose Hill 127 F3
Rossall Beach 175 D5
Roughlee 170 B5
Rowlands 50 D2
Royal Oak 6 F4
Rufford 39 C3
Runshaw Moor 59 E4
Rush Bed 86 A6
Ryelands 218 C2

S

Sabden 145 F8
St Annes 89 D6
St Michael's on Wyre .157 C7
Salesbury 122 D6
Saltcotes 91 D5
Salterforth 194 D7
Salwick 115 E3
Samlesbury 119 E1
Samlesbury Bottoms 99 D6
Sandham's Green 111 C8
Sand Side 205 D2
Sandylands 216 B2
Sawley 230 C1
Scaitcliffe 104 B5
Scale Hall 218 A2
Scarisbrick 23 E7
Scarth Hill 16 C2
School Lane 97 F2
Scorton 204 E6

Scotforth 215 A3
Scout 86 E2
Scronkey 201 E3
Seven Stars 59 D8
Shadsworth 102 D3
Sharneyford 88 D5
Sharoe Green 117 E7
Shawclough 52 C3
Shawfield 52 A2
Shaworth 71 D6
Shaw Green 59 D2
Sherfin 85 B7
Sherwood 118 A6
Shevington 19 F5
Shevington Moor 29 A2
Shevington Vale 19 E7
Shirdley Hill 23 A6
Shireshead 207 E3
Shore 109 C2
Shorey Bank 82 A2
Shuttleworth 50 E8
Silverdale 224 C3
Simonstone 145 E1
Singleton 154 E1
Skelmersdale 18 A1
Skerton 218 C4
Skippool 153 F3
Skitham 179 B4
Slaidburn 229 C7
Slyne 218 D8
Smallwood Hey 201 B5
Smith Green 210 C3
Snape Green 36 E1
Sollom 57 B2
Sough 195 A8
Sough 65 B7
Southfield 149 B6
Southport 35 C3
South Shore 110 C8
Southward Bottom 108 A8
Sower Carr 177 D4
Spen Brook 169 D2
Spotland Fold 52 C1
Spring Hill 103 F5
Spring Side 86 B3
Spring Vale Darwen 65 C7
Spring Vale Haslingden ..85 A2
Squires Gate 110 B5
Stacksteads 70 B8
Staghills 86 D1
Staining 131 E5
Stake Pool 201 E4
Stake Pool 202 A5
Stalmine 177 C7
Stalmine Moss Side ...177 E7
Stanah 176 E2
Standish 29 F2
Stanhill 103 B4
Stanley 17 E3
Stanley Gate 7 E7
Stanworth 80 C4
Staynall 177 A4
Stodday 214 C2
Stoneyholme 127 F8
Stopper Lane 192 A8
Street 226 A6
Strongstry 68 C2
Stubbins 68 B1
Stydd 141 E4
Summerseat 50 C2
Sunderland 209 B4
Sunny Bower 123 B1
Swillbrook 136 B2
Swiss Clough 86 F1
Syke 52 F4
Syke Side 85 B1

T

Tagg Wood 50 A5
Tanhouse 9 D8
Tanners 50 B7

Tanterton 117 A6
Tardy Gate 77 B8
Tarleton 57 A7
Tarleton Moss 56 C7
Tarlscough 38 D1
Tarnbrook 233 B2
Tatham 238 D8
Tawd Bridge 9 B7
Tawd Valley Park 18 A2
Tewitfield 240 A4
The Greaves 214 F6
The Straits 76 D1
The Wrangling 101 D3
Thistleton 133 C8
Thorney Holme 169 E5
Thornton 176 C3
Thornton-in-Craven ...197 A6
Thornton in Lonsdale .242 F4
Thorpe Green 78 E4
Tockholes 81 A2
Tonacliffe 52 C6
Tong End 71 C2
Tontine 10 D5
Top of Ramsgreave ...122 C3
Top o' th' Lane 78 F3
Topping Fold 33 D3
Torrisholme 218 A4
Tosside 236 C2
Town Bent 103 D2
Town End 155 C8
Town Green 6 D7
Town Head 196 A1
Townsend Fold 68 E8
Town's Moor 101 E3
Trawden 172 C2
Treales 114 D6
Trough Gate 71 D8
Trunnah 176 B3
Tunstall 241 E4
Turner Green 120 C2
Turpin Green 77 B1
Turton Bottoms 48 D4
Twiston 192 A4

U

Up Holland 10 C7
Upper Thurnham 210 B2

V

Vale 109 C1

W

Waddington 189 C4
Wade Hall 59 E7
Walker Fold 164 C8
Walker's Hill 111 A7
Walk Mill 107 F8
Wallbank 52 B7
Walmer Bridge 74 F5
Walton-le-Dale 97 D4
Walton Summit 78 B8
Wapping 196 A2
Warbreck 152 D7
Warton Carnforth 223 D5
Warton Freckleton 92 D6
Warton Bank 92 C5
Water 87 A8
Waterbarn 70 A8
Waterfall 101 C2
Waterfoot 69 E8
Waterloo 81 B8
Waterside Colne 171 E4
Waterside Darwen 82 E3
Waterslack 224 E6
Waverledge 124 A4

Weeton 132 F2
Weeton Camp 132 D5
Weir 88 A7
Weld Bank 43 C5
Well Bank 85 A3
Wennington 241 E1
Wensley Fold 101 C4
Wesham 114 A6
West Bradford 189 F5
Westby 112 E4
West End Morecombe ..217 B3
West End Oswaldtwistle .103 C5
West Gillibrands 8 E8
Westhead 16 D4
Westhouse 242 E5
West Pimbo 9 D4
Whalley 144 B5
Whalley Banks 144 D3
Whalleys 18 A5
Wharles 134 F4
Wheatley Lane 169 F1
Wheelton 62 A7
Whin Lane End 155 A8
Whinny Heights 102 A2
Whitebirk 102 C6
Whitechapel 160 D7
Whitefield 148 C8
Whitehall 65 B5
Whiteholme 152 E7
White Lund 217 E2
White Stake 76 B8
Whitewell 228 D2
Whitewell Bottom 86 F5
Whittington 241 D7
Whittlefield 127 D7
Whittle-le-Woods 61 C7
Whittlestone Head 65 F4
Whitworth 71 D1
Wigglesworth 236 F4
Willacy Lane End 135 E3
Wilpshire 122 E5
Winewall 172 C4
Winmarleigh 203 E4
Wiswell 144 F7
Within Grove 125 E1
Withnell 80 B1
Withnell Fold 79 C3
Witton 101 B3
Woodgate Hill 33 D4
Woodhey 50 B3
Woodnook 104 B4
Woodplumpton 136 E2
Wood Road 50 C1
Woodsfold 135 E6
Wood Top 85 E1
Woodvale 21 B2
Worsthorne 129 B5
Worston 190 D2
Wray 238 D6
Wrayton 241 E3
Wrea Green 113 B3
Wrightington 28 B5
Wrightington Bar 28 F7
Wycoller 173 A3
Wymott 58 F6

Y

Yealand Conyers 225 F1
Yealand Redmayne ...225 E4
Yealand Storrs 225 C5
York 123 D8

A

A K Bsns Pk PR9 . . . . .36 A6
Aalborg Pl LA1 . . . . .214 F7
Abbey Cl Formby L37 . . . . . .12 B2
 Skelmersdale WN8 . . . . .10 C7
Abbey Cres BB3 . . . . .65 C8
Abbey Dale
 Appley Bridge WN6 . . . . .19 D7
 Burscough L40 . . . . .25 F3
Abbey Dr WN5 . . . . .10 C6
Abbey Farm BB7 . . . . .144 B6
Abbey Farm Cvn Pk L40 . .16 C8
Abbey Fields BB7 . . . . . . .144 C5
Abbey Fold L40 . . . . .25 D5
Abbey Gdns PR8 . . . . .35 A4
Abbey La L40 . . . . .25 C1
Abbey Lane Ind Est L40 . . .25 C1
Abbey Mews BB7 . . . . .144 C5
Abbey Pl BB3 . . . . .82 C1
Abbey Rd Blackpool FY4 . .110 D5
 Whalley BB7 . . . . .144 C5
Abbey St Accrington BB5 . .104 C6
 Accrington,Scaitcliffe BB5 . .104 C5
 Bacup OL13 . . . . .87 F4
 Preston PR2 . . . . .96 D8
Abbey Terr Barrow BB7 . . .166 D1
 Billington BB7 . . . . .144 A3
Abbey View Whalley BB7 . .144 C4
 Withnell PR6 . . . . .80 A1
Abbey Village Prim Sch
 PR6 . . . . .80 C1
Abbey Wlk PR1 . . . . .96 D3
Abbeydale LA3 . . . . .217 B2
Abbeyfield 3 BB11 . . . . . .128 B4
Abbeyfield Cl LA1 . . . . . . .215 A3
Abbeyfield Ho
 Barnoldswick BB18 . . . . . . .196 A3
 10 Burnley BB11 . . . . .127 E5
Abbeystead WN8 . . . . .9 C7
Abbeystead Dr LA1 . . . . . .215 A3
Abbeystead Ho 8 LA1 . .215 A3
Abbeystead La LA2 . . . . . . .232 E2
Abbeystead Rd LA2 . . . . . .232 C1
Abbeyville FY4 . . . . .110 C6
Abbeywood WN8 . . . . .9 C6
Abbot Mdw PR1 . . . . .96 D4
Abbot Wlk BB7 . . . . .167 A8
Abbots Cl Formby L37 . . . . .12 A1
 Kirkham PR4 . . . . .114 C4
 Rawtenstall BB4 . . . . .86 A4
Abbots Croft BB7 . . . . . . .144 C5
Abbots Ho 21 LA1 . . . . . .214 F8
Abbots Row FY8 . . . . .90 D6
Abbots Way Formby L37 . . . .9 A4
 Lancaster LA1 . . . . .214 C8
Abbotsford L39 . . . . .15 F5
Abbotsford Ave BB2 . . . . . .101 D1
Abbotsford Rd FY3 . . . . . . .131 A3
Abbotsway PR1 . . . . .96 C6
Abbott Brow BB2 . . . . .121 E3
Abbott Clough Ave BB1 .102 E4
Abbott Clough Cl BB1 . . . .102 E4
Abbott Croft PR2 . . . . .117 A7
Abbott St 17 BL6 . . . . .32 B4
Abbotts Cl PR5 . . . . .97 F3
Abbotts Wlk FY7 . . . . .199 A5
Abel St BB10 . . . . .128 A8
Abercorn Pl FY4 . . . . .110 B5
Abercrombie Rd FY7 . . . . . .198 F7
Abercrombie Rd FY7 . . . . . .198 F7
Aberdare Cl BB1 . . . . .101 E7
Aberdeen Dr PR2 . . . . .117 B1
Aberdeen Gdns OL12 . . . . .52 D4
Aberdeen Rd LA1 . . . . .215 A7
Abernethy St BL6 . . . . .32 D2
Abingdon Dr PR2 . . . . .117 B1
Abingdon Gr LA3 . . . . .213 A4
Abingdon Rd BB12 . . . . . . .126 D7
Abingdon St FY1 . . . . .130 B5
Abinger St BB10 . . . . .148 C1
Abington Dr PR9 . . . . .55 A5
Abner Row BB8 . . . . .194 D1
Abraham Altham Ct
 BB10 . . . . .148 F3
Abraham St
 Accrington BB5 . . . . .104 B5
 Blackburn BB2 . . . . .101 E2
 13 Horwich BL6 . . . . .32 B4
Abrams Fold PR9 . . . . .54 F5
Abrams Gn PR9 . . . . .54 F5
Acacia Cl 4 FY5 . . . . .176 D1
Acacia Rd PR2 . . . . .118 E2
Acacia Wlk 4 BB1 . . . . . .102 B5
Accrington & Rossendale
 Coll BB5 . . . . .104 D5
Accrington & Rossendale
 Coll Rawtenstall Campus
 BB4 . . . . .85 F2
Accrington Huncoat Prim
 Sch BB5 . . . . .125 F2
Accrington Rd
 Blackburn BB1 . . . . .102 C4
 Burnley BB11 . . . . .127 C5
 Hapton BB11 . . . . .126 E3
 Whalley BB6,BB2 . . . . .144 E4
Accrington Sta BB5 . . . . . .104 B6
Accrington Victoria Hospl
 BB5 . . . . .104 B7
Acer Gr PR2 . . . . .118 F3
Ackhurst Bsns Pk & Ind Est
 PR7 . . . . .42 F8
Ackhurst La WN5 . . . . .9 D5
Ackhurst Rd PR7 . . . . .42 F8
Ackroyd St 10 OL14 . . . . .109 B1
Acorn Appartments
 FY2 . . . . .152 C6

Acorn Ave BB5 . . . . .103 F3
Acorn Bank PR3 . . . . .181 C8
Acorn Bsns Ctr L33 . . . . . . .1 B1
Acorn Cl Kingsfold PR1 . . . .96 B2
 Lancaster LA1 . . . . .214 F4
 Leyland PR25 . . . . .60 A8
Acorn Gdn LA3 . . . . .217 C2
Acorn Mdw LA5 . . . . .221 A4
Acorn Mews FY4 . . . . .131 D1
Acorn St Bacup OL13 . . . . .87 F2
 Blackburn BB1 . . . . .102 B4
Acorn Venture Urban Farm★
 L33 . . . . .1 D2
Acornfield Rd L33 . . . . .1 D2
Acorns The L39 . . . . .15 C3
Acre Ave BB5 . . . . .103 F3
Acre Cl BL0 . . . . .68 D3
Acre Ct 11 LA1 . . . . .218 D2
Acre Gate FY4 . . . . .110 E7
 Southport PR8 . . . . .34 F3
Acre Gr Much Hoole PR4 . . .74 F1
Acre Mill Rd OL13 . . . . .70 D8
Acre Moss La LA4 . . . . . . .217 A4
Acre St Brierfield BB10 . . . .149 A3
 Burnley BB10 . . . . .148 B1
 Whitworth OL12 . . . . .71 D1
Acre View OL13 . . . . .70 D7
Acrefield Blackburn BB2 . . .101 A7
 Clayton Brook PR5 . . . . .78 C5
 Newburgh WN8 . . . . .27 A1
 Padiham BB12 . . . . .146 C1
Acregate WN8 . . . . .9 C7
Acregate La PR1 . . . . .118 D1
Acremount BB12 . . . . .145 D2
Acres La Great Altcar L37 . . .3 F8
 Maghull L31,L39 . . . . .4 E7
 Preesall FY6 . . . . .200 A3
Acres The BB6 . . . . .144 E8
Acresbrook Rd BB12 . . . . . .146 F6
Acresfield Adlington PR7 . . .30 F6
 Colne BB8 . . . . .172 A5
Acresfield Cl BL6 . . . . .31 C3
Acreswood Cl PR7 . . . . .29 E8
Active Way BB11 . . . . .128 A6
Acton Rd LA1 . . . . .130 E1
Ada St Blackburn BB2 . . . . .101 C5
 Burnley BB10 . . . . .148 B1
 Nelson BB9 . . . . .148 E6
 Ramsbottom BL0 . . . . .50 B5
Adamson St
 Burnley BB12 . . . . .127 C6
 Padiham BB12 . . . . .146 C1
Addenbrooke Cl LA1 . . .214 E4
Addington Rd LA2,LA6 . . . .237 B7
Addington St BB1 . . . . .102 A4
Addison Cres FY3 . . . . .130 D6
Addison Ct FY6 . . . . .199 D5
Addison Rd FY7 . . . . .199 A3
Addison St
 Accrington BB5 . . . . .104 C7
 Blackburn BB1 . . . . .101 C5
Addle St LA1 . . . . .215 A4
Adelaide Ave FY5 . . . . .153 C8
Adelaide Ct 5 FY1 . . . . . .130 C5
Adelaide La BB5 . . . . .104 C5
Adelaide St
 Accrington BB5 . . . . .104 C5
 Adlington PR6 . . . . .31 A8
 Blackpool FY1 . . . . .130 B5
 8 Burnley BB11 . . . . .127 D6
 7 Clayton-le-M BB5 . . . . . .125 A1
 Fleetwood FY7 . . . . .199 B5
 Preston PR1 . . . . .97 B8
 2 Ramsbottom BL0 . . . . . . .50 A4
 Rawtenstall BB4 . . . . .86 A7
Adelaide St W FY1 . . . . . .130 B4
Adelaide Terr BB2 . . . . .101 C5
Adelphi Ho 1 PR1 . . . . . . .117 E1
Adelphi Pl 2 PR1 . . . . . . .96 F8
Adelphi St
 6 Blackpool FY1 . . . . .130 B5
 Burnley BB11 . . . . .128 A4
 Lancaster LA1 . . . . .215 A6
 Preston PR1 . . . . .117 E1
 Standish WN6 . . . . .29 E2
Adlington Ave FY6 . . . . . . .153 B3
Adlington Prim Sch PR7 . .30 F7
Adlington South Bsns Village
 PR6 . . . . .31 A7
Adlington St BB11 . . . . . . .128 A6
Adlington Sta PR6 . . . . .31 A7
Admiral Cl FY8 . . . . .110 E1
Admiral St BB10 . . . . .128 B5
Admiral Way PR2 . . . . .95 D7
Admirals Sound FY5 . . .175 C2
Admiralty Cl L40 . . . . .25 C2
Adrian St FY1 . . . . .130 B1
Adstone Ave FY3 . . . . .130 F7
Agate St BB1 . . . . .122 F1
Ager St OL13 . . . . .70 C8
Agglebys Rd FY6 . . . . .176 F8
Agnes Ing La LA2 . . . . .238 D7
Agnes St Blackburn BB2 . . .101 C3
 12 Preston PR1 . . . . .97 A8
Agnew Rd FY7 . . . . .198 F4
Agnew St FY8 . . . . .91 A3
Aiken Ct PR4 . . . . .114 A5
Aikengill Rd LA2 . . . . .239 D4
Ailsa Ave FY4 . . . . .130 F2
Ailsa Cl PR3 . . . . .137 B8
Ailsa Rd BB1 . . . . .102 D3
Ailsa Wlk LA3 . . . . .212 F2
Aindow Ct PR8 . . . . .34 E3
Ainley St 10 FY1 . . . . .130 C6
Ainscough Brook Ho 1
 PR2 . . . . .118 F3
Ainscough Bsns Pk WN6 . .28 F6

Ainsdale & Birkdale Hills
 Nature Reserve★ PR8 . .21 B7
Ainsdale Ave
 Blackpool FY2 . . . . .152 E5
 Brierfield BB10 . . . . .148 C5
 Edgworth BL7 . . . . .48 E6
 Fleetwood FY7 . . . . .175 D7
 Thornton FY5 . . . . .176 D1
Ainsdale Cl LA1 . . . . .218 B3
 Darwen BB3 . . . . .65 B5
 Preston PR2 . . . . .116 A2
 Whitworth OL12 . . . . .52 D7
Ainsdale High Sch PR8 . . .21 C6
Ainsdale Sand Dunes
 National Nature Reserve★
 PR8 . . . . .20 E3
Ainsdale St John's CE Prim
 Sch PR8 . . . . .21 D4
Ainsdale Sta PR8 . . . . .21 C5
Ainse Rd BL6 . . . . .31 B3
Ainslie Cl BB6 . . . . .124 B5
Ainslie Rd PR2 . . . . .117 E3
Ainslie St 3 BB12 . . . . . . .127 C6
Ainspool La PR3 . . . . .181 A3
Ainsworth Ave PR8 . . . . . . .35 F4
Ainsworth Fold PR4 . . . . . .113 B3
Ainsworth Mall 3 BB1 . . .101 C5
Ainsworth St BB1 . . . . .101 C5
Aintree Cres PR8 . . . . .35 F4
Aintree Dr BB3 . . . . .82 A7
Aintree Rd Blackpool FY4 . .130 D1
 Thornton FY5 . . . . .153 B8
Air Hill Terr 8 OL12 . . . . . .52 C1
Airdrie Cres BB11 . . . . .127 D4
Airdrie Pl FY2 . . . . .152 E6
Aire Cl LA3 . . . . .217 F3
Airedale LA2 . . . . .211 B4
Airedale Ave FY3 . . . . .130 E3
Airedale Ct FY6 . . . . .153 C4
Airegate L31 . . . . .5 B2
Airey Ho PR3 . . . . .163 D1
Airey St BB5 . . . . .104 D3
Airton Garth BB9 . . . . .170 C3
Aisled Barn Visitor Ctr★
 BB8 . . . . .173 A3
Aitken Cl BL0 . . . . .50 B5
Aitken St Accrington BB5 . .104 C7
 Haslingden BL0 . . . . .68 C5
Ajax St 3 BL0 . . . . .50 B5
Akeman Ct LA3 . . . . .217 B3
Alamein Rd LA5 . . . . .223 E1
Alan Gr LA3 . . . . .212 F6
Alan Haigh Ct BB8 . . . . . .171 D6
Alan Ramsbottom Way
 BB6 . . . . .124 E4
Alandale Cl PR25 . . . . .60 B7
Alaska St BB2 . . . . .101 E2
Albany Ave FY4 . . . . .110 B5
Albany Cl FY6 . . . . .131 E8
Albany Ct PR7 . . . . .43 E8
Albany Dr
 Bamber Bridge PR5 . . . . . . .97 D2
 Copster Green BB1 . . . . . . .122 C8
Albany High Sch PR7 . . . . .43 E5
Albany Rd Blackburn BB2 . .101 B6
 3 Fleetwood FY7 . . . . .198 F4
 Lytham St Anne's FY8 . . . . .90 C5
 Morecambe LA4 . . . . .216 F4
 Southport PR9 . . . . .53 C1
Albany The BB3 . . . . .81 E4
Albatros St PR1 . . . . .118 B1
Albemarle Ct 2 BB7 . . . . .166 D8
Albemarle St BB7 . . . . .166 D8
Albert Ct Lancaster LA1 . .214 E4
 Southport PR9 . . . . .53 D1
Albert Ho BB4 . . . . .86 D1
Albert Pl Blackburn BB3 . . .81 F7
 Southport PR8 . . . . .35 B8
Albert Rd
 Barnoldswick BB18 . . . . . . .196 B2
 Blackpool FY1 . . . . .130 C5
 Colne BB8 . . . . .171 D4
 Formby L37 . . . . .2 B8
 Fulwood PR2 . . . . .117 D3
 Lancaster LA1 . . . . .218 D1
 Leyland PR25 . . . . .60 C8
 Rawtenstall BB4 . . . . .86 A7
 Rufford L40 . . . . .39 A3
 Southport PR9 . . . . .53 D1
Albert Sq 11 FY7 . . . . .199 B5
Albert St Accrington BB5 . .104 C5
 Blackburn BB2 . . . . .101 C2
 Brierfield BB9 . . . . .148 B5
 Burnley BB11 . . . . .128 B6
 Bury BL9 . . . . .33 A2
 3 Carnforth LA5 . . . . .223 D1
 Carnforth,Millhead LA5 . . .223 D3
 11 Chorley PR7 . . . . .43 D7
 2 Church BB5 . . . . .103 E6
 Clayton-le-M BB5 . . . . .124 F2
 Darwen BB3 . . . . .65 B5
 Earby BB18 . . . . .197 B2
 Egerton BL7 . . . . .47 D3
 Fleetwood FY7 . . . . .199 B4
 Great Harwood BB6 . . . . . .124 D4
 Hoddlesden BB3 . . . . .82 F1
 Horwich BL6 . . . . .32 B4
 Kirkham PR4 . . . . .113 F6
 Lytham St Anne's FY8 . . . . .91 C3
 Nelson BB9 . . . . .148 B8
 Oswaldtwistle BB5 . . . . . . .103 E4
 Padiham BB12 . . . . .126 C8
 Ramsbottom BL0 . . . . .50 B6
 Rishton BB1 . . . . .124 B1
 Wheelton PR6 . . . . .62 A7

Albert St continued
 Whitewell Bottom BB4 . . . . .86 E5
 Whitworth OL12 . . . . .52 C8
Albert Terr Bacup OL13 . . . .87 F3
 9 Barrowford BB9 . . . . . . .170 D3
 Calder Vale PR3 . . . . .182 E8
 9 Preston PR1 . . . . .118 A1
 Rawtenstall BB4 . . . . .86 A2
 Southport PR8 . . . . .35 A5
Alberta Cl BB2 . . . . .101 B8
Albion Ave FY3 . . . . .130 F6
Albion Ct BB11 . . . . .127 E4
Albion Mews LA1 . . . . .218 E1
Albion Mill 5 BB4 . . . . . . .86 D8
Albion Rd Blackburn BB2 . .101 D1
 Earby BB18 . . . . .197 B2
Albion St Accrington BB5 . .104 B6
 Bacup OL13 . . . . .88 A3
 7 Bacup,Stacksteads OL13 .70 C8
 Blackburn BB2 . . . . .101 C1
 Brierfield BB9 . . . . .148 B5
 Burnley BB11 . . . . .127 E5
 Chorley PR7 . . . . .43 C7
 11 Clitheroe BB7 . . . . .166 F8
 3 Nelson BB9 . . . . .148 B8
 7 Padiham BB12 . . . . .126 D7
Albion Terr BB11 . . . . .127 F5
Albrighton Cl PR5 . . . . .77 B7
Albrighton Cres PR5 . . . . . .77 B7
Albrighton Rd PR5 . . . . . . .77 C7
Albyn Bank Rd PR1 . . . . . . .97 B7
Albyn St E PR1 . . . . .97 B7
Alcester Ave PR1 . . . . .96 C5
Alconbury Cres FY5 . . . . . .175 C2
Aldate Gr PR2 . . . . .117 A2
Aldcliffe Cotts LA1 . . . . . .214 D5
Aldcliffe Hall Dr LA1 . . . . .214 D5
Aldcliffe Mews LA1 . . . . . .214 D5
Aldcliffe Rd
 Lancaster LA1 . . . . .214 E6
 7 Preston PR2 . . . . .116 E1
Alden Cl BB4 . . . . .68 A6
Alden Rd BB4,BL8 . . . . .67 F5
Alden Rise BB4 . . . . .68 A6
Alden Terr 6 LA1 . . . . .218 D3
Alder Ave Bury BL9 . . . . . . .33 C3
 Rawtenstall BB4 . . . . .86 B2
Alder Bank
 Blackburn BB2 . . . . .101 B4
 Newton-w-S PR4 . . . . .115 A2
 Thornton FY5 . . . . .176 C1
Alder Cl Leyland PR26 . . . . .59 B8
 Thornton FY5 . . . . .176 C1
Alder Coppice PR2 . . . . . . .116 E3
Alder Ct Fleetwood FY7 . . .198 C2
 Lancaster LA1 . . . . .214 D8
Alder Dr
 Charnock Richard PR7 . . . . .42 D7
 Gregson Lane PR5 . . . . .98 E1
Alder Gr Blackpool FY3 . . . .130 E7
 Coppull PR7 . . . . .42 F1
 Huncoat BB5 . . . . .125 E2
 Lancaster LA1 . . . . .214 D8
 Lytham St Anne's FY8 . . . . .91 A4
 Poulton-le-F FY6 . . . . .153 D1
Alder Grange Com & Tech
 Sch BB4 . . . . .86 A4
Alder Hill Croft BB18 . . . . .197 C2
Alder Hill St BB18 . . . . . . .197 B2
Alder La Formby L37,L39 . . .12 E7
 Moss Edge PR3 . . . . .179 A1
 Parbold WN8 . . . . .27 C1
Alder Meadow Cl OL12 . . . .52 A1
Alder Rd PR2 . . . . .119 A4
Alder St Bacup OL13 . . . . . .87 F3
 4 Blackburn BB1 . . . . .102 A7
 Burnley BB12 . . . . .127 C7
 Rawtenstall BB4 . . . . .86 B3
Alderbank BB6 . . . . .31 F3
Alderbrook Dr WN8 . . . . . . .27 C2
Alderdale Ave PR8 . . . . .21 A5
Alderfield PR1 . . . . .96 D3
Alderford Cl BB7 . . . . .166 C4
Alderlee Park Cvn Site
 PR8 . . . . .36 A2
Alderley WN8 . . . . .9 C6
Alderley Ave FY4 . . . . .110 B5
Alderley Hts LA1 . . . . .211 D7
Alderman Foley Dr OL12 . .52 A2
Alderman Rd LA1 . . . . .214 F4
Alderney Cl BB2 . . . . .101 B3
Alders The PR3 . . . . .204 C1
Aldersleigh Cres PR5 . . . . .98 D1
Alderson Cres L37 . . . . .11 F4
Alderville Cl PR4 . . . . .92 F6
Alderway BL0 . . . . .68 C1
Alderwood BB4 . . . . .86 B2
Alderwood Gr BL0 . . . . .68 D4
Aldfield Ave PR2 . . . . .116 C1
Aldingham Ct LA4 . . . . . . .217 B3
Aldingham Wlk LA4 . . . . . .217 A5
Aldon Gr PR4 . . . . .95 A1
Aldon Rd FY6 . . . . .153 C7
Aldren's La LA1 . . . . .218 D3
Aldwych Ave FY3 . . . . .130 E3
Aldwych Ct PR2 . . . . .117 A2
Aldwych Dr
 Bamber Bridge PR5 . . . . . . .77 D7
 Preston PR2 . . . . .117 A2
Aldwych Pl BB1 . . . . .122 F2
Alert St PR2 . . . . .117 C2
Alexander Cl
 Accrington BB5 . . . . .104 E1
 Burscough L40 . . . . .25 F3
Alexander Ct FY6 . . . . .153 D3

A K B – Alm 247

Alexander Dr L31 . . . . .5 D3
Alexander Gr BB12 . . . . . . .127 B6
Alexander Pl PR2 . . . . .139 D1
Alexander St BB9 . . . . .171 A2
Alexander Wharf 4 L31 . . .5 C7
Alexandra Cl
 Clayton-le-M BB5 . . . . .124 E3
 Skelmersdale WN8 . . . . . . .17 E1
Alexandra Ct 4 LA1 . . . . .214 F8
Alexandra Hall 8 LA1 . . .214 F8
Alexandra Ho PR1 . . . . . . .118 C1
Alexandra Mews
 1 Ormskirk L39 . . . . .15 E6
 8 Southport PR9 . . . . .35 C8
Alexandra Pavilions 6
 PR1 . . . . .118 A1
Alexandra Pl BB6 . . . . .124 D6
Alexandra Rd
 Bamber Bridge PR5 . . . . . . .97 D3
 Blackburn BB2 . . . . .101 C6
 Blackpool FY1 . . . . .130 B3
 Burscough L40 . . . . .25 D4
 Carnforth LA5 . . . . .223 D1
 Formby L37 . . . . .11 B1
 Kirkham PR4 . . . . .114 A6
 Lancaster LA1 . . . . .218 D3
 Longridge PR3 . . . . .140 A7
 Lytham St Anne's FY8 . . . . .90 A7
 Morecambe LA4 . . . . .216 E3
 Southport PR9 . . . . .35 D8
 Thornton FY5 . . . . .153 C8
Alexandra Sq LA1 . . . . . . .211 B7
Alexandra St
 Clayton-le-M BB5 . . . . .124 E3
 Preston PR1 . . . . .97 C7
Alexandra View 7 BB3 . . . .81 F2
Alexandria Dr FY8 . . . . .89 F5
Alexandria St BB4 . . . . .85 F4
Alford Fold PR2 . . . . .117 D7
Alfred St Blackpool FY1 . . .130 C5
 Bury BL9 . . . . .33 A1
 Darwen BB3 . . . . .65 B6
 Egerton BL7 . . . . .47 D3
 Lancaster LA1 . . . . .215 A8
 10 Rawtenstall BB4 . . . . . . .86 A3
 Whitworth OL12 . . . . .71 D2
Algar St 9 BB9 . . . . .170 D3
Alice Ave PR25 . . . . .77 A1
Alice Ingham Ct 18 OL12 . .52 C1
Alice Sq 5 PR1 . . . . .118 A1
Alice St Accrington BB5 . . .104 D7
 Barnoldswick BB18 . . . . . . .196 B2
 8 Darwen BB3 . . . . .65 A8
 Morecambe LA4 . . . . .217 C5
 Oswaldtwistle BB5 . . . . . . .103 E3
Alicia Ct OL12 . . . . .52 E1
Alicia Dr OL12 . . . . .52 E1
Alisan Rd FY6 . . . . .153 B5
Alker La PR7 . . . . .61 B3
Alker St PR7 . . . . .43 C7
Alkincoats Rd BB8 . . . . . . .171 C5
All Hallows RC High Sch
 PR1 . . . . .96 A3
All Hallows Rd FY2 . . . . . .152 D5
All Saint's Cl BB5 . . . . . . .103 B4
All Saints CE Prim Sch
 Appley Bridge WN6 . . . . . . .28 C1
 Clayton-le-M BB5 . . . . .124 F2
All Saints Cl
 Padiham BB12 . . . . .126 F7
 Rawtenstall BB4 . . . . .106 A1
All Saints RC High Sch
 BB4 . . . . .85 D1
All Saints Rd FY2 . . . . .152 E6
All Saints' Rd FY8 . . . . .89 E6
Allan Critchlow Way
 BB1 . . . . .124 B2
Allan St OL13 . . . . .87 F1
Allandale FY4 . . . . .110 C5
Allandale Ave FY5 . . . . . . .175 F4
Allandale St
 5 Burnley BB12 . . . . .127 B6
 Colne BB8 . . . . .171 F5
Allengate PR2 . . . . .117 F4
Allerton Cl BB3 . . . . .82 A2
Allerton Dr BB12 . . . . .127 D6
Allerton Rd
 Bamber Bridge PR5 . . . . . . .97 D4
 Southport PR9 . . . . .53 E1
Alleys Gn BB7 . . . . .189 C1
Alleytroyds BB5 . . . . .103 E5
Alliance Bsns Pk BB5 . . . .104 A5
Alliance St 104 F1
Allington Cl PR5 . . . . .97 E3
Allison Gr BB3 . . . . .171 F6
Allonby Ave FY5 . . . . .175 E4
Allotment La PR3 . . . . .157 C7
Allsprings Cl BB6 . . . . .124 D6
Allsprings Dr BB6 . . . . .124 D6
Alma Ave BB8 . . . . .194 D1
Alma Cl WN8 . . . . .10 C7
Alma Ct Skelmersdale WN8 .10 C7
 Southport PR8 . . . . .21 F7
Alma Dr PR7 . . . . .42 E4
Alma Hill WN8 . . . . .10 C7

248 Alm – Ash

Alma Hill Est WN8 10 C7
Alma Ho LA1 214 F6
Alma Ind Est 25 OL12 52 F1
Alma Par WN8 10 C7
Alma Pl Accrington BB5 84 E8
Clitheroe BB7 166 D7
Alma Rd Lancaster LA1 214 F6
Laneshaw Bridge BB8 172 D6
Skelmersdale WN8 10 C7
Southport PR8 35 A4
Alma Row PR5 98 E1
Alma St Bacup OL13 88 A2
Blackburn BB2 101 D5
9 Clayton-le-M BB5 124 F3
Padiham BB12 126 C8
Preston PR1 118 A1
13 Rochdale OL12 52 F1
Alma Terr BB11 106 B4
Almelo Ho 1 PR1 117 E2
Almhouses BD23 197 A5
Almond Ave
Burscough Bridge L40 25 E6
4 Bury BL9 33 C3
Almond Brook Rd WN6 29 C1
Almond Cl
Abbey Village PR6 80 B2
Fulwood PR2 118 D6
Higher Penwortham PR1 96 B3
Almond Cres BB4 68 F8
Almond St BB3 65 A8
Almonry The L40 17 B7
Almshouse Bglws L39 6 A6
Almshouses Aughton L39 6 A7
14 Lancaster LA1 214 F7
35 Lancaster LA1 214 F8
6 Rawtenstall BB4 85 E2
Alnwick Cl BB12 127 E7
Alpha St Darwen BB3 65 B8
10 Nelson BB9 170 F2
Salterforth BB18 194 E8
Alpic Dr FY5 152 C7
Alpine Ave
Bamber Bridge PR5 77 B7
Blackpool FY4 110 E5
Alpine Cl
Bamber Bridge PR5 77 B7
Hoddlesden BB3 82 E1
Alpine Gr BB2 81 B8
Alpine Hts PR3 181 B6
Alpine Lodge FY8 89 E5
Alpine Rd PR6 61 E3
Alpine View LA5 221 A6
Alsop St PR1 117 F2
Alston Ave FY5 175 D4
Alston Cl BB7 145 F7
Alston Ct Longridge PR3 140 B6
Southport PR8 21 E6
Alston Dr LA4 217 F5
Alston Hall Coll PR3 120 B8
Alston La PR3 140 A2
Alston Lane RC Prim Sch PR3 139 F2
Alston Rd FY2 152 E2
Alston St PR1 118 D1
Alt Rd Formby L37 12 B2
Hightown L38 3 A4
Altcar La Formby L37 11 F1
Haskayne L39 14 A2
Maghull L31 4 F5
Runshaw Moor PR25 59 E5
Altcar Rd L37 12 B2
Altham Bsns Pk BB5 125 E6
Altham Cvn Pk BB5 125 C1
Altham Ind Est BB5 125 D6
Altham La BB5 125 F4
Altham Rd
Morecambe LA4 217 C3
Southport PR8 35 E2
Altham St
2 Burnley BB10 128 A8
6 Padiham BB12 126 D8
Altham St James CE Prim Sch BB5 125 D6
Altham Wlk LA4 217 C3
Althorp Cl 6 FY1 130 C7
Althorpe Dr PR8 35 E3
Altom St BB1 101 E6
Alton Cl L38 2 F2
Altys La L39 15 F3
Alum Scar La BB2 100 A6
Alvern Ave PR2 117 D4
Alvern Cres PR2 117 D4
Alvina La L33 1 A5
Alwin St 8 BB11 127 E5
Alwood Ave FY3 130 F6
Amber Ave BB1 122 F2
Amber Dr PR6 43 E6
Amberbanks Gr FY1 130 B2
Ambergate Fulwood PR2 116 F6
Skelmersdale WN8 9 B7
Amberley St BB2 101 C2
Amberwood PR4 113 F5
Amberwood Dr BB2 101 A1
Ambledene PR5 78 A5
Ambleside Ave
Barnoldswick BB18 196 A3
3 Euxton PR7 60 D1
Knott End-on-S FY6 199 F6
2 Rawtenstall BB4 85 E2
Ambleside Cl
Accrington,Hillock Vale BB5 104 E8
Bamber Bridge PR5 97 E2
Blackburn BB1 102 A6
Ambleside Dr BB3 82 C3
Ambleside Rd
Blackpool FY4 131 D1
Fulwood PR2 118 E5
Lancaster LA1 218 F2
Lytham St Anne's FY8 110 E1
Maghull L31 5 D2
Ambleside Wlk PR2 118 E5
Ambleway PR5 97 C4
Ambrose Hall La PR4 136 E3
Ambrose St PR25 77 B2
Amelia St BB1 102 B6
Amersham WN8 9 C7
Amersham Cl PR4 75 F8
Amersham Gr BB10 148 D4
Amethyst St BB1 122 F2
Amounderness Way
Cleveleys FY5 175 F4
Fleetwood FY7 199 A3
Thornton FY5 153 C7
Ampleforth Dr PR5 97 A1
Ams Trad Est PR4 75 D7
Amy Johnson Way FY4 110 E4
Amy St OL12 52 B1
Ancenis Ct PR4 114 B5
Anchor Ave BB3 81 F4
Anchor Ct PR1 96 F7
Anchor Dr PR4 95 D2
Anchor Gr BB3 81 E5
Anchor Ho 1 BB1 101 F4
Anchor Rd BB3 81 F4
Anchor Ret Pk 1 BB11 128 A6
Anchor St PR9 35 B7
Anchor Way FY8 110 E1
Anchorage Ave PR4 72 F1
Anchorage Mews FY7 199 B3
Anchorage Rd FY7 199 B3
Anchorsholme La
Cleveleys FY5 152 F8
Thornton FY5 153 A8
Anchorsholme La E FY5 175 E1
Anchorsholme La W FY5 175 C1
Anchorsholme Prim Sch FY5 152 E8
Ancliffe La LA2,LA5 221 B2
Andelen Cl BB11 126 C3
Anders Dr L33 1 A5
Anderson Cl Bacup OL13 87 F1
Lancaster LA1 215 B6
Anderson Rd BB1 123 A7
Anderson St 9 FY1 130 C4
Anderton Cl BB4 69 F7
Anderton La BL6 31 E4
Anderton Prim Sch PR6 31 B8
Anderton Rd Euxton PR7 60 D1
Higham BB12 146 F5
Anderton St Adlington PR7 31 A7
Chorley PR7 43 C7
Anderton Way PR3 181 D6
Andertons Way PR2 118 D5
Andreas Cl PR8 35 B4
Andrew Ave BB4 85 F1
Andrew Cl Blackburn BB2 81 B8
Ramsbottom BL8 49 F1
Andrew Rd BB9 171 B1
Andrew St Bury BL9 33 A2
Preston PR1 118 C1
Andrews Cl L37 11 E1
Andrews La L37 11 E1
Andrews Yort L37 11 E1
Anemone Dr BB4 67 F8
Angel Way 3 BB8 171 E5
Angela St BB2 101 B1
Angelbank BL6 31 F2
Anger's Hill Rd FY4 130 F1
Angle St BB10 128 A8
Anglesey Ave BB12 127 A7
Anglesey St BB2 81 B8
Anglezarke Rd PR6 31 A7
Anglezarke Woodland Trail* PR6 44 D6
Anglian Cl BB5 103 C5
Angus St OL13 70 C8
Aniline St PR6 43 E8
Ann St Barrowford BB9 170 D3
Brierfield BB9 148 B6
4 Clayton-le-M BB5 124 F3
Skelmersdale WN8 8 E8
Anna's Rd FY4 111 E3
Annan Cres FY4 131 C1
Annandale Gdns WN8 10 A7
Annarly Fold BB10 129 A5
Annaside Cl 2 FY4 110 E7
Anne Ave PR8 21 E6
Anne Cl 6 BB10 128 B5
Anne St 2 BB11 128 B5
Annesley Ave FY3 130 E8
Annie St Accrington BB5 104 C7
Ramsbottom BL0 50 A4
5 Rawtenstall BB4 86 A2
Annis St PR1 97 C8
Ansbro Ave PR4 93 C6
Ansdell & Fairhaven Sta FY8 90 D4
Ansdell Gr Fulwood PR2 117 C3
Southport PR9 54 A4
Ansdell Prim Sch FY8 90 C5
Ansdell Rd Blackpool FY1 130 D2
Horwich BL6 32 C4
Ansdell Rd N FY8 90 D4
Ansdell Rd S FY8 90 D3
Ansdell St 3 PR1 118 C1
Ansdell Terr BB2 101 E1
Anselm Ct FY2 152 B3
Anshaw Cl BL7 46 C5
Anson Cl FY8 110 D1
Anson Rd PR4 114 B2
Anstable Rd LA4 217 E5
Anthony Rd LA1 214 E7
Antigua Dr BB3 81 F6
Antrim Rd FY2 152 C1
Anvil Cl WN5 10 D5
Anvil St OL13 70 E8
Anyon La LA2 207 E6
Anyon St BB3 82 B2
Anzio Rd PR4 132 E5
Apartments The PR9 35 B8
Apiary The PR26 58 A6
Appealing La FY8 110 E2
Apple Cl 2 BB2 101 C4
Apple Ct 3 BB2 101 C4
Apple St BB2 101 C4
Apple Tree Cl Euxton PR7 60 D3
St Michael's on W PR3 157 C8
Apple Tree Way BB5 103 E5
Appleby Bsns Ctr BB1 102 A5
Appleby Cl
Accrington BB5 104 D5
Gregson Lane PR5 98 E1
Appleby Dr BB9 170 D4
Appleby Rd FY2 152 D1
Appleby St
Blackburn BB1 102 A5
Nelson BB9 148 D8
Preston PR1 117 F1
Applecross Dr BB10 128 E4
Applefields PR25 60 B7
Applegarth
Barnoldswick BB18 196 C3
Barrowford BB9 170 B1
Applegarth Rd LA3 213 A8
Applegarth St 3 BB18 197 B1
Applesike PR4 95 A1
Appleton Cl FY6 153 A2
Appleton Rd WN8 17 F2
Appletree Cl
Kingsfold PR1 96 C2
Lancaster LA1 215 A3
Appletree Dr LA1 215 A3
Applewood Cl FY8 90 F3
Appley Bridge Sta WN6 19 C7
Appley Cl WN6 28 C2
Appley La N WN6 28 C1
Appley La S WN6,WN8 19 C6
Approach Way BB11 127 F2
Apsley Brow L31 5 A8
Apsley Fold PR3 140 B6
Aquaduct Street Ind Est PR1 117 D1
Aqueduct Mill PR1 117 D1
Aqueduct Rd BB2 101 D1
Aqueduct St PR1 117 E1
Arago St BB5 104 C7
Aragon Cl L31 5 E3
Arbories Ave 4 BB12 126 B8
Arbory Dr BB12 126 B8
Arbory The PR4 112 E7
Arbour Dr BB2 81 D6
Arbour La Kirkby L33 1 B2
Shevington Moor WN6 29 B1
Arbour Lane End PR3 162 E7
Arbour St 11 Bacup OL13 88 A3
Southport PR8 35 C6
Arboury St BB12 126 B8
Arcade BB5 104 C5
Arcadia 9 BB8 171 E5
Arcadia Ave L31 5 D3
Arch St Burnley BB11 127 F6
4 Darwen BB3 82 A1
Archbishop Temple CE High Sch & tech Coll PR2 117 F5
Archer Hill LA5 223 D3
Archery Ave BB8 194 D1
Archery Gdns PR3 181 C8
Arches The BB7 144 B6
Arcon Ho 5 Coppull PR7 42 E1
Lancaster LA1 214 F5
Lytham St Anne's FY8 91 B4
Arcon Rd PR7 42 E1
Ardee Rd PR1 96 D6
Arden Cl Slyne LA2 218 C8
Southport PR8 21 A5
Arden Gn FY7 198 E4
Ardengate LA1 214 F4
Ardleigh Ave PR8 35 E3
Ardley Rd BL6 32 C4
Ardmore Rd FY2 152 D2
Ardwick St BB10 128 A8
Argameols Cl PR8 35 F5
Argarmeols Gr L37 11 E5
Argarmeols Rd L37 11 E6
Argosy Ave FY3 130 F8
Argosy Ct 1 FY3 131 A8
Argyle Ct PR9 53 D1
Argyle Rd 7 Leyland PR25 77 A1
Poulton-le-F FY6 153 E3
Southport PR9 53 D2
Argyle St Accrington BB5 104 B6
8 Colne BB8 171 D5
Darwen BB3 81 F5
Heywood OL10 33 F1
3 Lancaster LA1 215 A7
Argyll Ct FY2 152 C1
Argyll Rd Blackpool FY2 152 C1
Preston PR1 118 A1
Ariel Way FY7 198 E4
Arkholme Ave FY1 130 D2
Arkholme CE Prim Sch LA6 241 B3
Arkholme Cl LA5 223 E2
Arkholme Ct LA4 217 B3
Arkholme Dr PR4 94 F1
Arkwright Ct FY4 111 C7
Arkwright Fold BB2 81 C8
Arkwright Rd PR1 117 F2
Arkwright St
Burnley BB12 127 C7
Horwich BL6 32 C2
Arley Gdns BB12 127 F7
Arley La WN1,WN2 30 D2
Arley Rise BB2 121 E2
Arley St PR6 43 D8
Arley Wood Dr PR7 43 A6
Arlington Ave FY4 110 B7
Arlington Cl
Ramsbottom BL9 50 C2
Southport PR8 21 A5
Arlington Rd BB3 64 F8
Armadale Rd FY2 152 E1
Armaside Rd PR4 116 D4
Armitstead Ct 8 FY7 198 F2
Armitstead Way 5 FY7 198 F2
Armstrong St Horwich BL6 32 C2
Preston PR2 117 B2
Arncliffe Ave BB5 103 F4
Arncliffe Gr BB9 170 C3
Arncliffe Rd
Burnley BB10 128 E5
Morecambe LA3 216 D1
Arndale Cl FY7 198 C2
Arndale Ctr
Morecambe LA4 217 A5
6 Nelson BB9 148 E8
Arndale Rd PR3 140 A7
Arnhem Rd
Carnforth LA5 223 E1
Preston PR1 97 D8
Arnian Ct L39 6 C7
Arno St 9 PR1 97 B7
Arnold Ave FY4 110 C7
Arnold Cl Blackburn BB2 102 A1
Brierfield BB9 148 C5
Burnley BB11 127 E2
Fulwood PR2 118 E2
Arnold Pl 1 PR7 43 A5
Arnold Rd FY8 91 D4
Arnold Sch FY4 110 C7
Arnold St 2 BB5 104 C6
Arnott Rd Blackpool FY4 130 E1
Fulwood PR2 117 C2
Arnside Ave
Blackpool FY1 130 D1
Lytham St Anne's FY8 90 C7
Arnside Cl
Clayton-le-M BB5 124 E2
Coupe Green PR5 98 E4
Lancaster LA1 215 B3
Arnside Cres
Blackburn BB2 80 E8
Morecambe LA4 217 C6
Arnside Rd
Broughton PR3 137 D2
Preston PR2 116 E2
Southport PR9 35 C7
Arnside Terr PR9 35 C7
Arran Ave BB1 102 D2
Arran Cl LA3 212 E7
Arran St BB11 127 D5
Arrow La LA2 219 D7
Arrowsmith Cl PR5 98 E2
Arrowsmith Ct 7 BL6 32 E1
Arrowsmith Dr PR5 98 E2
Arrowsmith Gdns FY5 175 E5
Arroyo Way PR2 118 B4
Arthur St Bacup OL13 88 B3
Barnoldswick BB18 196 A3
Blackburn BB2 101 C4
Brierfield BB9 148 B6
Burnley BB11 127 E6
Clayton-le-M BB5 124 F3
Earby BB18 195 A7
6 Fleetwood FY7 199 B5
Great Harwood BB6 124 D6
18 Nelson BB9 170 E1
Preston PR1 96 E7
Arthur St N 5 FY7 199 B5
Arthur Way BB2 101 C4
Arthurs La FY6 177 D2
Artle Pl LA1 218 C2
Artlebeck Cl LA2 237 C3
Artlebeck Gr LA2 237 C3
Artlebeck Rd LA2 237 C3
Arundel Ave FY2 152 B5
Arundel Dr FY6 153 C5
Arundel Pl 35 PR1 97 A7
Arundel Rd Longton PR4 95 A1
Lytham St Anne's FY8 90 C4
Southport PR8 21 F8
Arundel St BB1 124 A2
Arundel Way PR25 60 C8
Ascot Cl Lancaster LA1 215 B4
Southport PR8 34 E5
Ascot Gdns LA2 218 D8
Ascot Rd Blackpool FY3 130 E6
Thornton FY5 153 B8
Ascot Way BB5 104 D5
Ash Ave Galgate LA2 210 F4
Haslingden BB4 85 C3
Kirkham PR4 114 A4
Ash Bank Cl PR3 137 B8
Ash Brow WN8 27 B1
Ash Cl Appley Bridge WN6 19 D7
Barrow BB7 166 D1
Elswick PR4 156 A1
Ormskirk L39 15 D5
Rishton BB1 103 B8
Ash Coppice PR2 116 D2
Ash Ct PR4 115 D2
Ash Dr Freckleton PR4 93 A5
Poulton-le-F FY6 153 E2
Thornton FY5 176 C1
Warton LA5 223 E6
Warton PR4 92 D6
Ash Dr *continued*
West Bradford BB7 189 D7
Ash Field PR6 78 C3
Ash Gr Bamber Bridge PR5 97 F1
Barnoldswick BB18 196 B2
Chorley PR7 43 C5
Darwen BB3 82 B2
Formby L37 11 C1
Garstang PR3 181 B8
8 Horwich BL6 32 E1
Kirkham PR4 114 B7
Lancaster LA1 214 F5
Longton PR4 74 F8
New Longton PR4 75 F6
Orrell WN5 10 F6
Preesall FY6 200 A4
Ramsbottom BL0 49 F3
3 Rawtenstall BB4 86 A3
Skelmersdale WN8 17 D1
St Michael's on W PR3 157 C7
Water BB4 87 A8
Wrea Green PR4 113 C3
Ash Holme PR1 118 C3
Ash La Clifton PR4 115 E2
Great Harwood BB6 124 B6
Longridge PR3 140 B8
Ash Lea Gr FY6 177 C7
Ash Mdw PR2 116 E3
Ash Rd Coppull PR7 29 E8
Elswick PR4 156 A1
Ash St Bacup OL13 87 F3
Blackburn BB1 102 A7
Blackpool FY4 110 C6
Burnley BB11 128 B5
Bury BL9 33 A2
Fleetwood FY7 199 A4
Great Harwood BB6 124 C6
Nelson BB9 148 F8
Oswaldtwistle BB5 103 D4
Southport PR8 35 C5
Trawden BB8 172 C2
Ash Tree Gr
Hest Bank LA5 220 F3
Nelson BB9 149 A7
Ash Tree Wlk 18 BB9 170 D3
Ashborne Dr BL9 50 D2
Ashbourne Cl 7 LA1 218 D3
Ashbourne Cres PR2 117 A5
Ashbourne Dr LA1 218 D3
Ashbourne Gr LA3 217 C2
Ashbourne Rd LA1 218 D3
Ashbrook Cl PR4 73 E3
Ashbrook St LA1 214 D8
Ashburn Cl BL6 32 D1
Ashburnham Rd BB8 171 A2
Ashburton Ct 7 FY1 130 B7
Ashburton Rd FY1 130 B7
Ashby St PR7 43 D6
Ashcombe Gate FY5 153 D7
Ashcroft LA3 216 E1
Ashcroft Ave L39 15 F6
Ashcroft Cl LA2 237 B3
Ashcroft Pl BB7 189 E5
Ashcroft Rd Formby L37 11 F1
Kirkby L33 1 C3
Ashdale Cl Coppull PR7 29 D8
Formby L37 11 C2
Ashdale Gr FY5 176 E2
Ashdale Pl LA1 218 C2
Ashdene OL12 52 D4
Ashdown Cl Carleton FY6 153 B5
Southport PR8 35 E4
Ashdown Dr PR6 78 C2
Ashdown Mews PR2 118 E6
Asheldon St 1 PR1 118 D1
Ashen Bottom BB4 68 D6
Ashendean View BB12 146 D1
Ashfield PR2 117 F8
Ashfield Ave
Lancaster LA1 214 D7
Morecambe LA4 217 F6
Ashfield Cl BB9 170 C1
Ashfield Cotts 2 LA2 239 D8
Ashfield Ct Blackpool FY2 152 E6
Fulwood PR2 116 F6
Ashfield Rd Adlington PR6 31 B8
Blackpool FY2,FY5 152 E6
Burnley BB11 127 F6
Chorley PR7 43 B7
Ashfield Rise PR3 181 D2
Ashfield Terr WN6 19 C8
Ashfields PR26 76 B1
Ashford Ave LA1 214 E3
Ashford Cl LA1 214 F3
Ashford Cres PR3 137 C3
Ashford Rd
Lancaster LA1 214 F3
Preston PR2 116 E2
Ashford St Heywood OL10 33 F2
Nelson BB9 148 E7
Ashgrove PR1 118 E1
Ashiana Lodge 15 BB9 148 E8
Ashlands Cl BL0 68 D2
Ashleigh Ct PR2 118 A7
Ashleigh Mews FY3 130 E4
Ashleigh Prim Sch BB3 65 A6
Ashleigh St Darwen BB3 65 B6
Preston PR1 97 C7
Ashley Cl Blackpool FY2 152 D2
Thornton FY5 153 B7
Ashley Ct Accrington BB5 103 F5
Poulton-le-F FY6 153 C3
Whitworth OL12 71 D2
Ashley Gdns LA2 211 A3
Ashley La PR3 139 C8
Ashley Mews PR2 117 C1
Ashley Rd
Lytham St Anne's FY8 110 F1

Ashley Rd *continued*
Skelmersdale WN8 18 B3
Southport PR9 35 C7
Ashley St BB12 127 F7
Ashmead Rd WN8 18 A4
Ashmead View WN8 18 A4
Ashmeadow Gr LA6 221 F5
Ashmeadow La PR6 62 F8
Ashmeadow Rd LA6 221 F5
Ashmoor St PR1 117 E1
Ashmore Gr FY5 175 D1
Ashmount Dr OL12 52 F2
Ashness Cl Fulwood PR2 117 F8
Horwich BL6 31 F3
Ashton Ave FY6 199 D5
Ashton Cl PR2 96 A8
Ashton Ct
Knott End-on-S FY6 199 D5
Lancaster LA1 214 F7
Ashton Dr Lancaster LA1 218 C2
Nelson BB9 148 F6
Ashton Garden Ct FY8 89 E7
Ashton Ho BB3 65 B8
Ashton La BB3 65 A8
Ashton Meml★ LA1 215 B7
Ashton Prim Sch PR2 116 E2
Ashton Rd Blackpool FY1 130 C3
8 Darwen BB3 65 B8
Lancaster LA1,LA2 214 E4
Morecambe LA4 217 C5
Southport PR8 34 F1
Ashton St Longridge PR3 140 A8
8 Lytham St Anne's FY8 91 A3
7 Preston PR2 96 D8
Ashton Wlk 12 LA1 214 F8
Ashton-on-Ribble High Sch
PR2 116 F2
Ashtongate PR2 116 F1
Ashtree Ct Fulwood PR2 117 A4
Higher Walton PR5 98 C3
Ashtree Gr PR1 96 B4
Ashtrees L40 40 C2
Ashtrees Way 2 LA5 223 D2
Ashurst Cl WN8 18 A4
Ashurst Ct L37 11 E2
Ashurst Gdns WN8 18 B4
Ashurst Rd
Clayton-le-W PR25 77 D1
Shevington Moor WN6 29 B2
Skelmersdale WN8 18 B4
Ashville Terr BB2 81 D8
Ashwall St WN8 8 E8
Ashwell Pl FY5 152 C7
Ashwood WN8 18 C3
Ashwood Ave
Blackburn BB3 81 D6
Ramsbottom BL0 50 D7
Ashwood Cl FY8 90 E4
Ashwood Ct LA1 214 F5
Ashwood Rd PR2 117 D7
Ashworth Cl BB2 101 C5
Ashworth Ct
5 Blackpool FY3 130 D7
Preston PR1 97 B6
Ashworth Dr LA2 220 E2
Ashworth Gr PR1 97 C6
Ashworth Hospl L31 6 B2
Ashworth La
Newchurch BB4 86 F3
Preston PR1 97 C6
Ashworth Rd
Blackpool FY4 111 C8
Newchurch BB4 86 F2
Rochdale OL11 51 E2
Ashworth St
Accrington BB5 104 E2
16 Bacup OL13 88 A3
6 Bacup,Stacksteads OL13 70 D8
3 Bamber Bridge PR5 97 F2
Forest Holme BB4 87 A7
1 Preston PR1 97 B7
Rawtenstall BB4 69 F8
8 Rishton BB1 124 B1
Ashworth Terr
2 Bacup OL13 70 B8
7 Darwen BB3 82 A1
Askrigg Cl
Accrington BB5 104 E5
Blackpool FY4 111 A7
Asland Cl PR5 77 F8
Asland Gdns PR9 54 C4
Asmall Cl L39 15 D6
Asmall La
Haskayne L39,L40 14 E8
Ormskirk L39,L40 15 B7
Aspden St PR5 97 E1
Aspels Cres PR1 96 C4
Aspels Nook PR1 96 C4
Aspels The PR1 96 C4
Aspen Dr BB10 128 C7
Aspen Fold BB5 103 B5
Aspen Gdns
3 Chorley PR7 43 B6
Rochdale OL12 52 A1
Aspen Gr L37 11 C1
Aspen La Earby BB18 197 B2
Oswaldtwistle BB5 103 C4
Aspendale Cl PR4 74 F8
Aspinall Cl Horwich BL6 32 C1
Kingsfold PR1 96 D2
Aspinall Cres L37 12 F1
Aspinall Ct BL6 32 C2
Aspinall Fold BB1 101 E8
Aspinall Rd WN6 29 B1
Aspinall St BL6 32 D1
Aspinall Way BL6 32 C1
Aspley Gr BB8 172 C3
Asshawes The PR6 43 F1
Assheton Pl PR2 118 E4
Assheton Rd BB2 101 A5
Asten Bldgs BB4 69 F7
Aster Ch BB3 82 A7
Astland Gdns PR4 73 F2
Astland St FY8 89 E6
Astley Cres PR4 93 C6
Astley Ct LA1 214 D6
Astley Ctr The 2 PR7 43 D6
Astley Gate BB2 101 E5
Astley Hall★ PR7 61 A1
Astley Hall Dr BL0 50 C4
Astley Ho BB11 128 B6
Astley Hts BB3 65 A7
Astley Rd PR7 61 C1
Astley St Chorley PR7 61 C1
Darwen BB3 65 A7
Longridge PR3 140 A7
Astley Terr BB3 65 A7
Aston Ave FY5 176 A2
Aston Manor PR9 55 A5
Aston St PR4 132 E6
Aston Way PR26 76 C2
Aston Wlk BB2 82 A8
Asturian Gate PR3 140 F6
Athelstan Fold PR2 117 C3
Athens View BB10 128 C5
Atherton Rd PR25 59 D8
Atherton St Adlington PR7 31 A6
Bacup OL13 70 C8
Atherton Way OL13 70 B8
Athletic St BB10 128 C5
Athlone Ave FY2 152 C2
Athol Gr PR6 43 E6
Athol St Nelson BB9 148 F8
Ramsbottom BL0 50 C7
Athol St N BB11 127 D5
Athol St S BB11 127 D5
Athole Gr PR9 35 F7
Atholl St 12 PR1 96 D8
Atkinson Art Gal PR8 35 B7
Atkinson Cl 15 PR1 96 F8
Atkinson Liby PR8 35 B7
Atkinson St
Brierfield BB10 148 F3
Colne BB8 171 C3
Colne BB8 171 D4
Atlas Rd BB3 82 B1
Atlas St BB5 125 A1
Atrium Ct 10 BB11 128 B4
Aubigny Dr PR2 117 D4
Auburn Gr FY1 130 D2
Auckland St BB3 65 B7
Audenlea FY5 175 F3
Audenshaw Rd LA4 217 C4
Audley Cl
Lytham St Anne's FY8 90 D5
14 Nelson BB9 148 E8
Audley Inf & Jun Schs
BB1 102 A3
Audley La BB1 102 A4
Audley Range BB1 102 B4
Audley St BB1 102 A5
Audlum Ct 5 BL9 33 A3
Aughton Brow LA2 237 E6
Aughton Christ Church CE
Prim Sch L39 15 C3
Aughton Ct LA1 218 D4
Aughton Hall Cotts L39 15 C6
Aughton Mews PR8 35 A5
Aughton Park Dr L39 15 D2
Aughton Park Sta L39 15 D2
Aughton Rd Aughton LA2 237 E6
Southport PR8 35 A5
Aughton St
Fleetwood FY7 199 B5
Ormskirk L39 15 E4
Aughton St Michael's CE
Prim Sch L39 15 B1
Aughton Town Green Sch
L39 6 C8
Aughton Wlk 2 PR1 117 F1
Augusta Cl OL12 52 E2
Augusta St
Accrington BB5 104 C4
Rochdale OL12 52 E1
Auster Cres PR4 114 B2
Austin Cres PR2 117 B4
Austin Gr FY1 130 B1
Austin St 6 Bacup OL13 87 F2
5 Burnley BB11 127 E5
Austin Way FY4 112 A7
Austin's La BL6 32 F1
Austins Cl PR25 60 A8
Austwick Rd 4 LA1 218 B2
Austwick Way BB5 104 E5
Avallon Way BB3 82 C1
Avalon Cl 5 BB12 126 F7
Avalon Dr PR4 93 C7
Avalwood Ave PR4 75 B8
Avebury Cl Blackburn BB2 82 A8
Horwich BL6 32 F1
Aveling Dr PR9 55 A6
Avelon Cl L31 5 B5
Avenham Cl PR9 55 B5
Avenham Colonnade
PR1 97 A6
Avenham Ct 19 PR1 97 A7
Avenham Gr 5 FY1 130 B6
Avenham La PR1 97 A7
Avenham Pl
Newton-w-S PR4 114 F2
6 Preston PR1 97 A6
Avenham Rd
1 Chorley PR7 43 C7
Preston PR1 97 A7
Avenham St PR1 97 A7
Avenham Terr 11 PR1 97 A6
Avenue Par BB5 104 D6
Avenue Rd
Hurst Green BB7 164 E1
Normoss FY3 131 B7
Avenue The Adlington PR6 31 A8
Banks PR9 54 F5
Barley BB12 169 C5
Burnley BB10,BB11 128 D3
Carleton FY6 153 C4
Churchtown PR3 181 A3
Fulwood PR2 117 A6
Garstang PR3 204 B1
Higher Penwortham PR1 96 B5
Leyland PR25 60 A6
Ormskirk L39 15 D6
Ormskirk L39 15 E6
Orrell WN5 10 D3
Preston PR2 116 D1
Southport PR8 36 F5
Avery Gdns FY6 153 B6
Aviemore Cl
5 Blackburn BB1 102 A4
2 Ramsbottom BL0 50 A2
Avocet Ct PR26 76 A1
Avon Ave FY7 175 D8
Avon Bridge PR2 117 C8
Avon Cl BB2 101 D3
Avon Ct BB12 127 D7
Avon Dr
Barnoldswick BB18 196 C3
Bury BL9 33 A8
Avon Gdns PR4 116 D5
Avon Gn FY7 198 E4
Avon Ho 12 PR1 97 D8
Avon Pl FY1 130 C8
Avon St FY8 89 E6
Avondale Ave
Blackburn BB1 102 E5
Burnley BB12 127 C7
Avondale Cl BB3 81 E2
Avondale Cres FY4 110 F7
Avondale Dr
Bamber Bridge PR5 77 B8
Ramsbottom BL0 49 F3
Tarleton PR4 57 A8
Avondale Mews BB3 81 E3
Avondale Prim Sch BB3 81 E2
Avondale Rd Chorley PR7 43 C7
Darwen BB3 81 E3
Lancaster LA1 215 A6
Lytham St Anne's FY8 89 C8
Morecambe LA3 216 E3
Nelson BB9 148 D7
Southport PR9 35 B8
Avondale Rd N PR9 53 C1
Avondale St Colne BB8 172 A5
Standish WN6 29 E2
Avondale The PR9 53 B1
Avonhead Cl BL6 31 F3
Avonside Ave FY5 176 A3
Avonwood Cl BB3 81 E2
Avroe Cres FY4 110 D4
Axeholme Ct BL6 31 F3
Aylesbury Ave FY4 130 D1
Aylesbury Ho L31 5 B4
Aylesbury Wlk BB10 148 D3
Ayr Cl PR8 35 F4
Ayr Ct FY7 175 E7
Ayr Gr BB11 127 D3
Ayr Rd BB1 102 D3
Ayr St LA1 215 B7
Ayrefield Gr WN6 19 D6
Ayrefield La WN8 19 C4
Ayrton Ave FY4 110 D7
Ayrton St BB8 171 E5
Ayrton View LA2 218 E4
Ays-Garth Rd LA1 214 D8
Aysgarth Ave PR2 117 F7
Aysgarth Ct 1 FY4 110 F7
Aysgarth Dr
Accrington BB5 104 D6
Darwen BB3 81 E2
Lancaster LA1 218 D4
Azalea Cl
Clayton-le-W PR25 77 E2
Fulwood PR2 118 C6
Azalea Gr LA4 217 E5
Azalea Rd BB2 101 B6

B

Babbacombe Ave FY4 110 B6
Babylon La PR6 31 B8
Back Albert Rd BB8 171 D4
Back Albert St Bury BL9 33 A2
10 Padiham BB12 126 C8
Back Alfred St 11 BL0 50 B5
Back Altham St 5
BB12 126 D8
Back Andrew St 14 BL9 33 A2
Back Andrew St N 13
BL9 33 A2
Back Arthur St 15 BB5 124 F3
Back Ash St 8 BL9 33 A2
Back Ashburton Rd 14
FY1 130 C7
Back Ashby St 1 PR7 43 D6
Back Atkinson St BB8 171 C4
Back Avondale Rd (E)
LA3 216 E3
Back Avondale Rd (W)
LA3 216 E3
Back Bath St PR8 35 B8
Back Bell La 8 Bury BL9 33 A3
Bury BL9 33 B3
Back Benson St BL9 33 A1
Back Blackburn Rd E
BL7 47 D3
Back Bolton Rd BB3 65 B7
Back Bond St BB8 171 D5
Back Bond St W BL9 33 A2
Back Boundary St 14
BB8 171 D4
Back Bourne's Row PR5 98 E1
Back Bridge St 2 BL0 50 C6
Back Broading Terr
BB4 106 A3
Back Brook St N 13 BL9 33 A4
Back Brow WN8 10 C7
Back Brown St BB8 171 C4
Back Burnley Rd BB5 104 C6
Back Calton St LA4 217 B6
Back Cambridge St 10
BB8 171 D4
Back Canada St 3 BL6 32 B3
Back Carr Mill St BB4 85 B5
Back Cedar St 2 BL9 33 B3
Back Cedar St N 1 BL9 33 B3
Back Cemetery Terr 12
OL13 70 D8
Back Chapel St
1 Barnoldswick BB18 196 B2
4 Colne BB8 171 D4
Horwich BL6 32 C3
Back Chesham Rd N 5
BL9 33 A4
Back Chesham Rd S 7
BL9 33 A4
Back Chester St BL9 33 A4
Back Church St
Barrowford BB9 170 D3
8 Blackpool FY1 130 B5
5 Great Harwood BB6 124 C5
3 Hapton BB12 126 C4
1 Newchurch BB4 86 E1
Back Clarendon Rd FY1 130 B2
Back Clayton St 9 BB9 170 D1
Back Club St PR5 77 E7
Back Colne Rd BB18 196 A1
Back Commons BB7 189 D1
Back Constablelee BB4 85 F4
Back Cookson St 12
FY1 130 C6
Back Cop La FY7 199 A4
Back Cowm La OL12 71 C3
Back Crescent St LA4 217 A5
Back Crown St BL6 32 A4
Back Curzon St FY8 90 A7
Back Darwen Rd N BL7 47 E1
Back Deal St BL9 33 B2
Back Delamere St N BL9 33 A5
Back Delamere St S BL9 33 A5
Back Derby St 6 BB8 171 D5
Back Drinkhouse La
PR26 58 B1
Back Duckworth St
4 Bury BL9 33 A4
12 Darwen BB3 82 A1
Back Duke St 1 BB8 171 D4
Back Duncan St BL6 32 C3
Back Earl St 2 BB8 171 D4
Back East Bank 1 BB9 170 D4
Back Eaves St FY1 130 B7
Back Elm St 10 BL9 33 B2
Back Emmett St BL6 32 B3
Back Epsom Rd FY5 152 F8
Back Fazakerley St 14
PR7 43 C8
Back Fir St BL9 33 B2
Back Fletcher St BL9 33 A2
Back Forest Rd PR8 35 D6
Back Garston St BL9 33 A4
Back George St BL6 32 C3
Back Gisburn Rd BB9 170 E7
Back Glen Eldon Rd FY8 89 E7
Back Green St LA4 217 B6
Back Grimshaw St 8
PR1 97 A7
Back Grove Terr 10 LA4 217 F4
Back Hall St BB8 171 D4
Back Halstead St 2 BL9 33 A4
Back Hamilton St 1 BL9 33 A4
Back Harry St BB9 170 D3
Back Haslam St BL9 33 A4
Back Headroomgate Rd
FY8 89 F8
Back Heys BB5 103 E3
Back Heywood St E 15
BL9 33 A2
Back Heywood St W BL9 33 A1
Back High St Belmont BL7 46 C5
Blackpool FY1 130 B6
Chapeltown BL7 48 C4
Back Hill St 15 BB4 86 A7
Back Holly St BL9 33 A2
Back Holly St S 9 BL9 33 A2
Back Hope St OL13 87 F4
Back Hunter St 1 LA5 223 D2
Back Huntley Mount Rd
BL9 33 B3
Back Hurst St BL9 33 A1
Back Ingham St BL9 33 A1
Back Ingham St E BL9 33 A1
Back Kershaw St 10 BL9 33 A2
Back Knowlys Rd 2
LA3 212 F8
Back La Accrington BB5 104 E1
Appley Bridge WN6 19 E8
Bolton Green PR7 42 B7
Bretherton PR26 57 E5
Burscough Bridge L40 25 E6
Carnforth LA5,LA6 221 E7
Clayton Green PR6 78 A2
Clayton Green PR6 78 B1
Back La *continued*
Cumeragh Village PR3 139 B6
Gisburn BB7 231 C3
Great Eccleston PR3 156 B5
Greenhalgh PR4 133 B4
Grindleton BB7 190 B8
Haskayne L39 13 D3
Higham BB12 146 E6
Leyland PR25 60 C7
Longridge PR3 161 B6
Longton PR4 74 E8
Maghull L39 5 E6
Mawdesley L40 40 D1
Nelson BB10 149 F7
Newburgh L40,WN8 26 E2
Newton BB7 228 F6
Preesall FY6 200 A2
Rathmell BD24 236 F6
Rawtenstall BB4 86 A3
Rimington BB7 191 E8
Royal Oak L39 7 B2
Sabden BB12,BB7 146 C6
Skelmersdale,Digmoor WN8 9 D6
Skelmersdale,Holland Moor
WN8 9 E7
Stalmine FY6 177 E6
Trawden BB8 172 B2
Tunstall LA6 241 D4
Warton LA5 223 D5
Whitworth OL12 71 C3
Wiswell BB7 144 F8
Wray LA2 238 C6
Wrayton LA6 241 E2
Back La E L40 40 F1
Back Lathom St 9 BL9 33 A4
Back Laurel St 2 BL9 33 B2
Back Leach St BB8 171 C4
Back Lee St BB4 85 B2
Back Lines St 2 LA4 217 B5
Back Longworth Rd BL7 47 D3
Back Lord St
Blackpool FY1 130 B6
7 Lancaster LA1 218 D1
4 Rawtenstall BB4 86 A7
Back Lune St BB8 171 E4
Back Manor St 1 BL9 33 A2
Back Marine Rd LA4 216 F4
Back Marine Rd E LA4 217 D6
Back Mason St 17 BL9 33 A2
Back Moon Ave 5 FY1 130 B2
Back Morecambe St
LA4 217 B6
Back Moss La L40 25 F7
Back Mount 8 PR7 43 C8
Back Myrtle St 4 BL9 33 B2
Back Myrtle St S BL9 33 B2
Back Nelson St BL6 32 D3
Back New St 5 LA5 223 D2
Back Nook Terr 2 OL12 52 F3
Back North Cres FY8 89 E6
Back O The Town La L38 3 E3
Back Oddfellows Terr
BB4 86 F3
Back Oram St BL9 33 A4
Back Ormrod St 11 BL9 33 A2
Back Owen's Row BL6 32 C3
Back Oxford St BL9 33 A1
Back Parkinson St BB2 101 B2
Back Parsonage St 10
BL9 33 A3
Back Patience St 10
OL12 52 C1
Back Percy St BL9 33 B3
Back Peter St
8 Barrowford BB9 170 D4
3 Bury BL9 33 A3
Back Pine St 1 BL9 33 B2
Back Pleasant St 5
FY1 130 B7
Back Queen St
Great Harwood BB6 124 C5
12 Lancaster LA1 214 F7
1 Morecambe LA4 217 B5
Back Railway View PR7 31 A7
Back Rawlinson St 19
BL6 32 B4
Back Read's Rd FY1 130 C4
Back Regent St 1 BB4 85 B3
Back Rhoden Rd BB5 103 D2
Back Richard Burch St 1
BL9 33 A3
Back Rings Row BB4 106 A1
Back Rochdale Old Rd N 1
BL9 33 C3
Back Rochdale Old Rd S
Bury BL9 33 C3
Bury,Fairfield BL9 33 D3
Back Rochdale Rd BL9 33 B2
Back Rochdale Rd S 18
BL9 33 A2
Back Rushton St 6 OL13 70 E8
Back Salford St BL9 33 A4
Back Sandy Bank Rd BL7 48 D5
Back School La
Skelmersdale,Chapel House
WN8 17 D2
Skelmersdale,Up Holland
WN8 10 C7
Back Seed St 8 PR1 96 F8
Back Shannon St 4
FY1 130 B3
Back Shaw-Street BL9 33 B3
Back Shuttleworth St 7
BB12 126 C8

Back Skipton Rd 8 BB18 196 B2
Back Skull House La WN6 19 D8
Back South Cross St E 16 BL9 33 A2
Back Spencer St BB4 86 A7
Back Springfield Rd N FY8 89 E6
Back Square St BL0 50 C6
Back St LA3 209 D8
Back St Anne's Rd W FY8 89 E6
Back St John St OL13 87 F3
Back Stanley St BL0 50 B5
Back Starkie St PR1 96 F6
Back Sun St 9 LA1 214 F8
Back Teak St 5 BL9 33 B2
Back Tinline St 12 BL9 33 A2
Back Union St BL7 47 D2
Back Virginia St PR8 35 B6
Back Warbreck Rd 2 FY1 130 B6
Back Wash La BL9 33 B2
Back Wash La S 7 BL9 33 A2
Back Water St
10 Accrington BB5 104 C6
Egerton BL7 47 D2
Back Waterloo Rd 8 FY1 130 B1
Back Wellington St BB5 104 C5
Back West Cres FY8 89 E6
Back West End Rd N LA4 216 F4
Back Willow St BB12 127 E6
Back Winterdyne Terr LA3 216 E4
Back Wood St BL6 32 C3
Back Woodfield Rd 4 FY1 130 B2
Back Wright St BL6 32 B4
Back York St
Clitheroe BB7 166 F8
Rawtenstall BB4 86 A7
Back Zion St 16 BB8 171 D4
Backhouse St 1 BB5 103 E4
Backs The PR3 140 A6
Bacon St 8 BB9 148 E8
Bacup & Rawtenstall Gram Sch BB4 69 F8
Bacup Mus★ OL13 87 F3
Bacup Old Rd OL13 87 F7
Bacup Rd
Rawtenstall BB4,OL13 69 E8
Rawtenstall,Lower Cloughfold BB4 86 C2
Sharneyford OL14 88 E5
Walk Mill BB11 107 E6
Bacup Thorn Prim Sch OL13 87 F3
Baddon Cl LA4 217 C3
Baden Terr BB2 101 D1
Badge Brow BB5 103 E5
Badger Cl BB12 146 D1
Badger Rd PR26 77 A4
Badger St BL9 33 A3
Badger Wells Cotts BB7 146 A8
Badgers Cl BB5 104 E8
Badgers Croft PR2 118 F1
Badgers Rake L37 11 C5
Badgers Way PR5 97 B3
Badgers Wlk PR7 61 A3
Badgers Wlk E FY8 91 C3
Badgers Wlk W 12 FY8 91 B3
Badgers Wood PR3 159 C7
Bagganley La Chorley PR6 61 E4
Great Knowley PR6 61 F2
Bagnold Rd PR1 118 D1
Bagot St FY1 130 B1
Baildon Rd OL12 52 B1
Bailey Bank BB7 165 A7
Bailey Ct FY3 130 E6
Bailey La Heysham LA3 212 E8
Tosside BD23 236 B3
Bailey St Burnley BB11 127 E5
Earby BB18 197 C2
Bailrigg Chase LA1 215 B1
Bailrigg La LA1 215 A1
Baines Ave FY3 152 F1
Baines Endowed CE Prim Sch FY4 130 F1
Baines Sch FY6 153 D1
Bairstow St
3 Barnoldswick BB18 196 B3
Blackpool FY1 130 B3
13 Preston PR1 96 F7
Baker St 12 Bacup OL13 87 F3
Blackburn BB1 102 B4
Burnley BB11 127 E5
Coppull PR7 42 E1
Lancaster LA1 218 D3
4 Leyland PR25 77 B2
Nelson BB9 170 E1
Ramsbottom BL0 50 B5
Baker's La PR9 53 F3
Bakers Ct FY4 110 F7
Bakers Mews PR4 57 A6
Bala Cl BB1 101 E6
Balaclava St BB1 101 E6
Balcarres Cl PR25 77 A1
Balcarres Pl PR25 60 A8
Balcarres Rd Chorley PR7 43 B5
Leyland PR25 60 A8
Preston PR2 117 C2
Leyland PR25 77 B1
Balderstone Cl BB10 148 D2
Balderstone Hall La BB2 120 C6
Balderstone La BB10 148 E2
Balderstone Rd
Freckleton PR4 93 B7
Preston PR1 96 D5
Baldwin Gr FY1 130 D2
Baldwin Hill 3 BB7 166 D8
Baldwin Rd BB7 166 D8
Baldwin St Bacup OL13 70 B8
7 Bamber Bridge PR5 97 E1
5 Barrowford BB9 170 D4
Blackburn BB2 101 C3
Baldwin's Bldgs 14 BB4 86 A3
Balfour Cl Brierfield BB9 148 D5
Thornton FY5 153 D7
Balfour Ho 5 BB2 101 C4
Balfour Rd Fulwood PR2 117 E3
5 Rochdale OL12 52 C1
Southport PR8 35 E5
Balfour St Blackburn BB2 101 C4
Great Harwood BB6 124 E5
Leyland PR25 77 A1
Balham Ave FY4 110 E5
Ball Grove Dr BB8 172 B5
Ball La LA2 237 C3
Ball St Blackpool FY1 130 B1
3 Nelson BB9 170 D1
Poulton-le-F FY6 153 D3
Ball's Pl PR8 35 B7
Ballam Rd
Lower Ballam FY8 112 C3
Lytham St Anne's FY8 91 B4
Preston PR2 116 E1
Ballam St BB11 128 A4
Ballantrae Rd BB1 102 D3
Ballater St BB11 127 D3
Balle St BB3 65 A8
Balliol Cl BB12 126 D6
Ballot Hill Cres PR3 159 A5
Balm St BL0 50 A4
Balmer Gr FY1 130 D3
Balmoral PR7 30 E6
Balmoral Ave
Blackburn BB1 123 A4
Clitheroe BB7 166 C6
Leyland PR25 60 C8
Morecambe LA3 216 E3
Balmoral Cl Horwich BL6 32 E2
Ramsbottom BL8 50 A1
Southport PR9 54 B3
Balmoral Cres BB1 102 F4
Balmoral Ct PR7 43 B8
Balmoral Dr Brinscall PR6 62 E8
Formby L37 11 E1
Southport PR9 54 B3
Balmoral Pl FY5 153 C8
Balmoral Rd
Accrington BB5 104 D7
5 Bamber Bridge PR5 97 D3
Blackpool FY4 110 B8
Chorley PR7 43 B8
Darwen BB3 65 B6
Eccleston PR7 41 C7
Haslingden BB4 85 A1
Lancaster LA1 215 A7
Lytham St Anne's FY8 90 A5
3 Maghull L31 5 C1
Morecambe LA3,LA4 216 F3
New Longton PR4 96 A1
Balmoral Terr FY7 199 B5
Balniel Cl PR7 43 A7
Balshaw Ave PR7 60 D2
Balshaw Cres PR25 76 F2
Balshaw House Gdns PR7 60 D2
Balshaw La PR7 60 D1
Balshaw Lane Com Prim Sch PR7 60 E1
Balshaw Rd Leyland PR25 76 F1
Lowgill LA2 239 E3
Balshaw St 4 PR5 97 E2
Balshaw's CE High Sch PR25 60 B7
Baltic Bldgs 5 BB4 69 E8
Baltic Flats 4 BB4 69 E8
Baltic Rd 6 BB4 69 E8
Baltimore Rd FY8 90 B6
Bamber Ave FY2 152 C4
Bamber Bridge Sta PR5 77 E8
Bamber Gdns PR9 36 A8
Bamber St 2 PR7 43 B5
Bamber's Wlk PR4 113 E7
Bambers La FY4 111 C6
Bambers La N FY4 111 C7
Bamburgh Cl FY4 111 A7
Bamburgh Dr BB12 127 E7
Bamford Cl BL9 33 E4
Bamford Cres BB5 104 D4
Bamford Pl OL12 52 E1
Bamford Rd BL0 51 B6
Bamford St Burnley BB11 128 A6
Nelson BB9 149 A8
Bamfords Fold PR26 57 F5
Bampton Dr PR4 116 D4
Bamton Ave FY4 110 C7
Banastre PR7 61 A2
Banastre Rd PR8 35 B5
Banastre St 10 BB5 125 A1
Banbury Ave
Blackpool FY2 152 D1
Oswaldtwistle BB5 103 C4
Banbury Cl
3 Accrington BB5 104 A7
Blackburn BB2 80 F8
Banbury Dr PR2 117 E4
Banbury Rd
Longshaw WN5 10 D2
Banbury Rd continued
Lytham St Anne's FY8 90 A6
Morecambe LA3 217 C3
Bancroft Ave FY5 176 C2
Bancroft Fold BB18 196 A1
Bancroft Mill Engine Steam Mus★ BB18 196 B1
Bancroft Rd BB10 128 C8
Bancroft St 4 BB1 101 F5
Band La PR3 180 D1
Bangor Ave FY2 152 D4
Bangor St BB1 101 F7
Bank Ave WN5 10 D5
Bank Bottom BB3 82 A1
Bank Bridge PR4 57 B5
Bank Brow WN8 19 A8
Bank Cl Galgate LA2 210 F3
Longton PR4 75 A8
Bank Cott 2 LA2 239 B8
Bank Cotts BB7 144 B4
Bank Croft PR4 75 A8
Bank Fold BB9 170 E4
Bank Hall Cotts BB7 230 C1
Bank Hall Terr BB10 128 A7
Bank Head La PR5 98 D1
Bank Hey Cl BB1 123 A1
Bank Hey La N BB1 122 F3
Bank Hey La S BB1 123 A1
Bank Hey St FY1 130 B5
Bank House La
Bacup OL13 87 F2
Silverdale LA5 224 C3
Westhouse LA6 242 E4
Bank House St BB9 170 E4
Bank La Blackburn BB1 102 D4
Warton PR4 92 D4
Bank Mdw BL6 32 C4
Bank Mill St 3 BB4 85 B2
Bank Nook PR9 53 E3
Bank Par Burnley BB11 128 A6
Middleworth Green PR1 96 D3
Preston PR1 97 A6
Bank Pas PR8 35 A7
Bank Pl PR2 117 C1
Bank Rd Lancaster LA1 218 D3
Roby Mill WN8 19 D4
Bank Sq PR8 35 B8
Bank St Accrington BB5 104 C5
Adlington PR7 31 A7
14 Bacup OL13 87 F2
Bank Lane BL0 50 E7
Barnoldswick BB18 196 C2
Brierfield BB9 148 B6
Chapeltown BL7 48 C4
Chorley PR7 43 C8
10 Church BB5 103 E6
Darwen BB3 82 A1
Haslingden BB4 85 B3
11 Nelson BB9 170 E1
Padiham BB12 146 C1
Rawtenstall BB4 86 A2
Trawden BB8 172 C1
Bank Terr Heapey PR6 62 C4
Simonstone BB12 125 E8
Whitworth OL12 52 C8
Bank Top Baldingstone BL9 50 F1
Blackburn BB2 101 C4
Burnley BB11 128 A6
Roby Mill WN8 19 C4
Bank View FY6 177 C1
Bank View Cotts BB7 230 C1
Bankcroft Cl BB12 126 E8
Bankfield Burnley BB11 128 A6
Skelmersdale WN8 9 C7
Bankfield Ct FY5 153 B8
Bankfield Gr FY1 130 E3
Bankfield La PR9 54 B2
Bankfield St Bacup OL13 70 D8
Colne BB8 171 B4
Trawden BB8 172 B4
Bankfield Terr
2 Bacup OL13 70 D8
Barnoldswick BB18 196 C3
Bankhouse Mews BB9 170 E4
Bankhouse Rd BB9 170 E1
Bankhouse St
Burnley BB11 127 F6
Burnley BB11 128 A6
Banks Bridge Cl BB18 196 C4
Banks Cres LA3 212 F6
Banks Hill BB18 196 A4
Banks Meth Prim Sch PR9 55 B7
Banks Rd Fulwood PR2 117 C3
Southport PR9 54 D6
Banks Rise 10 LA2 239 D8
Banks St Blackpool FY1 130 B6
Lane Bottom BB10 149 B3
Banks Way 12 LA2 239 D8
Banksands La PR3 201 E7
Banksbarn WN8 9 C7
Banksfield Ave PR2 117 C3
Banksfield Pl PR5 78 A7
Bankside Blackburn BB2 101 E2
Clayton Green PR6 78 B1
Hightown L38 2 F3
Parbold WN8 27 B2
Bankside Cl Bacup OL13 87 E1
Goodshaw Chapel BB4 106 A1
Bankside La OL13 87 F2
Bankwood WN6 19 E6
Banner Cl PR7 41 B6
Bannerigg Brow LA6 243 A5
Bannerman Terr PR6 61 D2
Bannister Brook Ho PR25 77 A2
Bannister Cl
Higher Walton PR5 98 B4
Bannister Cl continued
Trawden BB8 172 B3
Bannister Ct
Blackpool FY2 152 B4
17 Nelson BB9 148 E8
Bannister Dr PR25 76 E1
Bannister Gn PR7 41 C3
Bannister Hall Cres PR5 98 B4
Bannister Hall Dr PR5 98 B4
Bannister Hall La PR5 98 B4
Bannister La
Eccleston PR7 41 C5
Hill Dale L40,WN6 27 E6
Leyland PR26 76 E4
Bannister St
11 Chorley PR7 43 C7
Lytham St Anne's FY8 91 B3
Bannister's Bit 4 PR1 96 C2
Bannistre Cl 1 FY8 90 A8
Bannistre Ct PR4 57 A6
Bannistre Mews PR4 57 A6
Bar Cotts BB12 145 E1
Bar St BB10 128 B8
Bar Terr OL12 52 C7
Barbara Castle Way BB1 101 E5
Barberry Bank BL7 47 E2
Barbon Pl LA1 218 C2
Barbon St Burnley BB10 148 C2
14 Padiham BB12 146 C1
Barbondale Rd LA6,LA10 243 E8
Barbrook Cl WN6 29 B2
Barclay Ave
Blackpool FY4 130 F2
Burnley BB11 127 C4
Barclay Rd PR3 140 A7
Barcroft Gn BB10 128 E1
Barcroft St BB8 171 C5
Barden Com Inf Sch BB10 148 A1
Barden Croft BB5 124 F4
Barden High Sch BB10 148 A2
Barden Jun Sch BB10 148 A1
Barden La BB10,BB12 148 A2
Barden Pl PR2 118 D4
Barden Rd BB5 103 F4
Barden St 3 BB10 148 B1
Barden View BB10 148 A2
Bardsea Pl PR2 116 F3
Bardsley Cl WN8 10 A7
Bardsway FY5 176 A3
Bardsway Ave FY3 130 F6
Bare Ave LA4 217 E6
Bare La LA4 217 E5
Bare Lane Sta LA4 217 E6
Barford Cl
Skelmersdale WN8 10 A7
Southport PR8 21 A6
Barford Gr BL6 32 F1
Bargee Cl BB1 101 F3
Barham St 6 FY1 130 B2
Barker Brow BB1,PR7 142 A3
Barker Cl LA6 240 B7
Barker La BB2 122 C2
Barker Sq LA2 211 A6
Barker Terr BB7 189 E1
Barkerfield Cl BB12 146 F5
Barkerhouse Rd BB10, BB9 149 B8
Barkfield Ave L37 11 E4
Barkfield La L37 11 D4
Barley Bank St BB3 81 F2
Barley Cl BB2 101 D5
Barley Cop La LA1 218 B4
Barley Gr BB10 128 C6
Barley Holme Rd BB4 86 A8
Barley La BB9 169 B7
Barley New Rd BB12 169 E5
Barley St BB12 126 C7
Barley Vistors Ctr★ BB12 169 C5
Barley Way 10 BB2 101 D5
Barleydale Rd BB9 170 E5
Barleyfield PR5 78 C3
Barlow Cres FY3 130 E4
Barlow Ct BL7 48 E5
Barlow St Accrington BB5 104 A6
Bacup OL13 70 B7
Horwich BL6 32 C2
Preston PR1 117 E1
Preston PR1 117 F2
11 Rawtenstall BB4 86 A3
Barlow's La L39 22 D5
Barlows Bldgs 5 BB4 85 F1
Barmouth Ave FY3 131 A3
Barmouth Cres BB1 122 E1
Barmouth Ct PR2 117 A3
Barmskin La PR7 41 B2
Barn Acre BL6 31 E1
Barn Cl PR4 56 A2
Barn Croft
3 Clitheroe BB7 166 D7
Higher Penwortham PR1 96 B4
1 Leyland PR26 76 B1
Barn Gill Cl BB1 101 F3
Barn Hey PR4 95 A1
Barn Hey Dr PR26 76 E3
Barn Hey Rd L33 1 A2
Barn Mdw
Clayton Brook PR5 78 B6
Edgworth BL7 48 D5
Barn Meadow Cres BB1 124 C1
Barn View PR6 30 F8
Barnacre Cl
Fulwood PR2 118 A8
Lancaster LA1 215 B2
Barnacre Rd PR3 140 A8
Barnard Cl BB5 103 C4
Barnbrook St BL9 33 A3
Barncroft Dr BL6 32 F3
Barnes Ave BB4 85 F2
Barnes Cl BL0 50 A3
Barnes Dr Cleveleys FY5 175 E5
Maghull L31 5 C3
Barnes Rd
Morecambe LA3 216 E3
Ormskirk L39 15 E3
Skelmersdale WN8 17 E1
Barnes Sq 1 BB5 124 F2
Barnes St Accrington BB5 104 C6
Burnley BB11 128 A6
Church BB5 103 E6
Clayton-le-M BB5 124 F3
Haslingden BB4 85 B4
Barnfield
6 Bamber Bridge PR5 77 A8
Kirkham PR4 114 A5
Much Hoole PR4 74 E3
Barnfield Ave BB10 128 F6
Barnfield Bsns Ctr BB9 148 F6
Barnfield Cl
4 Cleveleys FY5 175 F4
Colne BB8 172 A5
Egerton BL7 47 E2
Barnfield Dr WN8 9 E7
Barnfield Manor FY6 154 D3
Barnfield St
Accrington BB5 104 D5
Rochdale OL12 52 F2
Barnfield Way BB5 125 E5
Barnmeadow La BB6 124 C5
Barnoldswick CE Prim Sch BB18 196 B2
Barnoldswick La LA6 242 D3
Barnoldswick Rd
Beverley BB8,BB9 170 F7
Kelbrook BB18 194 F6
Barns La PR3 161 C8
Barns The Formby L37 12 A1
Weeton PR4 133 A2
Barnsfold PR2 117 D6
Barnside Euxton PR7 60 C3
Whitworth OL12 52 B8
Barnside Est BB8 172 F7
Barnstaple Way PR4 116 F6
Barnwood Cres BB18 197 C1
Barnwood Rd BB18 197 B1
Baron Rd FY1 130 C1
Baron St Darwen BB3 81 F2
Rawtenstall BB4 86 D1
Barons Cl BB3 82 A7
Barons Way
Blackburn BB3 82 A6
Euxton PR7 60 D2
Barracks Rd BB11 127 D6
Barret Hill Brow BB7 230 B4
Barret St BB18 197 A1
Barrett Ave PR8 35 A2
Barrett Ct 6 BL9 33 A2
Barrett Rd PR8 35 A2
Barrett St 5 BB10 128 A8
Barrington Ct BB5 103 F7
Barrington Dr PR8 21 B5
Barrison Gn L40 24 E2
Barritt Rd BB4 85 F2
Barronwood Ct PR4 57 A5
Barrow Nook La L39 7 E2
Barrow Sch BB7 166 D2
Barrow's La PR3 156 B5
Barrowcroft Cl WN1 30 B1
Barrowford Rd
Barrowford BB9 170 B1
Colne BB8 171 B5
Fence BB12 147 C7
Barrowford Sch BB9 170 D3
Barrowford St Thomas Prim Sch BB9 170 C3
Barrows La LA3 212 E7
Barrows La E PR3 156 B5
Barry Ave PR2 117 A3
Barry Gr LA3 212 F6
Barry St BB12 127 C7
Bartholomew Rd LA4 217 C4
Bartle La PR4 116 C7
Bartle Pl PR2 116 E1
Bartle Rd FY8 90 A8
Bartle St BB11 127 D5
Bartlett Ho PR8 35 B3
Barton Ave Blackpool FY1 130 B2
Knott End-on-S FY6 199 E5
Barton Ct LA1 215 A4
Barton Gdns LA1 215 B5
Barton Heys Rd L37 11 D1
Barton La PR3 137 E7
Barton Mans FY8 89 C7
Barton Rd Lancaster LA1 215 A4
Lytham St Anne's FY8 89 D8
Barton Row LA6 240 B7
Barton Sq FY6 199 E5
Barton St BB2 101 E5
Barton St Lawrence CE Prim Sch PR3 137 B7
Barton Streety BB2 101 E5
Bartons Cl PR9 54 D5
Barwood Lea Mill 14 BL0 50 C6
Bashall Gr PR25 77 B3
Basil St Colne BB8 171 D4
Preston PR1 118 C2
Basnett St BB10 148 C1
Bass La BL9 50 D3
Bassenthwaite Rd FY3 131 C2
Basset Cl OL12 52 E3
Basset Gdns OL12 52 E3
Bassett Way OL12 52 E2
Bastwell Rd BB1 101 F7
Bateman Gr LA4 217 B5

Bateman Rd LA4 217 B5
Bateman St BL6 32 D2
Bates St BB5 124 E3
Bath Mill La LA1 215 A8
Bath Mill Sq 7 LA1 215 A8
Bath Rd FY8 91 B3
Bath Springs L39 15 F5
Bath St Accrington BB5 104 B4
Blackburn BB2 101 C4
Blackpool FY4 130 B1
Colne BB8 171 E5
Lancaster LA1 215 A8
Lytham St Anne's FY8 91 B3
Morecambe LA4 217 A5
Nelson BB9 148 F8
2 Preston PR2 117 D1
Southport PR8 35 B8
Bacup OL13 88 A2
Bath St N PR9 35 B8
Bathurst Ave FY3 131 A7
Bathurst St 3 BB2 101 D5
Batridge Rd BL7 48 A7
Battersby St BL9 33 D3
Battismore Rd LA4 217 B5
Battle Way L37 12 B2
Bawdlands BB7 166 D8
Bawhead Rd BB18 197 B1
Baxenden St John's CE Prim Sch BB5 104 E1
Baxter St WN6 29 F1
Baxtergate LA4 217 B6
Bay Cl LA3 212 D6
Bay Horse Dr LA1 215 B3
Bay Horse La PR4 135 D4
Bay Horse Rd LA2 211 E4
Bay Rd Fulwood PR2 118 E2
Heysham LA3 212 D6
Bay St BB1 102 A7
Bay The FY5 175 C5
Bay Tree Farm PR2 95 D8
Bay Tree Rd PR6 78 B3
Bay View LA6 237 B8
Bay View Ave LA2 218 C8
Bay View Cotts LA3 212 E6
Bay View Cres LA2 218 C8
Bay View Dr LA3 212 F8
Bayard St BB12 127 A6
Baycliffe Cres LA4 217 A5
Bayley Fold BB7 166 E8
Bayley St BB5 124 E3
Bayliss Cl PR2 118 F3
Baylton Ct PR3 181 D2
Baylton Dr PR3 181 D2
Baynes Cotts 4 LA2 239 B8
Baynes St BB3 82 F1
Bayside FY7 199 B4
Bayswater FY2 152 C4
Baytree Cl
Bamber Bridge PR5 77 C8
Southport PR9 54 D5
Baytree Gr BL0 50 B2
Baytree Wlk OL12 71 C1
Baywood St BB1 101 F7
Bazil Gr LA3 209 D7
Bazil La LA3 209 D7
Bazley Rd FY8 90 D3
Beach Ave Cleveleys FY5 175 D3
Lytham St Anne's FY8 90 C3
Beach Priory Gdns PR8 35 A6
Beach Rd Cleveleys FY5 175 D3
Fleetwood FY7 198 E3
Lytham St Anne's FY8 89 D7
Pilling Lane FY6 200 B7
Southport PR8 34 F6
Beach St
Lytham St Anne's FY8 91 A3
Morecambe LA4 217 E7
Beacham Rd PR8 35 E7
Beachcomber Dr FY5 175 C3
Beachley Rd PR2 117 A4
Beachley Sq BB12 127 D7
Beachmews PR8 34 F6
Beacon Ave PR2 117 D5
Beacon Cl BB8 171 C3
Beacon Crossing WN8 27 C2
Beacon Ct PR3 138 D5
Beacon Ctry Pk★ WN8 18 F2
Beacon Dr PR3 138 D6
Beacon Fell Ctry Pk★ PR3 183 F2
Beacon Fell Cvn Pk PR3 162 D1
Beacon Fell Rd PR3 183 E2
Beacon Flats PR3 140 C8
Beacon Gr Fulwood PR2 117 D4
Garstang PR3 181 B6
Beacon Hill High Sch FY2 152 D1
Beacon Hts WN8 10 A8
Beacon La L40,WN8 18 D4
Beacon Lodge 10 PR2 118 F4
Beacon Rd
Poulton-le-F FY6 154 A3
Shevington Moor WN6 29 B2
Beacon Sch WN8 9 E8
Beacon St PR7 43 D7
Beacon View
Appley Bridge WN6 19 C8
Longridge PR3 162 B3
Beacon View Dr WN8 10 B7
Beacons The WN6 19 D7
Beaconsfield Ave PR1 118 E1
Beaconsfield Ct 4 L39 15 F5
Beaconsfield Rd PR9 35 F6
Beaconsfield St
Accrington BB5 104 D5
Great Harwood BB6 124 C5
16 Haslingden BB4 85 B3
Beaconsfield Terr
Catterall PR3 181 E2
Chorley PR6 61 D2
Beale Cl BB1 102 B1
Beale Rd BB9 148 B8
Beamish Ave BB2 81 D8
Beamont Dr PR1 96 D8
Bean Ave FY4 110 E8
Bear St BB12 126 F6
Beardshaw Ave FY1 130 D2
Beardsworth St BB1 102 A7
Beardwood BB2 101 A8
Beardwood Brow BB2 101 B7
Beardwood Dr BB2 101 A7
Beardwood Fold BB2 101 A7
Beardwood High Sch BB2 101 A6
Beardwood Hospl The BB2 101 A6
Beardwood Mdw BB2 101 A7
Beardwood Pk BB2 101 B7
Bearncroft WN8 9 D6
Bearswood Croft PR6 78 B2
Bearwood Way FY5 176 C2
Beatie St BB9 148 B6
Beatrice Ave BB12 127 C7
Beatrice Mews 11 BL6 32 B4
Beatrice Pl BB2 82 A8
Beatrice St 8 BL6 32 B4
Beattock Pl FY2 152 F6
Beatty Ave PR7 43 B6
Beatty Cl FY8 110 D1
Beatty Rd PR8 35 E5
Beauclerk Rd FY8 90 B6
Beaufort L37 12 A2
Beaufort Ave FY2 152 C5
Beaufort Cl Ormskirk L39 15 A1
Simonstone BB12 145 E2
Beaufort Gr LA4 217 D5
Beaufort Rd
Morecambe LA4 217 E5
Weir OL13 88 A7
Beaufort St Nelson BB9 148 E7
Rochdale OL12 52 C1
Beauley Ave BB12 145 E2
Beauly Cl 3 BL0 50 A2
Beaumaris Ave BB2 101 A1
Beaumaris Cl 2 BB4 85 B1
Beaumaris Rd PR25 60 C8
Beaumont Ave BL6 32 C4
Beaumont Coll (The Spastics Society) LA1 218 D4
Beaumont Cres L39 15 D2
Beaumont Ct
8 Blackpool FY1 130 C6
Lytham St Anne's FY8 90 A8
Beaumont Gdns FY6 153 A5
Beaumont Ho L39 15 D2
Beaumont Pl LA1 218 D4
Beaumont Rd BL6 32 C4
Beaumont St LA1 218 D4
Beaumont Way BB3 82 C1
Beaver Cl BB1 122 F5
Beaver Terr 14 OL13 88 A3
Beavers La WN8 9 D6
Bebles Rd L39 15 C3
Becconsall La PR4 73 F3
Beck Ct FY7 198 D1
Beck Gr FY5 175 E4
Beck Side LA2 237 C3
Beck View 7 LA1 215 A3
Beckdean Ave FY6 153 D2
Beckenham Ct BB10 148 D3
Beckett Ct 18 PR1 96 F8
Beckett St 5 BB3 65 A8
Becks Brow BD23 236 F3
Becks Crossing BB8 172 C2
Beckside Barley BB12 169 C5
Trawden BB8 172 C3
Beckside Mews LA6 240 B3
Beckway Ave FY3 130 F7
Bedale Pl FY5 175 E1
Beddington St 6 BB9 170 D1
Bedford Ave FY5 175 D3
Bedford Cl BB5 103 C4
Bedford Ct PR8 35 A2
Bedford Mews BB3 81 F4
Bedford Pl Lancaster LA1 215 A4
Padiham BB12 126 D7
Bedford Rd
Blackpool FY1 130 C8
Fulwood PR2 118 A4
6 Lytham St Anne's FY8 91 D4
Southport PR8 35 A2
Bedford St
6 Barrowford BB9 170 C1
Blackburn BB2 101 C2
Darwen BB3 81 F4
Egerton BL7 47 D2
Bedford Terr Bury BL9 33 A4
Haslingden BB4 68 A8
Bedfordshire Ave BB12 127 B7
Bee La PR1 96 E1
Bee Mill PR3 141 D3
Beech Ave Adlington PR6 31 B8
Bilsborrow PR3 159 A5
Blackpool FY3 130 E5
Darwen BB3 82 B2
Earby BB18 197 A1
Euxton PR7 60 C4
Galgate LA2 210 F4
Horwich BL6 32 E1
Kirkham PR4 114 B4
Leyland PR25 60 A7
Parbold WN8 27 C2
Poulton-le-F FY6 153 D4
Warton PR4 92 D6
Beech Bank PR4 155 F1
Beech Cl Bacup OL13 88 A3
Clitheroe BB7 166 D8
Oswaldtwistle BB5 103 C2
Rishton BB1 103 B8
Rufford L40 39 C4
Skelmersdale WN8 17 E1
Whitworth OL12 71 C1
Wilpshire BB1 122 E6
Beech Cres BB5 125 A1
Beech Ct Fulwood PR2 117 E7
Silverdale LA5 224 C2
Beech Dr Formby L37 11 D4
Freckleton PR4 93 A5
Fulwood PR2 117 D8
Haslingden BB4 85 C2
Kirkham PR4 113 E4
Longridge PR3 140 A7
Newton-w-S PR4 114 F2
Poulton-le-F FY6 153 D2
Whalley BB7 144 A7
Beech Gdns PR6 78 B1
Beech Gr Accrington BB5 104 A4
2 Barnoldswick BB18 196 C2
Blackburn BB3 81 D6
Brierfield BB10 148 C4
Chatburn BB7 190 D5
Knott End-on-S FY6 199 E6
Morecambe LA4 217 E5
Preston PR2 117 B1
Ramsbottom BL8 50 A1
Slyne LA2 218 C6
Southport PR9 35 F7
Warton LA5 223 D5
Beech Grove Cl BL9 33 B4
Beech Ho Southport PR8 35 A5
Chorley PR7 42 F6
Beech Ind Est 3 OL13 88 A3
Beech Mdw L39 16 A4
Beech Mount
Blackburn BB1 122 F3
Waddington BB7 189 B4
Beech Rd Aughton L39 6 A6
Elswick PR4 155 F1
Garstang PR3 181 B8
Halton LA2 219 C7
Leyland PR25 77 A2
Beech St Accrington BB5 104 C5
Bacup OL13 88 A3
Barnoldswick BB18 196 B1
Blackburn BB1 102 A7
Bury BL9 33 B2
Clayton-le-M BB5 124 F1
Clitheroe BB7 166 D8
Edgworth BL7 48 D5
Great Harwood BB6 124 C6
Lancaster LA1 214 D8
10 Nelson BB9 170 E1
Padiham BB12 126 D7
1 Preston PR1 96 D6
Ramsbottom BL0 50 C3
Rawtenstall BB4 86 A3
Beech St S PR1 96 E6
Beech Terr Ingleton LA6 242 F3
1 Preston PR1 96 E6
Beech Tree Ave WN6 19 D8
Beech Tree Cl BB9 148 E7
Beech Tree Sch PR5 78 B4
Beech Wlk PR6 61 A7
Beechacre BL0 50 D5
Beecham St LA4 217 B6
Beechcroft Cleveleys FY5 175 C4
1 Maghull L31 5 D1
Beeches Ct FY5 176 C1
Beeches The
Clayton Green PR6 78 C3
Singleton FY6 154 D1
Tarleton PR4 57 A7
Beechfield Hill Dale WN8 27 C5
Lancaster LA1 214 D7
Maghull L31 5 E1
Beechfield Ave
Blackpool FY3 130 E3
Knott End-on-S FY6 200 A5
Wrea Green PR4 113 C4
Beechfield Ct PR25 60 B8
Beechfield Gdns PR8 34 F6
Beechfield Mews PR9 35 C7
Beechfield Rd PR25 60 B8
Beechfields PR7 41 B6
Beechill Cl PR5 97 E3
Beeching Cl LA1 214 F6
Beechthorpe Ave BB7 189 B4
Beechtrees WN8 9 D7
Beechway Fulwood PR2 118 A4
Higher Penwortham PR1 96 B3
Maghull L31 6 B2
Beechway Ave L31 6 B2
Beechwood WN8 18 C3
Beechwood Ave
Accrington BB5 104 D3
Bamber Bridge PR5 97 D4
Burnley BB11 127 F3
Clitheroe BB7 166 E6
Fulwood PR2 117 C4
Ramsbottom BL0 50 D6
Shevington WN6 19 F5
Beechwood Cres WN5 10 E6
Beechwood Croft PR6 78 A3
Beechwood Ct
Blackburn BB1 101 F7
Coppull PR7 29 F8
Maghull L31 5 F1
Skelmersdale WN8 9 D6
Beechwood Dr
Blackburn BB2 80 E8
Formby L37 11 C1
Ormskirk L39 15 D5
Thornton FY5 153 B8
Beechwood Gdns LA1 215 A2
Beechwood Gr FY2 152 E4
Beechwood Mews BB1 82 A8
Beechwood Rd
12 Blackburn BB1 102 A7
Chorley PR7 43 E6
Beeford Dr WN5 10 E5
Beenland St 3 PR1 118 D1
Beeston Ave FY6 153 C5
Beetham Ct BB5 124 E2
Beetham Cvn Pk LA5, LA7 225 C8
Beetham Pl FY3 130 E6
Begonia St BB3 82 B1
Begonia View BB3 82 A7
Beightons Wlk OL12 52 D4
Bela Cl 3 LA1 218 A2
Bela Gr FY1 130 D2
Belfield WN8 9 D6
Belfield Rd BB5 104 C4
Belford Ave FY5 175 F4
Belford St BB12 127 F7
Belfry Cl PR7 60 D4
Belfry Cres WN6 29 F2
Belfry Mans BB6 143 C6
Belfry The FY8 91 D5
Belgarth Rd BB5 104 C7
Belgrave Ave
Higher Penwortham PR1 96 B3
Kirkham PR4 114 A7
Belgrave Cl
Blackburn BB2 101 B3
3 Lytham St Anne's FY8 90 D6
Belgrave Cres BL6 32 D3
Belgrave Ct
Burnley BB12 127 F7
Leyland PR25 59 F8
Belgrave Pl
Poulton-le-F FY6 153 B2
Southport PR8 34 F3
Belgrave Rd
Blackpool FY4 130 E1
Colne BB8 171 D6
Darwen BB3 65 A8
5 Leyland PR25 77 A1
Poulton-le-F FY6 153 B3
Southport PR8 34 F3
Belgrave Sq 9 BB3 82 A1
Belgrave St
Brierfield BB9 148 A6
Burnley BB12 127 F7
Nelson BB9 170 F1
Rising Bridge BB5 85 A8
Rochdale OL12 52 D1
Belgravia Apartments PR9 53 B1
Bell La Bury BL9 33 A3
Claughton PR3 182 C4
Clayton-le-M BB5 125 B4
Bell St BB4 85 B3
Bell Villas PR5 99 C3
Bell's Cl L31 5 C4
Bell's La L31 5 B3
Bell-Aire Park Homes LA3 212 F5
Bellamy Ave LA4 217 A3
Belle Field Cl PR1 97 A1
Belle Isle Ave OL12 52 C6
Belle View Pl FY3 130 D5
Belle Vue Ave LA1 215 A5
Belle Vue Dr LA1 215 A5
Belle Vue La BB7 189 B4
Belle Vue Pl BB11 127 E6
Belle Vue St
Blackburn BB2 101 C5
Burnley BB11 127 E6
Bellfield Rd LA4 217 C5
Bellflower Cl PR25 77 E3
Bellingham Rd FY8 91 B4
Bellis Ave PR9 53 F2
Bellis Way PR5 97 B2
Bells Arc 10 BB10 128 A8
Bells Bridge La PR3 203 F2
Bells La PR5 98 E3
Belmont Ave
Blackpool FY1 130 C4
Fulwood PR2 118 D2
Orrell WN5 10 D3
Poulton-le-F FY6 153 B3
Belmont Cl Brinscall PR6 62 E8
Burscough L40 25 E3
Fulwood PR2 118 D2
Lancaster LA1 218 B3
Belmont Cres PR2 118 D2
Belmont Ct PR3 140 B7
Belmont Dr PR6 61 E1
Belmont Gr BB10 128 D5
Belmont Pl PR7 29 C6
Belmont Rd Adlington PR6 31 B7
Belmont BB3,BL7 64 A2
Fleetwood FY7 199 A3
Fulwood PR2 117 C2
Great Harwood BB6 124 B5
Horwich BL6 32 C7
Leyland PR25 59 D8
Lytham St Anne's FY8 90 C5
Rivington BL6 45 C3
Belmont Sch BB4 85 E2
Belmont St PR8 35 A5
Belmont Terr
7 Barrowford BB9 170 D3
Foulridge BB8 194 E1
Belmont Way OL12 52 E2
Belper St BB1 102 A6
Belsfield Dr PR4 73 E4
Belshaw Ct BB11 127 A3
Belthorn Prim Sch BB1 82 F6
Belthorn Rd BB1 82 E6
Belton Hill PR2 117 D8
Belvedere Ave
Ramsbottom BL8 50 A1
Rawtenstall BB4 87 A1
Belvedere Ct
1 Lytham St Anne's FY8 90 D4
Thornton FY5 153 C8
Belvedere Dr Chorley PR7 43 B8
Formby L37 11 F1
Belvedere Pk L39 6 C7
Belvedere Rd
Adlington PR6 31 B8
Blackburn BB1 123 A3
Burnley BB10 128 B6
2 Leyland PR25 77 B2
Southport PR8 21 C5
Thornton FY5 153 C8
Belverdale Gdns FY4 110 F5
Belvere Ave FY4 110 D6
Belvoir St OL12 52 C1
Ben La
Barnoldswick BB18 196 D3
Rainford Junction L39 8 A1
Ben Lane Ct L39 8 B2
Benbow Cl FY8 110 D2
Bence Rd PR1 97 B6
Bence St BB8 171 E5
Bench Carr OL12 52 E1
Benenden Pl 9 FY5 176 A2
Bengal St PR7 61 D1
Bengarth Rd PR9 35 F8
Benjamin Hargreaves CE Prim Sch BB5 104 D5
Bennett Ave FY1 130 C4
Bennett Dr WN5 10 D4
Bennett House Sch The PR6 61 E1
Bennett Rd FY5 176 A3
Bennett St 4 BB9 170 F2
Bennett's La FY4 110 F6
Bennington St BB1,BB2 101 F3
Bennison Ct PR9 53 C1
Benson Ave LA4 217 D4
Benson Ho BB1 102 C8
Benson La PR4 135 F3
Benson Rd FY3 152 E1
Benson St Blackburn BB1 102 B7
Bury BL9 33 A1
Edgworth BL7 48 E5
Benson's La PR4 158 C1
Bent Est OL13 88 A7
Bent Gap La BB2 101 C4
Bent La Colne BB8 172 B6
Leyland PR25 60 C8
Bent St Blackburn BB2 101 D4
Haslingden BB4 68 D8
4 Oswaldtwistle BB5 103 D3
Bentcliffe Gdns BB5 104 D4
Bentgate Cl BB4 68 D8
Bentham Ave
Burnley BB10 148 B3
Fleetwood FY7 198 C1
Bentham Cl BB2 101 B1
Bentham Hall Cotts LA2 239 D8
Bentham Moor Rd LA6 242 D2
Bentham Pl WN6 29 F2
Bentham Rd
Blackburn BB2 101 B1
Ingleton LA6 242 E3
Lancaster LA1 215 A2
Standish WN6 29 F2
Bentham St Coppull PR7 42 E1
Southport PR8 35 B5
Bentham Sta LA2 239 D7
Bentham's Way PR8 35 C2
Bentinck Ave FY4 110 B5
Bentinck Rd FY8 89 C8
Bentinck St 9 OL12 52 C1
Bentlea Rd BB7 231 B3
Bentley Dr Kirkham PR4 113 E5
Peel Hill FY4 112 A6
Bentley Gn FY5 176 D2
Bentley La
Andertons Mill L40,PR7 41 A1
Bispham Green L40 27 E8
Bury BL9 51 A1
Bentley Mews OL12 52 E2
Bentley Park Rd PR4 74 F7
Bentley St 7 Bacup OL13 87 F3
Blackburn BB1 102 C5
Darwen BB3 65 C7
Nelson BB9 148 D7
Rochdale OL12 52 E2
Bentley Wood Way BB11 126 F4
Bentmeadows OL12 52 E1
Benton Rd PR2 118 D4
Bents BB8 172 B6
Bents La LA6 243 A3
Bentwood Rd BB4 85 A3
Beresford Dr PR9 53 F1
Beresford Gdns PR9 53 F2
Beresford Rd BB1 101 D7
Beresford St
8 Blackpool FY1 130 C7
9 Burnley BB11 127 D6
Nelson BB9 148 F6
Bergen St BB11 127 B5
Bergerac Cres FY5 152 F6
Berkeley Cl Chorley PR7 43 D5
Nelson BB9 148 E7
Berkeley Colonnade PR2 118 A4
Berkeley Cres BB12 146 C1

Berkeley Ct LA3 . . . .**212** E6
Berkeley Dr
Clayton-le-W PR5 . . . .**77** E4
Simonstone BB12 . . . .**145** E2
Berkeley St
Brierfield BB9 . . . .**148** A5
Nelson BB9 . . . .**148** E7
Preston PR1 . . . .**117** E1
Berkley Cl PR4 . . . .**113** E5
Berkshire Ave BB12 . . . . .**127** B7
Berkshire Cl BB1 . . . .**122** F7
Bernard St OL12 . . . .**52** E3
Berne Ave BL6 . . . .**32** A3
Berridge Ave BB4 . . . .**127** A6
Berriedale Rd BB9 . . . . . .**171** A1
Berry Cl WN8 . . . .**17** F2
Berry Field � PR1 . . . .**96** C3
Berry Ho Cotts L40 . . . .**38** A5
Berry House Rd L40 . . . . . .**38** A4
Berry La PR3 . . . .**140** A7
Berry Sq BL6 . . . .**31** D3
Berry St
Bamber Bridge PR5 . . . . . .**77** A8
Brierfield BB9 . . . .**148** A5
Burnley BB11 . . . .**127** F4
Preston PR1 . . . .**97** A7
Skelmersdale WN8 . . . .**17** F2
Berry's La FY6 . . . .**153** C4
Berrys La BB7 . . . .**144** C2
Bertha St BB5 . . . .**104** D6
Bertram Ave LA4 . . . . . .**217** A4
Bertrand Ave FY3 . . . . . .**131** A7
Berwick Ave
Cleveleys FY5 . . . .**175** F4
Southport PR9 . . . .**21** D5
Berwick Dr Burnley BB12 **127** E7
Fulwood PR2 . . . .**117** D4
Berwick Rd
Blackpool FY4 . . . .**110** C5
Lytham St Anne's FY8 . . . . .**89** F7
Preston PR1 . . . .**97** A6
Berwick St PR1 . . . .**118** E1
Berwick Way LA3 . . . . . .**212** E7
Berwen Ave LA4 . . . .**217** D6
Berwyn Cl BL6 . . . .**32** C5
Berwyn Ct PR8 . . . .**35** D4
Beryl Ave Blackburn BB1 **122** F7
Cleveleys FY5 . . . .**175** E1
Besant Cl BB1 . . . .**102** B1
Bescar Brow La L40 . . . . .**23** F7
Bescar La L40 . . . .**37** B1
Bescar La Sta L40 . . . .**37** B2
Bescot Way �12 FY5 . . . . .**152** F7
Bessie St ᴸᴮ BB18 . . . . . .**196** B2
Best St PR4 . . . .**113** F5
Bethel Ave FY2 . . . .**152** D4
Bethel Rd BB1 . . . .**102** A7
Bethel St
Barnoldswick BB18 . . . . .**196** B3
Colne BB8 . . . .**171** B4
Bethesda Cl BB2 . . . .**101** D3
Bethesda Rd FY1 . . . . . .**130** B4
Bethesda St
Barnoldswick BB18 . . . . .**196** B2
Burnley BB11 . . . .**127** F6
Betony LA4 . . . .**217** F6
Betony Cl OL12 . . . .**52** D3
Bett La PR6 . . . .**79** C1
Beulah Ave LA4 . . . .**217** D5
Bevan Pl BB9 . . . .**170** F2
Beverley Ave
Longshaw WN5 . . . .**10** E1
Poulton-le-F FY6 . . . .**131** D4
Beverley Cl
Clitheroe BB7 . . . .**166** E6
Preston PR2 . . . .**96** C8
Southport PR9 . . . .**54** C5
Wrea Green PR4 . . . .**113** A3
Beverley Ct
ᴣ Lytham St Anne's FY8 . .**90** A4
Morecambe LA4 . . . .**217** E5
Beverley Dr BB7 . . . .**166** D6
Beverley Gr FY4 . . . .**110** C7
Beverley Rd BB9 . . . .**170** E4
Beverley Rd N FY8 . . . . . .**90** A8
Beverley Rd S FY8 . . . . . .**90** A8
Beverley St
ᴸ Blackburn BB2 . . . . . .**101** B1
Burnley BB11 . . . .**127** E5
Beverly Cl FY5 . . . .**153** B8
Bevington Cl BB11 . . . . . .**127** E5
Bewcastle Dr L40 . . . .**16** C3
Bexhill Rd PR7 . . . .**117** A4
Bexley Ave FY2 . . . .**130** D8
Bexley Pl FY8 . . . .**90** E5
Bezza La BB2,PR5 . . . . . .**120** C5
Bhailok St ᴣ PR1 . . . .**96** E8
Bibby Dr FY3 . . . .**131** E5
Bibby Rd PR9 . . . .**54** A1
Bibby's La FY5 . . . .**153** B8
Bickerstaffe CE Sch L39 . . .**7** E5
Bickerstaffe St ᴀ FY1 . . .**130** B3
Bickerton Rd PR8 . . . .**34** F4
Bicknell St BB1 . . . .**101** E6
Bideford Ave FY3 . . . . . .**131** A6
Bideford Way PR4 . . . . . .**116** F6
Bidston St PR1 . . . .**97** E8
Big Fold BL6 . . . .**31** D2
Bigdale Dr L33 . . . .**1** A3
Billinge Ave BB2 . . . .**101** B5
Billinge Cl BB2 . . . .**101** B5
Billinge End BB2 . . . .**101** A6
Billinge End Rd
Blackburn BB2 . . . .**100** F5
Pleasington BB2 . . . .**100** B4

Billinge Hospl WN5 . . . . . .**10** D2
Billinge Side BB2 . . . . . .**100** F5
Billinge St BB1 . . . .**102** B4
Billinge View BB2 . . . . . .**100** F5
Billington Ave BB4 . . . . . .**86** A5
Billington Gdns BB7 . . . . .**144** A4
Billington Rd BB11 . . . . . .**127** B3
Billington St ᴸ PR4 . . . . .**113** F6
Billington St E ᴣ PR4 . . . .**113** F6
Bilsberry Cotts BB7 . . . . .**164** F1
Bilsborough Hey PR1 . . . . . .**96** E2
Bilsborough Mdw PR2 . . . .**116** E3
Bilsborrow La
Bilsborrow PR3 . . . .**159** C4
Inglewhite PR3 . . . .**160** A4
Binbrook Pl PR7 . . . .**43** A7
Bingley Ave FY3 . . . .**130** F6
Bingley Cl PR6 . . . .**78** C2
Binns Nook Rd OL12 . . . . . .**52** F2
Binns St BB4 . . . .**86** A7
Binyon Ct LA1 . . . .**214** F6
Binyon Rd LA1 . . . .**214** F5
Birbeck Rd L33 . . . .**1** A3
Birbeck Wlk L33 . . . .**1** A3
Birch Ave Burscough L40 . .**25** E4
Clayton-le-W PR25 . . . . . .**77** D3
Cleveleys FY5 . . . .**175** C2
Euxton PR7 . . . .**60** C4
Galgate LA2 . . . .**211** A4
Haslingden BB4 . . . .**85** C3
Higher Penwortham PR1 . . . .**96** A3
Newton-w-S PR4 . . . .**114** A3
Preston PR2 . . . .**117** A2
Birch Cl Huncoat BB5 . . . .**125** E2
Maghull L31 . . . .**5** F1
Whitworth OL12 . . . .**52** C6
Birch Cres
Gregson Lane PR5 . . . .**98** E1
Oswaldtwistle BB5 . . . . . .**103** F3
Birch Dr LA5 . . . .**224** C4
Birch Field PR6 . . . .**78** B3
Birch Gn L37 . . . .**11** D4
Birch Gr Barrow BB7 . . . .**166** D1
Lancaster LA1 . . . .**214** D8
Ramsbottom BL0 . . . .**50** A3
Stalmine FY6 . . . .**177** D7
Birch Green Rd WN8 . . . . .**18** C3
Birch Hall Ave BB3 . . . . . .**81** A4
Birch Hall La BB18 . . . . . .**197** D2
Birch La PR3 . . . .**184** C1
Birch Rd Chorley PR6 . . . . .**61** E2
Coppull PR7 . . . .**42** E1
Garstang PR3 . . . .**181** C8
Birch St Accrington BB5 . . .**104** B6
Bacup OL13 . . . .**87** F3
Fleetwood FY7 . . . .**199** A4
ᴸ Lytham St Anne's FY8 . . .**91** C3
Skelmersdale WN8 . . . .**8** E8
Southport PR8 . . . .**35** B4
Birch Terr BB5 . . . .**104** C5
Birch Tree Gdns FY3 . . . .**131** B2
Birch Tree Way ᴀ BL6 . . . .**32** E1
Birch View BB7 . . . .**166** D1
Birch Villas OL12 . . . .**52** C5
Birch Way FY6 . . . .**153** C4
Birch Wlk ᴸ BB1 . . . .**102** B4
Birchall Lodge �⁶ PR2 . . . .**118** F4
Birchbank Gdns BB1 . . . . .**102** A7
Birchenlee La BB8 . . . . . .**171** E2
Birches End OL12 . . . .**52** C5
Birches Rd BL7 . . . .**48** D4
Birches The L37 . . . .**11** E5
Birchfield PR4 . . . .**74** F4
Birchfield Ave BL9 . . . .**33** E1
Birchfield Dr PR3 . . . . . .**140** A8
Birchfield Way L31 . . . .**5** B5
Birchill Rd L33 . . . .**1** C2
Birchin La PR6 . . . .**78** D1
Birchover Cl PR2 . . . .**117** A5
Birchtree Ave LA3 . . . . . .**216** C1
Birchway Ave FY3 . . . . . .**130** E6
Birchwood PR26 . . . .**76** C1
Birchwood Ave PR4 . . . . . .**95** B1
Birchwood Cl FY8 . . . . . .**90** A8
Birchwood Dr Coppull PR7 .**42** E2
Fulwood PR2 . . . .**117** D7
Hambleton FY6 . . . .**177** C2
Birchwood Way L33 . . . . . .**1** A5
Bird i' th' Hand Cotts ᴣ
L39 . . . .**15** E6
Bird St Brierfield BB9 . . . .**148** B5
Preston PR1 . . . .**96** D6
Birdy Brow BB7 . . . .**165** A6
Birk St PR1 . . . .**96** E7
Birkacre Brow PR7 . . . . . .**42** F2
Birkacre Rd PR7 . . . .**42** F4
Birkbeck Pl FY7 . . . .**198** D2
Birkbeck Way BB10 . . . . .**148** A1
Birkdale Ave
Blackpool FY2 . . . .**152** E5
Fleetwood FY7 . . . .**175** E7
Longton PR4 . . . .**74** F8
Lytham St Anne's FY8 . . . .**110** F1
Birkdale Cl Euxton PR7 . . . .**60** D4
Lancaster LA1 . . . .**218** B3
Longton PR4 . . . .**74** F8
Thornton FY5 . . . .**153** D8
Birkdale Cop PR8 . . . .**35** E1
Birkdale Dr PR2 . . . .**116** E2
Birkdale High Sch PR8 . . . .**21** E7
Birkdale Prim Sch PR8 . . . .**35** B3
Birkdale Sta PR8 . . . .**34** F4
Birkdale Trad Est PR8 . . . .**35** A2
Birkett Dr PR2 . . . .**119** A3
Birkett Rd PR2 . . . .**119** A3
Birkett Rd BB5 . . . .**104** D7
Birkett's Pl LA4 . . . .**217** C5
Birkey La L37 . . . .**11** F2

Birklands Ave LA4 . . . . . .**217** C4
Birkrig WN8 . . . .**9** D6
Birks Brow PR3 . . . .**162** D3
Birkside Way FY4 . . . . . .**131** C1
Birkwith La LA2 . . . .**239** C7
Birley Cl WN6 . . . .**19** F8
Birley Ct PR8 . . . .**35** B5
Birley Pl BB10 . . . .**128** A8
Birley St Blackburn BB1 . .**101** F5
Blackburn BB1 . . . .**101** F6
Blackpool FY1 . . . .**130** B5
Kirkham PR4 . . . .**114** B5
ᴸ Preston PR1 . . . .**97** A7
Birleywood WN8 . . . .**9** D6
Birnam Gn FY7 . . . .**198** E4
Birtle Rd BL9 . . . .**33** E6
Birtwistle Ave BB6 . . . . . .**171** D6
Birtwistle Cl BB9 . . . .**148** B5
Birtwistle Ct BB18 . . . . . .**196** C1
Birtwistle Fold ᴣ BB8 . . . .**171** E5
Birtwistle Hyde Pk ᴣ
BB8 . . . .**171** D5
Birtwistle Standroyd Bglws
BB8 . . . .**172** A5
Birtwistle Terr BB6 . . . . . .**143** C1
Bisham Cl BB3 . . . .**65** C8
Bishop David Sheppard CE
Prim Sch PR9 . . . .**36** B7
Bishop Martin CE Prim Sch
WN8 . . . .**9** D6
Bishop Rawstorne CE
Language Coll The
PR26 . . . .**58** C2
Bishop St Accrington BB5 **104** C5
Burnley BB10 . . . .**148** B1
Nelson BB9 . . . .**148** D8
Bishopdale Cl
Blackburn BB2 . . . .**80** D7
Morecambe LA3 . . . .**217** F3
Bishopdale Rd LA1 . . . . . .**214** D7
Bishopgate ᴸ⁵ PR1 . . . .**97** A8
Bishops Gate BB8 . . . .**90** D7
Bishopsgate
Blackpool FY3 . . . .**153** B3
Lancaster LA1 . . . .**215** A4
Bishopstone Cl BB2 . . . . . .**82** A8
Bishopsway PR1 . . . .**96** D3
Bison Pl PR26 . . . .**76** C2
Bispham Ave PR26 . . . . . .**76** E4
Bispham Ct WN5 . . . .**10** D2
Bispham Endowed CE Jun
Sch FY2 . . . .**152** D4
Bispham Hall Bsns Pk
WN5 . . . .**10** C2
Bispham High Sch FY2 . . .**152** E2
Bispham Hospl FY2 . . . . . .**152** F6
Bispham Rd
Blackpool FY2 . . . .**152** D3
Blackpool,Warbreck FY3 . . .**130** E8
Carleton FY5,FY6 . . . . . .**153** A6
Cleveleys FY5 . . . .**175** C2
Cleveleys,Whiteholme FY5 . .**152** F6
Nelson BB9 . . . .**148** E6
Southport PR9 . . . .**35** F7
Bispham St ᴸ PR1 . . . .**96** F8
Bittern Cl FY3 . . . .**131** B6
Bivel St BB12 . . . .**127** D6
Bk Alfred St BL0 . . . .**50** B5
Bk Commercial St BB9 . . .**148** B6
Bk Dawson St BL9 . . . .**33** A4
Bk Owen St BB5 . . . .**104** C7
Bk Scotland Rd ᴸ BB9 . . .**148** D8
Bk Shepherd St BL9 . . . . . .**33** A1
Black Abbey St BB5 . . . . .**104** C5
Black Bull La PR2 . . . . . .**117** D5
Black Croft PR **78** B3
Black Horse St
Blackrod BL6 . . . .**31** C3
ᴀ Chorley PR7 . . . .**43** B6
Black House La
Chipping PR3 . . . .**185** B1
Lane Bottom BB10 . . . . . .**149** D3
Black La Nateby PR3 . . . . .**180** A8
Ramsbottom BL0 . . . .**51** B7
Black Lane Croft ᴣ
BB7 . . . .**189** E1
Black Lane Ends BB8 . . . .**195** F3
Black Moor Rd L40 . . . . . .**40** A2
Black Moss La
Ormskirk L39 . . . .**15** E3
Scarisbrick L40 . . . .**23** D6
Black Moss Rd BB9 . . . . .**169** E8
Black Moss Sch WN8 . . . . .**17** C2
Black-A-Moor La L39 . . . . .**14** A2
Blackacre La L39,L40 . . . . .**15** E8
Blackamoor Rd BB1 . . . . . .**82** C8
Blackberry Hall Cres
LA3 . . . .**213** A8
Blackberry Way PR1 . . . . . .**96** B2
Blackbrook Cl PR2 . . . .**62** A2
Blackburn Brow PR6 . . . . . .**61** E3
Blackburn Cathedral ★
BB1 . . . .**101** E4
Blackburn Mus & Art Gall ★
BB1 . . . .**101** E5
Blackburn Old Rd
Blackburn BB1 . . . .**123** D3
Great Harwood BB1,BB6 . . .**123** F5
Hoghton PR5 . . . .**99** C2
Blackburn Rd
Accrington BB5 . . . .**104** C6
Blackburn BB1 . . . .**102** E8
Church BB5 . . . .**103** F6

Blackburn Rd continued
Clayton-le-M BB5 . . . . . .**124** E1
Darwen BB3 . . . .**81** E4
Edenfield BL0,BB4 . . . . . .**68** D5
Egerton BL7 . . . .**47** C4
Great Harwood BB6 . . . . .**124** C4
Great Knowley PR6 . . . . . .**61** E4
Haslingden BB4,BB5 . . . . . .**85** B5
Higher Walton PR5 . . . . . .**98** B3
Higher Wheelton PR6 . . . . .**79** C1
Longridge PR3 . . . .**140** D7
Oswaldtwistle BB5,BB1 . . .**103** C5
Padiham BB12 . . . .**126** A8
Ribchester PR3 . . . .**141** E3
Rishton BB1 . . . .**124** A1
Wheelton PR6 . . . .**61** F6
Whittlestone Head BB3,BL7 . .**66** B2
Blackburn Royal Infmy
BB2 . . . .**101** D2
Blackburn St
Blackburn BB1 . . . .**101** E6
ᴸ Burnley BB11 . . . .**127** F6
Chorley PR6 . . . .**43** E7
Blackburn Sta BB1 . . . . . .**101** F4
Blackburn Trad Pk BB1 . . .**101** F6
Blackcar La L29 . . . .**4** A3
Blacker St BB10 . . . .**148** A2
Blackfen Pl FY2 . . . .**130** D8
Blackfield Rd PR4 . . . .**93** B6
Blackgate La Holmes PR4 . .**56** C3
Tarleton PR4 . . . .**56** E5
Blackhorse Ave BL6 . . . . . .**31** C2
Blackhorse La BL6 . . . .**31** C3
Blackhurst Ave PR4 . . . . . .**95** F2
Blackhurst Ct PR4 . . . .**75** B8
Blackhurst Rd L31 . . . .**5** C5
Blackleach Ave PR2 . . . . .**139** D1
Blackleach La PR4 . . . . . .**135** F1
Blackledge Cl WN5 . . . . . .**10** E5
Blackley Gr L33 . . . .**1** A6
Blacko Bar Rd BB9 . . . . . .**170** E2
Blacko Prim Sch BB9 . . . .**170** D8
Blackpool & Fleetwood
Tramway ★ FY2 . . . .**152** B3
Blackpool & The Fylde Coll
Blackpool FY1 . . . .**130** C4
Blackpool FY1 . . . .**130** D4
Blackpool,Whiteholme FY2 **152** E4
Blackpool & The Fylde Coll
(Nautical) FY7 . . . .**175** E7
Blackpool & The Fylde Coll
Ansdell Campus FY8 . . . . .**90** C5
Blackpool Airport FY4 . . . .**110** D3
Blackpool Central Pier ★
FY1 . . . .**130** A3
Blackpool Lifeboat Visitor
Ctr ★ FY1 . . . .**130** A4
Blackpool North Pier ★
FY1 . . . .**130** A5
Blackpool North Sta
FY1 . . . .**130** C6
Blackpool Old Rd
Little Eccleston PR4 . . . . .**156** A5
Poulton-le-F FY6 . . . .**153** B5
Blackpool Pleasure Beach ★
FY4 . . . .**110** B7
Blackpool Pleasure Beach
Sta FY4 . . . .**110** B6
Blackpool Rd
Blackpool FY2 . . . .**152** D4
Carleton FY6 . . . .**153** A4
Clifton PR4 . . . .**94** E8
Longridge PR3 . . . .**140** A7
Lytham St Anne's FY8 . . . . .**90** D5
Newton-w-S PR4 . . . .**115** B2
Preston PR1,PR2 . . . .**117** C2
Preston,Larches PR2 . . . . .**116** E1
St Michael's on W PR3 . . . .**157** B6
Wrea Green PR4 . . . .**113** C6
Blackpool Rd N FY8 . . . . . .**90** F2
Blackpool Sixth Form Coll
FY3 . . . .**153** A2
Blackpool South Pier ★
FY4 . . . .**110** A8
Blackpool South Sta
FY4 . . . .**130** B1
Blackpool St
ᴸ Church BB5 . . . .**103** E5
ᴣ Darwen BB3 . . . .**65** B6
Blackpool Twr ★ FY1 . . . . .**130** B5
Blackpool Zoo ★ FY3 . . . .**131** A4
Blackrod Brow BL6 . . . . . .**31** B4
Blackrod By-Pass Rd
BL6 . . . .**31** C2
Blackrod CE Prim Sch
BL6 . . . .**31** C2
Blackrod Sta BL6 . . . .**31** E2
Blacksmiths Row FY8 . . . . .**90** D7
Blacksnape Rd BB3 . . . . . .**82** D2
Blacksticks La PR3 . . . . . .**184** D1
Blackstone Rd PR6 . . . .**61** E1
Blackthorn Cl
Cleveleys FY5 . . . .**175** F5
Newton-w-S PR4 . . . .**114** F2
Preston PR2 . . . .**116** D1
Rochdale OL12 . . . .**52** E2
Blackthorn Cres OL13 . . . . .**87** F3
Blackthorn Croft PR6 . . . . .**78** A2
Blackthorn Dr PR1 . . . .**96** B3
Blackthorn La OL13 . . . . . .**87** F3
Blackthorn Mews OL12 . . . .**52** E2
Blackwood Cl OL13 . . . .**70** C8
Blackwood Pl LA1 . . . .**215** B5
Blackwood Rd OL13 . . . . . .**70** B7
Blades St LA1 . . . .**214** E4
Blaguegate La WN8 . . . . . .**17** B2
Blainscough Rd PR7 . . . . . .**29** E8
Blair Gr PR9 . . . .**35** F7

Blair St OL12 . . . .**52** D1
Blairgowrie Gdns L39 . . . . .**16** A4
Blaisdale Ave FY3 . . . . . .**130** F6
Blake Ave PR5 . . . .**77** A7
Blake Gdns BB6 . . . .**124** B4
Blake St BB5 . . . .**104** B6
Blakehall WN8 . . . .**9** D7
Blakeley Cres BB18 . . . . . .**196** B3
Blakewater Rd BB1 . . . . . .**102** C7
Blakey Moor BB2 . . . .**101** D5
Blakey St BB11 . . . .**128** B6
Blakiston St FY7 . . . .**199** A4
Blanche St ᴸ PR2 . . . . . .**117** C1
Blandford Ave FY5 . . . . . .**175** C1
Blandford Cl PR8 . . . .**34** F5
Blandford Rise BL6 . . . .**32** F1
Blannel St BB11 . . . .**127** E6
Blascomay Sq ᴸᴮ BB8 . . . .**171** D4
Blashaw La PR1 . . . .**96** A5
Blaydike Moss PR26 . . . . . .**76** B1
Blaydon Ave FY5 . . . .**175** E4
Blaydon Pk WN8 . . . .**9** D7
Blea Cl BB12 . . . .**127** B8
Blea Tarn Pl ᴣ LA4 . . . . .**217** D4
Blea Tarn Rd LA2 . . . .**215** C2
Bleachers Dr ᴣ PR25 . . . . .**76** E1
Bleak La L40 . . . .**26** D5
Bleakholt Rd BL0 . . . .**68** F1
Bleara Rd BB18 . . . .**195** D7
Bleasdale Ave
Blackpool FY5 . . . .**152** E8
Clitheroe BB7 . . . .**166** C7
Kirkham PR4 . . . .**114** A5
Poulton-le-F FY6 . . . .**153** C2
Staining FY3 . . . .**131** C6
Bleasdale CE Prim Sch
PR3 . . . .**184** A7
Bleasdale Cl
ᴣ Bamber Bridge PR5 . . . .**77** F8
Leyland PR25 . . . .**60** B7
Ormskirk L39 . . . .**6** D7
Bleasdale Ct PR3 . . . .**140** B7
Bleasdale Gr LA3 . . . .**216** E1
Bleasdale House Com Specl
Sch LA5 . . . .**224** C3
Bleasdale La PR3 . . . .**183** C6
Bleasdale Rd
Cumeragh Village PR3 . . . .**138** F6
Knott End-on-S FY6 . . . . .**199** D5
Lytham St Anne's FY8 . . . . .**91** C4
Whitechapel PR3 . . . .**183** D1
Bleasdale St E PR1 . . . . . .**118** C1
Blelock St PR1 . . . .**97** A7
Blenheim Ave
Blackpool FY1 . . . .**130** D4
Kirkham PR4 . . . .**113** F5
Blenheim Cl
Bamber Bridge PR5 . . . . . .**77** C8
ᴸ Blackburn BB1 . . . . . .**122** E1
Blenheim Dr
Thornton FY5 . . . .**176** C2
Warton PR4 . . . .**92** D6
Blenheim Pl FY8 . . . .**110** C1
Blenheim Rd PR8 . . . .**21** B6
Blenheim St Colne BB8 . . .**172** A5
ᴸᴮ Rochdale OL12 . . . .**52** C1
Blenheim Terr BB8 . . . . . .**194** E1
Blenheim Way PR4 . . . . . .**116** E6
Blessed Sacrament RC Prim
Sch PR2 . . . .**118** F3
Blind La Burton in L LA6 . . .**242** C3
Gisburn BB7 . . . .**231** C3
Higham BB12 . . . .**147** A6
Blindman's La L39 . . . .**15** C7
Bloom St ᴣ BL0 . . . .**50** A4
Bloomfield Ct PR1 . . . . . .**117** E2
Bloomfield Grange PR4 . . . .**96** C2
Bloomfield Pk LA5 . . . . . .**223** D1
Bloomfield Rd
Blackpool FY1 . . . .**130** C2
Withnell PR6 . . . .**80** A1
Bloomfield Road Football Gd
(Blackpool FC) FY1 . . . . .**130** C2
Blossom Ave
Blackpool FY4 . . . .**110** F7
Oswaldtwistle BB5 . . . . . .**103** E5
Blossoms The
Fulwood PR2 . . . .**118** C6
Poulton-le-F FY6 . . . .**153** F3
Blowick Bsns Pk PR9 . . . . .**36** A6
Blowick Ind Pk PR9 . . . . . .**36** A6
Blucher St BB8 . . . .**171** E4
Blue Bell La OL14 . . . . . .**109** D2
Blue Bell Pl PR1 . . . .**97** A7
Blue Gates BB7 . . . .**229** B3
Blue Moor PR4 . . . .**135** A2
Blue Scar La BB7 . . . .**230** D7
Blue Stone La L40 . . . .**40** F4
Bluebell Ave BB4 . . . .**68** A8
Bluebell Cl
Blackpool FY2 . . . .**152** D2
Cleveleys FY5 . . . .**175** F5
Hesketh Bank PR4 . . . . . .**73** E4
Lucas Green PR6 . . . .**61** C5
Bluebell Gr BB11 . . . .**127** C5
Bluebell Way
Fulwood PR2 . . . .**118** F6
Walton Summit PR5 . . . . . .**78** A8
Bluebell Wood PR25 . . . . . .**76** F3
Bluecoat Cres PR4 . . . . . .**115** A2
Bluestone La L31 . . . .**5** E1
Blundell Ave Formby L37 . .**11** B4
Hightown L38 . . . .**2** F3
Southport PR8 . . . .**34** F2
Blundell Cres PR8 . . . .**34** F2
Blundell Dr PR8 . . . .**34** F2
Blundell Gr L38 . . . .**2** F3
Blundell La Blackrod BL6 . .**31** A2

Blundell La *continued*
Higher Penwortham PR1 ...96 B6
Southport PR9 ...54 C2
Blundell Links Ct PR8 ...21 C4
Blundell Rd Fulwood PR2 117 E3
Hightown L38 ...2 F3
Lytham St Anne's FY8 ...110 F1
Blundell St FY1 ...130 B3
Blythe Ave FY5 ...175 E5
Blythe Cotts L40 ...25 E1
Blythe La L40 ...25 E1
Blythe Mews PR8 ...22 A8
Blythewood WN8 ...9 D7
Board St BB10 ...148 A1
Boarded Barn PR7 ...60 C3
Boardman Ave FY1 ...130 D2
Boardman St BL6 ...31 D2
Boarsgreave La BB4 ...69 F6
Bobbin Cl BB5 ...104 A5
Bobbin Mill Cl 11 OL14 .109 B1
Bobbin Mill Cotts PR3 ..181 F2
Bobbin St OL14 ...109 C1
Bobbiners La PR9 ...55 A3
Bobby Langton Way L40 .25 E5
Bocholt Way BB4 ...86 A2
Bodiam Rd BL8 ...49 F2
Bodie Hill LA2 ...209 E5
Bodkin La PR3 ...154 F7
Bodmin Ave PR9 ...54 B5
Bodmin St PR1 ...118 D1
Boegrave Ave PR5 ...77 A8
Bog Height Rd BB3 ...81 C6
Bogburn La PR7 ...29 D6
Boland St BB1 ...102 A7
Bold La L39 ...6 B7
Bold St Accrington BB5 ..104 D6
Bacup OL13 ...87 F1
Blackburn BB1 ...101 E6
Bury BL9 ...33 A3
Colne BB8 ...171 E4
Fleetwood FY7 ...199 B5
Morecambe LA3 ...216 E4
Preston PR1 ...117 D1
Southport PR9 ...35 B8
Bold Venture Cotts BB7 190 C4
Bold Venture Way BB5 .125 A3
Boleyn Ct FY3 ...131 A2
Boleyn The L31 ...5 E3
Bolland Cl 6 BB7 ...166 F8
Bolland Prospect BB7 ..166 F7
Bolland St BB18 ...196 B3
Bolton Ave
Accrington BB5 ...125 D1
Carleton FY6 ...153 C5
Lancaster LA1 ...218 D4
Bolton Cl L37 ...12 A2
Bolton Com Coll Horwich Campus BL6 ...32 D2
Bolton Croft PR26 ...59 B8
Bolton Gr BB9 ...170 D3
Bolton La LA5 ...221 C4
Bolton Mdw PR26 ...59 A8
Bolton Rd
Abbey Village PR6 ...80 B3
Adlington BL60,PR6 ...31 D6
Blackburn BB2 ...101 D2
Blackburn,Ewood BB2 ...81 E7
Chorley PR6 ...43 E4
Darwen BB3 ...65 B7
Darwen,Cadshaw BB3 ...65 C3
Edgworth BL7 ...48 D5
Hawkshaw BL8 ...49 D2
Riley Green PR5,PR6 ...79 E6
Southport PR8 ...35 A4
Bolton Rd N BL0 ...68 D2
Bolton Rd W BL0,BL8 ...50 A4
Bolton St Blackpool FY1 ..130 B2
Chorley PR7 ...43 C7
Colne BB8 ...171 C4
5 Newchurch BB4 ...86 E1
Ramsbottom BL0 ...50 B6
Bolton's Cop PR9 ...55 D5
Bolton's Ct 24 BB1 ...101 E5
Bolton's Meanygate PR4 56 C7
Bolton-by-Bowland CE Prim Sch BB7 ...230 D4
Bolton-le-Sands CE Prim Sch LA5 ...221 B4
Boltons Croft PR4 ...115 E7
Boltons Ct PR1 ...97 A7
Bombay St BB2 ...101 C3
Bonchurch St BB1 ...102 C4
Bond Cl BL6 ...32 C3
Bond St Blackpool FY4 ...110 B7
13 Burnley BB10 ...128 A8
Bury BL9 ...33 A2
Colne BB8 ...171 D5
Darwen BB3 ...82 A2
Edenfield BL0 ...68 E2
Lancaster LA1 ...215 A8
Nelson BB9 ...148 D7
Bond's La Adlington PR7 ..30 F7
Banks PR9 ...55 A7
Bonds La Bonds PR3 ...181 C6
Elswick PR4 ...156 A2
Bone Croft PR6 ...78 B3
Bone Hill La PR3 ...202 D1
Bonfire Hill Cl BB4 ...86 B7
Bonfire Hill Rd BB4 ...86 A7
Bonney St FY5 ...176 B3
Bonny Grass Terr BB7 ..144 A4
Bonny St FY1 ...130 B4
Bonsall St BB2 ...101 B2
Boome St FY4 ...110 C6
Boon Town LA6 ...240 C7
Boon Wlks LA6 ...240 C7
Boot St BB18 ...197 B2
Boot Way BB11 ...128 A5
Booth Bridge La BD23 ..197 B5
Booth Cres BB4 ...87 A1
Booth Ct 4 BB10 ...128 A8
Booth Rd OL13 ...70 B8
Booth St Accrington BB5 .104 C4
10 Bacup OL13 ...87 F2
Carnforth LA5 ...223 D1
Haslingden BB4 ...85 A4
10 Nelson BB9 ...148 D8
Rawtenstall BB4 ...69 E8
Southport PR8 ...35 B8
Booth's La L39 ...14 F4
Booth's Par PR2 ...117 F7
Boothfield House Cvn Pk FY6 ...200 A6
Boothley Rd FY1 ...130 D6
Boothman Pl BB9 ...170 E2
Boothman St BB2 ...101 D2
Boothroyden FY1 ...130 B8
Bootle St PR1 ...118 C1
Borage Cl FY5 ...176 A5
Bordeaux Cres FY5 ...152 F6
Border Ct 6 LA1 ...218 B1
Bores Hill WN1 ...30 C4
Borough Rd BB3 ...82 A1
Borrans Lane Cvn Pk LA3 ...212 F4
Borron La LA6 ...240 C3
Borrowdale L37 ...11 F5
Borrowdale Ave
Blackburn BB1 ...102 C3
Fleetwood FY7 ...198 E4
Nelson BB9 ...148 F7
Borrowdale Cl
4 Accrington BB5 ...125 D1
Brierfield BB10 ...148 C3
Borrowdale Dr BB10 ...148 C4
Borrowdale Gr LA4 ...217 D5
Borrowdale Rd
Blackpool FY4 ...131 B1
Lancaster LA1 ...215 A8
Leyland PR25 ...60 B7
Borwick Ave LA5 ...223 E6
Borwick Cl LA5 ...223 E6
Borwick Ct Borwick LA6 .240 B4
Morecambe LA4 ...217 B3
Borwick Dr LA1 ...218 B2
Borwick La LA6 ...240 B3
Borwick Mews LA6 ...240 B3
Borwick Rd LA6 ...240 D3
Bosburn Dr BB2 ...121 C2
Boscombe Ave LA3 ...216 E2
Boscombe Rd FY4 ...110 B6
Bosley Arc 2 FY1 ...130 B5
Bosley Cl BB3 ...65 D8
Bostock St 21 PR1 ...97 A7
Boston Ave FY2 ...152 D6
Boston Rd Bacup OL13 ...87 F3
Lytham St Anne's FY8 ...90 B6
Boston St BB9 ...148 F6
Bostons BB6 ...124 B5
Bostonway FY4 ...110 F8
Bosworth Dr PR8 ...21 B4
Bosworth Pl FY4 ...110 B4
Bosworth St BL6 ...32 B4
Botanic Gardens Mus* PR9 ...54 B2
Botanic Rd PR9 ...54 B2
Botany Bay* PR6 ...61 E3
Botany Brow PR6 ...61 E2
Bott House La BB8,BB9 .171 A2
Bottom o' th' Knotts Brow BL7 ...48 E3
Bottom O'Th' Moor BL6 .32 F3
Bottom O'Th' Rann BB1 ...82 F6
Bottom's Row BB4 ...69 F6
Bottomdale Cvn Pk LA2 218 D8
Bottomdale Rd LA2 ...218 E8
Bottomgate BB1 ...102 B5
Bottomley Bank La BB4 .86 B8
Bottomley St BB9 ...148 E8
Bottoms La LA5 ...224 D3
Botton Rd LA2 ...239 C1
Boulder St 10 BB4 ...86 A7
Bouldsworth Rd BB10 ..128 E5
Boulevard PR1 ...97 B5
Boulevard Gdns FY8 ...90 A4
Boulevard The
Blackburn BB1 ...101 E4
Lytham St Anne's FY8 ...90 A4
Boulsworth Cres BB9 .171 B1
Boulsworth Dr BB8 ...172 C1
Boulsworth Gr BB8 ...172 A5
Boulview Terr BB8 ...172 B5
Boundary Cl Eccleston PR7 41 B6
New Longton PR4 ...75 F8
Boundary Ct FY3 ...153 A1
Boundary La
Becconsall PR4 ...73 E1
Burscough L40 ...25 F4
Hale Nook FR6,PR3 ...178 B7
Holmes PR4,PR9 ...55 E6
Kirkby L33 ...1 F2
Shevington Moor WN6 ...29 A3
Boundary Meanygate
Becconsall PR4 ...73 D1
Holmes PR4 ...55 F7
Boundary Prim Sch FY3 130 F8
Boundary Rd
Accrington BB5 ...104 D7
Fulwood PR2 ...117 D3
Lancaster LA1 ...214 F6
Lytham St Anne's FY8 ...91 E5
Boundary St
Burnley BB10 ...148 C2
Colne BB8 ...171 D4
Leyland PR25 ...77 B2
Boundary St *continued*
Southport PR8 ...35 B4
Bourbles La FY6 ...200 D4
Bourne Brow PR3 ...159 E5
Bourne May Rd FY6 ...199 D5
Bourne Rd FY5 ...176 B5
Bourne Way FY5 ...176 A4
Bourne's Row PR5 ...98 E1
Bournemouth Rd FY4 ...110 B6
Bournesfield PR5 ...98 E1
Bovington Ave FY5 ...152 F8
Bow Brook Rd PR25 ...77 C1
Bow Hills La BB7 ...231 C6
Bow La Leyland PR25 ...77 B1
Preston PR1 ...96 E7
Bow St PR25 ...77 B2
Bowden Ave BB2 ...100 C1
Bowen St BB2 ...101 B2
Bower Cl BB2 ...101 B2
Bower St Blackburn BB2 .101 B2
Bury BL9 ...33 C3
Bowerham Com Prim Sch LA1 ...215 A6
Bowerham La LA1 ...215 B3
Bowerham Rd LA1 ...215 A5
Bowerham Terr 1 LA1 .215 A6
Bowers La PR3 ...180 E7
Bowers The PR7 ...43 D4
Bowes Lyon Pl FY8 ...90 C7
Bowfell Ave LA4 ...217 D5
Bowfell Cl FY4 ...131 D1
Bowfield's La BB2 ...120 F4
Bowgreave Cl 1 FY4 ...111 A6
Bowgreave Dr PR3 ...181 D4
Bowker St BL0 ...68 C5
Bowker's Green La L39 ...6 E4
Bowland Ave
Burnley BB10 ...128 E5
Chorley PR6 ...43 D8
Fleetwood FY7 ...175 D8
Lancaster LA1 ...211 B8
Bowland Cl
Carnforth LA5 ...223 C1
Longridge PR3 ...140 B8
Bowland Cres FY3 ...131 A8
Bowland Ct
4 Clitheroe BB7 ...166 E8
9 Southport PR9 ...35 C8
Bowland Dr LA1 ...218 B2
Bowland Gate La BB7 ..189 E7
Bowland High Sch BB7 .230 B1
Bowland Ho 7 BB1 ...101 F6
Bowland Pl Fulwood PR2 119 A3
Lytham St Anne's FY8 ...90 C6
Bowland Rd
Fulwood PR2 ...119 A3
Garstang PR3 ...204 C1
Heysham LA3 ...213 A8
Bowland View
Brierfield BB9 ...148 D4
Garstang PR3 ...204 C1
Glasson LA2 ...209 E4
Bowland Wild Boar Pk* BB7 ...186 E6
Bowlers Cl PR2 ...118 C5
Bowlers Wlk OL12 ...52 F2
Bowling Gn The BL0 ...68 D3
Bowling Green Cl
Darwen BB3 ...65 B7
Southport PR8 ...35 F5
Bowling Green Cotts BB6 ...143 C6
Bowling Green Cvn Pk LA5 ...223 C1
Bowlingfield PR2 ...117 A6
Bowness Ave
Blackpool FY4 ...131 D1
Fleetwood FY7 ...198 C1
Lytham St Anne's FY8 ...110 F2
Nelson BB9 ...148 E6
Rochdale OL12 ...52 C1
Southport PR8 ...21 C3
Thornton FY5 ...176 B2
Bowness Cl BB1 ...102 A6
Bowness Rd
Lancaster LA1 ...218 E1
Padiham BB12 ...146 C2
Preston PR1 ...119 A1
Bowood Ct FY3 ...131 B7
Bowran St PR1 ...96 F8
Box St BL0 ...50 D6
Boxer Pl PR26 ...76 C2
Boxwood Dr BB2 ...80 F8
Boxwood St BB1 ...101 F8
Boyd Cl WN6 ...29 F1
Boyes Ave PR3 ...181 D2
Boyle St BB1 ...101 F6
Boys La PR2 ...117 C5
Brabiner La PR2,PR3 ...139 B4
Brabins Endowed Sch PR3 ...185 E3
Bracebridge Dr PR8 ...35 F2
Bracewell Ave FY6 ...154 A3
Bracewell Cl BB9 ...148 E8
Bracewell La BD23 ...231 F3
Bracewell Rd PR2 ...118 E5
Bracewell St
Barnoldswick BB18 ...196 B3
Burnley BB10 ...148 B1
Nelson BB9 ...148 F8
Bracken Cl Blackburn BB2 .80 F8
Chorley PR6 ...43 E8
Bracken Dr PR4 ...93 D7
Bracken Gr BB4 ...68 A8
Bracken Hey BB7 ...167 A8
Bracken Lea Fold 3 OL12 ...52 B2
Bracken Way FY2 ...152 D2
Brackenbury Cl 5 PR5 ..77 A7
Brackenbury Rd PR1, PR2 ...117 E3
Brackenbury St PR1 ...117 F2
Brackendale BB2 ...101 C1
Brackenthaite Rd LA5, LA7 ...225 B7
Brackenway L37 ...12 A6
Bracknel Way L39 ...15 A1
Braconash Rd PR25 ...76 E2
Bradda Rd BB2 ...101 E1
Braddon St 2 PR1 ...118 D1
Brade St PR9 ...54 C4
Brades Ave FY5 ...176 D2
Brades La PR4 ...93 D7
Bradford Gr LA3 ...212 F6
Bradford St BB5 ...104 D6
Bradkirk La PR5 ...78 B8
Bradkirk Pl PR5 ...78 A7
Bradley Ct BB7 ...163 E8
Bradley Fold 5 BB9 ...170 E1
Bradley Gdns BB12 ...127 B5
Bradley Hall Rd BB9 ...170 F1
Bradley Hall Trad Est WN6 ...29 F2
Bradley Hill Trad Est WN6 ...30 A2
Bradley La Eccleston PR7 .41 D6
Standish WN6 ...29 F2
1 Standish WN6 ...29 E1
Bradley Pl 8 PR8 ...35 B7
Bradley Prim Sch BB9 ..170 E1
Bradley Rd BB9 ...170 E1
Bradley Rd E BB9 ...170 E1
Bradley Smithy Cl OL12 ..52 E2
Bradley St Colne BB8 ...171 F5
Southport PR9 ...35 C8
Bradley View 12 BB9 ...170 E1
Bradman Rd L33 ...1 D3
Bradshaw Brow L40 ...40 E2
Bradshaw Cl
Blackburn BB1 ...101 E8
Nelson BB9 ...148 E7
Stalmine FY6 ...177 C7
Standish WN6 ...29 D1
Bradshaw Ct PR9 ...36 A7
Bradshaw La
Corner Row PR4 ...133 D1
Eagland Hill PR3 ...179 A7
Mawdesley L40 ...40 E2
Parbold WN8 ...27 C1
Scronkey PR3 ...201 E2
Bradshaw Rd BL7 ...48 E1
Bradshaw Row BB5 ...103 F6
Bradshaw St Church BB5 103 F6
7 Lancaster LA1 ...215 A7
Nelson BB9 ...148 D7
Bradshaw St E 3 BB5 ..104 C6
Bradshaw St W BB5 ...103 F6
Bradshaw's La PR8 ...21 D6
Bradshawgate Dr LA5 ..224 C4
Bradwood Ct BB4 ...85 A2
Brady St BL6 ...32 A4
Bradyll Ct BB6 ...143 C6
Braefield Cres PR2 ...118 F2
Braemar Ave
Southport PR9 ...53 F2
Thornton FY5 ...153 C7
Braemar Ct 2 LA4 ...217 E4
Braemar Dr BL9 ...33 D2
Braemar Wlk FY2 ...152 F6
Braeside BB2 ...101 C6
Braewood Cl BL9 ...33 C3
Braganza Way LA1 ...214 C8
Braid Cl PR1 ...96 D1
Braid's La PR3 ...182 A7
Braidhaven WN6 ...19 E7
Braidwood Ct FY8 ...89 D7
Braintree Ave PR1 ...96 E2
Braith Cl FY4 ...110 F8
Braithwaite St 3 FY1 ...130 B7
Bramble Cl PR4 ...113 E6
Bramble Ct Kingsfold PR1 .96 E2
1 Thornton FY5 ...176 A2
Bramble St BB10 ...148 A1
Bramble Way
Burscough L40 ...25 F4
Parbold WN8 ...27 C1
Brambles The
Barrow BB7 ...166 D1
Blackburn BB2 ...101 A8
Blackpool FY8 ...110 B4
Coppull PR7 ...42 F2
Fulwood PR2 ...118 D6
Bramblewood PR26 ...58 B2
Bramblings The FY6 ...153 B2
Bramcote Cl L33 ...1 A4
Bramcote Rd L33 ...1 A4
Bramhall Rd WN8 ...17 F2
Bramley Ave
Burnley BB12 ...127 C8
Fleetwood FY7 ...198 E4
Bramley Cl 8 BB5 ...103 E5
Bramley Ct 2 WN6 ...29 E1
Bramley Gdns FY6 ...153 A2
Bramley View BB7 ...144 D8
Brampton Ave FY5 ...175 F4
Brampton Dr LA4 ...217 F5
Brampton St 2 PR2 ...117 C1
Bramwell Rd PR4 ...93 B6
Bramworth Ave BL0 ...50 B6
Branch Rd
Blackburn BB2,BB3 ...81 E7
Burnley BB11 ...128 B4
2 Clayton-le-M BB5 ...124 F3
Mellor Brook BB2 ...121 C2
Waddington BB7 ...189 B4
Branch St Bacup OL13 ...70 D8
Branch St *continued*
Nelson BB9 ...148 F8
Brancker St 3 PR7 ...43 A5
Brandiforth St PR5 ...97 F2
Brandlesholme Rd BL8 ..50 A1
Brandon Cl WN8 ...10 A7
Brandreth Delph WN8 ...27 C3
Brandreth Dr WN8 ...27 C2
Brandreth Pk WN8 ...27 D4
Brandreth Pl WN6 ...29 F1
Brandwood
Higher Penwortham PR1 ...96 A4
6 Newchurch BB4 ...86 E1
Brandwood Ct BL7 ...48 E5
Brandwood Fold BL7 ...48 E5
Brandwood Gr BB10 ..128 C6
Brandwood Pk OL13 ...70 B8
Brandwood Rd OL13 ...70 B8
Brandwood St BB3 ...82 B1
Brandy House Brow BB2 ...101 F2
Branksome Ave FY5 ...175 F3
Branksome Dr LA4 ...217 D4
Branston Rd FY4 ...130 E1
Branstree Rd FY4 ...131 C1
Brant Ct FY7 ...198 C1
Brant Rd PR1 ...119 A1
Brantfell Dr BB12 ...127 B8
Brantfell Rd
Blackburn BB1 ...101 D7
Great Harwood BB6 ...124 D6
Brantwood BB5 ...124 E2
Brantwood Ave
Blackburn BB1 ...102 F5
Morecambe LA4 ...217 E6
Brantwood Dr
Lancaster LA1 ...215 A2
Leyland PR25 ...77 B1
Brassey St BB12 ...127 C7
Brathay Pl FY7 ...198 D2
Bray St PR2 ...117 C1
Brays Heys 2 FY5 ...176 C1
Brays Rd FY8 ...112 B1
Brayshaw Pl PR2 ...118 E4
Brazil Cl LA3 ...217 A2
Brazley Ave BL6 ...32 E1
Bread St 4 BB12 ...127 D6
Bream Wood PR4 ...113 E4
Brearlands BD23 ...197 B6
Brearley St OL13 ...70 D8
Breck Cl FY6 ...153 E5
Breck Dr FY6 ...153 E5
Breck Prim Sch The FY6 ...153 F5
Breck Rd Blackpool FY3 ..130 E4
Poulton-le-F FY6 ...153 F6
Breckside Cl FY6 ...153 E5
Brecon Ave BB5 ...103 C4
Brecon Cl FY1 ...130 D3
Brecon Rd BB1 ...102 C5
Bredon Ave PR7 ...60 E1
Bredon Cl FY8 ...91 D5
Bredon Ct L37 ...11 E4
Breeze Cl Foulridge BB8 .194 E1
Thornton FY5 ...176 A4
Breeze Mount PR5 ...77 C8
Breeze Rd PR8 ...34 E2
Brenbar Cres OL12 ...71 D1
Brendjean Rd LA4 ...217 C4
Brendon Wlk FY3 ...130 F8
Brennand Cl
Bamber Bridge PR5 ...77 F8
Lancaster LA1 ...218 A2
Brennand St
Burnley BB10 ...148 B1
Clitheroe BB7 ...189 E1
Brent St BB10 ...148 C3
Brentlea Ave LA3 ...212 E7
Brentlea Cres LA3 ...212 E7
Brenton Bsns Complex 2 BL9 ...33 A2
Brentwood FY7 ...198 E2
Brentwood Ave
Blackpool FY5 ...152 D8
Burnley BB11 ...127 E3
Poulton-le-F FY6 ...153 C3
Brentwood Cl L38 ...2 F2
Brentwood Ct PR9 ...53 D1
Brentwood Rd
Adlington PR6 ...31 B8
Nelson BB9 ...171 A1
Bretherton Cl PR26 ...59 C8
Bretherton Cotts FY5 ..153 E8
Bretherton Ct L40 ...25 F3
Bretherton Endowed CE Prim Sch PR26 ...57 F5
Bretherton Rd PR26 ...58 B4
Bretherton Terr 9 PR25 .77 B1
Brett Cl BB7 ...167 A7
Brettarch Dr LA1 ...214 E5
Brettargh Cl LA1 ...214 E6
Brettargh Dr LA1 ...214 E6
Bretton Fold PR8 ...35 F5
Brewery Arc 42 LA1 ...214 F8
Brewery La Formby L37 ..11 F6
19 Lancaster LA1 ...214 F8
Brewery St
6 Blackburn BB2 ...101 D5
Longridge PR3 ...140 B7
Breworth Fold La PR6 ..79 A3
Briar Ave PR7 ...60 C4
Briar Bank Row PR2 ...118 A8
Briar Cl OL12 ...52 A1
Briar Croft PR4 ...75 A7
Briar Field FY2 ...152 F6

Briar Gr PR2 ....117 A4
Briar Hill Cl **3** BB1 ..102 A4
Briar Lea Rd LA6 .....221 E5
Briar Mews **1** FY5 ...176 C1
Briar Rd Blackburn BB1 ..101 F8
  Southport PR8 ....21 D4
  Thornton FY5 ....176 C1
Briar St OL13 ....88 A1
Briarcroft BB3 ....82 A6
Briarfield BL7 ....47 D2
Briarfield Rd FY5 ....153 B5
Briars Brook L40 .....26 A3
Briars Gn WN8 ....18 B4
Briars La Maghull L31 ...5 E1
  Ring o'Bells L40 .....26 A3
Briars The Fulwood PR2 .118 D6
  Southport PR8 ....34 F1
Briarscroft LA5 ......223 E6
Briarwood PR4 ....93 A6
Briarwood Cl
  Leyland PR25 ....59 E8
  Weeton PR4 ....132 F2
Briarwood Ct FY5 ...153 B7
Briarwood Dr FY2 ...152 E5
Briary Croft L38 ....2 D2
Brick Kiln La L40 .....39 B3
Brick St **9** Burnley BB11 .127 F6
  Bury BL9 ....33 A3
Brickcroft La PR26 ...58 B3
Brickhouse Gdns PR3 .185 E3
Brickhouse La FY6 ...177 C4
Brickmakers Arms Yd
  L39 ....15 D6
Bridge Ave L39 ....15 E5
Bridge Bank **4** PR5 ..97 C6
Bridge Cl
  Bamber Bridge PR5 ...77 A8
  6 Newchurch BB4 ....86 F1
Bridge Croft
  Bolton-le-S LA5 ....221 A4
  Clayton-le-M BB5 ...124 E4
Bridge Ct
  3 Bamber Bridge PR5 ..77 A8
  Clitheroe BB7 ......189 F2
  2 Lytham St Anne's FY8 .91 D4
Bridge End
  Bamber Bridge PR5 ...77 C8
  Barley BB12 ......169 C5
  Whalley BB7 ......144 C4
Bridge End Cl BB4 ....68 A7
Bridge End St OL14 ..109 C1
Bridge Farm Dr L31 ...5 F2
Bridge Gr PR8 ....35 B6
Bridge Hall Dr BL9 ...33 C4
Bridge Hall Fold BL9 .33 C2
Bridge Hall La BL9 ...33 D2
Bridge Ho
  6 Blackburn BB2 ....101 B1
  18 Lancaster LA1 ....218 D2
  3 Lytham St Anne's FY8 .91 D4
  Ormskirk L39 ....15 E4
Bridge Hos Accrington BB5 84 E8
  Whitewell Bottom BB4 .86 F7
Bridge House Marina & Cvn
  Pk PR3 ....181 A8
Bridge House Rd FY4 .110 F8
Bridge La LA1 ....214 F8
Bridge Mill Ct PR6 ...43 F6
Bridge Mill Rd BB9 ..148 C8
Bridge Mills BL0 .....68 E3
Bridge Rd
  3 Bamber Bridge PR5 ..77 C8
  Chatburn BB7 ......190 D5
  Fleetwood FY7 .....199 B4
  Lancaster LA1 .....214 F5
  Lytham St Anne's FY8 ..90 E4
  Morecambe LA4 ....217 C5
  Nether Kellet LA6 ..221 E4
  Preston PR1 ....117 C2
Bridge Row PR3 .....157 C7
Bridge St
  14 Accrington BB5 ....104 C6
  Bamber Bridge PR5 ...77 E7
  Blackburn BB1 .....101 E4
  Brierfield BB9 .....148 B5
  Burnley BB11 ......128 A6
  Bury BL9 ....33 A3
  Church BB5 ....103 E6
  Colne BB8 ....171 C4
  Darwen BB3 ....82 A1
  Garstang PR3 ......181 C6
  6 Great Harwood BB6 .124 C5
  Haslingden BB4 ....68 C6
  Higher Walton PR5 ...98 B3
  Horwich BL6 ....32 C4
  Newchurch BB4 .....86 F1
  Ormskirk L39 ....15 E4
  Padiham BB12 .....126 B8
  Ramsbottom BL0 ....50 C6
  Rawtenstall BB4 ....69 E7
  Rishton BB1 ....124 B2
  Southport PR8 ......35 B6
  Water BB4 ....87 A8
  Wheelton PR6 ......62 A7
  Whitworth OL12 .....71 C1
Bridge Terr
  6 Preston PR5 ......97 C6
  Whalley BB7 ......144 B7
Bridge Wills La PR9 ..54 C5
Bridgefield Cl BB1 ..124 B2
Bridgefield Dr BL9 ...33 C2
Bridgefield St **8** BB12 .126 C4
Bridgehall Dr WN8 ...10 B7
Bridgemill Rd BB1 ..101 F4
Bridgend Ct PR2 ....116 F3

Bridgend Dr PR8 ......21 B4
Bridgeside FY8 ....110 B4
Bridget St **22** LA1 ....214 F8
Bridgewater Ave **7** FY5 152 F7
Bridgewater Cl BB11 ..126 F4
Bridgewater Ct **6** BB2 .101 C4
Bridgeway PR5 ....77 C8
Bridle Path The BB18 .194 D7
Bridleway
  Lytham St Anne's FY8 ..90 E7
  Newchurch BB4 ......86 F2
Brief St BB10 ....128 A8
Brier Cres BB9 ......148 D6
Brier Dr LA3 ....212 E7
Brier Heights Cl BB9 .148 D5
Briercliffe
  Blackpool FY3 .....130 C2
  Colne BB8 ....171 B3
Briercliffe Bsns Ctr
  BB10 ....148 E3
Briercliffe Prim Sch
  BB10 ....148 E3
Briercliffe Rd
  Brierfield BB10 ....148 D2
  Burnley BB10 ......148 C1
  9 Chorley BB6 ....61 D1
Briercliffe St BB8 ...171 B3
Brierfield
  New Longton PR4 .....75 F8
  Skelmersdale WN8 ....9 D6
Brierfield Sta BB9 ..148 B5
Brierholme Ave BL7 ..47 E1
Brierley Ave FY3 ...130 E2
Brierley La PR4 .....136 B8
Brierley Rd PR5 ......78 A7
Brierley St PR2 .....117 C1
Briers Brow PR6 .....62 B7
Briers The PR7 ......41 C6
Briery Cl PR2 ....118 C4
Briery Hey PR5 ......78 C6
Briery St **2** LA1 .....218 B1
Brieryfield Rd PR1 ...96 D8
Brigg Field BB5 .....124 F4
Briggs Fold BL7 .....47 E2
Briggs Fold Cl BL7 ..47 E2
Briggs Fold Rd BL7 ..47 E2
Briggs Rd PR2 ......117 C2
Brighouse Cl L39 ....15 D6
Bright St Blackburn BB1 .102 B6
  Blackpool FY4 ....110 B8
  2 Burnley BB10 .....148 B1
  Bury BL9 ....33 A3
  Clitheroe BB7 .....166 F8
  Colne BB8 ....171 D5
  Colne,Cotton Tree BB8 .172 B5
  Darwen BB3 ....81 F2
  Egerton BL7 ....47 D2
  Oswaldtwistle BB5 ..103 D3
  Padiham BB12 .....126 D8
  13 Rawtenstall BB4 ....86 A3
  Southport PR9 ......35 F7
Bright Terr BB8 .....172 B2
Bright's Cl BB7 ....229 A5
Brighton Ave
  Blackpool FY4 ....110 B8
  Cleveleys FY5 .....175 D4
  Lytham St Anne's FY8 ..89 F7
Brighton Cres PR2 ..117 A3
Brighton Rd
  Brierfield BB10 ....148 C3
  Southport PR8 ......35 A3
Brighton St Bury BL9 ..33 B3
  7 Chorley PR6 ....43 E8
  Cornholme OL14 ....109 C1
Brighton Terr
  Blackburn BB2 ....101 B6
  Darwen BB3 ....81 E2
Brightstone Cl PR9 ...55 B5
Brightwater BL6 .....31 F2
Brigsteer Cl BB5 ...124 E2
Brindle Cl
  9 Lancaster LA1 ....218 A2
  Longridge PR3 .....140 B7
  Walton Summit PR5 ...78 B8
Brindle Fold PR5 .....78 C7
Brindle Gregson Lane Prim
  Sch PR5 ....98 E1
Brindle Hts PR6 ......78 F5
Brindle Rd
  Bamber Bridge PR5 ...97 F2
  Walton Summit PR5,PR6 .78 C7
Brindle St Blackburn BB2 101 C1
  Chorley PR7 ....43 C6
  Preston PR1 ....97 C8
Brindle St James' CE Prim
  Sch PR6 ....78 F5
Brindley Cl BB11 ....126 F4
Brindley St BL6 ......32 C2
Brink's Row BL6 .....32 D5
Brinklow Cl PR8 .....21 A5
Brinscall Terr PR6 ...62 F7
Brinwell Rd FY4 ....131 B1
Brisbane Pl FY5 .....152 F7
Brisbane St **8** BB5 ..125 A1
Bristol Ave Blackpool FY2 152 E4
  Fleetwood FY7 .....175 C8
  Leyland PR25 ....77 C3
Bristol Cl **9** BB1 ...102 A4
Bristol St Burnley BB11 .127 D3
  Colne BB8 ....171 E6
  Morecambe LA4 ....217 C4
Bristow Ave PR2 ....117 B2
Britannia Ave OL13 ..88 A2
Britannia Com Prim Sch
  OL13 ....71 C8
Britannia Cotts BB5 .103 A1
Britannia Pl **2** FY1 .130 B1

Britannia St BB6 ....124 C5
Britannia Way
  Blackpool FY4 ....111 E8
  Haslingden BB4 .....68 A8
Britannia Wharf PR2 ..96 B8
British Commercial Vehicle
Mus★ PR25 ....77 A1
British in India Mus★
  BB8 ....171 E5
British Lawnmower Mus★
  PR8 ....35 B5
Britten Cl BB2 ......102 A2
Britten St BB3 ....81 F2
Britwell Cl BB2 ......82 A8
Brixey St PR1 ....96 D6
Brixham PI **4** FY4 ..110 B6
Brixton Rd PR1 ......97 B7
Broad Clough Villas
  OL13 ....87 F5
Broad Croft PR4 ......95 A1
Broad Gate BB3 ....82 B2
Broad Ing OL12 ....52 C1
Broad Ing Cl BB10 ..128 E1
Broad La Formby L37 ..12 E2
  Hale Nook PR3 ....178 D5
  Haskayne L39 ......14 B2
  Kirkby L32 ....1 A1
  Maghull L29 ....4 C2
  Whalley BB7 ......144 B5
  Winmarleigh PR3 ...203 F5
Broad Lane Gypsy Camp
  L37 ....12 D8
Broad Mdw
  Bamber Bridge PR5 ...77 A8
  Chipping PR3 .....185 D3
Broad Meadow La PR26 .57 F4
Broad Oak Ave BR3 ..181 D6
Broad Oak Cl PR6 ....31 A8
Broad Oak Cotts CP6 ..44 D3
Broad Oak Gn PR1 ....96 B3
Broad Oak High Sch BL9 33 B2
Broad Oak Ind Est BB5 .104 D4
Broad Oak La Bury BL9 ..33 D3
  Higher Penwortham PR1 .96 B3
Broad Oak Rd BB5 ..104 D5
Broad Oak Terr BL9 ..33 E3
Broad Sq **8** PR25 ...60 A8
Broad St **3** Leyland PR25 .60 A8
  13 Nelson BB9 ....148 D8
Broadacre Caton LA2 .237 C3
  Shevington Moor WN6 ..29 B2
  Skelmersdale WN8 ....10 A6
Broadacre Cl LA2 ...237 C3
Broadacre PI LA2 ...237 C3
Broadacre View LA2 .237 C3
Broadbent Dr BL9 ....33 E4
Broadfield Accrington BB5 .84 B8
  Broughton PR3 .....137 B2
  Oswaldtwistle BB5 ..103 F2
Broadfield Ave
  Blackpool FY4 ....110 F5
  Poulton-le-F FY6 ..153 F3
Broadfield Dr
  Kingsfold PR1 ......96 D2
  Leyland PR25 ....76 E1
Broadfield Rd BB5 ..104 A3
Broadfield Sch BB5 .103 F2
Broadfield St BB5 ...103 F3
Broadfields PR7 ......61 B2
Broadfleet Ct PR3 ..201 C6
Broadfold Ave BB1 ..102 B7
Broadgate PR1 ....96 D6
Broadgate Foot Cvn Pk
  LA3 ....212 F4
Broadgreen Cl PR25 ..76 F1
Broadhead Rd BB3,BL7 ..66 F5
Broadhurst La WN6 ...28 E7
Broadhurst Rd FY5 ..152 E8
Broadhurst Way BB9 .148 C4
Broadith La PR3 ....160 E1
Broadlands PR8 ......34 E3
Broadlands Dr LA5 ..220 F3
Broadlands Pl FY8 ...90 F4
Broadlands Sch BB1 ..82 B8
Broadlea Gr OL12 ....52 C2
Broadley Fold OL12 ..52 B6
Broadley St BB4 ......86 A3
Broadmead WN8 ......27 B2
Broadness Dr BB9 ..148 E6
Broadoak Rd L31 ......5 E1
Broadoaks BL9 ....33 D3
Broadpool La FY6 ...177 C1
Broadriding Rd WN6 ..19 E6
Broadstone Cl OL12 ..52 A1
Broadstone Ct LA1 ..215 C7
Broadtree Cl BB2 ...121 C3
Broadwater Ave FY7 .175 F8
Broadwater Gdns FY7 .175 E8
Broadway
  Blackburn BB1 ....122 C4
  Blackpool FY4 ....110 C7
  Fleetwood FY7 .....198 E2
  Fulwood PR2 ......117 D7
  Haslingden BB4 .....68 B8
  Horwich BL6 ....32 D3
  Lancaster LA1 ....218 D2
  Leyland PR25 ....60 B8
  Morecambe LA4 ....217 D4
  Nelson BB9 ....148 D8
  Preston PR2 ......116 F2
Broadway Cl PR2 .....21 B5
Broadway Cres BB4 ..68 A8

Broadway Pl
  Barrowford BB9 ....170 D3
  Nelson BB9 ....171 A1
Broadway St BB2 ....101 B1
Broadwood Cl PR1 ...96 B4
Broadwood Dr PR2 ..117 F7
Broadwood Way FY8 ..90 E4
Brock Ave FY7 ......198 D2
Brock Bank BB4 ......86 F4
Brock Cl LA1 ....218 C3
Brock Clough Rd BB4 ..86 F4
Brock Mill La PR3 ..183 B2
Brock Rd Chorley PR6 ..61 D1
  Lane Heads PR3,PR4 ..156 E3
Brock Side PR3 .....159 C6
Brock St LA1 ....214 F8
Brockbank Ave LA1 .214 C8
Brockenhurst St BB10 .128 C5
Brockholes Brow PR1,
  PR2 ....119 A1
Brockholes Cres PR2 .153 E2
Brockholes View PR1 ..97 C7
Brockholes Way PR3 .181 F1
Brockholes Wood Com Prim
  Sch PR1 ....119 A1
Brocklebank Rd PR9 ..53 E2
Brocklehurst Ave BB5 .104 B3
Brocklewood Ave FY6 .131 D8
Brockway FY6 ......153 D2
Brockway Ave FY3 ..130 F6
Broderick Ave **1** FY2 .152 E1
Brodick Rd BB1 .....102 D3
Brodie Cl FY4 ......110 F6
Brogden La BB18 ...231 E2
Brogden St **4** BB18 ..196 B3
Brogden View BB18 .196 A4
Broken Bank Head BB7 .235 A2
Broken Banks BB8 ..171 C4
Broken Stone Rd BB3 ..81 A6
Bromilow Rd WN8 ....17 C1
Bromley Cl FY2 .....152 E1
Bromley Cross BL7 ..48 E1
Bromley Ct **5** FY2 ..152 E1
Bromley Gn PR6 .....61 F4
Bromley Ho BB2 ....101 C5
Bromley Rd FY8 .....89 F6
Bromley St
  Blackburn BB2 ....101 C5
  Preston PR1 ....96 B8
Brompton Ave L33 .....1 A5
Brompton Cl FY8 .....90 D5
Brompton Rd
  Poulton-le-F FY6 ..131 D8
  Southport PR8 ......35 E7
Bromsgrove Ave FY2 .152 E4
Bromsgrove Rd BB10 .128 B8
Bronte Ave BB10 ...128 D6
Bronte Cl OL12 ......52 A1
Brooden Dr BB9 ....148 C4
Brook Ave Maghull L31 ..5 E2
  Morecambe LA3 ....216 F3
  Scorton PR3 ......204 E7
Brook Croft PR2 ....117 B4
Brook Ct **8** BB4 .....86 A7
Brook Farm Cl L39 ...15 E4
Brook Field Way BB18 .197 B1
Brook Gr Cleveleys FY5 .175 E4
  Morecambe LA3 ....216 F3
Brook Hey PR4 ......74 F8
Brook Hey Dr L33 .....1 A3
Brook Hey Wlk L33 ....1 A3
Brook Ho
  Lytham St Anne's FY8 ..91 A3
  Southport PR8 ......35 C5
Brook La
  Charnock Richard PR7 ..42 C4
  Farington PR26,PR4 ..76 D6
  Much Hoole PR4 ....74 E3
  Ormskirk L39 ....15 E4
Brook Mdw PR4 .....116 F7
Brook Mill Ind Est PR4 .113 B4
Brook Pl PR2 ......116 D2
Brook Rd
  Lytham St Anne's FY8 ..91 C3
  Morecambe LA3 ....216 F3
Brook Side L31 ....5 E1
Brook St Adlington PR6 ..44 A1
  4 Barnoldswick BB18 .196 B2
  Blackburn BB2 ....101 B2
  Blackpool FY4 ....130 E1
  Bury BL9 ....33 A3
  Clitheroe BB7 .....189 F1
  Colne BB8 ....171 D5
  Earby BB18 ....197 B2
  Fleetwood FY7 .....175 E8
  Haslingden BB4 .....85 B5
  Higher Walton PR5 ...98 B3
  Kirkham PR4 ......113 F6
  Lancaster LA1 ....214 F7
  Nelson BB9 ....148 B8
  Oswaldtwistle BB5 ..103 E4
  Padiham BB12 .....126 D7
  Preston PR1 ....117 C2
  Rishton BB1 ....124 B1
  Southport PR9 ......54 D4
  Wheelton PR6 ......62 A7
Brook St N PR2 .....117 D3
Brook Vale Ct PR3 ..157 C2
Brook Villas
  Waddington BB7 ...189 B4
  West Bradford BB7 .189 D7
Brookbank BB9 .....170 E4
Brookdale Adlington PR6 ..44 A1
  Belmont BL7 ....46 C5
  New Longton PR4 ....76 A6
  Rochdale OL12 ......52 A1
Brookdale Ave FY5 .152 E6
Brookdale Cl PR25 ...60 B6

Brooke Cl Accrington BB5 104 E2
  Southport PR9 ......36 E3
Brooke St PR6 ....43 E7
Brookes La BB7 .....144 C5
Brookes St **10** OL13 ..70 D8
Brookes The **6** PR6 ..43 E7
Brookfield Croston PR26 ..58 B3
  Mawdesley L40 .....40 C2
  Mellor BB2 ....121 E2
  Parbold WN8 ....27 C2
Brookfield Ave
  Blackpool FY4 ....111 A6
  Fulwood PR2 ......118 C4
  Thornton FY5 .....176 C1
Brookfield Cl LA5 ..221 B5
Brookfield Com Prim Sch
  PR2 ....118 E5
Brookfield Ct PR3 ..185 E3
Brookfield Dr PR2 ..117 E8
Brookfield Ho BL0 ...49 F3
Brookfield La L39 .....6 A5
Brookfield Park Prim Sch
  WN8 ....17 D2
Brookfield Pl PR5 ...78 A6
Brookfield Rd
  Shevington Moor WN6 ..29 B2
  Skelmersdale WN8 ..10 B7
  Thornton FY5 .....176 C1
Brookfield Sch FY6 .153 F5
Brookfield St
  2 Blackburn BB1 ....101 E6
  4 Cornholme OL14 ..109 C1
  Preston PR1 ....117 C2
Brookfield Terr
  Hampson Green LA2 .207 E8
  Lytham St Anne's FY8 ..91 B4
Brookfield View LA5 .221 B5
Brookford Cl BB12 ..127 D8
Brookholme Ct LA1 .214 C7
Brookhouse Bsns Ctr **10**
  BB1 ....101 F6
Brookhouse Cl
  Blackburn BB1 ....101 F6
  Gregson Lane PR5 ...98 F2
Brookhouse Dr PR5 ..98 F2
Brookhouse Gdns **12**
  BB1 ....101 F6
Brookhouse La BB1 .101 F6
Brookhouse Prim Sch
  BB1 ....101 F7
Brookhouse Rd
  Caton LA2 ....237 C3
  Ormskirk L39 ....15 D6
Brookhouse St PR2 ..117 C1
Brookland LA6 .....242 C3
Brookland Cl BB5 ..124 F4
Brookland St BB4 ....86 D1
Brookland Terr BB4 ..69 F7
Brooklands Chipping PR3 185 F3
  Horwich BL6 ....32 C3
  Ormskirk L39 ....16 A6
  Preston PR2 ......117 A1
Brooklands Ave
  Burnley BB11 ......128 B3
  Fulwood PR2 ......117 E2
  Haslingden BB4 .....68 B7
  Kirkham PR4 ......114 A5
Brooklands Cl LA1 ..215 A4
Brooklands Dr
  Bonds PR3 ....181 C6
  Heysham LA3 .....212 F6
  Orrell WN5 ....10 D5
Brooklands Gr L40 ...25 F3
Brooklands Rd
  Burnley BB11 ......128 B3
  Lytham St Anne's FY8 ..90 C6
  Ramsbottom BL0 ....50 A2
  Skelmersdale WN8 ..10 C7
Brooklands Terr BB1 .102 A7
Brooklands The PR4 .113 B4
Brooklands Way FY4 .111 E7
Brooklyn Ave FY3 ..130 E8
Brooklyn Rd BB1 ...122 F5
Brooks Rd L37 ......11 D2
Brooks Way L37 .....11 D2
Brooksbottom Cl BL0 ..50 C4
Brookshaw St BL9 ...33 A4
Brookside
  Brockhall Village BB6 .143 C5
  Coppull PR7 ....42 F1
  Downham BB7 .....191 B5
  Euxton PR4 ....60 C2
  Kirkham PR4 ......113 F6
  Sabden BB7 ....145 F7
  Thornton FY5 .....176 C3
Brookside Cl Leyland PR26 76 E3
  Ramsbottom BL0 ....50 A3
  Whalley BB7 ......144 C5
Brookside Cotts PR6 ..62 D3
Brookside Cres
  Ramsbottom BL8 ....49 E1
  West Bradford BB7 .189 D7
Brookside Ctr FY5 ..176 C3
Brookside Dr LA2 ..226 A8
Brookside Ind Est BB5 .103 C5
Brookside La BB5 ..103 B3
Brookside Prim Sch
  BB7 ....166 F8
Brookside Rd
  Fulwood PR2 ......117 D7
  Southport PR8 ......35 C2
  Standish WN1 ....30 B1
Brookside St BB5 ...103 C3
Brookside View BB5 .103 B4
Brookview PR2 .....118 B5
Brookville OL12 .....71 C1
Brookway Blackburn BB2 ..81 B8

Brookway continued
Longton PR4 . . . . .74 F8
Wrea Green PR4 . . . . . . .113 A4
Broom Cl Burscough L40 . . .25 F4
Clayton-le-W PR25 . . . . . .77 E3
Broom Field PR3 . . . . . .181 D4
Broom Hill Coppice
PR3 . . . . .204 C2
Broome Cl PR8 . . . . . . .35 B3
Broome Rd PR8 . . . . . . .35 B3
Broomfield Mill St PR1 . .117 F1
Broomfield Pl
Blackburn BB2 . . . . .101 B3
Standish WN6 . . . . .29 E1
Broomfield Rd
Fleetwood FY7 . . . . .198 F2
Standish WN6 . . . . .29 E1
Broomflat Cl WN6 . . . . .29 E1
Broomholme WN6 . . . . .0 D7
Brotherod Hall Rd OL12 . .52 C2
Brothers St BB2 . . . . . .101 A1
Brotherston Dr BB2 . . . .81 C8
Brotherton Mdws 🗗
BB7 . . . . .166 F8
Brough Ave FY2 . . . . . .152 F2
Brougham St BB12 . . . . .127 F7
Broughton Ave
Blackpool FY3 . . . . .130 C4
Southport PR8 . . . . .35 D4
Broughton Bsns & Ent Coll
PR3 . . . . .137 C2
Broughton Cl BB2 . . . . .102 A1
Broughton Gr LA3 . . . . .217 C2
Broughton in Amounderness
CE Prim Sch PR3 . . . . .137 D1
Broughton St
🛈 Burnley BB12 . . . . . . .127 D6
🛈 Darwen BB3 . . . . .81 F2
Preston PR1 . . . . .117 E2
Broughton Tower Way
PR2 . . . . .118 A8
Broughton Way FY6 . . . .153 C6
Brow Cl PR3 . . . . .156 A6
Brow Edge BB4 . . . . . . .86 D1
Brow Hey PR5 . . . . .78 B6
Brow The PR4 . . . . .73 E4
Brow View BB10 . . . . . .128 B8
Browfoot Cl LA5 . . . . . .223 F1
Browgate PR4 . . . . . . .190 F8
Browgill Pl 🛈 LA1 . . . . .218 B2
Browhead Cl BB10 . . . . .128 B8
Browhead Rd BB10 . . . . .128 B8
Brown Birks Rd BB5 . . . .104 E8
Brown Birks St 🛈 OL14 . .109 B1
Brown Edge Cl PR8 . . . . .36 A2
Brown Hill La BB8 . . . . .171 F7
Brown Hill Row BB8 . . . .171 F7
Brown La
Bamber Bridge PR5 . . . . . .98 A2
Higher Walton PR5 . . . . . .98 A3
Brown Sq 🛈 BB11 . . . . .128 A6
Brown St Accrington BB5 . .104 E4
Bacup OL13 . . . . .87 F4
Bamber Bridge PR5 . . . . . .77 F8
Blackburn BB1 . . . . .101 E5
Blackrod BL6 . . . . .31 C2
Burnley BB11 . . . . .127 F6
Chorley PR6 . . . . .43 D8
Clitheroe BB7 . . . . .166 D7
Fleetwood FY7 . . . . .199 A3
🛈 Ramsbottom BL0 . . . . . .50 B5
Thornton FY5 . . . . .176 B3
Brown St E BB8 . . . . . .171 D5
Brown St W BB8 . . . . . .171 C4
Brown's La Kirkham PR4 . .113 D3
Thornton FY6 . . . . .176 E7
Brownedge Cl PR5 . . . . .97 C1
Brownedge La PR5 . . . . .97 C1
Brownedge Rd PR5 . . . . .77 B8
Brownedge St Mary's RC
High Sch PR5 . . . . . . .97 C1
Brownedge Wlk PR5 . . . .97 D1
Brownhill Ave BB10 . . . .128 C6
Brownhill Dr BB1 . . . . .123 A1
Brownhill La PR4 . . . . . .75 D7
Brownhill Rd
Blackburn BB1 . . . . .122 F3
Leyland PR25 . . . . .76 F1
Brownhill Sch OL12 . . . .52 E1
Brownhill View OL12 . . . .52 E1
Browning Ave
🛈 Lytham St Anne's FY8 . . .91 D4
Oswaldtwistle BB5 . . . . . .103 C5
🛈 Thornton FY5 . . . . . . .176 A3
Browning Cl BB8 . . . . . .171 D6
Browning Cres PR1 . . . . .118 D2
Browning Rd PR1 . . . . . .118 D2
Browning St BB3 . . . . . .82 F1
Brownley St Chorley PR6 . .43 E7
Clayton Green PR6 . . . . . .78 B1
Brownlow La WN5 . . . . . .10 C1
Brownlow Rd BL6 . . . . . .32 C5
Brownlow St
Blackburn BB1 . . . . .102 D4
Clitheroe BB7 . . . . .166 E2
Brownlow Terr BB2 . . . . .100 C1
Brownroyd BB18 . . . . . .197 C2
Browns Hey PR7 . . . . . . .61 A2
Brownside Mill Rd BB10 . .128 F6
Brownside Rd BB10 . . . . .128 F5
Brows Cl L37 . . . . .11 E3
Brows La L37 . . . . .11 E3
Browsholme LA1 . . . . . .218 A2
Browsholme Ave
Burnley BB10 . . . . .128 C6
Fulwood PR2 . . . . .118 C5
Browsholme Cl
Carnforth LA5 . . . . .223 C1

Browsholme Cl continued
Normoss FY3 . . . . .131 B8
Browsholme Hall ★ BB7 . .187 E7
Browsholme Rd BB7 . . . .229 C1
Broxfield Ct FY8 . . . . . .89 D6
Broxton Ave WN5 . . . . . .10 C7
Broyd View LA1 . . . . . .214 F5
Bruce St
🖬 Barnoldswick BB18 . . . .196 B3
Blackburn BB1 . . . . .102 B6
Burnley BB11 . . . . .127 D5
Brun Gr FY1 . . . . .130 E1
Brun St BB11 . . . . .127 D5
Brun Terr BB10 . . . . . .128 F5
Bruna La PR3 . . . . .181 B4
Brundhurst Fold BB2 . . . .121 E2
Brunel Dr BB1 . . . . . . .102 A4
Brunel St Burnley BB12 . .127 C7
Horwich BL6 . . . . .32 C2
Brunel Way FY4 . . . . . .111 C7
Brunel Wlk BB1 . . . . . .101 F4
Brungerley Ave BB7 . . . .189 E1
Brunshaw Ave BB10 . . . .128 D5
Brunshaw Prim Sch
BB10 . . . . .128 D4
Brunshaw Rd BB10 . . . . .128 D6
Brunswick Ave BL6 . . . . .32 E2
Brunswick Dr BB8 . . . . .171 A3
Brunswick Pl 🖬 PR2 . . . .117 C1
Brunswick Rd LA3 . . . . .216 E3
Brunswick St
Blackburn BB2 . . . . .101 D4
🖬 Blackpool FY1 . . . . . .130 B4
Burnley BB11 . . . . .128 A4
🖬 Chorley PR6 . . . . .43 D8
Darwen BB3 . . . . .65 B8
Nelson BB9 . . . . .148 E7
Brunswick Terr
Accrington BB5 . . . . . . .104 B6
Bacup OL13 . . . . .70 D8
Brunton Ho 🖬 LA1 . . . . .215 A5
Brunton Rd LA1 . . . . . .214 F6
Brunton's Warehouse
LA1 . . . . .218 C1
Brush St BB11 . . . . . . .127 C5
Brussells Rd BB3 . . . . . .82 C1
Bryan Rd FY3 . . . . .130 D5
Bryan St BB2 . . . . .101 E2
Brydeck Ave PR1 . . . . . .96 E4
Bryer St 🖬 LA1 . . . . . .214 F4
Bryer's Croft BB1 . . . . .122 F6
Bryn Gr LA2 . . . . .220 E2
Bryning Ave
Blackpool FY2 . . . . .152 C4
Wrea Green PR4 . . . . . . .113 B3
Bryning Fern La PR4 . . . .113 F4
Bryning Hall La
Saltcotes,Moss Side FY8 . . .112 F1
Warton PR4 . . . . .92 B8
Wrea Green FY8,PR4 . . . . .113 A1
Bryning La
Newton-w-S PR4 . . . . . . .114 F2
Wrea Green PR4 . . . . . . .113 A4
Bryning with Warton St
Paul's CE Prim Sch PR4 . .92 D6
Bryony Cl Cleveleys FY5 . .175 D5
Orrell WN5 . . . . .10 D5
Bryony Ct LA3 . . . . . . .217 B2
Buccleuch Ave BB7 . . . .166 D8
Buccleuch Cl BB7 . . . . . .166 D8
Buccleuch Rd 🖬 BB9 . . . .170 C1
Buccleuch St BB11 . . . . .127 E5
Buchanan St
Blackpool FY1 . . . . .130 C6
Chorley PR6 . . . . .43 D7
🖬 Ramsbottom BL0 . . . . . .50 B6
Buck St Burnley BB11 . . .127 E5
Colne BB8 . . . . .171 E5
Grindleton BB7 . . . . . . .190 B7
Buckden Cl FY5 . . . . . . .175 C1
Buckden Gate BB9 . . . . .170 C3
Buckden Pl LA3 . . . . . . .212 F4
Buckden Rd 🖬 BB5 . . . . .103 F4
Buckfast Dr L37 . . . . . . .12 B2
Buckholes La PR6 . . . . . .79 C1
Buckhurst Rd BL9 . . . . . .51 C3
Buckingham Ave
Horwich BL6 . . . . .32 E2
Kingsfold PR1 . . . . .96 E2
Buckingham Cl BB4 . . . . .85 A1
Buckingham Dr BB12 . . . .145 D2
Buckingham Gr
Church BB5 . . . . .103 F7
Formby L37 . . . . .11 C4
Morecambe LA3 . . . . . . .216 F3
Buckingham Pl LA3 . . . . .216 F3
Buckingham Rd
Lytham St Anne's FY8 . . . . .90 D4
🖬 Maghull L31 . . . . .5 D1
Morecambe LA3,LA4 . . . . .216 F3
Buckingham St PR6 . . . . .43 D7
Buckingham Way FY6 . . .153 C5
Bucklands Ave PR2 . . . . .117 D2
Buckley Cres FY5 . . . . . .152 D7
Bucknell Pl FY5 . . . . . . .152 F7
Buckshaw Hall Cl PR7 . . . .61 B2
Buckshaw Prim Sch PR7 . .61 A2
Buckthorn Cl PR6 . . . . . .61 C6
Buckton Cl PR4 . . . . . . .116 F6
Bude Cl PR4 . . . . .116 F6
Buff St 🖬 BB3 . . . . .65 A8
Buffalo Rd PR26 . . . . . . .77 A4
Bulcock St BB10 . . . . . .148 C5
Bulk Rd LA1 . . . . .218 C1
Bulk St LA1 . . . . .214 F8
Bull Cop LA3 . . . . .12 B3
Bull Park La FY6 . . . . . .154 C8
Bull St BB11 . . . . .128 A6

Bullens La L40 . . . . .23 E7
Buller Ave PR1 . . . . .96 E4
Buller St
🛈 Lancaster LA1 . . . . . .218 D3
Rawtenstall BB4 . . . . .86 A2
Bullfinch Dr BL9 . . . . . . .33 B5
Bullfinch St 🛈 BB1 . . . . .118 B1
Bullion The BB12 . . . . . .169 C5
Bulmer St PR2 . . . . .117 C2
Buncer La BB2 . . . . .101 A4
Bungalows The
Burnley BB11 . . . . .127 E4
🛈 Earby BB18 . . . . .197 B1
Great Eccleston PR3 . . . . .156 C5
Bunker St PR4 . . . . .93 C6
Bunkers Hill Cl BB2 . . . . .81 B8
Bunting Pl 🛈 FY5 . . . . . .175 F1
Bunyan St 🛈 OL12 . . . . .52 F1
Buoymaster LA1 . . . . . .218 C1
Burbank Cl FY4 . . . . . . .110 F5
Burdett St BB11 . . . . . .127 D5
Burdock Wlk LA3 . . . . . .217 B2
Burford Cl Blackburn BB2 . .80 E8
Blackpool FY3 . . . . .131 A7
Burford Dr LA3 . . . . . . .213 A7
Burgate FY4 . . . . .110 D5
Burgess Ave FY4 . . . . . .110 E7
Burgess Gdns L31 . . . . . . .5 C2
Burgess St
🛈 Blackburn BB1 . . . . . .102 C5
🛈 Haslingden BB4 . . . . . .85 B3
Burgess' La L37 . . . . .13 A2
Burgh Hall Rd PR7 . . . . . .43 A3
Burgh La PR7 . . . . .43 C4
Burgh La S PR7 . . . . .43 B2
Burgh Mdws PR7 . . . . . . .43 C4
Burgh Wood Cl PR7 . . . . .42 F6
Burgh Wood Way PR7 . . . .43 A6
Burghley Brow PR3 . . . . .181 D1
Burghley Cl PR6 . . . . . . .78 C2
Burghley Ct 🛈 PR25 . . . . .77 B1
Burgundy Cres FY5 . . . . .152 F7
Burholme Cl PR2 . . . . . .119 A2
Burholme Pl PR2 . . . . . .119 A2
Burholme Rd PR2 . . . . . .119 A2
Burleigh Rd 🛈 PR1 . . . . .96 E7
Burleigh St BB11 . . . . . .127 E5
Burlingham Cvn Pk PR3 . .204 B1
Burlington Ave
Formby L37 . . . . .12 B3
Morecambe LA4 . . . . . . .217 D5
Burlington Ctr FY4 . . . . .110 B7
Burlington Ctr The FY8 . . .89 E6
Burlington Gdns PR25 . . . .60 B8
Burlington Gr LA4 . . . . .217 D5
Burlington Ho 🛈 FY6 . . . .153 D3
Burlington Rd
Blackpool FY4 . . . . .110 B6
Southport PR8 . . . . .34 F3
Burlington Rd W FY4 . . . .110 A6
Burlington St
Blackburn BB2 . . . . .101 C5
Chorley PR7 . . . . .43 D7
Nelson BB9 . . . . .148 C7
Burn Gr FY5 . . . . .175 E4
Burn Hall Ind Est FY7 . . .176 A6
Burnage Gdns FY4 . . . . .110 D7
Burned House La FY6 . . . .200 D2
Burnedge Cl OL12 . . . . . .71 D2
Burneside Cl LA4 . . . . . .217 C4
Burnfell Rd 🛈 LA1 . . . . .218 A2
Burnham Cl BB11 . . . . . .127 E5
Burnham Ct
Blackpool FY3 . . . . .130 E5
Morecambe LA3 . . . . . . .216 E1
Burnham Gate BB11 . . . .127 E5
Burnham Trad Pk 🛈
BB11 . . . . .127 E6
Burnley Ave PR8 . . . . . . .21 D5
Burnley Barracks Sta
BB12 . . . . .127 E6
Burnley Bsns Ctr 🛈
BB11 . . . . .128 A6
Burnley Central Sta
BB12 . . . . .127 F7
Burnley Cl BB11 . . . . . .102 B5
Burnley Coll BB11 . . . . .128 A7
Burnley General Hospl
BB10 . . . . .148 C2
Burnley Habergham High Sch
BB12 . . . . .126 F7
Burnley Ivy Bank High Bsns &
Enterprise Coll BB12 . . .126 F7
Burnley La BB11,BB5 . . . .126 A2
Burnley Manchester Road Sta
BB11 . . . . .127 F5
Burnley Rd
Accrington,Hillock Vale
BB5 . . . . .104 D8
🛈 Accrington,Lower Fold
BB5 . . . . .104 C6
Baldingstone BL9 . . . . . . .50 E1
Blackburn BB1 . . . . .102 C6
Brierfield BB9,BB10 . . . . .148 B5
Brierfield,Harle Syke BB10 . .148 F5
Burnley BB10,BB11 . . . . .128 D1
Clayton-le-M BB5 . . . . . .125 C5
Colne BB8,BB9 . . . . . . .171 B3
Edenfield BL0 . . . . .68 D5
Gisburn BB7 . . . . .231 B3
Hapton BB11,BB5 . . . . . .126 B1
Holme Chapel BB10,OL14 . .108 C4
Padiham BB12 . . . . .126 D8
Rawtenstall BB4 . . . . .85 F5
Rawtenstall,Goodshaw Fold
BB4 . . . . .106 A2

Southport PR8 . . . . .21 C5
Trawden BB8 . . . . .172 B1
Weir BB11,BB4 . . . . . . .107 C3
Whalley BB6 . . . . .144 F3
Burnley Rd E Water BB4 . .107 A2
Whitewell Bottom BB4 . . . .86 F4
Burnley St BB1 . . . . . . .102 C5
Burns Ave
Lytham St Anne's FY8 . . . . .91 D4
Oswaldtwistle BB5 . . . . . .103 D5
Thornton FY5 . . . . .176 A3
Burns Cl WN5 . . . . .10 D1
Burns Dr BB5 . . . . .104 E2
Burns Pl FY4 . . . . .110 F8
Burns Rd FY4 . . . . .199 A5
Burns Rd Burnley BB12 . . .127 F7
Hapton BB12 . . . . .126 C4
Nelson BB9 . . . . .170 D1
Padiham BB12 . . . . .126 D7
Preston PR1 . . . . .118 D2
Burns Way BB6 . . . . . . .124 B4
Burns Wlk BB2 . . . . .82 C1
Burnsall Ave
Blackpool FY3 . . . . .153 A1
Heysham LA3 . . . . .212 F8
Burnsall Cl BB10 . . . . . .148 E3
Burnsall Pl
Barrowford BB9 . . . . . . .170 D3
Fulwood PR2 . . . . .118 E4
Burnsall Rd 🛈 BB5 . . . . .103 F4
Burnside
Barrowford BB9 . . . . . . .170 D3
🛈 Lancaster LA1 . . . . . .214 F8
Burnside Ave
Blackpool FY4 . . . . .110 E5
Calder Vale PR3 . . . . . . .182 E4
Fleetwood FY7 . . . . .198 C2
Fulwood PR2 . . . . .118 F3
Burnside Way PR1 . . . . . .96 D3
Burnslack Rd PR2 . . . . . .118 F3
Burrans Mdw 🛈 BB8 . . . .171 D4
Burrell Ave BB8 . . . . . . .171 D6
Burrington Cl PR2 . . . . . .118 D6
Burrow Heights La LA2 . . .210 F8
Burrow Rd
Over Burrow LA6 . . . . . . .241 D7
Preston PR1 . . . . .118 A1
Burrow's La FY6 . . . . . . .176 F5
Burscough Bridge Prim Sch
L40 . . . . .25 E5
Burscough Bridge St John's
CE Prim Sch L40 . . . . . .25 F5
Burscough Bridge Sta
L40 . . . . .25 E5
Burscough Ind Est L40 . . . .25 D5
Burscough Junc Sta L40 . . .25 F4
Burscough Lordsgate
Township CE Prim Sch
L40 . . . . .25 E5
Burscough Priory High Sch
L40 . . . . .25 E5
Burscough Rd L39 . . . . . .15 F7
Burscough St L39 . . . . . .15 E7
Burscough Village Prim Sch
L40 . . . . .25 F5
Burton Ave LA1 . . . . . . .218 A3
Burton Ct FY7 . . . . .175 C8
Burton Gdns BB9 . . . . . .148 B5
Burton Hill LA6 . . . . . . .242 C3
Burton Lodge PR7 . . . . . .199 B1
Burton Morewood CE Prim
Sch LA6 . . . . .240 C7
Burton Pk LA6 . . . . .240 B7
Burton Rd Blackpool FY4 . .130 F1
Low Bentham LA2 . . . . . .239 B8
Rishton BB1 . . . . .124 C1
Burton St Burnley BB11 . .128 B5
Rishton BB1 . . . . .124 C1
Burwain Castle Rd
BD23 . . . . .197 F8
Burwains Ave BB8 . . . . . .194 D1
Burwell Ave Coppull PR7 . . .29 D8
Formby L37 . . . . .11 D1
Rochdale OL12 . . . . .52 D4
Burwell Cl Kirkby L33 . . . . .1 A3
Burwen Cl BB11 . . . . . . .127 D3
Burwood Cl 🛈 PR1 . . . . .96 F2
Burwood Dr
Blackpool FY3 . . . . .131 A6
Fulwood PR2 . . . . .118 E3
Bury & Rochdale Old Rd
BL9 . . . . .33 F4
Bury Bsns Ctr BL9 . . . . . .33 A4
Bury Fold BB3 . . . . .65 A6
Bury Fold La BB3 . . . . . .65 A6
Bury La PR6 . . . . .79 F3
Bury New Rd
Heywood BL9,OL10 . . . . . .33 E2
Ramsbottom BL0 . . . . . . .50 D6
Bury Old Rd Edenfield BL0 . .68 F1
Heywood BL9,OL10 . . . . . .33 E1
Nangreaves BL0,BL9 . . . . .50 F4
Bury Rd Edenfield BL0 . . . .68 D3
Haslingden BB4 . . . . .85 B3
Rawtenstall BB4 . . . . .68 E7
Southport PR8 . . . . .35 B3
Turton Bottoms BL7 . . . . . .48 E3
Bury Row BB7 . . . . .145 F8
Bury St Darwen BB3 . . . . .82 A1
Oswaldtwistle BB5 . . . . . .103 D3
Buseph Barrow 🛈 LA4 . . .217 C4
Buseph Ct 🛈 LA4 . . . . . .217 C4
Buseph Dr LA4 . . . . .217 C4
Bush La Freckleton PR4 . . . .93 B5
Freckleton PR4 . . . . .93 B6
Bush St BB10 . . . . .148 B1
Bushburn Dr BB6 . . . . . .143 C1
Bushby's La L37 . . . . .11 C2
Bushby's Pk L37 . . . . .11 D2

Bushell Pl PR1 . . . . .97 A6
Bushell St PR1 . . . . .117 F1
Bushell's Hosp PR3 . . . . .138 E6
Bushey La WA11 . . . . .8 E2
Bussel Rd PR1 . . . . .96 E2
Butcher Brow PR5 . . . . . .97 E5
Butchers La L39 . . . . .6 B3
Bute Ave FY1 . . . . .130 B7
Bute Rd BB1 . . . . .102 B3
Bute St BB11 . . . . .127 D3
Butler Pl PR1 . . . . .117 F2
Butler Rd FY1 . . . . .130 B3
Butler St Blackpool FY1 . .130 C6
🛈 Burnley BB10 . . . . . . .128 A8
Preston PR1 . . . . .96 F7
Ramsbottom BL0 . . . . . . .50 A5
Rishton BB1 . . . . .124 C1
Butlers Farm Ct PR25 . . . .59 D7
Butlers Mdw PR4 . . . . . . .92 E6
Butt Hill La PR3 . . . . . . .182 E4
Butt's La PR3 . . . . .156 F5
Butterbergh 🛈 LA2 . . . . .239 D8
Buttercross Cl BB11 . . . . .127 D2
Butterfield Gdns L39 . . . . .15 D3
Butterfield St
🛈 Barrowford BB9 . . . . . .170 D3
🛈 Lancaster LA1 . . . . . .214 F8
Butterlands PR1 . . . . .97 F8
Buttermere Ave
Chorley PR7 . . . . .43 B6
Colne BB8 . . . . .171 F6
Fleetwood FY7 . . . . .198 C2
🛈 Morecambe LA4 . . . . . .217 D4
Buttermere Cl
🛈 Bamber Bridge PR5 . . . .97 E2
🛈 Blackburn BB1 . . . . . .101 F6
Formby L37 . . . . .11 D3
Fulwood PR2 . . . . .118 C4
Maghull L31 . . . . .5 E1
Buttermere Cres WA11 . . . .8 F2
Buttermere Ct LA1 . . . . .218 F1
Buttermere Dr
Knott End-on-S FY6 . . . . .199 F5
Oswaldtwistle BB5 . . . . . .103 D5
Ramsbottom BL0 . . . . . . .50 B7
Buttermere Rd
Burnley BB10 . . . . .128 F5
Lancaster LA1 . . . . .218 F1
Longridge PR3 . . . . .139 C5
Butterwick Field BL6 . . . . .31 F3
Butterworth Brow
Brinscall PR6 . . . . .63 A7
Chorley PR7 . . . . .43 A4
Butterworth Cl PR4 . . . . .114 A6
Button St PR3 . . . . .160 C6
Butts Barnoldswick BB18 . .196 B4
Great Harwood BB6 . . . . .124 B5
Butts Cl FY5 . . . . .152 C4
Butts Gr BB7 . . . . .189 E2
Butts La
High Bentham LA2 . . . . . .239 E8
Southport PR8 . . . . .35 F5
Butts Mount BB6 . . . . . .124 C5
Butts Rd FY5 . . . . .176 C4
Buxton Ave FY2 . . . . . . .152 C4
Buxton St Accrington BB5 . .104 A5
Morecambe LA4 . . . . . . .217 C4
Whitworth OL12 . . . . . . .71 C7
Bye La L39 . . . . .6 F8
Bye Rd BL0 . . . . .50 E8
Bye-Pass Rd LA5 . . . . . .221 A4
Byerworth La N PR3 . . . . .181 C4
Byerworth La S PR3 . . . . .181 C4
Byfield Ave FY5 . . . . . . .152 E2
Bygone Times ★ PR7 . . . . .41 C5
Byland Cl Blackpool FY4 . .110 C5
Formby L37 . . . . .12 B3
Read BB12 . . . . .145 D1
Bymbing Cl PR5 . . . . .77 C8
Byre View PR6 . . . . .30 F8
Byrom St Blackburn BB2 . .101 D4
Southport PR9 . . . . .35 F7
Byron Ave
Bolton-le-S LA5 . . . . . . .221 A5
Lytham St Anne's FY8 . . . . .91 D4
Thornton FY5 . . . . .176 A3
Warton PR4 . . . . .92 E6
Byron Cl Accrington BB5 . .104 E2
Formby L37 . . . . .11 F4
🛈 Orrell WN5 . . . . .10 F7
Oswaldtwistle BB5 . . . . . .103 D5
Tarleton PR4 . . . . .56 F5
Byron Cres PR7 . . . . .29 D7
Byron Gr BB18 . . . . .196 A3
Byron Rd Colne BB8 . . . . .171 F5
Maghull L31 . . . . .5 D3
Morecambe LA3 . . . . . . .216 E3
Ramsbottom BL8 . . . . . . .49 F2
Byron Sq BB6 . . . . .124 B4
Byron St Blackpool FY4 . .130 B1
Chorley PR6 . . . . .43 D8
Fleetwood FY7 . . . . .199 A5
Padiham BB12 . . . . .126 F7
Byron Terr BB2 . . . . . . .101 B3
Byton Wlk L33 . . . . .1 A4

C

Cabin End Row BB1 . . . .102 E4
Cabin La Halsall L39 . . . . .22 C5
Holmeswood L40 . . . . . . .38 A6
Maghull L31 . . . . .4 F4
Southport,Churchtown Moss
PR9 . . . . .54 F3

Cable Ct PR2 ....118 B8
Cable St Formby L37 .....12 A4
 Lancaster LA1 ....214 F8
 Southport PR8 ....35 B7
Cabus Cross Roads PR3 204 A5
Cabus Nook La PR3 .....204 B6
Cabus Terr PR3 ....204 C2
Cadby Ave FY3 ....130 F3
Cadley Ave PR2 ....117 B3
Cadley Cswy PR2 ....117 C4
Cadley Dr PR2 ....117 B3
Cadogan Pl **5** PR1 .....97 A6
Cadogan St BB9 ....170 D2
Cadshaw Cl BB1 ....101 E8
Cadwell Rd L31 ....5 B5
Caernarfon Cl PR7 .....176 D2
Caernarvon Ave BB12 ..127 A7
Caernarvon Cl BL8 ....49 F1
Caernarvon Rd BB4 ......85 A1
Cage La PR4 ....76 B8
Cairn Ct **6** FY4 ....110 C5
Cairn Gr FY4 ....110 C4
Cairndale Dr PR25 ....60 B6
Cairns Cl BB9 ....170 C3
Cairnsmore Ave PR1 ....118 F1
Cairo St BB12 ....127 C6
Caister Cl WN8 ....9 E8
Calcott St BB11 ....127 E2
Caldbeck Cl BB9 ....148 E6
Caldbeck Rd LA1 ....218 F1
Calder Ave Billington BB7 144 E5
 Chorley PR7 ....43 B5
 Cleveleys FY5 ....175 F2
 Darwen BB3 ....81 D4
 Fleetwood FY7 ....198 D3
 Freckleton PR4 ....93 A5
 Fulwood PR2 ....117 F6
 Longridge PR3 ....140 A4
 Ormskirk L39 ....15 E4
 Whalley BB7 ....144 A7
 Withnell PR6 ....80 A1
Calder Banks BB1 ......101 F7
Calder Cl Bury BL9 ......33 A8
 Carnforth LA5 ....223 B1
 Kirkby L33 ....1 A6
 Kirkham PR4 ....114 C5
 Lytham St Anne's FY8 ..110 F2
 Nelson BB9 ....170 D1
Calder Ct BB5 ....125 E6
Calder Dr Catterall PR3 .181 D2
 Maghull L31 ....5 F2
Calder House La PR3 ...181 A4
Calder Pl Billington BB7 .144 A4
 Great Harwood BB6 ...124 E6
Calder Rd Blackpool FY2 152 C1
 Rawtenstall BB4 ......86 A4
Calder St Blackburn BB1 101 F7
 Burnley BB11 ....127 F6
 Colne BB8 ....171 C4
 Nelson BB9 ....170 D1
 Padiham BB12 ....126 C8
 Preston PR2 ....117 C1
Calder Terr BB9 ....148 B8
Calder Vale
 Barrowford BB9 ......170 D2
 Whalley BB7 ....144 C4
Calder Vale Rd BB12 ...127 E6
Calder Vale St John CE Prim
 Sch PR3 ....226 C1
Calder View BB9 ....170 E5
Calder View Sch BB12 ..127 F8
Calder Way LA3 ....217 F2
Calderbank Cl **1** PR26 ..76 A1
Calderbrook Ave BB11 .127 C8
Calderbrook Pl BB11 ...127 E8
Caldershaw Bsns Ctr
 OL12 ....52 B2
Caldershaw Ctr The
 OL12 ....52 B2
Caldershaw La OL12 .....52 A2
Caldershaw Prim Sch
 OL12 ....52 A1
Caldershaw Rd OL11,
 OL12 ....52 A1
Calderstones Dr BB7 ..144 A7
Calderstones Hospl
 BB7 ....144 A7
Caldervale Ave FY6 ....153 C3
Caldew Cl BB5 ....104 E8
Caldicott Way FY6 .....153 C6
Caldy Dr BL8 ....50 A3
Caleb St **6** BB9 ......170 E1
Caledonian Ave **1** FY3 .130 E7
Calendar St **1** BB1 ...101 E5
Calendine Cl FY5 ......175 F5
Calf Croft Pl FY8 ....91 A4
Calf Hall La BB18 ......196 A2
Calf Hall Rd BB18 .....196 A2
Calf Hey BB5 ....124 F4
Calf Hey La OL12 ....52 D8
Calf Hey Rd BB4 ....84 B2
Calfcote La PR3 ....140 B7
Calgary Ave BB1 ......101 B8
Calico Cl BB5 ....103 B4
Calico Dr PR3 ....181 D3
Calico St BB2 ....101 D1
Calico Wood Ave WN6 ..19 F6
Calkeld La **7** LA1 ....214 F8
Calla Dr PR3 ....181 C8
Callander Sq OL10 ......33 F1
Callender St BL0 ....50 B6
Callon St PR1 ....97 E8
Caltha Dr BB3 ....82 A7
Caltha St **8** BL0 ......50 B6
Calva Cl BB12 ....127 B8

Calverley St **6** PR1 ...118 D1
Calverley Way OL12 .....52 E4
Calvert Ct PR5 ....97 D5
Calvert Pl FY3 ....131 A7
Cam Cl **1** PR1 ....77 F8
Cam La Clayton Green PR6 .78 A4
 Thornton-in-C BD23 ..197 B6
Cam St PR1 ....118 C2
Cam Wood Fold PR6 .....78 A3
Cambell's Ct PR8 ....34 E7
Camberley Cl PR8 ......34 E5
Camborne Ave LA5 ....221 C8
Camborne Ct FY3 ......131 B2
Camborne Pl PR4 ....93 B6
Cambray Rd FY1 ....152 C1
Cambrian Cl BB1 ......122 F3
Cambrian Ct PR9 ....35 D8
Cambrian Way BB4 ......85 B1
Cambridge Arc **5** PR8 ..35 B7
Cambridge Ave
 Lancaster LA1 ....215 B5
 Southport PR9 ....53 F2
Cambridge Cl
 7 Blackburn BB1 ...101 F4
 Padiham BB12 ....126 D6
 Preston PR1 ....117 E2
Cambridge Ct
 Preston PR1 ....117 E2
 Southport PR9 ....53 F2
Cambridge Dr
 Blackburn BB1 ....102 E4
 Garstang PR3 ....181 B7
 Padiham BB12 ....126 D6
Cambridge Gdns PR9 ....53 F2
Cambridge Rd
 9 Bamber Bridge PR5 ..77 F8
 Blackpool FY1 ....130 D5
 Cleveleys FY5 ....175 C3
 Fleetwood FY7 ....198 E3
 Formby L37 ....11 D1
 Lytham St Anne's FY8 ...90 E3
 Morecambe LA3 ......216 E3
 Orrell WN5 ....10 F8
 Skelmersdale WN8 .....17 E1
 Southport PR9 ....53 E2
Cambridge St
 Accrington BB5 ......104 D6
 Blackburn BB1 ....101 F4
 Brierfield BB9 ....148 B5
 3 Burnley BB11 ....127 D5
 10 Chorley PR7 ......43 C7
 9 Colne BB8 ....171 D4
 Darwen BB3 ....82 C1
 Great Harwood BB6 ...124 D5
 Haslingden BB4 ....85 B1
 Nelson BB9 ....148 D7
 Preston PR1 ....117 E2
Cambridge Wlk PR1 ....117 E2
Cambridge Wlks **6** PR8 ..35 B7
Camden Pl PR1 ....96 F6
Camden Rd FY3 ....130 E6
Camden St
 11 Barrowford BB9 ...170 D3
 Nelson BB9 ....148 D5
Camellia Dr PR25 ....77 E2
Camelot Theme Pk★
 PR7 ....41 F4
Cameron Ave FY3 ......130 E7
Cameron Croft **6** PR6 ..43 D8
Cameron St BB10 ....148 A1
Camforth Hall La PR3 ..139 A7
Camms View BB4 ....68 A8
Camomile Cl PR7 ....61 A3
Camp St BB10 ....148 E3
Campbell Ave **2** FY3 ..130 E7
Campbell St
 Blackburn BB1 ....122 F1
 4 Padiham BB12 ....126 F1
 Preston PR1 ....97 B8
 Read BB12 ....145 D1
 Rochdale OL12 ....52 E2
Campion Cl FY5 ....175 F5
Campion Ct BB5 ....103 E4
Campion Dr
 Haslingden BB4 ....68 A8
 Preston PR2 ....116 C1
Campion Way
 Morecambe LA3 ......217 B2
 Rochdale OL12 ....52 C3
Campions The PR2 .....116 C1
Camwood PR5 ....78 B4
Camwood Dr PR5 ......97 B1
Canada Cres FY2 ......152 E3
Canada St BL6 ....32 B3
Canal Bank
 Appley Bridge WN6 ....19 C7
 Burscough Bridge L40 ..25 B6
 Ring o'Bells L40 ....26 C2
Canal Bank Cotts L31 ....5 C7
Canal Bank Pygons Hill
 L31 ....5 C7
Canal Gdns LA5 ......221 B6
Canal Leach PR26 ......57 F6
Canal Mews BB9 ....148 D8
Canal Pl LA5 ....223 E1
Canal Row WN2 ....30 C1
Canal Side BB9 ....170 D2
Canal St Adlington PR7 ..31 A6
 3 Blackburn BB2 ....101 B1
 19 Burnley BB11 .....127 F6
 Church BB5 ....103 E6
 Clayton-le-M BB5 .....124 F2
Canal Wlk PR6 ....43 F8
Canalside BB1 ....101 D1
Canalside Craft Ctr★
 LA2 ....211 A3
Canberra Cl FY5 ......152 F7
Canberra La PR4 ......116 E4

Canberra Rd PR25 ......60 B8
Canberra Way PR4 .....92 E6
Candlemakers Croft **3**
 BB7 ....166 F8
Candlemakers Ct BB7 ..166 E8
Candlestick Pk BL9 .....33 D4
Cann Bridge St PR5 ....98 B4
Canning Rd PR9 ....36 A6
Canning St Burnley BB12 127 F7
 Padiham BB12 ....126 D7
Cannock Ave FY3 ......130 E8
Cannock Gn L31 ....5 B1
Cannon Hill PR2 ......117 C1
Cannon St
 Accrington BB5 ......104 B5
 11 Chorley PR7 ......43 C8
 10 Nelson BB9 ......170 F1
 Preston PR1 ....96 F7
 6 Ramsbottom BL0 ...50 A4
Canon Cl WN6 ....29 F2
Canon St BL0 ....33 A4
Canterbury Ave
 Blackpool FY3 ....130 F3
 Lancaster LA1 ....215 B5
Canterbury Cl
 Brinscall PR6 ....62 E8
 Carleton FY6 ....153 C5
 Formby L37 ....11 F5
 Garstang PR3 ....181 A7
 Morecambe LA3 ......217 B2
 Southport PR8 ....34 F4
Canterbury Rd **11** PR1 .118 D1
Canterbury St
 Blackburn BB2 ....101 E4
 Chorley PR6 ....43 E6
Canterbury Way PR3 ...181 A7
Cantlow Fold PR8 ......21 A4
Cantsfield Ave PR2 ....117 B4
Canute St PR1 ....118 A1
Cape St BB4 ....86 A2
Capernwray Ct LA6 ...240 D3
Capernwray Rd LA6 ...240 B2
Capesthorne Dr PR7 ....43 B5
Capilano Pk L39 ....6 C8
Capitol Trad Est L33 .....1 C2
Capitol Way PR5 ....97 C5
Capstan Cl FY8 ....110 E1
Captain St Horwich BL6 ..32 B4
 Weir OL13 ....88 A7
Captain's Row **3** LA1 ..218 D1
Carawood Cl WN6 ......19 D7
Carcroft Ave FY2 ......152 D4
Cardale PR4 ....95 D2
Cardiff St WN8 ....17 D1
Cardigan Ave
 Burnley BB12 ....127 A7
 10 Clitheroe BB7 ....166 E8
 Oswaldtwistle BB5 ....103 C4
Cardigan Pl **1** BB7 ..166 D8
Cardigan Pl FY4 ......110 A5
Cardigan Rd PR8 ....34 F1
Cardigan St Preston PR2 117 D1
 Rochdale OL12 ....52 E3
Cardinal Allen RC High Sch
 FY7 ....175 E8
Cardinal Gdns FY8 .....90 D6
Cardinal Newman Coll
 PR1 ....97 B7
Cardinal Pl FY5 ....175 E3
Cardinal St BB10 ......148 B1
Cardwell Cl PR4 ....92 C5
Cardwell Pl BB2 ......101 E5
Cardwell St BB12 .....126 D7
Carfax Fold OL12 ....52 B2
Carfax Rd L33 ....1 A4
Carfield WN8 ....9 E6
Carham Rd BB1 ....101 E8
Carholme Ave BB10 ...128 C6
Caribou The LA2 ......209 F5
Carisbrooke Ave FY4 ...111 A7
Carisbrooke Cl FY6 ...153 C6
Carisbrooke Dr PR9 ....53 F1
Carl Oway Ave PR2 ...118 C5
Carl's Way L33 ....1 A6
Carleton Ave
 Blackpool FY3 ....152 F1
 Fulwood PR2 ....118 D4
 Simonstone BB12 ....145 E2
Carleton Dr PR1 ....96 A4
Carleton Gate FY6 ....153 C4
Carleton Gdns FY6 ....153 B5
Carleton Green Com Prim
 Sch FY6 ....153 C6
Carleton Rd Colne BB8 .171 A3
 Great Knowley PR6 ....61 F3
Carleton St
 Morecambe LA4 ......217 A4
 Nelson BB9 ....148 E7
Carleton Way FY6 .....153 C5
Carley St BB3 ....81 E2
Carlin Gate FY2 ......152 B2
Carlinghurst Rd BB2 ..101 D4
Carlisle Ave
 Fleetwood FY7 ....198 D1
 Higher Penwortham PR1 ..96 A4
Carlisle Gr **1** FY4 ...176 E2
Carlisle Ho **34** PR1 ...97 A7
Carlisle Pl PR6 ....31 A8
Carlisle Rd
 Accrington BB5 ......104 D7
 Southport PR8 ....35 A4
Carlisle St Blackburn BB1 101 F4
 Preston PR1 ....97 A8
 Rochdale OL12 ....52 E3
Carlisle Terr LA5 .....223 D3
Carlton Ave
 Clayton Green PR6 ....78 B2
 Rawtenstall BB4 ....85 F1
 Water BB4 ....87 C7

Carlton Cl BL6 ....31 D2
Carlton Ct BB8 ....171 B5
Carlton Dr PR1 ....97 B5
Carlton Gdns BB1 .....101 E6
Carlton Gr Blackpool FY2 152 B4
 7 Horwich BL6 ....32 D1
Carlton Pl BB7 ....166 F7
Carlton Rd
 Blackburn BB1 ....101 E6
 Burnley BB11 ....127 C5
 Leyland PR25 ....59 F8
 Lytham St Anne's FY8 ..89 F7
 Southport PR8 ....21 C6
Carlton St Bacup OL13 ..148 B5
 Brierfield BB9 ....148 B5
 Preston PR2 ....96 D8
Carlton Wharf LA1 ....218 C1
Carluke St BB1 ....102 C5
Carlyle Ave FY4 ......110 B6
Carlyle St BB10 ....148 C3
Carmel Cl L39 ....15 D2
Carnarvon Rd
 Blackburn BB2 ....101 B5
 3 Preston PR1 ....96 D7
 Southport PR8 ....34 F1
Carneghie Ct PR8 ......34 F4
Carnfield Pl PR5 ....78 B8
Carnforth Ave FY2 ....152 E5
Carnforth Brow LA5 ..223 F2
Carnforth Christ Church CE
 Prim Sch LA5 ....223 D1
Carnforth Cl BB2 .....102 A1
Carnforth Dr BL8 ......50 B7
Carnforth High Sch LA5 223 E1
Carnforth Sta LA5 ....223 D2
Carnoustie Cl
 Fulwood PR2 ....117 B7
 Southport PR8 ....34 F4
Carnoustie Ct PR1 ......96 A6
Caroline Cl LA3 ......212 F8
Caroline Ct BB11 .....127 B4
Caroline St
 6 Blackpool FY1 ....130 B3
 Preston PR1 ....97 C8
Carr Bank Ave BL0 .....50 B7
Carr Bank Dr BL0 ......50 B7
Carr Bank Rd BL0 .....50 B7
Carr Barn Brow PR5 ....78 C6
Carr Bridge Residential Pk
 FY4 ....112 A6
Carr Brook Cl PR6 .....61 B8
Carr Cl Cold Row FY6 ..177 C4
 Poulton-le-F FY6 .....153 E2
 Smallwood Hey PR3 ..201 C5
Carr Dene Ct PR4 .....114 C5
Carr End La FY6 ......177 C6
Carr Field PR5 ....78 C4
Carr Fold PR5 ....50 B7
Carr Gate FY5 ....175 C4
Carr Hall Dr BB9 ......170 C1
Carr Hall Gdns BB9 ...170 B1
Carr Hall Rd BB9 .....170 B1
Carr Hall St BB4 ....85 A5
Carr Head BB8 ....172 C4
Carr Head La PR6 .....153 E2
Carr Head Prim Sch
 FY6 ....153 E2
Carr Hey **5** FY5 .....176 A2
Carr Hill 11–18 High Sch
 PR4 ....144 B4
Carr Holme Gdns PR3 .204 C1
Carr House La
 Bretherton PR26 ......57 D6
 Heskin Green WN6 .....41 F1
 Ince Blundell L38 ......3 E4
 Lancaster LA1 ....214 E7
Carr La Blackburn BB2 ..100 F6
 Chorley PR7 ....43 D5
 Cold Row FY6 ....177 C4
 Croston PR5 ....40 B8
 Heysham LA3 ....212 E7
 Kirkham PR4 ....114 C6
 Leyland PR25 ....77 A3
 Maghull L31 ....4 F5
 Middleton LA3 ....212 C3
 Much Hoole PR4,PR5 ..75 A1
 Rawtenstall,Hall Carr BB4 .86 A1
 Rawtenstall,Hugh Mill BB4 .69 F7
 Ring o'Bells L40 ....26 B3
 Singleton FY6 ....154 C1
 Smallwood Hey PR3 ..201 C4
 Southport PR8 ....21 F7
 Tarleton PR4 ....56 F7
 Warton PR4 ....92 B6
Carr Mdw PR5 ....78 C6
Carr Mill St BB4 ....85 B5
Carr Moss La Halsall L39 ..22 D2
 Haskayne L39 ....14 B8
Carr Mount **7** BB4 .....85 F1
Carr Pl PR5 ....78 B7
Carr Rd
 Barnoldswick BB18 ...196 A3
 Barrowford BB9 ......170 C1
 Blackpool FY5 ....152 D6
 Burnley BB11 ....127 E3
 Clayton Green PR6 ....78 B2
 Colne BB8 ....171 E6
 Cornholme OL14 ......108 F1
 Darwen BB3 ....65 B8
 Fleetwood FY7 ....199 A4
 Hambleton FY6 ......177 C2
 Horwich BL6 ....32 B5
 Kirkham PR4 ....114 B4
 Rawtenstall BB4 ....85 F1
 Water BB4 ....87 C7

Carr Royd Est FY6 ....154 A3
Carr Side La L29 ....4 A3
Carr St Bamber Bridge PR5 ..77 E8
 Blackburn BB1 ....101 E6
 Chorley PR6 ....61 E1
 Preston PR1 ....97 B7
 Ramsbottom BL0 ......50 B7
Carr View BB8 ....172 C1
Carr's Cres L37 ....11 E1
Carr's Cres W L37 .....11 D1
Carradice Cl BB9 .....148 D8
Carradon Dr WN6 ....29 C2
Carrfield Villas **4** OL14 109 A1
Carrick Mews FY3 ....131 B2
Carrier's Row BB8 ....172 E6
Carrington Ave BB2 ....81 C8
Carrington Gr LA4 ....217 C5
Carrington Rd
 Adlington PR7 ....30 F7
 Chorley PR7 ....43 C7
Carrol St PR1 ....118 B1
Carroll Cres L39 ....15 F7
Carron La PR3 ....160 A4
Carrs Croft BB7 ......191 E8
Carrs Ind Est BB4 .....85 A4
Carrs Wood BB2 .....100 F6
Carrside BB9 ....148 B8
Carrwood Dr PR4 .....114 A4
Carrwood Gn BB12 ...126 C8
Carrwood Hey BL0 .....50 A4
Carrwood Pk PR8 ......35 B4
Carrwood Rd PR5 ......97 B3
Carrwood Way PR5 .....97 B2
Carry La PR3 ....171 E4
Carshalton Rd FY1 ....130 B8
Carslidge St PR1 ......118 B1
Carson Rd FY4 ....131 A1
Cart Gate FY6 ....200 B3
Carter Ave BB11 .....126 C4
Carter Fold BB2 .....121 C2
Carter St Accrington BB5 ..104 B4
 7 Blackpool FY1 ....130 B5
 Burnley BB12 ....127 C7
Carter's Charity Prim Sch
 FY6 ....200 C7
Carter's La BB7 ......231 A5
Carterville Cl FY4 ....111 A7
Cartford Cl PR3 ......156 A6
Cartford Farm Cvn Pk
 PR4 ....156 A6
Cartford La PR3 ......156 A6
Cartmel Ave
 Accrington BB5 ......104 A3
 Fleetwood FY7 ....198 D1
 Lancaster LA1 ....211 B8
 Maghull L31 ....5 E2
Cartmel Cl PR8 ....35 F3
Cartmel Dr Burnley BB12 127 B8
 Coupe Green PR5 .....98 A4
 Formby L37 ....12 B2
Cartmel Pl
 Morecambe LA4 ......217 D4
 Preston PR2 ....116 F2
Cartmel Rd
 Blackburn BB2 ....101 A3
 Lancaster LA1 ....218 F2
 Leyland PR25 ....59 D8
Cartmell La
 Lytham St Anne's FY8 ..91 E8
 Nateby PR3 ....180 C2
Cartmell Rd
 Blackburn FY4 ....131 D1
 Lytham St Anne's FY8 ..89 F7
Cartwright Ct LA1 ....214 E5
Carus Ave BB3 ....82 E1
Carus Pk LA6 ....241 B2
Carus St BB3 ....82 F1
Carvel Way L40 ....25 F3
Carvers Brow PR26 .....58 B1
Carwags La PR3 ......161 C8
Carwood Gr BL6 ....32 D1
Carwood La PR6 ....61 C8
Caryl Rd FY8 ....89 D8
Caryle Gr LA4 ....217 E6
Caspian Way LA1 .....214 E4
Casserley Rd BB8 .....171 F6
Casson Gate OL12 .....52 E1
Castercliff Bank BB8 ..171 C3
Castercliffe Com Prim Sch
 BB9 ....171 B1
Castercliffe Rd BB9 ...149 B8
Casterton PR7 ....60 C2
Casterton Ave BB10 ..148 C3
Casterton Prim Sch
 BB10 ....148 C3
Castle Ave FY6 ....153 B6
Castle Bank LA5 .....224 C4
Castle Cl BB8 ....171 E6
Castle Cres BL6 ....32 C5
Castle Ct LA1 ....214 E8
Castle Dr Adlington PR7 ..30 E6
 Formby L37 ....11 F1
Castle Fold PR1 ....96 F2
Castle Gardens Cres
 FY6 ....153 B5
Castle Gate BB7 ......166 E8
Castle Gr BL0 ....50 B6
Castle Hill LA1 ....214 E8
Castle Hill Rd BL9 ......33 D5
Castle House La PR7 ...30 E6
Castle La Bonds PR3 ..181 D6
 Staining FY3 ....131 D5
 Westhead L40 ....16 E5
Castle Mount PR2 ....117 C2
Castle Par **5** LA1 ....214 E8
Castle Park Mews LA1 .214 E8
Castle Pk Hornby LA2 .238 B7
 Lancaster LA1 ....214 E8

Castle Rd BB8 ....172 A7
Castle St Blackburn BB1 ..102 B5
Brierfield BB9 ....148 B6
Burnley BB12 ....127 F7
6 Chorley PR7 ....43 D7
Clitheroe BB7 ....166 E8
7 Hapton BB12 ....126 C4
Nelson BB9 ....148 E8
Preston PR1 ....117 F1
Ramsbottom BL9 ....50 D2
Southport PR9 ....35 B8
Castle The BB8 ....172 A7
Castle View
Barnoldswick BB18 ....196 B1
Clitheroe BB7 ....166 E8
Castle View Cvn Pk LA6 240 D2
Castle View Ho 11 BB7 ..166 E8
Castle Wlk
Higher Penwortham PR1 ..96 C7
Southport PR8 ....35 A6
Castle Wlks PR26 ....58 B2
Castlecroft Ave BL6 ....31 D2
Castlegate FY1 ....130 B1
Castlehey WN8 ....9 E6
Castlerigg Dr BB12 ....127 B8
Castlerigg Pl FY1 ....131 C1
Castleton Rd PR1 ....118 B1
Castletown Dr OL13 ....88 B1
Cat Tail La PR8 ....36 E1
Catches La OL11 ....52 B1
Catforth Ave FY4 ....131 B1
Catforth Prim Sch PR4 ..136 A4
Catforth Rd Catforth PR4 135 F5
Preston PR2 ....116 E1
Catharine's La L39 ....15 F1
Cathedral Dr LA3 ....217 D2
Cathedral RC Prim Sch The
LA1 ....215 A7
Catherine Cl PR4 ....113 F7
Catherine St
6 Chorley PR7 ....43 C6
Kirkham PR4 ....113 F6
5 Preston PR1 ....97 B8
Catherine St E BL6 ....32 B4
Catherine St W BL6 ....32 B5
Cathrow Dr PR4 ....76 A7
Cathrow Way FY5 ....176 D2
Catley Cl PR6 ....61 C5
Catlow Ct BB10 ....149 C5
Catlow Hall St BB5 ....103 E4
Catlow Row BB10 ....149 C6
Catlow Terr BB7 ....166 E1
Cato St 4 BL0 ....50 A4
Caton Ave FY7 ....198 D1
Caton Cl
Clayton-le-W PR25 ....77 E2
Longridge PR3 ....140 B5
Southport PR9 ....53 F4
Caton Com Prim Sch
LA2 ....237 C3
Caton Gr FY3 ....130 F7
Caton Green Rd LA2 ....237 D3
Caton Rd LA1 ....218 F4
Caton St Paul's CE Prim Sch
LA2 ....237 D3
Cattan Gn L37 ....12 B3
Catterall Cl FY1 ....130 D7
Catterall Gates La PR3 .181 C3
Catterall La PR3 ....181 C1
Catterall St BB2 ....81 C8
Catterick Fold PR8 ....35 F3
Cattle St BB6 ....124 C5
Caunce Ave PR9 ....55 A6
Caunce St FY1,FY3 ....130 D6
Caunce's Rd PR9 ....37 C5
Causeway BB9 ....148 D2
Great Harwood BB6 ....124 B5
Causeway Ave PR2 ....117 C4
Causeway Croft BB7 ....189 F1
Causeway Head BB4 ....68 A8
Causeway La
Haskayne L37 ....13 B1
Rufford L40 ....39 B2
Causeway St 2 BB3 ....65 C7
Causeway The
3 Chorley PR6 ....43 E8
Southport PR9 ....54 C5
Wymott PR26 ....58 F6
Causey Foot BB9 ....148 D2
Cavalry Way BB11 ....127 D6
Cave St 1 Blackburn BB2 101 B1
2 Preston PR1 ....97 D8
Cavell Cl BB1 ....102 B1
Cavendish Cres PR2 ....118 F3
Cavendish Ct
Bolton-le-S LA5 ....221 A5
Southport PR9 ....35 A8
Cavendish Dr PR2 ....118 F3
Cavendish Mans FY5 ..175 C4
Cavendish Pl
6 Bamber Bridge PR5 ..97 D3
Blackburn BB2 ....101 B3
Cavendish Rd
Blackpool FY2 ....152 C4
Lytham St Anne's FY8 ..89 D8
Morecambe LA3 ....216 E3
2 Preston PR1 ....118 C1
Southport PR8 ....34 F3
Cavendish St
Barnoldswick BB18 ....196 B1
1 Chorley PR6 ....43 E1
Darwen BB3 ....81 F3
Lancaster LA1 ....214 D8
Cavendish Wlk PR9 ....35 B8
Cavour St BB2 ....127 F7
Cawthorne Prim Sch
LA2 ....232 F1
Cawthorne St LA1 ....214 E8

Caxton Ave FY2 ....152 C5
Caxton Rd PR2 ....118 B8
Cecil Cl FY8 ....91 A3
Cecil St
Barnoldswick BB18 ....196 B3
Blackpool FY1 ....130 C7
4 Lytham St Anne's FY8 ..91 A3
Oswaldtwistle BB5 ....103 A4
Rishton BB1 ....124 C2
Cecilia Rd BB2 ....101 A2
Cecilia St PR1 ....118 D1
Cedar Ave
5 Bamber Bridge PR5 ..77 B8
Cleveleys FY5 ....175 E2
Euxton PR7 ....60 C4
Fleetwood FY7 ....175 E8
Haslingden BB4 ....85 C3
Horwich BL6 ....32 E1
Knott End-on-S FY6 ....200 A5
Poulton-le-F FY6 ....131 D8
Preston PR2 ....117 A2
Rawtenstall BB4 ....85 E2
Warton PR4 ....92 D6
Cedar Cres Kirkham PR4 .114 A4
Ormskirk L39 ....15 D4
Ramsbottom BL0 ....50 C7
Cedar Ct Blackburn BB1 .101 F7
7 Leyland PR25 ....77 B1
Cedar Farm Galleries ★
L40 ....40 C1
Cedar Field PR6 ....78 C1
Cedar Gr Longton PR4 ....95 A1
Orrell WN5 ....10 F6
Skelmersdale WN8 ....17 C1
Cedar Ho PR7 ....42 F6
Cedar Lo FY4 ....118 E2
Fulwood PR2 ....214 D8
Lancaster LA1 ....130 B5
Cedar Sq 5 FY1 ....104 D6
Cedar St Accrington BB5 .101 F8
Blackburn BB1 ....128 B5
Burnley BB11 ....33 A3
Bury BL9 ....33 B3
Bury BL9 ....216 F4
Morecambe LA4 ....52 F1
Rochdale OL12 ....35 D4
Southport PR8 ....96 B3
Cedar Way PR1 ....155 F1
Cedar Wlk PR4 ....196 A1
Cedars Inf Sch BB1 ....101 F8
Cedars The Chorley PR6 ..43 B4
Eccleston PR7 ....41 B7
New Longton PR4 ....75 F8
Cedarwood Cl FY8 ....90 E4
Cedarwood Dr PR25 ....59 E8
Cedarwood Pl LA1 ....215 C7
Cedric Pl FY2 ....152 C4
Celia St BB10 ....128 C5
Cemetery La
Burnley BB11 ....127 A4
Preesall Park FY6 ....200 B1
Cemetery Rd Darwen BB3 .65 B5
Earby BB18 ....197 B2
Padiham BB12 ....126 C7
Preston PR1 ....118 C1
Ramsbottom BL0 ....50 A4
Southport PR8 ....35 C4
Cemetery View PR7 ....31 A6
Centenary Way BB11 ....148 A8
Central 12 Ret Pk PR9 ....35 C7
Central Ave
Clitheroe BB7 ....166 D7
Edenfield BL0 ....68 D2
Gregson Lane PR5 ....98 E2
Kirkham PR4 ....113 F6
Lancaster LA1 ....218 D4
Oswaldtwistle BB5 ....103 C4
Southport PR8 ....21 F8
Central Ave N FY5 ....175 F3
Central Beach FY8 ....91 B3
Central Bldgs 16 BB6 ..146 C1
Higher Penwortham PR1 ..96 A4
Lytham St Anne's FY8 ....90 C5
Morecambe LA4 ....216 C1
Central Lancaster High Sch
LA1 ....218 F1
Central Sq
7 Haslingden BB4 ....85 B3
Maghull L31 ....5 D2
Central St BL0 ....50 C6
Central View OL13 ....88 A2
Centre Dr PR6 ....78 B4
Centurian Way BB1 ....82 B6
Centurion Ct BB1 ....82 B7
Centurion Ho 1 PR4 ..114 B5
Centurion Ind Est PR25 ..77 B3
Centurion Rd PR25,
PR26 ....77 A4
Ceres Way LA1 ....214 C8
Chad St BB8 ....171 A2
Chadderton Ct 19 PR1 ..97 A8
Chaddock St 26 PR1 ....97 A7
Chadfield Rd FY1 ....130 C3
Chadwich Gdns 1 PR5 ..77 A7
Chadwick St
Blackburn BB2 ....101 D3
3 Blackpool FY1 ....130 C3
Bury BL9 ....33 E4
Chadwick Terr OL12 ....52 D4
Chaffinch Cl FY5 ....175 F5
Chaffinch Ct FY3 ....131 B6

Chaffinch Dr BL9 ....33 C4
Chaigley Ct BB7 ....165 A8
Chaigley Farm Cotts
BB7 ....165 A8
Chaigley Rd PR3 ....140 B8
Chain Caul Rd PR2 ....95 C3
Chain Caul Way PR2 ....95 F8
Chain House La PR4 ....76 D7
Chain La FY3,FY4 ....131 E4
Chalfont St BB6 ....124 B2
Chalfont Field PR2 ....117 C5
Challan Hall Cotts LA5 .224 E5
Challan Hall Mews LA5 .224 E5
Challenge Way BB1 ....102 C7
Chamber St BB4 ....87 A8
Chambres Rd PR8 ....35 D5
Chambres Rd N PR8 ....35 D6
Champagne Ave FY5 ..152 F7
Chancel Pl BB3 ....65 C8
Chancel Way BB3 ....65 C8
Chancery Cl PR7 ....42 F1
Chancery Rd PR7 ....61 B2
Chancery Wlk 3 BB11 .128 A6
Chandler St 6 PR1 ....96 F8
Chandlers Croft PR4 ....73 E4
Chandlers Ford FY6 ....153 E4
Chandlers Rest PR3 ....91 D3
Chandley Ct PR8 ....21 C5
Change Cl OL13 ....88 B4
Changford Gn L33 ....1 A3
Changford Rd L33 ....1 A3
Channel Way PR2 ....96 C8
Channing Rd FY8 ....90 C4
Chapel Alley L37 ....11 F3
Chapel Brow Leyland PR25 77 B2
Longridge PR3 ....140 B5
Chapel Cl Clitheroe BB7 .166 B8
Hest Bank LA2 ....220 D1
Kirkham PR4 ....113 F7
Overton LA3 ....209 D8
Trawden BB8 ....172 B2
West Bradford BB7 ....189 E5
Whalley BB7 ....144 C5
Chapel Ct Brierfield BB10 149 A3
Ormskirk L39 ....15 F4
Chapel Fields BL7 ....48 C4
Chapel Fold
Longridge PR3 ....140 A6
Salterforth BB18 ....194 D7
Chapel Gdns
Catterall PR3 ....181 D2
Hesketh Bank PR4 ....73 C4
Ramsbottom BL8 ....49 D1
Chapel Grange BL7 ....48 C4
Chapel Hill
Longridge PR3 ....140 A6
Salterforth BB18 ....194 D7
Chapel Hill La BB4 ....86 A4
Chapel Hill Trad Est
PR3 ....140 A6
Chapel Ho Burnley BB11 .127 C5
4 Maghull L31 ....5 D1
Ormskirk L39 ....15 E4
Rishton BB1 ....124 C1
Chapel House Rd BB9 ..148 E7
Chapel La Banks PR9 ....55 B7
Burscough L40 ....25 E2
Burton in L LA6 ....242 C1
Catforth PR4 ....135 D4
Coppull PR7 ....42 E1
Formby L37 ....11 F3
Galgate LA2 ....211 B5
Hoghton PR5 ....99 D2
Holmeswood L40 ....38 B6
Langho BB6 ....143 B2
Longton PR4 ....75 C8
New Longton PR4 ....75 E8
Out Rawcliffe PR3 ....178 B2
Overton LA3 ....209 D8
Parbold WN8 ....27 D1
Ramsbottom BL8 ....50 A6
West Bradford BB7 ....189 E5
Wheelton BL7 ....62 B5
Chapel Mdw PR4 ....75 C8
Chapel Mdws PR4 ....57 A5
Chapel Mews
2 Earby BB18 ....197 B1
Ormskirk L39 ....15 F4
Chapel Park Rd PR4 ....75 C8
Chapel Rd Blackpool FY4 .111 B7
Fulwood PR2 ....118 A4
Hesketh Bank PR4 ....73 C4
Chapel Rise BB7 ....144 B4
Chapel Sq LA2 ....237 D3
Chapel St
10 Accrington BB5 ....104 C5
Adlington PR7 ....30 F6
14 Bacup OL13 ....70 C8
Barnoldswick BB18 ....196 B2
Belmont BL7 ....46 C5
Belthorn BB1 ....82 F6
Blackburn BB1 ....101 D4
Blackpool FY1 ....130 B4
Blackrod BL6 ....31 D2
Brierfield BB9 ....148 B6
Brinscall PR6 ....62 F8
Burnley BB11 ....128 A6
Chorley PR7 ....43 C8
Clayton-le-M BB5 ....124 E3
Colne BB8 ....171 D4
Coppull PR7 ....42 E1
Darwen BB3 ....65 A8
Earby BB18 ....197 B2
Egerton BL7 ....47 D3
Foulridge BB8 ....194 E1
Galgate LA2 ....211 A4
Great Eccleston PR3 ....156 B5

Chapel St continued
Haslingden BB4 ....85 B3
Higham BB12 ....146 F5
Horwich BL6 ....32 C3
3 Lancaster LA1 ....214 F8
Longridge PR3 ....140 B5
Lytham St Anne's FY8 ..91 A3
Morecambe LA4 ....217 A5
Nelson BB9 ....148 E8
Newchurch BB4 ....86 A1
Ormskirk L39 ....15 F4
Oswaldtwistle BB5 ....103 A4
Poulton-le-F FY6 ....153 D3
Preston PR1 ....96 F7
Rawtenstall BB4 ....86 A8
Rishton BB1 ....124 C2
Slaidburn BB7 ....229 C7
Southport PR8 ....35 B7
Whitworth OL12 ....52 C8
Worsthorne BB10 ....129 A5
Chapel Street 3 FY6 ..153 D3
Chapel The BB4 ....86 A3
Chapel View
Goodshaw Chapel BB4 ..106 A1
Overton LA3 ....209 D8
Chapel Way PR7 ....29 F8
Chapel Wlk Coppull PR7 ..42 E1
Longton PR4 ....75 D8
2 Padiham BB12 ....146 C1
Warton LA5 ....223 E6
Chapel Wlks
Kirkham PR4 ....114 B4
5 Preston PR1 ....96 F7
Chapel Yd PR5 ....97 D5
Chapelhouse Wlk L37 ..12 A3
Chapels BB3 ....82 A3
Chapels Brow BB3 ....82 A3
Chapelside La BB3 ....80 F3
Chapelside 4 BB10 ....128 B5
Chapelside BB3 ....181 D2
Chapeltown Rd BL7 ....48 C2
Chapman Cl PR3 ....156 C5
Chapman Ct
Barnoldswick BB18 ....196 B3
Fleetwood FY7 ....199 B4
Chapman Rd
Fulwood PR2 ....118 A3
Hoddlesden BB3 ....82 F1
Chapter Rd BB3 ....65 C8
Chardonnay Cres 2
FY5 ....152 F7
Charlbury Gr LA3 ....213 A7
Charles Ave PR8 ....21 E6
Charles Cl PR4 ....73 E3
Charles Cres PR5 ....98 C3
Charles Gr LA3 ....140 A7
Charles La BB4 ....85 A2
Charles St Blackburn BB2 153 D3
Blackpool FY1 ....130 C6
Clayton-le-M BB5 ....124 E2
Colne BB8 ....171 E5
Darwen BB3 ....82 A2
Egerton BL7 ....47 D2
Great Harwood BB6 ....124 C4
Lancaster LA1 ....214 F6
Morecambe LA4 ....217 C5
Nelson BB9 ....170 E2
Oswaldtwistle BB5 ....103 E3
Charles Way PR2 ....116 E1
Charlesbye Ave L39 ....16 B6
Charlesbye Cl L39 ....16 B6
Charleston Ct 3 PR5 ....97 E2
Charlesway Ct 1 PR2 ..116 E1
Charlesworth Cl L31 ....5 B5
Charley Wood Rd L33 ....1 C1
Charlotte Pl 32 PR1 ....97 A7
Charlotte St
Blackburn BB1 ....101 E6
Burnley BB11 ....127 F5
Chapeltown BL7 ....48 C4
Preston PR1 ....97 A7
4 Charlotte's La PR4 ....56 E2
Charley Cl PR1 ....96 C2
Charnley Fold Bglws PR5 97 F3
Charnley Fold Ind Est
PR5 ....97 F3
Charnley Fold La PR5 ....97 F3
Charnley Rd FY1 ....130 C4
Charnley St
Blackburn BB2 ....101 C2
1 Lancaster LA1 ....218 B1
2 Preston PR1 ....96 F7
Charnley's La PR4 ....54 E2
Charnock WN8 ....9 E6
Charnock Ave WN6 ....9 C2
Charnock Back La PR6 ....44 C6
Charnock Brow PR7 ....42 C7
Charnock Fold PR1 ....118 A4
Charnock Ho PR7 ....61 C2
Charnock Moss BB5 ....86 F2
Charnock St Chorley PR6 .43 D7
9 Kirkham PR4 ....113 F6
8 Leyland PR25 ....77 B1
Preston PR1 ....117 F2
Charnwood Ave FY3 ....131 A7
Charnwood Cl BB2 ....101 A8
Charter Brook BB6 ....124 C5
Charter La PR7 ....42 D3
Charter St BB5 ....104 C5
Charterhouse Ct FY7 ..198 D4
Charterhouse Pl BB2 ..101 B3
Chartwell Cl PR6 ....78 C2
Chartwell Rd PR8 ....21 B6

Chartwell Rise 5 PR5 ....77 C8
Chasden Cl PR6 ....61 C5
Chase Cl PR5 ....34 F4
Chase Keys PR9 ....54 A1
Chase The Burnley BB12 .127 D8
Cottam PR4 ....116 D5
3 Leyland PR25 ....77 C2
Normoss FY3 ....131 C7
Silverdale LA5 ....224 D2
Thornton FY5 ....176 A4
Chatburn Ave
Burnley BB10 ....128 D5
Clitheroe BB7 ....189 F1
Chatburn CE Prim Sch
BB7 ....190 D5
Chatburn Cl
Great Harwood BB6 ....124 E5
Normoss FY3 ....131 B8
Rawtenstall BB4 ....86 A4
Chatburn Gdns OL10 ....33 F2
Chatburn Old Rd BB7 ..190 D5
Chatburn Park Ave BB9 148 A6
Chatburn Park Dr
Brierfield BB9 ....148 A6
Clitheroe BB7 ....190 A2
Chatburn Rd
Chatburn BB7 ....190 D5
Clitheroe BB7 ....190 A3
Fulwood PR2 ....118 F4
Longridge PR3 ....140 A7
Chatburn St BB2 ....101 C5
Chatham Ave FY4 ....110 E1
Chatham Cres BB8 ....171 E6
Chatham Pl
5 Chorley PR6 ....43 E8
Preston PR1 ....118 B2
Chatham St Colne BB8 ..171 E6
Nelson BB9 ....170 D1
Chatsworth Ave
Blackpool FY2 ....152 C6
Fleetwood FY7 ....198 D2
Warton PR4 ....92 D6
Chatsworth Cl
Barrowford BB9 ....170 E1
4 Blackburn BB1 ....122 E1
Chorley PR7 ....43 B8
2 Thornton FY5 ....176 D1
Chatsworth Ct PR6 ....43 F1
Chatsworth Rd
Bamber Bridge PR5 ....97 D3
Lancaster LA1 ....214 F4
1 Leyland PR25 ....77 A1
Lytham St Anne's FY8 ..89 D7
Morecambe LA4 ....216 F4
Southport PR8 ....21 B6
Chatsworth St
Preston PR1 ....97 D8
Rochdale OL12 ....52 E3
Chatteris Pl FY5 ....175 C1
Chatterton BL0 ....68 C2
Chatterton Dr BB5 ....104 E2
Chatterton Old La BL0 ..68 C2
Chatterton Rd BL0 ....68 C1
Chaucer Ave FY5 ....175 F2
Chaucer Cl PR7 ....41 B6
Chaucer Gdns BB6 ....124 B4
Chaucer Rd FY7 ....199 A4
Chaucer St PR1 ....118 D2
Cheam Ave PR7 ....43 C6
Cheapside Blackpool FY1 .130 B5
6 Chorley PR7 ....43 C7
Formby L37 ....12 A2
11 Lancaster LA1 ....214 F8
1 Low Bentham LA2 ..239 B8
8 Preston PR1 ....96 F7
Cheddar Ave FY4 ....110 D6
Cheddar Dr PR2 ....118 D6
Chedworth Ave LA3 ....213 A7
Cheetham Hill OL12 ....71 D3
Cheetham Mdw PR26 ....59 B8
Cheetham St BB2 ....101 C5
Chelburn Gr BB10 ....128 C6
Chelford Ave FY3 ....130 E8
Chelford Cl 4 PR1 ....96 F2
Chelmsford Cl LA1 ....215 B5
Chelmsford Gr PR7 ....43 B7
Chelmsford Pl PR7 ....43 B7
Chelmsford Wlk PR26 ..59 A8
Chelsea Ave FY2 ....152 E1
Chelsea Cl 3 FY2 ....152 E1
Chelsea Mews
4 Blackpool FY2 ....152 E1
Lancaster LA1 ....218 D2
Chelston Dr BB4 ....68 A7
Cheltenham Ave BB5 ..104 C8
Cheltenham Cres
Lytham St Anne's FY8 ..91 D5
Thornton FY5 ....153 D8
Cheltenham Dr WN5 ....10 D2
Cheltenham Rd
Blackburn BB2 ....101 C5
Blackpool FY1 ....130 B7
Lancaster LA1 ....214 F5
Cheltenham Way PR8 ....35 F3
Chelwood Cl FY6 ....200 A5
Chennel Ho 4 LA1 ....214 E8
Chepstow Gdns PR3 ....181 D6
Chepstow Rd FY3 ....130 F4
Chequer Cl WN8 ....9 F5
Chequer La WN8 ....9 F6
Chequers BB5 ....124 F2
Chequers Ave LA1 ....215 B4
Chequers Way FY5 ....176 D2
Cheriton Field PR2 ....117 C7
Cheriton Gdns BL6 ....32 B5

Cheriton Pk PR8 ....**35** E3
Cherries The PR7 ......**60** D3
Cherry Ave BL9 ....**33** C3
Cherry Cl
 2 Blackburn BB1 ......**102** B5
 Fulwood PR2 ....**118** D6
 Kirkham PR4 ....**113** E5
Cherry Cres
 Oswaldtwistle BB5 .....**103** D2
 Rawtenstall BB4 ....**68** F8
Cherry Dr BB6 ....**143** C6
Cherry Gn L39 ....**15** B1
Cherry Gr
 Abbey Village PR6 ......**80** B2
 Burscough Bridge L40 ...**25** E6
 Longridge PR3 ....**140** A7
Cherry La PR4 ....**93** B4
Cherry Lea BB2 ......**100** F2
Cherry Orch PR3 .....**140** B6
Cherry Rd PR8 ....**21** D2
Cherry St BB1 ....**102** B5
Cherry Tree Cl
 Fisher's Row PR3 ......**201** E5
 Hest Bank LA5 ....**220** F2
 Heysham LA3 ....**212** E6
 Knott End-on-S FY6 ...**200** A6
Cherry Tree Ct
 Blackpool FY4 ....**131** B1
 10 Fleetwood FY7 ......**199** B5
 Standish WN6 ....**29** D2
Cherry Tree Dr LA1 ...**214** F4
Cherry Tree Gdns
 Blackpool FY4 ....**111** A8
 Nelson BB9 ....**149** A8
Cherry Tree Gr PR6 ....**61** C3
Cherry Tree La
 3 Blackburn BB2 ....**80** E8
 Ormskirk L39 ....**15** B1
 Rawtenstall BB4 ....**68** F8
Cherry Tree Mews
 BB11 ....**127** D3
Cherry Tree Rd FY4 ...**131** A1
Cherry Tree Rd N FY4 .**131** A1
Cherry Tree Sta BB2 ..**100** F1
Cherry Tree Terr BB2 .**100** F1
Cherry Tree Way
 Haslingden BB4 ....**68** B7
 5 Horwich BL6 ....**32** E1
Cherry Trees PR5 .....**97** C3
Cherry Vale PR4 ....**73** F2
Cherry View L33 ....**1** A5
Cherry Wood PR1 ......**96** A3
Cherryclough Way BB2 .**81** B8
Cherrycroft WN8 ....**9** E6
Cherrydale FY2 ....**152** D5
Cherryfields PR7 ....**60** D4
Cherryfold Com Sch
 BB11 ....**127** D4
Cherrywood Ave
 Cleveleys FY5 ....**175** C1
 Lytham St Anne's FY8 ...**90** E4
Cherrywood Cl PR25 ....**59** E8
Cheryl Dr FY5 ....**153** B8
Chesham Cres BL9 ......**33** A3
Chesham Dr PR4 ....**75** F8
Chesham Fold Rd BL9 ...**33** B4
Chesham Ind Est BL9 ...**33** A4
Chesham Lodge PR3 ...**156** B5
Chesham Prim Sch BL9 .**33** A5
Chesham Rd BL9 ....**33** A5
Chesham St PR3 ......**156** B5
Cheshire Ct
 Ramsbottom BL0 ....**50** D6
 Southport PR9 ....**53** E1
Cheshire House Cl PR26 .**76** F7
Chesmere Croft PR1 ....**96** B5
Chesmere Dr PR1 ......**96** B5
Chessington Gn BB10 ..**148** D3
Chester Ave Chorley PR7 .**43** E4
 Cleveleys FY5 ....**175** E2
 2 Clitheroe BB7 ....**189** E1
 Poulton-le-F FY6 ....**153** C4
 Southport PR9 ....**35** F8
Chester Cl Blackburn BB1 **102** A3
 Garstang PR3 ....**181** B7
 Morecambe LA3 ....**217** B2
Chester Cres BB4 ....**68** B8
Chester Ct FY5 ....**176** C3
Chester Dr BL0 ....**50** A4
Chester Pl Adlington PR6 .**31** A8
 Great Eccleston PR3 ...**156** C5
 Lancaster LA1 ....**215** A5
Chester Rd
 Blackpool FY3 ....**130** D6
 Preston PR1 ....**118** C1
 Southport PR9 ....**35** F8
Chester St
 Accrington BB5 ....**104** A5
 Blackburn BB1 ....**102** A4
 Bury BL9 ....**33** A4
Chesterbrook PR3 .....**141** E4
Chesterfield Cl PR8 .....**21** C4
Chesterfield Rd
 Blackpool FY1 ....**130** C7
 Southport PR8 ....**21** C5
Chesters The PR9 ......**53** D2
Chestnut Ave
 Blackpool FY4 ....**110** F5
 Bolton-le-S LA5 ....**221** A5
 Bury BL9 ....**33** B2
 Caton LA2 ....**237** C3
 Chorley PR6 ....**61** E2
 Euxton PR7 ....**60** C4
 Higher Penwortham PR1 .**96** A4
 Chestnut Bsns Pk BB12 **127** B5

Chestnut Cl
 Bamber Bridge PR5 ......**97** E2
 Blackpool FY2 ....**152** D2
 Garstang PR3 ....**204** D1
 Halsall L39 ....**23** C1
 Kirkham PR4 ....**114** B5
Chestnut Cotts BB7 ...**191** A5
Chestnut Cres
 Barrow BB7 ....**166** D1
 Fulwood PR2 ....**118** E2
 Longton PR4 ....**74** F8
Chestnut Ct Leyland PR25 .**60** A7
 Ormskirk L39 ....**15** F6
Chestnut Dr
 Barnoldswick BB18 .....**196** A1
 Fulwood PR2 ....**117** D7
 Morecambe LA4 ....**217** F6
 Rawtenstall BB4 ....**68** F8
 Whalley BB7 ....**144** A7
Chestnut Gdns
 Blackburn BB1 ....**101** F7
 Thornton FY5 ....**176** B3
Chestnut Gr
 Accrington BB5 ....**104** A4
 Clayton-le-M BB5 .....**125** A4
 Darwen BB3 ....**65** A5
 Lancaster LA1 ....**214** D8
Chestnut Grange L39 ...**15** D3
Chestnut Rise BB11 ...**127** F4
Chestnut St PR8 ....**35** C5
Chestnut Way L37 ......**11** C1
Chestnut Wlk **5** BB1 ..**102** B5
Chestnuts The PR7 .....**42** F2
Chethams Cl FY5 ......**176** A2
Chevassut Cl BB9 ......**170** C1
Cheviot Ave
 Burnley BB10 ....**128** E5
 Cleveleys FY5 ....**175** F4
 Lytham St Anne's FY8 ...**91** E5
Cheviot Cl Horwich BL6 ..**32** C5
 Ramsbottom BL0 ....**50** C4
Cheviot St PR1 ....**96** C8
Chew Gdns FY6 ....**153** B3
Chichester Cl
 Burnley BB10 ....**128** B6
 Thornton FY5 ....**176** A2
Chicken St BB2 ....**101** C4
Chiddingford Ct FY1 ...**130** D3
Childrey Wlk BB2 ....**82** A8
Chilgrove Ave BL6 ......**31** D1
Chiltern Ave
 Blackpool FY4 ....**110** D7
 Burnley BB10 ....**128** E5
 Euxton PR7 ....**60** D1
 Poulton-le-F FY6 ......**153** C3
Chiltern Cl Horwich BL6 ..**32** C5
 Lytham St Anne's FY8 ...**91** E5
 Ramsbottom BL0 ....**50** C4
Chiltern Ct **4** LA1 ....**215** A5
Chiltern Mdw PR25 .....**77** D1
Chiltern Rd
 Ramsbottom BL0 ....**50** C4
 Southport PR8 ....**21** B6
Chilton Cl L31 ....**5** D1
Chilton Ct **5** L31 ....**5** D1
Chilton Mews **2** L31 ....**5** D1
Chimes The Kirkham PR4 **114** A4
 Tarleton PR4 ....**57** A5
China St Accrington BB5 .**103** F6
 Lancaster LA1 ....**214** F8
Chindit Cl L37 ....**11** D2
Chindits Way PR2 .....**118** B4
Chingford Bank BB10 ..**148** D3
Chingle Cl PR2 ....**118** E6
Chippendale Mews PR3 **181** C8
Chipping Ave PR8 ......**21** A5
Chipping Ct **4** FY3 ....**131** A8
Chipping Gr
 Burnley BB10 ....**128** D4
 Normoss FY3 ....**131** A8
Chipping La PR3 ......**140** A8
Chipping Manor PR9 ....**55** A6
Chipping St **3** BB12 ..**146** D1
Chirk Dr PR4 ....**176** D2
Chisacre Dr WN6 ....**19** D7
Chisholm Cl WN6 ......**29** A7
Chisholme Cl BL8 ......**49** F2
Chislehurst Ave FY4 ...**130** D1
Chislehurst Gr BB10 ...**148** D4
Chislehurst Pl FY8 ......**90** E5
Chislett Cl L40 ....**25** D4
Chisnall Ave WN6 ......**28** F6
Chisnall La Coppull PR7 ..**29** C6
 Heskin Green PR7 ......**41** F2
 Wrightington Bar WN6 ...**29** A5
Chiswell Gr FY5 ....**153** D8
Chiswick Gr FY3 ......**131** B2
Chitheroe Rd PR3 .....**163** C1
Chive Cl FY2 ....**152** F3
Chorcliffe Ho **7** PR7 ...**43** C8

Chorley & District Hospl
 PR7 ....**61** C2
Chorley All Saints CE Prim
 Sch PR7 ....**43** B3
Chorley Astley Park Sch
 PR7 ....**43** B8
Chorley Bsns & Tech Ctr
 PR7 ....**60** E4
Chorley Cl PR8 ....**54** F5
Chorley Hall Rd PR7 ....**61** C2
Chorley Info Ctr PR7 ....**43** C8
Chorley La PR7 ....**42** D3
Chorley New Rd BL6 ....**32** D2
Chorley New Road Prim Sch
 BL6 ....**32** D2
Chorley North Ind Est
 PR6 ....**61** D3
Chorley Old Rd
 Clayton Green PR6 ......**78** C2
 Horwich BL6 ....**32** E3
 Whittle-le-W PR6 ....**61** C8
Chorley Rd Adlington PR6 .**31** A8
 Adlington,Blackrod BL6,PR7 **31** B5
 Bamber Bridge PR5 ......**97** B3
 Blackpool FY3 ....**152** F2
 Hill Dale L40,WN8 ......**27** D6
 Ollerton Fold BB2,PR6 ...**79** E4
 Parbold WN8 ....**27** C4
 Standish WN1 ....**30** C3
Chorley Southlands High Sch
 PR7 ....**43** A5
Chorley St PR6 ....**31** B8
Chorley St James CE Prim
 Sch PR6 ....**43** E7
Chorley Sta PR6 ....**43** D8
Chorley West Bsns Pk
 PR7 ....**42** F8
Chorlton Cl BB10 ......**148** D2
Chorlton Gdns BB1 ....**101** F7
Chorlton St BB1 ....**101** F7
Chorlton Terr BB7 .....**166** D1
Christ Church CE Prim Sch
 BB8 ....**172** B5
Christ Church Hall BB5 .**104** C4
Christ Church Sq **1**
 BB5 ....**104** C5
Christ Church St
 2 Accrington BB5 .....**104** C5
 6 Bacup OL13 ....**88** A3
 Preston PR1 ....**96** F7
Christ The King RC High Sch
 PR1 ....**97** B6
Christ The King RC Prim Sch
 Blackpool BB11 ....**131** A7
 Burnley BB11 ....**127** E3
Christ The King Sch PR8 .**35** B2
Christian Rd PR1 ....**96** F7
Christiana Hartley Maternity
 Hospl PR8 ....**35** D5
Christie Ave LA4 ......**217** D4
Christie Park (Morecambe
 FC) LA4 ....**217** D4
Christines Cres L40 .....**25** E4
Christleton Cl BB10 ....**148** D3
Church & Oswaldtwistle Sta
 BB5 ....**103** E5
Church Alley BB5 ......**124** F2
Church Ave
 Accrington BB5 ....**104** E2
 Higher Penwortham PR1 .**96** C6
 Lancaster LA1 ....**214** F4
 Preston PR1 ....**97** E8
Church Bank Church BB5 **103** E7
 Over Kellet LA6 ....**237** B8
Church Bank Gdns LA6 .**240** C7
Church Bank St **20** BB3 ..**82** A1
Church Brook Ho **8** PR1 **96** E4
Church Brow
 Bolton-le-S LA5 ....**221** A3
 Clitheroe BB7 ....**189** E1
 Halton LA2 ....**219** C6
 Walton-le-D PR5 ....**97** E5
Church Brow Cl LA5 ...**221** A3
Church Brow Gdns **5**
 BB7 ....**189** E1
Church Cl Clitheroe BB7 ..**189** E1
 Dolphinholme LA2 .....**226** A8
 Formby L37 ....**12** A3
 Freckleton PR4 ....**93** A6
 Mellor BB2 ....**121** D2
 Ramsbottom BL0 ....**50** B5
 Read BB12 ....**145** D2
 Southport PR9 ....**36** A8
 Waddington BB7 ....**189** B4
Church Close Ct L37 ....**12** A3
Church Cotts LA6 ......**241** C7
Church Ct
 Bolton-le-S LA5 ....**221** A3
 Edenfield BL0 ....**68** D4
 Kirkham PR4 ....**114** A5
 16 Lancaster LA1 .....**218** D2
 Preston PR1 ....**118** C2
Church Dr
 Lytham St Anne's FY8 ...**90** F3
 Orrell WN5 ....**10** D5
 Whalley BB7 ....**144** A7
Church Fields Bescar L40 .**23** F7
 Ormskirk L39 ....**15** E5
Church Fold
 Charnock Richard PR7 ...**42** E4
 Coppull PR7 ....**29** F8
Church Gdns
 Longridge PR3 ....**140** B7
 Warton PR4 ....**92** E6
Church Gn Formby L37 ...**11** C2
 Skelmersdale WN8 ......**17** F1
Church Gr LA3 ....**209** E8
Church Hall BB5 ......**103** F7
Church Hill
 Nether Kellet LA6 .....**221** F5
 Whittle-le-W PR6 ....**61** C7
Church Hill Ave LA5 ...**223** D5
Church Hill Rd
 Blackburn BB1 ....**102** A7
 Ormskirk L39 ....**15** D6
Church Ho **7** L39 ......**15** E5
Church House Mus PR3 **137** D1
Church La
 Accrington BB5 ....**125** A1
 Aughton L39 ....**6** A7
 Bilsborrow PR3 ....**159** A4
 Broughton PR3 ....**137** D1
 Charnock Richard PR7 ...**42** D4
 Edenfield BL0 ....**68** D4
 Farington PR4,PR26 ....**76** F7

Church La continued
 Goosnargh PR3 ....**138** D6
 Great Harwood BB6 ....**124** C6
 Great Mitton BB7 .....**165** E3
 Hambleton FY6 ....**177** D1
 Kelbrook BB18 ....**195** A6
 Maghull L31 ....**5** A8
 Mellor BB2 ....**121** E2
 Morecambe LA4 ....**217** B6
 Newchurch BB4 ....**86** E1
 Newton-w-S PR4 ......**115** B3
 12 Padiham BB12 .....**146** C1
 Tunstall LA6 ....**241** E4
 Whalley BB7 ....**144** C5
 Whitechapel PR3 ......**160** E7
 Winmarleigh PR3 .....**203** E4
 Wrightington Bar WN6 ...**28** D8
Church Mdws BB8 ....**171** D5
Church Pk Lea Town PR4 **115** F3
 Overton LA3 ....**209** D8
Church Raike PR3 .....**185** C3
Church Rd
 Bamber Bridge PR5 .....**77** E7
 Bamber Bridge PR5 .....**77** F6
 Banks PR9 ....**55** A6
 Bickerstaffe L39 ....**7** E6
 Kirkham PR4 ....**113** F7
 Leyland PR25 ....**60** F3
 Lytham FY8 ....**90** F3
 Lytham St Anne's FY8 ...**90** B6
 Rufford L40 ....**39** C4
 Shuttleworth BL0 ....**50** E8
 Singleton FY6 ....**154** F1
 Skelmersdale WN8 ......**17** F1
 Tarleton PR4 ....**57** A5
 Thornton FY5 ....**176** A2
 Thornton-in-C BD23 ...**197** A5
 Warton PR4 ....**92** E6
 Weeton PR4 ....**132** F1
 Wharles PR4 ....**134** F2
Church Row Preston PR1 .**97** A7
 Wrea Green PR4 ......**113** B4
Church Row Chambers
 PR4 ....**75** A8
Church Sq BB10 ......**129** B5
Church St
 Accrington BB5 ....**104** C5
 Adlington PR7 ....**31** A7
 Bacup OL13 ....**70** C8
 Barnoldswick BB18 ....**196** B2
 Barrowford BB9 ....**170** D4
 Belmont BL7 ....**46** C4
 Blackburn BB1 ....**101** E5
 Blackpool FY1 ....**130** C5
 Blackrod BL6 ....**31** C2
 Brierfield BB9 ....**148** B5
 Brierfield,Harle Syke BB10 **148** F2
 Burnley BB11 ....**128** A6
 Bury BL9 ....**33** A3
 Chorley PR7 ....**43** C7
 Church BB5 ....**103** E6
 Churchtown PR3 ......**181** A2
 Clayton-le-M BB5 .....**124** F2
 1 Clitheroe BB7 .....**166** E8
 Colne BB8 ....**171** D5
 Croston PR26 ....**58** B1
 Darwen BB3 ....**82** A1
 Fleetwood FY7 ....**199** B4
 Garstang PR3 ....**181** C7
 Goodshaw Chapel BB4 .**106** A1
 Great Harwood BB6 ....**124** C5
 Halton LA2 ....**219** B6
 2 Hapton BB12 ......**126** C4
 Haslingden BB4 ....**85** B4
 Higher Walton PR5 .....**98** B3
 Horwich BL6 ....**32** C3
 Kirkham PR4 ....**114** B5
 Lancaster LA1 ....**214** E8
 Lancaster LA1 ....**214** F8
 Leyland PR25 ....**77** B2
 Longridge PR3 ....**140** B7
 Morecambe LA4 ....**217** B6
 Newchurch BB4 ....**86** E1
 Ormskirk L39 ....**15** E5
 Orrell,Far Moor WN5 ...**10** E5
 Oswaldtwistle BB5 .....**103** D3
 Padiham BB12 ....**126** C8
 2 Poulton-le-F FY6 ...**153** D3
 Preston PR1 ....**97** A7
 5 Ramsbottom BL0 ....**50** C6
 Rawtenstall BB4 ....**69** E8
 Read BB12 ....**145** D2
 Rishton BB1 ....**124** A1
 Skelmersdale WN8 ......**10** C7
 Slaidburn BB7 ....**229** C2
 Southburn PR9 ....**35** C7
 Standish WN6 ....**29** E1
 Trawden BB8 ....**172** C2
 Whittington LA6 ......**241** C7
 Whitworth OL12 ....**52** C8
 Ribchester PR3 ....**141** D3
Church Terr **21** BB3 ....**82** A1
Church View Aughton L39 .**6** A7
 Gisburn BB7 ....**231** B3
 Salesbury BB1 ....**122** E6
 Stalmine FY6 ....**177** C7
 Tarleton PR4 ....**57** A5
 Trawden BB8 ....**172** C2
Church View Ct **1** L39 ..**15** E5
Church Way Formby L37 ..**11** C2
 Nelson BB9 ....**148** D6
Church Wlk
 Blackburn BB1 ....**122** F3
 Euxton PR7 ....**60** C2
 Fulwood PR2 ....**118** D4
 Kirkham PR4 ....**113** F7
 Tarleton PR4 ....**57** A6

Church Wlks **3** L39 ....**15** E5
Churchfield PR2 ....**117** F6
Churchfields PR8 ....**34** F3
Churchgate
 Goosnargh PR3 ....**138** D6
 Southport PR9 ....**53** F1
Churchgate Mews PR9 ..**54** A1
Churchill Ave
 Rishton BB1 ....**103** A8
 Southport PR9 ....**53** F2
Churchill Cl **2** FY5 ....**176** B2
Churchill Ct FY3 ......**130** D6
Churchill Dr PR2 ......**118** D4
Churchill Rd
 Barrowford BB9 ....**170** B1
 Brinscall PR6 ....**63** A8
 Fulwood PR2 ....**118** C4
Churchill St OL12 ....**52** C1
Churchill Way
 Leyland PR25 ....**77** A2
 Nelson BB9 ....**148** B8
Churchlands La WN6 ....**29** F1
Churchside PR4 ....**75** F8
Churchtown Cres OL13 ..**88** B1
Churchtown Ct **2** PR9 ..**54** A2
Churchtown Gdns **1**
 PR9 ....**54** A2
Churchtown Prim Sch
 PR9 ....**54** B2
Churchward Sq BL6 .....**32** C2
Churton Gr WN6 ....**29** B2
Cicely Ct **6** BB1 ......**101** F4
Cicely La BB1 ....**101** F5
Cicely St BB1 ....**101** F4
Cinder La Lancaster LA1 .**214** F3
 Lewth PR4 ....**136** A6
 Mere Brow PR4 ....**55** F2
Cinderbarrow La LA5,
 LA6 ....**240** A6
Cinnamon Brow WN8 ....**10** C6
Cinnamon Ct **3** PR1 ....**96** C2
Cinnamon Hill Dr N PR5 .**97** D3
Cinnamon Hill Dr S PR5 .**97** D3
Cintra Ave PR2 ....**117** D3
Cintra Terr PR2 ....**117** D3
Circus The **10** BB3 .....**82** A1
Cirrus Dr L39 ....**15** A1
City Ct PR1 ....**97** A8
City Heights Cl **21** LA1 .**215** A8
City Mus* LA1 ....**214** F8
Clairane Ave PR2 ......**117** E6
Clairville PR8 ....**34** F5
Clancut La PR7 ....**42** F2
Clanfield PR2 ....**117** E7
Clara St Preston PR1 .....**97** C7
 Whitworth OL12 ....**71** D1
Clare Ave BB8 ....**171** A2
Clare Rd LA1 ....**218** C4
Clare St Blackpool FY1 ..**130** B1
 Burnley BB11 ....**127** D6
Claremont Ave
 Chorley PR7 ....**43** B7
 Clitheroe BB7 ....**166** F7
 Southport PR8 ....**35** A4
Claremont Com Prim Sch
 FY1 ....**130** C8
Claremont Cres LA4 ...**216** F4
Claremont Ct
 Blackpool FY1 ....**130** C7
 Lytham St Anne's FY8 ...**89** E5
Claremont Dr
 Clitheroe BB7 ....**166** F7
 Ormskirk L39 ....**15** D3
Claremont Gdns PR8 ....**35** A4
Claremont Pl FY8 ....**89** E8
Claremont Rd
 Accrington BB5 ....**104** B8
 Blackpool FY1 ....**130** C8
 Chorley PR7 ....**43** B3
 Morecambe LA4 ....**216** F4
 Southport PR8 ....**35** A4
Claremont St
 Brierfield BB9 ....**148** A6
 Burnley BB12 ....**127** D6
 Colne BB8 ....**172** A5
Claremont Terr BB9 ...**148** A5
Claremount Ave PR25 ...**60** B8
Clarence Ave
 Cleveleys FY5 ....**175** D3
 4 Haslingden BB4 ....**85** A1
 Knott End-on-S FY6 ...**199** E5
Clarence Cl **10** BL9 ....**33** A4
Clarence Ct
 15 Blackpool FY4 ....**130** B1
 5 Morecambe LA4 ...**217** E6
 Southport PR8 ....**35** A4
Clarence House Sch L37 .**11** F6
Clarence Pk BB2 ......**101** B7
Clarence Rd
 Accrington BB5 ....**104** A4
 Southport PR8 ....**35** A4
Clarence St
 Barnoldswick BB18 ....**196** C1
 Blackburn BB1 ....**101** D6
 Burnley BB12 ....**128** B4
 4 Chorley PR7 ....**43** D7
 Colne BB8 ....**172** A5
 Darwen BB3 ....**81** F3
 Lancaster LA1 ....**215** A4
 Leyland PR25 ....**77** B2
 Longridge PR3 ....**140** A8
 Morecambe LA4 ....**217** B5
 Oswaldtwistle BB5 .....**103** C3
 Rawtenstall BB4 ....**86** A7
 Rochdale OL12 ....**52** D2
 Trawden BB8 ....**172** C2
Clarendon Gr L31 ....**5** C5

Clarendon Rd
Blackburn BB1 101 F8
Blackpool FY1 130 B2
Lancaster LA1 218 D3
Lytham St Anne's FY8 90 A8
Clarendon Rd E
Blackburn BB1 102 A8
Morecambe LA4 216 F4
Clarendon Rd N FY8 89 F8
Clarendon Rd W LA3 216 E4
Clarendon St
Accrington BB5 104 D6
Bury BL9 33 A4
10 Chorley PR6 43 E7
Colne BB8 172 B5
Preston PR1 97 A6
Claret St BB5 104 A5
Clark St Morecambe LA4 217 B6
Poulton-le-F FY6 153 F3
Clarke Holme St 3 BB4 86 F2
Clarke St 6 BB1 124 B1
Clarke Wood Cl BB7 144 F8
Clarke's Cotts L40 27 A8
Clarke's La OL12 52 E1
Clarkes Croft BL9 33 C3
Clarkfield Cl L40 25 F3
Clarkfield Dr LA4 217 D5
Clarksfield Rd LA5 221 A4
Clarrick Terr LA6 242 F3
Claton-le-Wold CE Prim Sch PR6 77 F2
Claughton Ave PR25 77 E1
Claughton Dr LA1 215 A3
Claughton Ind Est PR3 181 E1
Claughton Mans 5 FY4 110 D8
Claughton St 13 BB10 148 B1
Claughton Terr LA2 237 F5
Clawthorpe Cotts LA6 240 C8
Clay Brow Rd WN8 9 E6
Clay Gap La FY6,PR3 177 F4
Clay La LA3 213 B8
Clay St BB11 127 C5
Claybank 10 BB12 146 C1
Claybank Fold 9 BB12 146 C1
Clayburn Cl PR6 61 E2
Claylands Dr LA5 221 A4
Claypool Prim Sch BL6 32 F1
Claypool Rd BL6 32 E1
Clayton Ave Leyland PR25 59 D7
Rawtenstall BB4 68 E8
Clayton Brook Prim Sch PR5 78 B5
Clayton Brook Rd PR5 78 C6
Clayton Cl 11 BB9 170 D1
Clayton Cres FY4 110 E6
Clayton Ct PR3 140 B7
Clayton Gdns L40 25 E4
Clayton Gr BB1 122 D6
Clayton Green Rd PR6 78 B3
Clayton Hall Dr BB5 124 F4
Clayton Lodge BB5 124 F4
Clayton Mews WN8 17 D1
Clayton Row BB6 143 D1
Clayton St
1 Accrington BB5 125 A1
6 Bamber Bridge PR5 97 E1
Barnoldswick BB18 196 C2
Blackburn BB2 101 E4
Colne BB8 171 E4
Great Harwood BB6 124 C5
18 Nelson BB9 170 D1
7 Oswaldtwistle BB5 103 E5
Skelmersdale WN8 17 D1
Clayton Street Ind Units BB9 170 D1
Clayton Villa Fold PR6 78 A3
Clayton Way
Blackburn BB2 81 D7
Clayton-le-M BB5 125 A3
Clayton's Gate 11 PR1 96 F8
Clayton-le-Moors Ind Est BB5 124 E2
Clayton-le-Woods CE Prim Sch PR6 78 A2
Clayton-le-Woods Manor Road Prim Sch PR6 78 B2
Claytongate
Blackpool FY4 111 A7
Coppull PR7 42 F2
Claytongate Dr PR1,PR5 97 A2
Claytonhalgh PR3 141 E3
Cleator Ave FY2 152 C1
Cleaver Cotts L38 3 A6
Cleaver St Blackburn BB1 101 F5
Burnley BB10 128 B8
Clecken La PR3 182 D2
Clegg Ave FY5 175 D3
Clegg St 6 Bacup OL13 70 C8
Brierfield BB9 148 B5
Burnley BB10 128 A8
Haslingden BB4 85 B3
Kirkham PR4 114 A5
Nelson BB9 148 E6
Skelmersdale WN8 17 D1
Whitworth OL12 71 C2
Worsthorne BB10 129 A5
Clegg St E 9 BB10 128 A8
Clegg's Ave OL12 71 C2
Clegg's Ct OL12 71 C2
Clematis Cl PR7 61 A3
Clematis St BB2 101 B6
Clemens Ct BB3 81 E3
Clement St
Accrington BB5 104 C5
4 Darwen BB3 65 A8
Clement View 14 BB9 148 D8
Clementina St OL12 52 F1
Clements Dr BB9 148 C4
Clengers Brow PR9 54 A3
Clent Ave L31 5 C3
Clent Gdns L31 5 C3
Clent Rd L31 5 C3
Clerk Hill Rd BB7 144 F5
Clerkhill St BB1 102 B5
Clery St BB1 127 A5
Cleve Way L37 12 B2
Clevedon Rd
Blackpool FY1 130 B7
Fulwood PR2 117 A4
Cleveland Ave PR2 118 C4
Cleveland Cl BL0 50 C3
Cleveland Dr LA1 214 D7
Cleveland Rd
Leyland PR25 76 F2
Lytham St Anne's FY8 91 B3
Cleveland St Chorley PR7 43 C8
Colne BB8 171 F6
2 Coppull PR7 42 E1
Cornholme OL14 109 B1
Clevelands Ave
Morecambe LA3 216 F3
Silverdale LA5 224 C4
Clevelands Gr
Burnley BB11 127 E4
Morecambe LA3 216 F3
Clevelands Mt BB11 127 E4
Clevelands Rd BB11 127 F4
Clevelands Wlk LA3 216 F3
Cleveleys Ave
Cleveleys FY5 175 D3
Fulwood PR2 117 C4
Lancaster LA1 218 A2
Southport PR9 54 A4
Cleveleys Rd
Accrington BB5 104 B8
Blackburn BB2 101 F1
Coupe Green PR5 98 E3
Southport PR9 54 A3
Cleves Ct FY3 131 A2
Cleves The L31 5 E3
Clieves Hills La L39 14 E3
Clifden Ct L37 11 F3
Cliff Ave BL9 50 C2
Cliff Ct FY2 152 B4
Cliff Mount BL0 50 B7
Cliff Pl FY2 152 B4
Cliff Rd PR9 53 D1
Cliff St Colne BB8 171 B3
Padiham BB12 146 D1
Preston PR1 96 E6
Rishton BB1 124 B2
Cliff View OL14 109 B2
Cliffe Ct PR1 97 D8
Cliffe Dr PR6 61 B8
Cliffe La BB6 124 C6
Cliffe Pk BB6 124 C6
Cliffe St BB9 170 E1
Clifford Ave Longton PR4 95 A1
Morecambe LA4 217 D6
Clifford Rd Blackpool FY1 130 C7
Southport PR8 35 A2
Clifford St
Barnoldswick BB18 196 C2
Chorley PR7 43 D8
Colne BB8 171 E5
Cliffs The LA3 216 D2
Clifton Ave
Accrington BB5 104 C7
Blackpool FY4 131 C1
Leyland PR25 60 B8
Preston PR2 117 A2
Warton PR4 92 E6
Clifton Cl FY5 176 C1
Clifton Cres
Blackpool FY3 131 A2
Preston PR1 118 C2
Clifton Ct
1 Blackpool FY4 110 B6
3 Lytham St Anne's,Lytham FY8 91 C3
2 Lytham St Anne's,St Annes FY8 89 E6
Clifton Dr Blackpool FY4 110 B5
Blackrod BL6 31 C3
Great Harwood BB6 124 C6
Higher Penwortham PR1 96 C5
Lytham St Anne's FY8 90 D3
Morecambe LA4 217 E5
Clifton Dr N FY8 110 B2
Clifton Dr S FY8 89 E5
Clifton Gdns FY8 90 C6
Clifton Gn PR4 115 D2
Clifton Gr Chorley PR7 43 B7
Preston PR1 118 C3
Wilpshire BB1 122 F4
Clifton Grange FY8 89 D7
Clifton Ho PR2 118 C4
Clifton Hospl FY8 90 B5
Clifton La PR4 115 D2
Clifton Lodge FY8 89 E5
Clifton Par 4 FY8 91 B3
Clifton Pk Ret Ctr FY4 111 D8
Clifton Pl Freckleton PR4 93 B6
Fulwood PR2 117 B2
Clifton Prim Sch FY8 90 C6
Clifton Rd Blackpool FY4 111 C8
Brierfield BB9 148 C4
Burnley BB12 127 C7
Fleetwood FY7 199 A3
Formby L37 12 A5
Southport PR8 35 F6
Clifton Sq 5 FY8 91 B3
Clifton St Accrington BB5 104 A4
Blackpool FY1 130 B5
Burnley BB12 127 F6
Colne BB8 171 D5
Clifton St *continued*
Darwen BB3 81 F4
Earby BB18 195 A8
Lytham St Anne's FY8 91 B3
5 Preston PR1 96 D6
Rishton BB1 124 B1
Trawden BB8 172 C2
Clifton Terr BB3 82 E2
Clifton Wlk 8 FY8 91 B3
Clinkham Rd BB6 124 A5
Clinning Rd PR8 35 A2
Clinton Ave FY1 130 C4
Clinton St BB1 102 A6
Clippers Quay 2 BB1 101 F4
Clitheroe Castle★ BB7 166 E8
Clitheroe Castle Mus★ BB7 166 E8
Clitheroe Hospl BB7 190 A3
Clitheroe Pendle Prim Sch BB7 189 F1
Clitheroe Pl FY4 111 A8
Clitheroe Rd
Brierfield BB9 148 A5
Chatburn BB7 190 C3
Lytham St Anne's FY8 90 C6
Sabden BB7 167 E1
Waddington BB7 189 C3
West Bradford BB7 189 F5
Whalley BB7 144 C7
Clitheroe Royal Gram Sch
Clitheroe BB7 189 F1
Clitheroe BB7 190 A2
Clitheroe St
3 Padiham BB12 126 C8
Preston PR1 97 C7
Clitheroe Sta BB7 189 E1
Clitheroes La PR4 93 B6
Clive Ave FY8 110 E1
Clive Lodge PR8 34 F2
Clive Rd
Higher Penwortham PR1 96 B6
Southport PR8 34 F2
Clive St BB12 127 F8
Cliviger Holme CE Prim Sch BB10 108 B6
Clockhouse Ave BB10 148 D3
Clockhouse Ct BB10 148 D3
Clockhouse Gr BB10 148 D3
Clod La BB4 68 C8
Clods Carr La FY6 199 F3
Clog Heads BB8 172 C2
Clogger La BD23 197 F7
Cloister Dr BB3 82 C1
Cloister Gn L37 12 B2
Cloisters LA3 217 C2
Cloisters The
Blackpool FY3 130 E5
Formby L37 11 F3
2 Leyland PR25 77 C2
6 Preston PR2 96 D8
1 Rawtenstall BB4 69 E8
Tarleton PR4 57 A6
Whalley BB7 144 D5
Clorain Cl L33 1 A3
Clorain Rd L33 1 A3
Close The Banks PR9 55 A5
Clayton-le-M BB5 124 F4
Cleveleys FY5 175 D2
Cleveleys,Rossall Beach FY5 175 D4
Fulwood PR2 118 E6
Garstang PR3 204 B1
Ince Blundell L38 3 E3
Kirkham PR4 114 B4
New Longton PR4 76 A7
Rising Bridge BB5 85 A8
Weeton PR4 132 E2
Withnell Fold PR6 79 C3
Closes Hall Mews BB7 230 F5
Clough Acre PR7 61 A2
Clough Ave PR5 97 B3
Clough Bank BB7 190 D5
Clough End Rd BB4 85 B5
Clough Head Visitor Ctr★ BB4 84 A3
Clough Heads Cotts PR3 226 F1
Clough La
Hesketh Lane PR3 163 A7
Simonstone BB12 145 F1
Clough Rd Bacup OL13 88 A3
Nelson BB9 149 A8
Clough St 11 Bacup OL13 70 D8
Burnley BB11 127 D5
Darwen BB3 65 C6
5 Newchurch BB4 86 F1
Clough Terr BB18 196 B1
Clough The
Clayton Green PR6 78 A3
Darwen BB3 65 C6
Clougha Ave Halton LA2 219 D7
Lancaster LA1 215 B6
Cloughfield PR1 96 D1
Cloughfold Prim Sch BB4 86 C2
Cloughwood Cres WN6 19 D6
Clovelly Ave
Blackpool FY5 152 D6
Fulwood PR2 117 D3
Clovelly Dr
Higher Penwortham PR1 96 A5
Newburgh WN8 27 A1
Skelmersdale WN8 18 A8
Southport PR8 21 E8
Clover Ave FY8 111 A1
Clover Cres BB12 127 D8
Clover Ct Blackpool FY2 152 F6
Southport PR8 35 B5
Clover Dr PR4 93 D7
Clover Field PR6 78 B2
Clover Hill Rd BB9 148 F7
Clover Mews FY3 130 E6
Clover Rd PR7 43 A5
Clover St OL13 88 A3
Clover Terr BB3 82 A3
Cloverfield PR1 96 B4
Cloverfields 5 BB1 102 A6
Cloverhill Ho BB9 148 F7
Club La PR3 185 E3
Club St Bamber Bridge PR5 77 F7
Cornholme OL14 109 B1
Clucas Gdns L39 15 E6
Clyde St Blackburn BB2 101 B3
4 Blackpool FY1 130 B7
Preston PR2 96 C8
Clydesdale Pl PR26 76 C2
Clyffes Farm Cl L40 24 A7
Co-operation St
Bacup OL13 88 A2
1 Newchurch BB4 86 F2
Rawtenstall,Cloughfold BB4 86 B2
3 Rawtenstall,Crawshawbooth BB4 86 A7
Co-operative Bldgs BB10 107 F8
Co-operative St
1 Bamber Bridge PR5 77 E8
22 Barnoldswick BB18 196 B2
Haslingden BB4 67 F7
Coach Ho PR7 60 A5
Coach Ho Ct L40 25 E3
Coach House Mews PR3 181 C7
Coach Mews LA4 216 F4
Coach Rd Bickerstaffe L39 7 F1
Church BB5 103 E5
Warton LA5 223 D7
Coal Clough La BB11 127 E4
Coal Clough Rd OL14 109 B2
Coal Hey 12 BB4 85 B3
Coal Hey St 13 BB4 85 B3
Coal Pit La
Accrington BB5 103 F4
Bacup OL13 88 B3
Barnoldswick BB7 193 B7
Colne BB8 171 F4
Gisburn BB7 231 D2
Rawtenstall BB4 87 A4
Skelmersdale L39 8 D4
Tockholes BB3 81 B3
Coal Rd BL0 51 C8
Coal St 12 BB11 127 F6
Coastal Dr LA2 220 E2
Coastal Rd
Hest Bank LA2,LA5 220 F2
Morecambe LA4 217 F8
Southport,Birkdale PR8 34 C3
Southport,Woodvale PR8 21 A4
Coastal Rise LA2 220 E2
Coastline Mews PR9 54 A4
Coates Ave BB18 196 C3
Coates Fields BB18 196 C4
Coates La BB18 196 D4
Coates Lane Prim Sch BB18 196 D3
Cob Castle Rd BB4 84 E3
Cob La BB8,BB18 195 B4
Cob Moor Ave WN5 10 D1
Cob Moor Rd WN5 10 D1
Cob Wall BB1 102 A6
Cobb's Brow La WN8 18 B6
Cobb's Clough Rd L40 17 F5
Cobbled Court Yd LA1 214 E7
Cobbs Brow Prim Sch WN8 18 A3
Cobbs La BB5 83 E8
Cobden Ct 4 BB1 101 E5
Cobden Ho BB4 86 D1
Cobden Rd PR9 36 A6
Cobden St Bacup OL13 71 B8
Barnoldswick BB18 196 B1
Brierfield BB10 148 F3
Burnley BB10 128 B8
4 Bury BL9 33 A3
Chorley PR6 61 E1
10 Darwen BB3 65 A8
Egerton BL7 47 D2
Hapton BB12 126 C4
Nelson BB9 148 D7
Padiham BB12 146 D1
Cobham Ct 2 BB4 86 E1
Cobham Rd BB5 104 D5
Cobourg Cl BB2 101 F2
Cochran St 25 BB3 82 A1
Cock Hall La OL12 52 C8
Cock Robin PR26 58 C2
Cock Robin La PR3 181 D2
Cocker Ave FY6 154 A2
Cocker Bar Rd PR26 58 D8
Cocker La PR26 76 C1
Cocker Rd PR5 78 B7
Cocker Sq 3 FY1 130 B6
Cocker St Blackpool FY1 130 B6
Darwen BB3 65 C7
Cocker Trad Est FY1 130 C7
Cockerham Parochial CE Prim Sch LA2 206 D4
Cockerham Rd
Forton LA2,PR3 207 B4
Garstang PR3 204 B1
Cockerham Wlk FY3 131 A8
Cockerill St BB4 85 B4
Cockerill Terr BB7 166 D1
Cockersand Ave PR4 95 C1
Cockersand Dr LA1 215 A3
Cockhall La OL12 71 C1
Cockhill La BB8 172 B8
Cocking Yd LA6 240 C7
Cockle Dick's La PR9 53 E2
Cockleach Lane Ends PR3 162 A2
Cockridge Cl BB2 81 B7
Codale Ave FY2 152 D5
Coddington St BB1 102 B5
Coe La PR4 57 A5
Cog La BB11 127 D4
Cog St BB11 127 D5
Colbran St Burnley BB10 128 B8
12 Nelson BB9 170 F2
Colburne Cl L40 25 F5
Colchester Ave LA1 215 B5
Colchester Dr 6 FY5 175 F4
Colchester Rd
Blackpool FY3 130 F3
Southport PR8 35 F3
Cold Bath St 4 PR1 96 E8
Cold Well La LA7 224 F8
Coldale Ct 5 FY4 110 B6
Coldstream Pl BB2 101 E2
Coldweather Ave BB9 148 F5
Cole Cres L39 6 C8
Colebatch PR2 117 D5
Coleman St 4 BB9 148 F8
Colenso Rd
Blackburn BB1 101 D7
Fulwood PR2 117 C2
Coleridge Ave FY5 176 A3
Coleridge Cl Colne BB8 171 D6
Cottam PR4 116 E4
Coleridge Dr BB5 104 E2
Coleridge Ho LA2 218 C4
Coleridge Pl BB6 124 B4
Coleridge Rd
Blackpool FY1 130 D6
Longshaw WN5 10 D1
Ramsbottom BL8 49 F2
Coleridge St BB2 101 C3
Coles Dr LA5 224 B8
Coleshill Ave BB10 128 D5
Colesville Ave FY5 176 B1
Colin St
Barnoldswick BB18 196 B3
Burnley BB11 127 D5
Colinmander Gdns L39 15 C3
Colinton WN8 9 E7
Colldale Terr BB4 85 B2
College Ave
Cleveleys FY5 175 C1
Formby L37 11 E4
College Cl Formby L37 11 D4
Longridge PR3 140 A5
Padiham BB12 126 D6
Southport PR8 35 A3
College Croft BD24 236 F7
College Ct
Accrington BB5 104 A6
4 Blackpool FY1 130 C4
Preston PR1 117 F2
College Gate FY5 175 C5
College Path L37 11 D5
College Rd WN8 19 B1
College St
Accrington BB5 104 A6
7 Cornholme OL14 109 C1
Collegiate High Sch Sports Coll FY3 153 A1
Collier St BB5 104 E2
Collier's Row BB1 102 F1
Colliers St BB5 103 E5
Collin's Hill La PR3 185 A3
Colling St 9 BL0 50 B5
Collinge Fold La BB4 85 F4
Collinge St
Padiham BB12 126 C7
Rawtenstall BB4 85 F4
Collingham Pk LA1 215 A2
Collingwood BB5 124 E2
Collingwood Ave
Blackpool FY3 130 E6
Lytham St Anne's FY8 110 E1
Collingwood Pl FY3 130 E6
Collingwood Rd PR7 43 B7
Collingwood St
Colne BB8 171 C4
Standish WN6 29 E1
Collingwood Terr 7 LA2 239 D8
Collins Ave FY2 152 E3
Collins Dr BB5 104 E2
Collins Rd PR5 97 F1
Collins Rd N PR5 97 F2
Collinson St PR1 118 C1
Collisdene Rd WN5 10 E6
Collison Ave PR7 43 C8
Colloway Ho LA3 212 E6
Collyhurst Ave FY4 110 E6
Colman Ct PR1 96 D6
Colnbrook WN6 29 B1
Colne & Broughton Rd BD23 197 C6
Colne La BB8 171 E4
Colne Rd
Barnoldswick BB18 196 A1
Barrowford BB8,BB9 170 F4
Brierfield BB9 148 B6
Burnley BB10,BB11 128 A8
Burnley,Burnley Lane BB10 148 B3
Kelbrook BB18 195 A7
Trawden BB8 172 B2
Colne Sta BB8 171 C4

Colonnade The LA1 ...215 C7
Colt House CI PR25 ...60 A7
Colthurst Dr BB7 ...190 A2
Coltsfoot Dr PR6 ...61 D2
Coltsfoot Wlk LA3 ...217 B2
Columbia Way BB2 ...101 B8
Columbine CI Chorley PR7 61 A3
  Rochdale OL12 ...52 C3
Colville Ave 1 FY4 ...110 C5
Colville Rd BB3 ...81 E4
Colville St BB10 ...128 A8
Colwall CI L33 ...1 A2
Colwall Rd L33 ...1 A2
Colwall Wlk L33 ...1 A2
Colwyn Ave
  Blackpool FY4 ...130 E1
  Morecambe LA4 ...217 D6
Colwyn Pl PR2 ...117 A3
Colyton CI PR6 ...43 E8
Colyton Rd PR6 ...43 E8
Colyton Rd E 2 PR6 ...43 E8
Combermere Gr LA3 ...212 E5
Combermere Rd LA3 ...212 E6
Comer Gdns L31 ...5 C3
Comet Dr PR26 ...76 C2
Comet St OL13 ...88 A7
Commerce St Bacup OL13 87 F2
  Haslingden BB4 ...85 A4
Commercial Rd
  Chorley PR7 ...61 C1
  Great Harwood BB6 ...124 C5
  Nelson BB9 ...148 E8
Commercial St
  Bacup OL13 ...70 D8
  Barnoldswick BB18 ...196 B2
  10 Blackpool FY1 ...130 B1
  Brierfield BB9 ...148 B6
  7 Church BB5 ...103 E6
  12 Great Harwood BB6 ...124 C5
  Oswaldtwistle BB5 ...103 D3
  Rawtenstall BB4 ...106 A3
  Rishton BB1 ...124 B1
Common Bank Employment
  Area PR7 ...42 F8
Common Bank La PR7 ...42 F8
Common Edge Rd FY4 ...110 F6
Common End PR7 ...30 E5
Common Garden St 38
  LA1 ...214 F8
Common La PR9 ...55 C1
Common The
  Adlington PR7 ...30 E5
  Parbold WN8 ...27 C3
Commons La BB2 ...121 B5
Commonside FY8 ...90 D4
Commonwealth CI FY8 ...90 C8
Como Ave BB11 ...127 C4
Company St 7 BB1 ...124 B1
Compley Ave FY6 ...153 C2
Compley Gn FY6 ...153 C2
Compression Rd LA3 ...212 E2
Compston Ave BB4 ...106 A1
Compton CI FY6 ...153 C5
Compton Gn PR2 ...117 D7
Compton Rd PR8 ...35 B3
Comrie Cres BB11 ...127 D3
Concorde Ho 1 FY1 ...130 C4
Concourse Sh Ctr The
  WN8 ...18 B1
Conder Ave FY5 ...175 F2
Conder Brow LA5 ...223 E2
Conder Green Rd LA2 ...210 F3
Conder Pl LA1 ...218 C2
Conder Rd PR2 ...116 E1
Condor Gr Blackpool FY1 130 D3
  Lytham St Anne's FY8 ...89 E8
Conduit St BB9 ...170 D1
Coneygarth La
  Tunstall LA6 ...241 D4
  Whittington LA6 ...241 D6
Congleton CI FY4 ...131 B1
Congress St PR7 ...61 C1
Conifer Ct L37 ...11 F2
Conifers The Barton PR3 ...137 B8
  Hambleton FY6 ...177 B2
  Kirkham PR4 ...114 B5
  Maghull L31 ...5 C3
Conisber CI BL7 ...47 E1
Coniston Ave
  Accrington BB5 ...103 F4
  Adlington PR6 ...31 B8
  Barnoldswick BB18 ...196 A3
  Carleton FY7 ...153 B4
  Euxton PR7 ...60 D1
  Fleetwood FY7 ...198 E4
  Hambleton FY6 ...177 C2
  Knott End-on-S FY8 ...199 F6
  Lytham St Anne's FY8 ...110 F2
  Orrell WN5 ...10 F7
  Padiham BB12 ...146 C2
  Preston PR2 ...117 D2
  Thornton FY5 ...179 B1
Coniston CI
  Longridge PR3 ...140 A5
  Ramsbottom BL0 ...50 C7
Coniston Cres FY5 ...176 B1
Coniston Ct
  Morecambe LA4 ...217 C6
  Southport PR8 ...21 C3
Coniston Dr
  Bamber Bridge PR5 ...97 E2
  Darwen BB3 ...82 C2
Coniston Gr BB8 ...172 A6
Coniston Ho PR1 ...96 B4

Coniston Rd
  Blackburn BB1 ...102 A8
  Blackpool FY4 ...110 C7
  Blackrod BL6 ...31 D3
  Bolton-le-S LA5 ...221 A4
  Carnforth LA5 ...221 B1
  Chorley PR7 ...43 B6
  Formby L37 ...11 D2
  Fulwood PR2 ...118 C4
  Lancaster LA1 ...218 E2
  Morecambe LA4 ...217 C6
Coniston St 8 BB12 ...127 C6
Coniston Way Bacup OL13 88 A4
  Croston PR26 ...58 B3
  Rainford Junction WA11 ...8 F2
  Rishton BB1 ...123 F1
Connaught Dr FY5 ...176 D2
Connaught Rd
  Heysham LA3 ...212 D1
  Lancaster LA1 ...215 B5
  Preston PR1 ...96 F5
Consett Ave FY5 ...175 C5
Constable Ave
  Bamber Bridge PR5 ...77 A7
  Burnley BB11 ...127 F3
Constable Lee Cres BB4 ...86 A4
Constable St 8 PR1 ...97 A8
Convent CI
  Bamber Bridge PR5 ...97 D1
  Leyland PR25 ...77 C2
  Ormskirk L39 ...15 E2
Convent Cres FY3 ...131 A8
Conway Ave
  Bamber Bridge PR5 ...97 A1
  Blackburn BB1 ...101 E7
  Cleveleys FY5 ...175 D2
  Clitheroe BB7 ...166 C6
  Leyland PR25 ...60 C8
  Normoss FY3 ...131 B7
Conway CI Catterall PR3 ...181 D2
  Euxton PR7 ...60 E1
  Haslingden BB4 ...85 B1
  Ramsbottom BL0 ...50 B6
Conway Cres
  Barnoldswick BB18 ...196 C3
  Ramsbottom BL8 ...49 F2
Conway Ct
  Gregson Lane PR5 ...98 D2
  4 Lytham St Anne's FY8 ...89 E6
Conway Dr Bury BL9 ...33 D2
  Fulwood PR2 ...117 C6
  Oswaldtwistle BB5 ...103 B4
Conway Gr BB10 ...148 C3
Conway Ho 7 PR1 ...97 D8
Conway Rd Eccleston PR7 ...41 C7
  Rawtenstall BB4 ...86 C2
Conyers Ave PR8 ...34 F3
Cook Gdns BB1 ...102 B4
Cook Green La PR3 ...141 C7
Cook House Rd BB8 ...171 E6
Cook St BL9 ...33 A2
Cooke St BL6 ...32 D4
Cookson CI PR4 ...93 B6
Cookson Rd FY5 ...176 B3
Cookson St FY1 ...130 C5
Cookwood Ho 13 PR1 ...96 D8
Coolham La BB18 ...197 D1
Coolidge Ave LA1 ...214 D7
Coombes The PR2 ...117 F5
Coop St FY1 ...130 B3
Cooper Ct FY5 ...175 D3
Cooper Hill CI PR5 ...97 D5
Cooper Hill Dr PR5 ...97 D5
Cooper Rd PR1 ...96 D8
Cooper St Bacup OL13 ...87 F4
  Burnley BB11 ...128 A5
  Horwich BL6 ...32 B4
  Nelson BB9 ...170 E1
Cooper's La PR7 ...28 E5
Cooper's Way FY1 ...130 D7
Cooperage The BB5 ...103 D3
Coopers CI 5 BB5 ...103 D3
Coote La PR4,PR5 ...76 F7
Cop La Fleetwood FY7 ...199 A4
  Higher Penwortham PR1 ...96 C4
Cop Lane CE Prim Sch
  PR1 ...96 C3
Cop Royd Terr BB10 ...128 F1
Cop The FY5 ...175 D6
Copeland Dr WN6 ...29 F1
Copeland Pl FY8 ...91 C4
Copp La PR3,PR4 ...156 A2
Copper Beech CI PR4 ...74 E3
Copper Beeches
  Blackburn BB2 ...101 A6
  Kingsfold PR1 ...96 D2
Copperas La BL6 ...31 B1
Copperfield CI BB10 ...128 E6
Copperfield St BB1 ...101 F3
Copperwood Way PR7 ...42 F7
Coppice Ave BB5 ...104 D7
Coppice Brow LA5 ...223 F2
Coppice CI Chorley PR6 ...61 E1
  Nelson BB9 ...171 A2
Coppice Dr
  Longshaw WN5 ...10 D2
  Whitworth OL12 ...52 D7
Coppice La PR6 ...62 C3
Coppice Leys 11 L37 ...11 E3
Coppice St BL9 ...33 C3
Coppice The
  Blackburn BB2 ...101 A4
  Clayton-le-M BB5 ...124 F4
  Fulwood PR2 ...117 A6
  Kirkham PR4 ...114 A6
  Longton PR4 ...75 A7

Coppice The continued
  Morecambe LA4 ...217 E5
  Ramsbottom BL0 ...50 A4
Coppingford CI OL12 ...52 A2
Coppins Gn FY6 ...153 E1
Coppull CE Prim Sch
  PR7 ...42 F1
Coppull Ent Ctr PR7 ...42 E2
Coppull Hall La PR7 ...43 A1
Coppull Moor La PR7 ...29 E6
Coppull Rd Chorley PR7 ...43 A4
  Maghull L31 ...5 C4
Copse Rd FY7 ...198 F2
Copse The
  Accrington BB5 ...103 F5
  Chapeltown BL7 ...48 C2
  Chorley PR7 ...43 B4
Copse View Bsns Pk 12
  FY7 ...198 F2
Copster Dr PR3 ...140 B7
Copster Hill CI BB1 ...82 D8
Copthurst Ave BB12 ...146 F6
Copthurst La PR6 ...61 F7
Copthurst St 18 BB12 ...146 C1
Coptrod Head CI OL12 ...52 E4
Copy Bottom BB10 ...108 C4
Copy La LA2 ...237 C3
Copy Nook BB1 ...102 A5
Coral CI FY4 ...131 A1
Corbridge CI
  Blackpool FY3 ...111 A7
  Carleton FY6 ...153 C5
Corbridge Ct BB7 ...189 E1
Corcas La FY8 ...176 F8
Cork Rd LA1 ...215 B5
Cork St BL9 ...33 A2
Corka La FY8 ...112 F1
Corlass St 10 BB9 ...170 D3
Corless Cotts LA2 ...226 A8
Corn Mill La FY7 ...199 B4
Corn Mill Lo L31 ...5 C2
Corn Mill Mews BB7 ...144 C5
Corn Mill Yd BB5 ...124 F2
Corn Mkt LA1 ...214 F8
Cornbrook WN8 ...9 E7
Corncroft PR1 ...96 C3
Cornel Gr BB11 ...127 C4
Cornelian St BB1 ...122 F2
Cornelian Way FY3 ...131 A1
Corner Bank CI PR4 ...112 F7
Cornerhouse The 13 BL0 ...50 C6
Corners The FY5 ...175 C4
Cornfield PR4 ...116 E6
Cornfield CI PR4 ...73 E4
Cornfield Gr BB12 ...127 A8
Cornfield St BB3 ...82 B2
Cornflower CI PR6 ...61 D2
Cornford Rd FY4 ...111 B8
Cornhill Arc BB5 ...104 B6
Cornholme BB10 ...148 E2
Cornholme Jun & Infs Sch
  OL14 ...109 A1
Cornholme Terr 9
  OL14 ...109 B1
Cornmill Terr 6 BB18 ...196 B3
Cornthwaite Rd PR2 ...117 E3
Cornwall Ave
  Blackburn BB1 ...102 E4
  Blackpool FY2 ...152 C4
  Cleveleys FY5 ...175 F4
Cornwall Cres WN1 ...30 E1
Cornwall Pl
  Blackpool FY3 ...131 B2
  Church BB5 ...103 F7
Cornwall Rd BB1 ...124 A1
Cornwall Way PR8 ...21 C2
Corona Ave L31 ...5 C5
Coronation Ave
  Blackburn BB2 ...80 C7
  Formby L37 ...12 A2
  Forton PR3 ...207 B3
  Padiham BB12 ...126 C7
Coronation Cres 5 PR1 ...97 B7
Coronation Ct PR26 ...58 B3
Coronation Gr BB4 ...86 E1
Coronation Mount LA6 ...242 C3
Coronation Pl 6 BB9 ...170 D3
Coronation Rd
  Brierfield BB9 ...148 C5
  Cleveleys FY5 ...175 C2
  Kirkham PR4 ...114 A5
  Lytham St Anne's FY8 ...90 C4
  Maghull L31 ...5 D3
Coronation St
  Barnoldswick BB18 ...196 C2
  Blackpool FY1 ...130 B4
  Great Harwood BB6 ...124 D6
Coronation Terr BB6 ...143 C1
Coronation Way LA1 ...218 C4
Coronation Wlk PR8 ...35 A7
Corporation Ct 4 OL13 ...70 D8
Corporation St
  Accrington BB5 ...104 A5
  11 Blackburn BB2 ...101 E5
  Blackpool FY1 ...130 B5
  6 Clitheroe BB7 ...166 D8
  Preston PR1 ...96 F8
  4 Southport PR8 ...35 B7
Corpus Christi RC High Sch
  PR2 ...117 A4
Corranstone CI BL6 ...32 B3
Corriander CI FY2 ...152 F3
Corrib Rd FY2 ...152 D2
Corringham Rd LA4 ...217 B5

Corston Gr BL6 ...31 D1
Corwen CI PR1 ...101 E7
Cosford St PR4 ...132 E6
Cosgate CI WN5 ...10 E5
Cotswold Ave PR7 ...60 D1
Cotswold CI Eccleston PR7 41 D6
  Ramsbottom BL0 ...50 C4
Cotswold Dr BL6 ...32 C5
Cotswold Rd
  Blackpool FY4 ...152 D1
  Chorley PR7 ...43 C6
  Lytham St Anne's FY8 ...91 D5
Cottage CI L39 ...15 D4
Cottage Fields PR7 ...43 B5
Cottage Gdns PR5 ...78 B8
Cottage La
  Bamber Bridge PR5 ...97 F3
  Ormskirk L39 ...15 D5
Cottage Mews L39 ...15 D5
Cottage Wlk OL12 ...52 C4
Cottam Ave PR2 ...117 A4
Cottam CI
  Lytham St Anne's FY8 ...110 F2
  Whalley BB7 ...144 C5
Cottam Ct PR2 ...117 A2
Cottam Gn PR4 ...116 F6
Cottam Hall La PR2 ...116 F5
Cottam La PR2 ...117 A2
Cottam Pl FY6 ...153 C2
Cottam Prim Sch PR4 ...116 D5
Cottam St PR7 ...43 C6
Cottam Way PR4 ...116 D4
Cottesloe Pl BB9 ...170 C3
Cottesmore CI OL12 ...52 C6
Cottesmore Pl FY3 ...131 A6
Cottom Croft BB5 ...124 F4
Cotton Ct Colne BB8 ...171 C3
  Preston PR1 ...97 A8
Cotton Dr L39 ...15 D6
Cotton Hall St BB3 ...82 A7
Cotton St Accrington BB5 104 B5
  Burnley BB12 ...127 D7
  Padiham BB12 ...126 C7
Cotton Tree La BB8 ...172 A5
Cottys Brow PR9 ...53 F3
Coudray Rd PR9 ...53 E1
Coulston Ave FY2 ...152 B3
Coulston Rd LA1 ...215 B6
Coultate St 7 BB4 ...127 C6
Coulter Beck La LA6 ...242 A7
Coulthurst St 1 BL0 ...50 B6
Coulton Rd BB9 ...148 B5
Counsell Ct 3 FY5 ...176 B2
Countess CI PR4 ...114 A7
Countess Cres FY2 ...152 C3
Countess Rd BB3 ...82 A7
Countess St BB5 ...104 A6
Countess Way PR7 ...60 D2
Countessway 3 PR5 ...97 E1
Country Mews BB2 ...100 F7
County Ave LA1 ...211 B8
County Brook La BB8,
  BB18 ...194 C4
County CI PR26 ...77 A4
County Rd Kirkby L32 ...1 A1
  Ormskirk L39 ...15 E6
County St LA1 ...214 E8
Coupe Gn PR5 ...98 E4
Coupland CI OL12 ...52 C8
Courage Low La WN6 ...28 D5
Course La L40,WN8 ...26 D1
Court Gr BB1 ...122 E6
Court Hey L31 ...5 E1
Court Mews PR9 ...54 A1
Court Rd PR9 ...35 C8
Court Royal FY8 ...90 E3
Court The Fulwood PR2 ...117 C2
  Higher Penwortham PR1 ...96 C4
  Southport PR9 ...35 B8
Courtfield L39 ...15 D7
Courtfield Ave FY2 ...130 D8
Courtfields 3 FY1 ...130 C4
Courtgreen L39 ...15 D7
Courtyard The
  8 Bacup OL13 ...88 A3
  1 Kirkham PR4 ...113 F5
Courtyard Wks L33 ...1 C2
Cousin's La L40 ...39 A3
Cove Dr LA5 ...224 C4
Cove Rd LA5 ...224 B4
Cove The Cleveleys FY5 ...175 C4
  Lytham St Anne's FY8 ...90 D3
  Morecambe LA4 ...217 E7
Covell Ho 3 LA1 ...214 E8
Coventry St 2 PR7 ...43 C6
Coverdale Dr BB2 ...80 D7
Coverdale Rd LA1 ...214 D8
Coverdale Way 4 BB12 127 D7
Covert The FY5 ...175 F4
Coveway Ave FY3 ...130 E6
Cow Gate La BD23 ...231 E2
Cow La BB11 ...127 C6
Cow Well La PR6 ...61 B8
Cowan Brae BB1 ...101 D6
Cowdrey Mews 8 LA1 ...218 B1
Cowell Way 9 BB2 ...101 D5
Cowes Ave BB4 ...85 C2
Cowgarth La BB18 ...197 A1
Cowgill St 17 Bacup OL13 ...88 A3
  Earby BB18 ...197 B1
Cowhill La BB1 ...102 F7
Cowley Cres BB12 ...146 C8
Cowley Rd Blackpool FY4 ...110 F8
  Fulwood PR2 ...118 E4
Cowling Brow PR6 ...43 E7

Cowling Brow Ind Est
  PR6 ...43 F6
Cowling La PR25 ...76 D1
Cowling Rd PR6 ...43 F6
Cowm Park Way N OL12 .71 D2
Cowm Park Way S OL12 .71 C1
Cowm St OL12 ...71 E5
Cowpe Rd BB4 ...69 F7
Cowper Ave 1 BB7 ...189 C1
Cowper Pl BB7 ...230 C1
Cowper St Blackburn BB1 101 F7
  Burnley BB11 ...127 C5
Cowslip Way PR6 ...61 D2
Cowtoot La OL13 ...88 A4
Cox Green CI BL7 ...47 D3
Cox Green Rd BL7 ...47 E2
Coxfield WN6 ...19 D7
Coyford Dr PR9 ...54 A4
Crab Tree La PR3 ...177 E6
Crabtree Ave Bacup OL13 ...88 A1
  Higher Penwortham PR1 ...96 A3
  Newchurch BB4 ...86 F2
Crabtree Bldgs BB4 ...86 F4
Crabtree CI L40 ...25 D4
Crabtree La L40 ...25 D6
Crabtree Orch 3 FY5 ...176 B3
Crabtree Rd FY5 ...176 B3
Crabtree St
  Blackburn BB1 ...102 B5
  Brierfield BB9 ...148 B5
  Colne BB8 ...171 C4
  Whitewell Bottom BB4 ...86 F4
Cracoe Gill BB9 ...170 C3
Craddock Rd BB8 ...171 E5
Crag Ave BL9 ...50 D2
Crag Bank Cres LA5 ...221 C8
Crag Bank La LA5 ...223 C8
Crag Bank Rd
  Carnforth LA5 ...223 B1
  Crag Bank LA5 ...221 C8
Crag Fold BL9 ...50 D2
Crag La BL9 ...50 D2
Crag Rd Lancaster LA1 ...218 F1
  Warton LA5 ...223 A6
Crag View BB4 ...69 D7
Cragg Bottom Rd BD22 ...174 F1
Cragg Row BB18 ...194 D7
Cragg St
  1 Blackpool FY1 ...130 B3
  Colne BB8 ...171 C5
Cragg's Row 18 PR1 ...96 F8
Craggs Hill LA6 ...237 B8
Craggs La LA2 ...239 D3
Craig St LA3 ...216 D3
Craigflower Ct PR5 ...78 C7
Craigholme House Pk
  LA5 ...223 B1
Craiglands Ave LA3 ...216 D2
Craiglands Ct LA1 ...214 C5
Crail Pl OL10 ...33 F1
Crake Ave FY7 ...198 C2
Crake Bank 4 LA1 ...218 A2
Crambe Hts BB3 ...82 A7
Cranberry Bottoms BB3 ...65 E5
Cranberry Chase 4 BB3 ...65 C7
Cranberry CI BB3 ...65 D6
Cranberry Fold Ct BB3 ...65 D5
Cranberry La BB3 ...65 D6
Cranberry Rise BB4 ...106 A2
Cranborne CI Horwich BL6 32 F1
  Standish WN6 ...29 D1
Cranborne St 10 PR1 ...97 C8
Cranborne Terr BB2 ...101 C6
Cranbourne Dr
  Chorley PR6 ...43 E7
  Church BB5 ...104 E8
Cranbourne Gr FY5 ...153 E7
Cranbourne St
  5 Bamber Bridge PR5 ...77 E8
  Chorley PR6 ...43 D7
  Colne BB8 ...171 E6
Cranbrook Ave
  Blackpool FY2 ...152 E5
  Oswaldtwistle BB5 ...103 C4
Cranbrook St BB2 ...101 D2
Cranbury CI FY5 ...175 D3
Crane St PR7 ...29 D6
Cranes La L40 ...16 A7
Cranesbill CI FY5 ...199 F6
Cranfield View BB3 ...65 C6
Crangle Fold BB7 ...190 A2
Crank Rd WN5 ...10 D1
Crankshaw St 22 BB4 ...86 A3
Cranleigh Ave FY2 ...152 C3
Cranleigh CI BL6 ...31 D3
Cranmer St 5 BB11 ...127 E6
Cranshaw Dr BB1 ...101 F8
Cranston Rd L33 ...1 C2
Cranwell Ave LA1 ...215 B5
Cranwell CI 2 BB1 ...102 A4
Cranwell Ct PR4 ...113 F5
Craven CI PR2 ...117 F7
Craven Cnr 8 FY5 ...152 F7
Craven Ct BL6 ...32 D2
Craven Dr PR5 ...77 D7
Craven St Accrington BB5 104 A5
  6 Barnoldswick BB18 ...196 C2
  Brierfield BB9 ...148 B5
  Burnley BB11 ...128 A5
  Bury BL9 ...33 C3
  Clitheroe BB7 ...166 E7
  Colne BB8 ...172 A5
  Nelson BB9 ...148 C8
  Rawtenstall BB4 ...85 F2
Craven St E BL6 ...32 D2
Craven's Ave BB2 ...81 D6
Craven's Brow BB2 ...81 E7
Cravendale Ave BB9 ...170 F3

Cravens Hollow BB2 . . . .81 D6
Cravens Hollows BB2 . . . .81 E6
Crawford Ave
Adlington PR7 . . . . .30 E5
Blackpool FY2 . . . . .152 D5
Chorley PR7 . . . . .43 B7
Leyland PR25 . . . . .60 B8
Maghull L31 . . . . .5 B3
Preston PR1 . . . . .118 F1
Crawford Rd WN8 . . . . .9 D2
Crawford St BB9 . . . . . . .170 E1
Crawford Village Prim Sch
WN8 . . . . .9 E3
Crawshaw Dr BB4 . . . . . . .86 A6
Crawshaw Grange BB4 . .86 A7
Crawshaw La BB10 . . . . .149 D6
Crawshaw St BB5 . . . . . .104 B6
Crawshaw's Bldgs BB4 . . .86 A1
Crawshawbooth Prim Sch
BB4 . . . . .86 A8
Crediton Ave PR9 . . . . . . .54 B5
Crediton Cl BB2 . . . . .81 C8
Crescent Ave
Cleveleys FY5 . . . . .175 D2
Formby L37 . . . . .11 E1
Crescent Ct FY4 . . . . . . .110 A5
Crescent E FY5 . . . . .175 D2
Crescent Gn L39 . . . . .15 B1
Crescent Rd
Poulton-le-F FY6 . . . . .153 E4
Southport PR8 . . . . .34 F3
Crescent St PR1 . . . . . . .118 C1
Crescent The
Bamber Bridge PR5 . . . . . . .77 C8
Bamber Bridge,School Lane
PR5 .97 F2
Blackburn BB2 . . . . .100 E1
Blackpool FY4 . . . . .110 B7
Brierfield BB10 . . . . .148 B4
Bury BL9 . . . . .33 A3
Carleton FY6 . . . . .153 C4
Chorley PR7 . . . . .61 C2
Clitheroe BB7 . . . . .166 D7
Colne BB8 . . . . .171 E6
Dunsop Bridge BB7 . . . . . .228 C5
Fleetwood FY7 . . . . .175 E8
Freckleton PR4 . . . . .93 C5
Hest Bank LA2 . . . . .220 D1
Horwich BL6 . . . . .32 E1
Lytham St Anne's FY8 . . . . .89 E6
Preesall FY6 . . . . .200 B4
Preesall Park FY6 . . . . . . .200 D1
Preston,Ashton-on-R PR2 .117 B2
1 Preston,Lea PR2 . . . . .116 D1
Southport PR9 . . . . .54 C3
Warton PR4 . . . . .92 C4
Whalley BB7 . . . . .144 A6
Whitworth OL12 . . . . .52 C8
Worsthorne BB10 . . . . . . .129 A5
Crescent W FY5 . . . . . . .175 D2
Cressell Pk WN6 . . . . .29 B1
Cresswood Ave FY5 . . . .175 D1
Crestway Blackpool FY3 . .130 F6
Tarleton PR4 . . . . .57 A8
Creswell Ave PR2 . . . . . .116 F3
Creswick Ave BB11 . . . . .127 F3
Creswick Cl BB11 . . . . . .127 F3
Crewdson St BB3 . . . . . . .81 F2
Crewgarth Rd LA3 . . . . .217 B2
Cribden End La BB4 . . . .85 D4
Cribden La BB4 . . . . .85 E5
Cribden St BB4 . . . . .85 F4
Criccieth Cl 3 BB4 . . . . . .85 B1
Criccieth Pl FY5 . . . . . . .176 D2
Crichton Pl FY4 . . . . .110 B5
Cricket Path Formby L37 . .11 F5
Southport PR8 . . . . .34 F3
Cricketers Gn PR7 . . . . . .41 B6
Crimbles La LA2 . . . . . . .206 B2
Crime Well La LA3 . . . . .212 E7
Crimea St OL13 . . . . .88 A2
Crinan Sq OL10 . . . . .33 F1
Cringle Way BB7 . . . . . .190 A2
Cripple Gate WN6 . . . . . .29 A2
Cripple Gate La PR5 . . . .99 C4
Critchley Cl PR4 . . . . .74 F3
Croasdale 7 LA1 . . . . . .218 A2
Croasdale Ave
Brierfield BB10 . . . . .148 E2
Fulwood PR2 . . . . .118 E4
Croasdale Cl LA5 . . . . . .223 C1
Croasdale Dr
Cleveleys FY5 . . . . .175 F4
Clitheroe BB7 . . . . .166 F7
Parbold WN8 . . . . .27 C3
Croasdale Sq BB1 . . . . .102 A3
Croasdale Wlk FY3 . . . . .131 B8
Crockleford Ave PR8 . . . .35 E3
Crocus Cl BB4 . . . . .67 F8
Crocus Field PR25 . . . . . .60 A7
Croft Acres BL0 . . . . .68 D2
Croft Ave Burscough L40 . .25 F3
Orrell WN5 . . . . .10 D5
Slyne LA2 . . . . .218 C8
Croft Bank PR1 . . . . .96 C3
Croft Butts La PR4 . . . . .93 C6
Croft Cl BB4 . . . . .86 A5
Croft Ct Fleetwood FY7 . .198 E2
Freckleton PR4 . . . . .93 B6
Southport PR9 . . . . .54 C4
Thornton FY5 . . . . .176 C3
Croft Field L31 . . . . .5 E1
Croft Gdns PR4 . . . . . . .114 A4
Croft Head Rd BB1 . . . . .123 B1
Croft Hey L40 . . . . .39 B4
Croft Heys L39 . . . . .15 B1
Croft Ho FY6 . . . . .153 D4
Croft La BB12 . . . . .146 F6
Croft Manor PR4 . . . . .93 C6
Croft Mdw PR5 . . . . .78 C6
Croft Rd PR6 . . . . .43 E7
Croft St Bacup OL13 . . . . . .87 F3
Burnley BB11 . . . . .128 A5
Bury BL9 . . . . .33 A2
Clitheroe BB7 . . . . .166 E7
18 Darwen BB3 . . . . .82 A1
Earby BB18 . . . . .197 C2
Great Harwood BB6 . . . . .124 C4
Morecambe LA4 . . . . .217 C5
10 Preston PR1 . . . . .96 D8
Preston PR1 . . . . .96 E8
Croft The Blackburn BB1 .101 D7
Burton in L LA6 . . . . .242 C3
Caton LA2 . . . . .237 C3
Cleveleys FY5 . . . . .175 D2
Colne BB8 . . . . .171 E7
Eccleston PR7 . . . . .41 C7
Euxton PR7 . . . . .60 B3
Fleetwood FY7 . . . . .198 E2
Garstang PR3 . . . . .204 B1
Goosnargh PR3 . . . . .138 D6
Great Plumpton PR4 . . . . .112 E7
Hoghton PR5 . . . . .99 B2
Lytham St Anne's FY8 . . . .111 B1
Maghull L31 . . . . .5 B5
Orrell WN5 . . . . .10 D3
Poulton-le-F FY6 . . . . .153 D2
Thornton-in-C BD23 . . . . .197 B5
Warton LA5 . . . . .223 E6
Croft Way FY5 . . . . .153 C8
Crofters Bank BB4 . . . . .106 A1
Crofters Fold
Galgate LA2 . . . . .211 B4
Morecambe LA3 . . . . .216 E1
Crofters Gn Euxton PR7 . .60 C3
Preston PR1 . . . . .117 E2
Crofters La L33 . . . . .1 A5
Crofters Mdw PR26 . . . . .76 E3
Crofters Mews 12 FY1 . .130 C7
Crofters Wlk
4 Kingsfold PR1 . . . . .96 D2
Lytham St Anne's FY8 . . . . .90 E7
Croftgate PR2 . . . . .117 F5
Croftland Gdns LA5 . . . .221 B6
Croftlands Borwick LA6 . .240 B3
Orrell WN5 . . . . .10 D4
Ramsbottom BL0 . . . . .50 A3
Warton LA5 . . . . .223 E6
Crofton Ave FY2 . . . . . . .152 D5
Crofts Cl PR4 . . . . .114 C5
Crofts The PR4 . . . . .95 A1
Croftson Ave L39 . . . . . . .15 F7
Croftwood Terr BB2 . . . .101 A1
Croich Gn BL8 . . . . .49 B2
Croichbank BL8 . . . . .49 B2
Croichley Fold BL8 . . . . .49 D2
Cromarty Sq OL10 . . . . . . .33 F1
Crombleholme Rd PR1 .118 E1
Cromer Ave BB10 . . . . . .148 C1
Cromer Gr BB10 . . . . . . .148 C1
Cromer Pl Blackburn BB1 .101 E7
Fulwood PR2 . . . . .117 A4
Cromer Rd Blackpool FY2 152 E4
Lytham St Anne's FY8 . . . .111 A1
Southport PR8 . . . . .34 E2
Cromer St OL12 . . . . .52 E1
Cromfield L39 . . . . .15 C2
Cromford Wlk 9 PR1 . . . .97 C8
Crompton Ave FY4 . . . . .110 E7
Crompton Ct 20 PR1 . . . .97 A8
Crompton Pl BB2 . . . . . .101 C5
Crompton St PR1 . . . . . .118 C1
Cromwell Ave 1 PR1 . . . .96 C3
Cromwell Cl L39 . . . . .15 C2
Cromwell Mews PR3 . . .181 C8
Cromwell Rd
Blackpool FY1 . . . . .130 C7
Fulwood PR2 . . . . .118 D3
Higher Penwortham PR1 . . .96 C3
Lancaster LA1 . . . . .214 E6
Cromwell St
Accrington BB5 . . . . .104 B8
20 Blackburn BB1 . . . . . . .102 A4
Burnley BB12 . . . . .127 F8
Foulridge BB8 . . . . .194 D1
4 Preston PR1 . . . . .118 A1
Cromwell Terr 12 BB9 . . .170 D3
Cromwell Way PR1 . . . . . .97 A1
Cronkeyshaw Ave OL12 . .52 E2
Cronkeyshaw Rd OL12 . . .52 F1
Cronkshaw St BB10 . . . .128 A7
Cronshaw Dr BB6 . . . . . .143 C1
Crook Dale La FY6 . . . . .177 E7
Crook Gate La PR3 . . . . .178 E1
Crook Nook LA3 . . . . . . .213 B2
Crook O'Lune Cvn Pk
LA2 . . . . .219 F5
Crook St Adlington PR7 . . .30 F7
Chorley PR7 . . . . .43 B5
Preston PR1 . . . . .97 B8
Crookall Cl 7 FY7 . . . . .198 F2
Crooked La PR1 . . . . .97 A8
Crooked Shore OL13 . . . . .87 F3
Crookfield Rd BL7 . . . . . .64 B3
Crookhalgh Ave BB10 . . .128 F6
Crookhey Gdns LA2 . . . .206 E3
Crookhey Hall Sch LA2 . .206 E3
Crookings La PR1 . . . . . . .96 A6
Crooklands Dr PR3 . . . .181 C8
Crookleigh Pl LA3 . . . . .216 D2
Cropper Gdns PR4 . . . . . .73 D3
Cropper Rd FY4 . . . . . . .111 C6
Cropper Rd N FY4 . . . . .111 C7
Cropper's La L39 . . . . . . .16 A1
Cropton Rd L37 . . . . .11 F3
Crosby Cl BB3 . . . . .65 B6
Crosby Ct FY8 . . . . .110 F1
Crosby Gr FY3 . . . . .130 F3
Crosby Pl PR2 . . . . .117 A4
Crosby Rd Blackburn BB2 101 E1
Lytham St Anne's FY8 . . . .110 F1
Southport PR8 . . . . .35 A3
Crosby St OL12 . . . . .52 F2
Crosfield Ave BL9 . . . . . .50 C2
Crosier Wlk PR4 . . . . . . .116 E5
Crosland Rd L32 . . . . .1 A1
Crosland Rd N FY8 . . . . . .90 A8
Crosland Rd S FY8 . . . . . .90 A8
Crosley Cl BB5 . . . . .104 B3
Cross Bank 9 BB12 . . . .126 D8
Cross Barn Gr BB3 . . . . . .65 B8
Cross Barn La L38 . . . . . . .3 E3
Cross Barn Wlk 5 BB3 . . .65 B8
Cross Bldgs 17 BB4 . . . . .86 A7
Cross Brow PR7 . . . . .42 C8
Cross Edge BB5 . . . . . . .104 A1
Cross Field PR4 . . . . .95 C1
Cross Flatts Cres BB18 .194 E8
Cross Fold BB7 . . . . . . .190 B8
Cross Gates BB6 . . . . . . .124 C5
Cross Gn L37 . . . . .12 A2
Cross Green Cl L37 . . . . .12 A2
Cross Green Rd PR2 . . .117 E6
Cross Hagg St BB8 . . . . .171 C4
Cross Hall Ct L39 . . . . . .16 A4
Cross Halls PR1 . . . . .96 C3
Cross Helliwell St 17
BB8 . . . . .171 D4
Cross Hill Ct LA5 . . . . . .221 A4
Cross Hill Four Lane Ends
PR3 . . . . .226 B6
Cross Hill La BB7 . . . . . .231 B1
Cross Hos PR7 . . . . .42 C8
Cross Keys Dr PR6 . . . . . .61 C7
Cross La
Barley Green BB12 . . . . . .169 C4
Halsall L39 . . . . .23 C1
Low Bentham LA2 . . . . . . .239 B8
Orrell WN5 . . . . .10 D3
Ramsbottom BL8 . . . . .50 A6
Salterforth BB18 . . . . .194 E8
Treales PR4 . . . . .134 D1
Waddington BB7 . . . . .188 E5
Cross Meanygate L40 . . .38 C5
Cross Rd LA2 . . . . .239 B7
Cross School St 5 BB8 171 D4
Cross Skelton St 6
BB8 . . . . .171 E5
Cross St Accrington BB5 .104 C5
4 Bacup OL13 . . . . .88 A3
Blackburn BB3 . . . . .81 F7
Blackpool FY1 . . . . .130 B7
Brierfield BB9 . . . . .148 B5
Brierfield,Harle Syke BB10 148 F3
Chorley PR7 . . . . .61 C1
Clayton-le-M BB5 . . . . . . .124 E3
Clitheroe BB7 . . . . .166 D8
Darwen BB3 . . . . .65 B7
Earby BB18 . . . . .197 A1
Fleetwood FY7 . . . . .199 B5
Great Harwood BB6 . . . . .124 D5
Higham BB12 . . . . .146 F6
3 Leyland PR25 . . . . .77 B2
Longridge PR3 . . . . .140 A6
Lytham St Anne's FY8 . . . . .89 D8
Morecambe LA4 . . . . .217 C5
Nelson BB9 . . . . .148 D8
Oswaldtwistle BB5 . . . . . .103 D4
Preston PR1 . . . . .96 F7
Ramsbottom BL0 . . . . .50 C6
16 Rawtenstall BB4 . . . . . .86 A7
Southport PR8 . . . . .35 B6
Standish WN6 . . . . .29 E1
Worsthorne BB10 . . . . . . .129 B6
Cross St N BB4 . . . . .85 B5
Cross St S BB4 . . . . .85 B4
Cross St W BB8 . . . . . . .171 B4
Cross Swords Cl PR7 . . . .43 A5
Cross The L38 . . . . .3 E4
Cross Way FY5 . . . . . . .175 D4
Crossdale Ave LA3 . . . . .216 D2
Crossdale Sq 10 LA1 . . .215 A8
Crosse Hall La PR6 . . . . .43 F7
Crosse Hall St PR6 . . . . .43 F7
Crossens Way PR9 . . . . . .54 C6
Crossfield Rd WN8 . . . . . . .9 C8
Crossfield St BB2 . . . . . .101 F3
Crossgill Pl 7 LA1 . . . . .218 B2
Crosshall Brow L40 . . . . .16 C4
Crosshill Rd BB2 . . . . . .101 B5
Crosshill Specl Sch
BB1 . . . . .102 C2
Crosshills 5 BB12 . . . . .146 C1
Crossings The PR5 . . . . . .99 B2
Crossland Rd FY4 . . . . .130 E1
Crossland St BB5 . . . . . .104 A5
Crosslands LA6 . . . . . . .241 D7
Crossley Fold BB11 . . . .127 D4
Crossley House Ind Est
PR1 . . . . .96 E4
Crossways BB7 . . . . . . .189 D7
Croston Ave PR6 . . . . .31 A8
Croston Barn La PR3 . . .181 A8
Croston Cl 6 BB1 . . . . .102 B5
Croston Close Rd BL9,
OL12 . . . . .51 C4
Croston Dr L40 . . . . .39 B6
Croston La PR7 . . . . .42 B2
Croston Rd
Croston L40,PR26 . . . . .39 C7
Farington PR26 . . . . .76 F6
Garstang PR3 . . . . .181 B8
Leyland PR26 . . . . .76 E4
Croston St BB1 . . . . .102 C5
Croston Sta PR26 . . . . . . .58 B3
Croston's Brow PR9 . . . . .53 F3
Crow Foot Row BB18 . . .196 B1
Crow Hills Rd PR1 . . . . . .96 A6
Crow La Ramsbottom BL0 .50 C6
Skelmersdale WN8 . . . . . . .18 F3
Town End PR3 . . . . .155 E8
Crow Orch Prim Sch
WN8 . . . . .17 F2
Crow Orchard Rd WN6 . .29 A1
Crow Park La BB7 . . . . .231 C4
Crow Tree Ave 4 OL13 . . .70 B8
Crow Trees Brow BB7 . .190 D4
Crow Trees Gdns BB7 . .190 D5
Crow Trees La BL7 . . . . . .48 C7
Crow Wood Ave BB12 . . .127 D7
Crow Wood Ct BB12 . . . .127 E7
Crow Wood Rd BB4 . . . . .68 D6
Crow Woods BL0 . . . . . . .68 D5
Crowborough Cl BL6 . . . .32 F1
Crowder Ave FY5 . . . . . .176 B2
Crowell Way PR5 . . . . . . .97 E3
Crowland Cl PR9 . . . . . . .36 A6
Crowland St PR9 . . . . . . .36 A6
Crowland Way L37 . . . . . .12 B2
Crowle St PR1 . . . . .97 D8
Crown Bldgs PR8 . . . . . . .21 F8
Crown Cl L37 . . . . .12 A2
Crown Gdns BL7 . . . . .48 D6
Crown La Fleetwood FY7 .199 B4
Horwich BL6 . . . . .32 A4
Swillbrook PR4 . . . . .136 B2
Crown Mews 3 PR4 . . . .114 A5
Crown Point BL7 . . . . . . .48 D6
Crown Point Rd BB11 . . .127 E1
Crown St Accrington BB5 .104 A5
3 Chorley PR7 . . . . .43 C8
Darwen BB3 . . . . .65 A8
Leyland PR25 . . . . .77 B3
Preston PR1 . . . . .96 F8
Crown Way BB8 . . . . . . .171 C5
Crowndale BL7 . . . . .48 D7
Crownest Ind Est BB18 .196 C3
Crownest Rd BB18 . . . . .196 C3
Crownlee PR1 . . . . .96 A3
Crowshaw Dr OL12 . . . . .52 E3
Crowther Ct BB10 . . . . . .129 B6
Crowther St
Burnley BB11 . . . . .128 B4
Clayton-le-M BB5 . . . . . . .124 E3
Crowthorn Rd BL7 . . . . . .67 A1
Crowtrees 3 LA2 . . . . . .239 B8
Crowtrees Gr BB9 . . . . . .169 F5
Crowtrees Rd BB7 . . . . .145 F8
Croxteth Cl L31 . . . . .5 E3
Croxton Ct PR9 . . . . .53 E1
Croxton Wlk 10 BL6 . . . . .32 B4
Croyde Cl PR9 . . . . .54 B5
Croyde Rd FY8 . . . . .90 A5
Croydon Rd 5 FY3 . . . . .130 E7
Croydon St BB2 . . . . . . .101 C5
Crummock Pl 2 FY4 . . . .131 C1
Crummock Rd PR1 . . . . .119 A1
Crumpax Ave PR3 . . . . .140 A8
Crumpax Cft PR3 . . . . . .140 A8
Crumpax Gdns PR3 . . . .140 A7
Crumpax Mdw PR3 . . . .140 A8
Crystal Gr FY8 . . . . .89 E8
Crystal Lodge 3 FY8 . . . .90 C4
Crystal Mews FY1 . . . . .130 B1
Crystal Rd Blackpool FY1 .130 B1
Thornton FY5 . . . . .176 B5
Cub St PR26 . . . . .77 A4
Cuba Ind Est BL0 . . . . . .50 C8
Cuba St 2 BB9 . . . . .148 D8
Cuckoo Brow BB1 . . . . .101 D8
Cuckoo La Bury BL9 . . . . .33 C2
Bury BL9 . . . . .33 C3
Skitham PR3 . . . . .179 B3
Cuckstool La BB12 . . . . .147 E6
Cudworth Rd FY8 . . . . . .110 F1
Cuerdale La PR5 . . . . . . .98 D6
Cuerdale St BB10 . . . . . .148 E3
Cuerden Ave PR25 . . . . . .59 D7
Cuerden Church Sch PR5 77 F8
Cuerden Cl PR5 . . . . .77 E4
Cuerden Residential Cvn Pk
PR25 . . . . .77 E3
Cuerden Rise PR5 . . . . . .77 C7
Cuerden St Chorley PR6 . .43 E7
Colne BB8 . . . . .171 B3
Cuerden Valley Pk* PR5 .77 F3
Cuerden Way PR5 . . . . . . .77 D7
Culbeck La PR7 . . . . .59 F2
Culshaw St
3 Blackburn BB1 . . . . . . .102 A5
Burnley BB10 . . . . .128 C5
Culshaw Way L40 . . . . . . .23 F7
Culvert La WN8 . . . . .27 A2
Cumberland Ave
Blackpool FY1 . . . . .130 D4
Burnley BB12 . . . . .127 A6
Clayton-le-M BB5 . . . . . . .125 A3
Cleveleys FY5 . . . . .175 E4
Leyland PR25 . . . . .59 E7
Cumberland Cl BB3 . . . . .65 C6
Cumberland Rd PR8 . . . . .35 D5
Cumberland St
12 Blackburn BB1 . . . . . .102 A4
5 Colne BB8 . . . . .171 E5
Nelson BB9 . . . . .170 E1
Cumberland View 2
LA1 . . . . .215 A6
Cumberland View Cl
LA3 . . . . .216 D3
Cumberland View Rd
LA3 . . . . .216 D3
Cumbrian Ave FY3 . . . . .130 E7
Cumbrian Way BB12 . . . .127 B8
Cumeragh La PR3 . . . . .139 C6
Cummins Ave L37 . . . . . . .11 E5
Cumpstey St BB2 . . . . . .101 E3
Cunliffe Ave BL0 . . . . . . .50 A4
Cunliffe Cl BB1 . . . . . . .123 B1
Cunliffe Ct BB5 . . . . . . .124 F2
Cunliffe Ho BB4 . . . . .86 D1
Cunliffe La BB7 . . . . . . .144 F8
Cunliffe Rd
Blackburn BB1 . . . . .123 C1
Blackpool FY1 . . . . .130 D2
Cunliffe St Chorley PR7 . . .43 D7
11 Preston PR1 . . . . .97 A8
Ramsbottom BL0 . . . . .50 C7
Cunnery Mdw PR25 . . . . .77 E1
Cunningham Ave PR7 . . .43 A6
Cunningham Ct LA1 . . . .214 E5
Cunningham Gr BB12 . . .127 B6
Cunscough La L31,L39 . . . .6 D3
Curate St Chorley PR6 . . .61 E1
Great Harwood BB6 . . . . .124 C5
Curlew Cl Blackburn BB1 .101 E8
2 Cleveleys FY5 . . . . . . .175 F4
Leyland PR25 . . . . .59 C7
Oswaldtwistle BB5 . . . . . .103 D3
Curlew Gdns BB11 . . . . .127 C5
Curlew Gr LA3 . . . . .212 F5
Curlew La L40 . . . . .38 E2
Curteis St BL6 . . . . .32 B4
Curtis Dr 1 FY7 . . . . . . .198 D3
Curtis St 8 BB4 . . . . .86 A3
Curve St OL13 . . . . .87 F1
Curven Edge BB4 . . . . . .68 A7
Curwen Ave LA3 . . . . . .212 E6
Curwen La PR3 . . . . .160 C2
Curwen St 7 PR1 . . . . . .118 C1
Curzon Pl BB2 . . . . .101 C3
Curzon Rd
Lytham St Anne's FY8 . . . . .90 A7
Poulton-le-F FY6 . . . . .153 E3
Southport PR8 . . . . .35 E5
Curzon St
10 Burnley BB11 . . . . . . .127 F6
1 Clitheroe BB7 . . . . . . .166 D7
Colne BB8 . . . . .171 E4
Cusson Rd L33 . . . . .1 B1
Custom House La FY7 . .199 C5
Customs Way PR2 . . . . . .96 C8
Cut La Haskayne L39,L40 . .14 F6
Rishton BB1 . . . . .123 F1
Rochdale OL12 . . . . .52 A1
Cutgate Rd OL12 . . . . . . .52 B1
Cutler Cl BB2 . . . . .101 C5
Cutler Cres OL13 . . . . . . .70 D7
Cutler La Bacup OL13 . . . .70 D7
Hesketh Lane PR3 . . . . . .162 C8
Cutt Cl PR26 . . . . .58 F6
Cutts La FY6 . . . . .177 F2
Cyclamen Cl PR25 . . . . . .77 E2
Cygnet Cl L39 . . . . .15 C2
Cygnet Ct L33 . . . . .1 A2
Cypress Ave FY5 . . . . . .175 E2
Cypress Cl
Clayton-le-W PR25 . . . . . . .77 E2
Fulwood PR2 . . . . .119 A4
Cypress Gr
Bamber Bridge PR5 . . . . . . .77 B8
7 Blackpool FY3 . . . . . . .130 D7
Cypress Rd PR8 . . . . .35 F6
Cypress Ridge BB2 . . . . . .80 F1
Cyprus Ave FY8 . . . . .90 B4
Cyprus Rd LA3 . . . . .212 E7
Cyprus St BB3 . . . . .65 B6

D

D'urton La PR2,PR3 . . . . .137 F1
Daffodil Cl Haslingden BB4 68 A8
Rochdale OL12 . . . . .52 E3
Dagger Rd PR4 . . . . .115 C8
Daggers Hall La FY4 . . . .110 E8
Daggers La FY6 . . . . .200 B3
Dahlia Cl Blackburn BB3 . .82 B7
Clayton-le-W PR25 . . . . . . .77 E2
Rochdale OL12 . . . . .52 D3
Dailton Rd WN8 . . . . .10 A7
Daisy Bank 11 Bacup OL13 87 F3
Lancaster LA1 . . . . .215 D7
Daisy Bank Cl PR25 . . . . .76 D1
Daisy Bank Cres BB10 . . .128 E5
Daisy Bank St 18 OL14 . .109 B1
Daisy Croft PR2 . . . . .95 D8
Daisy Fold PR6 . . . . .61 E2
Daisy Hill BB4 . . . . .86 A3
Daisy Hill Dr PR6 . . . . . . .31 A8
Daisy Hill Fold PR7 . . . . .60 D1
Daisy La Blackburn BB1 . .101 F6
Preston PR1 . . . . .118 C3
Ring o'Bells L40 . . . . .26 B4
Daisy Mdw PR5 . . . . .78 B5
Daisy St Blackburn BB1 . .102 A6
Colne BB8 . . . . .171 D4
4 Lancaster LA1 . . . . . . .218 D3
Daisy Wy PR8 . . . . .35 C2
Daisyfield Mill BB1 . . . .102 A5
Daisyfield Prim Sch
BB1 . . . . .102 A6
Daisyfield St BB3 . . . . . . .81 E5
Daisyfields PR4 . . . . . . .116 F7
Dalby Cl Blackpool FY5. . .152 F7
Preston PR1 . . . . .118 D3
Dalby Cres BB2 . . . . . . .101 A1
Dalby Lea BB2 . . . . .101 A1

Dale Ave **1** Euxton PR7 . . . .60 D1
Longton PR4 . . . . .74 E8
Slyne LA2 . . . . .218 C8
Dale CI Burnley BB12 . . . . .127 D6
Maghull L31 . . . . .5 C2
Parbold WN8 . . . . .27 B2
Dale Cres BB2 . . . . .80 E7
Dale Dyke Wlk FY6 . . . . . . .153 B3
Dale La L33 . . . . .1 B4
Dale Mill BB4 . . . . .86 F2
Dale St Accrington BB5 . . . .104 A6
Bacup OL13 . . . . .87 F3
8 Bacup,Stacksteads OL13 70 C8
Blackburn BB1 . . . . .101 D4
Blackpool FY1 . . . . .130 B3
Brierfield BB9 . . . . .148 A5
Burnley BB12 . . . . .127 D6
Colne BB8 . . . . .171 C5
Earby BB18 . . . . .197 B3
Haslingden BB4 . . . . .85 B3
Lancaster LA1 . . . . .215 A4
Nelson BB9 . . . . .148 C8
4 Oswaldtwistle BB5 . . . . .103 E4
Preston PR1 . . . . .97 B8
Ramsbottom BL0 . . . . .68 C1
Dale St E BL6 . . . . .32 D2
Dale St W BL6 . . . . .32 D2
Dale Street Mews **7**
FY1 . . . . .130 B3
Dale Terr BB10 . . . . .190 D5
Dale View Billington BB7 . .144 B4
Blackburn BB2 . . . . .81 E6
Chorley PR7 . . . . .43 C4
Earby BB18 . . . . .197 A1
6 Rawtenstall BB4 . . . . . . .85 F1
Dalecrest WN5 . . . . .10 E1
Daleford CI FY5 . . . . .153 C8
Dalegarth CI FY4 . . . . .131 C1
Dalehead Rd PR25 . . . . .60 B7
Dales Ct FY4 . . . . .110 D6
Dales The BB6 . . . . .123 A8
Dales View Pk Cvn Pk
BB18 . . . . .194 B7
Dales Wlk L37 . . . . .12 A6
Dalesford BB4 . . . . .85 B1
Dalesview Cres LA3 . . . . . .212 F7
Dalesway BB9 . . . . .170 C3
Dalewood Ave FY4 . . . . . . .130 E1
Dalglish Dr BB2 . . . . .81 D7
Dalkeith Ave FY3 . . . . .131 A2
Dalkeith Rd BB9 . . . . .148 C8
Dall St BB11 . . . . .128 A4
Dallam Ave LA4 . . . . .217 C6
Dallam Dell FY5 . . . . .176 B4
Dallas Ct LA4 . . . . .217 F4
Dallas Rd Lancaster LA1 . .214 E7
5 Morecambe LA4 . . . . . .217 F4
Dallas St PR1 . . . . .117 E2
Dalmore Rd PR2 . . . . .117 A3
Dalton Ave FY4 . . . . .110 D5
Dalton CI Blackburn BB1 . .102 B5
Ramsbottom BL0 . . . . .50 A4
Dalton La LA6 . . . . .240 C7
Dalton Rd Lancaster LA1 . .215 A8
Morecambe LA3 . . . . .216 D3
Dalton Sq LA1 . . . . .214 F8
Dalton St Burnley BB10 . . .127 D3
Lytham St Anne's FY8 . . . . .89 D4
Nelson BB9 . . . . .170 E1
Dalton St Michael's CE Prim
Sch WN8 . . . . .18 D5
Dalweb Ind Pk PR9 . . . . . . .55 C3
Dam Head Rd BB18 . . . . . .196 B2
Dam La L40 . . . . .24 C6
Dam Side
2 Barnoldswick BB18 . . .196 B3
Colne BB8 . . . . .171 D4
Dam Top BB4 . . . . .86 B2
Dam Wood La L40 . . . . .24 C5
Dame Fold Higham BB12 . .146 F6
12 Padiham BB12 . . . . . . .126 C8
Damfield La L31 . . . . .5 C1
Damside Cotts LA2 . . . . . . .211 B5
Damside St LA1 . . . . .214 F8
Damsom CI BB6 . . . . .143 C6
Danbers WN8 . . . . .9 F6
Dancer La BB7 . . . . .231 B1
Dandy Row BB3 . . . . .82 C3
Dandy Wlk BB1 . . . . .101 E4
Dandy's Meanygate PR4 .56 A8
Dane Mews FY6 . . . . .131 E8
Dane St BB10 . . . . .128 A7
Danes Ct PR4 . . . . .114 C5
Danes Dr PR5 . . . . .97 D1
Danesbury PI **4** FY1 . . . .130 C5
Daneshouse Rd BB10 . . . .128 A8
Danesmoor Dr BB9 . . . . . . .33 B4
Danesway Adlington PR7 . .43 F1
Bamber Bridge PR5 . . . . . . .97 D1
Higher Penwortham PR1 . . .96 A4
Daneswood Ave OL12 . . . . .52 C8
Daneswood CI OL12 . . . . . .52 C8
Daneway PR8 . . . . .21 B6
Danewerke St **9** PR1 . . . .97 A8
Daniel Fold CI 52 B2
Daniel Fold La PR3 . . . . . .181 D2
Daniel St
10 Clayton-le-M BB5 . . . .124 F3
Whitworth OL12 . . . . .71 D2
Daniell St BB1 . . . . .124 A1
Daniels La WN5 . . . . .9 C7
Danson Gdns **3** FY2 . . . .130 E8
Danvers St BB1 . . . . .124 B2
Daram Ho **3** FY1 . . . . . . .130 D2
Darbishire Rd PR7 . . . . . . .198 F4

Daresbury Ave PR8 . . . . . . .21 A5
Darfield WN8 . . . . .9 F7
Dark La Blackrod BL6 . . . . .31 B3
Earby BB18 . . . . .197 E2
Johnson's Hillock PR6 . . . . .61 E6
Maghull L31 . . . . .5 E1
Mawdesley L40 . . . . .40 E3
Newchurch BB4 . . . . .86 E1
Ormskirk L40 . . . . .16 C6
Dark Wood La PR5 . . . . . . .99 B6
Darkinson La
Lea Town PR4 . . . . .115 F1
Preston PR4 . . . . .116 F1
Darkwood Cres BB7 . . . . . .190 D5
Darley Ave FY4 . . . . .110 E7
Darley Ct BB7 . . . . .89 D7
Darley St BL6 . . . . .32 E5
Darlington Ct PR7 . . . . .42 D4
Darlington St PR7 . . . . .42 E1
Darmond Rd L33 . . . . .1 A3
Darnbrook Rd BB18 . . . . . .196 A2
Darnhill Com Sch OL10 . . .33 F1
Darnley St BB10 . . . . .128 C5
Dart St PR2 . . . . .96 C8
Dartford CI **1** BB1 . . . . . .102 A4
Dartmouth CI PR4 . . . . .113 F5
Darululoom Islamia BL8 . .49 F1
Darwen CI PR3 . . . . .140 B7
Darwen Ent Ctr BB3 . . . . . .82 A3
Darwen L Ctr BB3 . . . . .82 A1
Darwen Moorland High Sch
BB3 .82 B3
Darwen Rd BL7 . . . . .47 C1
Darwen St Blackburn BB2 101 E4
Higher Walton PR5 . . . . .98 B4
2 Padiham BB12 . . . . . . .126 C8
Preston PR1 . . . . .97 C7
Darwen St Barnabas CE Prim
Sch BB3 . . . . .65 C6
Darwen St Peter's CE Prim
Sch BB3 . . . . .65 B8
Darwen Sta BB3 . . . . .82 A1
Darwen Vale High Sch
BB3 .81 E5
Darwen View PR5 . . . . .97 E5
Darwin Ct PR9 . . . . .53 E1
Darwin St BB10 . . . . .148 A2
Daub Hall La PR5 . . . . .98 E3
Daub La L40 . . . . .40 A1
Dauntesey Ave FY3 . . . . . .131 A6
Davenham Rd
Darwen BB3 . . . . .81 E3
Formby L37 . . . . .11 F3
Davenport Ave FY2 . . . . . .152 C5
Daventry Ave FY2 . . . . . . .152 B4
David Crosley Ho **2**
BB18 . . . . .196 B2
David St Bacup OL13 . . . . . .70 D8
11 Barrowford BB9 . . . . . .170 D4
Burnley BB11 . . . . .127 F4
16 Rochdale OL12 . . . . . . .52 F1
David St N **15** OL12 . . . . . .52 F1
Davidson St **15** LA1 . . . . .215 A8
Davies Rd BB1 . . . . .102 D6
Davis St PR3 . . . . .140 A8
Davitt CI **4** BB4 . . . . .85 B3
Davy Field Brow BB1 . . . . .82 B6
Davy Field Rd BB1 . . . . . . .82 B6
Dawber Delph WN6 . . . . . . .19 D8
Dawber's La PR7 . . . . .59 E2
Dawlish Ave FY3 . . . . .130 F8
Dawlish CI BB2 . . . . .81 C8
Dawlish Dr PR9 . . . . .54 A5
Dawlish Lodge FY8 . . . . . . .89 D7
Dawlish PI PR2 . . . . .117 A3
Dawnay Rd PR2 . . . . .118 E3
Dawson Ave
Simonstone BB12 . . . . .145 E2
Southport PR9 . . . . .54 C5
Dawson Gdns L31 . . . . .5 C2
Dawson La PR6,PR7,PR25 .60 E7
Dawson PI PR5 . . . . .78 A7
Dawson Rd
Lytham St Anne's FY8 . . . . .110 F1
Ormskirk L39 . . . . .15 F1
Dawson Sq BB11 . . . . .128 A4
Dawson St BL9 . . . . .33 A4
Dawson Wlk PR1 . . . . .117 F1
Day St BB9 . . . . .148 E1
Daybrook WN8 . . . . .9 F7
Dayfield WN8 . . . . .10 B7
Dayton PI FY4 . . . . .110 C6
De Lacy Ho BB2 . . . . .101 C5
De Lacy St Clitheroe BB7 .166 D8
Preston PR2 . . . . .117 D2
De Vitre Cotts LA1 . . . . . . .214 E4
De Vitre St **7** LA1 . . . . . . .218 E1
De-Haviland Way WN8 . . . .9 F8
Deakin's Terr BL7 . . . . .46 C5
Deakins Bsns Pk BL7 . . . . .47 D1
Deal PI FY8 . . . . .110 F1
Deal St Blackburn BB1 . . . .101 F4
9 Bury BL9 . . . . .33 B2
Dean Brow PR3 . . . . .141 F8
Dean CI Edenfield BL0 . . . . .68 D3
Skelmersdale WN8 . . . . .10 C7
Dean Ct FY7 . . . . .175 D8
Dean Edge Rd BD22 . . . . .174 F1
Dean Fold BB4 . . . . .87 B4
Dean Hall La PR7 . . . . .59 D2
Dean Head La BL6 . . . . .45 A4
Dean La
Billington BB6,BB7 . . . . . . .144 C1
Samlesbury PR5 . . . . .119 F3
Tockholes BB3 . . . . .81 B1
Water BB4 . . . . .87 B8
Dean Mdw **5** BB7 . . . . . .166 D7
Dean Mill BB11 . . . . .128 A5

Dean Rd BB4 . . . . .85 B1
Dean St
Bamber Bridge PR5 . . . . . . .97 E1
Blackpool FY4 . . . . .110 B8
Burnley BB11 . . . . .127 E6
Darwen BB3 . . . . .81 F4
2 Padiham BB12 . . . . . . .146 D1
Trawden BB8 . . . . .172 C2
Dean Terr **4** PR4 . . . . . . .114 A5
Dean Wood Ave WN5 . . . . .10 E8
Dean Wood CI PR7 . . . . . . .43 A6
Deancroft LA3 . . . . .216 E2
Deanfield BB7 . . . . .190 B2
Deanfield St BB7 . . . . .190 A2
Deanpoint LA3 . . . . .217 C3
Deans Ct L37 . . . . .11 F5
Deans La L40,WN8 . . . . . . .26 E3
Deansgate Blackpool FY1 .130 B5
Morecambe LA4 . . . . .217 B5
Deansgate La L37 . . . . .12 B5
Deansgate La N L37 . . . . . .12 A6
Deansgrave BB4 . . . . .85 B1
Deansgreave Rd OL13 . . . .71 B7
Dearden Clough **1** BL0 . .68 E2
Dearden Fold BL0 . . . . .68 E2
Dearden Nook BB4 . . . . . . .86 A1
Dearden Way WN8 . . . . .10 A7
Deardengate BB4 . . . . .85 B3
Deardengate Croft **11**
BB4 .85 B3
Deben CI WN6 . . . . .29 D1
Deborah Ave PR2 . . . . .118 A7
Dee Rd LA1 . . . . .218 B2
Dee St FY8 . . . . .89 E6
Dee St Cott **5** FY8 . . . . . .89 E6
Deepdale Ave FY6 . . . . . . .153 B5
Deepdale Ct BB9 . . . . .170 C3
Deepdale Dr BB10 . . . . . . .148 C4
Deepdale Gn BB9 . . . . .170 C3
Deepdale Ho **5** PR1 . . . . .118 B1
Deepdale Inf Sch PR1 . . . .118 B2
Deepdale Jun Sch PR1 . . .118 B2
Deepdale La PR4 . . . . .115 C3
Deepdale Mill PR1 . . . . . . .118 B1
Deepdale Mill St PR1 . . . .118 B1
Deepdale Rd
Blackpool FY4 . . . . .131 C1
Fleetwood FY7 . . . . .199 A3
Preston PR1 . . . . .118 B2
Deepdale Sh Pk PR1 . . . . .118 C3
Deepdale St **8** PR1 . . . . . .97 B8
Deeply Vale La BL9 . . . . . . .51 C2
Deer Chace BB12 . . . . .147 D8
Deer Park La LA2 . . . . .238 B7
Deer Park Rd BB10 . . . . . .128 C4
Deer Pk BB5 . . . . .104 E8
Deerfold PR7 . . . . .61 B2
Deerhurst Rd FY5 . . . . .152 E7
Deerplay CI BB10 . . . . .148 E2
Deerplay Dr OL13 . . . . .88 A8
Deerstone Ave BB10 . . . . .128 C6
Deerstone Rd BB9 . . . . . . .149 B8
Deeside FY4 . . . . .110 E5
Deganwy Ave BB1 . . . . . . .101 E7
Deighton Ave **6** PR25 . . . .60 A8
Deighton CI WN5 . . . . .10 E5
Deighton Rd PR7 . . . . .43 B6
Delamere Ave LA3 . . . . . . .212 E6
Delamere CI
Accrington BB5 . . . . .125 B1
Blackburn BB2 . . . . .101 B2
Delamere PI PR6 . . . . .43 D8
Delamere Rd
Brierfield BB10 . . . . .148 F3
Skelmersdale WN8 . . . . .17 F2
Southport PR8 . . . . .21 B5
Delamere St BB3 . . . . .33 A5
Delamere Way WN8 . . . . . .10 A7
Delany Dr PR4 . . . . .93 A6
Delaware Rd **8** FY3 . . . . .152 E1
Delaware St PR1 . . . . .118 D1
Delf La Haskayne L39 . . . . .14 A4
Shore OL14 . . . . .109 C3
Delfby Cres L32 . . . . .1 A1
Delius CI BB2 . . . . .102 A1
Dell Gdns OL12 . . . . .52 B2
Dell La **4** BB12 . . . . .126 C4
Dell Mdw OL12 . . . . .52 C5
Dell Rd OL12 . . . . .52 B3
Dell Side Way OL12 . . . . . .52 C2
Dell The
Appley Bridge WN6 . . . . . . .19 D7
Blackburn BB2 . . . . .81 D6
Fulwood PR2 . . . . .117 D7
Knowley PR6 . . . . .62 A3
Skelmersdale WN8 . . . . .10 B7
Horwich BL6 . . . . .32 C1
Wrea Green PR4 . . . . .113 B3
Dellar St **1** OL12 . . . . .52 C1
Dellfield La L31 . . . . .5 E1
Dellway The PR4 . . . . .95 D2
Delma Rd BB10 . . . . .128 C5
Delph App BB1 . . . . .102 C4
Delph Ave BB7 . . . . .47 D3
Delph Brook Way BL7 . . . .47 D2
Delph CI Blackburn BB1 . .102 C4
Ormskirk L39 . . . . .15 C1
Delph Common Rd L39 . . .15 C1
Delph Ct **3** BB6 . . . . .124 C5
Delph Dr L40 . . . . .25 F4
Delph La Blackburn BB1 . .102 C3
Blackburn BB1 . . . . .102 C4
Charnock Green PR7 . . . . . .42 D6
Coppull PR7 . . . . .42 E5
Formby L37 . . . . .11 C3
Garstang PR3 . . . . .181 B7
Oakenclough PR3 . . . . .183 B7
Ormskirk L39 . . . . .15 C1
Delph Lane Est BB1 . . . . . .102 C4

Delph Mount
Great Harwood BB6 . . . . . .124 B6
Haslingden BB4 . . . . .85 B4
Delph Park Ave L39 . . . . . .15 D6
Delph Rd BB6 . . . . .124 B6
Delph Side Com Prim Sch
WN8 .9 C8
Delph St Darwen BB3 . . . . .82 B3
Haslingden BB4 . . . . .85 B4
Delph The WN8 . . . . .27 C3
Delph Top L39 . . . . .16 A6
Delph Way PR6 . . . . .61 C7
Delphene Ave FY5 . . . . . . .152 D6
Delphinium Way BB3 . . . . .82 A7
Delphside CI WN5 . . . . .10 D5
Delphside Rd WN5 . . . . . . .10 D5
Delta La **2** FY7 . . . . .199 A4
Delta Park Ave PR4 . . . . . .73 E4
Delta Park Dr PR4 . . . . .73 E4
Deltic Way L33 . . . . .1 B1
Delves La BB3 . . . . .149 E2
Demming CI PR2 . . . . .95 C8
Denbigh Ave
Cleveleys FY5 . . . . .175 E1
Southport PR9 . . . . .53 F3
Denbigh Dr PR25 . . . . .77 B1
Denbigh Dr BB7 . . . . .189 F2
Denbigh Gr BB7 . . . . .127 A7
Denby CI PR5 . . . . .97 C3
Dene Bank Rd BB5 . . . . . .103 E3
Dene The Blackburn BB2 . .101 B7
Hurst Green BB7 . . . . .142 E8
Denebank **7** 152 D5
Denefield Ho PR8 . . . . .35 B6
Deneway Ave FY3 . . . . . . .130 F6
Denford Ave Leyland PR25 60 D8
Lytham St Anne's FY8 . . . . .90 A4
Denham La PR6 . . . . .78 E2
Denham Way FY7 . . . . .198 F2
Denham Wood Way PR7 .42 F6
Denholme WN8 . . . . .9 F7
Denholme Gr FY2 . . . . .152 E5
Denis St LA1 . . . . .215 A8
Denmark Rd
Lytham St Anne's FY8 . . . . .90 D4
Southport PR9 . . . . .54 A2
Denmark St LA1 . . . . .214 D7
Dennis Gr LA4 . . . . .217 A4
Denny Ave LA1 . . . . .218 C2
Denny Bank LA2 . . . . .219 C5
Denny Beck La LA2 . . . . . .219 C5
Denshaw WN8 . . . . .9 F7
Denstone Ave FY2 . . . . . . .152 D4
Dent Dale BB5 . . . . .104 D5
Dent Row **8** BB11 . . . . . .127 F5
Dent St BB8 . . . . .171 B3
Denton St
Barnoldswick BB18 . . . . . .196 A3
7 Rochdale OL12 . . . . . . .52 F1
Denville Ave FY5 . . . . .152 F8
Denville Rd
Blackburn BB2 . . . . .101 D5
Preston PR1 . . . . .118 C1
Denville St **5** BB2 . . . . . .101 D5
Depot Rd Blackpool FY3 . .152 E1
Kirkby L33 . . . . .1 D4
Derbe Rd FY8 . . . . .89 F5
Derby CI BB3 . . . . .65 B5
Derby Cres PR4 . . . . .135 C8
Derby Ct L37 . . . . .11 E5
Derby Hill PR4 . . . . .133 A1
Derby Hill Cres L39 . . . . . .16 A5
Derby Hill Rd L39 . . . . .16 A5
Derby Ho Kirkham PR4 . . .114 A6
6 Lancaster LA1 . . . . . . .218 D1
Derby PI PR6 . . . . .31 A8
Derby Rd Blackpool FY1 . .130 B7
Cleveleys FY5 . . . . .175 C3
Formby L37 . . . . .11 E5
Fulwood PR2 . . . . .117 E5
Garstang PR3 . . . . .181 B7
Kirkham PR4 . . . . .114 A6
Lancaster LA1 . . . . .218 D1
Longridge PR3 . . . . .140 A7
Lytham St Anne's FY8 . . . . .90 C5
Poulton-le-F FY6 . . . . .153 D4
Skelmersdale WN8 . . . . .8 C8
Southport PR9 . . . . .35 C7
Derby Sq PR1 . . . . .97 D8
Derby St Accrington BB5 . .104 C6
Blackburn BB1 . . . . .102 A6
Brinscall PR6 . . . . .63 A8
Burnley BB11 . . . . .127 F5
Clitheroe BB7 . . . . .166 F8
Colne BB8 . . . . .171 D5
Horwich BL6 . . . . .32 C1
Leyland PR25 . . . . .77 B2
Morecambe LA4 . . . . .217 A5
Nelson BB9 . . . . .170 E1
Ormskirk L39 . . . . .15 F5
Preston PR1 . . . . .97 A8
Ramsbottom BL0 . . . . .50 D6
Rishton BB1 . . . . .124 C1
Derby St W L39 . . . . .15 E5
Derbyshire Almshouses The
BB2 . . . . .101 B6
Derbyshire Ave PR3 . . . . . .181 B8
Derek Rd PR6 . . . . .78 C1
Derham St BB2 . . . . .101 E3
Derry Rd PR2 . . . . .118 E3
Dertern La LA5 . . . . .221 A7
Derwent Ave
Burnley BB9 . . . . .148 A2
Fleetwood FY7 . . . . .198 D2
Formby L37 . . . . .11 D2
Morecambe LA4 . . . . .217 C5
Padiham BB12 . . . . .146 C2
Southport PR9 . . . . .53 F1

Derwent CI Colne BB8 . . . .172 A6
Darwen BB3 . . . . .82 C1
Freckleton PR4 . . . . .93 A6
Haslingden BB4 . . . . .85 B4
Horwich BL6 . . . . .32 C2
Knott End-on-S FY6 . . . . . .199 F6
Maghull L31 . . . . .5 F2
Rishton BB1 . . . . .123 F1
Derwent Cres BB7 . . . . . . .166 C7
Derwent Ct LA1 . . . . .218 A2
Derwent Dr
Freckleton PR4 . . . . .93 A6
Longridge PR3 . . . . .139 F5
Derwent Hall **3** PR1 . . . .117 E1
Derwent Ho **9** PR1 . . . . . .97 D8
Derwent PI
Blackpool FY5 . . . . .152 D8
Poulton-le-F FY6 . . . . .153 D1
Derwent Rd Chorley PR7 . . .43 C5
Lancaster LA1 . . . . .215 B8
Lytham St Anne's FY8 . . . . .111 A1
Orrell WN5 . . . . .10 F8
Derwent St
6 Darwen BB3 . . . . .81 F2
11 Rochdale OL12 . . . . . .52 F1
Derwentwater PI PR1 . . . .117 F2
Dever Ave PR25 . . . . .76 D1
Devere Gdns FY8 . . . . .89 E6
Devon Ave
Fleetwood FY7 . . . . .198 E3
Oswaldtwistle BB5 . . . . . . .103 B6
Skelmersdale WN8 . . . . .10 B6
Devon CI PR5 . . . . .97 D3
Devon Cres BB4 . . . . .68 B8
Devon Dr WN1 . . . . .30 B1
Devon Farm Way L37 . . . . .12 B3
Devon Gr BB12 . . . . .127 A7
Devon PI **1** Church BB5 . .103 E5
Lancaster LA1 . . . . .215 A4
Devon Rd BB1 . . . . .102 C5
Devon St Blackpool FY4 . .130 D1
Colne BB8 . . . . .171 E6
Darwen BB3 . . . . .65 B6
Devona Ave FY4 . . . . .131 B1
Devonport CI PR5 . . . . .97 E3
Devonport Rd BB2 . . . . . . .101 C5
Devonport Way PR6 . . . . . .43 E8
Devonshire Ave FY5 . . . . .176 B2
Devonshire Ct
9 Blackpool FY3 . . . . . .130 D7
17 Chorley PR7 . . . . .43 C8
Devonshire Dr
Clayton-le-M BB5 . . . . .125 A3
Garstang PR3 . . . . .181 B8
Devonshire Ho FY3 . . . . . .130 D6
Devonshire Jun Sch
FY3 . . . . .131 A7
Devonshire Mews FY3 . . .176 B1
Devonshire PI PR1 . . . . . . .118 C1
Devonshire Prim Sch
FY3 . . . . .130 D6
Devonshire Rd
Blackpool FY2 . . . . .152 D6
Burnley BB10 . . . . .128 A8
Chorley PR7 . . . . .43 C7
Fulwood PR2 . . . . .118 A4
Lytham St Anne's FY8 . . . . .89 D7
Morecambe LA3 . . . . .216 F3
Rishton BB1 . . . . .124 A1
Southport PR9 . . . . .36 A4
Devonshire Road Hospl
FY1 . . . . .130 D7
Devonshire Sq FY3 . . . . . .130 D5
Devonshire Square Mews **5**
FY3 . . . . .130 D5
Devonshire St
Accrington BB5 . . . . .104 B7
Lancaster LA1 . . . . .214 F5
Devron Mill BB6 . . . . .124 D4
Dew Forest BB3 . . . . .181 D4
Dew Meadow CI OL12 . . . .52 E2
Dewberry Fields WN8 . . . .10 B7
Dewhirst Rd OL12 . . . . .52 F4
Dewhirst Way OL12 . . . . . .52 F4
Dewhurst Ave FY4 . . . . . . .110 E8
Dewhurst CI BB3 . . . . .65 C6
Dewhurst Clough Rd BL7 47 D2
Dewhurst Ct BL7 . . . . .47 D3
Dewhurst Ind Est PR2 . . . .117 D1
Dewhurst Rd BB6 . . . . .142 F1
Dewhurst Row PR5 . . . . . . .77 D2
Dewhurst St
Blackburn BB1 . . . . .102 A4
Colne BB8 . . . . .171 D4
Darwen BB3 . . . . .65 B6
Preston PR1 . . . . .117 D1
Dexter Way WN8 . . . . .10 B6
Deycroft Ave L33 . . . . .1 A4
Deycroft Wlk L33 . . . . .1 A4
Deyes Ct L31 . . . . .5 E1
Deyes End L31 . . . . .5 E1
Deyes High Sch L31 . . . . . . .5 D1
Deyes La Maghull L31 . . . . . .5 D1
Maghull,Moss Side L31 . . . . .5 F1
Diamond Jubilee Rd L40 .39 C4
Diana Ct **10** LA1 . . . . .214 F7
Dianne Rd FY5 . . . . .176 D2
Dib Rd BB5 . . . . .73 B5
Dibbs Pocket PR4 . . . . .93 D7
Dicconson Terr **6** FY6 . . .91 B3
Dicconson Way L39 . . . . . .16 A5
Dicconson's La L39 . . . . . .14 D4
Dick La PR6 . . . . .62 E7
Dick's La L40 . . . . .16 F4
Dickens Ave BB18 . . . . . . .196 A3
Dickens Rd PR7 . . . . .29 E8
Dickens St BB1 . . . . .102 A3
Dickensons Field **3** PR1 .96 E2

Dicket's La WN8 ....17 A2
Dickie's La FY4 ....111 B7
Dickie's La S FY4 ....111 C6
Dickinson Cl
  Blackburn BB2 ....101 C3
  Formby L37 ....11 F2
Dickinson Ct
  ■ Horwich BL6 ....32 B4
  Southport PR8 ....35 A2
Dickinson Rd L37 ....11 F2
Dickinson St BB2 ....101 D3
Dickinson St W BL6 ......32 B4
Dickson Ave PR1 ....118 D2
Dickson Hey PR4 ....75 F8
Dickson Rd FY1 ....130 B7
Dickson St Burnley BB12 .127 C6
  Colne BB8 ....171 E6
  ■ Preston PR1 ....97 B7
Didsbury St BB1 ....102 C5
Digham Ave FY5 ....152 D6
Digmoor Dr WN8 ....9 C7
Digmoor Rd WN8 ....9 D6
Dill Hall La BB5 ....103 F7
Dilworth Bottoms PR3 ..141 A8
Dilworth Ct PR3 ....140 C7
Dilworth La PR3 ....140 C7
Dimmock St BB2 ....101 C2
Dimple Pk BL7 ....47 D3
Dimple Rd BL7 ....47 C6
Dimples La PR3 ....181 E5
Dinckley Gr FY1 ....130 D3
Dinckley Sq BB2 ....101 B6
Dinely St PR8 ....103 F6
Dingle Ave
  Appley Bridge WN6 ......19 E8
  Blackpool FY3 ....130 F8
  Skelmersdale WN8 ....10 C8
Dingle Cl L39 ....15 C1
Dingle Rd WN8 ....10 B7
Dingle The Fulwood PR2 .117 D7
  Knowley PR6 ....62 A3
Dinmore Ave FY3 ....131 A8
Dinmore Pl FY3 ....131 A7
Dinorwic Rd PR8 ....35 A2
Dirty Leech OL12 ....52 F6
Disraeli St BB10 ....148 A2
Ditchfield L37 ....12 A2
Division La FY4 ....111 C3
Dixey St BL6 ....32 A3
Dixon Rd PR3 ....140 B7
Dixon St Barrowford BB9 170 C3
  Blackburn BB2 ....101 C4
  Horwich BL6 ....32 B3
Dixon's Farm Mews
  PR4 ....115 D1
Dixons La PR2 ....139 C2
Doals Gate OL13 ....88 A8
Dob Brow PR7 ....42 F4
Dob La PR4 ....75 A4
Dobbin Cl BB4 ....86 C2
Dobbin Gate BB4 ....86 C2
Dobbin La BB4 ....86 C2
Dobbs Dr L37 ....12 A4
Dobson Ave FY8 ....89 E8
Dobson Cl WN6 ....28 E2
Dobson Rd FY3 ....131 B7
Dobson St ■ BB3 ....81 F2
Dobson's La FY6 ....177 E6
Dock Rd FY8 ....91 D4
Dock St Blackburn BB1 ..102 A5
  Fleetwood FY7 ....199 B4
Docker La LA6 ....241 C5
Docker Park Farm★
  LA6 ....241 A4
Dockinsall La PR3 .....178 D3
Dockray Ct ■ BB8 .....171 E5
Dockray St BB8 ....171 E5
Dockray Yd ■ BB8 ....171 E5
Docky Pool La FY4 ....111 A6
Doctor's La Eccleston PR7 .41 B6
  Great Altcar L37 ....12 E2
  Sollom PR4 ....56 F3
Doctors Row PR3 ......140 A6
Dodd Way PR5 ....78 A6
Dodd's La L31 ....5 D2
Dodgeons Cl FY6 ......153 C2
Dodgson La BB18 .....197 F2
Dodgson Pl PR1 ......118 C1
Dodgson Rd PR1 .....118 C1
Dodney Dr PR2 ....116 C1
Dodworth Ave PR8 .....35 E5
Doe Mdw WN8 ....27 A1
Doeholme Rake LA2 ...232 F1
Dog Pits La OL13 ......88 A6
Dole La Abbey Village PR6 .80 C1
  Chorley PR7 ....43 C8
Doles La PR26 ....58 A7
Dolls House & Fleetwood
  Mus The★ FY7 ....199 C5
Dolly's La PR9 ....36 F3
Dolphinholme CE Prim Sch
  LA2 ....226 A8
Dolphinholme Mill LA2 .226 A8
Dombey St
  Blackburn BB1 ....102 A3
  Blackburn BB1 ....102 A4
Dominica Ave BB3 ......81 F6
Dominion Ct BB11 .....127 B4
Dominion Rd BB2 .....101 C8
Don St FY8 ....89 E7
Doncaster Rd FY3 ......89 E7
Donnington Lodge PR8 .34 F6
Donnington Rd
  Carleton FY6 ....153 C6
  Lytham St Anne's FY8 ..89 F7
Donshort Mews ■ BB9 .170 C1
Doodstone Ave PR5 ....97 B1

Doodstone Cl PR5 ....97 B1
Doodstone Dr PR5 ......97 B1
Doodstone Nook PR5 ...97 B1
Dora St BL0 ....50 A4
Dorchester Ave BB5 ...103 C4
Dorchester Cl
  Blackburn BB1 ....102 B3
  Thornton FY5 ....153 C8
Dorchester Dr L33 ......1 C1
Dorchester Gdns LA3 ..217 C2
Dorchester Rd
  Blackpool FY1 ....130 B8
  Garstang PR3 ....181 B8
  Skelmersdale WN8 .....10 A7
Doric Gn WN5 ....10 D1
Doris Henderson Way
  LA1 ....217 F1
Doris St Burnley BB11 .128 B7
  Chorley PR6 ....61 D1
Dorking Rd PR6 ....61 F4
Dorman Rd PR2 ....118 E3
Dorothy Ave ■ PR25 ...77 A1
Dorothy St Blackburn BB2 .81 C8
  ■ Ramsbottom BL0 .....50 B5
Dorrington Rd LA1 ....214 F5
Dorritt Rd FY4 ....110 E6
Dorritt St ■ BB1 ......102 A4
Dorset Ave
  ■ Bamber Bridge PR5 ..97 D3
  Cleveleys FY5 ....175 D4
  Darwen BB3 ....81 F3
  Padiham BB12 ....126 D7
  Southport PR8 ....21 C2
Dorset Dr Blackburn BB1 .102 E4
  Clitheroe BB7 ....189 F2
  Haslingden BB4 ....68 A8
Dorset Rd
  Lytham St Anne's FY8 ..89 E8
  Preston PR1 ....118 A1
  Rishton BB1 ....124 A1
  Standish WN1 ....30 B1
Dorset St
  ■ Blackpool FY4 ......130 D1
  Burnley BB12 ....127 A6
Dotcliffe Rd BB18 .....195 A6
Double Row ■ BB12 ...126 B8
Doughty St BB8 ......171 D4
Douglas Ave
  Becconsall PR4 ....73 F1
  Blackpool FY3 ....130 D7
  ■ Heysham LA3 ......212 F7
  Horwich BL6 ....32 C5
  Skelmersdale WN8 .....10 B7
  Stalmine FY7 ....177 C7
Douglas Cl
  Bamber Bridge PR5 ....77 F7
  Blackburn BB2 ....81 D7
  Horwich BL6 ....32 C5
  Rufford L40 ....39 C3
Douglas Ct Fulwood PR2 .117 D3
  Southport PR8 ....21 C2
Douglas Dr Freckleton PR4 93 B6
  Heysham LA3 ....212 F7
  Maghull L31 ....5 F7
  Ormskirk L39 ....15 D7
  Orrell WN5 ....10 F7
  Shevington WN6 ......19 F5
Douglas Gr BB3 ....81 D4
Douglas Hall ■ PR1 ...117 E1
Douglas Ho PR7 ....43 D5
Douglas La PR3 ......139 D1
Douglas Leatham Ho ■
  FY1 ....130 D3
Douglas Pl
  Blackburn BB1 ....122 F1
  Fleetwood FY7 ....198 D3
Douglas Rd Bacup OL13 .88 A1
  Brierfield BB10 ....149 A3
  Fulwood PR2 ....117 D3
  Shevington Moor WN6 ..29 A2
  Southport PR9 ....54 C4
Douglas Rd N PR2 ....117 D3
Douglas Sq ■ OL10 ....33 F1
Douglas St Colne BB8 ..171 E6
  Lytham St Anne's FY8 ..89 D6
  Preston PR2 ....96 C8
  Ramsbottom BL0 ......50 B5
Douglas Way BB10 ....149 A3
Doultons The PR5 .....97 C3
Dove Ave ■ PR1 ....96 E4
Dove Cl ■ FY5 ....175 F1
Dove Dr BL9 ....33 B4
Dove La BB3 ....81 F2
Dove St
  Lytham St Anne's FY8 ..89 D6
  Preston PR1 ....118 D1
Dove Tree Ct FY4 ....131 B1
Dovecote PR6 ....78 A3
Dovedale Ave
  Blackpool FY3 ....131 C2
  Fulwood PR2 ....117 A5
  Maghull L31 ....5 C2
  Thornton FY5 ....176 B3
Dovedale Cl
  Brierfield BB10 ......148 C4
  Fulwood PR2 ....117 A4
  Leyland PR25 ....60 A6
Dovedale Dr
  Burnley BB12 ....127 C6
  Standish WN6 ....29 E2
Dovedale Gdns PR3 ...140 B6
Dover Cl Blackburn BB1 .102 C4
  Ramsbottom BL8 ......50 A1
  Warton PR4 ....92 E7
Dover Ct FY1 ....130 D2
Dover Gdns FY1 ......153 B5
Dover La PR5,PR6 ......79 C8
Dover Rd Blackpool FY1 .130 E2

Dover Rd continued
  Lytham St Anne's FY8 ...89 F8
  Southport PR8 ....34 F2
Dover St Accrington BB5 .104 A4
  Blackburn BB3 ....81 F7
  Nelson BB9 ....170 E1
Dovestone Dr FY6 ....153 B3
Dovetree Cl PR5 ....97 A3
Dowbridge PR4 ....114 C4
Dowbridge Way PR4 ..114 C5
Downes Gr LA4 ......217 D4
Downeyfield Rd LA3 ..213 C3
Downfield Cl BL0 ......50 B6
Downham Ave
  Great Harwood BB6 ...124 F6
  Rawtenstall BB4 ......69 E5
Downham Cotts ■ LA2 .211 A4
Downham Dr BB5 .....104 A3
Downham Pl BB5 .....128 D5
Downham Pl
  Lytham St Anne's FY8 ..90 C5
  ■ Preston PR2 ....116 E2
Downham Rd
  Chatburn BB7 ....190 E5
  Leyland PR25 ....76 D1
Downham St BB2 .....101 C4
Downham Wlk WN5 ....10 D1
Downholland Moss La
  L37 ....12 C4
Downholland-Haskayne CE
  Prim Sch L39 ....13 E3
Downing Ct PR3 ......137 C3
Downing St PR1 ....97 E8
Downley Cl OL12 ......52 B2
Downs The FY6 ....153 D4
Dowry St BB5 ....104 C6
Dragon Cl WN8 ....9 E8
Dragon St ■ BB12 ...126 C8
Drake Cl
  Lytham St Anne's FY8 .110 E1
  Ormskirk L39 ....15 C2
Drakelowe Ave FY4 ..110 F6
Drakes Croft PR2 .....117 C3
Drakes Hollow PR5 ....97 D4
Drammen Ave BB11 ...127 B5
Draperfield PR7 ....43 A4
Drapers Ave PR7 ......41 C6
Draw Well Rd L33 ......1 D2
Draycombe La E FY4 ..110 D2
Draycombe Dr LA3 ...216 E2
Draycot Ave FY3 ....130 F8
Drayton Rd LA3 .....213 A7
Drew St BB11 ....127 B5
Drewitt Cres PR9 .....54 D4
Drewton Ave LA3 ....216 D2
Drinkhouse La PR26 ...58 A1
Drinkhouse Rd PR26 ..58 B1
Driscoll St ■ PR1 ....97 D8
Drive The Bacup OL13 ..87 F2
  Brockhall Village BB6 .143 C5
  Carnforth LA5 ....223 A1
  Edenfield BL0 ....68 D3
  Fulwood PR2 ....118 B4
  Hest Bank LA2 ......220 E1
  Heysham LA3 ....212 F7
  Longton PR4 ....75 A8
  Walton-le-D PR5 ......97 F5
Driver St ■ BB4 ......86 A7
Driving Gate BB4 ....106 A1
Dronsfield Rd PR2 ...117 F4
Drovers Way LA6 ....240 D7
Drovers Wlk LA3 ....212 F7
Druids Cl BL7 ....47 D3
Drumacre La E PR4 ...75 D6
Drumacre La W PR4 ..75 A6
Drumhead Rd PR6 .....61 D2
Drummersdale La L40 ..24 D7
Drummond Ave FY3 ..130 E7
Drumpton Ave PR3 ...178 C2
Dryberad La PR3 .....178 C2
Dryburgh Ave FY3 ...130 F3
Dryden Gr BB6 ......124 F3
Dryden Rd FY7 ......199 A4
Dryden St
  ■ Clayton-le-M BB5 ..124 F3
  Padiham BB12 ....126 E7
Dryfield La BL6 ....32 A5
Duchess Ct FY2 .....152 B3
Duchess Dr FY2 .....152 B3
Duchess St BB3 ......81 F7
Duchy Ave PR2 ......118 B4
Duck St
  Smallwood Hey PR3 ..201 A4
  Wray LA2 ....238 D6
Duckett St ■ BB11 ..127 E6
Ducketts La PR3 .....159 B8
Duckshaw Rd BB3 .....64 F6
Duckworth Cl PR3 ...181 D3
Duckworth Dr PR3 ...181 D3
Duckworth Hall BB5 .103 A3
Duckworth Hall Brow
  BB5 ....103 B1
Duckworth Hill La BB5 .103 B1
Duckworth La
  Rawtenstall BB4 ......68 E8
  Tarleton PR4 ....56 F8
Duckworth St
  Barrowford BB9 ......170 D2
  Blackburn BB3 ....101 D3
  ■ Bury BL9 ....33 A4
  Church BB5 ....103 E6
  Darwen BB3 ....81 F3
Duddle La PR5 ....97 D2
Duddon Ave Darwen BB3 .81 D2
  Fleetwood FY7 ....198 D2
  Maghull L31 ....5 F2
Duddon St LA3 ......217 F2

Dudley Ave
  Blackpool FY2 ....152 D1
  Oswaldtwistle BB5 ...103 C4
Dudley Cl PR4 ....95 A1
Dudley St Brierfield BB9 .148 C5
  Colne BB8 ....171 F5
  Morecambe LA4 .....217 C4
Duerden St BB9 .....148 D7
Duffins Ct OL12 ......52 D3
Dugdale Ct FY4 .....110 F5
Dugdale La BB7,BD23 .235 F1
Dugdale St BB11 ....128 A5
Dugdales Cl FY4 ....111 E7
Dugie St BL0 ....50 B7
Duke Ave PR8 ....35 C4
Duke of Sussex St BB2 .81 B8
Duke St
  Bamber Bridge PR5 ...77 E7
  Blackburn BB2 ......101 D5
  Blackpool FY1 ......130 B1
  Brierfield BB10 .....148 F3
  Burton in L LA6 ....242 C3
  Chorley PR7 ....43 C6
  Clayton-le-M BB5 ...125 A2
  Colne BB8 ....171 D4
  Colne,Cotton Tree BB8 .172 B5
  Formby L37 ....11 F2
  Great Harwood BB6 ..124 B5
  Heysham LA3 ....212 E7
  High Bentham LA2 ...239 D8
  Lancaster LA1 ......218 C1
  Oswaldtwistle BB5 ...103 D3
  Preston PR1 ....97 B7
  Ramsbottom BL0 ......50 A4
  Rawtenstall BB4 ......69 E8
  Rochdale OL12 ....52 F1
  Southport PR8 ....35 B5
Duke St Prim Sch PR7 .43 C6
Duke's Wood La WN8 ..9 D3
Dukes Brow
  Blackburn BB2 ......101 C6
  Great Harwood BB6 ..124 B5
Dukes Ct BB2 ....101 B6
Dukes Dr BB3 ....82 F1
Dukes Mdw PR2 ....117 A5
Dukes Way L37 ....11 F2
Dulas Gn L32 ....1 A1
Dulas Rd L32 ....1 A1
Dumb Tom's La LA6 ..242 F1
Dumbarton Cl ■ PR4 .111 A6
Dumbarton Rd LA1 ..215 A4
Dumfries Cl FY2 ....152 F5
Dunald Mill La LA2,LA6 .237 B6
Dunbar Cl FY4 ......111 A6
Dunbar Cres PR8 .....21 F8
Dunbar ■ Heysham LA3 .212 E7
Dunbar Rd Fulwood PR2 .116 F3
  Southport PR8 ....34 F1
Duncan Ave FY2 ....152 C4
Duncan Cl
  Brownside BB10 .....128 E3
  Lytham St Anne's FY8 .110 E1
Duncan Pl FY7 ......198 E4
Duncan St Burnley BB12 .127 A5
Dundas St BB8 ......171 C4
Dundee Cl OL10 ......33 F1
Dundee Dr BB1 ....102 A4
Dundee La BL0 ....50 B6
Dundee St LA1 ......215 A4
Dunderdale Ave BB9 .148 C2
Dunderdale St PR3 ..140 B7
Dundonald St PR1 ...97 C8
Dundonnell Rd BB9 ..171 A1
Dunedin Rd BL8 ......49 F2
Dunelt Ct ■ FY1 ....130 C2
Dunelt Rd FY1 ......130 C2
Dunes Ave FY4 .....110 B5
Dunes Dr L37 ....11 C4
Dunes Ho FY4 ....89 F1
Dungeon La WN8 .....18 C7
Dunham Dr PR6 ......61 C6
Dunkeld St ■ LA1 ...215 A7
Dunkenhalgh Way
  Church BB5 ....103 E7
  Clayton-le-M BB5 ...124 E1
Dunkenshaw Cres LA1 .215 B2
Dunkirk Ave
  Carnforth LA5 ......221 E8
  Fulwood PR2 ....117 C3
Dunkirk La Leyland PR26 .59 C8
  New Longton PR26 ....76 A1
Dunkirk Mews PR25 ..59 D8
Dunkirk Rd PR8 ......34 F2
Dunlin Ave LA3 .....212 F5
Dunlin Cl FY5 ......176 A5
Dunlin Dr FY4 ....90 E7
Dunlop Ave PR8 ......21 C6
Dunmail Ave ■ FY3 .130 F2
Dunmore St PR1 .....97 B8
Dunnock La PR4 ....116 E4
Dunnockshaw Community
  Woodland Trail★
  BB11 ....106 C6
Dunny Shop Ave BB5 .104 A4
Dunoon Cl PR2 ......116 E4
Dunoon Dr BB1 ......102 D3
Dunoon St BB11 ....127 C6
Dunrobin Dr PR7 .....60 D1
Dunscar Dr PR6 ......61 B4
Dunsop Cl
  ■ Bamber Bridge PR5 .77 E8
  ■ Blackpool FY1 ....130 D1
Dunsop Ct ■ FY1 ...130 C2
Dunsop Gdns LA3 ...217 F2

Dunsop Rd PR2 ......118 D4
Dunsop St BB1 ......101 F7
Dunster Ave BB5 ....103 C5
Dunster Gr PR8 .....166 C6
Dunster Rd PR8 .....21 C6
Dunvegan Cl ■ FY4 .111 A6
Durban Cl LA3 .....175 C4
Durban Gr BB11 ....127 E4
Durham Ave
  Burnley BB12 ....127 B7
  Cleveleys FY5 ......175 E3
  Lancaster LA1 .....215 A4
  Lytham St Anne's FY8 ..89 E7
Durham Cl Blackburn BB1 .101 F4
  Leyland PR25 ....59 E7
  Morecambe LA4 ....217 B2
Durham Dr
  Oswaldtwistle BB5 ...103 F3
  Ramsbottom BL0 .....50 B3
  Wilpshire BB1 ......122 F6
Durham Gr ■ PR3 ...181 B7
Durham Rd
  Blackpool FY1 ......130 D5
  Darwen BB3 ....81 F2
  Wilpshire BB1 ......122 F7
Durham St
  Accrington BB5 .....104 D7
  Skelmersdale WN8 ...17 C1
  Thornton FY1 ......130 D2
Durn St ■ OL14 ....109 A1
Dutch Barn Cl PR7 ...61 B2
Dutton Ct ■ BB3 .....81 F7
Dutton Lee Cotts PR3 .142 A7
Dutton Rd FY3 .....130 D5
Dutton St ■ BB5 ...104 C6
Duttonfield Cl PR26 ..76 E3
Duttons Way BB1 ...102 D1
Duxbury Cl L31 ....5 E3
Duxbury Dr BL9 ......33 C2
Duxbury Hall Rd PR7 ..43 E3
Duxbury Ho ■ PR7 ..43 D7
Duxbury Jubilee Pk★
  PR7 ....43 D3
Duxbury St BB3 ......65 B6
  Earby BB18 ....197 C2
Dye House La ■ LA1 .214 F8
Dyer St 113 F5
Dyers La L9 ....15 E4
Dyke La PR3 ....201 A3
Dyke Nook BB7 .....166 F6
Dykes La LA5 ......225 C4
Dymock Rd PR1 ....118 D1
Dymock Rd N PR1 ..118 D1
Dyneley Ave BB10 ..128 F4
Dyneley Rd BB1 ....102 C7
Dyson St BB2 ......101 E2

E

Eachill Gdns BB1 ...103 B8
Eachill Rd ■ BB1 ...124 B1
Eager La L31 ....5 B8
Eagle Brow Cl FY5 ..176 B4
Eagle St Accrington BB5 .104 B5
  Blackburn BB1 ......102 C4
  ■ Nelson BB9 ......170 F1
  Oswaldtwistle BB5 ...103 C2
Eagles The FY6 .....153 E5
Eagley Bank OL12 ....71 C8
Eagley Rd BB9 .....148 C4
Ealand Chase BL6 ....31 F3
Ealing Gr PR6 ....61 F3
Eamont Ave PR9 .....54 B5
Eamont Pl FY7 .....198 D2
Eanam BB1 ....101 F5
Eanam Old Rd BB1 ..101 F5
Earby Lead Mining Mus★
  BB18 ....197 B2
Earby Rd BB18 ......194 F8
Earby Springfield Prim Sch
  BB18 ....197 C2
Earcroft Way BB3 .....81 E5
Eardley Rd LA3 .....212 F4
Earhart Cl WN8 ....9 E8
Earl Rd BL0 ....50 B6
Earl St
  Barnoldswick BB18 ..196 C2
  Blackburn BB1 ......101 E6
  Burnley BB10 ......128 B8
  Clayton-le-M BB5 ...124 F2
  Colne BB8 ....171 D4
  Great Harwood BB6 ..124 B5
  Lancaster LA1 ......218 D1
  ■ Nelson BB9 ......170 F1
  Preston PR1 ....96 F8
  Ramsbottom BL0 .....50 D6
Earlesdon Ave BB18 .196 F1
Earls Ave PR5 ....77 E8
Earls Dr BB3 ....82 E1
Earls Way PR7 ....60 D2
Earlsway FY3 ......131 D5
Earnock Ave 18 E1
Earnsdale Ave BB3 ...81 D2
Earnsdale Cl BB3 .....81 E2
Earnsdale Rd BB3 ....81 E3
Earnshaw Ave OL12 ..52 E3
Earnshaw Dr PR25 ...76 D1
Earnshaw Rd OL13 ...87 F3
Earnshaw Row ■ OL13 .87 F3
Easby St L37 ....12 A2
Easdale Ave LA4 ...217 E5
Easedale Cl
  Burnley BB12 ....127 B8

Easedale Cl continued
Hest Bank LA5 . . . . .220 F2
Easedale Dr PR8 . . . . .21 B4
Easington LA1 . . . . .218 A2
Easington Cres FY3 . . . . . .131 B8
East Ave BB18 . . . . .196 B2
East Bank
2 Barrowford BB9 . . . . .170 D4
Water BB4 . . . . .107 A1
East Bank Ave BB4 . . . . .85 B2
East Bank Rd FY8 . . . . .89 E5
East Beach FY8 . . . . .91 C3
East Boothroyden FY1 . .130 B8
East Cecil St FY8 . . . . .91 A4
East Chorley Business Ctr 3
PR6 . . . . .43 D8
East Cliff PR1 . . . . .96 F4
East Cliff Rd PR1 . . . . .96 F6
East Cliffe FY8 . . . . .91 C3
East Cres BB5 . . . . .104 B8
East Croft BB9 . . . . .171 B2
East Ct FY5 . . . . .175 D5
East Dene WN8 . . . . .27 B2
East End St BB8 . . . . .171 C4
East Gate BB4 . . . . .85 B3
East Gate Cl FY8 . . . . .110 C4
East Hills St 21 BB18 . . . . .196 B2
East Holme FY8 . . . . .91 C4
East La Galgate LA2 . . . . .211 B6
Maghull L29 . . . . .4 B2
East Lancashire Rd BB1 122 F3
East Lancashire Rly★
Ramsbottom BL0 . . . . .50 C5★
Ramsbottom BL0 . . . . .50 C5
East Lodge Pl BB10 . . . . . .128 E1
East Mead Blackpool FY3 .130 F3
Ormskirk L39 . . . . .15 B2
East Meade L31 . . . . .5 C2
East Mount WN5 . . . . .10 F6
East Par
19 Barnoldswick BB18 . . . .196 B2
17 Rawtenstall BB4 . . . . . . .86 A3
East Park Ave
Blackburn BB1 . . . . .101 D7
Darwen BB3 . . . . .64 F8
East Park Ct BB1 . . . . .101 D6
East Park Dr FY3 . . . . .131 A6
East Park Rd BB1 . . . . .101 D6
East Rd Fulwood PR2 . . . . .118 A3
Lancaster LA1 . . . . .215 A8
Maghull L31 . . . . .5 F1
East Sq PR4 . . . . .95 A1
East St Bamber Bridge PR5 .77 E2
Blackburn BB2 . . . . .101 C3
Blackburn,Feniscowles BB2 80 D8
Brierfield BB9 . . . . .148 C3
Edenfield BL0 . . . . .68 D4
Hapton BB12 . . . . .126 C4
Haslingden BB4 . . . . .68 A7
Leyland PR25 . . . . .77 B1
Leyland PR25 . . . . .77 B2
Morecambe LA3 . . . . .216 E4
10 Nelson BB9 . . . . .170 D1
Padiham BB12 . . . . .146 C1
18 Preston PR1 . . . . .97 A8
Rawtenstall BB4 . . . . .85 F5
Southport PR9 . . . . .35 D7
East Terr PR7 . . . . .60 D4
East Topping St 3 FY1 . .130 B5
East View Bacup OL13 . . . . .87 F2
3 Bamber Bridge PR5 . . . . . .77 A7
Fulwood PR2 . . . . .118 F5
9 Galgate LA2 . . . . .211 A4
Grimsargh PR2 . . . . .139 B1
Grindleton BB7 . . . . .190 B7
Pendleton BB7 . . . . .167 B4
Preston PR1 . . . . .97 A8
9 Preston,Frenchwood
PR5 . . . . .97 C5
Ramsbottom BL0 . . . . .50 C3
Ramsbottom,Stubbins BL0 . .68 C1
Read BB12 . . . . .145 D2
Rising Bridge BB5 . . . . .85 A8
Trawden BB8 . . . . .172 C2
Winmarleigh PR3 . . . . .203 F6
East View Ct LA1 . . . . .218 B3
East View Terr
Abbey Village PR6 . . . . .80 B3
14 Barnoldswick BB18 . . . .196 B2
East Ward Com Prim Sch
BL9 . . . . .33 B2
East Way PR6 . . . . .43 D8
East Wlk BL7 . . . . .47 D2
Eastbank Ave FY4 . . . . . . .111 A7
Eastbank St PR8 . . . . .35 B6
Eastbank Street Sq 9
PR8 . . . . .35 B7
Eastbourne Cl PR2 . . . . . .116 F5
Eastbourne Rd
Blackpool FY4 . . . . .110 B4
Southport PR8 . . . . .35 A3
Eastcliff LA2 . . . . .237 F5
Eastcott Cl BB2 . . . . .82 A8
Eastern Ave BB10 . . . . . . .148 C1
Eastfield Dr Longton PR4 . .95 A1
West Bradford BB7 . . . . . . .189 F6
Eastgate Accrington BB5 .104 C6
Fulwood PR2 . . . . .117 E4
Morecambe LA3 . . . . .217 E2
Ribchester PR3 . . . . .141 E4
Whitworth OL12 . . . . .52 C7
Eastham Hall Cvn Pk FY8 91 E6
Eastham Pl BB11 . . . . .128 B6
Eastham St Burnley BB10 128 B5
Clitheroe BB7 . . . . .189 E1

Eastham St continued
Lancaster LA1 . . . . .215 A7
Preston PR1 . . . . .117 E1
Eastlands Heysham LA3 . .213 A7
Leyland PR26 . . . . .59 C7
Eastleigh WN8 . . . . .18 D1
Eastmoor Dr BB7 . . . . .166 F7
Easton Cl PR2 . . . . .118 D6
Easton Ct FY8 . . . . .89 F6
Eastpines Dr FY5 . . . . .152 F8
Eastside FY4 . . . . .110 F8
Eastway Freckleton PR4 . . . .93 A6
Fulwood PR2 . . . . .118 B6
Maghull L31 . . . . .5 E1
Eastway Bsns Village
PR2 . . . . .118 B8
Eastwood Ave
Blackpool FY3 . . . . .130 E8
2 Fleetwood FY7 . . . . .198 F3
Eastwood Cl 6 BL9 . . . . . .33 B2
Eastwood Cres BB4 . . . . . . .86 C2
Eastwood Rd PR25 . . . . .76 C1
Eastwood St
Barnoldswick BB18 . . . . . . .196 C3
2 Blackburn BB1 . . . . .102 A6
Rawtenstall BB4 . . . . .86 C2
Eastwood Terr BB18 . . . . .196 C3
Eaton Ave FY1 . . . . .130 C1
Eaton Ct FY8 . . . . .89 F6
Eaton Pl PR4 . . . . .113 F5
Eaton Way FY6 . . . . .131 E8
Eaves Ave BB11 . . . . .127 D2
Eaves Cl BB5 . . . . .125 F1
Eaves Green La PR3 . . . . .138 F8
Eaves Green Rd PR7 . . . . . .43 B5
Cuddy Hill PR4 . . . . .136 D7
Fulwood PR2 . . . . .117 E3
Eaves Lane Hospl PR6 . . . . .43 E8
Eaves Rd FY8 . . . . .111 A1
Eaves St FY1 . . . . .130 B7
Eavesdale WN8 . . . . .9 E8
Evesham Cl PR5 . . . . .97 A1
Eaveswood Cl PR5 . . . . .97 E1
Ebenezer Terr BB7 . . . . . .144 B4
Ebony St 11 BB1 . . . . .102 A7
Ebor Lo PR8 . . . . .35 A5
Ebor St BB10 . . . . .148 B2
Eccles Rd L37 . . . . .11 D1
Eccles St Accrington BB5 .104 B7
Blackburn BB2 . . . . .101 E3
Preston PR1 . . . . .118 C1
Ramsbottom BL0 . . . . .50 B6
Eccles's La L40 . . . . .27 B7
Ecclesgate Rd FY4 . . . . . . .111 A5
Eccleshill Cotts BB3 . . . . . .82 C4
Eccleshill Gdns BB3 . . . . . .82 C4
Eccleshill Rd BB3 . . . . .81 F6
Eccleshill St 1 BB12 . . . . .126 C8
Eccleston Prim Sch PR7 . .41 B6
Eccleston Rd FY1 . . . . .130 D1
Eckersley Cl BB2 . . . . .81 D8
Eclipse Rd BB2 . . . . .80 D8
Ecroyd Rd PR2 . . . . .111 A5
Ecroyd St Leyland PR25 . . .77 A1
Nelson BB9 . . . . .148 C8
Edale Ave BB4 . . . . .85 C2
Edale Cl PR25 . . . . .60 A7
Edale Ct PR1 . . . . .117 F1
Edale Dr WN6 . . . . .29 E2
Eddington Rd FY8 . . . . .90 B4
Eddleston Cl FY3 . . . . .131 D5
Edelston Rd 5 FY1 . . . . . .130 C6
Eden Ave Edenfield BL0 . . .68 D3
Fleetwood FY7 . . . . .198 D2
Lytham St Anne's FY8 . . . . .90 E3
Morecambe LA4 . . . . .217 F5
Southport PR9 . . . . .53 F3
Eden Cl BB9 . . . . .170 D4
Eden Ct BL0 . . . . .68 D2
Eden Gdns PR3 . . . . .140 B8
Eden Hall PR1 . . . . .117 E1
Eden La BL0 . . . . .68 D2
Eden Mount Way LA5 . . . .223 F2
Lancaster LA1 . . . . .214 F4
Eden Pk Blackburn BB2 . .101 A8
Lancaster LA1 . . . . .214 F4
Eden St Accrington BB5 . .104 A5
Blackburn BB1 . . . . .102 A5
9 Blackpool FY1 . . . . .130 C6
Edenfield BL0 . . . . .68 D2
Leyland PR25 . . . . .60 A8
Edenfield PR4 . . . . .74 F4
Edenfield Ave FY6 . . . . . . .153 F2
Edenfield CE Prim Sch
BL0 . . . . .68 D4
Edenfield Ct PR8 . . . . .35 E3
Edenfield Rd
Ramsbottom OL11,OL12 . . . .51 E4
Rochdale OL11,OL12 . . . . . .52 B1
Edenfield St OL11,OL12 . . . .52 B1
Edenhurst WN8 . . . . .9 E8
Edenhurst Apartments
BB4 . . . . .68 D8
Edenhurst Cl L37 . . . . .11 C2
Edenhurst Dr L37 . . . . .11 C2
Edensor Terr BB3 . . . . .81 F2
Edenvale Ave FY2 . . . . . . .152 B4
Edenvale Cres LA1 . . . . . .218 C3
Edenvale Rd LA1 . . . . .218 C3
Edenway PR2 . . . . .117 D2
Edgar St Accrington BB5 . .104 B6
Huncoat BB5 . . . . .125 E2
Nelson BB9 . . . . .170 F2
16 Ramsbottom BL0 . . . . . .50 B5
Edgar St W 17 BL0 . . . . . . .50 B5
Edge End BB6 . . . . .124 B5
Edge End Ave BB9 . . . . . . .148 D6
Edge End High Sch BB9 148 D6

Edge End La
Brierfield BB9 . . . . .148 D6
Great Harwood BB6 . . . . . . .124 B6
Edge End Rd BB6 . . . . .124 B5
Edge End Terr BB2 . . . . .80 B3
Edge Gate La PR6 . . . . .63 A6
Edge Hall Rd WN5 . . . . .10 E5
Edge Hill Coll PR7 . . . . .43 A8
Edge Hill Univ Coll L39 . .16 A3
Edge La Bacup OL13 . . . . . .71 C8
Barnoldswick BB18 . . . . . . .231 F1
Edgworth BL7 . . . . .48 A8
Rawtenstall BB4 . . . . .86 D3
Edge Yate La BB4 . . . . .86 B5
Edgecott Cl LA3 . . . . .213 A7
Edgefield PR7 . . . . .61 B2
Edgefield Ct FY3 . . . . .131 B8
Edgehill Cl PR2 . . . . .117 D4
Edgehill Cres PR25 . . . . . . .76 C2
Edgehill Dr PR2 . . . . .117 D4
Edgeley Ct 1 BB12 . . . . . .127 D7
Edgemoor Cl OL12 . . . . .71 E5
Edgeside BB6 . . . . .124 B5
Edgeside La BB4 . . . . .86 F2
Edgeware Rd BB2 . . . . . . .101 C6
Edgeway Pl 3 FY5 . . . . . .176 C1
Edgeway Rd FY4 . . . . .110 C5
Edgeworth Vale BL7 . . . . . .48 E6
Edgley Ct PR4 . . . . .95 E2
Edgley Dr L39 . . . . .16 A5
Edgworth Gr BB10 . . . . . . .128 C6
Edgworth Views BL7 . . .48 D8
Edinburgh Cl PR25 . . . . . . .77 C1
Edinburgh Dr BB5 . . . . . . .103 F3
Edinburgh Rd Formby L37 11 E1
Haslingden BB4 . . . . .84 F1
Edisford Prim Sch BB7 .166 C7
Edisford Rd
Clitheroe BB7 . . . . .166 C8
Waddington BB7 . . . . .189 B4
Edison St BB3 . . . . .81 F1
Edith St
Barnoldswick BB18 . . . . . . .196 B3
Blackburn BB1 . . . . .102 A4
Nelson BB9 . . . . .148 F8
Shuttleworth BL0 . . . . .50 E8
Edleston Lodge 2 PR2 . . .118 F4
Edleston St BB5 . . . . .103 F4
Edmondson Pl 4 FY7 . . . .198 F2
Edmondson St BB18 . . . . .196 B3
Edmondson's La BD23 . . .197 F8
Edmonton Dr BB2 . . . . . . .101 A8
Edmonton Pl FY2 . . . . .152 F3
Edmund Gennings Ct
BB7 . . . . .190 D5
Edmund St
5 Accrington BB5 . . . . . . .104 C5
6 Blackburn BB2 . . . . .81 D7
Burnley BB10 . . . . .148 B1
Darwen BB3 . . . . .82 B1
3 Preston PR1 . . . . .97 B8
Edmundson St
Blackburn BB2 . . . . .101 C5
6 Church BB5 . . . . .103 E4
Edward Ct PR4 . . . . .57 A5
Edward Ct 9 BB5 . . . . . . .103 E6
Edward Sq 10 PR1 . . . . . .118 A1
Edward St
Accrington BB5 . . . . .104 E1
13 Bacup OL13 . . . . .88 A3
Bamber Bridge PR5 . . . . . . .77 E8
Barnoldswick BB18 . . . . . . .196 C3
Blackpool FY1 . . . . .130 B5
Burnley BB11 . . . . .128 A6
3 Carnforth LA5 . . . . .223 D2
Chorley PR6 . . . . .43 D7
8 Church BB5 . . . . .103 E6
Darwen BB3 . . . . .82 A2
8 Earby BB18 . . . . .197 B2
7 Great Harwood BB6 . . . .124 C5
Haslingden BB4 . . . . .85 B6
Horwich BL6 . . . . .32 A3
Lancaster LA1 . . . . .215 A8
2 Leyland PR25 . . . . .60 A8
Lytham St Anne's FY8 . . . . .89 F7
Morecambe LA4 . . . . .217 A5
Nelson BB9 . . . . .170 F2
Preston PR1 . . . . .96 F8
Rawtenstall BB4 . . . . .86 A8
4 Rishton BB1 . . . . .124 B1
Thornton FY5 . . . . .176 B4
Walton-le-D PR5 . . . . .97 C5
Whitworth OL12 . . . . .71 D2
Edward VII Quay PR2 . . . .96 B7
Edwell Ave FY4 . . . . .110 D8
Edwin Waugh Gdns OL12 52 D3
Edwinstowe Rd FY5 . . . . . .90 D6
Egan St PR1 . . . . .97 A8
Egbert St PR1 . . . . .118 A1
Egerton WN8 . . . . .9 D8
Egerton Gr PR7 . . . . .43 B6
Egerton Lodge BL7 . . . . . . .47 E1
Egerton Prim Sch BL7 . . .47 D3
Egerton Rd Belmont BL7 . .46 E4
Blackpool FY1 . . . . .130 B7
Leyland PR25 . . . . .76 F2
Preston PR1 . . . . .117 B1
Egerton Vale BL7 . . . . .47 D2
Egremont Ave FY5 . . . . . . .175 D5
Egypt Mount BB4 . . . . .85 D2
Egypt Terr 3 BB4 . . . . .85 E2
Eider Cl FY7 . . . . .175 F5
Eidsforth La PR3 . . . . .226 A1
Eidsforth Rd LA4 . . . . .217 B6
Eight Acre Ave BB7 . . . . . .145 F8
Eight Acre La Formby L37 .12 B6
Yealand Redmayne LA5 . . . .225 E4
Eildon Dr FY6 . . . . .153 D1

Elaine Ave FY4 . . . . .130 F1
Elbow La L37 . . . . .11 F3
Elbow St PR7 . . . . .43 C7
Elbut La BL9 . . . . .33 F5
Elcho St PR1 . . . . .118 A2
Elder Ave L40 . . . . .25 F4
Elder Cl Clayton Green PR6 78 C2
Warton PR4 . . . . .92 E6
Elder Ct BB5 . . . . .104 E8
Elder St BB9 . . . . .170 F2
Elderberry Cl FY5 . . . . . . .175 F5
Elderbrook Cl PR4 . . . . . . .73 E4
Elderwood Ave FY5 . . . . . .153 B7
Eldon Ct FY8 . . . . .89 F7
Eldon Gr LA3 . . . . .212 F7
Eldon Ho PR6 . . . . .43 D7
Eldon Prim Sch PR1 . . . .117 E2
Eldon Rd BB1 . . . . .101 D7
Preston PR1,PR2 . . . . .117 D2
Eldons Croft PR8 . . . . .21 D5
Eldwick St BB10 . . . . .148 C1
Eleanor St Blackburn BB1 101 F5
3 Nelson BB9 . . . . .170 E1
Electricity St BB5 . . . . . . .104 B6
Elgar St BB2 . . . . .102 A2
Elgin Cres BB11 . . . . .127 D4
Elgin Pl FY3 . . . . .131 A7
Elgin St 4 Lancaster LA1 215 A7
Preston PR1 . . . . .118 A2
Elijah St 4 PR1 . . . . .97 D8
Elim Ct 4 FY8 . . . . .91 C3
Elim Gdns BB2 . . . . .101 C1
Elim Pl BB2 . . . . .101 C1
Elim View BB10 . . . . .148 D2
Eliza St Burnley BB10 . . . .128 B5
Ramsbottom BL0 . . . . .50 D6
Elizabeth Ave PR8 . . . . . . .21 E6
Elizabeth Cl FY3 . . . . .131 D5
Elizabeth Ct
Blackpool FY3 . . . . .130 D6
9 Lancaster LA1 . . . . .214 F7
Poulton-le-F FY6 . . . . .153 D3
Elizabeth Dr BB4 . . . . .68 A8
Elizabeth Ho BB3 . . . . .82 B1
Elizabeth Sq 8 PR1 . . . . .118 A1
Elizabeth St
Accrington BB5 . . . . .103 F5
Blackburn BB1 . . . . .101 F5
Blackpool FY1 . . . . .130 C6
Burnley BB11 . . . . .128 A5
Edenfield BL0 . . . . .68 D3
6 Fleetwood FY7 . . . . .199 B5
Nelson BB9 . . . . .170 E1
Padiham BB12 . . . . .126 C7
Preston PR1 . . . . .96 F8
Whitewell Bottom BB4 . . . . .86 F4
Elker Cotts BB7 . . . . .143 F4
Elker La BB7 . . . . .143 F5
Elker Mews BB7 . . . . .143 F3
Elkfield Dr FY3 . . . . .153 A1
Elkin Rd LA4 . . . . .217 D5
Elland Pl FY1 . . . . .130 B1
Elland Rd BB9 . . . . .148 C6
Ellel Hall Gdns LA2 . . . . .210 F3
Ellel St John the Evangelist
CE Prim Sch LA2 . . . . . .211 A3
Ellen Ct PR1 . . . . .117 F2
Ellen St Bamber Bridge PR5 97 E1
Darwen BB3 . . . . .65 A7
11 Nelson BB9 . . . . .148 D8
Preston PR1 . . . . .117 E1
Preston PR1 . . . . .117 F2
Ellenrod Dr OL12 . . . . .52 A2
Ellenrod La OL12 . . . . .52 A2
Ellenshaw Cl Darwen BB3 .82 B1
Rochdale OL12 . . . . .52 A2
Eller Brook Cl PR6 . . . . . . .43 F1
Eller Brook Ho L39 . . . . . .15 E6
Ellerbeck Ave PR2 . . . . . . .118 E5
Ellerbeck Cl BB10 . . . . . . .148 E3
Ellerbeck Rd
Accrington BB5 . . . . .104 B7
Cleveleys FY5 . . . . .175 C5
Darwen BB3 . . . . .82 B1
Ellerbrook Dr L40 . . . . .25 F3
Ellerbrook Way L39 . . . . . .15 E6
Ellerigg La LA6 . . . . .243 A6
Ellershaw Ho 12 LA1 . . . .218 D2
Ellerslie Rd PR2 . . . . .117 B1
Ellesmere Ave Colne BB8 171 F5
Thornton FY5 . . . . .176 B1
Ellesmere Gr LA4 . . . . .217 A3
Ellesmere Rd
Blackpool FY4 . . . . .130 E1
Darwen BB3 . . . . .81 E3
Morecambe LA4 . . . . .216 F4
Elletson St FY6 . . . . .153 D4
Elliott Ave BB3 . . . . .65 B6
Elliott Cl PR1 . . . . .117 E6
Elliott Gdns WN6 . . . . .19 E7
Elliott St Burnley BB10 . . .128 C5
Preston PR1 . . . . .117 E1
Preston PR1 . . . . .117 E2
Elliott Wlk PR1 . . . . .117 E2
Ellis Dr LA4 . . . . .217 E6
Ellis St
Barnoldswick BB18 . . . . . . .196 B2
1 Burnley BB11 . . . . .127 E5
19 Ramsbottom BL0 . . . . . .50 B5
Ellisland Rd LA1 . . . . .131 C1
Ellison Fold BB5 . . . . .124 E3
Ellison Fold La BB3 . . . . . . .82 C1
Ellison Fold Terr BB3 . . . . .82 B1
Ellison St Accrington BB5 104 B6
Darwen BB3 . . . . .82 A2

Ellwood Ave
Lancaster LA1 . . . . .218 E4
Morecambe LA3 . . . . .217 C2
Ellwood Ct LA3 . . . . .217 D2
Ellwood Gr LA3 . . . . .217 D2
Elm Ave Blackpool FY3 . . .130 E5
Galgate LA2 . . . . .210 F4
Poulton-le-F FY6 . . . . .153 D3
Preston PR2 . . . . .117 A2
Warton PR4 . . . . .92 C6
Elm Brow PR3 . . . . .162 C4
Elm Cl Barnoldswick BB18 196 A1
Haslingden BB4 . . . . .85 B3
Rishton BB1 . . . . .103 B8
Salterforth BB18 . . . . .194 E8
Elm Ct Poulton-le-F FY6 . .153 D3
Skelmersdale WN8 . . . . .17 E1
Elm Dr
3 Bamber Bridge PR5 . . . . . .97 F1
Formby L37 . . . . .11 D1
Elm Gr Chorley PR6 . . . . . . .61 E2
Clayton-le-W PR25 . . . . .77 D3
Darwen BB3 . . . . .82 B3
Fulwood PR2 . . . . .118 E2
6 Horwich BL6 . . . . .32 E1
Kirkham PR4 . . . . .114 B7
Morecambe LA4 . . . . .217 E7
Skelmersdale WN8 . . . . .17 E1
Elm Mill BB10 . . . . .128 A8
Elm Park Dr PR8 . . . . .21 E5
Elm Pl L39 . . . . .15 E4
Elm Rd Burscough L40 . . . .25 E3
Southport PR8 . . . . .35 B4
Elm St 7 Bacup OL13 . . . . .88 A3
Blackburn BB1 . . . . .102 A4
Burnley BB10 . . . . .128 A8
Bury BL9 . . . . .33 B2
Colne BB8 . . . . .171 E6
Edenfield BL0 . . . . .68 E3
Fleetwood FY7 . . . . .199 A4
Great Harwood BB6 . . . . . . .124 C4
Haslingden BB4 . . . . .85 B3
9 Nelson BB9 . . . . .170 E1
Ramsbottom BL0 . . . . .50 D6
Rawtenstall BB4 . . . . .86 A3
Rochdale OL12 . . . . .52 F1
Whitworth OL12 . . . . .71 D2
Elm Tree Gr BB6 . . . . .143 C5
Elmbank Ave FY5 . . . . .152 C7
Elmcroft LA38 . . . . .3 A3
Elmdale Cl L37 . . . . .11 D2
Elmer's Gn WN8 . . . . .18 D2
Elmer's Green La WN8 . . . .18 C4
Elmers Wood Rd WN8 . . . .18 D2
Elmfield Dr PR5 . . . . .78 C6
Elmfield Hall Flats BB5 . .103 F7
Elmfield St BB5 . . . . .103 F7
Elmhurst Rd FY8 . . . . .90 B8
Elmpark Gate OL12 . . . . . . .52 B3
Elmpark Gr OL12 . . . . .52 B3
Elmpark Vale OL12 . . . . . . .52 B3
Elmpark View OL12 . . . . . . .52 B3
Elmpark Way OL12 . . . . . . .52 B3
Elmridge WN8 . . . . .9 D8
Elmridge Cres FY2 . . . . . . .152 F3
Elms Ave Cleveleys FY5 . . .175 E2
Lytham St Anne's FY8 . . . . .90 E3
Elms Ct LA4 . . . . .217 E7
Elms Dr Morecambe LA4 . .217 E7
Wrea Green PR4 . . . . .113 B4
Elms Rd LA4 . . . . .217 E7
Elms The
Clayton Green PR6 . . . . .78 C1
Maghull L31 . . . . .5 D3
Southport PR8 . . . . .35 C5
Southport,Birkdale PR8 . . . .34 F6
Elmsdale Cl LA1 . . . . .218 C2
Elmsfield Pk L39 . . . . .6 A6
Elmside Cl FY5 . . . . .176 D2
Elmslack Ct LA5 . . . . .224 C4
Elmslack La LA5 . . . . .224 C4
Elmsley St PR1 . . . . .117 E2
Elmslie Gdns FY3 . . . . . . .130 E3
Elmstead WN8 . . . . .9 D8
Elmswood Cl FY8 . . . . .90 F4
Elmwood Chorley PR7 . . . . .61 B1
Longridge PR3 . . . . .140 A8
Skelmersdale WN8 . . . . .18 C3
Elmwood Ave
1 Leyland PR25 . . . . .76 E1
Preesall FY6 . . . . .200 B4
Elmwood Cl BB5 . . . . .104 D6
Elmwood Ct PR4 . . . . .132 F2
Elmwood Dr
Higher Penwortham PR1 . . . .96 B4
Thornton FY5 . . . . .176 C1
Elmwood Gdns LA1 . . . . . .215 A2
Elmwood St BB11 . . . . .127 D5
Elsby Ave FY5 . . . . .153 C8
Elsie St 10 BL0 . . . . .50 A4
Elsinore Cl FY7 . . . . .198 F5
Elslack La BD23 . . . . .197 F7
Elson Rd L37 . . . . .11 D1
Elston Ave FY3 . . . . .131 A8
Elston Gn PR2 . . . . .139 E1
Elston La PR2 . . . . .119 F7
Elston Lodge 7 PR2 . . . . .118 F4
Elswick WN8 . . . . .9 C8
Elswick Gdns BB2 . . . . . . .121 D3
Elswick Gn PR9 . . . . .54 A5
Elswick Ind Pk PR4 . . . . . .156 A1
Elswick Lodge BB2 . . . . . .121 E3
Elswick Pl Blackpool FY4 .110 E5
Lytham St Anne's FY8 . . . . .90 B8
Elswick Rd Leyland PR25 . .59 D8
Preston PR2 . . . . .116 E1
Southport PR9 . . . . .53 F4

Elswick St BB3 82 B1
Elsworth Cl L37 2 C8
Elterwater FY6 199 E5
Elterwater Pl
Blackpool FY3 131 C2
Lancaster LA1 218 E1
Eltham Ct FY3 153 B1
Elton Rd BB1,BB4 83 B5
Elton St 3 PR2 117 C1
Elvaston Rd FY6 153 C6
Elvington Rd L38 3 A2
Elwood Grange FY8 89 C8
Ely Cl Darwen BB3 82 C1
Wilpshire BB1 122 F6
Ely Mews PR9 54 A2
Embankment Rd BL7 48 C5
Emerald Ave BB1 122 F2
Emerald Cl FY5 152 F7
Emerald Cotts BL8 49 F3
Emerald St BB1 122 F2
Emerson Ave FY4 110 D7
Emerson Cl L38 3 A4
Emerson Rd PR1 118 D2
Emerson St LA1 215 A4
Emesgate La LA5 224 C3
Emily St
Bamber Bridge PR5 77 A8
Blackburn BB1 102 A6
Burnley BB11 128 A4
Emlsett Rd PR5 97 F3
Emma St BB5 103 F6
Emmanuel Christian Sch
OL12 52 D1
Emmanuel Holcombe CE
Prim Sch BL8 50 A6
Emmanuel Rd PR9 53 F2
Emmanuel St PR1,PR2 117 E2
Emmaus Rd LA3 212 F6
Emmett St Horwich BL6 32 B3
Preston PR1 117 F1
Emmott Ct BB8 172 E6
Emmott La BB8 172 D6
Emnie La PR26,PR25 59 C7
Empire Gr 2 FY3 130 D7
Empire Ho BB5 104 B6
Empire St BB6 124 D6
Emporium The 7 BB7 166 E8
Empress Ave PR2 117 E4
Empress Cl L31 5 B1
Empress Dr FY2 152 B1
Empress St
Accrington BB5 103 F6
Blackburn BB3 81 F7
Colne BB8 171 E5
Empress Way PR7 60 E2
End St BB8 171 B4
Endcliffe Rd LA4 217 C5
Endeavour Cl PR2 96 B7
Enderley Ct FY5 176 C1
Ending Rake OL12 52 C4
Endsleigh Gdns FY4 110 E6
Endsleigh Gr LA1 218 A3
Enfield Cl Eccleston PR7 41 C5
Huncoat BB5 125 E2
Enfield Rd
Accrington BB5 125 D2
Blackpool FY1 130 C7
Engine La L37 3 E8
England Ave
Blackburn BB2 81 D8
Blackpool FY2 152 C4
English Martyrs' Pl PR1 117 F2
English Martyrs' RC Prim Sch
PR1 117 E1
Ennerdale WN8 9 D8
Ennerdale Ave
Blackburn BB1 102 C3
Fleetwood FY7 198 C1
Maghull L31 5 E2
Morecambe LA4 217 D4
Ennerdale Cl
Clitheroe BB7 166 C7
Formby L37 11 D3
Forton PR3 207 B3
Knott End-on-S FY6 199 F6
Lancaster LA1 218 F2
Leyland PR25 60 A7
Oswaldtwistle BB5 103 D5
Ennerdale Dr
Ormskirk L39 15 B2
Walton-le-D PR5 97 E5
Ennerdale Rd
Blackpool FY4 131 C1
Burnley BB10 128 E5
Chorley PR7 43 A6
Clitheroe BB7 166 C7
Formby L37 11 E3
Longridge PR3 139 F5
Ennismore St BB10 148 C1
Enoch Brow BB2 80 C8
Ensign Ct FY8 110 C4
Enstone WN8 18 D1
Enterprise Ct BB5 125 D1
Enterprise Dr PR26 77 A4
Enterprise Way
Fleetwood FY7 176 A6
Nelson BB8 170 F3
Enterprise Workshops
Kirkby L33 1 B1
Southport PR9 36 A6
Entwisle Rd BB5 104 B8
Entwistle Hall La BL7 48 B8
Entwistle St BB3 82 A1
Entwistle Sta BL7 48 B8
Ephraim St PR1 97 C7
Epping Ave BB5 125 B1
Epping Cl FY2 152 E5
Epping Pl PR6 43 D8
Epsom Cl PR6 61 F4
Epsom Croft PR6 31 B7
Epsom Gr L33 1 A6
Epsom Rd FY5 152 F8
Epsom Way BB5 104 D5
Epworth St BB3 65 B6
Equity St BB3 65 A8
Erdington Rd FY1 130 C3
Eric Morecambe Ho 9
LA4 217 F4
Ericson Dr PR8 35 B5
Erith Gr FY2 152 C5
Ermine Cl BB2 82 A8
Ermine Pl LA3 217 E3
Ernest St Bacup OL13 71 C8
6 Church BB5 103 E6
Clayton-le-M BB5 124 F1
Cornholme OL14 109 C1
Ernlouen Cl BB2 81 A8
Erskine Rd PR6 61 E1
Escar St 9 BB11 127 F5
Escott Gdns 11 BB10 128 A8
Escowbeck Ho LA2 237 B3
Esher Pond PR2 117 C6
Eshton Terr BB7 166 E7
Esk Ave Edenfield BL0 68 D5
Fleetwood FY7 198 D2
Eskbank WN8 9 C8
Eskbrook WN8 18 C1
Eskdale WN8 9 B8
Eskdale Ave
Fleetwood FY7 198 D1
Ormskirk L39 15 C2
Eskdale Cl Blackpool FY4 130 F1
Brierfield BB10 148 B4
Formby L37 11 D2
Fulwood PR2 117 F8
Eskdale Cres BB2 80 E8
Eskdale Ct FY5 175 D1
Eskdale Dr Formby L37 11 D2
Kirkham PR4 114 A7
Maghull L31 5 E2
Eskdale Gdns BB12 146 C2
Eskdale Gr FY6 199 F6
Eskdale Pl LA4 217 D4
Eskdale Rd Leyland PR25 60 C7
Longridge PR3 139 F6
Eskew La LA2 239 B8
Eskham Cl PR4 113 E6
Eskrigge Cl 4 LA1 218 D4
Eskrigge La LA2 238 A8
Esp La BB18 231 F1
Esplanade
Knott End-on-S FY6 199 D6
Preston PR1 97 B5
Southport PR8 34 F7
Esplanade Mews FY6 199 E5
Esplanade The
Fleetwood FY7 199 A5
Rishton BB1 103 A8
Essex Ave Burnley BB12 127 B7
Heywood OL10 33 E1
Essex Cl BB2 101 D3
Essex Pl FY2 152 F2
Essex Rd
3 Morecambe LA4 217 F4
4 Rishton BB1 124 A1
Southport PR8 22 A8
Standish WN1 30 B1
Essex St Accrington BB5 104 D6
Barnoldswick BB18 196 B2
Colne BB8 171 E4
Darwen BB3 82 C1
Horwich BL6 32 D1
Nelson BB9 170 E1
Preston PR1 118 A1
Essie Terr BB18 196 B1
Essington Ave LA4 217 A4
Est Bank Rd BL0 50 A3
Esther St BB1 102 C5
Esthwaite Gdns LA1 218 F1
Ethel St
Barnoldswick BB18 196 C2
Whitworth OL12 71 D2
Ethersall Rd BB9 148 E6
Eton Ave BB5 104 C7
Eton Cl BB12 126 E6
Eton Ct PR9 53 C1
Eton Pk PR2 118 C5
Eton Way WN5 10 F8
Ettington Dr PR8 21 A5
Ettrick Ave FY7 198 D3
Europa Dr PR26 77 A4
Europa Way LA1 214 C8
Euston Gr LA4 217 B5
Euston Rd LA4 217 B5
Euston St PR1 96 E7
Euxton Balshaw La Sta
PR7 60 D1
Euxton CE Prim Sch PR7 60 C2
Euxton Hall Ct PR7 60 C2
Euxton Hall Gdns PR7 60 C1
Euxton Hall Hospl PR7 60 C1
Euxton Hall Mews PR7 60 C2
Euxton La Chorley PR7 61 B3
Euxton PR7 60 E4
Euxton St Mary's RC Prim Sch
PR7 60 C3
Evans St Burnley BB11 127 F4
Horwich BL6 32 D4
Preston PR2 117 D1
Evanstone Cl 5 BL6 32 B3
Eve St BB9 171 A2
Evelyn Rd BB3 81 E5
Evelyn St BB10 148 A1
Evenwood WN8 18 D1
Evenwood Ct WN8 18 C1
Everard Cl L40 23 F7
Everard Rd PR8 35 D4
Everest Cl FY8 111 A1
Everest Ct 2 PR4 113 F6
Everest Dr FY2 152 C5
Everest Rd FY8 111 A2
Evergreen Ave PR25 60 A7
Evergreen Cl PR7 43 B5
Evergreens The
Blackburn BB2 80 F8
Cottam PR4 116 E4
Formby L37 11 D4
Eversham Cl PR9 55 A5
Eversholt Cl BB12 147 D7
Eversleigh Ave FY5 176 A3
Eversleigh St PR1 117 E1
Eversley WN8 18 D1
Everton BB2 102 A1
Everton Rd
Blackpool FY4 110 C6
Southport PR8 35 A4
Everton St BB3 81 F1
Every St Brierfield BB9 148 B6
Burnley BB11 127 E5
Nelson BB9 148 D8
Ramsbottom BL0 50 D6
Evesham Ave PR1 96 E2
Evesham Cl
5 Accrington BB5 104 A7
Blackpool FY5 152 E7
Heysham LA3 213 A6
Hutton PR4 95 C1
Evesham Manor PR9 55 A6
Evesham Rd
Lytham St Anne's FY8 90 A5
Normoss FY3 131 B7
Evington WN8 18 D1
Ewell Cl PR6 61 F4
Ewood BB2 101 D1
Ewood Cvn Site BB2 101 D1
Ewood La BB4 68 C7
Ewood Park (Blackburn
Rovers FC) BB2 81 D8
Exchange St
Accrington BB5 103 F5
18 Blackburn BB1 101 E5
Blackpool FY1 130 B6
Colne BB8 171 D4
Darwen BB3 82 A2
Edenfield BL0 68 D3
Exchange The 2 BB8 171 D5
Exe St PR1 118 B2
Exeter Ave LA1 215 B6
Exeter Dr FY5 176 A2
Exeter Pl 2 PR2 116 E2
Exeter St Blackburn BB2 101 D2
3 Blackpool FY4 130 C1
Exmoor Cl PR9 54 B6
Exmouth St BB11 128 A5
Exton St BB9 148 A5
Extwistle Rd BB10 129 B7
Extwistle Sq BB10 128 E5
Extwistle St
Burnley BB10 128 B8
Nelson BB9 148 D7
Eyes La Bretherton PR26 57 E3
Newburgh WN8 27 A3

F

Factory Brow
Blackrod BL6 31 D3
Scorton PR3 204 E6
Factory Hill Horwich BL6 32 D4
5 Lancaster LA1 218 E1
Factory La Adlington PR6 31 B8
Barrowford BB9 170 D4
Middleforth Green PR1 96 F3
17 Padiham BB12 146 C1
Factory St BL0 50 C7
Fair Elms LA1 214 D7
Fair Haven Ct 2 FY8 90 D4
Fair Hill BB4 68 A7
Fair Oak Cl PR2 118 F3
Fair View OL13 71 C8
Fair View Cres OL13 88 B3
Fair View Rd BB11 128 B5
Fair Way FY6 177 C7
Fairacres WN6 29 B1
Fairbairn Ave BB12 127 C8
Fairbairn St BL6 32 B3
Fairbank Gr LA4 217 A3
Fairbank Wlk BB4 106 A2
Fairburn WN8 18 B3
Fairclough Rd
Accrington BB5 104 A3
Thornton FY5 176 A3
Fairfax Ave FY2 152 E5
Fairfax Cl PR3 181 D6
Fairfax Pl PR5 97 D2
Fairfax Rd PR2 118 E4
Fairfield PR3 181 C8
Fairfield Ave
Newchurch BB4 86 F2
Normoss FY3 131 B7
Poulton-le-F FY6 153 D3
Fairfield Cl Carnforth LA5 223 E1
Clitheroe BB7 166 C7
Lancaster LA1 214 E8
Ormskirk L39 15 E7
Fairfield Com Prim Sch
BL9 33 D3
Fairfield Ct
Fleetwood FY7 198 F2
Poulton-le-F FY6 153 D4
Fairfield Dr
Brierfield BB10 148 C3
Bury BL9 33 D3
Fairfield Dr *continued*
Clitheroe BB7 166 C7
Ormskirk L39 15 E7
Preston PR2 117 B2
Fairfield General Hospl
BL9 33 E4
Fairfield Gr LA3 216 E2
Fairfield Rd
Blackpool FY1 130 C8
Fulwood PR2 118 D4
Lancaster LA1 214 E8
Leyland PR25 59 F8
Morecambe LA3 216 E2
Nelson BB9 149 B8
Poulton-le-F FY6 131 F7
Southport PR8 21 C5
Fairfield St
Accrington BB5 103 F4
5 Bamber Bridge PR5 77 B7
Fairham Ave 6 PR1 96 D2
Fairhaven WN8 18 C3
Fairhaven Ave FY7 175 D7
Fairhaven Cl 6 FY5 176 D1
Fairhaven La FY8 89 E5
Fairhaven Lake* FY8 90 C3
Fairhaven Rd
Blackburn BB2 101 F1
Leyland PR25 76 D1
Lytham St Anne's FY8 89 F5
Middleforth Green PR1 96 E5
Southport PR9 54 B4
Fairhaven Way LA4 217 D5
Fairheath Rd LA2 239 B4
Fairhill Terr BB4 68 A7
Fairholme Rd BB11 128 B3
Fairholmes Cl 1 FY5 176 B3
Fairholmes Ct 2 FY5 176 B3
Fairholmes Way FY5 176 B3
Fairhope Ave
Lancaster LA1 218 C3
Morecambe LA4 217 F6
Fairhope Ct BB2 101 C6
Fairhurst Ave WN6 29 D3
Fairhurst Ct FY5 175 D3
Fairhurst St FY1 130 C6
Fairhurst's Dr WN8 27 B2
Fairlawn Rd FY8 90 F3
Fairlea Ave LA4 217 F6
Fairlie WN8 18 C3
Fairmont Dr FY6 177 D2
Fairsnape Ave PR3 140 B7
Fairsnape Dr PR3 181 B6
Fairsnape Rd FY8 91 D4
Fairstead WN8 18 C3
Fairthorn Wlk L33 1 A3
Fairview Ave FY8 90 A7
Fairview Cl PR4 74 F5
Fairview Dr Adlington PR6 30 F8
Adlington PR6 44 A1
Fairway Chorley PR7 61 C2
Fleetwood FY7 198 C1
Higher Penwortham PR1 96 B6
Poulton-le-F FY6 153 A2
Southport PR8 53 C2
Whitworth OL12 52 C7
Fairway Gdns FY6 199 D5
Fairway Rd FY4 110 E8
Fairways Fulwood PR2 118 A6
Horwich BL6 32 C3
Lytham St Anne's FY8 90 A6
Fairways Ave PR3 137 C3
Fairways Ct Formby L37 11 C5
Wilpshire BB1 122 F5
Fairways Dr BB11 127 E2
Fairways The WN8 18 D3
Fairweather Ct BB12 146 D1
Fairwinds Ave PR4 73 D4
Falcon Ave BB3 81 E3
Falcon Cl Blackburn BB1 101 D8
Bury BL9 33 B4
Falcon Ct BB5 124 F2
Falcon Dr FY6 153 B2
Falcon St PR1 118 B2
Falinge Fold OL12 52 D1
Falinge Park High Sch
OL12 52 D1
Falinge Rd OL12 52 E1
Falkirk Ave FY2 152 C6
Falkland WN8 18 C3
Falkland Ave FY4 130 F2
Falkland Rd PR8 35 D5
Falkland St PR1 96 F7
Falkus Ct 6 FY6 153 D3
Fall Barn Rd BB4 86 B2
Fall Kirk LA2 240 F1
Fallbarn Cres BB4 86 A1
Fallbarn Rd BB4 86 B2
Fallowfield Cl PR4 113 E6
Fallowfield Dr
Burnley BB12 127 D8
Rochdale OL12 52 D2
Fallowfield Rd FY8 90 C6
Falmouth Ave
Fleetwood FY7 175 C8
Haslingden BB4 85 C2
Falmouth Rd FY1 130 C2
Falshaw Dr BL9 50 E1
Falstone Ave BL0 50 C4
Far Croft PR5 97 A1
Far East View 16 BB18 196 B2
Far Field PR1 96 D3
Far La PR1 96 C2
Far Moor La LA1 215 C8
Far Nook PR6 61 B7
Faraday Ave BB7 166 D8
Faraday Dr PR2 118 C7
Faraday Rise OL12 52 B1
Faraday St BB12 127 D7
Faraday Way FY2,FY6 153 A6
Fareham Cl
Bamber Bridge PR5 97 F3
Fulwood PR2 118 A4
Fareham Dr PR9 55 A5
Farfield Dr BB3 81 F6
Farholme La OL13 70 D8
Faringdon Ave FY4 110 E5
Farington Ave PR25 59 D7
Farington Gate PR25 77 B2
Farington Prim Sch PR25 77 B3
Farington Rd PR5,PR26 77 A6
Farington St Paul's CE Prim
Sch PR26 76 F7
Farleton Cl LA5 223 C5
Farleton Ct 3 LA1 218 D4
Farleton Old Rd LA2 238 A5
Farley La Roby Mill WN8 19 A3
Skelmersdale WN8 18 F3
Farm Ave Adlington PR6 31 A8
Bacup OL13 87 F4
Farm Cl Southport PR9 36 A8
Thornton FY5 176 B2
Farm House Cl
Blackburn BB1 102 C4
Lucas Green PR6 61 C6
Farm Meadow Rd WN5 10 E5
Farmdale Dr L31 5 E1
Farmdale Rd LA1 215 B5
Farmend Cl PR4 75 B8
Farmer Parr's Animal World
(Mus)* FY7 175 F7
Farmer's Row BB2 81 B7
Farnborough Rd PR8 21 F8
Farnborough Road Inf & Jun
Schs PR8 22 A8
Farnell Pl FY4 110 D6
Farnham Way FY6 153 C5
Farnlea Dr LA4 217 E5
Farnworth Rd FY5 176 D1
Faroes Cl BB2 101 F1
Farrer Ave LA1 211 B7
Farrer St BB9 148 C7
Farrier Rd L33 1 A2
Farriers Fold 4 LA3 212 F7
Farriers Yd LA2 237 C3
Farringdon Cl PR1 118 F1
Farringdon Cres PR1 118 F1
Farringdon La PR2 118 F3
Farringdon Pl PR1 118 F1
Farrington Cl
1 Blackburn BB2 101 C1
Burnley BB11 127 C3
Farrington Ct BB11 127 C3
Farrington Dr L39 15 E6
Farrington Pl BB11 127 C3
Farrington Rd BB11 127 B3
Farrington St PR7 43 C8
Farthings The PR7 60 F1
Faulkner Cl PR8 21 C6
Faulkner Gdns PR8 21 C6
Faulkner's La PR3 207 B1
Favordale Rd BB8 172 A5
Fawcett WN8 18 B3
Fawcett Cl BB2 101 D3
Fawcett Rd L31 5 D3
Fayles Gr FY4 131 A1
Fazackerley St PR2 117 C1
Fazakerley St 13 PR7 43 C8
Fearn Dene 2 OL12 52 B2
Fearnhead Ave BL6 32 B5
Fearnlea Cl 1 OL12 52 B2
Fearns Com Sports Coll
OL13 87 A1
Fearns Moss BB4,OL13 87 A1
Fecitt Brow BB1 102 D4
Fecitt Rd BB2 101 B6
Federation St BB18 196 A3
Feilden Pl BB2 80 D8
Feilden St BB2 101 D5
Feildens Farm La BB2 121 B3
Felgate Brow FY3 130 E5
Felix St BB11 128 B7
Fell Brow PR3 140 B6
Fell Cl 5 PR5 77 F8
Fell End Cvn Pk LA7 225 E8
Fell Rd Casterton LA6 243 C2
Morecambe LA4 217 F4
Waddington BB7 189 A6
Fell View Brierfield BB10 148 D3
Caton LA2 237 C3
Chorley PR6 43 E6
Garstang PR3 181 C8
Grimsargh PR2 139 C2
Southport PR9 54 D6
Weir OL13 88 A8
West Bradford BB7 189 D7
Whalley BB7 144 A7
Fell View Cl PR3 181 C8
Fell Way FY6 177 D7
Fellborough Lodge 5
FY8 90 A8
Fellery St PR7 43 C8
Fellfoot Lodge PR2 119 A4
Fellfoot Rd LA6 243 A3
Fellgate LA3 217 E2
Fells View BB7 144 A4
Fellside Cl BL8 49 F1
Fellside View LA3 212 F7
Fellstone Vale PR6 80 A1
Fellstone View PR6 80 A1
Fellway Cl 7 PR5 77 C8
Felstead WN8 18 B2
Felstead St PR1 97 D8
Felton Way PR4 74 F3

Feltons WN8 . . . . .18 B2
Fenber Ave FY4 . . . . .110 C7
Fencegate BB12 . . . . .147 C7
Fengrove PR4 . . . . .75 A8
Fenham Carr La LA1 . . . .215 C7
Feniscliffe Dr BB2 . . . . . .101 A2
Feniscowles Prim Sch
BB2 . . . . .80 C8
Fennel Cl FY2 . . . . .152 F4
Fenney Ct WN8 . . . . .18 C1
Fennyfold Terr BB12 . . . . .126 C6
Fensway PR4 . . . . .95 D2
Fenton Ave BB18 . . . . . . .196 D3
Fenton Rd Blackpool FY1 130 C6
Fulwood PR2 . . . . .118 C4
Fenton St LA1 . . . . .214 E8
Fenwick St BB11 . . . . .127 D3
Ferguson Gdns OL12 . . . . .52 F3
Ferguson Rd FY1 . . . . . . .130 E2
Ferguson St BB2 . . . . .81 D7
Fermor Rd Becconsall PR4 73 E1
Preston PR1 . . . . .118 C4
Fern Ave BB5 . . . . .103 F3
Fern Bank Carnforth LA5 223 D1
Chorley PR6 . . . . .61 D3
Lancaster LA1 . . . . .215 A5
Maghull L31 . . . . .5 E1
Nelson BB9 . . . . .148 E7
Fern Breck Cotts FY6 . .200 A2
Fern Cl
2 Bamber Bridge PR5 . . . .77 B8
Skelmersdale WN8 . . . . . . .17 E1
Fern Ct FY7 . . . . .198 C1
Fern Gore Ave BB5 . . . . .104 A3
Fern Gr FY1 . . . . .130 C3
Fern Hill La OL12 . . . . .52 A3
Fern Isle Cl OL12 . . . . .52 B8
Fern Lea Bolton-le-S LA5 .221 A4
Nelson BB9 . . . . .148 E8
Fern Lea St BB4 . . . . .69 D8
Fern Mdw PR6 . . . . .78 C2
Fern Rd BB11 . . . . .127 E4
Fern St Bacup OL13 . . . . . .87 F3
Colne BB8 . . . . .171 F6
Newchurch BB4 . . . . .86 F1
Ramsbottom BL0 . . . . .50 D7
Fern Terr BB4 . . . . .85 A3
Fernbank Ave BB18 . . . . .196 A3
Fernbank Ct BB9 . . . . . . .148 E7
Ferncliffe Dr LA3 . . . . . . .216 D2
Ferndale
4 Blackburn BB1 . . . . . .102 A6
Skelmersdale WN8 . . . . . . .18 C2
Ferndale Ave FY4 . . . . . . .110 D7
Ferndale Cl
Freckleton PR4 . . . . .93 D7
Leyland PR25 . . . . .60 B7
Thornton FY5 . . . . .176 C2
Ferndale Dr WN6 . . . . .19 E7
Ferndale St BB10 . . . . . . .128 C8
Ferngrove BL9 . . . . .33 B4
Fernhill Ave BB18 . . . . . . .196 A3
Fernhill Cl OL13 . . . . .70 E8
Fernhill Cres **1** OL13 . . . . .70 E8
Fernhill Dr OL13 . . . . .70 E8
Fernhill Gr **2** OL13 . . . . . .70 E8
Fernhill Pk OL13 . . . . .70 E8
Fernhill Way **4** OL13 . . . . .70 E8
Fernhills BL7 . . . . .47 E2
Fernhurst Ave FY4 . . . . . .130 D1
Fernhurst Gate L39 . . . . . .15 B1
Fernhurst St BB2 . . . . .81 D8
Fernlea Ave
Barnoldswick BB18 . . . . . .196 B2
Oswaldtwistle BB5 . . . . . . .104 A3
Fernlea Cl BB2 . . . . .81 B8
Fernlea Dr BB5 . . . . .124 F4
Fernleigh PR26 . . . . .59 A8
Fernleigh Cl FY2 . . . . .152 D4
Fernley Rd PR8 . . . . .35 A5
Ferns The Bacup OL13 . . . .88 A1
Bamber Bridge PR5 . . . . . . .97 C3
Preston PR2 . . . . .117 C2
Fernside Way OL12 . . . . . .52 A1
Fernstone Cl BL6 . . . . .32 A3
Fernview Dr FY7 . . . . .50 A1
Fernville Terr **9** OL13 . . . .70 D8
Fernwood Ave FY5 . . . . . .153 B8
Fernwood Cl FY8 . . . . .90 E4
Ferny Knoll Rd WA11 . . . . .8 F4
Fernyhalgh Ct PR2 . . . . . .118 D6
Fernyhalgh Gdns PR2 . . . .118 D6
Fernyhalgh La PR2 . . . . . .118 D7
Fernyhalgh Pl PR2 . . . . . .118 D6
Ferrier Bank PR4 . . . . .92 D5
Ferrier Cl **1** BB1 . . . . .102 C5
Ferry Rd PR2 . . . . .95 F8
Ferry Side La PR9 . . . . . . .54 C5
Ferry View Ct FY7 . . . . . .199 C5
Ffrances Pas **81** LA1 . . . . .214 F4
Fiddler's La Chipping PR3 184 F4
Clayton Green PR6 . . . . . . .78 B2
Fidler La PR26 . . . . .76 F5
Field Cl L40 . . . . .25 F3
Field Edge La PR3 . . . . . . .201 E5
Field Maple Dr PR2 . . . . . .118 F3
Field Rd LA3 . . . . .212 D6
Field St Blackburn BB2 . . . .101 B2
Blackpool FY1 . . . . .130 C2
Padiham BB12 . . . . .126 C7
Skelmersdale WN8 . . . . . . .18 C2
Field Top OL13 . . . . .88 A7
Field Wlk L39 . . . . .16 B5
Fielden St Burnley BB11 . . .127 D5

Fielden St continued
Chorley PR6 . . . . .43 E8
5 Leyland PR25 . . . . .76 D1
Fieldfare Cl
Middleworth Green PR1 . . .96 C3
Thornton FY5 . . . . .176 A5
Fieldfare Ct PR7 . . . . .42 F5
Fieldhouse Ave FY5 . . . . .176 D2
Fieldhouse Ind Est OL12 . .52 F2
Fieldhouse Rd OL12 . . . . . .52 F2
Fieldhouse Sch OL12 . . . . .52 F1
Fielding Cres BB2 . . . . . . .101 A1
Fielding La
Great Harwood BB6 . . . . . .124 B5
Oswaldtwistle BB5 . . . . . . .103 E3
Fielding Pl PR6 . . . . .31 B8
Fielding Rd FY1 . . . . .130 D8
Fielding St BB1 . . . . .124 C1
Fieldings Bldgs **9** BB4 . . . .85 E2
Fieldings The L31 . . . . .5 B4
Fieldlands PR8 . . . . .36 A2
Fields End BB6 . . . . .123 C8
Fields Rd BB4 . . . . .85 C1
Fields The PR7 . . . . .41 B7
Fieldsend LA3 . . . . .213 A7
Fieldside Ave PR7 . . . . .60 C1
Fieldside Cl PR5 . . . . .97 C3
Fieldview WN8 . . . . .10 A7
Fieldway FY8 . . . . .110 E2
Fife Cl PR6 . . . . .43 E6
Fife St Accrington BB5 . . . .104 A4
Barrowford BB9 . . . . .170 C1
Fifth Ave Blackpool FY4 . . .110 C7
Burnley BB10 . . . . .148 B3
Bury BL9 . . . . .33 D4
Filberts Cl PR2 . . . . .117 C3
Filberts The PR2 . . . . .117 C3
File St PR7 . . . . .43 C7
Filey Pl Blackpool FY1 . . . .130 B6
Fulwood PR2 . . . . .117 A4
Filey Rd FY8 . . . . .111 A1
Filton Gr LA3 . . . . .217 E3
Finch Cl BB1 . . . . .101 E6
Finch La
Appley Bridge WN6 . . . . . .28 B1
Cottam PR4 . . . . .116 E4
Finch Mill Ave WN6 . . . . . .19 D7
Finch St **5** BB3 . . . . .81 F7
Finch's Cotts **6** PR1 . . . .96 E4
Finches The FY6 . . . . .153 B2
Finchley Rd FY1 . . . . .130 B8
Findon WN6 . . . . .29 A2
Fine Jane's Way PR9 . . . . .36 B8
Finney Park Dr PR2 . . . . . .95 D8
Finnington Cotts BB2 . . . . .80 A6
Finnington La BB2 . . . . . . .80 A6
Finsbury Ave
Blackpool FY1 . . . . .130 D2
Lytham St Anne's FY8 . . . . .90 B4
Finsbury Pl BB2 . . . . .81 D8
Finsley Gate BB11 . . . . . . .128 A5
Finsley St BB10 . . . . .148 E3
Finsley View BB10 . . . . . . .148 F3
Fir Cl PR7 . . . . .198 C2
Fir Cotes L31 . . . . .5 E1
Fir Ct BB5 . . . . .104 E8
Fir Gr Blackpool FY1 . . . . .130 E2
Warton PR4 . . . . .92 D6
Fir Grove Rd **11** BB11 . . . .128 E4
Fir St Burnley BB10 . . . . . .128 B5
Bury BL9 . . . . .33 A2
Haslingden BB4 . . . . .85 B3
Nelson BB9 . . . . .148 F8
Ramsbottom BL0 . . . . .50 D7
Southport PR8 . . . . .35 F6
Fir Tree Ave PR2 . . . . .117 B4
Fir Tree Cl Hest Bank LA5 .220 F2
Much Hoole PR4 . . . . .74 E3
Skelmersdale WN8 . . . . . . .9 D7
Fir Tree La Haskayne L39 .14 F3
Ormskirk L39 . . . . .15 A2
Fir Tree Pl FY5 . . . . .152 F8
Fir Tree Way **3** BL6 . . . . .32 E1
Fir Trees Ave
Bamber Bridge PR5 . . . . . . .77 A8
Fulwood PR2 . . . . .119 A4
Fir Trees Cl BB8 . . . . .149 A8
Fir Trees Cres **1** PR5 . . . .77 A8
Fir Trees Gr BB12 . . . . . . .146 E5
Fir Trees La BB12 . . . . . . .146 E5
Fir Trees Pl PR2 . . . . .118 F4
Fir Trees Rd PR5 . . . . .97 A1
Firbank PR7 . . . . .60 C2
Firbank Ave PR4 . . . . .57 A7
Firbank Rd LA1 . . . . .218 E1
Firbeck WN8 . . . . .18 C1
Fircroft WN6 . . . . .29 A2
Firfield Cl PR4 . . . . .113 E5
Firs Cl L37 . . . . .11 D5
Firs Cres L37 . . . . .11 D5
Firs La L39 . . . . .14 E3
Firs Link L37 . . . . .11 D4
Firshill Cl FY5 . . . . .153 B8
First Ave Blackpool FY4 . . .110 C7
Church BB5 . . . . .104 A8
Clifton PR4 . . . . .115 C1
Poulton-le-F FY6 . . . . .153 E3
Preesall Park FY6 . . . . .200 C1
Preston PR2 . . . . .117 A2
West Bradford BB7 . . . . . . .189 D7
Wrea Green PR4 . . . . .113 B4
First Terr LA1 . . . . .209 B5
Firswood Cl FY8 . . . . .90 E4
Firswood Rd L40,WN8 . . . .17 C3
Firtree Cl PR7 . . . . .43 C3
Firtrees Dr BB2 . . . . .80 F8
Firwood WN8 . . . . .18 D3
Firwood Cl PR3 . . . . .140 A8

Firwood La PR5 . . . . .99 B5
Fish House La PR3 . . . . . .185 B5
Fish La L40 . . . . .38 B2
Fish Rake La BL0,BB4 . . . . .68 E6
Fisher Dr Orrell WN5 . . . . . .10 C7
Southport PR9 . . . . .35 F7
Fisher St FY1 . . . . .130 C6
Fisher's La FY4 . . . . .111 A5
Fisher's Slack La FY6 . . . .155 D3
Fishergate PR1 . . . . .96 F7
Fishergate Ct **12** PR1 . . . .96 E3
Fishergate Ctr PR1 . . . . . . .96 F7
Fishergate Hill PR1 . . . . . .96 E6
Fishergate Wlk **7** PR1 . . . .96 F7
Fishermans Cl L37 . . . . . . .11 B6
Fishermans Reach PR4 .113 D4
Fishmoor Dr BB2 . . . . .81 F8
Fishwick La PR6 . . . . .79 B1
Fishwick Par PR1 . . . . .97 D8
Fishwick Prim Sch PR1 . .118 E1
Fishwick Rd PR1 . . . . .97 C8
Fishwick View PR1 . . . . . . .97 D8
Fitchfield PR1 . . . . .96 F2
Fitzgerald St PR1 . . . . . . .118 C1
Fitzroy Rd FY2 . . . . .152 D3
Fitzroy St PR1 . . . . .96 E7
Five Acres PR26 . . . . .76 E4
Five Ashes La LA2 . . . . . . .210 F7
Five Lane Ends
Hampson Green LA2 . . . . .207 D8
Preesall FY6 . . . . .200 A2
Singleton FY6 . . . . .154 D4
Flag La Bamber Bridge PR1 96 F1
Bretherton PR26 . . . . .58 A5
Runshaw Moor PR26,PR7 . .59 D4
Flag St OL13 . . . . .70 E8
Flagg La PR6 . . . . .43 F5
Flakefleet Ave FY7 . . . . . .198 E1
Flamstead WN8 . . . . .18 C1
Flare Rd LA3 . . . . .212 D6
Flash La LA2 . . . . .39 B4
Flat La L40 . . . . .225 E3
Flatfield Way L31 . . . . .5 E1
Flatman's La L39 . . . . .13 E1
Flats Ret Pk The PR5 . . . . .97 C5
Flats The Chorley PR7 . . . . .43 B6
Kirkham PR4 . . . . .114 B4
3 Kirkham PR4 . . . . .114 B5
Flax Cl BB4 . . . . .68 A8
Flax La L40 . . . . .25 F2
Flax Moss Cl BB4 . . . . .68 A8
Flax St **8** BL0 . . . . .50 A4
Flaxfield Rd L37 . . . . .12 A3
Flaxfield Way PR4 . . . . . . .114 A5
Flaxfields L40 . . . . .25 F3
Flaxton WN8 . . . . .18 C1
Fleet La LA2 . . . . .238 A8
Fleet St Blackpool FY1 . . . .130 C4
Chorley PR7 . . . . .43 C7
Horwich BL6 . . . . .32 D3
Longridge PR3 . . . . .140 A7
Lytham St Anne's FY8 . . . . .89 D8
Nelson BB9 . . . . .170 E1
4 Preston PR1 . . . . .96 F7
Fleet Street La PR3 . . . . . .141 A6
Fleet Wlk **5** BB11 . . . . . . .128 A6
Fleetgreen LA1 . . . . .218 C3
Fleetwood Charles Saer Com
Prim Sch FY7 . . . . .198 D2
Fleetwood Chaucer Com
Prim Sch FY7 . . . . .199 A4
Fleetwood Cl
Blackburn BB2 . . . . .101 F1
Southport PR9 . . . . .53 F3
Fleetwood Cres PR9 . . . . . .55 A6
Fleetwood Ct PR9 . . . . .53 D1
Fleetwood Dr PR9 . . . . .55 A6
Fleetwood Flakefleet Prim
Sch FY7 . . . . .198 E2
Fleetwood High Sch
FY7 . . . . .198 D2
Fleetwood Hospl FY7 . . . .199 B5
Fleetwood Old Rd PR4 . . .133 E3
Fleetwood Rd
Blackpool FY5 . . . . .152 D7
Burnley BB10 . . . . .148 C2
Carleton FY7 . . . . .153 B5
Esprick PR4 . . . . .133 D5
Fleetwood FY7 . . . . .175 E8
Kirkham PR4 . . . . .113 F7
Padiham BB12 . . . . .126 D8
Southport PR9 . . . . .53 E3
Fleetwood Rd N FY5 . . . . .176 B3
Fleetwood Rd S FY5 . . . . .153 B7
Fleetwood Sh & L Village
FY7 . . . . .199 A3
Fleetwood St
6 Leyland PR25 . . . . .77 B2
Preston PR2 . . . . .117 D1
Fleming Ho **8** LA1 . . . . . .218 D2
Fleming Sq
Blackburn BB2 . . . . .101 E4
Longridge PR3 . . . . .140 B7
Flensburg Way PR26 . . . . .76 D4
Fletcher Ave PR4 . . . . .118 C6
Fletcher Rd Preston PR1 . .118 C1
Rishton BB1 . . . . .103 A8
Fletcher St
Blackburn BB2 . . . . .101 D3
Bury BL9 . . . . .33 A2
Nelson BB9 . . . . .148 F7
Fletcher's Dr L40 . . . . .25 E4
Flett St PR1 . . . . .117 C1
Fletton Cl OL12 . . . . .52 E2
Fletton Mews OL12 . . . . . .52 E2
Flimby WN8 . . . . .18 D1
Flimby Cl BB2 . . . . .81 F8
Flintoff Way PR1 . . . . .118 B3

Flintron Brow LA2 . . . . . . .233 A2
Flip Rd BB4 . . . . .85 A2
Flockton Ct **9** BL6 . . . . . . .32 B4
Flordon WN8 . . . . .18 D2
Florence Ave
Burnley BB11 . . . . .127 C4
Warton PR4 . . . . .92 D5
Florence Pl **1** BB1 . . . . . .102 A6
Florence St
Blackburn BB1 . . . . .102 A6
Blackpool FY4 . . . . .111 A6
Burnley BB11 . . . . .127 C5
1 Church BB5 . . . . .103 E6
Flower Fields PR3 . . . . . . .181 D2
Flower Scar Rd OL14 . . . . . .88 E6
Flowerfield PR4 . . . . .116 E6
Flowers Cl BB2 . . . . .81 D7
Floyd Rd PR2 . . . . .118 E3
Floyer St PR1 . . . . .97 B7
Fluke Hall La PR3 . . . . . . .201 B8
Fold BB9 . . . . .170 E5
Fold Gdns OL12 . . . . .52 B4
Fold House Cvn Pk PR3 201 D4
Fold The Rawtenstall BB4 . . .86 A7
Thornton-in-C BD23 . . . . . .197 B5
Fold View BL7 . . . . .47 E1
Folds BL6 . . . . .31 C3
Folds St BB12 . . . . .127 F8
Foldside PR4 . . . . .93 C7
Folkestone Cl
Cleveleys FY5 . . . . .175 F4
Warton PR4 . . . . .92 E7
Folkestone Rd
Lytham St Anne's FY8 . . . . .89 F8
Southport PR8 . . . . .35 F3
Folly La Barnoldswick BB8 193 F7
Lancaster LA1,LA2 . . . . . . .218 B4
Folly Terr BB4 . . . . .86 B8
Folly Wlk **20** OL12 . . . . . .52 F1
Fontwell WN6 . . . . .29 F1
Fooden La BB7 . . . . .230 E4
Foot Mill Cres OL12 . . . . . .52 D2
Foot Wood Cres OL12 . . . .52 D2
Footeran La LA5 . . . . .225 E3
Forbes Cl BB4 . . . . .85 A7
Ford La Goosnargh PR3 . . .160 F2
Silverdale LA5 . . . . .225 E4
Ford St Barrowford BB9 . . . .170 E4
Burnley BB10 . . . . .148 B1
Lancaster LA1 . . . . .218 B1
Fordham Cl PR8 . . . . .35 E3
Fordside Ave BB5 . . . . . . .124 E4
Fordstone Ave FY6 . . . . . .200 A4
Fordway Ave FY3 . . . . .130 F6
Fore St BB3 . . . . .81 F7
Foregate PR2 . . . . .117 E4
Foreside BB9 . . . . .170 E5
Forest Ave BB12 . . . . .147 E8
Forest Bank BB4 . . . . .86 A7
Forest Bank Rd BB4 . . . . . .86 A7
Forest Becks Brow BB7 230 D6
Forest Brook Ho PR2 . . . .117 C3
Forest Cl PR5 . . . . .97 C3
Forest Dr
Lytham St Anne's FY8 . . . . .90 F4
Shevington Moor WN6 . . . . .29 A2
Skelmersdale WN8 . . . . . . .18 C3
Forest Fold WN6 . . . . .19 E6
Forest Gate
Blackpool FY3 . . . . .130 E5
Morecambe LA3 . . . . .217 E5
Forest Gr PR3 . . . . .137 B8
Forest Ho BB9 . . . . .148 D7
Forest Holme Cl BB4 . . . . . .87 A7
Forest La BB9 . . . . .170 B2
Forest Pk LA1 . . . . .214 C7
Forest Rd PR8 . . . . .35 D6
Forest St Burnley BB11 . . . .128 B6
Forest Holme BB4 . . . . .87 A7
Nelson BB9 . . . . .170 D1
Forest View
14 Barrowford BB9 . . . . .170 D3
Brierfield BB9 . . . . .148 A5
Rochdale OL12 . . . . .52 D2
Forest Way PR2 . . . . .117 F6
Forester Dr BB12 . . . . .147 D8
Forester's Bldgs **9**
BB18 . . . . .196 B2
Foresters Hall **12** PR1 . . .96 F8
Forestry Houses BB7 . . . .228 C5
Forestway PR25 . . . . .59 F8
Forfar Gr BB11 . . . . .127 D3
Forfar St BB11 . . . . .127 D3
Forge Cl L40 . . . . .16 E4
Forge Cnr BB7 . . . . .144 C5
Forge La PR3 . . . . .181 E8
Forge St **3** OL13 . . . . .87 F2
Forges St PR25 . . . . .77 A1
Forgewood Cl LA2 . . . . . . .219 E6
Forgewood Dr LA2 . . . . . . .219 D6
Formby Ave FY7 . . . . .175 D7
Formby Bridge L37 . . . . . . .11 E2
Formby Bsns Pk L37 . . . . . .12 B3
Formby By-Pass
Formby L37 . . . . .12 B5
Hightown L37,L38 . . . . .3 B8
Formby Cl BB2 . . . . .81 F8
Formby Cres PR4 . . . . .74 F8
Formby Fields L37 . . . . . . .12 A2
Formby Gdns L37 . . . . .11 F4
Formby High Sch L37 . . . . .11 E4
Formby La Formby L37 . . . .12 B2
Haskayne L39 . . . . .14 E2
Formby Pl PR2 . . . . .116 E2
Formby Point Cvn Pk
L37 . . . . .11 B1
Formby Rd FY8 . . . . .110 F1
Formby St L37 . . . . .11 E2

Formby Sta L37 . . . . .11 E2
Forrest Ct **4** FY3 . . . . . . .130 E8
Forrest St BB1 . . . . .102 A5
Forrester Cl PR25 . . . . .76 E1
Forrestside BB2 . . . . .81 D7
Forshaw Ave
Blackpool FY3 . . . . .130 F8
Lytham St Anne's FY8 . . . . .89 D8
Forshaw Cl **6** FY7 . . . . . .198 F2
Forshaw Rd **3** PR1 . . . . . .96 D2
Forsythia Dr PR4 . . . . .78 B4
Fort Ave PR3 . . . . .141 D3
Fort St Accrington BB5 . . . .104 B6
Blackburn BB1 . . . . .102 A5
11 Clayton-le-M BB5 . . . .124 F3
Clitheroe BB7 . . . . .166 D7
Read BB12 . . . . .145 D2
Fort Street Ind Est BB1 .102 A6
Forton Primary Sch
PR3 . . . . .207 B3
Forton Rd **8** PR2 . . . . . . .116 E1
Forty Acre La PR3 . . . . . . .163 B5
Forward Ind Est PR25 . . . .76 E2
Foscote Rd L33 . . . . .1 A4
Fossdale Moss PR26 . . . . . .76 C1
Fosse Bank Ct BB2 . . . . . .82 A8
Fosse Cl BB1,BB2 . . . . . . .82 A8
Fosse Ct LA3 . . . . .217 E3
Foster Croft PR1 . . . . .96 C6
Foster Ct Bury BL9 . . . . . . .33 D4
Chorley PR6 . . . . .61 E1
Foster Rd
Barnoldswick BB18 . . . . . .196 A3
Formby L37 . . . . .11 D2
Foster St Accrington BB5 . .104 C7
Chorley PR6 . . . . .61 E1
Fosterfield Pl PR6 . . . . . . .61 E1
Fosters Cl PR9 . . . . .36 B8
Fosters Green Rd WN8 . . .18 D3
Fothergill St **1** BB8 . . . . .171 C5
Foul La PR8,PR9 . . . . .36 A5
Fouldrey Ave FY6 . . . . . . .153 F5
Foulds Cl BB8 . . . . .171 C4
Foulds Rd BB8 . . . . .172 B3
Foulds Terr BB8 . . . . .172 C2
Foulridge Wharf★ BB8 .194 D2
Foundary Gdns LA5 . . . . .223 D3
Foundry La Halton LA2 . . . .219 A7
Halton LA2 . . . . .219 B6
Foundry St **1** Bacup OL13 87 F2
Blackburn BB2 . . . . .101 D4
3 Burnley BB11 . . . . .127 F6
15 Chorley PR7 . . . . .43 C8
23 Darwen BB3 . . . . .82 A1
Haslingden BB4 . . . . .85 B2
Rawtenstall BB4 . . . . .85 F1
Fountain Pl BB5 . . . . .104 B5
Fountain Sq **3** BB9 . . . . .170 D3
Fountain St
Accrington BB5 . . . . .104 A5
Barnoldswick BB18 . . . . . .196 C2
Bury BL9 . . . . .33 A2
Colne BB8 . . . . .171 D4
Darwen BB3 . . . . .65 A8
Nelson BB9 . . . . .170 E1
Fountain St N **12** BL9 . . . .33 A3
Fountains Ave
Blackburn BB1 . . . . .102 B8
Read BB12 . . . . .145 D1
Fountains Cl PR7 . . . . .43 D5
Fountains Reach PR5 . . . .97 C3
Fountains The
Barrowford BB9 . . . . .170 D3
Ormskirk L39 . . . . .15 E6
Fountains Way
Formby L37 . . . . .12 B2
Oswaldtwistle BB5 . . . . . . .103 B5
Four Acre La PR3 . . . . . . .162 E5
Four Lane Ends
Barley BB7 . . . . .192 B2
Blackpool FY3 . . . . .131 A6
Bretherton PR26 . . . . .58 A7
Burton in L LA2 . . . . .242 C1
Carleton FY5 . . . . .153 B5
Charnock Richard PR7 . . . . .42 C4
Clitheroe BB7 . . . . .167 A6
Dolphinholme LA2 . . . . . . .226 A8
Gregson Lane PR5 . . . . . . .98 D2
Halsall L39 . . . . .23 D3
Halton LA2 . . . . .218 F7
Heapey PR6 . . . . .62 C4
Morecambe LA3 . . . . .216 D1
Simonstone BB12 . . . . . . .145 F4
Thornton FY5 . . . . .176 E1
Wray LA2 . . . . .238 E4
Four Lane Ends Rd OL13 .70 B8
Four Oaks Rd PR5 . . . . . . .78 B7
Fouracre BB2 . . . . .121 E2
Fourfields PR5 . . . . .97 E2
Fourth Ave Blackpool FY4 110 C7
Bury BL9 . . . . .33 D4
Fowler Ave PR26 . . . . .77 B6
Fowler Cl PR5 . . . . .99 C2
Fowler Height Cl BB2 . . . .81 B7
Fowler Hill La PR4 . . . . . .204 B5
Fowler Ind Pk BL6 . . . . . . .32 C2
Fowler La Farington PR26 .76 E1
Leyland PR5,PR26 . . . . . . .77 B5
Fowler St PR1 . . . . .117 D3
Fox Gr LA3 . . . . .216 E3
Fox Ind Est **2** FY2 . . . . . .152 E1
Fox La Coupe Green PR5 . . .98 E3
Leyland PR25 . . . . .59 E7
Fox Lane Ends PR4 . . . . . .113 A4
Fox St Accrington BB5 . . . .104 B6
Clitheroe BB7 . . . . .189 E1
Horwich BL6 . . . . .32 C2
Padiham BB12 . . . . .126 F6

Fox St continued
Preston PR1 . . . . .96 F7
Foxcote PR7 . . . . .61 C2
Foxdale Ave FY3 . . . . . .130 D7
Foxdale Cl Bacup OL13 . . .88 A1
Edgworth BL7 . . . . .48 E7
Southport PR8 . . . . .35 E3
Foxdale Gr PR1 . . . . . .118 D3
Foxdale Pl LA1 . . . . . .218 C2
Foxen Dole La BB12 . . . .147 A5
Foxes Farmserve FY6 . . .131 E7
Foxes Terr PR3 . . . . . .157 C7
Foxfield Ave LA4 . . . . .217 C3
Foxfield Cl BB5 . . . . . .103 D4
Foxfield Dr BB4 . . . . . .86 F4
Foxfields FY6 . . . . . . .177 C8
Foxfold WN8 . . . . .18 D3
Foxglove Ave L40 . . . . . .25 F4
Foxglove Cl
Hesketh Bank PR4 . . . . . .73 E4
Standish WN6 . . . . .29 D2
Walton Summit PR5 . . . . .78 B8
Foxglove Ct OL12 . . . . . .52 F3
Foxglove Dr Bury BL9 . . . .33 D3
Lucas Green PR6 . . . . . . .61 C5
Foxglove Way PR4 . . . . . .93 D7
Foxhall Rd FY1 . . . . . .130 B3
Foxhall Sq 8 FY1 . . . . .130 B3
Foxhill Bank Brow BB5 . .103 E5
Foxhill Cl L37 . . . . .11 C3
Foxhill Dr BB4 . . . . . . .86 F4
Foxhill Terr BB5 . . . . . .100 F2
Foxhole Rd Chorley PR7 . .42 F8
Euxton PR7 . . . . .60 F1
Foxholes Rd Horwich BL6 . .32 D4
Morecambe LA4 . . . . . .217 D6
Foxhouse La L31 . . . . .5 F1
Foxhouse St BB2 . . . . . .101 C5
Foxstones Cres BB2 . . . . .81 A8
Foxstones La BB10 . . . . .129 B2
Foxwell Cl BB4 . . . . . . .85 C2
Foxwood Chase BB5 . . . .104 E8
Foxwood Cl WN5 . . . . . . .10 E5
Foxwood Dr PR4 . . . . . .113 E5
Foxwood The PR7 . . . . . .42 C1
Frailey Cl PR8 . . . . .21 C4
France St Blackburn BB2 . .101 D4
Church BB5 . . . . .103 E6
Frances St 3 BB3 . . . . . .81 F2
Francis Ave BB9 . . . . . .170 E5
Francis St Blackburn BB2 . .101 B1
Blackpool FY1 . . . . . . .130 B6
Burnley BB10 . . . . .148 A1
3 Clayton-le-M BB5 . . .124 F3
Colne BB8 . . . . .171 B3
Preston PR2 . . . . .117 C1
Frank St
4 Accrington BB5 . . . .125 A1
Barnoldswick BB18 . . . .196 B2
Preston PR1 . . . . .117 F1
Frankland Ho 15 LA1 . . .218 D2
Franklands PR4 . . . . . . .95 A1
Franklands Dr PR2 . . . . .119 A5
Franklands Fold 1 PR1 . . .96 F8
Franklin Ainsworth Ho 2
BB6 . . . . .124 C5
Franklin Rd BB2 . . . . . .101 B3
Franklin St
2 Burnley BB12 . . . . .127 C6
Clitheroe BB7 . . . . . . .166 D7
27 Darwen BB3 . . . . . .82 A1
Lancaster LA1 . . . . . . .214 F5
Fraser Ave PR1 . . . . . . .96 E5
Fraser St Accrington BB5 .104 A4
Burnley BB10 . . . . .148 B1
Frazer Gr 13 LA1 . . . . .214 F8
Freckleton CE Prim Sch
PR4 . . . . .93 C7
Freckleton Ct FY8 . . . . . .91 C3
Freckleton Dr L33 . . . . . . .1 A5
Freckleton Rd
Kirkham PR4 . . . . .114 B3
Southport PR9 . . . . .53 F4
Freckleton St
Blackburn BB2 . . . . . . .101 E4
Blackpool FY1 . . . . . . .130 B4
Kirkham PR4 . . . . .114 B4
2 Lytham St Anne's FY8 . .91 C3
Freckleton Strike Lane Prim
Sch PR4 . . . . .93 B8
Frederick Row BB1 . . . .102 B5
Frederick St
Accrington BB5 . . . . . .104 A6
Barnoldswick BB18 . . . .196 A3
6 Blackburn BB2 . . . .101 E3
2 Blackpool FY4 . . . .110 D8
Chorley PR6 . . . . .43 E7
Darwen BB3 . . . . .82 A2
Oswaldtwistle BB5 . . . .103 E4
12 Ramsbottom BL0 . . .50 B5
Fredora Ave FY3 . . . . . .131 A2
Free La BB4 . . . . .68 A6
Free Trade St 16 BB11 . . .127 F6
Freeholds La
Waddington BB7 . . . . . .188 F6
Waddington BB7 . . . . . .188 F7
Freeholds Rd OL12 . . . . . .71 E6
Freeholds Terr OL12 . . . . .71 E6
Freeman's La PR7 . . . . . .42 E3
Freemantle Ave FY4 . . . .110 B4
Freetown Bsns Pk 11
BL9 . . . . .33 A4
Freightway LA3 . . . . . .217 E2
French Cl BB2 . . . . .101 E4
French Rd BB2 . . . . . . .101 B4
Frenchwood Ave
Lytham St Anne's FY8 . . . .90 F3

Frenchwood Ave continued
Preston PR1 . . . . .97 B6
Frenchwood Com Prim Sch
PR1 . . . . .97 B6
Frenchwood Knoll PR1 . . .97 B6
Frenchwood St 4 PR1 . . .97 A6
Freshfield Ave BB5 . . . .124 E3
Freshfield Ct L37 . . . . . . .11 E4
Freshfield Cvn Pk L37 . . . .11 E4
Freshfield Prim Sch L37 . . .12 A4
Freshfield Rd L37 . . . . . . .11 E4
Freshfield Sta L37 . . . . . .11 E5
Freshfields PR2 . . . . . .116 B3
Friar St BB1 . . . . .214 F8
Friar's Moss Rd LA2 . . . .232 A4
Friar's Pas 23 LA1 . . . .214 F8
Friargate Horwich BL6 . . .32 C4
Preston PR1 . . . . .96 F8
Friargate Wlk 6 PR1 . . . .96 F7
Friars The PR2 . . . . . . .117 E4
Friars Wlk L37 . . . . .12 B2
Friary PR4 . . . . .114 C4
Friday St PR6 . . . . .43 D8
Fieldhurst Rd OL14 . . . . .109 C5
Frinton Gr FY2 . . . . . . .152 E6
Frith's Ct PR5 . . . . .98 F1
Friths Ave PR5 . . . . .98 E1
Frobisher Dr FY8 . . . . . .110 D1
Frog La L40 . . . . .26 D3
Frome St PR1 . . . . .118 D1
Froom St PR6 . . . . .43 D8
Fry St BB9 . . . . .148 F8
Fryent Cl BL6 . . . . .31 D2
Fryer Cl PR1 . . . . .96 D1
Fulford Ave 1 PR2 . . . . .116 C1
Fulham St BB9 . . . . . . .170 F2
Full View BB2 . . . . .81 B8
Fullers Terr OL13 . . . . . . .87 F1
Fulmar Cres LA3 . . . . . .212 F5
Fulmar Terr BB5 . . . . . .103 E4
Fulmars The FY6 . . . . . .153 B2
Fulshaw Rd PR2 . . . . . .117 B2
Fulwood & Cadley Prim Sch
PR2 . . . . .117 D4
Fulwood Ave
Becconsall PR4 . . . . . . .73 E1
Blackpool FY3 . . . . . . .130 F8
Southport PR8 . . . . .35 D4
Fulwood Dr LA4 . . . . . .217 F6
Fulwood Hall Hospl
PR2 . . . . .118 C5
Fulwood Hall La PR2 . . . .118 B4
Fulwood High Sch & Arts Coll
PR2 . . . . .117 C6
Fulwood Hts PR2 . . . . . .118 C5
Fulwood Row PR2 . . . . .118 E6
Funchal Ave L37 . . . . . . .11 D1
Furlong Cres FY3 . . . . . .153 A1
Furlong Gn FY5 . . . . . . .153 D4
Furlong La FY6 . . . . . . .153 D5
Furness Ave
Blackburn BB1 . . . . . . .102 A4
Fleetwood FY7 . . . . . . .198 D1
Formby L37 . . . . .11 F3
Lancaster LA1 . . . . . . .211 B7
Normoss FY3 . . . . .131 A4
Ormskirk L39 . . . . .15 E4
Read BB12 . . . . .145 D1
Furness Cl Chorley PR7 . .43 D5
Southport PR8 . . . . .21 B3
Furness Ct 3 FY3 . . . . . .131 A4
Furness Dr
High Bentham LA2 . . . . .239 D8
Poulton-le-F FY6 . . . . . .154 A3
Furness Rd
7 Burnley BB10 . . . . .148 B1
3 Lancaster LA1 . . . . .218 B1
Furnessford Rd LA2 . . . .239 A6
Furnival Dr L40 . . . . . . .25 D4
Further Ends Rd PR4 . . . .93 B6
Further Field PR5 . . . . . .78 A8
Further Heights Rd 1
OL12 . . . . .52 F1
Further La BB2,PR5 . . . .100 C3
Further Wilworth BB1 . . .122 C2
Furthergate BB1 . . . . . .102 B5
Furthergate Ind Est
BB1 . . . . .102 B5
Fushetts La LA2 . . . . . .239 D8
Futura Pk BL3 . . . . .32 C1
Fylde Ave Lancaster LA1 .211 B7
Leyland PR26 . . . . .76 C4
Fylde Coast Hospl FY3 . . .130 F7
Fylde Ct FY6 . . . . .199 D5
Fylde Rd
Lytham St Anne's FY8 . . . .90 D5
Poulton-le-F FY6 . . . . . .153 E4
Preston PR1,PR2 . . . . . .117 D1
Southport PR9 . . . . .54 B4
Fylde Road Ind Est PR1 . .117 D1
Fylde St Kirkham PR4 . . . .114 A4
Preston PR1 . . . . .96 E8
Fylde View Cl FY6 . . . . .153 D2

G

Gabbot St PR7 . . . . .31 A7
Gable Mews L37 . . . . . . .12 A1
Gable The LA6 . . . . . . .240 B7
Gables Pl LA4 . . . . .217 D5
Gables The PR4 . . . . . . .116 E4
Gadfield St 2 BB3 . . . . . .65 B8
Gadsby St FY1 . . . . . . .130 B2
Gage St 32 LA1 . . . . . .214 F8
Gaghills Rd BB4 . . . . . . .86 F1
Gaghills Terr 3 BB4 . . . . .86 F1

Gainsborough Ave
Bamber Bridge PR5 . . . . .77 A7
Blackburn BB2 . . . . . . .101 C6
Burnley BB11 . . . . .127 F3
Morecambe LA4 . . . . . .217 D6
Gainsborough Rd
Blackpool FY1 . . . . . . .130 D4
Ramsbottom BL0 . . . . . .50 B1
Southport PR8 . . . . .34 E3
Gaisgill Ave LA4 . . . . . .217 B3
Gait Barrows Nature
Reserve* LA7 . . . . . .225 A7
Gale St OL12 . . . . .52 F3
Gales La LA3 . . . . .40 A3
Galgate Silk Mills Ind Est
LA2 . . . . .211 B4
Gall La OL14 . . . . .109 C3
Galleries The 1 BB9 . . . .148 E8
Gallery The 1 BB11 . . . .127 E4
Galligreaves St BB2 . . . .101 D3
Galligreaves The BB2 . . .101 D4
Galloway Cl 2 OL10 . . . . .33 F1
Galloway Cres FY2 . . . . .152 F5
Galloway Dr WN8 . . . . . .10 B6
Galloway Rd FY7 . . . . . .198 F5
Gallows La PR3 . . . . . . .142 A6
Galway Ave FY2 . . . . . .152 D3
Gamble Rd FY5 . . . . . . .176 B4
Gambleside Cl BB4 . . . . .106 A1
Game St BB6 . . . . .124 C5
Gamull La PR2 . . . . . . .118 F5
Gandy La OL12 . . . . .52 D4
Gannow Bsns Pk BB12 . .127 B6
Gannow La BB12 . . . . . .127 C6
Gantley Ave WN5 . . . . . .10 D3
Gantley Cres WN5 . . . . . .10 D3
Gantley Rd WN5 . . . . . . .10 D3
Ganton Cl PR8 . . . . .35 E3
Ganton Ct PR1 . . . . .96 A6
Garbett St BB5 . . . . . . .104 A4
Garden Ave PR4 . . . . . .113 B4
Garden City BL0 . . . . . . .50 A2
Garden Cl FY3 . . . . .131 A2
Garden Pl LA6 . . . . . . .240 C7
Garden Row OL12 . . . . . .52 D2
Garden St
Abbey Village PR6 . . . . . .80 C2
Accrington BB5 . . . . . .104 B7
11 Bacup OL13 . . . . . .70 C8
1 Bamber Bridge PR5 . . .77 B7
6 Barnoldswick BB18 . .196 B2
Blackburn BB2 . . . . . . .101 C4
Brierfield BB9 . . . . . . .148 B5
Colne BB8 . . . . .171 B4
Great Harwood BB6 . . . .124 C4
Higham BB12 . . . . .146 F5
Kirkham PR4 . . . . .114 A4
Lytham St Anne's FY8 . . . .89 E6
Nelson BB9 . . . . .148 E8
Oswaldtwistle BB5 . . . .103 D4
Padiham BB12 . . . . . . .146 C1
Preston PR1 . . . . .96 F7
Ramsbottom BL0 . . . . . .50 C6
Ramsbottom,Brooksbottoms
BL0 . . . . .50 C3
Garden Terr
17 Blackpool FY4 . . . .130 B1
Chorley PR7 . . . . .61 C1
Heysham LA3 . . . . .213 A2
BB8 . . . . .171 B4
Garden Vale Bsns Ctr 1
BB8 . . . . .171 B4
Garden View Pl 1 FY4 . . .130 E1
Garden Wlk
Cleveleys FY5 . . . . . . .175 D5
Preston PR1 . . . . .117 B1
Gardeners Mews 10
FY1 . . . . .130 C7
Gardeners Row BB7 . . . .145 F7
Gardeners View L33 . . . . . .1 A6
Gardenia Cl PR6 . . . . . . .78 B4
Gardens Gr LA4 . . . . . . .217 A4
Gardens The Halton LA2 . .219 B6
Turton Bottoms BL7 . . . . .48 D4
Gardiners Pl WN8 . . . . . . .8 E8
Gardner Arc LA3 . . . . . .216 E4
Gardner Bldgs LA3 . . . . .216 E4
Gardner Rd Formby L37 . . .12 B4
Lancaster LA1 . . . . . . .218 D2
Morecambe LA4 . . . . . .216 E3
Warton LA5 . . . . .223 D5
Gardner's La PR3 . . . . . .182 D3
Garfield Ave LA1 . . . . . .214 D7
Garfield Ct FY3 . . . . . . .131 C2
Garfield Dr LA4 . . . . . . .217 F4
Garfield St
Accrington BB5 . . . . . .104 D5
8 Cornholme OL14 . . . .109 C1
Fleetwood FY7 . . . . . . .199 B5
Garfield Terr PR6 . . . . . .61 D2
Garland Gr 2 FY3 . . . . . .198 D3
Garner Ave BB4 . . . . . . .81 D7
Garnet Cl 4 FY5 . . . . . .152 F7
Garnet St 3 LA1 . . . . . .215 A8
Garnett Gn L29 . . . . .15 D4
Garnett Pl WN8 . . . . .9 A7
Garnett Rd BB7 . . . . . . .166 C7
Garnett St
Barrowford BB9 . . . . . .170 D2
Darwen BB3 . . . . .82 B1
Morecambe LA4 . . . . . .217 B6
Ramsbottom BL0 . . . . . .50 B5
Garrick Gr FY3 . . . . . . .130 E7
Garrick Par PR8 . . . . . . .35 A6
Garrick St BB9 . . . . . . .170 E2
Garrison Rd PR2 . . . . . .118 B3
Gars End LA2 . . . . .238 D6
Gars The LA2 . . . . .238 D6

Garsdale Ave BB10 . . . .148 B4
Garsdale Cres PR2 . . . . . .97 E5
Garsdale Rd PR2 . . . . . .118 C4
Garsden Ave BB1 . . . . . .102 A3
Garstang Cl FY6 . . . . . .153 C2
Garstang Com Prim Sch
PR3 . . . . .181 C8
Garstang High Sch PR3 . .181 D5
Garstang New Rd FY4 . . .154 C3
Garstang Rd
Bilsborrow PR3 . . . . . . .159 A4
Bowgreave PR3 . . . . . . .181 D4
Catterall PR3 . . . . .181 E1
Chipping PR3 . . . . .185 C2
Cockerham LA2,PR3 . . . .206 E2
Fulwood PR1,PR2,PR3 . . .117 C5
Kirkham PR4 . . . . .113 F6
Little Eccleston PR3,FY6 . .155 D5
Newsham PR3 . . . . .137 B4
Singleton FY6 . . . . .154 C3
Southport PR9 . . . . .54 A5
St Michael's on W PR3 . . .157 C7
Stake Pool PR3 . . . . . . .202 B3
Garstang Rd E FY6 . . . . .153 A4
Garstang Rd N PR4 . . . . .113 F7
Garstang Rd S PR4 . . . . .113 F6
Garstang Rd W FY3,FY6 . .153 B2
Garstang St BB3 . . . . . . .82 A1
Garstang St Thomas' CE Prim
Sch PR3 . . . . .181 B6
Garston St BL9 . . . . .33 A4
Garstone Croft PR2 . . . .117 D6
Garswood Cl
Brierfield BB12 . . . . . . .147 F2
Maghull L31 . . . . .5 E3
Garth Edge OL12 . . . . . . .71 E6
Garton Ave FY4 . . . . . . .110 D6
Gas Field Rd LA3 . . . . . .212 E4
Gas House La LA2 . . . . .239 D8
Gas St Adlington PR6 . . . . .31 A6
Bacup OL13 . . . . .87 F2
8 Burnley BB11 . . . . .127 F6
Haslingden BB4 . . . . . . .84 F1
Longridge PR3 . . . . . . .140 A8
Gas Terr PR25 . . . . .77 B2
Gaskell Cl LA5 . . . . . . .224 C3
Gaskell Cres FY5 . . . . . .176 B4
Gaskell Ho LA1 . . . . . . .218 C4
Gaskell Rd PR1 . . . . .96 E5
Gaskell St PR6 . . . . .43 E8
Gate Ho PR1 . . . . .96 E7
Gate St BB1 . . . . .102 A5
Gatefield Ct BB11 . . . . . .128 A4
Gategill Gr WN5 . . . . . . .10 D3
Gateland BB18 . . . . . . .194 D8
Gates La L29 . . . . .4 C1
Gateside Ct 2 FY3 . . . . .131 A8
Gateside Dr FY3 . . . . . . .130 F8
Gateway Cl FY5 . . . . . . .153 D7
Gathurst La WN6 . . . . . . .19 F5
Gathurst Rd
Fulwood PR2 . . . . .117 C2
Orrell WN5 . . . . .10 E8
Gaulter's La FY6 . . . . . .200 C4
Gaw Hill La L39 . . . . . . .15 B3
Gaw Hill View L39 . . . . . .15 B3
Gawthorpe Edge BB12 . . .126 F8
Gawthorpe Hall* BB12 . . .146 F1
Gawthorpe Rd BB12 . . . .127 D7
Gawthorpe St 13 BB12 . . .146 C1
Gawthorpe View BB12 . . .146 F5
Gaydon Way FY5 . . . . . .152 E7
Gaylands La BB18 . . . . . .197 C2
Gayle Way 1 BB5 . . . . . .103 F4
Gaythorne Ave PR1 . . . . .97 F8
Geddes St BB2 . . . . .100 F2
Geldof Dr FY1 . . . . .130 B6
General St FY1 . . . . . . .130 B6
Geneva Rd PR2 . . . . . . .118 C4
Genoa St BB11 . . . . .127 F5
Geoffrey Lodge 13 PR2 . .118 F4
Geoffrey St Bury BL9 . . . .33 A4
Chorley PR6 . . . . .61 D1
Preston PR1 . . . . .97 D3
Ramsbottom BL0 . . . . . .50 A4
George Ave
Blackpool FY3 . . . . . . .130 F1
Great Harwood BB6 . . . .124 B4
George Dr PR8 . . . . .21 E5
George La BB12 . . . . . . .145 C2
George Rd BL0 . . . . .50 B5
George St Accrington BB5 .103 F4
4 Bacup OL13 . . . . . .70 C8
Barnoldswick BB18 . . . .196 C4
Blackburn BB2 . . . . . . .101 E4
Blackpool FY1 . . . . . . .130 C6
Burnley BB11 . . . . .127 F5
Chorley PR7 . . . . .43 C7
13 Clayton-le-M BB5 . . .124 F3
Clitheroe BB7 . . . . . . .166 D6
Darwen BB3 . . . . .82 A2
1 Earby BB18 . . . . . .197 B1
Great Harwood BB6 . . . .124 C5
Haslingden BB4 . . . . . . .85 B3
Horwich BL6 . . . . .32 C3
3 Lancaster LA1 . . . . .214 F7
Leyland PR25 . . . . .77 B2
Longridge PR3 . . . . . . .140 A8
11 Lytham St Anne's FY8 .91 B3
Morecambe LA4 . . . . . .217 C5
Oswaldtwistle BB5 . . . .103 E4
Preston PR1 . . . . .97 D3
Rishton BB1 . . . . .124 C5
Whalley BB7 . . . . .144 C5
Whitworth OL12 . . . . . .52 C8
George St W BB2 . . . . . .101 D4
George Terr WN5 . . . . . .10 D5

George's La Banks PR9 . . .55 F7
Horwich BL6 . . . . .32 E5
George's Rd PR1 . . . . . . .96 F7
George's Row 2 BB4 . . . .69 F8
Georgian Pl L37 . . . . . . .11 E4
Gerald Ct 4 BB12 . . . . . .128 A4
Gerard Way L33 . . . . .1 A2
German La
Bolton Green PR7 . . . . . .42 D7
1 Coppull PR7 . . . . . .42 E1
Gerrard Pl WN8 . . . . .8 F7
Gerrard St Lancaster LA1 .214 D6
Preston PR1 . . . . .96 E7
Gerrard's Fold PR6 . . . . .80 B2
Gerrard's Terr FY6 . . . . .153 C4
Gertrude St Nelson BB9 . .171 A2
Shawforth OL12 . . . . . . .71 E6
Ghants La FY6 . . . . .177 E2
Ghyll La BB18 . . . . .196 E5
Ghyll Mdws BB18 . . . . . .196 D4
Giant Axe (Lancaster FC)
LA1 . . . . .214 E8
Gib Hey La PR3 . . . . . . .161 F3
Gib Hill La BB4 . . . . . . .106 B2
Gib Hill Rd BB9 . . . . . . .171 B1
Gib La Blackburn BB2 . . . .81 A7
Hoghton PR5 . . . . .99 C3
Gibfield Rd BB8 . . . . . . .171 A4
Gibfield Sch BB8 . . . . . .171 B2
Gibfield St BB2 . . . . . . .101 B6
Gibraltar Rd PR4 . . . . . .132 C5
Gibraltar St BB2 . . . . . .101 B6
Gibson St FY3 . . . . .170 F2
Giddygate La L31 . . . . . . .6 B1
Gidlow Ave PR6 . . . . . . .31 A7
Gilbert Pl L40 . . . . .25 E4
Gilbert St Brierfield BB10 .148 E2
1 Chorley PR7 . . . . . .43 C6
Ramsbottom BL0 . . . . . .68 C1
Rawtenstall BB4 . . . . . . .86 C1
Gilbertson Rd PR7 . . . . . .43 E2
Gildabrook Rd FY4 . . . . .110 D5
Gilderdale Ct 2 FY8 . . . . .91 C4
Gildow St 1 PR1 . . . . . . .96 E8
Giles St Clitheroe BB7 . . .166 E7
Nelson BB9 . . . . .170 E1
Gilescroft Ave L33 . . . . . . .1 A4
Gilett Farm Cvn Pk FY4 . .111 F3
Gilhouse Ave PR2 . . . . . .116 C1
Gill Ct PR4 . . . . .110 B5
Gill La PR4 . . . . .75 C5
Gill Nook PR4 . . . . .75 A5
Gill St Burnley BB12 . . . .127 E6
Colne BB8 . . . . .171 B3
Nelson BB9 . . . . .170 D1
Gillcroft PR7 . . . . .41 B7
Giller Cl PR1 . . . . .96 F7
Giller Dr PR1 . . . . .96 F7
Giller Fold 1 PR1 . . . . . .96 F7
Gillett St 6 PR1 . . . . . . .118 C1
Gillhead Brow LA2 . . . . .242 D1
Gillians BB18 . . . . .194 B8
Gillians La BB18 . . . . . .194 B8
Gillibrand Cl PR1 . . . . . .96 C1
Gillibrand Ho PR7 . . . . . .61 C2
Gillibrand Prim Sch PR7 . .43 B6
Gillibrand St Chorley PR7 . .43 C7
Darwen BB3 . . . . .81 F3
Walton-le-D PR5 . . . . . . .97 D5
Gillibrand Wlks PR7 . . . . .43 C7
Gillibrands Rd WN8 . . . . . .9 A7
Gillies St Accrington BB5 .104 C6
Blackburn BB2 . . . . . . .101 C3
Gillison Cl LA6 . . . . . . .241 C2
Gillow Ave LA1 . . . . . . .211 B7
Gillow Cl LA1 . . . . .214 F5
Gillow Pk PR3 . . . . .155 F6
Gillow Rd PR4 . . . . .113 C4
Gills Croft BB7 . . . . . . .167 A4
Gilpin Ave L31 . . . . .5 E2
Gilpin Cl 2 LA1 . . . . . . .218 A2
Gilstead Ave LA3 . . . . . .213 A8
Gin Bow PR7 . . . . .43 D6
Gin Croft La BL0 . . . . . . .68 C4
Gingham Brow BL6 . . . . .32 E4
Girvan Gr BB11 . . . . . . .127 D5
Girvan Wlk 1 OL10 . . . . .33 F1
Gisburn Ave FY8 . . . . . . .90 C6
Gisburn Gr Blackpool FY3 .130 E7
Burnley BB10 . . . . .128 D5
Gisburn Old Rd
Barnoldswick BB7,BB9 . .193 C7
Foulridge BB9 . . . . . . .193 C4
Gisburn Prim Sch BB7 . . .231 B3
Gisburn Rd
Barnoldswick BB18 . . . .196 A3
Barrowford BB9 . . . . . .170 E5
Bolton-by-B BB7 . . . . . .230 E4
Fulwood PR2 . . . . .118 E4
Gisburn Road Prim Sch
BB18 . . . . .196 B2
Gisburn St
Barnoldswick BB18 . . . .196 A3
Blackburn BB2 . . . . . . .101 C4
BB7 . . . . .231 B4
Gisburne Park Hospl
BB7 . . . . .231 B4
Gladden Ho 7 WN8 . . . . . .8 E8
Glade The Blackburn BB2 . .81 D6
Morecambe LA4 . . . . . .217 C5
Glades The FY8 . . . . .91 C4
Gladesmoor Rd L33 . . . . . .1 B1
Gladeway FY5 . . . . .153 D7
Gladstone Cres OL13 . . . .88 A2
Gladstone Dr PR9 . . . . . .35 F6
Gladstone St Bacup OL13 . .88 A2
Blackburn BB1 . . . . . . .102 B6

Gladstone St *continued*
Blackpool FY4 130 C1
Bury BL9 33 B3
2 Cornholme OL14 109 B1
Great Harwood BB6 124 C5
Gladstone Terr
Abbey Village PR6 80 C1
16 Barrowford BB9 170 D3
Blackburn BB2 100 F1
3 Lancaster LA1 218 E1
Trawden BB8 172 B4
Gladstone Way 4 FY5 175 F1
Glaisdale Dr PR8 35 F3
Glamis Dr Chorley PR7 43 B8
Southport PR9 54 B3
Glamis Rd PR25 60 C8
Glamorgan Gr BB12 127 A7
Glangarry 7 FY8 91 C3
Glasson Cl BB2 101 F1
Glastonbury Ave FY1 130 E2
Gleb Mews PR4 115 D2
Glebe Cl Accrington BB5 104 B5
Burton-in-K LA6 240 C7
Fulwood PR2 117 F4
Maghull L31 5 B1
Standish WN6 29 F1
Glebe Cotts BB4 85 A6
Glebe Ct 20 LA1 215 A8
Glebe La Banks PR9 55 A7
Kirkham PR4 114 C4
Glebe Pl PR8 35 B7
Glebe Rd Skelmersdale WN8 9 A8
Standish WN6 29 F1
Glebe St Burnley BB11 128 B4
Great Harwood BB6 124 C5
Glebe The PR26 59 B8
Glebelands PR4 57 A5
Gledhill Way BL7 48 A1
Gledstone View BB18 196 A3
Glegside Rd L33 1 A2
Glen Cottage (Youth Hostel)
BB18 197 D2
Glen Cres OL13 70 A8
Glen Dr WN6 19 E8
Glen Eldon Rd FY8 89 E7
Glen Garth BB18 196 D3
Glen Gdns OL12 52 F2
Glen Gr PR2 118 F5
Glen Park Dr PR4 73 D4
Glen Rd BB4 69 F8
Glen Royd 1 OL12 52 C1
Glen Sq BB11 127 F2
Glen St Bacup OL13 70 E8
Blackpool FY3 130 E4
Burnley BB11 127 E6
Colne BB8 171 D6
Ramsbottom BL0 50 B7
Glen The Blackburn BB2 81 D6
Caton LA2 237 C3
Fulwood PR2 118 F2
Knott End-on-S FY6 199 E4
Glen Top OL13 70 A8
Glen View PR3 141 B8
Glen View Ave LA3 212 E6
Glen View Cres LA3 212 E6
Glen View Dr LA3 212 E6
Glen View Rd BB11 127 E2
Glen View St 1 OL14 109 B1
Glen Way BB9 148 B6
Glenapp Ave FY4 111 A6
Glenarden Ave FY5 152 F8
Glenavon Dr OL12 52 D3
Glenbeck Cl BL6 32 D1
Glenborough Ave OL13 70 C8
Glenbrook Cl BB2 81 B8
Glenburn High Sch WN8 9 B8
Glenburn Rd WN8 18 A1
Glencarron Cl BB3 65 F8
Glencoe Ave
Blackpool FY3 153 A1
Hoddlesden BB3 82 E1
Glencoe Cl OL10 33 F1
Glencourse Dr PR2 118 D5
Glencoyne Dr PR9 54 B5
Glencroft PR7 60 C3
Glencross Pl FY4 110 E7
Glendale Ave PR5 97 C1
Glendale Cl
Blackpool FY2 152 F5
Burnley BB11 128 A3
Leyland PR25 60 B7
Poulton-le-F FY6 153 C3
Glendale Cres PR5 97 C1
Glendale Dr BB2 121 E2
Glendale Gr
Fulwood PR2 118 D2
Kirkby L33 1 A5
Glendale Way L37 11 F2
Glenden Foot OL12 52 D2
Glendene Pk BB1 122 E5
Glendor Rd BB10 128 E5
Gleneagles Ave BB3 82 E1
Gleneagles Ct PR4 114 B4
Gleneagles Dr
Brockhall Village BB6 143 C6
Euxton PR7 60 D4
Fulwood PR2 117 B7
Higher Penwortham PR1 96 A6
Morecambe LA4 217 D6
Southport PR8 21 C3
Gleneagles Way 1 BL0 50 B5
Glenfield Ave FY2 152 E6
Glenfield Cl BB1 102 B7
Glenfield Cvn Site PR3 201 C5
Glenfield Park Ind Est
Blackburn BB1 102 B7
Nelson BB9 171 A1
Glenfield Rd BB9 171 A1
Glengreave Ave BB1 122 E3
Glenholme Gdns FY6 153 C2
Glenluce Cres BB1 102 D3
Glenluce Dr PR1 97 F8
Glenmarsh Way L37 12 B3
Glenmere Cres FY5 152 C7
Glenmore PR6 78 A3
Glenmore Ave FY5 176 B2
Glenmore Cl BB5 104 E2
Glenmore Rd BL0 49 F2
Glenpark Dr PR9 54 B4
Glenrose Terr PR8 35 A5
Glenroy Ave BB8 171 D6
Glenroyd Cl FY3 130 E3
Glenroyd Dr L40 25 E4
Glenshiels Ave BB3 65 E8
Glenside WN6 28 B2
Glentworth Rd E LA4 217 D3
Glentworth Rd W LA4 217 C3
Glenview Cl PR2 119 A3
Glenview Ct PR2 119 A3
Glenway PR1 96 C4
Glenwood St 3 FY3 130 D5
Global Way BB3 82 A5
Globe La BL7 47 D3
Globe Mill 7 BB4 86 F2
Glossop Cl FY2 152 C6
Gloucester Ave
Accrington BB5 104 A7
Blackpool FY1 130 D4
8 Clayton-le-M BB5 124 F3
Cleveleys FY5 175 D3
Horwich BL6 32 D2
Lancaster LA1 215 A4
Leyland PR25 77 C3
Gloucester Ct
5 Blackpool FY1 130 D4
Horwich BL6 32 D2
Gloucester Dr LA3 216 E3
Gloucester Rd
Blackburn BB1 102 D5
Chorley PR7 43 C6
Lytham St Anne's FY8 90 D4
Rishton BB1 103 A8
Southport PR8 34 F5
Glover Cl PR26 58 F6
Glover Rd PR7 29 D7
Glover St Horwich BL6 32 B4
Preston PR1 97 A7
Glover's Ct 23 PR1 97 A7
Glynn St BB5 103 F7
Godiva St BB10 148 A1
Godley St BB11 128 B6
Godwin Ave 7 FY3 130 E3
Goe La PR4 93 B6
Goit St Blackburn BB2 101 C2
Newchurch BB4 86 F1
Goitside BB9 170 E1
Golbourne St PR1 118 B1
Goldacre La BB6 124 A7
Goldburn Cl PR2 116 F6
Golden Hill 9 PR25 77 B2
Golden Hill La PR25 76 F2
Golden Hill PRU PR25 76 E2
Golden Way PR1 96 C3
Goldfield Ave BB10 128 F6
Goldfinch Dr BL9 33 C4
Goldfinch St PR1 118 B1
Goldhey St 13 BB1 102 A7
Goldsboro Ave FY3 130 F3
Goldshaw Ct BB12 169 C3
Goldstone Dr FY5 152 F7
Golf Rd L37 11 E5
Golf View PR2 117 A6
Golgotha Rd LA1 215 A6
Golgotha Village LA1 215 B7
Gonder La PR3 182 E3
Gooch St BL6 32 C2
Good Shaw Fold Cl BB4 106 A2
Good St PR1 96 E7
Goodall Cl BB18 197 B2
Goodenber Cres 15 LA2 239 D8
Goodenber Rd LA2 239 D8
Goodshaw Ave
Blackburn BB1 122 E1
Goodshaw Chapel BB4 106 A1
Goodshaw Ave N BB4 106 A2
Goodshaw Chapel★
BB4 106 B1
Goodshaw Cl BB1 101 E8
Goodshaw Fold Rd BB4 105 F2
Goodshaw La
Accrington BB5 105 C1
Goodshaw Chapel BB4 106 B2
Goodwood Ave
Blackpool FY2 152 D1
Fulwood PR2 117 F7
Slyne LA2 218 D8
Goodwood Ct LA1 215 B4
Goodwood Rd LA1 215 B4
Goose Cote Hill BL7 47 E1
Goose Foot Cl PR5 99 D7
Goose Foot Cott PR5 99 D4
Goose Foot La PR5 99 C6
Goose Green Ave PR7 42 F1
Goose Green La BB8 172 B2
Goose Hill St 18 OL13 87 F3
Goose House La BB3 82 A3
Goose Lane Cotts PR3 185 E1
Goosebutts La BB7 166 F7
Gooselands BD24 236 F6
Gooseleach La BB12 145 E1
Goosnargh La PR3 138 B7
Goosnargh Whitechapel Prim Sch PR3 160 D7
Gordale Cl
Barnoldswick BB18 196 A2
Blackpool FY4 111 A8
Gordon Ave
Accrington BB5 104 A4
Maghull L31 5 C3
Southport PR9 53 C1
Thornton FY5 176 B2
Gordon Ho 11 PR9 35 C8
Gordon Rd
Fleetwood FY7 198 F3
Lytham St Anne's FY8 90 D4
8 Nelson BB9 170 D1
Gordon St Bacup OL13 87 F4
14 Blackpool FY4 130 B1
Burnley BB12 127 F7
Chorley PR6 43 D7
Church BB5 103 E5
Clayton-le-M BB5 125 A2
Colne BB8 171 F5
Darwen BB3 82 A3
Preston PR1 117 E1
Rawtenstall BB4 85 F2
Southport PR9 35 C8
Worsthorne BB10 129 B6
Gordon Terr 1 LA1 215 A5
Gordon Way OL10 33 F1
Gordonstoun Cres WN5 10 F7
Gordonstoun Pl
Blackburn BB2 101 C3
8 Thornton FY5 176 A2
Gore Cl BL9 33 C1
Gore Dr L39 15 E3
Gores La L37 11 F5
Gores Rd L33 1 C1
Goring St PR7 43 D7
Gornall's Bldgs 7 BB4 85 E2
Gorple Gn BB10 129 B5
Gorple Rd BB10 129 D5
Gorple St BB10 148 E3
Gorrell Cl BB12 169 D2
Gorse Ave FY5 175 F3
Gorse Bank BL9 33 C3
Gorse Cl
Great Knowley PR6 61 E5
Tarleton PR4 57 A6
Gorse Gr Fulwood PR2 118 E3
Haslingden BB4 68 A8
Longton PR4 95 A1
Gorse La PR4 56 D5
Gorse Rd Blackburn BB2 101 B5
Blackpool FY3 130 E4
Gorse St BB1 102 B6
Gorse Way L37 11 C4
Gorsefield L37 12 A6
Gorsewood Rd PR25 76 E1
Gorsey Brow WN6 29 B2
Gorsey La Banks PR9 55 C7
Haskayne L39 13 B7
Hightown L38 3 B2
Mawdesley L40 40 C1
Gorsey Pl WN8 9 B7
Gorst La L40,PR9 25 A6
Gorsuch La L39,L40 23 D4
Gorton Fold BL6 32 C3
Gorton St FY1 130 C6
Gosforth Rd
Blackpool FY2 152 C1
Southport PR9 35 F8
Gough La
Clayton Brook PR5 78 C5
Walton Summit PR5 78 B6
Goulding Ave PR25 77 B1
Goulding St PR7 43 D6
Gowans La PR6 79 A8
Gower Ct PR26 76 D3
Gower Gdns L40 25 F3
Gower Gr PR4 75 A5
Goyt St FY8 89 F7
Grab La LA1 215 C7
Graburn Rd L37 11 F4
Gracamy Ave PR4 92 D5
Grace St BL6 32 B3
Gradwell St 2 PR1 96 E8
Grafton Ave
Accrington BB5 104 E2
Brierfield BB10 148 B5
Grafton Ct 3 Chorley PR7 43 B5
12 Darwen BB3 81 F2
Grafton Dr PR8 21 A5
Grafton Pl LA3 216 E3
Grafton Rd Fulwood PR2 118 F4
Morecambe LA3 216 E3
Grafton St Adlington PR7 30 F6
Blackburn BB2 101 D2
Blackpool FY1 130 C7
Clitheroe BB7 166 F8
Nelson BB9 170 F1
Preston PR1 96 E6
Grafton Terr 11 BB3 81 F2
Grafton Villas OL13 87 F1
Graham Ave
Appley Bridge WN6 28 C2
Bamber Bridge PR5 77 C8
Graham Rd PR3 204 C2
Graham St
Hoddlesden BB3 82 F1
Lancaster LA1 214 F6
Morecambe LA4 217 A5
1 Padiham BB12 126 D7
4 Preston PR1 118 B1
Grampian Way FY8 91 D5
Granary The FY5 176 A2
Granby Ave FY3 130 E8
Granby Cl PR9 53 F3
Granby St BB12 127 D6
Grand Manor Dr FY8 90 D7
Grane Pk BB4 85 A2
Grane Rd BB4 84 C2
Grane St BB4 85 B2
Grange Ave
Barrowford BB9 170 F5
Fulwood PR2 118 F4
Fulwood PR2 119 A4
Great Harwood BB6 124 C6
Rawtenstall BB4 86 B3
Southport PR9 35 E8
Thornton FY5 176 B2
Grange Cl
Great Harwood BB6 124 C6
Hoghton PR5 99 B4
Knott End-on-S FY6 199 F6
Oswaldtwistle BB5 104 A3
Rawtenstall BB4 86 B2
Grange Cres BB4 86 A2
Grange Ct 18 FY1 130 C7
Grange Dr Coppull PR7 29 D8
Coupe Green PR5 98 E4
Euxton PR7 60 C4
Grange Farm Cotts PR4 93 E5
Grange Gdns FY6 153 D2
Grange La
Accrington BB5 104 C5
Formby L37 11 E5
Hutton PR4 94 D3
Newton-w-S PR4 114 F2
Stalmine FY6 177 B7
Grange Park Cl PR1 96 A6
Grange Park Way BB4 84 F1
Grange Pl PR2 118 F4
Grange Rd Blackburn BB2 101 B2
Blackpool FY3 130 F7
Edgworth BL7 48 C1
Elswick PR4 155 F1
Fleetwood FY7 198 D3
Fulwood PR2 117 C3
Hambleton FY6 177 D1
Hightown L38 2 E6
Holme Chapel BB10 108 A7
Leyland PR25 76 D2
Lytham St Anne's FY8 89 E7
Rawtenstall BB4 86 B2
Singleton FY6 155 A3
Southport PR9 35 E7
Whitworth OL12 71 D3
Grange St
Accrington BB5 104 C5
Barnoldswick BB18 196 A3
Burnley BB11 127 E5
Clayton-le-M BB5 124 E3
Morecambe LA4 217 E6
2 Rawtenstall BB4 86 A2
Grange Terr 19 BB4 86 A3
Grange The Arnside LA5 224 A8
Cottam PR4 116 E5
Edgworth BL7 48 E5
Lytham St Anne's FY8 90 E3
Southport PR9 54 C3
Wilpshire BB1 122 F5
Grange View
Carnforth LA5 223 D3
Hest Bank LA5 220 F3
Grange View Rd LA6 221 F6
Grangefield PR4 94 F1
Granings The PR4 116 D6
Granny's Bay FY8 90 C3
Grant Cl LA1 214 D7
Grant Dr PR4 75 A5
Grant Mews BL0 50 B7
Grant Rd BB2 101 B3
Grant St Accrington BB5 104 A6
Burnley BB11 127 E5
Grantham Cl PR8 35 A1
Grantham Rd
5 Blackpool FY1 130 C7
Southport PR8 35 A1
Weeton Camp PR4 132 E6
Grantham St BB2 101 B2
Granton Cl L37 11 E3
Granton Wlk PR2 117 A4
Grants La BL0 50 C6
Granville Ave
Becconsall PR4 73 E2
Maghull L31 5 C2
Granville Cl L39 6 B8
Granville Ct Chorley PR6 61 E1
Southport PR9 53 D1
Granville Gdns BB5 104 D3
Granville Pk L39 6 C8
Granville Pk W L39 6 B8
Granville Rd
Accrington BB5 104 D3
Blackburn BB2 101 B5
Blackpool FY1 130 D5
Brierfield BB9 148 C6
Chorley PR6 61 E1
Darwen BB3 64 F8
Great Harwood BB6 124 D6
Lancaster LA1 218 C3
Morecambe LA3 216 E3
Southport PR8 34 D4
Granville St Adlington PR6 31 A7
Brierfield BB10 148 F2
14 Burnley BB10 128 A8
Colne BB8 171 E5
Haslingden BB4 68 A7
Grape La PR26 58 C1
Grasmere Ave
Blackburn BB1 122 C1
3 Fleetwood FY7 198 E4
Leyland PR25 77 A3
Orrell WN5 10 F8
Padiham BB12 146 C1
Skelmersdale WN8 10 B7
Grasmere Ave *continued*
Thornton FY5 176 B2
Grasmere Cl
Accrington,Hillock Vale
BB5 104 E8
Bamber Bridge PR5 97 D2
Colne BB8 172 A5
Euxton PR7 60 E1
Fulwood PR2 118 C4
8 High Bentham LA2 239 D8
Rishton BB1 124 A1
Grasmere Dr 9 LA2 239 D8
Grasmere Gr
Longridge PR3 139 F5
Whittle-le-W PR6 61 B7
Grasmere Rd
Blackpool FY1 130 D2
Formby L37 11 D3
Haslingden BB4 68 C8
Hightown L38 3 A4
Knott End-on-S FY6 199 F6
Lancaster LA1 215 A8
Lytham St Anne's FY8 110 E1
Maghull L31 5 D2
Morecambe LA4 217 E6
Grasmere St
Burnley BB10 148 A2
10 Rochdale OL12 52 F1
Grasmere Terr
Bacup OL13 87 F4
Chorley PR7 43 B5
Grassington Dr
Brierfield BB10 148 D3
Bury BL9 33 D1
Grassington Pl 4 FY5 152 F8
Grassington Rd FY8 90 C7
Gratton Pl WN8 9 A8
Grave-Yard La L39 7 A6
Gravel Cl PR9 54 F5
Gravel La Banks PR9 54 F5
Banks PR9 55 B3
Gravel The PR4 55 F2
Graver Weir Terr BB4 107 A1
Graving Dock Rd FY8 91 D4
Gravners Field FY5 176 D2
Grayrigg Dr LA4 217 B3
Grays Pl LA3 216 E2
Great Arley Sch FY5 176 B3
Great Avenham St 3
PR1 97 A6
Great Bolton St BB2 101 E3
Great Close La BD23,
BD24 236 D6
Great Croft Cl BB18 196 A3
Great Eaves Rd BL0 50 C7
Great Eccleston Copp CE Prim Sch PR3 156 A3
Great Flatt OL12 52 B1
Great George St
Colne BB8 171 D5
Preston PR1 118 A1
Great Gill PR4 75 A5
Great Greens La PR5 78 C5
Great Hanover St PR1 118 A1
Great Harwood Prim Sch
BB6 124 B5
Great Hay PR4 74 E2
Great Hey PR4 74 E2
Great House Barn Rivington★ BL6 31 F8
Great John St 20 LA1 214 F8
Great Lee OL12 52 D3
Great Lee Wlk OL12 52 D2
Great Mdw
Bamber Bridge PR5 77 A8
Chorley PR7 61 A2
Great Shaw St PR1 96 F8
Great Stone of Fourstones★
LA2 239 D5
Great Stones Cl BL7 47 E2
Great Townley St PR1 97 D8
Great Tunstead PR4 75 A7
Great Wood Cl PR7 42 F6
Great Wood Prim Sch
LA4 217 E5
Greave Cl Bacup OL13 88 B3
Rawtenstall BB4 86 A4
Greave Clough Cl 9
OL13 88 A3
Greave Clough Dr OL13 88 B3
Greave Cres 10 OL13 88 A3
Greave Rd OL13 88 B3
Greave Terr OL13 88 B3
Greaves Cl
Appley Bridge WN6 19 F8
Banks PR9 55 A6
Greaves Ct 3 LA1 215 A5
Greaves Dr LA1 214 F6
Greaves Hall Ave PR9 55 A5
Greaves Mdw PR1 96 E2
Greaves Mead LA1 214 F5
Greaves Rd LA1 214 F6
Greaves St
Great Harwood BB6 124 C4
Haslingden BB4 84 F2
9 Preston PR1 97 A7
Greaves The LA1 215 A6
Greaves-Town La PR2 116 E1
Grebe Cl FY3 131 B7
Grebe Wharf 2 LA1 218 E1
Green Acre PR3 138 D6
Green Acres PR4 93 C7
Green Ave FY4 110 C6
Green Bank
5 Bacup OL13 70 D8
Barnoldswick BB18 196 D4
Green Bank Bsns Pk
BB1 102 C7

Green Bridge N BB4 ....69 E7
Green Bridge S BB4 ....69 E7
Green Brook Cl BL9 ....33 A4
Green Cl BB11 ....127 E2
Green Close Pk BB2 ....101 C2
Green Dick's La PR3 ....200 E5
Green Dr
　Bamber Bridge PR5 ....97 C1
　Barton PR4 ....137 B8
　Cleveleys FY5 ....175 C5
　Clitheroe BB7 ....190 A2
　Fulwood PR2 ....117 E7
　Higher Penwortham PR1 ....96 B5
　Lytham St Anne's FY8 ....91 C5
　Poulton-le-F FY6 ....131 E8
Green End PR5 ....99 E7
Green End Ave BB18 ....197 B2
Green End Barn BB18 ....197 B1
Green End Cl 12 OL13 ....88 A3
Green End Rd BB18 ....197 B1
Green Gate Fulwood PR2 117 C3
　Hutton PR4 ....95 C1
Green Haworth CE Prim Sch
　BB5 ....104 B3
Green Head Cotts 6
　LA2 ....239 B8
Green Hey
　Lytham St Anne's FY8 ....91 D4
　Much Hoole PR4 ....74 E3
Green Heys Dr L31 ....5 F1
Green Hill OL13 ....88 A1
Green Hill La LA2,LA6 ....237 B6
Green Hill Rd OL13 ....88 A1
Green Howarth View
　BB5 ....104 A3
Green La Banks PR9 ....55 C4
　Bilsborrow PR3 ....159 B2
　Bispham Green L40 ....27 B7
　Blackburn BB2 ....101 A1
　Bretherton PR26 ....58 C7
　Chipping PR3 ....185 F3
　Coppull PR7 ....30 A8
　Cowan Bridge LA6 ....242 B6
　Downham BB7 ....191 B6
　Farington PR26 ....76 E7
　Formby L37 ....11 F5
　Freckleton PR4 ....93 B6
　Garstang PR3 ....181 A7
　Grindleton BB7 ....190 A7
　Halton LA2 ....219 F8
　Holmes PR4 ....56 C4
　Horton BD23 ....231 E5
　Horwich BL6 ....32 B5
　Kingsfold PR4 ....96 C1
　Lancaster LA1,LA2 ....218 E6
　Lancaster,Bailrigg LA1,
　LA2 ....211 A7
　Longridge PR3 ....140 B8
　Maghull L31 ....5 A2
　Maghull L31 ....5 C1
　Morecambe LA3 ....217 B2
　Ormskirk L39 ....15 E6
　Orrell WN5 ....10 D3
　Padiham BB12 ....126 C8
　Preesall FY6 ....200 C2
　Riley Green PR5 ....79 E8
　Samlesbury Bottoms PR5 ..99 B7
　Skelmersdale L40 ....18 A6
　Sollom PR4 ....56 D1
　Standish WN6 ....29 D1
　Woodsfold PR4 ....135 E6
Green La E PR3 ....204 C2
Green La The L40 ....25 F4
Green La W
　Freckleton PR4 ....93 B5
　Garstang PR3 ....204 B1
Green Lane Ave L39 ....15 E6
Green Link L31 ....5 B1
Green Mdw BB4 ....172 B2
Green Meadow La FY4 ....177 C1
Green Mount BB6 ....144 D8
Green Nook La PR3 ....139 F6
Green Oak Pl FY5 ....153 A8
Green Park Ct BB4 ....144 D8
Green Park Dr L31 ....5 B1
Green Park Prim Sch L31 ..5 B2
Green Pk BB7 ....144 C5
Green Pl PR5 ....78 A6
Green Rd BB8 ....171 D4
Green Ridge Cl BB9 ....148 D5
Green Row BB3 ....81 B6
Green St Adlington PR6 ....31 B8
　12 Barnoldswick BB18 ..196 B2
　Burnley BB10 ....148 B1
　Chorley PR7 ....43 A5
　Darwen BB3 ....82 A1
　Edenfield BL0 ....68 E3
　Great Harwood BB6 ....124 B5
　Lancaster LA1 ....218 E1
　Lytham St Anne's FY8 ....91 A3
　Morecambe LA4 ....217 B6
　Oswaldtwistle BB5 ....103 C2
　Padiham BB12 ....126 C7
　Rawtenstall BB4 ....86 A3
Green St E 17 BB3 ....82 A1
Green The Adlington PR6 ....43 F2
　Bispham Green L40 ....27 B8
　Bolton-le-S LA5 ....221 B5
　Churchtown PR3 ....181 A2
　Colne BB8 ....171 F6
　5 Darwen BB3 ....82 A1
　Eccleston PR7 ....41 C6
　Fulwood PR2 ....118 F2
　Hesketh Bank PR4 ....73 E3
　Nelson BB9 ....171 B2
　Parbold WN8 ....27 B2
　Ramsbottom BL8 ....49 F1
　Silverdale LA5 ....224 D2

Green The continued
　Weeton PR4 ....132 F2
　Wrea Green PR4 ....113 B3
Green Way 4 FY4 ....110 F7
Green Wlk Blackrod BL6 ..31 D1
　Earby BB18 ....197 A1
　Southport PR8 ....21 D5
Green's La Haskayne L31 ..14 C1
　Maghull L31 ....5 C8
　Stalmine FY6 ....177 F7
Greenacre Blackburn BB3 ..81 F6
　Westhead L40 ....16 E4
Greenacre Cl BL0 ....50 F2
Greenacre Ct LA1 ....215 B3
Greenacre Pk LA2 ....220 E2
Greenacre Rd LA2 ....220 E2
Greenacre St BB7 ....166 E7
Greenacres Chorley PR7 ....43 C5
　Edgworth BL7 ....48 E6
　Read BB12 ....145 D2
Greenacres Ave PR4 ....114 A4
Greenacres Dr PR3 ....181 D6
Greenacres The 95 D2
Greenbank
　4 Horwich BL6 ....32 D1
　Ormskirk L39 ....15 C2
　Poulton-le-F FY6 ....153 E3
　Whitworth OL12 ....52 C5
Greenbank Ave
　Maghull L31 ....5 C3
　Orrell WN5 ....10 D3
　Preston PR1 ....117 D2
Greenbank Dr
　Fence BB12 ....147 E8
　Southport PR8 ....34 E2
Greenbank High Sch BB4 34 E1
Greenbank Pk BB4 ....86 B2
Greenbank Pl PR1 ....117 E1
Greenbank Rd
　Blackburn BB1 ....102 B6
　Middlewood Green PR1 ....96 A4
　Rochdale OL12 ....52 F2
Greenbank Sch OL12 ....52 F1
Greenbank St
　Preston PR1 ....117 D2
　Preston PR1 ....117 E1
　Rawtenstall BB4 ....86 B2
Greenbank Terr BB3 ....81 F6
Greenbank Way BB1 ....102 C6
Greenbanks FY2 ....152 F3
Greenbarn Way BL6 ....31 D1
Greenberfield La BB18 ....196 C4
Greenbriar Cl FY3 ....152 F1
Greenbrook Cl BB12 ....126 F6
Greenbrook Rd BB12 ....126 F6
Greenbrook St 6 BL9 ....33 A4
Greencliffe La BB10 ....129 A1
Greencroft PR1 ....96 D3
Greendale Ave BB4 ....86 E2
Greendale Cl
　Fleetwood FY7 ....198 C2
　Southward Bottom BB10 ..108 A7
Greendale Dr LA5 ....223 D3
Greendale Mews 1
　PR2 ....116 E2
Greendale View BB7 ....190 B8
Greenfield Ave
　Chatburn BB7 ....190 D5
　Clitheroe BB7 ....166 C8
　Parbold WN8 ....27 B2
Greenfield Cl PR5 ....54 A3
Greenfield Ct 2 LA1 ....215 A7
Greenfield Dr PR5 ....77 A8
Greenfield Gdns 1 BB4 ..85 B2
Greenfield Ho 18 LA1 ....215 A8
Greenfield La PR3 ....161 A6
Greenfield Park (Cvn Pk)
　PR4 ....93 F8
Greenfield Rd
　Adlington PR6 ....31 A8
　Blackpool FY5 ....152 E8
　Burnley BB10 ....128 D4
　Chorley PR6 ....43 E8
　Colne BB8 ....171 A4
　Colne BB8 ....171 B4
　Fleetwood FY7 ....198 D4
　Southport PR8 ....36 C1
Greenfield St Darwen BB3 65 C6
　Haslingden BB4 ....85 B3
　12 Lancaster LA1 ....215 A8
　Rawtenstall BB4 ....86 A3
Greenfield Terr
　3 Cornholme OL14 ....109 A1
　Oswaldtwistle BB5 ....103 A1
Greenfield View BB3 ....82 A7
Greenfield Way PR2 ....117 B5
Greenfields Blackburn BB2 ..87 F8
　Caton LA2 ....237 C3
　Hesketh Bank PR4 ....73 D4
Greenfields Cres PR4 ....113 B4
Greenfinch CI FY3 ....131 B6
Greenfold Dr BB4 ....106 A2
Greenfoot 5 LA2 ....239 B8
Greenfoot La LA2 ....239 B8
Greenford Cl WN5 ....10 D6
Greenford Rd PR8 ....21 C4
Greengate FY5 ....176 D2
Greengate Cl 6 BB12 ....127 D7
Greengate La LA5 ....221 C8
Greenhalgh La
　Adlington PR6 ....31 B8
　Greenhalgh PR4 ....133 D4
Greenhall Cl PR3 ....181 D6
Greenham Ave L33 ....1 A6
Greenhaven WN8 ....10 B1
Greenhead Ave BB1 ....102 B7
Greenhead La BB12 ....147 D5

Greenhey Pl WN8 ....8 F8
Greenheys Ave BB4 ....153 B4
Greenheys Cres BL8 ....49 F1
Greenhill BB6 ....124 B5
Greenhill Ave PR4 ....114 A6
Greenhill Pl 2 FY1 ....130 C6
Greenholme Ave LA4 ....217 B3
Greenhurst Cl BB2 ....101 D4
Greenings La PR9 ....37 C3
Greenland Ave WN6 ....29 E1
Greenland La PR6 ....31 D5
Greenlands Cres PR2 ....118 E3
Greenlea Cl WN5 ....10 D5
Greenlea Dr LA4 ....217 D5
Greenloon's Dr L37 ....11 C3
Greenloon's Wlk L37 ....11 C2
Greenmead Cl PR4 ....116 E5
Greenmoor La PR3 ....141 B7
Greenmount Ave
　1 Kirkham PR4 ....114 A5
　1 Thornton PR4 ....176 A3
Greenmount Cl BL8 ....49 F2
Greenmount Dr BL8 ....49 F2
Greenmount Prim Sch
　BL8 ....49 F2
Greenock Cl BB11 ....127 D4
Greenock Dr OL10 ....33 F1
Greenock St BB11 ....127 D4
Greenpark Cl BL8 ....49 F1
Greens Arms Rd BB3,BL7 ..47 E7
Greens La Bacup OL13 ....88 A3
　Bacup,Nun Hills OL13 ....70 D7
　Haslingden BB4 ....68 C7
Greens The OL12 ....71 C1
Greenset Cl LA1 ....218 C4
Greenside Cottam PR4 ....116 D4
　Euxton PR7 ....60 C3
　Ribchester PR3 ....141 E3
Greenside Ave
　Blackburn BB2 ....81 A8
　Preston PR2 ....116 C1
Greenside Cl
　Hawkshaw BL8 ....49 B3
　Kirkby L33 ....1 A6
Greenside Dr BL8 ....49 F1
Greenside Gdns PR26 ....59 B7
Greenslate Ave WN6 ....19 E8
Greenslate Ct WN5 ....10 E3
Greensnook La OL13 ....88 A3
Greensnook Mews 5
　OL13 ....88 A3
Greensnook Terr 1
　OL13 ....88 A3
Greenstone Ave BL6 ....32 B3
Greensward Cl WN6 ....29 B1
Greensway PR3 ....137 C3
Greenthorn Cl BL7 ....48 E7
Greenthorne Terr 2 BB3 ..98 B3
Greenvale WN6 ....19 F4
Greenville Dr L31 ....5 C1
Greenwater Ct 7 LA1 ....218 D2
Greenway Catterall PR3 ....181 D3
　Eccleston PR7 ....41 B7
　Fulwood PR2 ....117 D7
　Higher Penwortham PR1 ..96 B4
　Horwich BL6 ....32 F3
Greenway Ave
　Clayton-le-M BB5 ....103 E6
Greenway Cl WN8 ....17 E2
Greenway Ho FY6 ....153 E3
Greenway Mews BL6 ....50 C4
Greenway St BB3 ....81 C3
Greenways Becconsall PR4 73 F1
　Lytham St Anne's FY8 ....90 B6
　Orrell WN5 ....10 D3
　Over Kellet LA6 ....237 B8
Greenwich Dr FY8 ....90 D5
Greenwood PR5 ....78 B4
Greenwood Ave
　Blackpool FY1 ....130 C2
　Hest Bank LA5 ....220 F2
　Horwich BL6 ....32 D1
Greenwood Cl
　Lytham St Anne's FY8 ....90 E4
　Ormskirk L39 ....15 C1
Greenwood Cres LA5 ....220 F2
Greenwood Ct PR5 ....77 A1
Greenwood Dr LA5 ....220 F2
Greenwood Gdns PR8 ....35 A5
Greenwood La WN6 ....29 E2
Greenwood Rd WN6 ....29 E2
Greenwood St
　1 Bamber Bridge PR5 ....97 E1
　Preston PR1 ....97 B7
Greenwood The BB2 ....81 D7
Greetby Hill L39,L40 ....16 A6
Greetby Pl WN8 ....9 A8
Greg Ho 13 LA1 ....218 D2
Gregareth Cl 5 LA1 ....218 A2
Gregory Ave FY2 ....152 C5
Gregory Fold BB4 ....68 A7
Gregory La L39 ....23 B3
Gregory Mdw PR3 ....181 B7
Gregory Pl LA1 ....91 A3
Gregory's Ct LA1 ....215 A4
Gregson Cl 4 FY4 ....110 F7
Gregson Dr 3 FY7 ....198 F2
Gregson La
　7 Blackburn BB2 ....101 D5
　Gregson Lane PR5 ....98 E1
　Higher Walton PR5 ....98 C2
Gregson Rd LA1 ....215 A7
Gregson St 5 Darwen BB3 ..65 A8
　Lytham St Anne's FY8 ....91 A3
Gregson Way PR2 ....118 D5
Gregson's Ave L37 ....11 E5
Grenada Cl BB3 ....81 F6

Grenfell Ave FY3 ....130 E7
Grenville Ave
　Bamber Bridge PR5 ....97 D2
　Lytham St Anne's FY8 ....110 E1
Gresham Rd FY5 ....175 D1
Gresham St BB4 ....86 F1
Gresley Ave BL6 ....32 B3
Gresley Ct LA1 ....214 F6
Gresley Pl FY2 ....152 E2
Gressingham Dr LA1 ....215 A4
Gressingham Ho 3 LA1 215 A3
Gressingham Wlk LA1 ....215 B3
Greta Heath LA6 ....242 C3
Greta Pl Fleetwood FY7 ....198 D3
　Lancaster LA1 ....218 C2
Gretdale Ave FY8 ....89 E8
Gretna Cres FY5 ....152 D8
Gretna Rd BB1 ....122 F1
Gretna Wlk BB1 ....122 F1
Grey Heights View PR6 ..43 E8
Grey St Barrowford BB9 ..170 D3
　Burnley BB10 ....128 A8
Greyfriars Ave PR2 ....117 D5
Greyfriars Cres PR2 ....117 D5
Greyfriars Dr PR1 ....96 C5
Greyfriars Rd PR8 ....21 D7
Greyhound Bridge Rd
　LA1 ....218 D1
Greystock Ave PR2 ....117 E6
Greystock Dr PR5 ....78 B8
Greystock Pl PR2 ....117 E6
Greystoke Ave BB2 ....80 E8
Greystoke Ct FY4 ....110 B5
Greystoke Pl FY4 ....110 B5
Greystokes LA3 ....15 D2
Greystonegill La LA2 ....239 C4
Greystones BB2 ....76 B1
Greystones Dr BB12 ....147 E8
Greythwaite Ct LA4 ....214 D6
Greywood Ave BL9 ....33 A4
Griffin Cl Burnley BB11 ....127 B5
　Bury BL9 ....33 B4
　Huncoat BB5 ....125 F1
Griffin Park Prim Sch
　BB2 ....101 B3
Griffin St BB2 ....101 B3
Griffiths Dr PR9 ....35 F8
Griffon Ho PR9 ....53 F2
Grime St Chorley PR7 ....43 D6
　Darwen BB3 ....81 F2
　7 Ramsbottom BL0 ....50 A4
Grimeford La BL6,PR6 ....31 C5
Grimeford Mill PR6 ....31 D6
Grimeshaw La LA1 ....219 B3
Grimrod Pl WN8 ....9 A7
Grimsargh St 10 PR1 ....118 D1
Grimsargh St Michaels CE
　Sch PR2 ....139 C1
Grimshaw Green La LA0,
　WN8 ....27 C6
Grimshaw La L39 ....15 E7
Grimshaw Pk BB2 ....101 F3
Grimshaw Ret Pk BB2 ....101 F3
Grimshaw St
　Accrington BB5 ....104 D4
　6 Barrowford BB9 ....170 D4
　Burnley BB11 ....128 A5
　5 Church BB5 ....103 E6
　2 Clayton-le-M BB5 ....124 F2
　Darwen BB3 ....65 B7
　Great Harwood BB6 ....124 C5
　Preston PR1 ....97 A7
Grindlestone Ct PR3 ....138 E6
Grindleton Cl FY3 ....131 B8
Grindleton Gr BB10 ....128 D5
Grindleton CE Prim Sch
　BB7 ....190 C8
Grindleton Rd
　1 Blackburn BB2 ....101 C4
　Grindleton BB7 ....190 B7
　West Bradford BB7 ....189 F6
Gringley Rd LA4 ....217 C3
Grinstead Cl PR8 ....34 F1
Grisedale Ave BB1 ....102 C2
Grisedale Cl L37 ....11 E3
Grisedale Dr BB12 ....127 B8
Grisedale Pl PR7 ....43 B5
Gristlehurst La BL9 ....33 F5
Gritstone Cl LA1 ....215 D8
Grizedale Cl
　Clayton-le-M BB5 ....124 E2
　Fulwood PR2 ....118 F2
Grizedale Cres PR2 ....119 A2
Grizedale Ct
　Blackpool FY3 ....130 E5
　8 Thornton FY5 ....176 B3
Grizedale Pl
　Fulwood PR2 ....118 F2
　Morecambe LA3 ....216 F4
Grizedale Rd
　Blackpool FY1 ....131 C1
　Lancaster LA1 ....218 F2
Grosvenor Cl PR8 ....34 E5
Grosvenor Ct
　Carnforth LA5 ....223 C1
　Cleveleys FY5 ....175 C4
　6 Lytham St Anne's FY8 ..90 A8
　Southport PR8 ....34 E4
Grosvenor Gdns PR8 ....34 F3
Grosvenor Ho PR9 ....36 A6
Grosvenor Lodge BB1 ..122 F6

Grosvenor Mews PR4 ....114 B4
Grosvenor Park Prim Sch
　LA3 ....217 F2
Grosvenor Pl
　Carnforth LA5 ....223 C1
　Preston PR2 ....117 B2
　Southport PR8 ....34 F3
Grosvenor Rd
　Carnforth LA5 ....223 D1
　Chorley PR7 ....43 B6
　Morecambe LA3 ....216 D3
　Southport PR8 ....34 E4
Grosvenor St
　Blackpool FY1 ....130 C5
　Burnley BB12 ....127 F4
　Colne BB8 ....171 F5
　Lytham St Anne's FY8 ....91 C3
　Preston PR1 ....97 B7
Grosvenor Way
　5 Blackburn BB1 ....101 E5
　Horwich BL6 ....32 A3
Groundwork Countryside
　Ctr★ BB4 ....85 E1
Grouse St OL12 ....52 F1
Grove Ave Adlington PR6 ..31 A7
　Longton PR4 ....74 F8
Grove Cres PR4 ....31 A7
Grove Ct Lancaster LA1 ....214 F4
　Oswaldtwistle BB5 ....103 C3
Grove La BB12 ....146 C1
Grove Mead L31 ....5 F1
Grove Mill PR7 ....41 C5
Grove Pk Ormskirk L39 ....15 F7
　Southport PR9 ....35 F8
Grove Rd Preston PR5 ....97 C6
　Skelmersdale WN8 ....10 C8
Grove St Accrington BB5 ....104 C4
　Bacup OL13 ....88 A3
　12 Bamber Bridge PR5 ..77 F8
　Barrowford BB9 ....170 D3
　Blackburn BB2 ....101 E2
　4 Burnley BB11 ....127 D5
　Bury BL9 ....33 C3
　Earby BB18 ....197 B2
　Leyland PR25 ....59 D8
　Lytham St Anne's FY8 ....89 F7
　Morecambe LA4 ....216 F4
　Nelson BB9 ....148 E8
　Oswaldtwistle BB5 ....103 D3
　Southport PR8 ....35 A4
Grove Terr PR8 ....35 A4
Grove The
　Appley Bridge WN6 ....28 C2
　Bilsborrow PR3 ....159 A5
　4 Burnley BB12 ....127 B6
　Carnforth LA5 ....223 B1
　Chipping PR3 ....185 D4
　Cleveleys FY5 ....175 E3
　Clitheroe BB7 ....189 F1
　Higher Penwortham PR1 ..96 B4
　Lancaster LA1 ....215 A4
　Ormskirk L39 ....6 C7
　Oswaldtwistle BB5 ....103 E5
　Preston PR1 ....117 B1
　Rufford L40 ....39 A3
　Whalley BB7 ....144 C5
Grovewood PR8 ....34 E5
Grovewood Dr WN6 ....19 E8
Grovewood Ho PR7 ....61 C2
Grundy Cl Bury BL9 ....33 A1
　Southport PR8 ....35 E5
Grundy La BL9 ....33 A1
Grundy Mews FY4 ....110 C2
Grundy St 7 PR25 ....77 B2
Grundy's La PR7 ....43 C1
Guardian Cl PR2 ....118 A4
Gubberford La PR3 ....204 D4
Guernsey Ave
　Blackburn BB2 ....101 F1
　Leyland PR7 ....60 F6
Guide La BB12 ....147 A7
Guide Rd BB4 ....73 E6
Guild Hall Arc 5 PR1 ....97 A7
Guild Park Hosp PR3 ....138 F5
Guild Row 7 PR1 ....97 A7
Guild Way PR1 ....96 D7
Guildford Ave
　Blackpool FY2 ....152 D6
　Great Knowley PR6 ....61 C4
Guildford Rd
　29 Preston PR1 ....97 A7
　Southport PR8 ....35 E1
Guildford St FY6 ....153 C6
Guildhall St PR1 ....96 F7
Guilford St BB9 ....148 B5
Guinea Hall Cl PR9 ....55 A5
Guinea Hall La PR9 ....55 A5
Guinea Hall Mews PR9 ..55 A5
Gulf La LA2,PR3 ....202 C2
Gummers Howe Wlk
　LA5 ....221 E8
Gurney St BB2 ....101 B3
Gutter La BL0 ....50 B7
Guy St BB12 ....146 C1
Guys Ind Est L40 ....39 A3
Guys Thatched Hamlet (Craft
　Ctr)★ PR3 ....158 F3
Guysyke BB8 ....171 C4
Gynn Ave FY1 ....130 B8
Gynn Sq FY1 ....130 B8

H

Habergham Dr BB12 ... 126 F8
Habergham High Sch BB12 ... 127 A7
Habergham St 19 BB12 ... 146 C1
Hackensall Rd FY6 ... 199 E5
Hacking Cl BB6 ... 143 C1
Hacking Dr PR3 ... 139 F5
Hacking St Bury BL9 ... 33 A2
Darwen BB3 ... 81 F1
5 Nelson BB9 ... 170 F2
Hacklands Ave PR2 ... 116 C1
Haddings La BB12 ... 147 A8
Haddon Ct FY2 ... 152 C5
Haddon Pl PR2 ... 117 D3
Haddon Rd FY2 ... 152 C5
Hadlee Terr LA1 ... 218 B1
Hadleigh Rd FY6 ... 153 C6
Hadrian Rd LA3 ... 217 E3
Hadstock Ave L37 ... 11 D1
Hagg La PR3 ... 156 C8
Hagg St BB8 ... 171 C4
Haig Ave Lancaster LA1 ... 214 D8
Leyland PR25 ... 76 F1
Preston PR2 ... 117 D2
Southport PR8 ... 35 E5
Tarleton PR4 ... 57 A7
Haig Rd FY1 ... 130 B1
Haigh Cl PR7 ... 43 A7
Haigh Cres Chorley PR7 ... 43 B7
Maghull L31 ... 5 C4
Haigh Ct PR8 ... 35 F6
Haigh Hall Cl BL0 ... 50 B4
Haighton Ct PR2 ... 118 A7
Haighton Dr PR2 ... 118 E6
Haighton Green La PR2 ... 138 E2
Hail St BL0 ... 50 A4
Hala Cres LA1 ... 215 A3
Hala Gr LA1 ... 215 A3
Hala Hill LA1 ... 215 B3
Hala Rd LA1 ... 215 A3
Hala Sq LA1 ... 215 A3
Halcyon Cl 6 OL12 ... 52 B2
Haldane Rd BB3 ... 81 E4
Haldane St BB10 ... 148 B2
Halden Rd LA3 ... 216 E3
Hale Carr Gr LA3 ... 216 E1
Hale Carr La LA3 ... 216 E1
Hale St BB11 ... 128 A4
Hales Rushes Rd PR3 ... 178 C4
Half Acre PR5 ... 77 A8
Half Acre La BL6 ... 31 C2
Halford Pl FY5 ... 152 E7
Halfpenny La
Andertons Mill PR7 ... 41 B3
Longridge PR3 ... 139 F8
Halifax Rd Brierfield BB9 ... 148 C5
Lane Bottom BB10 ... 149 D3
Nelson BB9,BB10 ... 148 E5
Southport PR8 ... 21 C5
Halifax St FY3 ... 130 F3
Hall Ave FY4 ... 130 C1
Hall Brow Cl L39 ... 16 B4
Hall Carr La PR4 ... 74 D6
Hall Carr Mill Cotts BB4 ... 86 B2
Hall Carr Rd BB4 ... 86 A1
Hall Cl Caton LA2 ... 237 B3
Rawtenstall BB4 ... 86 A6
Hall Coppice The BL7 ... 47 E1
Hall Croft PR4 ... 95 D2
Hall Dr Caton LA2 ... 237 B3
Heysham LA3 ... 213 A2
Morecambe LA4 ... 217 E4
Hall Fold OL12 ... 52 C8
Hall Garth Gdns LA6 ... 240 B1
Hall Gate PR7 ... 61 A2
Hall Gate La FY6 ... 177 C8
Hall Gdns OL12 ... 52 C2
Hall Gn WN8 ... 10 B7
Hall Gr LA3 ... 213 A2
Hall Greaves Cl LA3 ... 209 D8
Hall Green Cl WN8 ... 10 B7
Hall Green La L40,PR7 ... 41 A3
Hall Hill BB7 ... 228 D1
Hall Hill St 4 BB12 ... 146 C1
Hall La Appley Bridge WN6 ... 28 D2
Bickerstaffe L39 ... 7 E4
Bispham Green L40,WN8 ... 27 A6
Bracewell BD23 ... 231 F3
Great Eccleston PR3 ... 156 C4
Ince Blundell L38 ... 3 F3
Kirkby L33 ... 1 A8
Leyland PR25 ... 76 F2
Longton PR4 ... 74 E7
Maghull L31 ... 5 B7
Mawdesley L40 ... 40 D3
Orrell WN5 ... 10 F4
Rivington BL6 ... 45 A2
Royal Oak L33,L39 ... 7 B1
Skelmersdale L40 ... 17 A6
St Michael's on W PR3 ... 157 E6
Hall Mdws BB8 ... 172 C3
Hall More Cvn Pk LA7 ... 225 E7
Hall Park Ave BB10 ... 128 F4
Hall Park Ctr FY8 ... 90 F4
Hall Park Dr FY8 ... 90 E6
Hall Pk Haslingden BB4 ... 85 A6
Lancaster LA1 ... 214 F4
Hall Rd Bescar L40 ... 23 F6
Bescar L40 ... 24 B6
Fulwood PR2 ... 117 E5
Middleworth Green PR1 ... 96 E3
Hall Rd *continued*
Trawden BB8 ... 172 B3
Hall St Bacup OL13 ... 87 F3
Blackburn BB2 ... 101 E2
Burnley BB11 ... 128 A6
Clitheroe BB7 ... 166 E7
Colne BB8 ... 171 D4
Haslingden BB4 ... 85 B2
Morecambe LA4 ... 217 B6
Preston PR2 ... 117 C1
Ramsbottom BL0 ... 50 C2
12 Rawtenstall BB4 ... 86 A3
Southport PR9 ... 35 C7
Whitworth OL12 ... 52 B8
Whitworth OL12 ... 52 C8
Worsthorne BB10 ... 129 A5
Hall's Cotts FY4 ... 111 A6
Hallam Cres BB9 ... 149 A8
Hallam La LA3 ... 213 A2
Hallam Rd BB9 ... 149 A8
Hallam St 11 BB5 ... 125 A1
Hallam Way FY4 ... 111 E7
Hallbridge Gdns WN8 ... 10 B8
Hallcroft WN8 ... 18 C2
Halley Rd BB3 ... 81 E3
Halley St OL13 ... 88 A7
Hallfield Rd BB6 ... 124 D6
Hallgate Hill BB7 ... 229 B4
Halliwell Cres PR4 ... 95 E1
Halliwell Ct 7 PR7 ... 43 C7
Halliwell Hts PR5 ... 97 F3
Halliwell La PR6 ... 61 C4
Halliwell Pl 8 PR7 ... 43 C7
Halliwell St
Accrington BB5 ... 104 E2
Chorley PR7 ... 43 C7
Hallmoor Cl L39 ... 15 E2
Hallows Cl PR3 ... 157 C6
Hallows Farm Ave OL12 ... 52 D2
Hallows St BB10 ... 148 A2
Hallsall Dr LA4 ... 217 F6
Hallsalls Sq PR3 ... 156 B5
Hallwell St BB10 ... 128 A8
Hallwood Cl BB10 ... 148 B4
Hallwood Rd PR7 ... 43 A5
Halmot Ct 3 BB4 ... 86 E1
Halmote Ave BB12 ... 146 F5
Halsall Bldgs 6 PR9 ... 35 C8
Halsall Ct L39 ... 15 D6
Halsall Hall L39 ... 23 B1
Halsall Hall Dr L39 ... 23 B1
Halsall La Formby L37 ... 11 F3
Haskayne L39 ... 14 D6
Ormskirk L39 ... 15 D6
Halsall Manor Ct L39 ... 23 B1
Halsall Rd Halsall L39 ... 23 C2
Southport PR8 ... 22 A8
Halsbury St PR1 ... 97 B6
Halstead Cl BB9 ... 170 D4
Halstead La BB9 ... 170 D4
Halstead Rd PR2 ... 118 E5
Halstead St Burnley BB11 ... 127 F5
Bury BL9 ... 33 A4
Worsthorne BB10 ... 129 A6
Halstead Wlk BL9 ... 33 A5
Halton Ave
Clayton-le-W PR25 ... 77 D1
Cleveleys FY5 ... 175 E4
Halton Chase L40 ... 16 E4
Halton Ct LA4 ... 217 B3
Halton Gdns
Blackpool FY4 ... 110 F8
Cleveleys FY5 ... 175 F4
Halton Pl Fulwood PR2 ... 118 F4
Longridge PR3 ... 140 B8
Halton Rd Lancaster LA1 ... 218 E4
Maghull L31 ... 5 D3
Nether Kellet LA6 ... 221 E5
Halton St PR4 ... 132 E6
Hambledon Dr 6 PR1 ... 96 E2
Hambledon St 10 BB12 ... 126 D8
Hambledon Terr
Higham BB12 ... 146 F6
2 Padiham BB12 ... 126 F7
Hambledon View
Padiham BB12 ... 126 F7
Read BB12 ... 145 D1
Hambleton Cl PR4 ... 94 F1
Hambleton Cvn Pk FY6 ... 177 D4
Hambleton Prim Sch
FY6 ... 177 D2
Hameldon App BB11 ... 127 D5
Hameldon Ave BB5 ... 104 E2
Hameldon Cl BB11 ... 126 C2
Hameldon Rd
Goodshaw Chapel BB4 ... 106 A2
Hapton BB11 ... 126 D2
Hameldon View BB6 ... 124 D5
Hamer Ave
Blackburn BB1 ... 102 D5
Goodshaw Chapel BB4 ... 106 A1
Hamer Rd PR2 ... 117 D3
Hamer St 18 Darwen BB3 ... 65 A8
Ramsbottom BL0 ... 50 B2
Rawtenstall BB4 ... 86 A2
Hamerswood Dr PR3 ... 181 D2
Hamilton Ct
6 Blackpool FY1 ... 130 B4
8 Lytham St Anne's FY8 ... 91 D4
Hamilton Dr LA1 ... 218 A3
Hamilton Gr PR2 ... 118 E3
Hamilton Rd
Barrowford BB9 ... 170 C1
Chorley PR7 ... 43 C7
Fulwood PR2 ... 118 D4
Morecambe LA4 ... 218 A6
Nelson BB8 ... 171 A2
Hamilton St BB2 ... 101 D2
Hamilton Way OL10 ... 33 E1
Hamlet Cl BB2 ... 101 C3
Hamlet Gr PR4 ... 134 F4
Hamlet Rd FY7 ... 198 F4
Hamlet The Adlington PR7 ... 43 F1
Lytham St Anne's FY8 ... 110 F2
Hammer Terr BL0 ... 50 C3
Hammerton Gn 17 OL13 ... 87 F3
Hammerton Hall Cl LA1 ... 218 C4
Hammerton Hall La LA1 ... 218 C4
Hammerton Pl FY3 ... 131 A8
Hammerton St
Bacup OL13 ... 87 F4
Burnley BB11 ... 127 F5
Hammond Ave OL13 ... 70 D8
Hammond Ct PR1 ... 117 E1
Hammond Dr BB12 ... 145 C2
Hammond Rd L33 ... 1 C3
Hammond St Nelson BB9 ... 148 F7
Preston PR1 ... 117 E1
Preston PR1 ... 117 E2
Preston PR1 ... 117 F2
Hammond's Row 17 PR1 ... 97 A8
Hampden Ave BB3 ... 65 B7
Hampden Rd PR25 ... 77 A2
Hampden St
6 Burnley BB11 ... 128 B4
Hapton BB12 ... 126 C4
Hampsfell Dr LA4 ... 217 B3
Hampshire Cl BB1 ... 123 A7
Hampshire Pl FY4 ... 110 F6
Hampshire Rd
Bamber Bridge PR5 ... 97 E3
Rishton BB1 ... 124 A1
Hampson Ave PR25 ... 77 D1
Hampson Cotts LA2 ... 211 B1
Hampson Gr FY6 ... 200 A4
Hampson La LA2 ... 211 C1
Hampson St BL6 ... 32 B4
Hampson Terr PR3 ... 156 C5
Hampstead Cl FY8 ... 90 E6
Hampstead Mews 3
FY1 ... 130 C7
Hampstead Rd
Fulwood PR2 ... 118 D2
Standish WN6 ... 29 D1
Hampton Cl PR7 ... 43 B8
Hampton Ct FY8 ... 90 C8
Hampton Pl FY5 ... 175 E3
Hampton Rd
Blackpool FY4 ... 110 C8
Formby L37 ... 11 E1
Morecambe LA3 ... 216 E3
Southport PR8 ... 35 C5
Hampton St PR2 ... 117 C2
Hamptons The FY6 ... 153 D1
Hanbury St PR2 ... 117 C1
Hancock St BB2 ... 101 C3
Hand La L40 ... 40 F5
Handbridge The PR2 ... 117 E5
Handel St OL12 ... 52 B8
Handley Rd 4 FY1 ... 130 C6
Handsworth Ct 4 FY1 ... 130 C7
Handsworth Rd FY1 ... 130 C7
Handsworth Wlk PR8 ... 35 F3
Hanging Green La LA2 ... 220 E1
Hanley Cl FY6 ... 177 C7
Hanmer Pl 3 LA1 ... 215 A6
Hannah St
Accrington BB5 ... 104 B5
15 Bacup OL13 ... 88 A3
Darwen BB3 ... 65 B8
Hanover Cres FY2 ... 152 C5
Hanover St Colne BB8 ... 171 D5
Morecambe LA4 ... 217 B5
4 Preston PR1 ... 117 F1
Hansby Cl WN8 ... 9 E8
Hanson Bldgs 5 BB12 ... 126 C8
Hanson St Adlington PR7 ... 30 F6
Great Harwood BB6 ... 124 C4
Rishton BB1 ... 124 C1
Hanstock Cl WN5 ... 10 E5
Hants La L39 ... 15 E6
Happy Mount Ct LA4 ... 217 F7
Happy Mount Dr LA4 ... 217 E7
Hapton CE Methodist Prim
Sch BB11 ... 126 C4
Hapton Rd BB12 ... 126 C7
Hapton St
7 Padiham BB12 ... 126 D8
Thornton FY5 ... 176 B4
Hapton Sta BB11 ... 126 C4
Hapton Way BB4 ... 106 A2
Harbour Ave PR4 ... 92 E6
Harbour Cl 11 FY7 ... 198 F2
Harbour Ho 7 FY8 ... 91 D4
Harbour La Brinscall PR6 ... 62 D7
Edgworth BL7 ... 48 D5
Warton PR4 ... 92 E6
Harbour Trad Est 13
FY7 ... 198 F2
Harbour Way FY7 ... 199 B3
Harbury Ave PR8 ... 21 A4
Harcles Dr BL0 ... 50 B2
Harcourt Mews 12 BL6 ... 32 B4
Harcourt Rd
Accrington BB5 ... 104 D3
Blackburn BB2 ... 101 C6
Blackpool FY4 ... 110 D8
Lancaster LA1 ... 218 C3
Harcourt St
14 Bacup OL13 ... 87 F3
2 Burnley BB11 ... 127 D5
Preston PR1 ... 117 E1
Hard Knott Rise LA5 ... 221 E8
Hardacre La
Lucas Green PR6 ... 61 C5
Rimington BB7 ... 231 B2
Hardacre St L39 ... 15 F6
Hardaker Ct 1 FY8 ... 89 E6
Hardcastle Rd PR2 ... 117 E3
Harden Rd BB18 ... 195 A6
Hardhorn Ct FY6 ... 153 D3
Hardhorn Rd FY6 ... 153 D2
Hardhorn Way FY6 ... 153 D2
Harding Rd L40 ... 25 D4
Harding St PR6 ... 31 B8
Hardlands Ave 4 LA4 ... 217 F4
Hardman Ave
Rawtenstall BB4 ... 86 A1
Rawtenstall,Hugh Mill BB4 ... 69 A8
Hardman Cl
Blackburn BB1 ... 102 F4
Rawtenstall BB4 ... 69 F7
Hardman Dr BB4 ... 69 F7
Hardman St
Blackburn BB2 ... 101 C3
3 Blackpool FY1 ... 130 C6
Hardman Terr OL13 ... 70 D8
Hardman Way 24 BB3 ... 82 A1
Hardsough Fold BL0 ... 68 C5
Hardsough La BL0 ... 68 D5
Hardwen Ave 7 PR2 ... 116 C1
Hardwicke Ho 10 LA1 ... 214 E8
Hardwicke St 4 PR1 ... 97 A8
Hardy Ave
Barnoldswick BB18 ... 196 A3
Brierfield BB9 ... 148 B6
Hardy Cl PR2 ... 95 F8
Hardy Ct 13 BB9 ... 148 E8
Hardy Dr PR7 ... 43 A7
Hardy St Blackburn BB1 ... 122 F1
Brierfield BB9 ... 148 B6
Hare Clough Cl BB2 ... 101 F3
Hare Runs Ho LA1 ... 218 D3
Harebell Cl Blackburn BB2 ... 80 D8
Formby L37 ... 11 F1
Rochdale OL12 ... 52 D3
Hareden Brook Cl BB1 ... 101 F3
Hareden Cl 4 PR5 ... 77 F8
Hareden Rd PR2 ... 118 F2
Harefield Rise BB12 ... 127 D7
Hareholme La BB4 ... 86 D2
Hares La PR8 ... 36 D1
Harestone Ave PR7 ... 43 A5
Harewood PR7 ... 61 B2
Harewood Ave
Blackpool FY3 ... 153 A1
Lancaster LA1 ... 215 A3
Morecambe LA3 ... 216 E2
Simonstone BB12 ... 145 E2
Southport PR8 ... 21 C6
Harewood Cl FY6 ... 153 C5
Harewood Rd PR1 ... 118 C2
Hargate Ave OL12 ... 52 A2
Hargate Cl BL9 ... 50 C2
Hargate Rd FY5 ... 176 C2
Hargher St BB11 ... 127 D5
Hargreaves Ave PR25 ... 60 B8
Hargreaves Ct
Clitheroe BB7 ... 166 C7
Fulwood PR2 ... 116 F4
Whitewell Bottom BB4 ... 86 F6
Hargreaves Dr BB4 ... 85 F2
Hargreaves Fold La BB4 ... 87 A7
Hargreaves La 2 BB2 ... 101 E3
Hargreaves Rd BB5 ... 103 C4
Hargreaves St
9 Accrington BB5 ... 104 C5
Brierfield BB10 ... 148 F3
14 Burnley BB11 ... 127 F6
Colne BB8 ... 171 B4
Haslingden BB4 ... 85 B3
Hoddlesden BB3 ... 82 F1
Nelson BB9 ... 148 C7
Southport PR8 ... 35 C6
Thornton FY5 ... 176 B3
Whitewell Bottom BB4 ... 86 E5
Hargrove Ave
Burnley BB12 ... 127 D7
Padiham BB12 ... 146 C1
Harington Cl L37 ... 11 D3
Harington Gn L37 ... 11 D3
Harington Rd L37 ... 11 D4
Harland St PR2 ... 117 D3
Harland Way OL12 ... 52 B2
Harlech Ave FY1 ... 130 D1
Harlech Cl BB4 ... 85 B1
Harlech Dr Leyland PR25 ... 77 C1
Oswaldtwistle BB5 ... 103 C4
Harlech Gr FY5 ... 176 D2
Harleston Rd L33 ... 1 A3
Harleston Wlk L33 ... 1 A3
Harley Bank LA2 ... 239 C8
Harley Cl LA2 ... 239 C8
Harley Rd FY3 ... 130 E4
Harley St BB12 ... 127 C6
Harling Rd PR1 ... 118 D1
Harling St BB12 ... 127 B6
Harold Ave
8 Blackpool FY4 ... 111 A6
Burnley BB11 ... 127 C4
Harold St Burnley BB11 ... 127 D5
Colne BB8 ... 171 C4
Harold Terr PR5 ... 77 A8
Harper St BB18 ... 196 A3
Harper's La PR6 ... 61 D1
Harperley PR7 ... 61 B2
Harpers La BB12 ... 147 D8
Harridge Ave OL12 ... 52 C3
Harridge La L39,L40 ... 24 A1
Harridge St OL12 ... 52 C3
Harridge The OL12 ... 52 C3
Harrier Ct LA1 ... 214 E8
Harrier Dr Blackburn BB1 ... 101 D8
Skelmersdale WN8 ... 9 E8
Harriet St BB11 ... 127 E5
Harrington Ave FY4 ... 110 B5
Harrington Rd
Chorley PR7 ... 43 B8
Morecambe LA3 ... 216 E3
Harrington St
Accrington BB5 ... 125 A1
Preston PR1 ... 117 F1
Harris Ave FY1 ... 130 D1
Harris Cl OL10 ... 33 E1
Harris Ct 2 BB7 ... 166 E8
Harris Ctr PR2 ... 117 E5
Harris Mus & Art Gallery*
PR1 ... 97 A7
Harris Prim Sch PR2 ... 117 B7
Harris Rd WN6 ... 29 B3
Harris St Fleetwood FY7 ... 199 A4
2 Preston PR1 ... 97 A7
Harrison Ave FY5 ... 176 B2
Harrison Cres
Blackrod BL6 ... 31 C3
Morecambe LA3 ... 216 D1
Harrison Dr BB8 ... 171 C6
Harrison La PR4 ... 96 B2
Harrison Rd Adlington PR7 ... 31 A6
Chorley PR7 ... 43 C6
Fulwood PR2 ... 117 E6
Harrison St Bacup OL13 ... 71 B8
Barnoldswick BB18 ... 196 C1
Blackburn BB2 ... 101 D4
Blackpool FY1 ... 130 C3
Brierfield BB10 ... 148 F2
5 Cornholme OL14 ... 109 B1
Horwich BL6 ... 32 B4
Ramsbottom BL0 ... 50 C7
Harrison Terr BB7 ... 190 B8
Harrison Trading Est
PR1 ... 118 C1
Harrock La L40,WN6 ... 27 F6
Harrock Rd PR25 ... 77 D1
Harrod Dr PR8 ... 34 E3
Harrogate Cres BB10 ... 148 D2
Harrogate Rd FY8 ... 90 C7
Harrogate Way PR9 ... 54 C6
Harrop Pl PR2 ... 118 E4
Harrow Ave
Accrington BB5 ... 104 C7
Fleetwood FY7 ... 198 F3
Harrow Cl Orrell WN5 ... 10 F8
Padiham BB12 ... 126 E6
Harrow Dr BB1 ... 102 B3
Harrow Gr LA4 ... 217 F4
Harrow Pl Blackpool FY4 ... 110 A5
Lytham St Anne's FY8 ... 90 E5
Harrow St BB5 ... 103 E4
Harrow Stiles La OL13 ... 107 E1
Harrowdale Pk LA2 ... 219 D7
Harrowside FY4 ... 110 B6
Harrowside Brow 3
FY4 ... 110 B6
Harrowside W FY4 ... 110 A5
Harry Potts Way BB10 ... 128 B5
Harry St Barrowford BB9 ... 170 D3
Salterforth BB18 ... 194 D7
Harsnips WN8 ... 18 C2
Harswell Cl WN5 ... 10 E5
Hart St Blackburn BB1 ... 101 F4
Burnley BB11 ... 128 A6
Southport PR8 ... 35 E6
Hart's Houses BL6 ... 32 D5
Hart's La WN8 ... 9 F8
Hartford Ave FY1 ... 130 D2
Hartington Rd
Brinscall PR6 ... 63 A8
Darwen BB3 ... 81 E4
Preston PR1 ... 96 D7
Hartington St
Brierfield BB9 ... 148 B5
Colne,Cotton Tree BB8 ... 172 B5
Lancaster LA1 ... 215 B8
Rishton BB1 ... 124 A1
Hartland WN8 ... 18 C2
Hartland Ave PR9 ... 54 B5
Hartlands Cl BB10 ... 148 D3
Hartley Ave BB5 ... 104 A3
Hartley Cres PR8 ... 34 F2
Hartley Dr BB9 ... 149 A7
Hartley Gdns BB8 ... 172 C6
Hartley Homes BB8 ... 172 C6
Hartley Rd PR8 ... 34 F2
Hartley St
3 Blackburn BB1 ... 101 E6
2 Burnley BB11 ... 127 C5
Colne BB8 ... 171 D5
Earby BB18 ... 197 B1
Great Harwood BB6 ... 124 D6
2 Haslingden BB4 ... 85 B3
Horwich BL6 ... 32 B3
Nelson BB9 ... 148 E7
2 Oswaldtwistle BB5 ... 103 E4
Rochdale OL12 ... 52 B1
Hartleys Terr BB8 ... 171 E4
Hartmann St BB5 ... 104 A6
Hartshead WN8 ... 18 C2
Hartwood Gn PR6 ... 61 C3
Hartwood Rd PR9 ... 35 D7
Harvest Dr PR6 ... 61 C6
Harvesters Fold PR4 ... 134 F4
Harvey Longworth Ct
BB4 ... 106 A1
Harvey St 14 Nelson BB9 ... 170 E1
Oswaldtwistle BB5 ... 103 D4
Harvington Dr PR8 ... 21 B5
Harwich Rd FY8 ... 111 A1
Harwin Cl OL12 ... 52 D3
Harwood Ave FY8 ... 89 E8
Harwood Cl FY6 ... 177 C7
Harwood Gate BB1 ... 102 B6

Harwood La BB6 . . . . .124 E6
Harwood New Rd BB6 . . . . .124 E6
Harwood Rd Rishton BB1 124 A2
  Wilpshire BB1 . . . . .123 D4
Harwood St
  14 Blackburn,Cob Wall
  BB1 . . . . .102 A7
  Blackburn,Green Bank
  BB1 . . . . .102 B6
  Darwen BB3 . . . . .81 E2
Harwood's La BB3 . . . . .82 E1
Hasbury Dr FY5 . . . . .176 C2
Hasgill Ct LA1 . . . . .218 C1
Haskoll St LA6 . . . . .32 C1
Haslam Ct **1** BB10 . . . . . .148 B1
Haslam Dr L39 . . . . .15 D7
Haslam St BL9 . . . . .33 A4
Haslemere Ave **6** FY3 . .130 E3
Haslemere Ind Est PR25 . .76 F3
Haslingden Broadway Prim
  Sch BB4 . . . . .68 C8
Haslingden Grane (Trail)★
  BB4 .84 A2
Haslingden High Sch
  BB4 .68 B8
Haslingden Old Rd
  Blackburn BB1,BB5 . . . . . .102 E3
  Rawtenstall BB4 . . . . .85 C2
Haslingden Prim Sch
  BB4 .85 B2
Haslingden Rd
  Blackburn BB1,BB2 . . . . . .102 B2
  Oswaldtwistle BB5 . . . . .83 D7
  Rawtenstall BB4 . . . . .85 E4
Haslingden St James CE Prim
  Sch BB4 . . . . .85 B3
Haslow Pl FY3 . . . . .130 F7
Hassall Dr PR4 . . . . .156 A1
Hassett Cl PR1 . . . . .96 E6
Hastings Ave
  Blackpool FY2 . . . . .152 E5
  Warton PR4 . . . . .92 E7
Hastings Cl
  Blackburn BB1 . . . . .102 C4
  Thornton FY5 . . . . .176 C1
Hastings Pl FY8 . . . . .91 A3
Hastings Rd Kirkham PR4 114 B2
  Lancaster LA1 . . . . .214 F5
  Leyland PR25 . . . . .77 B2
  Preston PR2 . . . . .117 B1
  Southport PR8 . . . . .34 E1
  Thornton FY5 . . . . .176 C1
Hastings The LA1 . . . . . .214 F5
Haston Lee Ave BB1 . . . . .122 F3
Hasty Brow Rd LA2 . . . . . .218 B6
Hatfield Ave
  Fleetwood FY7 . . . . .198 F3
  Morecambe LA4 . . . . .217 F6
Hatfield Cl FY5 . . . . .176 C2
Hatfield Ct LA4 . . . . .217 F6
Hatfield Gdns **2** FY7 . . .198 E2
Hatfield Mews **2** FY7 . . .198 F2
Hatfield Rd
  Accrington BB5 . . . . .104 D7
  Fulwood PR2 . . . . .118 C3
  Southport PR8 . . . . .21 C6
Hatfield Wlk **1** FY7 . . . . .198 E2
Hathaway FY4 . . . . .110 E6
Hathaway Fold **4** BB12 126 D7
Hathaway Rd
  Fleetwood FY7 . . . . .198 E4
  Lancaster LA1 . . . . .218 C3
Hatlex Dr LA2 . . . . .220 E2
Hatlex Hill LA2 . . . . .220 E2
Hatlex La LA2 . . . . .220 E2
Hattersley St BB11 . . . . . .127 E6
Hatton St PR7 . . . . .30 F6
Haugh Ave BB12 . . . . .145 E4
Haulgh St BB10 . . . . .148 B2
Haunders La PR4 . . . . .74 B1
Havelock Cl BB2 . . . . .101 D3
Havelock Rd
  Bamber Bridge PR5 . . . . . .77 E7
  Middleforth Green PR1 . . . .96 E5
Havelock St
  Blackburn BB2 . . . . .101 C2
  5 Blackpool FY1 . . . . . .130 B4
  Burnley BB12 . . . . .127 B6
  Lancaster LA1 . . . . .215 A6
  Oswaldtwistle BB5 . . . . . . .103 D3
  11 Padiham BB12 . . . . . .146 C1
  Preston PR1 . . . . .117 D2
  Preston PR1 . . . . .117 E2
  Preston PR1 . . . . .117 F2
Haven Brow L39 . . . . .6 C8
Haven Rd FY8 . . . . .91 C3
Haven Sch FY5 . . . . .175 E4
Haven St BB10 . . . . .128 C5
Haven Wlk L31 . . . . .5 C4
Havenbrook Gr BL0 . . . . . . .50 A3
Haverbreaks Pl LA1 . . . . .214 E6
Haverbreaks Rd LA1 . . . . .214 E5
Haverholt Cl BB8 . . . . .171 C5
Haverholt Rd BB8 . . . . . . .171 C5
Haverthwaite Ave LA3 . . .212 F7
Havre Pk BB18 . . . . .196 C2
Hawarden Ave LA4 . . . . . .217 F6
Hawarden Rd **1** PR1 . . . .118 E1
Hawarden St BB9 . . . . . . .148 E7
Hawes Dr BB8 . . . . .171 F6
Hawes Side La FY4 . . . . . .110 E8
Hawes Side Prim Sch
  FY4 . . . . .110 E7
Hawes Terr BB10 . . . . . . .148 B2
Haweside St PR9 . . . . .35 C7
Haweswater Ave PR7 . . . . .43 B6
Haweswater Gr L31 . . . . . . .5 F2
Haweswater Pl **3** LA4 . .217 E4

Haweswater Rd **1** BB5 .125 D1
Hawick Gr OL10 . . . . .33 E1
Hawk Cl BL9 . . . . .33 B4
Hawk St Burnley BB11 . . .128 A6
  Carnforth LA5 . . . . .223 E2
Hawker Dr WN8 . . . . .9 E8
Hawkeshead Cl BB2 . . . . .101 B4
Hawkhurst Ave PR2 . . . . .117 D6
Hawkhurst Cres PR2 . . . . .117 D6
Hawkhurst Rd
  Middleforth Green PR1 . . . .96 E5
  Preston PR1 . . . . .118 B1
Hawking Pl FY2 . . . . .152 E1
Hawkins Cl PR1 . . . . .117 E1
Hawkins St
  Blackburn BB2 . . . . .101 B2
  Preston PR1 . . . . .117 E1
Hawks Gr BB4 . . . . .86 A1
Hawksbury Dr PR1 . . . . . . .96 D2
Hawksclough WN8 . . . . . . .18 D2
Hawkshaw Ave BB3 . . . . . .81 E3
Hawkshaw Bank Rd
  BB1 . . . . .101 D8
Hawkshaw La BL8 . . . . .49 B5
Hawkshaw St BL6 . . . . .32 B3
Hawkshead PR1 . . . . .96 E3
Hawkshead Ave PR7 . . . . . .60 D1
Hawkshead Cl L31 . . . . .5 E2
Hawkshead Dr LA4 . . . . . .217 C3
Hawkshead Rd
  Fulwood PR2 . . . . .118 C5
  Knott End-on-S FY6 . . . . . .199 F6
Hawkshead St
  Blackburn BB2 . . . . .101 B4
  Southport BB9,PR9 . . . . . . .35 D7
Hawkshead Terr FY4 . . . . .111 D8
Hawkshelth Cl BL7 . . . . . . .47 E1
Hawksley St BL6 . . . . .32 D2
Hawkstone Cl
  Huncoat BB5 . . . . .125 F1
  Thornton FY5 . . . . .153 D8
Hawkstone Ct LA4 . . . . . .217 F6
Hawkswood PR7 . . . . .41 B6
Hawkswood Gdns BB9 . . .148 A4
Hawksworth Ave LA3 . . . .216 E2
Hawksworth Cl L37 . . . . . . .12 A6
Hawksworth Dr L37 . . . . . .12 A6
Hawksworth Gr LA3 . . . . .216 E2
Hawksworth Rd BB5 . . . . .104 B8
Hawley Gn OL12 . . . . .52 D2
Hawley St Colne BB8 . . . . .171 C4
  Colne,Cotton Tree BB8 . . . .172 C5
Haworth Art Gallery★
  BB5 . . . . .104 D3
Haworth Ave
  Accrington BB5 . . . . .104 D3
  Ramsbottom BL0 . . . . .50 A2
  Rawtenstall BB4 . . . . .85 F2
Haworth Dr OL13 . . . . .70 C8
Haworth St
  Accrington BB5 . . . . .125 B1
  Edgworth BL7 . . . . .48 D5
  Oswaldtwistle BB5 . . . . . . .103 E4
  Rishton BB1 . . . . .124 B1
Haws Ave LA5 . . . . .223 D1
Haws Hill LA5 . . . . .223 D1
Hawthorn Ave Caton LA2 237 C3
  Darwen BB3 . . . . .82 C2
  Edenfield BL0 . . . . .68 D2
  Fleetwood FY7 . . . . .175 E8
  Orrell WN5 . . . . .10 F6
  Oswaldtwistle BB5 . . . . . . .103 F3
  Ramsbottom BL0 . . . . .50 A2
Hawthorn Bank BB5 . . . . .125 A3
Hawthorn Cl Caton LA2 237 C3
  Kirkham PR4 . . . . .113 E6
  Langho BB6 . . . . .123 D8
  Leyland PR26 . . . . .76 D2
  New Longton PR4 . . . . .76 A7
  Whalley BB7 . . . . .144 A7
Hawthorn Cres
  Preston PR1 . . . . .116 D1
  Skelmersdale WN8 . . . . . . .17 E1
Hawthorn Dr BB1 . . . . . . .103 B8
Hawthorn Gdns BB5 . . . . .125 A3
Hawthorn Rd Bacup OL13 . .88 A2
  Blackpool FY1 . . . . .130 C7
  Bolton-le-S LA5 . . . . .221 A6
  Fulwood PR2 . . . . .118 C2
  Morecambe LA4 . . . . .217 F4
Hawthorne Ave
  Brierfield BB10 . . . . .148 C5
  Garstang PR3 . . . . .181 B8
  Higher Walton PR5 . . . . . . .98 C3
  Horwich BL6 . . . . .32 E1
  Newton-w-S PR4 . . . . .114 F3
Hawthorne Cl
  Barrowford BB9 . . . . .170 B1
  Clayton Green PR6 . . . . . . .78 B3
  Nelson BB9 . . . . .149 B8
Hawthorne Cres L37 . . . . .12 A2
Hawthorne Dr BB18 . . . . . .196 C4
Hawthorne Gr
  17 Barrowford BB9 . . . . .170 D3
  Carleton FY5 . . . . .153 B5
  Southport PR9 . . . . .35 F7
Hawthorne Ind Est PR7 . .190 A1
Hawthorne Lea FY5 . . . . . .153 C8
Hawthorne Mdws BB4 . . .106 A1
Hawthorne Pl BB7 . . . . . . .189 B7
Hawthorne Rd
  Burnley BB11 . . . . .127 F4
  Thornton FY5 . . . . .153 C8
Hawthorne Terr BB8 . . . . .194 E1
Hawthornes The L40 . . . . . .39 B3
Hawthorns Jun Sch
  BB1 . . . . .101 F8

Hawthorns The
  Bilsborrow PR3 . . . . .159 A5
  Eccleston PR7 . . . . .41 B7
  Fulwood PR2 . . . . .117 F6
  Lancaster LA1 . . . . .215 A2
  Lytham St Anne's FY8 . . . .110 F2
  Newburgh WN8 . . . . .27 A1
  Woodplumpton PR4 . . . . . .136 E2
Haxey Wlk BL6 . . . . .31 F3
Haydock Ave BB5 . . . . .60 A8
Haydock Gr LA3 . . . . .216 D1
Haydock La BL7 . . . . .48 B1
Haydock Rd LA1 . . . . .215 B3
Haydock Sq **1** BB6 . . . .124 C5
Haydock St
  6 Bamber Bridge PR5 . . .97 E2
  7 Blackburn BB1 . . . . . .122 E1
  Burnley BB10 . . . . .148 C1
Haydocks La PR4 . . . . .116 D5
Haydon Ave PR5 . . . . .77 A7
Hayfell Ave LA4 . . . . .217 C3
Hayfell Cres LA2 . . . . .220 D1
Hayfell Gr LA2 . . . . .220 D1
Hayfield Ave
  Blackpool FY2 . . . . .152 E2
  Gregson Lane PR5 . . . . .98 A1
  Poulton-le-F FY6 . . . . .153 E3
Hayfield Cl
  Gregson Lane PR5 . . . . .98 A1
  Ramsbottom BL8 . . . . .49 F1
Hayfield Rd L39 . . . . .15 E7
Hayfields BB18 . . . . .194 E8
Hayhurst Cl BB7 . . . . .144 C6
Hayhurst Farm Terr
  BB7 . . . . .166 F7
Hayhurst Rd BB7 . . . . .144 C6
Hayhurst St PR1 . . . . .117 F2
Haylemere Ct PR8 . . . . . . .34 E5
Hayling Pl PR2 . . . . .117 A4
Haylot Dr LA2 . . . . .219 D2
Haylot Sq **9** LA1 . . . . . .215 A8
Haymans Gn L31 . . . . .5 E1
Haymarket FY8 . . . . .90 B6
Haymarket Lodge PR9 . . . .53 D1
Hayshaw Mews PR3 . . . . .207 D3
Haysworth St PR1 . . . . . . .117 F2
Hayward Gr WN6 . . . . .29 C2
Haywood Cl
  Accrington BB5 . . . . .104 B8
  Fulwood PR2 . . . . .118 A8
Haywood Rd BB5 . . . . .104 B8
Hazel Ave
  Bamber Bridge PR5 . . . . . .98 A1
  Bury BL9 . . . . .33 B2
  Clayton-le-M BB5 . . . . .124 F2
  Darwen BB3 . . . . .82 B2
  Fleetwood FY7 . . . . .175 F8
  Ramsbottom BL0 . . . . .50 B1
Hazel Bank **3** LA3 . . . . .212 F7
Hazel Cl
  Bamber Bridge PR5 . . . . . .97 D3
  Blackburn BB2 . . . . .101 C4
  Higher Penwortham PR1 . . .96 B3
  Knott End-on-S FY6 . . . . . .199 F6
Hazel Coppice PR2 . . . . . .116 E3
Hazel Ct Fulwood PR2 . . . .117 E3
  Ormskirk L39 . . . . .15 E5
Hazel Dene BB7 . . . . .189 C6
Hazel Gr Bacup OL13 . . . . .88 B3
  Bamber Bridge PR5 . . . . . .98 A1
  Blackburn BB1 . . . . .102 F5
  Blackpool FY3 . . . . .130 E5
  Chorley PR6 . . . . .61 C3
  Clayton-le-M BB5 . . . . .125 A2
  Clitheroe BB7 . . . . .166 C4
  Fulwood PR2 . . . . .119 A4
  Lancaster LA1 . . . . .214 D8
  Longridge PR3 . . . . .140 B8
  Rawtenstall BB4 . . . . .85 F4
  Southport PR8 . . . . .35 E7
  Tarleton PR4 . . . . .54 F8
Hazel Hall La BL0 . . . . .50 B1
Hazel La WN8 . . . . .18 B4
Hazel Mount BL7 . . . . .47 C2
Hazel St Ramsbottom BL0 . .50 A4
  Rising Bridge BB5 . . . . .85 A8
Hazelbank Gdns L37 . . . . .11 E5
Hazeldene Ave **2** BB4 . . .85 B2
Hazeldene Rd FY4 . . . . . . .198 F2
Hazelhead La PR3 . . . . . . .204 E2
Hazelhurst Cl BL0 . . . . .50 B4
Hazelhurst Com Prim Sch
  BL0 .50 A4
Hazelhurst Dr PR3 . . . . . . .181 A7
Hazelhurst Lodge **12**
  PR2 . . . . .118 F4
Hazelhurst Rd PR2 . . . . . . .119 A2
Hazelmere Rd
  Fulwood PR2 . . . . .117 D8
  Preston PR1 . . . . .117 A1
Hazelmoor BB1 . . . . .122 E6
Hazelmount Ave LA5 . . . .223 D3
Hazelmount Cres LA5 . . . .223 D3
Hazelmount Dr LA5 . . . . . .223 C3
Hazelrigg La LA2 . . . . .211 D7
Hazels The Coppull PR7 . . .42 E1
  Wilpshire BB1 . . . . .122 E6
Hazelwood
  Silverdale LA5 . . . . .224 C2
  Southport PR8 . . . . .34 C4
Hazelwood Ave L40 . . . . . . .25 E4
Hazelwood Cl
  Blackburn BB1 . . . . .123 A1
  Leyland PR25 . . . . .76 E1

Hazelwood Dr
  Hesketh Bank PR4 . . . . .73 E4
  Morecambe LA4 . . . . .217 F6
Hazelwood Gdns LA1 . . . .215 A2
Hazelwood Rd BB9 . . . . . .149 A8
Hazlehurst Cl L37 . . . . .11 C2
Hazlewood Cl FY5 . . . . . . .176 C2
Hazlewood Dr FY3 . . . . . . .130 E2
Head Dyke La PR3 . . . . . . .201 C3
Headbolt La Halsall PR8 . . .22 A4
  Kirkby L33 . . . . .1 A5
Headfort Cl FY2 . . . . .152 D2
Headingley Cl BB5 . . . . . . .125 F1
Headingly Ave WN8 . . . . . .17 C1
Headlands Cl LA2 . . . . .52 E1
Headlands The LA3 . . . . . .212 D7
Headley Rd PR25 . . . . .76 E1
Headroomgate Rd FY8 . . . .89 F8
Heads La BB18 . . . . .195 B6
Heald Brow BB18 . . . . . . .196 A4
Heald Cl Rochdale OL12 . . .52 C3
  Weir OL13 . . . . .88 A8
Heald Croft PR3 . . . . .181 D6
Heald Dr OL12 . . . . .52 C3
Heald House Rd PR25 . . . . .60 C7
Heald La OL13 . . . . .88 A8
Heald Rd BB10,BB12 . . . . .148 A2
Heald St Blackpool FY3 . . .130 D6
  6 Chorley PR6 . . . . .43 E8
Healdwood Cl BB12 . . . . . .147 F3
Healdwood Dr BB12 . . . . .147 F3
Healey Ave OL12 . . . . .52 D4
Healey Ct BB11 . . . . .127 F5
Healey Dell Cotts OL12 . .52 B4
Healey Dell Nature Reserve★
  OL12 . . . . .52 B4
Healey Gr OL12 . . . . .52 C5
Healey Hall Farm OL12 . . .52 C4
Healey Hall Mews OL12 . .52 C4
Healey La OL12 . . . . .52 E3
Healey Mount BB11 . . . . . .127 F4
Healey Prim Sch OL12 . . . .52 E3
Healey Row BB11 . . . . .127 F5
Healey St FY3 . . . . .130 D7
Healey Stones OL12 . . . . . .52 C4
Healey Wood Rd BB11 . . . .127 F4
Heaning Ave
  Accrington BB5 . . . . .104 D8
  Blackburn BB1 . . . . .102 D4
Heanor Dr PR8 . . . . .35 F3
Heap Bridge Village Prim Sch
  BL9 .33 D1
Heap Brow BL9 . . . . .33 D1
Heap Clough BB4 . . . . .84 C3
Heap Ct PR9 . . . . .35 E8
Heap St Brierfield BB9 . . .148 A5
  Burnley BB10 . . . . .148 B1
  Bury BL9 . . . . .33 D1
  Rawtenstall BB4 . . . . .86 A8
  Worsthorne BB10 . . . . .129 B6
Heapey Fold La PR6 . . . . . .44 C7
Heapey Ho 62 A3
Heapey Rd PR6 . . . . .61 F2
Heapfold **4** OL12 . . . . . .52 B2
Heaplands BL8 . . . . .49 F1
Heapworth Ave BL0 . . . . . .50 B6
Heartwood Cl BB2 . . . . . . .101 A8
Heasandford Ind Est
  Burnley BB10 . . . . .128 D8
  Burnley BB10 . . . . .148 D2
Heasandford Prim Sch
  BB10 . . . . .128 B8
Heath Ave BB4 . . . . .50 B1
Heath Gr LA3 . . . . .212 E6
Heath Hill Dr OL13 . . . . . . .70 C8
Heath St BB10 . . . . .128 B8
Heathbourne Rd OL13 . . . .70 C8
Heather Bank
  Burnley BB11 . . . . .127 C4
  Rawtenstall BB4 . . . . .68 F8
Heather Brow BB18 . . . . . .197 D2
Heather Cl Brierfield BB9 148 D4
  Burscough L40 . . . . .25 E4
  Chorley PR6 . . . . .43 E8
  Formby L37 . . . . .12 B5
  Haslingden BB4 . . . . .68 A6
  Horwich BL6 . . . . .32 B4
  Southport PR8 . . . . .21 D2
  Thornton FY5 . . . . .176 B1
Heather Gr PR2 . . . . .118 E3
Heather Lea Dr PR6 . . . . . .62 F8
Heatherfield PL7 . . . . .48 E6
Heatherfield Pl PR7 . . . . . .117 C1
Heatherlands
  Haslingden BB4 . . . . .68 A6
  Millgate OL12 . . . . .71 D4
Heatherlea Cl WN8 . . . . . . .10 C7
Heatherlea Rd BB12 . . . . .147 D7
Heatherleigh PR6 . . . . .76 D3
Heatherleigh Gdns BB2 . . .81 D6
Heathers The
  Clayton Brook PR5 . . . . . . .78 C4
  Knott End-on-S FY5 . . . . . .199 F5
Heatherside Rd BL0 . . . . . .50 C7
Heatherway PR2 . . . . .118 E6
Heatherways L37 . . . . .12 A6
Heathey La FY39,PR8 . . . . .23 A7
Heathfield PR6 . . . . .43 F1
Heathfield Ave OL13 . . . . .70 C8
Heathfield Cl L37 . . . . .12 A6
Heathfield Dr PR2 . . . . . . .118 E4
Heathfield Pk BB2 . . . . . . .100 F6
Heathfield Rd Bacup OL13 70 C8
  Fleetwood FY7 . . . . .198 E2
  Southport PR8 . . . . .21 F6
Heathfoot Ave LA3 . . . . . . .212 E6
Heathfoot Dr LA3 . . . . .212 E6
Heathgate Fence BB12 . . .147 D8
  Skelmersdale WN8 . . . . . . .18 C2

Har – Hen **271**

Heathland WN8 . . . . .10 B7
Heathrow Pl PR7 . . . . .43 A7
Heathway PR2 . . . . .117 F5
Heathway Ave FY3 . . . . . . .130 E6
Heathy La L39 . . . . .13 B8
Heatley Cl BB2 . . . . .101 D3
Heatley St PR1 . . . . .96 F8
Heaton Bottom Rd LA3 . . .213 E5
Heaton Cl
  Bamber Bridge PR5 . . . . . .97 D4
  Burscough L40 . . . . .25 D4
  Carleton FY6 . . . . .153 C5
  Morecambe LA4 . . . . .217 E3
  Skelmersdale WN8 . . . . . . .10 A7
  Thornton FY5 . . . . .153 C8
Heaton Ho LA1 . . . . .214 F5
Heaton Mount Ave PR2 . .117 F6
Heaton Pl PR1 . . . . .118 E1
Heaton Rd Lancaster LA1 214 F5
  Lytham St Anne's FY8 . . . . .90 A8
Heaton St
  3 Blackburn BB2 . . . . . .101 E4
  Leyland PR25 . . . . .76 E1
  Standish WN6 . . . . .29 E1
Heatons Bridge Rd L40 . . .24 D3
Heaviley Gr BL6 . . . . .32 A5
Hebden Ave FY1 . . . . .130 D1
Heber St BB11 . . . . .106 B4
Hebrew Rd BB10 . . . . .128 A8
Hebrew Sq **12** BB10 . . . .128 A8
Heckenhurst Ave BB10 . . .129 A6
Hector Rd BB3 . . . . .81 E5
Hedge Row PR4 . . . . .113 B3
Hedge Rows OL12 . . . . .71 C1
Hedgerow The BB2 . . . . . .101 A8
Hedgerows Rd PR26 . . . . . .59 A8
Heeley Rd FY8 . . . . .89 E8
Height Barn La OL13 . . . . .71 A8
Height Croft BB9 . . . . .148 E5
Height La PR3 . . . . .161 F7
Height Side La BB7 . . . . . . .86 B7
Heights Ave OL12 . . . . .52 E2
Heights Cl OL12 . . . . .52 E2
Heights Cotts BB5 . . . . . . .104 F4
Heights Ct OL12 . . . . .52 E1
Heights La OL12 . . . . .52 E1
Heights Rd BB9 . . . . .148 D6
Heights The BL6 . . . . .32 E1
Heightside Ave BB4 . . . . . .86 E2
Heightside Mews BB4 . . . .86 E2
Helen's Cl FY4 . . . . .110 E6
Helena St BB10 . . . . .128 B5
Helks Brow LA2 . . . . .239 B2
Hellifield PR2 . . . . .117 F7
Hellifield Rd
  Bolton-by-B BB7 . . . . .230 E5
  Gisburn BB7 . . . . .231 C4
Helm Cl BB11 . . . . .127 D2
Helmcroft **5** BB4 . . . . . .85 A1
Helmcroft Ct **1** BB4 . . . .85 B1
Helmn Way BB2 . . . . .170 F2
Helmsdale WN8 . . . . .18 C2
Helmsdale Cl BL0 . . . . .50 A4
Helmsdale Rd
  Blackpool FY4 . . . . .110 F4
  Nelson BB9 . . . . .171 A1
Helmshore Prim Sch
  BB4 .68 A7
Helmshore Rd
  Haslingden BB4 . . . . .68 A7
  Ramsbottom BL8,BB4 . . . . .68 A3
Helmshore Textile Mus★
  BB4 .67 F8
Helmside Ave LA4 . . . . . . .217 C3
Helmsley Gn **2** PR25 . . . .77 D3
Helston Cl Burnley BB11 . .127 B4
  Southport PR9 . . . . .54 E5
Helton Cl BB9 . . . . .170 D4
Helvellyn Dr BB12 . . . . . . .127 C8
Hemingway FY4 . . . . .110 D8
Hemingway Pl **1** BB9 . . .148 F8
Hemp St OL13 . . . . .87 F1
Hempshaw Ave BB4 . . . . .106 A2
Henderson Rd
  Fleetwood FY7 . . . . .198 F2
  Weeton Camp PR4 . . . . . . .132 E6
Henderson St PR1 . . . . . . .117 E2
Hendon Pl PR2 . . . . .116 E2
Hendon Rd BB9 . . . . .148 E8
Hendriff Pl **4** OL12 . . . . .52 F1
Hendry La BB3 . . . . .81 D7
Henfield Cl BB5 . . . . .125 A3
Henley Ave FY5 . . . . .175 D4
Henley Ct
  7 Blackpool FY2 . . . . . .152 E1
  Southport PR9 . . . . .53 E1
Henley Dr PR9 . . . . .53 F1
Henley Mews LA3 . . . . . . .216 E3
Henley St **9** OL12 . . . . . .52 F1
Hennel Ho PR5 . . . . .97 C4
Hennel La
  Bamber Bridge PR5 . . . . . .97 B2
  Bamber Bridge PR5 . . . . . .97 C3
  Bamber Bridge PR5 . . . . . .97 C4
Henrietta St Bacup OL13 . .87 F2
  Blackburn BB2 . . . . .101 C5
  Preston PR1 . . . . .97 B8
Henrietta Street Ind Est **2**
  OL13 . . . . .87 F2
Henry Gdns BB9 . . . . .148 B5
Henry St Accrington BB5 . .104 D3
  Bank Lane BL0 . . . . .50 D7
  Blackpool FY1 . . . . .130 C2
  Church BB5 . . . . .103 F6
  Clayton-le-M BB5 . . . . .125 A2

Henry St continued
Colne BB8 ....171 C4
Lancaster LA1 ....214 F7
Lytham St Anne's FY8 ...91 A3
2 Nelson BB9 ....170 D1
Rawtenstall BB4 ....85 F2
Rishton BB1 ....124 B1
Henry Whalley St BB2 ..101 A2
Henson Ave FY4 ....110 E6
Henthorn Cl 4 BB7 ......166 D7
Henthorn Rd BB7 ....166 C6
Henthorne St 1 FY1 .....130 C6
Henwick Hall Ave BL0 ...50 B4
Herbert St Bacup OL13 ..70 D8
Blackburn BB2 ....101 D2
Burnley BB11 ....127 E5
Horwich BL6 ....32 B4
Leyland PR25 ....77 A1
Padiham BB12 ....126 D7
Preston PR1 ....118 B1
Hereford Ave
8 Blackpool FY3 ......130 E3
Burnley BB12 ....127 B7
Garstang PR3 ....181 B8
Hereford Cl BB5 ....104 B7
Hereford Dr BB7 ....166 F7
Hereford Gr Cottam PR4 .116 D5
Skelmersdale WN8 ......10 B6
Hereford Rd
Blackburn BB1 ....102 C5
Nelson BB8,BB9 ....171 A2
Southport PR9 ....35 F7
Hereford St BB9 ....148 C8
Herevale Hall Dr BL0 ....50 B4
Heriot Cl 8 FY5 ....175 F1
Heritage The PR25 ......76 F3
Heritage Way
Cleveleys FY5 ....175 F1
Tarleton PR4 ....57 A5
Herkomer Ave BB11 .....127 E2
Herlebeck Rise LA1 .....218 F2
Hermitage WN6 ....19 E7
Hermitage St BB1,BB5 ..124 C1
Hermitage The FY5 .....175 F1
Hermitage Way FY8 ......90 D6
Hermon Rd FY5 ....175 E1
Hermon St 2 PR1 ....118 C1
Hern Ave PR5 ....77 A8
Heron Cl Blackburn BB1 .101 D8
Cleveleys FY5 ....175 F5
Heron Ct BB11 ....127 C5
Heron Dr LA4 ....217 C3
Heron Way Blackpool FY3 131 B6
Kirkham PR4 ....114 B4
Oswaldtwistle BB5 .....103 E3
Herons Ct L31 ....5 B4
Herons Reach BL0 ....68 B4
Herons Wharf WN6 ......19 D7
Heronsyke LA1 ....218 D4
Herring Arm Rd FY7 ....199 A2
Herschel Ave BB12 ......127 C8
Herschell St
2 Blackburn BB2 ......101 B1
Preston PR1 ....97 B6
Hertford St BB2 ....101 C2
Hesketh Ave Banks PR9 ..55 A6
Blackpool FY2 ....152 B4
Hesketh Cl Darwen BB3 ..65 C6
Fulwood PR2 ....118 E1
Hesketh Ct Blackpool FY2 152 B4
Great Harwood BB6 ....124 C6
Hesketh Dr Maghull L31 ...5 F1
Rufford L40 ....39 A3
Shevington Moor WN6 ..29 A2
Southport PR9 ....53 F1
Hesketh Gn L40 ....39 B4
Hesketh La Becconsall PR4 73 F1
Hesketh Lane PR3 .....162 D7
Tarleton PR4 ....57 A7
Hesketh Links Ct PR9 ...53 E2
Hesketh Lodge L37 ......11 E3
Hesketh Manor PR9 .....53 E2
Hesketh Pl FY7 ....199 B5
Hesketh Rd Burscough L40 25 D4
Fulwood PR2 ....118 E1
Heysham LA3 ....212 E8
Longridge PR3 ....140 A8
Lytham St Anne's FY8 ..111 A1
Southport PR9 ....53 D2
Hesketh St
Great Harwood BB6 ....124 C5
Preston PR1 ....117 C1
Hesketh-with-Becconsall All
Saints CE Sch PR4 ....73 E4
Heskin Cl L31 ....5 D4
Heskin Hall Ct L39 ......15 D8
Heskin La L39 ....15 D8
Heskin Pemberton's CE Prim
Sch CE Prim Sch PR7 ..41 E2
Hesley La BD24 ....236 E6
Hessam Hts LA3 ....212 F5
Hesse St 1 BB3 ....65 A8
Hest Bank La LA2 ....218 C7
Hest Bank Rd LA4 ....217 E6
Hester Cl L38 ....2 F4
Hestham Ave LA4 ....217 B4
Hestham Cres LA4 ......217 B4
Hestham Dr LA4 ....217 B5
Hestham Par LA4 ....217 B4
Hetherington Pl FY2 ....152 E2
Hetton Lea BB9 ....170 C3
Heversham WN8 ....18 C2
Heversham PR2 ....117 F7
Heversham Cl
Lancaster LA1 ....215 B3

Heversham Cl continued
Morecambe LA4 ....217 C3
Hewart Dr BL9 ....33 C3
Hewart St BB12 ....127 A7
Hewitt Bsns Pk WN5 ....10 E4
Hewitt Cl PR4 ....95 E1
Hewitt St 8 PR25 ....77 B2
Hewlett Ave PR7 ....42 D1
Hewlett Cl BL8 ....50 A1
Hewlett St PR7 ....42 E1
Hewngate PR5 ....98 E1
Hexham Ave FY5 ....175 E4
Hexham Cl BB5 ....104 C3
Hexham Rd LA4 ....217 F5
Hey Bottom La OL12 ....52 F6
Hey End PR4 ....75 F8
Hey Head Ave BB4 ......70 A8
Hey House Mews BL8 ....49 F4
Hey St BB9 ....170 E1
Heycrofts View BL0 ......68 E3
Heydon Cl L37 ....11 D1
Heyes Rd WN5 ....10 E4
Heyes St WN6 ....19 C7
Heyes The PR6 ....78 B2
Heyescroft L39 ....7 D6
Heyfold Gdns BB3 ....81 F3
Heyhead St BB9 ....148 C5
Heyhouses BB7 ....146 A8
Heyhouses Ct FY8 ....90 B8
Heyhouses Endowed CE Inf
Sch FY8 ....89 F7
Heyhouses Endowed CE Jun
Sch FY8 ....89 F8
Heyhouses La FY8 ....90 C7
Heyhurst Rd BB2 ....101 D5
Heymoor Ave BB6 ......124 D6
Heys BB5 ....103 D3
Heys Ave 5 BB4 ....85 A3
Heys Cl Blackburn BB2 ...81 C7
Rawtenstall BB4 ....86 C1
Heys Ct Blackburn BB2 ...81 C8
Oswaldtwistle BB5 .....103 E3
Heys La
Barley Green BB12 .....169 D5
Blackburn BB2,BB3 .....81 C7
Darwen BB3 ....81 F2
Great Harwood BB6 ....124 E5
Oswaldtwistle BB5 .....103 E3
Heys Lane Ind Est BB4 ..124 E5
Heys Bacup OL13 ....87 F1
Haslingden BB4 ....85 A3
Rawtenstall BB4 ....86 C1
Thornton FY5 ....176 B3
Heys The Coppull PR7 ...42 F2
Parbold WN8 ....27 C3
Southport PR9 ....34 D4
Heysham Ave LA3 ......212 F8
Heysham Bsns Pk LA3 ..212 E2
Heysham Cres BB2 .....101 F1
Heysham Hall Dr LA3 ...212 E6
Heysham Hall Gr LA3 ...212 E7
Heysham High Sch LA3 .216 F3
Heysham Mossgate Rd
LA3 ....212 F7
Heysham Nuclear Power Sta
Nature Reserve★ LA3 .212 D4
Heysham Pk LA3 ....212 F7
Heysham Port Sta LA3 .212 C5
Heysham Rd
4 Heysham LA3 ......212 E7
Morecambe LA3 ....216 D2
Southport PR9 ....35 F7
Heysham St 2 PR1 .....117 C1
Heywood Cl L37 ....11 E3
Heywood Com High Sch
OL10 ....33 E1
Heywood Rd PR2 ....116 E2
Heywood St
1 Blackpool FY1 ......130 B4
Bury BL9 ....33 A1
Great Harwood BB6 ....124 C4
Heyworth Ave BB2 ....81 C7
Hibbert Terr LA1 ....214 F3
Hibson Rd BB9 ....148 D8
Nelson,Little Marsden BB9 148 D7
Hic Bibi La PR7 ....29 C6
Hick's Terr 5 BB1 ......124 B1
Hickory St BB1 ....101 F7
Hickson Ave L31 ....5 C3
Hidings Court La LA4 ...217 B4
Hiers House La BB8 ....171 B5
Higgin St Burnley BB10 .128 B5
Colne BB8 ....171 D5
Worsthorne BB10 .....129 B5
Higgin's La L40 ....25 C4
High Bank PR6 ....62 A3
High Bank Cres BB3 .....65 A7
High Banks L31 ....5 C3
High Barn La OL12 ......71 C3
High Bentham Bsns Pk
LA2 ....239 D7
High Bentham Prim Sch
LA2 ....239 D8
High Cl BB12 ....126 E6
High Cop Cop PR6 ....78 F4
High Crag Ct LA5 ......223 E6
High Ct LA4 ....217 F5
High Fold BB18 ....195 A6
High Gate FY7 ....198 D3
High Gate La FY6 ......177 A6
High Gn PR25 ....76 F1
High La Bickerstaffe L39 ...7 C8
Laneshaw Bridge BD22 .174 A8
Ormskirk L39,L40 ......16 A8
Salterforth BB18 ......194 C5
High Legh FY8 ....90 C3
High Mdw PR5 ....97 B2
High Moor La WN6 ......28 B4

High Moss L39 ....15 E3
High Mount Ct 2 LA1 ..214 F7
High Mount Ho 1 LA1 ..214 F7
High Park Pl PR9 ....36 A8
High Park Rd PR9 ....36 A8
High Peak Rd OL12 ......52 C6
High Rd Halton LA2 .....219 C7
Lowgill LA2 ....239 C5
High St Accrington BB5 ..104 B4
Belmont BL7 ....46 C4
Blackburn BB1 ....101 E5
Blackpool FY1 ....130 B6
Brierfield BB9 ....148 B5
Burton in L LA6 ......242 C3
Chapeltown BL7 ....48 C4
10 Chorley PR7 ....43 C8
Clitheroe BB7 ....166 B8
Colne BB8 ....171 E5
Darwen BB3 ....82 A1
Elswick PR4 ....155 F1
Fleetwood FY7 ....199 B4
Garstang PR3 ....181 C7
Great Eccleston PR3 ..156 B5
Haslingden BB4 ....85 B4
Horwich BL6 ....32 B4
Lancaster LA1 ....214 F7
Mawdesley L40 ....40 B1
Nelson BB9 ....148 D7
Oswaldtwistle BB5 ....103 F3
Padiham BB12 ....146 D1
Rishton BB1 ....124 B1
Skelmersdale WN8 .....17 C1
Standish WN6 ....29 E1
Higham Gr FY3 ....130 F2
Higham Hall Rd BB12 ..146 F5
Higham Rd BB12 ....146 E4
Higham Side Rd PR4 ...135 C6
Higham St BB12 ....146 D1
Highbank BB1 ....122 F1
Highbank Ave FY4 ......111 A8
Highbank Hotel 7 PR2 .117 C1
Highbury Ave
Blackpool FY3 ....130 E8
Fleetwood FY7 ....198 F3
Highbury Gate PR4 .....156 A2
Highbury Pl BB1 ....101 D6
Highbury Rd FY8 ....110 E1
Highbury Rd E FY8 .....110 D1
Highbury Rd W FY8 ....110 D1
Highcroft BB1 ....17 F1
Highcroft Ave FY2 ......152 E5
Highcroft Way OL12 .....52 F4
Highcross Ave FY6 .....131 D8
Highcross Hill FY6 ......131 D8
Highcross Rd FY6 ......153 D1
Highdale LA3 ....213 A7
Higher Antley St BB5 ..104 A5
Higher Audley St BB1 ..101 F4
Higher Austin's BL6 .....32 F1
Higher Bank Rd PR2 ...117 F3
Higher Bank St
Blackburn BB2 ....101 B6
Withnell PR6 ....80 A1
Higher Barn BL9 ....33 E5
Higher Barn St 2 BB1 ..102 A5
Higher Blackthorn OL13 .87 F4
Higher Bold Venture
BB3 ....65 A6
Higher Booths La BB4 ..106 A1
Higher Change Villas
OL13 ....88 B4
Higher Chapel La BB7 ..230 A1
Higher Church St BB3 ...82 B1
Higher Cockcroft 14
BB1 ....101 E5
Higher Commons La
BB2 ....121 C4
Higher Compley Cvn Pk
FY6 ....153 C2
Higher Croft
Kingsfold PR1 ....96 C2
2 Kingsfold PR1 ......96 D2
Higher Croft Cotts BB3 ..81 F8
Higher Croft Rd BB2,BB3 .81 F8
Higher Cross Row 8
OL13 ....87 F3
Higher Cswy BB9 ......170 D3
Higher Dunscar BL7 .....47 C1
Higher Eanam BB1 .....102 A5
Higher Feniscowles La
BB2 ....80 B8
Higher Field BB6 ....123 C8
Higher Firs Dr BB5 .....125 A3
Higher Fold La BL0 ......50 E7
Higher Furlong PR4 ......74 F6
Higher Gate BB5 ....125 F1
Higher Gate Rd BB5 ....125 F1
Higher Gn FY6 ....153 E3
Higher Greenfield PR2 ..117 B5
Higher Heys BB5 ....103 E3
Higher Hill BB3 ....80 F2
Higher House Cl BB2 .....81 A7
Higher House La PR6 ....62 B2
Higher Knowles BL6 .....32 E2
Higher La Haslingden BB4 .85 B4
Holmes PR4 ....56 C3
Salterforth BB18 ......194 B7
Scorton PR3 ....204 F4
Skelmersdale,Dalton WN8 .18 C7
Skelmersdale,Up Holland
WN8 ....10 C7
Higher Lawrence St 14
BB3 ....82 B2
Higher London Terr BB3 .82 B2
Higher Mdw PR25 ....77 E1
Higher Mill St BB4 ......86 A3
Higher Moor Cotts FY2 .152 F2

Higher Moor Rd FY3 ...153 A2
Higher Moss La L37 .....13 A2
Higher Moulding BL9 ....33 E5
Higher Park Rd BB18 ...194 C8
Higher Peel St 8 BB5 ..103 D3
Higher Perry St BB3 .....82 B2
Higher Ramsgreave Rd
BB1 ....122 C3
Higher Rd
Knowle Green PR3 ....163 B3
Longridge PR3 ....162 E2
Tosside BD23 ....236 C5
Higher Reedley Rd BB9,
BB10 ....148 D5
Higher Row BL9 ....33 D3
Higher Saxifield BB10 ..148 E3
Higher South St BB3 ....82 A1
Higher Summerseat BL0 .50 B2
Higher Syke LA2 ....233 C2
Higher Tentre BB11 ....128 B5
Higher View LA4 ....110 C6
Higher Walton CE Prim Sch
PR5 ....98 C3
Higher Walton Mill PR5 ..98 B4
Higher Walton Rd PR5 ...97 E4
Higher Waterside BB3 ...82 E3
Higher Witton Rd BB2 ..101 B4
Highergate BB5 ....125 F2
Highfield Bacup OL13 ....87 F2
Brinscall PR6 ....62 F8
Great Harwood BB6 ...124 B5
Rawtenstall BB4 ....86 A7
Highfield Ave
Bamber Bridge PR5 ....97 C1
Brierfield BB9 ....148 B3
Foulridge BB8 ....194 E1
Fulwood PR2 ....118 C4
Inskip PR4 ....135 C8
Leyland PR25 ....77 C3
Highfield Cl Adlington PR6 .31 A7
Clifton PR4 ....115 C1
Oswaldtwistle BB5 ....103 F3
Tarleton PR4 ....57 A5
Highfield Cres
5 Barrowford BB9 ....170 D3
Morecambe LA4 ......216 F4
Nelson BB9 ....170 E3
Highfield Ct BB4 ....85 A2
Highfield Dr
Fulwood PR2 ....117 E8
Hest Bank LA2 ....220 D1
Kingsfold PR1 ....96 D2
Longridge PR3 ....140 B6
Longton PR4 ....74 F6
Highfield Gdns BB2 ....101 E2
Highfield Gr PR5 ....97 C2
Highfield High Sch FY4 .110 E6
Highfield Ind Est PR7 ....61 D2
Highfield La L40 ....24 D7
Highfield Mews BB3 .....65 B8
Highfield Pk
Haslingden BB4 ....85 A1
Maghull L31 ....5 D2
Highfield Prim Sch PR6 ..43 E8
Highfield Priory Sch
PR2 ....118 F5
Highfield Rd
Adlington PR6 ....31 A7
Blackburn BB2 ....101 E3
Blackpool FY6 ....110 E6
Blackrod BL6 ....31 E1
Carnforth LA5 ....221 E8
Clitheroe BB7 ....166 F7
Croston PR26 ....58 D2
Darwen BB3 ....82 B1
1 Earby BB18 ....197 B2
Edenfield BL0 ....68 D3
Ormskirk L39 ....15 E7
Rawtenstall BB4 ....86 D1
5 Rishton BB1 ......124 A1
Southport PR9 ....54 D3
Highfield Rd N
Adlington PR6 ....31 A8
Chorley PR7 ....61 C2
Highfield Rd S PR7 ......61 C1
Highfield St
4 Darwen BB3 ....65 B8
Haslingden BB4 ....85 A2
Highfield Terr LA2 ......239 C8
Highfurlong Sch FY3 ...153 A2
Highgale Gdns PR5 .....77 C7
Highgate Blackpool FY4 .110 D5
Goosnargh PR3 ....138 D6
Higher Penwortham PR1 .96 B5
Nelson BB9 ....148 D7
Highgate Ave PR2 ......117 E4
Highgate Cl Fulwood PR2 117 F4
Newton-w-S PR4 ......114 F3
Highgate Cres WN6 ......19 E7
Highgate La Warton PR4 ..92 E6
Whitworth OL12 ....52 C5
Highgate Pl FY8 ....90 D6
Highgate Rd Maghull L31 ..5 D3
Skelmersdale WN8 ......10 B7
Highgrove Ave PR7 ......41 F3
Highgrove Cl LA4 ......217 A4
Highgrove Ct PR26 ......58 F8
Highland Ave PR1 ....96 B4
Highland Brow LA2 .....211 A4
Highland Dr PR7 ....60 E6
Highland Lo WN6 ....29 D1
Highland Rd BL6 ....32 E1
Highmeadow WN8 ....10 A6
Highmoor BB9 ....148 F6
Highmoor Pk BB7 ......166 F6
Highrigg Dr PR3 ....137 F1
Highsands Ave L40 ......39 A3
Hightown BB4 ....86 E4

Hightown Rd BB4 ....86 F4
Hightown Sta L38 ....3 A4
Highways Ave PR7 ......60 D1
Highwoods Pk BB6 .....143 B5
Higson St BB2 ....101 D5
Hilary Ave FY2 ....152 C5
Hilary St BB10 ....148 A1
Hilbre Cl PR9 ....53 F1
Hilbre Dr PR9 ....53 F1
Hilderstone La LA5 .....240 A7
Hildrop Rd 7 BB9 ......170 F1
Hill Cl WN6 ....19 E8
Hill Cres PR4 ....115 A2
Hill Crest OL13 ....87 E1
Hill Crest Ave
Burnley BB10 ....128 F4
Fulwood PR2 ....117 E8
Hill Croft
Clayton Green PR6 .....78 A2
Kirkham PR4 ....114 B5
Hill End La BB4 ....86 C1
Hill Field Croft PR3 ....204 C1
Hill Hos 16 BB3 ....65 A8
Hill House Fold La WN6 .28 C5
Hill House La
Jack Green PR6 ....79 A7
Wrightington WN6 .....28 C5
Hill La Blackrod BL6 .....31 C2
Colne BB8 ....172 C7
Nether Kellet LA6 .....221 F4
Hill Pl BB9 ....148 D6
Hill Rd
Higher Penwortham PR1 .96 C5
Lancaster LA1 ....218 D3
Leyland PR25 ....77 C1
Hill Rd S PR1 ....96 D3
Hill Rise Haslingden BB4 .85 C1
1 Ramsbottom BL0 .....50 A4
Hill Rise View L39 ......15 A1
Hill Side LA1 ....214 E8
Hill St Accrington BB5 ..104 C5
Barnoldswick BB18 ...196 C2
Blackburn BB1 ....102 B5
Blackpool FY4 ....130 B1
Brierfield BB9 ....148 B5
Carnforth LA5 ....223 D1
3 Church BB5 ....125 D2
Colne BB8 ....171 D4
Fence BB9 ....147 F6
Oswaldtwistle BB5 ....103 D5
Padiham BB12 ....126 C8
Preston PR1 ....96 F8
Ramsbottom BL9 ......50 C3
Rawtenstall BB4 ....86 A7
Southport PR9 ....35 B7
Hill Top Barrowford BB9 .170 D4
Colne,Cotton Tree BB8 .172 C4
Foulridge BB8 ....194 C2
Longridge PR3 ....162 D2
New Longton PR4 ......76 A6
Trawden BB8 ....172 B2
Hill Top Cl Freckleton PR4 .93 D7
Yealand Redmayne LA5 .225 E4
Hill Top La Earby BB18 ..197 A2
Whittle-le-W PR6 ......61 D8
Hill View Beverley BB9 ..170 E7
7 Blackburn BB1 ......122 E1
2 Rawtenstall BB4 .....85 F1
Hill View Dr PR7 ....29 D8
Hill View Rd PR3 ......204 C1
Hill Wlk PR25 ....77 A2
Hillam La LA2 ....206 B7
Hillary Cres L31 ....5 D1
Hillary Ct L37 ....11 E2
Hillbrook Rd PR25 ......76 F2
Hillcliffe FY8 ....89 E5
Hillcrest Maghull L31 .....5 F1
Skelmersdale WN8 ......9 B8
Hillcrest Ave
Bolton-le-S LA5 ....221 A5
Fulwood PR2 ....117 A4
Longridge PR3 ....140 A7
Hillcrest Cl PR4 ....57 A8
Hillcrest Dr Bescar L40 ..23 F7
Longridge PR3 ....140 A4
Tarleton PR4 ....57 A8
Hillcrest Rd
Blackburn BB2 ....100 F2
Blackpool FY4 ....110 B4
Langho BB6 ....123 C8
Ormskirk L39 ....15 E6
Hillcroft Fulwood PR2 ..117 C7
High Bentham LA2 ....239 D7
Hildean WN8 ....10 C8
Hillingdon Rd BB10 ....148 D3
Hillingdon Rd N BB10 ..148 D3
Hillkirk Dr OL12 ....52 C3
Hillmount Ave LA3 .....212 F8
Hillock Cl L40 ....24 A7
Hillock La Bescar L40 ....24 A7
Skelmersdale WN8 .....18 D7
Warton PR4 ....92 E8
Hillocks The PR26 ......58 B1
Hillpark Ave
Fulwood PR2 ....117 D4
Gregson Lane PR5 ......98 D3
Hills Ct 2 LA1 ....218 D1
Hills The PR2 ....119 C7
Hillsborough Ave BB9 ..148 D5
Hillsea Ave LA3 ....212 F8
Hillside Burnley BB11 ..127 D4
Tarleton PR4 ....57 A6
Hillside Ave
Blackburn BB1 ....102 C4
Blackrod BL6 ....31 E1
Brierfield BB10 ....148 C5
15 Darwen BB3 ....65 A8
Egerton BL7 ....48 B1

Hillside Ave continued
Farington PR26 . . . . .76 F7
Fulwood PR2 . . . . .117 D4
Hill Dale WN8 . . . . .27 D5
Horwich BL6 . . . . .32 C4
Kirkham PR4 . . . . .114 C5
Ormskirk L39 . . . . .15 D3
Preesall FY6 . . . . .200 B4
Hillside Cl Blackburn BB1 **102** C4
Blackpool FY3 . . . . .130 E6
Brierfield BB9 . . . . .148 C5
Burnley BB11 . . . . .127 D2
Clitheroe BB7 . . . . .166 E6
Euxton PR7 . . . . .60 C1
Goodshaw Chapel BB4 . .106 A1
Great Harwood BB6 . . . .124 C6
Thornton FY5 . . . . .153 D8
Hillside Com Prim Sch
WN8 . . . . .9 D8
Hillside Cres Horwich BL6 32 C4
Weir OL13 . . . . .87 F7
Whittle-le-W PR6 . . . . . .61 C8
Hillside Ct L39 . . . . .15 D3
Hillside Dr Newchurch BB4 86 E2
Stalmine FY6 . . . . .177 C7
West Bradford BB7 . . . .189 F6
Hillside Gdns BB3 . . . . . .65 A7
Hillside Rd
Haslingden BB4 . . . . . . .85 C3
Low Bentham LA2 . . . . .239 C8
2 Preston PR1 . . . . .97 C6
Ramsbottom BL0 . . . . . .50 A5
Southport PR8 . . . . .34 E1
Hillside Sch PR3 . . . . . .140 D7
Hillside Sta PR3 . . . . . . .34 E1
Hillside View BB9 . . . . . .148 C5
Hillside Way OL12 . . . . . .71 C1
Hillside Wlk
Blackburn BB1 . . . . .102 C4
Rochdale OL12 . . . . .52 D4
Hillstone Ave OL12 . . . . .52 D4
Hillstone Cl BL8 . . . . . . .49 F2
Hillsview Rd PR8 . . . . . . .21 C4
Hilltop OL12 . . . . .52 C5
Hilltop Dr BB4 . . . . .68 C7
Hilltop Wlk L39 . . . . .15 C3
Hillview Rd PR4 . . . . . . .114 A6
Hillview Short Stay Sch
BB11 . . . . .127 C5
Hillylaid Rd FY5 . . . . . . .176 D2
Hilmont Terr BB1 . . . . . .101 F7
Hilmore Rd LA4 . . . . . . .217 A5
Hilstone La FY2 . . . . . . .152 D1
Hilton Ave
6 Blackpool FY1 . . . . . .130 B1
Horwich BL6 . . . . .32 A3
Lytham St Anne's FY8 . . . .90 C6
Hilton Ct FY8 . . . . .89 E5
Hilton Rd BB3 . . . . .65 B8
Hilton St BB3 . . . . .65 A8
Hilton's Brow PR6 . . . . . .79 B4
Hinchley Gn L31 . . . . .5 B1
Hind St Burnley BB10 . . .148 B2
4 Preston PR1 . . . . .96 E6
Hind's Head Ave WN6 . . .28 F6
Hindburn Ave L31 . . . . . . .5 F2
Hindburn Pl **2** LA1 . . . .218 C2
Hinde St LA1 . . . . .218 E1
Hindle Fold La BB6 . . . .124 C6
Hindle St Accrington BB5 .104 C6
Bacup OL13 . . . . .70 D8
Darwen BB3 . . . . .81 F2
Haslingden BB4 . . . . . . .85 B3
Hindley Beech **1** L31 . . . .5 C2
Hindley Cl PR2 . . . . .118 C2
Hindley Ct **3** BB9 . . . . .170 C1
Hindley St **5** PR7 . . . . .43 C6
Hinton St BB10 . . . . . . .128 B5
Hippings La BB4 . . . . . . .86 F1
Hippings Meth Prim Sch
BB5 . . . . .103 E3
Hippings Vale BB5 . . . . .103 D4
Hippings Way BB7 . . . . .189 E2
Hirst St **6** Burnley BB11 .128 B4
6 Cornholme OL14 . . . .109 B1
Padiham BB12 . . . . .146 C1
Hoarstones Ave BB12 . . .147 D7
Hob Gn BB2 . . . . .121 F2
Hob La BL7 . . . . .48 C7
Hobart Pl FY5 . . . . .152 F8
Hobart St BB11 . . . . . . .128 B6
Hobberley Dr WN8 . . . . . .9 E8
Hobbs La PR3 . . . . .183 A4
Hobcross La L40 . . . . . . .26 A2
Hobson St BB4 . . . . .85 F4
Hobson's La LA6 . . . . . .240 C4
Hockley Pl FY3 . . . . . . .130 F7
Hodder Ave
Blackpool FY1 . . . . .130 D1
Chorley PR7 . . . . .43 D5
Fleetwood FY7 . . . . .198 D2
Maghull L31 . . . . .5 F2
Morecambe LA3 . . . . . . .217 F3
Hodder Bridge Ct BB7 . . .165 B7
Hodder Brook PR2 . . . . .119 A3
Hodder Cl
6 Bamber Bridge PR5 . .97 E2
Fleetwood FY7 . . . . .198 D2
Hodder Ct BB7 . . . . .165 C4
Hodder Dr BB7 . . . . .189 D7
Hodder Gr Clitheroe BB7 .166 C7
Darwen BB3 . . . . .81 E4
Hodder Pl Blackburn BB1 101 F6
Lancaster LA1 . . . . .218 C4
Lytham St Anne's FY8 . . . .90 C7
Hodder St
Accrington BB5 . . . . . . .104 D6
1 Blackburn BB1 . . . . .101 E6

Hodder St continued
Brierfield BB10 . . . . .148 C3
Longridge PR3 . . . . .140 B7
Hodder Way FY6 . . . . . . .153 D2
Hoddlesden Fold BB3 . . . .82 F1
Hoddlesden Rd BB3 . . . . .82 E1
Hoddlesden St Paul's CE
Prim Sch BB3 . . . . .82 F1
Hodge Bank Bsn Pk
BB9 . . . . .170 D2
Hodge Brow BL6 . . . . . . .44 F4
Hodge La BB18 . . . . .194 B8
Hodge St PR8 . . . . .35 B7
Hodgefield BB7 . . . . .144 A4
Hodgson Ave PR4 . . . . . . .93 A5
Hodgson High Sch Tech Coll
FY6 . . . . .153 F3
Hodgson Pl FY6 . . . . .153 D2
Hodgson Rd FY1 . . . . . . .130 C8
Hodgson St Darwen BB3 . .82 B1
3 Oswaldtwistle BB5 . . .103 E4
Hodson St
Bamber Bridge PR5 . . . . .97 C1
Southport PR8 . . . . .35 C6
Hogarth Ave BB11 . . . . . .127 F3
Hogarth Cres PR4 . . . . . .134 F4
Hogg's La L37 . . . . .11 F1
Hoggs Hill La L37 . . . . . . .11 F1
Hoghton Ave OL13 . . . . . .71 A8
Hoghton Cl LA1 . . . . . . .214 D6
Hoghton Gr PR9 . . . . .35 C8
Hoghton La PR5 . . . . .98 D3
Hoghton Pl **3** PR9 . . . . .35 B7
Hoghton Rd Leyland PR25 .76 D1
Longridge PR3 . . . . .140 C7
Hoghton St
8 Bamber Bridge PR5 . .77 A8
Southport PR9 . . . . .35 C6
Hoghton Twr ★ PR5 . . . . .99 E1
Hoghton View PR1 . . . . . .97 C6
Holbeck Ave
Blackpool FY4 . . . . .110 F8
Morecambe LA4 . . . . . . .217 F4
Rochdale OL12 . . . . .52 D4
Holbeck St BB10 . . . . . . .148 A1
Holborn Dr L39 . . . . .15 C3
Holborn Hill L39 . . . . . . .15 C4
Holcombe Brook Prim Sch
BL0 . . . . .50 A2
Holcombe Ct BL0 . . . . . . .49 F2
Holcombe Dr BB10 . . . . .128 B6
Holcombe Gr PR6 . . . . . . .61 C5
Holcombe Lee BL0 . . . . . .50 A4
Holcombe Mews BL0 . . . . .49 F3
Holcombe Old Rd BL8,
BL0 . . . . .50 A5
Holcombe Prec BL0 . . . . .49 F3
Holcombe Rd
Blackpool FY2 . . . . .152 E1
Haslingden BB4 . . . . . . .67 F8
Ramsbottom BL8 . . . . . .49 F2
Holcombe Village BL8 . . . .50 A6
Holcroft Pl FY8 . . . . .90 F4
Holden Ave Bury BL9 . . . .33 C4
Ramsbottom BL0 . . . . . .50 A5
Holden Cl BB9 . . . . .170 C1
Holden Fold BB3 . . . . . . .82 B3
Holden La BB7 . . . . .230 B5
Holden Pl BB4 . . . . .84 F1
Holden Rd Brierfield BB9 148 A5
Brierfield,Reedley BB10 . .148 B3
Holden St Accrington BB5 .104 B5
Adlington PR7 . . . . .30 F7
Belthorn BB1 . . . . .82 F6
Blackburn BB2 . . . . .101 C4
Burnley BB11 . . . . .127 F5
Clitheroe BB7 . . . . .166 F8
Holden Way LA1 . . . . . . .214 F5
Holden Wood Dr BB4 . . . .84 F1
Hole House La BB7 . . . . .235 E2
Hole House St BB1 . . . . .102 C5
Holgate FY4 . . . . .110 F6
Holgate Dr WN5 . . . . . . .10 E6
Holgate St
Brierfield BB10 . . . . .148 B1
Great Harwood BB6 . . . .124 C5
Holhouse La BL8 . . . . . . .49 F2
Holker Bsns Ctr **2** BB8 .171 B4
Holker Cl Coupe Green PR5 98 E3
Lancaster LA1 . . . . .214 D6
Holker La PR26 . . . . .59 B4
Holker St Colne BB8 . . . .171 B4
Darwen BB3 . . . . .65 B8
Holland Ave
Bamber Bridge PR5 . . . . .97 E2
Rawtenstall BB4 . . . . . . .85 F3
Holland Bsns Pk L40 . . . .17 C4
Holland Ct WN8 . . . . .9 D2
Holland House Ct PR5 . . . .97 E2
Holland House Rd PR5 . . . .97 E3
Holland Lodge **4** PR2 . .118 F4
Holland Moor Prim Sch
WN8 . . . . .9 E7
Holland Moss WN8 . . . . . .9 A5
Holland Pl BB9 . . . . .170 D2
Holland Rd PR2 . . . . .117 C1
Holland St
Accrington BB5 . . . . . . .103 F6
Blackburn BB1 . . . . .101 D6
3 Burnley BB12 . . . . . .126 B8
Holland's La WN8 . . . . . . .17 A1
Holliers Cl L31 . . . . .5 E1
Hollies Blackburn BB2 . . .101 A8
Catterall PR3 . . . . .181 D2
Hollies Rd BB3 . . . . .123 A7
Hollies The PR8 . . . . .34 F6
Hollin Bank BB9 . . . . . . .148 B6

Hollin Bridge St BB2 . . . .101 D2
Hollin Cl BB4 . . . . .86 F4
Hollin Gr BB4 . . . . .86 A4
Hollin Hall BB8 . . . . .172 C1
Hollin Hill BB11 . . . . . . .128 B3
Rawtenstall BB4 . . . . . . .86 A4
Hollin Mill St BB9 . . . . . .148 B6
Hollin Rd BB11 . . . . .101 C2
Hollin Way
Rawtenstall,Constable Lee
BB4 . . . . .86 A4
Rawtenstall,Rush Bed BB4 .86 A6
Hollingreave Dr BB4 . . . . .86 A4
Hollingreave Rd BB11 . . .128 A4
Hollings PR4 . . . . .75 F7
Hollington St BB8 . . . . . .172 B5
Hollinhead Cres PR2 . . . .117 A4
Hollinhurst Ave PR1 . . . . .96 C6
Hollinhurst Brow LA2 . . .239 C2
Hollinhurst Wlk BB12 . . .146 E3
Hollins Ave BB10 . . . . . .128 F4
Hollins Cl Accrington BB5 104 C4
Hoghton PR5 . . . . .99 C3
Hollins Ct **1** BB18 . . . . .196 B3
Hollins Gr PR2 . . . . .117 B3
Hollins Grove St BB3 . . . .81 F3
Hollins Hill PR3 . . . . . . .207 C2
Hollins La
Accrington BB5 . . . . . . .104 C3
Edenfield BL0 . . . . .68 E2
Hollins Lane PR3 . . . . . .207 C2
Runshaw Moor PR26 . . . .59 C4
Silverdale LA5 . . . . .224 D1
Hollins Rd
Barnoldswick BB18 . . . . .196 A2
Darwen BB3 . . . . .81 F4
Nelson BB9 . . . . .171 A2
Preston PR1 . . . . .118 B2
Hollins Tech Coll The
BB5 . . . . .104 D2
Hollinshead St PR7 . . . . . .43 C8
Hollinshead Terr BB3 . . . .64 B7
Hollinview Cl BB4 . . . . . . .86 A5
Hollinwood Dr BB4 . . . . . .86 A5
Hollow Gill Brow BD24,
BD24 . . . . .236 F5
Hollowbrook Way **4**
OL12 . . . . .52 D2
Hollowell La BL6 . . . . . . .32 D1
Holloworth La L40 . . . . . .26 D2
Holloworth La PR4 . . . . .136 C5
Hollowhead Ave BB1 . . . .122 F5
Hollowhead Cl BB1 . . . . .122 F5
Hollowhead La BB1 . . . . .123 A5
Hollowrane LA6 . . . . .240 C7
Holly Ave BB4 . . . . .85 C1
Holly Bank
Accrington BB5 . . . . . . .104 C4
Edgworth BL7 . . . . .48 B7
Fulwood PR2 . . . . .117 C5
Warton LA5 . . . . .223 D5
Holly Cl Clayton Green PR6 78 B2
Skelmersdale WN8 . . . . .17 C1
Thornton FY5 . . . . .176 C3
Westhead L40 . . . . .16 E4
Holly Cres PR7 . . . . .42 E2
Holly Ct BB1 . . . . .101 F7
Holly Fold La L39,WA11 . .8 C7
Holly Gr Longridge PR3 . .140 A8
Tarleton PR4 . . . . .57 A7
Holly Ho **8** BB1 . . . . . . .128 B5
Holly La Ormskirk L39 . . .15 A4
Rufford L40 . . . . .39 C3
Skelmersdale L39,WA11 . . .8 A7
Holly Mews FY8 . . . . . . .110 F2
Holly Mount BB4 . . . . . . .68 A7
Holly Mount RC Prim Sch
BL8 . . . . .49 D1
Holly Pl PR5 . . . . .78 B6
Holly Rd Blackpool FY1 . .152 C1
Thornton FY5 . . . . .176 B3
Holly St Blackburn BB1 . .101 F7
Brierfield BB10 . . . . .128 B5
Bury BL9 . . . . .33 A2
Nelson BB9 . . . . .148 F8
Oswaldtwistle BB5 . . . . .103 D4
Ramsbottom BL0 . . . . . .50 C3
Holly Terr BB1 . . . . .101 F8
Holly Tree Cl BB3 . . . . . . .65 A6
Holly Tree Way BB2 . . . . .80 F8
Holly Wlk LA1 . . . . .214 D8
Hollybank PR2 . . . . .116 F5
Hollybrook Rd PR8 . . . . . .35 A5
Hollytree Cl BB4 . . . . . . .85 F5
Hollywood Ave
Blackpool FY3 . . . . .130 C8
Higher Penwortham PR1 . .96 C3
Hollywood Gr FY7 . . . . . .198 F4
Holman St **5** PR1 . . . . . .118 C1
Holmbrook Cl BB2 . . . . . .81 F8
Holmby St BB10 . . . . . . .148 B2
Holmdale Ave PR9 . . . . . .54 C4
Holme Ave FY7 . . . . .175 D8
Holme Bank BB4 . . . . . . .85 F1
Holme Cl BB18 . . . . .195 A4
Holme Cres BB8 . . . . . . .172 B4
Holme End BB12 . . . . . . .147 F4
Holme Hill BB7 . . . . .189 E2
Holme La Caton LA2 . . . .237 C3
Haslingden BB4 . . . . . . .68 D8
Rawtenstall BB4 . . . . . . .68 A5
Holme Mills Ind Est LA6 240 B8
Holme Pk LA2 . . . . .239 D7
Holme Rd
Bamber Bridge PR5 . . . . .77 E8

Holme Rd continued
Burnley BB12 . . . . .127 E7
Clayton-le-M BB5 . . . . .124 E4
Higher Penworth PR1,
PR2 . . . . .96 C7
Holme Slack Com Prim Sch
PR1 . . . . .118 C3
Holme Slack La PR1 . . . .118 C3
Holme St Accrington BB5 104 C6
Bacup OL13 . . . . .70 D8
Barrowford BB9 . . . . . . .170 D2
Colne,Cotton Tree BB8 . .172 B5
Darwen BB3 . . . . .65 A8
Nelson BB9 . . . . .148 E8
Holme Terr Nelson BB9 . .148 C8
Rawtenstall BB4 . . . . . . .68 A5
Holme The
Calder Vale PR3 . . . . . . .182 E8
Rawtenstall BB4 . . . . . . .68 A5
Holme Vale BB4 . . . . . . .68 A6
Holmebrook Dr BL6 . . . . .32 C1
Holmefield Ave FY5 . . . . .175 E2
Holmefield Cl FY5 . . . . . .175 E2
Holmefield Cl **8** BB9 . . .170 D3
Holmefield Gdns **15**
BB9 . . . . .170 D3
Holmefield Rd
Knott End-on-S FY6 . . . .199 E5
Lytham St Anne's FY8 . . . .90 A7
Holmehouse Lodge **15**
PR2 . . . . .118 F4
Holmes Ct Fulwood PR1 . .117 E3
Garstang PR3 . . . . .181 C8
Holmes Dr BB5 . . . . .87 F4
Holmes La OL13 . . . . . . .87 F3
Holmes Mdw **3** PR26 . . .76 B1
Holmes Rd FY5 . . . . .176 B3
Holmes Sq **7** BB11 . . . .128 B5
Holmes St Burnley BB11 . .128 B5
Forest Holme BB4 . . . . . .87 A7
Padiham BB12 . . . . .126 D8
Rawtenstall BB4 . . . . . . .86 B3
Holmes Terr BB4 . . . . . . .85 F5
Holmes The BB4 . . . . . . .85 F5
Holmestrand Ave BB11 . . .127 B4
Holmeswood PR4 . . . . . .114 A5
Holmeswood Cres PR3 . .137 B8
Holmeswood Meth Sch
L40 . . . . .38 C6
Holmeswood Pk BB4 . . . . .68 C8
Holmeswood Rd L40 . . . . .38 D6
Holmfield Cres **2** PR2 . .116 D1
Holmfield Pk L37 . . . . . . .11 D4
Holmfield Rd
Blackpool FY2 . . . . .152 B2
Fulwood PR2 . . . . .118 A4
Holmrook Rd PR1 . . . . . .118 B1
Holmsley St BB10 . . . . . .128 B5
Holmwood Cl OL13 . . . . . .11 D3
Holmwood Gdns L37 . . . . .11 D4
Holsands Cl PR2 . . . . . . .118 E6
Holst Gdns BB2 . . . . .102 A1
Holstein Ave OL12 . . . . . .52 D4
Holstein St PR1 . . . . .97 A8
Holt Ave PR7 . . . . .42 F2
Holt Brow PR25 . . . . .60 A6
Holt Coppice L39 . . . . . . .6 A7
Holt La PR6 . . . . .78 E3
Holt Mill Rd BB4 . . . . . . .69 D8
Holt Sq BB9 . . . . .170 E5
Holt St Orrell WN5 . . . . . .10 D5
9 Rawtenstall BB4 . . . . .69 E8
Rishton BB1 . . . . .124 C1
Whitworth OL12 . . . . . . .71 C1
Holt St W BL0 . . . . .50 B5
Holt's Terr OL12 . . . . . . .52 E2
Holts La FY8 . . . . .153 F2
Holy Cross RC High Sch
PR7 . . . . .43 C4
Holy Family RC Prim Sch
Blackpool FY1 . . . . .130 C8
Fulwood PR2 . . . . .116 F4
Southport PR9 . . . . .35 E7
Warton PR4 . . . . .92 F6
Holy Saviour RC Prim Sch
BB9 . . . . .170 D2
Holy Souls RC Prim Sch
BB1 . . . . .122 C1
Holy Trinity CE Prim Sch
Burnley BB11 . . . . .127 E5
Formby L37 . . . . .11 F3
Southport PR9 . . . . .35 C8
Holy Trinity RC Prim Sch
BB9 . . . . .148 C5
Holy Trinity Sch BB3 . . . .82 A1
Holy Trinity Stacksteads CE
Prim Sch OL13 . . . . . . .70 C8
Holyoake Ave FY2 . . . . . .152 E1
Holyoake St
Burnley BB12 . . . . .127 A6
2 Cornholme OL14 . . . .109 A7
Home Breeze Ho **1**
LA4 . . . . .217 E6
Home Farm Cl LA2 . . . . .238 D6
Home Farm Mews PR26 . .58 D1
Home Field PR3 . . . . .181 C8
Homeacre Ave BB7 . . . . .145 F8
Homechase Ho PR8 . . . . .34 F4
Homefylde RC **4** FY3 . . .130 D3
Homelinks FY7 . . . . .90 D3
Homer Ave PR4 . . . . .56 F7
Homesands Ho PR9 . . . . .35 D8
Homestead Cl **4** PR25 . .76 D1
Homestead Dr FY7 . . . . . .198 E1

Homestead The **9** FY8 . .91 A3
Homestead Way FY7 . . . .198 E1
Homewood Ave LA4 . . . .217 F6
Homfray Gr LA3 . . . . . . .217 E3
Honey Hole Rd 101 E2
Honey Holme La BB10 . .107 C5
Honey Moor Dr FY5 . . . .176 B4
Honeypot La FY6 . . . . . . .154 C4
Honeysuckle Cl PR6 . . . . .61 B5
Honeysuckle Gr PR4 . . . . .73 E4
Honeysuckle Pl FY2 . . . . .152 F6
Honeysuckle Row PR2 . . .118 E2
Honeysuckle Way OL12 . . .52 D3
Honeywood Cl BL0 . . . . . .50 A3
Honister Ave FY3 . . . . . .130 E6
Honister Cl **6** FY7 . . . . .198 D3
Honister Rd
Brierfield BB10 . . . . .148 B3
Lancaster LA1 . . . . .218 F2
Honister Sq FY8 . . . . . . .110 F2
Honiton Ave BB2 . . . . . . .81 C8
Honiton Way PR4 . . . . . .116 F4
Hoo Hill Ind Est FY3 . . . .130 E8
Hoo Hill La FY3 . . . . .130 E8
Hood St **4** BB5 . . . . . . .104 C6
Hoodhouse St BB11 . . . . .127 E4
Hookwood Ave FY5 . . . . .175 D1
Hoole La Banks PR9 . . . . .55 A6
Nateby PR3 . . . . .180 D3
Hoole St Michael CE Prim
Sch PR4 . . . . .74 C1
Hools La PR3 . . . . .201 A5
Hope Cl FY5 . . . . .176 B4
Hope La PR3 . . . . .162 C5
Hope Sq PR9 . . . . .35 D7
Hope St Accrington BB5 . .104 C5
Adlington PR6 . . . . .31 B8
Bacup OL13 . . . . .87 F4
Blackburn BB2 . . . . .101 D5
Brierfield BB9 . . . . .148 B5
Chorley PR7 . . . . .61 C1
Darwen BB3 . . . . .81 F1
Great Harwood BB6 . . . .124 C4
Haslingden BB4 . . . . . . .85 B2
Horwich BL6 . . . . .32 B4
Lancaster LA1 . . . . .215 A7
Lytham St Anne's FY8 . . . .90 A7
Morecambe LA3 . . . . . . .217 C4
Nelson BB9 . . . . .148 D8
12 Padiham BB12 . . . . .126 D8
4 Preston PR1 . . . . . . .96 F8
Ramsbottom BL0 . . . . . .50 B5
Rawtenstall BB4 . . . . . . .86 C1
Southport PR9 . . . . .35 C7
Worsthorne BB10 . . . . . .129 B6
Hope St N BL6 . . . . .32 B5
Hope Terr
10 Bamber Bridge PR5 . .77 A8
Blackburn BB2 . . . . .101 C6
Hopkinson St BB8 . . . . . .172 B5
Hopkinson Terr BB8 . . . . .172 C3
Hopton Rd FY1 . . . . .130 B2
Hopwood Ave BL6 . . . . . .32 C4
Hopwood St
Accrington BB5 . . . . . . .104 B4
4 Bamber Bridge PR5 . .77 E8
Bamber Bridge PR5 . . . . .77 E8
Blackburn BB2 . . . . .101 C6
8 Burnley BB11 . . . . . .127 E6
Preston PR1 . . . . .97 A8
Horace St **7** BB12 . . . . .127 D6
Horden Rake BB2 . . . . . . .80 E7
Horden View BB2 . . . . . . .80 E7
Hordley St BB12 . . . . . . .127 A6
Horeb Cl **5** BB12 . . . . . .126 D7
Hornbeam Cl PR1 . . . . . . .96 B3
Hornby Ave
Fleetwood FY7 . . . . .175 D8
Fulwood PR2 . . . . .118 C4
Hornby Bank Hornby LA2 238 B8
Nether Kellet LA6 . . . . . .221 F5
Hornby Croft PR26 . . . . . .59 B8
Hornby Ct
4 Blackburn BB2 . . . . .101 C4
Kirkham PR4 . . . . .114 B4
Lancaster LA1 . . . . .218 C4
Hornby Dr Lancaster LA1 215 A4
Newton-w-S PR4 . . . . . .114 F2
Hornby Hall Cl LA2 . . . . .238 B7
Hornby High Sch LA2 . . .238 B7
Hornby La PR4 . . . . .156 F2
Hornby Park Ct **1** FY3 . .130 D4
Hornby Rd Blackpool FY1 130 C4
Caton LA2 . . . . .237 C3
Chorley PR6 . . . . .43 E6
Longridge PR3 . . . . .140 B8
Lytham St Anne's FY8 . . . .89 E5
Southport PR9 . . . . .54 A4
Wray LA2 . . . . .238 D1
Wray LA2 . . . . .238 D6
Hornby St Burnley BB11 . .128 A5
Oswaldtwistle BB5 . . . . .103 E3
Hornby Terr LA4 . . . . . . .217 C6
Hornby's La
Hale Nook PR3 . . . . .178 A5
Moss Edge PR3 . . . . . . .178 D6
Hornchurch Dr PR7 . . . . . .43 A7
Horncliffe Cl BB4 . . . . . . .68 C4
Horncliffe Hts BB9 . . . . .148 B5
Horncliffe Rd FY4 . . . . . .110 B6
Horncliffe View BB4 . . . . .68 B4
Horne St BB5 . . . . .104 C6
Horning Cres BB10 . . . . .148 D2
Horns La PR3 . . . . .161 B3

Hornsea Cl Fulwood PR2 ...117 A4
Thornton FY5 ....176 D2
Hornsey Ave FY8 ....110 B4
Horridge Fold BL7 ......47 E3
Horrobin Fold BL7 ......48 C2
Horrobin La
  Chapeltown BL7 ....48 C2
  Rivington PR6,BL6 ......44 E1
Horrocks Fold PR4 ......74 E3
Horrocks Rd BL7 ....48 D6
Horrocksford Way LA1 .214 D6
Horse Park La PR3 .....202 A3
Horsebridge Rd FY3 ...131 B8
Horsefield Ave OL12 ....52 C6
Horses Health Farm★
  BD24 ....236 F6
Horsfall Ave **2** FY8 ...91 A3
Horsfall Cl BB8 ....104 B7
Horsfall Cl BB8 ....171 F5
Horton Ave BB10 ....148 B3
Horton Lodge BD23 ....231 E4
Horwich Bsns Pk BL6 ...32 B2
Horwich Heritage Ctr★
  BL6 ....32 C4
Horwich Parish CE Prim Sch
  BL6 ....32 C4
Hoscar Moss Rd L40 ....26 D3
Hoscar Sta L40 ....26 D4
Hospital Cotts PR3 ...140 F6
Hosticle La LA6 ....241 C7
Hothersall La PR3 ....140 D4
Hough La PR25 ....77 A1
Houghclough La PR3 ..184 F1
Houghton Ave **6** FY4 .110 D8
Houghton Cl
  Lytham St Anne's FY8 .110 F2
  Middleforth Green PR1 .96 C3
Houghton Ct Halton LA2 .219 C7
  7 Thornton FY5 ....176 B3
Houghton La WN6 ....19 E6
Houghton Rd PR1 ....96 C3
Houghton St **8** PR6 ...43 D8
Houghton's La WN8 ....18 C1
Houghtons Rd WN8 .....18 B3
Houldsworth Rd PR2 ..117 C3
Hounds Hill **2** FY1 ..130 B4
Hounds Hill Ctr FY1 ..130 B4
Houseman Pl FY4 ......110 E7
Hove Ave FY7 ....175 C8
Hove Cl BL8 ....49 F1
Hove Rd FY8 ....89 F6
Howard Brook Ho PR1 .118 F1
Howard Cl
  Accrington BB5 ....103 F5
  Lytham St Anne's FY8 .110 E1
  Maghull L31 ....5 F1
Howard Ct PR9 ....53 D1
Howard Dr PR4 ....56 F7
Howard Mews LA5 .....223 C1
Howard Rd PR7 ....43 C5
Howard St Blackpool FY1 130 C4
  Burnley BB11 ....127 D5
  Nelson BB9 ....148 C8
  Rishton BB1 ....124 A1
  26 Rochdale OL12 ...52 F1
Howards La WN5 ....10 F7
Howarth Ave BB5 ......103 F7
Howarth Cres FY6 .....153 E3
Howarth Rd PR2 ......117 D3
Howarth's St BB4 ......87 A8
Howden Hts FY6 ......153 B3
Howe Ave FY4 ....110 E8
Howe Croft BB7 ......166 F8
Howe Dr BL0 ....50 B2
Howe Gr PR7 ....43 A7
Howe Wlk **4** BB11 ..128 A6
Howells Cl L31 ....5 D2
Howgill Ave LA1 .....218 E4
Howgill Cl BB9 ....148 F6
Howgill La BB7 ......231 C1
Howgill Way FY9 ......91 D5
Howgills The PR2 ....118 A7
Howick CE Prim Sch PR1 95 F3
Howick Cross La PR1 ..95 E5
Howick Moor La PR1 ...96 A3
Howick Park Ave PR1 ..95 F4
Howick Park Cl PR1 ...95 F4
Howick Park Dr PR1 ...95 F4
Howick Row PR2 ....95 D5
Howorth Cl BB11 .....128 A3
Howorth Rd BB11 ....128 A3
Howsin St BB10 ......148 A1
Hoylake Cl PR2 ......117 B6
Hoyle Ave FY8 ....110 F2
Hoyle Bottom BB5 ...103 E1
Hoyle St Bacup OL13 ..70 E8
  Rising Bridge BB5 ....85 A8
  Whitworth OL12 ......71 D3
Hoyles La PR4 ....116 D6
Hozier St BB1 ....102 C5
Hubert Pl LA1 ....214 D8
Hubie St BB12 ....127 F7
Huck La FY8 ....91 E7
Hud Hey Ind Est BB4 ..85 B5
Hud Hey Rd BB4 ......85 B5
Hud Rake BB4 ....85 B4
Hudcar La BL9 ....33 A4
Hudson Ct PR5 ....78 C8
Hudson Pl BB2 ......101 B8
Hudson Rd FY1 ......130 D2
Hudson St
  Accrington BB5 .....104 C4
  Brierfield BB9 ......148 B5
  Burnley BB11 ....127 D5
  6 Cornholme OL14 .109 C1

Hudson St continued
  9 Preston PR1 ......97 A7
Hufling Ct **8** BB11 ..128 B4
Hufling La BB11 .....128 B4
Hugh Barn La PR4 .....75 F7
Hugh Bsns Pk BB4 .....69 E8
Hugh Rake BB4 ....85 F6
Hughes Ave BL6 ......32 A4
Hughes Cl **11** BL9 ...33 A3
Hughes Gr FY2 ......152 E1
Hughes St BB11 .....128 A5
Hull Rd FY1 ....130 B4
Hull St Burnley BB11 .128 B5
  Preston PR2 ....96 C8
Hullet Cl WN6 ....19 E8
Hulme Ave FY5 ......176 C2
Hulme St PR8 ....35 A7
Hulmes Bridge Bsns Ctr
  L39 ....23 D2
Hulton Dr BB9 ......148 E6
Humber Ave **2** FY3 .130 E8
Humber Sq BB10 .....148 C2
Humber St PR3 ......140 A7
Humblescough La PR3 180 D5
Humphrey St BB4 ....148 B6
Huncoat Ind Est BB5 .125 C1
Huncoat Ind Pk BB5 ..125 D1
Huncoat Sta BB5 ....125 E2
Hundred End La PR4,PR9 72 F1
Hungerford Rd FY8 ...89 F5
Hunslet St Burnley BB11 128 B6
  Nelson BB9 ....148 F7
Hunstanton Cl PR7 ....60 D5
Hunt Fold Dr BL8 ....49 F1
Hunt Rd L31 ....5 D1
Hunt St **2** PR1 .....96 D7
Hunter Ave PR4 ....57 A6
Hunter Rd PR4 ......114 B2
Hunter St Brierfield BB9 148 B5
  Carnforth LA5 ......223 C2
Hunter's La PR4 ......56 B3
Hunters Chase WN5 ..10 E1
Hunters Dr BB12 ....127 D8
Hunters Fold PR4 ....75 A5
Hunters Gate LA1 ...214 E5
Hunters Gn BL0 ......49 F3
Hunters Lodge
  Bamber Bridge PR5 ...97 C3
  Blackburn BB2 ......100 F1
Hunters Rd PR25 .....77 D1
Hunting Hill Cvn Pk
  LA5 ....223 C1
Hunting Hill Rd LA5 .223 B1
Huntingdon Ct **5** PR9 54 A2
Huntingdon Gr L31 .....5 C4
Huntingdon Hall Rd
  PR3 ....164 A2
Huntingdon Rd FY5 ..175 C1
Huntington Dr BB3 ...65 A7
Huntley Ave **4** FY3 .130 E7
Huntley La PR5 ......102 D1
Huntley Mount Rd BL9 .33 B3
Huntley St BL9 ....33 B3
Huntly Way OL10 .....33 E1
Huntroyde Ave BB12 .126 B8
Huntroyde Cl **2** BB12 127 D7
Hunts Field PR6 ......78 C2
Huntsmans Chase PR4 114 F6
Hurlston Ave WN8 ....9 C8
Hurlston Dr L39 ......15 E7
Hurlston Hall Country Cvn Pk
  L40 ....24 C2
Hurlston La L40 .....24 C1
Hurn Gr PR7 ....43 A7
Hurst Brook PR7 .....42 F1
Hurst Cres BB4 ......86 B3
Hurst Gn L40 ....40 C2
Hurst La BB4 ....86 B3
Hurst Pk PR1 ....96 C4
Hurst St BL9 ....33 A2
Hurst's La L39 ....7 B2
Hurstdene Cl FY6 ...153 F3
Hurstead St BB5 ....104 E1
Hurstleigh Dr LA3 ..213 A7
Hurstleigh Hts FY5 .176 E2
Hurstmere Ave FY4 .110 E8
Hurstway PR2 ....117 D7
Hurstway Cl PR2 ....117 D7
Hurstwood L37 ....11 E5
Hurstwood Ave
  Blackburn BB2 .....101 A1
  Burnley BB10 ......128 D5
Hurstwood Dr FY2 ..152 D2
Hurstwood Ent Pk BB4 .85 A2
Hurstwood Gdns BB9 148 D4
Hurstwood La BB10 ..129 B4
Hurtley St BB10 ....128 A8
Hut La PR6 ....44 B3
Hutch Bank Rd BB4 ..84 F2
Hutchinson Ct BB3 ..82 A2
Hutchinson St **4** BB2 101 E3
Huttock End La OL13 ..70 D8
Hutton CE Gram Sch
  PR4 ....95 D2
Hutton Cl LA6 ......240 C7
Hutton Cres LA4 ...217 A4
Hutton Ct WN8 ....17 D1
Hutton Dr BB12 ....127 E7
Hutton Gdns LA5 ...223 C4
Hutton Gr LA4 .....217 A4
Hutton Hall Ave PR4 .95 E1
Hutton Rd WN8 ......17 D1
Hutton St Blackburn BB1 102 B5
  Standish WN1 ....30 A3
Hutton Way
  5 Lancaster LA1 ..218 B1

Hutton Way continued
  Ormskirk L39 ....15 E5
Huyton Rd PR6,PR7 ...31 A6
Huyton Terr PR6 .....31 B6
Hyacinth Cl BB4 ......67 F8
Hyatt Cres WN6 ......29 C3
Hyde Rd Blackpool FY1 .130 B2
  Morecambe LA4 .....217 A4
Hydeaway Ct LA4 ...217 A4
Hygiene BB5 ....124 F2
Hynd Brook Ho BB5 ..104 A5
Hyndburn Bridge BB5 124 F5
Hyndburn Cl
  Carnforth LA5 ......223 F2
  Morecambe LA3 ....217 F3
Hyndburn Dr **2** BB3 ..81 D4
Hyndburn Park Prim Sch
  BB5 ....104 A6
Hyndburn Rd
  Accrington BB5 .....104 A6
  Church BB5 ....103 F6
  Great Harwood BB6 .124 F5
Hyndburn St BB5 ....103 F6
Hyning Rd LA5 .....223 E8
Hynings The BB6 ...124 B6
Hythe Cl Blackburn BB1 .102 C4
  Southport PR8 ....35 E3

I

Ibbison Ct FY1 ......130 C3
Icconhurst Cl BB5 ...104 E2
Ice St BB1 ....101 E7
Iddesleigh Rd **3** PR1 118 E1
Iddon Ct **6** FY1 ...130 C6
Idlewood Pl FY5 ....152 F8
Idstone Cl BB2 ......82 A8
Ightenhill Cty Prim Sch
  BB12 ....127 C6
Ightenhill Park La BB12 127 C6
Ightenhill Pk Mews **1**
  BB12 ....127 C7
Ightenhill St BB12 ..146 C1
Ilex Mill BB4 ....86 A2
Ilford Rd FY4 ......130 E1
Ilkley Ave
  Lytham St Anne's FY8 .90 C6
  Southport PR9 ......54 C6
Ilkley Gr FY5 ......152 E8
Illawalla The FY5 ..153 E6
Illingworth Rd PR1 .118 E1
Ilway PR5 ....97 E3
Imperial Gdns BB9 ..148 D8
Imperial St **2** FY1 .130 B7
Ince Cres L37 ....11 D3
Ince La PR7 ....41 C6
Inchfield
  Skelmersdale WN8 ...18 B1
  Worsthorne BB10 ...129 B6
India Mill Bsns Ctr **4**
  BB3 ....65 A8
India St Accrington BB5 .103 F6
  Darwen BB3 ....65 B8
  Ramsbottom BL0 .....50 C3
Industrial Cotts **10** BB4 69 F8
Industrial Pl **4** OL13 .87 F2
Industrial St Bacup OL13 88 A2
  Ramsbottom BL0 .....68 C5
Industry Rd **8** OL12 ..52 F1
Industry St Darwen BB3 .82 B2
  Whitworth OL12 ......71 D2
Infant St **11** BB5 ..104 C6
Infirmary Cl BB2 ...101 D2
Infirmary Rd BB2 ...101 D2
Infirmary St BB2 ...101 E2
Ing Dene Ave BB8 ..171 B4
Ing Dene Cl BB8 ....171 B4
Ingersol Rd BL6 .....32 E1
Infield Terr OL14 ...109 C1
Ingham Brow BL6 ....32 F4
Ingham St
  Barrowford BB9 ....170 D3
  Bury BL9 ....33 A1
  Padiham BB12 ......146 D1
Inglby BB1 ....102 D5
Ingle Cl **5** PR6 ....61 D1
Ingle Head PR2 ....117 D6
Ingle Nook BL6 .....128 F4
Ingle View LA6 ....242 C3
Ingleborough Dr BB18 .196 A2
Ingleborough Rd LA1 .218 B3
Ingleborough View
  Brinscall PR6 ....63 A8
  Carnforth LA5 .....221 E8
  14 High Bentham LA2 .239 D8
  Hornby LA2 ....238 B6
Ingleborough Way PR25 .77 C2
Ingleby Cl Cleveleys FY5 175 F5
  Standish WN6 ....29 D2
Inglehurst Rd BB11 .127 B5
Inglenook Cl **7** FY5 .175 F1
Ingleton Ave FY2 ...152 F4
Ingleton Cl BB5 ....104 D5
Ingleton Dr **1** LA1 .215 A4
Ingleton Ho **2** LA1 .215 A3
Ingleton Rd Fulwood PR2 118 E4
  Southport PR8 ....35 E3
Ingleway FY5 ....175 F3
Ingleway Ave FY5 ..130 F6
Inglewhite WN8 .....18 A2
Inglewhite Fold **2**
  BB12 ....126 D7
Inglewhite Rd PR3 ..161 C3
Inglewood Cl Bury BL9 ..33 C4
  Fleetwood FY7 .....198 C1
  Warton PR4 ....92 A2
Inglewood Gr FY2 ..152 E5

Ingol Com Prim Sch
  PR2 ....116 F4
Ingol Gdns FY6 ....177 C2
Ingol Gr FY6 ....177 C2
Ingol La FY6 ....177 C2
Ingot St PR1 ....96 D8
Ingram WN8 ....18 B1
Ings Ave
  Barnoldswick BB18 .196 B3
  Rochdale OL12 ......52 B2
Ings La BB18 ....52 C2
Ingthorpe Ave FY2 ..152 D5
Inkerman Rd PR4 ...132 F6
Inkerman St Bacup OL13 .88 A2
  9 Padiham BB12 ..126 C8
  Preston PR2 ....117 D2
  12 Rochdale OL12 ..52 F1
Inner Prom FY8 ......90 B3
Innes Sch OL12 ......52 C1
Inskip WN8 ....18 A2
Inskip Ct WN8 ......18 B2
Inskip Pl Blackpool FY4 110 E5
  Lytham St Anne's FY8 .90 A8
Inskip Rd Leyland PR25 .76 D2
  Preston PR2 ....116 E1
  Southport PR9 ......54 A4
  Wharles PR4 ....135 A5
Inskip St BB12 .....126 C8
Inskip St Peter's CE Sch
  PR4 ....135 B8
Institute St BB12 ..126 D8
Intack Cvn Pk LA6 ..237 A7
Intack La BB2 ......121 B2
Intack Prim Sch BB1 .102 D5
Intack Rd PR4 ....75 B8
Intake Cres BB8 ....171 F6
Intake La Maghull L39 ...4 B3
  Skelmersdale L39 ....8 B2
Interlink Express Stadium
(Accrington Stanley FC)
  BB5 ....104 B8
Inver Rd FY2 ....152 D3
Inverness Rd BB3 ...64 F8
Ipswich Pl FY5 .....175 C2
Ipswich Rd PR2 ....118 D2
Ireby Rd LA6 ......242 C3
Irene Pl BB2 ....101 B5
Irene St BB10 ......128 C5
Iris St BL0 ....50 B6
Iron St Blackburn BB2 .101 E3
  Horwich BL6 ....32 C2
Irongate PR5 ....77 C8
Ironside Cl PR2 ....118 B4
Irton Rd PR9 ....35 E8
Irvin Ave PR9 ......54 C5
Irvin St PR1 ....118 B1
Irvine St **8** BB9 ..170 F2
Irving Cl FY2 ......152 F5
Irving Pl BB2 ......101 B5
Irving St PR9 ....53 B1
Irwell WN8 ....18 A3
Irwell Ho **10** BB4 ...69 E8
Irwell St WN5 ....10 F7
Irwell St **7** Bacup OL13 .87 F2
  Burnley BB10 ......127 A6
  Longridge PR3 ......140 A7
  Longridge PR3 ......140 B8
  Lytham St Anne's FY8 .89 F7
  Ramsbottom BL0 .....50 C6
Irwell Terr **12** OL13 ..87 F2
Irwell Vale Rd BB4 ..68 C6
Irwell Vale Sta BL0 ..68 C5
Isa St **5** BL0 ......50 A4
Isabella St Longridge PR3 140 A8
  Rochdale OL12 ......52 F2
Isherwood Fold BL7 ..48 D7
Isherwood St
  Blackburn BB2 .....101 D1
  1 Preston PR1 ....118 B1
  Preston PR1 ....118 C1
Islamic Coll Jamea Al
  Kauthar LA1 ....214 F5
Island Cotts BL9 .....50 C2
Island La PR3 ......203 B3
Islay Rd FY8 ....90 E6
Isle of Man BB1 ....122 E4
Isle of Man St BB4 ...87 A7
Isleworth Dr PR7 ....43 B7
Islington BB2 ......101 B4
Islington Cl BB10 ..148 D3
Ivan St BB10 ....148 B2
Ivegate Colne BB8 ...171 C5
  Foulridge BB8 .....194 E1
Ivinson Rd BB3 .....82 B3
Ivory St **1** BB12 ..127 C6
Ivy Ave Blackpool FY4 ..110 C5
  Haslingden BB4 .....85 C3
Ivy Bank 118 D6
Ivy Cl Clayton-le-W PR25 .77 C2
  Ring o'Bells L40 ....26 A3
Ivy Cotts
  11 Rawtenstall BB4 ...69 F8
  Tockholes BB3 ......80 F3
Ivy Gdns FY5 ......176 A4
Ivy Gr **2** BB4 ......86 A3
Ivy House Ct PR5 ...78 B7
Ivy St Blackburn BB2 .101 E2
  Burnley BB10 ......148 B1
  Nelson BB9 ....171 A2
  Ramsbottom BL0 ....49 F3
  1 Rawtenstall BB4 ..69 F8
  Southport PR8 ....35 D6
Ivy Terr BB3 ....65 B6
Ivydale WN8 ....18 B2

J

j2 Bsns Pk BL9 ......33 C2

J

Jack La BD23 ......236 F4
Jack Walker Way BB2 ..81 D7
Jackdaw Rd BL8 .....49 F2
Jacks Key Dr BB3 ...65 C5
Jacksmere La L40,PR8 ..23 B8
Jackson Cl Haskayne L39 .13 F5
  Lancaster LA1 .....214 C7
Jackson Heights Rd BB1 .83 B4
Jackson Rd
  2 Chorley PR7 ....43 A5
  1 Leyland PR25 ...76 D1
Jackson St
  8 Bamber Bridge PR5 .77 F8
  Blackpool FY3 .....130 E7
  6 Burnley BB10 ..128 A8
  Chorley PR7 ....43 D6
  5 Clayton-le-M BB5 124 F3
Jackson Terr LA5 ..223 D3
Jackson's Banks Rd
  BB2 ....120 E6
Jackson's Common La
  L40 ....24 B1
Jackson's La L40 .....27 E7
Jacob St BB5 ....104 C5
Jacob's La PR4 .....115 A2
Jacson St **3** PR1 ...97 A7
Jade Cl L33 ....1 A3
Jagoe Mews BB18 ..197 A1
Jagoe Rd BB18 .....197 A1
James Ave Blackpool FY4 130 F1
  Great Harwood BB6 124 B5
James Pl Coppull PR7 ..29 E8
  Standish WN6 ......29 D2
James Sq WN6 ......29 D2
James St Bacup OL13 ..70 B7
  Bamber Bridge PR5 ..97 E1
  Barnoldswick BB18 .196 B1
  4 Barrowford BB9 ..170 D4
  Belthorn BB1 ....82 F6
  Blackburn BB1 .....101 E5
  Burnley BB10 ......148 A1
  Bury BL9 ....33 A1
  12 Clayton-le-M BB5 124 F3
  Colne BB8 ....171 E4
  1 Darwen BB3 .....82 A1
  Earby BB18 ....197 B1
  Egerton BL7 ....47 D3
  Great Harwood BB6 124 B5
  Haslingden BB4 .....85 A2
  Horwich BL6 ....31 F3
  Huncoat BB5 ....125 E2
  30 Lancaster LA1 ..214 F8
  Morecambe LA4 ...217 C5
  Oswaldtwistle BB5 .103 D3
  Preston PR1 ....97 B7
  Rawtenstall BB4 ....86 A2
  Rishton BB1 ....124 C1
  Salterforth BB18 ..194 D7
  Whitworth OL12 .....71 D2
James St W **6** BB3 ..82 A1
Jameson Rd FY7 ...199 A1
Jameson St **3** FY1 .130 C3
Jameston Rise **14** BL6 .32 B4
Jane La Catforth PR4 .135 E5
  Leyland PR26 ....76 A3
Jane St OL12 ....71 E6
Jane's Brook Rd PR8 ..35 C4
Jane's Mdw PR4 .....57 A5
Janice Dr PR2 ......117 D7
Janine Cl LA4 .....217 A4
Jannat Cl BB5 .....104 B5
Jarrett Rd L33 ....1 A4
Jarrett Wlk L33 .....1 A4
Jarvis Cl OL12 .....52 F1
Jasmine Rd PR5 ....97 A3
Jason Ct FY8 ....89 D7
Jasper St BB1 ......122 F1
Jefferson Cl LA1 ...214 D7
Jefferson Way OL12 ..52 F2
Jeffrey Ave PR3 ...140 B7
Jeffrey Hill Cl PR2 .119 C7
Jeffrey Sq FY1 ....130 D3
Jellicoe Cl FY8 ....110 E1
Jem Gate FY5 .....152 D8
Jemmett St PR1 ...117 E2
Jenny La Blackpool FY4 .111 C7
  Higher Wheelton PR6 ..79 C1
Jenny Nook LA3 ...213 A7
Jenny St BB9 ......148 D6
Jensen Cl LA1 .....214 E6
Jensen Dr FY4 .....112 A6
Jepheys Pl **17** OL12 .52 F1
Jepheys St OL12 ....52 F1
Jepp Hill **3** BB18 .196 B2
Jepps Ave PR3 .....137 B7
Jepps La PR3 ......137 B8
Jepson St **9** BB3 ...65 A8
Jepson Way FY4 ...110 F4
Jericho Rd BL9 .....33 E4
Jersey Ave FY2 ....152 E2
Jersey Fold PR7 .....60 E6
Jersey St BB2 .....101 B1
Jervis Cl FY8 ......110 D1
Jesmond Ave FY4 ..110 B7
Jesmond Ct FY8 .....89 F8
Jesmond Gr LA4 ...217 D3
Jessel St BB2 .....101 B2
Jesson Way LA5 ...223 C1
Jevington Way LA3 .213 A7
j2 Holme BB9 ....148 A5

Jib Hill Cotts BB10 .....148 D2
Jinny La BB12 ....169 E4
Jobling St BB8 ....171 B3
Jockey St BB11 ....127 C5
Joe Connolly Way 2
  BB4 ....69 E8
Joe La PR3 ....181 D2
John Cross CE Prim Sch
  PR3 ....159 A4
John Henry St OL12 ...71 D4
John Hill St 3 FY4 ....130 F2
John Kay Ct LA1 ......218 B3
John o' Gaunt St 15
  BB12 ....146 C1
John St
  2 Bamber Bridge PR5 ..97 E1
  Barnoldswick BB18 ...196 B1
  Barrowford BB9 ......170 E4
  Blackpool FY1 ....130 B2
  Brierfield BB9 ......148 B6
  4 Carnforth LA5 ....223 D2
  Church BB5 ....103 E7
  Clayton-le-M BB5 ....124 F3
  Colne BB8 ....171 C4
  Coppull PR7 ....42 E1
  Darwen BB3 ....81 F2
  Earby BB18 ....197 B1
  5 Galgate LA2 ......211 A4
  Haslingden BB4 ....85 B3
  Leyland PR25 ....77 A1
  Newchurch BB4 ....86 F1
  Oswaldtwistle BB5 ...103 D3
  Thornton FY5 ....176 B4
  Whitworth OL12 ....71 D2
John Wall Ct 8 BB7 ...166 B8
John William St 7 PR1 .97 C8
Johnny Barn Cl BB4 ...86 D2
Johnny Barn Cotts BB4 .86 D2
Johns Wood Cl PR7 ....42 F6
Johnson Cl
  Carnforth LA5 ....223 C1
  Lancaster LA1 ....214 C7
Johnson New Rd BB3 ...82 E2
Johnson Rd
  Blackpool FY4 ....130 F2
  Waterside BB3 ....82 D4
Johnson St PR9 ....35 B8
Johnson's Meanygate
  PR4 ....56 D7
Johnspool PR2 ....117 C6
Johnston Cl BB2 ......101 C5
Johnston St BB2 ......101 C5
Johnsville Ave FY4 ...110 E7
Joiner's Row BB2 .....101 E3
Joiners Alley 10 BB6 .124 C5
Jolly Tar La PR7 ......30 B7
Jonathan Cl BB4 ....68 A8
Jones St BL6 ....32 B4
Jones' Gr FY7 ....199 B5
Jones's Yd LA6 ....240 B7
Joseph St
  Barrowford BB9 ......170 D2
  Darwen BB3 ....82 B1
  3 Rochdale OL12 .....52 D2
Joy Pl OL12 ....52 F2
Joy St Ramsbottom BL0 .50 B6
  Rochdale OL12 ....52 F2
Joyce Ave FY4 ....130 F2
Jubilee Almshouses
  PR26 ....58 B1
Jubilee Ave Ormskirk L39 .15 F6
  Orrell WN5 ....10 C4
  Preesall FY6 ....200 A4
  Preston PR2 ....116 D1
Jubilee Bldgs 19 LA2 .239 D8
Jubilee Cl Darwen BB3 .82 D1
  Haslingden BB4 ....85 A1
Jubilee Ct
  1 Haslingden BB4 ....85 A1
  11 Lancaster LA1 ...214 E8
Jubilee Cts PR25 .....59 E8
Jubilee Dr Cleveleys FY5 .176 C4
  Skelmersdale WN8 ......8 E8
Jubilee La FY4 ....111 B5
Jubilee La N FY4 .....111 B6
Jubilee Pl PR6 ....61 D1
Jubilee Rd
  9 Bamber Bridge PR5 ..77 A8
  Church BB5 ....103 F7
  Formby L37 ....11 D1
  Haslingden BB4 ....85 A1
  Walmer Bridge PR4 ....74 F4
Jubilee St
  Accrington BB5 ......125 A1
  Blackburn BB1 ....101 E4
  Brierfield BB10 .....148 F3
  Darwen BB3 ....82 A1
  Oswaldtwistle BB5 ...103 E4
  Read BB12 ....145 D2
Jubilee Terr Clifton PR4 .115 C1
  Freckleton BB4 ....93 C7
  Goosnargh PR3 ....138 D5
  Langho BB6 ....143 D1
Jubilee Trad Est PR1 .117 E1
Jubilee Way Croston PR26 58 B3
  Lytham St Anne's FY8 ..90 C8
Jud Falls BB7 ....165 A3
Judd Holmes La PR3 ..162 D7
Jude St BB9 ....148 D8
Judeland PR7 ....61 A2
Judge Fields BB8 .....171 D6
Judges Lodgings Mus★
  LA1 ....214 E8
Judith St OL12 ....52 C3
Julia Mews 5 BL6 ....32 B4
Julia St BL6 ....32 B4
July St 17 BB1 ....102 A4
Jumbles Beck BL7 .....48 D2

Jumbles Ctry Pk★ BL7 .48 D2
Jumps La OL14 ....109 E1
Junction La L40 ....25 E3
Junction Rd Preston PR2 .96 D7
  Rainford Junction WA11 ..8 F1
Junction St
  Brierfield BB9 ......148 B6
  Burnley BB12 ....127 E6
  Burnley,Whittlefield BB12 .127 E7
  Colne BB8 ....171 A3
  Darwen BB3 ....65 B7
Junction Terr PR7 .....60 C5
June Ave 131 A1
June St 16 BB1 ....102 A4
June's Wlk PR4 ....75 A5
Juniper Cl FY6 ....200 A5
Juniper Croft PR6 .....78 A1
Juniper Ct BB5 ......104 E8
Juniper St 6 BB1 ....102 A7
Juno St PR1 ....170 D2
Jutland St PR1 ....97 A8

K

Kairnryan Cl FY2 .....152 F5
Kale Gr L33 ....1 A5
Kaley La BB7 ....190 E5
Kane St PR2 ....117 C1
Kate St 3 BL0 ....50 B6
Kateholm OL13 ....88 A7
Kay Brow BL0 ....50 C6
Kay Fold Lodge BB1 ..122 D2
Kay Gdns BB25 ....128 B5
Kay St Blackburn BB2 .101 E3
  Blackpool FY1 ....130 B4
  Brierfield BB9 ......148 B6
  Bury BL0 ....33 A3
  Chapeltown BL7 ....48 C4
  Clitheroe BB7 ....166 D6
  Darwen BB3 ....82 B1
  3 Oswaldtwistle BB5 .103 D3
  1 Padiham BB12 .....146 D1
  1 Preston PR1 ....96 E7
  Ramsbottom BL0,BL9 ...50 C3
  Rawtenstall BB4 ......86 A2
Kaymar Ind Est PR1 ...97 C7
Kayswell Rd LA4 .....217 F5
Kearsley Ave PR4 .....57 A6
Keasden Ave FY4 .....110 A7
Keasden Rd BB7 .....235 E6
Keating Ct 3 FY7 ....199 A3
Keats Ave Bolton-le-S LA5 221 A5
  Longshaw WN5 ....10 D1
  Rochdale OL12 ....52 A1
  Warton PR4 ....92 E6
Keats Cl Accrington BB5 .104 E2
  Colne BB8 ....171 D6
  Eccleston PR7 ....41 D5
  Thornton FY5 ....176 A4
Keats Fold 3 BB12 ...126 F7
Keats Rd BL8 ....49 F2
Keats Terr PR8 ....35 F6
Keats Way PR4 ....116 D4
Kebs Rd OL14 ....109 D3
Keele Cl FY5 ....176 A2
Keele Wlk BB1 ....101 F4
Keen Cl PR4 ....95 E2
Keeper's Hey FY5 ....176 A4
Keeper's La PR3 .....204 F1
Keepers Gate FY8 .....90 D7
Keepers Wood Way PR7 .42 F6
Keer Bank 1 LA1 ....218 A2
Keer Holme La LA6 ...240 E4
Keighley Ave BB8 ....171 D6
Keighley Rd Colne BB8 .171 F5
  Laneshaw Bridge BB8 .172 D6
  Trawden BB8 ....172 C4
Keirby Wlk BB11 .....128 A6
Keith Gr LA3 ....175 D1
Keith St BB12 ....127 C6
Kelbrook Dr BB11 ....127 E3
Kelbrook Prim Sch
  BB18 ....195 A6
Kelbrook Rd BB18 ....194 E7
Kelk Beck Cl L31 ......5 F2
Kellet Acre 4 PR5 ....77 A7
Kellet Ave PR25 ......77 D1
Kellet Ct 1 LA1 .....214 E8
Kellet La
  Bolton-le-S LA5,LA2 .221 C3
  Borwick LA6 ....240 B3
  Walton Summit PR5 ...78 B7
Kellet Rd Carnforth LA5 .223 E1
  Over Kellet LA6 ....240 A1
Kellet Road Ind Est LA5 223 F1
Kellett St 8 BB7 .....43 C8
Kelmarsh Cl FY3 .....131 B2
Kelne Ho 7 LA1 .....214 E8
Kelsall Ave BB1 .....102 B8
Kelsey St LA1 ....214 E8
Kelso Ave FY5 ....175 D1
Kelsons Ave FY5 .....176 C2
Kelswick Dr BB9 .....148 E6
Kelverdale Rd FY5 ...152 F8
Kelvin Rd FY5 ....152 C6
Kelvin St 3 BL1 ......81 F1
Kelwood Ave BL9 .....33 D5
Kem Mill La PR6 ......61 B8
Kemble Cl BL6 ....32 B5
Kemp Cl BB1 ....122 F3
Kemp St FY7 ....199 B4
Kemple View BB7 ....166 D6
Kempton Ave FY3 ....130 F3
Kempton Park Fold PR8 .35 F3
Kempton Rd LA1 .....215 B4
Kempton Rise BB1 ...101 F3
Kenbury Cl L33 ....1 A4

Kenbury Rd L33 ....1 A4
Kendal Ave
  Barrowford BB9 .....170 D4
  Blackpool FY3 ......153 A1
  Cleveleys FY5 ......175 D4
Kendal Cl WA11 ....8 F2
Kendal Dr Maghull L31 ..5 E2
  Morecambe LA3 ......217 E4
  Rainford Junction WA11 ..8 F2
Kendal Rd
  Lytham St Anne's FY8 .110 D1
  Ramsbottom BL0 ....50 A2
Kendal Rd W BL0 .....49 F2
Kendal Row BB7 ....82 F6
Kendal St Blackburn BB1 .101 E6
  Clitheroe BB7 ......189 F1
  5 Nelson BB9 ......170 D1
  Preston PR1 ....96 E8
Kendal Way PR8 ......21 B3
Kendall Cl BB2 ....81 D8
Kenilworth Ave FY7 ..198 E3
Kenilworth Cl BB12 ..126 E8
Kenilworth Ct FY8 ....89 F6
Kenilworth Dr
  Clitheroe BB7 ......166 C6
  Earby BB18 ....195 A8
Kenilworth Gdns FY4 .110 B7
Kenilworth Pl
  Fleetwood FY7 ......198 E3
  Lancaster LA1 ......215 A5
Kenilworth Rd
  Lytham St Anne's FY8 .89 F6
  Morecambe LA3 ......217 C3
  Southport PR8 ....21 B4
Kenlis Rd PR3 ....181 F4
Kenmay Way L33 ....1 A3
Kenmure Pl PR1 ......117 F2
Kennedy Cl LA1 .....214 D6
Kennedy Ho FY1 .....130 B1
Kennelwood Ave L33 ...1 A3
Kennet Dr PR2 ....117 F8
Kennett Dr PR7 ....77 B2
Kennington Prim Sch
  PR2 ....118 A4
Kennington Rd PR2 ..118 A4
Kensington Ave PR1 ..96 B6
Kensington Cl BL8 ....50 A1
Kensington Ct Formby L37 12 A3
  Morecambe LA4 .....217 B5
Kensington Dr BL6 ...32 D3
Kensington Gdns PR5 .97 C1
Kensington Ho LA1 ..214 F5
Kensington Ind Pk PR9 .35 C6
Kensington Pl BB11 .127 D4
Kensington Rd
  Blackpool FY3 ......130 E4
  Chorley PR7 ....43 B7
  Cleveleys FY5 ......175 C3
  Formby L37 ....11 E1
  Lancaster LA1 ......214 F5
  Lytham St Anne's FY8 .90 D4
  Morecambe LA4 .....217 B5
  Southport PR9 ....35 C6
Kensington St BB9 ..148 C7
Kent Ave
  2 Bamber Bridge PR5 .97 D3
  Cleveleys FY5 ......175 D4
  Formby L37 ....12 A1
Kent Ct BB9 ....170 D4
Kent Dr Blackburn BB1 .102 E4
  Clayton-le-W PR25 ...77 D1
Kent Ho LA1 ....214 F7
Kent Rd Blackpool FY1 .130 C3
  Formby L37 ....12 A1
  Southport PR8 ....35 A4
Kent St Blackburn BB1 .101 F4
  Burnley BB12 ....127 F7
  Fleetwood FY7 ......199 B5
  3 Lancaster LA1 ...218 D2
  Preston PR1 ....117 F2
Kent Way LA3 ....217 F3
Kent Wlk BB4 ....68 A8
Kent's Cl PR4 ....113 F7
Kentmere Ave
  Bamber Bridge PR5 ...97 E1
  Leyland PR25 ....77 A3
Kentmere Cl
  Burnley BB12 ....127 B8
  5 Fleetwood FY7 ...198 D3
Kentmere Dr
  4 Blackburn BB2 ....80 E8
  Blackpool FY4 ......131 C1
  Longton PR4 ....75 B8
Kentmere Gr 1 LA4 ..217 D4
Kentmere Rd LA1 ...218 E1
Kenton Cl LA4 ....11 F6
Kenwood Ave LA4 ...217 A4
Kenworthys Flats PR8 ..35 B8
Kenwyn Ave FY3 ....130 E3
Kenyon La Dinckley BB6 .142 F4
  Whittle-le-W PR6 ....61 F7
Kenyon Rd
  Morecambe LA4 .....217 F5
  Nelson BB9 ....148 B7
  Standish WN6 ....29 D2
Kenyon St
  6 Accrington BB5 ..104 C6
  Bacup OL13 ....71 B8
  Blackburn BB1 ......102 C6
  Bury BL0 ....33 A3
  Ramsbottom BL0 ......50 C6
  Rawtenstall BB4 ......86 A3
Kenyon's La L37 ......12 A3
Kenyons Lodge L31 ...15 E3
Keppel Pl BB11 ......127 E6
Kepple La PR3 ......181 B6
Kerenhappuch St 5 BL0 .50 B5

Kerfoot's La WN8 ......8 C8
Kerr Pl PR1 ....96 D8
Kershaw Cl 6 BB4 ....86 A7
Kershaw St 8 Bacup OL13 87 E4
  Bury BL9 ....33 A2
  Chorley PR6 ....61 E1
  Church BB5 ....103 E7
Kerslake Way L38 ......3 A4
Kerton Row PR8 ....34 F4
Keston Gr FY4 ....110 C5
Kestor La PR1 ....140 A7
Kestrel Cl Blackburn BB1 101 D8
  Cleveleys FY5 ......175 F5
  Knowley PR6 ....62 A3
Kestrel Ct PR9 ....35 D7
Kestrel Dr Bury BL9 ...33 B4
  Darwen BB3 ....81 D3
Kestrel Mews WN8 ...18 C4
Kestrel Pk WN8 ......18 C4
Kestrel Terr BB5 ....103 E3
Keswick Cl
  Accrington BB5 .....125 D1
  Maghull L31 ....5 E2
  Southport PR8 ....21 C3
Keswick Ct LA1 .....218 F1
Keswick Dr BB2 ....80 E8
Keswick Gr Heysham LA3 212 E5
  Knott End-on-S FY6 .199 F5
Keswick Rd
  Blackpool FY1 ......130 C3
  Burnley BB10 ....148 B2
  Lancaster LA1 ......218 F1
  Lytham St Anne's FY8 .89 E8
Keswick Way WA11 ....8 F2
Keswick Wlk LA1 ....218 F1
Kettering Rd PR8 ....21 B5
Kevin Ave FY6 ......153 F5
Kevin Gr LA3 ....213 D1
Kew Gdns
  Higher Penwortham PR1 .96 B5
  Leyland PR25 ....77 B3
Kew Gr FY5 ....175 D1
Kew House Dr PR8 ...36 A2
Kew Rd Formby L37 ...11 D1
  Nelson BB9 ....170 F2
  Southport PR8 ....35 B3
Kew Ret Pk PR9 ......36 A4
Kew Woods Prim Sch
  PR8 ....35 F3
Key View BB3 ....65 C5
Keynsham Gr BB12 ..127 D7
Khyber St BB8 ....171 C4
Kibble Cres BB10 ...148 C3
Kibble Gr BB9 ......148 D4
Kibboth Crew BL0 .....50 B7
Kidbrooke Ave FY4 ..110 B4
Kidder St BB2 ....81 D8
Kiddington Cl PR5 ....77 D8
Kiddrow La BB12 ....127 A7
Kidsgrove PR2 ......116 F5
Kielder Ct 3 FY8 .....91 C4
Kielder Dr BB2 ......127 E2
Kilbane St FY7 ......198 F1
Kilburn Rd WN5 .....10 C5
Kilcrash La PR3 .....180 D7
Kildale Cl L31 ....5 C2
Kildare Ave FY5 ....176 A4
Kildare Rd FY2 .....152 D3
Kilgrimol Gdns FY8 ..110 C1
Kilkerran Cl PR6 .....43 D8
Killer St 1 BL0 ......50 C6
Killiard La BB2 ......100 E3
Killingbeck Cl L40 ...25 D4
Killington St BB10 ..148 C2
Killingworth Mews 5
  BL6 ....32 C1
Killon St BL9 ....33 A1
Kilmory Pl FY2 ......152 F5
Kilmuir Cl PR2 ......118 C5
Kiln Bank OL12 ......71 C2
Kiln Bank La OL12 ....71 C2
Kiln Cl BB7 ....190 A2
Kiln Croft PR5 ....78 B3
Kiln Ct 1 LA1 ....218 D1
Kiln Hill BB1 ....146 F6
Kiln House Way BB5 .104 A3
Kiln La Hambleton FY6 .177 B2
  Paythorne BB7 .....231 C6
  Rimington BB7 .....230 F2
  Skelmersdale WN8 ...17 E1
  Wray LA2 ....238 D6
Kiln St Nelson BB9 ..148 D8
  Ramsbottom BL0 ......50 B5
Kiln Terr 8 OL13 .....70 D8
Kiln Wlk OL12 ....52 E2
Kilnbank Ave LA4 ...217 A5
Kilngate PR2 ....97 C3
Kilnhouse La FY8 ...111 A1
Kilns The BB11 ......128 B3
Kilruddery Rd PR1 ...96 E5
Kilsby Cl PR5 ....97 C3
Kilworth Ht PR1 ....117 C5
Kimberley Ave FY4 ..110 C5
Kimberley Cl BB10 ..148 F3
Kimberley Rd PR2 ..117 C2
Kimberley St Bacup OL13 70 A7
  Brierfield BB10 ....148 F3
  Coppull PR7 ....42 E1
Kimberly Cl PR4 ......93 B6
Kimble Cl BL8 ....49 F2
Kime St BB12 ....127 C6
Kincardine Ave 7 FY4 .111 A4
Kincraig Pl FY2 .....152 F6
Kincraig Prim Sch FY2 .152 F5
Kincraig Rd FY2 ....152 F5
Kindonan Ave 6 FY4 .111 A6

King Edward Ave
  Blackpool FY2 ......152 B1
  Lytham St Anne's FY8 ..90 A4
King Edward St BB5 ..103 C3
King Edward Terr BB9 170 D2
King Edward VII & Queen
  Mary Schs PR8 ....90 B4
King George Ave FY2 152 B1
King George Ct 19 OL13 .87 F3
King George V Coll PR8 .35 E5
King Henry Mews BB7 .230 D3
King La BB7 ....166 E8
King St Accrington BB5 .104 B6
  5 Bacup OL13 ......87 F2
  6 Bamber Bridge PR5 .77 B7
  Barnoldswick BB18 .196 B2
  Blackburn BB2 ......101 D4
  Blackpool FY1 ......130 C5
  Brierfield BB9 .....148 A5
  Brierfield,Harle Syke BB10 148 F3
  Carnforth LA5 ......223 D1
  Chorley PR7 ....43 D6
  5 Clayton-le-M BB5 .124 F2
  Clitheroe BB7 ......166 E8
  Colne BB8 ....171 E5
  Fleetwood FY7 .....199 A4
  15 Great Harwood BB6 .124 C5
  Haslingden BB4 ......85 B4
  High Bentham LA2 ..239 D8
  Horwich BL6 ....32 A4
  Lancaster LA1 .....214 F8
  Leyland PR25 ....77 A1
  Longridge PR3 .....140 B2
  Morecambe LA4 .....217 B5
  Padiham BB12 ......126 C8
  Ramsbottom BL0 .....50 C6
  Rawtenstall BB4 .....69 E8
  Southport PR8 ....35 A6
  Whalley BB7 ....144 C5
  Whitworth OL12 .....71 B4
King Street Terr BB9 148 A5
King William St BB1 ..101 E5
King's Bridge Cl 4 BB2 101 B1
King's Bridge St BB2 .101 B1
King's Cl FY6 ....153 E3
King's Cres 2 BB4 ..216 E3
King's Croft PR5 .....97 D5
King's Cswy BB9 ....148 E5
King's Dr LA5 ......223 E1
King's Highway
  Accrington BB5 ....105 B2
  Huncoat BB5 ....104 F8
King's Rd Accrington BB5 104 B7
  Blackburn BB2 .....101 B1
  Lytham St Anne's FY8 .89 E5
King's Sq FY1 ......130 C5
King's Wlk FY5 .....175 D5
Kingcraig Ct FY2 ...152 F4
Kingfisher Bank BB11 .127 C4
Kingfisher Cl
  Blackburn BB1 .....101 E8
  Chorley PR7 ....42 F5
  Maghull L31 ....5 B4
  Oswaldtwistle BB5 .103 E3
  Southport PR9 ....35 D8
Kingfisher Ctr Bacup OL13 70 B4
  10 Rawtenstall BB4 ..86 A3
Kingfisher Dr Bury BL9 .33 B4
  Poulton-le-F FY6 ...153 B2
Kingfisher Mews FY6 .153 B2
Kingfisher Pk WN8 ...18 C4
Kingfisher St PR1 ...118 B1
Kings Arc 37 LA1 ...214 F8
Kings Arms Cl 34 LA1 .214 F8
Kings Ave BB4 ....86 A4
Kings Cl L37 ....11 E2
Kings Cres PR25 .....77 A1
Kings Ct Fleetwood FY7 .199 B4
  Leyland PR25 ....77 A1
Kings Dr Fulwood PR2 .117 C2
  Hoddlesden BB3 ......82 F1
  Padiham BB12 ......126 E6
Kings Hey Dr PR9 ....53 F1
Kings Lea PR7 ....30 F1
Kings Mdw PR8 ....21 D3
Kings Meadow Prim Sch
  PR8 ....21 D3
Kings Meadow Cleveleys FY5 .175 C2
  Formby L37 ....11 E2
Kingsacre PR3 ......181 A3
Kingsbarn Cl PR2 ...118 C2
Kingsbridge Cl PR1 ..96 E2
Kingsbridge Wharfe
  BB2 ....101 B1
Kingsbury Ct PR25 ...21 B4
Kingsbury Ct WN8 ...18 C4
Kingsbury Pl BB10 ..148 D3
Kingsbury Sch
  Ormskirk L39 ....15 E5
  Skelmersdale WN8 ...17 D1
Kingscote Dr FY3 ...130 F2
Kingsdale Ave
  Brierfield BB10 ....148 C3
  Fulwood PR2 ....118 D5
  Morecambe LA3 ....216 E1
Kingsdale Cl Leyland PR25 60 B6
  Walton-le-D PR5 .....97 F5
Kingsdale Rd LA1 ...214 D7
Kingsfold Christian Sch The
  PR4 ....73 E2
Kingsfold Dr PR1 .....96 E2
Kingsfold Prim Sch PR1 .96 E2
Kingshaven Dr PR1 ...96 E2
Kingshotte Gdns BB9 .170 C3

Kingsland Gr
Blackpool FY1 ... 130 D3
12 Burnley BB11 ... 128 B4
Kingsland Rd BB11 ... 128 B4
Kingsley Ave BB12 ... 126 E7
Kingsley Cl Blackburn BB2 80 D7
Church BB5 ... 103 F7
Maghull L31 ... 5 C5
Thornton FY5 ... 176 A3
Kingsley Ct 5 FY1 ... 130 C4
Kingsley Dr PR7 ... 43 A5
Kingsley Rd
Blackpool FY3 ... 131 B2
Cottam PR4 ... 116 E6
Laneshaw Bridge BB8 ... 172 D6
Kingsley St BB9 ... 170 F2
Kingsmead
Blackburn BB1 ... 102 D4
Chorley PR7 ... 43 C5
Kingsmede FY4 ... 110 E6
Kingsmere Ave FY8 ... 110 F1
Kingsmill Ave BB7 ... 144 A8
Kingsmuir Ave PR2 ... 118 D4
Kingsmuir Cl LA3 ... 212 E7
Kingston Ave
Accrington BB5 ... 104 A4
Blackpool FY4 ... 110 C5
Kingston Cl FY6 ... 199 F6
Kingston Cres
Haslingden BB4 ... 68 A7
Southport PR9 ... 54 C5
Kingston Dr FY8 ... 90 D6
Kingston Mews 4 FY5 ... 176 B3
Kingston Pl BB3 ... 81 F7
Kingsway Accrington BB5 104 A8
Bamber Bridge PR5 ... 77 E8
Blackburn BB3 ... 82 A7
Blackpool FY4 ... 110 C7
Burnley BB11 ... 128 A6
Cleveleys FY5 ... 175 C2
Euxton PR7 ... 60 E2
Great Harwood BB6 ... 124 F6
Hapton BB11 ... 126 C3
Heysham LA3 ... 213 A8
Higher Penwortham PR1 ... 96 B6
Huncoat BB5 ... 125 F1
Lancaster LA1 ... 218 E1
Leyland PR25 ... 59 E7
Lytham St Anne's FY8 ... 90 C4
Preston PR2 ... 116 F2
Southport PR8 ... 35 A7
Kingsway Ave PR3 ... 137 C3
Kingsway Ct
2 Lytham St Anne's FY8 ... 90 C4
Morecambe LA3 ... 216 E1
Kingsway Sports Ctr LA1 ... 218 E1
Kingsway W PR1 ... 96 B6
Kingswood Cl FY8 ... 90 E4
Kingswood Coll L40 ... 24 A6
Kingswood Pk PR8 ... 34 F5
Kingswood Rd PR25 ... 77 A2
Kingswood St 6 PR1 ... 96 E7
Kinloch Way L39 ... 15 D6
Kinnerton Pl FY5 ... 152 F8
Kinross Cl Blackburn BB1 102 A4
1 Ramsbottom BL0 ... 50 A2
Kinross Cres FY4 ... 131 A1
Kinross St BB11 ... 127 D4
Kinross Wlk 7 BB1 ... 102 A4
Kintbury Rd FY8 ... 89 F4
Kintour Rd FY8 ... 90 E6
Kintyre Cl FY4 ... 110 F7
Kintyre Way LA3 ... 212 E7
Kipling Dr FY3 ... 131 B2
Kipling Pl BB6 ... 124 B4
Kirby Dr PR4 ... 93 B6
Kirby Rd Blackburn BB2 ... 101 D1
Blackpool FY1 ... 130 B2
Nelson BB9 ... 148 B8
Kirby's Cotts L39 ... 6 B3
Kirk Ave BB7 ... 166 C8
Kirk Head PR4 ... 74 E2
Kirk Hill Rd BB4 ... 85 C3
Kirk Ho BB5 ... 103 E6
Kirk Rd BB5 ... 103 E7
Kirk View BB4 ... 87 A1
Kirkbeck Cl LA2 ... 237 D3
Kirkby Ave
Clayton-le-W PR25 ... 77 E1
Cleveleys FY5 ... 175 E4
Kirkby Bank Rd L33 ... 1 C2
Kirkby Lonsdale Rd LA2 ... 219 D7
Kirkby Lonsdale Rd
Caton LA2,LA6 ... 237 B6
Over Kellet LA6 ... 240 B1
Kirkdale Ave
Lytham St Anne's FY8 ... 89 F7
Newchurch BB4 ... 86 E1
Kirkdale Cl BB3 ... 65 C6
Kirkdale Gdns WN8 ... 10 A7
Kirkdale Rd BB6 ... 123 C8
Kirkdene Ave BB8 ... 194 D1
Kirkdene Mews BB8 ... 194 D1
Kirkes Rd LA1 ... 215 A7
Kirkfell Dr BB12 ... 127 C8
Kirkfield PR3 ... 185 D3
Kirkgate Burnley BB11 ... 128 B4
Kirkham PR4 ... 114 B4
Kirkgate La LA6 ... 240 B4
Kirkham & Wesham Prim Sch PR4 ... 113 F5
Kirkham & Wesham Sta PR4 ... 113 F6
Kirkham Ave FY1 ... 130 E2
Kirkham By-Pass PR4 ... 114 B4
Kirkham Cl PR25 ... 76 D1
Kirkham Gram Jun Sch PR4 ... 113 F4
Kirkham Gram Sch PR4 113 F5
Kirkham Mus★ PR4 ... 114 A5
Kirkham Rd
Freckleton PR4 ... 93 B8
Kirkham PR4 ... 114 E6
Southport PR9 ... 54 A4
Weeton PR4 ... 132 F2
Kirkham St PR1 ... 96 E8
Kirkham Trad Pk PR4 ... 114 B4
Kirkhill Ave BB4 ... 85 C3
Kirklake Bank L37 ... 11 C2
Kirklake Rd L37 ... 11 D2
Kirkland & Catterall St Helen's CE Prim Sch PR3 ... 181 A2
Kirkland Pl PR2 ... 95 E8
Kirklands Chipping PR3 ... 185 E3
Hest Bank LA2 ... 220 E1
Kirklands Rd LA6 ... 237 B8
Kirklees Rd PR8 ... 34 F1
Kirkmoor Cl BB7 ... 189 D1
Kirkmoor Rd BB7 ... 166 E8
Kirkstall Ave
Blackpool FY1 ... 130 E2
Read BB12 ... 145 D1
Kirkstall Cl PR7 ... 43 D5
Kirkstall Dr
Barnoldswick BB18 ... 196 D3
Chorley PR7 ... 43 D5
Formby L37 ... 12 B2
Kirkstall Rd Chorley PR7 ... 43 D5
Southport PR8 ... 34 F2
Kirkstone Ave
Blackburn BB2 ... 80 E8
Fleetwood FY7 ... 198 D1
Kirkstone Dr
Blackpool FY5 ... 152 C7
Morecambe LA4 ... 217 D5
Kirkstone Rd FY8 ... 110 D1
Kirton Cres FY8 ... 90 C6
Kirton Pl FY5 ... 175 E1
Kit Brow La LA2 ... 211 D6
Kittiwake Cl 13 FY5 ... 175 F1
Kittiwake Rd PR6 ... 62 A3
Kittlingborne Brow PR5 ... 98 A3
Kitty La FY4 ... 111 B4
Knacks La OL12 ... 52 A5
Knaresboro Ave FY3 ... 130 F3
Knaresborough Cl FY6 ... 153 D5
Knebworth Cl PR6 ... 78 C2
Knight Cres BB3 ... 82 A6
Knighton Ave BB2 ... 101 C8
Knights Cl FY5 ... 175 F1
Knightsbrdige Cl PR4 ... 113 E6
Knightsbridge Ave
Blackpool FY4 ... 110 D6
Colne BB8 ... 171 B5
Knightsbridge Cl
Kirkham PR4 ... 113 E6
2 Lytham St Anne's FY8 ... 90 D6
Knightsbridge Ct PR9 ... 53 D1
Knightscliffe Cres WN6 ... 19 D6
Knitting Row La PR3 ... 178 A3
Knob Hall Gdns PR9 ... 53 F3
Knob Hall La PR9 ... 53 F3
Knoll La PR4 ... 75 A4
Knoll The LA2 ... 218 C8
Knot Acre PR4 ... 76 A8
Knot La
Newsholme BB7,BD23 ... 231 D5
Walton-le-D PR5 ... 97 F5
Knott Hill OL12 ... 71 D6
Knott Hill St OL12 ... 71 E6
Knott La LA5 ... 224 A8
Knott St BB3 ... 82 A1
Knotts Brow BL7 ... 48 F4
Knotts Dr BB8 ... 171 C3
Knotts La
Bolton-by-B BB7,BD23 ... 230 B8
Colne BB8 ... 171 D3
Padiham BB12 ... 126 E6
Knotts Mount BB8 ... 171 C3
Knowe Hill Cres LA1 ... 215 B3
Knowl Cl BL0 ... 50 C4
Knowl Gap Ave BB4 ... 85 A1
Knowl Mdw BB4 ... 68 A6
Knowle Ave
Blackpool FY2 ... 152 C1
Cleveleys FY5 ... 175 E2
Southport PR8 ... 21 C6
Knowle La BB3 ... 82 A3
Knowle The FY2 ... 152 C2
Knowles Brow BB7 ... 165 B3
Knowles Rd FY8 ... 89 E7
Knowles St
1 Chorley PR7 ... 43 C6
Preston PR1 ... 97 D8
Rishton BB1 ... 124 B1
Knowlesly Mdws BB3 ... 65 C6
Knowlesly Rd BB3 ... 65 B6
Knowley Brow PR6 ... 61 E2
Knowlmere St BB5 ... 104 B7
Knowlys Ave LA3 ... 212 F8
Knowlys Cres 4 LA3 ... 212 F8
Knowlys Dr 3 LA3 ... 212 F8
Knowlys Gr LA3 ... 212 F8
Knowlys Rd LA3 ... 212 E8
Knowsley Ave
Blackpool FY3 ... 130 E3
Leyland PR25 ... 77 C4
Knowsley Cl
Gregson Lane PR5 ... 98 F2
Lancaster LA1 ... 214 D6
Knowsley Cres
Shawforth OL12 ... 71 E6
Thornton FY5 ... 176 C2
Weeton PR4 ... 132 E2
Knowsley Dr PR5 ... 98 F2
Knowsley Gate FY7 ... 198 D4
Knowsley Gr 6 BL6 ... 32 D1
Knowsley Ind Pk L33 ... 1 C2
Knowsley La Edgworth BL7 66 E4
Rivington PR6 ... 44 E4
Knowsley Park Way BB4 ... 68 B8
Knowsley Rd
Haslingden BB4 ... 68 B8
Leyland PR25 ... 60 C8
Ormskirk L39 ... 15 F5
Southport PR9 ... 53 C1
Wilpshire BB1 ... 122 F5
Knowsley Rd Ind Est BB4 68 B8
Knowsley Rd W BB1 ... 122 E5
Knowsley Road Ind Est BB4 ... 85 B1
Knowsley St
3 Colne BB8 ... 171 D4
31 Preston PR1 ... 97 A7
Knox Gr FY1 ... 130 D3
Knunck Knowles Dr BB7 ... 189 E1
Knutsford Rd FY3 ... 131 B2
Knutsford Wlk L31 ... 5 D4
Knuzden Brook BB1 ... 102 D4
Korea Rd PR2 ... 118 B4
Kumara Cres FY4 ... 131 B1
Kyan St BB10 ... 148 B2
Kylbarrow La LA5 ... 225 F2
Kylemore Ave FY2 ... 152 D3
Kytson Cl 1 FY1 ... 130 D7

L

Laburnam Cotts PR3 ... 201 E5
Laburnum Ave
Bamber Bridge PR5 ... 77 B8
Lytham St Anne's FY8 ... 91 B5
Laburnum Cl
Burnley BB11 ... 127 D3
Preston PR1 ... 118 C3
Laburnum Dr
Fulwood PR2 ... 117 D8
Oswaldtwistle BB5 ... 103 F3
Skelmersdale WN8 ... 17 D1
Laburnum Gr
Burscough Bridge L40 ... 25 E6
Horwich BL6 ... 32 E1
Lancaster LA1 ... 214 D8
Maghull L31 ... 5 F1
Southport PR8 ... 35 F7
Laburnum Pk LA5 ... 221 C8
Laburnum Rd
Blackburn BB1 ... 102 A8
Chorley PR6 ... 61 D3
Haslingden BB4 ... 68 A7
2 Lancaster LA1 ... 218 D2
Laburnum St
6 Blackpool FY3 ... 130 D7
Haslingden BB4 ... 85 A3
Lacey Ct 19 BB4 ... 85 B3
Lachman Rd BB8 ... 172 B3
Lacy Ave PR1 ... 96 E2
Ladbrooke Gr BB11 ... 127 E2
Lade End LA3 ... 212 E8
Ladies Row PR4 ... 134 F4
Ladies Wlk LA1 ... 218 E2
Ladies Wlk Ind Est LA1 ... 218 E2
Lady Acre PR5 ... 78 A8
Lady Alice's Dr L40 ... 16 E8
Lady Anne Cl L40 ... 24 B7
Lady Cl BB3 ... 82 A6
Lady Crosse Dr PR6 ... 61 C7
Lady Green Ct L38 ... 3 E3
Lady Green La L38 ... 3 D4
Lady Hartley Ct BB8 ... 172 D6
Lady Hey Cres PR2 ... 116 C1
Lady Pl PR5 ... 97 E4
Lady St PR1 ... 96 F8
Lady Well Dr PR2 ... 118 C7
Lady's Wlk L40 ... 16 C6
Ladybank Ave PR2 ... 118 D7
Ladybower La FY6 ... 153 B3
Ladyman St 9 PR1 ... 96 E7
Ladysmith Ave BL9 ... 33 A5
Ladysmith Rd PR2 ... 117 C2
Ladywell St PR1 ... 96 E8
Lafford La WN8 ... 19 C2
Lagonda Dr
Blackpool FY4 ... 111 F6
Peel Hill FY4 ... 112 A6
Lagonda Way FY4 ... 111 F6
Laidley's Wlk FY7 ... 198 E5
Lairgill Row LA2 ... 239 E8
Laister Ct 7 LA4 ... 217 E6
Laithbutts La LA6 ... 221 F5
Laithe St Burnley BB11 ... 127 F4
Colne BB8 ... 171 C4
Lake Ave LA4 ... 216 F4
Lake Gr LA4 ... 216 F4
Lake Point FY8 ... 90 D3
Lake Rd
Lytham St Anne's FY8 ... 90 C4
Morecambe LA3 ... 216 F3
Lake Rd N FY8 ... 90 C4
Lake Side Cotts WN1 ... 30 C1
Lake View BL7 ... 46 C5
Lake View Rd BB8 ... 171 D7
Lakeber Ave LA2 ... 239 D8
Lakeber Cl 11 LA2 ... 239 D8
Lakeber Dr 13 LA2 ... 239 D8
Lakeland Cl
Billington BB7 ... 144 A3
Forton PR3 ... 207 B3
Lakeland Dr BB7 ... 144 A8
Lakeland Gdns PR7 ... 43 A5
Lakeland Ho LA4 ... 217 E7
Lakeland Way BB12 ... 127 B8
Lakes Dr WN5 ... 10 E6
Lakeside Ave WN5 ... 10 E3
Lakeside Ct PR9 ... 53 C1
Lakeview Ct PR9 ... 35 B8
Lakeway FY3 ... 130 F6
Lakewood Ave FY5 ... 175 D1
Lamaleach Dr PR4 ... 93 A6
Lamb Row BB7 ... 145 E7
Lamb's La PR3 ... 201 A4
Lambert Cl PR2 ... 118 E3
Lambert Rd Fulwood PR2 118 E3
Lancaster LA1 ... 218 C3
Lambert St BB8 ... 172 C2
Lamberts Mill Footwear Mus★ BB4 ... 86 B2
Lambeth Cl
Blackburn BB1 ... 102 A4
Horwich BL6 ... 32 D3
Lambeth Ct PR2 ... 117 E5
Lambeth St
Blackburn BB1 ... 102 A4
Colne BB8 ... 172 B5
Lambing Clough La BB7 142 E7
Lambourne WN8 ... 18 B4
Lambridge Cl LA4 ... 217 B3
Lambs Hill Cl 7 FY5 ... 176 D1
Lambs Rd FY5 ... 153 D8
Lambshear La L31 ... 5 C4
Lambton Gates BB4 ... 86 C2
Lamlash Rd BB1 ... 102 D4
Lammack Prim Sch BB1 ... 122 C1
Lammack Rd BB1 ... 101 C8
Lamour Pl 4 FY7 ... 198 D3
Lanark Ave FY2 ... 152 C6
Lanark Cl OL10 ... 33 F1
Lanark St BB11 ... 127 D4
Lancambe Ct LA1 ... 218 A2
Lancashire Ambulance Service HQ PR3 ... 137 C1
Lancashire Coll PR7 ... 43 A8
Lancashire Constabulary HQ PR4 ... 95 E1
Lancashire Enterprise Bsns Pk PR26 ... 77 A4
Lancashire Fire & Rescue HQ PR2 ... 117 D8
Lancashire Rd PR26 ... 77 A4
Lancashire St LA4 ... 216 E4
Lancaster & Lakeland Nuffield Hospl The LA1 ... 215 A7
Lancaster & Morecambe Coll LA1 ... 217 F3
Lancaster & Morecambe Coll (Annexe) LA4 ... 217 B5
Lancaster Ave
Accrington BB5 ... 104 B7
Clayton-le-W PR25 ... 77 E1
Great Eccleston PR3 ... 156 C5
Haslingden BB4 ... 68 B8
Horwich BL6 ... 32 D2
Lytham St Anne's FY8 ... 89 F4
Ramsbottom BL0 ... 50 A4
Thornton FY5 ... 176 C2
Lancaster Castle★ LA1 ... 214 E8
Lancaster Christ Church CE Prim Sch LA1 ... 215 B8
Lancaster Cl
Adlington PR6 ... 31 B7
Great Eccleston PR3 ... 156 C5
Knott End-on-S FY6 ... 199 F5
Maghull L31 ... 5 F1
Southport PR8 ... 34 E4
Lancaster Cres WN8 ... 17 E1
Lancaster Ct Chorley PR7 .61 C2
Parbold WN8 ... 27 C2
Lancaster Dallas Road Comm Prim Sch LA1 ... 214 E7
Lancaster Dr Banks PR9 ... 54 F5
Brinscall PR6 ... 62 E8
Clayton-le-M BB5 ... 125 A3
Clitheroe BB7 ... 166 C7
Padiham BB12 ... 126 D6
Lancaster Gate Banks PR9 54 F5
Fleetwood FY7 ... 198 D4
14 Lancaster LA1 ... 214 F8
Nelson BB9 ... 148 D7
Lancaster Gdns PR8 ... 34 E4
Lancaster Girls' Gram Sch LA1 ... 214 E7
Lancaster Ho
28 Preston PR1 ... 97 A7
Southport PR8 ... 34 E4
Lancaster L Pk★ LA1 ... 215 B6
Lancaster La
Clayton-le-W PR25 ... 77 E2
Parbold WN8 ... 27 C3
Lancaster Lane Sch PR25 ... 77 D1
Lancaster Maritime Mus★ LA1 ... 218 C1
Lancaster Moor Hospl LA1 ... 215 D8
Lancaster Pl
Adlington PR6 ... 31 A8
Blackburn BB1 ... 101 B5
Lancaster Rd
Blackpool FY3 ... 131 A3
Carnforth LA5 ... 221 B7
Caton LA2 ... 237 B3
Lancaster Rd *continued*
Cockerham LA2 ... 206 C6
Fisher's Row PR3 ... 201 E5
Formby L37 ... 11 E1
Garstang PR3 ... 204 C1
Hornby LA2 ... 238 B7
Knott End-on-S FY6 ... 199 F5
Lancaster LA3 ... 213 D3
Morecambe LA4 ... 217 C5
Morecambe,Torrisholme LA4 ... 217 F4
Moss Edge PR3 ... 178 E6
Preesall FY6 ... 200 C3
Preston PR1 ... 96 F8
Preston PR1 ... 97 A8
Ratten Row PR3 ... 156 A8
Slyne LA2 ... 218 D6
Southport PR8 ... 34 E4
Lancaster Rd N PR1 ... 117 F1
Lancaster Road Prim Sch LA4 ... 217 D4
Lancaster Royal Gram Sch LA1 ... 215 A8
Lancaster Royal Gram Sch (Annexe) LA1 ... 215 B7
Lancaster St
Blackburn BB2 ... 101 C4
Colne BB8 ... 171 D5
Coppull PR7 ... 42 F1
Oswaldtwistle BB5 ... 103 C3
Lancaster Sta LA1 ... 214 E8
Lancaster Way 16 PR1 ... 97 A8
Lancastergate PR25 ... 59 F8
Lanchester Ct PR25 ... 59 D6
Lanchester Gdns BB6 ... 143 C6
Lancia Cres FY4 ... 112 A6
Lancing Pl BB2 ... 101 C3
Land End L31 ... 6 C1
Land Gate OL12 ... 71 F5
Land La New Longton PR4 75 D5
Southport PR9 ... 54 D4
Landcrest Cl PR4 ... 114 B2
Landing La BB7 ... 229 F4
Landless St BB9 ... 148 A5
Landseer Ave FY2 ... 152 C4
Landseer Cl BB11 ... 127 E3
Landseer St PR1 ... 118 C1
Landsmoor Dr PR4 ... 95 A1
Lane Bottom BB18 ... 194 B8
Lane End BB11 ... 126 C2
Lane End La OL13 ... 88 A1
Lane End Rd OL13 ... 71 A8
Lane Ends Brierfield BB9 148 D6
Longridge PR3 ... 140 F8
Rivington PR6 ... 44 D4
Lane Ends Ct 2 FY4 ... 130 E1
Lane Foot Brow LA2 ... 239 D4
Lane Head LA2 ... 238 D6
Lane Head La OL13 ... 87 F3
Lane Ho BB8 ... 172 C1
Lane House Cl BB2 ... 81 B8
Lane Side OL13 ... 88 A4
Lane Side Terr BB5 ... 125 D6
Lane The Carleton FY6 ... 153 A3
Sunderland LA3 ... 209 A5
Lane Top
Colne,Cotton Tree BB8 ... 172 C5
Fence BB12 ... 147 D7
Lanedale PR4 ... 75 A8
Lanefield Dr FY5 ... 175 C4
Laneshaw Bridge Prim Sch BB8 ... 172 E6
Laneshaw Cl BB3 ... 81 E4
Laneside Altham BB5 ... 125 D6
Great Harwood BB6 ... 124 A6
Laneside Ave
Accrington BB5 ... 104 B8
Higham BB12 ... 146 F6
Laneside Ho 5 BB4 ... 85 B2
Laneside Rd BB4 ... 85 C2
Lang St Accrington BB5 ... 104 A6
Blackpool FY1 ... 130 C6
Langber End La LA6 ... 242 F1
Langcliffe Rd PR2 ... 118 E4
Langdale LA2 ... 237 C3
Langdale Ave
Clitheroe BB7 ... 166 C7
Croston PR26 ... 58 B3
Formby L37 ... 11 D2
Hesketh Bank PR4 ... 73 D4
Rawtenstall BB4 ... 85 E2
Langdale Cl
3 Accrington BB5 ... 125 D1
Bamber Bridge PR5 ... 97 D1
Blackburn BB2 ... 80 E8
Formby L37 ... 11 D2
Freckleton PR4 ... 93 A6
Thornton FY5 ... 176 B2
Langdale Cres PR2 ... 118 E3
Langdale Ct
Cleveleys FY5 ... 175 F1
3 Fleetwood FY7 ... 198 E2
4 Garstang PR3 ... 181 B7
Higher Penwortham PR1 ... 96 C4
Langdale Dr
Burscough L40 ... 25 E4
Maghull L31 ... 5 E2
Langdale Gdns PR8 ... 34 F1
Langdale Gr PR6 ... 61 B7
Langdale Pl
1 Blackpool FY4 ... 131 C1
Lancaster LA1 ... 218 E2
Langdale Rd
Blackburn BB2 ... 80 E8
Blackpool FY4 ... 131 C1
Carnforth LA5 ... 221 E8
Fulwood PR2 ... 118 E3
Lancaster LA1 ... 218 E2

Langdale Rd continued
Leyland PR25 . . . . .60 B6
Longridge PR3 . . . . .139 F5
Lytham St Anne's FY8 . . .110 D1
Morecambe LA4 . . . . . .217 D5
Padiham BB12 . . . . .146 C2
Langdale Rise BB8 . . . . .171 F6
Langden Brook Mews
LA3 . . . . .217 F2
Langden Brook Sq BB1 .102 A3
Langden Cres PR5 . . . . . .77 F8
Langden Dr PR2 . . . . . .119 A3
Langden Fold PR2 . . . . .139 D1
Langdon Way FY2 . . . . .152 E2
Langfield BB10 . . . . . . .129 B6
Langfield Ave FY4 . . . . .110 C5
Langfield Cl PR2 . . . . . .117 F8
Langford St BB5 . . . . . .104 E1
Langham Ave BB5 . . . . .104 B8
Langham Rd
Blackburn BB1 . . . . . . .101 D7
Standish WN6 . . . . .29 C1
Langham St BB12 . . . . .127 B6
Langho St BB2 . . . . . . .101 C1
Langho Sta BB6 . . . . . .143 C1
Langho Woods BB6 . . . .143 C5
Langholm Cl [6] PR25 . . . .76 C1
Langholme Cl BB9 . . . . .170 C1
Langholme Rd PR1 . . . . .96 B4
Langholme St BB9 . . . . .148 E6
Langholme Way OL10 . . . .33 F1
Langley Cl Hightown L38 . . .2 F2
Standish WN6 . . . . .29 E2
Langley Ct L40 . . . . .25 B5
Langley La PR3 . . . . . . .137 F6
Langley Pl L40 . . . . .25 B4
Langley Rd Burscough L40 25 B4
Lancaster LA1 . . . . .215 A7
Langport Cl PR2 . . . . . .117 F8
Langridge Way LA4 . . . .217 B3
Langroyd Rd BB8 . . . . . .171 E6
Langsford Cl BB18 . . . . .196 C2
Langshaw Dr BB7 . . . . .166 F6
Langshaw La LA2 . . . . .211 D5
Langstone Cl BL6 . . . . . .32 B3
Langthwaite Rd LA1,LA2 215 E5
Langton Ave WN6 . . . . . .29 E1
Langton Brow
Eccleston PR7 . . . . .41 D5
Longridge PR3 . . . . .140 B7
Langton Cl Blackburn BB2 .81 C7
Eccleston PR7 . . . . .41 D5
Lancaster LA1 . . . . .218 E4
Leyland PR26 . . . . .59 C8
Langton Pl WN6 . . . . . . .29 E1
Langton Rd PR4 . . . . . .114 A5
Langton St PR1 . . . . . . .96 D7
Langtree WN8 . . . . .18 B3
Langtree La Elswick PR4 .155 F2
Standish WN6 . . . . .29 D3
Langwood FY7 . . . . . . .198 E2
Langwood WA11 . . . . . . .9 C1
Langwyth Rd BB10 . . . .128 E5
Lansborough Cl PR26 . . . .59 B8
Lansbury Pl [3] BB9 . . . .170 F2
Lansdown Hill PR2 . . . . .117 C7
Lansdown Rd PR4 . . . . .114 A7
Lansdowne Cl
Burnley BB11 . . . . .127 F4
Ramsbottom BL0 . . . . . . .50 B5
Lansdowne Gr LA4 . . . .217 E7
Lansdowne Pl [1] FY1 . . .130 B6
Lansdowne Rd
Burnley BB11 . . . . .127 E4
Lytham St Anne's FY8 . . . .90 D5
Morecambe LA4 . . . . . .217 E4
Southport PR8 . . . . .35 E6
Lansdowne St BB2 . . . . .101 B3
Lansil Ind Est LA1 . . . . .218 E3
Lansil Way LA1 . . . . . . .218 E3
Lansil Wlk LA1 . . . . . . .218 E3
Lanterns The FY6 . . . . .153 D4
Lapford Cres L33 . . . . . . .1 A4
Lapford Wlk L33 . . . . . . .1 A4
Lappet Gr PR4 . . . . . . .116 E5
Lapwing Row FY6 . . . . . .90 E7
Lapwings The FY6 . . . . .153 B2
Larbreck Ave PR4 . . . . .156 A1
Larbreck Hall Cvn Pk
PR3 . . . . .155 C5
Larbreck Rd FY3 . . . . . .130 E7
Larch Ave PR6 . . . . .61 E2
Larch Cl Blackburn BB2 . . .80 F8
Freckleton PR4 . . . . .93 A5
Knott End-on-S FY6 . . . .200 A5
Rawtenstall BB4 . . . . .68 F8
Skelmersdale WN8 . . . . . .17 E1
Larch Dr PR6 . . . . .62 F7
Larch Gate PR5 . . . . . . .98 E2
Larch Gr
Bamber Bridge PR5 . . . . . .97 F1
Garstang PR3 . . . . .181 C8
Lancaster LA1 . . . . .214 D8
Larch Rd BB5 . . . . .103 F3
Larch St Blackburn BB1 . .102 A7
Burnley BB12 . . . . .127 C7
Bury BL9 . . . . .33 B2
Nelson BB9 . . . . .148 F8
Southport PR8 . . . . .35 E6
Larch Way L37 . . . . .11 D4
Larches Ave PR2 . . . . . .116 F1
Larches La PR2 . . . . . . .116 E1
Larches The BB1 . . . . . .101 F7
Larchgate PR2 . . . . . . .118 C2
Larchway PR3 . . . . .140 B8
Larchwood
Higher Penwortham PR1 . . .96 B4
Lancaster LA1 . . . . .215 B4

Larchwood continued
Preston PR2 . . . . .116 E1
Larchwood Cl PR4 . . . . . .90 F4
Larchwood Cres PR25 . . .76 E1
Largs Rd BB1 . . . . .102 C3
Lark Ave [3] PR1 . . . . . . .96 E4
Lark Cl FY3 . . . . .131 B3
Lark Ct FY7 . . . . .198 D1
Lark Hill Blackburn BB1 . .101 F6
Higher Walton PR5 . . . . . .98 B3
Lark Hill Pl OL12 . . . . . . .52 E1
Lark St [4] Burnley BB12 . .127 C7
Colne BB8 . . . . .171 E6
Darwen BB3 . . . . .65 B5
Larkfield PR7 . . . . .41 B6
Larkfield Cl BL8 . . . . . . .49 F1
Larkfield Ct PR9 . . . . . . .54 A3
Larkfield La PR9 . . . . . . .54 A3
Larkfield Prim Sch PR9 . .54 A3
Larkhill
Brockhall Village BB6 . . . .143 C5
Skelmersdale WN8 . . . . . .18 B4
Larkhill Ave BB10 . . . . . .148 C5
Larkhill Gr L38 . . . . .2 F3
Larkhill La L37 . . . . .11 C4
Larkhill Rd PR1 . . . . .97 B7
Larkhill St Blackpool FY1 130 C6
Preston PR1 . . . . .97 B7
Larkholme Ave FY7 . . . .198 E1
Larkholme La FY7 . . . . .198 E1
Larkholme Par FY7 . . . .198 D1
Larkholme Prim Sch
FY7 . . . . .175 D8
Larkspur Cl Blackburn BB2 80 D8
[3] Southport PR8 . . . . . . .35 D6
Last Drop Village The ★
BL7 . . . . .48 A1
Latham Ave
[9] Blackpool FY3 . . . . . .130 E3
Ormskirk L39 . . . . .16 A5
Latham Cres PR4 . . . . . .57 A6
Latham Row BL6 . . . . . . .31 C3
Latham St Burnley BB10 . .148 B1
Preston PR1 . . . . .97 A6
Lathom Ave
Morecambe LA4 . . . . . .217 D4
Parbold WN8 . . . . .27 B3
Lathom Cl L40 . . . . .25 A4
Lathom Dr L31 . . . . .5 E3
Lathom Gr LA4 . . . . . . .217 D4
Lathom High Sch WN8 . . .17 F3
Lathom La L40 . . . . .16 F2
Lathom Rd Bickerstaffe L39 .7 F8
Southport PR9 . . . . .53 C1
Lathom St [8] BL9 . . . . . .33 A4
Lathom St James CE Prim
Sch L40 . . . . .16 E4
Lathom Way PR3 . . . . . .181 D6
Latimer Pl [2] WN5 . . . . .10 F7
Latimer Dr PR4 . . . . . . .75 F7
Lauderdale Ave FY5 . . . .175 D1
Lauderdale Cres [1] PR2 118 F4
Lauderdale Rd PR2 . . . . .118 F4
Lauderdale St PR1 . . . . . .96 E6
Laund Gate BB12 . . . . . .147 D8
Laund Gr BB5 . . . . .104 D3
Laund Hey View BB4 . . . .85 B1
Laund La Haslingden BB4 . .85 C3
Ollerton Fold PR6 . . . . . . .79 E4
Laund Rd BB5 . . . . .104 D3
Laund St BB4 . . . . .85 F4
Laund The PR26 . . . . . . .76 A1
Laundry Rd N FY4 . . . . .111 A5
Laura St BL0 . . . . .50 C2
Laurel Ave Blackpool FY1 130 E2
Burscough Bridge L40 . . . .25 C4
Darwen BB3 . . . . .82 B2
Euxton PR7 . . . . .60 B3
Fleetwood FY7 . . . . .175 D1
Lytham St Anne's FY8 . . . .91 B5
Laurel Bank LA1 . . . . . .214 D1
Laurel Bank Ave PR2 . . .117 C3
Laurel Bank Terr BB2 . . . .80 F3
Laurel Dr
Skelmersdale WN8 . . . . . .17 E2
Thornton FY5 . . . . .153 B8
Laurel Gr PR8 . . . . .35 E7
Laurel St [4] Bacup OL13 . .87 F3
Burnley BB11 . . . . .128 B4
[3] Bury BL9 . . . . .33 B2
[10] Preston PR1 . . . . .97 A7
Laurels The Coppull PR7 . .42 F3
Kirkham PR4 . . . . .113 D4
Poulton-le-F FY6 . . . . . .153 F3
Laureston Ave LA3 . . . . .212 F6
Laurie Pl [2] OL12 . . . . . .52 F1
Laurier Ave [3] FY4 . . . . .110 C6
Laurier Rd BB10 . . . . . .148 B2
Lauriston Cl [4] FY4 . . . .111 A6
Lavender Cl PR2 . . . . . .118 C6
Lavender Gr PR7 . . . . . . .43 C5
Lavender Hill BB4 . . . . . .68 F8
Lavender Way FY6 . . . . .199 F5
Laverick Rd LA2 . . . . . .237 A5
Laverton Cl BL9 . . . . . . .33 E1
Laverton Rd FY8 . . . . . . .90 A4
Law St Cornholme OL14 . .109 B1
Newchurch BB4 . . . . .86 F1
Lawley Rd BB2 . . . . .101 A3
Lawn Ct [2] FY1 . . . . . . .130 D4
Lawn St BB10 . . . . .128 A8
Lawn Tennis Ct FY4 . . . .110 D5
Lawns Ave WN5 . . . . . . .10 C3
Lawns The PR9 . . . . .53 F2
Lawnsdale Cvn Pk FY8 . .112 E1

Lawnswood Ave
Lancaster LA1 . . . . .215 A3
Poulton-le-F FY6 . . . . . .153 C2
Lawnswood Cres FY3 . . .131 C2
Lawnswood Dr LA3 . . . . .217 C2
Lawnwood Ave PR7 . . . . .43 A5
Lawrence Ave
Bamber Bridge PR5 . . . . . .97 D2
Burnley BB11 . . . . .127 C4
Longridge PR3 . . . . .140 A7
Lytham St Anne's FY8 . . . .90 A6
Preston PR1 . . . . .97 B5
Simonstone BB12 . . . . . .145 E2
Lawrence Cl OL12 . . . . . .52 F1
Lawrence La PR7 . . . . . . .41 C7
Lawrence Rd Chorley PR7 .43 B7
Higher Penwortham PR1 . . .96 B5
Lawrence Row [4] FY7 . . .199 A4
Lawrence St
Blackburn BB2 . . . . .101 C4
[12] Blackpool FY4 . . . . . .130 B1
Fulwood PR2 . . . . .117 D3
Padiham BB12 . . . . .146 D1
Whitewell Bottom BB4 . . . .86 F4
Lawrie Ave BL0 . . . . .50 B5
Lawson Cl LA1 . . . . .214 F3
Lawson Gdns LA2 . . . . .218 C8
Lawson Pl LA2 . . . . .218 C8
Lawson Rd Blackpool FY3 131 A3
Horwich BL6 . . . . .32 C4
Lytham St Anne's FY8 . . . .111 A2
Lawson St [3] Chorley PR6 43 E7
Preston PR1 . . . . .96 F8
Rawtenstall BB4 . . . . . . .86 A8
Southport PR9 . . . . .36 A7
Lawsons Ct [4] FY5 . . . . .176 C1
Lawsons Rd FY5 . . . . . .176 C2
Lawswood Formby L37 . . . .11 F3
[6] Thornton FY5 . . . . . . .176 C1
Lawton Cl PR6 . . . . .79 B1
Laxey Gr PR1 . . . . .118 D3
Laxey Rd BB2 . . . . .101 C1
Laycock Gate FY3 . . . . .130 D6
Layton Prim Sch FY3 . . .130 E8
Layton Rd Blackpool FY3 130 E6
Preston PR2 . . . . .116 C1
Layton Sta FY2 . . . . . . .152 E1
Lazenby Ave FY7 . . . . . .198 C2
Lea Bank BB4 . . . . .86 D2
Lea Com Prim Sch PR2 116 D1
Lea Cres L39 . . . . .15 F7
Lea Ct L39 . . . . .15 F7
Lea Dr BB2 . . . . .81 E6
Lea La Cottam PR4 . . . . .116 B5
Gressingham LA2 . . . . . .237 F8
Heysham LA3 . . . . .212 E6
Lea Mount Dr BL9 . . . . . .33 D4
Lea Neeld's Endowed CE
Prim Sch PR4 . . . . . . .116 C4
Lea Rd Lucas Green PR6 . . .61 C5
Preston PR2,PR4 . . . . . .116 D3
Lea St Mary's RC Primary Sch
PR4 . . . . .115 F2
Lea Way Cl FY5 . . . . . . .153 D7
Leach Cres FY6 . . . . . . .110 F2
Leach La FY8 . . . . .110 E1
Leach Pl PR5 . . . . .78 B8
Leach St Blackburn BB2 . .101 E2
Colne BB8 . . . . .171 C4
Leaches Fold BL0 . . . . . . .50 D8
Leachfield Cl [2] LA2 . . . .211 A4
Leachfield Ind Est PR3 . .204 B1
Leachfield Rd LA2 . . . . .210 F4
Leacroft BB3 . . . . .82 A6
Lead Mines Clough ★
PR6 . . . . .45 A7
Leadale Pl PR2 . . . . .116 D2
Leadale Cl WN6 . . . . . . .29 D1
Leadale Gn PR25 . . . . . .76 E1
Leadale Rd PR25 . . . . . .76 E1
Leaford Ave FY3 . . . . . .130 E8
Leafy Cl PR25 . . . . .60 B7
Leagram Cres PR2 . . . . .119 A3
Leamington Ave
Baldingstone BL9 . . . . . . .50 E1
Burnley BB12 . . . . .148 C1
Southport PR8 . . . . .21 D5
Leamington Rd
Blackburn BB2 . . . . .101 B6
Blackpool FY1 . . . . .130 D5
Lytham St Anne's FY8 . . . .89 F6
Morecambe LA4 . . . . . .217 D3
Southport PR8 . . . . .21 D5
Leamington St BB9 . . . . .148 E7
Leander Gdns FY6 . . . . .153 D2
Leapers View LA6 . . . . .237 B8
Leaside Cl OL12 . . . . . . .52 D2
Leathercote PR3 . . . . . .181 C6
Leathwood L31 . . . . .5 E1
Leavengreave Ct OL12 . . .71 D4
Leaver St BB12 . . . . . . .127 A5
Leaverholme Cl BB10 . . .108 A7
Leavesley Rd FY1 . . . . . .130 D8
Lebanon St BB10 . . . . . .128 C5
Leck Ho [11] LA1 . . . . . . .215 A3
Leck St Peter's CE Prim Sch
LA6 . . . . .242 B7
Leckhampton Rd FY1 . . .130 B8
Leckonby St PR3 . . . . . .156 B5
Ledburn WN8 . . . . .18 B3
Ledbury Ave FY8 . . . . . . .90 B5
Ledbury Rd FY3 . . . . . . .131 B7
Ledson Gr L39 . . . . .6 B7
Lee Brook Cl BB4 . . . . . .86 A4
Lee Gr BB10 . . . . .128 F4
Lee Green St [3] BB10 . . .128 A8
Lee La Bispham Green L40 . .27 C7
Great Harwood BB1 . . . . .124 B3

Lee La continued
Horwich BL6 . . . . .32 B4
Whittlestone Head BL7 . . . .66 B2
Lee Rd Bacup OL13 . . . . . .70 E8
Blackpool FY4 . . . . .111 B8
Nelson BB9 . . . . .170 F1
Lee St Accrington BB5 . . .104 C6
Bacup OL13 . . . . .87 C7
Barrowford BB9 . . . . . . .170 D3
Rawtenstall BB4 . . . . . . .86 A4
Burnley BB10 . . . . .128 A8
Lee View OL13 . . . . .88 B1
Lee's St OL13 . . . . .71 C8
Leebrook Rd BB4 . . . . . . .85 F4
Leech House La LA2 . . . .211 A5
Leech Cl [15] BB1 . . . . .97 A8
Leeds Cl [15] BB1 . . . . .97 A8
Leeds Rd Blackpool FY1 . .130 D5
[4] Nelson BB9 . . . . .148 E8
Nelson BB9 . . . . .170 F1
Leehouse Dr FY6 . . . . . .131 D8
Leek St PR1 . . . . .97 E8
Leeming La LA6 . . . . . . .242 C3
Lees Cotts BL7 . . . . .48 C2
Lees Ct LA3 . . . . .212 E7
Lees La WN8 . . . . .18 E7
Lees Rd Adlington PR6 . . . .31 B8
Kirkby L33 . . . . .1 B2
Lees The BB10 . . . . .108 A7
Leesands Cl PR2 . . . . . .118 E5
Leeson Ave PR7 . . . . . . .42 D4
Leeswood WN8 . . . . .18 B3
Leet Rd BB12 . . . . .146 F5
Leeward Cl BB3 . . . . .81 F6
Leeward Rd PR2 . . . . . . .95 F8
Legh La PR4 . . . . .56 B4
Leicester Ave
Cleveleys FY5 . . . . .175 E3
Garstang PR3 . . . . .181 B7
Horwich BL6 . . . . .32 A3
Leicester Gate FY5 . . . . .175 E3
Leicester Lodge [3] PR2 .118 F4
Leicester Rd
Blackburn BB1 . . . . .102 C5
Blackpool FY1 . . . . .130 D5
Preston PR1 . . . . .118 A1
Leicester St PR9 . . . . . . .35 B8
Leigh Brow PR5 . . . . .97 B2
Leigh Pk BB12 . . . . .126 C3
Leigh Row PR7 . . . . .43 C7
Leighton Ave
Fleetwood FY7 . . . . .198 D3
Maghull L31 . . . . .5 D2
Leighton Ct LA1 . . . . . . .217 A3
Leighton Dr LA1 . . . . . . .214 D7
Leighton Hall ★ LA5 . . . .225 C1
Leighton Moss Nature
Reserve ★ LA5 . . . . . . .225 A3
Leighton Moss Visitor Ctr ★
LA5 . . . . .224 F2
Leighton St PR1 . . . . . . .96 E8
Leinster Rd LA1 . . . . . . .215 A5
Leisure Lakes Cvn Pk
PR4 . . . . .55 E1
Leith Ave FY5 . . . . .175 D2
Lemon Tree Ct FY8 . . . . .110 B4
Lemonius St BB5 . . . . . .104 C4
Lench Rd BB4 . . . . .69 D8
Lench St BB4 . . . . .69 F8
Lenches Fold BB8 . . . . . .171 D4
Lenches Rd BB8 . . . . . . .171 D3
Lendel Cl L37 . . . . .11 E3
Lennon St [3] PR7 . . . . . .43 C7
Lennox Ct FY4 . . . . .110 D6
Lennox Gate FY4 . . . . . .110 D7
Lennox Rd OL14 . . . . . . .109 A1
Lennox St [18] Preston PR1 .97 A7
Worsthorne BB10 . . . . . .129 A6
Lennox Wlk OL10 . . . . . . .33 F1
Lenton Ave L37 . . . . .11 D4
Lentworth Ave FY2 . . . . .152 D5
Lentworth Dr LA1 . . . . . .214 A4
Lentworth Ho [5] LA1 . . . .215 A3
Leo Case Ct [5] PR1 . . . . .97 D8
Leonard St
Barnoldswick BB18 . . . . .196 B2
Nelson BB9 . . . . .148 E7
Leonard Terr BB3 . . . . . .82 E3
Leopold Gr FY1 . . . . . . .130 B5
Leopold Rd BB2 . . . . . . .101 B6
Leopold St BB8 . . . . . . .171 B4
Leopold Way BB2 . . . . . .82 A8
Lesley Rd PR8 . . . . .35 E2
Leslie Ave Caton LA2 . . . .237 C3
Thornton FY5 . . . . .176 C2
Letchworth Dr PR7 . . . . .43 B6
Letchworth Pl [2] PR7 . . . .43 B6
Letcliffe Ctry Pk ★ BB18 194 B8
Lethbridge Rd PR8 . . . . .35 D5
Letitia St BL6 . . . . .32 A3
Levant St BB12 . . . . . . .126 C7
Leven Ave FY7 . . . . .198 D3
Leven Gr BB3 . . . . .81 E4
Leven St BB11 . . . . .128 B4
Levens Cl Banks PR9 . . . .55 A5
Blackburn BB2 . . . . .81 D5
Lancaster LA1 . . . . .214 D7
Poulton-le-F FY6 . . . . . .131 C6
Levens Ct LA3 . . . . .216 C2
Levens Dr
Clayton-le-W PR25 . . . . . .77 D2
Morecambe LA3 . . . . . .216 E2
Poulton-le-F FY6 . . . . . .153 C2
Levens Gr FY1 . . . . .130 D3
Levens St [12] PR1 . . . . . .118 C1
Levens Way LA5 . . . . . .224 D2
Levensgarth Ave PR2 . . .117 F2
Lever St BB2 . . . . .100 F7

Lever House La PR25 . . . .77 C2
Lever House Prim Sch
PR25 . . . . .77 C3
Lever Park Ave BL6 . . . . .32 B5
Lever Park Sch BL6 . . . . .32 C3
Lever St Blackpool FY3 . . .130 E4
[18] Ramsbottom BL0 . . . . .50 C6
Rawtenstall BB4 . . . . . . .86 B2
Levine Ave FY4 . . . . . . .131 A1
Lewis Cl PR7 . . . . .30 E6
Lewis Ct PR9 . . . . .35 D8
Lewis Dr OL10 . . . . .33 F1
Lewis St BB6 . . . . .124 D5
Lewis Textile Mus ★
BB1 . . . . .101 E5
Lewtas St FY1 . . . . .130 B6
Lewth La PR4 . . . . .136 B5
Lex St PR1 . . . . .97 C8
Lexton Dr PR9 . . . . .54 B3
Ley Ct LA1 . . . . .214 D8
Ley St BB5 . . . . .104 E2
Leybourne Ave PR8 . . . . .21 F7
Leyburn Ave
Blackpool FY2 . . . . .152 C5
Fleetwood FY7 . . . . .198 E2
Leyburn Cl
Accrington BB5 . . . . .104 C5
Fulwood PR2 . . . . .118 E5
Leyburn Rd Blackburn BB2 81 C7
Lancaster LA1 . . . . .218 D3
Leycester Dr LA1 . . . . . .218 A3
Leyfield PR1 . . . . .96 E2
Leyfield Cl FY3 . . . . .153 A1
Leyfield Rd PR25 . . . . . . .59 F8
Leyland Cl Southport PR9 .54 E5
Trawden BB8 . . . . .172 B5
Leyland La Leyland PR25 . .76 D2
Runshaw Moor PR26,PR25 .59 D4
Leyland Meth Inf Sch
PR25 . . . . .77 B1
Leyland Meth Jun Sch
PR25 . . . . .77 B1
Leyland Rd Burnley BB11 128 B6
Middlesworth Green PR1 . .96 E3
Southport PR9 . . . . .53 C1
Leyland St BB5 . . . . . . .104 E3
Leyland St Andrew's CE Inf
Sch PR25 . . . . .59 F8
Leyland St James CE Prim
Sch PR26 . . . . .59 B8
Leyland St Mary's RC Prim
Sch PR25 . . . . .76 F1
Leyland St Mary's RC Tech
Coll PR25 . . . . .59 E7
Leyland Sta PR25 . . . . . .77 B2
Leyland Way Leyland PR25 77 C1
Ormskirk L39 . . . . .15 F5
Leylands The FY8 . . . . . .90 F2
Leys Cl Elswick PR4 . . . .156 A1
Wiswell BB7 . . . . .144 F8
Leys Rd FY2 . . . . .152 D1
Leyster St LA4 . . . . .217 C5
Leyton Ave PR25 . . . . . . .59 D7
Leyton St OL12 . . . . .52 F2
Libby La PR3 . . . . .201 C6
Library Ave LA1 . . . . . . .211 B7
Library Mews FY4 . . . . . .110 E7
Library Rd PR6 . . . . .78 B4
Library St Chorley PR7 . . .43 C7
Church BB5 . . . . .103 E4
[15] Preston PR1 . . . . .97 A7
Lichen Cl PR7 . . . . .42 D4
Lichfield Ave LA4 . . . . . .217 D6
Lichfield Rd
Blackpool FY1 . . . . .130 C8
Chorley PR7 . . . . .43 C6
Preston PR2 . . . . .116 F2
Liddesdale Rd BB9 . . . . .171 B2
Liddington Cl BB2 . . . . . .82 A8
Liddington Hall Dr BL0 . . .50 B4
Lidget Ave PR2 . . . . . . .116 C1
Lidgett BB8 . . . . .172 A5
Lidum Park Ind Est FY8 . .91 E5
Liege Rd [4] PR25 . . . . . . .60 A8
Lifeboat Pl [13] FY7 . . . . .199 B5
Lifeboat Rd L37 . . . . .11 B1
Lifton Rd L33 . . . . .1 A2
Liggard St FY4 . . . . .91 C4
Lightbown Ave FY3 . . . . .130 E3
Lightbown Cotts BB3 . . . .81 E2
Lightbown St BB3 . . . . . .82 A3
Lightburne Ave FY8 . . . . .89 F5
Lightfoot Cl PR2 . . . . . . .117 D8
Lightfoot Green La PR4 . .117 B8
Lightfoot La PR2,PR4 . . .117 B7
Lighthorne Dr PR4 . . . . . .21 A4
Lighthouse Cl [4] FY7 . . . .199 B5
Lighthurst Ave PR7 . . . . .43 C6
Lighthurst La PR7 . . . . . .43 D5
Lightwood Ave
[2] Blackpool FY4 . . . . . .130 C1
Lytham St Anne's FY8 . . . .90 D3
Lilac Ave
[1] Blackpool FY1 . . . . . .130 D2
Haslingden BB4 . . . . . . .85 B3
Kingsfold PR1 . . . . .96 F2
Lytham St Anne's FY8 . . . .91 B5
Southport PR8 . . . . .21 D5
Lilac Cl PR4 . . . . .92 D5
Lilac Cres PR4 . . . . .134 F4
Lilac Gr Abbey Village PR6 .80 C2
Clitheroe BB7 . . . . .166 C7
Darwen BB3 . . . . .82 B3
Knott End-on-S FY6 . . . .199 E5
Preston PR1 . . . . .118 C3

Lilac Gr continued
Skelmersdale WN8 ....17 E1
Lilac Rd BB1 ....102 A8
Lilac St BB8 ....171 F6
Lilac Terr 3 OL13 ......70 D1
Lilacs The FY6 ....153 F3
Lilburn Cl BL0 ....50 C4
Lilford Cl PR4 ....57 A5
Lilford Rd BB1 ....101 D6
Lily Gr Lancaster LA1 ...215 A5
Preston PR1 ....118 C3
Lily St 16 Bacup OL13 ...87 F2
Blackpool FY1 ....130 C5
Darwen BB3 ....82 B1
Nelson BB9 ....148 F6
Lima Rd FY8 ....90 B6
Lima St BL9 ....33 B3
Limbrick
21 Blackburn BB1 ......101 E5
Blackburn BB1 ....101 E5
Limbrick Rd PR6 ....43 E7
Lime Ave Galgate LA2 ...211 A4
Kirkham PR4 ....114 B4
Oswaldtwistle BB5 .....103 D2
Lime Chase PR2 ....117 C8
Lime Cl PR1 ....96 B4
Lime Ct WN8 ....17 E1
Lime Gr Blackpool FY2 ...152 E2
Chorley PR7 ....43 C5
Garstang PR3 ....181 B8
Lancaster LA1 ....214 D8
Longridge PR3 ....140 A8
Lytham St Anne's FY8 ...89 E2
Poulton-le-F FY6 ......153 E2
Preston PR2 ....116 F2
Ramsbottom BL0 ....50 D7
Skelmersdale WN8 ......17 E1
Thornton FY5 ....176 C1
Lime Rd Accrington BB5 ...104 C7
Haslingden BB4 ....85 C3
Lime St Blackburn BB1 ...101 E6
Clitheroe BB7 ....189 F1
Colne BB8 ....171 E6
Great Harwood BB6 ....124 C6
Nelson BB9 ....148 C8
Southport PR8 ....35 E6
Lime Tree Gr BB4 ....86 A4
Lime Tree Way L37 ......11 C2
Limebrest Ave FY5 .....153 D8
Limechase Cl 9 FY4 ...111 A6
Limefield BB2 ....101 B5
Limefield Ave
Brierfield BB9 ....148 C6
Whalley BB7 ....144 C6
Limefield Ct BB2 ......101 B5
Limefield Dr WN8 ....9 E7
Limefield St BB5 ......104 D5
Limerick Rd FY2 ....152 D3
Limers Gate
Rochdale OL12 ....52 F5
Sharneyford OL14 ......88 E4
Limers La BB6 ....124 A6
Limes Ave Darwen BB3 ...65 A8
Euxton PR7 ....60 C4
Morecambe LA3 ....216 E3
Limestone Trail★ BB10 .108 E6
Limewood Cl
Accrington BB5 ....104 D6
Haslingden BB4 ....68 A7
Limey La BB11 ....106 E6
Limont Rd PR8 ....21 D5
Lina St BB5 ....103 F6
Linacre La L37 ....4 B7
Linadale Ave 4 FY5 ...176 B2
Linaker Dr L39 ....14 B8
Linaker Prim Sch PR8 ...35 B5
Linaker St PR8 ....35 B5
Linby St BB10 ....128 B5
Lincoln Ave
Cleveleys FY5 ....175 E3
Fleetwood FY7 ....198 E3
Lincoln Chase PR2 .....116 C1
Lincoln Cl Blackburn BB1 102 B4
Morecambe LA4 ....217 D3
Lincoln Ct
1 Accrington BB5 .....104 A7
Blackpool FY1 ....130 C4
Lincoln Ho 7 PR1 .....97 B7
Lincoln Pk BB7 ....190 E1
Lincoln Pl BB4 ....85 A3
Lincoln Rd
Blackburn BB1 ....102 B4
Blackpool FY1 ....130 C5
Earby BB18 ....197 B2
Lancaster LA1 ....214 E7
Southport PR8 ....35 A1
Lincoln St Burnley BB11 .128 A4
Cornholme OL14 ....109 B1
3 Haslingden BB4 ......85 A3
Preston PR1 ....118 B1
Lincoln Way
Clitheroe BB7 ....190 A2
Garstang PR3 ....181 B8
Lincoln Wlk PR1 ....118 B1
Lindadale Ave BB5 .....104 A4
Lindadale Cl BB5 ......104 A3
Lindale Ave PR2 ....139 E1
Lindale Cres BB10 ....148 A2
Lindale Gdns FY4 ......110 E6
Lindale Rd Fulwood PR2 .118 A4
Longridge PR3 ....139 F5
Lindbeck Ct FY4 ....111 C8
Lindbeck Rd FY4 ......131 C1
Lindbergh Ave LA1 .....214 E4
Lindel La 200 B2

Lindel Rd FY7 ....198 F2
Linden Ave
Blackburn BB1 ....101 D6
Cleveleys FY5 ....175 F3
Orrell WN5 ....10 E6
Ramsbottom BL0 ....50 D6
Linden Cl
Bamber Bridge PR5 .....97 B1
Barrowford BB9 ....170 B1
Cleveleys FY5 ....175 F2
Edenfield BL0 ....68 D2
Linden Cres BB3 ....82 C2
Linden Ct 7 Earby BB18 .197 B1
Orrell WN5 ....10 E6
Linden Dr
Bamber Bridge PR5 .....97 B1
Clitheroe BB7 ....166 F7
Linden Fold PR4 ......156 A1
Linden Gn FY5 ....175 F2
Linden Gr Chorley PR6 ...61 D3
Fulwood PR2 ....118 E3
Garstang PR3 ....181 C8
Orrell WN5 ....10 E6
Linden Lea Blackburn BB2 80 F8
Rawtenstall BB4 ....68 F8
Linden Mews FY8 ......110 F2
Linden Pl FY2 ....152 E3
Linden Rd Colne BB8 ...171 D5
Earby BB18 ....197 B1
Linden St BB10 ....128 B5
Linden Wlk WN5 ....10 E6
Lindens WN8 ....18 B4
Lindens The FY6 ......200 B4
Linderbreck La FY6 ....131 E8
Lindeth Cl
Nether Kellet LA6 .....221 F6
Silverdale LA5 ....224 C2
Lindeth Gdns 8 LA1 ...218 D3
Lindeth Rd LA5 ....224 C2
Lindholme WN8 ....18 C3
Lindisfarne Ave BB2 ...101 F1
Lindisfarne Cl BB12 ...127 E7
Lindle Ave PR4 ....95 E2
Lindle Cl PR4 ....95 E2
Lindle Cres PR4 ....95 E2
Lindle La PR4 ....96 A2
Lindley Ave FY5 ....10 C5
Lindley Croft FY5 ....176 E2
Lindley Dr WN8 ....27 C3
Lindley St
Bamber Bridge PR5 .....77 B8
Blackburn BB2 ....101 B2
Lindon Park Rd BB4 ....68 C7
Lindow Cl 13 LA1 ....214 F7
Lindow Sq LA1 ....214 E7
Lindow St LA1 ....214 F7
Lindred Rd BB9 ....148 B7
Lindsay Ave
Blackpool FY3 ....130 E3
Leyland PR25 ....77 B1
Lytham St Anne's FY8 ...90 B6
Poulton-le-F FY6 ......153 D2
Lindsay Cl Blackpool FY8 .110 A4
Morecambe LA3 ....217 C2
Lindsay Dr PR7 ....43 A7
Lindsay Pk BB10 ......128 F5
Lindsay St Burnley BB11 .128 A6
Horwich BL6 ....32 D1
Lindsey Ho 2 BB5 ....104 A7
Linedred La BB9 ......148 B7
Lines St LA4 ....217 B5
Linfield Terr FY4 .....110 E6
Lingart La PR3 ....204 D1
Lingdales L37 ....12 E5
Lingfield Ave BB4 .....166 E6
Lingfield Cl BB2 ....80 C8
Lingfield Rd FY7 .....198 F2
Lingfield Way BB2 .....80 D8
Linghaw La LA2 ....239 F8
Lingmell Ave LA2 .....100 F1
Lingmoor Dr BB12 .....127 A8
Lingmoor Rd LA1 ......218 F1
Lingwell Cl PR6 ....61 C5
Link 59 Bsns Pk BB7 ...190 A2
Links Ave PR9 ....53 F3
Links Ct FY8 ....89 E5
Links Dr LA2 ....239 D8
Links Field PR2 ....117 C3
Links Gate Fulwood PR2 .117 C3
Lytham St Anne's FY8 ...90 A6
Thornton FY5 ....153 D7
Links La BB2 ....80 C8
Links Lodge FY4 ....90 A6
Links Rd Blackpool FY1 .130 C8
Higher Penwortham PR1 ..96 B6
Kirkby L32 ....1 A1
Knott End-on-S FY6 ...199 D5
Lytham St Anne's FY8 ...89 E5
Links The FY5 ....175 C4
Links View FY8 ....90 C5
Linkside Ave BB9 .....149 B8
Linley Gr BL0 ....50 A2
Linnet Cl FY3 ....131 B6
Linnet Dr BL9 ....33 B4
Linnet La FY8 ....90 E7
Linnet St PR1 ....118 B2
Linslade Cres L33 ......1 A4
Linton Ave LA3 ....216 D1
Linton Dr BB11 ....127 D3
Linton Gdns BB9 .....170 C3
Linton Gr PR1 ....96 B5
Linton Rd PR2 ....117 D3
Lion Ct 11 BB5 .....103 E6
Lion La BL6 ....31 C2
Lion St BB5 ....103 E6
Lionel St BB12 ....127 C6
Lions Ct 1 FY8 .....91 D4
Lions Dr BB1 ....102 D1

Liptrott Rd PR7 ....43 A5
Lisbon Dr Burnley BB11 .127 E5
Darwen BB3 ....82 C1
Lisbon St 17 OL12 ....52 C1
Lismore Pk PR8 ....34 E4
Lister Croft BD23 .....197 A5
Lister Gr LA3 ....212 F8
Lister St Accrington BB5 .104 A6
3 Blackburn BB2 .....101 E3
Lister Well Rd BB18 ...194 A6
Litchford Ho BB4 ......86 C2
Little Acre Longton PR4 ..75 A8
Thornton FY5 ....153 D8
Little Banks PR5 ....78 B6
Little Brewery La L37 ...11 F6
Little Carr La PR7 .....43 D5
Little Cl Leyland PR26 ...76 E3
Middleforth Green PR1 ...96 C3
Little Coppins La FY6 ..153 E1
Little Digmoor Prim Sch
WN8 ....9 B6
Little Fell La LA2 .....215 A3
Little Fell Rd LA1,LA2 ...215 F6
Little Flatt OL12 ......52 B1
Little Hey La L37 ......12 B4
Little Hoole Prim Sch
PR4 ....75 A5
Little La Banks PR9 ....55 B7
Longridge PR3 ....140 A7
Southport PR9 ....54 B1
Little Meadow La L40 ...39 D4
Little Moor BB7 ......166 E6
Little Moor Clough BL7 ..47 E2
Little Moor View FY6 ...166 E6
Little Peel St 8 BB2 ...101 D5
Little Poulton La FY6 ..153 F4
Little Queen St BB8 ...171 C4
Little Scotland BL6 ....31 B2
Little St BB5 ....104 A6
Little Stones Rd BL7 ...47 E2
Little Toms La BB10 ...148 D3
Little Tongues La FY6 ..200 B4
Little Twining PR4 .....75 A7
Littledale Mews LA2 ...218 F6
Littledale Rd
Crossgill LA2 ....237 E1
Quernmore LA2 ......232 E3
Littlemoor Ho BB7 ....146 A8
Littlemoor Ho BB7 ....146 A7
Littlemoor Rd BB7 ....166 E7
Littleton Gr WN6 ......29 E2
Littleton Manor PR9 ...55 A5
Littlewood 7 PR7 ...198 E3
Littondale Gdns BB2 ...80 D7
Liverpool Ave PR8 .....21 D5
Liverpool New Rd PR4 ...74 F5
Liverpool Old Rd
Much Hoole PR4 ......74 C1
Much Hoole PR4 ......74 E3
Sollom PR4 ....57 B2
Southport PR8 ....21 C1
Walmer Bridge PR4 ....74 F5
Liverpool Rd
Bickerstaffe L39 ......7 C5
Blackpool FY1 ....130 D5
Burnley BB12 ....127 A6
Formby L37 ....12 A1
Higher Penwortham PR1 ..96 B5
Hightown L37 ....3 A8
Longton PR4 ....74 F7
Maghull L31 ....5 D4
Much Hoole PR4 ......74 D2
Ormskirk L39 ....15 B2
Preston PR1 ....96 D6
Royal Oak L39 ....6 F4
Rufford L40 ....39 C5
Skelmersdale WN8 ......8 C8
Sollom PR4 ....57 A3
Southport PR8 ....21 F8
Liverpool Rd N
Burscough Bridge L40 ...25 E5
Maghull L31 ....5 C2
Liverpool Rd S
Burscough L40 ....25 D2
Maghull L31 ....5 C1
Livesey Branch Rd BB2 ..81 D8
Livesey Fold PR6 ......80 A1
Livesey Hall Cl BB0 ...100 E1
Livesey St
11 Lytham St Anne's FY8 .91 A3
Padiham BB12 ....126 C8
Preston PR1 ....97 B7
Rishton BB1 ....124 C4
Livesley's La
Great Altcar L37 ......12 F2
Haskayne L37 ....13 A2
Livet Ave FY4 ....110 D7
Livingstone Rd
Accrington BB5 ......104 B8
Blackburn BB2 ....101 B4
Blackpool FY1 ....130 C4
Livingstone St BB9 ...148 B5
Livingstone Wlk BB9 ...148 B6
Lloyd Cl Lancaster LA1 .218 B1
Lloyd St Darwen BB3 ...81 F3
Whitworth OL12 ....71 C1
Lloyd Wlk 11 BB9 ...148 E8
Lloyd's Ave LA4 ......217 B4
Lobden Cres OL12 .....52 D8
Lochinch Cl FY4 ......111 A6
Lochinver Gr 7 OL10 ...33 F1
Lock Gate BB4 ....85 C1
Lock La PR4 ....57 B2
Lock St 10 BB5 .....103 E4

Locka La
Gressingham LA6 .....240 F3
Lancaster LA1 ....211 A8
Locke Ind Est 1 BL6 ...32 B3
Lockerbie Ave FY5 ....152 D8
Lockfield Dr BB18 ....196 C4
Lockhart Rd PR1 .....117 F2
Lockhurst Ave FY5 ....152 F8
Lockside BB2 ....101 D2
Lockside Rd PR2 ....95 F8
Lockwood Ave FY6 ....153 D4
Lockyer Ave BB12 ....127 D6
Locomotion Ind Est BL6 .32 B2
Lodge Bank Brinscall PR6 .62 F7
Horwich BL6 ....31 F3
Lodge Bank Est BL6 ...31 F3
Lodge Cl
2 Bamber Bridge PR5 ..97 F1
Blackpool FY5 ....152 C7
Freckleton PR4 ....93 B7
Lodge Ct Blackpool FY5 .152 C7
Inskip PR4 ....157 B1
Staining FY3 ....131 D5
Lodge La Bacup OL13 ...87 F1
Clifton PR4 ....115 D1
Elswick PR4 ....156 B1
Farington PR26 ....76 E6
Lytham St Anne's FY8 ...91 F5
Melling LA2 ....241 D1
Rainford Junction L39,WA11 .8 D1
Singleton FY6 ....154 D2
Lodge Mill La BL0 .....69 A1
Lodge Rd Catterall PR3 .182 A1
Orrell WN5 ....10 E4
Lodge St Accrington BB5 .104 C7
Lancaster LA1 ....214 D8
Preston PR1 ....96 E8
Ramsbottom BL0 ......50 C6
Shuttleworth BL0 .....50 C6
Lodge The FY8 ....90 E7
Lodge View
Farington PR26 ....76 E7
Longridge PR3 ....140 A6
Lodge Wood Cl PR7 ....43 A6
Lodges Ct 6 LA4 ...217 E6
Lodges Gr LA4 ....217 E6
Lodgeside BB5 ....124 F3
Lodgings The PR2 .....118 C5
Lodore Rd FY4 ....110 C6
Lofthouse Way FY7 ...199 A4
Loftos Ave FY4 ......110 D8
Logwood St BB1 ......101 F7
Lois Pl BB2 ....101 C5
Lomas La BB4 ....68 F8
Lomax Cl BB6 ....124 D6
Lomax Sq BB6 ....124 C5
Lomax St 7 Bury BL9 ...33 A3
Darwen BB3 ....82 A2
Great Harwood BB6 ...124 C5
Ramsbottom BL8 ......49 F1
Rochdale OL12 ....52 F1
Lomeshaye Bsns Village
BB9 ....148 B7
Lomeshaye Ind Est BB9 148 B7
Lomeshaye Jun Sch
BB9 ....148 C8
Lomeshaye Pl BB9 ....148 C8
Lomeshaye Rd BB9 ....148 D7
Lomeshaye Way BB9 ...148 C8
Lomond Ave
Blackpool FY3 ....130 F2
Lytham St Anne's FY8 ...90 B5
Lomond Cl PR7 ....60 D4
Lomond Gdns BB2 ....100 F1
London La PR8 ....22 D8
London Rd
Blackburn BB1 ....101 E6
Blackpool FY3 ....130 D6
Preston PR1 ....97 C6
London Sq 2 BB9 ...35 B7
Southport PR8,PR9 ....35 B7
London Terr BB3 ......82 B2
London Way PR5 ....97 C3
London Wlk BB1 ......101 E6
Londonderry Rd LA3 ...212 E5
Long Acre Cl LA5 ....221 C8
Long Acre Pl FY8 ......91 A4
Long Barn Brow PR5 ...99 E2
Long Barn Row PR5 ...99 E2
Long Bldg BB7 ....230 C1
Long Butts PR1 ....96 D2
Long Cl Clitheroe BB7 ..190 A2
Leyland PR26 ....59 A8
Long Copse PR7 ....60 F1
Long Croft Barton PR3 .137 B8
Longton PR4 ....95 A1
Long Croft Mdw PR7 ...61 B2
Long Cswy BB7 ....231 B2
Long Cswy The BB10 ...108 D7
Long Dales La Caton LA6 237 A6
Over Kellet LA6 ......237 A7
Long Gn BB18 ....197 C2
Long Hey La BB1,BB3 ...83 C2
Long Heys or Back La
WN8 ....18 F5
Long Ing La BB18 .....196 C2
Long La Abbeystead LA2 .232 F1
Banks PR9 ....55 B6
Bickerstaffe L39 ......7 B7
Chorley PR6 ....44 B4
Laneshaw Bridge BB8 ..172 D7
Low Bentham LA2 .....239 B7
Maghull L29 ....4 B1
Oakenclough PR3 .....226 B1
Ormskirk L39 ....6 F8
Pleasington BB2 .....100 B2
Quernmore LA2 ......232 A5

Long La continued
Skelmersdale WN8 ....9 E3
Street PR3 ....226 B5
Tockholes BB3 ....81 A3
Long Lane End LA2 ....211 E2
Long Level LA6 ......241 F8
Long Lover La BB7 ....192 C8
Long Marsh La LA1 ....218 B1
Long Mdw Chorley PR7 ...43 A5
Colne BB8 ....172 A5
Kirkham PR4 ....113 E5
Mellor Brook BB2 ....121 B2
Much Hoole PR4 ....74 F4
Long Meanygate PR9 ...37 C7
Long Moss PR26 ....59 A8
Long Moss La PR4 ......76 A6
Long Moss Mdws PR4 ...75 F6
Long Row Blackburn BB2 122 B2
Calder Vale PR3 .....182 E8
Long Wham La PR4 .....75 D1
Longacre
Clayton Brook PR5 .....78 C5
Longton PR4 ....74 F8
Southport PR9 ....53 F3
Longacres Dr OL12 ....71 D2
Longacres La OL12 ....71 D2
Longber La LA6 ......242 B3
Longbrook Ave PR5 .....97 E1
Longcliffe Dr PR8 .....21 C4
Longcroft Cotts BL9 ...50 F1
Longfield Formby L37 ...12 B5
Fulwood PR2 ....117 F8
Higher Penwortham PR1 ..96 B4
Longfield Ave Coppull PR7 42 E2
Poulton-le-F FY6 .....153 D4
Longfield Ct BB18 ....196 B1
Longfield Dr LA5 ....221 C8
Longfield Manor PR7 ...43 A5
Longfield Pl FY6 .....153 D4
Longfield Terr BB10 ...107 E8
Longfold Maghull L31 ...5 E1
Mere Brow PR4 ....55 F2
Longford Ave FY2 ....152 E5
Longford Rd PR8 ......35 C4
Longhey WN8 ....18 C4
Longholme Rd 9 BB4 ...86 A2
Longhouse La FY6 ....131 D8
Longlands Ave LA3 ...212 E4
Longlands Cres LA3 ...212 F8
Longlands La LA3 ....212 E7
Longlands Rd LA1 ....218 C3
Longley Cl PR2 ......117 F8
Longley La PR3 ......160 B2
Longmeadow La
Heysham LA3 ....213 A7
Thornton FY5 ....176 C3
Longmeanygate
Leyland PR26 ....76 D2
Leyland,Midge Hall PR26 .76 A2
Longmere Cres LA5 ...221 C8
Longmire Way LA4 ....217 A5
Longmoor La PR3 .....180 E6
Longridge Ave FY4 ...110 E5
Longridge CE Prim Sch
PR3 ....140 A7
Longridge Community Hospl
PR3 ....140 A7
Longridge Cty Prim Sch
PR3 ....139 F8
Longridge Dr OL10 .....33 F2
Longridge Fell Forest Wlk
(E)★ BB7 ....164 F6
Longridge Fell Forest Wlk
(W)★ PR3 ....164 A4
Longridge Heath BB9 ..148 B3
Longridge High Sch
PR3 ....140 A4
Longridge Lodge 14
PR2 ....118 F4
Longridge Rd
Hesketh Lane PR3 ....162 D6
Hurst Green BB7,PR3 ..142 D8
Longridge PR3 ....162 B3
Red Scar PR2 ....119 B6
Longroyd Rd BB18 ....197 B1
Longsands Com Prim Sch
PR2 ....118 D5
Longsands La PR2 ....118 E6
Longshaw Ave WN5 ....10 E1
Longshaw Cl
Longshaw WN5 ....10 E1
Rufford L40 ....39 A5
Longshaw Comm WN5 ...10 E1
Longshaw Inf Sch BB2 ..81 E8
Longshaw Jun Sch BB2 101 E1
Longshaw La BB2 .....101 D2
Longshaw Old Rd WN5 ...10 E1
Longshaw St BB2 .....101 D1
Longsight Ave
Accrington,Hillock Vale
BB5 ....104 E8
Clitheroe BB7 ....189 F1
Longsight Rd
Langho BB6 ....143 B2
Langho BB6 ....143 D2
Osbaldeston BB1,BB2 ..121 E4
Ramsbottom BL0 ....50 D2
Longstock Hall CP Sch
Avondale Unit PR5 ....77 B8
Longstock Hall Moor Hey Sch
PR5 ....97 A1
Longton Ave FY5 .....176 B2
Longton Brickcroft Nature
Reserve★ PR4 ....74 F6
Longton Brickcroft Visitor
Ctr★ PR4 ....74 F7
Longton Bsns Pk PR4 ...74 E4
Longton By-Pass PR4 ...75 C6

Longton Cl BB1 102 C5
Longton Ct PR8 21 C5
Longton Dr Formby L37 12 A6
Morecambe LA4 217 E4
Longton Prim Sch PR4 75 A8
Longton Rd
Blackpool FY1 130 C5
Burnley BB12 127 E8
Longton St
Blackburn BB1 102 C5
Chorley PR6 43 E8
Longton's Cotts LA6 240 B1
Longtons La BD23 236 B3
Longway FY4 110 F8
Longwood Cl FY8 90 E4
Longworth Ave
Blackrod BL6 31 C3
Burnley BB10 128 D6
Coppull PR7 42 F2
Longworth Clough BL7 47 D2
Longworth La BL7 47 C2
Longworth Rd
Billington BB7 144 B4
Egerton BL7 47 B3
Horwich BL6 32 C4
Longworth Rd N BL7 46 D5
Longworth St
5 Bamber Bridge PR5 97 E2
Chorley PR7 43 B6
Preston PR1 118 C1
Lonmore PR5 97 D3
Lonsdale Ave
Fleetwood FY7 198 E3
Lancaster LA1 211 B7
Morecambe LA4 217 E4
Ormskirk L39 15 F7
Lonsdale Cl PR25 60 A6
Lonsdale Cres 3 FY7 198 E3
Lonsdale Dr PR26 58 C3
Lonsdale Gdns 4 BB9 170 D3
Lonsdale Gr LA4 217 E4
Lonsdale Mews 5 PR5 77 A8
Lonsdale Pl LA1 215 A5
Lonsdale Rd
Blackpool FY1 130 B2
Formby L37 11 F3
Hest Bank LA2 220 D1
Morecambe LA4 217 E4
Preston PR1 118 C1
Southport PR8 35 D4
Lonsdale St
Accrington BB5 103 F5
Burnley BB12 127 C7
Nelson BB9 170 F1
Lord Ave OL13 87 C1
Lord Nelson Wharf PR2 96 B8
Lord Sefton Way L37 12 E2
Lord Sq BB1 101 E5
Lord St Accrington BB5 104 B6
Bacup OL13 87 F2
Blackburn BB2 101 E5
Blackpool FY1 130 B6
Brierfield BB9 148 B5
Burscough Bridge L40 25 E5
Bury BL9 33 A2
Bury,Heap Bridge BL9 33 C1
Chorley PR6 43 D7
Clayton Green PR6 78 C1
Colne BB8 171 C5
Darwen BB3 82 A2
Eccleston PR7 41 C5
Fleetwood FY7 199 B4
Great Harwood BB6 124 C4
Horwich BL6 32 B4
Lancaster LA1 218 D1
Lytham St Anne's FY8 89 E7
Morecambe LA4 217 B6
Oswaldtwistle BB5 103 E4
Preston PR1 97 A8
Rawtenstall BB4 86 A2
Rawtenstall,Crawshawbooth BB4 86 A7
Rishton BB1 124 B1
Southport PR8,PR9 35 B7
Lord St W
12 Blackburn BB2 101 E5
Southport PR8 35 A6
Lord Street Mall 10 BB1 101 E5
Lord Street Prim Sch BL6 32 B4
Lord Street Sch BB8 171 C5
Lord's Ave PR5 77 B7
Lord's Close Rd LA2 239 E2
Lord's Cres BB3 82 A6
Lord's La Kingsfold PR1 96 E1
Longridge PR3 162 B2
Lord's Lot Rd
Capernwray LA6 240 D1
Over Kellet LA6 240 C1
Lord's Wlk PR1 97 A8
Lords Croft PR6 78 A2
Lordsgate Dr L40 25 E3
Lordsgate La L40 25 C2
Lordsome Rd LA3 216 E2
Lorne Rd FY2 152 D2
Lorne St Chorley PR7 43 C7
Darwen BB3 81 F2
Lytham St Anne's FY8 91 D4
Lorne Way OL10 33 F1
Lorraine Ave PR2 117 E3
Lorton Cl Burnley BB12 127 B8
Fulwood PR2 117 F6
Lostock Gdns FY4 110 E6
Lostock Hall Com High Sch PR5 97 C1
Lostock Hall Com Prim Sch PR5 97 B1
Lostock Hall Sta PR5 77 B8
Lostock La PR5 77 D7
Lostock Mdw PR6 78 A1
Lostock Rd PR26 58 C3
Lostock Sq PR5 77 B7
Lostock View PR5 77 B7
Lothersdale Cl BB10 148 D3
Lothian Ave FY7 198 D3
Lothian Pl FY2 152 E5
Lottice La BB5,BB1 103 A1
Lotus Dr FY4 112 A6
Loud Bridge Back La PR3 161 D8
Loud Bridge Rd PR3 161 D7
Loughlin Dr L33 1 A5
Loughrigg Cl BB12 127 B7
Loughrigg Terr FY4 131 C1
Louie Pollard Cres BB6 124 D6
Louis St BL0 68 D5
Louis William St BB1 82 D8
Louise St FY1 130 B3
Loupsfell Dr LA4 217 C4
Lourdes Ave PR5 97 A1
Louvain St BB18 196 A3
Lovat Rd PR1 117 F2
Love Clough Rd BB4 105 F2
Love La BL0 68 E1
Loveclough Pk BB4 106 A3
Lovely Hall La BB1 122 D7
Low Bank BB12 126 E6
Low Bentham Com Prim Sch LA2 239 B8
Low Bentham Rd LA2 239 C8
Low Croft PR3 137 B2
Low Fold BB18 195 A6
Low Gn PR25 76 F1
Low Hill BB3 65 A6
Low La Leck LA6 242 B7
Morecambe LA4 217 F5
Low Mill LA2 237 B3
Low Moor La BB18 196 B1
Low Moor Rd FY2 152 E3
Low Rd Halton LA2 219 E7
Heysham LA3 213 A2
Low St LA6 242 C3
Lowcroft
High Bentham LA2 239 E8
Skelmersdale WN8 18 C3
Lowcross Rd FY6 153 E2
Lowe View BB4 87 A1
Lowe's La WN8 17 F8
Lower Alt Rd L38 2 F4
Lower Antley St BB5 103 F5
Lower Ashworth Cl BB2 101 C4
Lower Audley Ind Est BB2 101 F3
Lower Audley St BB1, BB2 101 F4
Lower Bank Rd PR2 117 F3
Lower Bank St PR6 80 A1
Lower Barn St BB3 65 C7
Lower Barnes St BB5 124 E4
Lower Burgh Rd PR7 43 A4
Lower Burgh Way PR7 43 B4
Lower Carr La L37 4 B7
Lower Chapel La BB7 190 B8
Lower Clough St BB9 170 D2
Lower Clowes BB4 68 E8
Lower Clowes Rd BB4 68 E8
Lower Cockcroft 13 BB2 101 E5
Lower Copthurst La PR6 61 E7
Lower Cribden Ave BB4 85 D2
Lower Croft 1 PR1 96 D2
Lower Croft St 3 BB18 197 B2
Lower Cross St 26 BB3 82 A1
Lower Darwen Prim Sch BB3 82 A6
Lower East Ave BB18 196 B3
Lower Eccleshill Rd BB3 82 A5
Lower Field PR26 76 F6
Lower Gate Rd BB5 125 F2
Lower Gn
Poulton-le-F FY6 153 E3
3 Rochdale OL12 52 C1
Lower Greenfield PR2 117 B5
Lower Hazel Cl BB2 101 C4
Lower Hey PR4 95 A1
Lower Hill BB3 80 F2
Lower Hill Dr PR6 44 A1
Lower Hollin Bank St BB2 101 D2
Lower House Gn BB4 87 A8
Lower House Rd PR26 59 D8
Lower La Freckleton PR4 93 D7
Haslingden BB4 85 B4
Kirkham PR4 114 C1
Longridge PR3 140 B7
Lower Laithe Cotts BB9 170 C2
Lower Laithe Dr BB9 170 C3
Lower Lune St 7 FY7 199 B5
Lower Makinson Fold 2 BL6 32 D1
Lower Manor La BB12 147 F2
Lower Mdw BL7 48 D6
Lower Mead BL7 47 F1
Lower Mead Dr BB12 147 F2
Lower North Ave BB18 196 B2
Lower Park St BB18 196 C2
Lower Parrock Rd BB9 170 C1
Lower Philips Rd BB1 102 C8
Lower Prom
Southport PR8 35 A7
Southport PR8 35 B8
Lower Rd Longridge PR3 140 E7
Shuttleworth BL0 50 E8
Lower Ridge Cl BB10 128 B6
Lower Rook St BB18 196 C2
Lower Rosegrove La BB12 127 A5
Lower School St 6 BB8 171 D4
Lower Tentre BB11 128 B5
Lower Timber Hill La BB11 128 A2
Lower Waterside Farm Cotts BB3 82 E3
Lower West Ave BB18 196 B2
Lower Wilworth BB1 122 E1
Lower Wlk FY2 152 C7
Lowerfield BB6 123 C8
Lowerfields BB12 126 F6
Lowerfold BB6 124 C6
Lowerfold Cl OL12 52 C4
Lowerfold Cres OL12 52 C4
Lowerfold Dr OL12 52 C4
Lowerfold Rd BB6 124 C6
Lowerfold Way OL12 52 C4
Lowergate BB7 166 E8
Lowerhouse Cres BB12 127 A6
Lowerhouse Fold BB12 127 A6
Lowerhouse Jun Sch BB12 127 A6
Lowerhouse La
Burnley,Rose Grove BB12 127 B6
Padiham BB12 126 F6
Lowes Ct
3 Blackpool FY1 130 B1
5 Thornton FY5 176 B3
Lowes Gn L37 12 B3
Lowes Rd BL9 33 A6
Lowesby Cl PR5 97 E3
Loweswater Cl BB5 104 F8
Loweswater Cres BB12 127 B8
Loweswater Dr 5 LA4 217 D4
Lowesway Blackpool FY4 110 F8
6 Thornton FY5 176 B3
Lowfield Cl PR4 114 F2
Lowfield Rd FY4 110 F7
Lowgill La LA2 239 C3
Lowick Cl PR5 98 E4
Lowick Dr FY6 153 D1
Lowland Way FY2 152 F6
Lowlands Rd
Bolton-le-S LA5 221 A5
Morecambe LA4 217 C4
Lowndes St PR1 117 E2
Lowood Gr PR2 116 D1
Lowood Lodge 7 FY8 91 A3
Lowood Pl BB2 101 A6
Lowrey Terr FY1 130 B2
Lowry Cl PR5 77 A7
Lowry Hill La L40 26 B2
Lowstead Pl FY4 110 E6
Lowstern Cl BL7 47 E1
Lowther Ave
Blackpool FY2 152 B2
Maghull L31 5 F2
Morecambe LA3 217 E3
Lowther Cres PR26 76 D2
Lowther Ct Blackpool FY2 152 B2
5 Lytham St Anne's FY8 91 A3
Lowther Dr PR26 76 D3
Lowther La BB8 194 D1
Lowther Pl BB1 102 A8
Lowther Rd
Fleetwood FY7 198 F4
Lancaster LA1 218 F1
Lowther St Colne BB8 171 E6
Nelson BB9 148 C8
Preston PR2 117 C1
Lowther Terr
Appley Bridge WN6 19 C8
Lytham St Anne's FY8 91 A3
Lowthian St 25 PR1 96 F8
Lowthorpe Cres PR1 118 B2
Lowthorpe Pl PR1 118 B2
Lowthorpe Rd PR1 118 B2
Lowthwaite Dr BB9 148 E6
Lowton Rd FY8 90 A8
Loxham Gdns FY4 110 D6
Loxley Gdns BB12 126 F6
Loxley Gn PR2 118 C6
Loxley Pl FY5 152 E7
Loxley Pl E FY5 152 F7
Loxley Rd PR8 35 D4
Loxwood Cl PR5 97 A3
Loynd St
11 Great Harwood BB6 124 C5
Ramsbottom BL0 50 D6
Loyne Pk LA6 241 D7
Loyne Sch The LA1 218 B2
Lubbock St BB12 127 C6
Lucas Ave PR7 42 D8
Lucas La E PR6 61 C6
Lucas La W PR6 61 C5
Lucas St BL9 33 A3
Lucerne Cl PR2 118 C4
Lucerne Rd PR2 118 C4
Lucy St Barrowford BB9 170 D3
Lancaster LA1 214 F8
Morecambe LA4 217 B6
Ludlow WN8 18 C4
Ludlow Dr L39 15 D7
Ludlow Gr FY2 152 F2
Ludlow St WN6 29 D3
Luke St 17 OL13 70 C8
Lulworth WN8 18 C4
Lulworth Ave
Blackpool FY3 131 A3
Preston PR2 117 D2
Lulworth Lodge PR8 34 F5
Lulworth Pl PR5 97 D2
Lulworth Rd
Fulwood PR2 118 A4
Southport PR8 34 F5
Lumb Carr Ave BL0,BL8 50 A4
Lumb Carr Rd BL0,BL8 50 A4
Lumb Cotts BL0 68 B4
Lumb Holes La BB4 69 E7
Lumb La BB4 86 F4
Lumb Scar 9 OL13 87 F2
Lund St Blackburn BB2 101 C4
2 Preston PR1 97 A8
Lunds Cl L40 16 E4
Lunds La PR4 74 D1
Lune Ave L31 5 E2
Lune Cl PR4 114 C5
Lune Dr Clayton-le-W PR25 77 E2
Morecambe LA3 217 F3
Lune Gr FY1 130 C3
Lune Ho
5 Lancaster LA1 218 D1
Lancaster,Abraham Heights LA1 214 F7
Lune Ind Est LA1 214 C8
Lune Rd Fleetwood FY7 198 F4
Lancaster LA1 218 B1
Lune Sq LA1 218 D1
Lune St Colne BB8 171 E4
Lancaster LA1 218 D1
Longridge PR3 140 B8
Padiham BB12 126 D8
Preston PR1 96 F7
Lune Terr LA1 218 D1
Lune Valley LA1 218 F4
Lune View FY6 199 E6
Lune View Cvn Pk LA2 219 C6
Lunedale Ave FY1 130 C1
Lunesdale Cl FY8 90 C7
Lunesdale Ct
Butt Yeats LA2 238 B6
Lancaster LA1 218 F1
Lunesdale Dr PR3 207 B3
Lunesdale Rd 2 PR4 114 A5
Lunesdale Terr LA2 237 E4
Lunesdale View LA2 219 D7
Luneside LA1 214 C8
Lunt La L29 4 D1
Lunt Rd L29 4 C1
Lupin Cl Accrington BB5 104 A7
Lucas Green PR6 61 B5
Lupin Rd BB5 104 B7
Lupton Dr BB9 170 D4
Lupton Pl LA1 218 B3
Lupton St PR7 43 C6
Lutner St BB11 128 A5
Luton Rd Cleveleys FY5 175 E1
Preston PR2 116 F2
Lutwidge Ave PR1 118 C1
Lyceum Ave 3 FY3 130 D4
Lychfield Dr PR5 77 E7
Lychgate 21 PR1 97 A8
Lydd Gr PR7 43 A7
Lyddesdale Ave FY5 152 D8
Lydgate Brierfield BB10 148 E2
Chorley PR7 43 A5
Lydia St BB5 104 B4
Lydiate La
Bilsborrow PR3 159 C6
Leyland PR25 77 C4
Newtown PR7 59 B1
Lydiate Lane End PR7 59 B2
Lydiate Prim Sch L31 5 C4
Lydiate Station Rd L31 4 E5
Lydric Ave PR5 98 E2
Lyelake La L40 16 F2
Lymbridge Dr BL6 31 D1
Lyme Gr FY6 199 E5
Lymm Ave LA1 218 A3
Lyncroft Cres FY3 130 E7
Lyndale WN8 18 B4
Lyndale Ave
Bamber Bridge PR5 97 C2
Haslingden BB4 85 B2
Wilpshire BB1 123 A7
Lyndale Cl Leyland PR25 60 B6
Rawtenstall BB4 86 A7
Wilpshire BB1 123 A7
Lyndale Ct FY7 199 B5
Lyndale Cvn Site FY4 111 F6
Lyndale Gr PR5 97 C2
Lyndale Rd BB11 126 C3
Lyndale Terr BB7 231 B3
Lynden Ave LA4 217 E5
Lyndeth Cl PR2 118 E6
Lyndhurst Maghull L31 5 D1
Skelmersdale WN8 18 B4
Lyndhurst Ave
Blackburn BB1 102 E5
Blackpool FY4 130 D1
Lyndhurst Dr PR2 116 E2
Lyndhurst Gr BB6 124 E6
Lyndhurst Rd
Blackburn BB2 101 E2
Burnley BB10 128 C5
Darwen BB3 81 F3
Southport PR8 35 B2
Lyndon Ave BB6 124 E6
Lyndon Ct BB6 124 E6
Lyndon Ho BB6 124 E6
Lynfield Rd BB6 124 E6
Lynn Gr 6 FY1 130 B7
Lynn Pl PR2 118 D2
Lynslack Terr LA5 224 B8
Lynthorpe Rd
Blackburn BB2 101 E2
Nelson BB9 171 A1
Lynton Ave
Blackpool FY4 110 D8
Leyland PR25 60 C8
Lynton Ct FY7 175 C8
Lynton Dr PR8 34 E1
Lynton Rd Accrington BB5 103 F4
Lynton Rd *continued*
Southport PR8 34 E1
Lynwood Ave
Blackpool FY3 130 E8
Clayton-le-M BB5 124 F4
Darwen BB3 81 E4
Grimsargh PR2 139 C2
Ormskirk L39 15 C3
Lynwood Cl
Clayton-le-M BB5 124 F4
Colne BB8 171 D7
Darwen BB3 81 E3
Skelmersdale WN8 9 D7
Whalley BB7 144 A7
Lynwood Dr FY6 177 C7
Lynwood End L39 15 C3
Lynwood Rd
Blackburn BB2 101 B6
Huncoat BB5 125 E2
Lyons La PR6 43 D7
Lyons La S PR7 43 D7
Lyons Rd PR8 35 A5
Lystra Ct FY8 89 F5
Lyth Rd LA1 218 F2
Lythall Ave FY8 91 D4
Lytham CE Prim Sch FY8 91 B4
Lytham Cl Fulwood PR2 117 D3
Lancaster LA1 215 C7
Lytham Ct PR7 60 D4
Lytham Hall★ FY8 90 F4
Lytham Hall Park Prim Sch FY8 90 F3
Lytham Heritage Ctr★ FY8 91 B3
Lytham Lifeboat Mus★ FY8 91 C2
Lytham Rd Blackburn BB2 101 F1
Blackpool FY1,FY4 110 C6
Brierfield BB10 148 C2
Freckleton PR4 93 B6
Fulwood PR2 117 D3
Saltcotes,Moss Side FY8 112 E1
Southport PR9 54 A4
Warton FY8,PR4 92 D5
Lytham St Chorley PR6 43 E7
Rochdale OL12 52 E3
Lytham St Anne's High Tech Coll FY8 90 C5
Lytham St Anne's Local Nature Reserve★ FY8 110 B1
Lytham St Annes Way FY8 90 D7
Lytham Sta FY8 91 A3
Lytham Windmill (Mus)★ FY8 91 C2
Lythcoe Ave PR2 117 C4
Lythe Fell Ave LA2 219 D7
Lythe Fell Rd LA2 234 F8
Lythe La LA2 239 E2
Lytles Cl L37 12 A2
Lytton St BB12 126 F7

M

Maaruig Cvn Pk FY6 200 A6
Mabel Ct FY4 110 B8
Mabel St Colne BB8 171 F5
2 Rochdale OL12 52 D2
Maberry Cl WN6 19 D7
Macaulay St BB11 127 C5
Macauley Ave FY4 110 F8
Macbeth Rd FY7 198 E4
Mackay Croft 4 PR6 43 D8
Mackenzie Cl 5 PR6 43 D8
Maclaren Cl FY3 131 D5
Macleod St BB9 148 D8
Maddy St 2 PR1 96 D8
Madeley Gdns OL12 52 C1
Maden Rd OL13 87 F2
Maden St BB5 103 E6
Maden Way OL13 87 F2
Madison Ave
Blackpool FY2 152 B5
Hest Bank LA5 220 E2
Madryn Ave L33 1 A2
Maesbrook Cl PR9 55 B5
Mafeking Ave BL9 33 A5
Mafeking Rd PR2 117 C2
Magdalen Ave FY5 175 D1
Maggots Nook Rd WA11 9 A1
Maghull Homes The L31 5 B1
Maghull La L31 6 B1
Maghull Smallholdings Est L31 5 F3
Magnolia Cl PR2 118 C6
Magnolia Dr PR25 77 E2
Magnolia Rd PR1 96 B3
Magpie Cl BB11 127 C5
Maharishi School of the Age of Enlightenment L40 18 A5
Maida Vale FY5 152 D8
Maiden Cl Rawtenstall BB4 69 F8
Skelmersdale WN8 17 C2
Maiden St BB4 85 B6
Main Ave LA3 212 F3
Main Cl LA3 209 D8
Main Dr FY6 153 E2
Main Rd Bolton-le-S LA5 221 B5
Galgate LA2 211 A3
Hest Bank LA2 220 F1
Nether Kellet LA6 221 F5
Main Sprit Weind PR1 97 A7
Main St Bolton-by-B BB7 230 D4
Burton-in-K LA6 240 B7

Main St continued
Cockerham LA2 ....206 D4
Downham BB7 ....191 B5
Gisburn BB7 ....231 C3
Grindleton BB7 ....190 B8
Heysham LA3 ....212 E8
High Bentham LA2 ......239 D8
Hornby LA2 ....238 B7
Kelbrook BB18 ....195 A6
Lancaster LA1 ....218 D2
Low Bentham LA2 ......239 B8
Overton LA3 ....209 D8
Rathmell BD24 ....236 F6
Warton LA5 ....223 D5
Whittington LA6 ....241 D7
Wray LA2 ....238 D6
Mains La
Bispham Green L40 ....27 A6
Poulton-le-F FY6 ......154 B4
Mainway LA1 ....218 D2
Mairscough La L39 .....14 B5
Maitland Ave FY5 .....175 D1
Maitland Cl 5 PR1 .....97 C8
Maitland Pl BB4 ....86 A1
Maitland St
18 Bacup OL13 ....87 F2
4 Preston PR1 ....97 C8
1 Preston PR1 ....97 C8
Majestic Bldgs 24 BB18 .196 B5
Majestic Mews WN5 .....10 D5
Major St Accrington BB5 .104 B4
Ramsbottom BL0 ....50 B6
Rawtenstall BB4 ....86 A7
Makinson Ave BL6 ....32 E1
Makinson La BL6 ....32 F4
Makinsons Row 11 LA2 .211 B4
Malcolm Pl FY7 ....198 E4
Malcolm St PR1 ....118 D1
Malden St PR25 ....77 A1
Maldern Ave FY6 ......153 C5
Maldon Pl PR2 ....118 D2
Malham Ave
5 Accrington BB5 ......103 F4
Blackpool FY4 ....110 D8
Malham Cl Lancaster LA1 218 B3
Southport PR8 ....35 E3
Malham Gdns BB1 .....101 F3
Malham Pl PR2 ....118 E4
Malham Rd BB10 ......148 D3
Malham View Cl BB18 ..196 A1
Malham Wend BB9 .....170 C3
Malkin Cl BB9 ....170 E8
Malkin La BB7 ....165 F6
Mall The Burnley BB11 ..128 A6
Fulwood PR2 ....118 E2
Lytham St Anne's FY8 ....90 C7
Mallard Cl Heysham LA3 .212 F4
Leyland PR25 ....59 D8
Ormskirk L39 ....15 C2
Thornton FY5 ....176 A4
Mallard Ct Blackpool FY3 131 B6
Lancaster LA1 ....214 E8
Mallard Dr BL6 ....32 A3
Mallard Ho L31 ....5 B4
Mallard Pl BB5 ....103 D3
Mallards The PR9 ......54 C3
Mallards Wlk PR5 ......78 A5
Mallee Ave PR9 ....54 A3
Mallee Cres PR9 ....54 A3
Malley La PR4 ....136 C8
Mallom Ave PR7 ....60 E1
Mallory Ave L31 ....5 B4
Mallow Wlk LA3 ....217 B2
Mallowdale FY5 ....176 A4
Mallowdale Ave LA3 ....213 A8
Mallowdale Rd LA1 ....218 B2
Malt Kiln Brow PR3 ....185 E4
Malt Kiln Gr PR3 ......156 A5
Malt St BB5 ....104 B7
Maltby Pl 2 FY4 ....130 F2
Malthouse Bsns Ctr L39 .15 C6
Malthouse Ct
Ormskirk L39 ....15 E6
3 Preston PR2 ....117 D1
Malthouse The 4 PR2 ..117 D1
Malthouse Way PR1 .....96 D3
Maltings The Longton PR4 .74 F8
Middleworth Green PR1 ...96 D4
Thornton FY5 ....176 A4
Whittington LA6 ......241 D7
Maltkiln La
Bispham Green L40,WN8 ..27 C2
Ormskirk L39 ....6 E8
Malton Dr PR5 ....77 A7
Malvern Ave
Blackburn BB2 ....101 D1
Blackpool FY1 ....130 D2
Lancaster LA1 ....215 A6
Oswaldtwistle BB5 ....103 C4
Padiham BB12 ....126 D6
Preston PR1 ....97 B6
Stalmine FY6 ....177 C7
Malvern Cl
6 Accrington BB5 .....104 A7
Bamber Bridge PR5 .....77 C8
Horwich BL6 ....32 C4
Malvern Ct
6 Nelson BB9 ....148 F8
Southport PR8 ....35 A6
Malvern Gdns PR8 ......35 A6
Malvern Rd
Lytham St Anne's FY8 ....90 D5
Nelson BB9 ....171 A1
Preston PR1 ....97 B6
Malvern St Preston PR1 ..97 B5

Malvern St continued
Standish WN6 ....29 D3
Malvern Way BB4 ....68 A7
Manby Cl PR5 ....98 E3
Manchester Mill Ind Est
PR1 ....97 C8
Manchester Rd
Accrington BB5 ....104 D3
Barnoldswick BB18 ....196 B1
Blackpool FY3 ....130 D6
Blackrod BL6 ....31 E1
Burnley BB10 ....127 E3
Clow Bridge BB11 .....106 D6
Hapton BB11,BB12 ....126 C4
Haslingden BB4 ....85 B2
Haslingden,Ewood Bridge
BB4 ....68 D7
Nelson BB9 ....148 D7
Preston PR1 ....97 B7
Ramsbottom BL0,BL9 ....50 E4
Southport PR9 ....35 C7
Mancknols St BB9 .....149 A7
Mancknols Walton Cottage
Homes BB9 ....149 B8
Mandela Ct BB1 ......101 E6
Mandeville Rd PR8 ......21 B5
Mandeville Terr BL8 .....49 E2
Manfield WN8 ....18 A3
Mangholes BB4 ....85 B7
Manion Ave L31 ....5 B5
Manion Cl L31 ....5 B5
Manitoba Cl BB2 ......101 B8
Manley Cl BL9 ....50 C2
Manner Sutton St BB1 .101 F5
Manning Rd
4 Preston PR1 ....118 E1
Southport PR8 ....35 E6
Manor Burscough L40 ....25 D2
Fulwood PR2 ....118 B4
Higher Penwortham PR1 ..96 B4
Ribchester PR3 ....141 D3
Slyne LA2 ....218 C8
Manor Brook 1 BB5 ...104 C6
Manor Cl Burton in L LA6 242 C3
Coupe Green PR5 ......98 F3
Slyne LA2 ....218 C8
Manor Cres
Burscough L40 ....25 D2
Slyne LA2 ....218 D8
Manor Ct
11 Blackpool FY1 .....130 C7
3 Blackpool,Hawes Side
FY4 ....130 E1
Caton LA2 ....237 D4
Fulwood PR2 ....117 B7
4 Southport PR9 ......54 A2
Manor Ctyd LA3 ......212 E8
Manor Dr Burscough L40 ..25 D2
Cleveleys FY5 ....175 D3
Kirkham PR4 ....114 C4
Slyne LA2 ....218 C8
Manor Farm LA6 ......241 D7
Manor Fields BB7 .....144 C5
Manor Gdns L40 ....25 D2
Manor Gr
Higher Penwortham PR1 ..96 A4
Morecambe LA4 ....216 F2
Skelmersdale WN8 ......17 F1
Manor House Cl
Leyland PR26 ....59 B8
Maghull L31 ....5 C1
Manor House Cotts BB3 .65 E8
Manor House Cres PR1 .118 B3
Manor House Dr WN8 ....9 E3
Manor House Park Flats
FY5 ....175 D4
Manor La Hest Bank LA2 .220 F1
Higher Penwortham PR1 ..96 B4
Manor Lodge L37 ....11 E4
Manor Mews FY6 ......153 E4
Manor Pk PR2 ....118 C4
Manor Pl BB5 ....103 F7
Manor Rd Blackburn BB2 .101 B5
Blackpool FY1 ....130 D4
Burnley BB12 ....127 B7
Burscough L40 ....25 D2
Clayton Green PR6 .....78 B3
Clitheroe BB7 ....166 D7
Colne BB8 ....171 E7
Darwen BB3 ....64 F8
Fleetwood FY7 ....198 E4
Garstang PR3 ....204 C1
Horwich BL6 ....32 D4
Inskip PR4 ....135 C8
Shevington WN6 ....19 F6
Slyne LA2 ....218 D8
Southport PR9 ....54 A2
Whalley BB7 ....144 C5
Wrea Green PR4 ......113 B4
Manor St Accrington BB5 .104 D7
Bacup OL13 ....87 F1
Bury BL9 ....33 A2
Nelson BB9 ....148 F8
Ramsbottom BL0 ....50 B7
Manor Way Coppull PR7 ..29 D8
Wrea Green PR4 ......113 B3
Manor Wood
Fleetwood FY7 ....198 E4
Kirkham PR4 ....114 B7
Manorcroft PR4 ....74 F8
Manse Ave WN6 ....28 F5
Mansell Way BL6 ....32 D1
Mansergh St BB10 .....148 C2
Mansfield Ave BL6 ....32 D1
Mansfield Cres BB9 ....148 C6
Mansfield Dr PR5 ....98 E3
Mansfield Gr BB9 .....148 B6

Mansfield High Sch
BB9 ....148 B6
Mansfield Rd FY3 ......130 D8
Mansion House Bldgs 2
BB4 ....86 A7
Mansion St S BB5 ......104 D6
Manston Gr PR7 ....43 A7
Manx Jane's La PR9 ....54 A4
Manxman Rd BB2 ......101 F1
Many Brooks Ho PR5 ...98 E1
Maple Ave Blackpool FY3 130 D5
Brinscall PR6 ....62 F7
Burscough L40 ....25 E4
7 Bury BL9 ....33 B2
6 Clitheroe BB7 .....166 D7
Fleetwood FY7 ....175 F8
Haslingden BB4 ....85 C3
Horwich BL6 ....32 E1
Morecambe LA3 ....216 E2
Thornton FY5 ....153 C8
Maple Bank BB10 ......128 C2
Maple Cl Formby L37 ....11 C1
Newton-w-S PR4 ......114 F2
Whalley BB7 ....144 D6
Wilpshire BB1 ....122 E6
Maple Cres
8 Preston PR1 ....96 E7
Rishton BB1 ....103 B8
Maple Ct
Clayton-le-W PR25 .....77 D3
Garstang PR3 ....204 C1
Maple Dr
Bamber Bridge PR5 .....97 F1
Oswaldtwistle BB5 ....103 F3
Poulton-le-F FY6 .....153 E2
Maple Gr Chorley PR6 ...61 D3
Fulwood PR2 ....119 A4
Grimsargh PR2 ....139 D1
Higher Penwortham PR1 ..96 B4
Lancaster LA1 ....214 D8
Ramsbottom BL0 ....50 D6
Warton PR4 ....92 D6
Maple Rd PR3 ....204 C1
Maple St Blackburn BB1 .102 A7
Clayton-le-M BB5 .....124 F1
Great Harwood BB6 ...124 D6
3 Rishton BB1 ....124 B1
Southport PR8 ....35 E6
Maplebank 3 PR2 .....116 C1
Maples The PR26 ....58 F6
Maplewood
Skelmersdale WN8 ......18 A4
Southport PR9 ....53 F2
Maplewood Ave FY6 ...200 A5
Maplewood Cl
Chorley PR7 ....43 C6
Leyland PR25 ....59 E8
Lytham St Anne's FY8 ...90 F4
Maplewood Gdns LA1 ..215 A2
Marabou Dr BB3 ....81 E3
Marathon Pl PR26 ......76 C3
Marble Ave 5 FY5 .....152 F7
Marble Ct BB5 ....103 E4
Marble Pl PR8 ....35 B7
Marble Pl Sh Ctr PR8 ...35 B7
Marble St BB5 ....103 E4
March St BB12 ....127 F8
Marchbank Rd WN8 .....17 D1
Marchwood Rd FY3 ....131 B8
Marcroft Ave FY4 ......110 E7
Mardale Ave
Blackpool FY4 ....131 C1
Morecambe LA4 ....217 D5
Mardale Cl PR8 ....21 B4
Mardale Cres PR25 .....60 B7
Mardale Rd
1 Lancaster LA1 .....218 E1
Longridge PR3 ....139 F5
Preston PR1 ....119 A1
Maresfield Rd PR1 ......96 E5
Margaret Rd PR1 ....96 E4
Margaret St
Blackburn BB1 ....102 D4
Oswaldtwistle BB5 ....103 C2
1 Preston PR1 ....97 A8
Rawtenstall BB4 ....85 F4
Margate Ave FY4 ......110 E6
Margate Rd Fulwood PR2 117 A4
Lytham St Anne's FY8 ...89 F8
Maria Ct 9 BB11 ......128 A4
Maria Sq BL7 ....46 D4
Maria St BB3 ....65 B6
Marians St L39 ....15 E7
Maricourt Ave BB1 ....102 D5
Marilyn Ave 4 PR5 .....77 B8
Marina Ave
2 Blackpool FY1 .....130 D2
Poulton-le-F FY3 .....131 D8
Marina Cl PR5 ....97 A1
Marina Dr
Bamber Bridge PR5 .....97 A1
Fulwood PR2 ....117 E7
Marina Gr PR5 ....97 A1
Marina Mews FY7 .....199 B3
Marina Rd L37 ....11 F1
Marine Ave BB11 ......127 C4
Marine Cl LA3 ....216 E4
Marine Dr Hest Bank LA2 220 D1
Lytham St Anne's FY8 ...90 D3
Southport PR8 ....34 E7
Southport,Marshside PR8,
PR9 ....53 D4
Marine Gate Mans PR9 .35 B8
Marine Ind Ctr FY8 .....91 D4
Marine Par
Fleetwood FY7 ....198 C1
Southport PR8 ....35 A8

Marine Rd E LA4 ....217 C6
Marine Rd W LA3,LA4 ..216 F4
Marine Road Central
LA4 ....217 A5
Mariners Cl FY7 ....198 E1
Mariners Way PR2 ......96 B8
Marino Cl FY3 ....153 D8
Maritime Ct PR8 ....35 B7
Maritime St FY7 ......198 F2
Maritime Way PR1 ......95 F7
Mark Cl PR1 ....96 F1
Mark Rd L38 ....2 F4
Mark Sq PR4 ....57 A6
7 Bury BL9 ....33 B2
6 Clitheroe BB7 .....166 D7
Burnley BB10 ....148 B1
Mark's Ave PR26 ....76 E5
Markazul Uloom Sch
BB2 ....101 F2
Market Ave 2 BB1 .....101 E5
Market Chambers BL0 ...50 C7
Market Cross 5 L39 ....15 E5
Market Ho PR7 ....31 A6
Market Pl Adlington PR7 ..31 A7
12 Chorley PR7 ....43 C8
3 Clitheroe BB7 .....166 D7
10 Colne BB8 ....171 E5
Edenfield BL0 ....68 D3
Garstang PR3 ....181 C7
Longridge PR3 ....140 B7
4 Poulton-le-F FY6 ..153 D3
Ramsbottom BL0 ....50 C7
Standish WN6 ....29 E1
Market Sq Burnley BB11 .128 A6
4 Kirkham PR4 ......114 B5
10 Lancaster LA1 ....214 F8
Lytham St Anne's FY8 ...91 A3
Nelson BB9 ....148 D8
Market St Adlington PR7 ..31 A6
Bacup OL13 ....87 F2
7 Barnoldswick BB18 .196 B2
Blackpool FY1 ....130 B5
Carnforth LA5 ....223 D2
Chorley PR7 ....43 C7
Church BB5 ....103 E5
Colne BB8 ....171 E5
Darwen BB3 ....82 A1
Edenfield BL0 ....68 D4
Hambleton FY6 ....177 C2
Kirkham PR4 ....113 F6
Lancaster LA1 ....214 F8
Millgate OL12,OL13 ....71 D4
Morecambe LA4 ....217 A5
9 Nelson BB9 ....148 D8
Preston PR1 ....96 F8
5 Rawtenstall BB4 ....69 F8
Southport PR8 ....35 B7
Standish WN6 ....29 E1
Whitworth OL12 ....52 C6
Market St W PR1 ....96 F8
Market Street La 7
BB2 ....101 E4
Market Way
1 Blackburn BB1 .....101 E5
6 Ormskirk L39 ......15 E5
Marketgate 28 LA1 ....214 F8
Markham Dr PR8 ....35 E2
Markham Rd BB2 ......101 B3
Markham St PR2 ......117 C1
Markland St
3 Preston PR1 ....96 E7
6 Ramsbottom BL0 ....50 C7
Marklands Rd BL6 ......32 E5
Markross St BB4 ....86 A2
Marl Ave PR1 ....96 B4
Marl Cop PR26 ....58 A6
Marl Croft PR1 ....96 D2
Marl Gr WN5 ....10 D4
Marl Hill Cres PR2 ....119 A2
Marl Pits BB4 ....86 B3
Marl Rd L33 ....1 C3
Marland WN8 ....18 A4
Marlborough Rd FY3 ...130 C4
Marlborough WN8 ......18 A4
Marlboro Rd FY3 ......130 C4
Marlborough Ave
Cleveleys FY5 ....175 D5
Maghull L31 ....5 D3
Warton PR4 ....92 D6
Marlborough Cl
Ramsbottom BL0 ....50 C3
Whitworth OL12 ....52 C7
Marlborough Ct WN8 ...18 A4
Marlborough Dr
Bamber Bridge PR5 .....97 D3
Fulwood PR2 ....117 D7
Marlborough Gdns 5
PR9 ....35 C8
Marlborough Rd
Accrington BB5 ....104 C7
Lytham St Anne's FY8 ..110 E1
Morecambe LA3 ....216 E3
Southport PR9 ....35 C7
Marlborough St
Burnley BB11 ....128 A4
Chorley PR6 ....61 C1
14 Rochdale OL12 .....52 C1
Marled Hey BL7 ....48 D5
Marles Ct BB10 ....128 B8
Marlfield PR4 ....74 F4
Marlfield Rd PR2 ......116 F5
Marlhill Rd FY3 ....131 B8
Marlin St 7 BB9 ......170 F2
Marlow Ct PR7 ....30 F6
Marlowe Ave
Accrington BB5 ....104 E2
Padiham BB12 ....126 F7
Marlowe Cres BB6 .....124 B4
Marlton Rd BB2 ....101 D1

Marlton Way LA1 ......214 E8
Marmaduke Cotts LA6 ..241 D4
Marple Cl BB4 ....29 B2
Marquis Cl BB3 ....81 F7
Marquis Dr PR4 ....93 C7
Marquis St PR4 ....113 F5
Marron Cl PR25 ....59 E8
Mars St BL7 ....48 E6
Marsden Com Prim Sch
BB9 ....148 D7
Marsden Cres BB9 .....149 A8
Marsden Cl BB10 ......148 C3
Marsden Dr BB9 ......148 D6
Marsden Gr BB9 ......148 C5
Marsden Hall Rd BB9 ..149 A8
Marsden Hall Rd N BB9 .171 B1
Marsden Hall Road S
BB9 ....149 A8
Marsden Height Cl BB9 148 F5
Marsden Mall 5 BB9 ..148 E8
Marsden Pl BB9 ......149 A8
Marsden Rd
Blackpool FY4 ....110 D8
Brierfield BB10 ......148 C3
Southport PR9 ....35 E7
Marsden Sq BB4 ....85 B4
Marsden St
Accrington BB5 ....104 B4
Blackburn BB2 ....101 B2
6 Haslingden BB4 ....85 A3
Kirkham PR4 ....114 B5
Marset Cl OL12 ....52 A1
Marsett Pl PR2 ....118 E5
Marsh Brows L37 ....11 E2
Marsh Cl LA2 ....206 B4
Marsh Cres LA4 ....217 F4
Marsh Ct 2 FY5 ......176 A2
Marsh Dr PR4 ....93 D7
Marsh Gate BB3 ....82 D1
Marsh Gates PR4 ....93 D7
Marsh Hos LA2 ....206 B4
Marsh House La BB3 ....82 C1
Marsh La Brindle PR6 ...79 B5
Cockerham LA2 ....206 B4
Glasson LA2 ....209 D3
Hambleton FY6 ....177 C1
Ince Blundell L37,L38 ...3 E6
Longton PR4 ....74 D8
Ormskirk L40 ....24 D1
Preston PR1 ....96 E7
5 Preston PR1 ....96 F8
Withnell Fold PR6 .....79 A4
Marsh Mill Thornton FY5 .176 B2
* Thornton FY5 ......176 B2
Marsh Moss La L40 .....25 C7
Marsh Rd Banks PR9 ....72 D1
Hesketh Bank PR4 .....73 F4
Thornton FY5 ....176 B2
Marsh St Blackburn BB1 .101 E6
Horwich BL6 ....32 A4
4 Lancaster LA1 .....218 B1
Marsh Terr BB3 ....82 A2
Marsh View PR4 ....114 F2
Marsh Way Clitheroe BB7 189 F2
Kingsfold PR1 ....96 C2
Marshall Ave BB5 .....125 C4
Marshall Gr PR2 ......117 A4
Marshall's Brow PR1 ....96 E3
Marshall's Cl Maghull L31 .5 C4
5 Middleworth Green PR1 .96 E4
Marshallsay L37 ....12 A2
Marsham Ct PR3 ......181 D6
Marsham Gr BB3 ....82 C1
Marshaw Pl PR3 ......181 A6
Marshaw Rd LA1 ......218 B2
Marshdale Rd FY4 .....110 F7
Marshes La The PR4 ....38 A8
Marshside Nature Reserve ★
PR9 ....53 E5
Marshside Prim Sch PR9 54 A5
Marshside Rd PR9 ......53 F4
Marston Cl PR2 ....117 C7
Marston Cres L38 ....3 A2
Marston Moor PR2 ....117 C7
Mart La L40 ....25 E5
Martholme Ave BB5 ...125 A3
Martholme Cl BB6 .....124 D6
Martholme La BB6 .....124 F8
Martin Ave FY8 ....110 C4
Martin Croft Rd BB4 ....85 A5
Martin Dr BB3 ....65 C6
Martin Field Rd PR1 ....96 C3
Martin La
Drummersdale L40 .....24 E6
Rochdale OL12 ....52 B1
Martin Mere ★ L40 .....38 B1
Martin St Burnley BB10 .148 B1
Bury BL9 ....33 D3
Turton Bottoms BL7 ....48 D4
Martin Top La BB7 ....192 C7
Martindale Cl BB1 .....102 C2
Martindales The PR6 ....78 B3
Martinfield PR2 ....117 F8
Martinfields BB10 .....148 C4
Martinique Dr BB3 ......81 F6
Martins Ave PR7 ....43 C7
Martins La WN8 ....9 D7
Martland Ave WN6 ......19 F5
Marton Dr Blackpool FY4 110 D8
Burnley BB11 ....127 E3
Morecambe LA4 ......217 F6
Marton Fold FY4 ......111 A4
Marton Mere Cvn Pk
FY3,FY4 ....131 C2
Marton Pl LA4 ....217 F6
Marton Prim Sch FY4 ..110 F7
Marton Rd PR2 ....95 F8

Marton St 4 LA1 ....214 F7
Marton View FY3 ....130 E4
Marton Wlk 4 BB3 ....65 B6
Marwick Cl WN6 ....29 D2
Mary Ave PR8 ....21 E6
Mary Brown Cotts BB7 .190 C8
Mary St Blackburn BB1 ..102 A4
  5 Burnley BB10 ....128 B5
  Carnforth LA5 ....223 D3
  Colne BB8 ....171 C4
  Lancaster LA1 ....214 F8
  Ramsbottom BL0 ....50 B5
  Rishton BB1 ....124 B1
Mary St E BL6 ....32 B4
Mary St W Horwich BL6 ..32 A4
  Longridge PR3 ....140 A8
Mary Towneley Fold
  BB10 ....128 C4
Marybank Cl PR2 ....118 C5
Maryland Cl LA5 ....224 D2
Masefield Ave
  Padiham BB12 ....126 E7
  Thornton FY5 ....176 A3
Masefield Cl
  Brockhall Village BB6 .143 B5
  Great Harwood BB6 ..124 B4
Masefield Pl PR5 ....97 D2
Mason Cl PR4 ....93 C6
Mason Hill View PR2 ..118 A4
Mason House Cres PR2 117 A5
Mason Row BL7 ....47 E2
Mason St
  7 Accrington BB5 ....104 C6
  Bury BL9 ....33 A2
  Chorley PR6 ....61 E2
  Colne BB8 ....171 D5
  Egerton BL7 ....47 E1
  Horwich BL6 ....32 B3
  Oswaldtwistle BB5 ....103 D3
Masonfield PR5 ....78 B5
Masonfield Cres LA1 ..215 D7
Masongill Fell La LA6 ..242 E7
Masons Ct 1 FY7 ....198 E3
Masons Way 8 BB18 ..196 B3
Masonwood PR2 ....118 A6
Massam's La L37 ....11 F6
Massey Croft OL12 ....52 C8
Massey La BB9 ....148 A5
Massey St Brierfield BB9 .148 A4
  Burnley BB11 ....128 A6
  Bury BL9 ....33 B3
Masterson Ave BB12 ..145 D2
Matcham Ct 11 FY1 ..130 B5
Matchmoor La BL6 ....32 F4
Mather Ave BB5 ....104 B8
Mather St FY3 ....130 D7
Mathias Ct LA4 ....217 B6
Matlock Ave PR8 ....35 B4
Matlock Cl PR8 ....35 B4
Matlock Cres PR8 ....35 B4
Matlock Gr BB10 ....148 C2
Matlock Pl PR2 ....117 A5
Matlock Rd PR8 ....35 B4
Matlock St 13 BB3 ....81 F2
Matrix Pk PR7 ....60 D7
Matterdale Rd PR25 ....60 B7
Matthew St BB8 ....171 E4
Matthew St BB2 ....101 B2
Matthews Ct FY4 ....110 D7
Matthias St LA4 ....217 B6
Mattock Cres LA4 ....217 F5
Maud St Barrowford BB9 .170 D2
  Chorley PR7 ....43 B6
Maudland Bank PR1 ....96 E8
Maudland Rd
  Blackburn FY1 ....130 C2
  Preston PR1 ....96 E8
Maudsley St
  Accrington BB5 ....104 C6
  Blackburn BB1 ....101 F5
Maureen Ave 3 PR5 ....77 B8
Maurice Gr FY2 ....152 E1
Maurice St BB9 ....148 D8
Mavis Dr PR7 ....42 E2
Mavis Rd BB2 ....101 A5
Mawdesley St Peter's CE
  Prim Sch L40 ....40 C3
Mawdsley Cl L37 ....12 B3
Mawdsley Terr L39 ....15 F7
Maxwell Gr FY2 ....152 E2
Maxwell St BL9 ....33 B3
May Bell Ave FY5 ....175 E4
May La Bilsborrow PR3 ..159 C8
  Claughton PR3 ....182 E1
May St Barrowford BB9 .170 D2
  Blackburn BB1 ....102 A4
  Edgworth BL7 ....48 E6
  Nelson BB9 ....170 F2
May Terr BB7 ....144 A4
Maybank Cl PR9 ....54 A1
Maybury Ave BB12 ....127 B5
Maybury 21 BL0 ....50 B5
Maycroft Ave FY6 ....153 B5
Mayfair BL6 ....32 D3
Mayfair Cl Haslingden BB4 68 A7
  Hightown L38 ....2 F2
  Lytham St Anne's FY8 ..90 D6
Mayfair Cres BB1 ....122 F5
Mayfair Ct PR9 ....53 D1
Mayfair Dr FY5 ....153 C8
Mayfair Gdns 5 FY5 ..176 C1
Mayfair Rd Blackpool FY1 130 E2
  Burnley BB10 ....128 E5
  Nelson BB9 ....171 A1
Mayfayre Ave L31 ....5 B5
Mayfield Darwen BB3 ....65 B7
  Woodsfold PR4 ....135 E4

Mayfield Ave
  Adlington PR6 ....31 A7
  Bamber Bridge PR5 ....77 C8
  Blackpool FY4 ....110 C5
  Clitheroe BB7 ....166 F7
  Formby L37 ....11 C1
  Fulwood PR2 ....117 A5
  Fulwood PR2 ....117 B4
  Haslingden BB4 ....85 A1
  5 Kirkham PR4 ....114 A5
  Lancaster LA1 ....218 C3
  Oswaldtwistle BB5 ....103 F4
  Thornton FY5 ....176 A4
Mayfield Ct L37 ....11 F5
Mayfield Dr LA4 ....217 E6
Mayfield Fold BB11 ....128 B3
Mayfield Gdns BB5 ....103 F4
Mayfield Pl 10 FY7 ....198 F2
Mayfield Prim Sch FY8 ..89 C8
Mayfield Rd
  Blackburn BB1 ....122 E3
  6 Chorley PR6 ....61 D1
  High Bentham LA2 ....239 D7
  Leyland PR25 ....60 A7
  Lytham St Anne's FY8 ..89 E8
  Preston PR2 ....117 B1
  Ramsbottom BL0 ....50 A2
  Skelmersdale WN8 ....10 B7
Mayfield Sch PR7 ....43 C6
Mayfield St BB2 ....101 E3
Mayflower Ave PR1 ....96 A3
Mayflower Cotts WN1 ....30 C1
Mayflower Gr PR3 ....181 E1
Mayflower Ind Est L37 ..12 A1
Mayflower St BB2 ....101 B2
Mayhall Ct L31 ....5 D2
Maylands Pl BB9 ....170 C3
Maylands Sq LA4 ....217 C4
Maynard St PR1,PR2 ....117 D2
Mayo Dr PR4 ....57 A6
Mayor Ave FY1 ....130 C2
Maypark PR5 ....78 A5
Mayson St BB1 ....101 E4
Maytree Wlk WN8 ....18 B4
Mayville Rd BB9 ....148 B6
McCall Cl PR4 ....113 A3
McDonald Rd LA3 ....212 D5
McKenzie St PR5 ....60 B8
Mead Ave PR25 ....60 B8
Meadow Ave
  Fleetwood FY7 ....198 E1
  Knott End-on-S FY6 ....200 A6
  Southport PR8 ....35 C4
Meadow Bank
  Kingsfold PR1 ....96 C3
  Maghull L31 ....5 B2
  3 Ormskirk L39 ....15 F5
Meadow Bank Ave
  BB10 ....148 B5
Meadow Bank Cotts BB4 85 E3
Meadow Bank Mews 2
  BB9 ....170 F2
Meadow Bank Rd 15
  BB9 ....148 D8
Meadow Brook Ho 1
  PR1 ....118 A1
Meadow Brow PR9 ....54 D5
Meadow Cl
  Billington BB7 ....144 A3
  Blackpool FY2 ....152 D2
  Brierfield BB10 ....148 C4
  Clifton PR4 ....115 C2
  Foulridge BB8 ....194 D1
  Huncoat BB5 ....125 F1
  Skelmersdale WN8 ....9 D7
  Westhead L40 ....16 E4
  Wrea Green PR4 ....113 B3
Meadow Clough WN8 ..18 B4
Meadow Cotts OL12 ....71 D3
Meadow Court Rd LA4 .217 C3
Meadow Cr PR4 ....113 F6
Meadow Cres FY6 ....153 A3
Meadow Croft
  Nether Kellet LA6 ....221 F4
  West Bradford BB7 ....189 E5
Meadow Ct
  11 Oswaldtwistle BB5 ..103 E4
  Preston PR6 ....96 E6
  Treales PR4 ....135 A1
Meadow Dr
  Bolton-le-S LA5 ....221 A5
  Ormskirk L39 ....15 C2
  Warton PR4 ....92 C5
Meadow Field PR1 ....96 E2
Meadow Gate BB3 ....82 B2
Meadow Gdns BB1 ....124 B1
Meadow Head Ave OL12 52 D6
Meadow Head Cl BB2 ..101 A1
Meadow Head La
  Longton PR4 ....74 F7
  Tockholes BB3 ....81 B4
Meadow Ho 7 PR1 ....97 A8
Meadow La
  Clayton Brook PR5 ....78 B4
  Croston PR26 ....57 C1
  Hesketh Bank PR4 ....73 F4
  Hoscar L40 ....26 C6
  Knott End-on-S FY6 ....199 F4
  Lytham St Anne's FY8 ..91 A4
  Maghull L31 ....5 F1
  Rufford L40 ....39 D3
  Southport PR8 ....21 D3
Meadow Pk Galgate LA2 .210 F4
  Garstang PR3 ....204 C2
  Haslingden BL0 ....68 C4
  Kirkham PR4 ....113 E6
  Staining FY3 ....131 D5

Meadow Pk continued
  Tarleton PR4 ....57 B6
Meadow Reach PR1 ....96 B2
Meadow Rise BB2 ....81 A8
Meadow St
  Accrington BB5 ....104 C6
  Adlington PR7 ....31 A6
  Barnoldswick BB18 ....196 A4
  17 Burnley BB11 ....127 F6
  Darwen BB3 ....65 B6
  Great Harwood BB6 ....124 C4
  Lancaster LA1 ....214 D8
  Leyland PR25 ....77 A1
  Padiham BB12 ....146 C1
  Preston PR1 ....97 A8
  Wheelton PR6 ....62 A7
Meadow Terr BB3 ....81 E5
Meadow Vale
  Blackburn BB2 ....81 E6
  Leyland PR26 ....59 A8
Meadow View
  Adlington PR6 ....30 F8
  Clitheroe BB7 ....166 C8
  Farleton LA2 ....238 A6
  Great Plumpton PR4 ....112 F7
  Lancaster LA1 ....218 B3
  Rochdale OL12 ....52 A1
  Southport PR8 ....35 D4
Meadow Way
  Arkholme LA6 ....241 B3
  Bacup OL13 ....87 F2
  Barnoldswick BB18 ....196 D4
  Blackrod BL6 ....31 E1
  Coppull PR7 ....29 D8
  Edgworth BL7 ....48 E6
  Garstang PR3 ....204 C2
  Ramsbottom BL9 ....50 C2
Meadoway
  Accrington BB5 ....104 A7
  Longton PR4 ....74 F8
  Tarleton PR4 ....57 A5
Meadowbarn Cl PR4 ..116 E5
Meadowbridge Cl L40 ..16 E4
Meadowbrook
  Blackpool FY3 ....131 C2
  Burscough L40 ....25 D2
Meadowbrook Cl BL9 ..33 C4
Meadowcroft
  Blackburn BB3 ....82 A6
  Euxton PR7 ....60 B3
  Formby L37 ....11 B3
  Lytham St Anne's FY8 ..111 A1
  Skelmersdale WN8 ....18 A4
Meadowcroft Ave
  Catterall PR3 ....181 D3
  Cleveleys FY5 ....175 E2
  Hambleton FY6 ....177 C1
Meadowcroft Bsns Pk
  PR4 ....96 B1
Meadowcroft Cl BB4 ..86 A5
Meadowcroft Gr LA3 ..216 E1
Meadowcroft Rd PR25 ..59 D7
Meadowfield
  Fulwood PR2 ....117 F8
  Halton LA2 ....219 C7
  Skelmersdale WN8 ....10 A7
Meadowfield Cl
  Halton LA2 ....219 C7
  Whalley BB7 ....144 A7
Meadowfields BB2 ....81 D7
Meadowhead Cty Inf Sch
  BB2 ....101 B1
Meadowhead Jun Sch
  BB2 ....101 B1
Meadowland Cl PR26 ..76 E3
Meadowlands
  Charnock Richard PR7 ..42 D4
  Clitheroe BB7 ....166 C8
  Haslingden BB4 ....85 C2
Meadows Ave Bacup OL13 87 F4
  Cleveleys FY5 ....175 E2
  Haslingden BB4 ....85 C2
Meadows Cl LA5 ....225 E4
Meadows Dr BB4 ....106 A1
Meadows The
  Arnside LA5 ....224 C8
  Bamber Bridge PR5 ....97 F3
  Billington BB7 ....144 A4
  Burnley BB12 ....127 D8
  Cleveleys FY5 ....175 E2
  Colne BB8 ....171 D6
  Darwen BB3 ....81 E5
  Elswick PR4 ....155 F1
  Heskin Green PR7 ....41 E2
  Hollins Lane PR3 ....207 C2
  2 Leyland PR26 ....76 B1
  3 Maghull L31 ....5 D1
  Oswaldtwistle BB5 ....103 F3
  Whitworth OL12 ....71 C1
  Yealand Redmayne LA5 .225 E3
Meadowside
  Claughton LA2 ....237 F5
  Croston PR26 ....58 A2
  Grindleton BB7 ....190 C8
  Lancaster LA1 ....214 F7
  Walmer Bridge PR4 ....75 A5
Meadowside Ave BB5 ..124 E3
Meadowside Dr PR5 ....98 E1
Meadowside Rd LA4 ..217 B3
Meads Rd PR2 ....117 B1
Meadup Ct LA3 ....217 A2
Meadway Becconsall PR4 .73 F2
  Blackpool FY1 ....130 F1
  Clayton Green PR6 ....78 B3
  Higher Penwortham PR1 ..96 A3
  Padiham BB12 ....126 B7
  Ramsbottom BL0 ....68 C1
  Skelmersdale WN8 ....18 A4
Meadway Cl BL6 ....32 D3

Meagles La PR3,PR4 ..155 E3
Mealhouse La 6 PR7 ..43 C8
Mealrigg La LA6 ....241 A7
Meanwood Ave FY4 ....110 F5
Meanwood Brow 15
  OL12 ....52 C1
Meanwood Prim Sch
  OL12 ....52 C1
Meanygate PR5 ....97 E1
Mearbeck Pl 6 LA1 ..218 B2
Mearley Brook Fold
  BB7 ....166 F7
Mearley Rd PR2 ....118 E4
Mearley St BB7 ....166 F7
Mearley Syke BB7 ....166 F8
Mearsbeck LA3 ....216 E3
Meath Rd PR1 ....96 D6
Mede The PR4 ....114 B3
Medina Cl BB5 ....104 B5
Medlar Cl PR4 ....113 A6
Medlar Ct PR4 ....114 A6
Medlar Gate PR4 ....114 A6
Medlar La PR4 ....133 A4
Medlar-with-Wesham CE
  Prim Sch PR4 ....113 F6
Medley St OL12 ....52 F1
Medlock Ave FY7 ....198 D2
Medlock Pl FY7 ....198 D2
Medway PR2 ....117 F6
Medway Ave FY7 ....175 D8
Medway Cl PR5 ....97 B7
Medway Dr BL6 ....32 D3
Medway Ho 6 PR1 ....97 D8
Meeting House La LA1 .214 E8
Meins Croft BB2 ....101 A6
Meins Rd BB2 ....100 F6
Melba Rd PR7 ....118 E3
Melbert Ave PR2 ....117 C3
Melbourne Ave
  Blackpool FY5 ....152 E8
  Fleetwood FY7 ....175 E8
Melbourne Cl BB3 ....32 C3
Melbourne Gr BB3 ....32 C3
Melbourne Rd 11 LA1 .215 A8
Melbourne St
  6 Accrington BB5 ....125 A1
  7 Darwen BB3 ....65 B6
  2 Newchurch BB4 ....86 F1
  Oswaldtwistle BB5 ....103 D3
  Padiham BB12 ....126 D7
  19 Preston PR1 ....96 F8
Melbreck BB2 ....18 A4
Melbury Dr BL6 ....32 F1
Meldon Grange LA3 ..213 A8
Meldon Rd LA3 ....213 A7
Meldreth Cl L37 ....11 C1
Melford Cl PR6 ....61 F3
Melford Dr WN5 ....10 D3
Melfort Cl BB4 ....100 F1
Melia Cl BB4 ....85 F2
Melita St BB3 ....65 B8
Melling Brow LA6 ....241 C2
Melling Ct 3 Colne BB8 .171 C5
  Morecambe LA4 ....217 A3
Melling Ho 4 LA1 ....215 A3
Melling Mews PR3 ....181 C8
Melling Rd Hornby LA2 .238 B7
  Southport PR9 ....35 E7
Melling St 17 PR1 ....96 F8
Melling St Wilfrid CE Prim
  Sch LA1 ....241 D2
Melling's La FY8 ....111 A1
Mellings Ave WN5 ....10 E1
Mellings Fold 3 PR1 ..97 C6
Mellings Wood FY8 ..111 A1
Mellishaw La LA3 ....217 D1
Mellor Brow BB2 ....121 D2
Mellor Cl Burnley BB11 .127 D3
  Standish WN6 ....29 C2
Mellor Ct PR3 ....140 B7
Mellor La BB2 ....121 F3
Mellor Pl 6 PR1 ....97 B7
Mellor Rd Kirkham PR4 .114 A5
  Leyland PR25 ....76 D2
Mellwood Ave FY3 ....152 F1
Melrose Ave
  Blackpool FY3 ....130 E8
  Burnley BB11 ....127 E6
  Fulwood PR2 ....118 C5
  Morecambe LA4 ....217 C5
  Oswaldtwistle BB5 ....103 F4
  Southport PR9 ....54 B5
Melrose Gdns PR26 ....58 C2
Melrose St 10 Darwen BB3 .81 F2
  Lancaster LA1 ....215 A7
  Ramsbottom BL0 ....50 B2
Melrose Terr OL13 ....88 A7
Melrose Way PR7 ....43 D5
Melton Gr FY8 ....90 E3
Melton Pl Blackpool FY5 .152 E4
  Leyland PR25 ....77 B1
Melville Ave
  Barnoldswick BB18 ....196 A3
  Darwen BB3 ....65 A7
Melville Dr BB2 ....101 E4
Melville Gdns BB3 ....65 A8
Melville Rd
  Blackpool FY2 ....152 C4
  Heysham LA3 ....212 C1
Melville St Burnley BB10 .148 C1
  Darwen BB3 ....65 A8
Melvin Ho PR9 ....35 B4
Memorial Gdns PR3 ..159 A4
Memory Cl PR4 ....93 B7
Menai Dr PR2 ....117 D2
Mendip Cl Horwich BL6 ..32 C5
  Lytham St Anne's FY8 ..91 E5

Mendip Rd PR25 ....77 D1
Menivale Cl PR9 ....54 E5
Meols Cl L37 ....11 E2
Meols Cop High Sch PR8 35 F5
Meols Cop Rd PR8,PR9 ..35 E4
Meols Cop Ret Pk PR9 ..36 A4
Meols Cop Sta PR9 ....35 F7
Meols Ct PR9 ....55 A6
Meolsgate Ave PR4 ....57 A7
Mercer Cres BB4 ....68 A8
Mercer Ct Adlington PR7 ..43 F1
  Maghull L31 ....5 A3
Mercer Dr BB6 ....124 E6
Mercer Ho 5 BB5 ....125 A1
Mercer Rd PR5 ....97 A1
Mercer St
  16 Clayton-le-M BB5 ....124 F3
  Great Harwood BB6 ....124 D5
  1 Padiham BB12 ....126 F7
  Preston PR1 ....97 C8
Mercer's La L39 ....7 B4
Merchants Ho 4 BB1 ..101 F4
Merchants Landing BB1 101 F3
Merchants Quay 1 BB1 101 F3
Merclesden Ave BB9 ..171 B1
Mercury Way WN8 ....9 E7
Mere Brook FY3 ....131 E5
Mere Brow La PR4 ....56 A2
Mere Cl Broughton PR3 ..137 F3
  Skelmersdale WN8 ....17 F2
Mere Ct Burnley BB11 ..128 B4
  Burscough Bridge L40 ..25 E5
Mere Fold PR7 ....42 D3
Mere La Banks PR9 ....55 A2
  Holmeswood PR4 ....38 A7
  Rufford L40 ....38 E3
Mere Park Ct FY3 ....131 A2
Mere Rd Blackpool FY3 .130 C3
  Formby L37 ....11 D2
Mere Sands Wood Nature
  Reserve ★ L40 ....38 C4
Meredith St BB9 ....148 E7
Merefell Rd LA5 ....221 A6
Merefield PR7 ....61 A1
Merefield Sch PR8 ....21 B4
Merefold BL6 ....31 F3
Mereland Cl WN5 ....10 E6
Mereland Rd FY3 ....131 A2
Merepark Dr PR9 ....54 B4
Meres Way PR8 ....35 B2
Mereside PR4 ....74 F7
Mereside Prim Sch FY4 131 C1
Merewood WN8 ....18 A4
Meriden Cl PR8 ....21 B5
Merlecrest Dr PR4 ....57 A8
Merlewood Ave PR9 ..54 B3
Merlin Cl PR6 ....62 A3
Merlin Ct BB5 ....103 D3
Merlin Dr BB5 ....103 D3
Merlin Gr Leyland PR25 .59 C8
  Padiham BB12 ....126 E6
Merlin Rd BB2 ....101 B6
Merlyn Rd FY5 ....175 E1
Merrick Ave PR1 ....97 F8
Merrilox Ave L31 ....5 D3
Merry Trees La PR4 ..116 E5
Merryburn Cl PR2 ....118 A4
Merscar La L40 ....24 D6
Mersey Ave Darwen BB3 .81 D3
  Formby L37 ....11 E6
  Maghull L31 ....5 F2
Mersey Rd Blackpool FY4 110 B8
  Fleetwood FY7 ....198 F4
  Orrell WN5 ....10 E1
Mersey St Bacup OL13 ..88 A1
  Burnley BB12 ....127 A6
  Longridge PR3 ....140 B8
  Preston PR2 ....96 C8
Merton Ave PR2 ....117 F6
Merton Gr PR6 ....61 F3
Merton St Burnley BB12 .127 F7
  4 Nelson BB9 ....170 D1
Messenger St BB9 ....149 A7
Meta St BB2 ....101 E2
Metcalf Dr BB5 ....125 D6
Metcalfe Cl BB2 ....81 D8
Metcalfe St BB12 ....127 B5
Mete St PR1 ....97 D8
Methuen Ave
  Coupe Green PR5 ....98 E3
  Fulwood PR2 ....117 E6
Methuen Cl PR5 ....98 E3
Methuen St PR5 ....98 F3
Metropolitan Bsns Pk
  FY3 ....131 B2
Metropolitan Dr FY3 ..131 B2
Mettle Cote OL13 ....88 A1
Mewith La LA2 ....239 C6
Mews The 1 Darwen BB3 .65 C7
  Lancaster LA1 ....215 B6
  1 Padiham BB12 ....146 C1
  Southport PR8 ....35 A5
Mexford Ave FY2 ....130 D8
Meyler Ave FY1 ....130 E8
Michael Pl LA4 ....217 D5
Michael Wife La BL0 ..68 A8
Michael's La L39 ....22 C3
Michaels Cl L39 ....22 C3
Michaelson Ave LA4 ..217 E4
Mickering La L39 ....6 C5

Mickleden Ave PR2 . . . . .117 F7
Mickleden Rd FY4 . . . . .131 C1
Micklefield Ct **2** PR25 . . . .76 D1
Micklegate FY5 . . . . .152 C7
Mickleton Dr PR8 . . . . .21 A5
Middle Hey PR4 . . . . .74 E3
Middle Hill OL12 . . . . .52 F4
Middle Holly Rd PR3 . . . . .204 C8
Middle La LA2 . . . . .211 A6
Middle Meanygate PR4 . .56 C7
Middle Moss La
  Great Altcar L37 . . . . .12 F3
  Haskayne L37 . . . . .13 A3
Middle St Blackpool FY1 . .130 B3
  Colne BB8 . . . . .171 C4
  Lancaster LA1 . . . . .214 F8
  Whitworth OL12 . . . . .71 D1
Middle Turn BL7 . . . . .48 D7
Middle Withins La L37,L38 .4 A7
Middlecot Cl WN5 . . . . .10 E5
Middlefield PR26 . . . . .59 A8
Middleforth Gn PR1 . . . . . .96 E4
Middleforth Ind Est **4**
  PR1 . . . . .96 E4
Middlegate LA3 . . . . .217 C2
Middlegate BB4 . . . . .106 A1
Middlesex Ave BB12 . . . . .127 B7
Middleton Ave FY7 . . . . . . .198 D1
Middleton Dr BB9 . . . . . . .170 E6
Middleton Rd
  Heysham LA3 . . . . .212 C5
  Heysham,Middleton LA3 . .213 D2
Middleton Way LA1 . . . . . .212 F6
Middlewood WN8 . . . . .18 A4
Middlewood Cl
  Eccleston PR7 . . . . .41 C6
  Ormskirk L39 . . . . .6 C1
Middlewood Dr L39 . . . . . . .6 C1
Middlewood Rd L39 . . . . . . .6 C1
Midfield BB6 . . . . .123 C8
Midge Hall La Bescar PR9 .37 C3
  Leyland PR4,PR5 . . . . .75 F4
Midgeland Rd FY4 . . . . . . .111 B5
Midgeland Terr FY4 . . . . . .111 C5
Midgery La PR2 . . . . .118 B7
Midgley St BB8 . . . . .171 C6
Midhurst Dr PR8 . . . . .21 B4
Midland St
  12 Accrington BB5 . . . . .104 C5
  Nelson BB9 . . . . .170 E1
Midland Terr LA5 . . . . .223 D3
Midsummer St BB2 . . . . . .101 C5
Midville Pl **15** BB3 . . . . . .82 A1
Milbanke Ave PR4 . . . . . . .114 A5
Milbeck Cl PR3 . . . . .139 F5
Milbourne Rd BL9 . . . . .33 A4
Milbourne St FY1 . . . . . . .130 C5
Milburn Ave FY5 . . . . .175 F5
Mildred Cl FY5 . . . . .176 A3
Mile End Cl BB8 . . . . .194 D1
Mile End Row BB2 . . . . . .101 A6
Mile Rd FY6 . . . . .155 A1
Mile Stone Mdw PR7 . . . . .60 D4
Miles Ave OL13 . . . . .70 D8
Miles La WN6 . . . . .19 E6
Miles St PR1 . . . . .117 F2
Miles Wlk PR1 . . . . .117 E2
Milestone Mdw PR7 . . . . . .60 D4
Milestone Pl LA2 . . . . .237 C3
Miletas Pl FY8 . . . . .90 C4
Milford Ave FY2 . . . . .152 D1
Milford Cl L37 . . . . .11 C1
Milford St Colne BB8 . . . .171 C4
  6 Rochdale OL12 . . . . . .52 F1
Milk St BL0 . . . . .50 B5
Milking La BB3 . . . . .82 A6
Milking Stile La LA1 . . . . .214 D8
Mill Bank WN6 . . . . .19 D7
Mill Brook PR3 . . . . .181 D3
Mill Brook Pl BB7 . . . . . . .166 D1
Mill Brow Haskayne L39 . . .14 A7
  Lowgill LA2 . . . . .239 C2
Mill Brow Rd BB18 . . . . . .197 C2
Mill Cl PR4 . . . . .135 C4
Mill Cotts BB3 . . . . .82 F3
Mill Ct PR3 . . . . .140 B8
Mill Dam Cl L40 . . . . .25 C2
Mill Dam La L40 . . . . .16 D8
Mill Entrance BB5 . . . . . . .124 F2
Mill Field
  Clayton-le-M BB5 . . . . . .124 F4
  Parbold WN8 . . . . .27 C1
Mill Gap St **17** BB3 . . . . .65 A8
  15 Rawtenstall BB4 . . . . .86 A3
Mill Gdns **6** LA2 . . . . . . .239 D8
Mill Gn BB8 . . . . .171 D4
Mill Haven PR2 . . . . .117 D3
Mill Hey Ave FY6 . . . . . . .153 E1
Mill Hey La L40 . . . . .39 C3
Mill Hill
  Oswaldtwistle BB5 . . . . . .103 E4
  Preston PR1 . . . . .96 E4
Mill Hill Bridge St BB2 . .101 B2
Mill Hill Cotts BL6 . . . . . . .44 F1
Mill Hill Gr LA3 . . . . .213 A2
Mill Hill La BB11 . . . . .126 B3
Mill Hill St BB2 . . . . .101 B2
Mill Hill Sta BB2 . . . . .101 B2
Mill Ho **19** LA1 . . . . .215 A8
Mill Ho Mews **17** LA1 . . .215 A8
Mill House La Brindle PR6 .78 F8
  Longridge PR3 . . . . .141 A8

Mill House View WN8 . . . . .10 C7
Mill La Appley Bridge WN6 .19 C7
  Bacup OL13 . . . . .88 B3
  Becconsall PR4 . . . . .73 F2
  Blackburn BB2 . . . . .101 E4
  Bolton Green PR7 . . . . . . .42 A8
  Bolton Green PR7 . . . . . . .60 A1
  Bolton-le-S LA5 . . . . .221 A6
  Burscough L40 . . . . .25 E4
  Carnforth LA5 . . . . .223 D4
  Caton LA2 . . . . .237 B3
  Clayton Green PR6 . . . . . .78 C1
  Coppull PR7 . . . . .42 E2
  Darwen BB3 . . . . .64 A5
  Earby BB18 . . . . .197 D2
  Eccleston PR7 . . . . .41 C5
  Elswick PR4 . . . . .156 B1
  Fleetwood FY7 . . . . .199 B4
  Fulwood PR2 . . . . .117 C4
  Gisburn BB7 . . . . .231 B4
  Goosnargh PR3 . . . . .138 E6
  Great Harwood BB6 . . . . .125 A6
  Halton LA2 . . . . .219 D6
  Hambleton FY6 . . . . .177 E1
  Haskayne L39 . . . . .14 F1
  Hesketh Lane PR3 . . . . . .162 C8
  Heskin Green PR7 . . . . . . .42 A2
  Horwich BL6 . . . . .32 D4
  Leyland PR25 . . . . .59 D8
  Leyland,Earnshaw Bridge
    PR26 . . . . .76 E3
  Low Bentham LA2 . . . . . .239 C7
  Parbold WN8 . . . . .27 C1
  Skelmersdale WN8 . . . . . . .17 F2
  Skelmersdale,Up Holland
    WN8 . . . . .10 A8
  Southport PR9 . . . . .54 A1
  Staining FY3 . . . . .131 D5
  Stalmine FY6 . . . . .177 D7
  Waddington BB7 . . . . . . .189 A8
  Walton-le-D PR5 . . . . .97 D5
  Warton PR4 . . . . .92 F6
  Wrea Green PR4 . . . . . . .113 A3
Mill Lane Cres PR3 . . . . . . .14 F1
Mill Lane Ind Est BB7 . . . .231 B3
Mill Leat Cl WN8 . . . . .27 C2
Mill Leat Mews WN8 . . . . .27 C2
Mill Nook OL12 . . . . .52 F3
Mill Rd Orrell WN5 . . . . . . .10 D5
  Southport PR8 . . . . .21 D5
Mill Row BB4 . . . . .85 F5
Mill St Accrington BB5 . . . .104 F1
  Adlington PR6 . . . . .31 B8
  Bacup OL13 . . . . .87 F3
  Barnoldswick BB18 . . . . .196 A2
  Barrowford BB9 . . . . .170 D4
  Church BB5 . . . . .103 F6
  Clayton-le-M BB5 . . . . . .124 F2
  Coppull PR7 . . . . .42 E1
  Great Harwood BB6 . . . . .124 C5
  Haslingden BB4 . . . . .85 B5
  Lancaster LA1 . . . . .215 A8
  Leyland PR25 . . . . .59 D8
  Leyland,Seven Stars PR25 .59 D8
  Nelson BB9 . . . . .148 A4
  Ormskirk L39 . . . . .15 F5
  Oswaldtwistle BB5 . . . . . .103 D3
  Padiham BB12 . . . . .126 C8
  Preesall FY6 . . . . .200 B3
  Preston PR1 . . . . .96 D8
  Ramsbottom BL0 . . . . .50 A4
  Southport PR8 . . . . .35 C6
  West Bradford BB7 . . . . . .189 E5
  Wheelton PR6 . . . . .62 A7
Mill The Leyland PR26 . . . .76 D2
  Preston PR1 . . . . .96 F8
Mill View Mew 93 B7
Mill View Ct L39 . . . . .7 E6
Mill Wood Cl PR6 . . . . .79 C3
Mill Yd BL9 . . . . .33 A3
Millar Barn La BB4 . . . . . . .69 F8
Millar's Pace PR9 . . . . .54 B5
Millbank Fulwood PR2 . . . .117 C3
  4 Preston PR1 . . . . .97 B8
Millbank Brow L40 . . . . . . .25 F3
Millbank La L31,L39 . . . . . .5 F3
Millbrook BB12 . . . . .147 E8
Millbrook Cl
  Skelmersdale WN8 . . . . . .17 E2
  Wheelton PR6 . . . . .62 A7
Millbrook Ct BB7 . . . . .189 E5
Millbrook Mews **1** FY8 . .91 C3
Millbrook Row PR6 . . . . . . .44 B1
Millbrook St BB3 . . . . .81 F7
Millbrook Way PR1 . . . . . . .96 C3
Millcombe Way PR5 . . . . . .97 E3
Millcroft Chorley PR7 . . . . .61 A2
  Fulwood PR2 . . . . .117 D4
Millcroft Ave WN5 . . . . . . .10 D5
Milldyke Cl FY4 . . . . .110 F6
Millenium Ct FY8 . . . . .110 B4
Miller Ave PR6 . . . . .80 B2
Miller Cl BB5 . . . . .103 C5
Miller Cres FY6 . . . . .154 E1
Miller Ct
  14 Lancaster LA1 . . . . .218 D2
  Lancaster,Haverbreaks
    LA1 . . . . .214 E5
Miller Field PR1 . . . . .116 E3
Miller Fold Ave BB5 . . . . .104 B3
Miller Ho **4** PR1 . . . . .97 A7
Miller La Catforth PR4 . . . .135 E4
  Cottam PR4 . . . . .116 E5
Miller Rd PR1,PR2 . . . . . . .118 C2
Miller St
  4 Blackpool FY1 . . . . .130 B1
  11 Preston PR1 . . . . . . .97 C8
  Ramsbottom BL9 . . . . .50 C2

Miller's Brow PR3 . . . . . . .207 E3
Millers Ct L39 . . . . .15 F5
Millers Nook WN8 . . . . .10 B7
Millersdale Cl FY5 . . . . . . .153 E7
Millersgate PR4 . . . . .116 E4
Millet Terr BL9 . . . . .33 C7
Millett St BL0 . . . . .50 D7
Millfield Cl PR4 . . . . .92 F6
Millfield High Sch FY5 . . .153 C8
Millfield Rd
  Blackpool FY4 . . . . .110 F6
  Chorley PR7 . . . . .61 C1
Millfold OL12 . . . . .71 D2
Millgate BL7 . . . . .47 D2
Millgate Rd **18** BB4 . . . . .86 A3
Millgate Terr OL12 . . . . . . .71 E5
Millgreen Cl WN8 . . . . .10 A7
Millham St BB1 . . . . .101 E6
Millholme Dr LA2 . . . . . . .239 D7
Millhouse Lo PR8 . . . . .21 D5
Millhouse St BL0 . . . . .50 E8
Millington Ave FY4 . . . . . .110 E8
Millom Ave FY2 . . . . .152 D4
Millom Cl FY7 . . . . .175 C8
Millrace Ct **5** LA1 . . . . . .218 D2
Millrose Cl WN8 . . . . .17 F2
Mills St OL12 . . . . .71 D1
Millstone Ct **3** LA1 . . . . .218 D3
Millthorne Ave BB7 . . . . . .166 D7
Millthorne Ho **9** BB7 . . .166 D8
Millwood Cl BB2 . . . . .101 A1
Millwood Glade PR7 . . . . . .61 B1
Millwood Rd PR5 . . . . .97 B3
Milman Cl L39 . . . . .15 D3
Milne St BL0 . . . . .68 C5
Milner Rd Darwen BB3 . . . .81 E4
  Lytham St Anne's FY8 . . . .90 E4
Milner St Burnley BB10 . . .128 A8
  Preston PR1 . . . . .118 A2
Milnshaw Gdns BB5 . . . . .104 B7
Milnshaw La BB5 . . . . .104 B6
Milnthorpe Ave FY5 . . . . . .175 C5
Milton Ave Blackpool FY3 .130 F5
  Clitheroe BB7 . . . . .189 E1
  2 Thornton FY5 . . . . . .176 A3
Milton Cl
  Bamber Bridge PR5 . . . . . .97 D2
  Darwen BB3 . . . . .82 C1
  Great Harwood BB6 . . . . .124 B4
  Haslingden BB4 . . . . .68 A7
Milton Cres Kirkham PR4 . .114 A5
  Poulton-le-F FY6 . . . . . . .131 D8
Milton Ct PR7 . . . . .42 E1
Milton Dr L39 . . . . .16 A4
Milton Gr
  Barnoldswick BB18 . . . . .196 A3
  Longshaw WN5 . . . . .10 D1
  Orrell WN5 . . . . .10 F6
Milton Rd Colne BB8 . . . . .171 D5
  Coppull PR7 . . . . .29 E8
Milton St
  3 Barrowford BB9 . . . .170 D4
  1 Blackburn BB1 . . . . .102 A5
  Brierfield BB9 . . . . .148 B5
  Brierfield,Harle Syke BB10 148 F3
  Clayton-le-M BB5 . . . . . .124 F3
  Fleetwood FY7 . . . . .199 A4
  Nelson BB9 . . . . .170 D1
  Oswaldtwistle BB5 . . . . . .103 E4
  Padiham BB12 . . . . .126 E7
  Ramsbottom BL0 . . . . .50 B6
  Southport PR9 . . . . .36 A7
Milton Terr PR6 . . . . .61 D2
Milton Way L31 . . . . .5 B1
Mimosa Cl PR7 . . . . .61 A3
Mimosa Rd PR2 . . . . .118 E2
Mincing La BB2 . . . . .101 E4
Minden Rd PR2 . . . . .132 E5
Minehead Ave BB10 . . . . .148 D2
Minerva Rd LA1 . . . . .214 C8
Minnie Cl L40 . . . . .71 D2
Minnie St BB2 . . . . .101 C6
Minor St **13** BB4 . . . . . . .86 A7
Minstead Ave L33 . . . . .1 A2
Minster Cres BB3 . . . . .65 C8
Minster Dr LA3 . . . . .217 B2
Minster Pk PR4 . . . . .116 E5
Minstrel Wlk FY6 . . . . .153 D4
Mint Ave BB9 . . . . .170 D4
Mint St BL0 . . . . .68 C2
Mintholme Ave PR5 . . . . . . .98 E2
Mintor Rd L33 . . . . .1 A2
Mire Ash Brow BB2 . . . . . .121 D1
Mire Ridge BB8 . . . . .172 A3
Mirfield Gr **11** FY4 . . . . .130 D1
Miry La WN8 . . . . .27 C2
Mission Cotts L40 . . . . .26 B8
Mission The BB8 . . . . .172 C6
Mitcham Rd FY4 . . . . .111 B8
Mitchell St Burnley BB12 .127 C6
  Clitheroe BB7 . . . . .166 D7
  4 Colne BB8 . . . . .171 D5
Mitella St BB10 . . . . .128 C5
Mitre St BB11 . . . . .127 E6
Mitten's La L37 . . . . .12 A4
Mitten's La L37 . . . . .12 B3
Mitton Ave
  Barrowford BB9 . . . . .170 F6
  Rawtenstall BB4 . . . . .86 A4
Mitton Cl Blackburn BB2 . .101 C1
  Heywood OL10 . . . . .33 F2
Mitton Dr PR2 . . . . .119 A3
Mitton Gr BB10 . . . . .128 D5
Mitton Hos BB9 . . . . .170 F6

Mitton Rd
  Great Mitton BB7 . . . . . . .165 F2
  Whalley BB7 . . . . .144 B7
Mitton St BB1 . . . . .101 F7
Mizpah St BB10 . . . . .128 C5
Mizzy Rd OL12 . . . . .52 F1
Moira Cres PR2 . . . . .118 F4
Moleside Cl BB5 . . . . .104 D6
Mollington Rd BB2 . . . . . .101 B7
Molly Wood La BB11 . . . . .126 F5
Molyneux Ct **16** PR1 . . . .97 A8
Molyneux Dr FY4 . . . . . . .110 D7
Molyneux Pl FY8 . . . . .91 A4
Molyneux Rd L39 . . . . .6 C7
Mona Pl PR1 . . . . .96 E8
Mona Rd BB2 . . . . .101 E1
Monarch Cres FY8 . . . . . . .90 B8
Monarch St BB5 . . . . .103 E4
Money Close La LA3 . . . . .212 D4
Moneyclose Gr LA3 . . . . . .212 D5
Monk Hall St BB10 . . . . . .128 A7
Monk St Accrington BB5 . .104 A6
  2 Clitheroe BB7 . . . . .166 D7
Monk's La FY6 . . . . .200 A1
Monkroyd Ave BB18 . . . . .196 A2
Monkroyd Rd BB8 . . . . . . .172 F7
Monks Carr La L37,L38 . . .4 A6
Monks Cl L37 . . . . .12 A1
Monks Dr Formby L37 . . . . .12 A1
  Longridge PR3 . . . . .140 A6
  Withnell PR6 . . . . .80 A1
Monks Gate FY8 . . . . .90 D7
Monks La L40 . . . . .25 D7
Monks Wlk PR1 . . . . .96 C6
Monkswell Ave LA5 . . . . . .221 A5
Monkswell Dr LA5 . . . . . . .221 A5
Monkswood Ave LA4 . . . . .217 E5
Monmouth Ct PR2 . . . . . . .116 F3
Monmouth Rd BB1 . . . . . .102 C5
Monmouth St
  5 Burnley BB12 . . . . . .127 D6
  Colne BB8 . . . . .172 A5
Monroe Dr **3** FY7 . . . . . .198 D3
Montagu Mews L37 . . . . . . .11 E5
Montagu Rd L37 . . . . .11 E5
Montague Cl BB2 . . . . . . .101 D4
Montague Rd BB11 . . . . . .127 E5
Montague St
  Blackburn BB2 . . . . .101 C5
  Blackpool FY4 . . . . .110 B8
  Brierfield BB9 . . . . .148 B6
  4 Clitheroe BB7 . . . . .166 D8
  Colne BB8 . . . . .171 E6
Montcliffe Cotts BL6 . . . . .32 E5
Montcliffe Rd PR6 . . . . . . .61 E1
Monteagle Dr LA2 . . . . . . .238 B7
Monteagle Sq LA2 . . . . . . .238 B7
Montfield Hey BB9 . . . . . . .148 A5
Montford Ct BB12 . . . . . . .147 F6
Montford Rd BB9 . . . . .147 F6
Montgomery Ave PR9 . . . . .36 B6
Montgomery Cl BB5 . . . . .104 E2
Montgomery Gr BB12 . . . .127 C7
Montgomery High Sch
  FY2 . . . . .152 D5
Montgomery St **7** PR5 . .77 F8
Monthall Rise LA1 . . . . . . .218 F1
Montjoly St PR1 . . . . .97 C7
Monton Rd BB3 . . . . .81 E4
Montpelier Ave FY2 . . . . . .152 C5
Montreal Ave FY1 . . . . . . .130 D4
Montreal Rd BB2 . . . . .101 C8
Montrose Ave
  Blackpool FY1 . . . . .130 C3
  Ramsbottom BL0 . . . . .50 A2
Montrose Cl PR6 . . . . .43 E6
Montrose Cres LA3 . . . . . .212 E7
Montrose Dr PR9 . . . . .53 F1
Montrose St
  Blackburn BB2 . . . . .101 C3
  Brierfield BB9 . . . . .148 B6
  Burnley BB11 . . . . .127 F4
Montrose Terr **17** BB18 . .196 B2
Moody La BB10 . . . . .40 E1
Moody St **5** WN6 . . . . . . .29 E1
Moon Ave **7** FY1 . . . . . .130 B2
Moon Bay Wharf LA3 . . . .212 D6
Moon St PR5 . . . . .77 E8
Moons Acre LA3 . . . . .239 D8
Moor Ave
  Appley Bridge WN6 . . . . . .19 E8
  Higher Penwortham PR1 . .96 A4
Moor Cl Darwen BB3 . . . . . .65 D8
  Lancaster LA1 . . . . .215 A8
  Southport PR8 . . . . .21 D2
Moor Close La LA6 . . . . . .240 B1
Moor Dr WN8 . . . . .9 D7
Moor Edge BB7 . . . . .144 B6
Moor End Prim Sch
  BB5 . . . . .103 D4
Moor Field
  New Longton PR4 . . . . . . .76 A7
  Whalley BB7 . . . . .144 B6
Moor Gate **14** LA1 . . . . .215 A8
Moor Hall La PR4 . . . . . . .114 F4
Moor Hall St PR1 . . . . .117 E2
Moor Hey Cotts PR26 . . . . .58 A6
Moor La
  Billington BB6,BB7 . . . . . .144 B2
  Butt Yeats LA2 . . . . .238 C5
  Clitheroe BB7 . . . . .166 E8
  Darwen BB3 . . . . .82 B3
  Haslingden BB4 . . . . .84 F6
  Hutton PR4 . . . . .95 D1
  Ince Blundell L38,L23 . . . .3 E2
  Lancaster LA1 . . . . .215 A8
  Langho BB6 . . . . .123 E8
  Maghull L29 . . . . .4 D1

Moor La continued
  Padiham BB12 . . . . .146 C1
  Preston PR1 . . . . .117 F1
  Salterforth BB18 . . . . . . .194 C6
  Southport PR8 . . . . .21 C2
  Waddington BB7 . . . . . . .229 D2
  West Bradford BB7 . . . . . .189 D7
  Whalley BB7 . . . . .144 B6
  Wiswell BB7 . . . . .144 F7
Moor Nook Com Prim Sch
  PR2 . . . . .119 A3
Moor Park Ave
  Blackpool BB9 . . . . .152 E4
  Preston PR1 . . . . .118 A2
Moor Park High Sch
  PR1 . . . . .118 A2
Moor Park Inf & Jun Sch
  FY2 . . . . .152 E3
Moor Platt Cl BL6 . . . . .32 F3
Moor Rd
  Barber's Moor PR26 . . . . .58 D3
  Chorley PR7 . . . . .43 B5
  Haslingden BB4 . . . . .67 F5
  Orrell WN5 . . . . .10 E6
  Ramsbottom BL8 . . . . .50 A6
  Rivington PR6 . . . . .44 E7
Moor Side La BB7 . . . . . . .144 F8
Moor St Clayton-le-M BB5 .124 F3
  Kirkham PR4 . . . . .114 A5
  33 Lancaster LA1 . . . . .214 F8
  Ormskirk L39 . . . . .15 F5
Moor View Bacup OL13 . . .88 A4
  Bacup,Brandwood OL13 . .70 B7
  Rawtenstall BB4 . . . . .69 F6
  Salterforth BB18 . . . . . . .194 E8
Moor Way BL8 . . . . .49 C3
Moorbottom Rd BL8 . . . . . .49 E5
Moorbrook Sch PR2 . . . . . .117 E3
Moorbrook St PR1 . . . . . . .117 E1
Moorcroft Blackburn BB3 . .82 A6
  Broughton PR3 . . . . .137 B2
  Edenfield BL0 . . . . .68 D2
Moorcroft Cres PR2 . . . . . .118 D3
Moore Dr BB12 . . . . .146 F5
Moore St Blackpool FY4 . .130 B1
  Colne BB8 . . . . .171 C5
  Nelson BB9 . . . . .148 F2
  Padiham BB12 . . . . .126 F7
  Preston PR1 . . . . .97 C7
Moore Tree Dr FY4 . . . . . .111 A8
Moorend BB7 . . . . .166 F7
Moores La WN6 . . . . .29 D2
Moorfield BL7 . . . . .48 D6
Moorfield Ave
  Accrington,Hillock Vale
    BB5 . . . . .104 F8
  Blackburn BB1 . . . . .122 E3
  Blackpool FY3 . . . . .130 E6
  Carleton FY6 . . . . .153 B4
Moorfield Cl
  Clayton-le-M BB5 . . . . . .125 B3
  Fulwood PR2 . . . . .117 E8
  Preston PR1 . . . . .96 A2
Moorfield Dr
  Clayton-le-M BB5 . . . . . .125 B3
  Fulwood PR2 . . . . .118 E3
  Lytham St Anne's FY8 . . . .91 A4
Moorfield Ind Est BB5 . . . .125 B3
Moorfield La L40 . . . . .24 C3
Moorfield Pl **3** OL12 . . . .52 F1
Moorfield Rd PR25 . . . . . . .59 C8
Moorfield Sch PR1 . . . . . . .118 A3
Moorfield Way BB5 . . . . . .125 B3
Moorfields Blackpool FY2 .152 F4
  Chorley PR7 . . . . .61 C1
Moorfields Ave PR2 . . . . . .117 E8
Moorgate Accrington BB5 .104 B2
  Blackpool FY4 . . . . .110 F6
  Bury BL9 . . . . .33 A3
  Fulwood PR2 . . . . .117 F5
  Ormskirk L39 . . . . .15 E4
Moorgate Gdns **2** BB2 . .101 C1
Moorgate La BB6 . . . . .143 A5
Moorgate Rd BB18 . . . . . .196 B2
Moorgate Ret Pk **13** BL9 .33 A3
Moorgate St BB2 . . . . .101 C1
Moorhead Gdns PR4 . . . . . .92 E7
Moorhead High Sch
  BB5 . . . . .104 A7
Moorhead St **2** BB8 . . . .171 C5
Moorhen Pl **14** FY5 . . . . .175 F1
Moorhey Cres
  Higher Penwortham PR1 . .96 B5
  Walton Summit PR5 . . . . . .78 A8
Moorhey Dr PR1 . . . . .96 B5
Moorhouse Ave BB5 . . . . .104 A4
Moorhouse Cl BB5 . . . . . .104 A4
Moorhouse St
  Accrington BB5 . . . . .104 A4
  1 Blackpool FY1 . . . . .130 B7
  Burnley BB11 . . . . .127 C5
Moorhouses L38 . . . . .2 F7
Moorings The
  Burnley BB12 . . . . .127 E7
  4 Chorley PR6 . . . . . . .43 E8
  Hest Bank LA2 . . . . .220 D1
  Maghull L31 . . . . .5 D1
Moorland Ave
  Blackburn BB2 . . . . .80 D7
  Clitheroe BB7 . . . . .189 F3
  Darwen BB3 . . . . .81 D2
  Earby BB18 . . . . .197 C1
  Fulwood PR2 . . . . .118 D4
  Poulton-le-F FY6 . . . . . . .153 E4
  Whitworth OL12 . . . . .52 C7
Moorland Cl BB9 . . . . .170 F6
Moorland Cres
  Clitheroe BB7 . . . . .189 F2

Moorland Cres *continued*
Fulwood PR2 118 D4
Whitworth OL12 52 C7
Moorland Dr
Brierfield BB9 148 D4
Horwich BL6 32 F3
Moorland Gate PR6 43 F6
Moorland Gdns FY6 153 E4
Moorland Rd
Blackburn BB2 81 C7
Burnley BB11 127 F3
Clitheroe BB7 189 F2
Langho BB6 143 C1
Lytham St Anne's FY8 90 A7
Poulton-le-F FY6 153 F4
Moorland Rise BB4 85 C2
Moorland Sch Ltd BB7 189 E3
Moorland St OL12 52 E1
Moorland Terr OL12 52 A1
Moorland View BB9 148 E6
Moorlands PR1 117 E3
Moorlands Gr LA3 216 E3
Moorlands Terr OL13 88 A1
Moorlands The OL13 88 A8
Moorlands View BL0 68 D5
Moorside Melling LA6 241 D2
Wharles PR4 134 D3
Moorside Ave
Blackburn BB1 102 D4
Brierfield BB9 148 D4
Fulwood PR2 118 F3
Horwich BL6 32 C4
Moorside Cl LA6 241 D2
Moorside Com Prim Sch WN8 9 E7
Moorside Cres OL13 88 A4
Moorside Dr
Clayton-le-M BB5 125 A2
Preston PR1 96 B2
Moorside La PR4 136 C4
Moorside Prim Sch LA1 215 B4
Moorside Rd Caton LA2 237 D3
Edgworth BL7 66 D1
Moorsview BL0 50 B6
Moorthorpe Cl BB3 65 A6
Moorview Cl BB10 148 E2
Moorview Ct 2 FY4 110 F7
Moorway FY6 153 F4
Moray Cl BL0 50 A4
Morecambe Bay Com Prim Sch LA4 217 B5
Morecambe Bay Nature Reserve (RSPB)★ LA5 220 D5
Morecambe High Sch LA4 217 C6
Morecambe Rd
Blackburn BB2 101 F1
Lancaster LA3,LA1 218 A2
Morecambe Rd Sch LA3 217 F3
Morecambe St E LA4 217 B6
Morecambe St W LA4 217 B6
Morecambe Sta LA4 217 A5
Moresby Ave FY3 131 B7
Moreton Dr
Poulton-le-F FY6 153 D2
Staining FY3 131 D5
Moreton Gn 2 LA3 212 F7
Moreton Pk BB7 144 E2
Moreton St BB5 104 B6
Morewood Dr LA6 240 C7
Morland Ave
Bamber Bridge PR5 77 A7
Kirkham PR4 113 F7
Morley Ave BB2 101 A1
Morley Cl LA1 218 C3
Morley Croft PR26 76 E3
Morley La PR3 202 A5
Morley Rd Blackpool FY4 130 E1
Lancaster LA1 218 C3
Southport PR9 35 E8
Morley St 1 BB12 126 D8
Morningside LA1 214 E7
Mornington Ct PR1 118 F1
Mornington Rd
Adlington PR6 31 B8
Higher Penwortham PR1 96 B5
Lytham St Anne's FY8 91 E4
Preston PR1 118 F1
Southport PR9 35 C7
Morris Cl PR25 60 A8
Morris Cres PR2 118 D2
Morris Ct PR2 118 D2
Morris Hey L39 23 D3
Morris Rd Chorley PR6 61 E1
Fulwood PR2 118 D2
Skelmersdale WN8 10 A7
Morrison St PR6 61 D2
Morse St BB10 128 D5
Morston Ave FY2 152 E1
Mort St BL6 32 B4
Mortimer Gr LA3 213 A8
Morton St 22 BB1 101 E5
Morven Gr PR8 35 E7
Moscow Mill St BB5 103 E5
Mosedale Dr BB12 127 B8
Moseley Ave BB18 196 F1
Moseley Cl BB11 128 A2
Moseley Rd BB11 128 A3
Mosley Ave BL0 50 B2
Mosley St
Barnoldswick BB18 196 B2
Blackburn BB2 101 E2
4 Leyland PR25 77 A1
Nelson BB9 148 D8
Preston PR1 97 C8
Southport PR8 35 B4
Mosman Pl BB9 170 C3
Moss Acre Rd PR1 96 E2
Moss Ave Orrell WN5 10 D3
Preston PR2 117 A2
Moss Bank Coppull PR7 42 E1
Ormskirk L39 15 D2
Moss Bank Ct L39 15 D2
Moss Bank Pl FY4 110 F8
Moss Bridge L40 26 C3
Moss Bridge La L40 26 C2
Moss Bridge Pk PR5 77 C8
Moss Cl Chorley PR6 43 E8
Haslingden BB4 68 A8
Moss Cotts L40 17 A3
Moss Delph La L39 15 C1
Moss Dr BL6 32 F3
Moss Edge Cotts FY8 111 A2
Moss Edge La
Blackpool FY4 111 A3
Lytham St Anne's FY8 111 B2
Moss End Way L33 1 D3
Moss Fold Rd BB3 81 E5
Moss Gate BB1 102 B6
Moss Gdns PR8 35 C2
Moss Gn L37 12 B4
Moss Hall La FY8 90 E7
Moss Hall Rd
Accrington BB5 104 C8
Bury BL9 33 D1
Moss Hey La PR4 56 A3
Moss House La
Great Plumpton PR4 112 C7
Much Hoole PR4 75 B2
Stake Pool PR3 202 A4
Stalmine FY6 177 D8
Moss House Rd
Blackpool FY4 111 A6
Broughton PR4 137 B2
Moss La
Appley Bridge WN6 28 E3
Bamber Bridge PR5 77 B8
Banks PR9 55 D6
Becconsall PR4 73 C1
Bickerstaffe L39 7 F2
Blackburn BB1,BB5 102 F3
Blackrod BL6 31 F2
Bretherton PR26 58 C8
Burscough L40 26 A7
Catforth PR4 135 D5
Chipping PR3 186 A1
Clayton-le-W PR25 77 D2
Coppull PR7 42 E1
Croston PR5 40 A8
Duncombe PR3 158 D2
Farington PR26 76 D5
Formby L37,L39 12 E5
Garstang PR3 181 B7
Glasson LA2 209 E1
Hambleton FY6 177 D1
Hightown L38,L23 3 C2
Holme Mills LA5 240 A8
Inskip PR4 157 B3
Kingsfold PR1 96 E1
Kirkby,Northwood L33 1 B3
Leyland PR25 77 C2
Lucas Green PR6 61 D5
Maghull L31 5 E2
Maghull,Lydiate L31 5 D5
Morecambe LA4 217 A5
New Longton PR4 75 E7
Silverdale LA5 224 F5
Skelmersdale WN8 8 F6
Southport PR9 36 C8
St Michael's on W PR3 157 B8
Walmer Bridge PR4 75 C4
Wymott PR26 58 F5
Moss La E PR4 115 A8
Moss La W PR4 114 F7
Moss Lane View WN8 8 F6
Moss Lea PR4 57 A7
Moss Nook
Burscough Bridge L40 25 E6
Ormskirk L39 15 C2
Moss Pl LA1 218 E4
Moss Rd Lancaster LA3 213 E7
Orrell WN5 10 D3
Southport PR8 35 C2
Moss Side
Barnoldswick BB18 196 C2
Formby L37 12 B4
Moss Side La
Hale Nook FR6,PR3 178 C7
Lane Heads PR3 156 E5
Mere Brow PR4 55 F4
Stalmine FY6 177 E7
Wrea Green PR4 113 A3
Moss Side Prim Sch PR26 76 B1
Moss Side St OL12 71 E5
Moss Side Sta FY8 112 D1
Moss Side Way PR26 59 C8
Moss St
Bamber Bridge PR5 77 B8
Blackburn BB1 102 A6
7 Clitheroe BB7 166 D8
Great Harwood BB6 124 C4
Preston PR1 96 E8
Ramsbottom BL9 50 D2
Moss Terr PR6 61 E5
Moss View Maghull L31 5 F1
Ormskirk L39 15 E4
Southport PR8 21 E5
Moss Way 3 FY4 110 F7
Moss Wood Cl PR7 43 A6
Mossbank 7 BB1 102 A6
Mossbourne Rd FY6 153 C2
Mossbrook Dr PR4 116 F5
Mossdale 6 BB1 102 A6
Mossdale Ave PR2 118 D4
Mossfield Cl
Bamber Bridge PR5 77 B8
Bury BL9 33 B3
Mossfield Rd PR6 43 E8
Mossfields WN6 28 F6
Mossgate Cty Prim Sch
Heysham LA3 212 F8
Morecambe LA3 216 E1
Mossgiel Ave PR8 21 B5
Mosshill Cl L31 5 C3
Mosslands PR25 76 D1
Mosslawn Rd L32 1 A1
Mosslea Dr PR3 137 B8
Mossom La FY5 152 D7
Mossway PR4 75 F7
Mossy Lea Fold WN6 29 A3
Mossy Lea Rd WN6 28 F5
Mostyn Ave BB18 197 B1
Mostyn St BB3 81 E4
Motherwell Cres PR8 35 F3
Mottram Cl PR6 61 C5
Mottram Mews 7 BL6 32 B4
Mottram St BL6 32 B4
Moulden Brow BB2 80 B7
Moulding Cl BB2 101 B4
Mounsey Rd PR5 77 F8
Mount Ave
Lancaster LA1 218 D3
Morecambe LA4 217 F7
Rawtenstall BB4 69 F8
Mount Carmel RC High Sch BB5 104 A4
Mount Carmel Sch L39 15 D2
Mount Cres Orrell WN5 10 F6
Over Town BB10 108 A8
Mount Gdns LA4 217 E7
Mount House Cl L37 12 B5
Mount House Rd L37 12 B5
Mount La Burnley BB10 128 F1
Over Town BB10 108 A8
Shore OL14 109 C3
Mount Pleasant
Adlington PR6 31 A8
Arnside LA5 224 C8
16 Bacup OL13 70 C8
Blackburn BB1 101 F5
Brinscall PR6 63 A8
Chatburn BB7 190 D5
Edgworth BL7 48 D5
High Bentham LA2 239 D8
Nangreaves BL9 50 F3
Nelson BB10 149 C6
7 Preston PR1 96 F8
Rawtenstall BB4 85 E2
Sabden BB7 146 A7
Slaidburn BB7 229 B7
Sollom PR4 57 A3
Whittle-le-W PR6 61 C8
Worsthorne BB10 129 A5
Mount Pleasant La LA5 221 B5
Mount Pleasant Prim Sch BB5 124 F2
Mount Pleasant St
3 Burnley BB11 127 F5
Cornholme OL14 109 A1
3 Horwich BL6 32 D1
6 Oswaldtwistle BB5 103 E4
Mount Rd Burnley BB11 127 F4
Fleetwood FY7 199 A5
Mount St Accrington BB5 104 B4
13 Barrowford BB9 170 D3
Blackpool FY1 130 B6
Brierfield BB9 148 B5
Clayton-le-M BB5 125 A2
Fleetwood FY7 199 A4
Great Harwood BB6 124 C6
Horwich BL6 32 D2
Preston PR1 96 F7
Ramsbottom BL0 50 B6
Rawtenstall BB4 85 E2
Southport PR9 35 D7
Mount St James BB1 102 F4
Mount Terr BB4 86 A2
Mount The
Blackburn BB2 101 C6
Skelmersdale WN8 9 B8
Mount Trinity 3 BB1 101 F5
Mount Zion Ct OL14 109 A1
Mountain Ash OL12 52 B3
Mountain Ash Cl OL12 52 B3
Mountain La BB5 104 C4
Mountain Rd PR7 29 E8
Mountbatten Cl PR2 96 B7
Mountbatten Rd PR7 43 B6
Mountfield Ct WN5 10 F7
Mountside Cl OL12 52 F2
Mountside View OL12 52 D3
Mountwood WN8 18 A4
Mountwood Lo PR8 21 C5
Mowbray Ave BB2 101 F2
Mowbray Dr
Blackpool FY3 152 F1
Burton-in-K LA6 240 C7
Mowbray Pl 1 FY7 198 E4
Mowbray Rd FY7 198 E4
Mowbreck Ct PR4 114 A6
Mowbreck La PR4 114 B7
Mowbrick La LA2 220 D1
Mowgrain View 2 OL13 87 F3
Muirfield PR1 96 A6
Muirfield Cl Euxton PR7 60 D4
Fulwood PR2 117 B6
Muirfield Dr PR8 21 C4
Mulberry Ave PR1 96 A3
Mulberry Cl PR4 115 C1
Mulberry Cotts 10 LA2 211 A4
Mulberry Ct 1 BL6 32 D1
Mulberry La LA1 215 A2
Mulberry Mews
Blackpool FY2 152 F6
5 Kirkham PR4 114 B5
Mulberry St BB1 102 B5
Mulberry Wlk 3 BB1 102 B5
Mulgrave Ave PR2 117 A1
Mullion Cl PR9 54 B5
Muncaster Rd PR1 117 F2
Munro Ave WN5 10 E6
Munro Cres PR2 118 E3
Munster Ave FY2 152 D3
Murchison Gr FY5 175 E1
Murdock Ave PR2 117 D2
Murdock St BB2 101 B4
Murray Ave PR26 76 E5
Murray St Burnley BB10 148 B1
Leyland PR25 77 B1
Preston PR1 117 E1
Musbury Cres BB4 86 A1
Musbury Mews BB4 84 F1
Musbury Rd BB4 67 F7
Musbury View BB4 84 F1
Musden Ave BB4 68 A7
Museum of Lancashire★ PR1 97 B8
Museum St 19 BB1 101 E5
Myers St
Barnoldswick BB18 196 B1
Burnley BB10 128 A8
Myerscough Ave
Blackpool FY4 110 F5
Lytham St Anne's FY8 89 D8
Myerscough Coll PR3 158 D5
Myerscough Hall Dr PR3 158 E5
Myerscough Planks PR3 159 A2
Myerscough Smithy Rd BB2 120 E4
Myndon St LA1 218 D3
Myra Ave LA4 217 C4
Myra Rd FY8 90 B4
Myrtle Ave Blackpool FY3 130 D5
Burnley BB11 127 D4
Cleveleys FY5 175 F5
Poulton-le-F FY6 153 E5
Myrtle Bank Rd
9 Bacup OL13 87 F3
Blackburn BB2 81 C8
Myrtle Cotts OL13 88 A2
Myrtle Dr PR4 114 C4
Myrtle Gdns BL9 33 B2
Myrtle Gr
1 Barnoldswick BB18 196 C2
Burnley BB10 128 F4
Haslingden BB4 85 A1
Morecambe LA3 216 F3
Southport PR9 35 E7
Myrtle St N BL9 33 B2
Myrtle St S 8 BL9 33 B2
Mystic Mews 8 L39 15 E5
Mythop Ave FY8 91 C4
Mythop Cl 1 FY8 91 C4
Mythop Ct FY4 131 D1
Mythop Pl PR2 116 F1
Mythop Rd
Lytham St Anne's FY8 91 C4
Weeton FY4,PR4 132 C2
Mythop Village FY4 131 F2
Mytton St BB12 126 D8
Mytton View BB7 166 D7

N

Naarian Ct BB1 101 F7
Nab La Blackburn BB2 101 D5
Oswaldtwistle BB5 103 B4
Nab Rd PR6 61 E1
Nab View BB7 144 A4
Nab Wood Dr PR7 43 A6
Nab's Head La PR5 99 E8
Nabbs Fold BL8 49 F3
Nabbs Way BL8 50 A1
Naburn Dr WN5 10 E5
Nairn Ave WN8 18 B5
Nairn Cl Blackpool FY4 111 A7
Standish WN6 29 D1
Nairne St BB11 127 D5
Nancy St BB3 82 B1
Nansen Rd
Blackburn BB2 101 B3
Fleetwood FY7 199 A3
Nantwich Ave OL12 52 F3
Napier Ave Blackpool FY4 110 B6
Tarleton PR4 56 F8
Napier Cl FY8 110 E1
Napier St
6 Accrington BB5 104 C5
Nelson BB9 148 E7
Napier Terr PR8 35 A5
Naples Rd BB3 82 C1
Naptha La PR4 76 C6
Narcissus Ave BB4 68 A8
Nares Rd BB2 101 B3
Nares St PR2 117 C1
Narrow Croft Rd L39 15 B1
Narrow La Leyland PR5 75 F2
Ormskirk L39 15 B1
Narrow Lane (Clieves Hills) L39 14 E6
Narrow Moss La L39,L40 15 E8
Narrowgates Cotts BB12 169 C5
Narvik Ave BB11 127 B4
Nasmyth St BL6 32 C3
Nateby Ave FY4 110 E5
Nateby Cl Longridge PR3 139 F8
Nateby Cl *continued*
Lytham St Anne's FY8 90 B7
Nateby Crossing La PR3 181 A8
Nateby Ct 2 FY4 110 B6
Nateby Hall La PR3 203 F1
Nateby Pl PR2 116 F1
Nateby Prim Sch PR3 180 C6
National Football Mus The★ PR1 118 B2
Nave Cl BB3 82 C1
Navena Ave FY7 198 E2
Navigation Bsns Village PR2 96 A8
Navigation Ho 6 BB1 101 F3
Navigation Way
Blackburn BB1 101 F3
1 Fleetwood FY7 199 A3
Preston PR2 96 A7
Naylor's Terr BL7 46 C5
Naylorfarm Ave WN6 19 F5
Naze Ct Freckleton PR4 93 B6
4 Newchurch BB4 86 E1
Naze La PR4 93 B6
Naze La E PR4 93 C5
Naze Lane Ind Est PR4 93 C4
Naze Rd BB4 86 E1
Naze View Ave 4 BB4 86 F2
Neales Fold PR9 54 D5
Neapsands Cl PR2 118 D5
Near Mdw PR6 78 C3
Neargates PR7 42 D3
Neath Cl
Bamber Bridge PR5 97 E3
Blackburn BB1 101 E7
Ned's La
Smallwood Hey PR3 201 A5
Stalmine FY6 177 D5
Neddy Hill LA6 240 B7
Neddy La BB7 144 A4
Nedens Gr L31 5 C3
Nedens La L31 5 C3
Needham Ave LA4 217 A3
Needham Rise LA4 217 A3
Needham Way WN8 18 B5
Needless Hall La BD23 231 E7
Nell Carrs BL0 50 E8
Nell La PR5 77 E4
Nell's La L39 5 F5
Nelson & Colne Coll
Barrowford BB9 170 D2
Colne BB8 171 A5
Colne BB8 171 D5
Nelson Ave PR25 77 B1
Nelson Cres PR2 116 D2
Nelson Ct Fleetwood FY7 198 F3
Preston PR2 95 E8
Southport PR8 34 F4
Nelson Dr PR2 116 D2
Nelson Gdns PR4 135 C8
Nelson Rd
2 Blackpool FY1 130 B2
Brierfield BB10 149 A4
Chorley PR7 43 C7
Fleetwood FY7 198 F3
Nelson Sq BB11 127 F5
Nelson St Accrington BB5 104 C5
Bacup OL13 71 C8
3 Bamber Bridge PR5 77 E8
Clitheroe BB7 166 B8
7 Colne BB8 171 D5
1 Darwen BB3 81 F2
Great Harwood BB6 124 D6
Horwich BL6 32 D3
7 Kirkham PR4 113 F5
Lancaster LA1 214 F8
Lytham St Anne's FY8 91 D3
Morecambe LA4 217 A5
Southport PR8 35 A6
Nelson Sta BB9 148 E8
Nelson Terr Church BB5 103 F6
Preston PR1 96 D8
Nelson Way PR2 95 E8
Nene Cl PR25 60 B7
Neps La BB7 231 C6
Neptune St BB11 127 F6
Neptune Way BB3 82 B6
Nesswood Ave FY4 110 E6
Neston St PR1 97 E8
Nether Beck LA6 240 A2
Nether Kellet Com Prim Sch LA6 221 E4
Nether Kellet Rd LA6 237 B8
Nether View LA2 241 E1
Netherby St BB11 127 E4
Netherfield Cl BB12 127 D7
Netherfield Gdns 9 BB9 148 E8
Netherfield Rd BB9 148 E8
Netherheys Cl BB8 171 B5
Netherlands Rd LA4 217 C4
Netherley Rd PR7 29 E8
Netherton Ho 13 BB6 124 C5
Nethertown Cl BB7 144 B6
Netherwood Gdns BB6 143 B5
Netherwood Rd BB10 128 D7
Netherwood St BB10 148 E2
Nethway Ave FY3 130 F6
Netley Ave OL12 52 F3
Network 65 Bsns Pk BB11 126 F4
Neverstitch Cl WN8 17 F2
Neverstitch Rd WN8 17 D2
Nevett St PR1 97 D8
Nevill St PR8 35 B7

Neville Ave FY5 ....175 E1
Neville Dr FY5 ....153 B8
Neville St PR3 ....140 A1
Nevy Fold Ave BL6 ......32 F3
New Acres Carnforth LA5 223 D1
Newburgh WN8 ....27 A1
New Bank Rd BB2 ....101 B6
New Barn BB4 ....68 B6
New Barn La BB4 ....69 A8
New Bath St BB8 ....171 C6
New Bonny St FY1 ......130 B4
New Briggs Fold BL7 ....47 E2
New Brown St 17 BB9 ...170 D1
New Brunswick St BL6 ...32 B3
New Bury Cl BB5 ....103 C3
New Century Apartments
  BL0 ....50 C7
New Chapel La BL6 ......32 F2
New Chapel St BB2 .....101 B2
New Church Cl 14 BB5 ..124 F3
New Church Ho 6 FY1 ..130 C4
New Church Mews 5
  BB10 ....148 B1
New Cock Yd 25 PR1 ....97 A7
New Court Dr BL7 ....47 E3
New Court Way L39 .....15 F5
New Cswy L37,L38 ....3 B8
New Cut Cl PR8 ....22 A8
New Cut La L39,PR8 .....22 D6
New Fold WN5 ....10 C4
New Foul La PR8 ....36 A4
New Garden Fields BB4 ..87 A7
New Garden St 1 BB2 ..101 E3
New Ground Ct BB10 ....148 C3
New Hague BB18 ....194 F3
New Hall Ave FY4 ......111 B5
New Hall Ave N FY4 ....111 B6
New Hall Dr PR8 ....36 C1
New Hall Hey Bsns Pk
  BB4 ....85 F1
New Hall Hey Rd BB4 ....85 F1
New Hall La PR1 ....97 C8
New Hall Rd BL9 ....33 E4
New Hall St BB10,BB12 .148 A1
New Hey La PR4 ....114 E5
New House La PR3 ......203 F3
New House St BB8 .....171 E5
New Inn Yd LA4 ....217 B6
New La
  Burscough Bridge L40 ..25 B6
  Burton-in-K LA6 ......240 B7
  Duncombe PR3 ....158 F8
  Eagland Hill PR3 .....179 D7
  Great Mitton BB7 .....165 E6
  Haskayne L39 ....13 E3
  Middleworth Green PR1 .96 E3
  Newtown PR7 ....59 A1
  Ormskirk L39 ....15 E2
  Oswaldtwistle BB5 ....103 C2
  Smallwood Hey PR3 ...201 B2
  Southport PR9 ....54 E3
  Tarleton PR4 ....56 D6
  Thornton FY5 ....153 C7
New Lane Head PR26 .....59 A2
New Lane Pace PR9 .....55 B8
New Lane Sta L40 ....25 B7
New Line OL13 ....71 B8
New Line Ind Est OL13 ..71 A8
New Links Ave PR2 .....117 A6
New Longton All Saints CE
  Prim Sch PR4 ....75 F7
New Market St
  15 Blackburn BB1 ....101 E5
  Chorley PR7 ....43 C8
  Clitheroe BB7 ....166 E8
  Colne BB8 ....171 D5
New Market The FY1 ...130 B1
New Meadow Cl BB1 .....82 A8
New Meadow La L37 ....3 F8
New Miles La WN6 ....19 F5
New Mill St
  Blackburn BB1 ....101 F6
  Eccleston PR7 ....41 C6
New Moss La PR6 ....61 C5
New Oxford St BB8 ....171 E6
New Palace Ct BB12 ...127 B7
New Park St 2 BB2 ....101 D5
New Pastures 4 PR5 ....77 C8
New Plough Yd BB6 ....124 D5
New Quay Rd LA1 ......214 B8
New Rd Adlington PR6 ..31 D8
  Bamber Bridge PR5 ....97 B1
  Blackpool FY8 ....110 B4
  Burnley BB11 ....128 B2
  Coppull PR7 ....42 F3
  Croston PR5 ....40 B7
  Earby BB18 ....197 B2
  Formby L37 ....12 A5
  Ingleton LA6 ....242 F4
  Lancaster LA1 ....214 F8
  Newchurch BB4 ....86 F2
  Rufford L40 ....39 B3
  Silverdale LA5 ....224 F1
  Staynall FY6 ....177 B4
  Warton LA5 ....223 A6
  Whitworth OL12 ....71 B1
New Rough Hey FY6 ....116 F6
New Row Altham BB5 ...125 E6
  Trawden BB8 ....172 C4
New Row Cotts PR3 ....163 D1
New Scotland St BB9 ..170 E1
New St Blackrod BL6 ....31 D2
  Brinscall PR6 ....62 F8
  2 Burnley BB12 .....126 B8
  Carnforth LA5 ....223 D2

New St continued
  Caton LA2 ....237 D3
  Colne BB8 ....171 B3
  Eccleston PR7 ....41 C6
  Halton LA2 ....219 C6
  Haskayne L39 ....14 B8
  14 Haslingden BB4 ....85 B3
  Lancaster LA1 ....214 F8
  Mawdesley L40 ....40 C2
  Morecambe LA4 ......217 A5
  Nelson BB9 ....170 F1
  Rochdale OL12 ....52 E2
New Summerseat House Sch
  BL0 ....50 B2
New Taylor Fold BB10 ..148 F3
New Way Royal Oak L39 ..7 C2
  Whitworth OL12 ....71 C1
New Wellington St BB2 101 C1
New Wellington Gdns
  BB2 ....101 C1
Newark Pl Fulwood PR2 .117 D8
  4 Preston PR2 ......116 E2
Newark Rd OL12 ....52 F3
Newark Sq OL12 ....52 F3
Newark St BB5 ....103 F5
Newarth La PR4 ....73 E3
Newbeck Cl BL6 ....32 F3
Newbigging Ave 5 BB4 .86 F2
Newburgh CE Prim Sch
  WN8 ....27 A1
Newburn Cl WN8 ....18 B5
Newbury Ave 3 FY4 ...110 D8
Newbury Ct PR2 ....117 C8
Newbury Gn PR2 ....117 C8
Newbury Rd
  Lytham St Anne's FY8 .90 A4
  Skelmersdale WN8 .....18 B5
Newby Ave
  Fleetwood FY7 ....198 D1
  Poulton-le-F FY6 ....153 D1
Newby Back La BB7 ....231 A4
Newby Burnley BB11 ...127 E2
  Southport PR8 ....21 B3
Newby Ct L37 ....11 F3
Newby Dr
  Clayton-le-W PR25 ....77 E2
  Lancaster LA1 ....218 D3
  Skelmersdale WN8 .....18 B5
Newby La BB7 ....192 B8
Newby Pl Blackpool FY4 131 B1
  Fulwood PR2 ....118 D4
Newby Rd BB5 ....104 E8
Newcastle Ave
  Blackpool FY3 ....130 D4
  Cleveleys FY5 ....175 F4
Newcastle St BB2 .....101 C3
Newchurch CE Prim Sch
  BB4 ....86 E1
Newchurch Cl BB2 .....101 F2
Newchurch Old Rd OL13 .87 E1
Newchurch Rd
  Bacup OL13 ....70 C8
  Rawtenstall BB4 ......86 C2
Newcombe Rd BL0 ....50 B2
Newcroft LA5 ....223 E6
Newfield Ct FY8 ....89 F6
Newfield Dr
  Blackburn BB1,BB2 ....82 A8
  Nelson BB9 ....148 E8
Newfield Rd PR5 ....78 A7
Newfield Sch BB1 ......82 B8
Newgate Fulwood PR2 ..117 E4
  Morecambe LA3 ......217 E2
Newgate Ave WN6 ....19 E8
Newgate La PR4 ....76 C8
Newgate Rd WN8 ....9 F7
Newhaven Dr PR3 ......181 D2
Newhouse Rd
  Accrington BB5 ......125 D1
  Blackpool FY4 ....130 F2
Newington Ave BB1 ....122 F3
Newlands PR7 ....41 C6
Newlands Ave
  Blackpool FY3 ....130 D2
  Burscough L40 ....25 F4
  Clitheroe BB7 ....166 C7
  Higher Penwortham PR1 96 B5
  Lancaster LA1 ....215 B5
  Rochdale OL12 ....52 F3
Newlands Cl
  5 Blackburn BB2 .....80 E8
  Rochdale OL12 ....52 F3
Newlands Rd
  Lancaster LA1 ....215 C5
  Lytham St Anne's FY8 .90 C5
  Morecambe LA4 ......217 C4
  Quernmore LA1 ....215 E6
Newlands Way FY6 ....153 C1
Newlyn Ave
  Blackpool FY4 ....110 E5
  Maghull L31 ....5 E1
Newlyn Ct FY4 ....110 E5
Newlyn Dr WN8 ....9 D7
Newlyn Pl PR2 ....116 F5
Newman Gr FY5 ....175 E5
Newman Rd 2 FY1 ....130 D8
Newman St BB10 ......148 B1
Newmarket Ave LA1 ...215 B3
Newmarket St LA4 ....217 E7
Newport Ct PR2 ......116 F3
Newport St BB9 ......170 E1
News La WA11 ....8 F2
Newsham Hall La PR4 ..136 F3
Newsham Pl LA1 ......215 A5
Newsham Rd LA1 ......215 A5
Newsham St 1 PR2 ....117 D1
Newsome St PR25 ......77 A1

Newstead Dr WN8 ....18 B5
Newstet Rd L33 ....1 C2
Newthorn BB5 ....104 A1
Newton Ave
  Poulton-le-F FY6 ....153 C2
  Preston PR1 ....98 A8
Newton Bluecoat CE Prim
  Sch PR4 ....115 A2
Newton Cl Freckleton PR4 .93 C7
  Leyland PR26 ....59 B8
Newton Ct PR2 ....117 B1
Newton Dr
  Accrington BB5 ......104 D3
  Blackpool FY3 ....130 C5
  Holme Chapel BB10 ...108 A7
  Ramsbottom BL8 ....50 A1
  Skelmersdale WN8 .....18 B5
Newton Dr E FY3 ......131 B7
Newton Gr FY5 ....153 D7
Newton Hall Holiday Ctr
  FY3 ....131 C6
Newton Ho PR1 ....97 A8
Newton Pl FY3 ....131 A7
Newton Rd
  Lytham St Anne's FY8 .90 A7
  Preston PR2 ....117 B2
Newton St Blackburn BB1 102 B5
  Burnley BB10 ....127 C7
  Clitheroe BB7 ....166 D7
  Darwen BB3 ....82 B3
  Oswaldtwistle BB5 ...103 C5
  2 Preston PR1 ....97 B8
  Southport PR9 ....36 A7
Newton Terr LA1 .....218 E3
Newtown BB18 ....196 B2
Newtown St BB8 ......171 E5
Nib La PR1 ....76 E8
Nichol St PR7 ....61 C1
Nicholas St
  Brierfield BB10 .....148 E3
  Burnley BB11 ....128 A5
  Colne BB8 ....171 C4
  Darwen BB3 ....81 F1
Nicholl Cl FY8 ....89 D6
Nicholl St 1 BB4 ....128 A8
Nicholson Cres LA4 ..217 D5
Nick Hilton's La PR6 ..44 D3
Nickey La BB2 ....121 F2
Nickleton Brow PR4 ...44 C2
Nickson Weind PR3 ...181 C7
Nicksons La FY6 ......200 B4
Nicola Cl OL13 ....88 A7
Nightfield La BB2 ....120 F6
Nightingale Cl
  Blackburn BB1 ....102 B1
  Whalley BB7 ....144 A7
Nightingale Cres 4
  BB11 ....127 C5
Nightingale Dr FY6 ..153 B2
Nightingale Rd BL6 ....31 C3
Nightingale St PR6 ....31 A8
Nile Cl PR2 ....95 E4
Nile St 5 Lancaster LA1 214 F8
  12 Nelson BB9 ....170 D1
  Preston PR1 ....97 A7
Nimes St PR1 ....97 D8
Nine Elms PR2 ....117 C6
Nineteen Acre La LA5 .225 F4
Nineveh St 12 BB8 ...171 E5
Nipe La WN5 ....9 B5
Nithside FY4 ....131 C1
Niton Cl BB4 ....85 C1
Nixon La PR26 ....59 A8
Nixon's La PR8 ....21 E7
Nixons Ct PR26 ....58 F8
Nixons La WN8 ....9 D7
Noble St 13 Darwen BB3 .65 A8
  Great Harwood BB6 ..124 C4
  Rishton BB1 ....124 B1
Noblett Ct 9 FY7 ....198 F2
Noblett St BB1 ....101 F5
Noel Gate L39 ....15 B1
Noel Jones Ct FY8 ....89 E7
Noel Rd LA1 ....218 C3
Noel Sq PR2 ....118 E1
Noels Villa PR3 .....138 E4
Noggarth Rd BB12 ....169 F2
Nolan St PR8 ....35 C5
Nook Cotts PR3 ......180 C6
Nook Cres PR3 ....139 C1
Nook Croft BB18 .....197 C2
Nook Farm Ave OL12 ...52 F3
Nook Field PR3 ......138 D6
Nook Glade PR2 ......139 C1
Nook La
  Bamber Bridge PR5 ....77 D6
  Blackburn BB2 ....100 F1
  Churchtown PR3 .....181 A3
  Mawdesley L40 ....40 E5
  Oswaldtwistle BB5 ...103 B2
Nook Terr Blackburn BB2 .101 A1
  1 Rochdale OL12 .....52 F3
Nook The
  Appley Bridge WN6 ...19 E7
  Bolton-le-S LA5 ....221 A4
  Staining FY3 ....131 D5
Nookdales Cotts LA6 .242 F1
Nookfield Cl FY8 ......91 A4
Nooklands PR2 ....117 E4
Noon Sun St OL12 ......52 F1
Noor St PR1 ....118 A1
Nora St BB9 ....170 D3
Norbreck Cl BB2 ....81 F8
Norbreck Cl FY5 .....152 C6
Norbreck Dr PR2 .....116 E1
Norbreck Prim Sch FY5 152 D8
Norbreck Rd FY5 .....152 C7

Norburn Cres L37 .....11 F2
Norbury Cl PR9 ....54 C5
Norcliffe Rd FY2 ....152 C5
Norcote Lodge L37 ....11 E4
Norcross Brow PR6 ....63 B8
Norcross La FY5 .....153 A7
Norcross Pl PR2 .....116 F1
Norden Ct
  Great Harwood BB6 ..124 E5
  1 Rishton BB1 ......124 B1
Norden High Sch BB1 .124 C2
Norden View BB1 .....124 A2
Norfield L39 ....15 F5
Norfolk Ave
  Blackpool FY2 ....152 B3
  Burnley BB12 ....127 B7
  Cleveleys FY5 ....175 E3
  Morecambe LA3 ......216 F2
  Padiham BB12 ....126 D6
Norfolk Cl
  7 Clayton-le-M BB5 .124 F3
  Leyland PR25 ....59 E7
Norfolk Gr
  Accrington BB5 ......104 A7
  Southport PR8 ....34 F1
Norfolk Rd
  Bamber Bridge PR5 ....97 D4
  Blackpool FY3 ....131 A2
  Longshaw WN5 ....10 E1
  Lytham St Anne's FY8 .91 C5
  Preston PR1 ....118 A1
  Southport PR8 ....34 F1
Norfolk St
  Accrington BB5 ......104 D7
  Blackburn BB2 ....101 C2
  Colne BB8 ....171 C6
  Darwen BB3 ....82 B1
  Lancaster LA1 ....218 D2
  Nelson BB9 ....170 D1
  Rishton BB1 ....124 A1
Norham Cl BB12 ......127 E7
Norkeed Rd FY5 ......152 C7
Norland Dr LA3 ......212 F8
Norman Cl FY5 ....175 F1
Norman Rd BB5 ....103 C5
Norman St
  Burnley BB10 ....128 A7
  Bury BL9 ....33 B4
  Fulwood PR2 ....117 D3
  Preston PR1 ....117 E2
Normandie Ave FY2 ..152 D3
Normandy Rd PR4 ....137 B3
Normanhurst LA3 ......16 A4
Normington Cl L31 ....5 C4
Normoss Ave FY3 ....131 A7
Normoss Rd FY3 .....131 C7
Norris House Dr L39 ..6 C8
Norris Way L37 ....12 B3
Norse Cotts PR26 .....57 E6
North Albert St 12 FY7 199 B5
North Albion St FY7 ..199 A4
North Ave
  Barnoldswick BB18 ..196 B2
  Ramsbottom BL0 ......49 F1
North Bank Ave BB1 ..122 E1
North Church St FY7 ..199 B5
North Cliff St 6 PR1 ..96 E6
North Cliffe Sch BB6 .124 B6
North Clifton St 7 FY8 .91 B3
North Cres FY8 ....89 E6
North Croft PR3 .....181 C8
North Ct Blackpool FY5 152 C8
  Cleveleys FY5 ....175 D5
North Dr
  Appley Bridge WN6 ...28 C2
  Blackpool FY5 ....152 D6
  Cleveleys FY5 ....175 D5
  Inskip PR4 ....157 C1
  Kirkham PR4 ....113 F6
  Lancaster LA1 ....211 B8
North Dunes L38 ....2 F4
North East Ave PR6 ...63 A8
North East Dr LA1 ...211 B8
North End Football Gd
  (Preston North End FC)
  PR1 ....118 B2
North End La L38 ......3 A6
North Gr 1 PR5 ....77 C8
North Highfield PR2 ..118 E6
North Ho 10 PR6 ......35 B7
North Houses La FY8 .111 D1
North Leach Dr BB3 ...21 A5
North Meade L31 ....5 C2
North Meadowside PR4 .75 A6
North Mersey Bsns Ctr
  L33 ....1 D4
North Moor La L39 ....23 E2
North Moss La L37 ....12 D7
North Nook La PR3 ...183 E3
North Par 7 BB18 ....196 B3
North Park Ave BB5 ..170 C1
North Park Dr FY3 ...130 F5
North Perimeter Rd L33 .1 D4
North Prom FY8 ....89 D7
North Quarry Bsns Pk
  WN6 ....1 D3
North Rd Blackburn BB1 102 C3
  Bretherton PR26 ......58 B7
  Carnforth LA5 ....223 D1
  Lancaster LA1 ....214 F8
  Preston PR1 ....117 F1
  Rawtenstall BB4 ......86 C2
  Southport PR9 ....54 C4
North Ribble St 7 PR5 .97 C6

North Road Prim Sch
  LA5 ....223 D1
North Spine LA1 .....197 B8
North Sq Blackpool FY3 130 D6
  Cleveleys FY5 ....175 D5
North St
  Barnoldswick BB18 ..196 B1
  Brierfield BB10 .....148 F3
  Burnley BB10 ....148 A1
  Chorley PR7 ....61 D7
  2 Clitheroe BB7 ....189 F1
  Colne BB8 ....171 E6
  Fleetwood FY7 ......199 B5
  Hapton BB12 ....126 C5
  Haslingden BB4 ....85 C1
  Morecambe LA4 ......217 B5
  14 Nelson BB9 ......170 D1
  Newchurch BB4 ....86 E1
  Padiham BB12 ....146 C1
  Preston PR1 ....96 F8
  Ramsbottom BL0 ......68 C2
  Rawtenstall BB4 ......86 A2
  Southport PR9 ....35 C8
  Water BB4 ....87 A8
  Whitworth OL12 ....71 C1
North Syke Ave PR2 ..116 C1
North Union View PR5 .76 F1
North Vale PR5 ....43 F1
North Valley Rd BB8 .171 D5
North Valley Ret Pk
  BB8 ....171 D5
North View Kirkham PR4 113 F5
  Ramsbottom BL0 ......50 B2
  Ramsbottom,Strongstry BL0 68 C2
  Rawtenstall BB4 ......86 A8
  Whitworth OL12 ....71 D1
North View Cl PR3 ...156 C5
North Warton St FY8 ..91 C3
North West Dr LA1 ...211 A8
Northall PR4 ....74 E2
Northam Cl PR9 ....54 A5
Northbrook Gdns PR25 .76 E1
Northbrook Prim Sch
  PR25 ....76 F1
Northbrook Rd PR25 ..76 F1
Northcliffe BB6 .....124 B6
Northcote Rd
  Langho BB6 ....143 C3
  Preston PR1 ....96 D7
Northcote St Darwen BB3 .65 B6
  4 Haslingden BB4 ....85 B2
  8 Leyland PR25 ......77 A1
Northdene WN8 ....27 B2
Northenden Rd PR7 ....42 E1
Northern Ave PR4 .....74 E2
Northern Prim Sch OL13 .87 F6
Northern Terr LA5 ...224 F5
Northfield
  Skelmersdale WN8 .....18 B4
  Southport PR9 ....53 C1
Northfield Ave FY1 ..130 B8
Northfield Cl L33 .....1 A4
Northfield Rd
  Blackburn BB1 ....101 E7
  Rising Bridge BB5 ....85 A8
Northfleet Ave FY7 ..198 E2
Northfold Com Prim Sch
  FY5 ....152 D6
Northgate Blackburn BB2 101 E5
  Blackpool FY2 ....152 C4
  Goosnargh PR3 ......138 D6
  Leyland PR25 ....77 B2
  Lytham St Anne's FY8 .89 D6
  Morecambe LA3 ......217 E2
  Whitworth OL12 ....52 C7
Northgate Cl BL6 .....32 C1
Northgate Dr PR6 .....61 E2
Northlands Fulwood PR2 117 E6
  Leyland PR26 ....59 C7
Northleach Ave 2 PR1 .96 F2
Northside PR7 ....60 C3
Northumberland Ave
  Blackpool FY2 ....152 B1
  Cleveleys FY5 ....175 E5
Northumberland Cl BB3 .65 C6
Northumberland St
  2 Chorley PR7 ....43 D7
  Morecambe LA4 ......217 A5
Northway Broughton PR3 137 C3
  Fleetwood FY7 ......198 D1
  Fulwood PR2 ....117 D7
  Maghull L31,L39 ......5 E4
  Ormskirk L39 ....15 A1
  Skelmersdale WN8 .....18 B4
Northway Prim Sch L31 .5 E3
Northways WN6 ....29 D2
Northwood Cl
  Burnley BB12 ....127 D2
  Lytham St Anne's FY8 .90 E4
Northwood Way FY6 ..153 D2
Norton Ave LA3 ......216 D3
Norton Ct FY8 ....89 F4
Norton Dr LA3 ....216 E2
Norton Gr LA3 ....216 D2
Norton Pl LA3 ....216 D2
Norton Rd Garstang PR3 204 C2
  Morecambe LA3 ......216 D2
  Rochdale OL12 ....52 F3
Norton St 1 BB12 ....126 C4
Norton Vale FY5 .....176 D2
Norway Ho 11 BB8 ....171 D5
Norwich Pl
  Blackpool FY2 ....152 D5
  33 Preston PR1 ......97 A7
Norwich St BB1 ......101 F7
Norwood Ave
  Becconsall PR4 ....73 F2
  Blackburn BB1 ....101 E2

Norwood Ave continued
Blackpool FY3 . . . . .130 E8
Southport PR9 . . . . .35 E7
Norwood Cl PR6 . . . . .31 A8
Norwood Cres PR9 . . . . . . .35 E7
Norwood Ct 13 LA1 . . . . . .215 A8
Norwood Cty Prim Sch
PR9 .35 E7
Norwood Dr LA4 . . . . . . .217 F3
Norwood Gdns PR9 . . . . . .35 F7
Norwood Rd
Lytham St Anne's FY8 . . . .89 C8
Southport PR8,PR9 . . . . . . .35 F6
Notre Dame Gdns BB1 . .102 A6
Nottingham Rd PR1 . . . .118 A1
Nottingham St BB1 . . . . .102 A4
Novak Pl 6 LA4 . . . . . . .217 F4
Nowell Gr BB12 . . . . .145 D2
Nowell St 17 BB6 . . . . . .124 C5
Noyna Ave BB8 . . . . .194 E1
Noyna Rd BB8 . . . . .194 E1
Noyna St BB8 . . . . .171 E6
Noyna View BB8 . . . . . . .171 E7
Nun's St LA1 . . . . .215 A8
Nurseries The Formby L37 . .12 A2
Hesketh Bank PR4 . . . . . . .73 E3
Nursery Ave L39 . . . . .16 A6
Nursery Cl Coppull PR7 . .42 E4
Leyland PR25 . . . . .59 F8
Nursery Cl Becconsall PR4 73 F1
Formby L37 . . . . .11 F2
Nursery La PR4 . . . . .75 E8
Nursery Nook BB3 . . . . . . .82 D5
Nursery Rd L31 . . . . .5 C4
Nuthall Rd PR8 . . . . .35 F3
Nuttall Ave
Great Harwood BB6 . . . . .124 C4
Horwich BL6 . . . . .32 A3
Nuttall Cl BL0 . . . . .50 C5
Nuttall Hall Cotts BL0 . .50 D5
Nuttall Hall Rd BL0 . . . . .50 D5
Nuttall La BL0 . . . . .50 C4
Nuttall Rd Blackpool FY1 .130 D2
Ramsbottom BL0 . . . . .50 D4
Nuttall St Accrington BB5 104 C5
Bacup OL13 . . . . .88 B3
Blackburn BB2 . . . . .101 D1
Blackburn,Ewood BB2 . . . .81 D8
7 Burnley BB11 . . . . .128 B4
Bury BL9 . . . . .33 A1
Rawtenstall BB4 . . . . .86 B3
Nuttall St Mews 3 BB5 104 C5
Nutter Cres BB12 . . . . . .146 F5
Nutter Rd Accrington BB5 104 C7
Cleveleys FY5 . . . . .175 D3
2 Preston PR1 . . . . .96 E7

O

O'Hagan Ct BB9 . . . . . . .148 B6
Oak Ave Blackpool FY4 . .110 D8
Euxton PR7 . . . . .60 D3
Galgate LA2 . . . . .210 F4
Higher Penwortham PR1 . . .96 B3
9 Horwich BL6 . . . . .32 E1
Kirkham PR4 . . . . .114 B4
Longridge PR3 . . . . .140 A7
Morecambe LA4 . . . . .217 F6
Ormskirk L39 . . . . .15 D4
Ramsbottom BL0 . . . . .50 A2
Rising Bridge BB5 . . . . . . .85 A8
Thornton FY5 . . . . .153 C8
Oak Bank Accrington BB5 125 D2
Gregson Lane PR5 . . . . . . .98 E1
Oak Cl Barrow BB7 . . . . .166 D1
Millgate OL12 . . . . .71 D4
Rishton BB1 . . . . .103 B8
Oak Cres WN8 . . . . .17 D1
Oak Croft PR6 . . . . .78 B2
Oak Dr Burscough L40 . . .25 F3
Chorley PR6 . . . . .61 C3
Freckleton PR4 . . . . .93 A5
Halton LA2 . . . . .219 D7
Oak Gates BL7 . . . . .47 E1
Oak Gn L39 . . . . .15 F5
Oak Gr Darwen BB3 . . . . .82 B5
Garstang PR3 . . . . .181 C7
New Longton PR4 . . . . . . .76 A6
Oak Hill Cl BB5 . . . . .104 C4
Oak La Accrington BB5 . .104 D5
Newton-w-S PR4 . . . . . . .114 F2
Oak Rd PR3 . . . . .181 B8
Oak Ridge BB7 . . . . .189 D7
Oak St Accrington BB5 . .104 C5
Bacup OL13 . . . . .88 A3
Brierfield BB9 . . . . .148 B6
Burnley BB12 . . . . .127 C6
Clayton-le-M BB5 . . . . . . .124 F1
Clow Bridge BB11 . . . . . .106 B4
Colne BB8 . . . . .171 F6
Fleetwood FY7 . . . . .199 A4
Great Harwood BB6 . . . . .124 C6
Millgate OL12 . . . . .71 D5
2 Nelson BB9 . . . . .170 E1
Oswaldtwistle BB5 . . . . . .103 D3
Preston PR1 . . . . .97 A7
Ramsbottom BL0 . . . . .50 B5
Southport PR8 . . . . .35 E6
Oak Terr BB18 . . . . .196 C3
Oak Tree Ct WN8 . . . . . . .18 D3
Oak Tree Dr PR4 . . . . . . .113 C4
Oak View Leyland PR25 . .76 E2
Millgate OL12 . . . . .71 D4
Oakdene Ave BB5 . . . . . .125 E1
Oaken Bank BB10 . . . . . .148 E3
Oaken St OL13 . . . . .88 B3

Oakenclough Cotts PR3 226 C2
Oakenclough Rd
Bacup OL13 . . . . .88 B3
Bleasdale PR3 . . . . .183 F4
Oakeneaves Ave BB11 . .127 D2
Oakengate PR2 . . . . .118 C7
Oakengates WN6 . . . . .29 F1
Oakenhead Cl PR3 . . . . .160 D7
Oakenhead St PR1 . . . . .118 E1
Oakenhead Wood Old Rd
BB4 .85 E3
Oakenhurst Rd BB2 . . . . .101 D4
Oakenshaw Ave OL12 . . . .52 C6
Oakenshaw View OL12 . . .52 C6
Oakfield Fulwood PR2 . . .117 F7
Preston PR2 . . . . .117 B1
Oakfield Ave
Barnoldswick BB18 . . . . . .196 A3
Clayton-le-M BB5 . . . . . . .124 C4
Huncoat BB5 . . . . .125 C1
Oakfield Cl BL6 . . . . .32 F2
Oakfield Cres BB5 . . . . . .103 F4
Oakfield Dr Formby L37 . .11 D4
Leyland PR26 . . . . .59 B8
Oakfield House Sch
PR4 . . . . .115 C5
Oakfield Rd
Blackburn BB2 . . . . .81 D7
Hightown L38 . . . . .2 F3
Oakfields L39 . . . . .16 A5
Oakford Cl PR9 . . . . .55 B5
Oakgate Cl PR7 . . . . .56 F5
Oakgrove FY4 . . . . .110 D6
Oakham Ct 12 PR1 . . . . . .97 A7
Oakhill Cl L31 . . . . .5 D2
Oakhill Coll BB7 . . . . . . .144 D6
Oakhill Cottage La L31 . . .5 D4
Oakhill Dr L31 . . . . .5 D4
Oakhill Rd L31 . . . . .5 D3
Oakhurst Ave BB5 . . . . . .125 E1
Oakland Ave FY5 . . . . . . .152 D6
Oakland Glen PR5 . . . . . . .97 A3
Oakland St
4 Bamber Bridge PR5 . . . .97 E1
Nelson BB9 . . . . .148 E8
Oaklands Ave
Barrowford BB9 . . . . .170 D3
Tarleton PR4 . . . . .57 A7
Oaklands Ct LA1 . . . . . . .214 C5
Oaklands Dr
Higher Penwortham PR1 . . .96 A4
Rawtenstall BB4 . . . . .85 E2
Oaklands Gr PR2 . . . . . . .116 F1
Oaklands Rd BL0 . . . . .68 D2
Oaklea WN8 . . . . .29 A2
Oakleaf Cl PR3 . . . . .138 C6
Oakleaf Ct FY5 . . . . .175 D4
Oakleaf Way FY4 . . . . . . .131 D1
Oaklee Gr L33 . . . . .1 A4
Oakleigh WN8 . . . . .9 D2
Oakleigh Terr 8 OL14 . .109 B1
Oakley Rd
Morecambe LA3 . . . . .216 D2
Rawtenstall BB4 . . . . .85 F2
Oakley St BB4 . . . . .85 E2
Oakmere PR6 . . . . .78 C3
Oakmere Ave PR6 . . . . . . .79 D2
Oakmere Cl BB2 . . . . .81 C6
Oakmoor Ave FY2 . . . . . .152 E4
Oakridge Cl PR2 . . . . . . .117 F7
Oaks Bar BB1 . . . . .122 C8
Oaks Brow BB1 . . . . .122 C7
Oaks The
Bamber Bridge PR5 . . . . . .97 B3
Chorley PR7 . . . . .43 B4
Leyland PR26 . . . . .59 A7
Poulton-le-F FY6 . . . . .153 D4
Southport PR8 . . . . .34 F6
St Michael's on W PR3 . . .157 C7
Oaksfield BB3 . . . . .81 E5
Oakshaw Dr OL12 . . . . . . .52 A1
Oakshott Pl PR5 . . . . .78 B7
Oaktree
Clayton-le-W PR25 . . . . . . .77 D4
Fulwood PR2 . . . . .117 A4
Oaktree Cl PR2 . . . . .117 A4
Oakville Rd LA3 . . . . .212 E5
Oakway PR3 . . . . .140 A8
Oakwood WN8 . . . . .18 D3
Oakwood Ave
Bamber Bridge PR5 . . . . . .97 C4
Blackburn BB1 . . . . .123 B1
Lytham St Anne's FY8 . . . .90 E4
Shevington WN6 . . . . .19 F5
Southport PR8 . . . . .21 D6
Oakwood Cl
Blackpool FY4 . . . . .110 F4
Brierfield BB10 . . . . .148 D3
Darwen BB3 . . . . .81 E5
Thornton FY5 . . . . .176 D2
Oakwood Dr
Fulwood PR2 . . . . .117 D8
Southport PR8 . . . . .21 E5
Oakwood Gdns LA1 . . . . .215 A4
Oakwood Gr LA5 . . . . . . .220 F2
Oakwood Rd
Accrington BB5 . . . . .104 D3
Chorley PR7 . . . . .43 B6
Coppull PR7 . . . . .42 C7
Oakwood View PR7 . . . . . .43 B4
Oakworth Ave PR2 . . . . . .118 F5
Oasis Cl L40 . . . . .39 B3
Oasis Wildlife Ctr★ LA7 126 D7
Oat St BB12 . . . . .126 D7
Oban Cres PR1 . . . . .118 D3
Oban Ct PR2 . . . . .139 D1
Oban Dr BB1 . . . . .102 C3

Oban Pl FY2 . . . . .152 E6
Oban St BB10 . . . . .128 C8
Observatory Rd BB2 . . . .102 A2
Occupation La
Singleton FY6 . . . . .154 D4
Stalmine FY6 . . . . .177 C7
Ocean Bvd FY4 . . . . .110 A7
Ocean Ct FY6 . . . . .199 D5
Ocean Way FY5 . . . . .175 C3
Odell Way PR5 . . . . .97 E3
Off Botanic Rd PR9 . . . . .54 A1
Off Mount Pleasant St 7
BB5 . . . . .103 E4
Offerton St BL6 . . . . .32 A3
Ogden Cl BB4 . . . . .68 A7
Ogden Dr BB4 . . . . .68 A7
Old Acre L38 . . . . .2 F3
Old Back La BB7 . . . . . . .144 F7
Old Bank La
Blackburn BB1,BB2 . . . . . .102 B2
Blackburn BB2 . . . . .102 A2
Old Bank St 4 BB2 . . . . .101 E4
Old Boundary Way L39 . .15 F6
Old Bridge La FY6 . . . . . .154 B7
Old Bridge Way PR6 . . . . .61 D1
Old Buckley La PR3 . . . . .141 D7
Old Carr Mill St BB4 . . . .85 B5
Old Chapel The BB1 . . . . .85 D7
Old Clitheroe Rd PR3 . . .163 E3
Old Cock Yd PR1 . . . . .97 A7
Old Croft PR2 . . . . .117 D8
Old Dawber's La PR7 . . . .60 B1
Old Engine Ho The 12
BL0 .50 C6
Old Engine La
Ramsbottom BL0 . . . . .50 D6
Skelmersdale WN8 . . . . . . .17 C2
Old Farmside BB2 . . . . . . .81 D7
Old Forge FY8 . . . . .90 D7
Old Gates Dr BB2 . . . . . . .80 F8
Old Gn BL8 . . . . .49 F1
Old Greaves Town La
PR2 . . . . .116 E1
Old Greenwood La BB6 . .32 D1
Old Ground St 8 BL0 . . . .50 C6
Old Hall Bsns Pk PR9 . . .36 A5
Old Hall Cl
Bamber Bridge PR5 . . . . . .77 E8
7 Morecambe LA4 . . . . . .217 F4
Roughlee BB9 . . . . .170 B5
Old Hall Dr
Bamber Bridge PR5 . . . . . .77 E8
Huncoat BB5 . . . . .125 F1
Old Hall La
Charnock Green PR7 . . . . .42 B6
Pleasington BB2 . . . . .100 C2
Old Hall Pk PR3 . . . . .137 E3
Old Hall Sq BB10 . . . . . . .129 A5
Old Hall St BB10 . . . . . . .128 A8
Old Hey Croft 5 PR1 . . . .96 D2
Old Hive PR3 . . . . .185 D4
Old House La FY6 . . . . . .111 D7
Old Kiln OL13 . . . . .70 D8
Old La Bispham Green L40 .27 D8
Earby BB18 . . . . .197 B2
Formby L37 . . . . .11 F6
Haskayne L39 . . . . .13 E3
Horwich BL6 . . . . .32 F7
Kelbrook BB18 . . . . .194 F4
Maghull L31 . . . . .5 E4
Salterforth BB18 . . . . .194 B5
Shawforth OL12,OL13 . . . .71 E6
Old Lancaster La PR2 . . .117 C1
Old Lancaster Rd PR1 . . .181 B2
Old Langho Rd BB6 . . . . .143 C5
Old Laund St BB12 . . . . .147 E8
Old Links St PR1 . . . . .36 B8
Old Lodge La PR3 . . . . . .159 A8
Old Lord's Cres BL6 . . . . .32 B5
Old Lostock La PR5 . . . . . .77 E7
Old Mains La FY6 . . . . . .153 F6
Old Market Ct LA4 . . . . . .217 B6
Old Meadow Ct 3 FY3 . .130 E3
Old Meadow La PR5 . . . .130 E3
Old Meadows Rd OL13 . . .88 A5
Old Mill Cl PR4 . . . . .74 F5
Old Mill Dr BB8 . . . . .171 F4
Old Mill Hill L39 . . . . .15 D3
Old Mill La Formby L37 . .11 F4
Hill Dale L40 . . . . .27 F6
Old Mill Terr PR6 . . . . . . .61 E1
Old Mill The PR5 . . . . .97 F2
Old Millstones PR1 . . . . . .96 D7
Old Moor Rd LA2 . . . . . . .238 F8
Old Moss La L39 . . . . .13 C5
Old Nab Rd BB6 . . . . .123 E8
Old Oak Gdns PR5 . . . . . .97 A2
Old Oliver La BD24 . . . . .236 C5
Old Orch PR7 . . . . .117 D5
Old Park La PR9 . . . . .36 A4
Old Parsonage La PR3 . .126 B8
Old Penny Gdns LA4 . . . .217 E4
Old Pepper La WN6 . . . . .29 B2
Old Pope La PR4 . . . . .76 B8
Old Prescot Cl L31 . . . . . . .6 C2
Old Quarry La BL7 . . . . . .47 F1
Old Raike BD23 . . . . .236 C4
Old Rake BL6 . . . . .32 C5
Old Rd BD23 . . . . .197 C6
Old Rectory Gn L39 . . . . . .6 A7
Old Rectory The LA2 . . . .206 C5
Old Roman Rd BB12,BB7 145 A3
Old Rough La L33 . . . . .1 A2
Old Row Barrow BB7 . . . . .166 D1
Kirkham PR4 . . . . .114 B4
4 Rawtenstall BB4 . . . . . . .85 C2
Old Sawmill The BD24 . .236 E7

Old Sch Mews 8 BB4 . . . .85 B3
Old School Cl PR26 . . . . . .59 A8
Old School Dr PR4 . . . . . . .75 B8
Old School Ho The
Blackburn BB1 . . . . .82 D8
Higher Walton PR5 . . . . . . .98 B3
Old School La
Adlington PR7 . . . . .30 E5
Bamber Bridge PR5 . . . . . .77 C6
Euxton PR7 . . . . .60 D3
Tockholes BB3 . . . . .80 F2
Old School Mews 12
OL13 . . . . .70 C8
Old School Row 3
BB12 . . . . .127 B6
Old School The LA2 . . . . .219 C6
Old St BB4 . . . . .86 F1
Old Station Ct PR2 . . . . . .139 D1
Old Station Ct 8 BB7 . . .166 E8
Old Stone Trough La
BB18 . . . . .195 A5
Old Swan Cl BL7 . . . . .47 E2
Old Tom's La PR6 . . . . . . .177 E8
Old Town St WN8 . . . . .8 D8
Old Town Cl L37 . . . . .11 E4
Old Town Hall Mews
LA4 . . . . .217 B6
Old Town La L37 . . . . .11 E4
Old Town Way WN8 . . . . . . .8 D8
Old Trafford Cvn Pk
LA3 . . . . .212 F4
Old Trafford Pk LA3 . . . .213 A4
Old Tram Rd
Bamber Bridge PR5 . . . . . .77 F7
Preston PR1,PR5 . . . . .97 A4
Old Vicarage PR1 . . . . .97 A8
Old Vicarage Ct FY5 . . . . .89 F5
Old Vicarage Rd BL6 . . . .32 F3
Old Will's La BL6 . . . . .32 B6
Old Worden Ave PR7 . . . . .60 E4
Oldbury PR1 . . . . .97 A8
Olde Stoneheath Ct PR6 .44 B4
Oldfield 7 Kingsfold PR1 . .96 D2
Much Hoole PR4 . . . . .74 F4
Oldfield Ave
Blackpool FY2 . . . . .152 C4
Darwen BB3 . . . . .81 E3
Oldfield Carr La FY6 . . . .153 E1
Oldfield Cl FY6 . . . . .153 E1
Oldfield Cres FY6 . . . . . . .153 E3
Oldfield Rd BB5 . . . . .85 A7
Oldham St Burnley BB11 .127 C6
Morecambe LA4 . . . . .217 B6
Olivant St BB12 . . . . .127 C7
Olive Bank BB6 . . . . .143 D1
Olive Cl PR6 . . . . .61 C5
Olive Gr Blackpool FY3 . .130 E5
Skelmersdale WN8 . . . . . . .17 E1
Southport PR8 . . . . .35 E7
Warton PR4 . . . . .92 C6
Olive La BB3 . . . . .82 B2
Olive Rd LA1 . . . . .218 D2
Olive St OL13 . . . . .70 E8
Olive Terr BB4 . . . . .85 F5
Oliver Ct FY6 . . . . .199 E5
Oliver Pl LA5 . . . . .223 E2
Oliver St 10 OL13 . . . . . . .70 C8
Oliver's Pl PR2 . . . . .118 B8
Olivers Pl PR2 . . . . .118 A8
Oliverson's CE Prim Sch
PR3 . . . . .138 D6
Ollerton La BB6 . . . . .79 E4
Ollerton La End PR6 . . . . .79 E3
Ollerton Rd FY8 . . . . .90 D5
Ollerton St PR6 . . . . .44 A1
Ollerton Terr PR6 . . . . .79 E3
Olympia St BB10 . . . . . . .128 C5
Olympic Way FY4 . . . . . . .111 C8
Omerod St BB4 . . . . .87 A8
Omrod Pl 1 FY1 . . . . . . .130 B2
Onchan Dr OL13 . . . . .88 B1
Onchan Rd BB2 . . . . .101 E1
One Ash Cl OL12 . . . . .52 F2
Onslow Cres PR8 . . . . .35 A2
Onslow Rd FY3 . . . . .130 F7
Ontario Cl BB2 . . . . .101 A8
Oozebooth Terr BB1 . . . .101 E7
Oozehead La BB2 . . . . . . .101 B5
Opal Cl 6 FY5 . . . . .152 D7
Opal St BB1 . . . . .122 F2
Openshaw Dr BB1 . . . . . .101 E8
Openshaw St BL9 . . . . . . .33 A1
Oporto Cl BB11 . . . . .127 C5
Oram Rd PR5 . . . . .78 F8
Oram St BL9 . . . . .33 A4
Orange St BB5 . . . . .104 B8
Orchard Ave
Blackpool FY4 . . . . .110 C6
Bolton-le-S LA5 . . . . .221 A6
New Longton PR4 . . . . . . .76 A7
Poulton-le-F FY6 . . . . .153 E1
Orchard Bridge 6 BB12 127 F6
Orchard Cl Becconsall PR4 73 F3
Blackburn BB2 . . . . .81 D6
Euxton PR7 . . . . .60 D3
Freckleton PR4 . . . . .93 A6
Fulwood PR2 . . . . .117 A5
Silverdale LA5 . . . . .224 B2
Slyne LA2 . . . . .218 D8
Thornton FY5 . . . . .176 B4
Wrea Green PR4 . . . . .113 B2
Orchard Croft 2 PR5 . . . .77 A8
Orchard Ct Fulwood PR2 .117 D5
Maghull L31 . . . . .5 F1
Orchard Dr
Fleetwood FY7 . . . . .198 E1
Lucas Green PR6 . . . . .61 C5
Oswaldtwistle BB5 . . . . . .103 F5

Orchard End PR3 . . . . . . .156 C5
Orchard Grange PR1 . . . . .96 A5
Orchard La
Lancaster LA1 . . . . .214 D7
Longton PR4 . . . . .74 F8
Southport PR8 . . . . .21 D4
Orchard Lo L39 . . . . .15 F6
Orchard Mill Dr PR26 . . . .58 B2
Orchard Pl PR4 . . . . .74 E3
Orchard Rd FY8 . . . . .89 E6
Orchard St
5 Barnoldswick BB18 . . . .196 B2
Great Harwood BB6 . . . . .124 C4
1 Leyland PR25 . . . . .77 B1
26 Preston PR1 . . . . .96 F8
Orchard The
Burnley BB11 . . . . .127 C4
Clitheroe BB7 . . . . .189 C4
Croston PR26 . . . . .58 C3
Kirkham PR4 . . . . .114 F6
Little Eccleston PR3 . . . . .156 A5
Ormskirk L39 . . . . .15 D5
Warton PR4 . . . . .92 E6
Woodplumpton PR4 . . . . .136 E1
Wray LA2 . . . . .238 D6
Orchard View L39 . . . . . . .15 D1
Orchard Wlk
Grimsargh PR2 . . . . .139 C2
Ramsbottom BL8 . . . . .49 F1
Orchards The
Barnoldswick BB18 . . . . . .196 C3
Carleton FY6 . . . . .153 B5
Orrell WN5 . . . . .10 E5
Overton LA3 . . . . .209 D8
Southport PR8 . . . . .21 A4
Orchid Cl WN8 . . . . .10 B6
Orchid Way OL12 . . . . . . .52 D6
Ord Ave FY4 . . . . .130 F1
Ord Rd PR2 . . . . .117 C2
Orders La PR4 . . . . .114 A4
Ordnance St BB1 . . . . . . .102 A5
Oregon Ave FY3 . . . . .130 E8
Oriole Cl 9 BB1 . . . . .101 F6
Orion Bldgs 1 FY5 . . . . .175 D2
Orkney Cl BB1 . . . . .102 D3
Orkney Rd 1 FY1 . . . . . .130 C2
Orme Ho L39 . . . . .16 A5
Orme St 1 FY1 . . . . .130 C3
Ormerod Bldgs 1 OL13 . .70 D8
Ormerod Rd BB10,BB11 . .128 B3
Ormerod St
Accrington BB5 . . . . .104 B5
Burnley BB11 . . . . .128 A5
Colne BB8 . . . . .171 C4
Haslingden BB4,BB5 . . . . .85 B7
5 Nelson BB9 . . . . .148 F8
Rawtenstall BB4 . . . . .86 A2
Thornton FY5 . . . . .176 B4
Worsthorne BB10 . . . . . . .129 A5
Ormerod Terr
Barrow BB6 . . . . .144 D8
Foulridge BB8 . . . . .194 E1
Ormond Ave
Blackpool FY1 . . . . .130 B8
Westhead L40 . . . . .16 E4
Ormond St BL9 . . . . .33 A3
Ormonde Cres L33 . . . . . . .1 A2
Ormont Ave FY5 . . . . .175 E2
Ormrod St BL9 . . . . .33 A2
Ormrods The BL9 . . . . . . .33 F5
Orms Way L37 . . . . .11 E3
Ormsby Cl WN6 . . . . .29 E2
Ormskirk & District General
Hospl L39 . . . . .16 A4
Ormskirk Asmall Prim Sch
L39 .15 D6
Ormskirk Bsns Pk L39 . . .15 F6
Ormskirk CE Prim Sch
L39 .16 A6
Ormskirk Coll L39 . . . . . . .15 F4
Ormskirk Lathom Park CE
Prim Sch L40 . . . . .17 A8
Ormskirk Old Rd L39 . . . . .7 F7
Ormskirk Rd
Bickerstaffe L39 . . . . .7 E7
Preston PR1 . . . . .97 A8
Rainford Junction WA11 . . .8 D1
Skelmersdale,Chapel House
WN8 . . . . .17 C1
Skelmersdale,Tanhouse WN8 .9 D7
Skelmersdale,Up Holland
WN8 . . . . .10 A7
Ormskirk Sch
Ormskirk L39 . . . . .15 F4
Ormskirk L39 . . . . .16 B5
Ormskirk St Anne's RC Prim
Sch L39 . . . . .15 E4
Ormskirk Sta L39 . . . . . . .15 F5
Ormskirk West End Prim Sch
L39 .15 E5
Ormston Ave BL6 . . . . . . .32 C5
Orpen Ave BB11 . . . . .127 F3
Orpington Sq BB10 . . . . .148 C3
Orrell Cl 3 PR25 . . . . .76 D1
Orrell Gdns WN5 . . . . .10 F6
Orrell Hill La L38 . . . . .3 C4
Orrell Holgate Prim Sch
WN5 . . . . .10 E5
Orrell La L40 . . . . .25 D5
Orrell Newfold Com Prim Sch
WN5 . . . . .10 D7
Orrell Rd WN5 . . . . .10 E7
Orrell RU FC WN5 . . . . . . .10 E5
Orrell Water Pk★ WN5 . .10 E4

Orrest Rd PR1 . . . . .119 A1
Orton Ct BB9 . . . . .170 D4
Orwell Cl L37 . . . . .11 D1
Osbaldeston La BB2 . . . .121 D5
Osbert Croft PR4 . . . . . . .95 A1
Osborne Ave FY5 . . . . . .175 F1
Osborne Cres LA3 . . . . . .216 F3
Osborne Dr PR6 . . . . .78 C2
Osborne Gr
  Cleveleys FY5 . . . . . . .175 D5
  Morecambe LA4 . . . . . .217 A3
Osborne Rd
  Bamber Bridge PR5 . . . .97 D3
  Blackburn BB2 . . . . . . .101 B6
  Blackpool FY4 . . . . . . .110 B8
  Cleveleys FY5 . . . . . . .175 D5
  Formby L37 . . . . .11 E1
  Lytham St Anne's FY8 . . .89 F5
  Morecambe LA3,LA4 . . .216 F2
  Southport PR8 . . . . .21 B6
Osborne St **11** PR1 . . . . .96 E7
Osborne Terr Bacup OL13 .70 D8
  Darwen BB3 . . . . .81 E2
  11 Rawtenstall BB4 . . . . .85 E2
  Spen Brook BB12 . . . . .169 D2
  Whitewell Bottom BB4 . . .86 F4
Osborne Way BB4 . . . . . .85 A1
Osbourne Way PR1 . . . . .118 A1
Oscar St **4** FY4 . . . . . . .130 F2
Oslo Rd BB11 . . . . .127 B5
Osprey Cl Blackburn BB1 .101 D8
  Knowley PR6 . . . . .62 A3
Oswald Rd
  Lytham St Anne's FY8 . . .91 D4
  Preston PR2 . . . . .117 C1
Oswald St
  Accrington BB5 . . . . . . .104 D6
  Blackburn BB1 . . . . . . .101 E6
  Burnley BB12 . . . . .127 F8
  Oswaldtwistle BB5 . . . . .103 D3
  Rishton BB1 . . . . .124 C2
Oswaldtwistle Mills Shopping
  Village★ BB5 . . . . .103 E4
Otley Rd FY8 . . . . .90 B7
Ottawa Cl BB2 . . . . .101 A8
Otterburn Cl FY3 . . . . . . .153 B1
Otterburn Gr BB10 . . . . . .128 D6
Otterburn Rd BB2 . . . . . . .81 C7
Otters Cl PR2 . . . . .118 F2
Ottershaw Gdns BB1 . . . .101 E8
Ottery Cl PR9 . . . . .54 A5
Otway St PR1 . . . . .117 E2
Oulton Cl L31 . . . . .5 B4
Our Lady & St Anselm's RC
  Prim Sch OL12 . . . . . . .71 D2
Our Lady & St Edward's RC
  Prim Sch PR2 . . . . .117 D8
Our Lady & St Gerard's RC
  Prim Sch PR5 . . . . .77 A8
Our Lady & St Hubert's RC
  Prim Sch BB6 . . . . .124 E6
Our Lady & St John RC Arts
  Coll BB1 . . . . .102 C3
Our Lady & St Paul's RC Prim
  Sch OL10 . . . . .33 F1
Our Lady Of Compassion RC
  Prim Sch L37 . . . . .12 A3
Our Lady of Lourdes RC Prim
  Sch
  Carnforth LA5 . . . . .223 E1
  Southport PR8 . . . . .35 A1
Our Lady of Perpetual
  Succour RC Prim Sch
  BB2 . . . . .81 E8
Our Lady of the Assumption
  RC Prim Sch FY4 . . . . .110 F5
Our Lady Queen of Peace RC
  High Sch WN8 . . . . .17 F4
Our Lady Star of the Sea RC
  Prim Sch FY8 . . . . .89 F6
Our Lady's RC High Sch
  Fulwood PR2 . . . . .117 C4
  Lancaster LA1 . . . . .218 D1
Ousby Ave LA3 . . . . .217 B2
Ousby Rd LA3 . . . . .217 B2
Ouseburn Rd BB2 . . . . . . .81 C8
Ousle Rock BB12 . . . . . . .169 E2
Out La PR26 . . . . .58 C2
Out Moss La LA4 . . . . . . .217 B4
Out Rawcliffe CE Prim Sch
  PR3 . . . . .178 F2
Outer Prom FY7 . . . . .198 E3
Outgate Rd PR4 . . . . . . .116 D4
Outlet La L31,L39 . . . . .6 F1
Outlook The L38 . . . . .2 F4
Outram Ho PR5 . . . . .97 D1
Outram La **2** BB1 . . . . .122 E1
Outram Way PR5 . . . . . . .77 E8
Outterside St PR7 . . . . . . .31 A6
Outwood Rd BB11 . . . . . .128 B4
Oval The Burnley BB11 . . .127 C3
  Shevington WN6 . . . . . .19 F5
Ovangle Rd LA3 . . . . .217 F2
Over Hos BL7 . . . . .48 B6
Over Town BB10 . . . . . . .129 A1
Overdale Gr FY3 . . . . .131 A8
Overdell Dr OL12 . . . . . . .52 C4
Overfield Way OL12 . . . . . .52 F2
Overshores Rd BL7 . . . . . .48 B8
Overton Rd PR2 . . . . .95 E8
Overton St Helen's CE Sch
  LA3 . . . . .213 D1
Ovington Dr PR8 . . . . .35 E3
Owen Ave L39 . . . . .15 F6
Owen Ct BB5 . . . . .124 F3

Owen Rd LA1 . . . . .218 D2
Owen St Accrington BB5 .104 C7
  Burnley BB12 . . . . .127 A5
  Darwen BB3 . . . . .82 A3
  Preston PR1 . . . . .97 B8
Owen's La L39 . . . . .13 E2
Owen's Row BL6 . . . . .32 C3
Owens St PR6 . . . . .43 E7
Owlet Hall Rd BB3 . . . . . . .81 E2
Owsten Ct BL6 . . . . .31 F3
Owtram St **2** PR1 . . . . . .97 C8
Ox Hey BB5 . . . . .124 F4
Ox Hey Ave PR2 . . . . . . .116 C1
Ox Hey Cl BL0 . . . . .50 C7
Ox St **15** BL0 . . . . .50 B5
Oxcliffe Ave LA3 . . . . . . .216 D1
Oxcliffe Gr LA3 . . . . .216 D1
Oxcliffe New Farm Caravans
  LA3 . . . . .216 D1
Oxcliffe Rd LA3 . . . . .216 D1
Oxendale Rd L37 . . . . . . .176 D2
Oxenholme Ave FY5 . . . .175 D4
Oxenhurst Rd FY3 . . . . . .131 A8
Oxford Ave BB5 . . . . .125 A3
Oxford Cl Blackburn BB1 .101 F4
  Padiham BB12 . . . . . . .126 D6
Oxford Ct
  4 Lytham St Anne's FY8 .90 A4
  Southport PR8 . . . . .34 F4
Oxford Dr Blackburn BB1 .102 E4
  Kirkham PR4 . . . . .114 C4
Oxford Gdns PR8 . . . . . . .34 E4
Oxford Pl
  9 Burnley BB11 . . . . . .128 B5
  Lancaster LA1 . . . . .218 C3
Oxford Rd
  Bamber Bridge PR5 . . . .77 D8
  Blackpool FY1 . . . . .130 D5
  Burnley BB11 . . . . .128 B5
  Cleveleys FY5 . . . . .175 D3
  Fleetwood FY7 . . . . . . .198 E3
  Fulwood PR2 . . . . .117 D4
  Lytham St Anne's FY8 . . .89 E8
  Lytham St Anne's,Ansdell
  FY8 . . . . .90 D4
  Nelson BB9 . . . . .171 A2
  Orrell WN5 . . . . .10 F8
  Skelmersdale WN8 . . . . .17 E1
  Southport PR8 . . . . .34 E4
Oxford St Accrington BB5 104 B6
  Adlington PR7 . . . . .31 A6
  Brierfield BB9 . . . . .148 B5
  Bury BL9 . . . . .33 A1
  Carnforth LA5 . . . . .223 D1
  9 Chorley PR7 . . . . . . .43 C7
  Colne BB8 . . . . .171 E5
  Darwen BB3 . . . . .81 F4
  Lancaster LA1 . . . . .218 D3
  Morecambe LA4 . . . . . .217 B6
  Preston PR1 . . . . .97 A6
Oxford Way
  Fleetwood FY7 . . . . . . .198 E3
  Rochdale OL12 . . . . .52 E2
Oxheys Cl BB10 . . . . .128 F6
Oxheys Ct **2** PR1 . . . . .117 E2
Oxheys Ind Est PR1 . . . . .117 D2
Oxheys St PR1 . . . . .117 D2
Oxhill Pl FY5 . . . . .152 F7
Oxhouse Rd WN5 . . . . . . .10 D4
Oxley Cl PR4 . . . . .113 F5
Oxley Rd LA1 . . . . .118 C1
Oxley Rd N PR1 . . . . . . .118 D1
Oystercatcher Gate FY8 . .90 E7

P

Paa La BB7 . . . . .231 C7
Packet La LA5 . . . . .221 A4
Pad Cote La BD22 . . . . . .174 A8
Paddington Ave PR26 . . . .59 A8
Paddington Barn PR3 . . . .157 C7
Paddock Ave PR26 . . . . . .59 A8
Paddock Dr FY3 . . . . .131 C2
Paddock La BB1 . . . . . . .102 D4
Paddock Rd WN8 . . . . .9 C5
Paddock St **9** BB5 . . . .103 E4
Paddock The
  Blackburn BB2 . . . . . . .101 A8
  Carleton FY6 . . . . .153 C5
  Formby L37 . . . . .12 A5
  Fulwood PR2 . . . . .118 A6
  4 Kingsfold PR1 . . . . . .96 E2
  Ormskirk L39 . . . . .15 C3
  Oswaldtwistle BB5 . . . . .103 E4
  Ramsbottom BL0 . . . . . .50 B7
  Rufford L40 . . . . .39 C4
  Sawley BB7 . . . . .230 C1
  Southport PR8 . . . . .21 C4
  Thornton FY5 . . . . .153 B8
Padgate Pl BB11 . . . . . . .127 B4
Padiham Gawthorpe High
  Sch BB12 . . . . .126 E8
Padiham Green CE Prim Sch
  BB12 . . . . .126 C8
Padiham Prim Sch
  BB12 . . . . .126 D8
Padiham Prim Sch Annexe
  BB12 . . . . .126 E8
Padiham Rd
  Burnley BB12 . . . . .127 E6
  Burnley,Whittlefield BB12 .127 C7
  3 Burnley,Whittlefield
  BB12 . . . . .127 D6
  Padiham BB12 . . . . . . .126 F7
  Sabden BB7 . . . . .146 A7
Padstow Ct PR9 . . . . .54 A5
Padway PR1 . . . . .96 D2

Page Ct L37 . . . . .11 F3
Pagefield Cres BB7 . . . . .167 A7
Pages Ct PR5 . . . . .77 B7
Paignton Ave BB1 . . . . . .101 D7
Painley Cl FY8 . . . . .91 A4
Painter Wood BB7 . . . . . .144 B4
Paisley St BB11 . . . . .127 D5
Palace Ct LA3 . . . . .216 F3
Palace Gdns BB12 . . . . . .127 B7
Palace Rd PR8 . . . . .34 C5
Palace St Burnley BB12 . .127 C7
  Bury BL9 . . . . .33 A2
Palais Bldgs **3** L40 . . . . .25 E5
Palatine Cl BB1 . . . . .215 A5
Palatine High Sch FY4 . . .110 C8
Palatine Rd
  Blackburn BB2 . . . . . . .101 C5
  Blackpool FY1 . . . . .130 C4
  Cleveleys FY5 . . . . .175 D4
  Southport PR8 . . . . .34 F5
Palatine Sq BB11 . . . . . . .127 E5
Palatine St **10** BL0 . . . . .50 C6
Paley Rd **1** PR1 . . . . . . .96 D7
Palfrey Cl FY6 . . . . .153 B6
Pall Mall Blackburn BB2 . .100 E5
  Chorley PR7 . . . . .43 C6
Palladium Bldgs **7** FY1 130 B1
Palm Ct WN8 . . . . .17 E2
Palm Dr FY6 . . . . .153 B6
Palm Gr PR8 . . . . .35 E6
Palm St Blackburn BB1 . . .102 A7
  5 Burnley BB11 . . . . . .127 D5
Palma St **4** OL14 . . . . . .109 B1
Palmaston Cl LA1 . . . . . . .214 E6
Palmer Ave FY1 . . . . .130 C2
Palmer Gr **3** LA4 . . . . . .217 E6
Palmer St BB1 . . . . .101 D6
Palmerston Cl BL0 . . . . . . .50 C4
Palmerston Rd PR9 . . . . . .35 F6
Palmerston St BB12 . . . . .126 D7
Palmetto View **1** PR1 . . .90 D7
Pankhurst Cl BB1 . . . . . . .102 B1
Pansy St N BB5 . . . . .104 B7
Pansy St S BB5 . . . . .104 B7
Panton St BL6 . . . . .32 D1
Parade The LA5 . . . . .223 B1
Paradise Cl PR6 . . . . .61 C8
Paradise La
  1 Blackburn BB2 . . . . .101 E4
  Formby L37 . . . . .12 A6
  Leyland PR26 . . . . .76 B1
Paradise St
  Accrington BB5 . . . . . . .104 B5
  Barrowford BB9 . . . . . . .170 E5
  Blackburn BB2 . . . . . . .101 D4
  Haslingden BB4 . . . . .67 F7
  11 Burnley BB11 . . . . .127 F6
  Great Knowley PR6 . . . . .61 F3
  2 Newchurch BB4 . . . . .86 F2
  Ramsbottom BL0 . . . . . .50 C7
Paradise Terr **2** BB2 . . .101 E4
Paragon Way LA1 . . . . . .214 C8
Parbold Cl Blackpool FY3 152 F1
  Burscough L40 . . . . .25 E3
Parbold Douglas CE Prim Sch
  WN8 . . . . .27 D3
Parbold Hill WN8 . . . . .27 E2
Parbold Our Lady & All Saints
  RC Prim Sch WN8 . . . . .27 C2
Parbold Sta WN8 . . . . .27 C2
Pardoe Cl PR4 . . . . .73 E3
Pardoe Ct L40 . . . . .25 F3
Paris BB1 . . . . .122 E4
Parish St **11** BB12 . . . . .126 C8
Park Ave
  Barnoldswick BB18 . . . .196 B1
  Barrowford BB9 . . . . . . .170 C1
  Blackburn BB1 . . . . . . .101 D6
  Burnley BB11 . . . . .127 E4
  Chatburn BB7 . . . . .190 D5
  Clitheroe BB7 . . . . .189 E1
  Euxton PR7 . . . . .60 D2
  Fleetwood FY7 . . . . . . .198 F3
  Formby L37 . . . . .11 F1
  Great Harwood BB6 . . . .124 D5
  Haslingden BB4 . . . . .85 B1
  Lancaster LA1 . . . . .215 B7
  Longshaw WN5 . . . . .10 E1
  Lytham St Anne's FY8 . . .90 E3
  Maghull L31 . . . . .5 D3
  Much Hoole PR4 . . . . . . .74 E2
  New Longton PR4 . . . . . .75 F8
  Ormskirk L39 . . . . .15 E5
Park View
  Accrington BB5 . . . . . . .104 A7
  Carnforth LA5 . . . . .223 D3
  Gisburn BB7 . . . . .231 B3
  Middleworth Green PR1 . .96 D4
  Newchurch BB4 . . . . .86 F1
  Padiham BB12 . . . . . . .126 C8
Park View Terr
  Abbey Village PR6 . . . . .80 C1
  Salterforth BB18 . . . . . .194 D7
Park Wall Rd L29,L38 . . . . .4 B2
Park Way Colne BB8 . . . . .171 C6
  Formby L37 . . . . .11 F1
  Middleworth Green PR1 . .96 D4
Park Wlk PR2 . . . . .118 A4
Park Wood Dr BB4 . . . . . . .85 E2
Parkbourn L31 . . . . .6 A2
Parkbourn Dr L31 . . . . .6 A2
Parkbourn N L31 . . . . .6 A2
Parkbourn Sq L31 . . . . .6 A2
Parkdale Gdns BB2 . . . . . .81 D6
Parke Gdns PR3 . . . . .79 C3

Park Gate Rd BB1 . . . . . .142 D1
Park Hall L Ctr PR7 . . . . . .42 A4
Park Hall Rd PR7 . . . . .41 F3
Park Head BB7 . . . . .144 F2
Park Hey Dr WN6 . . . . . . .19 E7
Park High Sch BB8 . . . . . .171 F6
Park Hill
  Barnoldswick BB18 . . . .196 C1
  21 Rochdale OL12 . . . . .52 F1
Park Hill Rd PR3 . . . . .181 C7
Park Ho
  4 Lancaster LA1 . . . . .218 D1
  Longridge PR3 . . . . . . .140 A7
Park La Brierfield BB9 . . . .148 C5
  Caton LA2 . . . . .237 B5
  Galgate LA2 . . . . .211 A6
  Garstang PR3 . . . . .204 A4
  Great Harwood BB6 . . . .124 D6
  Holmes PR4 . . . . .56 B2
  Horwich BL6 . . . . .32 D3
  Kirkham PR4 . . . . .114 A7
  Maghull L31 . . . . .5 D3
  Middleworth Green PR1 . .96 E3
  Oswaldtwistle BB5 . . . . .103 E3
  Preesall FY6 . . . . .200 B3
  Wennington LA2 . . . . . .238 E8
Park Lane Dr **3** LA1 . . . . .6 B2
Park Lee Hospl BB2 . . . . .101 E2
Park Lee Rd BB2 . . . . . . .101 E2
Park Link L39 . . . . .15 B1
Park Mews BB7 . . . . .231 B3
Park Mill Pl PR1 . . . . .118 A1
Park Pl Blackburn BB2 . . .101 B3
  Blackburn,Feniscowles BB2 80 D7
  24 Preston PR1 . . . . . . .97 A7
  Walton-le-D PR5 . . . . . . .97 C4
Park Prim Sch
  Colne BB8 . . . . .171 F5
  Skelmersdale WN8 . . . . .17 E1
Park Rd Accrington BB5 . .104 A6
  Adlington PR7 . . . . .30 F6
  Bacup OL13 . . . . .87 F1
  Barnoldswick BB18 . . . .196 B1
  Blackburn BB2 . . . . . . .101 E3
  Blackpool FY1 . . . . .130 D3
  Burnley BB10 . . . . .128 E1
  Chorley PR7 . . . . .43 C8
  Coppull PR7 . . . . .42 E1
  Darwen BB3 . . . . .65 B6
  Edgworth BL7 . . . . .48 E5
  Formby L37 . . . . .11 E1
  Fulwood PR2 . . . . .118 A4
  Gisburn BB7 . . . . .231 B3
  Great Harwood BB6 . . . .124 D5
  Haslingden BB4 . . . . .67 F7
  Kirkham PR4 . . . . .113 F4
  Lancaster LA1 . . . . .215 A8
  Leyland PR25 . . . . .60 A7
  Longshaw WN5 . . . . .10 F1
  Lytham St Anne's FY8 . . .89 E6
  Mellor Brook BB2,PR5 . .121 A1
  Middleworth Green PR1 . .96 D4
  Newchurch BB4 . . . . .86 F1
  Ormskirk L39 . . . . .15 A5
  Padiham BB12 . . . . . . .126 C8
  Poulton-le-F FY6 . . . . . .153 E4
  Ramsbottom BL0 . . . . . .49 F3
  Rishton BB1 . . . . .124 C1
  Silverdale LA5 . . . . .224 D4
  Southport PR9 . . . . .35 D8
  Thornton FY5 . . . . .176 B1
Park Rd W PR9 . . . . .53 C1
Park Road Ind Est OL13 . .87 F1
Park Sch FY3 . . . . .130 E4
Park Side BB18 . . . . .195 A8
Park Sq LA1 . . . . .215 A8
Park St Accrington BB5 . . .104 C6
  Barnoldswick BB18 . . . .196 B1
  Barrowford BB9 . . . . . . .170 D4
  Chorley PR7 . . . . .61 C1
  Clitheroe BB7 . . . . .166 E7
  Eccleston PR7 . . . . .41 C6
  Great Harwood BB6 . . . .124 D5
  Haslingden BB4 . . . . .85 B3
  Haslingden,Bridge End BB4 .67 F7
  Lytham St Anne's FY8 . . .91 B3
  Morecambe LA4 . . . . . .217 E6
Park Stone Rd PR3 . . . . . .137 C3
Park Street E BB9 . . . . . .170 E4
Park Terr Blackburn BB1 . .101 D7
  Great Harwood BB6 . . . .124 D6
Park View
  Accrington BB5 . . . . . . .104 A7
Park View Ave PR2 . . . . . .117 B2
Park View Cl BB9 . . . . . . .148 B7
Park View Ct **2** FY4 . . . .110 C8
Park View Rd FY8 . . . . . . .91 B4

Parke Rd PR6 . . . . .62 E8
Parker Ave BB7 . . . . .166 E6
Parker Cres L39 . . . . .15 F7
New Longton PR4 . . . . . .76 C6
Parker St
  Accrington,Higher Baxenden
  BB5 . . . . .104 E2
  Accrington,Hillock Vale
  BB5 . . . . .104 E8
  3 Blackpool FY1 . . . . .130 C5
  Brierfield BB10 . . . . . . .148 F3
  Burnley BB11 . . . . .128 A6
  Bury BL9 . . . . .33 A2
  Chorley PR7 . . . . .61 C1
  Colne BB8 . . . . .171 C5
  Lancaster LA1 . . . . .215 A8
  11 Nelson BB9 . . . . . .170 F2
  Preston PR2 . . . . .117 C2
  Rishton BB1 . . . . .124 C2
Parker Terr BB7 . . . . .231 B3
Parkers Fold PR3 . . . . . . .181 C2
Parkers Wood Cl PR7 . . . .43 A6
Parkes Way PR3 . . . . .81 D7
Parkfield Ave PR2 . . . . . .117 B2
Parkfield Cl Leyland PR26 .59 C8
  Ormskirk L39 . . . . .15 C4
  5 Preston PR2 . . . . . .116 C1
Parkfield Cres **6** PR2 . .116 C1
Parkfield Dr
  Lancaster LA1 . . . . .215 A6
  Preston PR2 . . . . .95 C8
Parkfield Gr L31 . . . . .5 C1
Parkfield View PR2 . . . . . .95 C8
Parkgate PR3 . . . . .138 D5
Parkgate Dr
  Lancaster LA1 . . . . .215 C7
  Leyland PR25 . . . . .59 C7
Parkhead La PR3 . . . . . . .182 A8
Parkhill Gr OL14 . . . . .109 A1
Parkinson Fold BB4 . . . . . .68 C6
Parkinson La PR3 . . . . . . .162 B8
Parkinson St
  Blackburn BB2 . . . . . . .101 C2
  Burnley BB11 . . . . .128 A4
  Foulridge BB8 . . . . .194 D1
  Haslingden BB4 . . . . .85 A3
Parkinson Way **1** FY4 . .130 C1
Parkland Cl FY5 . . . . .175 C1
Parkland Gr LA3 . . . . .216 E2
Parkland View BB11 . . . . .127 E2
Parklands
  Skelmersdale WN8 . . . . .18 D2
  Southport PR9 . . . . .35 E8
Parklands Ave PR1 . . . . . .96 A4
Parklands Cl PR1 . . . . .96 A4
Parklands Dr PR2 . . . . . . .117 E8
Parklands Gr PR2 . . . . . . .117 E8
Parklands High Sch PR7 . .43 A8
Parklands The PR3 . . . . . .181 D3
Parklands Way BB2 . . . . . .81 B8
Parks The LA4 . . . . .217 E7
Parkside Morecambe LA4 217 C3
  Preston,Holme Slack PR1 .118 B3
  Preston,Lea PR2 . . . . . .116 D2
  Whitworth OL12 . . . . . . .71 D2
Parkside Ave PR7 . . . . . . .43 C8
Parkside Cl **12** OL14 . . .109 B1
Parkside Cres WN5 . . . . . .10 F6
Parkside Ct
  Morecambe LA4 . . . . . .217 C3
  Southport PR9 . . . . .53 D1
Parkside Dr PR6 . . . . .61 B6
Parkside La PR3 . . . . .181 A7
Parkside Rd
  Cornholme OL14 . . . . . .109 B1
  Lytham St Anne's FY8 . . .90 A7
  Nelson BB9 . . . . .149 B8
Parkside View FY5 . . . . . .176 A4
Parkstone Ave
  Carleton FY6 . . . . .153 B5
  Thornton FY5 . . . . .153 D8
Parksway FY6 . . . . .199 D5
Parkthorn Rd PR2 . . . . . . .95 C8
Parkview Cl LA4 . . . . .217 B3
Parkview Flats FY5 . . . . . .89 C6
Parkway Blackpool FY3 . .131 A6
  Shevington Moor WN6 . . .29 A2
Parkwood BL7 . . . . .47 D2
Parkwood Ave BB12 . . . . .127 D7
Parkwood Ct BB4 . . . . .85 E2
Parkwood Mews **1** BB9 170 F2
Parliament St
  Burnley BB11 . . . . .128 B5
  11 Colne BB8 . . . . . . .171 E5
  19 Darwen BB3 . . . . . . .82 A1
  Lancaster LA1 . . . . .218 D1
  Morecambe LA4 . . . . . .216 E4
  Skelmersdale WN8 . . . . .10 C7
Parlick Ave **2** BB4 . . . . .140 B7
Parlick Rd Fulwood PR2 . .119 C3
  Garstang PR3 . . . . .181 B6
Parr Cottage Cl PR7 . . . . .41 C7
Parr La PR7 . . . . .41 C7
Parr's La L39 . . . . .15 D1
Parramatta St **8** BB4 . . . .86 A2
Parrock Cl PR1 . . . . .96 E3
Parrock Par BB4 . . . . .86 A7
Parrock Rd BB9 . . . . .170 C2
Parrock St
  Barnoldswick BB18 . . . .196 B2
  19 Nelson BB9 . . . . . .170 E1
  1 Rawtenstall BB4 . . . . .86 A7
Parrox Fold FY6 . . . . .200 A5
Parrox La PR4 . . . . .114 C2
Parrys Way FY6 . . . . .153 E4
Parsley Cl FY2 . . . . .152 F3
Parson La BB7 . . . . .166 E8

Par – Pin 287

Parson's Brow 4 PR7 . . . 43 C7
Parson's Bullough Rd
PR6,BL6 . . . 44 E5
Parsonage Ave PR3 . . . 141 D3
Parsonage Brow WN8 . . . 10 A8
Parsonage Cl 3 Bury BL9 33 A2
Morecambe LA3 . . . 217 C2
Skelmersdale WN8 . . . 10 A7
Parsonage Cotts 9 BB7 166 E8
Parsonage Dr BB9 . . . 148 C5
Parsonage Gdns PR4 . . . 57 A5
Parsonage La PR3 . . . 185 C1
Parsonage Rd BB1 . . . 123 A4
Parsonage St Bury BL9 . . . 33 A3
2 Church BB5 . . . 103 E5
Colne BB8 . . . 171 C4
Part St PR8 . . . 35 B6
Parth St BL9 . . . 33 D1
Partnership Way BB1 . . . 102 D2
Partridge Ave FY5 . . . 176 A4
Partridge Dr BB5 . . . 104 F1
Partridge Hill 4 BB12 . . . 146 D1
Partridge Hill St 5
BB12 . . . 146 D1
Passmonds Cres OL11,
OL12 . . . 52 B1
Past La Lane Ends BB7 . . . 230 A5
Lane Ends BB7 . . . 230 A7
Pasture Cl
Barnoldswick BB18 . . . 196 C4
Burnley BB11 . . . 127 E3
Pasture Dr Bonds PR3 . . . 181 D6
Foulridge BB8 . . . 194 D1
Pasture Field FY6 . . . 153 B6
Pasture Field Cl PR26 . . . 76 C1
Pasture Gr BB7 . . . 144 A7
Pasture La
Barrowford BB9 . . . 170 C5
Hest Bank LA5 . . . 220 E4
Pasturegate BB11 . . . 127 E3
Pasturegate Ave BB11 . . . 127 E4
Pasturelands BB4 . . . 106 A1
Pasturelands Dr BB7 . . . 144 A3
Pastures The
Blackburn BB2 . . . 101 A8
Grimsargh PR2 . . . 139 D1
Southport PR9 . . . 54 D5
Paterson St BB2 . . . 101 E3
Pathfinders Dr LA1 . . . 214 E4
Patience St 11 OL12 . . . 52 C1
Patmos St BL0 . . . 50 D6
Paton St OL12 . . . 52 D3
Patrick Ave BB12 . . . 145 D2
Patrick Cres BB4 . . . 86 C2
Patten St Blackburn BB1 . . . 102 C5
Colne BB8 . . . 171 D4
Preston PR1 . . . 96 F8
Patterdale Ave
Blackburn BB1 . . . 102 C3
Blackpool FY3 . . . 130 F2
Fleetwood FY7 . . . 198 D1
Oswaldtwistle BB5 . . . 103 D5
Thornton FY5 . . . 176 B3
Patterdale Cl
Brierfield BB10 . . . 148 C4
Southport PR8 . . . 21 B3
Patterdale Cres L31 . . . 5 E2
Patterdale Rd LA1 . . . 218 F1
Patterson Ct 8 FY8 . . . 91 C3
Pattison Cl OL12 . . . 52 D3
Paul's La Hambleton FY6 . 177 C2
Southport PR9 . . . 53 F3
Paulhan St BB10 . . . 148 B2
Pavey Cl FY4 . . . 110 F8
Pavilion Cl OL12 . . . 52 F2
Pavilion View PR26 . . . 58 B2
Pavilions The
Blackpool FY4 . . . 110 D4
Preston PR2 . . . 96 C7
Paxton Pl WN8 . . . 9 C4
Paxton St BB5 . . . 104 B6
Paynter Cl Barrow BB7 . . . 166 D1
Clayton-le-M BB5 . . . 125 A2
Paythorne Ave BB10 . . . 128 D5
Paythorne Cl FY3 . . . 153 B1
Peabody St BB3 . . . 82 A2
Peace Pl FY5 . . . 176 B4
Peace St BB11 . . . 127 D5
Peacehaven WN8 . . . 17 E1
Peachtree Cl PR2 . . . 118 D6
Peacock Cres LA2 . . . 220 E1
Peacock Dr PR3 . . . 204 D1
Peacock Hall Rd PR25 . . . 59 D7
Peacock Hill Cl PR2 . . . 119 C7
Peacock La LA2 . . . 220 E1
Peahall La PR3 . . . 202 A4
Pear Ave BL9 . . . 33 C3
Pear Pl 16 OL14 . . . 109 B1
Pear St 17 OL14 . . . 109 B1
Pear Tree Ave PR7 . . . 42 F3
Pear Tree Cl 2 PR5 . . . 97 E2
Pear Tree Cres PR5 . . . 97 E2
Pear Tree Croft PR4 . . . 75 A8
Pear Tree Ctyd PR4 . . . 115 E2
Pear Tree La PR7 . . . 60 E3
Pear Tree Rd PR6 . . . 78 B3
Pear Tree Sch PR4 . . . 114 A5
Pear Tree St 7 PR5 . . . 97 E2
Pearfield PR25 . . . 77 A2
Pearl Ave 6 FY2 . . . 152 E1
Pearl Brook Ind Est 4
BL6 . . . 32 B3
Pearl St Accrington BB5 . . . 103 F5
Blackburn BB1 . . . 122 F1
Pearson St
Blackburn BB2 . . . 101 D4
Bury BL9 . . . 33 B3
Peart St BB10 . . . 148 B2
Peartree Rd PR26 . . . 58 B3
Pebble Ct FY5 . . . 175 C3
Pechell St 5 PR2 . . . 117 C1
Pedder Ave LA3 . . . 213 C1
Pedder Dr LA3 . . . 213 D1
Pedder Gr LA3 . . . 213 D1
Pedder La FY6 . . . 177 B1
Pedder Rd LA3 . . . 213 C1
Pedder St
Morecambe LA4 . . . 217 A5
Preston PR2 . . . 96 E8
Pedder's La
Blackpool FY4 . . . 110 D7
Preston PR2 . . . 117 A1
Pedders Gr PR2 . . . 96 A8
Pedders La PR2 . . . 96 A8
Pedders Way PR2 . . . 96 A8
Peebles Gr BB11 . . . 127 D3
Peel Ave Blackpool FY3 . . . 130 D7
Heysham LA3 . . . 212 E6
Lancaster LA1 . . . 218 D2
Ramsbottom BL0 . . . 50 A5
Peel Bank Rd BB5 . . . 103 B4
Peel Brow BL0 . . . 50 D6
Peel Brow Sch BL0 . . . 50 D6
Peel Cl BB2 . . . 81 E8
Peel Cres LA1 . . . 214 D8
Peel Dr OL13 . . . 88 B1
Peel Gdns BB8 . . . 171 C5
Peel Hall Rd BL0 . . . 50 B2
Peel Hall St PR1 . . . 118 B1
Peel Hill FY4 . . . 111 E7
Peel Ho LA1 . . . 218 C1
Peel Mount
Blackburn BB1 . . . 102 F4
Ramsbottom BL0 . . . 50 A4
Peel Mount Cl BB1 . . . 102 F4
Peel Park Ave
Accrington BB5 . . . 104 D7
Clitheroe BB7 . . . 166 F7
Peel Park Cl
Accrington BB5 . . . 104 D7
Clitheroe BB7 . . . 166 F7
Peel Park Prim Sch
BB5 . . . 104 D7
Peel Pl BB9 . . . 170 F6
Peel Rd Blackpool FY4 . . . 111 F4
Colne BB8 . . . 171 B4
Fleetwood FY7 . . . 198 F3
Skelmersdale WN8 . . . 9 E5
Peel St Accrington BB5 . . . 104 C6
Adlington PR6 . . . 31 B8
Blackburn BB2 . . . 101 C2
Chorley PR7 . . . 43 C7
Clitheroe BB7 . . . 166 E8
Haslingden BB4 . . . 85 A3
6 Oswaldtwistle BB5 . . . 103 D3
Padiham BB12 . . . 126 D8
Preston PR2 . . . 96 E8
Rawtenstall BB4 . . . 86 C2
Southport PR8 . . . 35 F6
Peel Twr* BL8 . . . 49 F5
Peel Wlk L31 . . . 5 B2
Peerart Ct BB8 . . . 171 C4
Peers Clough Rd BB4 . . . 86 F7
Peet Ave L39 . . . 15 D4
Peet's La PR9 . . . 54 A1
Peg Way PR4 . . . 92 F6
Peg's La FY8 . . . 91 B8
Pegbank La LA6 . . . 241 A8
Pelham Ave 3 FY3 . . . 130 E8
Pelham St 3 BB1 . . . 102 A6
Pemberton Dr LA4 . . . 217 F5
Pemberton Pl LA4 . . . 217 F5
Pemberton St BB1 . . . 122 E1
Pembroke Ave
Blackpool FY2 . . . 152 B3
Morecambe LA4 . . . 217 D6
Pembroke Cl BL6 . . . 32 A4
Pembroke Ct
Blackpool FY2 . . . 152 B3
13 Darwen BB3 . . . 82 A1
14 Rochdale OL12 . . . 52 F1
Pembroke Pl Chorley PR7 . 43 B6
Leyland PR25 . . . 60 A8
Pembroke Rd FY8 . . . 90 D4
Pembroke St
Accrington BB5 . . . 104 D6
Bacup OL13 . . . 87 F1
Blackburn BB2 . . . 101 E3
11 Burnley BB10 . . . 148 B1
Pembury Ave PR1 . . . 96 F3
Pen-y-ghent Way BB18 196 A2
Penarth Ct PR2 . . . 116 F3
Pendle Ave Bacup OL13 . . . 88 A3
Chatburn BB7 . . . 190 E5
Clayton-le-M BB5 . . . 124 F4
Lancaster LA1 . . . 211 B6
Pendle Bridge BB12 . . . 147 F3
Pendle Cl Bacup OL13 . . . 88 A2
Blackpool FY3 . . . 152 F1
Pendle Comm Hospl
BB9 . . . 170 E1
Pendle Ct
Barnoldswick BB18 . . . 196 C3
5 Clitheroe BB7 . . . 166 F8
Kirkham PR4 . . . 114 A6
Longridge PR3 . . . 140 A7
Skelmersdale WN8 . . . 9 D3
Pendle Dr Blackburn BB2 101 F2
Horwich BL6 . . . 32 C5
Ormskirk L39 . . . 16 A6
Whalley BB7 . . . 144 A7
Pendle Fields BB12 . . . 147 D7
Pendle Heritage Ctr*
BB9 . . . 170 E4
Pendle Hill Cl PR2 . . . 119 C7
Pendle Ho BB1 . . . 101 F5
Pendle Ind Est BB9 . . . 148 F7
Pendle Pl
Lytham St Anne's FY8 . . . 91 C4
Skelmersdale WN8 . . . 9 D4
Pendle Rd Brierfield BB9 148 A5
Clayton-le-W PR25 . . . 77 D1
Clitheroe BB7 . . . 167 A7
Downham BB7 . . . 191 D3
Great Harwood BB6 . . . 124 F6
Lancaster LA1 . . . 218 B3
Pendle Row BB12 . . . 169 C5
Pendle St Accrington BB5 104 A5
Barrowford BB9 . . . 170 C3
Blackburn BB1 . . . 102 A5
Nelson BB9 . . . 170 D1
Padiham BB12 . . . 126 D8
Pendle St E BB7 . . . 145 F7
Pendle St W BB7 . . . 145 F7
Pendle Terr BB7 . . . 191 E8
Pendle Trad Est BB7 . . . 190 C4
Pendle View
Barley BB12 . . . 169 C6
Brockhall Village BB6 . . . 143 C6
Clayton-le-M BB5 . . . 125 A3
Foulridge BB8 . . . 194 E1
Grindleton BB7 . . . 190 B7
Higham BB12 . . . 146 F6
Huncoat BB5 . . . 125 F2
West Bradford BB7 . . . 189 D7
Pendle Way
Burnley BB12 . . . 127 E6
7 Nelson BB9 . . . 148 E8
Pendlebury Cl PR4 . . . 75 B8
Pendlehurst St BB11 . . . 127 E4
Pendlemist View BB8 . . . 171 C3
Pendleside BB9 . . . 148 B8
Pendleside Cl BB7 . . . 145 F7
Pendleton Ave
Accrington BB5 . . . 103 F4
Rawtenstall BB4 . . . 86 A4
Pendleton Rd
Pendleton BB7 . . . 167 A2
Wiswell BB7 . . . 144 F8
Penfold L31 . . . 5 E1
Pengarth Rd BL6 . . . 32 C4
Penguin St PR1 . . . 118 B2
Penhale Cl LA3 . . . 212 E6
Penhale Ct LA3 . . . 212 E6
Penhale Gdns LA3 . . . 212 E6
Penhill Cl 4 FY2 . . . 130 D8
Penistone St 6 BB12 . . . 127 D6
Penketh Pl WN8 . . . 9 C5
Penn St BL6 . . . 32 C3
Pennine Ave PR7 . . . 60 D1
Pennine Cl
8 Blackpool FY1 . . . 130 C4
Horwich BL6 . . . 32 C5
Pennine Cres BB9 . . . 148 C5
Pennine Gdns PR3 . . . 181 A7
Pennine Gr BB12 . . . 146 C2
Pennine Pl WN8 . . . 9 B6
Pennine Rd Bacup OL13 . . . 88 A2
Chorley PR6 . . . 43 E8
Horwich BL6 . . . 32 C5
Pennine View
Dolphinholme LA2 . . . 226 A8
Fleetwood FY7 . . . 199 B4
Glasson LA2 . . . 209 E4
Great Eccleston PR3 . . . 156 C5
Kirkham PR4 . . . 114 C5
Morecambe LA4 . . . 217 B4
Pennine Way
Barnoldswick BB18 . . . 196 A2
Brierfield BB9 . . . 148 C5
Great Eccleston PR3 . . . 156 C5
Stalmine FY6 . . . 177 D7
Pennines The PR2 . . . 118 A7
Pennington Ave L39 . . . 15 E6
Pennington Ct
Heysham LA3 . . . 212 E6
Ormskirk L39 . . . 15 F6
Pennington La WN2 . . . 30 E1
Penny House La BB5 . . . 104 C7
Penny St Blackburn BB1 . . . 101 F5
Lancaster LA1 . . . 214 F7
3 Preston PR1 . . . 97 A8
Penny Stone Rd LA2 . . . 219 C7
Pennyfarthing La 7
FY5 . . . 176 A2
Pennystone Rd FY2 . . . 152 B4
Penrhos Ave FY7 . . . 198 E1
Penrhyn Rd LA1 . . . 218 A2
Penrith Ave
Cleveleys FY5 . . . 175 D4
Heysham LA3 . . . 212 F8
Southport PR8 . . . 21 C3
Penrith Cres Colne BB8 . 171 B3
Maghull L31 . . . 5 E2
Penrith Rd BB8 . . . 171 A3
Penrod Way LA3 . . . 212 D5
Penrose Ave FY4 . . . 130 F1
Penrose Pl WN8 . . . 9 E4
Penshaw Cl 6 BB1 . . . 122 E1
Penswick Ave FY5 . . . 175 E1
Pentland Rd L33 . . . 1 A4
Penwell Fold WN8 . . . 9 E8
Penwortham Broad Oak Prim
Sch PR1 . . . 96 C2
Penwortham Brow PR1 . . . 96 C6
Penwortham Ct PR1 . . . 96 D4
Penwortham Girls' High Sch
PR1 . . . 96 C5
Penwortham Hall Gdns
PR1 . . . 96 E3
Penwortham Middleforth CE
Prim Sch PR1 . . . 96 D3
Penwortham Prim Sch
PR1 . . . 96 A5
Penwortham St Teresa's RC
Prim Sch PR1 . . . 96 A5
Penwortham Way
Farington PR26,PR4 . . . 76 D7
Kingsfold PR1 . . . 96 C1
Penzance St BB2 . . . 101 B2
Peplow Rd LA3 . . . 213 A8
Pepper La WN6 . . . 29 B3
Perch Pool La PR9 . . . 36 F4
Percival Ct 2 PR8 . . . 35 A6
Percival St
Accrington BB5 . . . 103 F5
Blackburn BB1 . . . 101 F7
Darwen BB3 . . . 81 F3
Percy Rd LA1 . . . 214 F6
Percy St Accrington BB5 . 104 D6
Blackburn BB2 . . . 101 B2
Blackpool FY1 . . . 130 C7
Bury BL9 . . . 33 B3
9 Chorley PR7 . . . 43 D7
Colne BB8 . . . 171 E6
Fleetwood FY7 . . . 198 F4
Nelson BB9 . . . 148 E7
Oswaldtwistle BB5 . . . 103 B5
Preston PR1 . . . 97 A8
Ramsbottom BL0 . . . 50 B5
Shawforth OL12 . . . 71 E6
Peregrine Dr BB3 . . . 81 D3
Peregrine Pl PR25 . . . 76 D2
Peridot Cl BB1 . . . 122 F2
Perimeter Rd L33 . . . 1 E2
Peronne Cres BB1 . . . 102 D5
Perpignan Way 16 LA1 . . . 214 F8
Perry St BB3 . . . 82 B2
Perryn Pl WN6 . . . 29 F1
Pershore Gdns FY3 . . . 131 B8
Pershore Gr PR8 . . . 21 A4
Pershore Rd FY8 . . . 90 B5
Persia St BB5 . . . 103 F6
Perth Cl FY5 . . . 152 F7
Perth St Accrington BB5 . 104 B4
Blackburn BB2 . . . 101 C3
Burnley BB11 . . . 127 D5
Lancaster LA1 . . . 215 A7
8 Nelson BB9 . . . 170 F1
Perthshire Gr PR7 . . . 60 F6
Peter Birtwistle Cl BB8 . 171 E5
Peter Grime Row BB5 . . . 125 F2
Peter La LA5 . . . 225 E1
Peter Martin St 3 BL6 . . . 32 B4
Peter St
9 Barrowford BB9 . . . 170 D4
Blackburn BB1 . . . 102 A6
Blackpool FY1 . . . 130 D5
Chorley PR7 . . . 43 C8
Colne BB8 . . . 171 E4
5 Lancaster LA1 . . . 214 F7
Rawtenstall BB4 . . . 86 A2
Peterfield Rd 1 PR1 . . . 96 E2
Peterhouse Sch PR9 . . . 54 B3
Peters Ave L40 . . . 25 E4
Petersan Ct PR6 . . . 61 C3
Petersbottom La LA2 . . . 239 E4
Petre Cres BB1 . . . 103 B8
Petre Rd BB5 . . . 124 F2
Petrel Cl BB1 . . . 101 D8
Petunia Cl PR25 . . . 77 E2
Petworth Rd PR8 . . . 21 B6
Pharos Ct 8 FY7 . . . 199 B5
Pharos Gr 2 FY7 . . . 199 B5
Pharos Pl FY7 . . . 199 B5
Pharos St FY7 . . . 199 B5
Pheasant Wood Dr FY5 . 175 F5
Pheasantford Gn BB10 . . . 128 B8
Pheasantford St BB10 . . . 128 B8
Philip Ave PR4 . . . 114 B4
Philip Dr PR8 . . . 21 F6
Philip St
Barnoldswick BB18 . . . 196 B2
Darwen BB3 . . . 82 B1
Philips Rd Blackburn BB1 102 B8
Weir OL13 . . . 88 A7
Phillip St FY4 . . . 130 F2
Phillip's Cl L37 . . . 11 F2
Phillip's La L37 . . . 11 F2
Phillips La BB8 . . . 171 B3
Phillipstown BB4 . . . 86 E4
Phoenix St
8 Lancaster LA1 . . . 218 D1
Rochdale OL12 . . . 52 C1
Phoenix Way BB11 . . . 127 C5
Phyllis St OL12 . . . 52 B1
Physics Ave LA1 . . . 211 B7
Piazza The LA1 . . . 215 C7
Piccadilly LA1 . . . 214 F3
Piccadilly Cl LA1 . . . 214 F3
Piccadilly Gr LA1 . . . 214 F3
Piccadilly Rd BB11 . . . 127 E5
Piccadilly Sq 2 BB11 . . . 127 E5
Piccadilly St BB4 . . . 85 B3
Pickard Cl BB18 . . . 196 D4
Pickard St LA1 . . . 214 F6
Pickering Cl FY8 . . . 90 B7
Pickering Fold BB1 . . . 82 B7
Pickering St BB9 . . . 148 B5
Pickerings The 2 PR5 . . . 77 C8
Pickles Dr L40 . . . 25 D4
Pickles St BB12 . . . 127 D7
Pickmere Ave FY4 . . . 110 E8
Pickmere Cl FY5 . . . 176 A4
Pickthorn Cl LA1 . . . 218 B4
Pickup Fold 3 BB3 . . . 65 C7
Pickup Fold Rd BB3 . . . 65 C7
Pickup Rd BB1 . . . 103 A8
Pickup St Accrington BB5 103 F5
11 Bacup OL13 . . . 87 F2
Blackburn BB1 . . . 102 A5
Clayton-le-M BB5 . . . 124 F3
Picton St BB2 . . . 81 B8
Pier Ct FY8 . . . 89 D7
Pier Ho 3 BB1 . . . 101 F3
Pier St FY1 . . . 130 B3
Pierce Cl Lancaster LA1 . 214 D7
Padiham BB12 . . . 146 C1
Piercefield Ct L37 . . . 12 A5
Piercefield Rd L37 . . . 11 F5
Piercy Higher Mount
BB4 . . . 86 F3
Piercy Mdw BB4 . . . 86 F3
Piercy Mount BB4 . . . 86 F3
Piercy Rd BB4 . . . 86 F3
Piercy Terr BB4 . . . 86 F3
Pierpoint II FY8 . . . 89 D7
Pierston Ave FY2 . . . 152 C1
Pike Ct FY7 . . . 198 C2
Pike View BL6 . . . 32 D4
Pikelaw Pl WN8 . . . 9 C5
Pikestone Ct 9 PR6 . . . 43 E8
Pilgrim St BB9 . . . 148 F6
Pilkington Dr BB5 . . . 125 A3
Pilkington Rd PR8 . . . 35 D5
Pilkington St
6 Blackburn BB1 . . . 101 E4
14 Ramsbottom BL0 . . . 50 B5
Pilling Ave
Accrington BB5 . . . 104 E2
Lytham St Anne's FY8 . . . 90 C7
Pilling Cl Chorley PR7 . . . 43 D6
Southport PR9 . . . 53 F5
Pilling Cres FY3 . . . 131 A8
Pilling Ct FY3 . . . 153 A1
Pilling Field BL7 . . . 47 E1
Pilling La Chorley PR7 . . . 43 D6
Maghull L31 . . . 5 A5
Pilling Lane FY6 . . . 200 B7
Pilling Pl WN8 . . . 9 C5
Pilling St Haslingden BB4 . 85 B6
3 Rawtenstall BB4 . . . 69 F8
Pilling St John's CE Prim Sch
PR3 . . . 201 C6
Pilmuir Rd BB2 . . . 101 E1
Pilot St BB5 . . . 104 B7
Pimbo La WN8 . . . 9 F3
Pimbo Rd WN8 . . . 9 C5
Pimhole Rd BL9 . . . 33 B2
Pimlico BB7 . . . 189 F3
Pimlico Link Rd BB7 . . . 190 C2
Pimlico Rd BB7 . . . 189 F2
Pinch Clough Rd BB4 . . . 86 F5
Pincock Brow PR7 . . . 42 C8
Pincock St PR7 . . . 42 C8
Pinder Cl BB7 . . . 189 B4
Pinder St BB9 . . . 170 F2
Pine Ave Blackpool FY1 . . . 130 E2
Much Hoole PR4 . . . 74 D4
Ormskirk L39 . . . 15 F7
Pine Cl Fulwood PR2 . . . 118 F4
Halton LA2 . . . 219 C6
Newburgh WN8 . . . 27 A1
Rishton BB1 . . . 103 B8
Skelmersdale WN8 . . . 17 F1
Pine Cres
Oswaldtwistle BB5 . . . 103 F3
Poulton-le-F FY6 . . . 153 E2
Pine Crest L39 . . . 15 B2
Pine Dr L39 . . . 15 F6
Pine Gr Chorley PR6 . . . 61 D3
Clitheroe BB7 . . . 166 D7
Garstang PR3 . . . 204 C1
Ormskirk L39 . . . 15 F7
Southport PR9 . . . 35 D7
Pine Lake* LA6 . . . 240 A3
Pine St Bacup OL13 . . . 88 A1
Blackburn BB1 . . . 102 A7
Burnley BB11 . . . 128 B5
Bury BL9 . . . 33 B2
Darwen BB3 . . . 65 B8
Haslingden BB4 . . . 85 C3
Lancaster LA1 . . . 218 C1
Morecambe LA4 . . . 217 C4
Nelson BB9 . . . 148 F8
Pine St N BL9 . . . 33 B3
Pine St S BL9 . . . 33 B2
Pine Way PR4 . . . 114 B7
Pine Wlks PR2 . . . 116 C1
Pines Cl PR5 . . . 78 C4
Pines The Leyland PR26 . . . 59 A8
Southport PR8 . . . 34 F6
Pineway PR2 . . . 117 C4
Pinewood Blackburn BB2 . . 80 F8
Skelmersdale WN8 . . . 18 D3
Pinewood Ave
Blackpool FY2 . . . 152 E4
Broughton PR3 . . . 137 C3
Caton LA2 . . . 237 C3
Formby L37 . . . 11 D1
Hest Bank LA5 . . . 220 F2
Knott End-on-S FY6 . . . 200 A5
Morecambe LA4 . . . 217 F6
Thornton FY5 . . . 153 B7
Pinewood Cl Formby L37 . 11 D2
Lancaster LA2 . . . 214 E2
Southport PR8 . . . 36 C1
Pinewood Cotts 1 LA2 . 239 D8
Pinewood Cres
Leyland PR25 . . . 59 E8
Lytham St Anne's FY8 . . . 90 D4
Orrell WN5 . . . 10 E6
Ramsbottom BL0 . . . 50 B2
Pinewood Dr
Accrington BB5 . . . 104 E6
Nelson BB9 . . . 149 A7
Pinfold Barrowford BB9 . . 170 E5

Pinfold continued
Longton PR4 . . . . .75 A8
Pinfold Cl Fulwood PR2 . .118 E1
Southport PR8 . . . . .21 B3
Pinfold La Inskip PR4 . . . .157 C2
Lancaster LA1 . . . . .218 D2
Longridge PR3 . . . . .140 B4
Pinfold L40 . . . . .23 F3
Southport PR8 . . . . .21 B3
Pinfold Pl
5 Kirkham PR4 . . . . .113 F5
Nelson BB9 . . . . .171 F1
Skelmersdale WN8 . . . . .9 D4
Pinfold Prim Sch L40 . . . .24 A3
Pinfold St PR1 . . . . .97 E8
Pingle Croft PR6 . . . . .78 A2
Pingwood La L33 . . . . .1 A5
Pink Pl BB2 . . . . .101 B3
Pink St BB12 . . . . .127 C6
Pinnacle Dr BL7 . . . . .47 E2
Pinner La BB4 . . . . .85 F7
Pinners Cl BL0 . . . . .50 B7
Pintail Cl Moss Side PR26 .76 A1
5 Rochdale OL12 . . . . . . .52 B2
Pintail Way FY8 . . . . .90 E7
Pioneer Cl BL6 . . . . .32 C4
Pioneer St BL6 . . . . .32 C4
Piper Cotts LA4 . . . . .217 C3
Piper Lea BB4 . . . . .87 A1
Piper's La L6 . . . . .240 C8
Pippin Bank OL13 . . . . . . .87 F1
Pippin St Burscough L40 . .25 A2
Thorpe Green PR6 . . . . . . .78 E5
Pit Hey Pl WN8 . . . . .9 C5
Pitt St Lancaster LA1 . . . .214 F8
11 Padiham BB12 . . . . . . .126 D8
Preston PR1 . . . . .96 C7
Southport PR9 . . . . .35 F6
Pittman Ct PR2 . . . . .118 B8
Pittman Way PR2 . . . . . . .118 C7
Pitts House La PR9 . . . . . .36 B8
Pittsdale Ave FY4 . . . . . . .131 A2
Pitville St BB3 . . . . .81 F3
Place The FY1 . . . . .130 B7
Place-de-Criel 12 BB9 . .148 C8
Plain Pl BB2 . . . . .101 E3
Plainmoor Dr FY5 . . . . . . .152 F4
Plane St Bacup OL13 . . . . .87 F4
Blackburn BB1 . . . . .102 A7
Plane Tree Cl BB11 . . . . . .127 E5
Plane Tree Rd 7 BB1 . . .102 A7
Planet Earth Ctr (Obsy &
Planetarium)★ OL14 . . . .88 F4
Plant St
Oswaldtwistle BB5 . . . . . .103 D3
Preston PR2 . . . . .117 C1
Plantain Wlk LA3 . . . . . . .217 B2
Plantation Ave
Arnside LA5 . . . . .224 C8
Knott End-on-S FY6 . . . . .199 E5
Plantation Gr LA5 . . . . . . .224 C8
Plantation La LA2 . . . . . . .232 D1
Plantation Rd
Accrington BB5 . . . . .104 E6
Blackburn BB2 . . . . .101 B1
Burscough L40 . . . . .25 B4
Edgworth BL7 . . . . .48 F7
Plantation Sq BB5 . . . . . .104 D6
Plantation St
Accrington BB5 . . . . .104 D6
Bacup OL13 . . . . .70 C8
Burnley BB10 . . . . .128 A7
6 Nelson BB9 . . . . .170 F1
Rawtenstall BB4 . . . . .86 B2
Plantation The BD23 . . . .236 B3
Plantation View
Bacup OL13 . . . . .87 F6
Ramsbottom BL0 . . . . .50 C3
Platt Cl BB5 . . . . .104 A5
Platt La WN1 . . . . .30 B3
Platt St FY1 . . . . .130 C6
Platten Gr LA4 . . . . .217 C5
Platts La L40 . . . . .25 D2
Platts Lane Ind Est L40 . .25 D2
Pleasant Gr FY5 . . . . .176 B2
Pleasant Pl 4 BB11 . . . . .127 F5
Pleasant St
Blackpool FY1 . . . . .130 B7
Haslingden BB4 . . . . .85 B3
3 Lytham St Anne's FY8 . .91 B3
Pleasant View
Bacup OL13 . . . . .70 C7
15 Barnoldswick BB18 . .196 B2
Blackpool FY4 . . . . .111 A4
Coppull PR7 . . . . .42 F2
Earby BB18 . . . . .197 C1
Hoddlesden BB3 . . . . .82 F1
Leyland PR26 . . . . .76 C3
Newchurch BB4 . . . . .86 F1
Tockholes BB3 . . . . .81 A1
Withnell PR6 . . . . .80 A1
Pleasington Ave PR3 . . . .181 D6
Pleasington Cl
Blackburn BB2 . . . . .101 A4
Blackpool FY4 . . . . .111 A4
Pleasington Gr BB10 . . . .128 D5
Pleasington La BB2 . . . . . .80 C8
Pleasington Nature
Reserve★ 100 D3
Pleasington Rd BB2 . . . . .100 C1
Pleasington St BB2 . . . . .100 C1
Pleasington Sta BB2 . . . .100 C1
Pleasureland★ PR8 . . . . .34 F7
Pleck Farm Ave BB1 . . . .101 E8
Pleck Pl FY6 . . . . .153 B6

Pleck Rd BB5 . . . . .104 C6
Pleckgate Fold BB1 . . . .122 E1
Pleckgate High Sch
BB1 . . . . .122 D1
Pleckgate Rd BB1 . . . . . .122 E1
Plessington Ct PR3 . . . . .140 A7
Plevna Rd PR1 . . . . .97 C8
Plex La L39 . . . . .14 C5
Plex Moss La L39 . . . . . . .13 D8
Plock Gn PR7 . . . . .43 C5
Plough La L40 . . . . .17 A4
Ploughlands The 2
PR2 . . . . .116 E1
Plover Cl FY5 . . . . .176 A5
Plover Dr Bury BL9 . . . . . .33 B4
Heysham LA3 . . . . .212 F5
Plover St Burnley BB12 . .127 D6
Preston PR1 . . . . .118 A1
Plover View 2 BB12 . . . .127 D6
Plovers Way FY3 . . . . .131 B6
Plox Brow PR4 . . . . .57 A6
Plumbe St BB11 . . . . .128 A5
Plumpton Ave FY4 . . . . . .110 F5
Plumpton Field PR4 . . . .136 E2
Plumpton La
Great Plumpton PR4 . . . . .112 E7
Halsall L39 . . . . .22 C4
Plumpton Rd PR2 . . . . . .117 C2
Plumtree Cl PR2 . . . . . . .118 C6
Plunge Rd BL0 . . . . .68 E3
Plungington Rd PR1,PR2 117 E2
Plymouth Ave FY7 . . . . . .175 C8
Plymouth Gr PR6 . . . . .43 E8
Plymouth Rd FY2,FY3 . . .152 E1
Poachers Trail FY6 . . . . . .90 D7
Poachers Way FY5 . . . . . .176 A4
Pochard Pl 6 FY5 . . . . . .175 F1
Pocklington St BB5 . . . . .104 D2
Poets' Rd BB12 . . . . .126 F7
Pointer Cl LA1 . . . . .214 F6
Pointer Gr LA2 . . . . .219 D7
Pointer The LA1 . . . . .214 F6
Poland St BB5 . . . . .103 F5
Pole La PR4 . . . . .93 F5
Pole St Preston PR1 . . . . . .97 A8
Standish WN6 . . . . .29 E1
Polefield PR2 . . . . .117 E7
Pol²ce St BB3 . . . . .82 A1
Police Yd 18 LA2 . . . . . . .239 D8
Pollard Pl LA1 . . . . .218 E4
Pollard Row BB12 . . . . . .169 C1
Pollard St
Accrington BB5 . . . . .104 C7
Burnley BB11 . . . . .127 D5
4 Nelson BB9 . . . . .170 E1
6 Preston PR1 . . . . .96 E8
Pollards La BL9 . . . . .50 C2
Pollux Gate FY8 . . . . .90 C4
Polly Gn OL12 . . . . .52 F3
Polperro Dr PR4 . . . . .93 A6
Pomfret St
Blackburn BB2 . . . . .101 D3
Burnley BB11 . . . . .127 E6
Pompian Brow PR26 . . . . .57 E6
Pond Cl PR4 . . . . .57 A5
Pond Gdns FY6 . . . . .153 B6
Pond St LA5 . . . . .223 D2
Pond Terr LA5 . . . . .223 D2
Pont St BB9 . . . . .148 D7
Pontville Residential Sch
L39 . . . . .15 D3
Pool Ct FY7 . . . . .198 D1
Pool Foot La FY6 . . . . . . .154 E4
Pool Hey La PR8,PR9 . . . .36 B3
Pool House Com Prim Sch
PR2 . . . . .117 A6
Pool House Ct PR2 . . . . . .117 A6
Pool House La PR2 . . . . . .117 A5
Pool La PR4 . . . . .93 A4
Pool St PR9 . . . . .54 D5
Poole Rd PR2 . . . . .118 A4
Poole St BB1 . . . . .102 C5
Poolhill Cl FY5 . . . . .152 E7
Poolside Wlk PR9 . . . . . . .54 C4
Poot Hall OL12 . . . . .52 F3
Pope La Fulwood PR2 . . . .119 A3
Kingsfold PR1 . . . . .96 C2
White Stake PR4 . . . . .76 B8
Pope Wlk PR1 . . . . .96 D3
Poplar Ave
Bamber Bridge PR5 . . . . . .97 F1
Blackpool FY3 . . . . .130 D5
Bury BL9 . . . . .33 B3
Euxton PR7 . . . . .60 C4
Great Harwood BB6 . . . . .124 D6
Horwich BL6 . . . . .32 E1
Kirkham PR4 . . . . .114 A4
Longton PR4 . . . . .75 B8
4 Rochdale OL12 . . . . . . .52 C1
Warton PR4 . . . . .92 D6
Poplar Bank PR9 . . . . .53 D1
Poplar Cl
Bamber Bridge PR5 . . . . . .97 F1
Oswaldtwistle BB5 . . . . . .103 F3
Rishton BB1 . . . . .103 B8
Poplar Ct FY8 . . . . .89 E5
Poplar Dr Coppull PR7 . . .42 F1
Freckleton PR4 . . . . .93 A5
Higher Penwortham PR1 . . .96 C5
Longridge PR3 . . . . .140 A8
Skelmersdale WN8 . . . . . . .17 F1
Poplar Gr
Bamber Bridge PR5 . . . . . .97 F1
Fulwood PR2 . . . . .119 A4
Ramsbottom BL0 . . . . .50 D7
Poplar St Blackburn BB1 .101 F7
2 Blackburn BB1 . . . . . .102 A7

Poplar St continued
Chorley PR7 . . . . .43 D6
Haslingden BB4 . . . . .85 B3
Nelson BB9 . . . . .170 F1
Southport PR8 . . . . .35 E6
Poplar Terr BB4 . . . . .85 F6
Poplars The Adlington PR7 30 F6
Burscough L40 . . . . .25 E2
Poppy Ave PR6 . . . . .61 D2
Poppy Cl PR8 . . . . .35 B2
Poppy La L39 . . . . .16 B1
Poppyfield PR4 . . . . .116 F6
Poppyfields PR4 . . . . .73 E4
Porritt Ave LA1 . . . . .214 D8
Porritt St Bury BL9 . . . . . .33 A4
Bury BL9 . . . . .33 B4
Porritt Way BL0 . . . . .50 C7
Port Royal Ave LA1 . . . . .214 C8
Port Way Heysham LA3 . .212 D5
Preston PR2 . . . . .96 C7
Portal Gr BB2 . . . . .127 B6
Porter Pl 2 PR1 . . . . .97 A6
Porter St Accrington BB5 .103 F5
Preston PR1 . . . . .118 B1
Porter St E 4 PR4 . . . . . .113 F5
Porters Row FY6 . . . . . . .177 C7
Portfield Bar BB7 . . . . . .144 F3
Portfield La BB6 . . . . .144 F3
Portfield Rd BB7 . . . . .144 E4
Porthcawl Ct PR2 . . . . . . .116 F3
Portland Cotts PR6 . . . . . .62 D8
Portland Ct FY4 . . . . .111 A1
Portland Dr LA3 . . . . .217 B2
Portland Ind Est 12 BL2 .33 A4
Portland Pl BL6 . . . . .32 C3
Portland Rd
Blackpool FY1 . . . . .130 D4
Langho BB6 . . . . .123 C8
Portland St
Accrington BB5 . . . . .104 A4
Barrowford BB9 . . . . .170 D3
Blackburn BB2 . . . . .101 C3
Bury BL9 . . . . .33 A4
1 Chorley PR6 . . . . .43 D8
Colne BB8 . . . . .171 F5
Darwen BB3 . . . . .65 B6
Lancaster LA1 . . . . .214 F7
Nelson BB9 . . . . .148 D8
Preston PR1 . . . . .96 D7
Southport PR8 . . . . .35 B5
Portman St PR1 . . . . .118 B1
Portree Cl PR2 . . . . .118 C5
Portree Cres BB1 . . . . . . .102 D3
Portree Rd FY2 . . . . .152 E5
Portsmouth Ave BB10 . . .148 C2
Portsmouth Cl 7 FY5 . . .175 F4
Portsmouth Dr PR6 . . . . . .43 E8
Portway FY2 . . . . .152 E6
Post Horse La LA2 . . . . . .238 B7
Post La PR4 . . . . .92 F6
Post Office Ave 1 PR9 . . .35 B7
Post Office Bldgs 18
BB18 . . . . .196 B2
Post Office Row
St Michael's on W PR3 . . .157 C7
Tunstall LA6 . . . . .241 D4
Westhouse LA6 . . . . .242 F4
Post Office Yd 8 BB8 . . .171 E5
Postern Gate Rd LA2 . . .232 A8
Pot Gn BL0 . . . . .50 A3
Pot House La Darwen BB3 82 C3
Oswaldtwistle BB5 . . . . . .103 F2
Potter La
Coupe Green PR5 . . . . .98 D5
Samlesbury PR5 . . . . .119 E2
Potter Pl WN8 . . . . .9 D5
Potter St 5 BL9 . . . . .33 A3
Poulton Ave
Accrington BB5 . . . . .104 A8
Lytham St Anne's FY8 . . . .90 B8
Poulton Cres PR5 . . . . . . .98 D3
Poulton Ct PR9 . . . . .35 F7
Poulton Dr FY6 . . . . .153 F3
Poulton Gdns FY6 . . . . . .153 F3
Poulton Gr 3 FY7 . . . . . .199 A4
Poulton Old Rd FY3 . . . . .152 F1
Poulton Rd
Blackpool FY3 . . . . .130 E8
Carleton FY6 . . . . .153 C5
Fleetwood FY7 . . . . .198 F4
Morecambe LA4 . . . . .217 B5
Southport PR9 . . . . .35 F7
Poulton Sq LA4 . . . . .217 B6
Poulton St
Fleetwood FY7 . . . . .199 A4
Kirkham PR4 . . . . .114 B5
Preston PR2 . . . . .117 C1
Poulton-le-Fylde Sta
FY6 . . . . .153 D4
Poulton-le-Sands CE Prim
Sch LA4 . . . . .217 B6
Powder House La LA1,
LA4 . . . . .218 A4
Powderworks La L31 . . . . .6 C3
Powell Ave FY4 . . . . .110 D8
Powell St
Barnoldswick BB18 . . . . .196 B3
Burnley BB11 . . . . .127 E4
Darwen BB3 . . . . .82 B3
Powis Dr PR4 . . . . .57 A8
Powis Rd PR2 . . . . .96 B8
Powys Cl BB4 . . . . .85 B1
Poynter Gdns 4 PR1 . . . .118 C1
Poynton St BL9 . . . . .33 A1
Prairie Cres BB4 . . . . . . .148 B1
Pratt St BB10 . . . . .148 B1
Preesall Cl
Lytham St Anne's FY8 . . . .90 B7

Preesall Cl continued
Preston PR2 . . . . .116 E1
Southport PR9 . . . . .53 F4
Preesall Fleetwood's Charity
CE Prim Sch FY6 . . . . .200 B3
Preesall Mill Ind Est
FY6 . . . . .200 B2
Preese Gdns PR4 . . . . . . .156 A1
Preesall Moss La FY6 . . .200 D2
Preesall Rd PR2 . . . . .116 E1
Premier Bsns Pk BB6 . . .124 D6
Premier Way FY6 . . . . . . .153 F3
Prenton Gdns FY5 . . . . . .153 A7
Prescot Cl BL9 . . . . .33 A1
Prescot Gn L39 . . . . .15 D3
Prescot Pl Blackpool FY3 131 A2
Thornton FY5 . . . . .176 C2
Prescot Rd L31,L39 . . . . . . .6 D6
Prescott Ave L40 . . . . . . .39 A3
Prescott Rd WN8 . . . . .9 F4
Prescott St BB10 . . . . . . .128 C5
Presfield Sch PR9 . . . . . . .54 A3
Press Rd FY8 . . . . .89 D8
Prestbury Ave FY4 . . . . . .110 C5
Southport PR8 . . . . .21 B5
Prestbury Cl BL9 . . . . .33 A1
Prestbury Dr LA3 . . . . . . .217 B2
Preston Beck BB18 . . . . .197 B2
Preston Coll Winckley
Building PR1 . . . . .96 F7
Preston Coll, Fulwood
Campus PR2 . . . . .117 F5
Preston College, Park
Campus PR1 . . . . .117 F2
Preston Ent Ctr 5 PR1 .117 F1
Preston Grange Prim Sch
PR2 . . . . .119 A4
Preston Greenlands Com
Prim Sch PR2 . . . . .118 C3
Preston Lancaster New Rd
PR3 . . . . .181 B4
Preston Lancaster Old Rd
PR3 . . . . .181 D2
Preston Lancaster Rd
Bilsborrow PR3 . . . . .159 A6
Cabus PR3 . . . . .204 C5
Forton LA2,PR3 . . . . .207 C5
Galgate LA2 . . . . .211 A5
Preston Muslim Sec Sch
PR1 . . . . .118 B1
Preston New Rd
Blackburn BB2 . . . . .101 B5
Blackpool FY3,FY4 . . . . . .131 C2
Clifton PR4 . . . . .94 C7
Freckleton PR4 . . . . .93 D7
Little Plumpton PR4 . . . . .112 C6
Mellor Brook BB2,PR5 . . .120 D1
Samlesbury,PR5 . . . . .119 E1
Southport PR9 . . . . .54 B4
Preston Nook PR7 . . . . . . .41 C5
Preston Old Rd
Blackburn BB2 . . . . .80 D8
Blackpool FY3 . . . . .131 A2
Clifton PR4 . . . . .115 C1
Freckleton PR4 . . . . .93 C6
Preston Rd
Charnock Richard PR7 . . . .42 C4
Chorley PR6,PR7 . . . . .61 C2
Clayton Brook PR5,PR6,PR7 78 B4
Grimsargh PR2,PR3 . . . . .139 C2
Inskip PR4 . . . . .135 D7
Leyland PR25 . . . . .77 B2
Longridge PR3 . . . . .140 A5
Longridge PR3 . . . . .140 E6
Lucas Green PR6 . . . . .61 C4
Lytham St Anne's FY8 . . . .91 D4
Ribchester PR3 . . . . .141 B5
Southport PR8 . . . . .35 F9
Standish PR7,WN6 . . . . . . .29 D5
Preston St Carnforth LA5 223 D2
1 Chorley PR6 . . . . .61 D1
Darwen BB3 . . . . .81 F3
Fleetwood FY7 . . . . .199 B4
Kirkham PR4 . . . . .114 B5
16 Rochdale OL12 . . . . . .52 C1
Preston Sta PR1 . . . . .96 E7
Prestwich St BB11 . . . . . .127 E5
Prestwood Pl WN8 . . . . . . .9 F4
Pretoria St 2 OL12 . . . . . .52 C1
Price Cl LA1 . . . . .218 C3
Price St 9 Blackpool FY1 130 B1
Bury BL9 . . . . .33 A1
Prickshaw OL12 . . . . .52 B6
Prickshaw La OL12 . . . . . .52 B6
Priestfield Bank BB8 . . . .171 B5
Priesthouse Cl L37 . . . . . .12 A3
Priesthouse La L37 . . . . . .12 A3
Priestield FY5 . . . . .153 A7
Priestley Nook 4 BB5 . .104 C5
Priestley St BB8 . . . . .171 C4
Primet Bridge BB8 . . . . . .171 C4
Primet Bsns Ctr 4 BB8 .171 B4
Primet High Sch BB8 . . . .171 B3
Primet Hill BB8 . . . . .171 C4
Primet Hts BB8 . . . . .171 B3
Primet Prim Sch BB8 . . .171 B3
Primet St BB8 . . . . .171 C4
Primrose Ave FY4 . . . . . . .110 D6
Primrose Bank
1 Bacup OL13 . . . . .70 C8
Blackburn BB1 . . . . .101 F6
Blackpool FY2 . . . . .152 F6
Primrose Cl
Blackburn BB2 . . . . .101 B2
Formby L37 . . . . .12 B5
Hesketh Bank PR4 . . . . . . .73 E4
Southport PR9 . . . . .54 C6

Primrose Cotts
Calder Vale PR3 . . . . .182 E7
Middleton LA3 . . . . .213 A2
Primrose Ct
1 Blackburn BB1 . . . . . .101 F5
6 Lancaster LA1 . . . . . . .215 A7
Morecambe LA4 . . . . .217 B5
Primrose Dr
2 Blackburn BB1 . . . . . .101 F5
Bury BL9 . . . . .33 D4
Primrose Gr PR1 . . . . .118 C3
Primrose Hill Colne BB8 .171 F5
Mellor BB1,BB2 . . . . .122 A3
3 Preston PR1 . . . . .97 B7
Primrose Hill Prim Sch
PR7 . . . . .60 B4
Primrose Hill Rd PR7 . . . .60 B4
Primrose Hill Sch BB10 .148 D2
Primrose La Preston PR1 118 C3
Standish WN6 . . . . .29 D2
Primrose Rd
Clitheroe BB7 . . . . .166 D6
Preston PR1 . . . . .118 C3
Primrose Row PR7 . . . . . .59 F1
Primrose St
Accrington BB5 . . . . .104 A4
9 Bacup OL13 . . . . .70 C8
Brierfield BB9 . . . . .148 B5
Burnley BB10 . . . . .148 C1
Chorley PR6 . . . . .43 D8
Clitheroe BB7 . . . . .166 D7
Darwen BB3 . . . . .65 B8
6 Morecambe LA4 . . . . .217 B5
Primrose Terr
Blackburn BB2 . . . . .101 B2
Blackpool FY4 . . . . .111 A4
1 Darwen BB3 . . . . .65 B8
Langho BB6 . . . . .143 C1
Primrose Way
Carleton FY6 . . . . .153 B6
Church BB5 . . . . .103 E2
Primula Dr BB3 . . . . .82 A7
Prince Ave LA5 . . . . .223 C1
Prince Charles Gdns PR8 34 F4
Prince Lee Mdws BB3 . . . .65 B8
Prince St Bacup OL13 . . . .71 D7
11 Burnley BB11 . . . . . . .127 E5
Darwen BB3 . . . . .81 F1
Ramsbottom BL0 . . . . .50 C6
Prince's Pk WN6 . . . . .19 F4
Prince's Rd PR5 . . . . .97 E5
Prince's St BB2 . . . . .101 D4
Princes Cres LA4 . . . . . . .217 C7
Princes Ct
Higher Penwortham PR1 . . .96 B6
Lytham St Anne's FY8 . . . .89 D7
Princes Dr PR2 . . . . .117 E6
Princes Gdns LA4 . . . . . . .217 E5
Princes Rd
Higher Penwortham PR1 . . .96 B6
Lytham St Anne's FY8 . . . .90 D4
Princes Reach PR2 . . . . . .96 A7
Princes St Rishton BB1 . .124 B1
Southport PR8 . . . . .35 A6
Princes Way
Cleveleys FY5 . . . . .175 C1
Fleetwood FY7 . . . . .198 D3
Princess Alexandra Way
LA3 . . . . .212 D5
Princess Ave
Clitheroe BB7 . . . . .189 F1
Kirkham PR4 . . . . .113 F6
Lancaster LA1 . . . . .214 F6
Poulton-le-F FY6 . . . . . . .153 D3
Princess Ct
5 Blackpool FY1 . . . . . .130 B3
4 Morecambe LA4 . . . . .217 E6
Princess Gate PR9 . . . . . . .53 F2
Princess Gdns BB2 . . . . . .80 C7
Princess Par FY1 . . . . . . .130 B6
Princess Rd Adlington PR6 31 B8
Cleveleys FY5 . . . . .175 C2
Princess St
Accrington BB5 . . . . .103 F6
17 Bacup OL13 . . . . .87 F2
10 Bamber Bridge PR5 . . .77 F8
2 Bamber Bridge,Lostock Hall
PR5 . . . . .77 B7
Blackburn BB2 . . . . .101 C2
Blackpool FY1 . . . . .130 B3
Burnley BB12 . . . . .126 B8
Chorley PR7 . . . . .43 D6
4 Church BB5 . . . . .103 E6
Colne BB8 . . . . .171 C4
Great Harwood BB6 . . . . .124 D5
Haslingden BB4 . . . . .85 B2
Leyland PR25 . . . . .77 B1
Nelson BB9 . . . . .148 D7
Preston PR1 . . . . .97 B7
27 Rochdale OL12 . . . . . .52 F1
Whalley BB7 . . . . .144 C5
Whitworth OL12 . . . . .52 C8
Princess Way
Burnley BB12 . . . . .127 F7
Euxton PR7 . . . . .60 E2
Princeway FY4 . . . . .110 C2
Pringle Bank LA5 . . . . . . .223 D6
Pringle Ct PR3 . . . . .181 C7
Pringle St BB1 . . . . .102 A3
Pringle Wood PR3 . . . . . .137 C2
Prinny Hill Rd BB4 . . . . . .85 A3
Printer's Ct BL7 . . . . .48 D4
Printers Fold BB12 . . . . . .126 E6
Printshop La BB3 . . . . .65 A6
Prior's Cl BB2 . . . . .101 A6
Prior's Oak Cotts PR1 . . .96 C6
Priors Wlk BB7 . . . . .230 C1

Priorsgate LA3 217 C2
Priorswood Pl WN8 9 F4
Priory Cl Blackburn BB1 102 E4
Burscough L40 25 D5
Formby L37 12 B2
Higher Penwortham PR1 96 C6
6 Lancaster LA1 214 E8
Leyland PR25 77 C2
Morecambe LA3 217 C2
Newchurch BB4 86 E2
Pleasington BB2 100 C2
Tarleton PR4 57 A6
Priory Cres PR1 96 C6
Priory Ct
7 Blackpool FY1 130 C5
Burnley BB11 128 B2
Lytham St Anne's FY8 89 E7
Priory Dr BB3 65 C8
Priory Gate FY4 110 C5
Priory Gdns PR8 34 F4
Priory Gr L39 15 D4
Priory Grange
Darwen BB3 65 C8
Southport PR8 35 A4
Priory La
Higher Penwortham PR1 96 C6
Hornby LA2 238 B7
Priory Mews
Lytham St Anne's FY8 90 D7
Southport PR8 34 F6
Priory Nook WN8 10 C7
Priory Pl BB3 65 C8
Priory Rd WN8 10 C7
Priory St 5 Nelson BB9 170 F1
Preston PR2 96 D8
Priory Tech Coll PR1 96 A5
Priory Way BB18 196 A2
Priory Wlk 6 LA1 215 A8
Pritchard St
Blackburn BB2 101 E2
Burnley BB11 127 E5
Private La BB4 68 C8
Procter Moss Rd
Lower Green Bank LA2 232 B3
Quernmore LA2 215 D1
Procter St BB2 101 F3
Procter's Brow LA2 239 B5
Proctor Cl BB9 148 F5
Proctor Rd L37 11 C4
Progress Ave BB1 102 A7
Progress Bsns Pk PR4 114 A4
Progress Ct FY3 131 B8
Progress Rd BB9 170 F3
Progress St Chorley PR6 43 E8
Darwen BB3 82 B1
Progress Way FY4 111 B6
Promenade Ainsdale PR8 20 F6
Blackpool FY1,FY4 130 B5
Blackpool,Bispham FY2 152 B6
Cleveleys FY5 175 C5
Southport PR8,PR9 35 B8
Promenade N FY5 175 C3
Promenade Rd FY7 199 A5
Promenade S FY5 175 C2
Prospect Ave
Bamber Bridge PR5 77 B8
Darwen BB3 81 E2
Hest Bank LA2 220 E1
Prospect Bldgs 5 BB9 148 D8
Prospect Ct PR3 140 B6
Prospect Dr LA2 220 E1
Prospect Farm Cvn Pk
BB8 171 D3
Prospect Gdns BB3 81 E2
Prospect Gr LA4 217 C4
Prospect Hill
Haslingden BB4 85 A2
4 Rawtenstall BB4 86 A3
Prospect Pl
7 Middleworth Green PR1 96 E4
Preston PR2 117 B1
Skelmersdale WN8 9 F5
Prospect Rd BB4 86 A3
Prospect St
Great Harwood BB6 124 D5
Lancaster LA1 215 A7
Newchurch BB4 86 F1
Prospect Terr Bacup OL13 70 E7
10 Barrowford BB9 170 D4
Belthorn BB1 82 F6
Brinscall PR6 63 A8
Clow Bridge BB11 106 B4
Huncoat BB5 125 E2
Newchurch BB4 86 F1
Prospect View
Bamber Bridge PR5 77 A7
9 Rawtenstall BB4 86 A3
Provence Ave BB6 143 C6
Providence St BB1 102 A8
Prudy Hill FY6 153 D4
Prunella Dr BB3 82 A7
Pudding La OL14 109 C2
Pudding Pie Nook La
PR3 137 F4
Puddle House La FY6 131 F8
Pudsey Rd OL14 109 B2
Pump House La PR26 58 F6
Pump St Blackburn BB2 101 D4
Burnley BB11 127 E6
Clitheroe BB7 166 D8
Preston PR1 97 A8
Punnell's La L31 4 F5
Punstock Rd BB3 81 F1
Purbeck Dr BL6 32 F1
Pye Busk LA2 239 E8
Pye Busk Cl LA2 239 E8
Pye's Cotts L39 5 E7
Pygon's Hill La L31 5 D6

Q

Quaile Holme Rd FY6 199 D5
Quaker Brook La PR5 99 A3
Quaker La BB3 82 A2
Quakerfields BB3 82 A2
Quakers Terr WN6 29 D3
Quakers View BB9 148 A5
Quakers' Pl WN6 29 E1
Quality Row BB7 164 E1
Quarlton Dr BL8 49 B3
Quarry Bank
Garstang PR3 181 C6
Haslingden BB4 84 F1
Quarry Bank St 3 BB12 127 C7
Quarry Dr L39 15 C1
Quarry Farm Ct BB7 190 D5
Quarry Hill OL12 52 E3
Quarry Hill Nature Reserve*
BB9 148 F6
Quarry Mount L39 16 A6
Quarry Mount Mews
LA1 215 A7
Quarry Rd Brinscall PR6 62 F7
Caton LA2 237 E3
Chorley PR6 43 E6
Halton LA2 219 C6
Lancaster LA1 215 A7
Quarry St
13 Accrington BB5 104 C5
Bacup OL13 88 A2
Blackburn BB1 101 F5
Hapton BB11 126 C2
Padiham BB12 146 D1
Ramsbottom BL0 50 D6
Rochdale OL12 52 E1
Shawforth OL12 71 E6
Quarrybank 3 FY5 152 F8
Quarryside Dr L33 1 A3
Quay W FY8 89 E5
Quayle Ave FY4 110 E8
Quayside
5 Blackburn BB1 101 F4
Fleetwood FY7 199 B3
Quebec Ave FY2 152 E3
Quebec Rd BB2 101 B8
Queen Anne St
4 Haslingden BB4 85 A3
Southport PR8 35 B7
Queen Elizabeth Cres
BB5 104 D5
Queen Elizabeth Ct LA4 217 A5
Queen Elizabeth's Gram Sch
BB2 101 C6
Queen Elizabeth's Gram Sch
(Annexe) BB2 101 D6
Queen Ho BB4 86 D1
Queen Mary Ave FY8 90 A5
Queen Mary Sch FY8 90 A4
Queen Mary Terr BB7 144 B7
Queen Sq LA1 214 F7
Queen St
12 Accrington BB5 104 C6
Bacup OL13 87 F2
5 Bacup,Stacksteads OL13 70 C8
4 Bamber Bridge PR5 77 B7
Barnoldswick BB18 196 B1
Barrowford BB9 170 D4
Blackpool FY1 130 B6
Brierfield BB10 148 F2
Burnley BB11 127 F5
Bury BL9 33 A2
Carnforth LA5 223 D1
Clayton-le-M BB5 124 F3
Clitheroe BB7 166 C8
Colne BB8 171 C4
Darwen BB3 81 F2
Fleetwood FY7 199 A4
Great Harwood BB6 124 D5
Hoddlesden BB3 82 F1
Horwich BL6 32 B3
Lancaster LA1 214 F7
Lytham St Anne's FY8 91 A3
Morecambe LA4 217 B5
Nelson BB9 170 E1
Ormskirk L39 15 E4
Oswaldtwistle BB5 103 E4
Padiham BB12 126 C8
Preston PR1 97 B7
Ramsbottom BL0 50 B6
Rawtenstall BB4 86 A2
Whalley BB7 144 C5
Queen St E 3 PR7 43 D6
Queen Street Mill*
BB10 148 F2
Queen Vera Rd 4 FY1 130 B5
Queen Victoria Hospl
LA4 217 B5
Queen Victoria Rd
Blackpool FY1 130 C2
Burnley BB10 148 B1
Queen Victoria St BB2 101 B2
Queen's Cl Clitheroe BB7 166 E7
Poulton-le-F FY6 153 E3
Queen's Cres PR4 114 B4
Queen's Ct FY2 152 B2
Queen's Dr Carnforth LA5 223 E1
Oswaldtwistle BB5 103 F3
Queen's Gr PR7 43 C8
Queen's Lancashire
Regiment Mus The*
PR2 118 B4
Queen's Lancashire Way
BB11 127 F6
Queen's Park Hospl
BB2 102 A2
Queen's Park Rd
Blackburn BB1 102 A3
Burnley BB10 128 C7
Queen's Park Tech Coll
BB1 102 C2
Queen's Prom FY2 152 B5
Queen's Rd
Accrington BB5 104 C7
Blackburn BB1 102 B3
Burnley BB10 148 B2
Chorley PR7 43 C8
Darwen BB3 65 B6
Formby L37 11 D2
Fulwood PR2 117 E3
Lytham St Anne's FY8 89 F5
Walton-le-D PR5 97 E4
Queen's Sq
Hoddlesden BB3 82 F1
Poulton-le-F FY6 153 D3
7 Rawtenstall BB4 86 A2
Queen's Terr
3 Bacup OL13 70 E8
Blackburn BB2 101 B1
Fleetwood FY7 199 C5
Queens Ave L37 11 E5
Queens Croft L37 11 D2
Queens Ct Fulwood PR2 117 E3
Ormskirk L39 15 E4
Queens Ctyd 7 PR9 35 C8
Queens Dr Fulwood PR2 117 D6
Longridge PR3 140 A7
Morecambe LA4 217 E6
Staining FY3 131 E5
Queens Drive Prim Sch
PR2 117 D5
Queens Garth BD23 197 B5
Queens Gn L39 13 F5
Queens Jubilee Nature
Trail* PR8 34 E5
Queens Pl Kirkham PR4 113 F7
Ramsbottom BL9 50 C2
Queens Rd Clitheroe BB7 166 E7
Orrell WN5 10 C5
Southport PR9 35 C8
Queens Rd W BB5 104 A7
Queens Ret Pk PR1 97 B7
Queens Sq 1 FY1 130 B5
Queens Wlk FY5 175 D4
Queensberry Rd BB11 127 E5
Queensborough Rd BB5 104 B7
Queensbury Rd FY5 175 C2
Queenscourt Ave PR1 96 E2
Queenscourt Hospice
PR8 35 F4
Queensdale Cl PR5 97 E4
Queensgate Chorley PR7 43 B7
Nelson BB9 148 D7
Queensway
Bamber Bridge PR5 97 E1
Blackburn BB2 81 A8
Blackpool FY4 110 C7
Brinscall PR6 62 F8
Church BB5 103 F7
Clitheroe BB7 166 E7
Euxton PR7 60 E2
Higher Penwortham PR1 96 B6
Leyland PR25 59 E7
Lytham St Anne's FY4,FY8 111 B2
Newchurch BB4 86 E1
Poulton-le-F FY6 153 D3
Preston PR2 116 F2
Shevington WN6 19 F4
Waddington BB7 189 B4
Warton PR4 92 E7
Queensway Cl PR1 96 B6
Queensway Ct FY8 111 A1
Queensway Ind Est FY8 111 A2
Quernmore Ave FY3 131 A3
Quernmore Brow LA2 232 B5
Quernmore CE Prim Sch
LA2 232 A7
Quernmore Dr
Glasson LA2 209 E4
Kelbrook BB18 195 A5
Quernmore Ind Est PR4 93 C6
Quernmore Rd
Caton LA2 237 B2
Kirkby L33 1 A3
Lancaster LA1,LA2 215 D7
Quernmore Wlk L33 1 A3
Quillet The LA5 224 F3
Quin St PR25 77 A1
Quinton Cl PR8 21 A4

R

Rabbit La Burscough L40 24 F4
Cow Ark BB7 187 F6
Raby Sq LA4 217 B6
Raby St
4 Morecambe LA4 217 B5
1 Rawtenstall BB4 86 A2
Radburn Brow PR6 78 B3
Radburn Cl PR6 78 B3
Radcliffe Ct BB12 127 A6
Radcliffe Rd FY7 198 F2
Radeclyffe St BB7 189 E1
Radfield Ave 14 BB3 65 A8
Radfield Head BB3 64 F8
Radfield Rd BB3 64 F8
Radford Bank Gdns 12
BB3 65 A8
Radford Gdns BB3 65 A7
Radford St BB3 65 A8
Radley Ave FY3 130 E8
Radnor Ave
Burnley BB12 127 A7
Radnor Ave *continued*
Cleveleys FY5 175 F1
Radnor Cl BB5 103 C4
Radnor Dr PR9 53 F3
Radnor St Accrington BB5 104 B7
5 Preston PR1 96 E8
Radway Cl FY5 152 F7
Radworth Cres FY4 131 B1
Raeburn Ave BB11 127 E3
Raedale Ave BB10 148 B4
Raeside Ct FY8 90 A4
Raglan Rd Burnley BB11 127 E5
Morecambe LA3 216 E3
Raglan St 8 Colne BB8 171 D4
4 Nelson BB9 148 D8
Preston PR2 117 D2
Raikes Hill 2 FY1 130 C5
Raikes Hill Dr LA2 218 C8
Raikes Mews 6 FY1 130 C5
Raikes Par FY1 130 C5
Raikes Rd
Great Eccleston PR3 156 C5
Preston PR1 118 C1
Thornton FY5 153 E8
Rail Cl WA11 8 F2
Railgate OL13 71 C8
Railton Ave BB2 81 A8
Railway App L39 15 F5
Railway Ave PR9 54 F5
Railway Cotts Coppull PR7 42 F1
Preston PR4 116 C3
Salwick PR4 115 C4
Railway Crossing La
LA1 214 C5
Railway Gr 5 BB1 102 A7
Railway Path L39 15 E4
Railway Pl LA2 209 F5
Railway Rd
Adlington PR6,PR7 31 A7
Blackburn BB1 101 E5
Brinscall PR6 63 A8
Chorley PR6 61 D1
Darwen BB3 82 A1
Haslingden BB4 85 B4
Ormskirk L39 15 F5
Skelmersdale WN8 8 E8
Railway St Bacup OL13 70 B8
23 Barnoldswick BB18 196 B2
Brierfield BB9 148 B5
Burnley BB11 127 F7
Chorley PR7 43 D7
Foulridge BB8 194 D1
Lancaster LA1 214 F6
Leyland PR25 77 B2
Nelson BB9 148 E7
Ramsbottom BL0 50 C6
Ramsbottom,Summerseat
BL0,BL9 50 C2
Southport PR8 35 B5
Railway Terr
Brierfield BB9 148 B5
Entwistle BL7 48 B8
Great Harwood BB6 124 C4
10 Kirkham PR4 113 F6
Rawtenstall BB4 85 F1
Simonstone BB12 125 E8
Southport PR8 35 A5
Railway View
5 Accrington BB5 104 C6
Billington BB7 144 B4
Blackburn BB2 101 B2
Brierfield BB9 148 B6
Croston PR26 58 A2
3 Darwen BB3 65 B8
Railway View Ave BB7 189 E1
Railway View Rd BB7 189 E1
Rainford Junc WA11 8 F2
Rainford Rd L39,WA11 8 C4
Rainhall Cres BB18 196 D3
Rainhall Rd BB18 196 B2
Rake 4 BL0 50 B6
Rake Fold BL0 50 A6
Rake Foot BB4 85 B3
Rake La PR4 92 D5
Rake The LA2 232 E1
Rake Top OL12 52 C1
Rake Top Ave BB12 146 F6
Rakehead La OL13 70 B8
Rakehouse Brow LA2 232 F2
Rakes Bridge BB3 82 A7
Rakes House Rd BB9 170 F2
Rakes La BD23 231 F5
Rakes Rd LA2 237 E4
Raleigh Ave FY4 110 B5
Raleigh Cl FY8 110 D1
Raleigh Rd PR2 117 E6
Raleigh St BB12 126 E7
Ralph St BB5 104 C8
Ralph's Wife's La PR9 54 E6
Ramparts The LA1 218 E2
Ramper Gate FY5 175 D2
Rams Clough La BB5 84 A8
Ramsay Cl FY8 110 D1
Ramsay Ct FY6 199 D5
Ramsbottom Cottage Hospl
BL0 50 C5
Ramsbottom Heritage Ctr*
BL0 50 B7
Ramsbottom La BL0 50 C7
Ramsbottom Rd
Hawkshaw BL8,BL7 49 A3
Horwich BL6 32 C3
Ramsbottom St BB5 104 B7
Ramsbottom Sta BL0 50 C6
Ramsbottom Stubbins Prim
Sch BL0 68 D1
Ramsden St LA5 223 D2
Ramsey Ave Bacup OL13 88 A1
Ramsey Ave *continued*
Blackpool FY3 130 D7
Preston PR1 118 D3
Ramsey Gr BB10 148 C2
Ramsey Rd BB2 101 D1
Ramsgate Cl PR4 92 E7
Ramsgate Rd FY8 90 A8
Ramsgreave & Wilpshire Sta
BB1 122 F4
Ramsgreave Ave BB1 122 D2
Ramsgreave Dr BB1 122 D1
Ramsgreave Rd BB1 122 E4
Ramshill Ave FY6 153 B5
Ramson Ct LA3 217 B2
Ranaldsway PR25 59 D8
Randal St BB1 101 E6
Randall St 10 BB10 148 B1
Randolph St 21 BB1 102 A4
Ranelagh Dr PR8 21 F7
Range High Sch L37 2 C8
Ranger St BB5 104 B5
Rangeway Ave FY4 110 C7
Ranglet Rd PR5 78 B7
Rangletts Ave PR7 43 C6
Ranglit Ave PR2 116 C1
Rankin Ave PR4 73 F2
Rankin Cl BB18 196 C2
Rankin Dr BB3 82 E1
Ranlea Ave LA4 218 A6
Ranleigh Dr WN8 27 A1
Rannoch Dr BB2 100 F1
Ranslett Ct L37 12 A3
Rantreefold Rd LA2 239 C4
Rapley La PR4 136 A8
Ratcliffe Fold 5 BB4 85 B3
Ratcliffe St Darwen BB3 65 B8
10 Haslingden BB4 85 B3
Ratcliffe Wharf La PR3 207 B1
Rathbone Rd L38 2 F4
Rathlyn Ave FY3 130 E7
Rathmell CE Prim Sch
BD24 236 E7
Rathmell Cl FY3 153 B1
Rathmill Sike BB7 230 B1
Rathmore Cres PR9 54 B3
Ratten La PR4 95 D3
Raven Ave BB4 68 A7
Raven Cl PR7 42 F5
Raven Croft BB4 68 B8
Raven Meols La L37 11 F2
Raven Meols Hills Nature
Reserve* L37 2 B7
Raven Oak La BB10 129 B5
Raven Pk BB4 68 B8
Raven Rd BB2 101 B5
Raven St 3 Nelson BB9 170 F1
Preston PR1 118 C2
Raven's Cl FY3 131 B7
Ravendale Cl OL12 52 A1
Ravenglass Ave L31 5 D2
Ravenglass Cl
Blackburn BB2 102 A1
Blackpool FY4 110 E7
Kirkham PR4 114 A7
Ravenhead Dr WN8 10 A7
Ravenhead Way WN8 9 F6
Ravenhill Dr PR7 61 C1
Ravens Cl LA1 218 C3
Ravens Close Brow LA2 241 F1
Ravens Gr BB10 148 C4
Ravens The L37 11 F2
Ravens Wood BB2 101 B5
Ravenscroft L37 11 F2
Ravenscroft Ave L39 15 E4
Ravenscroft Cl BB1 123 A1
Ravenscroft Way BB18 196 C3
Ravensthorpe PR7 61 A1
Ravenswing Ave BB2 101 B7
Ravenswood
Fulwood PR2 118 E2
Great Harwood BB6 124 B6
Ravenswood Ave FY3 131 B7
Ravenwood Ave FY4 110 D5
Rawcliffe Dr PR2 95 E8
Rawcliffe Rd
12 Chorley PR7 43 C7
Ratten Row PR3 156 C7
Rawcliffe St
Blackpool FY4 110 B8
Burnley BB11 128 A6
Rawlinson Ct PR9 35 D8
Rawlinson Gr PR9 53 F1
Rawlinson La PR6 43 E1
Rawlinson Rd PR9 53 E1
Rawlinson St
1 Darwen BB3 65 B6
16 Horwich BL6 32 B4
5 Kirkham PR4 113 F6
Raws St BB11 128 A6
Rawson Ave BB5 104 A4
Rawson St 12 BB10 148 B1
Rawsons Rake BL0,BL8 50 A6
Rawsthorne Ave
Edenfield BL0 68 D2
Haslingden BB4 85 B2
Rawstorne Cl PR4 93 A6
Rawstorne Cres PR4 95 E1
Rawstorne Rd PR1 96 B5
Rawstorne St BB2 101 C4
Rawstron St OL12 71 C1
Rawtenstall Balladen Com
Prim Sch BB4 68 F8
Rawtenstall Cribden House
Com Specl Sch BB4 85 E1
Rawtenstall Rd BB4 85 C1

Rawtenstall Sta BB4 .....85 F1
Rawtenstall Water Prim Sch
BB4 ....87 A8
Rawtenstall Waterfoot Prim
Sch BB4 ....69 F8
Rawthey Rd **5** LA1 ....218 B2
Ray La PR3 ....181 F4
Raybourne Ave FY6 ....153 C3
Raygill Ave BB11 ......127 D3
Raygill Pl **3** LA1 .....218 B2
Raylees BL0 ....50 C4
Raymond Ave FY2 ......130 D8
Raynor St BB2 ....101 D5
Rays Dr LA1 ....214 F3
Read St **2** BB5 ......125 A1
Read St John's CE Prim Sch
BB12 ....145 C2
Read's Ave FY1 ....130 C4
Reading Cl **14** BB1 ...102 A4
Reads Ct **7** FY1 .....130 C4
Reaney Ave **3** FY1 ...110 E2
Rear West Lodge FY6 ...177 C1
Record St LA1 ....196 B1
Rectory Cl Chorley PR7 ..43 C8
Croston PR26 ....58 C2
Darwen BB3 ....65 C8
Newchurch BB4 ....86 E1
Tarleton PR4 ....57 A5
Rectory Gdns LA2 .....206 C5
Rectory Hill BL9 ....33 D4
Rectory La Bury BL9 ....33 D4
Standish WN1,WN6 .....30 A1
Rectory Paddock LA2 ..219 C6
Rectory Rd Blackpool FY4 130 E1
Burnley BB12 ....127 F7
Southport PR9 ....54 A1
Red Bank Rd FY2 .....152 C4
Red Barnes L37 ....11 F5
Red Bridge La LA5 ....224 F4
Red Cat La L40 ....25 E7
Red Cross St **5** PR1 ..96 E7
Red Delph La WA11 .....8 D1
Red Fold L39 ....15 C2
Red House La PR7 ......41 B6
Red La Colne BB8 .....171 B7
Eccleston PR7 ....41 E6
Red Lees Ave BB10 ...128 F4
Red Lees Rd BB10 ....129 A2
Red Lion Cl **2** L31 .....5 C1
Red Lion N Ctr L31 .....5 C1
Red Lion St
Burnley BB11 ....128 A5
Earby BB18 ....197 C2
Red Marsh Dr FY5 ....176 C3
Red Marsh Ind Est FY5 .176 C3
Red Rake BB1 ....101 C7
Red Rose Ct BB2 .....101 D4
Red Rose Lodge FY4 ..130 F1
Red Sands L39 ....15 D3
Red Scar Ind Est PR2 ..119 B5
Red Scar St BB8 ......171 C4
Red Shell La BB1,BB5 ...83 B7
Red Spar Rd BB10 ....148 D3
Redcar Ave Cleveleys FY5 175 F5
Fulwood PR2 ....117 A4
Redcar Ct PR8 ....35 F3
Redcar Rd Blackpool FY1 130 B8
Lancaster LA1 ....215 B3
Redcliffe Gdns LA1 .....15 E3
Redcross St OL12 ......52 F1
Redcross St N OL12 ....52 F1
Rede Ave FY7 ....198 C2
Redearth Rd BB3 ......65 A8
Redearth St BB3 ......65 A8
Redeswood Ave FY5 ..152 E8
Redfearn Wood OL12 ...52 B2
Redgate Formby L37 ....12 A2
Ormskirk L39 ....15 D5
Redgate Cl BB11 ......128 B3
Redgate Dr L37 ....12 B2
Redgate Prim Sch L37 ..12 A2
Redhill PR4 ....95 C1
Redhill Gr PR6 ....61 E3
Redhills Dr PR8 ....35 F3
Redisher Cl BL0 ....49 F3
Redisher Croft BL0 .....49 F3
Redisher La BL8 ....49 E3
Redlam BB2 ....101 B3
Redlam Brow BB2 .....101 C3
Redman Rd BB10 .....148 B4
Redmayne Dr LA5 .....223 F2
Redmayne St **3** PR1 ..97 D8
Redness BB9 ....148 E6
Redruth Dr
Carnforth LA5 ....223 C1
Crag Bank LA5 ....221 C8
Redruth St BB12 ......127 D6
Redstart Pl **12** FY5 ...175 F1
Redvers Rd BB3 ....81 E5
Redvers St Burnley BB10 148 B1
Lancaster LA1 ....214 D8
Redvers Terr FY1 .....130 B8
Redwing Ave
1 Cleveleys FY5 ....175 F4
Great Harwood BB6 ...124 B6
Redwing Rd BL8 ....49 F2
Redwood Ave
Leyland PR25 ....76 E1
Maghull L31 ....5 C3
Redwood Chase PR4 ..113 E4
Redwood Cl
Blackpool FY4 ....110 C4
Rochdale OL12 ....52 B3

Redwood Dr Chorley PR7 .43 D6
Longridge PR3 ....140 A8
Morecambe LA4 ......217 C6
Ormskirk L39 ....15 D4
Rawtenstall BB4 ....68 F8
Redwood Gdns FY5 ...176 E2
Redwood Hts LA1 .....215 C7
Reedley Dr
Brierfield BB10 ....148 C4
Clayton Brook PR5 .....78 C4
Redfield Pl PR5 ....78 A6
Reedley Dr
Brierfield BB10 ....148 C4
Brierfield,Reedley BB10 .148 C4
Reedley Farm Cl BB10 .148 B5
Reedley Gr BB10 .....148 B3
Reedley Prim Sch BB10 148 C4
Reedley Rd BB9,BB10 ..148 C5
Reedmace Wlk LA3 ....217 B2
Reeds Brow WA11 ......9 C1
Reeds Cl BB4 ....86 A6
Reeds La BB4 ....86 A6
Reeds The Lancaster LA1 218 A1
Ormskirk L39 ....15 D6
Reedsholme Cl BB4 ....86 A6
Reedy Acre Pl FY8 .....90 F4
Reedy Moor Terr BB8 ..194 C1
Reedyford Cott BB9 ...170 D2
Reedyford Rd BB9 ....170 E2
Reedymoor La BB8 ....194 C1
Reeford Gr BB7 ......166 D7
Reeth Way **3** BB5 ....103 F4
Reeval BB18 ....197 C2
Reeveswood PR7 ......41 B6
Regal Ave FY4 ....110 C6
Regal Ct PR8 ....21 D5
Regal Terr **5** LA1 ....218 D3
Regency Ave PR5 ......77 D8
Regency Ct Kirkham PR4 .113 E5
Whalley BB7 ....144 A7
Regency Gdns
Blackpool FY1 ....152 D2
Southport PR8 ....34 E4
Regent Ave Colne BB8 ..171 E6
Lytham St Anne's FY8 ..90 D6
Regent Cl Padiham BB12 .126 C7
Southport PR8 ....34 F4
Regent Ct
4 Blackpool FY1 ....130 B6
Fulwood PR2 ....117 E5
Lytham St Anne's FY8 ..89 D8
2 Southport PR9 .....35 C8
Regent Dr PR2 ....117 D4
Regent Gr PR2 ....117 E5
Regent Mews PR8 .....34 F4
Regent Pl BB9 ....170 E2
Regent Rd
Bamber Bridge PR5 ....97 D4
Blackpool FY1 ....130 C5
Chorley PR7 ....43 C7
Church BB5 ....103 F7
6 Leyland PR25 .....77 A1
Morecambe LA3 ......216 F3
Southport PR8 ....34 F4
Regent Rd E FY1 .....130 C5
Regent St Bacup OL13 ..88 A2
Blackburn BB1 ....101 E5
Brierfield BB9 ....148 B5
Coppull PR7 ....42 E1
Haslingden BB4 ....85 B3
Lancaster LA1 ....214 E7
Longridge PR3 ....140 A7
Nelson BB9 ....170 F2
Preston PR1 ....96 F6
Ramsbottom BL0 ......50 A4
Rochdale OL12 ....52 F1
Waddington BB7 .....189 B4
Regents Cl BB2 ......100 C2
Regents Terr FY6 .....153 E2
Regents View BB1 ....122 E1
Regentsway **6** PR5 ...77 E8
Reginald St BB8 ......171 C5
Reigate PR6 ....61 F3
Reiver Rd PR26 ....76 C3
Renacres Hall Hospl L39 .23 B5
Renacres La L39 ....23 B5
Rendel St BB12 ......127 C7
Rendsburg Way **15** LA1 214 F8
Renfrey Cl L39 ....15 E8
Rennie Cl PR3 ....181 D6
Rennie Ct LA1 ....214 E5
Rennie St BB10 ......128 C5
Renshaw St
Bamber Bridge PR5 ....97 E2
Bury BL9 ....33 C3
Renshaw St **8** BB10 .148 B1
Renwick Ave FY4 .....110 D8
Repton Ave
Blackpool FY1 ....130 C4
Morecambe LA4 ......217 F4
Reservoir Rd FY5 .....176 C3
Reservoir St
Burnley BB11 ....127 F4
Darwen BB3 ....81 F1
Reta Dr FY5 ....176 A3
Retford Rd L33 ....1 A2
Revidge Rd BB1,BB2 ..101 C7
Revoe Prim Sch FY1 ..130 C3
Revoe St FY1 ....130 C3
Rewe Cl BB2 ....81 C8

Rexington Bldgs BB11 ..127 C4
Reynolds St
Burnley BB11 ....127 E3
Lancaster LA1 ....218 F1
Rhoda St BB9 ....170 F1
Rhoden Rd Leyland PR26 ..76 C1
Oswaldtwistle BB5 ....103 D2
Rhodes Ave
Blackburn BB1 ....101 D8
Haslingden BB4 ....68 A7
Rhodesway PR5 ....98 E2
Rhuddlan Ave BB4 .....85 B1
Rhuddlan Gdns FY5 ..176 D2
Rhyddings High Sch
BB5 ....103 E4
Rhyddings High Sch (Annexe)
BB5 ....103 E5
Rhyddings St BB5 ....103 E4
Rhyddings The BL9 .....33 E7
Rhyl Ave BB1 ....101 E7
Rhyl St FY7 ....199 B5
Ribble Ave
Brierfield BB10 ....148 C2
Darwen BB3 ....81 E4
Freckleton PR4 ....93 A6
Great Harwood BB6 ...124 E6
Grindleton BB7 ....190 B7
Maghull L31 ....5 E2
Southport PR9 ....54 C4
Whalley BB7 ....144 A7
Ribble Bank PR1 ....96 B6
Ribble Bank St PR1 ....96 E7
Ribble Brook Ho PR1 ..117 F1
Ribble Cl Freckleton PR4 .93 A6
Middleworth Green PR1 ..96 E4
3 Preston PR1 ....96 E6
Withnell BB6 ....80 A1
Ribble Cres Kirkham PR4 114 B5
5 Preston PR1 ....97 C6
Ribble Ct **2** PR1 .....96 D6
Ribble Discovery Ctr★
FY8 ....90 C3
Ribble Dr Baldingstone BL9 50 F1
Hesketh Bank PR4 .....73 E4
West Bradford BB7 ...189 D7
Ribble Hall PR1 ......117 F1
Ribble Ho Blackburn BB1 .101 F5
11 Preston PR1 ......97 D8
Ribble La BB7 ....190 D6
Ribble Lodge **10** FY8 ..91 A3
Ribble Rd Blackpool FY1 .130 C4
Fleetwood FY7 ....198 F4
Leyland PR25 ....59 D8
Shevington Moor WN6 ..29 B2
Ribble St Bacup OL13 ..71 A8
Blackburn BB1 ....101 E6
Lytham St Anne's FY8 ..89 D6
Padiham BB12 ....126 D8
Preston PR1 ....96 E7
Ribble View PR4 ......189 F4
Ribble View Cl PR4 ....92 F6
Ribble Way PR4 ......166 C8
Ribblesdale Ave
Accrington BB5 ......104 B8
Clitheroe BB7 ....189 E2
Wilpshire BB1 ....123 A7
Ribblesdale Cl
Blackpool FY4 ....111 A8
Kirkham PR4 ....114 A5
Ribblesdale Ct
Gisburn BB7 ....231 B3
5 Morecambe LA4 ...217 B5
Ribblesdale Dr
Forton PR3 ....207 B3
Grimsargh PR2 ....139 C1
**Ribblesdale High Sch
Technology Coll** BB7 ..166 E7
Ribblesdale Pl
Barrowford BB9 ......170 E6
Blackburn BB2 ....101 C5
Chorley PR7 ....43 B7
Preston PR1 ....96 F6
Ribblesdale Rd PR3 ...141 A5
Ribblesdale St BB10 ..128 B8
Ribblesdale View BB7 .190 E5
Ribbleton Ave PR2 ....118 E2
Ribbleton Avenue Inf Sch
PR1 ....118 D2
**Ribbleton Avenue Meth Jun
Sch** PR1 ....118 D2
Ribbleton Dr BB5 ....104 C8
Ribbleton Gr BB7 ....144 A7
Ribbleton Hall Cres **2**
PR2 ....118 F3
Ribbleton Hall Dr PR2 .118 F3
Ribbleton Hall High Sch
PR2 ....118 F3
Ribbleton Hospl PR2 ..118 F2
Ribbleton La PR1 .....118 C1
Ribbleton Pl **6** PR1 ...97 B8
Ribbleton St **9** PR1 ...97 B8
Ribby Ave Kirkham PR4 .113 F5
Wrea Green PR4 ......113 C4
Ribby Pl Blackpool FY4 .131 B1
Ribby Rd Kirkham PR4 ..113 F4
Wrea Green PR4 ......113 C4
Ribby-with-Wrea CE Prim
Sch PR4 ....113 B4
Ribchester Ave
Blackpool FY4 ....131 B1
Burnley BB10 ....128 D5
Ribchester Rd
Copster Green BB1 ...142 A1
Dinckley BB6,PR3 ....142 C4
Longridge PR3 ....141 B5

Wilpshire BB1 ....122 E6
Ribchester Roman Bath Ho★
PR3 ....141 E3
**Ribchester St Wilfrid's CE
Prim Sch** PR3 .....141 E3
Ribchester Way BB9 ..148 D4
Rice Gr FY1 ....130 D8
Richard Burch St **2** BL9 .33 A3
**Richard Durning's Endowed
Prim Sch** L40 ....27 D7
Richard St Brierfield BB9 148 B5
Burnley BB11 ....128 B5
Shuttleworth BL0 ......50 E7
Weir OL13 ....88 A7
**Richard Thornton's CE Prim
Sch** LA2 ....242 B3
Richard's St **7** PR4 ..113 F6
Richard's Way **4** PR4 .110 E2
Richards Rd WN6 ......29 B3
Richards Way **7** LA1 .175 F1
Richards Wlk **7** LA1 ..218 B1
Richardson Cl PR4 .....93 C6
Richardson St FY1 ....130 B4
Richmond Ave
Accrington BB5 ......104 B5
Barnoldswick BB18 ...196 A3
Burnley BB10 ....128 F4
Burscough L40 ....25 E3
Cleveleys FY5 ....175 E2
Haslingden BB4 ....85 C2
Lancaster LA1 ....218 D4
Morecambe LA4 ......217 D4
Wrea Green PR4 ......113 B3
Richmond Cl Brinscall PR6 62 E8
Hightown L38 ....2 F2
Richmond Cres BB1 ..102 E5
Richmond Ct
8 Blackpool FY1 ....130 B7
Burscough L40 ....25 E3
Chorley PR7 ....43 C6
Leyland PR26 ....76 B1
Richmond Gr L31 ......5 E3
Richmond Hill **28** BB1 .101 E5
Richmond Hill La PR3 ..207 D2
Richmond Hill St BB5 ..104 B5
Richmond Ho Chorley PR7 43 C6
9 Lancaster LA1 ....218 D3
11 Preston PR1 ......97 A7
Richmond Ind Est BB5 .104 B5
Richmond Mews L40 ...25 E3
Richmond Pk BB3 .....82 A2
Richmond Rd
Accrington BB5 ......104 A4
Barnoldswick BB18 ...196 A3
Barrowford BB9 .....170 C1
Blackpool FY1 ....130 B7
Chorley PR6 ....43 E6
Eccleston PR7 ....41 C7
Lytham St Anne's FY8 ..89 E6
Southport PR8 ....34 F2
Richmond St
Accrington BB5 ......104 A5
Accrington BB5 ......104 B5
Burnley BB11 ....127 E5
Horwich BL6 ....32 B3
2 Preston PR1 ....97 B7
Richmond Terr
17 Blackburn BB1 ...101 E5
Clitheroe BB7 ....166 D7
Darwen BB3 ....82 D2
Rickard Rd BB9 ......148 E6
Ridding La BB7 ......144 B5
Riddings Ave BB10 ...128 F6
Riddings La BB7 .....144 C6
Riddiough Ct OL12 ....52 C8
Ridehalgh La BB10 ...149 F2
Ridehalgh St BB8 ....171 B3
Ridge Ave BB10 ......128 D6
Ridge Cl PR9 ....54 C5
Ridge Ct Burnley BB10 .128 C7
Longridge BB3 ....140 C8
Ridge Gr LA3 ....212 F8
Ridge La Lancaster LA1 .218 E1
Lancaster,Ridge LA1 ..219 A2
Roughlee BB12 ....169 F4
Ridge Prim Sch LA1 ..218 F1
Ridge Rd Burnley BB11 .128 B6
Chorley PR6 ....43 E7
Ridge Row BB10 .....128 D6
Ridge Sq LA1 ....218 F1
Ridge St
Barnoldswick BB18 ...196 B2
Lancaster LA1 ....218 E1
Ridge Way PR1 ....96 E4
Ridgeford Gdns PR2 ..117 D5
Ridgemont PR2 ......117 C6
Ridgeway
Barrowford BB9 .....170 C3
Barrowford BB9 .....170 D3
Great Harwood BB6 ..124 B6
Ridgeway Ave BB2 ....82 A8
Ridgeway Dr Maghull L31 ..5 B3
Thornton FY5 ....153 D8
Ridgeway The
Fleetwood FY7 ....198 D3
Nelson BB9 ....148 D7
Ridgeways BB4 ....85 C2
Ridgmont Cl BL6 ......32 C3
Ridgmont Dr BL6 ......32 F3
Ridgway BL6 ....31 C2
Ridgway Ct FY8 ....90 A7
Ridgwood Ave FY3 ...130 A5
Riding Barn St BB5 ...103 F7
Riding Cl BB18 ....196 C2
Riding Head La BL0 ....50 F8
Riding La L39 ....13 E4
Riding St Burnley BB11 .127 E5

Riding St continued
Preston PR1 ....117 F1
Southport PR8 ....35 B6
Ridings The
Burnley BB12 ....127 D8
Lucas Green PR6 ......61 C6
Southport PR9 ....54 A3
Ridley La
Barber's Moor PR26 ...58 D3
Maghull L31 ....5 D1
Mawdesley L40 ....40 F2
Ridley Rd PR2 ....117 C2
Ridley St **2** FY3 ....130 D5
Rifle St BB4 ....85 B2
Rigby Ave BL6 ....31 C2
Rigby Cl PR4 ....93 C6
Rigby Rd Blackpool FY1 .130 B3
Maghull L31 ....5 B3
Rigby St Colne BB8 ...171 C5
Nelson BB9 ....148 D8
Preston PR1 ....97 C8
Rigg Ho **10** LA1 .....218 D2
Rigg La Quernmore LA2 .232 B7
Whitechapel PR3 .....184 B1
Rigg St BB9 ....148 E8
Riley Ave FY8 ....89 F5
Riley Cl PR25 ....60 A8
Riley Ct FY8 ....89 F4
Riley Green Switch Rd
BB2,PR5 ....79 F7
Riley St Accrington BB5 .104 B4
Bacup OL13 ....87 F5
Brierfield BB9 ....148 B5
Burnley BB11 ....128 B4
Earby BB18 ....197 C2
Rimington Ave
Accrington BB5 ......104 A3
Burnley BB10 ....128 C5
Colne BB8 ....171 C6
Rimington Cl BB2 ....101 F2
Rimington Cvn Pk BB7 .231 B1
Rimington La BB7 ....191 D7
Rimington Pl
Lytham St Anne's FY8 ..90 B6
Nelson BB9 ....171 B1
Rimmer Gn PR8 ....36 D1
Rimmer's Ave Formby L37 .16 D7
Southport PR8 ....35 B6
Ring Dyke Way FY8 ....91 A4
Ring Lows La OL12 .....52 F4
Ring O'Bells La L40 ....26 B2
Ring Way PR1 ....96 F7
Rings St BB4 ....106 A2
Ringstone Cres BB9 ..149 B8
Ringstones La LA2 ....239 D4
Ringtail Cl L40 ....25 B4
Ringtail Ind Est L40 ...25 B2
Ringtail Pl L40 ....25 B4
Ringtail Rd L40 ....25 B4
Rington Ave FY6 .....153 B6
Ringway Chorley PR7 ..43 A7
Cleveleys FY5 ....175 E4
Ringwood Ave BL0 .....50 A4
Ringwood Cl
Accrington BB5 ......125 B1
Lytham St Anne's FY8 ..90 F3
Ringwood Rd PR1 ....118 C2
Ripley Cl L31 ....5 E1
Ripley Dr FY8 ....90 B6
Ripley St Thomas' CE High
Sch LA1 ....214 F6
Ripon Ave **1** LA1 ...218 D4
Ripon Brook PR1 .....118 F1
Ripon Cl Cleveleys FY5 .175 E5
Great Eccleston PR3 ..156 C5
Southport PR8 ....35 F3
Ripon Hall Ave BL0 ....50 B4
Ripon Pl LA3 ....212 F8
Ripon Rd Blackpool FY4 .130 D4
Lytham St Anne's FY8 ..90 D5
Oswaldtwistle BB5 ...103 C5
Ripon St Blackburn BB1 .102 B4
Nelson BB9 ....148 D7
Preston PR1 ....117 E2
Ripon Terr PR1 ......118 F1
Rise The LA5 ....221 B6
Risedale Dr PR3 .....140 B7
Risedale Gr BB2 ......83 A7
Rishton Meth Prim Sch
BB1 ....124 B1
Rishton Rd
Clayton-le-M BB5 ....124 E3
Wilpshire BB1 ....123 C5
Rishton St FY1 ......130 C4
Rishton Sta BB1 .....103 A8
Rising Bridge Rd BB4,
BB5 ....85 A7
Ritherham Ave FY5 ...175 D3
River Bank Terr BB5 ..125 E6
River Cl L37 ....12 B1
River Dr BB12 ....126 D8
River Hts PR5 ....77 C8
River Lea Gdns BB7 ..166 F8
River Par PR1 ....96 D6
River Rd FY5 ....176 B3
River St Bacup OL13 ..87 A3
Blackburn BB1 ....101 F4
Colne BB8 ....171 D4
Darwen BB3 ....81 F2
Lancaster LA1 ....218 C1
Preston PR1 ....96 F1
Ramsbottom BL0 ......50 C6
Trawden BB8 ....172 C3
River View Glasson LA2 .209 E5
Tarleton PR4 ....57 A8
River Way BB9 ......170 D4
Rivermead Ct PR3 ...204 C1

Rivermead Dr PR3 .....181 C8
Rivermeade PR8 ....35 D4
Rivers Edge The OL12 ...71 C1
Rivers St WN5 ....10 E6
Rivers View Fold LA2 ..226 A8
Riversedge Rd PR25 .....59 C8
Riversgate FY7 ....198 F4
Riverside
Bamber Bridge PR5 ....77 E7
Clitheroe BB7 ....166 B8
Hightown L38 ....2 F4
Preston PR1 ....96 E5
Riverside Ave PR26 ......76 E4
Riverside Cl Halton LA2 .219 C6
Leyland PR26 ....76 E4
Riverside Cres PR26 .....58 A2
Riverside Ct OL12 ....71 D4
Riverside Cvn Site PR9 ..55 D3
Riverside Dr
Hambleton FY6 ....177 B1
Ramsbottom BL0 ....50 B2
Riverside Fold BB12 ....169 E5
Riverside Ind Est BB5 ..124 D2
Riverside Ind Pk PR3 ...181 C2
Riverside Lofts LA1 ....218 C1
Riverside Mews BB4 ......86 F4
Riverside Mill 3 BB8 ...171 B4
Riverside Park Ind Est
LA1 ....218 F4
Riverside Pk BB4 ....86 F4
Riverside Rd PR1 ....96 E5
Riverside Terr 4 BB18 ..197 B1
Riverside View BB5 ....124 E4
Riverside Wlk BB4 ......68 A7
Riversleigh Ave
Blackpool FY1 ....152 C1
Lytham St Anne's FY8 .....90 E3
Riversleigh Ct FY8 ......90 E3
Riversway Blackpool FY3 .130 F6
4 Lancaster LA1 ....218 D2
Poulton-le-F FY6 ....153 F5
Preston PR2,PR4 ....95 D8
Riversway Bsns Village
PR2 ....96 A8
Riversway Dr BB3 ....81 F6
Riversway Enterprise
Workshops PR2 ....95 E8
Riversway Managed
Workshops PR2 ....95 F8
Riversway Motor Pk PR2 95 D7
Riverview Ct LA4 ......217 B3
Riverway Cl PR5 ....77 D8
Rivington & Blackrod High
Sch BL6 ....32 B6
Rivington & Blackrod High
Sch (Annexe) BL6 ......32 B4
Rivington Ave
Adlington PR6 ....31 B7
Blackpool FY2 ....152 D5
Rivington Cl
Poulton-le-F FY6 ....153 D3
Southport PR8 ....35 A3
Tarleton PR4 ....56 F8
Rivington Ctry Pk★ BL6 .32 A8
Rivington Dr
Burscough L40 ....25 E3
Skelmersdale WN8 ....10 C7
Rivington Hall Cl BL0 ...50 C4
Rivington Ho 2 BL6 .....32 B4
Rivington La
Adlington PR6 ....31 D6
Horwich BL6 ....32 A7
Rivington BL6 ....44 F1
Rivington Park Ind Sch
BL6 ....44 F1
Rivington Pl PR7 ....29 D6
Rivington Prim Sch BL6 .44 F1
Rivington Rd
Belmont BL6,BL7 ....46 B4
Chorley PR6 ....61 E1
Rivington St
Blackburn BB1 ....102 B4
Blackrod BL6 ....31 D2
Rochdale OL12 ....52 F1
Rivington View PR6 ....61 E1
Rixton Gr FY5 ....176 B4
Roach Bridge Cotts PR5 .98 E6
Roach Rd PR5 ....99 B4
Roach St BL9 ....33 C1
Road La OL12 ....52 D4
Robbin's Bridge L31 ......5 E5
Robert St Accrington BB5 104 C7
Barnoldswick BB18 ......196 B2
Blackburn BB2 ....101 E3
Colne BB8 ....171 E5
15 Darwen BB3 ....81 F2
Great Harwood BB6 ......124 D6
43 Lancaster LA1 ....214 F8
Newchurch BB4 ....86 F2
Oswaldtwistle BB5 ......103 D3
Ramsbottom BL0 ....68 C1
Roberts Ct Leyland PR25 ..59 F8
Warton LA5 ....223 D6
Roberts St 2 Chorley PR7 43 C7
Nelson BB9 ....148 F8
7 Rawtenstall BB4 ....86 A3
Robertson Ct FY7 ......198 F1
Robin Bank Rd BB3 ......82 A2
Robin Cl PR7 ....42 D3
Robin Croft LA2 ....241 A1
Robin Hey PR26 ....76 B1
Robin Hill Dr WN6 ......29 B2
Robin Hill La WN6 ......29 C3
Robin Hood La WN6 ......28 B3
Robin House La BB10 ..149 C4
Robin La
High Bentham LA2 ......239 D8
Hill Dale WN8 ....27 C5
Robin La continued
Rimington BB7 ....231 B1
Robin Rd BL0 ....50 B2
Robin St PR1 ....118 D1
Robins Cl FY6 ....153 A4
Robins La Blackpool FY6 .153 A4
Carleton FY6 ....153 A6
Robinson Ct BB18 .....196 A3
Robinson La BB9,BB10,
BB12 ....148 A4
Robinson St
Blackburn BB1 ....102 B7
Burnley BB10 ....128 A8
Chatburn BB7 ....190 E5
Colne BB8 ....171 C5
Foulridge BB8 ....194 D1
Fulwood PR2 ....117 D3
18 Horwich BL6 ....32 B4
Robson St BB9 ....148 B6
Robson Way FY3 ....153 A2
Roby Mill WN8 ....19 B3
Roby Mill CE Prim Sch
WN8 ....19 B3
Rochdale Infmy OL12 ....52 F1
Rochdale Old Rd BL9 ....33 D4
Rochdale Rd Bacup OL13 .88 A1
Bury BL9 ....33 B2
Edenfield BL0 ....68 F2
Ramsbottom BL0,BL9 .....51 B7
Rochester Ave
Cleveleys FY5 ....175 F4
Morecambe LA4 ....217 D3
Rochester Cl OL13 ......88 A7
Rochester Dr BB10 .....148 C3
Rochford Ave FY5 ......175 E1
Rock Bridge Fold BB4 ...86 E5
Rock Brow PR3 ....163 B7
Rock Fold BL7 ....47 F1
Rock Gdns PR5 ....99 B3
Rock Hall Rd BB4 ....85 B3
Rock La Burnley BB11 ...128 B3
Tockholes BB3 ....81 A3
Trawden BB8 ....172 C3
Rock m' Jock LA2 ......237 B3
Rock St Accrington BB5 ..104 E2
Clitheroe BB7 ....166 E8
18 Haslingden BB4 ....85 B3
Horwich BL6 ....32 B3
Shuttleworth BL0 ....50 E7
Thornton FY5 ....176 B4
Rock Terr Egerton BL7 ....47 F1
Pendleton BB7 ....167 B4
11 Rawtenstall BB4 ....86 A7
Rock Villa Rd PR6 ....61 C8
Rock Water (Bird
Conservation Ctr)★
BB10 ....129 C2
Rockburgh Cres PR4 ....75 A5
Rockcliffe Ave OL13 .....87 E1
Rockcliffe Dr OL13 ......87 E1
Rockcliffe Rd OL13 ......87 F1
Rockcliffe St 5 BB4 .....86 A3
Rockcliffe Villas OL13 ...70 E8
Rockfield Gdns 2 L31 .....5 C2
Rockfield Rd BB5 ......104 D6
Rockfield St BB2 ....101 E3
Rockhaven Ave BL6 ......32 C4
Rockingham Rd FY2 ....152 D3
Rockliffe La OL13 ....88 A1
Rockliffe Rd OL13 ....87 F1
Rockliffe St BB2 ....101 E2
Rockville BB9 ....170 E5
Rockville Ave FY5 ......152 F8
Rockwood Cl BB10 .....148 E3
Roddlesworth La PR6 .....63 E8
Roddlesworth Nature Trail★
BB3 ....64 B8
Roddlesworth Vistor Ctr★
BB3 ....64 B8
Rodhill La BB7 ....230 B3
Rodney Ave FY8 ....110 E1
Rodney St Blackburn BB2 101 C3
3 Preston PR1 ....96 F8
Rodwell Wlk FY3 ....130 F8
Roe Greave Rd BB5 ....103 D3
Roe Hey Dr PR7 ....42 F2
Roe La PR9 ....35 E8
Roe Lee Park Prim Sch
BB1 ....122 F2
Roe Lee Pk BB1 ....122 F2
Roe St OL12 ....52 C1
Roe-Park Mews PR9 .....35 E8
Roebuck Cl BB2 ....101 D3
Roebuck Prim Sch PR2 117 D2
Roebuck St PR2 ....117 C2
Roeburn Dr LA3 ....217 F2
Roeburn Pl LA1 ....218 C2
Roeburn Terr LA2 ......238 D6
Roeburndale Cres LA3 .213 A8
Roedean Ave LA4 ....217 F4
Roedean Cl Maghull L31 ...5 D2
12 Thornton FY5 ....176 A2
Roehampton Cl 11 FY5 .176 A2
Rogerley Cl FY8 ....91 A4
Rogersfield BB6 ....123 B8
Rolleston Rd BB2 ......101 B4
Roman Cres LA2 ....237 C3
Roman Mus★ PR3 ....141 E3
Roman Rd
Blackburn BB1,BB2 ....82 B8
Preston PR1 ....97 B7
Whittlestone Head BB3 ....66 A4
Roman Way
Cleveleys FY5 ....175 F1
Clitheroe BB7 ....167 A8
Kirkham PR4 ....114 C4
Red Scar PR2 ....119 C6
Roman Way Ind Est
PR2 ....119 C6
Rome Ave BB11 ....127 C4
Romford Rd PR1 ....118 C2
Romford St 2 BB12 ....127 C7
Romiley Dr WN8 ....17 F2
Romney Ave
Barrowford BB9 ....170 D3
Blackpool FY4 ....130 D1
Burnley BB11 ....127 E3
Fleetwood FY7 ....198 E3
Romney St BB9 ....148 D7
Romney Wlk BB1 ....102 C4
Romsey Ave L37 ....12 B2
Ronald St Blackburn BB1 .102 C5
Burnley BB12 ....127 A5
Ronaldsway Nelson BB9 .171 B2
Preston PR1 ....118 D3
Ronaldsway Cl OL13 .....88 B1
Ronbury Cl 1 BB9 .....170 C1
Roney St BB2 ....101 C5
Ronwood Cl PR4 ....155 F1
Ronwood Ct PR2 ....96 B8
Roocroft Sq BL6 ....31 C2
Roods The LA5 ....223 E6
Rook Hill Rd OL13 ....70 B8
Rook St
Barnoldswick BB18 ......196 B2
Colne BB8 ....171 D5
Nelson BB9 ....170 E1
Preston PR1 ....118 B1
3 Ramsbottom BL0 ....50 C6
Rookery Ave WN6 ....19 E8
Rookery Cl Chorley PR7 ...43 A6
Kingsfold PR1 ....96 F2
Rookery Dr PR1 ....96 F2
Rookery Rd
Barnoldswick BB18 ......196 C3
Southport PR9 ....53 F1
Rookwood PR7 ....41 B6
Rookwood Ave PR7 ....61 C2
Rooley Moor Rd
Bacup OL12,OL13 ....70 C4
Rochdale,Shawfield OL12 ..52 A3
Rochdale,Spotland Fold
OL12 ....52 C1
Rooley St OL12 ....52 C1
Rooley View OL13 ....87 E1
Roosevelt Ave LA1 .....214 D7
Roots La PR4 ....135 E2
Rope Wlk PR3 ....181 C7
Ropefield Way OL12 .....52 E3
Rosary Ave FY4 ....130 E1
Roscoe Ave FY5 ....176 D2
Roscoe Lowe Brow PR6 .31 D7
Rose Acre La LA5 .....225 F2
Rose Ave Blackpool FY1 ..130 D2
Burnley BB11 ....127 E4
Fulwood PR2 ....117 C3
Rose Bank Lancaster LA1 215 A5
Rawtenstall BB4 ....86 A3
Rose Bank St OL13 ......87 F3
Rose Cl PR25 ....77 E2
Rose Cotts
Low Bentham LA2 ....239 B8
Preesall FY6 ....200 C3
Rose Cres
Skelmersdale WN8 ....17 E1
Southport PR8 ....21 C2
Rose Ct 1 FY7 ....198 F4
Rose Fold
Middleworth Green PR1 ...96 D4
Thornton FY5 ....176 B4
Rose Fold Cotts PR1 ....96 D4
Rose Gdns PR4 ....73 E4
Rose Gr LA2 ....210 F4
Rose Grove Sta BB11 ...127 B5
Rose Hill Euxton PR7 .....60 C4
Ramsbottom BL0 ....50 B6
Southport PR8,PR9 ....35 D6
Rose Hill Ave BB1 .....102 A4
Rose Hill Rd BB2 ......100 C1
Rose Hill St Bacup OL13 ..87 F2
Darwen BB3 ....65 B8
Rawtenstall BB4 ....106 A1
Rose Hill Terr 7 BB3 ....65 B8
Rose La PR1 ....118 C3
Rose Lea PR2 ....118 D6
Rose Mount BB4 ....86 F1
Rose Pl Accrington BB5 ..104 B4
Ormskirk L39 ....15 D2
Rose St Accrington BB5 ..104 B4
Bacup OL13 ....87 F2
7 Blackburn BB2 ....101 E3
Darwen BB3 ....82 B1
Leyland PR25 ....77 B3
Morecambe LA4 ....217 B6
Newchurch BB4 ....86 E2
14 Preston PR1 ....97 A7
Rose Terr PR2 ....117 B2
Rose Vale St BB4 ....86 B2
Roseacre FY4 ....110 C5
Roseacre Cl BB4 ....86 F4
Roseacre Dr PR4 ......156 A1
Roseacre Pl
Lytham St Anne's FY8 .....90 B8
5 Preston PR2 ....116 E1
Roseacre Prim Sch FY4 110 C5
Roseacre Rd PR4 ......134 D6
Rosebank
Clayton-le-M BB5 ......125 A3
Edenfield BL0 ....68 D1
2 Preston PR2 ....116 C1
Rosebank Ave 3 FY4 ...110 C5
Rosebay Ave BB2 ....80 D8
Rosebay Cl L37 ....12 A3
Roseberry Ave PR4 .....116 E5
Roseberry Cl BL0 ....50 C3
Rosebery Ave
Blackpool FY4 ....110 B6
Lancaster LA1 ....215 A5
Lytham St Anne's FY8 .....90 B4
Morecambe LA4 ....217 C4
Rosebery St
Burnley BB10 ....148 B2
Cornholme OL14 ....109 B1
Southport PR9 ....36 A6
Rosecroft Cl L39 ....15 E6
Rosedale Ave
Blackpool FY4 ....131 A2
Heysham LA3 ....213 A8
Rosedale St BB4 ....85 F5
Rosedene LA2 ....218 D7
Rosedene Cl PR4 ......116 E5
Rosefinch Way FY3 ....131 B3
Rosegarth LA2 ....218 D7
Rosegrove Cvn Pk FY6 .200 A6
Rosegrove Inf Sch
BB12 ....127 A6
Rosegrove La BB11 ....127 B5
Rosehill Ave
Burnley BB11 ....127 E4
12 Nelson BB9 ....170 F1
Rosehill Bsns Pk 1 PR9 .35 D6
Rosehill Com Inf Sch
BB11 ....127 F3
Rosehill Dr L39 ....15 C2
Rosehill Jun Sch BB11 .127 E3
Rosehill Mans L39 ......15 C2
Rosehill Mt BB11 ......127 E4
Rosehill Rd Burnley BB11 127 F3
Nelson BB8 ....171 A2
Roseland Ave BB9 .....148 C6
Roseland Cl L31 ....5 B4
Roselea Dr PR9 ....54 C4
Roselyn Ave FY4 ....110 C5
Rosemary Ave
Blackpool FY4 ....110 C5
Cleveleys FY5 ....175 F3
Rosemary Ct Formby L37 .11 F3
1 Kingsfold PR1 ....96 C2
Rosemary La Formby L37 .11 F3
Haskayne L39 ....14 B4
8 Lancaster LA1 ....214 F8
Swillbrook PR4 ....136 A1
Rosemeade Ave PR5 .....77 B8
Rosemede Ave FY4 .....130 F2
Rosemount OL13 ....88 A4
Rosemount Ave
Barnoldswick BB18 ......196 A3
Burnley BB11 ....127 E4
Knott End-on-S FY6 .....200 A5
Rosendale Cl OL13 ......88 B3
Rosendale Cres OL13 ....88 B3
Roseway Blackpool FY4 ..110 C5
Lytham St Anne's FY8 .....90 B6
Poulton-le-F FY6 ....153 C3
Preston PR2 ....117 A1
Rosewood Cottam PR4 ..116 E5
Southport PR9 ....53 F2
Rosewood Ave
Blackburn BB1 ....101 F8
Burnley BB11 ....127 E3
Haslingden BB4 ....85 C3
Higher Walton PR5 ....98 C3
Rosewood Cl Chorley PR7 43 D6
Lytham St Anne's FY8 .....90 E4
1 Thornton FY5 ....176 D1
Rosewood Dr Chorley PR7 43 E6
Higher Walton PR5 ....98 B3
Roshaw PR2 ....139 C1
Rosklyn Rd PR6 ....43 E7
Rosley St BB8 ....172 B5
Ross St Brierfield BB9 ..148 B5
Darwen BB3 ....65 A6
Rossall Cl
Coupe Green PR5 ....98 E3
Fleetwood FY7 ....175 D8
Padiham BB12 ....126 D6
Rossall Ct Cleveleys FY5 .175 C5
Fleetwood FY7 ....198 E3
Rossall Dr PR2 ....117 C4
Rossall Gate FY7 ......175 C8
Rossall Gdns FY5 ......175 D4
Rossall Grange La FY7 .198 D3
Rossall Hospl FY7 .....175 C8
Rossall La FY7 ....175 E7
Rossall Rd Blackpool FY3 130 D7
Chorley PR6 ....61 E1
Cleveleys FY5 ....175 D3
Fulwood PR2 ....117 C4
Lancaster LA1 ....218 A2
Lytham St Anne's FY8 .....90 D4
Rossall Sch FY7 ....175 C6
Rossall St PR2 ....117 C1
Rossall Terr BB2 ....101 E1
Rossendale Ave
Burnley BB11 ....127 E2
Lancaster LA1 ....211 B8
Morecambe LA4 ....217 C6
Rossendale Ave N FY5 .176 B2
Rossendale Ave S FY5 ..176 B1
Rossendale General Hospl
BB4 ....85 D2
Rossendale Mus★ BB4 ..85 E2
Rossendale Rd
Burnley BB11 ....127 C3
Lytham St Anne's FY8 .....90 A7
Rossendale Sch BL0 .....51 A7
Rosser Ct 18 BB9 ......148 E8
Rossett Ave FY4 ....131 C1
Rossetti Ave BB11 ......127 F3
Rossington Ave FY2 ....152 E5
Rosslyn Ave FY6 ....200 A6
Rosslyn Cres FY6 ......200 B5
Rosslyn Cres E FY6 ....200 B5
Rossmoyne Rd LA1 .....215 A4
Rostle Top Rd 6 BB18 ..197 B1
Rostrevor Cl 4 PR26 ....76 B1
Rostron Cres L37 ....11 E1
Rostron Rd BL0 ....50 B6
Rostron's Bldgs BB4 .....86 D1
Rothay Ave FY7 ....198 D2
Rothbury Pl FY8 ....91 C4
Rotherhead Cl BL6 ......31 F2
Rotherwick Ave PR7 ......43 B7
Rothesay Cres LA3 .....212 D5
Rothesay Rd
Blackburn BB1 ....102 D3
Brierfield BB9 ....148 C6
Heysham LA3 ....212 D5
Rothley Ave PR8 ....21 A4
Rothsay Rd LA3 ....212 E5
Rothwell Ave BB5 ......104 C4
Rothwell Cl L39 ....15 D5
Rothwell Cres PR2 .....118 F4
Rothwell Ct PR25 ....77 A2
Rothwell Dr
Fleetwood FY7 ....198 D3
Ormskirk L39 ....15 B2
Southport PR8 ....21 A4
Rothwell Lodge 5 PR2 .118 F4
Rothwell Rd PR6 ....31 B7
Rothwell St BL0 ....50 B6
Rotten Row Caton LA2 ..237 D3
Southport PR8 ....34 F6
Rough Hey Gate BB5 ...103 F2
Rough Hey Ind Est PR2 .119 B7
Rough Hey Pl PR2 .....119 B7
Rough Hey Rd PR2 .....119 B7
Rough Heys BB5 ....104 A2
Rough Heys La FY4 ....110 E7
Rough Hill La BL9 ....33 E4
Rough Lea Rd FY5 .....175 D2
Rough Lee Rd BB5 .....104 C4
Roughlee CE Prim Sch
BB12 ....169 F4
Roughlee Gr BB10 .....128 D5
Roughlee Old Hall BB9 .170 A5
Roughlee St BB9 ....170 D2
Roughlee Terr BB11 ....106 B4
Roughwood Dr L33 ....1 A4
Round Acre
Bamber Bridge PR1 ....97 A1
Nab's Head PR5 ....99 E7
Round Barn BL7 ....66 B3
Round Hill Pl BB10 ....128 E1
Round Mdw PR26 ....76 C1
Round Meade The L31 .....5 C2
Round Wood PR1 ....96 C7
Roundel St BB10 ....148 B2
Roundell Rd BB18 .....196 C3
Roundhay FY4 ....110 F8
Roundhill La BB4 ....85 A7
Roundhill Rd BB4,BB5 ...84 E6
Roundhill View BB5 .....85 A8
Roundhouse The 44
LA1 ....214 F8
Roundway FY7 ....175 C8
Roundway Down PR2 ..117 C7
Roundway The L38 ....2 F3
Roundwood Ave BB10 ..148 A4
Row The Heapey PR6 .....62 D3
Silverdale LA5 ....224 E3
Rowan Ave Fulwood PR2 .119 A4
2 Horwich BL6 ....32 E1
Oswaldtwistle BB5 ......103 D2
Rowan Bank LA2 ....219 C7
Rowan Cl Blackburn BB1 .123 B1
Bonds PR3 ....181 D6
Burscough Bridge L40 .....25 F6
Higher Penwortham PR1 ..96 B3
Rochdale OL12 ....52 B3
Rowan Croft PR6 ....78 B1
Rowan Dr BL9 ....33 B3
Rowan Gr Burnley BB10 .128 C6
Chorley PR6 ....61 C3
Rowan La WN8 ....18 B4
Rowan Tree Cl BB5 ....104 D7
Rowangate PR2 ....118 C7
Rowans The Adlington PR6 31 A8
Aughton L39 ....6 A7
Poulton-le-F FY6 ......153 A2
Rowberrow Cl PR2 .....118 D6
Rowen Pk BB2 ....101 B8
Rowland Ave BB9 ......149 A8
Rowland Cl FY5 ....175 F2
Rowland La FY5 ....175 F2
Rowland St BB5 ....104 A5
Rowlands Rd BL9 ....50 D2
Rowley La BB10 ....128 D6
Rowley Trad Est FY8 ....89 D7
Rowntree Ave FY7 .....198 F3
Roworth Cl PR5 ....97 E3
Rowsley Rd FY8 ....89 D7
Rowton Heath PR2 .....117 C7
Roxburgh Rd FY4 ......111 A6
Roxton Cl BL6 ....32 B5
Roy St OL14 ....109 A1
Royal Albert Cotts LA1 .214 E4
Royal Ave Blackpool FY3 .130 F3
Fulwood PR2 ....117 E6
Kirkham PR4 ....114 B4
Leyland PR25 ....59 E7
Royal Bank Rd FY3 .....130 E3
Royal Beach Ct FY8 .....89 D7
Royal Birkdale Golf Club The
PR8 ....34 D2
Royal Brook Ho 7 PR1 ..118 A1
Royal Cl L37 ....12 A1
Royal Cres L37 ....12 A1

Royal Cross Prim Sch
PR2 . . . . .116 E1
Royal Ct Brierfield BB10 . .148 F3
11 Lancaster LA1 . . . . . .214 F7
Royal Dr PR2 . . . . .117 D3
Royal Fold LA3 . . . . .212 E8
Royal Gdns BL0 . . . . .50 A3
Royal Lancaster Infmy
LA1 . . . . .214 F7
Royal Lytham & St Anne's
Golf Course FY8 . . . . . .90 B5
Royal Oak Ave BB1 . . . . .122 E1
Royal Oak Bldgs 16 BB10 .130 B1
Royal Oak Cotts BB9 . . . .170 B4
Royal Oak Mdw LA2 . . . .238 B8
Royal Pl FY8 . . . . .90 C8
Royal Preston Hospl The
PR2 . . . . .117 F6
Royal Rd LA4 . . . . .217 C6
Royal Terr PR8 . . . . .35 A7
Royal Troon Ct PR4 . . . . .114 A4
Royal Umpire Cvn Pk
PR26 . . . . .58 E2
Royalty Ave PR4 . . . . .96 A1
Royalty Gdns PR4 . . . . . . .76 A8
Royalty La PR4 . . . . .76 A8
Royalty Mall LA4 . . . . . . .217 A5
Royds Ave
Accrington BB5 . . . . . . .104 C3
Morecambe LA3 . . . . . . .216 D2
Royds Gr LA3 . . . . .216 D1
Royds Rd OL13 . . . . .70 A7
Royds St Accrington BB5 .104 C4
Bury BL9 . . . . .33 D4
Lytham St Anne's FY8 . . .89 E5
Royle Rd
4 Burnley BB12 . . . . . .127 F6
Burnley BB12 . . . . .127 F7
Chorley PR7 . . . . .43 C8
Royle St 1 FY1 . . . . . . .130 B1
Roylen Ave FY8 . . . . . . .153 B5
Royles Brook Cl 9 FY5 .176 B3
Royles Ct FY5 . . . . .176 B2
Roynton Rd BL6 . . . . .32 B7
Royshaw Ave BB1 . . . . . .101 E8
Royshaw Cl BB1 . . . . . . .101 E8
Royston Cl BL8 . . . . .49 F1
Royston Rd FY6 . . . . .153 F5
Royton Dr PR6 . . . . .61 C5
Ruby St Blackburn BB1 . .122 F2
Ramsbottom BL0,BL9 . . . .50 C3
Rudd St BB4 . . . . .85 A3
Ruddington Rd PR8 . . . . . .35 E2
Rudman St OL12 . . . . .52 E2
Rudyard Ave PR6 . . . . .29 E2
Rudyard Dr BB3 . . . . .65 D8
Rudyard Pl Blackpool FY3 130 F7
Lytham St Anne's FY8 . . .89 E8
Ruecroft Cl WN6 . . . . .19 D8
Ruff La L39,L40 . . . . .16 B4
Rufford Ave L31 . . . . .5 E3
Rufford CE Sch L40 . . . . .39 B4
Rufford Cl PR7 . . . . .43 B3
Rufford Cotts L40 . . . . . . .38 C6
Rufford Dr PR9 . . . . .54 B4
Rufford New Hall L40 . . . .39 B5
Rufford Park La L40 . . . . .39 A5
Rufford Rd
Bispham Green L40 . . . . .39 F1
Lytham St Anne's FY8 . . .90 D5
Southport PR9 . . . . .54 C4
Rufford Sta L40 . . . . .39 D4
Rufus St PR1 . . . . .118 C2
Rugby Ave BB5 . . . . .104 C2
Rugby Dr WN5 . . . . .10 F8
Rugby St 9 FY4 . . . . . . .130 D1
Rumley's Fold BB11 . . . . .127 E2
Runcorn Ave FY2 . . . . . . .152 F2
Rundle Rd PR2 . . . . .117 D3
Runnymede Ave FY5 . . . .175 D2
Runriggs The FY5 . . . . . .176 B1
Runshaw Ave WN6 . . . . . .19 E8
Runshaw Coll PR7 . . . . . . .60 E4
Runshaw Hall PR7 . . . . . . .60 A5
Runshaw Hall La PR7 . . . .60 B5
Runshaw La Euxton PR7 . .60 B3
Runshaw Moor PR7 . . . . . .59 E3
Runshaw Sixth Form Coll
PR25 . . . . .60 B6
Rupert St Carnforth LA5 . .223 D3
Nelson BB9 . . . . .148 C7
Rochdale OL12 . . . . .52 C1
Rush Hey Bank BB11 . . . .107 D8
Rushbed Cotts BB4 . . . . . .86 A6
Rushbed Dr BB4 . . . . .86 A6
Rushden Rd L32 . . . . .1 A1
Rushes Farm Cl BB5 . . . .103 C4
Rushey Cl BB4 . . . . .86 A6
Rushley Dr LA2 . . . . .220 D1
Rushley Way LA2 . . . . . . .220 D1
Rushmoor Cl BB4 . . . . . .106 A1
Rushton Ave BB18 . . . . . .197 B1
Rushton Cl BB9 . . . . .171 B2
Rushton St 5 Bacup OL13 .70 E8
Barrowford BB9 . . . . . . .170 D3
Great Harwood BB6 . . . .124 B4
Rushworth Bldgs OL13 . . .70 C8
Rushworth St E 6 BB10 148 B1
Rushy Field BB5 . . . . . . .124 F5
Rushy Hey PR5 . . . . .62 A7
Rushy Hill View 19 OL12 .52 C1
Ruskin Ave
9 Blackpool FY1 . . . . .130 B2
Colne BB8 . . . . .171 D6

Ruskin Ave continued
Leyland PR25 . . . . .77 A1
Oswaldtwistle BB5 . . . . .103 C5
Padiham BB12 . . . . .126 E7
Thornton FY5 . . . . .176 A3
Ruskin Cl PR4 . . . . .56 F6
Ruskin Dr BB5 . . . . .104 C5
Ruskin Gr Bolton-le-S LA5 221 A5
Hapton BB11 . . . . .126 C4
Ruskin Ho LA1 . . . . .218 C4
Ruskin Pl BB9 . . . . .170 F2
Ruskin Rd Freckleton PR4 .93 B6
2 Lancaster LA1 . . . . .218 D3
Preston PR1 . . . . .97 B6
Ruskin St Burnley BB10 . .148 A2
Rusland Ave FY4 . . . . . . .131 D1
Rusland Dr PR5 . . . . .98 E4
Ruslands Gdns LA4 . . . . .217 C4
Russell Ct Burnley BB11 . .128 B4
Lytham St Anne's FY8 . . .89 F6
Southport PR9 . . . . .54 B4
Russell Dr LA4 . . . . .218 A4
Russell Mews 40 LA1 . . .214 F8
Russell Pl BB6 . . . . .124 B5
Russell Rd Carnforth LA5 .223 E1
Southport PR9 . . . . .36 A6
Russell Sq PR6 . . . . .61 D1
Russell Sq W 6 PR6 . . . .61 D1
Russell St
Accrington BB5 . . . . . . .104 C5
Bacup OL13 . . . . .87 F4
Blackburn BB2 . . . . .101 E3
39 Lancaster LA1 . . . . .214 F8
6 Nelson BB9 . . . . . . .148 D8
Russell Terr BB12 . . . . . .126 C7
Russia St BB5 . . . . .103 F6
Ruth St Edenfield BL0 . . . .68 D2
Whitworth OL12 . . . . .71 D1
Rutherford Pl FY8 . . . . . .110 B4
Ruthin Cl BB1 . . . . .101 E7
Ruthin Ct PR2 . . . . .116 F3
Ruthin Dr FY5 . . . . .176 D2
Rutland Ave
1 Bamber Bridge PR5 . . .97 D3
Blackburn BB1 . . . . .102 E4
Burnley BB12 . . . . .127 A6
Cleveleys FY5 . . . . .175 D4
Fleetwood FY7 . . . . .198 F3
Freckleton PR4 . . . . .93 C7
Lancaster LA1 . . . . .215 A5
Poulton-le-F FY6 . . . . . .153 C3
Rutland Cl
Clayton-le-M BB5 . . . . . .124 F1
Garstang PR3 . . . . .181 B8
Rutland Cres L39 . . . . . . .15 E7
Rutland Ct FY8 . . . . .90 D5
Rutland Pl 8 BB12 . . . . .126 D7
Rutland Rd
Lytham St Anne's FY8 . . .90 D5
Southport PR8 . . . . .35 D5
Rutland St
Accrington BB5 . . . . . . .103 F5
Blackburn BB2 . . . . .101 B3
Colne BB8 . . . . .171 F5
1 Nelson BB9 . . . . . . .170 F1
Preston PR1 . . . . .97 C8
Rutland Wlk BB4 . . . . . . .68 A8
Ryan Cl PR25 . . . . .76 E1
Ryburn Ave
Blackburn BB2 . . . . .101 B4
Blackpool FY4 . . . . .130 E1
Ryburn Rd L39 . . . . .15 E4
Rycliffe St BB12 . . . . . . .146 C1
Rydal Ave
Bamber Bridge PR5 . . . . .97 D2
Blackpool FY1 . . . . .130 C3
Darwen BB3 . . . . .65 A8
Fleetwood FY7 . . . . .198 E4
Formby L37 . . . . .11 D3
Freckleton PR4 . . . . .93 A6
Kingsfold PR1 . . . . .96 C3
5 Orrell WN5 . . . . .10 F7
Poulton-le-F FY6 . . . . . .153 D3
Thornton FY5 . . . . .176 B1
Rydal Cl
5 Accrington BB5 . . . .125 B5
Blackrod BL6 . . . . .31 C3
Brierfield BB10 . . . . .148 C4
Fulwood PR2 . . . . .118 C4
Padiham BB12 . . . . .146 C1
Rydal Ct LA4 . . . . .217 B5
Rydal Gr
Knott End-on-S FY6 . . . .199 D6
Morecambe LA3 . . . . . . .216 D2
Rydal Mount BB1 . . . . . . .82 F6
Rydal Pl Chatburn BB7 . .190 C3
Chorley PR7 . . . . .43 C6
Colne BB8 . . . . .172 A5
Rydal Rd Blackburn BB1 .102 A7
Hambleton FY6 . . . . .177 C2
Haslingden BB4 . . . . .68 C8
Hest Bank LA5 . . . . .220 F4
Lancaster LA1 . . . . .215 A5
Lytham St Anne's FY8 . . .89 E8
Morecambe LA3 . . . . . . .216 D2
Preston PR1 . . . . .118 D2
Rydal St BB10 . . . . .148 A2
Ryddingwood PR1 . . . . . . .96 B6
Ryde Cl BB4 . . . . .85 C1
Ryden Ave Cleveleys FY5 175 D3
Leyland PR25 . . . . .77 C1
Ryden Rd BB1 . . . . .122 D6

Ryder Cl L39 . . . . .15 C2
Ryder Cres Ormskirk L39 . .15 C1
Southport PR8 . . . . .21 E7
Ryding Cl PR26 . . . . .76 E3
Ryding's La PR9 . . . . .55 D8
Rydinge The L37 . . . . .12 A6
Rydings The BB6 . . . . . . .143 A1
Rye Gdns BB2 . . . . .81 D6
Rye Gr 3 BB2 . . . . .80 B6
Rye Moss La L37 . . . . .4 B8
Rye St PR1 . . . . .118 A1
Ryecroft PR6 . . . . .62 A7
Ryecroft Ave FY6 . . . . . . .177 C1
Ryecroft La BL7 . . . . .46 C5
Ryecroft Pl FY6 . . . . .177 C2
Ryefield PR6 . . . . .62 A7
Ryefield Ave
Haslingden BB4 . . . . .85 B2
Kingsfold PR1 . . . . .96 D2
Ryefield Ave W BB4 . . . . .85 B2
Ryefield Pl BB4 . . . . .85 B2
Ryeground La L37 . . . . . . .12 A5
Ryeheys Rd FY8 . . . . .89 E8
Ryelands Cres PR2 . . . . . .95 E8
Ryelands Prim Sch LA1 .218 B2
Ryelands Rd LA1 . . . . . . .218 C2
Ryknild Way LA3 . . . . . . .217 F3
Ryland Ave FY6 . . . . .153 C3
Rylands Rd PR7 . . . . .43 B7
Rylands St BB10 . . . . . . .148 B1
Ryldon Pl FY4 . . . . .131 A2
Rylstone Dr
Barnoldswick BB18 . . . . .196 A2
Morecambe LA3 . . . . . . .216 D1
Rymers Gn L37 . . . . .11 E4
Ryscar Way FY2 . . . . .152 F6
Rysdale Cres LA4 . . . . . . .217 C4
Ryson Ave FY4 . . . . .130 F1

S

Sabden Brook Ct BB7 . . .146 A8
Sabden Pl 7 FY8 . . . . . . .90 C7
Sabden Prim Sch BB7 . . .145 F8
Sabden Rd Higham BB12 .146 F6
Padiham BB12 . . . . .146 A4
Whalley BB7 . . . . .145 A4
Sabden Wlk BB2 . . . . . . .101 F2
Saccary La BB1,BB2 . . . .122 A4
Sackville Gdns BB9 . . . . .148 A5
Sackville St
Barnoldswick BB18 . . . . .196 B1
Blackpool FY4 . . . . .110 C6
Brierfield BB9 . . . . .148 B5
10 Burnley BB11 . . . . . .127 F5
6 Bury BL9 . . . . .33 A3
Chorley PR6 . . . . .43 E7
Nelson BB9 . . . . .148 F7
Sacred Heart RC Prim Sch
Blackburn BB2 . . . . .101 B6
Chorley PR6 . . . . .43 E7
Church BB5 . . . . .103 F6
Colne BB8 . . . . .171 D7
Preston PR2 . . . . .117 C1
Thornton FY5 . . . . .176 B3
Saddle Lodge 11 PR2 . . .118 F4
Saddler Nook La LA6 . . . .241 C8
Saddlers Mews 5 BB7 . .166 E8
Sadler St 3 BB5 . . . . . . .103 E5
Sadlers Row FY8 . . . . . . .90 D7
Saer Cl 7 FY2 . . . . .198 D3
Saffron Cl 4 BB9 . . . . . .170 C1
Sagar Dr PR4 . . . . .93 A6
Sagar Fold Colne BB8 . . .171 F5
Ormskirk L39 . . . . .6 D8
Sagar Holme Terr BB4 . . .86 E5
Sagar La OL14 . . . . .109 D3
Sagar St Eccleston PR7 . . .41 C6
Nelson BB9 . . . . .148 E8
Sage Cl FY2 . . . . .152 F3
Sage Cl PR1 . . . . .96 C2
Sage La PR1 . . . . .118 B3
Sahara Fold 1 BB1 . . . . .102 A7
SS John Fisher & Thomas
More RC High Sch
BB8 . . . . .171 B2
SS Peter & Paul RC Prim Sch
L40 . . . . .40 F2
St Aidan's Ave
Blackburn BB2 . . . . .101 D2
Darwen BB3 . . . . .65 B8
St Aidan's CE Prim Sch
Bamber Bridge PR5 . . . . .97 F1
Blackburn BB2 . . . . .101 C2
St Aidan's CE Tech Coll
FY6 . . . . .200 B3
St Aidan's Cl BB2 . . . . . .101 C1
St Aidan's Rd 8 PR5 . . . .97 E2
St Aidans Pk 9 PR5 . . . . .97 E2
St Alban's Cl 2 BB1 . . . .101 F6
St Alban's Pl PR7 . . . . . . .43 D5
St Alban's RC Prim Sch
BB1 . . . . .101 F6
St Alban's Rd
Blackpool FY1 . . . . .130 D4
Darwen BB3 . . . . .81 E4
Lytham St Anne's FY8 . . .89 F7
St Albans Rd
Morecambe LA4 . . . . . . .217 F6
Rishton BB1 . . . . .103 A8
St Ambrose Terr PR25 .77 B2
St Andrew's Ave
Cleveleys FY5 . . . . .175 D2
Preston PR2 . . . . .117 D2
St Andrew's CE Prim Sch
Oswaldtwistle BB5 . . . . .103 D4
Preston PR2 . . . . .117 B1

St Andrew's CE Prim Sch
continued
Ramsbottom BL0 . . . . . . .50 B5
St Andrew's Cl
Leyland PR25 . . . . .60 A7
Oswaldtwistle BB5 . . . . .103 D4
St Andrew's Ct FY5 . . . . .175 D2
St Andrew's Ct 1 BB5 . .103 D4
St Andrew's Pl
Blackburn BB1 . . . . .101 D6
Southport PR8 . . . . .35 B6
St Andrew's Rd PR1 . . . .118 A2
St Andrew's Rd N FY8 . . .89 E7
St Andrew's Rd S FY8 . . .89 E6
St Andrew's St
Blackburn BB1 . . . . .101 D6
4 Burnley BB10 . . . . . .148 B1
St Andrews Cl
Colne BB8 . . . . .171 C3
Euxton PR7 . . . . .60 C4
Lancaster LA1 . . . . .215 C3
St Andrews Ct FY8 . . . . . .89 E7
St Andrews Gr LA4 . . . . .217 D6
St Andrews Maghull CE Prim
Sch L31 . . . . .5 D1
St Andrews Rd BB6 . . . . .143 C6
St Andrews Way PR25 . . .60 A8
St Ann's Ct BB7 . . . . . . .166 B8
St Ann's Sq BB7 . . . . . . .166 C8
St Ann's St 5 BB2 . . . . .101 E3
St Anne & St Joseph's RC
Prim Sch BB5 . . . . . . .104 D5
St Anne's Ave LA4 . . . . . .217 F5
St Anne's CE Prim Sch
BB4 . . . . .86 F3
St Anne's Cl Caton LA2 . .237 C3
Formby L37 . . . . .11 C5
St Anne's Coll Gram Sch &
Jun Sch FY8 . . . . .89 E5
St Anne's Cres BB4 . . . . .86 F3
St Anne's Ct WN6 . . . . . . .19 F5
St Anne's Dr BB12 . . . . . .147 D7
St Anne's on-the-sea Sta
FY8 . . . . .89 E7
St Anne's Path L37 . . . . . .11 F6
St Anne's Pl 18 LA1 . . . .214 F8
St Anne's Pleasure Island
Family Fun Pk★ FY8 . . .89 E5
St Anne's RC Prim Sch
Blackburn BB2 . . . . .101 D4
Leyland PR25 . . . . .59 D8
St Anne's RC Sch PR4 . .113 A6
St Anne's Rd Formby L37 .11 F6
Leyland PR25 . . . . .77 C3
Ormskirk L39 . . . . .15 D4
St Anne's Rd E FY8 . . . . .89 E7
St Anne's Rd W FY8 . . . . .89 E6
St Anne's St
Padiham BB12 . . . . .126 C7
Preston PR1 . . . . .118 A2
St Anne's Way BB12 . . . .147 D7
St Annes Cl
5 Blackburn BB1 . . . . .101 E3
4 Church BB5 . . . . . . .103 E5
St Annes Ct FY4 . . . . . . .130 C1
St Annes Rd
Blackpool FY4 . . . . .110 D7
4 Chorley PR6 . . . . . . .43 E7
Great Eccleston PR3 . . . .156 C5
Horwich BL6 . . . . .32 C4
Southport PR9 . . . . .53 F4
St Anthony's Cl PR2 . . . .117 C4
St Anthony's Cres PR2 . .117 C4
St Anthony's Dr PR2 . . . .117 C4
St Anthony's Pl 7 FY1 . .130 C7
St Anthony's RC Prim Sch
PR2 . . . . .117 C4
St Anthony's Rd PR1 . . . .118 A2
St Anthonys Pl PR4 . . . . .114 A4
St Antony's RC Prim Sch
BB1 . . . . .102 C3
St Augustine of Canterbury
RC Prim Sch BB12 . . . .127 B6
St Augustine's RC High Sch
Billington BB7 . . . . .144 A4
St Augustine's RC Prim Sch
PR1 . . . . .97 A7
St Austell Dr BL8 . . . . . . .49 F2
St Austell Pl LA5 . . . . . . .221 C8
St Austin's Pl PR1 . . . . . .97 A7
St Austin's Rd PR1 . . . . . .97 A7
St Barnabas St
Blackburn BB2 . . . . .101 C5
2 Darwen BB3 . . . . . . .80 B6
St Barnabas' & St Paul's CE
Prim Sch BB2 . . . . . . .101 D5
St Barnabas' Pl PR1 . . . .101 D5
St Bartholomew's CE Prim
Sch OL12 . . . . .52 C8
St Bartholomew's Parish CE
Sch BB6 . . . . .124 C6
St Bede's Ave FY1 . . . . . .130 B1
St Bede's RC High Sch
Blackburn BB2 . . . . .81 A8
Lytham St Anne's FY8 . . .91 C4
Ormskirk L39 . . . . .15 D4
St Bedes Cl L39 . . . . .15 D3
St Bee's Cl BB2 . . . . .101 F1
St Benet's Cl PR5 . . . . . . .97 D1
St Bernadette's RC Prim Sch
FY2 . . . . .152 D2
St Bernadettes RC Prim Sch
LA1 . . . . .215 B4
St Bernard Ave FY3 . . . . .130 F4
St Bernard's RC Prim Sch
PR2 . . . . .116 D1
St Bernard's Rd FY6 . . . .199 E6

St Brides Cl BL6 . . . . .32 A4
St Catherine Cl FY3 . . . . .153 B1
St Catherine's CE Prim Sch
BL6 . . . . .32 A3
St Catherine's Dr PR2 . . .117 C4
St Catherine's RC Prim Sch
PR25 . . . . .77 C2
St Catherines Cl 4 PR25 .77 C2
St Catherines Ct 26 LA1 214 F8
St Catherines Way PR5 . .77 C7
St Cecilia St BB6 . . . . . . .124 D5
St Cecilia's RC High Sch
PR3 . . . . .140 A6
St Celia's Way LA4 . . . . .217 E6
St Chad's Ave BB7 . . . . .190 D5
St Chad's CE Prim Sch
FY6 . . . . .153 D3
St Chad's Dr LA1 . . . . . . .218 D4
St Chad's RC Prim Sch
PR6 . . . . .61 F6
St Chad's Rd
Blackpool FY1 . . . . .130 B2
Preston PR1 . . . . .118 C1
St Chads Cl FY6 . . . . . . .153 D3
St Charles' RC Sch BB1 124 B1
St Charles' Rd BB1 . . . . .124 B1
St Christines Ave PR25 . . .77 C4
St Christopher's CE High Sch
BB5 . . . . .104 A7
St Christopher's Rd
PR1 . . . . .118 A2
St Christopher's Way
LA4 . . . . .217 D6
St Clair Dr PR9 . . . . .54 A1
St Clair Rd BL8 . . . . .49 F3
St Clare's RC Prim Sch
PR2 . . . . .117 F7
St Clares Ave PR2 . . . . . .118 A6
St Clement St
Blackburn BB1 . . . . .102 B4
Blackburn BB1 . . . . .102 B5
St Clement's Ave FY3 . . .130 C5
St Clements Ave PR25 . . .77 C3
St Clements Cl 3 BB1 . .102 B4
St Clements Cl BB9 . . . . .170 C1
St Crispin Way BB4 . . . . .85 A2
St Cuthbert's CE Prim Sch
Darwen BB3 . . . . .81 E3
Halsall L39 . . . . .23 B1
St Cuthbert's Cl
Fulwood PR2 . . . . .117 D3
1 Lytham St Anne's FY8 . .91 A3
3 Southport PR9 . . . . . .54 A2
St Cuthbert's Ct 6 FY8 . .91 A3
St Cuthbert's RC Prim Sch
FY4 . . . . .110 C8
St Cuthbert's Rd
Bamber Bridge PR5 . . . . .97 A1
Preston PR1 . . . . .118 A2
Southport PR9 . . . . .54 A2
St Cuthberts Cl BB3 . . . . .81 E3
St David's Ave
Blackburn BB2 . . . . .80 E7
Cleveleys FY5 . . . . .175 D2
St David's Gr FY8 . . . . . . .89 D8
St David's Rd
Leyland PR25 . . . . .77 C2
Preston PR1 . . . . .118 A2
St David's Rd N FY8 . . . . .89 D8
St David's Rd S FY8 . . . . .89 F6
St David's Wood BB5 . . . .104 D7
St Deny's Croft 3 BB7 . .189 E1
St Edmund Hall Cl BL0 . . .50 D7
St Edmund's RC Prim Sch
WN8 . . . . .17 F1
St Edmund's Rd FY4 . . . .130 C1
St Edmund's St BB6 . . . .124 D5
St Edward's RC Prim Sch
BB3 . . . . .81 E4
St Frances Cl 4 BB1 . . . .101 F3
St Francis CE Prim Sch
BB2 . . . . .100 F1
St Francis Cl PR2 . . . . . .118 A7
St Francis CE Prim Sch
PR3 . . . . .161 A2
St Francis' Rd BB2 . . . . .101 A3
St Gabriel Cl WN8 . . . . . .19 C3
St Gabriel's Ave BB1 . . . .122 F3
St Gabriel's CE Prim Sch
BB1 . . . . .122 E2
St George Ct FY1 . . . . . .130 D6
St George's Ave
Blackburn BB2 . . . . .101 B1
Cleveleys FY5 . . . . .175 D2
Lytham St Anne's FY8 . . .89 E7
St George's CE High Sch
FY4 . . . . .111 A8
St George's CE Prim Sch
PR7 . . . . .43 E5
St George's La
Cleveleys FY5 . . . . .175 D2
Lytham St Anne's FY8 . . .89 E6
St George's Pl PR9 . . . . . .35 D7
St George's Quay LA1 . . .218 C1
St George's Rd
Blackpool FY4 . . . . .110 C6
Formby L37 . . . . .11 E4
Hightown L38 . . . . .2 F5
Lytham St Anne's FY8 . . .89 E6
Preston PR1 . . . . .118 A2
St George's Sh Ctr PR1 . .96 F7
St George's Sq FY8 . . . . .89 D7
St George's St PR5 . . . . . .43 C7
St George's Terr BB4 . . . .70 A6
St Georges Cl BB8 . . . . . .171 C3
St Georges Pk PR4 . . . . .113 C6
St Georges Rd BB9 . . . . .148 F7

St Georges Terr BB3 ...81 F1
St Gerrard's Rd PR5 ...97 A1
St Giles St 7 BB12 ...146 C1
St Giles Terr 6 BB12 ...146 C1
St Gregory Rd PR1 ...118 B2
St Gregory's Pl PR7 ...43 C5
St Gregory's RC Prim Sch
Chorley PR7 ...43 C5
Maghull L31 ...5 C4
Preston PR1 ...118 B3
St Helen's Cl PR3 ...181 A2
St Helen's Rd
Clayton Green PR6 ...78 C1
Overton LA3 ...209 E8
St Helens Cl BB5 ...103 F3
St Helens Rd L39 ...16 A2
St Helens Well PR4 ...57 A5
St Helier Cl BB2 ...81 C8
St Helier's Pl PR3 ...137 A7
St Heliers Rd FY1 ...130 C1
St Hilda's CE Prim Sch FY6 ...153 B5
St Hilda's Cl PR7 ...43 C4
St Hilda's RC Girls' High Sch BB11 ...127 C3
St Hilda's Rd FY8 ...89 D8
St Hilda's Way PR7 ...43 C4
St Hubert's Rd BB6 ...124 C4
St Hubert's St BB6 ...124 D5
St Ignatius' Pl 6 PR1 ...97 A8
St Ignatius' RC Prim Sch PR1 ...97 A8
St Ignatius' Sq 5 PR1 ...97 A8
St Ives Ave Blackpool FY1 130 E3
Freckleton PR4 ...93 A6
St Ives Cres PR2 ...117 A4
St Ives Rd BB1 ...102 D4
St Jame's CE Prim Sch BB3 ...82 B2
St Jame's Terr PR5 ...99 E7
St James CE Prim Sch BB3 ...82 A7
St James Cl
Bamber Bridge PR5 ...77 B8
Church BB5 ...103 E7
3 Haslingden BB4 ...85 B3
Ormskirk L40 ...16 C3
St James Ct
1 Bamber Bridge PR5 ...77 B8
Blackburn BB1 ...101 E7
Heysham LA3 ...212 E7
9 Lancaster LA1 ...214 E8
Standish WN6 ...29 D2
St James Ho BB5 ...104 B5
St James Lodge
Leyland PR26 ...59 B8
Lytham St Anne's FY8 ...90 A5
St James Mews BB5 ...103 E7
St James Pl
4 Padiham BB12 ...126 D8
Southport PR8 ...35 B5
St James RC Sch WN8 ...18 B4
St James Rd
Blackpool FY4 ...110 C6
Church BB5 ...103 E7
St James Row BB4 ...86 A3
St James Sq 15 OL13 ...87 F3
St James St Bacup OL13 ...87 F2
Brierfield BB9 ...148 B5
1 Rawtenstall BB4 ...86 A3
Southport PR8 ...35 B6
St James' CE Prim Sch BB1 ...101 E7
St James' Cres BB3 ...82 B2
St James' Lanehead CE Prim Sch BB10 ...148 D2
St James' RC Prim Sch WN5 ...10 D4
St James' Rd
10 Barnoldswick BB18 ...196 B2
Orrell WN5 ...10 D4
St James' Sq 11 BB18 ...196 B2
St James' St
Accrington BB5 ...104 B5
Blackburn BB2 ...101 C1
Rawtenstall,Waterfoot BB4 ...69 E8
St James's CE Prim Sch BB7 ...166 E7
St James's Dr LA6 ...240 B7
St James's Gdns PR26 ...59 B8
St James's La 6 BB11 ...128 A6
St James's Pl
Blackburn BB1 ...101 E7
9 Chorley PR6 ...43 E7
St James's Rd
Blackburn BB1 ...101 E7
Preston PR1 ...117 F2
St James's Row 13 BB11 127 F6
St James's St
Burnley BB11 ...127 F6
8 Chorley PR6 ...43 E7
Clitheroe BB7 ...166 E7
Burnley BB11 ...128 A6
St James-the-Less RC Prim Sch BB4 ...85 F3
St Jerome's RC Prim Sch L37 ...11 C3
St John Ave FY7 ...198 D2
St John Bosco RC Prim Sch L31 ...5 B2
St John RC Jun Sch BB10 ...148 C3
St John Rigby RC Sixth Form Coll WN5 ...19 F2
St John Southworth RC Prim Sch BB9 ...148 D7
St John St Bacup OL13 ...87 F3
Colne BB8 ...171 E5
St John St *continued*
Horwich BL6 ...32 B3
St John Stone RC Prim Sch PR8 ...21 D2
St John the Baptist RC Prim Sch BB12 ...126 C7
St John Vianney RC Prim Sch FY1 ...130 E2
St John with St Augustine CE Prim Sch BB5 ...104 C7
St John with St Michael CE Prim Sch OL12 ...71 E5
St John's Ave Darwen BB3 65 B8
Morecambe LA3 ...216 E2
Poulton-le-F FY6 ...153 E5
Silverdale LA5 ...224 C3
Thornton FY5 ...176 D1
St John's CE Meth Prim Sch PR6 ...62 E7
St John's CE Prim Sch
Blackpool FY1 ...130 C5
Great Harwood BB6 ...124 C4
Higham BB12 ...147 A6
Nelson BB9 ...149 B8
Southport PR9 ...54 C5
St John's Cl
Accrington BB5 ...104 E2
5 Rawtenstall BB4 ...86 A7
Read BB12 ...145 D2
St John's Ct
5 Bacup OL13 ...87 F3
8 Blackpool FY1 ...130 C5
6 Burnley BB12 ...127 C6
6 Lytham St Anne's FY8 ...91 C3
St John's Gn PR25 ...76 E1
St John's Gr
Morecambe LA3 ...216 E2
Silverdale LA5 ...224 C3
St John's Pl Nelson BB9 ...149 A8
16 Preston PR1 ...97 A7
St John's RC Inf Sch BB10 ...148 B1
St John's RC Prim Sch
Burscough L40 ...25 E2
Poulton-le-F FY6 ...153 E4
St John's Rd
5 Burnley BB12 ...127 C6
Morecambe LA3 ...216 D2
Padiham BB12 ...126 C7
Southport PR8 ...34 F1
Walton-le-D PR5 ...97 D5
St John's Sh Ctr PR1 ...97 A8
St John's St Darwen BB3 ...65 B8
Great Harwood BB6 ...124 C4
Lytham St Anne's FY8 ...91 C3
Rawtenstall BB4 ...69 F8
St John's Stonefold CE Prim Sch BB5 ...85 A7
St John's Terr LA3 ...217 C2
St Johns Ave
Kirkham PR4 ...113 F4
Smallwood Hey PR3 ...201 C5
St Johns Cl PR6 ...61 B7
St Johns Ct Fulwood PR3 137 F1
Southport PR8 ...21 D4
St Johns RC Prim Sch WN8 ...18 C1
St Johns Wood FY8 ...90 E3
St Joseph & St Bede RC Prim Sch BL9 ...33 B4
St Joseph's Con Ctr WN8 19 B2
St Joseph's RC High Sch & Sports Coll BL6 ...32 E1
St Joseph's RC Inf Sch PR6 ...61 D1
St Joseph's RC Prim Sch
Adlington PR6 ...31 B8
Bacup OL13 ...87 D1
Barnoldswick BB18 ...196 B3
Chorley PR6 ...61 D2
Darwen BB3 ...65 A8
Gregson Lane PR5 ...98 E1
Hurst Green BB7 ...164 F1
Kirkham PR4 ...113 F7
Lancaster LA1 ...218 D3
Preston PR1 ...118 C1
Ramsbottom BL0 ...50 B6
Withnell PR6 ...80 A1
St Joseph's RC Prim Sch Wrightington WN6 ...29 A3
St Joseph's Terr 1 PR1 118 C1
St Josephs Cl FY3 ...130 E5
St Josephs Pl PR6 ...61 D1
St Josephs Prep Sch BB12 ...127 A8
St Jude's Ave PR5 ...97 D1
St Judes Ave PR25 ...77 C4
St Katherines Dr BL6 ...31 C3
St Kentigern's RC Prim Sch FY3 ...130 D5
St Kitts Cl BB3 ...81 E6
St Laurence's CE Prim Sch PR7 ...61 C1
St Lawrence Ave BB2 ...101 B8
St Lawrence St BB6 ...124 C5
St Lawrence's Ave PR3 ...137 B8
St Leger Ct 11 BB5 ...104 C5
St Leonard Ct 6 LA1 ...218 E1
St Leonard's Ave BL6 ...32 F1
St Leonard's CE Prim Sch
Bamber Bridge PR5 ...97 C4
Padiham BB12 ...146 C1
St Leonard's CE Sch BB6 ...143 E2
St Leonard's Cl PR2 ...117 A3
St Leonard's Ct FY8 ...89 D8
St Leonard's Gate LA1 ...214 F8
St Leonard's Rd FY3 ...131 A3
St Leonard's Rd E FY8 ...89 E8
St Leonard's Rd W FY8 ...89 D8
St Leonard's St 8 BB12 146 C1
St Leonards CE Prim Sch BB2 ...121 A5
St Louis Ave FY3 ...130 F7
St Lucia Cl BB3 ...81 F6
St Luke & St Philip's CE Prim Sch BB2 ...101 D3
St Luke's Bldg 2 PR8 ...35 D6
St Luke's CE Prim Sch
Formby L37 ...11 D1
Lancaster LA1 ...218 D3
Slyne LA2 ...218 C8
St Luke's Church Rd L37, L38 ...2 C8
St Luke's Ct 1 FY4 ...110 C6
St Luke's Dr Formby L37 ...11 C2
Orrell WN5 ...10 E4
St Luke's Gr PR9 ...35 E7
St Luke's Pl 9 PR1 ...118 C1
St Luke's RC Prim Sch WN8 ...9 E6
St Luke's Rd
Blackpool FY4 ...110 C6
Southport PR9 ...35 D7
St Lukes Ct 2 LA1 ...214 E8
St Margaret's CE Prim Sch LA2 ...238 B7
St Margaret's Ct
1 Blackburn BB1 ...102 B5
1 Fleetwood FY7 ...199 A4
St Margaret's Gdns BB11 ...126 C4
St Margaret's Rd
Bolton-le-S LA5 ...221 B6
1 Leyland PR25 ...77 C2
Morecambe LA4 ...217 D6
St Margarets Cl PR2 ...117 A4
St Margarets Way BB1 ...102 B5
St Maria Goretti RC Prim Sch PR2 ...118 F5
St Marie's RC Prim Sch L33 ...1 A3
St Maries RC Prim Sch Standish WN6 ...29 E2
St Mark's CE Prim Sch
Bury BL9 ...33 A4
Scarisbrick L40 ...23 D7
St Mark's Pl
Blackburn BB2 ...101 B4
1 Blackpool FY3 ...130 E8
St Mark's Pl E 5 PR1 ...96 D8
St Mark's Pl W 4 PR1 ...96 D8
St Mark's Rd
Blackburn BB2 ...101 B4
Preston PR1 ...96 D8
St Marks RC Prim Sch WN8 ...9 E8
St Marlow Ave 3 PR25 ...77 C3
St Martin's Coll LA1 ...215 B6
St Martin's Ct FY5 ...175 F2
St Martin's Dr BB2 ...80 D8
St Martin's Rd
Blackpool FY4 ...110 C6
Lancaster LA1 ...215 A7
Preston PR1 ...118 A2
St Martins Cl FY6 ...153 B5
St Mary & St Michael RC Prim Sch PR3 ...181 C6
St Mary CE Prim Sch BB2 ...121 D2
St Mary Cl FY3 ...153 B1
St Mary Magdalen's CE Prim Sch BB5 ...104 B7
St Mary Magdalen's RC Prim Sch PR1 ...96 E4
St Mary Magdalene's RC Prim Sch BB12 ...127 D8
St Mary's & St Andrews RC Prim Sch PR3 ...137 A5
St Mary's & St Benedicts RC Prim Sch PR5 ...97 E1
St Mary's & St Joseph's RC Prim Sch BB1 ...101 F3
St Mary's Ave
Bamber Bridge PR5 ...97 D1
Barnoldswick BB18 ...196 D3
St Mary's CE Prim Sch
Eccleston PR7 ...41 C6
Hawkshaw BL8 ...49 C2
Spen Brook BB12 ...169 C3
St Mary's Cl PR5 ...97 D1
St Mary's Coll BB1 ...101 E7
St Mary's Ct
Clayton-le-M BB5 ...124 F2
Mellor BB2 ...121 E2
Preston PR1 ...97 B8
Rawtenstall BB4 ...85 F2
St Mary's Dr BB6 ...143 D1
St Mary's Gate
Burnley BB11 ...128 B5
Euxton PR7 ...60 C3
St Mary's Gdns
Mellor BB2 ...121 E2
Southport PR8 ...21 F7
St Mary's Par LA1 ...214 E8
St Mary's Rawtenstall CE Prim Sch BB4 ...85 F3
St Mary's RC Coll FY3 ...130 F7
St Mary's RC Prim Sch
Accrington BB5 ...103 F4
Bacup OL13 ...88 B2
Burnley BB10 ...128 B6
Chipping PR3 ...185 E3
Chorley PR7 ...43 A7
Claughton PR3 ...182 D1
Clayton-le-M BB5 ...124 F3
St Mary's RC Prim Sch *continued*
Fleetwood FY7 ...199 A5
Great Eccleston PR3 ...156 B5
Haslingden BB4 ...85 C2
Horwich BL6 ...32 D2
Morecambe LA4 ...217 C6
Osbaldeston BB2 ...121 D4
Sabden BB7 ...145 F7
St Mary's RC Prim Sch Scarisbrick L40 ...24 A7
St Mary's RC Sch BB6 ...143 C1
St Mary's Rd
Bamber Bridge PR5 ...97 E1
Great Eccleston PR3 ...156 B5
Heysham LA3 ...212 E8
St Mary's St
4 Clitheroe BB7 ...189 E1
Nelson BB9 ...148 C8
Preston PR1 ...97 B8
St Mary's St N 7 PR1 ...97 B8
St Mary's Terr 6 BB4 ...86 A2
St Mary's Way BB4 ...86 A2
St Mary's Wlk 16 PR7 ...43 C8
St Marys Cl
Blackburn BB1 ...102 B5
Longridge PR3 ...140 A8
8 Preston PR1 ...97 C8
St Marys Wharfe BB1 ...101 F3
St Matthew St BB11 ...127 E5
St Matthew's CE Prim Sch BB1 ...101 F4
St Matthew's CE Sch PR1 ...97 D8
St Matthew's Ct 9 BB11 ...127 E5
St Matthew's RC Prim Sch WN8 ...9 D7
St Michael & All Angels CE Prim Sch BB8 ...171 E8
St Michael & St John's RC Prim Sch BB7 ...166 E8
St Michael Rd L39 ...5 F7
St Michael with St John CE Prim Sch BB1 ...101 E6
St Michael's CE High Sch PR7 ...61 C1
St Michael's CE Prim Sch PR4 ...114 B5
St Michael's Cl
Blackburn BB2 ...80 E7
Bolton-le-S LA5 ...221 A4
Chorley PR7 ...61 B1
Southport PR9 ...53 F1
St Michael's Cres LA5 ...221 A4
St Michael's Ct
Barrowford BB9 ...170 C2
1 Blackburn BB1 ...101 F6
St Michael's Gr
Bolton-le-S LA5 ...221 A4
Morecambe LA4 ...217 C4
St Michael's La LA5 ...221 A4
St Michael's Pl
Bolton-le-S LA5 ...221 A4
Newsham PR3 ...137 B5
St Michael's Rd
Duncombe PR3 ...158 D4
4 Leyland PR25 ...77 C3
Preston PR1 ...118 A2
St Michael's St BB1 ...101 F7
St Michael's Terr PR26 ...58 B2
St Michael's-on-Wyre CE Prim Sch PR3 ...157 C6
St Michaels Cl PR2 ...117 D3
St Michaels Pk L39 ...6 A7
St Michaels Rd
Blackpool FY2 ...152 D3
Kirkham PR4 ...114 C5
St Mildred's Way LA3 ...212 E6
St Monica's Way FY4 ...131 D1
St Nicholas Arcs 13 LA1 214 F8
St Nicholas Cres LA5 ...221 B6
St Nicholas Gr PR4 ...113 B4
St Nicholas La LA5 ...221 A6
St Nicholas Rd
Blackpool FY4 ...111 B5
Church BB5 ...103 F7
St Nicholas' Ave BB7 ...145 F8
St Nicholas' CE Prim Sch
Blackpool FY4 ...111 A4
Church BB5 ...103 F7
St Ogg's Rd LA4 ...217 C3
St Oswald Ho LA1 ...215 A6
St Oswald St LA1 ...215 A6
St Oswald's CE Prim Sch BB1 ...102 E4
St Oswald's Cl
Blackburn BB1 ...102 E4
Preston PR1 ...118 C2
St Oswald's RC Prim Sch
Accrington BB5 ...104 A3
Longton PR4 ...75 B8
St Oswald's RC Prim Sch Coppull PR7 ...29 D8
St Oswald's Rd BB1 ...102 E4
St Patrick's Pl PR5 ...97 E4
St Patrick's RC Prim Sch
Heysham LA3 ...213 A8
Southport PR9 ...54 A2
Walton-le-D PR5 ...97 E4
St Patrick's Rd N FY8 ...89 E7
St Patrick's Rd S FY8 ...89 F6
St Patrick's Wlk LA3 ...212 E7
St Paul's Ave
Blackburn BB2 ...101 D5
Lytham St Anne's FY8 ...90 B4
Preston PR1 ...118 A1
St Paul's CE Prim Sch
Adlington PR6 ...31 A7
Bury BL9 ...33 B4
Nelson BB9 ...148 D6
Oswaldtwistle BB5 ...103 E4
Ramsbottom BL0 ...50 C6
St Paul's Cl Adlington PR6 31 A8
Clitheroe BB7 ...166 C8
St Paul's Constable Lee CE Prim Sch BB4 ...86 A4
St Paul's Ct
5 Burnley BB11 ...127 F5
12 Oswaldtwistle BB5 ...103 E4
10 Preston PR1 ...97 A8
St Paul's Dr Caton LA2 ...237 D3
Lancaster LA1 ...214 F5
St Paul's Pas PR8 ...35 A6
St Paul's RC Prim Sch BB2 ...80 D8
St Paul's Rd
Blackpool FY1 ...130 B8
Lancaster LA1 ...214 F5
Nelson BB9 ...148 E6
Preston PR1 ...118 A1
1 Rishton BB1 ...124 A1
St Paul's Sq Preston PR1 ...97 A8
Southport PR8 ...35 A6
St Paul's St
Blackburn BB2 ...101 D5
Bury BL9 ...33 A3
Clitheroe BB7 ...166 C8
Oswaldtwistle BB5 ...103 E4
4 Ramsbottom BL0 ...50 C6
Southport PR8 ...35 A6
St Paul's Terr
Clitheroe BB7 ...166 C8
Hoddlesden BB3 ...82 E2
St Paul's Villas BL9 ...33 A3
St Paul's Wlk 4 FY8 ...90 C4
St Pauls Cl PR26 ...76 F7
St Pauls Mans 4 PR8 ...35 A6
St Peter & St Paul's CE Prim Sch BB1 ...124 A2
St Peter St
Blackburn BB2 ...101 E4
2 Rishton BB1 ...124 A1
St Peter's Ave Formby L37 11 D4
Haslingden BB4 ...85 B2
St Peter's CE Prim Sch
Accrington BB5 ...104 A2
Burnley BB11 ...128 A6
Chorley PR6 ...61 E2
Formby L37 ...12 A5
Fulwood PR2 ...117 F7
Heysham LA3 ...212 E7
St Peter's Cl Darwen BB3 ...65 B8
Formby L37 ...11 D4
Salesbury BB1 ...122 D6
St Peter's Pl
Fleetwood FY7 ...199 B4
7 Haslingden BB4 ...85 B2
St Peter's RC Cath★ LA1 ...215 A8
St Peter's RC High Sch WN5 ...10 F7
St Peter's RC Prim Sch
Blackburn BB2 ...101 B2
Lytham St Anne's FY8 ...91 C5
Newchurch BB4 ...86 E2
St Peter's Rd
Lancaster LA1 ...215 A8
Newchurch BB4 ...86 E2
Southport PR8 ...35 A3
St Peter's Sq 8 PR1 ...96 E8
St Peter's St Chorley PR6 ...61 E1
1 Preston PR1 ...96 F8
St Peters Mews 16 LA1 ...215 A8
St Philip St BB10 ...148 A1
St Philip's CE Prim Sch
Nelson BB9 ...148 E8
Southport PR8 ...35 C5
St Philip's Ct BB2 ...101 C3
St Philip's Rd PR1 ...118 A2
St Philip's St
Blackburn BB2 ...101 B3
13 Nelson BB9 ...170 E1
St Pius X Prep Sch PR2 117 E4
St Richards RC Prim Sch WN8 ...17 D1
St Saviour's Cl PR5 ...77 F7
St Saviour's Com Prim Sch OL13 ...71 A8
St Saviours Ct OL13 ...87 F1
St Silas's CE Prim Sch BB2 ...101 B6
St Silas's Rd BB2 ...101 B6
St Stephen's Ave
8 Blackburn BB1 ...102 A7
Blackpool FY2 ...152 B2
St Stephen's CE Inf Sch BB1 ...102 B7
St Stephen's CE Jun Sch BB1 ...102 B7
St Stephen's CE Prim Sch
Burnley BB11 ...128 B4
Preston PR1 ...96 E6
St Stephen's Rd
9 Blackburn BB1 ...102 A7
Hightown L38 ...2 F4
Preston PR1 ...118 B2
Standish WN6 ...29 C1
St Stephen's St 2 BB11 128 B4
St Stephen's Way BB8 ...171 F6
St Stephens Rd PR4 ...113 F4

St Stephens' CE Prim Sch
PR9 ....55 A5
St Teresa's Ave FY5 .....175 D1
St Teresa's RC Prim Sch
Cleveleys FY5 ....175 D1
Preston PR1 ....118 E1
Southport PR8 ....35 A4
Up Holland WN8 ....19 B1
St Theodore's RC Sports Coll
& Sixth Form BB10 ......128 B7
St Theresa's Dr PR2 ....117 C4
St Theresas Ct 2 PR4 ...114 E5
St Thomas CE Prim Sch
Blackburn BB1 ....102 B5
Maghull L31 ....5 D4
St Thomas Cl
Blackpool FY3 ....153 B1
Haslingden BB4 ....68 A7
St Thomas Ct 4 BL9 .....33 A2
St Thomas More Wlk
LA1 ....214 D8
St Thomas Rd PR4 ....114 A4
St Thomas St BB1 ....102 B4
St Thomas the Martyr CE
Prim Sch WN8 ....10 B7
St Thomas' CE Prim Sch
Bury BL9 ....33 B1
Lytham St Anne's FY8 ....89 F6
St Thomas' Pl PR1 ......117 F1
St Thomas' Rd
Lytham St Anne's FY8 ....89 F6
Preston PR1 ....118 A2
St Thomas' St PR1 ......117 F1
St Thomas's Ct WN8 .....10 C7
St Thomas's Rd
Chorley PR7 ....43 C8
Rawtenstall BB4 ....86 A7
St Thomas's Sq 4 PR7 ...43 C8
St Veronica's RC Prim Sch
BB4 ....68 B7
St Vincent Ave FY1 .....130 E3
St Vincent's RC Prim Sch
OL12 ....52 A1
St Vincent's Way PR8 ....35 A4
St Vincents Cl BB3 ......81 F6
St Vincents Rd PR2 .....117 F5
St Walburga's Rd FY3 ...130 F7
St Walburge Rd PR2 ......96 E8
St Walburges Gdns 8
PR2 ....96 D8
St Wilfred's Dr OL12 ....52 D4
St Wilfred St 3 PR1 .....96 F7
St Wilfrid's CE High Sch &
Tech Coll BB2 ....101 D3
St Wilfrid's CE Prim Sch
LA2 ....219 C7
St Wilfrid's Pk LA2 ....219 C7
St Wilfrid's Pl WN6 .....29 F1
St Wilfrid's RC Prim Sch
PR3 ....140 A8
St Wilfrid's Rd WN6 .....29 F1
St Wilfrid's Terr PR3 ...140 A7
St Wilfrid's Way 6 WN6 ..29 F1
St Williams RC Prim Sch
PR3 ....201 E4
St Wulstan's RC Prim Sch
Fleetwood FY7 ....198 E3
Great Harwood BB6 ......124 C5
Salcombe Ave FY2 ....152 F2
Salcombe Dr PR9 ....54 A5
Salcombe Rd FY8 ....110 C1
Salem Mews LA3 ....212 E8
Salem St BB4 ....85 B3
Salerno St BB11 ....127 C4
Sales's La BL9 ....51 B3
Salesbury CE Prim Sch
BB1 ....122 D7
Salesbury View BB1 .....122 F4
Salford Cl BB1 ....101 E5
Salford Ct PR8 ....21 C5
Salford Rd Galgate LA2 ..211 A3
Southport PR8 ....21 C5
Salford St PR9 ....33 A4
Salisbury Ave FY6 ......199 E5
Salisbury Cl LA3 ....217 B2
Salisbury Ct
Knott End-on-S FY6 .....199 E5
Lancaster LA1 ....214 D8
Salisbury Rd
Blackpool FY1 ....130 C4
Brinscall PR6 ....62 F8
Darwen BB3 ....81 E3
Horwich BL6 ....32 F1
Lancaster LA1 ....214 D8
Preston PR1 ....96 D7
Salisbury St
3 Chorley PR7 ....43 D7
Colne BB8 ....171 C6
Great Harwood BB6 ......124 E6
15 Haslingden BB4 ......85 B3
5 Preston PR1 ....118 D1
Southport PR9 ....36 A6
Sallowfields WN5 ....10 D5
Sally's La PR9 ....54 B2
Salmesbury Ave FY2 .....152 F2
Salmon St PR1 ....97 C7
Salmons Leap PR4 ....113 E4
Salmsbury Hall Cl BL0 ...50 C4
Salop Ave FY2 ....152 C4
Salt Aire Sports Ctr
LA1 ....218 A1
Salt Ayre La
Lancaster LA1 ....218 B1
Morecambe LA1 ....217 B1
Salt Marsh Cl FY6 ......177 B1

Salt Marsh La FY6 ......177 B1
Salt Pit La L40 ....40 F3
Saltash Rd FY5 ....176 B5
Saltburn St BB12 ....127 B6
Saltcotes Pl FY8 ....91 D4
Saltcotes Rd FY8 ....91 D7
Salter Fell Rd LA1 .....218 B2
Salter St PR1 ....117 F1
Salterford La BB10 .....129 A4
Salterforth La
Barnoldswick BB18 ......196 E2
Salterforth BB18 ....194 D7
Salterforth Prim Sch
BB18 ....194 D8
Salterforth Rd BB18 ....197 A1
Salthill Ind Est BB7 ...190 A2
Salthill Rd BB7 ....189 F1
Salthill View BB7 ......189 F1
Salthouse Ave FY1 ......130 C3
Saltpit La L31 ....5 E1
Salus St BB10 ....148 C1
Salwick Ave FY2 ....152 D5
Salwick Cl PR9 ....53 F5
Salwick Pl
Lytham St Anne's FY8 ....90 A8
Preston PR2 ....116 E1
Salwick Rd PR4 ....135 B3
Salwick Sta PR4 ....115 C5
Sambourn Fold PR8 ....21 A5
Samlesbury Aerodrome
BB2,PR5 ....120 F3
Samlesbury CE Prim Sch
PR5 ....119 D1
Samlesbury Hall ★ PR5 ..120 E2
Samuel St Bury BL9 ......33 A3
Preston PR1 ....97 D8
Sanctuary The 5 FY4 ....93 F4
Sand Beds BL0,BB4 ....69 B5
Sand La LA5 ....223 C4
Sandbank Cotts OL12 .....71 C2
Sandbank Gdns OL12 ......71 C2
Sandbeds La LA2 ....238 A8
Sandbrook Gdns WN5 ......10 D5
Sandbrook Rd Orrell WN5 ..10 D5
Southport PR8 ....21 D4
Sandbrook Way PR8 ....21 C3
Sandcastle (L Pool) ★
FY4 ....110 A8
Sanderling Cl
Cleveleys FY5 ....152 F8
Lytham St Anne's FY8 ....90 E7
Sanderling Rd L33 ....1 A3
Sanders Gr LA4 ....217 A4
Sanderson La PR7 ....28 A8
Sanderson St 9 BL9 .....33 A3
Sandersons Way FY4 .....110 F8
Sandfield 4 FY5 ....176 A2
Sandfield Cotts L39 .....15 D2
Sandfield Ho 6 LA1 .....215 A3
Sandfield Pk L39 ....15 D2
Sandfield Rd OL13 ....88 A1
Sandfield St 11 PR25 ....77 B1
Sandford Dr L31 ....5 D2
Sandford Rd WN5 ....10 C5
Sandgate Blackpool FY4 ..110 D5
Chorley PR7 ....43 D5
Lytham St Anne's FY8 ....89 C7
Sandham St 7 PR6 ....43 D8
Sandhams Way FY4 ....111 D8
Sandheys Dr PR9 ....53 F1
Sandhill St BB3 ....65 B5
Sandhills L38 ....2 F3
Sandhills Ave FY4 ......110 B5
Sandhills Cl BB18 ......194 E8
Sandholme La PR3 ....182 A4
Sandholme Villas BB18 ..197 A1
Sandhurst Ave
Blackpool FY2 ....152 C5
Lytham St Anne's FY8 ....89 E7
Sandhurst Cl Formby L37 ..11 C1
9 Kirkham PR4 ....113 F5
Sandhurst Ct FY8 ....89 D6
Sandhurst Grange FY8 ....89 E7
Sandhurst St BB11 ......128 B6
Sandhurst Way L31 ....5 B5
Sandicroft Ave FY6 .....177 C1
Sandicroft Pl FY6 ......200 B4
Sandicroft Rd FY1 ......152 C1
Sandilands Gr L38 ....2 F3
Sandiway Ct PR9 ....35 E8
Sandiway Dr BB10 ....148 F3
Sandiways L31 ....5 E1
Sandiways Cl FY5 ....153 C8
Sandon Pl FY4 ....110 C4
Sandon Rd PR8 ....34 F1
Sandon St Blackburn BB2 ..101 C3
Darwen BB3 ....82 B2
Sandon Terr BB1 ....101 C3
Sandown Cl PR4 ....113 E5
Sandown Ct
30 Preston PR1 ....97 A7
1 Southport PR9 ....35 C8
Sandown Rd
Haslingden BB4 ....85 C2
Lancaster LA1 ....215 B3
Thornton FY5 ....176 B1
Sandpiper Cl
8 Blackburn BB1 ....101 F6
Normoss FY3 ....131 B6
Sandpiper Ct FY5 ....175 C2
Sandpiper Pl 10 FY5 ....175 F1
Sandpiper Sq 5 BB11 ....127 C5
Sandridge Ave PR7 ....43 B7
Sandridge Pl FY4 ....110 B4
Sandringham Ave
Leyland PR25 ....77 C1
Thornton FY5 ....176 B1

Sandringham Cl
Adlington BB5 ....30 E6
5 Barrowford BB9 ......170 C1
Blackburn BB1 ....122 E1
Tarleton PR4 ....57 A6
Whalley BB7 ....144 A7
Sandringham Ct
Lytham St Anne's FY8 ....90 C6
Morecambe LA4 ....217 A4
Southport PR8 ....35 B8
Sandringham Dr
Brinscall PR6 ....62 F8
Ramsbottom BL8 ....50 A1
Sandringham Gr 2 BB4 ...85 A1
Sandringham Lodge 2
FY5 ....175 D2
Sandringham Park Dr
PR4 ....76 A8
Sandringham Rd
Bamber Bridge PR5 ......97 D3
Chorley PR7 ....43 B8
Darwen BB3 ....81 E4
Eccleston PR7 ....41 C7
Formby L37 ....11 E1
Horwich BL6 ....32 E2
Lytham St Anne's FY8 ....90 A5
Morecambe LA4 ....217 A4
Southport PR8 ....34 E3
Southport,Ainsdale PR8 ...21 C5
Sandringham Way PR4 ....116 E6
Sands Cl BB1 ....124 B2
Sands Rd BB1 ....124 B2
Sands The BB7 ....144 C5
Sands Way FY1 ....130 C3
Sandsdale Ave PR2 .....118 C5
Sandside Dr LA4 ....217 C3
Sandwell Ave FY5 ......176 C2
Sandwich Cl BB1 ....102 C4
Sandwick Cl PR2 ....117 E7
Sandy Bank Rd BL7 ......48 D5
Sandy Brook Ho PR2 ....117 F7
Sandy Cl FY5 ....175 C3
Sandy Gate La PR4 .....137 B2
Sandy La Accrington BB5 ..104 E5
Adlington PR7 ....30 F6
Barrowford BB9 ....170 D2
Bispham Green L40 ......39 F2
Blackburn BB3 ....81 E6
Blackpool FY1 ....111 A4
Brindle PR5,PR6 ....79 C6
Brinscall PR6 ....62 E8
Clayton Green PR6 ......78 C3
Fleetwood FY7 ....175 D7
Hambleton FY6 ....177 C1
Hightown L38 ....3 A3
Holmeswood L40 ....38 D5
Holmeswood L40 ....38 E5
Leyland PR25 ....60 A8
Lower Bartle PR4 ......116 D7
Maghull,Holt Green L39 ...6 B6
Maghull,Lydiate L31 .....5 C5
Mawdesley L40 ....40 A1
Newburgh WN8 ....26 F1
Ormskirk L40 ....16 D7
Orrell WN5 ....10 D4
Out Rawcliffe PR3 .....178 F1
Pleasington BB2 ....100 C2
Preesall FY6 ....200 B4
Skelmersdale WN8 ....17 D1
Sollom L40 ....39 A8
Thorpe Green PR6 ....78 E4
Sandy La Dr WN8 ....17 D1
Sandy Pl 7 PR25 ....60 B8
Sandy Way L40 ....38 D4
Sandybeds Cl BB5 ......104 D2
Sandybrook Cl PR2 .....118 C5
Sandycroft PR2 ....118 F2
Sandyfields PR4 ....116 E6
Sandyforth Ave FY5 ....176 B3
Sandyforth La PR4 .....117 A8
Sandygate BB11 ....127 F6
Sandyhall La BB9 ......170 A2
Sandylands Arc LA3 ....216 A2
Sandylands Com Prim Sch
LA3 ....216 B3
Sandylands Prom LA3 ....216 D3
Sanfield Cl L39 ....15 E6
Sangara Dr BB3 ....81 F7
Sangness Dr PR3 ....35 E3
Sansbury Cres BB9 .....171 A2
Santon Cl PR4 ....114 A7
Sanvino Ave PR8 ....21 D5
Sapphire St BB1 ....122 F1
Sarah La PR26 ....57 F5
Sarah St Bacup OL13 ....71 C8
Darwen BB3 ....82 B1
Sarahs Fold FY6 ....177 C2
Sark Gdns BB2 ....101 F1
Sarmatian Fold PR3 ....141 D3
Sarscow La PR26 ....58 E2
Saswick Ct PR4 ....134 B7
Saul St PR1 ....96 F8
Saul's Dr LA5 ....224 A8
Saunder Ave PR8 ....128 A5
Saunder Height La BB4 ..86 E3
Saunders Cl BB4 ....86 A7
Saunders Mews PR7 ......43 C3
Saunders Rd BB2 ....101 C5
Saunders St PR9 ....53 C1
Saunders' La Hutton PR4 ..95 D2
New Longton PR4 ....95 E1
Savick Ave PR2 ....116 D1
Savick Cl PR5 ....77 F8
Savick Ct PR2 ....117 C4
Savick Rd PR2 ....117 D4
Savick Way PR2 ....116 E3
Saville Ave FY6 ....153 B6

Saville Rd Blackpool FY1 ..130 C1
Maghull L31 ....5 C3
Saville St PR7 ....43 C5
Savon Hook L37 ....12 B1
Savoy Ave LA3 ....217 C3
Savoy St Accrington BB5 ..103 F5
4 Preston PR1 ....96 E7
Sawdon Ave PR8 ....35 E3
Sawley Abbey ★ BB7 ....230 C1
Sawley Ave
Accrington BB5 ....104 D7
Blackpool FY4 ....110 D5
Lytham St Anne's FY8 ....90 C6
Read BB12 ....145 D1
Sawley Cl BB3 ....65 C8
Sawley Cres PR2 ....118 F2
Sawley Dr BB6 ....124 E6
Sawley Rd Chatburn BB7 ..190 E6
Grindleton BB7 ....190 C8
Sawley BB7 ....230 C1
Sawmills Ind Est FY1 ...130 D6
Sawrey Ct BB5 ....124 E2
Sawthorpe Wlk FY4 .....153 B3
Sawyer St 5 OL12 ....52 F1
Saxby Gr FY4 ....130 F1
Saxenholme PR8 ....34 F5
Saxifield St BB10 .....148 E3
Saxon Cl
Oswaldtwistle BB5 .....103 C5
Thornton FY5 ....153 C8
Saxon Hey PR2 ....117 C3
Saxon Hts LA3 ....212 F5
Saxon Lodge PR8 ....34 F5
Saxon St BB10 ....128 A7
Scafell Ave LA4 ....217 D5
Scafell Cl BB12 ....145 D1
Lytham St Anne's FY8 ...111 A2
Scafell Rd Lancaster LA1 ..218 E2
Lytham St Anne's FY8 ...111 A2
Scaffold La L38 ....3 D4
Scaitcliffe St BB5 ....104 B5
Scale Farm Rd LA1 .....218 A2
Scale Hall La
Lancaster LA1 ....218 B2
Newton-w-S PR4 ....115 A2
Scar End Cl OL13 ....88 A8
Scar St B2 ....101 B3
Scarborough Rd
Blackburn BB2 ....102 A1
Lytham St Anne's FY8 ...111 A1
Scargill Rd LA5,LA6 ....221 F1
Scarisbrick Ave
Parbold WN8 ....27 C2
Southport PR8 ....35 A7
Scarisbrick Cl L31 ......5 E3
Scarisbrick Ct PR8 .....35 C6
Scarisbrick New Rd PR8 ..35 D5
Scarisbrick Pk L40 .....24 A6
Scarisbrick St
Ormskirk L39 ....15 E6
Southport PR9 ....35 B7
Scarlet Dr PR4 ....95 F2
Scarlett St BB11 ......127 E5
Scarr Dr OL12 ....52 F3
Scarr La BB2 ....101 A6
Scarr Terr OL12 ....71 D2
Scarsdale Ave FY4 .....110 C5
Scarth Hill La L39 .....16 A2
Scarth Hill Mans L39 ....1 E2
Scarth La BB12 ....126 B5
Scarth Pk WN8 ....9 C7
Scawfell Rd PR7 ....43 B5
Sceptre Way PR5 ....78 B6
Schleswig St PR1 ....97 A8
Schleswig Way PR26 ....59 C7
Schofield Ave FY3 .....131 B7
Schofield Cl BB4 ......85 F2
Schofield Rd BB4 ......85 F2
Schofield St Darwen BB3 ..81 F2
Haslingden BB4 ....68 A6
3 Rawtenstall BB4 ....69 E8
Schola Green La
Morecambe LA4 ....217 B4
Morecambe LA4 ....217 B5
Scholars Ct FY8 ....89 E5
Scholars Gn PR2 ....116 C1
Scholefield Ave BB9 ...148 E5
Scholefield La BB9 ....148 F5
Scholes Bank BL6 ......32 A5
Scholes St BB3 ....81 F2
Scholey Head La BB10 ..108 A8
School Ave L37 ....11 F3
School Brow PR6 ....61 B7
School Cl Ormskirk L39 ..15 C1
Southport PR8 ....35 B2
School Ct Egerton BL7 ...47 E2
Ramsbottom BL0 ....68 D2
School Field PR5 ....78 B5
School Fields BB18 ....197 B3
School Hillocks Cotts 4
PR5 ....77 A8
School Ho The BB10 ....148 D2
School House Gn L39 ....15 F5
School House Gr L40 ....25 D5
School House La BB5 ...104 B1
School House Mews 7
PR6 ....43 E7
School La
Bamber Bridge PR5 .....97 F2
Blackburn BB1 ....82 D8
Brinscall PR6 ....62 E8
Burnley BB11 ....128 A7
Burscough Bridge L40 ...25 D7
Catforth PR4 ....136 A4
Earby BB18 ....197 B2
Edgworth BL7 ....48 D8
Euxton PR7 ....60 D3

School La continued
Farington PR5 ....76 F7
Formby L37 ....11 F3
Forton LA2,PR3 ....207 B3
Freckleton PR4 ....93 C7
Hammerton Mere BB7 ....235 E3
Haskayne L39 ....13 F4
Inskip PR4 ....157 D1
Kirkham PR4 ....114 B5
Laneshaw Bridge BB8 ...172 E6
Leyland PR25 ....77 A1
Leyland,Moss Side PR26 ..59 A8
Longton PR4 ....75 A8
Lytham St Anne's FY8 ...91 A3
Maghull L31 ....6 A1
Mawdesley L40 ....40 C1
Mereclough BB10 ......129 A1
Newton-w-S PR4 ....115 A2
Ollerton Fold PR6 ......79 F4
Out Rawcliffe PR3 .....178 F2
Pilling PR3 ....201 C6
Preesall FY6 ....200 B3
Roby Mill WN8 ....19 B3
Simonstone BB12 ......145 F1
Skelmersdale,Chapel House
WN8 ....17 E1
Skelmersdale,Up Holland
WN5,WN8 ....10 C7
Standish WN6 ....29 D1
Westhead L40 ....16 B3
Winmarleigh PR3 ......203 F6
Wray LA2 ....238 D6
School Rd Blackpool FY4 ..111 B5
Heysham LA3 ....212 E7
Hightown L38 ....2 F4
Thornton FY5 ....153 C8
School St Accrington BB5 ..104 B6
Bacup OL13 ....70 B8
Bamber Bridge PR5 .....97 F2
Bury BL9 ....33 B1
Colne BB8 ....171 D4
Darwen BB3 ....82 A1
Great Harwood BB6 ....124 C4
Horwich BL6 ....32 C3
Kelbrook BB18 ....195 A6
Leyland PR25 ....77 B2
Nelson BB9 ....148 C8
Preston PR1 ....96 E7
Ramsbottom BL0 ....50 B5
Rawtenstall BB4 ....86 A8
Rishton BB1 ....124 B1
Walmer Bridge PR4 .....74 B5
Whitewell Bottom BB4 ...86 F4
School Terr
Salterforth BB18 ......194 D8
Whitworth OL12 ....71 D1
School View BL7 ....48 D8
School Villas LA2 .....211 B5
Schoolfold PR4 ....73 E4
Schoolhouse Fold BB11 ..126 C3
Schoolhouse La LA2 ....219 D7
Schwartzman Dr PR9 ....55 A6
Scorton Ave FY3 ......130 F7
Scorton CE Prim Sch
PR3 ....204 E6
Scorton Hall Pk PR3 ...204 E6
Scorton Ho LA1 ....215 A2
Scotch Green La PR3 ...160 A6
Scotforth Ct 1 LA1 ....215 A3
Scotforth Rd
Lancaster LA1 ....215 A4
Preston PR1 ....97 C8
Scotforth St Paul's CE Prim
Sch LA1 ....215 A4
Scotland Bank Terr BB2 ..81 C8
Scotland La BL9 ....33 D8
Scotland Pl 11 BL0 ....50 C6
Scotland Rd
Carnforth LA5 ....223 E3
8 Nelson BB9 ....148 D8
15 Nelson BB9 ....170 D1
Scotshaw Brook Ind Est
BB3 ....81 E7
Scotswood Ave FY4 .....110 D6
Scott Ave Accrington BB5 ..104 E2
Morecambe LA4 ....216 F3
Simonstone BB12 ......145 E2
Scott Cl Blackpool FY4 ..110 F8
Maghull L31 ....5 D1
Oswaldtwistle BB5 .....103 D5
Scott Dr L39 ....15 F7
Scott Gr LA4 ....217 A4
Scott Laithe La BB7 ...230 E3
Scott Mews FY4 ....110 F8
Scott Park Rd BB11 ....127 E4
Scott Rd LA3 ....216 F3
Scott St Clayton-le-M BB5 ..124 F3
Nelson BB9 ....170 D1
Padiham BB12 ....126 F7
Southport PR9 ....36 A7
Scott's Terr BB11 .....127 D6
Scott's Wood PR2 ......117 C7
Scout Rd Edenfield BL0 ..69 A2
Egerton BL7 ....47 B1
Newchurch BB4 ....86 F3
Scow Croft La PR6 ......62 D4
Scowcroft Dr LA4 .....217 C5
Scriffen La LA2 ....211 D3
Scudamore Cres 6 FY4 ..130 D1
Sea View Lancaster LA1 ..215 A5
Longridge PR3 ....161 D2
Walmer Bridge PR4 .....74 F5
Sea View Cl LA2 ....218 B8
Sea View Dr LA2 ....218 B8
Sea Wall FY7 ....198 C3
Seabank Rd
Fleetwood FY7 ....199 A5
Southport PR9 ....35 B8

Seaborn Dr LA4 ......217 E6
Seaborn Gr LA4 ....217 D6
Seaborn Rd LA4 ......217 D6
Seabourne Ave FY4 ...110 B7
Seabrook Dr FY5 .....152 E8
Seacole Cl BB1 ....102 B1
Seacrest Ave FY1 .....130 C8
Seacroft Cres PR9 .....54 B5
Seafield L37 ....12 A1
Seafield Rd
  Blackpool FY1 ....130 B8
  Lytham St Anne's FY8 ...90 F3
  Southport PR8 ....21 C6
Seafore Cl L31 ....5 B4
Sealand Ave L37 ....11 E2
Sealand Cl L37 ....11 D2
Seascale Cl BB2 ......102 A1
Seasiders Way FY1 ....130 B3
Seathwaite Ave
  Blackpool FY4 ....131 C1
  Morecambe LA3 ......216 E2
Seathwaite Way BB5 ..104 E8
Seaton Ave FY5 ......175 E4
Seaton Cres FY8 ......89 C8
Seaton Pl WN8 ....17 E3
Seaton Way PR9 ....54 A5
Seattle Ave FY2 ......152 E4
Seaview Way FY7 .....199 B3
Seawell Ave LA3 .....216 D2
Second Ave
  Blackpool FY4 ......110 C7
  Bury BL9 ....33 D4
  Church BB5 ....104 A8
  Preesall Park FY6 ...200 D1
Second Terr LA3 ......209 B4
Sedberg St PR2 ......117 D3
Sedbergh Ave FY4 ....130 F1
Sedbergh Cl BB5 .....104 D5
Sedbergh Jun Sch LA2 .239 B8
Sedburgh St BB10 ....148 C2
Seddon Pl WN8 ....17 E3
Sedge Ct LA3 ....217 B2
Sedgefield PR4 ....74 E8
Sedgefield Cl FY4 ....110 F6
Sedgeley Mews PR4 ...93 A6
Sedgley Ave PR4 ......93 A6
Sedgwick St PR1 .....118 A1
Sedwell Cl FY8 ....90 F4
Seed St Blackpool FY1 .130 C6
  Preston PR1 ....96 F8
Seedall Ave BB7 .....166 D7
Seedhill Terr 13 BB9 ..170 D1
Seedlee Rd PR5 ....78 A6
Sefton Ave
  4 Burnley BB11 ......127 E5
  Orrell WN5 ....10 D5
  Poulton-le-F FY6 ....153 D1
Sefton Cl
  Clayton-le-M BB5 ...125 A3
  Darwen BB3 ....65 C6
  Orrell WN5 ....10 D5
Sefton Ct FY8 ....89 D7
Sefton Dr Bury BL9 ....33 A6
  Lancaster LA1 ......218 B2
Sefton Gdns L39 ....6 D7
Sefton La BL6 ....32 D1
Sefton Rd
  Bamber Bridge PR5 ...97 D3
  Formby L37 ....11 E2
  Lytham St Anne's FY8 ..89 F7
  Morecambe LA3 .....216 E3
  Orrell WN5 ....10 D5
Sefton St Brierfield BB9 ..148 B5
  Colne BB8 ....171 F5
  Southport PR8 ....35 C5
Sefton Terr 3 BB11 ...127 E5
Sefton View WN5 ......10 D5
Segar St
  19 Great Harwood BB6 ..124 C5
  Kirkham PR4 ....113 F6
Segar's La PR8,L39 ...21 E4
Segars La PR8 ....21 D5
Selborne Mews BB2 ..101 B3
Selborne St
  Blackburn BB2 ......101 B3
  Preston PR1 ....97 B6
Selbourne Rd FY1 ....130 D6
Selbourne Terr BB18 ..197 C2
Selby Ave Blackpool FY4 .110 D5
  Cleveleys FY5 ......175 F4
  2 Lancaster LA1 ....218 D4
Selby Cl BB5 ....104 E3
Selby Dr L37 ....12 B2
Selby Pl WN8 ....17 D2
Selby Rd PR4 ....113 F5
Selby St Colne BB8 ..171 C5
  Nelson BB9 ....148 E7
  Preston PR1 ....117 D1
Seldon St 11 Colne BB8 ..171 D4
  15 Nelson BB9 ......170 E1
Selkirk Cl 6 BB1 .....102 A4
Selkirk Dr PR5 ....97 D2
Selkirk St BB11 ......127 C4
Sellers St PR1 ....118 C1
Selous Rd BB3 ....101 B3
Selside Dr LA4 ....217 B3
Selworthy Rd
  Southport PR8 ....34 D3
  Southport PR8 ....34 E3
Senior Ave FY4 ......130 F1
Seniors Dr FY5 ......175 F3
Sephton Dr L39 ....15 F7
Sephton St 7 PR5 ....77 A7
Sergeant St 11 PR5 ...77 F8
Serpentine Rd BB11 ..127 F4
Serpentine The
  3 Lytham St Anne's FY8 ..91 A3
  Ormskirk L39 ....6 D8

Sett End Rd W BB1 ...102 C1
Sett End Road N BB1 .102 D2
Settle La LA3 ....231 B7
Settle Pl FY8 ....90 C7
Settle Terr BB10 .....148 C2
Seven Acres PR5 ......78 C5
Seven Houses BB1 ...102 D4
Seven Sands PR4 .....95 A1
Seven Stars Prim Sch
  PR25 ....59 D7
Seven Stars Rd PR25 ..59 D7
Seven Trees Ave BB1 ..102 A8
Sevenoaks Ave PR8 ...21 B5
Sevenoaks Ct 2 FY5 .152 E8
Sevenoaks Dr FY5 ...152 F8
Seventh Ave FY4 ....110 C6
Severn Ave FY7 .....175 D8
Severn Ct LA3 ....217 F2
Severn Dr PR5 ....97 C2
Severn Hill PR2 .....117 C8
Severn Ho 10 PR1 ....97 D8
Severn Rd FY4 ....110 B7
Severn St PR3 ......140 A7
Seville Ct FY8 ....90 D3
Seymour Ave LA3 ....212 F7
Seymour Ct PR1 .....117 D2
Seymour Dr L31 ....5 E3
Seymour Gr LA3 .....212 F7
Seymour Rd
  Blackpool FY1 ....130 C2
  Fulwood PR2 ....117 C3
  Lytham St Anne's FY8 ..90 D4
Seymour Rd Chorley PR6 .43 E8
  5 Fleetwood FY7 ....198 F4
  5 Lancaster LA1 ....215 M4
Shacklady Rd L33 .....1 A4
Shackleton Rd PR4 ..114 B2
Shackleton St
  Burnley BB10 ....128 B8
  Cornholme OL14 ....109 C1
Shade La PR7 ....43 D1
Shade Row FY6 ......200 B3
Shadsworth Bsns Pk
  BB1 ....102 C5
Shadsworth Cl BB1 ..102 C4
Shadsworth Cty Inf Sch
  BB1 ....102 D4
Shadsworth Jun Sch
  BB1 ....102 C2
Shadsworth Rd BB1 ..102 C3
Shady La
  Clayton-le-W PR5,PR25 ..77 E3
  Slyne LA2 ....218 C8
Shaftesbury Ave
  Blackpool FY2 ......152 C2
  Burnley BB11 ....127 F3
  Cleveleys FY5 ......175 D5
  Darwen BB3 ....81 E3
  Great Harwood BB6 ..124 E6
  Higher Penwortham PR1 ..96 B6
  New Longton PR4 ....75 F8
  Normoss FY3 ....131 B6
  Southport PR8 ....22 A4
Shaftesbury Cl FY8 ...90 D5
Shaftesbury Gr PR8 ...35 A1
Shaftesbury Pl
  Chorley PR7 ....43 B8
  Lancaster LA1 ......214 F4
Shaftesbury Rd PR8 ...35 A1
Shakeshaft St 11 BB1 .102 A4
Shakespeare Ave BB6 .124 B4
Shakespeare Prim Sch
  FY7 ....198 E4
Shakespeare Rd
  Fleetwood FY7 ......198 E4
  Lancaster LA1 ......218 C4
  Preston PR1 ....118 D1
Shakespeare St
  Padiham BB12 ......126 D7
  Southport PR8 ....35 B5
Shakespeare Terr PR6 .61 D7
Shakespeare Way BB2 .101 C3
Shalbourn Rd FY8 .....90 A4
Shale St BB12 ....127 D6
Shalgrove Field PR2 ..117 C7
Shalom Lodge FY8 ....89 F5
Shannon Sq BB10 ...148 C2
Shannon St FY1 .....130 B3
Shap Cl Accrington BB5 .104 E3
  Barrowford BB9 ....170 D4
Shap Ct FY7 ....198 D1
Shap Gr BB10 ....148 A3
Shard La FY6 ....154 B8
Shard Rd FY6 ....154 B6
Shards Ct 17 LA1 ....218 D4
Sharley Fold PR3 ....140 B7
Sharman Ave FY8 ...110 F1
Sharneyford Prim Sch
  OL13 ....88 C5
Sharoe Bay Ct PR2 ..117 F6
Sharoe Green Hospl
  PR2 ....117 F4
Sharoe Green La PR2 .117 F7
Sharoe Green Pk PR2 .118 A5
Sharoe Mount Ave PR2 .117 F7
Sharow Gr FY1 .....130 D3
Sharp St
  1 Barrowford BB9 ...170 D3
  Burnley BB10 ....148 B8
Sharpe's Ave LA1 ...215 A5
Sharpes Mill LA1 ....214 F7
Sharples Ct PR3 ....140 A8
Sharples Gn BL7 .....48 D6
Sharples Mdw BL7 ...48 D6
Sharples St
  Accrington BB5 .....103 F5

Sharples St continued
  Blackburn BB2 ......101 D3
Sharrats Path PR7 ....42 F4
Sharrock St 7 PR8 ...35 B7
Shaw Bridge St 4 BB7 .166 F8
Shaw Brook Cl BB1 ..103 A8
Shaw Brook Rd PR25 ..59 E6
Shaw Brow PR6 ......61 B7
Shaw Cl Blackburn BB2 .101 D5
  Shirdley Hill L39 ....23 A6
Shaw Clough Rd BB4 ..86 F3
Shaw Clough St BB4 ..86 F3
Shaw Cres L37 ....12 B3
Shaw Hall Cvn Site L40 .24 B7
Shaw Hill PR6 ....61 B7
Shaw Hill Dr PR6 .....61 B6
Shaw Hill St PR7 .....43 C7
Shaw La Haskayne L39 .13 E6
  Nether Kellet LA6 ..221 F4
  Shore OL14 ....109 C3
Shaw Rd Blackpool FY1 .130 B1
  Horwich BL6 ....32 B5
Shaw Sq 4 BB18 ....197 B2
Shaw St Blackburn BB2 .101 D5
  Bury BL9 ....33 B3
  Colne BB8 ....171 D4
  Haslingden BB4 ......85 B6
  2 Lancaster LA1 ....215 A8
  2 Preston PR1 ....118 A1
Shaw's Ave PR8 ......35 A1
Shaw's La PR3 ......201 A3
Shaw's Rd PR8 ....35 A1
Shawbridge Ct PR4 ..166 F8
Shawbrook Cl PR7 ....60 C5
Shawbury Cl BL6 .....31 D1
Shawcliffe La BB6,BB7 .144 B2
Shawclough Cl OL12 ..52 D3
Shawclough Com Prim Sch
  OL12 ....52 E3
Shawclough Rd OL12 ..52 D3
Shawclough Way OL12 .52 D3
Shawes Dr PR3 ....31 C7
Shawfield 4 BB4 ......85 F1
Shawfield La OL12 ....52 A2
Shawhead Cotts BB8 .195 E1
Shaws Garth L39 ......23 A6
Shay La Longridge PR3 .139 F6
  Slaidburn BB7 ......229 B7
Shay Lane Ind Est PR3 .139 F5
Shay The 10 FY5 ....152 F7
Shays Dr BB7 ....167 A7
Shear Bank Cl BB1 ..101 D6
Shear Bank Gdns BB1 .101 D6
Shear Bank Rd BB1 ..101 D6
Shear Brow BB1 .....101 D7
Shearwater Dr BB1 ..101 F6
Shed St Colne BB8 ...171 C4
  Oswaldtwistle BB5 ..103 D3
  Whitworth OL12 ......71 D1
Sheddon Gr BB10 ...128 E5
Sheep Gap OL12 ......52 B1
Sheep Gn BB4 ....85 B8
Sheep Hill Brow PR6 ..78 A3
Sheep Hill La
  Clayton Green PR6 ...78 A3
  Clayton Green PR6 ...78 B3
  Clayton-le-W PR6,PR25 ..77 F2
Sheep House La BL6 ..45 A3
Sheephill La PR4 .....76 A7
Sheffield Dr PR2 .....116 D1
Sheldon Ave WN6 .....29 E2
Sheldon Ct 1 PR1 ....117 F1
Shelfield La BB10 ....149 F7
Shelfield Rd BB9 ....171 B1
Shelley Cl
  Bolton-le-S LA5 ....221 A5
  Coppull PR7 ....29 F8
Shelley Dr
  Accrington BB5 .....104 E2
  Eccleston PR7 ....41 D5
  Ormskirk L39 ....15 D6
Shelley Gdns BB6 ...124 B4
Shelley Gr Blackpool FY5 .152 D8
  Darwen BB3 ....82 C1
  Southport PR8 ....35 F6
Shelley Mews PR2 ...117 C2
Shelley Rd PR2 ......117 C2
Shellfield Rd PR9 .....54 A4
Shellingford Cl WN6 ..19 D7
Shelton Dr PR8 ....21 A4
Shenley Way PR9 .....54 D5
Shenstone Rd FY3 ...130 F7
Shepherd Rd FY8 .....90 A7
Shepherd Rd N FY8 ...90 A8
Shepherd St Bacup OL13 .87 F3
  Bury BL9 ....33 A1
  Darwen BB3 ....82 C1
  9 Lytham St Anne's FY8 .91 B3
  Preston PR1 ....117 D1
Shepherd's Ave PR3 .181 D4
Shepherd's La L39 ...14 E5
Shepherds Cl
  Blackrod BL6 ....31 C3
  Ramsbottom BL8 .....49 F1
Shepherds Gn BB4 ...87 A8
Shepherds Way PR6 ..43 B8
Sheppard St FY1 ....130 B4
Sheraton Pk PR2 ....117 A6
Sherborne Lodge 9
  PR2 ....118 F4
Sherbourne Cl FY6 ..153 D5
Sherbourne Cres PR1 .118 D5
Sherbourne Dr FY5 ..153 C5
Sherbourne Rd
  Accrington BB5 .....104 E3
  Blackpool FY1 ......130 C2
  Hambleton FY6 .....177 C2

Sherbourne St 5 PR6 ..43 D7
Sherburn Rd PR1 .....96 E3
Sherburn St PR1 .....118 A3
Sherburne Ave 4 PR4 .113 F5
Sherdley Rd PR5 ......77 B7
Sherfin Side BB5 ......85 B7
Sherfin Nook BB5 .....85 B7
Sheridan Rd BB8 ....172 D6
Sheridan St
  Brierfield BB10 .....148 B8
  6 Nelson BB9 ......170 F2
Sheriff St OL12 ....52 E1
Sheringham Ave FY5 .152 D7
Sheringham Way FY6 .153 E3
Sherrat St WN8 ....17 D1
Sherringham Rd PR8 ..34 E2
Sherwood Ave
  Blackpool FY3 ....130 E8
  Ormskirk BB9 ....15 C2
Sherwood Ct BB10 ...128 C5
Sherwood Dr WN8 ....18 D3
Sherwood Ho PR8 ....21 C5
Sherwood Lodge PR4 ..34 F5
Sherwood Pl Chorley PR6 .43 D8
  2 Cleveleys FY5 ....175 F1
Sherwood Prim Sch
  PR2 ....118 A7
Sherwood Rd
  Blackburn BB8 ......102 B3
  Lytham St Anne's FY8 ..90 C6
Sherwood Way
  Accrington BB5 .....125 A1
  Fulwood PR2 ....118 A7
Shetland Cl
  Blackburn BB1 .....102 C3
  Wilpshire BB1 ......122 F7
Shetland Rd FY1 ....130 C2
Shevington Com Prim Sch
  WN6 ....19 E8
Shevington Cswy PR26 .58 B2
Shevington La WN6 ...29 B1
Shevington Moor WN6 .29 A2
Shevington Vale Prim Sch
  WN6 ....19 E8
Shilton St BL0 ....50 B5
Shipley Cl FY3 ......153 B1
Shipley Rd FY3 ......153 B1
Shipper Bottom La BL0 .50 D5
Shirdley Cres PR3 ....21 C3
Shire Bank Cres PR2 .117 E5
Shire La BB7 ....142 D8
Shireburn Ave BB7 ..166 C7
Shireburn Cotts BB7 .164 E1
Shireburn Rd L37 ....11 D5
Shires The BB2 ......81 D6
Shireshead Cres LA1 .215 A2
Shirewell Rd WN5 ....10 E5
Shirley Cres FY2 ....152 D6
Shirley Gdns BB3 .....80 F2
Shirley Hts FY6 .....153 D4
Shirley La PR4 ....95 A1
Shop La Accrington BB5 .104 D5
  Higher Walton PR5 ...98 B4
  Maghull L31 ....5 C1
Shore Ave BB10 .....148 F2
Shore Cl LA5 ....224 C2
Shore Cotts LA5 ....224 D2
Shore Gn Cleveleys FY5 .175 F3
  Silverdale LA5 .....224 B2
Shore New Rd OL14 .109 B1
Shore Rd Ainsdale PR8 ..20 F6
  Blackpool FY5 ......152 C8
  Hesketh Bank PR4 ...73 C4
  Heysham LA3 ......212 D6
  Silverdale LA5 .....224 B2
  Southport PR8 ....21 B6
Shore The LA5 ......220 F5
Shorefield Mount BL7 ..47 E1
Shorefields Cvn Pk LA3 .208 E7
Shoreside Prim Sch PR8 .21 B4
Shorey Bank BB11 ...128 A6
Shorrock Cl BB2 .....101 B1
Shorrock St BB3 .....65 A8
Shorrocks Ave PR3 ..157 C8
Short Clough Cl BB4 ..86 A6
Short Clough La BB4 ..86 A6
Short Croft La L37 ...12 D1
Short La PR3 ....137 F5
Short St Bacup OL13 ..70 B8
  Colne BB8 ....171 D4
Shorten Brook Dr BB5 .125 E6
Shorten Brook Way
  BB5 ....125 E6
Shortlands Dr LA3 ...212 E7
Shortlands The BB12 .146 C2
Shortridge Rd FY4 ..110 B8
Showfield BB10 .....129 B6
Showley Brook Cl BB1 .122 F4
Showley Ct BB1 .....122 E6
Showley Rd BB1 ....122 A6
Shrewsbury Cl PR4 ..114 C2
Shrewsbury Dr
  Lancaster LA1 ......215 B5
  Thornton PR5 ....176 A2
Shropshire Dr BB1 ..122 F6
Shuttle Cl BB1 ......104 A6
Shuttleworth Mead Bsns Pk
  BB12 ....126 B7
Shuttleworth Rd PR1 .117 F2
Shuttleworth St
  Burnley BB10 ....148 B2
  Earby BB18 ....197 B2
  6 Padiham BB12 ....126 C8
  Rishton BB1 ....124 B2
Shuttling Fields La PR5 .98 D2
Sibbering Brow Preston Rd
  PR7 ....42 C7

Siberia Mill BB10 ....148 F3
Sibsey St LA1 ....214 E7
Siddow's Ave BB7 ...166 D7
Side La BB7 ....192 C7
Sidebeet La BB1 ....102 E7
Sidegarth Gate LA2 .237 C7
Sidegarth La LA2 ....237 D7
Sidford Ct FY3 ......130 F8
Sidgreaves La PR4 ..116 B4
Siding La Kirkby L33 ...1 C7
  Rainford Junction WA11 ..8 D1
Siding Rd PR7 ....199 A3
Siding St OL13 ....70 C8
Sidings Bsns Pk The
  BB7 ....144 C6
Sidings Rd LA3 .....212 F2
Sidings The Bacup OL13 .71 A8
  Colne BB8 ....171 C4
  Darwen BB3 ....65 B7
  Whalley BB7 ....144 C6
Sidmouth Ave BB4 ...85 C2
Sidmouth Rd FY8 ...110 C1
Sidney Ave Becconsall PR4 .73 F3
  Blackpool FY2 ......152 E6
Sidney Rd PR9 ....35 F8
Sidney Terr 4 LA1 ..215 A8
Siemens St BL6 ......32 C2
Silbury Cl BB2 ....82 A8
Silcock's Cotts FY5 .176 F1
Silk Mill La PR3 .....160 B3
Silloth Cl BB2 ......101 F1
Silly La LA2 ....239 D2
Silsden Ave PR2 ....118 D5
Silsden Cl FY3 ......153 B1
Silver Birch Way L31 ..5 B5
Silver Ridge Cvn Pk
  LA7 ....225 E8
Silver St Clifton PR4 .115 D1
  Hurst Green BB7 ...164 E1
  8 Preston PR1 .....97 A6
  Ramsbottom BL0 .....50 C6
Silverburn 4 FY8 ....90 A8
Silverdale Becconsall PR4 .73 F3
  Blackpool FY2 ......152 E6
  Southport PR8 ....34 E4
Silverdale Ave
  Fleetwood FY7 ......198 D1
  Heysham LA3 ......212 F7
Silverdale Cl
  Blackburn BB2 ....81 F3
  Brierfield BB10 .....148 B3
  Clayton-le-M BB5 ...124 C5
  Coupe Green PR5 ....98 E4
  Leyland PR25 ....60 B6
Silverdale Ct PR8 ....35 E4
Silverdale Dr PR2 ...118 E5
Silverdale Moss Rd LA5 .224 D7
Silverdale Rd
  Arnside LA5 ....224 C8
  Chorley PR6 ....43 E7
  Lytham St Anne's FY8 ..90 C7
  Yealand Redmayne LA5 ..225 E4
Silverdale St John's CE Prim
  Sch LA5 ....224 C3
Silverdale Sta LA5 ..224 F3
Silvermere Cl 20 BL0 .50 B5
Silversmiths Row FY8 .90 D7
Silverstone Gr L31 ...5 B4
Silverthorne Dr PR9 ..53 F1
Silverwell St BL6 .....32 B4
Silverwood Ave FY4 ..110 D8
Silverwood Cl FY8 ...90 E4
Silverwood Ct 1 FY4 .110 D8
Silvester Rd PR7 ....43 C6
Silvester St BL6 .....31 D2
Silvia Way FY7 .....198 E4
Simfield Cl WN6 ......29 D1
Simmonds Way BB9 .148 D3
Simmons Ave PR5 ....97 B3
Simmons Way BB5 ..125 A3
Simmons' St BB2 ...101 D5
Simonstone Bsns Pk
  BB12 ....125 F7
Simonstone La BB12 .125 E8
Simonstone Rd BB12,
  BB7 ....145 F6
Simonstone St Peter's CE
  Prim Sch BB12 .....145 F1
Simonswood Ind Pk L33 ..1 B6
Simonswood La Kirkby L33 .1 A2
  Royal Oak L39 ....6 F3
Simonswood Wlk L33 ..1 A2
Simpson Cl BB18 ....196 D3
Simpson St
  Blackpool FY4 ......110 B8
  Hapton BB12 ....126 C4
  Oswaldtwistle BB5 ..103 D3
  9 Preston PR1 .....96 F8
Simpson St Ind Units
  BB12 ....126 C5
Sinclair Ct FY8 ......90 B7
Sineacre La
  Bickerstaffe L39 .....7 E1
  Kirkby L33,L39 ......1 E8
Singleton Ave
  Horwich BL6 ....32 C5
  Lytham St Anne's FY8 ..90 B8
  Read BB12 ....145 D2
Singleton CE Prim Sch
  FY6 ....154 E1
Singleton Cl PR2 ....117 F7
Singleton Ct 4 FY1 .130 B4
Singleton Rd
  Weeton PR4 ....132 F4
  Weeton Camp PR4 ..132 E6

Singleton Row 14 PR1 96 F8
Singleton St 3 FY1 130 B3
Singleton Way PR2 117 F7
Sion Brook Ho PR2 118 F4
Sion Cl PR2 118 F4
Sion Hill PR2 118 F4
Sir Frank Whittle Way FY4 110 D4
Sir Simon's Arc 27 LA1 214 F8
Sir Tom Finney Way PR1,PR2 118 B3
Six Acre La PR4 75 C6
Six Arches Cvn Pk PR3 204 D8
Sixfields 13 FY5 152 F7
Sixpenny La PR8 21 D1
Sixth Ave Blackpool FY4 110 C7
Bury BL9 33 D4
Size House Village 6 BB4 85 B2
Size St OL12 71 D1
Sizehouse St 22 PR1 96 F8
Sizer St PR1 117 F1
Sizergh Ct LA1 214 D7
Sizergh Rd LA4 217 E5
Skaithe The BB7 229 C7
Skeffington Rd PR1 118 C1
Skeleron La BB7 192 B6
Skelmersdale Coll WN8 18 B4
Skelmersdale Coll (Westbank Campus)
Skelmersdale WN8 18 B1
Skelmersdale WN8 9 B8
Skelmersdale Rd L39,WN8 8 B7
Skelmersdale Sports Ctr WN8 9 C7
Skelshaw Cl BB1 102 A3
Skelton St BB8 171 E5
Skelwith Rd FY3 131 B2
Skerton 1 LA1 218 D2
Skerton Com Prim Sch LA1 218 D2
Skerton Ct LA1 218 D2
Skerton High Sch LA1 218 D2
Skerton Ho 6 LA1 218 D2
Ski Rossendale* BB4 85 E3
Skiddaw Cl BB12 147 C1
Skiddaw Rd
Blackpool FY4 110 F8
Lancaster LA1 218 E2
Skiddaw St BB1 102 A5
Skip La PR4 95 B3
Skippool Ave FY6 153 E5
Skippool Rd FY5 153 E7
Skipton Ave
Carleton FY6 153 C5
Southport PR9 54 C6
Skipton Cl
Bamber Bridge PR5 97 F2
Blackpool FY4 130 F1
Skipton Cres PR2 118 E5
Skipton Gate LA6 242 C2
Skipton Old Rd
Colne BB8 172 C7
Foulridge BB8 194 E2
Skipton Rd
Barnoldswick BB18 196 D4
Colne BB8 171 E6
Earby BB18 197 B3
Foulridge BB8 194 E2
Lytham St Anne's FY8 90 B6
Trawden BB8 172 B3
Skipton Road Bsns Ctr BB18 196 B3
Skipton St
Morecambe LA4 217 A5
Nappa BB7 231 D7
Skitham La PR3 179 D4
Skull House La WN6 19 D8
Skye Cl OL10 33 F1
Skye Cres BB1 102 C3
Slack BB12 146 F6
Slack Booth BB8 172 C1
Slack Gate OL12 52 F8
Slack House Cotts L39 16 A3
Slack La LA2 209 C1
Slack's La PR6 44 B2
Slackey's La PR9 54 C4
Slackwood La LA5 224 E2
Slade La BB12 146 C1
Slade St PR1 96 E7
Sladen St OL12 52 F1
Slaidburn Ave
Burnley BB10 128 D5
Rawtenstall BB4 86 A4
Slaidburn Brennands Prim Sch BB7 229 C7
Slaidburn Cres PR9 54 B5
Slaidburn Dr
Accrington BB5 104 A4
Lancaster LA1 215 A3
Slaidburn Heritage Ctr* BB7 229 C7
Slaidburn Ind Est PR9 54 A5
Slaidburn Pl PR2 119 A2
Slaidburn Rd
Fulwood PR2 119 A2
Lowgill LA2 239 E4
Waddington BB7 189 A5
Slaidburn Wlk 5 FY3 131 A8
Slaidburn YH* BB7 229 C7
Slape La LA6 240 C8
Slate La WN8 17 C2
Slater Ave Colne BB8 171 D6
Horwich BL6 32 C4
Slater La
Leyland,Moss Side PR26 59 B8
Leyland,Seven Stars PR25 59 D8
Slater Rd FY5 175 C2
Slater St BB2 101 C1
Slinger Rd FY5 175 C3
Slip Inn La 29 LA1 214 F8
Slipper Lowe Brow BB3 64 A5
Sliven Clod Rd BB4 105 E2
Sluice La L40 39 B3
Slyne Hall Hts LA2 221 A1
Slyne Rd
Bolton-le-S LA2,LA5 221 A2
Lancaster LA1 218 D3
Morecambe LA4 218 A5
Slynewoods LA2 218 F7
Smalden La BB7 230 A3
Small La
Drummersdale L40 24 E8
Ormskirk L39 15 F4
Ormskirk,Clieves Hills L39 15 A3
Small La N L39 23 E2
Small La S L39 14 D6
Smalley Croft PR1 96 F3
Smalley St Burnley BB11 128 B4
Standish WN6 29 E1
Smalley Thorn Brow BB6 123 F6
Smalley Way BB2 101 E2
Smallshaw Ind Est BB11 127 C4
Smallshaw La BB11, BB12 127 B5
Smallshaw Rd OL12 52 A4
Smallwood Hey Rd PR3 201 C5
Smeaton St BL6 32 C2
Smethurst Hall Pk WN5 10 C2
Smethurst Hall Rd BL9 33 F4
Smethurst Rd WN5 10 C2
Smirthwaite St BB11 127 D5
Smith Ave PR4 73 F1
Smith Brow BL6 31 C3
Smith Cl PR2 139 C1
Smith Croft PR26 59 B8
Smith La BL7 47 F1
Smith Rd FY5 175 D2
Smith St Adlington PR7 30 F6
13 Bamber Bridge PR5 77 F8
Barnoldswick BB18 196 A1
Burnley BB12 127 E6
Bury BL9 33 A3
Chorley PR7 43 D6
Colne BB8 171 C4
3 Kirkham PR4 113 F5
Nelson BB9 148 F8
Ramsbottom BL0 50 B5
Skelmersdale WN8 17 D1
Whittle-le-W PR6 61 C8
Worsthorne BB10 129 B5
Smith's La PR4 57 A1
Smithills Cl PR6 61 E1
Smithills Hall Cl BL0 50 C5
Smithy Bridge St 9 BB5 103 D3
Smithy Brow
Abbeystead LA2 232 F1
Andertons Mill WN6 28 C8
Haslingden BB4 85 B4
Newburgh WN8 27 A1
Smithy Brow Ct BB4 85 B4
Smithy Cl Brindle PR6 78 F5
Formby L37 12 B4
Garstang PR3 181 C8
Stalmine FY6 177 C7
Smithy Cvn Pk PR3 204 A5
Smithy Fold
Rochdale OL12 52 C1
Wrea Green PR4 113 B4
Smithy Gn L37 12 B4
Smithy La Aughton L39 6 A6
Brindle PR6 78 F6
Claughton PR3 182 B2
Foulridge BB8 171 B8
Haskayne L39 14 A6
Heysham LA3 212 E6
Holmeswood L40 38 C6
Hurlston Green L40 24 B3
Lytham St Anne's FY8 90 C6
Mawdesley L40 40 C2
Much Hoole PR4 74 E2
Preesall FY6 200 B3
Staining FY3,FY6 131 E6
Stalmine FY6 177 C7
Westhouse LA6 242 E4
Smithy Lane Ends L40 24 D6
Smithy Mews 9 FY1 130 C7
Smithy Row BB7 164 E1
Smithy St
2 Bamber Bridge PR5 77 E8
9 Haslingden BB4 85 B3
7 Ramsbottom BL0 50 C6
Smithy Wlk 2 L40 25 E5
Smithyfield Ave BB10 128 F6
Snaefell Rd BB2 101 E1
Snape Gn Carr Cross PR8 23 D8
Southport PR8 36 E1
Snape La LA5 225 F1
Snape Rake La PR3 183 D4
Snape St BB3 81 F3
Snapewood La PR3 204 B3
Snell Cres BB8 171 F6
Snell Gr BB8 171 F6
Sniddle Hill La BB3 64 E8
Snipe Cl Cleveleys FY5 175 F5
Normoss FY3 131 B6
Snipewood PR7 41 B6
Snodworth Rd BB6 123 D7
Snow Hill PR1 96 F8
Snow St BB1 101 F6
Snowden Ave LA3 216 D3
Snowden St 1 BB12 127 B6
Snowdon Ave BB1 101 E7
Snowdon Cl FY1 130 D3
Snowdon Dr BL6 32 C5
Snowdon Rd FY8 111 A2
Snowdrop Cl
Clayton-le-W PR25 77 E2
Haslingden BB4 67 F8
Snowhill La PR3 204 F6
Snowshill Cres FY5 152 F7
Sod Hall La PR4 76 A5
Sollam's Cl 4 PR5 97 F2
Sollom La PR4 57 B2
Solway Ave BB2 100 F1
Solway Cl Blackpool FY2 152 C6
Middleworth Green PR1 96 E3
Somerby Rd LA4 217 C4
Somerford Cl BB12 127 D7
Somersby Cl PR5 97 E3
Somerset Ave
Blackpool FY1 130 D3
Chorley PR7 61 C1
Clitheroe BB7 189 F2
Darwen BB3 81 F3
Lancaster LA1 215 A6
Wilpshire BB1 122 F6
Somerset Cl BB5 103 F3
Somerset Ct FY1 130 D3
Somerset Dr PR8 21 C3
Somerset Gr Church BB5 103 F7
Rochdale OL12 52 A1
Somerset Pk PR2 117 B7
Somerset Pl BB9 171 A1
Somerset Rd
Leyland PR25 77 B2
Preston PR1 118 A1
Rishton BB1 124 A1
Somerset St BB11 128 A4
Somerset Wlk BB4 68 B8
Sorrel Cl Cleveleys FY5 175 F5
Knott End-on-S FY6 200 A6
Sorrel Ct 2 PR1 96 C2
Soudan St BB10 148 B2
Sough La Belthorn BB1 83 A7
Blackburn BB1,BB5 102 F2
Earby BB18 195 A7
Sough Rd BB3 65 B7
Soulby Cl 3 BB2 101 C1
South Ave
Barnoldswick BB18 196 B3
Chorley PR7 43 D6
Cleveleys FY5 175 C4
Morecambe LA4 217 C5
New Longton PR4 75 F8
South Cliff St 5 PR1 96 E6
South Clifton St FY8 91 B3
South Cross St BL9 33 A1
South Dr
Appley Bridge WN6 28 C2
Fulwood PR2 117 E7
Inskip PR4 135 C8
Lancaster LA1,LA2 211 B6
Padiham BB12 126 E8
South East Dr LA1 211 B7
South End PR1 96 E5
South Gr Barton PR3 137 B8
Fulwood PR2 117 E8
Morecambe LA4 217 C5
South Hey FY8 90 C6
South Holme FY8 91 B4
South King St FY1 130 C5
South Lawn FY1 130 E2
South Meade L31 5 B1
South Meadow La PR1 96 E6
South Meadow St PR1 97 A8
South Moss Rd FY8 90 C7
South Par FY5 175 E1
South Park Dr FY3 130 F2
South Pk FY8 91 A4
South Prom FY8 89 E5
South Rd Bretherton PR26 57 F5
Coppull PR7 42 E1
Lancaster LA1 214 F7
Morecambe LA4 217 D5
Thornton FY5 176 D3
South Ribble Ind Est PR5 97 C5
South Ribble Mus* PR25 60 A8
South Ribble St 8 PR5 97 C6
South Shore Hospl FY4 110 C5
South Shore St
6 Church BB5 103 E5
Haslingden BB4 85 A3
South Spine LA1 211 B7
South Sq Blackpool FY3 130 D6
Cleveleys FY5 175 D5
South St Accrington BB5 104 C5
Accrington,Hillock Vale BB5 104 E8
Bacup OL13 88 A2
Burnley BB11 128 A6
16 Darwen BB3 82 A1
Great Eccleston PR3 156 B5
Haslingden BB4 85 C1
Lytham St Anne's FY8 91 D4
Newchurch BB4 86 E1
Ramsbottom BL0 50 D6
16 Rawtenstall BB4 86 A3
South Strand FY7 175 E7
South Terr
Abbey Village PR6 80 C2
Ormskirk L39 15 E4
Ramsbottom BL0 68 C2
South Valley Dr BB8 171 C3
South View
Bamber Bridge PR5 77 B7
South View *continued*
2 Bamber Bridge,Lostock Hall PR5 77 A7
Belmont BL7 46 C5
Bretherton PR26 57 F5
Cumeragh Village PR3 138 F6
Dolphinholme LA2 226 A8
Fisher's Row PR3 201 F4
4 Great Harwood BB6 124 C5
20 Haslingden BB4 85 B3
Kirkham PR4 114 A4
Nelson BB9 148 D7
Read BB12 145 E3
Saltcotes,Moss Side FY8 112 D1
South View St 5 OL14 109 C1
South View Terr 1 PR25 60 A8
South Warton St FY8 91 C3
South West Dr LA1 211 B7
South Westby St 2 FY8 91 B3
Southbank Ave FY4 111 A7
Southbank Rd PR8 35 C5
Southbourne Ave FY6 153 C2
Southbourne Rd FY3 131 A2
Southbrook Rd PR25 76 F1
Southcliffe BB6 124 B6
Southcliffe Ave BB12 127 C7
Southdene WN8 27 B2
Southdown Dr FY5 153 D8
Southdowns Rd PR7 43 D6
Southern Ave
Burnley BB12 127 C7
Preston PR1 97 C6
Southern Cl PR3 140 A6
Southern Ct BB12 127 C8
Southern Par PR1 97 B6
Southern Rd PR8 35 A6
Southey Cl PR2 117 F7
Southey St 2 BB11 127 E6
Southfield PR4 74 E3
Southfield Cotts BB10 149 B6
Southfield Dr
New Longton PR4 75 F7
Poulton-le-F FY3 131 C8
West Bradford BB7 189 F5
Southfield Gdns PR4 74 E3
Southfield La BB8,BB10 149 C7
Southfield Rd BL0 50 A2
Southfield Sq BB9 148 F8
Southfield St BB9 148 F7
Southfield Terr BB8 172 E6
Southfleet Ave FY7 198 E1
Southfleet Pl FY7 198 E1
Southfold Pl FY8 91 A4
Southgate Fleetwood FY7 175 D8
Fulwood PR2 117 D5
Morecambe LA3 217 E2
Preston PR1 117 F1
Whitworth OL12 52 C7
Southgates PR7 42 D3
Southlands PR4 114 A4
Southlands Ave PR5 97 C1
Southlands Dr PR26 59 C8
Southport & Formby District General Hospl PR8 35 E4
Southport Barn Cotts BB7 230 C1
Southport Botanic Gdns* PR9 54 B2
Southport Coll PR9 35 C7
Southport General Infmy PR8 35 D5
Southport New Rd
Banks PR4,PR9 55 D3
Holmes PR4 56 D3
Southport Old Rd L37 12 B7
Southport Rd Chorley PR7 43 A8
Formby L37 12 A5
Haskayne L39 14 A6
Hurlston L40 24 A2
Maghull L31,L39 5 B5
Newtown PR26,PR7 59 B2
Ormskirk L39,L40 15 D8
Scarisbrick L40,PR8 23 E7
Southport PR8 36 B2
Southport Residential Parkhomes PR8 36 A2
Southport Sta PR8 35 B7
Southport Terr PR6 43 E7
Southport Zoo* PR8 34 F7
Southside PR7 60 C3
Southway Fleetwood FY7 198 D1
Skelmersdale WN8 18 B1
Southwood Ave FY7 198 F3
Southwood Cl FY8 90 E4
Southwood Dr BB5 104 E3
Southworth Ave FY4 110 E7
Southworth St BB2 101 D2
Southworth Way FY5 175 E5
Sovereign Gate FY4 110 F5
Sow Clough Rd OL13 87 D1
Sower Carr La FY6 177 D4
Sowerby Ave FY4 110 D8
Sowerby Rd PR3 157 E3
Sowerby St 4 BB12 126 C8
Spa Ct LA4 217 E7
Spa Fold L40 17 A4
Spa Garth BB7 166 F8
Spa La L40,WN8 17 C4
Spa Rd PR1 96 D8
Spa St Burnley BB12 127 E7
Padiham BB12 126 D8
3 Preston PR1 96 D8
Spalding Ave PR3 181 D6
Spark La L40 39 B6
Sparrow Hill WN6,WN8 28 A2
Sparth Ave BB5 124 F3
Sparth Rd BB5 124 F3
Speakmans Dr WN6 19 C6
Speedie Cl BB2 81 D8
Speedwell Cl FY5 175 F5
Speedwell St BB2 101 B2
Speke St BB2 101 B2
Spen Brook Cotts BB12 169 C2
Spen Brow LA2 239 B6
Spen Cnr FY4 130 D1
Spen Farm FY4 111 C8
Spen La PR4 114 E6
Spen Pl FY4 110 F8
Spenbrook Rd BB12 169 C3
Spencer Ct FY1 130 C7
Spencer Gr BB6 124 B5
Spencer St
Accrington BB5 104 D6
Burnley BB10 148 A1
Ramsbottom BL0 50 B5
12 Rawtenstall BB4 86 A7
Spencer's La Halsall L39 22 B3
Orrell WN5 10 D7
Spencers Dr PR4 57 A8
Spencers Fold BB12 169 F1
Spencers La WN8 9 B7
Spendmore La PR7 42 E1
Spenleach La BL8 49 D3
Spenser Cl BB10 129 C4
Spenser St BB12 126 D7
Spey Cl Leyland PR25 59 E8
Standish WN6 29 D1
Speyside FY4 110 D7
Spindle Berry Ct BB5 104 C4
Spinnakers The FY8 89 E5
Spinners Ct LA1 214 F7
Spinners Gn OL12 52 F2
Spinners Sq PR5 77 E7
Spinney Brow PR2 118 D4
Spinney Cl
Lucas Green PR6 61 B6
New Longton PR4 75 F8
Ormskirk L39 15 D3
Spinney Croft PR3 140 A7
Spinney La LA5 224 C8
Spinney The Arnside LA5 224 C8
Blackburn BB2 101 A8
Burnley BB12 127 D8
Chapeltown BL7 48 C2
Chorley PR6 61 C3
Cleveleys FY5 152 F7
Formby L37 12 A5
Grindleton BB7 190 B7
Heysham LA3 213 A7
Lancaster LA1 215 B5
Poulton-le-F FY6 153 E4
Preston PR1 95 F3
Rochdale OL12 52 D3
Tarleton PR4 57 A7
Spinneyside BB2 101 D3
Spinning Ave BB1 82 D8
Spinnings The BL0 50 C3
Spire Cl BB3 65 D8
Spiredale Brow WN6 29 F2
Spires Gr PR4 116 E5
Spod Rd OL12 52 D1
Spodden Cotts OL12 71 D2
Spodden Fold OL12 52 C8
Spodden Mill OL12 71 D3
Spotland Tops OL12 52 B1
Spout Houses BB9 170 D8
Spout La LA2 241 F1
Spouthouse La BB5 125 F1
Spread Eagle St BB5 103 C5
Spring Ave BB6 124 C6
Spring Bank
Appley Bridge WN6 19 C8
Garstang PR3 181 C6
10 Preston PR1 96 E7
Rochdale OL12 52 D4
Silverdale LA5 224 C3
Whitworth OL12 71 D1
Spring Bank Terr BB2 101 C2
Spring Brook Ho BB5 124 F2
Spring Cl Kirkby L33 1 A5
Ramsbottom BL0 50 B6
Southport PR8 35 A5
Spring Field WA11 8 E2
Spring Garden St 41 LA1 214 F8
Spring Gardens Rd BB8 171 D4
Spring Gardens St 4 BB4 69 F8
Spring Gardens Terr 3 BB12 146 C1
Spring Gdns
8 Accrington BB5 104 C5
2 Bacup OL13 88 A3
11 Darwen BB3 65 A8
Freckleton PR4 93 B8
15 Horwich BL6 32 B4
Kingsfold PR1 96 F2
Leyland PR25 59 F8
Lytham St Anne's FY8 110 F1
Rawtenstall,Cowpe BB4 69 F6
7 Rawtenstall,Crawshawbooth BB4 86 A7
Spring Gr BB8 172 C6
Spring Hall BB5 124 F5
Spring Hill
6 Blackburn BB1 101 E5
Freckleton PR4 93 D7
Spring Hill Com Prim Sch BB5 104 A4
Spring Hill Com Prim Sch (Hannah St) BB5 104 B5
Spring Hill Rd
Accrington BB5 103 F4
Burnley BB11 127 F4
Spring La Blackburn BB2 101 B3
10 Colne BB8 171 D5

Spring La *continued*
Haslingden BB4 . . . .**85** B4
Nab's Head PR5 . . . .**99** C8
Spring Mdw PR25 . . . .**77** E1
Spring Mdws
Clayton-le-M BB5 . . . . .**125** A3
Darwen BB3 . . . .**65** D7
Spring Pl Colne BB8 . . . . .**171** D5
Whitworth OL12 . . . .**71** D3
Spring Rd WN5 . . . .**10** F8
Spring Row BB8 . . . .**172** C6
Spring Side Millgate OL12 **71** D4
Rawtenstall BB4 . . . .**69** F4
Spring Side Cotts BL7 . . .**47** A2
Spring St Accrington BB5 .**103** F4
Bacup OL13 . . . .**87** F1
Bank Lane BL0 . . . .**50** D7
1 Cornholme OL14 . . . . .**109** C1
Horwich BL6 . . . .**32** B4
6 Leyland PR25 . . . .**77** B1
Nelson BB9 . . . .**148** C2
5 Oswaldtwistle BB5 . . .**103** E4
Ramsbottom BL0 . . . .**50** B6
Rawtenstall BB4 . . . .**86** A8
Rishton BB1 . . . .**124** B2
Spring Terr
7 Bacup OL13 . . . .**70** D8
Goodshaw Chapel BB4 . .**105** F2
Langho BB6 . . . .**143** D1
Oswaldtwistle BB5 . . . . .**103** D4
Rochdale OL12 . . . .**52** A1
Spring Terr S 5 BB4 . . . .**85** E2
Spring Vale PR3 . . . .**207** B3
Spring Vale Garden Village
BB3 . . . .**65** C6
Spring Vale Rd BB3 . . . . . .**65** B7
Spring View
Blackburn BB2 . . . .**101** C5
Over Town BB10 . . . .**108** A8
Spring Villas 18 OL14 . . .**109** B1
Spring Wood Nature Trail★
BB7 . . . .**144** E5
Spring Wood St BL0 . . . . .**50** B7
Spring Yd 5 BB8 . . . .**171** D5
Springbank BB9 . . . .**170** E5
Springbank Ave FY5 . . . .**176** C2
Springbank Gdns BB4 . . . .**105** F2
Springbrook Ave FY5 . . . .**152** F8
Springburn Cl BL0 . . . .**32** D1
Springcroft 1 PR25 . . . . . .**77** C3
Springdale Rd BB12 . . . .**123** C8
Springfield Blacko BB9 . .**170** D8
High Bentham LA2 . . . . . .**239** E8
Springfield Ave
Accrington BB5 . . . .**103** F4
Bacup OL13 . . . .**88** A3
Blackburn BB2 . . . .**100** E1
Earby BB18 . . . .**197** C1
Kirkham PR4 . . . .**113** E5
Springfield Bank BB11 . . .**128** B5
Springfield Cl
Burscough L40 . . . .**25** D2
Formby L37 . . . .**11** C2
Whalley BB7 . . . .**144** D6
Springfield Com Prim Sch
BB10 . . . .**128** B5
Springfield Cres LA2 . . . .**239** E8
Springfield Ct 1 FY3 . . . .**130** E3
Springfield Dr
Newchurch BB4 . . . .**86** E1
Thornton FY5 . . . .**176** B4
Springfield Flats 7 BB3 . .**65** A8
Springfield Gdns
Nether Kellet LA6 . . . . . .**221** F5
Scorton PR3 . . . .**204** E6
Springfield Mews 2
BB5 . . . .**103** D3
Springfield Rd
Adlington PR6 . . . .**31** A8
Blackpool FY1 . . . .**130** B6
Burnley BB11 . . . .**128** A4
Burnley BB11 . . . .**128** B5
1 Chorley PR7 . . . .**43** C8
Coppull PR7 . . . .**29** E8
Great Harwood BB6 . . . .**124** B4
Horwich BL6 . . . .**32** D1
Leyland PR25 . . . .**59** D7
Lytham St Anne's FY8 . . .**89** E6
Maghull L39 . . . .**5** F6
Nelson BB9 . . . .**148** E6
4 Ramsbottom BL0 . . . . .**50** A2
Rawtenstall BB4 . . . .**86** B3
Springfield Rd N PR7 . . . .**29** E8
Springfield St
Blackburn BB2 . . . .**101** B3
Darwen BB3 . . . .**65** A8
Lancaster LA1 . . . .**214** F7
Morecambe LA4 . . . .**216** F4
Oswaldtwistle BB5 . . . . .**103** D4
Preston PR1 . . . .**117** E1
Springfield Terr
Adlington PR6 . . . .**31** B8
Blackburn BB2 . . . .**101** A1
Fleetwood FY7 . . . .**176** A6
Springfield View BB11 . .**106** C5
Springhill Ave OL13 . . . . .**70** D8
Springhill Villas OL13 . . . .**70** D8
Springmount BB18 . . . . .**197** C2
Springmount Dr WN8 . . . . .**27** C5
Springs Cres PR6 . . . .**61** E5
Springs Mews PR6 . . . . . .**61** E6
Springs Rd Chorley PR6 . . .**61** E6
Longridge PR3 . . . .**140** B8
Springsands Cl PR2 . . . . . .**118** E3
Springthorpe St 5 BB3 . . .**65** B6
Springvale BB5 . . . .**103** F4
Springvale Bsns Pk BB3 . .**65** B6
Springwater Ave BL0 . . . .**50** A3

Springwood Cl PR5 . . . . .**97** A3
Springwood Dr
Chorley PR7 . . . .**43** E5
Rufford L40 . . . .**39** A5
Springwood Rd BB10 . . . .**128** E5
Springwood Terr OL14 . . .**109** B1
Sprodley Dr WN6 . . . .**28** B2
Spruce Ave Bury BL9 . . . . .**33** B2
Lancaster LA1 . . . .**214** F4
Spruce Cl PR2 . . . .**118** C7
Spruce Ct BB5 . . . .**104** E4
Spruce St BL0 . . . .**50** B5
Spruce Way L37 . . . .**11** C5
Sprucewood Cl BB5 . . . . .**104** D6
Spurrier St PR26 . . . .**77** A4
Spymers Croft L37 . . . . . .**12** A6
Square House La PR9 . . . .**55** C6
Catforth PR4 . . . .**135** F4
Square La Burscough L40 . .**25** E3
Square St BL0 . . . .**50** C6
Square The
Blackpool FY3 . . . .**131** A2
Brinscall PR6 . . . .**62** F7
Burton-in-K LA6 . . . .**240** B7
Cleveleys FY5 . . . .**175** D5
Cumeragh Village PR3 . .**138** F5
Great Eccleston PR3 . . . .**156** B5
1 Leyland PR25 . . . .**77** B2
Scorton PR3 . . . .**204** E6
Waddington BB7 . . . . . .**189** B4
Walton-le-D PR5 . . . .**97** F5
Whalley BB7 . . . .**144** C5
Worsthorne BB10 . . . . . .**129** B5
Squire Rd BB9 . . . .**148** F8
Squire's Gate Rd PR2 . . .**117** C3
Squires Cl PR5 . . . .**98** E2
Squires Ct
7 Blackpool FY4 . . . . . .**110** C5
10 Lytham St Anne's FY8 . .**91** B3
Squires Gate Ind Est
FY4 . . . .**110** E4
Squires Gate La FY4 . . . .**110** D5
Squires Gate Sta FY8 . . .**110** D4
Squires Rd PR1 . . . .**96** C6
Squires Wood PR2 . . . . . .**118** D6
Squirrel Fold PR2 . . . . . .**118** F2
Squirrel Gn L37 . . . .**11** C5
Squirrel La BL6 . . . .**32** A4
Squirrel's Chase PR5 . . . . .**77** A7
Squirrels Chase PR4 . . . .**115** D1
Squirrels Cl BB5 . . . .**104** E8
Stable Cl Gisburn BB7 . . . .**231** B3
Kirkham PR4 . . . .**114** A6
Stable La PR6 . . . .**62** A7
Stable Yd PR3 . . . .**201** E3
Stables Cl BB4 . . . .**86** A6
Stables The Leyland PR7 . . .**60** A5
Whalley BB7 . . . .**144** B8
Whitworth OL12 . . . .**71** C1
Stack Croft PR6 . . . .**78** A2
Stack La OL13 . . . .**71** B8
Stackhouses The 2
BB11 . . . .**128** A6
Stadium Ave FY4 . . . .**110** E4
Staffa Cres BB1 . . . .**102** D4
Stafford Ave FY6 . . . .**153** D1
Stafford Cl PR4 . . . .**156** A1
Stafford Moreton Way
L31 . . . .**5** D1
Stafford Rd
11 Preston PR1 . . . .**118** A1
Southport PR8 . . . .**35** A1
Stafford St Burnley BB10 .**128** A7
Darwen BB3 . . . .**81** F4
Nelson BB9 . . . .**149** A8
Skelmersdale WN8 . . . . .**17** D1
Staghills Rd BB4 . . . .**86** D1
Stainburn Cl WN6 . . . .**19** E6
Stainforth Ave FY2 . . . . .**152** E5
Staining Ave PR2 . . . .**95** F8
Staining CE Prim Sch
FY3 . . . .**131** D5
Staining Old Rd FY3,FY6 .**131** D7
Staining Rd FY3 . . . .**131** C6
Staining Rd W FY3 . . . . . .**131** D5
Staining Rise FY3 . . . .**131** E5
Stainton Dr BB12 . . . .**127** E8
Stainton Gr 1 LA4 . . . . . .**217** E4
Stakepool Dr PR3 . . . . . .**201** E4
Stakes Hall Pl BB2 . . . . . .**101** C2
Stalls Rd LA3 . . . .**212** F2
Stalmine Ctry Pk FY6 . . . .**177** D5
Stalmine Hall Rd FY6 . . . .**177** C8
Stalmine Prim Sch FY6 . .**177** D7
Stamford Ave FY4 . . . . . .**110** D7
Stamford Ct FY8 . . . .**89** D8
Stamford Dr PR6 . . . .**61** C3
Stamford Pl 3 BB7 . . . . .**189** F1
Stamford Rd
Skelmersdale WN8 . . . . .**17** D2
Southport PR8 . . . .**35** B2
Stanagate PR4 . . . .**115** C1
Stanah Gdns FY5 . . . .**176** E2
Stanah Prim Sch FY5 . . . .**176** D1
Stanah Rd FY5 . . . .**176** E2
Stanalee La PR3 . . . .**160** B8
Stanbury Cl
Brierfield BB10 . . . .**148** E2
Bury BL9 . . . .**33** D1
Stanbury Dr BB10 . . . .**148** E2
Stancliffe St BB2 . . . .**101** C3
Standen Hall Cl BB10 . . . .**148** E3
Standen Hall Dr BB10 . . . .**148** E3
Standen Rd BB7 . . . .**166** F7
Standen Road Bglws
BB7 . . . .**166** F7
Standhouse La L39 . . . .**15** C2

Standing Stone La BB8,
BB9 . . . .**194** A2
Standish Com High Sch
WN6 . . . .**29** C2
Standish Ctr The 4 WN6 **29** E1
Standish St
Burnley BB11 . . . .**128** A6
Chorley PR7 . . . .**43** D7
Standish St Wilfred's CE Prim
Sch WN6 . . . .**29** F1
Standridge Clough La
BB18 . . . .**197** D1
Standroyd Dr BB8 . . . . . .**172** A5
Standroyd Rd BB8 . . . . . .**172** A5
Stanedge Cl BL0 . . . .**50** C4
Stanford Gdns BB2 . . . . .**102** A1
Stanford Hall Cres BL0 . . .**50** B4
Stang Top Rd BB9 . . . . . .**169** F6
Stangate LA3 . . . .**5** B2
Stanhill La BB5 . . . .**103** C4
Stanhill Rd BB1,BB5 . . . .**102** F4
Stanhill St BB5 . . . .**103** C3
Stanhope Ave LA3 . . . . . .**217** E3
Stanhope Ct LA3 . . . .**217** F3
Stanhope Rd 1 FY1 . . . . .**130** C7
Stanhope St
Burnley BB12 . . . .**127** F7
Darwen BB3 . . . .**82** A2
Preston PR1 . . . .**117** E2
Stanier Pl BL6 . . . .**32** C2
Stanifield Cl PR25 . . . .**77** B3
Stanifield La PR5,PR25 . . .**77** C5
Stankelt Rd LA5 . . . .**224** C2
Stanlawe Rd L37 . . . .**11** E6
Stanley Ave
Cleveleys FY5 . . . .**175** E2
Hutton PR4 . . . .**95** D2
Leyland PR25 . . . .**77** C4
Middleforth Green PR1 . .**96** E5
Poulton-le-F FY6 . . . . . .**153** D3
Southport PR8 . . . .**34** F3
Stanley Cl PR3 . . . .**140** B7
Stanley Croft PR4 . . . . . .**137** E3
Stanley Ct
Accrington BB5 . . . .**104** D7
Burscough Bridge L40 . . .**25** E5
Chipping BB7 . . . .**185** E3
Kirkham PR4 . . . .**114** B4
Stanley Dr Darwen BB3 . . .**65** B5
Hornby LA2 . . . .**238** B7
Stanley Fold PR5 . . . .**76** F8
Stanley Gate
Fleetwood FY7 . . . .**198** D3
Mellor BB2 . . . .**121** E2
Stanley Gr
Higher Penwortham PR1 . .**96** A5
Horwich BL6 . . . .**32** D1
Stanley High Sch PR9 . . . .**53** F4
Stanley Ho PR1 . . . .**96** E7
Stanley Mount 6 OL13 . . .**87** F3
Stanley Park FY3 . . . .**130** F3
Stanley Pl 9 Chorley PR7 . .**43** C8
Lancaster LA1 . . . .**214** D8
Preston PR1 . . . .**96** E7
Stanley Prim & Inf Sch
FY3 . . . .**131** B2
Stanley Range BB2 . . . . .**101** B1
Stanley Rd Blackpool FY1 .**130** C4
Fleetwood FY7 . . . .**198** F3
Formby L37 . . . .**11** E6
Kirkham PR4 . . . .**113** F7
Leyland PR25 . . . .**77** C4
Lytham St Anne's FY8 . . .**90** D3
Morecambe LA3 . . . .**216** E3
Skelmersdale WN8 . . . . .**10** B7
Stanley St
Accrington BB5 . . . .**104** D6
Bacup OL13 . . . .**87** F4
Brierfield BB9 . . . .**148** B6
6 Burnley BB11 . . . .**127** F5
Carnforth LA5 . . . .**223** D1
Colne BB8 . . . .**171** D5
Kirkham PR4 . . . .**114** B4
10 Leyland PR25 . . . .**77** B1
Longridge PR3 . . . .**140** A8
Morecambe LA4 . . . .**217** B6
Nelson BB9 . . . .**148** D8
Ormskirk L39 . . . .**15** F5
Oswaldtwistle BB5 . . . . .**103** D3
Preston PR1 . . . .**97** B8
Ramsbottom BL0 . . . .**50** B5
Rochdale OL12 . . . .**52** C1
Southport PR9 . . . .**35** B8
Stanley Terr PR1 . . . .**96** E7
Stanley Villas PR5 . . . .**99** B4
Stanley Way WN8 . . . .**17** E3
Stanleyfield Cl PR1 . . . . .**118** A1
Stanleyfield Rd PR1 . . . . .**118** A1
Stanmere Ct BL8 . . . .**49** B3
Stanmore Ave FY4 . . . . . .**110** F6
Stanmore Dr LA1 . . . .**214** E5
Stannanought Rd WN8 . . .**18** E2
Stanner Lodge FY8 . . . . . .**110** F2
Stanning Cl PR25 . . . .**59** E8
Stanrose Cl BL7 . . . .**47** E1
Stansfeld St BB2 . . . .**101** C3
Stansfield Ave L31 . . . .**5** F1
Stansfield Cl 7 BB9 . . . . .**170** D4
Stansfield Rd BB4 . . . .**69** E8
Stansfield St
2 Bacup OL13 . . . .**70** C8
Blackpool FY1 . . . .**130** C1
Burnley BB11 . . . .**128** A6
6 Darwen BB3 . . . .**65** A8
Nelson BB9 . . . .**148** E8
Stansfield Terr 14 OL14 .**109** B1
Stansford Ct PR1 . . . .**96** D4

Stansted Rd PR7 . . . .**43** A7
Stansy Ave LA3 . . . .**216** E1
Stanthorpe Wlk LA1 . . . .**148** A1
Stanworth Brow PR6 . . . . .**80** A5
Stanworth Rd BB9 . . . . . .**148** D8
Stanworth St BB10 . . . . . .**129** B5
Stanworth Terr PR6 . . . . . .**80** B4
Stanzaker Hall Dr PR3 . . .**158** D7
Stapleton Rd L37 . . . .**11** D1
Star Bank OL13 . . . .**70** D7
Star La BL6 . . . .**31** F3
Star St Accrington BB5 . . .**103** F5
Darwen BB3 . . . .**82** B1
Starbeck Ave FY4 . . . . . .**130** D1
Starfield Cl FY8 . . . .**91** A4
Starkie St
6 Blackburn BB1 . . . . . .**101** F5
Burnley BB11 . . . .**127** C5
Darwen BB3 . . . .**65** B8
12 Leyland PR25 . . . .**77** B1
Preston PR1 . . . .**96** F5
Starr Gate FY4 . . . .**110** B4
Starrgate Dr PR2 . . . .**116** E3
Startifants La PR3 . . . . . .**184** F4
Startifants Lane End
PR3 . . . .**185** A5
Startley Nook PR4 . . . .**76** B6
States Rd FY8 . . . .**90** B6
Statham Rd WN8 . . . .**17** D3
Statham Way L39 . . . .**15** C4
Station App
1 Burscough Bridge L40 . .**25** E5
Ormskirk L39 . . . .**15** F5
Station Ave WN5 . . . .**10** D5
Station Bldgs LA5 . . . . . .**223** D2
Station Brow PR25 . . . .**77** B2
Station Cl Rishton BB1 . . .**103** A8
Wilpshire BB1 . . . .**122** F4
Station Cotts LA6 . . . . . .**241** D2
Station Ct LA2 . . . .**238** F2
Station La
Burton-in-K LA6 . . . .**240** B7
Nateby PR3 . . . .**203** B1
Newsham PR3 . . . .**137** A5
Scorton PR3 . . . .**204** D7
Station Par OL14 . . . .**108** F1
Station Rd Adlington PR7 . .**31** A6
Bamber Bridge PR5 . . . . .**77** E8
Banks PR9 . . . .**54** F5
Barnoldswick BB18 . . . .**196** B2
Blackpool FY4 . . . .**110** B8
Blackrod BL6 . . . .**31** E1
Chapeltown BL7 . . . .**48** C4
Clitheroe BB7 . . . .**166** E8
Coppull PR7 . . . .**42** F1
3 Cornholme OL14 . . . . .**109** C1
Croston PR26 . . . .**58** B3
Fleetwood FY7 . . . .**199** A4
Foulridge BB8 . . . .**194** D1
Great Harwood BB6 . . . .**124** D5
Halton LA2 . . . .**219** C6
Haskayne L39 . . . .**13** C7
Haslingden,BB4 . . . .**85** B4
Haslingden,Bridge End BB4 .**68** A7
Hesketh Bank PR4 . . . . . .**73** F3
Hest Bank LA2 . . . .**220** D1
High Bentham LA2 . . . . .**239** D7
Hoghton PR5 . . . .**99** B2
Holme Mills LA6 . . . .**240** B8
Hornby LA2 . . . .**238** B7
Huncoat BB5 . . . .**125** E2
2 Lancaster LA1 . . . .**214** E8
Lancaster LA1 . . . .**214** E8
Lytham St Anne's FY8 . . .**91** B3
Maghull L31 . . . .**5** A6
Morecambe LA4 . . . .**217** B5
New Longton PR4 . . . .**75** F8
Ormskirk L39 . . . .**15** F6
Padiham BB12 . . . .**126** C8
Parbold WN8 . . . .**27** C2
Poulton-le-F FY6 . . . . . .**153** E4
Ramsbottom BL8 . . . .**49** F1
Rimington BB7 . . . .**191** E8
Rishton BB1 . . . .**124** A1
Rufford L40 . . . .**39** D4
Salwick PR4 . . . .**115** C4
Singleton FY6 . . . .**132** C8
Southport PR8 . . . .**21** C5
Thornton FY5 . . . .**176** D1
Walmer Bridge PR4 . . . . .**74** D4
Whalley BB7 . . . .**144** C5
Whitworth OL12 . . . .**71** D3
Whitworth,Broadley OL12 . .**52** C5
Wrea Green PR4 . . . .**113** B4
Station Road Ind Est
BB6 . . . .**124** E5
Station Sq FY8 . . . .**91** A3
Station Terr
Abbey Village PR6 . . . . . .**80** C2
Blackpool FY4 . . . .**110** B8
Station View BB6 . . . .**143** D1
Station Way
Garstang PR3 . . . .**181** C6
Hornby LA2 . . . .**238** B7
Staunton St LA5 . . . .**223** D3
Staveley Ave L40 . . . .**25** C4
Staveley Gr FY7 . . . .**198** D2
Staveley Pl PR2 . . . .**116** E2
Staveley Rd
Skelmersdale WN8 . . . . .**17** E3
Southport PR8 . . . .**21** D4
Staynall La FY6 . . . .**177** B4
Stead St BL0 . . . .**50** C6
Sted Terr BB1 . . . .**101** E6
Steeley La PR6 . . . .**43** D7
Steeple View PR2 . . . .**96** D8
Steer St BB10 . . . .**148** B1
Steeton Rd FY3 . . . .**153** B1

Stefano Rd 1 PR1 . . . .**97** C8
Steiner St BB5 . . . .**104** A6
Steiner's La BB5 . . . .**103** E7
Step Row OL13 . . . .**87** F5
Stephen St
Blackburn BB2 . . . .**101** B2
Lytham St Anne's FY8 . . .**89** E7
Stephendale Ave PR5 . . . .**78** B8
Stephens Gr LA3 . . . .**209** D8
Stephenson Dr BB12 . . . .**127** C7
Stephenson St
2 Chorley PR6 . . . .**43** E7
Horwich BL6 . . . .**32** B2
Stephenson Way L37 . . . . .**12** C3
Sterling Pl 3 OL10 . . . . . .**33** F1
Sterndale Ave WN6 . . . . . .**29** E2
Stevenson Ave 2 PR25 . . .**77** C3
Stevenson St E BB5 . . . . .**104** A5
Stevenson St W BB5 . . . .**103** F5
Steward Ave LA1 . . . .**215** B5
Stewart Cl LA5 . . . .**224** B8
Stewart Ct 9 LA1 . . . .**218** D2
Stewart St Blackburn BB2 . .**81** D8
Burnley BB11 . . . .**128** B4
11 Preston PR1 . . . .**96** E8
Stiles Ave PR4 . . . .**95** C1
Stiles The L39 . . . .**15** E5
Stirling Cl Chorley PR6 . . . .**43** E7
Clitheroe BB7 . . . .**166** C6
1 Leyland PR25 . . . .**77** C1
Stirling Ct
8 Blackpool FY1 . . . . . .**130** D7
Lane Bottom BB10 . . . . .**149** B4
Southport PR9 . . . .**54** A2
Stirling Dr BB1 . . . .**101** F4
Stirling Rd Blackpool FY3 .**130** D7
Lancaster LA1 . . . .**215** A7
Stirling St BB2 . . . .**101** B1
Stock Cl OL12 . . . .**52** E2
Stockbridge Cotts BB7 . . .**164** E5
Stockbridge Dr BB12 . . . .**126** E8
Stockbridge Rd BB12 . . . .**126** D7
Stockclough La BB2 . . . . . .**80** D6
Stockdale Cres PR5 . . . . . .**77** F8
Stockdove Way FY5 . . . . .**175** E3
Stockdove Wood FY5 . . . .**175** E3
Stockholm St BB11 . . . . . .**127** B5
Stockley Cres L39 . . . .**7** C6
Stockley Dr WN6 . . . .**19** E8
Stockpit Rd L33 . . . .**1** D2
Stocks Cl PR6 . . . .**79** B1
Stocks Ct
Heskin Green PR7 . . . . . .**41** E3
5 Poulton-le-F FY6 . . . .**153** D3
Stocks La
Barnoldswick BB7 . . . . .**193** A7
Carleton FY6 . . . .**153** A3
Heskin Green PR7 . . . . . .**41** E3
Stocks Lane End PR3 . . . .**181** D2
Stocks Park Dr BL6 . . . . . .**32** C3
Stocks Rd PR2 . . . .**117** C2
Stocks Resr & Gisburn Forest
Walks★ BB7 . . . .**235** E3
Stocks St 7 PR1 . . . .**96** E8
Stocksgate OL12 . . . .**52** B2
Stockwood Cl BB2 . . . . . .**101** A8
Stockydale Rd FY4 . . . . . .**111** A6
Stoke Ave FY1 . . . .**130** D7
Stokes Hall Ave PR25 . . . .**60** A8
Stone Bridge La BB5 . . . .**103** E3
Stone Cl BL0 . . . .**50** A4
Stone Croft PR1 . . . .**96** D2
Stone Cross Gdns PR3 . . .**181** D2
Stone Edge Rd BB9 . . . . .**170** E6
Stone Edge View BB9 . . . .**170** E6
Stone Fold BB5 . . . .**85** B8
Stone Hall La WN8 . . . .**19** C5
Stone Hill Dr BB1 . . . .**123** A1
Stone Hill La OL12 . . . .**52** A2
Stone Holme Terr BB4 . . . .**86** A8
Stone Mill Cotts BL7 . . . . .**48** D4
Stone Moor Bottom
BB12 . . . .**126** C6
Stone Pits BL0 . . . .**68** D3
Stone Row Head LA1 . . . .**215** C8
Stone St Haslingden BB4 . . .**84** F2
Rawtenstall BB4 . . . .**69** F8
Stonebarn Dr L31 . . . .**5** C3
Stonebridge Cl 6 PR5 . . . .**77** C8
Stonebridge Terr PR3 . . . .**140** A7
Stonechat Cl FY3 . . . .**131** B6
Stonecroft BB9 . . . .**170** E6
Stonecroft Rd PR25 . . . . . .**59** D7
Stonecrop WN6 . . . .**28** D2
Stonefield Longton PR4 . . . .**74** F8
Middleworth Green PR1 . .**96** E4
Stonefield Cotts BB2 . . . .**100** B2
Stonefold Ave PR4 . . . .**95** C1
Stonegate Fold PR6 . . . . . .**44** B1
Stonehill Cres OL12 . . . . . .**52** A3
Stonehill Dr OL12 . . . .**52** B3
Stonehill Rd OL12 . . . .**52** B3
Stoneholme Ind Est BB4 . .**86** A8
Stoneholme Rd BB4 . . . . . .**86** A8
Stonehouse Gn PR6 . . . . . .**78** B3
Stoneleigh Cl PR8 . . . .**21** C4
Stoneleigh Ct LA5 . . . . . .**224** C3
Stones Bank Rd BL7 . . . . . .**47** B5
Stones La PR3 . . . .**181** E3
Stoneway Rd FY5 . . . .**175** E1
Stonewell 17 LA1 . . . .**214** F8
Stoney Bank Rd BB18 . . . .**197** C2
Stoney Brow WN8 . . . .**19** B1
Stoney Butts PR2 . . . .**95** D8
Stoney Croft Dr LA5 . . . . .**223** E6

Stoney Ct BB8 ....194 E1
Stoney Holt PR25 ....77 E1
Stoney La Adlington PR7 .30 E4
 Bamber Bridge PR5 ....77 C6
 Foulridge BB8 ....194 E1
 Freckleton PR4 ....93 B5
 Galgate LA2 ....211 B3
 Hambleton FY6 ....177 C2
 Longridge PR3 ....161 C7
 Parbold WN6,WN8 .....27 E4
Stoney St BB11 ....128 B4
Stoneycroft BB10 ....129 A5
Stoneycroft Ave BL6 ....32 D4
Stoneycroft Cl BL6 ......32 D5
Stoneygate Cleveleys FY5 175 F1
 🛐 Preston PR1 ....97 A7
Stoneygate La WN6 .....28 B2
Stoneyholme Cty Prim Sch
 BB12 ....127 F8
Stoneyhurst Ave
 Burnley BB10 ....128 D5
 Thornton FY5 ....153 D8
Stoneyhurst Ht BB9 ....148 D4
Stoneyroyd OL12 ....71 D1
Stonor Rd PR7 ....30 F7
Stony Bank PR6 ....79 A6
Stony Croft Pl 🛂 FY4 ...110 C5
Stony Fold Brow BB3 ....64 A5
Stony Hill Ave FY4 ......110 C5
Stony La Cockerham PR3 .206 F2
 Hollins Lane PR3 .....207 B3
 Shore OL14 ....109 E2
Stonybutts 🛐 BB1 .....101 E5
Stonycroft Ave FY4 .....110 C5
Stonygate La PR3 ......141 D6
Stonyhurst PR7 ....43 C4
Stonyhurst Cl
 Blackburn BB2 ....101 D4
 Padiham BB12 ....126 E6
Stonyhurst Coll BB7 ....165 A3
Stonyhurst Coll Gdns★
 BB7 ....165 A2
Stonyhurst Rd BB2 .....101 D4
Stoop St BB11 ....127 C5
Stoopes Hill BB18 ......197 C2
Stoops Fold BB2 ....121 E2
Stoops La BB7 ....191 F8
Stopes Brow BB1,BB3 ...82 A7
Stopford Ave FY2 ......152 E2
Stopford Ct 🛐 BB5 ....124 F3
Stopgate La L33 ....1 C7
Stopper La BB7 ....192 B7
Store St Blackburn BB3 ..82 A7
 🛐 Haslingden BB4 ...85 B3
 Horwich BL6 ....32 C4
Storey Ave LA1 ....214 D8
Storey Hall LA1 ....214 E5
Storey Inst (Coll of F Ed)
 LA1 ....214 E8
Stork Cl FY5 ....175 F1
Stork St BB3 ....65 B8
Storrs La LA5 ....225 B4
Storwood Cl WN5 ......10 E5
Stott St 🛐 Nelson BB9 .148 B8
 Rochdale OL12 ....52 F1
Stour Lodge PR2 ....117 C6
Stourton Rd PR8 ....21 C4
Stourton St BB1 ......124 A2
Stout St BB2 ....101 D4
Strait La LA2 ....232 F1
Straits BB5 ....103 E4
Straits La BB12 ....145 D2
Straits The PR5 ....99 B2
Strand Rd PR1 ....96 D7
Strand St W PR2 ....96 C8
Strand The Blackpool FY1 130 B6
 Fleetwood FY7 ....175 D8
 Horwich BL6 ....32 D3
Strands Farm Ct LA2 ..238 B7
Strang St 🛐 BL0 ......50 C6
Strange St BB11 ....128 B4
Stransdale Cl 🛐 PR3 ..181 B7
Stratfield Pl 🛐 PR25 ...77 B1
Stratford Cl
 Lancaster LA1 ....218 C3
 Southport PR8 ....21 A6
Stratford Dr PR2 ......117 C4
Stratford Pl
 Blackpool FY1 ....130 E2
 🛂 Fleetwood FY7 ...198 E4
Stratford Rd Chorley PR6 .43 D8
 Lytham St Anne's FY8 ..90 B7
Stratford Way
 🛐 Accrington BB5 ...104 A7
 Colne BB8 ....171 F5
Strathaven Pl 🛐 OL10 ..33 F1
Strathclyde Rd BB1 ....102 A4
Strathdale FY4 ....110 C7
Strathmore Cl BL0 ......50 C4
Strathmore Gr PR7 ......43 B7
Strathmore Rd PR2 ....117 E3
Strathyre Cl FY2 ......152 F5
Stratton Ct BB9 ....148 E6
Stratton Gr BL6 ....32 B5
Strawberry Bank 🛐
 BB1 ....101 D5
Strawberry Fields PR7 ..61 B3
Strawberry Mews 🛐
 LA3 ....212 F8
Streatly Wlk BB2 ....82 A8
Street The PR6 ....44 E3
Strellas La LA5 ....221 C1
Stretford Pl OL12 ....52 E3
Stretton Ave FY4 ......110 E4
Stretton Dr PR9 ....35 F8

Stretton Rd BL0 ....50 A2
Strickens La PR3 ......182 C6
Strickland Dr LA4 .....217 E5
Stricklands La PR1 ......96 E4
Strike La PR4 ....93 B8
Strine The L40,PR4 .....57 A1
Stromness Gr 🛂 OL10 ..33 F1
Strongstry Rd BL0 ......68 C2
Stronsay Pl FY2 ....152 F6
Stroyan St BB10 ......128 C5
Strutt St 🛂 PR1 ......118 B1
Stryands PR4 ....95 C1
Stuart Ave Bacup OL13 ..70 D8
 Morecambe LA4 .....217 D6
Stuart Cl 🛮 Darwen BB3 .82 A1
 Fulwood PR2 ....118 E3
Stuart Pl FY3 ....153 A4
Stuart Rd Fulwood PR2 .118 E3
 Thornton FY5 ....176 C2
Stuart St Accrington BB5 .104 B7
 🛐 Barnoldswick BB18 .196 C3
Stubbins La Catterall PR3 181 F2
 Ramsbotton BL0 ......50 C8
 Sabden BB7 ....146 A1
Stubbins Vale Cvn Pk
 BB7 ....146 A7
Stubbins Vale Rd BL0 ...68 C1
Stubbins Vale Terr BL0 ..68 B1
Stubbylee La OL13 ......70 F8
Stubley Holme 🛐 OL14 .109 A1
Stubley La OL14 ....109 B1
Studfold PR7 ....61 B2
Studholme Ave PR1 .....96 E2
Studholme Cl 🛐 PR1 ...96 E2
Studholme Cres PR1 ....96 E2
Studley Ct PR9 ....53 D1
Stump Cross La BB7 ...230 F5
Stump Hall Rd BB12 ...146 F7
Stump La PR6 ....43 D8
Stunstead Cotts BB8 ..172 C2
Stunstead Rd BB8 .....172 C3
Sturgess Cl L39 ....15 F7
Sturminster Cl 🛐 PR1 ..96 E2
Styan St FY7 ....199 A4
Stydd La PR3 ....141 E4
Sudell Ave L31 ....5 F2
Sudell Cl BB3 ....82 C1
Sudell Cross 🛮 BB1 ...101 E5
Sudell La L31,L39 ....5 E6
Sudell Prim Sch BB3 ....82 B1
Sudell Rd BB3 ....82 B1
Sudellside St BB3 ....82 B1
Suffolk Ave BB12 ......127 A6
Suffolk Cl PR25 ....59 E6
Suffolk Rd Blackpool FY3 131 A2
 Preston PR1 ....118 A1
 Southport PR8 ....22 A8
Suffolk St BB2 ....101 C2
Sugar Stubbs La PR9 ...55 C4
Sugham La LA3 ....212 F8
Sulby Cl PR8 ....34 F3
Sulby Dr Fulwood PR2 ..118 F5
 Lancaster LA1 ....214 F6
Sulby Gr Fulwood PR2 ..119 A5
 Morecambe LA4 .....217 E6
Sulby Rd BB2 ....101 E1
Sullivan Dr BB2 ....102 A1
Sullom Side La PR3 ...182 C5
Sullom View PR3 ......181 C6
Sultan St BB5 ....104 D7
Sulyard St LA1 ....214 F8
Summer St Horwich BL6 .32 B4
 Nelson BB9 ....148 C7
 Skelmersdale WN8 ....18 A4
Summer Trees Ave PR7 116 D3
Summerdale Dr BL0 .....50 B8
Summerer Gr PR4 .....132 F6
Summerfield
 Leyland PR25 ....76 F3
 Thornton-in-C BD23 ..197 A5
Summerfield Cl PR5 ....97 B3
Summerfield Dr LA2 ..218 C7
Summerfields Coppull PR7 29 C7
 Lytham St Anne's FY8 .89 C8
Summerhill LA2 ....239 D7
Summerseat La BL0 ....50 A4
Summerseat Meth Prim Sch
 BL9 ....50 B2
Summerseat Sta BL9 ...50 C2
Summersgill Rd LA1 ..218 B2
Summerton Wlk BB3 ....82 E2
Summerville 🛮 FY4 ...110 C6
Summerville Ave FY3 ..131 E5
Summerville Wlk 🛮
 BB2 ....101 D5
Summerwood Cl FY2 ..152 D1

Sun St continued
 Ramsbottom BL0 ......50 B7
Sun Terr 🛮 OL14 .....109 B1
Sunacre Ct LA3 ......216 E3
Sunbank Cl OL12 ....52 D2
Sunbury Ave PR1 ....96 D3
Sunbury Dr PR8 ....21 B4
Suncliffe Rd BB9 ......148 D4
Suncourt PR8 ....34 F6
Sunderland Ave
 Cleveleys FY5 ....175 F4
 Hambleton FY6 ....177 D2
Sunderland Dr LA3 ....217 A2
Sunderland St BB12 ...127 B6
Sunfield Cl FY4 ....111 C4
Sunindale Ave BB4 .....87 A1
Sunningdale Ave 137 B3
Sunningdale Ave
 Blackpool FY4 ....131 A2
 Fleetwood FY7 ....175 D7
 Hest Bank LA2 ......220 D1
Sunningdale Cl PR4 ...114 A4
Sunningdale Cres LA2 .220 D1
Sunningdale Ct FY5 ....90 A6
Sunningdale Dr FY5 ...153 D8
Sunningdale Gdns
 Brierfield BB10 ......148 D3
 Formby L37 ....11 E3
Sunningdale Pl PR4 ...135 C8
Sunny Bank Kirkham PR4 113 F5
 Middleworth Green PR1 ..96 F3
Sunny Bank Ave
 Blackpool FY2 ....152 C4
 Newton-w-S PR4 .....115 A2
Sunny Bank Cl BB4 .....68 A6
Sunny Bank Cotts BB4 ..67 F5
Sunny Bank Mill 🛐 PR4 113 F5
Sunny Bank Rd
 Blackburn BB2 ......101 E1
 Haslingden BB4 ....68 A6
Sunny Bank Sch BB11 .127 E4
Sunny Bank Terr 🛐
 OL14 ....109 B1
Sunny Bower Cl BB1 ..123 B1
Sunny Bower Rd BB1 ..123 B1
Sunny Brow PR7 ....43 A2
Sunny Dr WN5 ....10 F6
Sunny Lea St BB4 ......85 F5
Sunny Rd PR9 ....54 A2
Sunny View PR6 ....80 C2
Sunnybank Dr BB5 ....103 C2
Sunnybank Rd LA5 ....221 A5
Sunnybank St
 Darwen BB3 ....82 A1
 🛮 Haslingden BB4 ...85 A3
Sunnycliff Ret Pk LA3 .217 D1
Sunnyfield Ave
 Morecambe LA4 .....217 E6
 Southward Bottom BB10 .108 A8
Sunnyfield La BB3 ......66 A8
Sunnyfields L39 ....16 A5
Sunnyhill PR2 ....118 C5
Sunnyhill Cl BB3 ....81 D2
Sunnyhurst BB3 ....81 D1
Sunnyhurst Ave FY4 ..110 D6
Sunnyhurst Cl BB3 .....81 D2
Sunnyhurst La BB3 .....81 D2
Sunnyhurst Rd BB2 ....101 D4
Sunnyhurst Wood Visitor
 Ctr★ BB3 ....81 D2
Sunnymede Dr L31 ......5 D3
Sunnymede Sch PR8 ...34 F6
Sunnymede Vale BL0 ...50 A3
Sunnymere Dr BB3 .....81 E2
Sunnyside
 🛐 High Bentham LA2 .239 D8
 Ormskirk L39 ....6 C7
 Southport PR8 ....34 F3
Sunnyside Ave
 Billington BB7 ....144 B4
 🛮 Blackburn BB2 .....80 E8
 Ribchester PR3 ......141 D3
 Warton PR4 ....92 E6
 Wilpshire BB1 ....123 A7
Sunnyside Camp Site
 LA3 ....217 A2
Sunnyside Cl
 Freckleton PR4 ....93 B7
 Lancaster LA1 ....214 E7
 Rawtenstall BB4 ......86 A6
Sunnyside Ct PR9 ......53 C1
Sunnyside Cvn Pk PR3 158 F5
Sunnyside La LA1 .....214 E7
Sunnyside Terr FY6 ...200 C3
Sunset Cl L33 ....1 A5
Super St BB5 ....124 E4
Surgeon's Ct PR1 ......96 F7
Surrey Ave Burnley BB12 .127 B7
 Darwen BB3 ....81 F3
Surrey Cl PR9 ....54 C5
Surrey Rd
 Barrowford BB9 .....170 D2
 Blackburn BB1 ......102 D5
Surrey St Accrington BB5 104 D6
 Preston PR1 ....97 C8
Sussex Ave BL9 ....33 E1
Sussex Cl Church BB5 .103 F7
 Standish WN1 ....30 B1
Sussex Dr Blackburn BB1 102 A4
 Garstang PR3 ....181 B7
 Haslingden BB4 ....68 B8
Sussex Rd Blackpool FY3 130 C6
 Rishton BB1 ....101 F8
 Southport PR8,PR9 ...35 D6
Sussex St
 🛮 Barnoldswick BB18 ..196 B2
 Burnley BB11 ....128 B4
 🛐 Nelson BB9 ......170 E1

Sussex St continued
 Preston PR1 ....118 A1
Sussex Wlk 🛮 BB1 ...102 A4
Sutch La L40 ....26 B5
Sutcliffe St Bacup OL13 .71 C8
 Brierfield BB10 ......148 F3
 🛮 Burnley BB11 .....127 F6
 🛐 Chorley PR7 ....43 D7
Sutcliffe Terr BB1 ......82 F6
Sutherland Cl BB1 ....123 A7
Sutherland Rd
 Blackpool FY1 ....130 C8
 Heywood OL10 ....33 F1
Sutherland St BB11 ...171 C4
Sutherland View 🛮 FY1 130 C7
Sutton Ave
 Brierfield BB10 ......148 D2
 Tarleton PR4 ....57 A8
Sutton Cres BB5 ......125 F1
Sutton Dr PR2 ....95 D8
Sutton Gr PR6 ....61 F4
Sutton La Adlington PR6 .31 B8
 Tarleton PR4 ....56 F5
Sutton Pl FY1 ....130 C4
Sutton Rd L37 ....11 E1
Sutton St Blackburn BB2 .80 D8
 Weeton Camp PR4 ..132 E6
Sutton's La L37 ....11 E1
Swain Cl OL12 ....52 E1
Swain St BB9 ....148 C8
Swainbank St BB11 ...128 B5
Swaine St BB9 ....148 C8
Swainson St
 🛮 Blackpool FY1 ....130 C6
 Lytham St Anne's FY8 ..90 F3
Swainstead Raike BD24 236 E8
Swaledale LA2 ....211 B4
Swaledale Ave BB10 ..148 B4
Swalegate L31 ....5 C2
Swallow Ave 🛮 PR1 ...96 E4
Swallow Cl Blackpool FY3 131 B2
 Thornton FY5 ....176 A4
Swallow Dr
 Blackburn BB1 ......101 E6
 Bury BL9 ....33 B4
Swallow Field PR4 ......74 E3
Swallow Pk 🛐 BB1 ...127 C5
Swallow Wharf 🛮 LA1 .218 E1
Swallowfields
 Blackburn BB1 ......101 E8
 Cottam PR4 ....116 E5
Swallowfold PR2 ......139 D1
Swan Alley 🛮 L39 .....15 F5
Swan Delph L39 ....15 C2
Swan Dr FY5 ....175 F1
Swan Farm Cl BB3 ......81 F7
Swan La L39 ....5 F6
Swan Mdw BB7 ....189 D1
Swan Rd BL8 ....49 F2
Swan St Blackburn BB2 .101 E3
 Darwen BB3 ....65 B6
 Preston PR1 ....97 C8
Swan Yd 🛮 LA1 ......215 A7
Swanage Ave FY4 ......110 B6
Swanage Rd BB10 .....148 C1
Swanfield Ct BB8 .....172 A5
Swanfield Terr BB8 ....172 A5
Swanpool La L39 ....15 C2
Swansea St PR2 ....96 C8
Swansey La PR6 ....78 C1
Swarbrick Ave PR2 ...139 D1
Swarbrick Cl FY1 .....130 D7
Swarbrick Ct PR3 .....140 B7
Swarbrick St PR4 .....114 A4
Sweet Briar Cl OL12 ...52 E2
Sweet Briar La OL12 ...52 E2
Sweetclough Dr BB12 .126 F6
Swift Cl Blackburn BB1 .101 F5
 Blackpool FY3 ......131 B3
Swift Gdns LA3 ......212 F5
Swift's Fold WN8 ....8 D8
Swilkin La FY5 ....177 E6
Swill Brook La 🛮 PR1 ..97 C6
Swinburn Gr WN5 .....10 F1
Swinburne Cl BB5 ....104 E2
Swinden Hall Rd BB9 .170 E2
Swinden La BB8 ......171 A2
Swindon Ave 🛮 FY4 ..110 D8
Swindon St BB11 .....127 D5
Swinglehurst Cotts PR3 185 E3
Swinglehurst La PR3 .185 E3
Swinless St BB10 .....128 B8
Swinshaw Cl BB4 .....106 A2
Swinside PR4 ....116 D4
Swiss St BB5 ....103 F6
Swithemby St BL6 ......32 A4
Sword Meanygate PR4 .56 C6
Sycamore Ave
 Blackpool FY4 ....110 F5
 Burnley BB12 ....127 B7
 Euxton PR7 ....60 D3
 Garstang PR3 ....181 B8
 Nelson BB9 ....148 B7
Sycamore Bglws BB7 ..231 C3
Sycamore Cl
 Blackburn BB1 ......101 F8
 Burnley BB12 ....127 C6
 Fulwood PR2 ....118 C6
 Mawdesley L40 ....40 C2
 Rishton BB1 ....103 B8
Sycamore Cres
 Caton LA2 ....237 C3
 Clayton-le-M BB5 ....125 A5
 🛮 Rawtenstall BB4 ...85 F1
Sycamore Ct PR7 ......43 B5
Sycamore Dr
 Kirkham PR4 ....113 D4
 Middleworth Green PR1 ..96 E3

Sycamore Dr continued
 🛮 Skelmersdale WN8 .17 E2
Sycamore Gdns
 Foulridge BB8 ....194 D1
 Heysham LA3 ....212 E6
Sycamore Gr
 Accrington BB5 .....104 C3
 Darwen BB3 ....82 B2
 Formby L37 ....11 C1
 Lancaster LA1 ....214 D8
Sycamore Rd
 Bilsborrow PR3 .....159 A5
 Blackburn BB1 ......101 F8
 Caton LA2 ....237 C3
 Chorley PR6 ....61 D2
 Fulwood PR2 ....118 E2
Sycamore Rise
 Brierfield BB9 ......148 D5
 Foulridge BB8 ....194 D1
Sycamore Trad Est FY4 110 F5
Sycamore Way BB18 ..196 A1
Sycamore Wlk 🛮 BL6 ..32 E1
Syd Brook La PR5,L40 ..40 E7
Sydenham Terr OL12 ...52 D3
Sydney Ave BB7 ......144 D5
Sydney St Accrington BB5 104 C6
 🛮 Burnley BB11 .....127 F6
 Clayton-le-M BB5 ....125 A1
 Darwen BB3 ....65 B7
 Hoddlesden BB3 ......82 F1
 Lytham St Anne's FY8 .89 F6
Sydney Terr BB8 ......172 C3
Syke Hill 🛮 PR1 ....97 A7
Syke House La PR3 ...160 E4
Syke La OL12 ....52 F4
Syke Rd OL12 ....52 F4
Syke Side Dr BB5 ....125 E6
Syke St PR1 ....97 A7
Sykefield BB9 ....148 A5
Sykelands Ave LA2 ...219 D7
Sykelands Gr LA2 ....219 D7
Sykes Cl BB18 ....194 E8
Sykes Gr LA2 ....219 D7
Sykes St BL9 ....33 A3
Sylvan Dr BB11 ......127 B4
Sylvan Gr PR5 ....98 A2
Sylvan Pl LA3 ....212 E6
Sylvancroft PR2 ......117 A5
Sylvester St LA1 .....214 E7
Symonds Rd PR2 .....117 E3

T

Tabby Nook PR4 ....55 F2
Tabby's Nook
 Newburgh WN8 ....27 A1
 Skelmersdale WN8 ....18 A8
Taberner Cl WN6 ......29 F1
Tabley La PR4 ....116 E2
Tabor St BB12 ....127 D6
Tadema Gr BB11 .....127 F2
Tadlow Cl L37 ....11 C1
Tag Croft PR2 ....116 F5
Tag Farm Ct PR2 .....116 F5
Tag La PR2 ....117 A4
Talaton Ct PR9 ....54 A5
Talbot Ave 🛮 BB5 ....124 F2
Talbot Cl Clitheroe BB7 .166 F7
 Rawtenstall BB4 ......68 E8
Talbot Ct
 🛮 Blackpool FY4 ....130 B1
 🛐 Lytham St Anne's FY8 .90 A8
 Euxton PR7 ....60 D2
 Southport PR8 ....35 B6
Talbot Gr BL9 ....33 A6
Talbot Ho PR7 ....61 C1
Talbot Rd Accrington BB5 104 A8
 Blackpool FY1,FY3 ...130 C6
 Leyland PR25 ....76 C2
 Lytham St Anne's FY8 .91 C4
 Middleforth Green PR1 ..96 E5
 Preston PR1 ....96 D7
Talbot Row 🛮 PR7 ....60 D1
Talbot St Brierfield BB10 .148 F2
 Burnley BB11 ....128 B6
 Chipping PR3 ....185 E3
 Chorley PR6 ....61 E1
 Colne BB8 ....171 D6
 Fulwood PR2 ....117 D4
 Rishton BB1 ....124 C1
 Southport PR8 ....35 A6
Talbot Terr 🛮 FY1 .....91 B3
Tall Trees LA1 ....218 D4
Tamar Cl PR25 ....60 B7
Tamar St PR1 ....97 E8
Tamneys The WN8 .....17 F1
Tan Hill Dr LA1 ....218 D3
Tan House Cl WN8 .....27 C3
Tan House La WN8 ....27 C3
Tan Pit Cotts WN8 .....19 C4
Tan Yard La PR3 .....140 C8
Tan Yd PR3 ....140 C8
Tancaster WN8 ....17 E1
Tanfield Nook WN8 ....27 C2
Tanfields WN8 ....17 F1
Tanglewood PR2 .....118 B5
Tanhouse 🛮 LA2 ....211 A4
Tanhouse La PR6 ......61 F6
Tanhouse Rd WN8 ......9 E7
Tanner Barn BB5 ....85 B7
Tanner St 🛐 BB11 ...127 F6
Tanners Croft 🛮 BL0 ..50 B6
Tanners St BL0 ....50 B6
Tanners Way FY8 ......90 D7
Tannersmith La L40 ...40 F5
Tanpits La LA6 ....240 B7

Tanpits Rd BB5 ....103 F6
Tansley Ave PR7 ....42 D1
Tansley Cl BL6 ....32 C2
Tansy La PR3 ....206 A1
Tanterton Hall Rd PR2 .117 A6
Tanyard Cl PR7 ....42 A4
Tape St **2** BL0 ....50 B6
Taper St BL0 ....50 B6
Tapestry St BB2 ....101 D1
Tarbert Cres BB1 ....102 D4
Tarbet St LA1 ....215 A4
Tardy Gate Trad Ctr PR5 .77 A8
Tarleton Ave BB11 ....128 B4
Tarleton Com Prim Sch
    PR4 ....56 F8
Tarleton High Sch PR4 .57 A7
Tarleton Holy Trinity CE Prim
    Sch PR4 ....57 A5
Tarleton Lodge FY8 ....89 F5
Tarleton Mere Brow CE Prim
    Sch PR4 ....55 F2
Tarleton Rd PR9 ....36 A8
Tarleton St BB11 ....128 B4
Tarlscough La L40 ....38 D1
Tarlswood WN8 ....17 F1
Tarn Ave BB5 ....124 F4
Tarn Brook Cl BB5 ....125 F1
Tarn Brow L39 ....15 C3
Tarn Cl PR1 ....95 F4
Tarn Cotts LA5 ....221 C6
Tarn Ct FY7 ....198 D1
Tarn Hows Cl **1** PR7 .43 B5
Tarn La LA6 ....240 B6
Tarn Rd Formby L37 ....11 D3
    Thornton FY5 ....153 D7
Tarnacre Hall Bsns Pk
    PR3 ....180 D1
Tarnacre Hall Mews
    PR3 ....180 D1
Tarnacre La PR3 ....180 E2
Tarnacre View PR3 ....181 C6
Tarnbeck Dr L40 ....40 D2
Tarnbrick Ave PR4 ....93 C7
Tarnbrook Cl
    Carnforth LA5 ....223 C1
    Hest Bank LA5 ....220 F2
Tarnbrook Cotts PR3 .201 E5
Tarnbrook Dr FY3 ....131 A7
Tarnbrook Rd
    5 Heysham LA3 ....212 F8
    2 Lancaster LA1 ....218 B2
Tarnside FY4 ....131 B1
Tarnside Rd WN5 ....10 E6
Tarnsyke Rd LA1 ....218 B2
Tarnwater La LA2 ....210 E7
Tarnway Ave FY5 ....153 D8
Tarradale PR4 ....94 F1
Tarragon Dr FY2 ....152 F4
Tarry Barn La BB7 ....167 A3
Tarvin Cl Brierfield BB10 .148 F3
    Southport PR9 ....54 D5
Tasker St **13** BB5 ....104 C6
Taskers Croft BB7 ....144 F8
Tatham St FY7 ....198 C1
Tatham Fells CE Prim Sch
    LA2 ....239 C4
Tattersall Sq BB4 ....86 F3
Tattersall St
    5 Blackburn BB2 ....101 E4
    Haslingden BB4 ....85 B6
    Oswaldtwistle BB5 ....103 D4
    2 Padiham BB12 ....126 D8
Tatton St BB8 ....171 B3
Tauheedul-Islam Girls' High
    Sch BB1 ....101 E6
Taunton Rd BB2 ....101 B5
Taunton St
    8 Blackpool FY4 ....130 D1
    Preston PR1 ....118 D1
Tavistock Dr PR8 ....21 B6
Tavistock St BB9 ....170 F1
Tawd Rd WN8 ....9 C8
Tay St Burnley BB11 ....127 D5
    3 Preston PR1 ....96 D6
Taybank Ave FY4 ....110 D7
Taydale Cotts BB10 .148 E3
Taylor Ave Newchurch BB4 .86 F2
    Ormskirk L39 ....16 A5
Taylor Cl BB2 ....101 C3
Taylor Ct BB4 ....85 A3
Taylor Gr LA4 ....217 F6
Taylor Holme Ind Est
    OL13 ....70 B8
Taylor St
    Barnoldswick BB18 .....196 A2
    Blackburn BB2 ....101 D3
    Brierfield BB9 ....148 B6
    Burnley BB10 ....128 A8
    Bury BL9 ....33 A3
    Chorley PR7 ....43 B5
    Clitheroe BB7 ....166 F8
    Darwen BB3 ....65 A8
    Haslingden BB4 ....85 B6
    2 Horwich BL6 ....32 B3
    Preston PR1 ....96 B6
    6 Rawtenstall BB4 ....86 A3
    Rochdale OL12 ....52 F1
    Skelmersdale WN8 ....17 C1
    Whitworth OL12 ....52 D8
Taylor St W BB5 ....104 B6
Taylor's Bldgs BB6 ....143 D1
Taylor's Ind Est PR3 .201 E5
Taylor's La
    Fisher's Row PR3 ....201 D6
    Holmes PR4 ....56 A6
Taylor's Meanygate PR4 .56 A7
Taylors Cl FY5 ....153 C5
Taylors Pl **18** OL12 ....52 F1

Taymouth Rd **5** FY4 ....111 A6
Taywood Cl FY6 ....153 F4
Taywood Rd FY5 ....176 A4
Teak St BL9 ....33 D7
Teal Cl Blackburn BB1 .101 D8
    Leyland PR25 ....59 D7
    Ormskirk L39 ....15 C2
    Thornton FY5 ....176 A4
Teal Ct FY3 ....131 B6
Teal La FY4 ....90 E7
Teanlowe Ctr FY6 ....153 D3
Tears La WN8 ....17 F8
Teasel Wlk LA3 ....217 B2
Tebay Ave Cleveleys FY5 .175 D4
    Kirkham PR4 ....114 C5
Tebay Cl L31 ....5 F2
Tebay Ct LA1 ....218 C4
Tedder Ave Burnley BB12 127 B6
    Southport PR9 ....36 A7
Teenadore Ave **1** FY4 .110 E7
Tees Ct FY7 ....198 D2
Tees St PR1 ....118 C2
Teesdale **8** LA2 ....211 A4
Teesdale Ave FY2 ....130 D8
Teil Gn PR2 ....118 E6
Telford St Burnley BB12 .127 C7
    Horwich BL6 ....32 D2
Telletholme Ind Est L40 .25 B3
Temperance St **8** PR6 .43 E8
Temperance Terr OL13 .87 F1
Temple Cl **2** BB1 ....102 B4
Temple Ct **10** PR1 ....96 F7
Temple Dr BB1 ....102 B4
Temple St
    10 Blackpool FY1 ....130 B5
    Burnley BB11 ....128 B5
    Colne BB8 ....171 E6
    Nelson BB9 ....148 F8
Temple Way PR6 ....61 D3
Templegate WN6 ....29 F2
Templemartin **2** WN8 .17 F2
Templeton Cl BB3 ....82 A2
Ten Row LA2 ....209 D3
Tenby **2** WN8 ....17 E2
Tenby Cl BB1 ....101 E7
Tenby Gr **6** OL12 ....52 C1
Tenby Rd **7** PR1 ....97 A6
Tenby St OL12 ....52 C1
Tennis St BB10 ....128 A8
Tennyson Ave
    Chorley PR7 ....43 C6
    Lytham St Anne's FY8 .91 D4
    Oswaldtwistle BB5 ....103 C4
    Padiham BB12 ....126 E7
    Read BB12 ....145 D2
    Thornton FY5 ....176 A3
    Warton PR4 ....92 D6
Tennyson Cl LA5 ....221 A5
Tennyson Dr
    Longshaw WN5 ....10 D1
    Ormskirk L39 ....15 D6
Tennyson Mill Ct PR1 .118 D1
Tennyson Pl
    Bamber Bridge PR5 ....97 D2
    Great Harwood BB6 ....124 B4
Tennyson Rd
    Blackpool FY3 ....130 D1
    Colne BB8 ....171 D5
    Fleetwood FY7 ....199 A4
    Preston PR1 ....118 D1
Tennyson St
    Brierfield BB10 ....148 F3
    Burnley BB11 ....127 D5
    6 Hapton BB12 ....126 C4
Tensing Ave FY2 ....152 D5
Tensing Rd L31 ....5 D1
Tenterfield St
    23 Preston PR1 ....96 F8
    6 Rawtenstall BB4 ....69 F8
Tenterheads BB7 ....69 F7
Terance Rd **2** FY4 ....110 E8
Tern Gr LA3 ....212 F5
Terra Cotta Bldgs BB4 .107 A1
Terrace Row BB7 ....144 C4
Terrace St PR1 ....118 C1
Terrace The **7** LA2 ....239 B8
Terry St BB9 ....171 A2
Tetbury Cl **8** BB2 ....80 E8
Teven St **5** PR5 ....97 E1
Teversham WN8 ....17 E2
Teviot **4** WN8 ....17 E2
Teviot Ave FY7 ....198 D3
Tewkesbury **3** WN8 .17 E2
Tewkesbury Ave FY4 ....110 D5
Tewkesbury Cl BB5 ....104 E3
Tewkesbury Dr FY8 ....91 D5
Tewkesbury St BB2 ....101 B1
Thames Ave BB10 ....148 C3
Thames Dr WN5 ....10 F7
Thames Ho **8** PR1 ....97 D8
Thames Prim Sch FY4 .110 B7
Thames Rd FY4 ....110 B7
Thames St PR4 ....114 F2
Thane Row BB11 ....107 D7
Thanet WN8 ....17 E2
Thanet Lee Cl BB10 ....128 E1
Thealby Cl WN8 ....17 E2
Theatre St PR1 ....96 F7
Thelma St BL0 ....50 B6
Thermdale Cl **3** PR3 .181 B7
Thetis Rd LA1 ....214 C8
Thickrash Brow LA2 ....239 D7
Third Ave Blackpool FY4 .110 C7
    Bury BL9 ....33 D4
    Preesall Park FY6 ....200 C1
Thirlmere Ct LA1 ....218 F1
Thirlmere Ave
    Burnley BB10 ....148 A2

Thirlmere Ave continued
    Carleton FY6 ....153 C4
    Colne BB8 ....171 F6
    Fleetwood FY7 ....198 C1
    Formby L37 ....12 A2
    Haslingden BB4 ....68 C8
    Horwich BL6 ....32 C2
    Padiham BB12 ....146 C2
    Skelmersdale WN8 ....10 B7
Thirlmere Cl
    2 Accrington BB5 ....125 D1
    Adlington PR6 ....31 B8
    6 Blackburn BB1 ....101 F6
    Knott End-on-S FY6 ....199 F6
    Longton PR4 ....75 B8
    Maghull L31 ....5 F2
Thirlmere Dr Darwen BB3 82 C2
    Longridge PR3 ....139 F5
    Morecambe LA4 ....217 A4
    Southport PR8 ....21 B3
    Withnell Fold PR6 ....79 D2
Thirlmere Gr LA4 ....217 B4
Thirlmere Rd
    Blackpool FY4 ....110 C7
    Blackrod BL6 ....31 C3
    Burnley BB10 ....128 E5
    Chorley PR7 ....43 B6
    Hightown L38 ....3 A4
    Lancaster LA1 ....218 F2
    Preston PR1 ....118 F1
Thirlmere Way BB4 ....106 A1
Thirsk WN8 ....17 E2
Thirsk Gr FY1 ....130 D2
Thirsk Rd LA1 ....215 D4
Thistle Break LA3 ....213 A7
Thistle Cl Chorley PR6 .43 E8
    Cleveleys FY5 ....175 F5
    Hesketh Bank PR4 ....73 E4
Thistle Ct L40 ....25 F6
Thistle St **15** OL13 ....87 F2
Thistlecroft PR2 ....117 A5
Thistlemount Ave BB4 .86 F1
Thistleton Mews **3** PR9 .35 C8
Thistleton Rd Preston PR2 95 E8
    Thistleton PR4 ....155 C1
Thomas Gr LA4 ....217 B5
Thomas St
    Blackburn BB2 ....101 D4
    Brierfield BB9 ....148 A5
    Burnley BB11 ....128 A5
    Colne BB8 ....171 C4
    2 Cornholme OL14 ....109 C1
    7 Haslingden BB4 ....85 A3
    Nelson BB9 ....148 E7
    9 Oswaldtwistle BB5 ....103 D3
    4 Preston PR1 ....97 B7
    Whitworth OL12 ....71 D2
Thomas Weind PR3 ....181 C7
Thomason Fold BL7 ....48 D6
Thompson Ave L39 ....16 B5
Thompson Dr BL9 ....33 C3
Thompson St
    Blackburn BB2 ....101 D4
    Darwen BB3 ....65 B7
    Horwich BL6 ....32 A3
    8 Kirkham PR4 ....113 F6
    Padiham BB12 ....126 D7
    Preston PR1 ....118 C1
Thompson Street Ind Est
    BB2 ....101 C4
Thonock Rd LA4 ....217 D3
Thorburn Dr OL12 ....52 B7
Thorn Bank BB3 ....88 A2
Thorn Cres OL13 ....88 A2
Thorn Dr OL13 ....88 A2
Thorn Gdns OL13 ....88 A2
Thorn Gr Blackpool FY1 .130 D2
    Colne BB8 ....171 E6
Thorn Hill Cl BB1 ....102 A5
Thorn La PR7 ....140 B2
Thorn St Bacup OL13 ....88 A2
    Burnley BB10 ....128 A8
    Clitheroe BB7 ....166 D8
    Great Harwood BB6 ....124 D6
    Preston PR1 ....118 C1
    Ramsbottom BL0 ....50 C3
    Rawtenstall BB4 ....85 F5
    Sabden BB7 ....146 A2
Thorn View BL9 ....33 C3
Thornbank FY3 ....131 B7
Thornbank Dr PR3 ....181 D2
Thornbeck Ave L38 ....2 F1
Thornber **1** WN8 ....17 F2
Thornber Cl BB10 ....148 C1
Thornber Gr FY1 ....130 D3
Thornber St BB2 ....101 C3
Thornbridge Ave L40 ....25 E3
Thornbury WN8 ....17 F2
Thornby **3** WN8 ....17 F2
Thorncliffe Dr BB3 ....65 D8
Thorndale **4** WN8 ....17 F2
Thorne St BB9 ....171 A2
Thorney Bank St **7**
    BB11 ....127 F5
Thorneybank Ind Est
    BB11 ....126 C2
Thorneycroft Cl FY6 ....153 B5
Thorneyholme RC Prim Sch
    BB7 ....228 C1
Thorneyholme Rd BB5 .104 C8
Thorneyholme Sq BB12 .169 E5
Thorneylea OL12 ....71 D1
Thornfield Lancaster LA1 214 F5
    Much Hoole PR4 ....74 E3
Thornfield Ave
    Fulwood PR2 ....118 F3

Thornfield Ave continued
    Longridge PR3 ....140 A8
    Newchurch BB4 ....86 E1
    8 Rawtenstall BB4 ....69 F8
    Thornton FY5 ....176 A4
Thornfield Cvn Pk FY3 .131 D5
Thorngate PR1 ....96 B4
Thorngate Cl PR1 ....96 B4
Thornham Ct FY3 ....130 C5
Thornhill L39 ....6 B8
Thornhill Ave
    Knott End-on-S FY6 ....200 A5
    Rishton BB1 ....103 A8
Thornhill Cl
    Blackpool FY4 ....110 F5
    Ormskirk L39 ....6 B8
Thornhill Rd Chorley PR6 .61 E2
    Leyland PR25 ....59 D8
    Ramsbottom BL0 ....50 A1
Thornhill St BB12 ....127 A6
Thornlea BB12 ....52 B2
Thornleigh Cl **10** FY5 .176 A2
Thornleigh Dr LA6 ....240 C7
Thornley Ave BB1 ....102 C6
Thornley Pl PR2 ....119 A3
Thornley Rd PR2 ....119 A3
Thornpark Dr **3** PR2 .116 D1
Thorns Ave LA2 ....220 D1
Thorns The L31 ....5 B2
Thornthwaite Rd PR4 .116 D4
Thornton WN8 ....17 F2
Thornton Ave
    Fulwood PR2 ....117 B4
    Lytham St Anne's FY8 .90 B8
    Morecambe LA4 ....217 C6
Thornton Cl
    Accrington BB5 ....104 A8
    Blackburn BB2 ....81 F8
    Rufford L40 ....39 C4
Thornton Cleveleys Baines
    Endowed Prim Sch
    FY5 ....176 C1
Thornton Cleveleys Burn
    Naze Prim Sch FY5 ...176 B3
Thornton Cleveleys Manor
    Beach Prim Sch FY5 .175 D3
Thornton Cleveleys Red
    Marsh Sch FY5 ....176 A3
Thornton Cleveleys Royles
    Brook Prim Sch FY5 ...176 A1
Thornton Cres
    Burnley BB10 ....128 E5
    Morecambe LA4 ....217 C5
Thornton Ctr FY5 ....176 C1
Thornton Dr
    Coupe Green PR5 ....98 D4
    Leyland PR26 ....76 C4
Thornton Gate FY5 ....175 D4
Thornton Gr LA4 ....217 C5
Thornton Hall Mews
    FY5 ....153 E7
Thornton Hts BD23 ....197 A5
Thornton in Craven Com
    Prim Sch BD23 ....197 B6
Thornton La Ingleton LA6 242 F5
    Morecambe LA4 ....217 C6
Thornton Manor Ct
    BD23 ....197 A5
Thornton Pl FY5 ....176 A4
Thornton Rd
    Burnley BB10 ....128 E5
    Morecambe LA4 ....217 C6
    Southport PR9 ....35 F7
Thorntrees Ave
    Newsham PR3 ....137 B5
    Preston PR2 ....116 D1
Thornway Ave FY5 ....153 D8
Thornwood WN8 ....17 F2
Thornwood Cl
    5 Blackburn BB1 ....122 E1
    Lytham St Anne's FY8 .90 E4
Thornylea BB12 ....81 D7
Thorough Way PR3 ....203 D2
Thoroughfare The LA5 .223 D5
Thoroughgood Cl L40 ....25 C7
Thorpe WN8 ....17 F2
Thorpe Ave LA4 ....217 F4
Thorpe Cl PR1 ....117 F1
Thorpe St BL0 ....50 B5
Thrang Brow La LA5 .225 C6
Threagill La LA5 ....223 F5
Three Lane Ends PR6 .62 C4
Three Nooks PR5 ....78 C5
Three Oaks Cl L40 ....26 B2
Three Point Bsns Pk BB4 85 A2
Three Pools PR9 ....54 C3
Three Rivers Woodland Pk
    BB7 ....189 D7
Three Tuns La L37 ....11 F3
Three Turns PR3 ....142 A8
Threefields PR2 ....117 A5
Threlfall PR7 ....60 F2
Threlfall Rd FY1 ....130 D1
Threlfall St **1** PR2 ....117 C1
Threlfall's La PR7 ....53 F2
Threshers Ct PR3 ....207 C2
Threshfield Ave LA3 .212 F8
Thrimby Ct LA4 ....217 B4
Thrimby Pl LA4 ....217 B4
Thropps La PR4 ....75 D6
Throstle Cl BB12 ....128 A7
Throstle Gr LA2 ....218 D8
Throstle Mill OL13 ....87 C1
Throstle Nest La PR3 .203 C1
Throstle
    Blackburn BB2 ....101 C4
    7 Nelson BB9 ....170 E1
Throstle Way **1** FY5 .175 F1

Throstle Wlk LA2 ......218 D8
Throup Pl BB9 ....170 E2
Thrum Fold OL12 ....52 D3
Thrum Hall La
    Rochdale OL12 ....52 D3
    Rochdale OL12 ....52 E3
Thrush Dr BL9 ....33 D4
Thrush St OL12 ....52 C1
Thrushgill Dr LA2 ....219 D7
Thurcroft Dr WN8 ....17 E2
Thurland Cl LA4 ....217 A3
Thurland Mill Cotts LA6 241 D3
Thurnham Glasson Christ
    Church CE Prim Sch
    LA2 ....209 E4
Thurnham Mews **7** LA1 214 F7
Thurnham Rd PR2 ....95 E8
Thurnham St LA1 ....214 F7
Thursby Ave FY4 ....110 D6
Thursby Cl PR8 ....21 B3
Thursby Pl **13** BB9 ....170 E2
Thursby Rd Burnley BB10 148 C1
    Nelson BB9 ....170 F2
Thursby Sq BB10 ....128 A8
Thursden Ave BB10 .148 F3
Thursden Pl BB9 ....171 B1
Thursfield Ave FY4 ....110 E8
Thursfield Rd BB10 ....128 B5
Thursford Gr BL6 ....31 D1
Thursgill Ave LA4 ....217 C3
Thurston WN8 ....17 E2
Thurston Rd PR25 ....77 A1
Thurston St BB11 ....128 B6
Thwaite Brow La LA5 .221 B6
Thwaite La LA2 ....239 C5
Thwaites Cl BB1 ....102 D2
Thwaites Rd BB5 ....103 C3
Thwaites St BB5 ....103 C3
Thyme Cl FY2 ....152 F3
Tib St **8** BL0 ....50 B6
Tiber Ave BB11 ....127 C4
Tiber St PR1 ....97 B7
Tibicar Dr E LA3 ....216 D1
Tibicar Dr W LA3 ....216 D1
Tiger The PR25 ....76 D2
Tilbury Gr WN6 ....19 D7
Tilcroft WN8 ....17 E2
Timber Brook PR7 ....61 D2
Timber St
    Accrington BB5 ....104 C5
    Bacup OL13 ....87 C5
    Brierfield BB9 ....148 B6
Timberhurst BL9 ....33 D2
Timbrills Ave BB7 ....145 F8
Timms Cl L37 ....11 F5
Timms La L37 ....11 F5
Tinacre Dr E LA3 ....216 D1
Tinckler's La PR7 ....41 A6
Tinedale View BB12 .146 D1
Tinker's La LA2 ....226 B7
Tinkerfield PR2 ....117 C1
Tinklers La BB7 ....229 E7
Tinline St BL9 ....33 A2
Tinniswood PR2 ....117 B1
Tinsley Ave PR8 ....35 E3
Tinsley's La
    Out Rawcliffe PR3 ....178 D4
    Southport PR8 ....36 A1
Tintagel WN8 ....17 E2
Tintagell Cl BB2 ....80 C7
Tintern Ave Chorley PR7 .43 D5
    Rochdale OL12 ....52 E2
Tintern Cl
    Accrington BB5 ....104 C2
    Read BB12 ....145 D1
Tintern Cres BB1 ....102 B8
Tintern Dr L37 ....12 B2
Tippet Cl BB2 ....102 A1
Titan Way PR26 ....76 B2
Tithe Barn La
    Knowley PR6 ....62 A4
    Runshaw Moor PR25,PR7 .59 F5
    Scorton PR3 ....204 E5
Tithebarn Gate FY6 ....153 D4
Tithebarn Hill LA2 ....209 E5
Tithebarn Pl FY6 ....153 D4
Tithebarn Rd PR8 ....35 E6
Tithebarn St
    Poulton-le-F FY6 ....153 D4
    6 Preston PR1 ....97 A7
    Preston PR1 ....97 A8
    Skelmersdale WN8 ....10 B7
Tittrington Brow BB7 .229 C2
Tiverton Ave WN8 ....17 E2
Tiverton Cl PR2 ....117 F8
Tiverton Dr Blackburn BB2 81 C8
    Brierfield BB10 ....148 F3
Tockholes CE Prim Sch
    BB3 ....81 A3
Tockholes Rd Darwen BB3 81 F2
    Tockholes BB3 ....81 A3
Tod Holes La BD23 ....236 E4
Todd Carr Rd BB4 ....86 F1
Todd Hall Rd BB4 ....84 F4
Todd La N PR5 ....97 C2
Todd La S PR5 ....77 C8
Todd's La PR5 ....55 A6
Todmorden Old Rd OL13 .88 B5
Todmorden Rd
    Bacup OL13 ....88 A4
    Burnley BB11 ....128 B3
    Cockden BB10 ....149 B1
    Lytham St Anne's FY8 .89 C8
Toll Bar Bsns Pk OL13 .70 C8
Toll Bar Cres LA1 ....214 F3

Toll Bar Ct LA6 ....240 C7
Tollgate PR1 ....96 E4
Tollgate Cres L40 ......25 C2
Tollgate Rd L40 ....25 B3
Tolsey Dr PR4 ....95 D2
Tom Benson Way PR2,
PR4 ....116 F4
Tom La BB4 ....86 F2
Tomlinson Rd
Heysham LA3 ....212 F6
Leyland PR25 ....76 F2
Preston PR2 ....117 C2
Tomlinson St BL6 ....32 B3
Tonacliffe Prim Sch
OL12 ....52 C6
Tonacliffe Rd OL12 .....52 C6
Tonacliffe Terr OL12 ...52 C7
Tonacliffe Way OL12 ....52 C6
Tong End OL12 ....71 C2
Tong Ho **20** OL13 ....88 A3
Tong La Bacup OL13 .....88 B2
Whitworth OL12 ....71 D1
Tongbarn WN8 ....17 C2
Tongues La FY6 ....200 C6
Tontine WN5 ....10 C5
Tontine Rd WN5,WN8 .....10 C5
Tontine St BB1 ....101 E5
Toogood La WN6 ....28 D6
Tootell St PR7 ....43 B6
Tootle La L40 ....39 A3
Tootle Rd PR3 ....140 B8
Top Acre PR4 ....95 C1
Top Acre Rd WN8 ....9 C7
Top Barn La BB4 ....86 E1
Top Locks L40 ....26 A4
Top o' th' Croft BB2 ...81 D8
Top of Fawna Rd PR3 ...163 D1
Top Of Heap OL10 ....33 F2
Top of Wallsuches BL6 ..32 F4
Top Row PR6 ....145 F8
Topaz St BB1 ....122 F2
Topaz Way PR6 ....43 E6
Topiary Gdns PR3 ......181 D4
Topping Fold Rd BL9 ....33 C3
Topping St Blackpool FY1 130 B5
Bury BL9 ....33 A3
Toppings The PR3 ......181 C6
Tor Ave BL8 ....49 F2
Tor End Rd BB4 ....67 F6
Tor Hey Mews BL8 ....49 F2
Tor View Haslingden BB4 .85 C1
Rawtenstall BB4 ....86 A1
Tor View Rd BB4 ....85 C1
Tor View Sch BB4 .....68 D8
Torcross Cl PR9 ....54 A5
Tormore Cl PR6 ....62 A3
Toronto Ave
Blackpool FY3 ....152 E3
Fleetwood FY7 ....198 E2
Toronto Rd BB2 ....101 C8
Torquay Ave
Blackpool FY3 ....131 A2
Brierfield BB10 ....148 D2
Torra Barn Cl BL7 ......47 E3
Torrentum Cl FY5 ......176 C1
Torridon Cl BB2 ....100 F1
Torrisholme Cty Prim Sch
LA4 ....217 F6
Torrisholme Rd LA1 ....218 B3
Torrisholme Sq **8** LA4 217 F6
Torside Gr FY6 ....153 B3
Torsway Ave FY3 ....130 F6
Torver Cl BB12 ....127 B8
Totnes Cl FY6 ....153 C5
Totnes Dr PR9 ....54 A5
Tottenham Rd BB3 ....81 F6
Tottington Rd BL7,BL8 ..48 F2
Tottleworth BB6 ....124 C3
Tottleworth Rd BB1 ....124 C2
Toulmin Cl PR3 ....181 D4
Tow Scar Rd LA6 ....242 F6
Towbreck Gdns FY6 .....131 B8
Ramsbottom BL0 ....50 A5
Tower Bldgs **10** PR9 ....35 C8
Tower Cl FY5 ....176 A4
Tower Cotts **3** LA3 ....212 F4
Tower Ct Chapeltown BL7 .48 C4
Lancaster LA1 ....214 F7
Tower Dene Prep Sch
PR9 ....53 F2
Tower End L37 ....11 C5
Tower Gn PR2 ....117 F2
Tower Hill Clitheroe BB7 189 F1
Ormskirk L39 ....16 A5
Tower Hill Rd WN8 ......10 B6
Tower La PR2 ....117 F7
Tower Nook WN8 ....10 A5
Tower Rd Blackburn BB2 100 E2
Darwen BB3 ....65 B8
Tower St **13** Bacup OL13 .87 F2
Blackpool FY5 ....130 B5
Chapeltown BL7 ....48 C4
Cornholme OL14 ....109 A1
Oswaldtwistle BB5 ....103 C5
Tower View Belthorn BB1 .83 A5
Blackpool FY2 ....152 D2
Blackrod BL6 ....31 C3
Darwen BB3 ....82 C1
Higher Penwortham PR1 ..96 C7
Towers Ave L31 ....5 C2
Towers Ct BB2 ....101 B3
Town Brook Ho **5** PR1 .117 E1
Town Brow PR25 ....77 F2

Town End
Bolton-le-S LA5 ....221 A3
Kirkham PR4 ....114 A5
Slaidburn BB7 ....229 C7
3 Thornton FY5 ......176 A2
Town End Cl L39 ....15 D4
Town Gate BB6 ....124 C5
Town Green Ct L39 ......6 C8
Town Green La L39 ......6 C8
Town Green Sta L39 .....6 C8
Town Hall Sq **8** BB6 ...124 C5
Town Hall St
16 Blackburn BB2 .....101 E5
9 Great Harwood BB6 ..124 C5
Town Head BB18 ....196 A1
Town Hill Bank BB12 ...146 D1
Town House Rd BB9 .....149 B8
Town La Coppull PR7 ....42 C1
Heskin Green PR7 ......41 C2
Much Hoole PR4 ....74 C1
Southport PR8 ....35 E3
Whittle-le-W PR6 ......61 D6
Town Lane (Kew) PR8 ....35 E3
Town View BB1 ....101 F4
Town Wlk BB1 ....101 F4
Towneley Ave
Blackpool FY4 ....110 E8
Huncoat BB5 ....125 F2
Towneley Cl LA1 ......214 D7
Towneley Hall (Art Gal &
Mus)★ BB11 ....128 C2
Towneley High Sch
BB11 ....128 C4
Towneley Ho PR3 ......140 A7
Towneley Par PR3 .....140 A7
Towneley Rd PR3 ......140 A7
Towneley Row PR3 .....140 A7
Towneley St BB10 .....148 B1
Townfield Ave BB10 ...128 F6
Townfield Cl PR4 ......74 F7
Townfield La LA2 .....218 C7
Townfields **1** BB11 ...128 B5
Towngate Eccleston PR7 .41 B7
Foulridge BB8 ....194 D1
Leyland PR25 ....59 F1
Leyland PR25 ....60 A8
Leyland PR25 ....77 A1
Townshouse Sch BB9 ..171 C1
Townlea Cl PR1 ....96 A3
Townley La PR1 ....95 D4
Townley St Brierfield BB9 148 B5
Brierfield,Harle Syke BB10 148 F3
Chorley PR6 ....43 D7
Colne BB8 ....171 E6
Morecambe LA4 ....217 B6
Townsend St
Haslingden BB4 ....85 A3
Rawtenstall BB4 ....69 F8
Townsfield LA5 ....224 C4
Townshill Wlk PR4 ....114 A6
Townsley St BB9 ......148 E6
*Townsmoor Ret Pk **8***
BB2 ....101 E3
Townsway PR5 ....77 C8
Towpath Wlk **2** LA5 ...223 D1
Toxhead Cl BL6 ....32 A3
Toy & Teddy Bear Mus of
Childhood★ FY8 ....89 D7
Tracks La WN5 ....10 D3
Trafalgar Cl PR2 .....117 D3
Trafalgar Ct PR8 ......34 F3
*Trafalgar Mall **3** BB9 148 E8*
Trafalgar Rd
Blackpool FY1 ....130 B2
Lancaster LA1 ....215 A6
Southport PR8 ....34 E3
Trafalgar St
Burnley BB11 ....127 F5
Chorley PR6 ....61 C1
Lytham St Anne's FY8 ..89 F7
Trafalgar Wharf PR2 ...96 B8
Trafford Gdns BB7 ....166 C4
Trafford St PR1 ......117 E2
Tramway La PR5 ....78 B6
Tranmere Ave LA3 .....216 D1
Tranmere Cres LA3 ....216 D1
Tranmere Rd FY4 ......130 E1
Tranmoor PR4 ....116 D1
Trans Brittania Enterprise Est
BB11 ....127 B3
Trap Hill L37 ....11 C2
Trapp La BB12 ....145 F2
Trash La Rimington BB7 .231 B1
Tockholes BB3 ....81 B2
Travellers Ct BB7 ....231 C3
Travers Lodge **8** PR2 .118 F4
Travers Pl PR2 ....96 C8
Travers St BL6 ....32 C1
Travis St BB10 ....128 A8
Trawden Cl BB5 ....104 C4
Trawden Cres PR2 .....118 E4
Trawden Forest Prim Sch
BB8 ....172 C2
Trawden Rd BB8 ....172 B4
Traylen Way OL12 ......52 A1
Treales CE Prim Sch
PR4 ....134 E2
Treales Rd PR4 ....115 B6
Trecastle Rd L33 ......1 A4
Tredgold St BL6 ....32 C2
Treen Cl PR9 ....54 B6
Treesdale Cl PR8 ......34 F4
Treetop Villas PR9 ....53 F4
Treetops Ave BL0 ......50 A3
Trefoil Cl FY5 ....176 A5
Tremellen St BB5 .....104 A6
*Trengrove St **7** OL12 ..52 C1*

Trent Ave L31 ....5 F2
Trent Cl
Burscough Bridge L40 ...25 F5
Morecambe LA3 ....217 F2
3 Thornton FY5 ......176 A2
Trent Rd Blackpool FY4 110 B7
Nelson BB9 ....149 A8
Trent St Longridge PR3 139 F7
Lytham St Anne's FY8 ...91 D3
Tresco Cl BB2 ....101 B1
Tretower Way FY5 .....176 D2
Trevarrick Ct BL6 .....32 E2
Trevelyan Dr WN5 ......10 D1
Trevor Dr BB1 ....101 F7
Trevor Rd Burscough L40 .25 E4
Southport PR8 ....21 C4
Triangle The
Accrington,Hillock Vale
BB5 ....104 E8
Fulwood PR2 ....117 E4
Trigg La PR6 ....62 D5
Trigge Ho PR7 ....61 C2
Trillium Way BB3 ......82 A7
Trinity & St Michael's CE
Prim Sch PR9 ....58 C2
Trinity Cl Brierfield BB9 148 C5
Freckleton PR4 ....93 B7
Padiham BB12 ....126 D6
Trinity Ct **3** BB1 ....101 F6
Trinity Fold **20** PR1 ..96 F8
Trinity Gdns
Southport PR8 ....35 A6
Thornton FY5 ....176 A3
Trinity Gn BL0 ....50 B2
Trinity Mews PR9 ......35 C7
Trinity Pl **24** PR1 ....96 F8
Trinity Rd PR7 ....43 B7
Trinity Sch WN8 ......17 F1
Trinity St **15** Bacup OL13 ..70 C8
Blackburn BB1 ....101 F6
Oswaldtwistle BB5 ....103 D3
Trinity Student Village
PR1 ....96 F8
Trinity Twrs **6** BB11 ..127 E6
Trinity Wlks PR4 ......57 A5
Trinket La LA2 ....238 E6
Tristan Ave PR4 ....75 A4
Troon Ave Blackburn BB1 102 C3
Thornton FY5 ....153 D8
Troon Cl PR7 ....60 D4
Troon Ct PR1 ....96 A6
Trough of Bowland★
BB7 ....227 D3
Trough Rd BB7 ....228 B5
Troughton Cres **1** FY4 110 E8
Trout Beck BB5 ....124 F4
Trout St **8** Burnley BB10 128 A8
Preston PR1 ....97 C7
Troutbeck Ave
Fleetwood FY7 ....198 D2
Forton PR3 ....207 B3
Maghull L31 ....5 E2
Troutbeck Cl
Burnley BB12 ....127 B8
Hawkshaw BL8 ....49 B2
Troutbeck Cres FY4 ...111 A4
Troutbeck Dr BL0 ......50 C7
Troutbeck Pl PR2 .....118 C5
Troutbeck Rd Chorley PR7 43 B5
Lancaster LA1 ....218 C1
Lytham St Anne's FY8 ..110 D1
Trower St PR1 ....97 B6
Troy St BB1 ....101 F7
Trumacar Com Prim Sch
LA3 ....212 F6
Trumacar La LA3 ......212 E5
Trumacar Terr LA3 ....212 F5
Truman Ave LA1 ....214 C7
Trumley Ct LA3 ....217 A2
Trundle Pie La L39 ....14 C6
Trunnah Gdns FY5 .....176 B3
Trunnah Rd FY5 ....176 B3
Truro Ave PR9 ....54 B5
Truro Pl **8** PR1 ......118 C1
Truro St **7** PR1 .....130 D1
Truscott Rd L40 ....25 D4
Tucker Hill BB7 ......189 E1
Tucker's Hill Brow WN2 .31 B1
Tudor Ave Preston PR1 .118 C1
Preston,Lea PR2 ......116 D1
Tudor Cl Carleton FY6 153 A4
1 Cleveleys FY5 .....175 F1
Darwen BB3 ....82 A2
Langho BB6 ....143 D1
Preston PR2 ....116 D1
Tudor Croft PR5 ....77 C7
Tudor Ct
Lytham St Anne's FY8 ...89 D8
Ormskirk L39 ....15 F6
Tudor Dr PR4 ....114 B2
Tudor Gate FY8 ....90 B8
Tudor Gdns L38 ....2 F4
Tudor Gr **2** LA4 .....217 D6
Tudor Mans PR3 ....34 F6
Tudor Pl FY4 ....110 B6
Tudor Rd
Lytham St Anne's FY8 ...89 D8
Southport PR8 ....21 B6
Tudor St FY25 ....76 F2
Tulip Gr OL12 ....52 E3
Tulketh Ave PR2 ......117 B1
Tulketh Brow PR2 .....117 C1
Tulketh Com Sports Coll
PR2 ....117 B4
Tulketh Cres PR2 .....117 C1
Tulketh Rd PR2 ....117 B1
Tulketh St PR8 ....35 F7
Tunbridge Pl **7** PR1 .118 D1
Tunbridge St **4** PR1 ..118 D1

Tunbrook Ave PR2 .....139 E1
Tunley Holme PR5 ......78 C5
Tunley La WN6 ....28 E5
Tunley Moss WN6 ......28 A8
Tunnel St Burnley BB12 127 D6
5 Darwen BB3 ....65 C7
Tunstall Dr BB5 ......125 B1
Tunstall Ho **10** LA1 ..215 A3
Tunstall St LA4 ......217 A5
Tunstead Ave BB12 ...125 E8
Tunstead Cres OL13 ...87 C1
Tunstead La Bacup OL13 .70 B8
Rawtenstall BB4,OL13 ..87 B1
Tunstead Mill Terr **3**
OL13 ....70 B8
Tunstead Rd OL13 .....87 C1
Tunstill Fold BB12 ...169 F1
Tunstill St BB10 .....148 B1
Turbary Rd LA6 ....242 E7
Turbary The PR2 ......117 C3
Turf Mdw BB4 ....106 A2
Turf Moor Football Gd
(Burnley FC) BB10 ....128 B6
Turf St BB11 ....128 B6
Turflands PR26 ....58 B1
Turkey Red Ind Est BB5 .84 F8
Turkey St Accrington BB5 104 D7
Out Rawcliffe PR3 ....178 A1
Turks Head Yd **22** PR1 .97 A7
Turn La BB3 ....64 F8
Turn Rd BL0 ....50 E8
Turnacre L37 ....12 B6
Turnberry WN8 ....17 D2
Turnberry Ave FY5 ...153 D2
Turnberry Cl
Kirkham PR4 ....114 A4
Morecambe LA4 ....217 D6
Turnberry Way PR9 ....54 D5
Turnbridge Rd L31 .....5 C3
Turnbury Cl PR7 ....60 D4
Turncroft Rd BB3 .....65 B8
Turner Ave PR5 ....77 A7
Turner Fold BB12 ....145 D3
Turner Rd BB9 ....148 B1
Turner St **4** Bacup OL13 70 C8
Clitheroe BB7 ....166 E7
3 Preston PR1 ....118 A1
Rochdale OL12 ....52 C1
Turner's Pl OL12 .....52 E3
Turnerford Cl BL7 ....47 E1
*Turney Crook Mews **9**
BB8 ....171 D5
Turnfield PR2 ....116 F6
Turning La PR8 ....36 A1
Turnpike BB4 ....86 F1
Turnpike Fold OL12 ..218 D5
Turnpike Gr BB5 .....103 C5
Turnpike Rd L39 ......15 A2
Turnpike The PR2 ....117 D6
Turnstone FY3 ....131 B6
Turpin Green La PR25 ..77 B1
Turstall Cotts LA2 ..237 B3
Turton & Edgworth
CE/Methodist Prim Sch
BL7 ....48 D5
Turton Belmont Com Prim
Sch BL7 ....46 C5
Turton Dr PR6 ....61 E1
Turton Gr BB10 ......128 D6
Turton Hollow Rd BB4 ..49 B1
Turton Rd BL8 ....49 B1
Turton Twr★ BL7 ......48 C3
Tuscan Ave BB11 .....127 C5
Tuscany Gr BB6 ......143 C6
Tuson Croft PR4 ......74 F8
Tuson Dr PR2 ....96 E8
Tuson Ho **2** PR1 .....96 E8
Tustin Ct PR1 ....96 C8
Tuxbury Dr FY5 ......153 D8
Tuxford Ct **1** FY8 ...90 D6
Tuxford Rd FY8 ....90 D6
Tweed St Blackburn BB2 .81 D8
4 High Bentham LA2 .239 D8
5 Lytham St Anne's FY8 .89 E6
Nelson BB9 ....149 A8
Tweed Street Ct **3** LA2 239 D8
Tweedys Ct PR3 ......185 C4
Twemlow Par
Heysham LA3 ....212 F8
Morecambe LA3 ....216 D1
Twenty Acre La PR4 ...75 B1
Twickenham Pl **4** FY8 .90 D6
Twig La L31 ....5 E5
Twin Lakes Ind Est PR26 58 A3
Twine Wlk LA6 ....242 C3
Twinegate OL12 ....52 E3
Twist Moor La PR6 ....63 B8
Twistfield Cl PR8 .....34 F5
Twiston La BB7 ......191 D5
Twitter La BB7 ....189 A3
Two Acre La PR1 ......96 C1
Two Brooks La BL8 ....49 B2
Two Gates Dr BB3 .....82 B2
Two Gates Wlk BB3 ...82 B2
Two Laws Rd BD22 ...174 C1
Two Saints Pl L39 ....15 E5
Twyford Ct L31 ....5 E1
Twyn Ghyll Cvn Site
BB7 ....231 B6
Tyldesley Rd FY1 ....130 B3
Tyne Ave FY3 ....130 D4
Tyne Cl FY5 ....175 E5
Tyne St
1 Bamber Bridge PR5 ..97 F1
4 Preston PR1 ....96 D6
Tynedale Pl FY3 .....153 A1
Tynedale Rd FY3 .....153 B1

Tynwald Rd BB2 ....101 F8
Tyrer Rd L39 ....15 F7
Tyrer's Ave L31 ....5 B5
Tyrers Cl L37 ....11 F2
Tyrone Ave FY2 ......152 D2
Tyseley Gr BB18 .....197 A1
Tythebarn St BB3 ......82 B1

U

Udale Pl **1** LA1 .....218 C2
Uggle La LA1 ....214 F3
Uldale Cl Nelson BB9 .148 E6
Southport PR8 ....21 B3
Ullswater Ave
Accrington BB5 ....125 D1
Fleetwood FY7 ....175 D8
Morecambe LA4 ......217 D4
Orrell WN5 ....10 D7
Rochdale OL12 ....52 C1
Thornton FY5 ....176 B1
Ullswater Cl
Blackburn BB1 ....101 F6
Hambleton FY6 ......177 C2
3 Rishton BB1 ....124 A1
Ullswater Cres
Carnforth LA5 ....221 E8
Thornton FY5 ....176 B1
Ullswater Rd
Blackpool FY4 ....110 C7
Burnley BB10 ....128 F5
Chorley PR7 ....43 B6
Fulwood PR2 ....118 C4
Lancaster LA1 ....215 A8
Ullswater Way BB4 ...106 A1
Ulnes Walton La PR26 .59 A6
Ulpha Cl BB12 ....127 B8
Ulster Cl LA1 ....215 B5
Ulster St BB11 ......127 D5
Ulverston Cl
Blackburn BB2 ....102 A1
Maghull L31 ....5 E2
Ulverston Cres FY8 ...90 C7
Ulverston Dr BB1 ....124 A1
Under Billinge La BB2 100 F4
Underbank Cl **3** OL13 .87 F3
Underbank Ho **1** OL13 .87 F3
Underbank Rd
Haslingden BB4 ....84 F3
Rising Bridge BB5 ....85 A7
Thornton FY5 ....176 F1
Underbank Way **2** BB4 .85 A3
Underley St BB10 ....148 C3
Underwood PR2 ......117 C3
Unicon Pk BB4 ....84 F3
Union Ct **13** OL13 ....70 C8
Union La PR3 ....178 C7
Union Pas **6** PR4 ...114 A5
Union Rd
Oswaldtwistle BB5 ...103 D3
Rawtenstall BB4 ......85 D2
Union St Accrington BB5 104 B6
Bacup OL13 ....87 F2
Bacup,Stacksteads OL13 .70 C8
Blackburn BB2 ....101 E3
Brierfield BB9 ......148 B5
Chorley PR7 ....43 C8
Clitheroe BB7 ....166 C8
Colne BB8 ....171 E5
Darwen BB3 ....82 A1
Egerton BL7 ....47 D2
Haslingden BB4 ....85 A3
Morecambe LA4 ......217 A5
10 Preston PR1 ....96 F8
Ramsbottom BL0 ......50 C6
Rawtenstall BB4 ......86 A3
Southport PR9 ....35 C8
Whittle-le-W PR6 .....61 C8
Whitworth OL12 ....52 C6
Union Terr
Clow Bridge BB4 .....106 A4
Rawtenstall BB4 ......86 B2
Unit Rd PR8 ....21 D5
Unity St
3 Barnoldswick BB18 196 C2
Blackburn BB2 ....101 E2
Kelbrook BB18 ......195 A6
Unity Trad Est BB2 ...101 D4
Unity Way BB4 ....85 F3
Univ of Central Lancashire
PR1 ....96 E8
Univ of Central Lancashire
Avenham Bldg PR1 ....97 A6
Univ of Lancaster LA1 211 B7
Unsworth Ave FY6 ...200 A4
Unsworth St OL13 .....70 D7
Up Brooks BB7 ....190 A1
Up Holland High Sch
WN5 ....10 C4
Up-Brooks Ind Est BB7 190 A1
Upholland Rd WN5 .....10 D2
Upholland Sta WN8 ....9 F4
Uplands Chase PR2 ...117 B6
Uplands Dr BB12 ....147 D7
Upper Ashmount BB4 ..86 C1
Upper Aughton Rd PR8 .35 B4
Upper Cliffe (Bersham Dr)
BB6 ....124 C6
Upper George St **22** OL12 52 F1
Upper Hill Way BB18 .194 B7
Upper Lune St FY7 ...199 B5
Upper Mead BL7 ......47 F1
Upper Westby St FY8 ..91 A3
Upphall La LA6 ......240 C4
Uppingham WN8 ....17 D1
Uppingham Dr BL0 ....50 B7
Upton Ave PR8 ....21 B6

Upton Barn L31 5 C2
Upwood Cl FY2 152 E5
Urban View PR6 62 F8
Ushers Mdw LA1 214 E7
Usk Ave FY5 176 D2

V

Vale Ave BL6 32 A3
Vale Cl WN6 19 E8
Vale Coppice Horwich BL6 32 A3
Ramsbottom BL0 50 C3
Vale Cotts BL6 31 F2
Vale Cres PR8 21 C2
Vale Croft WN8 10 A6
Vale Ct BB5 125 F1
Vale Gr L32 1 A1
Vale House Cl BB7 144 C5
Vale La L40 17 F5
Vale Rd LA1 218 C3
Vale Royal PR4 114 C5
Vale St Bacup OL13 88 A3
Blackburn BB2 101 E2
Darwen BB3 81 F2
Haslingden BB4 85 B4
Turton Bottoms BL7 48 D4
Vale Terr Calder Vale PR3 182 E8
Newchurch BB4 86 F3
Vale The
Appley Bridge WN6 19 D8
Fulwood PR2 117 F5
Valentia Rd FY2 152 D3
Valentines La PR2,PR4 116 E4
Valentines Mdw PR4 116 E4
Valeway Ave FY5 152 D8
Valiants Shireworld Equestrian Ctr PR3 179 A2
Valley Cl BB9 171 A1
Valley Ctr The 4 BB4 86 A2
Valley Dr
Barnoldswick BB18 196 D4
Padiham BB12 126 D8
Valley Gdns
2 Earby BB18 197 B2
Padiham BB11 126 F4
Valley Mill Ct BB8 172 E6
Valley Rd
Barnoldswick BB18 196 C2
Earby BB18 197 B2
Higher Penwortham PR1 96 D5
Hoghton PR5 99 F3
Longridge PR3 140 C7
Wilpshire BB1 122 F5
Valley St BB11 127 B4
Valley Terr BB12 145 E1
Valley View
Bamber Bridge PR5 97 A3
Chorley PR6 43 E7
Fulwood PR2 118 A4
Millgate OL12 71 D4
Valligates BB1 102 B7
Vance Rd FY1 130 B4
Vancouver Cres BB2 101 C8
Vandyck Ave BB11 127 E2
Vardon Rd BB2 101 B2
Varley St Colne BB8 171 F6
2 Darwen BB3 82 A1
Preston PR1 118 A2
Varlian Cl L40 16 C3
Vaughan Cl L37 11 D4
Vaughan Rd PR8 35 B4
Vaughan St BB9 148 F7
Vauxhall St BB2 101 B3
Vauze Ave BL6 31 D1
Vauze House Cl BL6 31 D2
Veevers St Brierfield BB9 148 A6
7 Burnley BB11 127 F6
Padiham BB12 126 D8
Velvet St BB2 81 D8
Venables Ave BB8 171 F6
Venice Ave BB11 127 C4
Venice St BB11 127 D5
Ventnor Pl PR2 117 A4
Ventnor Rd
Blackpool FY4 110 B6
1 Chorley PR7 43 B6
Haslingden BB4 85 C1
Venture Ct BB5 125 D5
Venture Rd FY7 176 A6
Venture St 19 OL13 88 A3
Verax St OL13 87 F1
Verbena Cl BB3 82 A7
Verbena Dr FY6 199 F6
Vermont Gr FY5 152 E8
Verna St 15 BL0 50 C6
Vernon Ave
Blackpool FY3 130 E3
Warton PR4 92 E6
Vernon Cres LA2 211 A3
Vernon Ct
4 Galgate LA2 211 A4
Southport PR8 35 D5
Vernon Lodge FY8 89 F5
Vernon Pk 3 LA2 211 A4
Vernon Rd
Laneshaw Bridge BB8 172 D6
Lytham St Anne's FY8 110 E1
Ramsbottom BL8 50 A1
Southport PR9 36 A8
Vernon St Blackburn BB2 101 E4
Darwen BB3 82 B1
Nelson BB9 148 E7
Preston PR1 117 F1
Verona Ave BB11 127 C5
Verona Ct 6 FY5 176 A2
Veronica St BB3 81 E4
Verulam Rd PR9 54 B3
Vesta St 6 BL0 50 B6
Vevey St PR25 77 A1
Viaduct Rd PR5 99 F2
Vicar La LA6 241 C2
Vicar St
5 Blackburn BB1 101 F5
Great Harwood BB6 124 C4
Vicarage Ave
5 Burnley BB12 126 B8
Caton LA2 237 C3
Cleveleys FY5 175 D3
Vicarage Cl Adlington PR6 31 A8
Burton-in-K LA6 240 C7
Euxton PR7 60 D3
Formby L37 11 D4
Fulwood PR2 117 F4
Lytham St Anne's FY8 89 F7
Morecambe LA3 217 C2
Ormskirk L40 16 B3
Wrea Green PR4 113 B4
Vicarage Dr BB3 65 C8
Vicarage Fold BB7 144 F7
Vicarage Gdns L40 25 D4
Vicarage La
Accrington BB5 104 E1
Banks PR9 54 F7
Blackpool FY4 130 E1
Burton-in-K LA6 240 C7
Churchtown PR3 181 A2
Fulwood PR2 117 F4
Newton-w-S PR4 115 A3
Ormskirk L40 16 C3
Samlesbury PR5 119 E1
Wilpshire BB1 122 F6
Rawtenstall BB4 85 F2
Vicarage Rd
Barnoldswick BB18 196 C3
Blackrod BL6 31 D2
Formby L37 11 D4
Kelbrook BB18 195 A6
Nelson BB9 148 D7
Orrell WN5 10 D4
Poulton-le-F FY6 153 E3
Vicarage Rd W BL6 31 C2
Vicarage St 3 PR6 61 D1
Vicarage Wlk L39 15 E5
Vicarsfields Rd PR25 60 A7
Viceroy Ct 3 PR8 35 A6
Vickers Dr WN8 9 E8
Victor Ave LA4 217 E6
Victoria Apartments 20 BB12 146 C1
Victoria Ave
Accrington BB5 104 D2
2 Blackburn BB2 80 E8
Brierfield BB9 148 B6
Chatburn BB7 190 E5
Lancaster LA1 214 F5
Victoria Bldgs
Darwen BB3 82 E3
Formby L37 11 E5
8 Low Bentham LA2 239 B8
1 Preston PR1 96 F7
Victoria Bridge Rd PR8 35 C6
Victoria Bsns & Ind Ctr BB5 104 B4
Victoria Cl BB7 144 A7
Victoria Cross 4 BB1 101 E6
Victoria Ct
7 Blackburn BB1 101 E5
Broughton PR3 137 C2
Chatburn BB7 190 D5
Croston PR26 58 B3
Fulwood PR2 117 E3
Horwich BL6 32 C3
Padiham BB12 126 E7
Southport PR8 34 F4
Victoria Dr BB4 85 B2
Victoria Gdns BB9 170 C2
Victoria Hospl FY3 131 A5
Victoria Lodge BB12 145 D2
Victoria Mans PR2 96 A7
Victoria Mews
7 Clitheroe BB7 166 D7
Morecambe LA4 217 C6
Victoria Par
Morecambe LA4 217 C6
Preston PR2 117 B1
7 Rawtenstall BB4 69 E8
Victoria Park Ave
Leyland PR25 59 D7
Preston PR2 116 D1
Victoria Park Dr PR2 116 D1
Victoria Park Miniature Rly★ PR8 34 E5
Victoria Pk WN8 17 C1
Victoria Pl Halton LA2 219 C6
6 Lancaster LA1 214 F7
Victoria Quay PR2 96 A7
Victoria Rd
Barnoldswick BB18 196 C2
Earby BB18 197 B2
Formby L37 11 D5
Fulwood PR2 118 A4
Horwich BL6 32 C2
Ince Blundell L38 3 E3
Kirkham PR4 113 F5
Lytham St Anne's FY8 89 F5
Ormskirk L39 15 C2
Padiham BB12 126 E7
Pleasington BB2 100 C1
Poulton-le-F FY6 153 E4
Preston PR5 97 D5
Victoria Rd E FY5 176 B1
Victoria Rd W FY5 175 E2
Victoria Sq FY5 175 D2
Victoria St
Accrington BB5 104 B5
Victoria St *continued*
13 Bacup OL13 70 D8
Bamber Bridge PR5 77 B8
Barrowford BB9 170 D3
25 Blackburn BB1 101 E5
Blackpool FY1 130 B5
Blackrod BL6 31 D2
1 Burnley BB11 127 F5
Burscough Bridge L40 25 E5
Carnforth LA5 223 D1
Chorley PR7 43 D7
Church BB5 103 E6
Clayton-le-M BB5 124 F2
Clayton-le-M BB5 124 F3
Clitheroe BB7 166 D7
9 Cornholme OL14 109 C1
22 Darwen BB3 82 A1
7 Earby BB18 197 B2
Fleetwood FY7 199 B5
Great Harwood BB6 124 D5
Haslingden BB4 85 A3
Longridge PR3 140 A7
Lytham St Anne's FY8 91 C3
Morecambe LA4 217 A5
Nelson BB9 148 D8
Oswaldtwistle BB5 103 D3
Preston PR1 117 E1
Ramsbottom BL0 50 B6
Rawtenstall BB4 86 C1
Rawtenstall,Waterfoot BB4 69 E8
Rishton BB1 124 B1
22 Rochdale OL12 52 F1
Southport PR8 35 B8
Wheelton PR6 62 A7
Whitworth OL12 52 C8
Victoria Terr
Abbey Village PR6 80 B2
12 Bamber Bridge PR5 77 A8
Billington BB7 144 A4
Calder Vale PR3 182 E8
2 Chorley PR6 61 D1
Glasson LA2 209 F5
5 Leyland PR25 60 A8
Mellor Brook BB2 121 C3
Tockholes BB3 80 F2
Wheelton PR6 62 A7
Victoria Way Formby L37 11 D5
Rawtenstall BB4 86 C2
Southport PR8 34 F7
Victoria Wharf LA1 218 C1
Victoria Works Ind Est BB11 127 B5
Victory Ave PR9 36 A7
Victory Cl BB9 148 E8
Victory Ctr The 2 BB9 148 E8
Victory Rd FY1 130 C6
Victory Wharf PR2 96 B8
View Rd BB3 81 E5
View St PR7 41 C7
Vihiers Cl BB7 144 C6
Viking Cl PR8 35 A4
Viking Way LA3 212 F5
Villa Way PR3 181 C6
Village Cl WN8 8 D8
Village Croft PR7 60 D3
Village Dr PR2 118 F2
Village Green La PR2 116 F6
Village Way
Blackpool FY2 152 D5
Hightown L38 2 F4
Skelmersdale WN8 8 D8
Villas Ct LA1 214 F7
Villas Rd L31 6 B2
Villas The PR4 116 E5
Villiers Ct PR1 117 E2
Villiers St Burnley BB11 127 C5
Bury BL9 33 A3
Padiham BB12 126 D7
Preston PR1 117 D2
Preston PR1 117 E2
Vincent Ct BB2 81 D8
Vincent Rd BB9 148 F8
Vincent St Blackburn BB2 81 D8
Colne BB8 171 F6
8 Lancaster LA1 215 A7
Vincit St BB10 128 C8
Vine Ct FY2 152 C1
Vine St Accrington BB5 104 A6
Brierfield BB9 148 B5
Chorley PR7 61 C1
Lancaster LA1 214 F6
Oswaldtwistle BB5 103 C3
Preston PR1 96 D8
Ramsbottom BL0 50 A4
Vinery The PR4 75 F8
Viola Cl WN6 29 D2
Violet St BB10 148 A1
Virginia Ave L31 5 D3
Virginia Gr L31 5 C3
Virginia St PR8 35 C6
Viscount Ave BB3 82 A6
Viscount Dr LA1 214 E4
Vivary Way BB8 171 B5
Vivian Dr PR8 35 A2
Vulcan Rd PR4 114 B1
Vulcan St 4 Nelson BB9 170 F1
Southport PR9 35 C7

W

Wackersall Rd BB8 171 B3
Waddington & West Bradford CE Prim Sch BB7 189 C5
Waddington Ave BB10 128 D6
Waddington Ct FY8 90 C6
Waddington Hospl (Almshouses) BB7 189 B5
Waddington Rd
Accrington BB5 104 D6
Clitheroe BB7 189 E1
Fulwood PR2 119 A2
Lytham St Anne's FY8 90 C7
West Bradford BB7 189 D5
Waddington St
Earby BB18 197 B2
3 Padiham BB12 126 D8
Waddow Gn BB7 166 C8
Waddow Gr BB7 189 C4
Waddow View BB7 189 B4
Wade Brook Rd PR26 58 F6
Wade St BB12 146 D1
Wades Croft PR4 93 C6
Wades Ct FY3 152 F1
Wadham Rd PR1 97 B6
Wagon Rd LA2,PR3 226 B8
Waidshouse Cl BB9 148 E6
Waidshouse Rd BB9 148 E6
Wain Ct BB2 101 B4
Waingap Cres OL12 52 D8
Waingap Rise OL12 52 F4
Waingap View OL12 52 D7
Waingate Grimsargh PR2 139 C1
Rawtenstall BB4 86 B3
Waingate Cl BB4 86 B3
Waingate Ct PR2 139 C1
Waingate La BB4 86 B3
Waingate Rd BB4 86 B3
Waitholme La LA5 240 A7
Wakefield Ave LA4 217 D6
Wakefield Dr LA1 215 A4
Wakefield Rd FY2 152 E4
Walden Rd BB1 122 F4
Waldon St PR1 97 E8
Waldron WN8 8 D8
Wales Rd BB4 86 F1
Wales Terr BB4 86 F1
Walesby Pl FY8 90 D5
Walgarth Dr PR7 43 B7
Walk Mill Pl BB10 128 E1
Walk The
Hesketh Bank PR4 73 C4
Southport PR8 35 A5
Walkdale PR4 95 D2
Walkden Barn Cotts BB5 103 A1
Walkden St 28 OL12 52 F1
Walker Ave BB5 104 A4
Walker Cl L37 11 F2
Walker Gr LA3 212 F7
Walker La PR2 117 B6
Walker Office Pk BB1 82 C8
Walker Park Ind Est BB1 82 C7
Walker Pl PR1 97 B7
Walker Rd BB1 82 C7
Walker St Blackburn BB1 101 F4
Blackpool FY1 130 B6
Clitheroe BB7 166 F8
Preston PR1 96 F8
Walker Way FY5 176 B4
Walkers Hill FY4 111 A7
Walkers Ind Est LA3 212 F3
Wall La PR3 155 E5
Wall St Blackpool FY1 130 C7
Newchurch BB4 86 E2
Wallace Hartley Mews 1 BB8 171 D5
Wallace La PR3 207 C4
Wallbank Dr OL12 52 C7
Wallbrook Ave WN5 10 D1
Wallcroft St WN8 8 E8
Walled Garden The PR6 61 B6
Wallend Rd PR2 95 D7
Waller Ave FY2 152 C5
Waller Hill BB8 194 D1
Walletts Rd PR7 43 B6
Wallhurst Cl BB10 129 B5
Walling's La LA5 224 B4
Wallstreams Ct BB10 129 B5
Wallstreams La BB10 129 B5
Wallsuches BL6 32 F4
Walmer Ct PR8 34 F4
Walmer Gn PR4 74 F5
Walmer Rd
Lytham St Anne's FY8 89 F8
Southport PR8 35 A3
Walmersley Old Rd BL9 50 F2
Walmersley Rd BL9 50 E2
Walmsgate BB18 196 B2
Walmsley Ave BB1 103 B8
Walmsley Bridge La
Bilsborrow PR3 159 E8
Claughton PR3 182 E1
Walmsley Brow BB7 144 B4
Walmsley CE Prim Sch BL7 47 E1
Walmsley Cl Church BB5 103 E6
Garstang PR3 181 C7
Walmsley Ct BB5 124 F1
Walmsley St Darwen BB3 82 B2
Fleetwood FY7 199 A4
18 Great Harwood BB6 124 C5
Rishton BB1 124 B1
Walney Gdns BB2 101 F1
Walney Pl FY3 131 A7
Walnut Ave Bury BL9 33 C3
Haslingden BB4 85 C3
Walnut Cl PR1 96 B3
Walnut St Bacup OL13 87 F3
Blackburn BB1 101 F7
3 Blackburn BB1 102 A7
Southport PR8 35 C4
Walpole Ave FY4 110 B5
Walpole St
Blackburn BB1 101 F4
9 Burnley BB10 148 B1
Walro Mews PR9 54 A3
Walsden Gr BB10 128 C6
Walsh Fold BL7 48 D2
Walsh St Blackburn BB2 101 E2
Horwich BL6 32 B4
Walshaw High Sch BB10 148 D1
Walshaw La BB10 148 D2
Walshaw St BB10 128 B8
Walter Ave FY8 111 A2
Walter Pl FY8 111 A2
Walter Robinson Ct FY3 130 D6
Walter St Accrington BB5 104 B6
Blackburn BB1 102 A4
Blackburn BB1 102 B4
Brierfield BB9 148 B5
Darwen BB3 65 B5
Huncoat BB5 125 E2
Oswaldtwistle BB5 103 D3
Walter Street Prim Sch BB9 148 B5
Waltham Ave FY4 110 D5
Waltham Cl BB5 104 E3
Waltham Ct LA2 219 C7
Walthew Gn WN8 19 C3
Waltho Ave L31 5 E1
Walton Ave
Higher Penwortham PR1 96 B3
Morecambe LA4 217 F5
Walton Cl OL13 88 A1
Walton Cottage Homes BB9 171 A1
Walton Cres BB2 102 A1
Walton Gn PR5 97 C4
Walton Gr LA4 217 F5
Walton High Sch BB9 171 A2
Walton La BB9 171 A1
Walton St Accrington BB5 125 A1
Adlington PR7 31 A6
Barrowford BB9 170 E4
Colne BB8 171 D4
8 Nelson BB9 170 E1
Southport PR9 35 C8
Walton Summit Rd PR5 78 A7
Walton View PR1 97 D8
Walton's Par PR1 96 E7
Walton-le-Dale Com Prim Sch PR5 97 D2
Walton-le-Dale High Sch PR5 97 F2
Walverden Ave 4 FY4 110 D8
Walverden Cres 3 BB9 148 F8
Walverden Prim Sch BB9 148 F8
Walverden Rd
Brierfield BB9 148 D5
Lane Bottom BB10 149 B4
Walverden Terr BB9 148 F7
Wanes Blades Rd L40 26 E5
Wanishar La L39 14 A5
Wansbeck Ave FY7 198 D2
Wansbeck Ho FY7 198 D2
Wansfell Rd BB7 166 C7
Wanstead Cres FY4 130 E1
Wanstead St PR1 97 E8
Warbreck Ct FY2 152 B1
Warbreck Dr FY2 152 B2
Warbreck Hill Rd FY2 152 D1
Warburton Bldgs BB4 84 F1
Warburton St BB4 84 F1
Warbury St PR1 118 E1
Warcock La OL13 88 B3
Ward Ave Cleveleys FY5 175 D3
Formby L37 11 D2
Oswaldtwistle BB5 103 C3
Ward Green Cross PR3 141 A7
Ward Green La PR3 141 A7
Ward St
Bamber Bridge PR5 77 B7
Belmont BL7 46 C5
5 Blackpool FY1 130 B1
Burnley BB11 127 E6
Chorley PR6 43 E7
Great Harwood BB6 124 C5
Kirkham PR4 114 A4
Ward's End PR1 97 A7
Warde St 10 BB9 148 E8
Wardle Ct PR6 61 C6
Wardle Dr FY5 175 F3
Wardle St OL13 70 D8
Wardley's La FY6 177 A3
Wareham Cl BB5 125 B1
Wareham Rd FY3 152 F1
Wareham St BB1 102 A7
Warehouse La BB8 194 D1
Waring Dr FY5 176 A2
Warings The
Heskin Green PR7 41 E4
Nelson BB9 148 E6
Warkworth Terr 18 OL13 88 A3
Warley Ave LA3 217 E4
Warley Dr LA3 217 E4
Warley Rd FY1 130 C8
Warley Wise La BB8 195 F3
Warmden Ave BB5 104 E3
Warmden Gdns BB1 102 A7
Warne Pl LA1 218 B1
Warner Rd PR1 118 D1
Warner St
Accrington BB5 104 C5
Haslingden BB4 85 B3
Warpers Moss Cl L40 25 F5
Warpers Moss La L40 26 A5
Warren Ave N FY7 198 F4

Warren Ave S FY7 . . . . . . .198 F4
Warren Cl LA2 . . . . .218 C8
Warren Ct PR8 . . . . .34 E5
Warren Dr Bacup OL13 . .71 C8
Barrowford BB9 . . . . . .170 C3
Blackpool FY5 . . . . . . .152 E7
Slyne LA2 . . . . .218 G8
Warren Fold BB7 . . . . .142 F8
Warren Gn L37 . . . . .11 D3
Warren Gr Blackpool FY5 .152 E8
Heysham LA3 . . . . .212 E5
Warren Rd Heysham LA3 .212 E5
Southport PR9 . . . . .36 A8
Warren St FY7 . . . . . . .199 B4
Warren The
Blackburn BB2 . . . . . . .101 A7
Fulwood PR2 . . . . .118 E6
Warrenhouse Rd L33 . . . . .1 B4
Warrenhurst Ho **1** FY7 . .198 F3
Warrenhurst Rd FY7 . . . .199 A4
Warrenside Cl BB1 . . . . .123 A4
Warrington St BB1 . . . . .102 A8
Warrington Terr BB6 . . . .144 D8
Warth La Ingleton LA6 . .242 F2
Rawtenstall BB4 . . . . . . .86 F2
Warton Archbishop Hutton's
Prim Sch LA5 . . . . . . .223 D5
Warton Ave LA3 . . . . . .212 E6
Warton Crag Nature
Reserve★ LA5 . . . . . .223 C6
Warton Old Rectory★
LA5 . . . . .223 D5
Warton Pl PR7 . . . . .43 A8
Warton Rd LA5 . . . . . . .223 D2
Warton St
Lytham St Anne's FY8 . .91 C3
2 Preston PR1 . . . . . . .96 E6
Wartonwood View **1**
LA5 . . . . .223 D1
Warwick Ave
Accrington BB5 . . . . . .104 B7
Clayton-le-M BB5 . . . . .124 F3
Cleveleys FY5 . . . . . . .175 F4
Darwen BB3 . . . . .81 E3
Lancaster LA1 . . . . . . .215 A5
Morecambe LA4 . . . . . .217 F6
Warwick Cl Church BB5 . .103 F7
Fulwood PR2 . . . . .117 E4
Ramsbottom BL8 . . . . . . .50 A1
Southport PR8 . . . . .35 B4
Warwick Dr
Barnoldswick BB18 . . . . .196 F1
Brierfield BB9 . . . . . . .148 D5
Clitheroe BB7 . . . . . . .189 D2
Padiham BB12 . . . . . . .126 D7
Warwick Ho **10** PR1 . . . .97 A6
Warwick Pl
Fleetwood FY7 . . . . . . .199 A5
Normoss FY3 . . . . .131 B8
Warwick Rd
Bamber Bridge PR5 . . . . .97 D4
Blackpool FY3 . . . . . . .130 D7
Eccleston PR7 . . . . .41 C7
Leyland PR25 . . . . .59 E7
Lytham St Anne's FY8 . .89 F6
Warwick St Adlington PR7 . .30 F6
Church BB5 . . . . .103 F7
Haslingden BB4 . . . . . . .85 B3
Longridge PR3 . . . . . . .140 A8
Nelson BB9 . . . . .148 E7
Preston PR1 . . . . .96 F8
Southport PR8 . . . . .35 B4
Wasdale Ave
Blackburn BB1 . . . . . . .102 C3
Maghull L31 . . . . .5 F2
Wasdale Cl Leyland PR25 . .60 B6
Padiham BB12 . . . . . . .146 C1
Wasdale Gr PR3 . . . . . .139 F5
Wasdale Rd FY4 . . . . . .111 A8
Wash La BL9 . . . . .33 B2
Washbrook Cl BB7 . . . . .166 D1
Washbrook Way L39 . . . . .15 E4
Washburn Ct LA3 . . . . .217 C2
Washington Ave
Blackpool FY2 . . . . . . .152 E2
3 Morecambe LA4 . . . .217 B5
Washington Cl LA1 . . . . .214 D7
Washington Ct FY2 . . . . .152 E2
Washington Dr LA5 . . . . .223 E6
Washington Hall Fire Brigade
Training Ctr PR7 . . . . . .60 F2
Washington La PR7 . . . . .60 F2
Washington St BB5 . . . . .104 C6
Waste La LA2 . . . . .226 C7
Wastwater Dr **4** LA4 . .217 E4
Watchyard La L37 . . . . . .12 A4
Water Fold BB4 . . . . . . .87 A8
Water Head PR2 . . . . . .117 B3
Water La Edenfield BL0 . .68 D2
Preston PR2 . . . . .117 D1
Southport PR9 . . . . .54 D5
Water Mdws BB2 . . . . . .81 D7
Water St
9 Accrington BB5 . . . .104 C6
Adlington PR7 . . . . .31 A6
1 Bamber Bridge PR5 . .97 F2
Brindle PR6 . . . . .78 F5
Chorley PR7 . . . . .61 C1
Clayton-le-M BB5 . . . . .124 F5
1 Colne BB8 . . . . . . .171 E5
Earby BB18 . . . . .197 B2
Egerton BL7 . . . . .47 D2
Great Harwood BB6 . .124 C5
Hapton BB12 . . . . .126 C4
Lancaster LA1 . . . . . . .218 D1

Water St continued
Nelson BB9 . . . . .148 E8
8 Ramsbottom BL0 . . . .50 B5
Rawtenstall BB4 . . . . . . .86 A8
Ribchester PR3 . . . . . . .141 E3
Whitworth OL12 . . . . . . .52 C8
Worsthorne BB10 . . . . . .129 B5
Water's Edge PR2 . . . . .116 F3
Waterbarn La OL13 . . . . .70 B8
Waterbarn St BB10 . . . . .148 B1
Waterdale FY2 . . . . . . .152 E5
Waterfall Mills BB2 . . . . .101 B2
Waterfall Terr BL7 . . . . . .46 C5
Waterfield Ave BB3 . . . . . .65 B6
Waterfold Bsns Pk BL9 . .33 B1
Waterfold La BL9 . . . . . .33 C1
Waterfoot Ave
Blackpool FY3 . . . . . . .130 E6
Southport PR8 . . . . .21 B3
Waterfoot Bsns Ctr **6**
BB4 . . . . .86 F2
Waterford Cl
Adlington PR6 . . . . .44 A1
Fulwood PR2 . . . . .118 C6
Waterford St BB9 . . . . .170 F1
Waterfront **2** BB1 . . . .101 F3
Waterfront Marine & Ind Est
FY8 . . . . .91 E3
Waterhead Cres FY5 . .152 C6
Waterhouse Gn PR6 . .61 B7
Waterhouse Nook PR7,
BL6 . . . . .31 A5
Watering Pool La PR5 . .97 B1
Waterleat Glade FY6 . .131 E8
Waterloo Cl BB2 . . . . . . .81 B8
Waterloo Prim Sch FY4 130 D1
Waterloo Rd
Blackpool FY4 . . . . . . .130 D1
Burnley BB11 . . . . .128 B4
Burnley BB11 . . . . .128 B5
Clitheroe BB7 . . . . . . .166 F8
Kelbrook BB18 . . . . . . .195 A6
Preston PR2 . . . . .117 C1
Southport PR8 . . . . .34 E2
Waterloo St
Accrington BB5 . . . . . .125 A1
Chorley PR7 . . . . .61 C1
Waterloo Terr PR2 . . . . .117 C1
Watermans Cl BB6 . . . . .32 C4
Watermede WN5 . . . . . .10 E3
Waters Edge
3 Blackburn BB1 . . . . .101 F4
Whalley BB7 . . . . .144 C4
Waters Edge Gn PR3 . .181 C6
Waters Reach
Cleveleys FY5 . . . . . . .175 C3
Lytham St Anne's FY8 . .90 D3
Waterside Blackpool FY2 152 D2
Lancaster LA1 . . . . . . .218 D1
Waterside Cl PR3 . . . . .181 B7
Waterside Ind Est BB8 171 E4
Waterside Mews BB12 126 D8
Waterside Pl LA4 . . . . .217 B3
Waterside Rd Colne BB8 171 D4
Haslingden BB4 . . . . . . .85 A2
Ramsbottom BL0,BL8,BL9 . .50 C3
Waterside Terr
10 Bacup OL13 . . . . . .87 F3
Waterside BB3 . . . . . . .82 C3
Waterslack Rd LA5 . . . .224 E6
Waterworks Cotts L39 . .6 F4
Waterworks Rd L39 . . . .16 A6
Watery Gate La PR3,PR4 156 D3
Watery La Darwen BB3 . .65 B6
Garstang PR3 . . . . . . .204 E1
Lancaster LA1 . . . . . . .218 B3
Preston PR2 . . . . .96 B8
Preston,Fishwick PR1 . .97 E7
Watery Lane Ind Est BB3 65 B6
Watford St **6** BB1 . . . .101 E6
Watkin La PR5 . . . . .77 B7
Watkin Rd PR6 . . . . .61 B8
Watkins Cl BB9 . . . . . .148 C4
Watling Cl LA3 . . . . . . .217 E3
Watling Gate BB6 . . . . .143 C6
Watling St BL8 . . . . . . .49 A1
Watling Street Rd
Fulwood PR2 . . . . .118 B3
Fulwood,Brookfield PR2 . .118 E5
Watson Ct FY4 . . . . . . .110 D7
Watson Gdns OL12 . . . . .52 D2
Watson Rd FY4 . . . . . . .110 D7
Watson St Blackpool BB2 101 B2
8 Oswaldtwistle BB5 . .103 E4
Watt St Burnley BB12 . .127 C7
Sabden BB7 . . . . .145 F7
Watton Beck Cl L31 . . . . .5 F2
Watts Cl **1** LA3 . . . . . . .1 A4
Watts St BL6 . . . . .32 C2
Wavell Ave PR9 . . . . . . .36 B7
Wavell Cl Accrington BB5 104 F1
Southport PR9 . . . . .36 B7
Wavell St BB12 . . . . . . .127 C6
Waverledge Bsns Pk
BB6 . . . . .124 B4
Waverledge Rd BB6 . .124 B4
Waverledge St BB6 . .124 C4
Waverley WN8 . . . . . . .17 D1
Waverley Ave
Blackpool FY1 . . . . . . .130 C8
Fleetwood FY7 . . . . . . .198 D3
Waverley Cl
Brierfield BB9 . . . . . . .148 D4
Read BB12 . . . . .145 D1
Waverley Dr
New Longton PR4 . . . . .75 F7
Tarleton PR4 . . . . .57 A6
Waverley Gdns PR2 . .118 E2

Waverley Pl BB2 . . . . . .101 B5
Waverley Rd
Accrington BB5 . . . . . .104 E3
Blackburn BB1 . . . . . . .102 F4
Preston PR1 . . . . .118 D1
Wilpshire BB1 . . . . . . .122 E4
Waverley St
1 Burnley BB11 . . . . .127 E6
Southport PR8 . . . . .35 A7
Waxy La PR4 . . . . .93 C7
Way Gate FY5 . . . . . . .175 D5
Way The LA3 . . . . .217 F3
Wayfarers Arc PR8 . . . . .35 B7
Wayman Rd FY3 . . . . . .130 D6
Wayoh Croft BL7 . . . . . .48 D6
Wayside FY6 . . . . .199 D5
Weald The PR4 . . . . . . .116 D5
Weasel La BB3 . . . . .81 B2
Weatherhill Cres BB9 . .148 E5
Weaver's Brow PR6 . . . .43 F5
Weaver Ave L40 . . . . . . .25 F5
Weavers Cl FY8 . . . . . . .90 D7
Weaver's Croft BB7 . .144 A4
Weavers Ct BB8 . . . . . .172 B2
Webb St BL6 . . . . .32 C3
Webber Ct BB11 . . . . . .127 A3
Webber Rd L33 . . . . .1 C1
Webster Ave FY4 . . . . . .110 E7
Webster Gdns PR4 . . . . .75 A4
Webster Gr LA4 . . . . . .218 A6
Webster St PR2 . . . . . .117 C1
Wedgewood Rd BB5 . .125 F1
Wedgwood Ct FY8 . . . . .90 A7
Weeton Ave
Blackpool FY4 . . . . . . .110 E5
Cleveleys FY5 . . . . . . .175 D3
Lytham St Anne's FY8 . .90 A8
Weeton Pl **4** PR2 . . . .116 F3
Weeton Prim Sch PR4 . .132 E6
Weeton Rd
Great Plumpton PR4 . .112 F7
Kirkham PR4 . . . . .113 F7
Kirkham,Weeton PR4 . .113 C8
Weeton PR4 . . . . .132 F2
Weeton Camp FY6,PR4 . .132 F7
Weeton St Michael's CE
Prim Sch PR4 . . . . . .132 E1
Weets View BB18 . . . . .196 C3
Weind The PR3 . . . . . . .156 B5
Weir La OL13 . . . . .88 A7
Weir St BB2 . . . . .101 E4
Weirden Cl PR1 . . . . . . .96 C1
Welbeck Ave
Blackburn BB1 . . . . . . .102 B8
Blackpool FY4 . . . . . . .130 E1
Fleetwood FY7 . . . . . . .198 F3
Welbeck Gdns FY7 . . . .198 F3
Welbeck Ho **4** FY7 . . . .198 F4
Welbeck Rd PR8 . . . . . .35 A4
Welbeck Terr BB8 . . . . .35 A4
Welbourne WN8 . . . . . .17 D1
Welburn Cl WN5 . . . . . .10 E5
Welburn Wlk FY5 . . . . .176 D2
Welbury Cl **5** BB18 . .197 B2
Weld Ave PR7 . . . . .43 C5
Weld Blundell Ave L31 . .5 B5
Weld Cl BB7 . . . . .11 D4
Weld Par PR8 . . . . .34 F4
Weld Rd PR8 . . . . .34 F5
Weldale PR8 . . . . .34 F4
Weldbank La PR7 . . . . .43 C5
Weldbank St PR7 . . . . .43 C5
Weldon Dr L39 . . . . . . .15 F4
Weldon St BB1 . . . . . . .127 E5
Well Ct Clitheroe BB7 . .189 F1
3 Standish WN6 . . . . .29 E1
Well Field BB5 . . . . . . .125 A2
Well Fold BB7 . . . . . . .166 F8
Well Head BB8 . . . . . . .172 B4
Well Head Rd BB12 . . . .169 A3
Well La Brinscall PR6 . .62 F7
Haskayne L39 . . . . . . .13 E6
Little Eccleston PR3 . .155 D6
Warton LA5 . . . . .223 E3
Yealand Redmayne LA5 . .225 E3
Well Orch PR5 . . . . . . .78 B5
Well St Burnley BB12 . .126 B8
Newchurch BB4 . . . . . . .86 F3
Rishton BB1 . . . . .124 B2
Well St N BB1 . . . . . . .68 C2
Well St W **6** BL0 . . . . .50 B5
Well Terr **1** BB7 . . . . .189 F1
Welland Cl FY2 . . . . . . .152 E4
Wellbrow Dr PR3 . . . . .140 B8
Wellbrow Terr OL12 . . . .52 D2
Wellcross Rd WN8 . . . . .10 B6
Wellesley St BB12 . . . . .126 F6
Wellfield PR4 . . . . .94 F1
Wellfield Ave PR25 . . . .76 F1
Wellfield Bsns Pk PR1 . .96 D8
Wellfield Dr BB12 . . . . .127 D7
Wellfield High Sch PR25 76 F1
Wellfield La L40 . . . . . .16 C3
Wellfield Methodist &
Anglican Church Sch
BB12 . . . . .127 D8
Wellfield Rd
Bamber Bridge PR5 . . . .77 A7
Blackburn BB2 . . . . . . .101 C6
Preston PR1 . . . . .96 D8
8 Padiham BB12 . . . . .126 D8
Sabden BB7 . . . . .145 F8
Southport PR8 . . . . .35 B7
Wellgate BB7 . . . . .166 F8
Wellhouse Rd BB18 . .196 B2
Wellhouse Sq **20** BB18 196 B2
Wellhouse St BB18 . . . .196 B2
Wellington Ave PR25 . .60 B8
Wellington Cl WN8 . . . . .9 E8

Wellington Ct
7 Accrington BB5 . . . .104 C5
3 Burnley BB10 . . . . .128 E5
Wellington Fold **3** BB3 . .82 A1
Wellington Mews BL7 . .48 D4
Wellington Pl PR5 . . . .97 D2
Wellington Rd
Blackburn BB2 . . . . . . .101 C3
Blackpool FY1 . . . . . . .130 B2
Lancaster LA1 . . . . . . .215 A5
Preston PR2 . . . . .117 C1
Turton Bottoms BL7 . . . .48 D4
Wellington St
Accrington BB5 . . . . . .104 C5
Barnoldswick BB18 . .196 B1
Chorley PR7 . . . . .61 C1
Clayton-le-M BB5 . . . .124 F2
Great Harwood BB6 . .124 C4
Kirkham PR4 . . . . .113 F5
Lytham St Anne's FY8 . .91 D3
16 Nelson BB9 . . . . . .170 D1
Preston PR1 . . . . .96 D8
19 Rochdale OL12 . . . .52 F1
1 Southport PR8 . . . . .35 A6
Wellington Street St Johns
BB1 . . . . .101 D6
Wellington Terr LA4 . .217 B5
Wellgate Gdns FY4 . .110 D6
Wellow Pl FY8 . . . . . . .90 C5
Wells Cl Morecambe LA3 217 B2
Thornton FY5 . . . . . . .176 A2
Wells Fold Cl PR6 . . . .78 C1
Wells St Haslingden BB4 . .85 B3
9 Preston PR1 . . . . . .118 D1
Welsby Rd PR25 . . . . . .59 D8
Welwyn Ave PR8 . . . . . .21 E6
Welwyn Pl FY5 . . . . . . .175 E1
Wembley Ave
Blackpool FY3 . . . . . . .130 E8
Higher Penwortham PR1 . .96 B6
Poulton-le-F FY6 . . . . .153 E3
Wembley Cl PR1 . . . . . .96 B5
Wembley Rd FY5 . . . . .176 B4
Wemyss Cl **1** LA3 . . . .212 E7
Wendover Rd FY6 . . . . .153 A6
Wenlock Cl BL6 . . . . . . .32 C6
Wenning Ave
High Bentham LA2 . . . .239 D7
Maghull L31 . . . . .5 E2
Wenning Ct LA3 . . . . . .217 F2
Wenning Pl LA1 . . . . . .218 C2
Wenning St BB9 . . . . . .148 F1
Wennington Hall Sch
LA2 . . . . .241 E1
Wennington Rd
Southport PR9 . . . . .35 F7
Wray LA2 . . . . .238 D6
Wennington Sta LA2 . .238 E8
Wensley Ave FY7 . . . . .198 E1
Wensley Bsns Pk BB2 . .101 B4
Wensley Cl BB11 . . . . .127 E3
Wensley Dr
Accrington BB5 . . . . . .104 D5
Lancaster LA1 . . . . . . .218 D1
Wensley Fold CE Prim Sch
BB2 . . . . .101 B5
Wensley Pl PR2 . . . . . .118 D4
Wensley Rd BB2 . . . . . .101 B4
Wensleydale Ave FY3 . .131 A7
Wensleydale Cl
Maghull L31 . . . . .5 B2
Thornton FY5 . . . . . . .153 D8
Wentcliffe Dr BB18 . . . .197 B1
Wentworth Ave
Fleetwood FY7 . . . . . . .175 D7
Inskip PR4 . . . . .135 C8
Wentworth Cl
Higher Penwortham PR1 . .96 A6
Southport PR8 . . . . .21 C4
Wentworth Cres **3** LA2 217 B2
Wentworth Ct PR4 . . . .114 B4
Wentworth Dr
Broughton PR3 . . . . . .137 C3
Euxton PR7 . . . . .60 D4
Lancaster LA1 . . . . . . .215 C7
Thornton FY5 . . . . . . .153 D8
Wentworth Mews FY8 . .90 A6
Wentworth Pl PR7 . . . .137 C3
Werneth Cl PR1 . . . . . .96 F1
Wescoe Cl WN5 . . . . . .10 E5
Wesham Cross PR4 . . . .113 F7
Wesham Hall Cl PR4 . .114 A6
Wesham Hall Rd PR4 . .114 A6
Wesham Park Hospl
PR4 . . . . .113 F7
Wesley Cl LA2 . . . . . . .239 D8
Wesley Ct
3 Fleetwood FY7 . . . .199 B5
16 Great Harwood BB6 124 C5
Wesley Dr LA3 . . . . . . .212 F7
Wesley Gr **5** BB12 . . . .127 D7
Wesley Mews FY4 . . . .111 A7
Wesley Pl Bacup OL13 . .87 E1
Higham BB12 . . . . . . .146 F6
Wesley St Accrington BB5 103 F6
Bamber Bridge PR5 . . . .77 E8
Blackburn BB1 . . . . . . .101 B1
Brierfield BB9 . . . . . . .148 B6
Oswaldtwistle BB5 . . . .103 E5
Sabden BB7 . . . . .145 F8
Southport PR8 . . . . .35 B7
Wesley Terr OL13 . . . . .88 A7
Wesleyan Row BB7 . .166 E8
Wessex Cl
Accrington,Hillock Vale
BB5 . . . . .104 C5
Standish WN1 . . . . .30 B1

West Ave
Barnoldswick BB18 . . . .196 B2
Fulwood PR2 . . . . .117 A6
West Bank PR7 . . . . . . .43 C5
West Bank Ave FY8 . . . .90 E3
West Beach FY8 . . . . . .91 A2
West Bourne BB4 . . . . .68 A8
West Bradford Rd
Clitheroe BB7 . . . . . . .189 F4
Grindleton BB7 . . . . . . .190 A6
Waddington BB7 . . . . .189 C5
West Bridge L31 . . . . . .5 C1
West Cliff PR1 . . . . .96 E6
West Cliff Terr PR1 . . . .96 E6
West Cliffe FY8 . . . . . . .91 C3
West Close Ave BB12 . .146 F5
West Close Rd BB18 . .196 B3
West Craven High Tech Coll
BB18 . . . . .196 C1
West Cres
Accrington BB5 . . . . . .104 B8
Broughton PR3 . . . . . .137 C3
West Ct FY5 . . . . .175 C5
West Dene WN8 . . . . . .27 B2
West Dr Clayton-le-W PR25 77 D3
Cleveleys FY5 . . . . . . .175 E3
Inskip PR4 . . . . .135 C8
Kirkham PR4 . . . . .113 E7
Lancaster LA1 . . . . . . .218 E2
Whalley BB7 . . . . .144 A7
West Dr W FY5 . . . . . .175 D3
West End
Great Eccleston PR3 . .156 A5
Higher Penwortham PR1 . .96 B6
West End Bsns Pk BB5 103 B5
West End La PR4 . . . . .92 B5
West End Prim Sch
Morecambe LA3 . . . . .216 F4
Oswaldtwistle BB5 . . . .103 C5
West End Rd LA4 . . . . .217 A4
West End Terr PR8 . . . .35 A7
West Exchange St **7**
BB8 . . . . .171 D4
West Field Rd BB18 . . . .196 A4
West Gate FY7 . . . . . . .198 D4
West Gdns **1** OL13 . . . .70 B8
West Gillibrands Ind Est
WN8 . . . . .8 E8
West Hall La LA6 . . . . .241 C7
West Hill BB9 . . . . . . .170 D7
West Ing La BD23 . . . . .231 D5
West La Downham BB7 . .191 A4
Formby L37 . . . . .11 F6
West Lancashire Light Rly★
PR4 . . . . .92 C5
West Leigh Rd BB1 . . . .101 C8
West Lodge FY6 . . . . . .177 C1
West Mdw PR2 . . . . . . .116 E3
West Meade L31 . . . . . .5 B2
West Moss La FY8 . . . .111 E1
West Mount WN5 . . . . . .10 F6
West Paddock PR25 . . . .59 E8
West Park Ave PR2 . . . .116 F2
West Park Dr FY3 . . . . .130 E4
West Park La PR2 . . . . .117 A2
West Park Rd BB2 . . . . .101 C6
West Pennine Bsns Pk
OL13 . . . . .87 F5
West Pk PR9 . . . . .53 D1
West Rd Fulwood PR2 . .117 F3
Lancaster LA1 . . . . . . .214 E8
Thornton FY5 . . . . . . .176 C3
West Sq FY7 . . . . .75 A8
West St **9** Blackpool FY1 130 B5
Burnley BB10 . . . . . . .128 C8
Chorley PR7 . . . . .43 C7
Colne BB8 . . . . .171 E4
Great Harwood BB6 . .124 C4
Lancaster LA1 . . . . . . .214 E8
Morecambe LA3 . . . . .216 E4
7 Nelson BB9 . . . . . .170 D1
Padiham BB12 . . . . . . .126 B8
7 Ramsbottom BL0 . . . .50 B5
Rawtenstall BB4 . . . . . .69 E8
Southport PR8 . . . . .35 A7
West Strand PR1 . . . . . .96 D8
West Street Com Prim Sch
BB8 . . . . .171 E4
West View Bacup OL13 . .70 B8
Bamber Bridge PR5 . . . .77 E7
Blackburn BB2 . . . . . . .101 B4
Blackpool FY1 . . . . . . .130 C3
Carnforth LA5 . . . . . . .223 D3
Clitheroe BB7 . . . . . . .166 D7
Darwen BB3 . . . . .82 B3
Elswick PR4 . . . . .155 F1
Garstang PR3 . . . . . . .181 C7
Glasson LA2 . . . . .209 E5
Grindleton BB7 . . . . . .190 B8
Haslingden BB4 . . . . . .85 B4
Haslingden,Bridge End BB4 . .68 A7
Hollins Lane PR3 . . . . .207 D2
Kirkham PR4 . . . . .113 F7
Longton PR4 . . . . .75 A8
4 Newchurch BB4 . . . .86 F1
Ormskirk L39 . . . . . . .15 F5
Oswaldtwistle BB5 . . . .103 C5
Over Town BB10 . . . . .108 A8
Parbold WN8 . . . . .27 C2
Preston PR1 . . . . .118 C2
Ramsbottom BL0 . . . . .68 C2
Waddington BB7 . . . . .189 B4
Wheelton PR6 . . . . . . .62 A7
West View Ave **8** FY1 130 B2
West View Pl BB2 . . . . .101 B6
West View Rd
Morecambe LA4 . . . . .217 A5
Whitewell Bottom BB4 . .86 F5

West View Terr
Billington BB7 . . . . .144 A4
Padiham BB12 . . . . .126 C7
1 Preston PR1 . . . . .96 D8
Tockholes BB3 . . . . .81 A2
West Way Chorley PR7 . . . .61 A2
Fleetwood FY7 . . . . .175 D8
West Wing L40 . . . . .17 B7
West Wlk BL7 . . . . .47 D2
Westbank Ave FY4 . . . . . .111 A4
Westboro Cl LA3 . . . . . . .216 D1
Westbourne Ave
Blackpool FY1 . . . . .130 C1
Burnley BB11 . . . . .127 D3
Wrea Green PR4 . . . . .113 B3
Westbourne Ave S
BB11 . . . . .127 E3
Westbourne Ct FY6 . . . . .199 D5
Westbourne Dr LA1 . . . . .214 D7
Westbourne Gdns PR8 . . .34 D4
Westbourne Pl LA1 . . . . .214 D8
Westbourne Rd
Chorley PR7 . . . . .43 B6
Cleveleys FY5 . . . . .175 D5
Heysham LA3 . . . . .213 A2
Knott End-on-S FY6 . . . . .199 D5
Lancaster LA1 . . . . .214 D7
Southport PR8 . . . . .34 D4
Warton LA5 . . . . .223 C4
Westbrook Cres PR2 . . . .117 A3
Westbury Cl
Blackpool FY5 . . . . .152 C7
Brierfield BB10 . . . . .148 E2
Westbury Gdns BB1 . . . . .102 C4
Westby Ave FY4 . . . . . . .110 E5
Westby Cl FY4 . . . . .111 D7
Westby Ct FY6 . . . . .153 D2
Westby Gr FY7 . . . . .199 B5
Westby Pl PR2 . . . . .116 F1
Westby Rd
Lytham St Anne's FY8 . . . . .89 E8
Westby PR4 . . . . .112 E5
Westby St FY8 . . . . .91 B3
Westby Way FY6 . . . . . . .153 D2
Westcliff Prim Sch FY5 .152 C5
Westcliffe BB6 . . . . .124 B6
Westcliffe Dr
Blackpool FY3 . . . . .130 E8
Morecambe LA3 . . . . .217 A4
Westcliffe Rd PR8 . . . . . .34 F5
Westcliffe Wlk BB9 . . . . .148 E7
Westcote St **6** BB3 . . . . .65 B6
Westcroft PR4 . . . . .74 E3
Westend Ave PR7 . . . . . . .42 D1
Westerdale Dr PR9 . . . . . .55 B5
Westerlong PR2 . . . . .116 D1
Western Ave BB11 . . . . . .127 E4
Western Ct OL13 . . . . .70 B8
Western Dr PR25 . . . . .76 D2
Western Rd OL13 . . . . .70 C8
Westfield
Bamber Bridge PR5 . . . . . .77 A8
1 Nelson BB9 . . . . .170 D1
Westfield Ave
Blackpool FY3 . . . . .153 A1
Fleetwood FY7 . . . . .198 E2
Normoss FY3 . . . . .131 B7
Read BB12 . . . . .145 D1
Westfield Cl BB7 . . . . . . .144 A7
Westfield Ct FY5 . . . . . . .176 B4
Westfield Dr
Bolton-le-S LA5 . . . . .221 A6
Fulwood PR2 . . . . .118 E4
Gregson Lane PR5 . . . . . . .98 D1
Leyland PR25 . . . . .76 E1
Warton PR4 . . . . .92 F5
West Bradford BB7 . . . . . .189 E6
Westfield Gr LA4 . . . . . . .217 A4
Westfield Rd FY1 . . . . . . .130 D1
Westfields PR26 . . . . .58 A2
Westgate
Barnoldswick BB18 . . . . . .196 A4
Burnley BB11 . . . . .127 E6
Fulwood PR2 . . . . .117 D5
Leyland PR25 . . . . .59 F8
Morecambe LA3,LA4 . . . . .217 C3
Read BB12 . . . . .145 C1
Skelmersdale WN8 . . . . . . .8 D8
Whitworth OL12 . . . . .52 B7
Westgate Ave
Morecambe LA3 . . . . .217 B2
Ramsbottom BL0 . . . . .50 A2
Westgate Cl OL12 . . . . . . .52 B7
Westgate Dr WN5 . . . . . . .10 D5
Westgate La LA6 . . . . . . .242 E5
Westgate Park Rd LA4 .217 C3
Westgate Prim Sch LA4 217 B3
Westgate Rd PR8 . . . . . . .110 C6
Westgate Trad Ctr **2**
BB11 . . . . .127 F6
Westham St LA1 . . . . .215 A4
Westhaven PR9 . . . . .35 D8
Westhaven Cres L39 . . . . .15 C1
Westhead Ave L33 . . . . . . .1 A1
Westhead Cl L33 . . . . .1 A1
Westhead Rd PR26 . . . . . .58 B2
Westhead Wlk
1 Fleetwood FY7 . . . . . . .198 F2
Kirkby L33 . . . . .1 A1
Westholme Ct PR9 . . . . . .53 C1
Westholme Lower Sch
BB2 . . . . .101 B6
Westholme Sch
Blackburn BB2 . . . . .100 E6
Blackburn BB2 . . . . .101 A4
Westhoughton Rd PR6,
PR7 . . . . .43 F1
Westland Ave BB3 . . . . . . .64 F8

Westlands PR26 . . . . .59 C7
Westlands Ct FY5 . . . . . .153 B8
Westleigh Rd PR2 . . . . . .116 F1
Westminster Ave LA4 . . .216 F4
Westminster Cl
Accrington BB5 . . . . .104 E3
Darwen BB3 . . . . .81 A3
Morecambe LA3 . . . . .217 B2
Read BB12 . . . . .145 D1
Westminster Dr PR8 . . . . .21 A4
Westminster Pl
Eccleston PR7 . . . . .41 A4
Hutton PR4 . . . . .95 D1
Westminster Rd
Blackpool FY1 . . . . .130 C8
Chorley PR7 . . . . .43 C7
Darwen BB3 . . . . .81 A3
Morecambe LA3,LA4 . . . . .216 E3
Westmoor Gr LA3 . . . . . .212 E5
Westmoreland Rd PR8 . . .35 D5
Westmoreland St BB9 . . .148 C8
Westmorland Ave
Blackpool FY1 . . . . .130 D3
Cleveleys FY5 . . . . .175 D4
Westmorland Cl
Darwen BB3 . . . . .65 C6
Higher Penwortham PR1 . . .96 B4
Leyland PR25 . . . . .59 E7
Westmorland St BB11 . . .127 D5
Weston Pl **4** FY1 . . . . . .130 D1
Weston St **9** PR2 . . . . . . .96 D8
Westover Ave LA5 . . . . . .223 E5
Westover Cl L31 . . . . .5 C1
Westover Gr LA5 . . . . . . .223 E5
Westover Rd Maghull L31 . .5 C1
Warton LA5 . . . . .223 E5
Westover St LA4 . . . . . . .217 A4
Westridge Ct PR9 . . . . . . .35 D8
Westside
Freckleton PR4 . . . . .93 A6
Fulwood PR2 . . . . .118 A4
Hightown L38 . . . . .2 A1
Maghull L31 . . . . .5 C2
Westway Ct PR2 . . . . .118 A4
Westway Sch BB12 . . . . . .127 F8
Westwell Gr **2** FY1 . . . .130 C4
Westwell Rd **4** PR6 . . . . .61 D1
Westwell St Darwen BB3 . .81 E4
14 Great Harwood BB6 . .124 C5
Westwood Ave
Blackpool FY3 . . . . .130 E4
2 Fleetwood FY7 . . . . . .198 E3
Poulton-le-F FY6 . . . . . . .153 E3
Rishton BB1 . . . . .124 A1
Westwood Cl PR8 . . . . . . .35 E3
Westwood Ct BB1 . . . . . .102 A6
Westwood Mews FY8 . . . .91 A3
Westwood Prim Sch PR5 78 C4
Westwood Rd
Burnley BB12 . . . . .127 C6
Clayton Brook PR5,PR6 . . .78 C4
Leyland PR25 . . . . .77 A2
Lytham St Anne's FY8 . . . . .91 A3
Westwood St BB5 . . . . . .104 B7
Wetherall St PR2 . . . . . . .117 D1
Wetherby Ave FY4 . . . . . .110 B5
Wetherfield Cl LA1 . . . . .218 E4
Weymouth Rd FY3 . . . . . .130 F3
Weythorne Dr BL9 . . . . . .33 F4
Whalley Abbey ★ BB7 . . .144 B5
Whalley Banks BB2 . . . . .101 D4
Whalley Banks Trad Est
BB2 . . . . .101 D4
Whalley CE Prim Sch
BB7 . . . . .144 C5
Whalley Cres Darwen BB3 .82 B1
Staining FY3 . . . . .131 C5
Whalley Dr Formby L37 . . .12 A2
Ormskirk L39 . . . . .6 D8
Rawtenstall BB4 . . . . .86 A4
Whalley Gdns OL12 . . . . .52 B1
Whalley La FY4 . . . . .111 A4
Whalley New Rd BB1 . . . .122 F1
Whalley Old Rd
Billington BB6,BB7 . . . . . .144 B3
Blackburn BB1 . . . . .102 A7
Sunny Bower BB1 . . . . . . .123 B1
Whalley Pl FY8 . . . . .90 B6
Whalley Range BB1 . . . . .101 F6
Whalley Rd
Accrington BB5 . . . . .104 B7
Bank Lane BL0 . . . . .50 E7
Barrow BB7 . . . . .166 D2
Billington BB6,BB7 . . . . . .143 F3
Burnley BB12 . . . . .126 B8
Clayton-le-M BB5,BB6 . . .124 F5
Clitheroe BB7 . . . . .166 D5
Heskin Green PR7 . . . . . . .41 D4
Hurst Green BB7 . . . . .165 B1
Lancaster LA1 . . . . .218 D4
Langho BB6 . . . . .143 D1
Langho BB6 . . . . .143 D2
Mellor Brook BB2 . . . . . . .121 C3
Read BB12 . . . . .145 C1
Rochdale OL12 . . . . .52 B1
Sabden BB7 . . . . .145 D6
Turner Green BB2,PR5 . . .120 C2
Wilpshire BB1,BB6 . . . . . .123 B7
Whalley St
2 Bamber Bridge PR5 . . .97 F2
Blackburn BB1 . . . . .101 E6
Burnley BB10 . . . . .148 A1
5 Chorley PR7 . . . . .43 C7
5 Clitheroe BB7 . . . . . . .166 D8
Whalley PR7 . . . . .144 B6
Whalley Terr BB3 . . . . . . .81 B4

Whalleys Rd WN8 . . . . . . .18 B5
Wham Bottom La OL12 . . .52 D4
Wham Brook Cl BB5 . . . . .103 B5
Wham Hey PR4 . . . . .76 A7
Wham La
New Longton PR4 . . . . . . .76 A7
Walmer Bridge PR4 . . . . . .75 D4
Whams La LA2 . . . . .207 D2
Wharf Ho **7** BB2 . . . . . .101 B1
Wharf St Blackburn BB1 . .101 F5
Lytham St Anne's FY8 . . . . .91 C3
Rishton BB1 . . . . .124 C1
Wharfdale Ave BB10 . . . .148 B4
Wharfe Cl LA3 . . . . .217 F3
Wharfedale
Blackpool FY4 . . . . .110 F7
Galgate LA2 . . . . .211 B4
Wharfedale Ave
Fulwood PR2 . . . . .118 C5
Thornton FY5 . . . . .176 B3
Wharfedale Cl
Blackburn BB2 . . . . .80 D7
Leyland PR25 . . . . .60 A7
Wharfedale Rd LA1 . . . . .214 D8
Wharton Ave FY5 . . . . . . .176 D1
Whave's La PR6 . . . . .79 D4
Wheat La L40 . . . . .26 A4
Wheat St Accrington BB5 .104 A6
Padiham BB12 . . . . .126 D7
Wheatacre WN8 . . . . .8 E8
Wheatcroft Ave BB12 . . . .147 D8
Wheatfield PR26 . . . . .59 A8
Wheatfield Cl **1** FY5 . . . .152 F7
Wheatfield Ct **8** LA1 . . .214 E8
Wheatfield St
Lancaster LA1 . . . . .214 E8
Rishton BB1 . . . . .124 B2
Wheathead La BB9 . . . . . .170 B8
Wheatholme St BB4 . . . . . .86 B2
Wheatlands Cres FY3 . . .131 C2
Wheatley Cl
3 Burnley BB12 . . . . . . .127 D7
Fence BB12 . . . . .147 D7
Wheatley Dr PR3 . . . . . . .140 B8
Wheatley Gr BB9 . . . . . . .170 C3
Wheatley Lane Prim Sch
BB12 . . . . .147 E8
Wheatley Lane Rd
Barrowford BB9 . . . . .170 B2
Fence BB12 . . . . .147 E8
Wheatsheaf Ave PR3 . . . .140 A7
Wheatsheaf Wlk
4 Ormskirk L39 . . . . . . .15 E5
Standish WN6 . . . . .29 D1
Wheel La PR3 . . . . .201 A6
Wheelton La PR25 . . . . . . .77 A3
Wheelwright Cl BB7 . . . . .231 B3
Wheelwrights Wharf L40 23 F4
Whelan Cl BB2 . . . . .81 D7
Whernside Ave FY4 . . . . .110 F7
Whernside Cl BB18 . . . . . .196 A2
Whernside Cres PR2 . . . .118 D5
Whernside Gr LA5 . . . . . .223 E5
Whernside Rd LA1 . . . . . .218 B3
Whernside Way PR25 . . . .77 C1
Whewell Row BB5 . . . . . .103 C5
Whimberry Ave BB4 . . . . .86 A1
Whimbrel Dr FY5 . . . . . . .176 A4
Whin Ave LA5 . . . . .221 B6
Whin Dr LA5 . . . . .221 B6
Whin Gr LA5 . . . . .221 B6
Whin La PR3 . . . . .155 B8
Whinberry Ave BB4 . . . . . .86 A1
Whinbrick Cotts PR4 . . . .113 B6
Whincroft BB11 . . . . .127 E2
Whinfell Dr LA1 . . . . .215 A3
Whinfield Ave
7 Chorley PR6 . . . . .61 D1
Fleetwood FY7 . . . . .198 E2
Whinfield La PR2 . . . . .96 A8
Whinfield Pl
Blackburn BB2 . . . . .101 A6
Preston PR2 . . . . .96 A8
Whinfield St **9** BB5 . . . . .125 A1
Whinney Brow PR3 . . . . .207 C3
Whinney Heys Rd FY3 . . .131 A6
Whinney Hill Rd BB5 . . . .125 C1
Whinney La
Blackburn BB2 . . . . .101 C8
Euxton PR7 . . . . .60 E3
Langho BB6 . . . . .143 D1
Mellor BB2 . . . . .122 B2
Whinneyfield La PR4 . . . .136 D2
Whinny La
Knott End-on-S FY6 . . . . .199 E4
Waddington BB7 . . . . . . .188 E6
Whinnysty La LA3 . . . . . .216 D1
Whinpark Ave FY3 . . . . . .131 A6
Whins Ave BB7 . . . . .145 E4
Whins La Read BB12 . . . . .145 E3
Wheelton PR6 . . . . .62 A8
Whins The BB7 . . . . .145 E7
Whinsands Cl PR2 . . . . . .118 D5
Whinsfell View LA4 . . . . .217 B5
Whipp St BB4 . . . . .166 D2
Whitaker Gn **8** BB4 . . . . .85 E2
Whitaker St BB5 . . . . . . .104 B7
Whitbarrow Sq **8** LA1 . .215 A8
Whitburn WN8 . . . . .17 D1
Whitburn Rd L33 . . . . .1 A4
Whitby Ave Fulwood PR2 .116 F5
Southport PR9 . . . . .54 D6
Whitby Dr BB2 . . . . .102 A1
Whitby Pl PR2 . . . . .116 F5
Whitby Rd
Lytham St Anne's FY8 . . . .111 A1
Morecambe LA4 . . . . .217 C5

White Acre Rd BB5 . . . . .104 E2
White Ash Est BB5 . . . . . .103 D4
White Ash La BB5 . . . . . . .103 C3
White Ash Sch BB5 . . . . . .103 D4
White Birk BL8 . . . . .49 F2
White Bull St **4** BB12 . . .127 C6
White Carr La Bury BL9 . . .51 B5
Cleveleys FY5 . . . . .153 A8
Hollins Lane PR3 . . . . . . .207 A4
Treales PR3 . . . . .134 C2
White Cross Ind Est LA1 214 F7
White Cross St LA1 . . . . . .214 F7
White Gate Fold PR7 . . . . .42 E3
White Gr BB8 . . . . .171 C6
White Hill Cl OL12 . . . . . . .52 D4
White Horse Cl BB6 . . . . . .32 C5
White Horse La PR3 . . . . .158 C1
White Hough Outdoor
Education Ctr BB12 . . . .169 E5
White House La
Bescar L40 . . . . .37 C1
Lane Heads PR3 . . . . .156 E4
White Lea PR3 . . . . .204 C1
White Lee Ave BB8 . . . . . .172 C2
White Lee La PR3 . . . . . . .183 C2
White Leys Cl BB18 . . . . .196 F1
White Lund Ave LA3 . . . . .217 C2
White Lund Rd LA3 . . . . . .217 C2
White Lund Trad Est
LA3 . . . . .217 D2
White Mdw PR2 . . . . .116 E3
White Moss La FY6 . . . . . .177 E4
White Moss Rd WN8 . . . . . .8 C7
White Moss Rd S WN8 . . . .8 D7
White Rd BB2 . . . . .101 A6
White St **2** Burnley BB12 .127 B6
Colne BB8 . . . . .171 B4
White Walls Cl BB8 . . . . . .171 A3
Whiteacre WN6 . . . . .29 A2
Whiteacre La BB6 . . . . . . .144 E8
Whitebeam Cl
Cleveleys FY5 . . . . .175 F5
Higher Penwortham PR1 . . .96 B3
Whitebeck La LA6 . . . . . . .240 B4
Whitebirk Dr BB1 . . . . . . .102 C8
Whitebirk Ind Est BB1 . . . .102 B8
Whitebirk Rd BB1 . . . . . . .102 D5
Whitecoats Dr FY8 . . . . . .91 D4
Whitecrest St FY5 . . . . . .175 F4
Whitecroft Ave **8** BB4 . . .85 B2
Whitecroft Cl BB4 . . . . . . .85 B2
Whitecroft La BB2 . . . . . .121 E2
Whitecroft Mdws BB4 . . . .85 B2
Whitecroft View BB5 . . . .104 C2
Whitefield Cl Hightown L38 .2 F1
Rufford L40 . . . . .39 C3
Whitefield Inf Sch BB9 . .148 C8
Whitefield Mdw **5** PR5 . .97 F1
Whitefield Pl LA3 . . . . . . .217 C2
Whitefield Prim Sch PR1 96 A4
Whitefield Rd PR1 . . . . . . .96 A4
Whitefield Rd E PR1 . . . . .96 B4
Whitefield Rd W PR1 . . . . .96 A4
Whitefield St BB12 . . . . . .126 C4
Whitefield Terr BB11 . . . .128 B3
Whitefriar Cl PR2 . . . . . . .117 A5
Whitegate LA3 . . . . .217 D3
Whitegate Dr FY3 . . . . . . .130 E3
Whitegate Gdns BB12 . . . .126 E2
Whitegate Lodge **5**
FY1 . . . . .130 E3
Whitehalgh La BB6 . . . . . .143 C1
Whitehall Ave WN6 . . . . . .19 E8
Whitehall Ct **3** FY1 . . . . .89 F8
Whitehall La Blackrod BL6 .31 D3
Grindleton BB7 . . . . .230 A1
Whitehall Rd
Blackburn BB2 . . . . .101 B1
Darwen BB3 . . . . .65 A5
Whitehall St Darwen BB3 . .65 B5
Nelson BB9 . . . . .170 F1
Rochdale OL12 . . . . .52 F1
Whitehaven Cl
Blackburn BB2 . . . . .102 A1
Southport PR8 . . . . .21 A3
Whitehaven St **7** BB11 . .127 E5
Whitehead Cl FY3 . . . . . . .131 D5
Whitehead Dr PR26 . . . . . .76 E3
Whitehead St
Blackburn BB2 . . . . .101 C5
21 Rawtenstall BB4 . . . . . .86 A3
Whitehey WN8 . . . . .8 E8
Whitehey Rd WN8 . . . . .8 E8
Whitehill Rd FY4 . . . . .111 E6
Whiteholme Dr FY5 . . . . . .153 D8
Whiteholme Pl **3** PR2 . . .116 E1
Whiteholme Rd FY5 . . . . .152 F7
Whitehough Pl BB9 . . . . . .171 B1
Whitehouse Ave L37 . . . . .12 A3
Whitehouse La L37 . . . . . .12 A3
Whiteledge Rd WN8 . . . . . .9 B6
Whitelees Way FY6 . . . . .153 D3
Whitelens Ave **4** BB4 . . .116 C1
Whiteley Ave BB2 . . . . . . .101 A1
Whiteley St BB4 . . . . .85 C1
Whiteleys La L40 . . . . .16 D2
Whitelow Rd BL0 . . . . .50 E5
Whitely Gr L33 . . . . .1 A6
Whitemoor Rd BB8 . . . . . .194 C2
Whitemoss OL12 . . . . .52 B2
Whitemoss Ave FY3 . . . . .131 B7
Whitendale **8** LA1 . . . . . .218 A4
Whitendale Cres BB1 . . . .102 A3
Whitendale Dr
Bamber Bridge PR5 . . . . . .77 F8
Hest Bank LA5 . . . . .220 F2
Whitendale Hall PR1 . . . .117 F1

Whitepits La LA2 . . . . . . .239 D5
Whiterails Dr L39 . . . . . . .15 D6
Whiterails Mews L39 . . . . .15 D6
Whiteray Rd **9** LA1 . . . . .218 B2
Whiteside Fold OL12 . . . . .52 A1
Whiteside St **7** FY1 . . . . .130 C6
Whiteside Way FY5 . . . . . .175 D7
Whitestock WN8 . . . . .8 E8
Whitethorn Cl PR6 . . . . . . .78 A2
Whitethorn Mews FY8 . . .111 A2
Whitethorn Sq **4** PR2 . . .116 C1
Whitethorne Mews FY5 . .153 C8
Whitewalls Dr BB8 . . . . . .171 A4
Whitewalls Ind Est
Colne BB8 . . . . .171 A3
Nelson BB9 . . . . .170 F2
Whitewell Cl PR3 . . . . . . .181 D3
Whitewell Dr BB7 . . . . . . .166 C7
Whitewell Pl **11** BB1 . . . .101 F6
Whitewell Rd BB5 . . . . . . .104 D8
Whitewell Vale BB4 . . . . . .86 F2
Whitewood Cl FY8 . . . . . . .90 E4
Whitley Ave
4 Blackpool FY3 . . . . . .130 D5
Cleveleys FY5 . . . . .175 C6
Whitley Rd WN8 . . . . .19 D3
Whitmoor St **7** LA4 . . . . .217 B5
Whitmore Dr PR2 . . . . . . .119 A2
Whitmore Gr PR2 . . . . . . .119 A2
Whitmore Pl PR2 . . . . . . .119 A2
Whitstone Dr WN8 . . . . . . .9 D7
Whittaker Ave FY3 . . . . . .130 E7
Whittaker Cl BB12 . . . . . .127 B8
Whittaker St BB5 . . . . . . .101 C5
Whittakers La BB7 . . . . . .189 F8
Whittam Ave FY4 . . . . . . .130 E1
Whittam Cres BB7 . . . . . .144 B6
Whittam Ct BB10 . . . . . . .129 B6
Whittam Rd Chorley PR7 . .43 B6
Whalley BB7 . . . . .144 B6
Whittam St BB7 . . . . .127 C5
Whitters La PR3 . . . . .203 D2
Whittingham Dr BL0 . . . . .50 C3
Whittingham La
Goosnargh PR3 . . . . .138 C5
Grimsargh PR2 . . . . .139 B2
Whittingham Rd PR3 . . . . .139 F7
Whittle Cl BB7 . . . . .189 F1
Whittle Dr L39 . . . . .15 E7
Whittle Gn PR4 . . . . .136 E3
Whittle Hill Egerton BL7 . .47 E3
Woodplumpton PR4 . . . . .136 E3
Whittle La WN6,WN8 . . . . .27 F4
Whittle Pk PR6 . . . . .78 B2
Whittle St Haslingden BB4 .85 A2
Rawtenstall BB4 . . . . .86 A3
Whittle-le-Woods CE Prim
Sch PR6 . . . . .61 B8
Whittlefield Prim Sch
BB12 . . . . .127 D7
Whittles St OL13 . . . . .71 B8
Whitton Mews **6** BL6 . . . .32 B4
Whittycroft Ave BB9 . . . . .170 E6
Whittycroft Dr BB9 . . . . . .170 E6
Whitwell Ave **4** FY4 . . . . .110 C5
Whitwell Cl WN6 . . . . .29 D2
Whitwell Gdns BL6 . . . . . .32 B5
Whitworth Com High Sch
OL12 . . . . .52 C8
Whitworth Dr PR7 . . . . . . .43 A7
Whitworth Rake OL12 . . . .52 D2
Whitworth Rd OL12 . . . . . .52 F2
Whitworth Sq OL12 . . . . . .52 D8
Whitworth St Horwich BL6 .32 C2
Kirkham PR4 . . . . .113 F6
Whitworth Water Ski Ctr ★
OL12 . . . . .71 C2
Whitworth Way BB18 . . . .196 C4
Wholesome La
Bescar PR9 . . . . .37 E3
New Longton PR4 . . . . . . .75 E5
Whytha Rd BB7 . . . . .192 D6
Wicken Tree Row BB12 . .145 F3
Wickentree Holt OL12 . . . .52 A1
Wickliffe St **9** BB9 . . . . .170 F1
Wicklow Ave FY8 . . . . . . .91 E5
Wicks Cres L37 . . . . .11 C4
Wicks Gdns L37 . . . . .11 D3
Wicks Gn L37 . . . . .11 C3
Wicks Green Cl L37 . . . . .11 C3
Wicks La L37 . . . . .11 D3
Wickworth St BB9 . . . . . .149 A7
Widford Wlk BL6 . . . . .31 E1
Widgeon Cl **5** FY5 . . . . . .175 F4
Widow Hill Rd BB10 . . . . .148 D1
Wigan La
Adlington PR7,WN1 . . . . . .30 D7
Chorley PR7 . . . . .43 E2
Wigan Rd
Bamber Bridge PR5 . . . . . .77 E7
Euxton PR7,PR25 . . . . . . .60 C5
Ormskirk L39 . . . . .16 A5
Skelmersdale WN8 . . . . . . .8 F8
Westhead L40 . . . . .16 E4
Wigeon Row FY8 . . . . .90 E7
Wiggins La L40 . . . . .38 B6
Wight Moss Way PR8 . . . .35 D3
Wignall St **8** PR1 . . . . . . .118 C1
Wignalls Mdw L38 . . . . . . .2 F3
Wigston Cl PR8 . . . . .21 B4
Wigton Ave PR25 . . . . .59 D7
Wilbraham St PR1 . . . . . .118 C1
Wilcove WN8 . . . . .17 F1
Wild La FY4 . . . . .111 D4
Wilderswood Ave BL6 . . . .32 C4

Wilderswood Cl PR6 ...78 C2
Wilderswood Ct BL6 ...32 D4
Wilding's La FY8 ...90 B8
Wildman St
▣ Blackpool FY3 ...130 D7
Preston PR1 ...117 E2
Wildoaks Dr FY5 ...153 D8
Wilds Pl BL0 ...50 B5
Wildwood Cl BL0 ...50 A4
Wilfield St ▣ BB11 ...127 E6
Wilford St FY3 ...130 E7
Wilfred Dr BL9 ...33 B4
Wilfred St BB5 ...104 C4
Wilkie Ave BB11 ...127 E2
Wilkinson Ave FY3 ...130 E4
Wilkinson Mount ▣
BB18 ...197 B2
Wilkinson St
Bamber Bridge PR5 ...77 B8
Barrowford BB9 ...170 C2
Clow Bridge BB11 ...106 B4
Haslingden BB4 ...85 B4
Higham BB12 ...146 F5
Nelson BB9 ...148 E7
Wilkinson Way FY6 ...199 F5
Willacy La PR4 ...135 E3
Willacy Par LA3 ...216 E2
Willaston Ave BB9 ...170 E8
Willey La LA2 ...206 D6
William Griffiths Ct
BB2 ...101 B2
William Henry St ▣ PR1 ...97 C8
William Herbert St ▣
BB1 ...101 F6
William Hopwood St ▣
BB1 ...102 A4
William St
Accrington BB5 ...104 C7
Bacup OL13 ...71 C8
▣ Bamber Bridge PR5 ...77 A8
Blackburn BB2 ...101 C4
▣ Blackpool FY3 ...130 E7
Brierfield BB9 ...148 B6
Carnforth LA5 ...223 D3
Clayton-le-M BB5 ...125 A1
Colne BB8 ...171 E4
▣ Darwen BB3 ...82 A1
▣ Earby BB18 ...197 B1
Horwich BL6 ...32 A3
▣ Nelson BB9 ...170 E1
Ramsbottom BL0 ...68 C1
Whitworth OL12 ...71 C1
William Thompson Rec Ctr
BB11 ...128 A5
William Young Cl PR1 ...118 C2
Williams Ave LA4 ...218 A6
Williams Dr BB2 ...102 A1
Williams La PR2 ...118 C7
Williams Pl ▣ BB9 ...148 F8
Williams Rd BB10 ...128 B8
Williamson Park Butterfly
Ho★ LA1 ...215 B7
Williamson Rd LA1 ...215 A8
Willis Rd BB2 ...101 A2
Willis St ▣ BB11 ...127 E5
Willoughby Ave FY5 ...175 C2
Willoughby St ▣ BB1 ...101 E6
Willow Ave BB4 ...86 A4
Willow Bank
Bilsborrow PR3 ...159 A5
Darwen BB3 ...65 A6
Willow Bank La BB3 ...81 F1
Willow Brook
Accrington BB5 ...104 B6
Shirdley Hill L39 ...23 A6
Willow Chase PR4 ...113 C4
Willow Cl Adlington PR6 ...31 B8
Bamber Bridge PR5 ...77 A8
Barrowford BB9 ...170 B1
Clayton-le-M BB5 ...124 C3
Forton PR3 ...207 B3
Freckleton PR4 ...93 A5
Gregson Lane PR5 ...98 E1
Higher Penwortham PR1 ...96 A4
Thornton FY5 ...176 D1
Willow Coppice PR2 ...116 E3
Willow Cres
Burscough Bridge L40 ...25 F6
Clayton-le-W PR25 ...77 F8
Fulwood PR2 ...118 E2
Willow Ct
Poulton-le-F FY6 ...154 A3
Standish WN6 ...29 E2
▣ Thornton FY5 ...176 D1
Willow Dr Barrow BB6 ...144 D8
Charnock Richard PR7 ...42 D3
Freckleton PR4 ...93 A5
Garstang PR3 ...204 C1
Nelson BB9 ...149 A8
Poulton-le-F FY6 ...131 D8
Skelmersdale WN8 ...17 E1
Wrea Green PR4 ...113 C4
Willow End L40 ...25 F4
Willow Field PR6 ...78 C3
Willow Field Chase PR5 ...99 B2
Willow Gn
▣ Ormskirk L39 ...15 C5
Preston PR2 ...96 A8
Rufford L40 ...39 A3
Willow Gr Blackpool FY3 ...130 D1
Formby L37 ...11 F4
Goosnargh PR3 ...138 D6
Hambleton FY6 ...177 B2

Willow Gr continued
Lancaster LA1 ...215 B8
Morecambe LA4 ...217 F6
Southport PR9 ...35 E7
West Bradford BB7 ...189 D7
Willow Hey
Skelmersdale WN8 ...17 F1
Tarleton WN8 ...57 A7
Willow Ho PR8 ...35 A5
Willow La LA1 ...214 C7
Willow Lane Com Prim Sch
LA1 ...214 D8
Willow Lodge FY8 ...90 C7
Willow Mill LA2 ...237 C3
Willow Mount BB1 ...122 F3
Willow Pk BB5 ...103 C2
Willow Pl PR4 ...155 F1
Willow Rd Chorley PR6 ...61 E2
Wymott PR26 ...58 E8
Willow St Accrington BB5 104 B6
Blackburn BB1 ...102 A7
Burnley BB12 ...127 E6
Bury BL9 ...33 B2
Clayton-le-M BB5 ...124 E3
Darwen BB3 ...81 F1
Fleetwood FY7 ...199 A4
Great Harwood BB6 ...124 C4
Haslingden BB4 ...85 B3
Rawtenstall BB4 ...69 E8
Willow Tree Ave
Broughton PR3 ...137 D3
Rawtenstall BB4 ...85 E2
Willow Tree Cres PR25 ...76 D1
Willow Tree Gdns ▣
FY5 ...176 D1
Willow Trees Dr BB1 ...122 C1
Willow Way PR4 ...75 F7
Willow Wlk WN8 ...18 B4
Willow-Dale FY5 ...176 D1
Willowbank Ave FY4 ...110 E6
Willowbank Cotts PR26 ...58 B2
Willowcroft Dr FY6 ...177 B1
Willowdene FY5 ...175 E1
Willowfield Rd LA3 ...213 A7
Willowgrove Pk FY6 ...200 B4
Willowhey PR9 ...53 F4
Willowmead Pk FY8 ...112 F2
Willowmead Way OL12 ...52 A2
Willows Ave
Cleveleys FY5 ...175 E1
Lytham St Anne's FY8 ...90 E3
Willows La
Accrington BB5 ...104 A3
Kirkham PR4 ...113 F5
Willows Park La PR3 ...140 B8
Willows RC Prim Sch The
PR4 ...113 F5
Willows The Chorley PR7 ...43 B4
Coppull PR7 ...29 E8
Kirkham PR4 ...113 E4
Lytham St Anne's FY8 ...90 E3
Mawdesley L40 ...40 C2
Mellor Brook BB2 ...121 C3
Southport PR8 ...34 F6
Whitworth OL12 ...52 C5
Wills Ave L31 ...5 C2
Willshaw Rd FY2 ...152 B1
Wilmar Rd PR25 ...77 C2
Wilmcote Gr PR8 ...21 B4
Wilmore Cl BB8 ...171 C5
Wilmot Rd PR2 ...118 C3
Wilpshire Banks BB1 ...122 F4
Wilpshire Rd BB1 ...123 E4
Wilsham Rd WN5 ...10 E5
Wilson Cl PR4 ...57 A7
Wilson Dr PR4 ...155 F1
Wilson Fold BB12 ...127 B6
Wilson Fold Ave BL6 ...32 F1
Wilson La LA3 ...212 E8
Wilson Sq FY5 ...152 D7
Wilson St Blackburn BB2 ...101 D2
Bury BL9 ...33 A1
Clitheroe BB7 ...166 E7
Foulridge BB8 ...194 D1
Horwich BL6 ...32 A4
Wilson's Endowed CE Prim
Sch LA2 ...237 B8
Wilton Cl Blackburn BB2 ...100 F8
Lancaster LA1 ...218 E4
Wilton Ct BB2 ...100 F7
Wilton Gr PR1 ...96 A4
Wilton Par FY1 ...130 B7
Wilton Pl ▣ PR25 ...77 B1
Wilton St
Barrowford BB9 ...170 D3
Brierfield BB9 ...148 B6
Burnley BB10 ...148 B1
Wiltshire Ave BB12 ...127 B7
Wiltshire Dr BB4 ...68 B8
Wiltshire Mews PR4 ...116 C5
Wilvere Ct FY5 ...152 C7
Wilvere Dr FY5 ...152 C8
Wilworth Cres BB1 ...122 E2
Wimberley Banks BB1 ...101 E6
Wimberley Gdns ▣ BB1 101 E6
Wimberley Pl ▣ BB1 ...101 E6
Wimberley St BB1 ...101 E7
Wimbledon Ave FY5 ...152 D7
Wimbledon Ct FY5 ...152 D6
Wimborne FY8 ...89 F5
Wimborne Cl BL6 ...32 F1
Wimbourne Pl FY4 ...110 B6
Wimbrick Cl L39 ...15 D4
Wimbrick Cres L39 ...15 D3
Winchcombe Rd FY5 ...152 C7
Winchester Ave
Accrington BB5 ...104 C7

Winchester Ave continued
▣ Blackpool FY4 ...130 D1
Chorley PR7 ...43 E4
Lancaster LA1 ...215 B5
Morecambe LA3 ...217 D6
Morecambe LA4 ...217 D6
Winchester Cl
Morecambe LA3 ...217 B2
▣ Orrell WN5 ...10 F7
Winchester Dr FY6 ...153 B6
Winchester Rd
Longshaw WN5 ...10 D1
Padiham BB12 ...126 D6
Winchester St BB1 ...102 A3
Winchester Way ▣ BB1 181 B7
Winckley Ct ▣ PR1 ...96 F7
Winckley Rd
Clayton-le-M BB5 ...124 C2
Preston PR1 ...96 F6
Winckley Sq PR1 ...96 F7
Winckley St ▣ PR1 ...96 F7
Winder Garth LA6 ...240 B1
Winder La PR3 ...207 B2
Windermere Ave
Accrington BB5 ...125 D1
Burnley BB10 ...148 A2
Clitheroe BB7 ...166 C7
Colne BB8 ...171 F6
Fleetwood FY7 ...175 D8
Leyland PR25 ...77 A3
Morecambe LA4 ...217 D4
Windermere Cl ▣ BB1 ...101 F6
Windermere Cres PR8 ...21 C3
Windermere Ct ▣ LA4 ...217 D4
Windermere Dr
Adlington PR6 ...44 B1
Darwen BB3 ...82 C3
Maghull L31 ...5 E2
Rainford Junction WA11 ...8 F2
Ramsbottom BL0 ...50 C7
Rishton BB1 ...124 A1
Windermere Ho PR1 ...96 B4
Windermere Rd
Bacup OL13 ...88 A3
Blackpool FY4 ...110 C8
Bolton-le-S LA5 ...221 A4
Carnforth LA5 ...221 E8
▣ Chorley PR6 ...43 E7
Fulwood PR2 ...118 C4
Hightown L38 ...3 A4
Lancaster LA1 ...215 B8
Orrell WN5 ...10 F8
Padiham BB12 ...146 C2
Preston PR1 ...119 A1
Windermere Sq FY8 ...110 F2
Windfield Cl L33 ...1 A6
Windflower Dr PR25 ...77 E3
Windgate Much Hoole PR4 ...74 E2
Skelmersdale WN8 ...17 F1
Tarleton PR4 ...57 B5
Windgate Fold PR4 ...57 A5
Windham Pl LA1 ...218 A3
Windholme ▣ LA1 ...218 A2
Windle Ash L31 ...5 C2
Windle Cl FY4 ...110 B4
Windmill Animal Farm★
L40 ...38 B4
Windmill Ave
Kirkham PR4 ...114 C4
Ormskirk L39 ...15 F5
Windmill Cl FY3 ...131 E5
Windmill Ct ▣ LA1 ...215 A3
Windmill Cvn Site FY4 ...111 E8
Windmill Ho
Blackpool FY4 ...110 F6
Southport PR9 ...53 F2
Windmill Hts WN8 ...10 A8
Windmill La PR6 ...79 B7
Windmill Pl FY4 ...110 F6
Windmill Rd WN8 ...9 F7
Windmill St LA1 ...214 D8
Windmill View PR4 ...114 A4
Windrows WN8 ...17 F1
Windrush Ave BL0 ...50 A2
Windrush The OL12 ...52 C4
Windsor Ave
Adlington PR7 ...30 F6
Blackpool FY4 ...110 B8
Church BB5 ...104 A8
Clitheroe BB7 ...166 C7
Fulwood PR2 ...117 B2
Haslingden BB4 ...85 A1
Lancaster LA1 ...215 B5
Longridge PR3 ...139 F7
Middleforth Green PR1 ...96 C3
Morecambe LA4 ...217 A3
New Longton PR4 ...96 A1
Newchurch BB4 ...86 E1
Thornton FY5 ...176 B2
Windsor Cl
Blackburn BB1 ...102 B3
Burscough L40 ...25 E3
Chorley PR7 ...43 B7
Leyland PR25 ...59 D7
Ramsbottom BL8 ...50 A1
Read BB12 ...145 D2
Windsor Ct
Poulton-le-F FY6 ...153 E3
Southport PR8 ...34 E4
Windsor Dr Brinscall PR6 ...62 E8
Fulwood PR2 ...117 D6
Horwich BL6 ...32 E2
Windsor Gdns PR3 ...181 B7
Windsor Gr LA4 ...217 A4
Windsor Lodge ▣ FY8 ...90 D4
Windsor Pl
Barnoldswick BB18 ...196 D3
▣ Fleetwood FY7 ...199 B5

Windsor Rd
Bamber Bridge PR5 ...97 D3
Blackburn BB2 ...101 B6
Blackburn,Knuzden Brook
BB1 ...102 E4
Chorley PR7 ...43 B7
Darwen BB3 ...81 F3
Eccleston PR7 ...41 C7
Formby L37 ...11 F1
Garstang PR3 ...181 B7
Great Harwood BB6 ...124 D5
Lytham St Anne's,Ansdell
FY8 ...90 A5
Lytham St Anne's,Ansdell
FY8 ...90 A4
▣ Maghull L31 ...5 C1
Morecambe LA3 ...216 F3
Normoss FY3 ...131 B7
Skelmersdale WN8 ...10 A8
Southport PR9 ...35 D7
Windsor St
Accrington BB5 ...104 C6
Burnley BB11 ...127 E6
Colne BB8 ...171 E5
Nelson BB9 ...149 A7
Windsor Terr FY7 ...199 B5
Windward Cl BB3 ...81 F6
Windy Bank BB8 ...171 E5
Windy Harbour Holiday Ctr
FY6 ...154 F5
Windy Harbour Rd
Singleton FY6 ...155 A4
Southport PR8 ...21 E7
Windy Hill LA2 ...239 E8
Windy St PR3 ...185 E3
Windyhill ▣ LA1 ...214 F8
Winery La PR5 ...97 C5
Winewall La BB8 ...172 C5
Winewall Rd BB8 ...172 B5
Wingate Ave
Blackpool FY5 ...152 D7
Morecambe LA4 ...217 D4
Wingate Pl FY5 ...152 D8
Wingate Wlk L33 ...1 A3
Wingate-Saul Rd LA1 ...214 E7
Wingates ▣ PR1 ...96 C3
Wingrove Rd FY7 ...198 F2
Winifred Ave BL9 ...33 F4
Winifred La L39 ...6 B8
Winifred St
Blackpool FY1 ...130 B4
Ramsbottom BL0 ...50 B5
Rochdale OL12 ...52 B1
Winmarleigh CE Prim Sch
PR3 ...203 E5
Winmarleigh Rd
Lancaster LA1 ...215 A2
Preston PR2 ...117 B1
Winmarleigh St ▣ BB1 ...102 C5
Winmarleigh Wlk BB1 ...102 C4
Winmoss Dr L33 ...1 A5
Winnipeg Cl BB2 ...101 B8
Winnipeg Pl FY2 ...152 E3
Winscar Wlk FY6 ...153 B3
Winsford Cres FY5 ...152 C8
Winsford Wlk BB11 ...127 B5
Winslow Ave FY6 ...153 B5
Winslow Cl ▣ PR1 ...96 E2
Winsor Ave PR25 ...60 B8
Winstanley Coll WN5 ...10 F3
Winstanley Gr ▣ FY1 ...130 C5
Winstanley Rd Orrell WN5 10 F3
Skelmersdale WN8 ...8 F8
Winster Cl PR5 ...98 E4
Winster Ct BB5 ...124 E2
Winster Pk LA1 ...218 A2
Winster Pl FY4 ...131 D1
Winster Wlk LA1 ...218 A2
Winsters The WN8 ...17 F1
Winston Ave
Cleveleys FY5 ...175 F2
Lytham St Anne's FY8 ...90 B6
Winston Cres PR8 ...35 E2
Winston Rd BB1 ...101 D7
Winter Gardens Arc
LA4 ...217 A5
Winter Hey La BL6 ...32 B3
Winter Hill Ct PR2 ...119 C7
Winterburn Rd BB2 ...81 C7
Winterley Dr BB5 ...125 E1
Winterton Rd BB3 ...82 A2
Winthorpe Ave LA4 ...217 D3
Winton Ave
Blackpool FY4 ...131 A1
Fulwood PR2 ...117 F6
Winton Gn BL6 ...32 F1
Winward Ho FY4 ...89 E5
Wiseman Cl LA4 ...217 C4
Wiseman St BB11 ...127 F6
Wisp Hill Gr LA2 ...219 D6
Wisteria Dr BB3 ...82 B7
Wiswell Cl
Brierfield BB10 ...148 E2
Rawtenstall BB4 ...86 A4
Wiswell La BB7 ...144 D6
Wiswell Shay BB7 ...144 E7
Witham Cl WN6 ...29 D1
Witham Rd WN8 ...17 D1
Withens Rd L31 ...5 D3
Withers St BB1 ...101 F4
Witherslack Cl LA4 ...217 B3
Withgill Piggery Cotts
BB7 ...165 E6
Within Gr BB5 ...104 D8
Withington La PR7 ...41 E2
Withins Field L38 ...2 F2
Withins La L37 ...4 A7
Withnell Fold PR6 ...79 C2

Withnell Fold Old Rd
PR6 ...79 E1
Withnell Fold Prim Sch
PR6 ...79 C3
Withnell Rd FY4 ...110 B8
Withy Ct PR2 ...117 E3
Withy Grove Cl PR5 ...97 F1
Withy Grove Cres PR5 ...97 F1
Withy Grove Rd PR5 ...97 F1
Withy Par PR2 ...117 E4
Withy Trees Ave PR5 ...97 F1
Withy Trees Cl PR5 ...97 F1
Witney Ave BB2 ...80 E8
Wittlewood Dr BB5 ...125 B1
Witton Ave FY7 ...198 E1
Witton Ctry Pk★ BB2 ...100 F4
Witton Ctry Pk Visitors Ctr★
BB2 ...100 F3
Witton Gr FY7 ...198 E1
Witton Par BB2 ...101 C3
Witton Park High Sch
BB2 ...101 A4
Witton St PR1 ...97 B8
Woborrow Rd LA3 ...212 E8
Woburn Cl BB5 ...104 E3
Woburn Gn PR25 ...77 B2
Woburn Rd FY1 ...130 C7
Woburn Way PR3 ...181 D2
Wold The PR6 ...62 A3
Wolfenden Gn BB4 ...69 F8
Wollaton Dr PR25 ...35 F3
Wolseley Cl PR25 ...60 A8
Wolseley Pl ▣ PR1 ...97 A7
Wolseley Rd PR1 ...96 E5
Wolseley St
Blackburn BB2 ...101 D1
Lancaster LA1 ...215 A8
Wolsey Cl FY5 ...175 E3
Wolsley Rd
Blackpool FY1 ...130 B1
Fleetwood FY7 ...198 F4
Wolverton WN8 ...8 F8
Wolverton Ave FY2 ...152 B2
Wood Bank
Haslingden BB4 ...67 F6
Kingsfold PR1 ...96 C3
Wood Cl BB9 ...170 A5
Wood Clough Platts
BB9 ...148 A5
Wood End
Brierfield BB12 ...147 F3
Kingsfold PR1 ...96 C1
Wood End Rd PR6 ...78 B2
Wood Gn Kirkham PR4 ...114 B7
Leyland PR25 ...76 E2
Wood Green Dr FY5 ...152 F8
Wood Hey Gr OL12 ...52 F4
Wood House La BB7 ...229 A8
Wood La Edenfield BL0 ...68 C2
Haskayne L37,L39 ...13 C1
Heskin Green PR7 ...41 E3
Hoscar L40 ...26 E5
Mawdesley L40 ...40 D5
Parbold WN8 ...27 D2
Wrightington Bar PR7,WN6 ...28 E8
Wood Lark Dr PR7 ...42 F5
Wood Lea Bank ▣ BB4 ...69 F8
Wood Lea Rd BB4 ...69 F8
Wood Nook ▣ BB4 ...86 A7
Wood Park Rd FY1 ...130 E1
Wood Road La BL8,BL9 ...50 C1
Wood St Blackpool FY1 ...130 B5
Brierfield BB9 ...148 B5
Burnley BB10 ...128 A8
Church BB5 ...103 E5
Colne BB8 ...171 E4
Darwen BB3 ...81 F1
Fleetwood FY7 ...175 E8
Great Harwood BB6 ...124 E5
Hapton BB12 ...126 C4
Horwich BL6 ...32 C3
▣ Lancaster LA1 ...214 F8
Lytham St Anne's FY8 ...89 E6
Poulton-le-F FY6 ...154 A3
Ramsbottom BL0 ...50 B5
Wood Street Livesey Fold ▣
BB3 ...81 F1
Wood Terr BB7 ...190 E5
Wood View
Blackburn BB2 ...100 F1
Burton in L LA6 ...242 C3
Wood View La FY6 ...177 C7
Wood's Brow PR3 ...141 B6
Wood's La PR3 ...180 A6
Woodacre Rd PR2 ...119 A2
Woodale Laithe BB9 ...170 C3
Woodbank Ave BB3 ...81 E2
Woodbank Ct ▣ FY5 ...152 F7
Woodbine Gdns BB12 ...127 C7
Woodbine Rd
Blackburn BB2 ...101 B6
Burnley BB12 ...127 C6
Woodbine Terr OL14 ...109 B1
Woodbridge Gdns OL12 ...52 C2
Woodburn Cl BB21 ...101 A8
Woodbury Ave
Blackburn BB2 ...101 D2
Fence BB12 ...147 D7
Woodcock Cl FY5 ...176 A5
Woodcock Est PR5 ...77 B6
Woodcock Fold PR7 ...41 C7
Woodcock Hill Rd BB2 ...100 B3
Woodcote Cl L33 ...1 A4
Woodcourt Ave BB11 ...127 D3
Woodcrest BB1 ...122 F5
Woodcroft
Appley Bridge WN6 ...19 E6

Woodcroft continued
Skelmersdale WN8 . . . . .8 F8
Woodcroft Ave BB4 . . . . . . .85 F5
Woodcroft Cl PR1 . . . . . . .96 C2
Woodcroft St SB4 . . . . . . .85 F5
Woodfall PR7 . . . . .61 B2
Woodfield PR5 . . . . .78 C6
Woodfield Ave
Accrington BB5 . . . . .104 D3
3 Blackpool FY1 . . . . . . .130 B2
Rochdale OL12 . . . . .52 E2
Woodfield Ct FY5 . . . . . . .176 B1
Woodfield Rd
Blackpool FY1 . . . . .130 B2
Chorley PR7 . . . . .61 C1
Ormskirk L39 . . . . .15 D3
Thornton FY5 . . . . .176 D1
Woodfield Terr BB9 . . . . .148 C5
Woodfield View BB7 . . . .144 C5
Woodfields
Hurst Green BB7 . . . . . . .165 B3
Simonstone BB12 . . . . . . .145 E3
Woodfold PR1 . . . . .96 B3
Woodfold Cl BB2 . . . . . . .121 C3
Woodfold La PR3 . . . . . . .204 C5
Woodfold Park Farm
BB2 . . . . .100 B8
Woodfold Pl BB2 . . . . . . .101 B5
Woodford Copse PR7 . . . .43 A7
Woodgate LA3 . . . . .217 F2
Woodgate Ave BB9 . . . . . .33 D4
Woodgate Hill Rd
Bury BL9 . . . . .33 C3
Bury,Woodgate Hill BL9 . . .33 D4
Woodgates Rd BB2 . . . . . .100 F5
Woodgrove Rd BB11 . . . . .128 B3
Woodhall Cres PR5 . . . . . .98 E4
Woodhall Gdns FY6 . . . . .177 C2
Woodhart La PR7 . . . . .41 C5
Woodhead Cl
Ramsbottom BL0 . . . . .50 C4
Rawtenstall BB4 . . . . .87 A2
Woodhead Rd BB12 . . . . .145 D2
Woodhey High Sch BL0 . . .50 A3
Woodhey Rd BL0 . . . . .50 A3
Woodhill Ave LA4 . . . . . . .217 A3
Woodhill Cl LA4 . . . . .217 A3
Woodhill La LA4 . . . . .217 A4
Woodhouse Rd FY5 . . . . . .153 E8
Woodhurst Dr WN6 . . . . . .29 D1
Woodland Ave
Bacup OL13 . . . . .87 F5
Bescar L40 . . . . .23 F7
Thornton FY5 . . . . .176 B2
Woodland Cl
Hambleton FY6 . . . . .177 D1
Wrea Green PR4 . . . . .113 B3
Woodland Cres FY6 . . . . .200 A6
Woodland Dr
Clayton-le-M BB5 . . . . . . .124 F5
Poulton-le-F FY6 . . . . . . .153 E1
Standish WN6 . . . . .29 E2
Woodland Gr
Blackpool FY3 . . . . .130 E4
Egerton BL7 . . . . .47 D2
Higher Penwortham PR1 . .96 B5
Woodland Pl BB3 . . . . . . .81 F7
Woodland Rd OL12 . . . . . .52 C2
Woodland Terr OL13 . . . . .87 F4
Woodland View
Bacup OL13 . . . . .87 F4
Brinscall PR6 . . . . .62 F7
Great Harwood BB6 . . . . .124 C6
Woodlands Ave
Bamber Bridge PR5 . . . . . .98 A2
Blackburn BB2 . . . . .100 E1
Fulwood PR2 . . . . .118 C2
Kingsfold PR1 . . . . .96 E2
8 Kirkham PR4 . . . . . . .113 F5
Woodlands Cl Formby L37 11 D2
Newton-w-S PR4 . . . . . . .114 F3
Ormskirk L39 . . . . .16 A4
Rawtenstall BB4 . . . . .86 D1
Southport PR9 . . . . .35 D8
Woodlands Com Prim Sch
WN8 . . . . .18 C2
Woodlands Cres PR3 . . . .137 B5
Woodlands Ct 5 FY8 . . . .90 D4
Woodlands Dr
Fulwood PR2 . . . . .117 E8
Kirkham PR4 . . . . .114 B7
Leyland PR25 . . . . .76 F1
Morecambe LA3 . . . . . . .216 E2
Shevington WN6 . . . . .19 F4
Silverdale LA5 . . . . .224 C4
Warton PR4 . . . . .92 C5
West Bradford BB7 . . . . .189 D7
Whalley BB7 . . . . .144 C5
Woodlands Gr
Darwen BB3 . . . . .81 D2
Grimsargh PR2 . . . . .139 E1
Morecambe LA3 . . . . . . .216 E2
Padiham BB12 . . . . .146 B1
Woodlands Mdw PR7 . . . .43 C3
Woodlands Pk BB7 . . . . .144 C5
Woodlands Prim Sch
L37 . . . . .11 D3
Woodlands Rd
Edenfield BL0 . . . . .68 D2
Formby L37 . . . . .11 D3
Lancaster LA1 . . . . .218 E4
Lytham St Anne's FY8 . . . .90 D4
Nelson BB9 . . . . .148 F8
Woodlands Sch PR2 . . . . .118 E2
Woodlands Specl Sch
FY3 . . . . .130 E4
Woodlands The
Brockhall Village BB6 . . . .143 C6

Woodlands The continued
Garstang PR3 . . . . .181 B8
6 Preston PR2 . . . . . . .116 E1
Southport PR8 . . . . .21 C5
Woodlands View LA6 . . . .237 B8
Woodlands Way
Longton PR4 . . . . .74 F8
Newsham PR3 . . . . .137 B5
Woodlea Chase BB3 . . . . .65 C3
Woodlea Cl PR9 . . . . .54 D5
Woodlea Gdns BB9 . . . . .148 C5
Woodlea Jun Sch PR25 . . .59 F8
Woodlea Rd
Blackburn BB1 . . . . .102 B4
Leyland BB9 . . . . .59 F8
Woodlee Rd PR4 . . . . .73 F2
Woodleigh Cl L31 . . . . .5 B5
Woodley Ave
Accrington BB5 . . . . .104 C4
Thornton FY5 . . . . .176 D1
Woodley Park Rd WN8 . . .18 B4
Woodman La LA2 . . . . . . .241 F6
Woodmancote PR7 . . . . . .61 B2
Woodmoss La PR8,L40 . . .36 E2
Woodnook Prim Sch
BB5 . . . . .104 C4
Woodnook Rd WN6 . . . . . .19 E8
Woodpecker Hill 3
BB11 . . . . .127 C5
Woodplumpton La PR3 . . .137 C2
Woodplumpton Rd
Burnley BB11 . . . . .127 F1
Fulwood PR2 . . . . .117 C3
Woodplumpton PR4 . . . . .136 E2
Woodplumpton,Moor Side
PR4 . . . . .136 D4
Woodplumpton St Anne's CE
Prim Sch PR4 . . . . .136 D2
Woodridge Ave FY5 . . . . .152 C8
Woodrow WN8 . . . . .8 E8
Woodrow Dr WN8 . . . . . . .27 A1
Woodroyd Dr BL9 . . . . . . .33 C3
Woodruff Cl FY5 . . . . . . .175 F5
Woodrush LA4 . . . . .217 F6
Woods Brow BB2 . . . . . . .120 D5
Woods Cl L39 . . . . .14 A4
Woods Gn PR1 . . . . .96 E6
Woods La PR3,PR4 . . . . . .135 E6
Woodsend Cl BB2 . . . . . . .82 A8
Woodside Chorley PR7 . . . .43 E4
Euxton PR7 . . . . .60 C3
Haslingden BB4 . . . . .85 C1
Leyland PR25 . . . . .77 C4
Woodside Ave
Clayton Green PR6 . . . . . .78 B1
Fulwood,Cadley PR2 . . . .117 E4
Fulwood,Ribbleton PR2 . . .118 E3
New Longton PR4 . . . . . . .75 F7
Rishton BB1 . . . . .102 F8
Southport PR8 . . . . .21 B3
Woodside Cl
Huncoat BB5 . . . . .125 F1
Skelmersdale WN8 . . . . . .10 C8
Woodside Cres BB4 . . . . . .86 D1
Woodside Dr
Blackpool FY3 . . . . .131 A5
Ramsbottom BL0 . . . . .50 A5
Standish WN6 . . . . .29 E2
Woodside Rd
Accrington,Hillock Vale
BB5 . . . . .104 E8
Huncoat BB5 . . . . .125 F1
Simonstone BB12 . . . . . . .145 E2
Woodside Terr BB9 . . . . .148 C8
Woodsley St BB12 . . . . . .127 B5
Woodstock Ave FY5 . . . . .153 C8
Woodstock Cl 8 PR5 . . . .77 C8
Woodstock Cres BB2 . . . . .80 E8
Woodstock Dr PR8 . . . . . .21 E4
Woodstock Gdns FY4 . . . .110 B7
Woodstock St 12 OL12 . . .52 C1
Woodtop 1 BB11 . . . . . . .127 D5
Woodvale Darwen BB3 . . . .81 F7
Leyland PR25 . . . . .59 A8
Woodvale Ct PR9 . . . . . . .55 A5
Woodvale Rd
Clayton Green PR6 . . . . . .78 B3
Southport PR8 . . . . .21 E2
Woodville Rd
Adlington PR6 . . . . .43 F1
Blackburn BB1 . . . . .102 A7
Brierfield BB9 . . . . .148 C6
2 Chorley PR7 . . . . .43 C8
Kingsfold PR1 . . . . .96 D2
Woodville Rd W 5 PR1 . . .96 C2
Woodville St
Lancaster LA1 . . . . .215 A8
Leyland PR25 . . . . .77 B2
Woodville Terr
Darwen BB3 . . . . .65 B6
Lytham St Anne's FY8 . . . .90 F3
Woodward Rd L33 . . . . .1 D4
Woodway PR7 . . . . .117 C4
Woodwell La LA5 . . . . . . .224 C1
Wookey Cl PR2 . . . . .118 D6
Wooley La BB5 . . . . .104 F2
Woolman Rd FY1 . . . . . . .130 C4
Woolpack BB8 . . . . .171 E3
Woolwich St BB1 . . . . . . .102 B5
Woone La BB7 . . . . .166 D7
Worcester Ave
4 Accrington BB5 . . . . . .104 A4
Garstang PR3 . . . . .181 B8
Lancaster LA1 . . . . .215 B5
Leyland PR25 . . . . .60 B8
Worcester Gdns PR4 . . . .116 D5
Worcester Pl PR7 . . . . . . .43 E3

Worcester Rd
Blackburn BB1 . . . . .102 C5
Blackpool FY3 . . . . .131 A3
Worden Cl PR25 . . . . .59 F7
Worden High Sch PR25 . . .76 E1
Worden La PR25 . . . . .60 A7
Worden Rd PR2 . . . . .117 D3
Wordsworth Ave
Blackpool FY3 . . . . .131 B2
Bolton-le-S LA5 . . . . .221 A5
Longshaw WN5 . . . . .10 C1
5 Lytham St Anne's FY8 . .91 D4
Orrell WN5 . . . . .10 A6
Padiham BB12 . . . . .126 E7
Thornton FY5 . . . . .176 A2
Warton PR4 . . . . .92 E6
Wordsworth Cl
Ormskirk L39 . . . . .15 D6
Oswaldtwistle BB5 . . . . . .103 C4
Wordsworth Ct 1 FY8 . . . .90 C4
Wordsworth Dr BB6 . . . . .124 B4
Wordsworth Gdns BB3 . . . .82 B5
Wordsworth Ho LA1 . . . . .218 C4
Wordsworth Pl PR5 . . . . . .97 D2
Wordsworth Rd
Accrington BB5 . . . . .104 A4
Colne BB8 . . . . .171 D5
Wordsworth St
Brierfield BB10 . . . . .148 F2
Burnley BB12 . . . . .127 C6
5 Hapton BB12 . . . . . . .126 C4
Wordsworth Terr PR6 . . . . .61 D2
Workshop St BB4 . . . . . . .212 F2
Worrall St 1 OL12 . . . . . . .52 C2
Worsicks Cotts FY6 . . . . .154 E1
Worsley Ave FY4 . . . . . . .110 C7
Worsley Cl FY6 . . . . .199 E5
Worsley Cl 13 BB5 . . . . . .103 E4
Worsley Rd FY8 . . . . .90 C5
Worsley St
Accrington BB5 . . . . .104 D4
Rising Bridge BB4 . . . . . . .85 A8
Worsten Ave BB2 . . . . . . .101 C1
Worsthorne Prim Sch
BB10 . . . . .129 A6
Worston Cl
Accrington BB5 . . . . .103 F4
Rawtenstall BB4 . . . . .86 A4
Worston La BB6 . . . . .124 F6
Worston Pl BB2 . . . . .101 C5
Worswick Cres 3 BB4 . . . .86 A2
Worthalls Rd BB12 . . . . . .145 D1
Worthing Cl PR8 . . . . .34 E5
Worthing Rd PR2 . . . . . . .117 A4
Worthington Rd FY4 . . . . .111 B4
Worthy St PR6 . . . . .43 E7
Wraith St BB3 . . . . .65 A8
Wray Cres
Wrea Green PR4 . . . . . . .113 C4
Wymott PR26 . . . . .58 F2
Wray Ct LA1 . . . . .218 C4
Wray Gr FY5 . . . . .152 D8
Wray with Botton Prim Sch
LA2 . . . . .238 D6
Wraywood Ct FY7 . . . . . .198 C1
Wren Ave PR1 . . . . .96 E5
Wren Cl Carleton FY6 . . . .153 A4
Thornton FY5 . . . . .153 D8
Wren Dr BL9 . . . . .33 B4
Wren Gr PR3 . . . . .130 C2
Wren St Burnley BB12 . . . .127 C6
Nelson BB9 . . . . .148 F8
Preston PR1 . . . . .118 B2
Wrennalls La PR7 . . . . . . .41 B5
Wright St Chorley PR6 . . . .43 E8
Horwich BL6 . . . . .32 B4
6 Kirkham PR4 . . . . . . .113 F6
Southport PR9 . . . . .35 C7
Weir OL13 . . . . .88 A7
Wright St W 4 BL6 . . . . . .32 B4
Wrightington Bar WN6 . . .28 E8
Wrightington Hospl
WN6 . . . . .28 D2
Wrightington Mossy Lea Prim
Sch WN6 . . . . .28 D2
Wrights Fold PR25 . . . . . .60 C8
Wrights Terr PR8 . . . . . . .35 B3
Wrigleys Cl L37 . . . . .11 F5
Wrigleys La L37 . . . . .11 F5
Written Stone La PR3 . . . .162 E1
Wroxham Cl BB10 . . . . . . .148 D2
Wroxton Cl FY5 . . . . .152 F7
Wycherley Rd OL12 . . . . . .52 B2
Wychnor PR2 . . . . .117 B7
Wycollar Cl BB5 . . . . .104 C4
Wycollar Rd BB2 . . . . . . .101 A6
Wycoller Ave BB10 . . . . . .128 D5
Wycoller Country Pk★
BB8 . . . . .173 B3
Wycombe Ave FY4 . . . . . .110 B6
Wyfordby Ave BB2 . . . . . .101 E4
Wyke Cop Rd PR8,PR9 . . . .36 D2
Wyke La PR8,PR9 . . . . .36 E6
Wyke Wood La PR9 . . . . . .36 F7
Wykeham Gr OL12 . . . . . . .52 B5
Wykeham Rd FY8 . . . . . . .91 B6
Wyllin Rd L31 . . . . .1 A2
Wymundsley PR7 . . . . .61 A2
Wyndene Cl PR3 . . . . .140 C8
Wyndene Gr PR4 . . . . .93 B6
Wyndham Gdns FY4 . . . . .110 D6
Wyndham Pl LA4 . . . . . . .217 F6
Wynfield PR5 . . . . .97 F2
Wynnstay Ave L31 . . . . .5 D3
Wynnwood Ave 1 FY1 . . .130 D8
Wynotham St BB10 . . . . . .148 C5
Wyre Ave PR4 . . . . .114 B5

Wyre Bank PR3 . . . . .157 B6
Wyre Cl
Great Eccleston PR3 . . . . .156 C5
Morecambe LA3 . . . . . . .217 F2
Wyre Cres BB3 . . . . .81 D4
Wyre Ct Fleetwood FY7 . . .198 E3
Poulton-le-F FY6 . . . . . . .154 A3
Wyre Estuary Ctry Pk★
FY5 . . . . .176 E3
Wyre Gr FY3 . . . . .130 C3
Wyre Ho LA1 . . . . .214 F7
Wyre La PR3 . . . . .204 D1
Wyre Rd FY5 . . . . .153 F6
Wyre Side Cl PR3 . . . . . . .181 C8
Wyre St Fleetwood FY7 . . .198 E3
Kirkham PR4 . . . . .113 F6
Lytham St Anne's FY8 . . . .90 A7
Padiham BB12 . . . . .126 D8
Preston PR2 . . . . .117 C1
Wyre Vale Cvn Pk PR3 . . .204 B1
Wyre View FY5 . . . . .199 E5
Wyredale Ct FY7 . . . . . . .198 F3
Wyredale Rd FY8 . . . . . . .89 C8
Wyrefields PR5 . . . . .154 A3
Wyresdale Ave
Accrington BB5 . . . . .104 A4
Blackpool FY2 . . . . .152 D4
Morecambe LA3 . . . . . . .216 E1
Poulton-le-F FY6 . . . . . . .153 C3
Southport PR8 . . . . .35 D4
Wyresdale Cres
Fulwood PR2 . . . . .118 D4
Glasson LA2 . . . . .209 E4
Scorton PR3 . . . . .204 E7
Wyresdale Ct LA1 . . . . . . .215 B7
Wyresdale Dr PR25 . . . . . .60 B6
Wyresdale Gdns LA1 . . . .215 B7
Wyresdale Rd
Knott End-on-S FY6 . . . . .199 D5
Lancaster LA1 . . . . .215 B6
Quernmore LA2 . . . . .232 A6
Wyreside PR3 . . . . .155 E8
Wyreside Dr FY6 . . . . . . .177 B2
Wyreside Ecology & Visitor
Ctr★ FY5 . . . . .176 E3
Wyreside Hall LA2 . . . . . .226 B7
Wytham St 6 BB12 . . . . . .126 D7
Wythburn Ave BB2 . . . . . . .80 E8
Wythburn Cl BB12 . . . . . .127 B8
Wythorpe Croft LA4 . . . . .217 B4
Wyvern Way FY6 . . . . . . .153 C5

Y

Yardley Ctr L33 . . . . .1 C1
Yardley Rd L33 . . . . .1 C1
Yare St 7 BB4 . . . . .69 F8
Yarlside La BD23 . . . . .231 E4
Yarm Pl BB11 . . . . .128 A6
Yarmouth Ave BB4 . . . . . . .85 C2
Yarraville St BB4 . . . . .86 A2
Yarrow Ave L31 . . . . .5 F2
Yarrow Cl Croston PR26 . . .58 B2
Withnell PR6 . . . . .80 A1
Yarrow Gate PR7 . . . . .43 E6
Yarrow Gr BL6 . . . . .32 B4
Yarrow Mill PR6 . . . . .43 E6
Yarrow Pl PR25 . . . . .59 D8
Yarrow Rd Chorley PR6 . . . .43 E6
Leyland PR25 . . . . .59 D8
Yarrow Valley Pk PR7 . . . .43 A2
Yarrow Wlk LA3 . . . . .217 B2
Yarwood St BL9 . . . . .33 A2
Yates Fold BB2 . . . . .101 F2
Yates St Blackpool FY1 . . .130 B6
Chorley PR7 . . . . .43 B5
Yeadon WN8 . . . . .18 B1
Yeadon Gr PR7 . . . . .43 A7
Yeadon Way FY1 . . . . . . .110 D7
Yealand CE Prim Sch
LA5 . . . . .225 E3
Yealand Dr LA1 . . . . .215 A4
Yealand Gr LA5 . . . . .223 E2
Yealand Rd LA5 . . . . .225 E2
Yeargate Ind Est BL9 . . . . .33 D2
Yellow Hall BB18 . . . . . . .195 A5
Yellow House La PR8 . . . . .35 B6
Yenham La LA3 . . . . .213 E1
Yerburgh Rd BB2 . . . . . . .121 C2
Yew Ct FY7 . . . . .198 C1
Yew Gn PR4 . . . . .114 B7
Yew St 10 Blackburn BB1 .102 A7
2 Bury BL9 . . . . .33 C3
Yew Tree Ave Euxton PR7 . .60 C1
Grimsargh PR2 . . . . .139 C2
Yew Tree Cl
Garstang PR3 . . . . .181 B8
Newton-w-S PR4 . . . . . . .114 F3
Wilpshire BB1 . . . . .122 E6
Yew Tree Dr
Blackburn BB2 . . . . .122 B1
Low Bentham LA2 . . . . . .239 C8
Oswaldtwistle BB5 . . . . . .103 F3
Yew Tree Gdns
Silverdale LA5 . . . . .224 C2
Stalmine FY6 . . . . .177 C8
Yew Tree Gr BB4 . . . . .68 C3
Yew Tree Rd
Blackpool FY3 . . . . .153 A1
Ormskirk L39 . . . . .15 E7
Yewbarrow Cl BB12 . . . . .147 C1
Yewdale WN8 . . . . .18 A1
Yewdale Ave LA4 . . . . . . .212 F6
Yewlands Ave
4 Bamber Bridge PR5 . . . .97 F1
Fulwood PR2 . . . . .117 E6

Yewlands Ave continued
Heskin Green PR7 . . . . . . .41 F3
3 Leyland PR25 . . . . . . .77 A1
Yewlands Cres PR2 . . . . . .117 E6
Yewlands Dr
Brierfield BB10 . . . . .148 B3
Fulwood PR2 . . . . .117 E6
Garstang PR3 . . . . .204 C1
2 Leyland PR25 . . . . . . .77 A1
Yewtree Ave PR2 . . . . . . .119 A4
Yewtree Cl PR7 . . . . .43 C5
Yewtree Gr PR5 . . . . .77 A7
York Ave Cleveleys FY5 . . .175 D2
Fleetwood FY7 . . . . .198 E3
Fulwood PR2 . . . . .117 E4
Haslingden BB4 . . . . .68 B8
Southport PR8 . . . . .35 A5
York Cl
4 Bamber Bridge PR5 . . . .97 D3
Clayton-le-M BB5 . . . . . . .124 F3
Formby L37 . . . . .11 F6
Leyland PR25 . . . . .59 E7
York Cres BB1 . . . . .122 F3
York Dr
Great Eccleston PR3 . . . . .156 C5
Kirkham PR4 . . . . .114 B2
Ramsbottom BL0 . . . . .50 A4
York Fields BB18 . . . . . . .196 B3
York Gdns PR8 . . . . .35 A5
York Gr PR3 . . . . .181 B7
York Ho Lancaster LA1 . . .215 A5
27 Preston PR1 . . . . . . .97 A7
York La BB6 . . . . .123 D8
York Pl Accrington BB5 . . .104 B7
Adlington PR6 . . . . .31 A8
Morecambe LA4 . . . . . . .217 C5
York Rd Blackpool FY2 . . .152 B4
Formby L37 . . . . .12 A3
Lancaster LA1 . . . . .215 A5
Langho BB1,BB6 . . . . . . .123 D6
Lytham St Anne's FY8 . . . .89 F5
Southport PR8 . . . . .34 F4
York St Accrington BB5 . . .104 B7
Bacup OL13 . . . . .87 F5
Barnoldswick BB18 . . . . .196 B2
Blackburn BB2 . . . . .101 E3
Blackpool FY1 . . . . .130 B3
Bury BL9 . . . . .33 A2
Chorley PR7 . . . . .43 D7
Church BB5 . . . . .103 E6
Clitheroe BB7 . . . . .189 F1
Colne BB8 . . . . .171 F5
Great Harwood BB6 . . . . .124 D5
Nelson BB9 . . . . .148 F8
Oswaldtwistle BB5 . . . . . .103 C3
Rawtenstall BB4 . . . . .86 A4
Rishton BB1 . . . . .124 A1
York Terr Blackburn BB2 . . .80 D8
4 Southport PR9 . . . . . . .35 C8
York View BB3 . . . . .81 B6
Yorke St 2 BB11 . . . . . . .127 F5
Yorkshire St
Accrington BB5 . . . . .104 C4
16 Bacup OL13 . . . . .87 F3
Blackpool FY1 . . . . .130 B3
Burnley BB11 . . . . .128 B6
Huncoat BB5 . . . . .125 E2
16 Nelson BB9 . . . . .148 E8
Yorkshire St E LA4 . . . . . .216 F4
Yorkshire St W LA3 . . . . .216 E4
Young Ave PR25 . . . . .77 C1
Young St Blackburn BB2 . .101 B2
Ramsbottom BL0 . . . . .50 B6

Z

Zama St 9 BL0 . . . . .50 A4
Zebudah St BB2 . . . . .101 C2
Zetland St Preston PR1 . . . .97 C7
Southport PR9 . . . . .35 D7
Zion Rd BB1 . . . . .102 A8
Zion St Bacup OL13 . . . . . .88 A3
Colne BB8 . . . . .171 D4

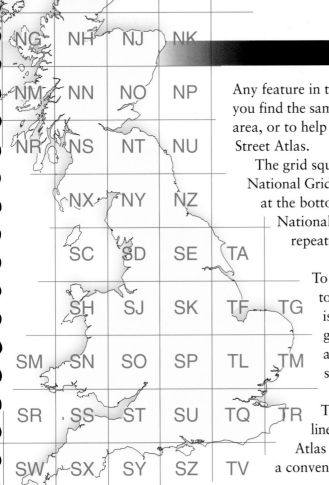

Any feature in this atlas can be given a unique reference to help you find the same feature on other Ordnance Survey maps of the area, or to help someone else locate you if they do not have a Street Atlas.

The grid squares in this atlas match the Ordnance Survey National Grid and are at 500 metre intervals. The small figures at the bottom and sides of every other grid line are the National Grid kilometre values (**00** to **99** km) and are repeated across the country every 100 km (see left).

To give a unique National Grid reference you need to locate where in the country you are. The country is divided into 100 km squares with each square given a unique two-letter reference. Use the administrative map to determine in which 100 km square a particular page of this atlas falls.

The bold letters and numbers between each grid line (**A** to **F**, **1** to **8**) are for use within a specific Street Atlas only, and when used with the page number, are a convenient way of referencing these grid squares.

Example *The railway bridge over DARLEY GREEN RD in grid square B1*

Step 1: Identify the two-letter reference, in this example the page is in **SP**

Step 2: Identify the 1 km square in which the railway bridge falls. Use the figures in the southwest corner of this square: Eastings **17**, Northings **74**. This gives a unique reference: **SP 17 74**, accurate to 1 km.

Step 3: To give a more precise reference accurate to 100 m you need to estimate how many tenths along and how many tenths up this 1 km square the feature is (to help with this the 1 km square is divided into four 500 m squares). This makes the bridge about **8** tenths along and about **1** tenth up from the southwest corner.

This gives a unique reference: **SP 178 741**, accurate to 100 m.

Eastings (read from left to right along the bottom) come before Northings (read from bottom to top). If you have trouble remembering say to yourself "Along the hall, THEN up the stairs"!

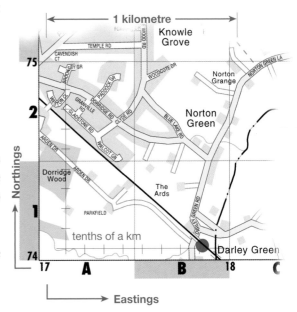

Addresses

Name and Address	Telephone	Page	Grid reference

Name and Address	Telephone	Page	Grid reference

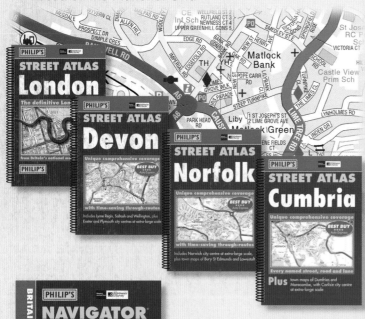